NEW AGE INTERNATIONAL

# WEBSTER'S STANDARD DICTIONARY



**NEW AGE INTERNATIONAL PUBLISHERS**

First Indian Sub-Continent Edition : 2008
by New Age International (P) Ltd., Publishers


Originally Published in United States of America.



Printed in India at Saras Graphics, Rai.
2 3 4 5 6 7 8 9 10
C-07-11-2098

ISBN(13):978- 81-224-2210-8
ISBN(10):81-224-2210-1
[redacted]

PUBLISHING FOR ONE WORLD
NEW AGE INTERNATIONAL (P) LIMITED, PUBLISHERS
4835/24, Ansari Road, Daryaganj, New Delhi - 110002
Visit us at www.newagepublishers.com

**a, A** *n.* first letter of the English alphabet *—indefinite article,* used before a word beginning with a consonant: *a house, a car, —adj.* per, for each: *twice a month;* first in order: *grade A quality, section A*

**aard´vark** *n.* a large burrowing African mammal that feeds on ants and termites; an ant bear

**aard´wolf** *n.* an African mammal of the hyena family that feeds on termites and larvae

**a·ba´** *n.* a sleeveless Arab robe

**a·back´** *adv.* pressed backward; to the rear; catching a headwind so as to force a sailing vessel backward **—taken aback** caught by surprise, disconcerted; caught by a wind change which reverses the sails

**ab´a·cus** *n.* an ancient device from the Orient for performing mathematical calculations by the use of rows of beads on rods

**a·baft´** *adv.* toward the stern of a ship; back *—prep.* further back than

**ab·a·lo´ne** *n.* an edible shellfish lined with mother-of-pearl that is used for buttons, beads, inlay, etc.

**a·ban´don** *n.* spontaneity, unrestrained enthusiasm or emotion *—vt.* to give up completely, to forsake or desert; to give in completely to emotion **—a·ban´don·ment** *n.*

**a·ban´doned** *adj.* left behind, forsaken; unrestrained; lacking modesty or moderation; shameless **—a·ban´don·er** *n.*

**a·base´** *vt.* to humble; to degrade; to dishonor

**a·base´ment** *n.* humiliation, shame

**a·bash´** *vt.* to disconcert or make confused; to embarrass **—a·bash´ed·´ly** *adv.*

**a·bash´ment** *n.* confusion, disorientation, embarrassment

**a·bate´** *vi., vt.* to lessen; to reduce in amount, force, etc. **—a·bat´a·ble** *adj.* **—a·bat´er** *n.*

**a·bate´ment** *n.* a lessening or alleviation, mitigation; in law, the conclusion of a suit **—a·bat´or** *n.*

**ab´a·tis** *n.* a defensive barricade of felled or bent trees

**a·bat·jour´** *n.* a device for deflecting sunlight; a skylight

**ab´at·toir** *n.* a slaughterhouse

**ab·ax´i·al** *adj.* facing away from the axis

**ab´ba·cy** *n.* the office or jurisdiction of an abbot

**ab´bess** *n.* the director of a nunnery

**ab´bey** *n.* a monastery or nunnery

**ab´bot** *n.* the director of a monastery

**ab´bot·cy, ab´bot·ship** *n.* the office and trappings of an abbot

**ab·bre´vi·ate** *vt.* to abridge or shorten

**ab·bre´vi·a´tion** *n.* a shortened form; a contraction of a word or phrase

**ABC´s** *n.* the basics; rudimentary elements; beginning knowledge

**ab´di·cate** *vi., vt.* to formally renounce, as a right or responsibility; to give up claim, as to a throne **—ab´di·ca´tion** *n.* **—ab´di·ca·tor** *n.*

**ab·do´men** *n.* the part of the human body comprising the lower portion of the trunk, from the diaphragm to the pelvic girdle

**ab·dom´i·nal** *adj.* pertaining to the abdomen **—ab·dom´i·nal·ly** *adv.*

**ab·du´cent** *adj.* of a muscle that pulls away from the median axis of the body

**ab·duct´** *vt.* to kidnap; to carry away by force

**ab·duc´tion** *n.* a kidnapping; the abducting of a person by force or deceit

**ab·duc´tor** *n.* a muscle that pulls away from the median axis of the body

**a·beam´** *adj., adv.* at right angles to the keel of a ship

**a·be·ce·dar´i·an** *adj.* primary, rudimentary *—n.* a beginning student, one learning the alphabet

**a·bed´** *adj.* in bed

**ab·er´rance, ab·er´ran·cy** *n.* deviation from the right or usual course **—ab·er´rant·ly** *adv.*

**ab·er´rant** *adj.* straying from what is right; abnormal *—n. a strange or* abnormal person **—ab·er´rant·ly** *adv.*

**ab´er·ra´tion** *n.* an abnormality; a deviation from the customary course or condition; delusion, derangement **—ab´er·ra´tion·al** *adj.*

**a·bet´** *vt.* assist; to support; to encourage, especially in wrongdoing **—a·bet´ment** *n.*

**a·bet´tor, a·bet´ter** *n.* one who assists; an accessory or collaborator

**a·bey´ance** *n.* temporary state of suspension; a hiatus

**a·bey´ant** *adj.* in a dormant state, inactive.

**ab·hor´** *vt.* to loathe; to look upon with repugnance

**ab·hor´rence** *n.* a hatred or loathing; a strong aversion

**ab·hor´rent** *adj.* detestable; causing a feeling of disgust **—ab·hor·rent·ly** *adv.*

**a·bid´ance** *n.* continuance

**a·bide´** *vi.* to dwell; to stay in a place; to remain unchanging *—vt.* to wait for; to endure: *the luggage will abide rough handling; to submit to: we will abide by your decision;* to accept the consequences of

**a·bid´ing** *adj.* continuing, steadfast **—a·bid´ing·ly** *adv.*

**a·bil´i·ty** *n.* power, faculty; competence; endowed with the necessary skill

**a·bi·o·gen´e·sis** *n.* the theory that life may be created from inorganic matter **—a·bi·o·ge·net´ic** *adj.* **—a·bi·o·ge·net´i·cal·ly** *adv.*

**a·bi·og´e·nist** *n.* one who believes in the spontaneous generation of life

**a·bi·ot´ic** *adj.* of inorganic matter, such as light or heat; not organic; not living

**ab·ject´, ab·ject** *adj.* wretched, degrading; disheartening, beyond all hope; without self esteem **—ab·ject´ly** *adv.* **—ab·ject´ness** *n.*

**ab·jec´tion** *n.* a wretched, degrading condition

**ab·jure´** *vt.* to renounce under oath; to recant or

retract, as an unpopular belief; to abstain from, as a practice: *to abjure traditional ceremony* —**ab·ju·ra´tion** *n.* —**ab·jur´a·to·ry** *adj.* —**ab·jur´er** *n.*

**ab·la´tion** *n.* the process of wearing away; erosion; the surgical excision of body tissue; disintegration of the nose cone of a space vehicle as it reenters the atmosphere —**ab·late** *vt., vi.*

**ab´la·tive** *adj.* in grammar, expressing separation or removal from source, *as freedom from fear*

**a·blaze´** *adj., adv.* on fire; aroused to passion or excitement; fervent

**a´ble** *adj.* possessing adequate ability; capable; qualified; one legally allowed, as by qualification or competence —**a´bly** *adv.*

**a´ble·bod´ied** *adj.* sound of body; physically capable

**a·bloom´** *adj.* in bloom; flowering

**ab´lu·ent** *adj.* used for cleaning —*n.* a cleansing agent

**ab·lu´tion** *n.* the act of washing, especially of the body; a bath; a ceremonial washing of the priest´s hands or of the chalice during a religious ceremony

**a´bly** *adv.* in a competent manner; proficiently

**ab´ne·gate** *vt.* to give up, as a privilege or desire —**ab´ne·ga·tor** *n.*

**ab·ne·ga´tion** *n.* rejection or renunciation of a belief or desire; selfdenial; disavowal

**ab·nor´mal** *adj.* unnatural; differing from the normal or average; not according to rule; curious, irregular, or odd

**ab·nor·mal´i·ty** *n.* an aberration; an oddity or anomaly; a malformation, a peculiarity

**ab·nor´mal·ly** *adv.* to an unusual degree; exceedingly, exceptionally

**ab·nor´mi·ty** *n.* a monstrosity or perversion

**a·board´** *adv.* into or on a conveyance, as a passenger or baggage; in agreement, as to support for a common cause —**all aboard** a warning to passengers to board, or that the vehicle, usually a train, is about to depart

**a·bode´** *n.* a dwelling; a place of habitation or residence

**a·bol´ish** *vt.* to put an end to; to invalidate —**a·bol´ish·er** *n.* —**a·bol´ish·ment** *n.*

**ab´o·li´tion** *n.* the act of terminating or eliminating, as the abolition of slavery in the U.S.

**ab·o·li´tion·ist** *n.* one who wishes to abolish, especially those who supported the abolition of slavery in the U.S.

**a·bom´i·na·ble** *adj.* hateful; horrible; that which is frightening or offensive —**a·bom´in·a·bly** *adv.*

**a·bom·i·na´tion** *n.* extreme disgust or abhorrence; any action, custom, practice, or thing which arouses feelings of disgust

**ab´o·rig´i·nal** *adj.* native or indigenous; primitive; pertaining to aborigines —*n.* a native inhabitant; an aborigine

**ab·o·rig´i·ne** *n.* a native or earliest known inhabitant of a region

**ab´o·rig´i·nes** *pl. n.* first inhabitants; the flora and fauna of an area

**a·bort´** *vi.* to bring forth young before the full term of development; to terminate prematurely, as a task or mission —*vt.* to cause to bring to an early, unsuccessful conclusion

**a·bor´tion** *n.* a miscarriage, usually intentional; any failure to evolve normally or as planned; the product of such failure, a monstrosity; a failed attempt —**a·bor´tion·ist** *n.*

**a·bor´tive** *adj.* useless; vain or futile; fruitless

**a·bound´** *vi.* to be plentiful; available in abundance

**a·bout´** *adv.* almost or approximately: *in about an hour,* around or in another direction: *turn about, wander about or look about* —*prep.* in or around an area: *somewhere about the office*; particular to or associated with: *she has an air about her*; approximating or near: *departing about noon, a group of about thirty*; in regard to: *a book about money management*

**a·bout´·face** *n.* in a military drill, a turn to the rear; any reversal of opinion or direction, especially one that is abrupt

**a·bove** *adv.* over; overhead; higher in rank —*adj.* foregoing or preceding: *the above paragraph* —*n.* that which is before or overhead —*prep.* rising over or higher: *the moon above the lake, boxes stacked above one another* —**above all** having precedence over everything else; the most important consideration

**a·bove´board** *adj., adv.* candid, forthright; in the open without anything concealed

**a·brade´** *vt.* to scrape or wear away by friction

**a·bra´sion** *n.* the act or result of a wearing away, as of stone by the force of the elements; an injury resulting from passing contact with a rough surface

**a·bra´sive** *adj.* wearing; capable of eroding; disagreeable or offensive, *as his abrasive manner* —*n.* a material which abrades, as sandpaper or emery —**a·bra´sive·ly** *adv.* **a·bra´sive·ness** *n.*

**a·breast´** *adv.* side by side

**a·bridge´** *vt.* to shorten; to condense, as a book or article, by reducing the material to fewer words; to lessen or deprive, as of civil rights

**a·bridg´ment** *n.* that which has been shortened; an abstract

**a·broad´** *adv.* away from one´s usual place; in a foreign land; widely circulated

**ab´ro·gate´** *vt.* to repeal or annul, esp. legally; to abolish —**ab´ro·ga´tion** *n.* —**ab´ro·ga·tor** *n.*

**a·brupt´** *adj.* happening suddenly or unexpectedly —**ab·rupt´ly** *adv.* —**ab·rupt´ness** *n.*

**ab´scess** *n.* a collection of pus in a body cavity

**ab·scis´sa** *n.* in a graph, the distance of a reference point from the Y-axis, parallel to the X-axis

**ab·scis´sion** *n.* the act of cutting off; severance or

removal; in public speaking, an abrupt pause for dramatic effect

**ab•scond´** *vi.* to leave quickly and secretly, esp. to avoid legal action

**ab´sence** *n.* a deficiency or inadequacy; the condition of being away; lack or want

**ab´sent** *adj.* not present; lacking or nonexistent; inattentive –**ab•sent´** *vt.* to keep oneself away –**ab´sent•ness** *n.* –**ab´sent•ly** *adv.*

**ab´sen•tee´** *n.* one who is missing, as from school or work –*adj.* referring to one not presently in residence: *an absentee landlord*; describing an action taken by one who is absent: *an absentee vote*

**ab´sen•tee´ism** *n.* the state of being absent; a measure of the frequency of absence from work, school, etc.

**ab´sent-mind´ed** *adj.* preoccupied, and thus unmindful of immediate demands; forgetful –**ab´sent•mind´ed•ly** *adv.* –**ab´sent•mind´ed•ness** *n.*

**ab´sinthe** *n.* wormwood; an anise flavored liqueur

**ab´so•lute** *adj.* complete; perfect; without restriction or reservation; pure and unadulterated; not related to or dependent on any arbitrary standard –*n.* **that which is perfect –ab´so•lute´ly** *adv.* –**ab•so•lute´ness** *n.*

**absolute zero** *n.* 459.6° F. below zero; the temperature at which a substance would be wholly deprived of heat

**ab´so•lu•tion** *n.* exoneration; vindication; forgiveness; in some churches, the ceremonial remission of sin

**ab´so•lut•ism** *n.* despotism; a principle that grants a ruler unlimited powers –**ab´so•lut•ist** *adj., n.* –**ab•so•lu•tis´tic** *adj.*

**ab•solve´** *vt.* to acquit of guilt or complicity; to free from an obligation; to pardon or remit from sin and its attendant punishment –**ab•solv´a•ble** *adj.* –**ab•solv´er** *n.*

**ab•sorb´** *vt.* **to swallow up or engross completely; to assimilate; to engage or occupy entirely –ab•sorb´a•ble** *adj.* –**ab•sorb•a•bil´i•ty** *n.* –**ab•sorb´er** *n.*

**ab•sor´bent** *adj.* absorbing or disposed to absorb –*n.* a substance that absorbs –**ab•sorb´en•cy** *n.*

**ab•sorb´ing** *adj.* stimulating or enticing, as *an absorbing story* –**ab•sorb´ing•ly** *adv.*

**ab•sorp´tion** *n.* the process of absorbing or being absorbed; concentration or preoccupation of the mind –**ab•sorp´tive** *adj.* –**ab•sorp´tive•ness, ab•sorp•tiv´i•ty** *n.*

**ab•stain´** *vi.* to forbear; to avoid or shun voluntarily

**ab•ste´mi•ous** *adj.* avoiding excess; temperate –**ab•ste´mi•ous•ly** *adv.*

**ab•sten•tion** *n.* temperance; foregoing –**ab•sten´tious** *adj.*

**ab´sti•nence** *n.* the practice of avoiding something, such as for intoxicating drink –**ab´sti•nent** *adj.* –**ab´sti•nent•ly** *adv.*

**ab´stract** *adj.* expressing a quality apart from the absolute or concrete; theoretical; difficult to understand; impersonal; of a style of art –*n.* an abridgement; a summary or essence; a non-specific idea or term –**ab•stract´** *vt.* to take from; to condense or summarize; to form a general notion of: *the abstract concept of equal rights* –*adj.* general; theoretical; considered apart from the specific or practical –**ab•stract´er** *n.* –**ab•strac´tion•al** *adj.* –**ab•strac´tion•ism** *n.*

**abstract art** a school of art that makes use of designs based on the relationship of elements rather than on the representation of objects

**ab•stract´ed** *adj.* disassociated or apart; obscure or puzzling; preoccupied –**ab•stract´ed•ly** *adv.*

**ab•strac´tion** *n.* preoccupation or absorption; a theory or ideal –**ab•strac´tive** *adj.*

**ab•struse´** *adj.* difficult to comprehend –**ab•struse´ly** *adv.* –**ab•struse´ness** *n.*

**ab•surd´** *adj.* irrational; preposterous; ridiculous –**ab•surd´ly** *adv.*

**ab•surd´i•ty** *n.* that which is preposterous or ridiculous

**a•bun´dance** *n.* a quantity in excess of need; plenty

**a•bun´dant** *adj.* plentiful; bountiful; more than enough –**a•bun´dant•ly** *adv.*

**a•buse´** *n.* improper use; misapplication; vicious or cruel treatment –*vt.* to use incorrectly; to harm by improper use: *abuse a privilege*; to injure by mistreating: *abuse an animal* –**a•bus´er** *n.*

**a•bu´sive** *adj.* characterized by abuse; serving to abuse as *abusive language* –**a•bu´sive•ly** *adv.* –**a•bu´sive•ness** *n.*

**a•but** *vi.* to touch or join; to border; to form a line of contact, with *on*, *upon*, or *against* –*vt.* to border on

**a•but´ment** *n.* a supporting element of a structure such as a bridge or wall; a buttress

**a•bys´mal** *adj.* bottomless; extreme: *abysmal despair* –**a•bys´mal•ly** *adv.*

**a•byss´** *n.* a bottomless gulf; a chasm; a tremendous depth

**ac•a•deme´, ac´a•deme** *n.* a place of learning; an academy; a scholarly environment

**ac´a•dem´ia** *n.* the academic world; institutions of learning collectively

**ac´a•dem´ic** *adj.* scholarly; of traditional learning rather than vocational; theoretical or hypothetical rather than practical –*n.* a student or scholar; a member of a learned society –**ac•a•dem´i•cal** *n.* –**ac•a•dem´i•cal•ly** *adv.*

**a•cad´e•my** *n.* a preparatory school; a society of scholars devoted to the advancement of art or science

**a cap•pel´la** *adj.* vocal music without instrumental accompaniment

**ac•cede´** *vi.* to come into an office; to give assent or agree to –**ac•ced´ence** *n.*

**ac•cel´er•ate** *vi.* to move more rapidly; to hurry –*vt.* to increase the speed of; to hasten the natural course of: *to accelerate growth with plant food*

**ac·cel´er·a´tion** *n.* a hastening of progress; the rate of increase in the speed of a body

**ac·cel´er·a´tor** *n.* a device that controls speed by regulating the flow of fuel, power, etc.; that which increases speed, flow, etc.

**ac´cent** *n.* voice stress on a syllable in the pronunciation of a word; a mark ( ´ )to indicate vocal stress; a manner of speaking which differs from place to place or from one language to another –*vt.* to stress; to speak or produce with an accent

**ac·cen´tu·ate** *vt.* to stress; to emphasize –**ac·cen´tu·a·tion** *n.*

**ac·cept´** *vt.* ro receive or take what is offered; to agree to or approve; to embrace as true, such as a belief; to take in as a member –**ac·cept´ance** *n.*

**ac·cept´a·ble** *adj.* satisfactory; worthy of being accepted; without need for further modification or negotiation, although not entirely pleasing: *an acceptable level of error* –**ac·cept´a·bil´i·ty** *n.* –**ac·cept´a·bly** *adv.*

**ac·cept´ed** *adj.* generally recognized or believed

**ac´cess** *n.* an approach or passage; permission to approach or enter; a means of obtaining –*vt.* to gain the use of, as a computer program or data

**ac·ces´si·ble** *adj.* easily approached or reached; easily influenced; allowing access; attainable –**ac·ces´si·bil´i·ty** *n.*

**ac·ces´so·ry, ac·ces´sa·ry** *adj.* extra or added; aiding, contributing; supplemental –*n.* an accomplice or abettor; something added as an incidental item of apparel –**ac·ces´so·rize** *vt.*

**ac´ci·dent** *n.* an unexpected occurrence, often unpleasant; a misadventure; an unintentional act

**ac·ci·den´tal** *adj.* happening by chance; fortuitous; incidental to the character of a thing –**ac·ci·den´tal·ly** *adv.*

**ac·claim´** *vt.* to applaud; to receive with approval; to approve by proclamation –*vi.* to applaud or shout approval –*n.* enthusiastic applause

**ac´cla·ma´tion** *n.* applause; general approval

**ac´cli·mate, ac·cli´ma·tize´** *vi., vt.* to grow accustomed to a new environment or circumstance

**ac·clam'a·to·ry** *adj.* expressing joy and adulation

**ac·cliv´i·ty** *n.* an upward slope, opposite of *declivity*

**ac´co·lade´** *n.* any honor or award; words of praise

**ac·com´mo·date´** *vi.* to become adjusted, as to a disability –*vt.* to supply food or lodging; to adapt; to be suitable for: *the room will accommodate four persons* –**ac·com´mo·dat·ing·ly** *adv.* –**ac·com´mo·da·tive** *adj.*

**ac·com´mo·da´tion** *n.* an adaptation; a reconciliation; a convenience; board or lodging; assistance; a willingness to provide assistance –**ac·com·mo·da´tion·al** *adj.*

**ac·com´pa·nist** *n.* one who plays a musical instrument or vocalizes to enhance the performance or presentation of another –**ac·com´pa·ni·ment** *n.*

**ac·com´pa·ny** *vt.* to go with; to escort; to play an instrument or sing with another; to supplement: *wine accompanied the meal*; to occur at the same time: *a cold accompanied by fever*

**ac·com´plice** *n.* an associate in crime; a knowing confederate

**ac·com´plish** *vt.* to perform; to fulfill, as an obligation; to complete

**ac·com´plished** *adj.* completed; fulfilled; proficient or expert: *an accomplished musician*; refined or cultivated

**ac·com´plish·ment** *n.* something completed; a worthly attainment

**ac·cord´** *n.* harmony or agreement; spontaneous desire –*vi.* to be in agreement; to harmonize –*vt.* to grant; to bring into harmony –**of one´s own accord** freely done, without urging –**according to** as per direction or plan; as reported

**ac·cord´ance** *n.* conformity; accord; harmony

**ac·cord´ing·ly** *adv.* consequently; as a result

**ac·cost´** *vt.* to confront; to approach and greet first

**ac·count´** *n.* a computation, a report or statement; a record of financial or commercial transactions –*vi.* to provide a reason; to explain; to be responsible –*vt.* to impute –**give a good account** to do well –**on account** on credit –**on no account** under no circumstance –**take into account** bear in mind

**ac·count´a·ble** *adj.* having liability; responsible; capable of being explained –**ac·count·a·bil´i·ty** *n.* –**ac·count´a·bly** *adv.*

**ac·count´an·cy** *n.* the office and duties of an accountant

**ac·count´ant** *n.* one experienced in the keeping of accounts; one whose business is to record or audit the financial records of an institution –**public accountant** an accountant whose services are available to the public for a fee –**certified public accountant** in the U.S., a public accountant who has been certified by a state examining body

**ac·count´ing** *n.* a settlement; a statement of the financial condition and transactions of an organization; the principles or profession of recording the financial transactions of an organization

**ac·cred´it** *vt.* to certify; to send with credentials

**ac·cre´tion** *n.* a growth; growth by accumulation or addition, as of sediment deposited along the course of a river or on a seashore

**ac·cru´al** *n.* an increase or accumulation; something that increases

**ac·crue´** *vi.* to increase; be added to, as interest

**ac·cu´mu·late** *vt.* to amass or pile up; to gather –*vi.* to increase –**ac·cu´mu·la·ble** *adj.* –**ac·cu´mu·la·tor** *n.*

**ac·cu´mu·la´tion** *n.* a collection; growth or increase

**ac·cu´mu·la·tive** *adj.* tending to increase –**ac·cu´mu·la·tive·ly** *adv.* –**ac·cu´mu·la·tive·ness** *n.*

**ac´cu·ra·cy** *n.* a measure of the degree of precision; correctness; exactness

**ac´cu·rate** *adj.* very exact; precise; capable of providing precise measurement; within established limits **–ac´cu·rate·ly** *adv.* **–ac´cu·rate·ness** *n.*

**ac·curs´ed, ac·curst´** *adj.* under a curse; deserving a curse **–ac·curs´ed·ly** *adv.*

**ac·cu·sa´tion, ac·cu´sal** *n.* the act of charging with a crime; arraignment

**ac·cuse´** *vi.* to verbalize charges *–vt.* to bring a charge against **–ac·cus´er** *n.* **–ac·cus´ing·ly** *adv.*

**ac·cused´** *n.* a person or persons charged with the commission of a crime

**ac·cus´tom** *vt.* to make or become familiar through use; to adapt to

**ac·cus´tomed** *adj.* habitual or usual; customary; characteristic

**ace** *n.* a single spot, as on a playing card or die; a person who excels, an expert; in tennis, a point won on the serve *–vt.* to score an ace

**ac´er·bate** *vt.* to make harsh or bitter; to intensify; to annoy

**a·cer´bic, a·cerb´** *adj.* sour tasting; harsh, as in manner or language **–a·cer´bi·ty** *n.*

**ac´e·tate´** *n.* a salt or ester of acetic acid; a type of fiber used in the making of textiles

**a·ce´tic** *adj.* sour; having the sour properties of vinegar; pertaining to or containing acetic acid or vinegar **–a·ce´ti·fy** *vi., vt.*

**acetic acid** *n.* a colorless sour acid which is the chief component of vinegar

**ac´e·tone** *n.* a colorless, flammable liquid ketone used as a solvent

**a·cet´y·lene** *n.* a colorless, flammable gas used as a fuel in welding

**a·ce´tyl·sal·i·cyl´ic acid** *n.* aspirin

**ache** *vi.* to hurt; to suffer throbbing pain; to suffer absence or loss: *to ache for a loved one*; to feel sympathy for *–n.* a dull protracted pain **–ach´i·ness** *n.* **–ach´ing·ly** *adv.* **–ach·y** *adj.*

**a·chieve´** *vi.* to reach an objective *–vt.* to accomplish; to complete successfully **–a·chiev´a·ble** *adj.* **–a·chiev´er** *n.*

**a·chieve´ment** *n.* the act of accomplishing; a notable act; a distinguished accomplishment

**ac´id** *adj.* sour and sharp to the taste; caustic or sarcastic, as of humor *–n.* a sour substance

**a·cid´ic** *adj.* having the properties of acid

**a·cid´i·fy** *vi.* to turn acid *–vt.* to transform into an acid **–a·cid´i·fi·ca´tion** *n.* **–a·cid´i·fi´er** *n.*

**a·cid´i·ty** *n.* sourness and tartness; degree of acid strength

**acid test** a test of quality, veracity, etc.; a severe test

**ac·knowl´edge** *vt.* to admit or confess; to certify as valid; to show appreciation; to confirm receipt of **–ac·knowl´edge·a·ble** *adj.*

**ac·knowl´edge·ment, ac·knowl´edg·ment** *n.* a confession; a recognition of responsibility; something said or done in response or appreciation; confirmation of receipt

**ac´me** *n.* the highest point; zenith

**ac´ne** *n.* a skin affliction, mainly in adolescents

**a´corn** *n.* the fruit of the oak tree

**a·cous´tic, a·cous´ti·cal** *adj.* pertaining to sound or the sense of hearing **–a·cous´ti·cal·ly** *adv.* **–ac·ous·ti´cian** *n.*

**a·cous´tics** *pl. n.* the scientific study of sound; the degree to which sound quality is maintained in a particular place

**ac·quaint´** *vt.* to make one aware of; to inform; to introduce **–be acquainted with** familiar, but not well known

**ac·quaint´ance** *n.* familiarity; knowledge; an associate; one who is known to another **–ac·quaint´ance·ship** *n.*

**ac´qui·esce´** *vi.* to agree or comply without enthusiasm; to submit to or accept as inevitable **–ac´qui·es´cence** *n.* **–ac´qui·es´cent** *adj.* **–ac·qui·es´cent·ly, ac·qui·esc´ing·ly** *adv.*

**ac·quire´** *vt.* to obtain or gain, esp. through personal effort **–ac·quir´a·ble** *adj.* **–ac·quir´er** *n.*

**ac´qui·si´tion** *n.* a thing gained, an appropriation

**ac·quis´i·tive** *adj.* prone to acquire, as property **–ac·quis´i·tive·ly** *adv.* **–ac·quis´i·tive·ness** *n.* **–ac·quis´i·tor** *n.*

**ac·quit´** *vt.* to pronounce innocent; to discharge a trust; to behave or act: *he acquitted himself well*

**ac·quit´tal** *n.* a discharge of duty; in law, a finding of not guilty as charged or of being set free by judgement of a court

**ac·quit´tance** *n.* a settlement of liability; a receipt or proof of such settlement

**a´cre** *n.* a land measure equal to 4,840 square yards

**a´cre·age** *n.* property; a number of acres comprising a single piece of property

**ac´rid** *adj.* sharp in taste or smell; pungent **–a·crid´i·ty** *n.* **–ac´rid·ly** *adv.* **–ac´rid·ness** *n.*

**ac·ri·mo´ni·ous** *adj.* sarcastic; caustic; acerbic

**ac´ri·mo·ny** *n.* sharp or bitter speech or temperament

**ac´ro·bat** *n.* an athlete skilled in gymnastics; a trapeze artist; a tumbler **–ac´ro·bat´ic** *adj.*

**ac´ro·bat´ics** *n.* gymnastics

**ac´ro·nym** *n.* a word formed from the initial letters or syllables of a group of words which make up the name of an organization, title, etc. as NASA for National Aeronautics and Space Administration

**ac·ro·pho´bi·a** *n.* a unnatural fear of heights **–ac´ro·phobe** *n.* **–ac·ro·pho´bic** *adj.*

**a·cross´** *adv.* from one side to the other; on the opposite side *–prep.* on or at the other side; from one side to the other; upon or in contact with: *I came across the papers yesterday*

**a·cros´tic** *n.* a written message whose initial letters form a word or another message

**a·cryl´ic** *adj.* of acrylic acid or any of the products made from it –*n.* a class of transparent resins; a substance obtained from an acrylic resin, as a paint, fiber, etc.

**act** *vi.* to behave oneself; to perform a function or produce an effect: *the acid will act on the metal* –*vt.* to play a part of the stage; to behave in a proper manner: *act like a gentleman*; to pretend to be something out of the ordinary: *don´t act like a fool* –**act as** to serve in a temporary capacity –**act on** follow an order or advice –**act up** to be troublesome –**get into the act** join in an activity –**put on an act** to pretend

**act´ing** *adj.* standing in for another, as *acting manager*, operating –*n.* a performance on the stage; an affectation

**ac´tion** *n.* putting forth or exerting energy; decisiveness: *a man of action*: the result of activity; a manner of movement: *the up and down action of a piston*; parts that move in a mechanism; a thing done; a law suit –**ac´tions** *pl. n.* one´s behaviour or conduct

**ac´tion·a·ble** *adj.* in law, forming the basis for a lawsuit or for prosecution –**ac´tion·a·bly** *adv.*

**ac´ti·vate** *vt.* to make active; to purify sewage by means of aeration –**ac´ti·va´tion** *n.* –**ac´ti·va·tor** *n.*

**ac´tive** *adj.* energetic, lively; busy; operative, as *an active volcano*; taking part, as *an active member*, –**ac´tive·ly** *adv.* –**ac´tive·ness** *n.*

**ac·tiv´i·ty** *n.* lively movement; a planned or specific undertaking or pursuit; a transaction

**ac´tiv·ism** *n.* involvement in social issues –**ac´tiv·ist** *n.*

**ac´tu·al** *adj.* existing in fact –*n.* a thing of substance; real –**ac´tu·al´i·ty** *n.*

**ac´tu·al·ise** *(Brit.)*, **ac´tu·al·ize** *(US)* *vt.* to make real; to portray realistically –**ac´tu·al·i·sa·tion, ac´tu·al·i·za·tion** *n.*

**ac´tu·al·ly** *adv.* truly, as a matter of fact

**ac´tu·ar·y** *n.* a statistician who calculates risk for investors or insurers –**ac·tu·ar´i·al** *adj.*

**ac´tu·ate** *vt.* to impel, to put in motion; to cause to act –**ac´tu·a·tion** *n.* –**ac´tu·a·tor** *n.*

**a·cu·i·ty** *n.* insight; discernment, especially of reasoning or of perception

**a·cu´men** *n.* quickness of understanding and acting; sharpness of intellect; soundness of judgment

**ac·u·punc·ture** *n.* an Oriental treatment for pain or illness in which fine needles are inserted through the skin at points determined to be beneficial according to the condition being treated –**ac´u·punc·tur·ist** *n.*

**a·cute´** *adj.* pointed, sharp; keen of mind; serious, critical, as an acute illness or disease; sharp or intense, as pain –**a·cute´ly** *adv.* –**a·cute´ness** *n.*

**acute angle** *n.* an angle of less than 90°

**ad** *n.* an advertisement

**ad´age** *n.* a proverb or maxim

**ad´a·mant** *adj.* unyielding; resolute in belief –**ad´a·mant·ly** *adv.*

**a·dapt´** *vi.* to grow adjusted to, as an environment –*vt.* to make suitable by adjusting or altering; to accommodate by changing oneself –**a·dapt´a·ble** *adj.* –**a·dapt·a·bil´i·ty** *n.*

**ad·ap·ta´tion** *n.* that which has been modified for a specific use; the process of modification

**a·dapt´er, a·dap´tor** *n.* a device for modifying an apparatus for a different or additional use; a connecting device that joins units whose connections are otherwise incompatible

**a·dap´tive** *adj.* capable of being modified –**a·dap´tive·ly** *adv.*

**add** *vi.* to produce an increase; to perform an addition; –*vt.* to increase in importance or size; to total a column of numbers; to speak or write more –**add up** to total; to seem reasonable or believable –**add´a·ble, add´i·ble** *adj.*

**ad´dend** *n.*, *pl.* **ad·den´da** in mathematics, a number which is to be added to an existing number, called the *augend*

**ad·den´dum** *n.* an addition; a thing to be added, usually at the end, such as an appendix

**ad´dict** *n.* one given to an obsession, as illegal drugs or alcohol –**ad·dict´** *vt.* to devote oneself to: *addicted to the latest fashions, addicted to work*; to be dependent on: *addieted to drugs*

**ad·dic´tion** *n.* psychological or physiological dependence on anything; a compulsion

**ad·dict´ed** *adj.* predisposed to a practice or substance

**ad·dic´tive** *adj.* habit-forming

**ad·di´tion** *n.* the process of finding the sum of two or more numbers; something added, as a room to a house; an increase –**ad·di´tion·al** *adj.*, *n.* –**ad·di´tion·al·ly** *adv.*

**ad´di·tive** *n.* an ingredient added to alter the flavor, performance, cost, etc. of a product –*adj.* tending to increase

**ad´dle** *vi.* to become disconnected or confused, as in speech –*vt.* to cause to become confused or disjointed; to muddle: *his thinking is addled by strong drink* –*adj.* confused, incoherent

**ad´dle·brained´** *adj.* confused; flustered; also **ad´dle·pat´ed**

**ad·dress´** *vt.* to speak or write to; to direct to specifically: *address a letter*, to direct attention or energy: *we´ll address this problem now* –*n.* a formal speech; one´s place of abode or work; the bearing or manner of a person; a specific location, as of a block of data, in a computer –**ad·dress´er** *n.*

**ad·dress´a·ble** *adj.* approachable; able to locate and use, as a block of data in computer memory.

**ad·dress·ee´** *n.* one who is addressed

**ad·duce´** *vt.* to cite as an example or proof **–ad·duc´i·ble** *adj.*

**ad·duct´** *vt.* to pull toward the median axis of the body **–ad·duc´tion** *n.*

**ad·duc´tor** *n.* of a muscle that pulls toward the median axis of the body

**ad´e·noid** *n.* a glandular tissue behind the nose at the upper part of the throat *–adj.* glandular

**a·dept´** *adj.* extremely skilled; proficient **–ad´ept** *n.* a person who is highly skilled; an expert **–a·dept´ly** *adv.* **–a·dept´ness** *n.*

**ad´e·quate** *adj.* barely satisfactory or sufficient; enough or suitable for immediate need **–ad´e·qua·cy** *n.* **–ad´e·quate·ly** *adv.* **–ad´e·quate·ness** *n.*

**ad·here´** *vi.* to stick fast; to follow closely: *adhere to the rules*; to follow faithfully or devotedly **–ad·her´ence** *n.* **–ad·her´ent** *n.*

**ad·he´sion** *n.* the act of sticking; the condition of being stuck; a close attachment

**ad·he´sive** *adj.* tending to stick; gummed *–n.* a substance which causes adhesion **–ad·he´sive·ness** *n.*

**adhesive tape** material coated with an adhesive, used for securing bandages, binding wounds, etc.

**ad hoc´** relating to a particular thing

**ad hoc committee** a committee formed for a particular purpose

**ad in´fi·ni´tum** to infinity; forever; unlimited

**ad´i·pose** *adj.* pertaining to fat **–ad·i·pose´ness, ad·i·pos´i·ty** *n.*

**ad·ja´cence ad·ja´cen·cy** *n.* the state of being near or neighboring

**ad·ja´cent** *adj.* near or joining; connected; neighboring **–ad·ja´cent·ly** *adv.*

**ad·jec·ti´val, ad´jec·ti·val** *adj.* like or performing the function of an adjective **–ad´jec·ti·val·ly** *adv.*

**ad´jec·tive** *n.* in grammar, a word that modifies a noun, as by color, size, location, etc.; a clause or phrase used as an adjective *–adj.* pertaining to or functioning as an adjective

**ad·join´** *vt.* to be in close proximity; to touch; to unite *–vi.* to lie close by; to be in contact

**ad·journ´** *vi., vt.* to end, as a meeting; to postpone proceedings; to move to another place; *adjourn to the living room* **–ad·journ´ment** *n.*

**ad·judge´** *vt.* to order by law; to decide judicially

**ad·ju´di·cate** *vi.* to perform the function of a judge *–vt.* to decide judicially **–ad·ju´di·ca´tion** *n.* **–ad·ju´di·ca·tive** *adj.* **–ad·ju´di·ca·tor** *n.* **–ad·ju´di·ca·to·ry** *adj.*

**ad´junct** *adj.* supplementary; additional *–n.* something added, as a peripheral device; a person assigned to another as a subordinate; a nonessential quality **–ad·junc´tive** *adj.* **–ad´junc´tive·ly** *adv.*

**ad·jure´** *vt.* to charge under oath; to appeal intently **–ad´ju·ra´tion** *n.* **–ad·jur´a·to·ry** *adj.* **–ad·jur´er, ad·ju´ror** *n.*

**ad·just´** *v.* to adapt or conform as to a new environment; *–vt.* to arrange or regulate so as to fit, match, or produce a desired result; to settle differences or arrive at an amount: *to adjust an insurance claim* **–ad·just´a·ble** *n.* **–ad·just´er, ad·just´or** *n.*

**ad·just´ment** *n.* the process or result of adjusting; the amount of settlement on a claim, as *an insurance adjustment*; an allowance in settlement of a claim, as for wear on a tire that is warranteed against damage

**ad´ju·tant** *n.* an assistant, usu. one who publishes or carries out the directives of a superior

**ad lib´** *adj.* created spontaneously: *ad lib remarks –adv.* spontaneously: *to compose ad lib –vi., vt.* to improvise *–n.*

**ad·min´is·ter** *vi.* to carry out the duties of a manager; to be of assistance *–vt.* to manage; to dispense, as a penalty; to conduct the taking of an oath, test, etc.; to provide assistance **–ad·min´is·tra·ble** *adj.* **–ad·min´is·trant**

**ad·min´is·trate** *vt.* to administer

**ad·min´is·tra´tion** *n.* the act of administering; the power or party in office and which runs the government; the term of the party in power; settlement of the estate of a deceased person by an executor or trustee **–ad·min´is·tra´tive** *adj.* **–ad·min´is·tra·tive·ly** *adv.* **–ad·min´is·tra´tor** *n.*

**ad´mi·ra·ble** *adj.* deserving admiration; comm-endable **–ad´mi·ra·bly** *adv.*

**ad·mi·ral·ty** *n.* the office and jurisdiction of an admiral; the branch of the judiciary that is responsible for maritime affairs

**ad·mi·ra´tion** *n.* wonder and appreciation of that which is rare, beautiful, etc.; something that engenders wonder, appreciation, approval, etc.

**ad·mire´** *vt.* to regard with wonder and appreciation; to esteem; to respect *–vi.* to feel or express admiration **–ad·mir´er** *n.* **–ad´mi·ra·bly** *adv.* **–ad·mir´ing·ly** *adv.*

**ad·mis´si·ble** *adj.* worthy of admission or consideration; allowable **–ad·mis´si·bil´i·ty** *n.* **–ad·mis´si·bly** *adv.*

**ad·mis´sion** *n.* the act of admitting the price paid for entrance; the right to enter; the confession of a deed or fault

**ad·mit´** *vt.* to allow to enter; to be the means to enter: *this pass will admit you*; to allow inclusion or membership, as to a club or professional society; to accede to or acknowledge, as an error in reasoning or in wrongdoing *–vi.* to afford entrance

**ad·mit´tance** *n.* right or permission to enter; the act of admitting; admission or entrance

**ad·mit´ted** *adj.* accepted as valid; confessed; acclaimed; acknowledged

**ad·mit´ted·ly** *adv.* confessedly

**ad·mix·ture** *n.* a combination; a blending of ingredients; the additional ingredient which is combined to form an admixture

**ad·mon´ish** *vt.* to counsel against error; to offer a mild rebuke; to instruct with authority —**ad·mon´ish·ing·ly** *adv.* —**ad·mon´ish·ment** *n.*

**ad´mo·ni´tion** *n.* a mild rebuke; a warning —**ad·mon´i·to´ry** *adj.*

**a·do´** *n.* activity, often overdone or unnecessary; bustle; commotion

**a·do´be** *adj.* made from sun-dried brick —*n.* a sun-dried brick; a building made from such bricks; the earth or clay of which such building blocks are made

**ad·o·les´cence** *n.* the period of growth from childhood to maturity

**ad·o·les´cent** *adj.* characteristic of youth; youthful; lacking maturity, often used pejoratively —*n.* a youth

**a·dopt´** *vt.* to take in and raise as one's own; to take up and follow, as a change in method or policy; to enact, as a law or ordinance —**a·dopt´a·ble** *adj.* —**a·dopt´er** *n.* —**a·dop´tion** *n.* —**a·dop´tive** *adj.*

**a·dor´a·ble** *adj.* delightful; enchanting —**a·dor´a·ble·ness** *n.* —**a·dor´a·bly** *adv.*

**ad´o·ra´tion** *n.* worship or reverence; deep affection, esteem, and dedication

**a·dore´** *vi., vt.* to cherish with unwavering affection; to be especially fond of —**a·dor´er** *n.* —**a·dor´ing·ly** *adv.*

**a·dorn´** *vt.* to decorate or embellish with ornaments; to beautify —**a·dorn´er** *n.* —**a·dorn´ment** *n.*

**ad·re´nal** *adj.* near the kidneys; of the adrenal glands —*n.* an adrenal gland

**adrenal gland** either of two small endocrine glands located above the kidneys

**ad·ren´al·in, ad·ren´al·ine** *n.* a stimulant secreted by the adrenal glands

**a·drift´** *adj., adv.* wandering; lacking direction or purpose

**a·droit´** *adj.* clever or resourceful, especially intellectually; expert —**a·droit´ly** *adv.* —**a·droit´ness** *n.*

**ad·sorb´** *vt.* to retain a gas or liquid on the surface, as contrasted with *absorb* —**ad·sorb´ent** *adj.* —**ad·sorp´tion** *n.* —**ad·sorp´tive** *adj.*

**ad´u·la´tion** *n.* base flattery; extravagant praise —**ad´u·late** *vt.* —**ad´u·la·to·ry** *adj.*

**a·dult´** *adj.* fully developed; full-grown; mature in manners and attitude; of or for a mature person. *adult education* —*n.* a fully grown person or animal; one who has attained legal majority

**a·dul´ter·ant** *n.* a substance that tends to contaminate

**a·dul´ter·ate´** *adj.* impure; contaminated —*vt.* to make impure by adding an undesirable substance; to lessen the value of by adding inferior ingredients —**a·dul´ter·a´tion** *n.* —**a·dul´ter·a·tor** *n.*

**a·dul´ter·ous** *adj.* characterized by or relating to adultery —**a·dul´ter·ous·ly** *adv.*

**a·dul´ter·y** *n.* sexual unfaithfulness by one who is married —**a·dul´ter·er** *n.*

**ad va·lo·rem** in proportion to the value, as *an ad valorem tax*

**ad·vance´** *adj.* before due: *an advance payment*; before the rest: *an advance party* —*n.* progress; an improvement; a prepayment or loan of money not yet due or earned —*vi.* to make progress or move forward; to rise in rank or value, etc. —*vt.* to put or move forward; to offer or promote, as a suggestion; to pay or loan money before it is due

**ad·vanced´** *adj.* at the front or ahead: *an advanced student*; late in the progression of events: *the advanced stage of a project*

**ad·vance·ment** *n.* furtherance or promotion: *the advancement of science*

**ad·van´tage** *n.* a circumstance favorable to success; superiority; a gain or benefit —*vt.* to benefit; to be of service to —**take advantage of** put to good use; to exploit

**ad´van·ta´geous** *adj.* providing advantage; beneficial —**ad´van·ta´geous·ly** *adv.* —**ad´van·ta´geous·ness** *n.*

**ad´vent** *n.* a coming, as of an important event

**ad·ven´ture** *n.* an exciting undertaking, often involving hazard; a speculative commercial venture —*vi.* to venture; to take risks —*vt.* to place at risk —**ad·ven´tur·er** *n.*

**ad·ven´ture·some** *adj.* inclined to take part in risky or hazardous activities —**ad·ven´ture·some·ly** *adv.* —**ad·ven´ture·some·ness** *n.*

**ad·ven´tur·ous** *adj.* inclined to take risks; characterized by risk; hazardous —**ad·ven´tur·ous·ly** *adv.* —**ad·ven·tur·ous·ness** *n.*

**ad´verb´** *n.* word that qualifies a verb, adjective, or other adverb, as to define time, place, manner, degree, etc. —**ad·verb´i·al** *adj.*

**ad´ver·sar´y** *n.* an opponent; one who is openly antagonistic —**ad´ver·sar´i·al** *adj.*

**ad´verse, ad·verse´** *adj.* acting against, as *adverse commentary*; unpropitious or unfavorable, as *adverse weather*, moving in opposition: *an adverse current* —**ad·verse´ly** *adv.* —**ad·verse´ness** *n.*

**ad·ver´si·ty** *n.* a state of hardship; difficult circumstances; misfortune

**ad´ver·tise´** *vi.* to proclaim publicly, as to create awareness of a product or business; to publicly request something such as living quarters or employment —*vt.* to give public notice of; to proclaim the quality or advantage of so as to sell —**ad´ver·tis·er** *n.*

**ad·ver·tise´ment** *n.* public notice in a periodical or the broadcast media to sell a product, announce an event, etc.

**ad´ver·tis·ing** *n.* any method of publicizing a product, event, etc.; the business of publicizing

**ad·vice´** *n.* counsel or guidance

**ad·vis´a·ble** *adj.* deserving of recommendation; opportune **—ad·vis´a·bil´i·ty, ad·vis´a·ble·ness** *n.* **—ad·vis´a·bly** *adv.*

**ad·vise´** *vi.* to offer advice *—vt.* to give advice; to recommend to; to notify or inform of **—ad·vis´er, ad·vi·sor** *n.*

**ad·vised´** *adj.* deliberately considered; prudent; informed **—ad·vise´ment** *n.*

**ad·vis´ed·ly** *adv.* with forethought; carefully; prudently

**ad·vi´so·ry** *adj.* having power to advise; offered as advice *—n.* a recommendation; an information bulletin, as *a weather advisory*

**ad´vo·ca·cy** *n.* the act of pleading a cause; support for a cause

**ad´vo·cate** *n.* one who pleads for another; one who argues a cause; a supporter; a lawyer *—vt.* to support or defend; to promote a cause or point of view; to argue in favor of **—ad´vo·ca·tor** *n.* **—ad·voc´a·to·ry** *adj.*

**adze, adz** *n.* a hand tool similar to an axe with the blade at right angles to its handle, used for trimming and dressing lumber, etc.

**ae´gis** *n.* in Greek mythology, the shield of Zeus; protective power; sponsorship or patronage

**aer´ate** *vt.* to oxygenate; to charge with gas; to purify by exposure to air, as for drinking water **—aer·a´tion** *n.* **—aer´a·tor** *n.*

**aer´i·al** *adj.* of or like air; performed in the air or by an aircraft, as *aerial photography*; living and growing in the air; insubstantial or spiritual *—n. (Brit.)* a device used for the transmission or reception of radio or television signals

**aer´i·al·ist** *n.* an aerial acrobat; a tightrope walker or trapeze artist

**aer·ie** *n.* the nest of a predatory bird, as the eagle; any dwelling at a high elevation

**aer´o·dy·nam´ics** *n.* the study of bodies moving in the air, esp. of the force of the atmosphere on objects in motion **—aer´o·dy·nam´i·cist** *n.*

**aer´o·nau´tics** *pl. n.* the science of aviation; the study of the design and operation of aircraft **—aer´o·naut** *n.* **—aer·o·nau´tic, aer·o·nau´ti·cal** *adj.* **—aer·o·nau´ti·cal·ly** *adv.*

**aer´o·plane** *(Brit.) n.* a fixed-wing aircraft

**aer´o·sol** *adj.* pertaining to a substance under pressure that is dispensed as a fine spray *—n.* a suspension of fine particles; a substance contained under pressure with an inert gas propellent which produces a fine spray when released

**aerosol bomb** *n.* container holding liquid under pressure to be released as spray or foam

**aer´o·space** *adj.* of the Earth's atmosphere and near outer space; of the science and technology of aeronautics and space flight *—n.*

**aerospace industry** the sector of commerce concerned with the design and manufacture of equipment for use in space

**aes´thete** *n.* a connoisseur of beauty, culture, fine art, etc.; one overly devoted to refinement and pretentious in appreciation of art and culture

**aes·thet´ic, aes·thet´i·cal** *adj.* appreciating the artistic or beautiful; characterized by fine taste **—aes·thet´i·cal·ly** *adv.*

**aes·thet´ics** *n.* the philosophical consideration or study of the expression of beauty and art, and the feelings they evoke **—aes·the·ti´cian** *n.* **—aes·thet´i·cism** *n.*

**a·far´** *adv.* remotely; from a distance

**af´fa·ble** *adj.* pleasant; friendly; courteous of manner; amiable **—af´fa·bil´i·ty** *n.* **—af´fa·bly** *adv.*

**af·fair´** *n.* a thing done or to be done; a bit of business; a social gathering; a minor dispute; a small matter; a vague or indefinite thing; a romantic liaison

**af·fect´** *vt.* to influence; to change; to arouse emotion; be partial to; to make a pretense of; to infect, as a disease *—n.* an emotion, as distinguished from thought or action

**af´fec·ta´tion** *n.* a calculated or elaborate pretense; an artificial manner

**af·fect´ed** *adj.* acted upon, as by a drug or disease; influenced emotionally; simulated so as to impress others; speaking or acting in an unnatural or insincere manner

**af·fec´tion** *n.* good or kind feelings for another; a fondness for anything; love **—af·fec´tion·al** *adj.* **—af·fec´tion·al·ly** *adv.*

**af·fec´tion·ate** *adj.* expressing fondness or love; loving **—af·fec´tion·ate·ly** *adv.*

**af´fi·da´vit** *n.* a written statement made under oath and notarized

**af·fil´i·ate** *vt.* to take in as a member; to join or associate with *—vi.* to become allied or associated *—n.* a person or organization allied with another as a member, partner, etc. **—af·fil´i·a´tion** *n.*

**af·fin´i·ty** *n.* any natural attraction; a close relationship; a platonic or spiritual attraction existing between persons; the force by which chemical elements are attracted to form compounds; in biology, a resemblance that suggests common origin

**af·firm´** *vt.* to declare or claim to be true; to ratify or confirm, as a legal judgment, a statute, etc. *—vi.* in law, to make a formal declaration not under oath **—af·firm´a·bly** *adv.* **—af·firm´a·ble** *adj.* **—af´fir·ma´tion** *n.*

**af·firm´a·tive** *adj.* positive, supportive *—n.* a word expressing confirmation or agreement **—af·firm´a·tive·ly** *adv.*

**affirmative action** a program of practical measures for correcting past discrimination, as in education or employment

**af·fix´** *vt.* to attach or fasten, as a label; to add, as the signature on a letter; to attribute, as responsibility or blame —**af´fix** *n.* something added

**af·fla´tus** *n.* articulation of divine knowledge; any creative impulse

**af·flict´** *vt.* to oppress; to rack with pain; to cause distress —**af·flict´er** *n.* —**af·flic´tive** *adj.* —**af·flic´tive·ly** *adv.*

**af·flic´tion** *n.* a state of pain or distress; that which causes suffering; a misfortune; a calamity

**af´flu·ence** *n.* wealth; abundance; a rich supply

**af´flu·ent** *adj.* wealthy; prosperous; generously supplied; abounding —*n.* a wealthy person; a sream or river that flows into another —**af´flu·ent·ly** *adv.*

**af·ford´** *vt.* to be able to pay or meet expenses; to undergo without inconvenience: *we can afford the time off now; to confer on or grant: it affords them pleasure* —**af·ford·a·bil´i·ty** *n.* —**af·ford´a·ble** *adj.* —**af·ford´a·bly** *adv.*

**af·front´** *n.* an intentional insult or indignity —*vt.* to insult flagrantly; treat with arrogance

**a·fi·cio·na´do** *n.* an enthusiastic fan, as of a sport

**a·field´** *adv.* to the field or off the usual path: said, often disapprovingly, of ideas or endeavors which are thought to have gone astray

**a·fire´** *adj.*, *adv.* on fire: often figuratively, of one who exhibits great enthusiasm for an idea or task

**a·float´** *adj.*, *adv.* resting on the surface of a liquid; drifting with no fixed plan; the state of an organization: *they will have a difficult time remaining afloat*

**a·foot´** *adj.*, *adv.* on foot; walking; on the move or progressing: *something is afoot*

**a·fore´men·tioned** *adj.* stated earlier; referred to previously

**a·fore´said** *adj.* said before

**a·fore´thought** *adj.* premeditated; considered earlier

**a·foul´** *adj.*, *adv.* entangled —**run afoul of** get into difficulty with

**a·fraid´** *adj.* filled with fear or apprehension: *afraid of the dark*; anxious about something: *afraid to show emotion*; regretful: *I´m afraid there´s been a mistake*

**a·fresh´** *adv.* once again; anew

**aft** *adj.* of the stern of a vessel —*adv.* toward the rear; astern

**af´ter** *adj.* subsequent; succeeding in time or place —*adv.* at a later time —*prep.* farther back, or later than: *salad was served after the soup*; in succession: *it happens time after time*; in pursuit of: *searching after knowledge*; concerning: *to inquire after someone* —*conj.* following the time that: *after dinner, we took a walk*

**aft´er·burn´er** *n.* a device in a jet engine that ignites unburned gas and increases thrust

**af´ter·ef·fect** *n.* a symptom which follows the initial effects of a medicine, an ailment, etc.

**af´ter·glow** *n.* the glow which remains after a light source has disappeared, as in the sky after sunset; an agreeable or pleasant feeling retained after an enjoyable experience

**af´ter-hours´** *adj.* following the normal business day; of an establishment that remains open past the legal closing time, as a club or tavern

**af´ter·im·age** *n.* the impression which remains after stimulus is removed

**af´ter·life** *n.* life after death

**af´ter·math** *n.* the consequence or result of an action

**af´ter·noon** *n.* the part of the day between noon and sunset

**af´ter·shock** *n.* tremors that follow in the wake of an earthquake

**af´ter·taste** *n.* a taste remaining in the mouth after eating a particular food

**af´ter·thought** *n.* a notion occurring after a decision or action

**af´ter·ward, af´ter·wards** *adv.* subsequently; in the time succeeding an event

**a·gain´** *adv.* one more; at another time; repeated; furthermore: *again the poor roads may delay us*

**a·gainst´** *prep.* in contact and pressing upon; in comparison to in opposition to

**a·gape´** *adj.*, *adv.* open-mouthed anything left open, as a door

**a´gar** *n.* a gelatinous substance obtained from seaweed employed as a culture medium and as a food product

**ag´ate** *n.* a variegated quartz; a child´s marble; in printing, 5¼ point type

**age** *n.* a distinct stage of life; a time in history; the condition of being old —*vi.* to ripen or mature —*vt.* to cause to grow old —**of age** old enough to be legally responsible

**a´ged** *adj.* advanced in years; characteristic of old age —*n.* elderly persons collectively —**aged´** *adj.* at the age of; brought to a desired state by time, as *an aged steals* —**ag´ed·ly** *adv.* —**ag´ed·ness** *n.*

**age´ism** *n.* discrimination based on age; undue preoccupation with age

**age´less** *adj.* seeming not to change with the passage of time; not limited by time; eternal —**age´less·ly** *adv.* —**age´less·ness** *n.*

**a´gen·cy** *n.* an active force; the means by which something is done; the business of acting for others; the office of an agent; a division of a governmental department

**a·gen´da** *n.*, *pl.* **a·gen´da** or **a·gen´dum** a catalogue of aims or goals; a schedule of duties, programs, or events to be discussed or carried out, especially of a business meeting

**a´gent** *n.* person or thing that serves to change; one

who acts for another; an authorized representative

**ag·glom´er·ate´** *adj.* densely clustered; gathered into a mass —*n.* things thrown together without discrimination; fused volcanic rock —*vi., vt.* to form into a mass —**ag·glom·er·a´tion** *n.* —**ag·glom´er·a·tive** *adj.*

**ag·glu´ti·nate** *adj.* joined together, as by adhesion —*vi., vt.* to join, as with glue; to form a new word or term by combining two words; to mass together, as cells, by adhesion —**ag·glu´ti·nant** *adj.*

**ag·glu·ti·na´tion** *n.* a mass formed by adhesion; a combination of word elements which form a new word —**ag·glu´ti·na·tive** *adj.*

**ag·gran´dize** *vt.* to make great or greater; to make to seem greater; to exalt —**ag·gran´dize·ment** *n.* —**ag·gran´diz·er** *n.*

**ag´gra·vate´** *vt.* to make worse; to make more burdensome; to exasperate or annoy —**ag´gra·va´tion** *n.* —**ag´gra·va·tor** *n.*

**ag´gre·gate´** *adj.* gathered together; forming a dense cluster; a mixture of mineral fragments existing naturally, as *aggregate rock* —*n.* a collection; an entire amount; a mixture of mineral fragments, as stones used in making concrete —*vt.* to bring together or collect into a mass; to total or amount to —**ag´gre·gate·ly** *adv.* —**ag´gre·ga´tion** *n.*

**ag·gres´sion** *n.* an unprovoked act of hostility; the instinct to act in a forceful manner; assertiveness

**ag·gres´sive** *adj.* characterized by or disposed to hostile or belligerent action; bold and assertive, as *an aggressive salesman* —**ag·gres´sive·ly** *adv.* —**ag·gres´sive·ness** *n.* —**ag·gres´sor** *n.*

**ag·grieve´** *vt.* to cause sorrow; to distress

**a·ghast´** *adj.* horrified; astonished

**ag´ile** *adj.* exhibiting physical quickness and dexterity; mentally alert —**ag´ile·ly** *adv.* —**ag´ile·ness, a·gil´i·ty** *n.*

**ag´i·tate´** *vi.* to stir public interest in by incessant discussion or debate —*vt.* to stir up, attempt to excite; to perturb or trouble; to shake or move sharply and irregularly —**ag´i·tat·ed·ly** *adv.* —**ag´i·ta´tion** *n.* —**ag´i·ta´tor** *n.*

**a·glow´** *adj., adv.* glowing

**ag·nos´tic** *adj.* claiming the inability to prove the existence of God, an afterlife, the mysteries of the universe, etc.; skeptical —*n.* one who embraces the theory of agnosticism; a doubter or questioner

**ag·nos´ti·cism** *n.* the doctrine that man does not have any valid knowledge; the theory that origins must remain unknown; the belief that the existence of God cannot be proved

**a·gog´** *adj., adv.* excited; agitated; in a state of impatient curiosity

**a·gon´ic** *adj.* forming no angle —**agonic line** an imaginary line along the surface of the earth where magnetic north and true north coincide

**ag´o·nize** *vi.* to sustain extreme distress; to struggle over —*vt.* to subject to torture; to cause torment, as *an agonizing decision* —**ag´o·niz·ing** *adj.* **ag´o·niz·ing·ly** *adv.*

**ag´o·ny** *n.* suffering caused by extreme physical or mental pain; an intense emotion; a violent effort

**ag·o·ra·pho´bi·a** *n*· the fear of open spaces

**a·grar´i·an** *adj.* pertaining to the distribution of lands; relating to or furthering agricultural interests —*n.* an advocate for the equitable distribution of farm land or farm income

**a·gree´** *vi.* to be of like mind; to consent; to correspond, be equal; to come to terms on, as of a contract —*vt.* to acknowledge

**a·gree´a·ble** *adj.* pleasurable to the senses; amiable; in accord with —**a·gree·a·bil·i·ty, a·gree´a·ble·ness** *n.* —**a·gree´a·bly** *adj.*

**a·greed´** *adj.*. brought into harmony; resolved by consent

**a·gree´ment** *n.* an understanding between two or more parties; a contract

**ag´ri·bus´i·ness** *n.* non-farm activities or enterprises associated with agriculture, such as the processing, packaging, and distribution of food, or the manufacturing of farm machinery

**ag´ri·cul´ture** *n.* the science or business that deals with the cultivation of the land, the breeding and raising of livestock, etc. —**ag·ri·cul´tur·al** *adj.* —**ag·ri·cul´tur·al·ly** *adv.*

**ag·ri·cul´tur·al·ist, ag·ri·cul´tur·ist** *n.* one who makes a study of or engages in the business of agriculture

**a·gron´o·my, ag·ro·nom´ics** *n.* the application of scientific principles to the raising of field crops —**ag·ro·nom´ic, ag·ro·nom´i·cal** *adj.* —**a·gron´o·mist** *n.*

**a·ground´** *adj., adv.* on the shore stranded —**run aground** of a vessel which touches land in shallow water

**a´gue** *n.* chills and fever

**ah** *interj.* an exclamation of surprise success, gratification, etc.

**a·ha´** *interj.* an exclamation of triumph, derision, etc.

**a·head´** *adv.* in advance; at the front; early or before due: *arrived ahead of time* —**get ahead** to improve one´s lot financially or socially

**a·hem´** *interj.* a sound made in the throat to gain attention

**aid** *n.* the act or effect of providing assistance; one who assists —*vi., vt.* to provide assistance to

**aide** *n.* a confidential assistant usually to a person of high rank in the military, business, politics, etc.

**AIDS** *Acquired Immune Deficiency Syndrome n.* a viral disease that attacks the body´s immune system

**ail** *vi.* be in poor health; to feel pain or distress —*vt.* to affect with pain or distress —**ail´ing** *adj.*

**ail´ment** *n.* a slight illness of body or mind

**aim** *vi.* to have a purpose: *aim to improve;* to point, as a firearm *—vt.* to point at or act against a person object, etc.: *aim your remarks to the audience —n.* the act of aiming an intention

**aim´less** *adj.* without purpose **—aim´less·ly** *adv.* — **aim´less·ness** *n.*

**air** *n.* the atmosphere that surrounds the earth; a light breeze; tune or melody; a characteristic appearance or manner; an affectation *—vt.* to ventilate or expose to the air; to announce abroad: *give air to one´s feelings* **—up in the air** undecided

**air bag** a safety device designed to protect the occupants of an automobile from being thrown forward in the event of a collision

**air´borne´** *adj.* carried by air; in the air, flying

**air´ brake´** *n.* a brake controlled by compressed air

**air cham´ber** *n.* a compartment filled with air such as in a hydraulic system in which air is compressed and expanded to regulate the flow of a fluid

**air´ con·di´tion·ing** *n.* the process by which the temperature and humidity of inside air can be regulated **–air´·con·di´tioned** *adj.* **–air con·di´tion·er** *n.*

**air´craft´** *n.* flying machine

**aircraft carrier** a ship for carrying airplanes which take off from and land on its deck

**air´drop** *n.* personnel or supplies delivered by parachute from an aircraft *—vt.* to discharge personnel or supplies by parachute from an aircraft

**air ex·press´** *n.* shipment by air, usually of small packages for overnight delivery

**air´frame´** *n.* the structural framework of an aircraft, excluding the engine

**air´freight´** *n.* freight shipped by air

**air gun** *n.* a weapon or tool that operates on compressed air

**air´hole, air´ hole** *n.* a hole made by air under pressure or by which air is allowed to escape; a breathing hole in ice covering a body of water

**air´ing** *n.* exposure to air, as to freshen or dry; a stroll outdoors; a public debate; a broadcast on radio or television

**air´lift´** *n.* the movement of supplies by air *—vt., vi.*

**air line** *n.* a tube, hose, pipe, etc. for supplying air, as for an internal combustion engine or a deep-sea diver

**air´line** *n.* an organization operating aircraft for the transport of passengers and cargo; the routes over which aircraft travel

**air´lock** *n.* an intermediate chamber with carefully controlled air pressure which provides a link between a vessel and it´s surrounding environment, as on a submarine or spacecraft

**air´mail´** *n.* mail carried by airplane *—vt.*

**air´plane´** *(US) n.* a fixed-wing aircraft

**air pocket** *n.* a vertical current of air which can cause aircraft passing through it to rise or fall suddenly

**air´port´** *n.* a base for aircraft

**air pres´sure** *n.* pressure of the atmosphere

**air pump** *n.* a device for compressing, moving, or removing air

**air´speed** *n.* the speed of an aircraft measured in relation to the surrounding air rather than to the ground

**air´space´** *n.* the area above a nation´s territory and that is subject to its jurisdiction

**air´strip** *n.* an airport; a stretch of straight, level ground used by aircraft to take off and land

**air´tight** *adj.* not allowing movement of air in or out; completely closed, with no weakness: *an airtight alibi*

**air´waves** *n. pl.* the medium through which radio and television signals travel

**air´worthy** *adj.* of an aircraft which is in proper condition for flight

**air´y** *adj.* open to the atmosphere; breezy; porous

**aisle** *n.* a narrow passageway between sections of seats, rows of people, etc.

**a·jar´** *adj., adv.* partly open, as a door

**a·kin´** *adj., adv.* related by blood; similar in some fashion

**à la** after the manner of

**al´a·bas´ter** *n.* a variety of whitish gypsum used for carved statuary, vases, etc. *—adj.* smooth and white, like alabaster

**à la carte** according to the bill of fare; items, usually food, that are priced and selected individually

**a·lac´ri·ty** *n.* willingness; readiness; prompt and lively **—a·lac´ri·tous** *adj.*

**à la mode´** according to the fashion; in food service, usually denoting a dish served with ice cream as *pie à la mode*

**a·larm´** *n.* a warning of danger; a device or sound which alerts or warns; a sudden fright or apprehension *—vt.* to warn of danger; to frighten

**a·larm´ing** *adj.* causing fright or apprehension — **a·larm´ing·ly** *adv.*

**a·larm´ist** *n.* one easily alarmed; one who attempts to excite others without just cause

**a·las´** *interj.* an expression of disappointment or sorrow

**al´ba·core** *n.* a tunny; a long-finned salt water food fish of the tuna family

**al´ba·tross´** *n.* sea bird of the South Seas; a symbol of hardship or affliction

**al·be´it** *conj.* although; even though; notwithstanding

**al·bi´no** *n.* a person, animal, or plant lacking natural pigmentation

**al´bum** *n.* a blank book for holding a collection of photographs, autographs, stamps etc.; a sound recording containing multiple selections

**al·bu´men** *n.* any of a number of proteins as found in

eggs, milk, etc. **—al•bu´mi•nous** *adj.*

**al´che•my** *n.* an ancient art dedicated to unlocking the mysteries of universal healing, eternal youth and the changing of base metals into gold

**al´co•hol** *n.* a clear liquid used as a solvent or intoxicant; the intoxicant contained in beer, wine and distilled liquor; any beverage containing alcohol

**al•co•hol´ic** *adj.* containing alcohol; caused by alcohol or alcoholism *—n.* one suffering from alcoholism

**al´co•hol•ism** *n.* a condition marked by the habitual and excessive consumption of alcoholic beverages

**al´cove** *n.* a recess connected to a large room; a secluded retreat

**ale** *n.* a type of beer

**ale´house** *n.* a place where beer is sold for consumption on premises

**a•lert´** *adj.* ready for action; bright lively *—n.* a warning signal; an attitude of preparedness *—vt.* to prepare for action; to warn of an impending threat **—on the alert** prepared; watchful **—a•lert´ly** *adv.* **—a•lert´ness** *n.*

**al•fres´co, al fres´co** *adj.* occurring out of doors, as *dining alfresco,* picnic *—adv.* in the open air

**al´gae** *pl. n., sing.* **al´ga** any of the number of simple organisms that live and grow in water

**al´ge•bra** *n.* a mathematical system that uses highly formalized rules of procedure and symbols to represent numbers **—al•ge•bra´ic, al•ge•bra´i•cal** *adj.* **—al•ge•bra´i•cal•ly** *adv.*

**al´go•rithm** *n.* a systematic method of problem solving; a set of computer instructions that has a specific beginning and end

**a´li•as** *n.* an assumed name

**al´i•bi** *n.* a defensive plea by one accused that establishes whereabouts at the time of a crime; an excuse

**a´li•en** *adj.* foreign; owing allegiance to another country; strange or unfamiliar; inconsistent or contrary: *conduct alien to his character —n.* a person who is not a citizen of the country in which he resides; a person of another country; a stranger

**al´ien•a•ble** *adj.* that can be legally transferred, as property

**al´ien•ate´** *vt.* to antagonize or estrange; to transfer property or title to another

**al´ien•a´tion** *n.* a feeling of not belonging; indifference

**a•light´** *adj., adv.* lighted, as a fire *—vi.* to get off or dismount; to descend and land or perch, as a bird from flight

**a•lign´** *vt.* to bring or arrange into a line; to adjust, as *to align the wheels of a car;* to identify with a cause: *aligned with the conservationists —vi.* to come into line **—a•lign´ment** *n.*

**a•like´** *adj.* matching in some way; equivalent *—adv.* in like manner

**al´i•ment** *n.* food, nourishment; something that provides nourishment **—al•i•men´tal** *adj.* **—al•i•men´tal•ly** *adv.*

**al•i•men´ta•ry** *adj.* pertaining to food or nutrition; supplying nutrition **—al•i•men•ta´tion** *n.*

**alimentary canal** the path traveled by food through the body

**al´i•mo•ny** *n.* an allowance for living expenses paid by one party to the other of a dissolved marriage

**a•line´** *vi.* to come into line *—vt.* to arrange or bring into line; to come or bring into agreement with **—a•line´ment** *n.*

**a•live´** *adj.* functioning; alert; in existence; animated **—alive with** abounding: *a campus alive with students*

**al´ka•li´** *n.* a soluble substance that neutralizes acids **—al´ka•line** *adj.* **—al•ka•lin´i•ty** *n.*

**al´ka•loid´** *n.* an alkaline substance in plants, etc.

**all** *adj.* entire; greatest possible: *in all respects;* primarily; *the giraffe is all neck and legs —n.* entirety: *he gave his all —pron.* everyone or each one; everything *—adv.* entirely; exclusively: *it's all about the economy;* for each; *the score is tied at one all* **—above all** most important **—after all** nevertheless **—all but** almost: *the job is all but finished* **—all in** tired **—all in all** all together; all things considered **—all out** without constraint: *an all out effort* **—at all** under any condition; in any way

**al•lay´** *vt.* to calm; to reduce in intensity, alleviate

**al´le•ga´tion** *n.* an assertion made without proof

**al•lege´** *vt.* to attest; to assert, especially without proof; to plead in support or denial of a claim **—al•lege´a•ble** *adj.* **—al•lege´er** *n.*

**al•leg´ed** *adj.* purported or asserted, but not proven **—al•leg´ed•ly** *adv.*

**al•le´giance** *n.* loyalty, as to a cause; an obligation of loyalty, as to a government or private organization

**al•le•gor´ic, al•le•gor´i•cal** *adj.* pertaining to or consisting of allegory **—al•le•gor´i•cal•ly** *adv.*

**al´le•go´ry** *n.* literature or art that uses people, animals, etc. as symbolic representations of abstract concepts; the symbols employed in such literature; any symbolic representation: *the owl is an allegory for wisdom*

**al´ler•gen** *n.* any substance capable of producing an allergic reaction

**al•ler´gic** *adj.* caused by an allergy; susceptible to, as an allergen; having an aversion: *he seems allergic to hard work*

**al´ler•gist** *n.* a physician who specializes in the diagnosis and treatment of allergies

**al´ler•gy** *n.* unusual sensitivity to certain substances, such as dust or pollen

**al•le´vi•ate´** *vt.* to relieve or make easier to bear; to lessen **—al•le´vi•a´tion** *n.* **—al•le´vi•a´tor** *n.*

**al•le´vi•a´tive, al•le´vi•a´to•ry** *adj.* tending to relieve, as in severity

**al´ley** *n.* a narrow street or passageway, esp. between or behind buildings **—al´ley·way** *n.*

**al·li´ance** *n.* a formal agreement, as between countries or persons; a union, as by treaty, blood, or marriage

**al·lied´** *adj.* closely related; associated or affiliated, as by treaty or relationship

**al´li·ga´tor** *n.* an American or Chinese reptile, similar to the crocodile with a shorter, wider snout

**al·lit´er·a´tion** *n.* a series of words beginning with the same consonant sound: "Peter Piper picked a peck..." **—al·lit´er·a·te** *vi., vt.* **—al·lit´er·a·tive** *adj.* **—al·lit´er·a·tive·ly** *adv.*

**al´lo·cate** *vt.* to allot or assign a share; to designate for a particular purpose

**al´lo·ca´tion** *n.* a thing or amount set aside

**al·lot´** *vt.* to apportion to; to distribute by lot **—al·lot´ment** *n.*

**all´-out´** *adj.* wholehearted, concentrated

**al·low´** *vt.* permit to have, happen, do, etc.; to acknowledge as true; to provide for: *allow extra money for incidentals* **—allow for** consider a condition: *allow for his inexperience* **—al·low´a·ble** *adj.*

**al·low´ance** *n.* that which is allowed; a fixed amount available or budgeted for a particular purpose: *an allowance for expenses*; a discount: *a trade-in allowance*; a variance to be reckoned due to circumstances: *make an allowance for traffic*

**al´loy** *n.* a mixture of metals; anything that that lessens value or purity *—vt.* to combine metals to make an alloy; to make metal less pure by mixing

**all´-time´** *adj.* unparalleled to the present

**al·lude´** *vi.* to refer to casually or indirectly

**al·lure´** *vt.* to tempt; to attract *—vi.* to be subtly attractive or seductive *—n.* appeal; the ability to attract; a quality that attract **—al·lur´er** *n.*

**al·lur´ing** *adj.* appealing; attractive; seductive **—al·lur´ing·ly** *adv.* **—al·lur´ing·ness** *n.*

**al·lu´sion** *n.* a casual or indirect reference **—al·lu´sive** *adj.* **—al·lu´sive·ness** *n.*

**al·lu´vi·um** *n.* soil deposited gradually by a moving body of water **—al·lu´vi·al** *adj.*

**al´ly** *n.* a person or group unified with another for a common purpose *—vt.* to unite for a purpose *—vi.* to enter into an alliance; to become united or associated

**al´ma·nac** *n.* a yearly calendar or book containing information about the weather and tides, astronomical information, etc.

**al´mond** *adj.* of the taste, color, etc of an almond *—n.* the edible kernel of the fruit of the almond tree of the tree itself

**al´most, al·most´** *adj., adv.* close to very nearly

**alms** *n., sing. & pl.* a donation made to a poor person

**a·lone´** *adj., adv.* unaccompanied; detached; excluding all others; *he alone knows why*; unique, without equal

**a·long´** *adv.* tracing the length of progressing beside or in the company of; advanced in distance of time: *well along the way —prep.* following the path of: *along the road* **—all along** the entire time; from the beginning **—get along** to persevere in spite of adversity; to live in harmony

**a·loof´** *adj.* distant; in a reserved manner *—adv.* apart, but nearby **—a·loof´ly** *adv.* **—a·loof´ness** *n.*

**a·loud´** *adv.* audibly; out loud

**al´pha·bet´** *n.* the symbols of a written language

**al´pha·bet´ic, al´pha·bet´i·cal** *adj.* of a written language; arranged in the order of the alphabet **—al·pha·bet·i·za´tion** *n.* **—al´pha·bet·ize** *vt.*

**al´pha·nu·mer´ic** *adj.* comprised of both letters and numbers

**al·read´y** *adv.* by this time or a time referred to

**al´tar** *n.* a place for sacred offerings; the front of a church or focus of any place of worship

**al´ter** *vt.* to modify; to adjust the fit of a garment; to castrate or spay *—vi.* to undergo change, as in appearance or manner **—al´ter·a·ble** *adj.* **—al·ter·a´tion** *n.*

**al´ter·cate´** *vi.* to quarrel; to argue bitterly **—al´ter·ca´tion** *n.*

**al´ter·nate** *adj.* every other; following by turns *—vt.* to arrange or use in turn *—vi.* to occur by turns; to take turns *—n.* a temporary substitute **—al´ter·nate·ly** *adv.* **—al´ter·nate·ness** *n.*

**al´ter·na´tion** *n.* a changing back and forth from one condition or state to another

**al·ter´na·tive** *adj.* providing a choice *—n.* a choice between two things; one of the options available; something that must be decided: *what is the alternative?* **—al·ter´na·tive·ly** *adv.*

**al·though´** *conj.* even though

**al·tim´e·ter** *n.* an instrument for measuring altitude

**al´ti·tude´** *n.* the height or elevation from a reference point, as above ground or sea level; in astronomy, the angle of a celestial body in relation to the horizon **—al·ti·tu´di·nal** *adj.*

**al´to´** *n.* the musical range between tenor and mezzo-soprano

**al´to·geth´er** *adv.* in all; all things being considered

**al´tru·ism** *n.* unselfish regard for the welfare of others **—al´tru·ist** *n.* **—al·tru·is´tic** *adj.* **—al·tru·is´ti·cal·ly** *adv.*

**a·lum´na** *n., pl.* **a·lum´nae** a female who has attended or graduated from a school

**a·lum´nus** *n., pl.* **a·lum´ni** a person, esp. a male, who has attended or graduated from a school

**al´ways** *adv.* for all time; every time

**A·M·, amplitude modulation** a means of radio broadcasting

**a·mal´gam** *n.* a combination of mercury and another metal; any mixture or combination

**a·mal´ga·mate** *vt.* to combine with mercury; to unite

or integrate: *amalgated industries* –*vi.* to become combined; to mix with another metal **–a·mal´ga·ma·tive** *adj.* **–a·mal´ga·ma·tor** *n.*

**a·man´u·en´sis** *n., pl.* **a·man´u·en´ses** one employed to copy manuscripts or to take dictation; a secretary

**a·mass´** *vt.* to accumulate for oneself, as wealth – **a·mass´a·ble** *adj.* **–a·mass´er** *n.* **–a·mass´ment** *n.*

**am´a·teur** *adj.* of that done or performed by one lacking professional skill or standing –*n.* one who engages in an activity for pleasure only, rather than for profit; one who lacks the skill of a professional **–am´a·teur·ism** *n.*

**am·a·teur´ish** *adj.* lacking the skill of a professional **–am·a·teur´ish·ly** *adv.* **–am·a·teur´ish·ness** *n.*

**a·maze´** *vt.* to fill with wonder or surprise; to astonish **–a·maz´ed·ly** *adv.* **–a·maz´ed·ness, a·maze´ment** *n.*

**am·bas´sa·dor** *n.* the highest ranking diplomat in an embassy **–am·bas·sa·do´ri·al** *adj.* **–am·bas´sa·dor·ship** *n.*

**am´bi·ance, am´bi·ence** *n.* the character of a place; atmosphere

**am´bi·dex´trous** *adj.* able to use both hands equally well; skillful, dexterous **–am·bi·dex·ter´i·ty, am´bi·dex´trous** *n.* **–am´bi·dex´trous·ly** *adv.*

**am´bi·ent** *adj.* encompassing; of the surrounding area

**am·big´u·ous** *adj.* not clear; vague; open to misinterpretation; possible to be understood in more than one way **–am´bi·gu´i·ty** *n.*

**am·bi´tion** *n.* a firm aspiration to attain a particular goal; a desired goal; passion or energy, as for work or play

**am·bi´tious** *adj.* marked by aspiration; desirous; eager; difficult: *an ambitious agenda* **–am·bi´tious·ly** *adv.* **–am·bi´tious·ness** *n.*

**am·biv´a·lent** *adj.* uncertain, especially as related to contradictory emotions; unsure how to proceed – **am·biv´a·lence** *n.* **–am·biv´a·len·cy** *adj.* **–am·biv´a·lent·ly** *adv.*

**am´bu·lance** *n.* a vehicle for transporting the sick or injured

**am´bu·lant** *adj.* moving about

**am´bu·late** *vi.* to walk or move from place to place **–am·bu·la´tion** *n.* **–am´bu·la·tive** *adj.*

**am´bu·la·to´ry** *adj.* able to walk; able to move about

**am´bus·cade´** *n.* an ambush; a hiding place –*vt.* to attack suddenly from hiding **–am´bus·cad·er** *n.*

**am´bush** *n.* a surprise attack from hiding; those hiding in wait; a deception or trap –*vt.* to lie in wait for; to attack from hiding

**a·mel´io·rate´** *vi., vt.* to make or become better; to improve **–a·mel´io·rant** *n.* **–a·me·lio·ra´tion** *n.* **–a·mel´io·ra·tive** *adj.*

**a·men´a·ble** *adj.* agreeable; responsive, as to advice or authority; open to criticism **–a·me·na·bil´i·ty, a·me´na·ble·ness** *n.* **–a·me´na·bly** *adv.*

**a·mend´** *vt.* to improve; to change or correct; to free of fault or error –*vi.* to improve one's behavior **–a·mend´a·ble** *adj.* **–a·mend´a·ble·ness** *n.* **–a·mend´er** *n.*

**a·mend´a·to·ry** *adj.* serving to correct or improve

**a·mend´ment** *n.* a correction; a removal of fault or error; an addition to a document which alters or adds to it

**a·mends´** *pl. n.* compensation for a wrong; an apology

**a·men´i·ty** *n.* a pleasant quality; something that makes one more comfortable

**A·mer·i·ca´na** *n.* things typically American; papers, antiques, etc. associated with American history and customs

**A·mer´i·can·ism** *n.* a manner of speech, custom, etc. peculiar to the people of the United States; a fondness for or loyalty to the U.S. and its institutions

**am´e·thyst** *n.* bluish-violet type of quartz; a bluish-violet color

**a´mi·a·ble** *adj.* friendly; good-natured **–a·mi·a·bil´i·ty, a´mi·a·ble·ness** *n.*

**am´i·ca·ble** *adj.* agreeable; of a congenial manner; **–am·i·ca·bil´i·ty, am´i·ca·ble·ness** *n.* **–am´i·ca·bly** *adv.*

**a·mid´, a·midst´** *prep.* among; in the middle of

**a·mi´no ac´id** organic acid containing the amino group $NH_2$, part of the protein molecule

**a·miss´** *adj.* out of order; improper, faulty –*adv.* wrongly; in an improper fashion **–take amiss** to be offended

**am´i·ty** *n.* friendly relations; good will

**am´me·ter** *n.* an instrument for measuring the strength of an electric current

**am´mu·ni´tion** *n.* any projectile fired from a weapon; an explosive used as a weapon; information used to attack or defend

**am·ne´si·a** *n.* loss of memory due to shock or injury **–am·ne´si·ac** *n., adj.* **–am·ne´sic, am·nes´tic** *adj.*

**am´nes·ty** *n.* an official pardon, esp. for a political offender –*vt.* to grant a pardon to

**am´ni·on** *n.* the membranous sac surrounding a fetus

**a·moe´ba** *n.* a one celled protozoan, characterized by indefinite shape and reproduction by splitting **–a·moe´bic** *adj.*

**a·mong´, a·mongst´** *prep.* in the midst of; included within an array

**a·mor´al** *adj.* without recognition or concern of ethical distinction; lacking a sense of right or wrong **–a·mo·ral´i·ty** *n.* **–a·mor´al·ly** *adv.*

**am´o·rous** *adj.* loving; passionate; suggesting desire: *an amorous gaze*; connected with love: *an amorous letter* **–am´o·rous·ly** *adv.* **–am´o·rous·ness** *n.*

**a·mor´phous** *adj.* lacking definite form or shape; unorganized **–a·mor´phism, a·mor´phous·ness** *n.* **–a·mor´phous·ly** *adv.*

**am´or·tise** *(Brit.)* **am´or·tize** *(US)* *vt.* to discharge a debt by regular payments **—am´or·tis·a·ble, am´or·tiz·a·ble** *adj.* **—am·or·ti·sa´tion, am·or·ti·za´tion** *n.* **—am´or·tise´ment, am´or·tize´ment** *n.*

**a·mount´** *n.* a total; a quantity; the entire value or effect *—vi.* to add up to; be equal to: *the lack of response amounts to rejection*

**am·per´age, am´per·age** *n.* the strength of an electrical current

**am´pere** *n.* standard unit for measuring the strength of an electric current

**am´per·sand** *n.* a symbol (&) representing the word *and*

**am·phet´a·mine** *n.* a stimulant used as a medication for colds, depression, etc.

**am·phib´i·an** *n.* an animal that functions equally well in water or on land; a craft able to navigate on land or water; an airplane designed to take off from either land or water

**am·phib´i·ous** *adj.* living or operating in water and on land **—am·phib´i·ous·ly** *adj.* **—am·phib´i·ous·ness** *n.*

**am´phi·the´a·ter** *n.* a round building or room with tiers of seats rising from a central open stage or arena

**am´ple** *adj.* large in capacity, size, etc.; more than enough; sufficient to meet ones needs **—am´ple·ness** *n.* **—am´ply** *adv.*

**am´pli·fi´er** *n.* an electronic device that strengthens electrical impulses

**am´pli·fy** *vt.* to increase or expand **—am´pli·fi·ca´tion** *n.*

**am´pli·tude´** *n.* extent, largeness, fullness

**am´pul, am´pule** *n.* a vial of medication, often for injection

**am´pu·tate´** *vt.* to cut off, usually by surgery **—am´pu·ta´tion** *n.* **—am´pu·tee´** *n.*

**a·muck´** *adj.* in a frenzy; crazed *—adv.* in a barbarous manner

**am´u·let** *n.* a magical charm or talisman

**a·muse´** *vt.* to occupy pleasantly to entertain; to induce a smile or laughter **—a·mus´a·ble** *adj.* **—a·mus´er** *n.*

**a·mus´ing** *adj.* entertaining; causing laughter **—a·mus´ing·ly** *adv.* **—a·mus´ing·ness** *n.*

**a·muse´ment** *n.* a diversion; that which brings pleasure; a feeling of enjoyment brought on by a diversion

**amusement** park a recreational area featuring rides, refreshments, shows, etc.

**an** *adj.*, indef. art. each or any; an article before words beginning with a vowel sound

**a·nach´ro·nism** *n.* the representation of something existing or occuring out of it proper order; something placed out of its appropriate time **—a·nach·ro·nis´tic, a·nach´ro·nous** *adj.*

**an·aer´obe** *n.* a microorganism that flourishes in the absence of oxygen **—an·aer·o´bic** *adj.* **—an·aer·o´bic·al·ly** *adv.*

**an´aes·the´si·a** *(Brit.)* *n.* a loss of sensation caused by disease; a loss of sensitivity to pain produced by an anaesthetic

**an´aes·the´si·ol·o·gy** *(Brit.)* *n.* the study of anaesthesia and its effects **—an·aes·the·si·ol´o·gist** *(Brit.)* *n.*

**an´aes·thet´ic** *(Brit.)* *adj.* pertaining to anaesthesia; producing anaesthesia: making insensitive to pain —n; an agent that produces a loss of feeling **—an´aes·thet´i·cal·ly** *adv.*

**an·aes´the·tise** *(Brit.)* *vt.* to render insensitive to pain, as by admistering an anaesthetic **—an·aes·the·ti´za·tion** *n.*

**an·aes´the·tist** *(Brit.)* *n.* one who administers anaesthetics

**an´a·gram´** *n.* a word or phrase made by rearranging the letters of another word or phrase **—an·a·gram·mat´ic, an·a·gram·mat´i·cal** *adj.* **—an·a·gram·mat´i·cal·ly** *adv.*

**an·al·ge´si·a** *n.* a deadening of pain without loss of consciousness

**an·al·ge´sic** *n.* a medication that relieves pain *—adj.* causing analgesia

**an´a·log** *(US)* *adj.* of data represented by a continuous variable, such as for a slide rule, sound level, etc. **—an·a·log´ic, an·a·log´i·cal** *adj.* **—an·a·log´i·cal·ly** *adv.*

**analog device** *(US)* a mechanism which represents physical relationships, as a thermometer or analog computer

**an´a·logue** *(Brit.)* *adj.* of data represented by a continuous variable, such as for a slide rule, sound level, etc.

**analogue device** *(Brit.)* a mechanism which represents physical relationships, as a thermometer or analogue computer

**a·nal´o·gous** *adj.* similar in certain ways **—a·nal´o·gous·ly** *adv.* **—a·nal´o·gous·ness** *n.*

**a·nal´o·gy** *n.* a partial similarity; a comparison based on some similarity between two things **—a·nal´o·gist** *n.*

**a·nal´y·sis** *n.* the division of a thing into parts for examination

**an´a·lyst** *n.* one skilled in careful examination or study, as *a systems analyst*; a psychoanalyst

**an´a·lyt´ic, an·a·lyt´i·cal** *adj.* pertaining to analysis; separating into basic parts; expert in analysis, as *an analytical mind*; psychoanalytic **—an·a·lyt´i·cal·ly** *adv.*

**an·a·lyt´ics** *n.* the branch of logic concerned with analysis

**an´a·lyse** *(Brit.)*, **an´a·lyze** *(US)* *vt.* to break down into parts for detailed study; to make a chemical or mathematical analysis; to psychoanalyze **—an·a·ly·sa´tion, an·a·ly·za´tion** *n.*

**an·a·phy·lac´tic** *adj.* pertaining to a severe reaction to a usually harmless substance introduced into the body for the second time —**an·a·phy·lac´ti·cal·ly** *adv.*

**an·a·phy·lax´is** *n.* abnormal sensitivity to a substance, such as a drug or sting; anaphylactic shock

**anaphylactic shock** a severe allergic reaction caused by the second exposure to usually harmless substance

**an·ar´chic, an·ar´chi·cal** *adj.* endorsing or promoting anarchy; lacking order —**an·ar´chi·cal·ly** *adv.*

**an´arch·y** *n.* the absence of government or governmental authority —**an´ar·chism** *n.*—**an´arch·ist** *n.* —**an·ar·chis´tic** *adj.*

**a·nath´e·ma** *n.* an ecclesiastical ban, as of a person or book for heresy; a denunciation or condemnation; a person so condemned; anything greatly disliked

**a·nat´o·mist** *n.* a specialist in or student of anatomy

**a·nat´o·mise** *(Brit.)*, **a·nat´o·mize** *(US) vt.* to dissect for study; to study and analyze in great detail —**a·nat·o·mi·sa´tion, a·nat·o·mi·za´tion** *n.*

**a·nat´o·my** *n.* the scientific study of the structure of an animal or plant; the physical structure of an organism; dissection of a plant or animal for study; any detailed study or analysis —**an·a·tom´ic, an·a·tom´i·cal** *adj.* —**an·a·tom´i·cal·ly** *adv.*

**an´ces·tor** *n.* a forefather; one from whom a person is descended; anything considered as a forerunner of a later form —**an·ces´tral** *adj.* —**an·ces´tral·ly** *adv.* —**an´ces·try** *n.*

**an´chor** *n.* a heavy device that can be lowered in the water to hold a ship or boat in place by its weight or by hooks that grip the bottom; any device that secures something in place —*vt.* to hold in place with an anchor; to fix firmly —*vi.* to lie at anchor, as of a ship; to be or become fixed in place

**an´chor·age** *n.* a place where ships lie at anchor; a fee charged for anchoring

**an´cho·rite** *n.* a religious recluse — **an·cho·rit´ic** *adj.*

**an´chor·per´son** *n.* the primary reporter for a newscast

**an´cient** *adj.* very old; antiquated —*n.* one who lived in the distant past; a very old person —**an´cient·ly** *adv.* —**an´cient·ness** *n.*

**an´cil·lar·y** *adj.* secondary; auxiliary

**and** *conj.* as well as; added to; to: *try and do better*

**and´i·ron** *n.* a metal support for wood in a fireplace

**an·drog´y·nous** *adj.* bearing both male and female characteristics; unisex: of a style that is not distinctly male or female, as in dress or appearance —**an·drog´y·nous·ly** *adv.* —**an·drog´y·ny** *n.*

**an´droid** *n.* an automaton that resembles a human

**an´ec·dot·al** *adj.* characterized by or consisting of anecdotes —**an´ec·dot·al·ly** *adv.*

**an´ec·dote** *n.* a short amusing story —**an·ec·dot´ic, an·ec·dot´i·cal** *adj.* —**an·ec·dot´i·cal·ly** *adv.*

**a·ne´mi·a** *n.* a deficiency of red blood corpuscles or hemoglobin in the blood

**a·ne´mic** *adj.* pertaining to or afflicted with anemia; listless; lacking vitality —**a·ne´mi·cal·ly** *adv.*

**an·e·mom´e·ter** *n.* a device for measuring the force of wind

**an·er·oid** *adj.* not using fluid, as *an aneroid barometer*

**an´es·the´si·a** *(US) n.* a loss of sensation caused by disease; a loss of sensitivity to pain produced by an anesthetic

**an´es·the´si·ol·o·gy** *(US) n.* the study of anesthesia and its effects —**an·es·the·si·ol´o·gist** *(US) n.*

**an´es·thet´ic** *(US) adj.* pertaining to anesthesia; producing anesthesia: making insensitive to pain —*n.* an agent that produces a loss of feeling — **an´es·thet´i·cal·ly** *(US) adv.*

**an·es´the·tist** *(US) n.* one who administers anesthetics

**an·es´the·tize** *(US) vt.* to render insensitive to pain, as by administering an anesthetic —*(US)* **an·es·the·ti´za·tion** *n.*

**an´eu·rysm, an´eu·rism** *n.* swelling in an artery at a point weakened by disease or injury

**a·new´** *adv.* again; freshly

**an´gel** *n.* a supernatural being; a guiding influence; a financial backer

**an´ger** *n.* strong displeasure or hostility; ire; wrath —*vt.* to make irate; to provoke —*vi.* to become angry

**an·gi´na pec´to·ris** a heart condition marked by severe pains in the chest

**an´gle** *n.* an ulterior motive; stratagem; point of view; fishing tackle; a figure made by the intersection of two lines or planes —*vi.* to attempt to obtain by cunning; to fish with a hook and line —**an´gu·lar** *adj.*—**an·gu·lar´i·ty** *n.*

**an´gler** *n.* a fisherman; one who schemes to achieve an end

**an´gli·cise** *(Brit.)*, **an´gli·cize** *(US) vi.* to become more like the English —*vt.* to appropriate an English trait or style

**an´gling** *n.* the skill of fishing with special hooked lures

**An·glo´phile** *n.* a devotee of England and its institutions

**an·gos·tu´ra bark** the bark of a South American tree used as a tonic or flavoring

**Angostura® bitters** a bitter flavoring, used primarily in beverages and desserts

**an´gry** *adj.* feeling or showing displeasure; threatening: *angry skies*; indicating anger: *an angry letter* —**an´gri·ly** *adv.* —**an´gri·ness** *n.*

**angst** *n.* feeling of trepidation or apprehension

**ang´strom, ang´strom u´nit** a factor for the measure of wavelength; a hundred millionth of a centimeter

**an´guish** *n.* severe misery, as from grief or pain —*vi.* be distressed —*vt.* to cause distress —**an´guished** *adj.*

**an´gu·lar** *adj.* of or like an angle; bony, gaunt; lacking grace: *angular gestures* —**an´gu·lar·ly** *adv.* —**an´gu·lar·ness** *n.*

**an·hy´drous** *adj.* of a chemical compound which contains no water

**an·i·mad·ver·sion** *n* severe criticism or condemnation

**an·i·mad·vert´** *vi* to comment, especially adversely or critically; to censure

**an´i·mal** *n.* a living creature distinguished from plants mainly by a need for complex organic nutrients and the inability to perform photosynthesis; the creatures of the earth, separate from man; a brutal human *—adj.* pertaining to animals; like an animal

**an´i·mate** *adj.* living; lively *—vt.* bring to life or make lifelike; to stimulate, inspire

**an´i·mated** *adj.* spirited; lively; vivacious **—an´i·mat·ed·ly** *adv.*

**an´i·ma´tion** *n.* the process of imparting life, spirit, interest, etc.; the condition of being alive; the process and technique of preparing animated cartoon drawings **—an´i·ma·tor** *n.*

**an´i·mism** *n.* the belief in a personal spirit or soul; the belief that inanimate objects possess a spirit or soul **—an´i·mist** *n.* **—an´i·mis´tic** *adj.*

**an´i·mos´i·ty** *n.* a strong feeling of hostility; hatred

**an´i·mus** *n.* animosity; an animating energy or purpose

**an´ise** *n.* a plant bearing aromatic seeds used for flavoring and medicine

**an´i·seed** *n.* anise seed; the seed of the anise plant valued for its flavor and aroma

**an´kle** *n.* the joint connecting the foot and the leg

**an´nals** *pl. n.* a chronological historical record; any historical account; a periodical that reports discoveries, etc. **—an´nal·ist** *n.* **—an·nal·is´tic** *adj.*

**an·neal´** *vt.* to heat and then cool slowly in order to make less brittle, as glass or metal; to strengthen by trial, as of determination

**an´ne·lid** *adj.* pertaining to any of a group of segmented invertebrates, as earthworms, leeches, etc. *—n.*

**an´nex** *n.* something added, as to a building; an auxiliary building **—an·nex´** *vt.* to add on; to incorporate into, as territory **—an´nex·a´tion** *n.*

**an·ni´hi·late** *vt.* to destroy entirely; to defeat utterly **—an·ni´hi·la·bil´i·ty** *n.* **—an·ni´hi·la·ble** *adj.* **—an·ni´hi·la·tor** *n.*

**an·ni´hi·la´tion** *n.* total destruction or elimination

**an´ni·ver´sa·ry** *n.* a date or celebration occurring at the same time each year; the celebration of a past event; the date of the event

**an´no·tate´** *vt.* to provide a commentary, such as explanatory notes of a literary work **—an·no·ta´tion** *n.* **—an´no·ta·tor** *n.* **—an´no·ta·tive** *adj.*

**an·nounce´** *vt.* to proclaim publicly; to make known; to give notice of the approach or appearance of; a radio or television speaker who delivers periodic messages, provides commentary, etc. **—an·nounce´ment** *n.* **—an·nounc´er** *n.*

**an·noy´** *vt.* to bother; to irritate by some action *—vi.* to be annoying **—an·noy´ance** *n.* **—an·noy´ing** *adj.* **—an·noy´ing·ly** *adv.*

**an´nu·al** *adj.* yearly; occurring once a year or every year *—n.* a publication that comes out once a year; a plant that lives only one season **—an´nu·al·ize** *vt.* **—an´nu·al·ly** *adv.*

**an·nu´i·ty** *n.* an annual allowance; the right to receive or the duty to pay an annual stipend; the periodic payment of money as an investment for future return

**an·nul´** *vt.* to make or declare invalid, as of a law or a marriage; to revoke or cancel **—an·nul´la·ble** *adj.* **—an·nul´ment** *n.*

**an´nu·lar** *adj.* formed like a ring; marked by rings **—an·nu·lar´i·ty** *n.* **—an´nu·late, an´nu·lat·ed** *adj.* **—an·nu·la´tion** *n.*

**an·nun´ci·ate** *vt.* to announce **—an·nun´ci·a·tor** *n.*

**an·nun·ci·a´tion** *n.* a proclamation; the act of proclaiming or announcing

**an´o·dyne´** *adj.* soothing; having power to soothe or eliminate pain *—n.* a medication that eases pain; anything that soothes or comforts

**a·noint´** *vt.* to sprinkle or rub with oil or ointment; to consecrate **—a·noint´er** *n.* **—a·noint´ment** *n.*

**a·nom´a·ly** *n.* a deviation from the norm; a peculiarity; one who is peculiar or difficult to categorize **—a·nom·a·lis´tic, a·nom·a·lis´ti·cal, a·nom´a·lous** *adj.* **—a·nom·a·lis´ti·cal·ly** *adv.*

**an·o´mic** *adj.* socially unstable or disorganized *—n.* one who is alienated from normal society

**an´o·mie, an´o·my** *n.* concern that the values of society have no personal relevance; a condition of society characterized by ineffectual norms or moral standards; individual disorientation that results in antisocial conduct

**a·non´y·mous** *adj.* of a work lacking the name of the donor or author; lacking distinctive characteristics **—an·o·nym´i·ty, a·non´y·mous·ness** *n.* **—a·non´y·mous·ly** *adv.*

**an·oth´er** *adj., pron.* one other; different, though similar in some aspect, as *another person, another car, another place*

**an´ser·ine** *adj.* of or like a goose; foolish or silly

**an´swer** *n.* any response to a question, inquiry, or request; an action in kind: retaliation; the solution to a problem *—vi.* to respond or reply; to prove sufficient to: *answer a need*; to be accountable: *answer for your actions*; to correspond: *he answers to your description* *—vt.* to speak, write, or act in response; to be sufficient; to correspond **—an´swer·er** *n.*

**an´swer·a·ble** ´ *adj.* accountable; capable of being responded to **—an·swer·a·bil´i·ty, an´swer·a·ble·ness** *n.* **—an´swer·a·bly** *adv.*

**answering machine** a device that responds to incoming telephone calls and records messages from the caller

**ant** *n.* a small communal insect

**ant·ac´id** *adj.* correcting acidity *–n.* an alkali; a remedy for acidity in the stomach

**an·tag´o·nism** *n.* animosity; mutual hostility or opposition

**an·tag´o·nist** *n.* an adversary; one who or that which opposes, as of a muscle or chemical **–an·tag·o·nis´tic** *adj.* **–an·tag·o·nis´ti·cal·ly** *adv.*

**an·tag´o·nize´** *vt.* to oppose or struggle against; to counteract

**ant´ bear** *n.* an aardvark

**an´te** *n.* the initial stake in a hand of poker; a prize or reward; an inducement to participate *–vt.* to contribute to the initial stake before a poker hand is dealt; to pay one´s share *–vi.* to pay up

**ante up** to pay as promised or obligated

**ant´eat·er** *n.* any of the mammals or birds that feed mainly on ants

**an´te·ce´dent** *adj.* going before, preceding *–n.* anything that logically precedes; in grammar, a noun or pronoun to which a relative pronoun refers **–an·te·cede´** *vt., vi.* **–an·te·ce´dence, an·te·ce´den·cy** *n.* **–an´te·ce´dent·ly** *adv.*

**an´te·cham·ber** *n.* a room which serves mainly as an entranceway to other rooms

**an´te·date** *vt.* to backdate; to occur earlier than

**an·te·di·lu´vi·an** *adj.* before the Biblical flood; antiquated *–n.* anything that lived before the Biblical flood; anything very old

**an´te·lope´** *n.* a graceful quadruped allied to the deer

**an´te·me·rid´i·an** *adj.* before noon

**an·ten´na** *n., pl.* **an·ten´nae, an·ten´nas** sense organs on the head of an insect, crab, etc.; a device used for the transmission or reception of radio or television signals

**an·te·pe´nult** *n.* the third syllable from the end of a word

**an·te·pe·nul´ti·mate** *adj.* the third from the end of anything

**an·te´ri·or** *adj.* toward or at the front; earlier in time

**an´te·room** *n.* a waiting room; an antechamber

**an´them** *n.* a hymn; a piece of joyous or triumphal music, often set to words from sacred writing **–national anthem** the official song of a nation or a people

**an´ther** *n.* part of the stamen in a flower that holds pollen

**an·thol´o·gise** *(Brit.)*, **an·thol´o·gize** *(US) vi.* to compile or publish an anthology *–vt.* to include in an anthology **–an·thol´o·gis·er, an·thol´o·gist, an·thol´o·giz·er** *n.*

**an·thol´o·gy** *n.* a collection of literary selections, as poems, novellas, etc.; an assortment or catalog, as of propositions or comments **–an·tho·log´i·cal** *adj.*

**an·tho·zo´an** *n.* a class of marine creatures that includes the corals and sea anemones **–an·tho·zo´an, an·tho·zo´ic** *adj.*

**an´thra·cite´** *n.* a hard coal that burns with a little flame and gives off substantial heat

**an´thrax** *n.* an infectious disease of man and some animals

**an´thro·poid** *adj.* similar to a human being; pertaining to man, apes and monkeys *–n.* any of the larger apes **–an´thro·poid´al** *adj.*

**an´thro·pol´o·gy** *n.* the scientific study of the customs, culture, etc. of man through the ages **–an·thro·po·log´ic, an·thro·po·log´i·cal** *adj.* **an·thro·po·log´i·cal·ly** *adv.* **–an·thro·pol´o·gist** *n.*

**an·thro·po·mor´phic** *adj.* having human form or characteristics **–an·thro·po·mor´phi·cal·ly** *adv.*

**an·thro·po·mor´phism** *n.* characterizing a spiritual being, natural phenomena, etc. as having human attributes

**an·thro·po·mor´phise** *(Brit.)*, **an·thro·po·mor´ phize** *(US)* to attribute human characteristics to *–vt., vi.* to attribute human qualities to things that are not human

**an´ti-** *prefix* against or opposed to

**an´ti·bi·ot´ic** *adj.* preventing the growth of bacteria *–n.* a substance that destroys bacteria and other microorganisms **–an´ti·bi·ot´i·cal·ly** *adv.*

**an´ti·bod´y** *n.* a protein produced in the body to neutralize harmful matter

**an´tic** *adj.* bizarre; incongruous *–n.* a caper or prank; a ridiculous act

**an·tic´i·pate´** *vt.* to expect; to foresee; to be prepared for; to act so as to forestall; to take or make use of too hastily, as profits not yet available *–vi.* to consider prematurely **–an·tic´i·pa´tion** *n.* **–an·tic´i·pa·tive** *adj.* **–an·tic´i·pa·to·ry** *adj.*

**an´ti·cli´max** *n.* a reduction in impressiveness or effectiveness; a decline in contrast to a previous rise **–an´ti·cli·mac´tic** *adj.* **–an´ti·cli·mac´ti·cal·ly** *adv.*

**an·ti·cli´nal, an·ti·clin´ic** *adj.* downward inclination on both sides from a median line, as an upward arch of rock stratum

**an·ti·cline** *n.* a rock stratum forming an upward bend

**an´ti·dote´** *n.* a substance used to counteract or neutralize a poison **–an·ti·dot´al** *adj.* **–an·ti·dot´al·ly** *adv.*

**an´ti·freeze** *n.* a liquid cooling agent with a low freezing point, used in automobile radiators to prevent freezing

**an´ti·gen, an·ti·gene´** *n.* a substance that stimulates the development of antibodies when introduced into an organism **–an·ti·gen´ic** *adj.* **–an·ti·gen´i·cal·ly** *adv.*

**an´ti·he·ro** *n.* an unlikely champion; one who does

not possess the usual qualities attributed to a hero —**an´ti·he·ro´ic** *adj.*

**an´ti·his´ta·mine´** *n.* any of a number of synthetic drugs used to treat cold symptoms and some allergies by preventing or reducing the action of histamine —**an´ti·his´ta·min´ic** *adj.*

**an·ti·log´a·rithm** *n.* the number that results from a base raised to a power by a logarithm

**an·ti·ma·cas´sar** *n.* a covering used to protect the backs and arms of chairs

**an·ti·mag·net´ic** *adj.* resistant to or protected from the influence of a magnetic field

**an´ti·mat´ter** *n.* particles composed of negative protons and positive electrons, the opposite of that in ordinary matter

**an´ti·mo·ny** *n.* a metallic element used primarily in alloys and pigments

**an·ti·neu·tri´no** *n.* the antiparticle of the neutrino, lacking electric charge

**an·ti·neu´tron** *n.* the antiparticle of the neutron, lacking electric charge

**an·ti·par´ti·cle** *n.* a subatomic particle with charge and magnetic property opposite to its corresponding particle

**an·ti·pas´to** *n.* an appetizer of delicacies, as smoked or salted fish and meat, cheese, fresh or pickled vegetables, etc.

**an·tip´a·thy** *n.* a strong or deep-seated aversion or dislike —**an·tip·a·thet´ic, an·tip·a·thet´i·cal** *adj.* —**an·tip·a·thet´i·cal·ly** *adv.*

**an´ti·phon** *n.* a verse chanted in response, often a group response to a leader; an arrangement of passages for alternate chanting or singing —**an·tiph´o·nal, an´ti·phon´ic, an´ti·phon´i·cal** *adj.* —**an´tiph´o·nal·ly** *adv.*

**an´ti·pode** *n.* an exact opposite

**an·tip´o·des** *pl. n.* the people or place on the opposite side of the globe; anything at the opposite extreme

**an·ti·py·ret´ic** *adj.* preventive or palliative for fever —*n.* a medicine to relieve fever

**an·ti·quar´i·an** *adj.* of antiquity or the collection of antiquities —*n.* a collector or dealer in antiquities —**an·ti·quar´i·an·ism** *n.*

**an´ti·quate** *vt.* to make old or obsolete; to make appear old —**an·ti·qua´tion** *n.*

**an´ti·quat·ed** *adj.* old-fashioned; out of date; no longer useful

**an·tique´** *adj.* old; made in an earlier time; in the style of an ancient time, esp. of ancient Greece or Rome —*n.* a relic; an object valued because of its age; the style of an ancient time —*vt.* to finish so as to resemble an antique —**an·tique´ly** *adv.* —**an·tique´ness** *n.*

**an·tiq´ui·ty** *n.* ancient history; an ancient relic

**an·ti·sep´sis** *n.* the prevention of infection by preventing the growth of or destroying harmful bacteria

**an´ti·sep´tic** *adj.* pertaining to antisepsis; thoroughly clean; capable of destroying harmful bacteria —*n.* a substance that destroys disease-causing microorganisms —**an´ti·sep´ti·cal·ly** *adv.*

**an·ti·so´cial** *adj.* adverse to social contact or society; opposed to social order; disruptive —**an·ti·so´cial·ly** *adv.*

**an·tith´e·sis** *n., pl.* **an·tith´e·ses** contrasting thoughts or expressions; the direct opposite: *joy is the antithesis of sorrow*

**an·ti·thet´ic, an·ti·thet´i·cal** *adj.* being in opposition or antagonistic —**an·ti·thet´i·cal·ly** *adv.*

**an´ti·tox´in** *n.* an antibody that acts against a disease; a preparation used in treating a disease —**an·ti·tox´ic** *adj.*

**an·ti·trust´** *adj.* opposition to practices that are in restraint of trade pertaining to the regulation of trusts, monopolies, etc.

**an·ti·ven´in** *n.* antitoxin which protects against snake bite or venom

**an´to·nym** *n.* a word opposite in meaning to another word —**an·to·nym´ic, an·ton´y·mous** *adj.*

**an´trum** *n., pl.* **an´tra** a cavity, esp. in a bone; a sinus cavity

**a´nus** *n.* the opening at the lower end of the alimentary canal

**an´vil** *n.* a heavy iron or steel block which forms a base for hammering metals, etc.; a fixed base which is struck to create an effect, as the lower contact of a telegraph key

**anx·i´e·ty** *n.* a feeling of uneasiness or worry; a cause for such feelings; extreme eagerness; a mental state marked by tension or dread

**anx´ious** *adj.* apprehensive regarding some uncertainty; impatient for the fulfillment of a desire —**anx´ious·ness** *n.* —**anx´ious·ly** *adv.*

**an´y** *adj.* one or some, without preference as to which —*pron.* one or more out of several —*adv.* at all: *feeling any better*

**an´y·bod·y** *pron.* any person —*n.* a person of importance

**an´y·how** *adv.* in any way whatever; in any case

**an´y·more** *adv.* at this time: *it's not done anymore*

**an´y·one** *pron.* any person

**an´y·thing** *adv.* at all; in any way: *is cricket anything like baseball?* —*n., pron.* a thing of any kind

**an´y·way** *adv.* in any event; nevertheless

**an´y·where** *adv.* in any place

**a·or´ta** *n.* the large artery from the left ventricle of the heart that carries blood to all of the body except the lungs

**a·part´** *adj.* separated; disassociated —*adv.* separately; independently —**apart from** with the exception of

**a·part´heid** *n.* the policy of racial discrimination in South Africa

**a·part´ment** *(US) n.* a room or rooms serving as living quarters

**ap´a·thy** *n.* a lack of emotion; unconcern; lacking interest **–ap´a·thet´ic, ap´a·thet´i·cal** *adj.* **–ap·a·thet´i·cal·ly** *adv.*

**ape** *n.* a large tailless primate, as a chimpanzee or gorilla; one who imitates; one who is rude or clumsy *–vt.* to imitate or mimic **–ape´like** *adj.* **–go ape** show great emotion, as anger or pleasure

**a·per·ri·tif´** *n.* a beverage, often wine, served before a meal

**ap´er·ture´** *n.* an opening; a hole or slit **–ap´er·tur·al** *adj.* **–ap´er·tured** *adj.*

**a´pex** *n.* a climax; the highest point

**a·pha´sia** *n.* loss of the ability to speak or understand language **–a·pha´si·ac, a·pha´sic** *adj., n.*

**a·phe´li·on** *n.* the point in an orbit farthest from the sun

**aph´o·rism** *n.* a wise saying; an adage **–aph´o·rist** *n.* **–aph·o·ris´tic, aph·o·ris´ti·cal** *adj.* **–aph·o·ris´ti·cal·ly** *adv.*

**aph·ro·dis´i·ac** *adj.* intensifying sexual desire *–n.* a food, beverage, etc. which is reputed to intensify sexual desire

**a·pi´an** *adj.* pertaining to bees

**a´pi·ar´y** *n.* a place where bees are kept **–a·pi·ar´i·an** *adj.* **–a´pi·a·rist** *n.*

**a·piece** *adv.* for each; to each

**a·plomb** *n.* self-confidence; assurance

**a·poc´a·lypse´** *n.* the symbolic destruction of evil; a prophetic revelation; total or near total destruction **–a·poc·a·lyp´tic, a·poc·a·lyp´ti·cal** *adj.* **–a·poc·a·lyp´ti·cal·ly** *adv.*

**a·poc´ry·pha** *pl. n.* writings of questionable authenticity

**a·poc´ry·phal** *adj.* not genuine; of dubious origin; fictitious **–a·poc´ry·phal·ly** *adv.*

**ap´o·gee** *n.* in the orbit of a satellite, the point farthest from the earth **–ap·o·ge´al, ap·o·ge´an** *adj.*

**a·po·lit´i·cal** *adj.* lacking interest in politics; of no importance politically **–a·po·lit´i·cal·ly** *adv.*

**a·pol´o·gist** *n.* one speaking in defense of a person or cause

**a·pol´o·gy** *n.* a formal argument or defense; an expression of regret **–a·pol·o·get´ic, a·pol·o·get´i·cal** *adj.* **–a·pol´o·get´i·cal·ly** *adv.* **–a·pol´o·gise, a·pol´o·gize** *vi.*

**ap·o·plec´tic** *n.* one subject to attacks of apoplexy **–ap·o·plec´tic, ap·o·plec´ti·cal** *adj.* exhibiting the symptoms of apoplexy **–ap·o·plec´ti·cal·ly** *adv.*

**a·pos´ta·sy** *n.* abandonment of one´s political or religious beliefs, principles, etc.

**a·pos´tate** *n.* one guilty of apostasy *–adj.*

**a·pos´ta·tize** *vi.* to abandon one´s political or religious beliefs, principles, etc.

**a·pos´tle** *n.* one of the twelve sent by Christ to preach the gospel; a missionary; any devoted advocate **–a·pos´tle·ship** *n.*

**a·pos´to·late** *n.* the office, duties, etc. of an apostle

**ap·os·tol´ic, ap·os·tol´i·cal** *adj.* pertaining to an apostle; in accordance with the practice of the apostles; of the line of succession from the Apostles; papal **–ap·os·tol´i·cism, a·pos·to·lic´i·ty** *n.*

**a·pos´tro·phe´** *n.* a mark (´) used to show omission of a letter, to form a possessive, or to form some plurals **–ap·os·troph´ic** *adj.* **–a·pos´tro·phize** *vi., vt.*

**a·poth´e·car·y** *n.* one who prepares prescription medicine **–apothecaries´ measure** the system of liquid measure used in preparing prescription medicine **–apothecaries´ weight** the system of weights used in preparing prescription medicine

**ap´o·thegm** *n.* a terse saying; a maxim **–ap·o·theg·mat´ic, ap·o·theg·mat´i·cal** *adj.* **–ap·o·theg·mat´i·cal·ly**

**a·poth´e·o·sis** *n.* the exaltation of a person to divine honors; deification **–a·po·the´o·size** *vt.*

**ap·pal´, ap·pall´** *vt.* to horrify or frighten; to stun **–ap·pal´ling, ap·pall´ing** *adj.* **–ap·pal´ling·ly, ap·pall´ing·ly** *adv.*

**ap´pa·ra´tus** *n.* a machine or equipment designed for a particular use

**ap·par´el** *n.* clothing

**ap·par´ent** *adj.* evident, visible; seeming to be, possible **–ap·par´ent·ly** *adv.* **–ap·par´ent·ness** *n.*

**ap·pa·ri´tion** *n.* a strange or unusual manifestation **–ap·pa·ri´tion·al** *adj.*

**ap·peal´** *vi.* to request aid or comfort; to be looked on favorably; *good food appeals to me*; to plead the rehearing of a case *–vt.* request a hearing in a higher court *–n.* a request for aid or support; a favorable quality; a petition to a higher power **–ap·peal·a·bil´i·ty** *n.* **–ap·peal´a·ble** *adj.* **–ap·peal´er** *n.* **–ap·peal´ing·ly** *adv.*

**ap·pear´** *vi.* to come into view; to seem to be; to be published or issued, as a book; to present oneself in a court of law

**ap·pear´ance** *n.* that which appears; a semblance; one´s demeanor or countenance; publication; attendance, as in court, before an audience, etc.

**ap·pease´** *vt.* to calm or soothe, as by granting concessions; to satisfy or please **–ap·pease´ment** *n.* **–ap·peas´a·ble** *adj.* **–ap·peas´er** *n.*

**ap·pel´lant** *adj.* regarding appeals *–n.* one who appeals

**ap´pel·la´tion** *n.* a name, title, or designation that identifies a person or thing **–ap·pel´la·tive** *adj., n.* **–ap·pel´la·tive·ly** *adv.*

**ap·pend´** *vt.* to add; to attach, as an addendum or supplement

**ap·pen´dage** *n.* a subordinate addition; a subsidiary part —**ap·pen´di·cal** *n.* —**ap·pen·dic´u·lar** *adj.*

**ap·pend´ant** *adj.* attached; allied in a subordinate position

**ap·pen·dec´to·my** *n.* removal of the appendix

**ap·pen´di·ci´tis** *n.* inflammation of the vermiform appendix

**ap·pen´dix** *n.*, *pl.* **ap·pen´dix·es** *or* **ap·pen´di·ces** an addition, such as supplementary material at the end of a book; an outgrowth, such as the vermiform appendix

**ap´per·tain´** *vi.* be relevant; to relate to

**ap´pe·tite´** *n.* a desire for food or drink; any compelling desire or longing

**ap´pe·tiz´er** *n.* a small amount of food or drink served before a meal to whet the appetite; a sample that stimulates the desire for more

**ap´pe·tiz´ing** *adj.* stimulating the appetite; tantalizingly attractive

**ap·plaud´** *vi.*, *vt.* to express approval, esp. by clapping the hands; to commend or praise —**ap·plaud´a·ble** *adj.* —**ap·plaud´a·bly, ap·plaud´ing·ly** *adv.* —**ap·plaud´er** *n.*

**ap·plause´** *n.* approval shown by clapping of hands

**ap´ple** *n.* the fruit of the apple tree; the apple tree; various exotic fruits or trees bearing little or no resemblance to the apple —**apple of his or her eye** one who is cherished

**ap´ple·jack** *n.* brandy distilled from apple cider

**ap´ple·sauce** *n.* a dish of cooked, spiced and puréed apples; slang for that which is nonsense or not believed

**ap·pli´ance** *n.* a device, usually mechanical or electrical, designed for a special purpose

**ap´pli·ca·ble** *adj.* pertinent; appropriate —**ap´pli·ca·bil´i·ty, ap´pli·ca·ble·ness** *n.* —**ap´pli·ca·bly** *adv.*

**ap´pli·cant** *n.* a candidate, as for a job opening

**ap·pli·ca´tion** *n.* something applied, as a medication; a formal request, as for employment or admission; the act of putting into effect, as of an ordinance, plan, etc.; close and consistent attention

**ap·pli´ca·to·ry** *adj.* that can be used; practical

**ap´pli·ca·tor** *n.* a device for applying a substance to a surface

**ap·plied´** *adj.* put into practice; of something practical in contrast to merely theoretical

**ap·pli·qué´** *n.* an ornament or embellishment —*vt.* to decorate by applying, as ornaments of one material to the surface of another

**ap·ply´** *vi.* to request: *apply for a loan*; *apply for admission*; to be relevant —*vt.* to put or spread on; to use; to devote to a particular use

**ap·point´** *vt.* to name or select

**ap·point·ee´** *n.* one selected for a position

**ap·point´ment** *n.* a scheduled meeting; a position for which one is selected

**ap·por´tion** *vt.* to distribute in shares —**ap·por´tion·er** *n.* —**ap·por´tion·ment** *n.*

**ap·pose´** *vt.* to arrange side by side or opposite —**ap·pos´i·tive** *adj.* —**ap·pos´i·tive·ly** *adv.*

**ap´po·site** *adj.* pertinent; fit for the purpose

**ap·po·si´tion** *n.* in immediate connection —**ap·po·si´tion·al** *adj.* —**ap·po·si´tion·al·ly** *adv.*

**ap·praise´** *vt.* to set a value for; to estimate the worth of —**ap·prais´al** *n.* —**ap·prais´er** *n.*

**ap·pre´ci·a·ble** *adj.* sufficient to be noticed; apparent; discernible —**ap·pre´ci·a·bly** *adv.*

**ap·pre´ci·ate** *vt.* to show gratitude; to recognize and understand, as the opinion of another; to increase in value

**ap·pre´ci·a´tion** *n.* awareness and recognition, such as for a favor from another, the value or beauty of a thing, etc.; the amount of an increase in value

**ap·pre´ci·a·tive** *adj.* able to or showing appreciation —**ap·pre´cia·tive·ly** *adv.* —**ap·pre´cia·tive·ness** *n.*

**ap´pre·hend´** *vt.* to capture; grasp mentally; await with dread —*vi.* to comprehend —**ap´pre·hen´sion** *n.*

**ap·pre·hen´si·ble** *adj.* capable of being understood —**ap·pre·hen·si·bil´i·ty** *n.* —**ap·pre·hen´si·bly** *adv.*

**ap·pre·hen´sive** *adj.* troubled or uneasy, especially about something pending; possessing awareness or understanding —**ap·pre·hen´sive·ly** *adv.* —**ap·pre·hen´sive·ness** *n.*

**ap·pren´tice** *n.* one learning a trade under the charge of a craftsman; any beginner or learner —*vt.* to accept as an apprentice —**ap·pren´tice·ship** *n.*

**ap·prise´, ap·prize´** *vt.* to notify or inform

**ap·proach´** *vi.* to draw near —*vt.* to come near; to be similar to; to start or restart: *approach a new job* —*n.* a means of access; a way of doing something —**ap·proach·a·bil´i·ty** *n.* —**ap·proach´a·ble** *adj.*

**ap´pro·ba´tion** *n.* approval; high regard —**ap´pro·ba·tive, ap·pro´ba·to·ry** *adj.*

**ap·pro´pri·ate´** *adj.* suitable or proper under the circumstances —*vt.* to take, often in an improper manner; set apart for a particular use: *monies appropriated to fund the school budget* —**ap·pro´pri·ate·ly** *adv.* —**ap·pro´pri·ate·ness** *n.* —**ap·pro´pri·a·tive** *adj.* —**ap·pro´pri·a´tion** *n.*

**ap·prov´al** *n.* consent; official sanction; favorably opinion —**on approval** of merchandise that may be examined or tested without obligation to buy

**ap·prove´** *vi.* to express approval —*vt.* to give consent; to view favorably —**ap·prov´a·ble** *adj.* —**ap·prov´ing·ly** *adv.*

**ap·prox´i·mate** *adj.* near in position or exactness —*vt.* to come near in position or kind —**ap·prox´i·mate·ly** *adv.* —**ap·prox·i·ma´tion** *n.*

**ap·pur´te·nance´** *n.* an adjunct or accessory —**ap·pur´te·nant** *adj.*

**a´pron** *n.* a covering to protect a person´s clothes; a covering to protect or adorn furniture; an overlapping piece to shield parts of a machine; the part of a theater stage in front of the curtain

**ap´ro·pos´** *adj.* appropriate *–adv.* with respect to, regarding

**apse** *n.* an extended portion of a building , especially a semicircular, domed recess at the altar of a church

**apt** *adj.* appropriate; likely, probably; competent, talented **–apt´ly** *adv.* **–apt´ness** *n.*

**ap´ti·tude** *n.* a natural gift; quickness of understanding

**aq´ua** *adj.* light blue-green *–n.* a blue-green color

**aq´ua·cul·ture** *n.* cultivation of plants in water; commercial cultivation of fish

**a·quar´i·um** *n.* a tank for water plants or animals; a building where sea life is kept for public exhibition

**aq´ua·tint** *n.* a type of etching in which tints or washes may be produced; the copper plate so produced; the print produced from such a plate

**aq´ua vi´tae** *n.* alcohol; distilled spirits, as whiskey, rum, etc.

**aq´ue·duct´** *n.* a conduit for carrying water

**a´que·ous** *adj.* watery; formed by or containing water

**aq´ui·line** *adj.* like an eagle, or its beak; curved or hooked like an eagle´s beak

**ar·a·besque´** *n.* an intricate scroll work design, often found in Arabian or moorish architecture; a ballet position in which the dancer extends one arm forward, and the other arm and leg backward

**Ar´a·bic** *adj.* pertaining to the language and culture of Arabia *–n.* any of the dialects of the language of the Middle East

**Arabic numerals** the figures 0, 1, 2, 3, 4, 5, 6, 7, 8, 9

**ar´a·ble** *adj.* of land capable of being plowed or cultivated *–n.* land suitable for cultivation **–ar·a·bil´i·ty** *n.*

**a·rach´nid** *n.* member of a class of arthropods, such as a spider, mite or scorpion

**Ar´a·ma´ic** *n.* of a group of Semitic languages, including that which was spoken in Palestine at the time of Christ

**ar´bi·ter** *n.* one qualified to judge a dispute

**ar´bi·trar·y** *adj.* based on opinion or chance; discretionary; capricious; autocratic **–ar´bi·trar´i·ly** *adv.* **–ar´bi·trar·i·ness** *n.*

**ar´bi·trate** *vi., vt.* to settle a dispute by submitting to the judgment of a third party **–ar´bi·tra·ble, ar´bi·tra·tive** *adj.*

**ar´bi·tra´tion** *n.* the referral of disputes to a disinterested party for settlement

**ar´bi·tra´tor** *n.* a judge; one chosen to settle disputes between parties

**ar´bor** *n.* a place shaded by low trees or vines

**ar·bo´re·al** *adj.* pertaining to trees; situated among trees **–ar·bo´re·al·ly** *adv.*

**ar·bo·res´cent** *adj.* treelike in structure; branching **–ar·bo·res´cence** *n.*

**ar·bo·re´tum** *n.* a botanical garden exhibiting trees

**ar´bor·vi´tae** *n.* a type of evergreen shrub or tree

**arc** *n.* a part of a curve

**ar·cade´** *n.* a covered passageway, often with shops along the sides

**ar·cane´** *adj.* secret; mysterious

**arch** *adj.* most distinguished; crafty *–n.* a curved structure, often supporting the wall above it *–vi.* to be curved like an arch *–vt.* to form into a curve

**ar´chae·ol´o·gy** *(Brit.)* *n.* the recovery and study of the places and artifacts of past cultures **–ar·chae·o·log´ic, ar·chae·o·log´i·cal** *adj.* **–ar·chae·ol´o·gist** *n.*

**ar·cha´ic** *adj.* ancient; old-fashioned

**arch´an·gel** *n.* an angel of highest rank

**ar´cha·ism** *n.* an obsolete expression; an antiquated style or usage **–ar´cha·ist** *n.* **–ar·cha·is´tic** *adj.*

**arch´bish´op** *n.* a church official who supervises bishops

**arch·bish´op·ric** *n.* the office of an archbishop

**arch·dea´con** *n.* a church official who oversees the temporal affairs of a diocese **–arch·dea´con·ate** *n.* **–arch·dea´con·ry** *n.* **–arch·dea´con·ship** *n.*

**arch´di´o·cese** *n.* the jurisdiction of an archbishop

**arch·en´e·my** *n.* a chief adversary

**ar´che·ol´o·gy** *(US)* *n. var. of archaeology* **–ar·che·o·log´ic, ar·che·o·log´i·cal** *adj.* **–ar·che·ol´o·gist** *n.*

**arch´er** *n.* one who shoots with a bow and arrow

**ar´cher·y** *n.* the art of shooting with bow and arrow

**ar´che·type** *n.* a standard pattern; model **–ar´che·typ·al, ar·che·typ´ic, ar·che·typ´i·cal** *adj.* **–ar·che·typ´i·cal·ly** *adv.*

**arch´fiend´** *n.* a principal demon

**ar·chi·pel´a·go** *n.* a sea with many small islands; a chain of islands

**ar´chi·tect´** *n.* one who designs and supervises the building of large structures; one who contrives or arranges: *the chief architect of peace* **–ar·chi·tec´tur·al** *adj.* **–ar·chi·tec´tur·al·ly** *adv.* **–ar´chi·tec´ture** *n.*

**ar´chive, ar´chives** *n.* a place where records are collected and stored **–ar·chi´val** *adj.*

**ar´chi·vist** *n.* one who maintains an archive

**arch´way** *n.* the passage under an arch

**arc lamp, arc light** a device that creates a high intensity light by means of an electric arc between two electrodes

**arc´tic** *adj.* of the polar regions

**ar´dent** *adj.* passionate; intensely enthusiastic; zealous **–ar´dent·cy** *n.* **–ar´dent·ly** *adv.*

**ar´dor** *n.* passion; enthusiasm

**ar´du·ous** *adj.* laborious; strenuous **–ar´du·ous·ly** *adv.* **–ar´du·ous·ness** *n.*

**a´re·a** *n.* a section of land; the extent or scope of anything

**area code** *(US)* a three digit prefix to a telephone number that identifies the locality to which a call is being placed

**a´re·a·way´** *n.* an open space in or around a building; a passageway

**a·re´na** *n.* an area where sporting events are staged, usually surrounded by seating; any sphere of conflict

**ar´gent** *adj.* like silver; gray-white *–n.* silver; that which has a silvery quality or color

**ar´gen·tine** *adj.* silvery *–n.* a silver-white metal of tin and zinc

**ar´gil** *n.* white clay or potter´s earth

**ar´gon** *n.* an inert gas used in the manufacture of light bulbs

**ar´got** *n.* the words and phrases peculiar to any group, trade, etc., generally not understood by those outside the group

**ar´gue** *vi.* to debate or dispute *–vt.* to attempt to prove by reason or evidence **–ar´gu·a·ble** *adj.* **ar´gu·a·bly** *adv.* **–ar´gu·er** *n.*

**ar´gu·ment** *n.* a reason offered as proof or confirmation; the art of reasoning; a discussion, debate, or quarrel; **–ar·gu·men·ta´tion** *n.*

**ar·gu·men´ta·tive** *adj.* disposed to argue, often unnecessarily; characterized by argument, as *an argumentative meeting;* moot or open to question, as *an argumentative view* **–ar·gu·men´ta·tive·ly** *adv.* **–ar·gu·men´ta·tive·ness** *n.*

**ar´gyle, ar´gyll** *n.* a design of solid blocks or diamonds overlaid with a contrasting design, from the tartan of the clan Campbell of Argyll; socks or stockings made in such a design

**a´ri·a** *n.* a melody; an elegant solo, as in an opera or oratorio

**ar´id** *adj.* dry, parched; desolate, barren; dull, uninteresting **–a·rid´i·ty, ar´id·ness** *n.*

**a·rise´** *vi.* to rise, as from sitting or lying down; to ascend upward; to originate or emanate from something

**ar´is·toc´ra·cy** *n.* government by a privileged minority; nobility; the upper class

**a·ris´to·crat´** *n.* a member of the aristocracy **–a·ris·to·crat´ic, a·ris·to·crat´i·cal** *adj* **–a·ris·to·crat´i·cal·ly** *adv.*

**a·rith´me·tic´** *n.* the art of calculating by numbers **–ar·ith·met´ic, ar·ith·met´i·cal** *adj.* **–ar·ith·met´i·cal·ly** *adv.*

**arithmetic mean** the sum of a group of values divided by the number of values in the group

**arithmetic progression** a sequence of values which, after the first, differ from the previous value by a constant quantity

**ark** *n.* the ship of Noah; a flat-bottomed boat or scow

**ark of the covenant** the chess containing the sacret tablets of the Hebrews

**arm** *n.* an upper limb of the human body; the part of a garment that covers the arm; the part of a chair that supports the arm; anything that looks like or functions like the human arm; a weapon *–vi.* to prepare for a conflict *–vt.* to provide with weapons; to provide anything needed for an encounter: *armed with information* **–an arm and a leg** an extremely high price **–arm´s length** sufficiently distant to preclude intimacy or conspiracy

**ar·ma´da** *n.* a fleet of warships

**Ar´ma·ged´don** *n.* any final, decisive battle

**ar´ma·ment** *n.* all of the weapons and military equipment contained in an arsenal, military installation, airplane, seagoing vessel, etc.; all of the forces equipped for battle in a given area or situation; the act of equipping for war

**ar´ma·ture** *n.* a piece of soft iron connecting the poles of a magnet; in a motor, the wrapped core which revolves through the magnetic field; arms or armor; protective devises for defense, as an animal´s shell or a plant´s thorns

**arm´chair** *n.* a chair with sides to support the arms

**ar´mis·tice** *n.* a truce; a temporary cessation of hostilities

**ar·moire´** a large cabinet or cupboard, originally for storing arms, now often used for dinnerware or clothing

**ar´mor** *n.* any protective covering; the armored vehicles of war *–vt.* to don armor

**ar´mored** *adj.* protected by armor; a military unit equipped with armored vehicles

**ar´mor·er** *n.* a manufacturer of arms; the custodian of small arms in a military unit

**ar´mor·y** *n.* place where arms are manufactured or stored

**ar´my** *n.* body of soldiers trained for war; a large number of anything

**a·ro´ma** *n.* a smell; an agreeable odor; a subtle, distinctive quality **–ar´o·mat´ic, ar´o·mat´i·cal** *adj.* **–ar·o·mat´i·cal·ly** *adv.*

**a·round´** *adv.* so as to surround or encompass; in the opposite direction; from place to place; in proximity *–prep.* encircling; on the other side of; in proximity **–to come around** to recover consciousness; to be persuaded

**a·rouse´** *vt.* to awaken; to stir up, excite **–a·rous´al** *n.*

**ar·peg´gi·o** *n.* the sounding of the notes of a chord in rapid succession

**ar·raign´** *vt.* to accuse; summon to face charges in court **–ar·raign´ment** *n.*

**ar·range´** *vt.* to put in a defined order; come to terms; to adapt or orchestrate a musical composition

—**ar•rang´er** *n.*

**ar•range´ment** *n.* that which has been arranged; the fashion in which something is ordered; a musical adaptation or orchestration

**ar´rant** *adj.* notoriously wicked —**ar´rant•ly** *adv.*

**ar•ray´** *n.* an orderly display; fine garments; an impressive gathering —*vt.* to gather in order; to adorn

**ar•rear´, ar•rears´** *n.* being behind, as in work or a debt; that which is behind —**in arrears** behind in making payment on a debt —**ar´rear´age** *n.*

**ar•rest´** *n.* capture —*vt.* to slow or stop, to capture and detain; to attract or engage, as the attention —**ar•rest´er, ar•res´tor** *n.*

**ar•rest´ing** *adj.* attracting attention; noteworthy —**ar•rest´ing•ly** *adv.*

**ar•rive´** *vi.* to reach a destination; to attain success —**ar•riv´al** *n.*

**ar´ro•gant** *adj.* overbearing; insolent; marked by excessive pride or vanity —**ar´ro•gance** *n.* —**ar´ro•gant•ly** *adv.*

**ar´row** *n.* a pointed shaft shot from a bow; a drawing in the shape of an arrow to show direction, etc.

**ar´row•root** *n.* a nutritious starch obtained from a tropical American plant, used in food preparation; the plant from which the starch is obtained

**ar•roy´o** *n.* steep-sided dry gulch; a stream which flows in such a gulch

**ar´se•nal** *n.* a place where arms and munitions are made or stored

**arson** *n* the setting of fire to a structure with criminal intent —**ar´son•ist** *n.*

**art** *n.* skill; any craft requiring skill; creative work —**arts** *pl. n.* the humanities

**ar•te´ri•al** *adj.* pertaining to the vessels that carry blood from the heart; corresponding to an artery, as in a course which has a complex of secondary paths: *an arterial highway*

**ar´ter•y** *n.* a vessel that carries blood from the heart; any main channel of communication or transportation

**art´ful** *adj.* crafty or cunning; ingenious or resourceful, esp. in deception —**art´ful•ly** *adv.* —**art´ful•ness** *n.*

**ar•thri´tis** *n.* painful inflammation of a joint —**ar•thrit´ic** *adj.* —**ar•thrit´i•cal•ly** *adv.*

**ar´thro•pod** *n.* any of a large group of invertebrates characterized by segmented limbs and bodies, including insects, spiders, crabs, etc. —**ar•throp´o•dous, ar•throp´o•dal** *adj.*

**ar´ti•choke´** *n.* an edible plant resembling the thistle

**ar´ti•cle** *n.* a written piece; a clause in a document; a separate item

**ar•tic´u•lar** *adj.* pertaining to the joints —**ar•tic´u•lar•ly** *adv.*

**ar•tic´u•late** *adj.* clearly spoken —*vi.* to speak clearly; to be jointed —*vt.* to speak clearly; to form with joints —**ar•tic´u•late•ly** *adv.* —**ar•tic´u•late•ness, ar•tic´u•la•cy** *n.* —**ar•tic´u•la´tion** *n.*

**ar´ti•fact´** *n.* an article fashioned by humans, especially a relic

**ar´ti•fice** *n.* a clever scheme

**ar´ti•fi´cial** *adj.* not natural; imitation; affected —**ar•ti•fi•ci•al´i•ty** *n.* —**ar•ti•fi´cial•ly** *adv.* —**ar•ti•fi•cial•ness** *n.*

**ar•til´ler•y** *n.* ordnance, cannon; the branch of military using ordnance

**ar´ti•san** *n.* a craftsman; one working at a skilled trade

**art´ist** *n.* one who is skilled, particularly one with a sense of style —**ar´tist•ry** *n.*

**ar•tiste´** *n.* a skillful performer, as a dancer or singer

**ar•tis´tic, ar•tis´ti•cal** *adj.* pertaining to arts; aesthetically pleasing; experienced in and receptive to art —**ar•tis´ti•cal•ly** *adv.*

**art´less** *adj.* without deception; natural; innocent; rough; unskilled; lacking taste —**art´less•ly** *adv.* —**art´less•ness** *n.*

**art´y** *adj.* affected; ostentatious —**art´i•ness** *n.*

**as** *adv.* equally—*this car is as fast as the other one*; for example—*to quote, as a verse*; *conj.* equal to—*such a plan as this cannot fail*; at the same time; in proportion—*the light grows brighter as he draws near*; in the manner that—*do as you are told*; because—*as it was raining, we drove slowly*

**as•cend´** *vi.* to move upward; to slope upward; to move from a lower to a higher place, position etc. —*vt.* to move upward on or along; to succeed, as to a throne —**as•cend´a•ble, as•cend´i•ble** *adj.* —**as•cend´er** *n.* —**as•cen´sion** *n.* —**as•cent´** *n.*

**as•cend´ant, as•cend´ent** *adj.* rising; commanding —*n.* a position of prominence or dominance —**as•cend´an•cy, as•cend´en•cy** *n.*

**as´cer•tain´** *vt.* to make certain —**as•cer•tain´a•ble** *adj.* —**as•cer•tain´a•bly** *adv.* —**as•cer•tain´ment** *n.*

**as•cet´ic** *adj.* austere; *n.* one who leads a life of austerity and self-denial —**as•cet´i•cal•ly** *adv.* —**as•cet´i•cism** *n.*

**as•cribe´** *vt.* to impute; to attribute as coming from or caused by

**a•scor´bic ac´id** *n.* vitamin C, a protection against scurvy, found in citrus fruits and some vegetables

**as´cot** *n.* a type of scarf worn in place of a necktie

**a•sex´u•al** *adj.* having no distinct sexual organs —**a•sex•u•al´i•ty** *n.* —**a•sex´u•al•ly** *adv.*

**ash** *n.* the pale, powdery residue left from burning; a tree cultivated for its tough, elastic wood

**a•shamed´** *adj.* a feeling of shame engendered by a failing or gaffe; impeded by fear of embarrassment —**a•sham´ed•ly** *adj.*

**ash´en** *adj.* pale in color, like ashes; pertaining to the wood of the ash tree

**a•shore´** *adv.* on the shore; aground

**ash´y** *adj.* like ashes; ash colored; covered with ashes

**a·side´** *adv.* to one side; apart

**as´i·nine** *adj.* like an ass; stupid or silly **–as´i·nine·ly** *adv.* **–as·i·nin´i·ty** *n.*

**ask** *vi.* to make inquiries *–vt.* to question; to inquire about; to make a request; to state a price

**a·skance´, a·skant** *adv* with suspicion or disapproval; with a sideways glance

**a·skew´** *adj., adv.* out of line; to one side

**a·slant´** *adj.* slanting; tilted *–adv.* in a slanting position *–prep.* across at an angle

**a·sleep´** *adj.* dormant; sleeping; dead *–adv.* into a state of rest

**a·so´cial** *adj.* avoiding social contact; self-centered

**asp** *n.* the European viper

**as·par´a·gus** *n.* a plant with tender, edible shoots

**as´pect** *n.* the appearance of a thing; consideration from a particular viewpoint

**as·per´i·ty** *n.* roughness or harshness

**as·perse´** *vt.* to accuse falsely; to slander **–as·per´sion** *n.*

**as´phalt´** *n.* a tarlike material used for paving, etc. **–as·phal´tic** *adj.* **–as·phal´tum** *n.*

**as·phyx´i·ate** *vt.* to suffocate **–as·phyx´i·a´tion** *n.*

**as´pic** *n.* a gelatin garnish or mold

**as´pir·ant** *adj.* aspiring *–n.* one who tries; a candidate

**as´pi·ra´tion** *n.* extreme desire; a thing desired

**as·pire´** *vi.* to long for or seek after something

**as´pi·rin** *n.* acetylsalicylic acid, taken as a remedy for headache, fever, etc.

**ass** *n.* a beast of burden; a stubborn or foolish person

**as·sail´** *vt.* to attack violently; to set on with vigor **–as·sail´a·ble** *adj.* **–as·sail´a·ble·ness** *n.* **–as·sail´ant, as·sail´er** *n.*

**as·sas´si·nate** *vt.* to murder; to attack by slander, inuendo, etc. **–as·sas´sin, as·sas·si·na´tor** *n.* **–as·sas·si·na´tion** *n.*

**as·sault´** *n.* a vicious attack *–vi., vt.* to make an attack upon **–as·sault´er** *n.*

**as·say´** *n.* a testing *–vt.* to test or analyze

**as·sem´blage** *n.* a gathering

**as·sem´ble** *vi., vt.* to gather together; to fit parts or put together **–as·sem´bly** *n.*

**assembly line** workers and machines arranged so as to permit the efficient fabrication of products on a large scale

**as·sent´** *n.* agreement; consent *–vi.* to agree **–as·sent´er, as·sen·tor** *n.* **–as·sent´ing·ly** *adv* **–as·sent´ive** *adv* **–as·sen´tive·ness** *n.*

**as·sert´** *vt.* to declare; to state with conviction **–as·sert´a·ble, as·sert´i·ble** *adj.* **–as·sert´er, as·ser´tor** *n.* **–as·ser´tion** *n.*

**as·ser´tive** *adj.* authoritative; insistent **–as·ser´tive·ly** *adv.* **–as·ser´tive·ness** *n.*

**as·sess´** *vt.* to set a value for; to impose an amouont, as a fine, tax, etc.; to evaluate, as a situation **–as·sess´a·ble** *adj.* **–as·sess´ment** *n.* **–as·ses´sor** *n.*

**as´set** *n.* property that has a market value; anything useful or appealing

**as·sev´er·ate** *vt.* to declare emphatically

**as·sid´u·ous** *adj.* painstaking; diligent **–as·sid´u·ous·ly** *adv.* **–as·sid´u·ous·ness** *n.*

**as·sign´** *vt.* to designate; to appoint; to ascribe **–as·sign´a·ble** *adj.* **–as·sign·ee´** *n.* **–as·sign´er, as·sign´or** *n.* **–as·signment** *n.*

**as·sig·na´tion** *n.* an appointment; a secret or illicit meeting

**as·sim´i·late** *vi.* to be absorbed; to become like *–vt.* to absorb and digest; adapt or conform **–as·sim·i·la´tion** *n.* **–as·sim´i·la·tive, as·sim´i·la·to·ry** *adj.*

**as·sist´** *n.* the act of helping *–vi.* to aid *– vt* to help; to work as a helper **–as·sis´tance** *n.* **–as·sis´tant** *n.*

**as·so´ci·ate´** *adj.* joined with others; linked *–n.* a co-worker; a thing linked in some way *–vt.* to bring into relationship; to unite, as in friendship; to connect in the mind: *associate poetry with romance* *–vi.* to join or be in company with **–as·so´ci·a´tion** *n.*

**as´si·nance** *n.* resemblance in sound; an approximation

**as·sort´** *vi.* to fall into like groups *–vt.* to classify; to divide into like groups

**as·sor´ted** *adj.* consisting of variety; diverse; sorted or classified

**as·sort´ment** *n.* a collection or accumulation

**as·suage´** *vt.* to alleviate; to calm; to satisfy

**as·sume´** *vt.* to undertake; to take for granted **–as·sum´a·ble** *adj.* **–as·sum´a·bly** *adv.*

**as·sump´tion** *n.* act of assuming; supposition **–as·sump´tive** *adj.*

**as·sur´ance** *n.* confidence; conviction; a positive or encouraging statement

**as·sure´** *vt.* to convey confidence; to offer a guarantee **–as·sur´ance** *n.*

**as·sured´** *adj.* undoubted; sure; confident **–as·sur´ed·ly** *adv.* **–as·sur´ed·ness** *n.*

**as´ter·isk** *n.* a star-like character (*) used to mark references

**asth´ma** *n.* a chronic illness that affects respiration

**asth·mat´ic** *n.* one suffering from asthma **–asth·mat´ic, asth·mat´i·cal** *adj.* affected with asthma **–asth·mat´i·cal·ly** *adv.*

**a·stig´ma·tism´** *n.* a visual defect causing distorted or blurred vision **–as·tig·mat´ic** *adj.*

**a·stir´** *adj., adv.* moving about

**as·ton´ish** *vt.* to stun, amaze **–as·ton´ish·ing** *adj.* **–as·ton´ish·ing·ly** *adv.*

**as·ton´ish·ment** *n.* surprise; amazement; a thing which causes such surprise

**a·stound´** *vt.* to overcome with amazement **–as·tound´ing** *adj.* **–as·tound´ing·ly** *adv.*

**as´tral** *adj.* of the stars

**a·stray´** *adj., adv.* off the correct path; straying into error or evil

**a·stride´** *adj., adv.* with one leg on each side *–prep.* with one leg on each side of

**as·trin´gent** *adj.* stern; severe; disposed to drawing together organic tissue **–as·trin´gen·cy** *n.* **–as·trin´gent·ly** *adv.*

**as´tro·dome** *n.* an enclosed field for sporting events, etc.; a transparent structure in some aircraft for making celestial observations

**as´tro·labe** *n.* an old navigational instrument used to obtain the altitude of planets and stars

**as·trol´o·gy** *n.* the belief that the stars can influence human affairs **–as·trol´o·ger** *n.* **–as·tro·log´ic, as·tro·log´i·cal** *adj.* **–as·tro·log´i·cal·ly** *adv.*

**as´tro·naut´** *n.* a space traveler

**as·tro·nau´tics** *pl. n.* the science of space travel

**as·tro·nom´ic, as·tro·nom´i·cal** *adj.* pertaining to astronomy; extremely numerous **–as·tro·nom´i·cal·ly** *adv.*

**as·tron´o·my** *n.* the study of stars, planets, etc. **–as·tron´o·mer** *n.*

**as´tro·phys´ics** *n.* the study of the physical properties of stars, planets, etc. **–as·tro·phys´i·cal** *adj.* **–as·tro·phys´i·cist** *n.*

**as·tute´** *adj.* exhibiting a keen mind; shrewd **–as·tute´ly** *adv.* **–as·tute´ness** *n.*

**a·sun´der** *adj.* disconnected *–adv.* in pieces

**a·sy´lum** *n.* sanctuary; home for the sick

**a·sym´me·try** *n.* lack of proportion

**a·sym·met´ric, a·sym·met´ri·cal** *adj.* disproportionate **–a·sym·met´ri·cal·ly** *adv.*

**at** *prep·* in the exact location; on or near; toward; in the condition of: *two people at odds*

**at´a·vism** *n.* retrogression to an earlier state **–at´a·vist** *n.* **–at·a·vis´tic** *adj.* **–at·a·vis´ti·cal·ly** *adj.*

**a·tax´i·a** *n.* failure to control muscular movement **–a·tax´ic** *adj., n.*

**at´el·ier** *n.* an artists studio

**a´the·ism** *n.* denial that gods exist **–a´the·ist** *n.* **–a·the·is´tic, a·the·is´ti·cal** *adj.* **–a·the·is´ti·cal·ly** *adv.*

**ath´lete** *n.* one trained in an endeavor requiring physical ability **–ath·let´ic** *adj.* **–ath·let´i·cal·ly** *adv.*

**ath´let´ics** *pl. n.* sporting contests, gymnastics, etc. collectively

**a·thwart´** *adv.* from side to side *–prep.* across the path of; in opposition to

**a·tilt´** *adj., adv.* tilted up; in lively conflict

**at´las** *n.* a book of maps

**at´mos·phere´** *n.* the air surrounding the earth; the general feeling or mood of an environment; decor **–at·mos·pher´ic, at·mos·pher´i·cal** *adj.***–at·mos·pher´i·cal·ly** *adv.*

**at·mos·pher´ics** *n.* broadcast interference caused by disturbance in the atmosphere

**a´toll** *n.* a coral island and its reef enclosing a lagoon

**at´om** *n.* a tiny particle; smallest combinable particle of an element **–a·tom´ic, a·tom´i·cal** *adj.* **–a·tom´i·cal·ly** *adv.*

**atomic clock** a precise instrument for the measurement of time

**atomic energy** energy liberated by the fission or fusion of atoms

**atomic number** the number of protons, etc. in an element which serves to identify the element

**atomic weight** the weight of an atom of an element relative to that of an atom of carbon

**at´om·ize´** *vt.* to separate into atoms; to make liquid into a fine spray **–at´om·iz·er** *n.*

**a·to·nal´i·ty** *n.* a lack of tonal quality **–a·ton´al, a·ton´al·ist, a·ton·al·is´tic** *adj.* **–a·ton´al·ly** *adv.* **–a·ton´al·ism** *n.*

**a·tone´** *vi.* to make amends **–a·ton´a·ble, a·tone´a·ble** *adj.* **–a·ton´er** *n.*

**a·tone´ment** *n.* reparation for wrong or injury

**a·top´** *adj., adv.* on or at the top

**a´tri·um** *n.* an entrance hall; an open area in the center of a building; one of the upper chambers of the human heart

**a·tro´cious** *adj.* cruel, wicked; offensive, tasteless **–a·tro´cious·ly** *adv.* **–a·tro´cious·ness** *n.* **–a·troc´i·ty** *n.*

**at´ro·phy** *n.* a wasting away, especially of muscles or other body tissue *–vi.* to waste away *–vt.* to cause to waste away **–a·troph´ic** *adj.*

**at·tach´** *vi.* to adhere *–vt.* to fasten on; to take by legal means **–at·tach´a·ble** *adj.* **–at·tach´ment** *n.*

**at·ta·che´** *n.* a person assigned to a diplomatic mission

**attache´case** *n.* a briefcase; a flat case with hinged lid for carrying business papers

**at·tack´** *n.* any hostile action *–vt.* to strike out against; to assault; to take up vigorously **–at·tack´er** *n.*

**at·tain´** *vi.* to arrive *–vt.* to reach or gain; to achieve or accomplish **–at·tain·a·bil´i·ty** *n.* **–at·tain´a·ble** *adj.* **–at·tain´ment** *n.*

**at·tain´der** *n.* the loss of all civil rights when a person is sentenced for a serious crime

**at·tar** *n.* a fragrant oil extracted from flower petals

**at·tempt´** *n.* a try *–vt.* to try; to make an effort **–at·tempt´a·bil·i·ty** *n.* **–at·tempt´a·ble** *adj.* **–at·tempt´er** *n.*

**at·tend´** *vi.* to heed; to give care *–vt.* to minister to; to accompany; to be present at

**at·tend´ance** *n.* one´s presence at a particular place and time; the record of one´s presence over a period of time, as in school; collectively, those who attend

**at·tend´ant** *adj.* present; waiting upon; following, as a consequence *–n.* one who waits upon; a servant; an accompaniment, as the result of action

**at·ten´tion** *n.* concentration; alertness; observation, notice; attentiveness

**at·ten´tive** *adj.* considerate, thoughtful **—at·ten´tive·ly** *adv.* **—at·ten´tive·ness** *n.*

**at·ten´u·ate** *vt., vi.* to make or become thin or fine; to reduce or become lessened in value, strength, quantity, severity, eta. **—at·ten´u·a·ble** *adj.* **—at·ten·u·a´tion** *n.*

**at·test´** *vt.* to testify; to certify under oath

**at´tic** *n.* an era or room directly beneath the roof and above the last full floor of a building

**at·tire´** *n.* clothing *—vt.* to dress

**at´ti·tude´** *n.* the posture or bearing of a person; the position of a thing in relation to a plane surface; a state of mind; a disposition

**at·tor´ney** *(US) n.* a lawyer

**at·tract´** *vt.* to draw or be drawn towards; to entice **—at·tract´a·ble** *adj.* **—at·tract´a·ble·ness, at·tract·a·bil´i·ty** *n.* **—at·tract´er, at·trac´tor** *n.* **—at·trac´tion** *n.*

**at·tract´ive** *adj.* possessing the power to entice, especially by charm or beauty **—at·tract´ive·ly** *adv.* **—at·tract´ive·ness** *n.*

**at´tri·bute´** *n.* a quality or characteristic**—at·tri´bute** *vt.* to impute as belonging **—at·trib´ut·a·ble** *adj.* **—at·tri·bu´tion** *n.*

**at·tri´tion** *n.* a wearing away; loss of personnel by resignation, retirement, etc.

**at·tune´** *vt.* to adjust; to bring into conformity with

**a·typ´i·c, a·typ´i·cal** *adj.* not characteristic; inconsistent with the normal or usual pattern **—a·typ´i·cal·ly** *adv.*

**au´burn** *adj., n.* a reddish-brown color

**auc´tion** *n.* a sale conducted by bidding*—vt.* to dispose of at such a sale **—auc·tion·eer´** *n.*

**au cou·rant´** *adj.* up to date; fashionable

**au·da´cious** *adj.* bold, daring; shameless **—au·da´cious·ly** *adv.* **—au·da´cious·ness, au·dac´i·ty** *n.*

**au´di·ble** *adj.* within the range of hearing; able to be heard **—au·di·bil´i·ty, au´di·ble·ness** *n.* **—au´di·bly** *adv.*

**au´di·ence** *n.* a formal interview; all who attend a show, concert, speech, etc.

**au´di·o** *adj.* pertaining to audible sound waves *—n.* that part of a device or occurrence concerned with sound

**audio frequency** a frequency of sound waves within the range of normal human hearing, about 20 to 20,000 cycles per second

**au´di·o·phile´** *n.* person interested in high-fidelity sound equipment

**au´di·o·vis´u·al** *adj.* embracing both sound and sight *—n.* material that incorporates both sound and sight

**au´dit** *n.* a verification of financial accounts *—vt.* to carefully examine so as to confirm the validity of; to attend a college course as a listener only

**au·di´tion** *n.* a tryout, as of an actor or dancer for a part *—vi.* a tryout to show one´s competence when applying for a job *—vt.* to try out, as for a job

**au´dit·or** *n.* one who examines the accounts of a business and certifies as to their accuracy; one who attends a college class, but does not participate for credit

**au´di·to´ri·um** *n.* room or building for large gatherings

**au´di·to·ry** *adj.* pertaining to the sense of hearing

**au´ger** *n.* a boring tool

**aug·ment´** *vi., vt.* to increase; to supplement **—aug·ment´a·ble** *adj.* **—aug·men·ta´tion** *n.* **—aug·men´tive, aug·men´ta·tive** *adj.*

**au grat´in** *adj.* cooked with cheese or bread crumbs

**au´gur** *vi., vt.* to predict from signs or omens; to be an omen

**au´gu·ry** *n.* the art of divination; an omen

**au·gust´** *adj.* inspiring reverence; imposing **—au·gust´ly** *adv.* **—au·gust´ness** *n.*

**au na·tu·rel´** *adj.* ungarnished, as food prepared without sauce; nude

**aunt** *n.* the sister of one´s parent or the wife of one´s uncle; an affectionate designation for an older female not related by blood or marriage

**au´ra** *n.* an invisible field or quality surrounding a person or object; a gentle breeze

**au´ral** *adj.* pertaining to the sense of hearing

**au´re·ate** *adj.* the color of gold

**au´ri·cle** *n.* one of the two atriums of the heart; the outer ear

**au·ric´u·lar** *adj.* pertaining to the sense of hearing

**au·rif´er·ous** *adj.* containing gold

**au·ro´ra** *n.* the dawn; a luminous display seen in the polar night sky

**aus´cul·tate** *vt.* to examine by listening, especially with a stethoscope **—aus·cul·ta´tion** *n.* **—aus´cul·ta·tive, aus·cul´ta·to·ry** *adj.*

**aus´pice** *n.* an omen, usually favorable; patronage

**aus·pi´cious** *adj.* favorable; fortunate **—aus·pi´cious·ly** *adv.* **—aus·pi´cious·ness** *n.*

**aus·tere´** *adj.* of a stern demeanor; plain in decor **—aus·ter´i·ty** *n.*

**au·then´tic** *adj.* genuine; official **—au·then´ti·cal·ly** *adv.* **—au´then·tic´i·ty** *n.*

**au·then´ti·cate´** *vt* to verify; to prove genuine **—au·then´ti·ca´tion** *n.* **—au·then´ti·ca´tor** *n.*

**au´thor** *n.* one who creates or originates **—au´thor·ship** *n.*

**au·thor·i·tar´i·an** *adj.* autocratic; strict *—n.* an advocate of authority over individual rights

**au·thor´i·ta·tive** *adj.* with authority **—au·thor´i·ta·tive·ly** *adv.* **—au·thor´i·ta·tive·ness** *n.*

**au·thor´i·ty** *n.* the power to command or act; one invested with such power

**au´thor·ise´** *(Brit.),* **au´thor·ize´** *(US) vt.* to give approval; to permit **—au·tho·ri·sa´tion, au·tho·ri·za´tion** *n.* **—au´thor·ised, au´thor·ized** *adj.*

**au´to·bi·og´ra·phy** *n.* the story of a person's life written by that person **—au´to·bi´o·graph´ic, au´to·bi´o·graph´i·cal** *adj.* **—au´to·bi´o·graph´i·cal·ly** *adv.*

**au·toc´ra·cy** *n.* absolute rule by a single person; a dictatorship; the rule of a dictator; a state governed by an absolute ruler

**au´to·crat´** *n.* an absolute ruler **—au·to·crat´ic, au·to·crat´i·cal** *adj.* **—au·to·crat´i·cal·ly** *adv.*

**au´to·graph´** *n.* a signature *—vt.* to write one's signature; to sign

**au´to·mate** *vt.* to operate by or adapt for automation

**au´to·mat´ic, au·to·mat´i·cal** *adj.* involuntary; self-operating **—au·to·mat´i·cal·ly** *adv.*

**au´to·ma´tion** *n.* machinery, devices, etc. that once programmed, operate with minimal human intervention

**au·tom´a·ton** *n.* a robot; a machine controlled by a computer or a concealed mechanism; a person whose actions appear mechanical

**au´to·mo·bile** *(US) n.* a passenger vehicle; a car

**au·to·nom´ic, au·to·nom´i·cal** *adj.* involuntary; acting without conscious control **—au·to·nom´i·cal·ly** *adv.*

**autonomic nervous system** that part of the nervous system which controls involuntary actions of the body, as heartbeat, flow of blood, glands, digestion, etc.

**au·ton´o·mous** *adj.* independent; acting without the supervision or control of another, *as an autonomous nation* **—au·ton´o·mous·ly** *adv.*

**au·ton´o·my** *n.* self government; the functioning of a group or part of an organization independent of its parent

**au´to·pi´lot** *n.* a device that can be set to maintain an aircraft's course and attitude

**au´top·sy** *n.* the medical examination of a dead body

**au´tumn** *n.* the season between summer and winter; fall **—au·tum´nal** *adj.* **—au·tum´nal·ly** *adv.*

**aux·il´ia·ry** *adj.* helping; supplementary *—n.* a supplemental person or thing

**a·vail´** *vi.* to assist or aid *—vt.* to be of value *—n.* benefit: *pleaded to no avail*

**a·vail´a·ble** *adj.* at one's disposal; obtainable **—a·vail´a·bil´i·ty, a·vail´a·ble´ness** *n.* **—a·vail´a·bly** *adv.*

**av´a·lanche´** *n.* a mass of snow, earth, etc. falling from a height; anything that comes in an abnormal quantity

**a·vant-garde´** *adj.* reflecting the most recent trends, as *avant-garde paintings —n.* those persons, as artists or writers, who promote, mirrror, or employ the most recent or unconventional techniques

**av´a·rice** *n.* greed; a passion for wealth **—av·a·ri´cious** *adj.* **—av·a·ri´cious·ly** *adv.* **—av·a·ri´cious·ness** *n.*

**av´a·tar** *n.* in Hindu legend, the incarnation of a god; any physical phenomenon

**a·venge´** *vt.* to exact punishment for a wrong or on behalf of another **—a·veng´er** *n.*

**av´e·nue** *n.* a wide street; an approach bordered with greenery or statuary; a means of access, as, through an intermediary, etc.

**a·ver´** *vt.* to declare to be true

**av´er·age** *adj.* of a median value; not exceptional: *an average student —n.* the value of several elements divided by the number of elements, as, the total cost of three items divided by three yields the average cost of the items *—vi.* to buy or sell so as to increase the average price; *vt.* to find or fix an average value **—av´er·age·ly** *adv.* **—av´er·age·ness** *n.*

**a·verse´** *adj.* opposed; reluctant **—a·verse´ly** *adv.* **—a·verse´ness** *n.*

**a·ver´sion** *n.* a dislike; a profound distaste; that which is distasteful **—a·ver´sive** *adj.*

**a·vert´** *vt.* to turn away; to ward off, prevent **—a·vert´ed·ly** *adv.* **—a·vert´a·ble, a·vert´i·ble** *adj.*

**a´vi·ar´y** *n.* a place for keeping birds

**a´vi·a´tion** *n.* the development and operation of aircraft **—a´vi·a·tor** *n.*

**av´id** *adj.* eager; extremely fervent or enthusiastic **—av´id·ly** *adv.* **—av´id·ness** *n.*

**av·o·ca´tion** *n.* a hobby; a sideline **—av·o·ca´tion·al** *adj.* **—av·o·ca´tion·al·ly** *adv.*

**a·void´** *vt.* to evade, shun; to keep from happening **—a·void´a·ble** *adj.* **—a·void´a·bly** *adv.* **—a·void´ance** *n.* **—a·void´er** *n.*

**av´oir·du·pois´** *n.* the common system of weights of the United States in which 16 ounces equal a pound

**a·vow´** *vt.* to declare openly; to confess **—a·vow´a·ble** *adj.* **—a·vow´a·bly** *adv.* **—a·vow´er** *n.*

**a·vow´al** *n.* acknowledgment; open admission

**a·vowed´** *adj.* readily acknowledged; openly declared **—a·vow´ed·ly** *adv.* **—a·vow´ed·ness** *n.*

**a·vun´cu·lar** *adj.* pertaining to an uncle

**a·wait´** *vt.* to watch for; to be ready for

**a·wake´** *adj.* not sleeping; alert *—vi.* to wake; to become aware *—vt.* to arouse; to make aware

**a·wak´en** *vi., vt.* to awake

**a·wak´en·ing** *adj.* stimulating; exciting *—n.* a rekindling of interest

**a·ward´** *n.* a judgment; a prize *—vt.* to grant by judgment

**a·ware´** *adj.* familiar with; conscious **—a·ware´ness** *n.*

**a·wash´** *adj., adv.* at or near water level; overflowing with water; inundated with anything, as *awash in job applications*

**a·way´** *adj.* at a distance *—adv.* distant; to the side;

diligently: *he's working away*; from one's keeping or possession; immediately: *fire away* —*interj.* begone

**awe** *n.* a feeling of wonder and fear —*vt.* to fill with wonder

**awe'some** *adj.* overwhelming; enkindling awe

**awe'strick·en, awe'struck** *adj.* stunned; impressed by awe

**aw'ful** *adj.* inspiring fear; dreadful; formidable

**aw'ful·ly** *adv.* in a dreadful manner; exceedingly, as *awfully bright*

**a·while'** *adv.* for a time, usually short-lived

**awk'ward** *adj.* clumsy; inconvenient; embarrassing —**awk'ward·ly** *adv.* —**awk'ward·ness** *n.*

**awl** *n.* a pointed tool for making small holes

**awn** *n.* a bristlelike part of some grasses

**awn'ing** *n.* a structural projection to ward off sun and rain

**awry'** *adj., adv.* not straight

**ax, axe** *n.* a tool for chopping wood

**ax'i·al** *adj.* along an axis

**ax'i·ol'o·gy** *n.* the study of values or the nature of value

**ax'i·om** *n.* an adage —**ax'i·o·mat'ic, ax'i·o·mat'i·cal** *adj.* —**ax·i·o·mat'i·cal·ly** *adv.*

**ax'is** *n*·, *pl.* **ax'es** a line around which an object rotates

**ax'le** *n.* a shaft on which a wheel is mounted

**az'i·muth** *n.* the arc of the horizon between the meridian of the observation point and a star sighting

**a·zo'ic** *adj.* referring to the time on earth before the appearance of life

**az'ure** *adj.* sky-blue —*n.*

**b, B** *n.* second letter of the English alphabet; not of the first order; second-rate, as *a B-movie*

**bab'ble** *n.* a rippling sound, as a *babbling brook* —*vi.* make incoherent noises; to prattle foolishly —*vt.* to disclose carelessly —**bab'bler** *n.*

**babe** *n.* an infant; one lacking in experience or knowledge

**ba'bel** *n.* a bedlam of speech or sounds

**ba'by** *adj.* childish; small —*n.* an infant; the youngest or smallest of a group; one who acts like a small child —*vt.* to handle gingerly, as something very delicate —**ba'by·ish** *adj.*

**baby doll** a short, sheer woman's nightgown

**baby food** purééd food for an infant

**baby grand** a small grand piano

**baby's-breath** a plant having small white or pink flowers

**ba'by·sit'** *vi., vt.* to care for children —**ba'by-sit·ter** *n.*

**bac'ca·lau're·ate** *n.* a bachelor of arts, science, etc. degree

**bac·cha·nal'** *adj.* a drunken revelry —*n.* a reveler; a riotous feast —**bac·cha·na'lia** *n.* —**bac·cha·na'lian** *adj.*

**back** *adj.* in the rear; isolated: *the back woods*; of an earlier period: *back payments* —*adv.* toward the rear; to a bygone place or condition —*n.* the posterior or hindmost part; the body from the neck to the base of the spine; the far side, away from the subject: *the back of the shelf*; the part of an object away from that which is normally used: *the back of a knife*; the part of a book where the leaves are joined and the cover is affixed —*vi.* to move backward —*vt.* to cause to move backward; to support or assist

**back'bit'er** *vt.* one who speaks ill of another

**back'bone** *n.* the spinal column; the main support: *the workers are the backbone of the organization*; courage; spunk

**back burner** of lower priority, as *to place the project on a back burner*

**back'drop** *n.* that which forms a background, as the curtain at the back of a stage

**back'er** *n.* a supporter; one who provides financial help or encouragement; an apologist

**back'fire** *n.* a line of fire deliberately set to halt the advance of a forest fire; premature explosion in an internal-combustion engine; a backward explosion in a gun —*vi.* to set a backfire; to give evidence of a backfire, as an explosive sound of an automobile exhaust; to achieve a result opposite to that anticipated

**back'gam'mon** *n.* a board game for two players, often involving wagers

**back'ground** *n.* that which is in the rear; that part of a picture, scene, etc. which is behind the main object, often serving to enhance; secondary; peripheral; one's past experience; sound which accompanies or serves to enhance a performance; a description of the events leading up to an event

**back'hand** *adj.* not straightforward or sincere —*adv.* with a backhand stroke —*n.* a movement made with the hand turned backward, as a tennis stroke

**back'hand·ed** *adj.* with the hand turned backward; insincere; ironic; turned in a direction opposite to the normal

**back'ing** *n.* financial or verbal support; a group of supporters; the act of moving backward; material added for additional strength

**back'lash'** *n.* a sharp recoil; a reaction

**back'log'** *n.* a reserve; orders to be filled or processed

**back'-ped·al** *vi.* to retreat from an earlier position, as of an opinion

**back seat** *n.* a seat in the rear of a theater, vehicle, etc.; a position of secondary importance

**back'side** *n.* the back part of a thing; the posterior or rump of a person or animal

**back'slap** *vi.* friendliness that is too effusive, often insincere —*vt.* to be overly friendly —**back'slap·per** *n.*

**back'slide** *vi.* to return to old ways, usually after

eschewing them

**back´spin** *n.* reverse rotation, as of a ball; the rebounded effect or results of an action

**back´stage** *adj.* situated off-stage so as to escape notice *–adv.* in any of the parts of a theater behind or to the side of the stage *–n.* the parts of the theater to the rear or sides of the stage, as wings, dressing rooms, etc.

**back´stairs´** *n.* stairs at the back of a dwelling, usually for the use of servants *–adj.* underhanded; indirect

**back´stop** *n.* a screen on a playing field to confine the game projectile such as a ball or puck *–vi.* to sustain or reinforce, as the opinions of another

**back´stretch** *n.* the part of a racecourse farthest from the spectators

**back talk** *n.* an insolent or argumentative response

**back´track** *vi.* to retrace one's steps; to retreat from an earlier statement or opinion

**back´up** *n.* support; an accumulation: something held in readiness for contingencies

**back´ward** *adj.* reversed; bashful; retarded in growth or development *–adv.* in the direction of the back; toward time past; in reverse order **–back´wards** *adv.* **–back´ward·ness** *n.*

**back´wa·ter** *n.* a place judged to be backward or undeveloped

**back´woods** *adj.* undeveloped; culturally deprived –n a sparsely settled area; an area which is not culturally advanced

**ba´con** *n.* cured meat from the back or side of a hog

**bac·te´ri·a** *n. pl., sing.* **bac·te´ri·um** a division of microorganisms that cause various diseases, fermentation, etc. **–bac·te´ri·al** *adj.* **–bac·te·ri·ol´o·gist** *n.* **–bac´te·ri·ol´o·gy** *n.*

**bac·te´ri·cide** *n.* a substance which destroys bacteria **–bac·te´ri·cid·al** *adj.*

**bad** *adj.* not satisfactory; unacceptable; evil; naughty: *a bad boy*; unlucky, as *a bad break*; offensive: *a bad attitude*; incorrect: *we received bad information*; detrimental, as a bad habit or illness; unfortunate; improper: *she chose a bad time to leave*; concerned, as, *to feel bad about* **–not bad, not half bad, not so bad** rather good, usually after low expectation *–n.* that which is bad; collectively, those who are bad

**badge** *n.* a symbol to show authority, rank, etc.

**badg´er** *n.* a burrowing mammal *–vt.* to tease or pester

**bad´i·nage** *n.* playful banter

**bad´ly** *adv.* incorrectly; offensively; detrimentally; severely or with intense desire, as *they need food badly*

**baf´fle** *vt.* to perplex, confuse or confound; to obstruct or impede **–baf´fle·ment** *n.* **–baf´fler** *n.* **–baf´fling** *adj.*

**bag** *n.* a sack, purse, suitcase, etc.; the amount a bag contains *–vi.* to bulge or hang loosely *–vt.* to place in a bag; to attain, as a prize or game in hunting **–in the bag** almost certain **–left holding the bag** left to be charged with responsibility or blame **–bag and baggage** completely; with all of one's possessions **–bag´ger** *n.*

**bag´a·telle´** *n.* a trifle

**ba´gel** *n.* a hard roll shaped like a doughnut

**bag´gage** *n.* luggage for traveling; a lascivious woman; a useless idea or practice

**bag´gy** *adj.* loose; ill-fitting

**bag´man** *n.* a person who collects or distributes illegal money, as bribes or wagers

**ba·guet´, ba·guette´** *n.* a crystal cut to a narrow, rectangular shape

**bail** *n.* security to insure one's appearance in court *–vt.* to free one who has given security; to remove water from a boat **–bail·ee´** *n.* **–bail´ment** *n.* **–bail´or** *n.*

**bail´iff** *n.* an officer of the court responsible for custody of prisoners, serving processes, etc.

**bail´i·wick** *n.* the office of a bailiff; one's special place or sphere of influence, knowledge etc.

**bail out** jump from an airplane with a parachute; to post bond; sell off a bad investment; to distance oneself from an unpleasant situation

**bails´man** *n.* one who posts bail for a fee

**bait** *n.* any enticement *–vt.* to lure or entice; to tease or provoke

**bake** *vi.* to become firm and dry by exposure to heat, as food baked in an oven or soil dried by the sun *–vt.* to cook with dry heat, as in an oven; to harden with heat, as pottery or soil

**bak´er** *n.* one skilled in the preparation of pastries, breads, etc.; one who makes and sells baked products **–baker´s dozen** thirteen, from an old custom of giving extra to avoid the penalties for short count or measure

**bak´er·y** *n.* a place for making baked goods; a shop where baked goods are sold

**baking powder** a mixture of baking soda and an acid salt used as a leavening agent

**baking soda** *(US)* sodium bicarbonate; a white crystalline compound used in cooking, cleaning, as an antacid, etc

**bak´sheesh, bak´shish** *n.* In certain Middle Eastern countries, a gratuity; a bribe

**bal·a·lai´ka** *n.* a three-stringed musical instrument of Russian origin

**bal´ance** *n.* a device for weighing; an amount owed; a state of equilibrium; the amount left after deducting that which has been or is to be used; a state of harmony, as in arrangement or design *–vi.* to be equal *–vt.* to compare; to compensate; to reconcile, as financial records

**balance of payments** the difference in the value of

payments and receipts for trade between nations
**balance of power** a comparison of the relative strength of nations or of a group of nations
**balance of trade** a comparison of the value of imports and exports of a country
**balance sheet** a statement of the financial condition of a business on a specific date
**bal´co·ny** *n.* a platform outside an upper window; an upper level of seats in a theater
**bald** *adj.* without hair or natural covering; unadorned **–bald´head·ed** *adj.* **–bald´ness** *n.*
**bal´der·dash** *n.* nonsense; meaningless words
**bald´faced** *adj.* audacious, brazen; obvious, as *a bald-faced lie*
**bale** *n.* a large bundle tied or wrapped for ease in handling *–vt.* to tie or wrap **–bal´er** *n.*
**ba·leen´** *n.* whalebone
**bale´ful** *adj.* noxious; harmful
**balk** *vi.* stop and refuse to proceed or take part
**balk´y** *adj.* prone to stop suddenly; reluctant to participate
**ball** *n.* a spherical object; any of a equal number of games that require a round object for throwing, hitting, etc.; a formal dance **–on the ball** qualified; alert
**bal´lad** *n.* a sentimental song; a song or poem that tells a story **–bal·lad·eer´** *n.* **–bal´lad·ry** *n.*
**bal·lis´tics** *n.* the study of the motion of projectiles **–bal·lis´tic** *adj.* **–bal·lis´ti·cal·ly** *adv.*
**bal·loon´** *n.* a bag inflated with gas so as to float in the air; a small inflated bag used as a toy or decoration; a large final payment on an installment loan **–bal·loon´ist** *n.*
**bal´lot** *n.* a paper for recording a vote; a vote cast; a list of those running for office
**ball´point pen´** a pen that distributes ink by means of a ball bearing point
**ball´room** *n.* a large room used for parties and dancing
**bal´ly·hoo** *n.* boisterous patter; any overblown promotion
**balm** *n.* an oinment for healing or soothing; anything soothing
**balm´y** *adj.* aromatic; having a healing or soothing effect; silly; slightly mad; very foolish **–balm´i·ly** *adv.* **–balm´i·ness** *n.*
**ba·lo´ney, bo·lo´gna** *n.* a large, mild sausage; idle or nonsensical talk
**bal´sa** *n.* a tree of tropical America; the very light wood from the balsa tree used in the construction of models and rafts
**bal´sam** *n.* the fragrant oleoresin obtained from various trees; a tree which exudes balsam; an aromatic ointment; any soothing or healing agent
**bal´us·ter** *n.* one of the small pillars which support a hand rail
**bal´us·trade** *n.* a hand rail and its supporting balusters
**bam·boo´** *n.* a tall hollow-stemmed grass
**bam·boo´zle** *vi.* to practice trickery or deception *–vt.* to mislead or deceive **–bam·boo´zle·ment** *n.* **–bam·boo´zler** *n.*
**ban** *n.* any prohibition, as of a motion picture, book, etc. in a community; an ecclesiastical sentence of excommunication or interdiction *–vt.* to forbid or prohibit; to impose an ecclesiastical ban
**ba´nal** *adj.* commonplace; trite **–ba·nal´i·ty** *n.* **–ba·nal´ly** *adv.*
**band** *n.* a flat strip of material used to bind, connect, reinforce, etc.; a broad stripe, contrasting to its surroundings in color, texture, etc.; a range of frequencies within set limits, as *a broadcast band;* a group of persons associated for a common purpose *–vi.* to associate *–vt.* to encircle or join with a strip of material; to unite
**band´age** *n.* material used to bind a wound *–vt.* to bind or cover with a bandage
**ban·dan´a, ban·dan´na** *n.* a large, brightly colored handkerchief
**ban´dit** *n.* a robber, thief; anyone who steals or defrauds
**band´lead·er, band´mas·ter** *n.* the leader of a group of musicians
**ban·do·leer´, ban·do·lier´** a broad belt with loops for holding rifle or shotgun cartridges
**band saw** a motor driven saw the blade of which consists of a toothed, endless belt
**band shell** *(US)* a bandstand for outdoor concerts
**band´stand** *n.* an outdoor platform, often of temporary construction, which serves as a stage for musicians or other entertainers
**band´wag·on** *n.* a decorated wagon which carries a band in a parade **–climb (or jump) on the bandwagon** change openly to an apparently winning position or candidate
**ban´dy** *adj.* curved or bowed *–vt.* to exchange quips; to pass along
**ban´dy·leg´ged** *adj.* bowlegged
**bane** *n.* a cause of distress or destruction; a deadly poison
**bang** *n.* a sudden loud noise; a show of enthusiasm *–vt.* to beat or strike loudly *–vi.* to make a loud noise; to strike noisily
**ban´ish** *vt.* to exile; to dismiss or drive away, as *to banish worries* **–ban´ish·ment** *n.*
**ban´is·ter, ban´nis·ter** *n.* a handrail along a staircase; a baluster
**ban´jo** *n.* a stringed instrument with a long narrow neck and circular sound box
**bank** *n.* a mound or heap; the edge of an inland body

of water; the sloping of a road, an airplane, etc. at a curve or turn; an institution where money is deposited, borrowed, etc.; a supply of anything held in reserve; like elements stored together: *a food bank* –*vi.* to incline an airplane; to do business with a bank –*vt.* to form a lateral slope; to cause to rebound at an angle, as in billiards; to deposit in a bank; to furnish financial backing –**bank a fire** to cover a fire so as to make it last longer by burning low –**bank on** to have complete faith in –**bank´a·ble** *adj.*

**bank account** an account held with a bank for the purpose of writing checks, accumulating funds, etc.; the funds available to the holder of such an account

**bank book** a book in which the transactions affecting a bank account are recorded

**bank´er** *n.* the owner or manager of a bank; a bank executive; the person who holds the stakes in a game of chance

**bank note** a promissory note issued by a bank

**bank´roll** *(US) n.* the money which one possesses –*vt.* to back financially –**bank´roll·er** *n.*

**bank´rupt** *adj.* insolvent; unable to pay one's debts; wanting of anything, as *morally bankrupt* –*n.* a person or company unable to honor its debts –*vt.* to cause to become bankrupt

**ban´ner** *n.* a flag; a cloth displaying a greeting, advertisement, etc.; a large newspaper headline

**ban´quet** *n.* a feast; a formal dinner

**ban·quette´** *n.* a bench for seating along a wall, as in a restaurant

**ban´shee** *n.* in Gaelic folklore, a spirit whose wailing predicts death

**ban´tam** *n.* a small domestic fowl

**ban´tam·weight** *n.* a boxer who weighs from 113 to 118 pounds

**ban´ter** *n.* light-hearted jesting –*vi.* to exchange good-natured jibes –*vt.* to tease good-naturedly –**ban´ter·ing·ly** *adv.*

**bap´tism** *n.* purification rite of the Christian Church; any initiatory rite or experience –**bap´tis´mal** *adj.* –**bap´tis´mal·ly** *adj.*

**bap´tise** *(Brit)*, **bap´tize** *(US) vt.* to consecrate or dedicate to a special purpose by a ceremony

**bar**[1] *n.* an oblong piece of rigid material; anything that blocks access; the legal profession or system; a stripe, as to denote rank; a division in a musical score –*vt.* to close off, as with a bar; to prevent or exclude

**bar**[2] *n. (Brit)* a room in a public house or club where drink is sold

**bar**[3] *n.(US)* an establishment where beverages or food are sold

**barb** *n.* a sharp spine on the shaft of an arrow, fishhook, etc.; a sharp retort

**bar·bar´i·an** *adj.* uncivilized –*n.* an uncivilized or uncultured person –**bar·bar´i·an·ism** *n.* –**bar·bar´ic** *adj.* –**bar·bar´i·cal·ly** *adv.*

**bar´bar·ism** *n.* a savage state, brutality

**bar·bar´i·ty** *n.* brutal or crude conduct; vulgarity

**bar´ba·rous** *adj.* lacking in culture; crude; brutal –**bar´ba·rous·ly** *adv.* –**bar´ba·rous·ness** *n.*

**bar´be·cue´** *n.* an outdoor celebration featuring food cooked over an open fire; the manner of cooking food over an open fire, often with a basting of well-seasoned sauce; any food cooked over an open fore –*vt.* to roast meat over a charcoal fire; to cook, usually meat, basted with a tangy sauce

**barbed** *adj.* having pointed ends; sharp or piercing, as *a barbed retort*

**barbed wire** a fencing wire with sharp pointed pieces at regular intervals

**bar´ber** *n.* one who trims the hair, beard, etc. –*vt.* to trim the hair or beard

**bard** *n.* a poet

**bare** *adj.* lacking clothing or covering; stark, plain; meager –*vt.* to uncover, expose –**bare´ness** *n.*

**bare´back** *adj.* riding an animal without a saddle –*adv.* without a saddle

**bare´faced** *adj.* with nothing concealed; impudent; obvious, as a *barefaced lie* –**bare´fac·ed·ly** *adv.* –**bare´fac·ed·ness** *n.*

**bare´hand´ed** *adj.* with nothing in the hands; without benefit of a tool or weapon other than the hands

**bare´ly** *adv.* only just; scarcely

**bar´gain** *n.* an understanding; a good price –*vi.* to negotiate

**barge** *n.* a boat that carries freight on inland waters –*vi.* to act clumsily

**bar´i·tone´** *n.* the musical range between bass and tenor

**bark** *n.* the covering of a woody plant; the sound made by a dog –*vt.* to strip the covering from a tree; to make or imitate the sound of a dog

**bar´keep** *n.* one who operates an establishment where alcoholic beverages are dispensed; a bar-tender

**bark´er** *n.* a person whose continuous patter is intended to attract patrons into an establishment

**barn** *n.* a farm building used for storing livestock, feed, etc.

**bar´na·cle** *n.* a type of crustacean that clings to submerged surfaces

**barn´storm** *vi.* to tour rural areas, usually for politicking, staging shows, etc. –**barn´storm·er** *n.*

**ba·rom´e·ter** *n.* an instrument that measures atmospheric pressure; anything that predicts change, esp. of statistical data –**bar·o·met´ric, bar·o·met´ri·cal** *adj.* –**bar·o·met´ri·cal** *adv.* –**ba·rom´e·try** *n.*

**bar´on** *n.* in British peerage, the rank above a baronet and below a viscount; one having great power in industry or finance

**bar´on·age, bar´o·ny** *n.* the sphere of influence of a baron

**ba·roque´** *adj.* characteristic of the ornate style in art and architecture popular in 16th and 17th century Europe; pertaining to anything from that period, as *baroque music* –*n.* the baroque form; anything characteristic of the baroque style

**bar´racks** *pl. n.* buildings for housing soldiers, workers, etc.

**bar·ra·cu´da** *n.* a large, voracious fish found in tropical seas

**bar·rage´** *n.* heavy artillary fire; anything overwhelming: *a barrage of accusations*

**barred** *adj.* blocked or decorated with bars; banned; not allowed

**bar´rel** *n.* a large cylindrical storage container; any cylinder, as *the barrel of a gun* –**over a barrel** at the mercy of another

**bar´ren** *adj.* incapable of reproducing; unproductive; desolate –**bar´ren·ly** *adv.* –**bar´ren·ness** *n.*

**bar·rette´** *(US) n.* a small appliance for keeping hair in place

**bar´ri·cade´** *n.* a barrier or blockade –*vt.* to create a barrier

**bar´ri·er** *n.* an obstruction

**bar´ris·ter** *n.* an attorney

**bar´tend´er** *n.* one who mixes and serves beverages at a tavern

**bar´ter** *n.* the exchange of goods or services –*vi., vt.* to trade

**ba´sal** *adj.* fundamental; a standard of reference

**ba·salt´** *n.* a dark volcanic rock

**base** *adj.* humble; cowardly; corrupt –*n.* a foundation; a starting place –*vt.* to form or place on a foundation; to establish a basis for –**base´ly** *adv.* –**base´ness** *n.*

**base´born** *adj.* illegitimate, born of lower class parents; common

**base´less** *adj.* with no foundation in fact; groundless; gratuitous –**base´less·ness** *n.*

**base´line** *n.* anything specified as a main point of reference

**base´ment** *n.* a foundation or floor below the main floor of a building

**bash** *n.* a shattering blow –*vt.* to strike with a heavy blow

**bash´ful** *adj.* timid; shy –**bash´ful·ly** *adv.* –**bash´ful·ness** *n.*

**ba´sic** *adj.* fundamental; forming the foundation for that which follows –**ba´si·cal·ly** *adv.*

**ba´sil** *n.* an aromatic plant of the mint family; the leaves of the plant, used to flavor food

**ba·sil´i·ca** *n.* an ancient Roman building with a long central nave and side aisles divided by columns; a church built after the style of the Roman basilica

**ba´sin** *n.* a wide, shallow container for wash water; an area drained by a body of water

**ba´sis** *n.* a fundamental principle; an essential quality or ingredient

**bask** *vi.* to relax in warmth; to revel in the glow of a pleasant situation: *to bask in the glory of ones deeds*

**bas´ket** *n.* a container made of woven material

**bas-re·lief´** *n.* a type of sculpture in which the subject is raised only slightly from the background

**bass** *adj.* of the lowest musical range, as *a bass guitar* –*n.* the lowest voice in music; a musical instrument in the lower range –**bass´ist** *n.*

**bass** *n.* any of a number of species of food and game fish

**bas´si·net´** *n.* a small basket which can hold a baby; a container for baby clothes, diapers, etc.

**bas·soon´** *n.* a double-reed bass wind instrument –**bas·soon´ist** *n.*

**bass´wood** *n.* the linden tree; the wood of the linden tree

**bas´tard** *adj.* born out of wedlock; unusual or irregular so as not to be usable; not the real thing or of inferior quality –*n.* an illegitimate child; any hybrid plant or animal; anything which deviates from the usual in size, quality, etc. –**bas´tard·ize** *vt.* –**bas·tard·i·za´tion** *n.* –**bas´tard·ly** *adv.* –**bas´tard·y** *n.*

**baste** *vt.* to sew with temporary stitches; to moisten food with drippings or other liquid while cooking –**bast´er** *n.*

**bas´ti·on** *n.* a strongly defended position

**bat** *n.* a cudgel; in some games, a stick for striking a ball; a nocturnal flying mammal –*vi.* in certain games, to take a turn at bat –*vt.* to strike with a bat

**batch** *n.* a quantity processed at one time, as *a batch of cookies*; a number of things collectively

**bate** *vi.* to diminish –*vt.* to lessen the intensity of; to take away

**bath** *n.* the act of cleansing the body by immersing in water or other liquid; liquid for bathing; a room or building set aside for bathing; a resort where natural springs, etc. are claimed to have healing power –**take a bath** to suffer a loss

**bathe** *vi.* to wash; to take a bath; to go into water; to be covered as with liquid –*vt.* to immerse in liquid; to wash; to cover, as though with liquid: *trees bathed in moonlight* –**bath´er** *n.*

**bath´robe** *(US) n.* a loose, casual garment, usually closed at the front with a belt

**ba·tik´, bat·tik´** *n.* a process for dying fabric in which portions are protected with melted wax, then the wax removed and the process repeated through a series of colors to obtain a complex, multicolored design; the fabric so dyed

**ba·tiste´** *n.* a fine, sheer fabric of cotton, silk or rayon

**bat·on´** *n.* a short staff borne as weapon or emblem of office

**bat·tal´ion** *n.* any large group united in a common cause

**bat´ten** *n.* a narrow strip of wood placed in the sail of a ship to keep it flat or to secure the tarpaulin cover of a hatchway; in the theater, a wood or metal strip used to stiffen a muslin flat or to hold a strip of lights *—vt.* to strengthen or secure with battens

**bat´ter** *n.* mixture used to make or coat baked or fried food *—vt.* to subject to repeated blows; to damage by beating or with use

**bat´ter·y** *n.* a number of things used together: *a battery of tests;* the illegal touching of a person; a device for storing an electrical charge

**bat´ting** *n.* a material used for stuffing pillows, comforters, etc.

**bat´ty** *adj.* a little crazy; odd

**bau´ble** *n.* a worthless trinket

**bawd** *n.* the operator of a brothel

**bawd´y** *adj.* racy; indecent; vulgar **—bawd´i·ly** *adv.* **—bawd´i·ness** *n.* **—bawd´ry** *n.*

**bawl** *n.* a loud outcry *—vi.* to sob noisily; to bellow or call out loudly **—bawl out** to berate

**bay** *adj.* reddish-brown *—n.* a reddish-brown horse; a wide inlet of the sea or a lake; a compartment or space used for storage as in a warehouse; the laurel, especially *Laurus nobilis* which provides the bay leaf for seasoning food; the cry of a dog, as in pursuit of game *—vi.* to cry out as a hound in pursuit **—at bay** cornered; held off: *keeping one's creditors at bay*

**bay´ou** *n.* a marshy inlet; a creek flowing through a delta

**bay window** an arrangement of windows that extends beyond the wall of a building

**ba·zaar´** *n.* a market or fair for selling a variety of goods

**beach** *n.* a sandy shore; a place for sunbathing, swimming, etc. *—vi., vt.* to strand a boat on land or on the bottom in shallow water

**bea´con** *n.* a warning signal, as a flag, fire, lamp, etc.

**bead** *n.* a small decorative ornament strung with others and worn around the neck or arm, or attached to a garment; a drop of liquid; the front sight of a rifle *—vi.* to gather in drops *—vt.* to decorate with beads **—draw a bead** take careful aim

**beak** *n.* a bird's bill; anything that is like a beak

**beak´er** *n.* a container with a lip formed for pouring

**beam** *n.* a large piece of wood or metal used for building; part of a balance; a shaft of light *—vi., vt.* to shine, radiate

**bean** *n.* the edible seed of any leguminous plant; the plant that bears the seeds; the head *—vt.* to hit on the head, as by something thrown

**bear** *vi.* to suffer a burden, to be productive; to have reference to *—vt.* to possess; to endure, as trouble or hardship; to produce offspring; to assume, as a responsibility **—bear down** to exert pressure **—bear in mind** remain conscious of **—bear out** or **bear witness** to confirm or support **—bear up** to maintain strength or attitude **—bear´a·ble** *adj.* **—bear´a·bly** *adv.* **—bear´er** *n.*

**bear** *n.* a large wild animal with shaggy hair; an ill-tempered person; one who expects a decline in stock prices

**beard** *n.* facial hair *—vt.* to take hold or pull the beard of; to defy boldly **—beard´ed** *adj.*

**bear´ing** *n.* mode of conduct; a part in a machine which is in contact with a moving part; a compass heading; relevance or significance: *this has little bearing on the matter*

**bear´ish** *adj.* rough; surly; inclined to sell stock in anticipation of a decline in prices **—bear´ish·ly** *adv.* **-bear´ish·ness** *n.*

**beast** *n.* any animal, other than a human; animal qualities in a person; one who is savage or brutal **—beast´li·ness** *n.* **—beast´ly** *adj.*

**beat** *adj.* exhausted *—n.* a blow; a repeated fluctuation, as of sound or the heart; area covered by a policeman, watchman, etc. *—vi.* to strike repeatedly or with force; to sound by striking; to pulsate *—vt.* to strike repeatedly; to shape by hammering; to mix by stirring forcefully; to beat another **—beat´er** *n.*

**be·a·tif´ic** *adj.* making happy; showing pleasure **—be·a·tif´i·cal·ly** *adv.*

**be·at´i·fi·ca´tion** *n.* a condition of blessedness **—be·at´i·fy** *vt.*

**be·at´i·tude´** *n.* perfect happiness

**beau** *n.* an escort; a sweetheart

**beau·ti´cian** *n.* one skilled in the arts of hairdressing, manicure, cosmetics, etc.

**beau´ti·ful** *adj.* pleasing to the senses

**beau´ti·fy´** *vt.* to make beautiful **—beau´ti·fi·ca´tion** *n.* **—beau´ti·fi·er** *n.*

**beau´ty** *n.* anything that by its quality pleases the senses **—beau´te·ous** *adj.* **—beau´te·ous·ly** *adv.* **—beau´te·ous·ness** *n.*

**beaux-arts´** *n.* fine arts

**bea´ver** *n.* a large aquatic rodent or its fur; a high hat, formerly made from beaver fur

**be´bop** *n.* a type of improvisational jazz

**be·calm** *vt.* to induce tranquility; to cease from moving for lack of wind, as of a sailing ship

**be·cause'** *conj.* for the reason that

**beck´on** *vi., vt.* to summon *—n.* a summoning gesture

**be·cloud'** *vt.* to obscure, as an issue, by presenting irrelevant or misleading information

**be·come´** *vi.* to come to be; to change into *—vt.* to suit

**be·com´ing** *adj.* attractive; suitable **—be·com´ing·ly** *adv.*

**bed** *n.* a piece of furniture, matting, place, etc. on which one sleeps or rests; a base or foundation; a specially prepared area, as *a flower bed* or *road bed* **—marriage bed** lying down together for the purpose of procreation

**be·daz´zle** *vt.* to blind; to impress or bewilder with brilliance

**bed´ding** *n.* linens for a bed; litter for an animal's bed; anything that forms a foundation

**be·deck´** *vt.* to adorn; to decorate

**be·dev´il** *vt.* to harass or torment; to bewitch **—be·dev´il·ment** *n.*

**bed´lam** *n.* a place or condition of great confusion

**bed´pan** *n.* a vessel used in bed by a sick person for urination, etc.

**be·drag´gle** *vi., vt.* to soil or soak

**bed´rid·den** *adj.* confined to bed

**bed´rock** *n.* solid rock beneath the surface material

**bed´room** *n.* a room for sleeping

**bedroom community** a residential area populated mostly by those who work outside the community

**bed´sore** *n.* an ulcer on the body caused by long confinement to bed

**bed´spread** *n.* a bed covering

**bed´spring** *n.* the springs which support the mattress of a bed

**bed´stead** *n.* the framework which supports springs, mattress, etc.

**bed´time** *n.* the time for going to bed *—adj.*

**bee** *n.* one of a family of insects which produce honey and are valuable for pollinating certain crops; a social gathering, usually in a rural area: *a quilting bee*

**bee´bread** *n.* a substance stored by bees for food

**beech** *n.* a tree with smooth, ash-gray bark which grows in temperate regions and produces an edible nut; the wood of the beech

**beef** *n.* an adult ox, cow, steer, etc or its flesh; muscle; a complaint

**beef´y** *adj.* large or muscular **—beef´i·ness** *n.*

**bee´hive** *n.* a nesting place for a colony of honey bees; a busy place

**bee´line** *n.* the shortest distance from one place to another **—make a beeline for** to rush directly and quickly to

**beer** *n.* an alcoholic beverage fermented from malts and hops; a beverage made from one of a variety of roots, as sassafras or ginger

**bees´wax** *n.* a substance secreted by honey bees, used to make the cells of a honeycomb

**beet** *n.* a fleshy root commonly used as a vegetable and in the production of sugar

**be·fall´** *vi.* to come about; to occur *—vt.* to happen to

**be·fore´** *adj.* preceding in time or place *—conj.* sooner than; rather than *—prep.* ahead of; in front of; in advance of

**be·foul´** *vt.* to contaminate or pollute **—be·foul´er** *n.* **—be·foul´ment** *n.*

**be·friend´** *vt.* to accept as a friend; to assist

**be·fud´dle** *vt.* to confuse

**beg** *vi., vt.* to ask for alms; to plead

**beg´gar** *n.* one who lives by begging; one who is impoverished *—vt.* to seem inadequate: *his answer beggars the question*; to impoverish

**beg´gar·ly** *adj.* like a beggar; poverty-stricken; squalid **—beg´gar·li·ness** *adv.*

**be·gin´** *vi., vt.* to start; to come into being

**be·gin´ner** *n.* a novice; one starting, as of school or to learn a sport

**be·gin´ning** *n.* onset; a starting time or place; the first part

**be·grudge´** *vt.* to envy another's pleasure; to give reluctantly **—be·grudg´ing·ly** *adv.*

**be·guile´** *vt.* to deceive by trickery; to defraud; to charm or delight **—be·guile´ment** *n.* **—be·guil´er** *n.* **—be·guil´ing·ly** *adv.*

**be·have´** *vi., vt.* to conduct oneself well **—be·hav´ior** *(US),* **be·hav´iour** *(Brit.)* *n.* **—be·hav´ior·al, be·hav´iour·al** *adj.*

**be·he´moth** *n.* a huge beast

**be·hest´** *n.* a decree or mandate; a command

**be·hind´** *adv.* toward the rear; past in place or time; in arrears *—prep.* at the back or far side of; following after; not in the open or revealed

**be·hold´** *vt.* to view

**beige** *adj.* of the light brownish-gray color of natural wool *—n.* the color of natural wool; a fabric of undyed, unbleached wool

**be´ing** *n.* anything that exists; conscious existence; the essential nature of a thing

**be·la´bor** *vt.* to denounce at length; to needlessly prolong an argument

**be·lat´ed** *adj.* past the proper time **—belat´ed·ly** *adv.* **—be·lat´ed·ness** *n.*

**belch** *vi.* to expel gas through the mouth; to expel violently

**be·lea´guer** *vt.* to harrass or annoy; to besiege

**bel´fry** *n.* a bell tower

**be·lie´** *vt.* to misrepresent; to prove false

**be·lief´** *n.* faith; trust; an expectation

**be·lieve´** *vi.* to have trust or faith *—vt.* to accept as true; to expect **—be·liev·a·bil´i·ty** *n.* **—be·liev´a·ble** *adj.* **—be·liev´a·bly** *adv.* **—be·liev´er** *n.*

**be·lit´tle** *vt.* to disparage

**bell** *n.* a hollow, metallic instrument which emits a tone when struck; anything shaped like a bell; the flared end of a wind instrument which provides amplification and resonance

**bel´la·don´na** *n.* deadly nightshade; a perennial herb which yields a number of poisonous alkaloids

**bell´boy** *n.* a hotel porter

**belle** *n.* a pretty female

**bel´li·cose´** *adj.* hostile; of an aggressive nature **—bel´li·**

cose·ly *adv.* **—bel´li·cose·ness** *n.* **—bel·li·cos´i·ty** *n.*

**bel·lig´er·ent** *adj.* warlike; at war *—n.* one engaged in war **—bel·lig´er·ence, bel·lig´er·en·cy** *n.*; **bel·lig´er·ent·ly** *adv.*

**bel´low** *vi., vt.* to cry out loudly *—n* a loud cry

**bel´lows** *pl. n.* a device for producing a stream of air, as for feeding a fire or playing a pipe organ

**bel´ly** *n.* the abdomen; the stomach and organs associated with it, as the intestines; any protrusion similar to the stomach

**bel´ly·ache** *n.* a pain in the stomach; *vi.* to complain

**bel´ly·but·ton** *n.* the navel

**belly dance** a dance characterized by gyrations of the hips and abdomen

**belly flop** a dive in which the stomach lands flat against the water

**bel´ly·ful** *n.* all that one can hold; all that one can endure

**belly laugh** boisterous laughter

**be·long´** *vi.* to be part of

**be·long´ings** *pl. n.* all that one owns

**be·lov´ed** *adj.* cherished *—n.* one who is loved

**be·low´** *adv.* in a lower place *—prep.* farther down; inferior level, as of rank, value, etc.

**belt** *n.* an article of clothing worn around the waist; a moveable band connecting two or more wheels in a machine; a moving line which transports parts or people from one place to another; a distinctive geographic zone: *the Bible belt, the wheat belt*; a blow; a shot of whiskey *—vt.* to encircle or secure with a belt; to strike **—below the belt** in boxing, an illegal punch, hence, any unfair act

**belt´way** *(US) n.* a roadway around a city

**be·moan´** *vi., vt.* to express sorrow; mourn

**be·muse´** *vt.* to absorb or preoccupy **—be·mus´ed·ly** *adv.* **—be·muse´ment** *n.*

**bench** *n.* a long hard seat; a work table; the office of a judge; judges collectively

**bench mark, bench´mark** *n.* a surveyor's marker used as a reference point; any standard for measuring quality, performance, etc.

**bend** *vi.* to turn; to yield, as from pressure; bow *—vt.* to curve or turn, incline; to subdue *—n.* a curved part **—bend´a·ble** *adj.*

**be·neath´** *adj., adv.* below; in a lower position *—prep.* below or under; subordinate; unbefitting: *it is beneath her dignity*

**ben´e·dick´, ben´e·dict´** *n.* a man recently married

**ben´e·dic´tion** *n.* an invocation of blessing **—ben·e·dic´tive, ben·e·dic´to·ry** *adj.*

**ben´e·fac´tion** *n.* the act of giving help; the help given **—ben´e·fac´tor** *n.*

**be·nef´i·cence** *n.* active goodness; a charitable act **—be·nef´i·cent** *adj.* **—be·nef´i·cent·ly** *adv.*

**ben´e·fi´cial** *adj.* advantageous; profitable **—ben·e·fi´cial·ly** *adv.*

**ben´e·fi´ci·ar·y** *n.* one who holds or receives a benefit or inheritance

**ben´e·fit** *n.* a thing that helps; an activity to benefit a cause; payments received for retirement, illness, unemployment, etc. *—vi.* to help *—vt.* to aid

**be·nev´o·lence** *n.* a bent to do good; a charitable act **—be·nev´o·lent** *adj.* **—be·nev´o·lent·ly** *adv.*

**be·nign´** *adj.* kindly; medically harmless **—be·nig·ni·ty** *n.* **—be·nign´ly** *adv.*

**be·nig´nant** *adj.* favorably inclined; agreeable **—be·nig´nan·cy —be·nig´nant·ly** *adv.*

**bent** *adj.* curved or warped; deformed; resolved: *bent on going —n.* a tendency; an inclination; an innate talent: *a bent for decorating*

**be·numb** *vt.* to daze or stun, as by shocking news; to deaden or paralyze, as with an anesthetic

**be·queath´** *vt.* to pass on, especially by will **—be·queath´al** *n.*

**be·quest´** *n.* a thing passed on

**be·rate´** *vt.* to reprimand or scold severely

**be·reave´** *vt.* to deprive of, especially by death **—be·reave´ment** *n.*

**be·ret´** *n.* a flat soft cap, usually of cloth

**ber´ry** *n.* a small juicy fruit

**ber·serk´** *adj., adv.* violent, rampaging; out of control *—n.* a berserker

**ber·serk´er** *n.* an early Norse warrior notable for viciousness and savagery

**berth** *n.* a sleeping place; a position in a ship's crew; room for ships to clear at sea; space to anchor

**be·seech´** *vt.* to ask earnestly; to implore; to beg **—be·seech´er** *n.* **—be·seech´ing·ly** *adv.*

**be·set´** *adj.* troubled; beleaguered *—vt.* to plague or torment; to embellish or decorate

**be·side´** *prep.* adjacent to; alongside

**be·sides´** *adv.* furthermore; else; in addition *—prep.*

**be·siege´** *vt.* to lay siege to; to overwhelm, as with information **—be·sieg´er** *n.*

**be·smirch´** *vt.* to defame; bring dishonor upon

**best** *adj.* finest; of premium quality *—adv.* to the highest degree *—vt.* to defeat.

**bes´tial** *adj.* of or like a beast; savage; brutal **—bes·ti·al´i·ty** *n.* **—bes´tial·ize** *vt.*

**be·stir´** *vt.* to stir to action

**be·stow´** *vt.* to give or endow **—be·stow´al** *n.*

**best´sell´er** *n.* that which is outselling all others of its type, as a book, record, etc.; often, that which is selling extremely well **—best´sell´ing** *adj.*

**bet** *vi., vt.* to wager *—n.* the act of wagering; the stake in a wager **—bet´tor, bet·ter** *n.*

**be´ta·torn´** *n.* an electron accelerator

**be·tray´** *vt.* to be disloyal or unfaithful; to lead astray **—be·tray´al** *n.* **—be·tray´er** *n.*

**be·troth´** *vt.* to commit oneself to marry; to promise in marriage, as a daughter **–be·troth´al** *n.*

**be·throthed´** *adj.* engaged to be married *–n.* the person to whom one is engaged; bound to a pledge of marriage

**bet´ter** *adj.* more appropriate or suitable; improved, such as for health; recovering *–adv.* in a more suitable fashion *–n.* one in authority or a superior position *–vt.* to improve upon or refine; to outdo **–bet´ter·ment** *n.*

**be·tween´** *adv.* in an intermediate position *–prep.* in or of that which separates or connects two things: *between friends, between light and dark, between events*

**bev´el** *adj.* biased; sloping *–n.* a sloping surface; an angle of more or less than 90°; a tool for measuring and marking angles *–vi.* to slant *–vt.* to cut at an angle

**bev´er·age** *n.* a liquid for drinking

**bev´y** *n.* a group

**be·wail´** *vt.* to lament

**be·ware´** *vi., vt.* to be on one's guard

**be·wil´der** *vt.* to confuse or confound, as by something mysterious or unexplainable; to astonish or shock **–be·wil´der·ed·ly, be·wil´der·ing·ly** *adv.* **–be·wil´der·ed·ness, be·wil´der·ment** *n.*

**be·witch´** *vt.* to enchant or charm; to captivate **–be·witch´ing** *adj.* **–be·witch´ing·ly** *adv.*

**be·yond´** *adv.* farther away *–prep.* farther than; greater than; surpassing

**bi·an´nu·al** *adj.* occurring twice each year **–bi·an´nu·al·ly** *adv.*

**bi´as** *n.* prejudice; partiality *–vt.* to influence

**Bible** *n.* the Scriptures

**bible** *n.* any book or writing recognized as sanctioned or approved **–bib´li·cal** *adj.* **–bib´li·cal·ly** *adv.*

**bib·li·og´ra·phy** *n.* a list of information sources for a given subject **–bib·li·og´ra·pher** *n.* **–bib´li·o·graph´ic, bib´li·o·graph´i·cal** *adj.*

**bib´li·o·phile** *n.* a collector of books

**bi·cam´er·al** *adj.* having two legislative bodies

**bicarbonate of soda** *(Brit.)* sodium bicarbonate; a white crystalline compound used in cooking, cleaning, as an antacid, etc.

**bi·cen·ten´ni·al** *adj.* occurring once in two hundred years *–n.* a two hundred year anniversary **–bi·cen·ten´a·ry** *adj., n.*

**bi´ceps** *n.* a muscle having two points of connection

**bick´er** *n.* a petty quarrel *–vi.* to quarrel

**bi·cus´pid** *n.* an adult tooth with a two-pointed crown **–bi·cus´pi·date** *adj.*

**bi´cy·cle** *n.* a two-wheeled vehicle propelled by the rider *–vi., vt.* to propel a bicycle **–bi´cy·cler, bi´cy·clist** *n.*

**bid** *n.* an amount offered; an attempt *–vt.* to request or order; to make an offer; to declare openly **–bid´der** *n.*

**bid´dy** *n.* a hen; a person considered a gossip

**bi·en´ni·al** *adj.* lasting two years; occurring every two years *–n.* a plant that lives two years **–bi·en´ni·al·ly** *adv.* **–bi·en´ni·um** *n.*

**bi´fo·cals** *pl. n.* eyeglasses with part of the lens for near vision and part for distant vision

**bi´fur·cate** *vi., vt.* to split into two parts **–bi´fur·cate, bi´fur·ca·ted** *adj.* forked; having two branches **–bi´fur·cat·ly** *adv.* **–bi·fur·ca´tion** *n.*

**big** *adj.* large in size, quantity, force, etc.; important ; massive; substantial; generous **–big´ness** *n.*

**big´a·mist** *n.* one who is married to two or more persons at one time **–big´a·mous** *adj.* **–big´a·mous·ly** *adv.* **–big´a·my** *n.*

**big´heart·ed** *adj.* generous **–big´heart·ed·ly** *adv.* **–big´heart·ed·ness** *n.*

**big´ot** *n.* an intolerant person **–big´ot·ed** *adj.* **–big´ot·ry** *n.*

**bi´jou** *n.* an ornament or bauble; a piece of jewelry; a trinket

**bike** *n.* a bicycle; a motorcycle **–bik´er** *n.*

**bi´ki´ni** *n.* a brief bathing suit

**bi·lat´er·al** *adj.* reciprocal; involving or affecting two parties **–bi·lat´er·al·ly** *adv.*

**bile** *n.* a digestive fluid secreted in the liver; bitterness, hostility

**bi·lin´gual** *adj.* capable of conversing in two languages **–bi·lin´gual·ism** *n.* **–bi·lin´gual·ly** *adv.*

**bil´ious** *adj.* of bile or an ailment of the liver; ill-tempered **–bil´ious·ly** *adv.* **–bil´ious·ness** *n.*

**bilk** *vt.* to cheat or swindle; to defraud **–bilk´er** *n.*

**bill** *n.* an invoice; *(US)* paper money; a draft of a law; the bony structure of a bird's jaw: a beak *–vt.* to make or tender an invoice **–bill´a·ble** *adj.*

**bill´board** *n.* a large outdoor signboard

**bil´lion** *(US) n.* one thousand million

**bill of fare** a restaurant menu

**bill of lading** a document listing the particulars relating to goods being shipped

**bill of sale** a document attesting to the transfer of property

**bil´low** *n.* a large wave; any surging mass *–vi., vt.* to surge or swell **–bil´low·i·ness** *n.* **–bil´low·y** *adj.*

**bi·month·ly** *adj., adv.* once every two months; of that occurring every two months, as *a bimonthly report –n.* a publication issued every two months

**bin** *n.* a receptacle for storing coal, corn, etc.

**bi´na·ry** *adj.* comprised of two parts; of a numbering system in base two

**binary star** a double star

**binary system** a numbering system in base two

**bind** *–vt.* to make fast; to fasten together; to obligate *–vi.* to tie; to be obligatory *–n.* a difficult situation

**bind´er** *n.* one who binds, especially books; something that holds together; a temporary agreement that remains in effect until execution of a final contract

**bind´ing** *adj.* obligatory, required *—n.* something used to hold together, as a strap, bandage, book cover, etc.

**bi·no´mi·al** *adj.* of a two part equation *—n.* a mathematical equation

**bi´o·as·tro·nau´tics** *n.* the study of living things in a weightless environment

**bi´o·chem´is·try** *n.* biological or physiological chemistry

**bi´o·de·grad´a·ble** *adj.* readily decomposed through bacterial action **—bi·o·de·grad·a·bil´i·ty, bi·o·deg·ra·da´tion** *n.* **—bi·o·de·grade´** *vt.*

**bi·o·e·col´o·gy** *n.* the study of the interrelationship of animals and plants to their environment

**bi·og´ra·phy** *n.* the story of a person's life **—bi·og´ra·pher** *n.* **—bi·o·graph´ic, bi·o·graph´i·cal** *adj.*

**biological clock** the natural cycles in the life of an organism

**biological warfare** the use of micro-organisms as a weapon of war

**bi·ol´o·gy** *n.* the science that deals with life forms **—bi·ol´o·gist** *n.* **—bi·o·log´ic, bi·o·log´i·cal** *adj.* **—bi·o·log´i·cal·ly** *adv.*

**bi´op·sy** *n.* the removal of tissue from the body for laboratory analysis

**bi´o·sphere** *n.* the living creatures of earth; the area in which earth's creatures exist

**bi´o·tin** *n.* a B vitamin

**bi·par´ti·san** *adj.* consisting of two political parties **—bi·par´ti·san·ism** *n.* **—bi·par´ti·san·ship** *n.*

**bi·par´tite** *adj.* having two parts or sections

**bi´ped´** *n.* an animal with two feet

**bi·po´lar** *adj.* having two poles; of opposing doctrines, characteristics, etc.

**birch´bark** *n.* the outer covering of the birch tree; a canoe made from the bark of the birch tree *—adj.* resembling the outer covering of the birch tree, especially the white birch

**birch beer** a beverage flavored with oil of birch

**bird** *n.* a warm-blooded, feathered animal with wings

**bird of prey** any of a variety of birds that catch and eat other animals

**birth** *n.* the act of coming into life; background or lineage

**birth´mark** *n.* an impression on the skin that is evident at birth; a blemish

**birth´right** *n.* the rights that come to one by virtue of being born into a family, country, etc.

**birth´stone** *n.* a gem associated with a particular birth month

**bisect´** *vt.* to divide into two parts **—bi·sec´tion** *n.* **—bi·sec´tion·al** *adj.* **—bi´sec´tor** *n.*

**bi·sex´u·al** *adj.* of both sexes; having both male and female organs

**bish´op** *n.* a ranking member of the clergy; a chess piece

**bish´op·ric** *n.* the office of a bishop

**bisque** *n.* a thick, creamed soup

**bit** *n.* a small scrap or quantity; a boring tool; a minor part in a play; the mouthpiece of a bridle

**bitch** *n.* a female dog *—vi.* to complain

**bite** *n.* the act of taking by the teeth; the amount taken; hurt or damage made by teeth; a stinging *—vi.* to grip; to hurt, as from a sting; to have a sharp taste; to take bait *—vt.* to seize with the teeth; to sting

**bit´ter** *adj.* having an acrid taste; cruel, harsh; resentful **—bit´ter·ly** *adv.* **—bit´ter·ness** *n.*

**bit´ters** *n.* a flavoring, medication or tonic made from bitter herbs

**bit´ter·sweet** *adj.* of a flavor that is both bitter and sweet; pleasure accompanied by sadness, as of memories that are both pleasant and painful

**bi·week´ly** *adj., adv.* occurring once every two weeks

**bi·year´ly** *adj., adv.* occurring once every two years

**bi·zarre´** *adj.* extremely unusual or unexpected **—bi·zarre´ly** *adv.* **—bi·zarre´ness** *n.*

**blab** *vi., vt.* to chatter, jabber; to reveal or tattle **—blab´ber** *n., vi.*

**black** *adj.* of the Afro-American peoples or their culture *—n.* technically, the absence of color; the opposite of white; an Afro-American **—black´en** *vi., vt.* **—black´en·er** *n.* **—black´ish** *adj.*

**black-and-blue** *adj.* bruised

**black and white** committed to writing; of a reproduction that is not in full color; of that expressed clearly or precisely

**black art** sorcery or witchcraft

**black´ball´** *vt.* to vote against, as a nominee for membership; to ostracize

**black´board´** *n.* a surface for drawing or writing with chalk

**black eye** discoloration around the eye following a blow; a disgrace or blemish; a blemish on one's reputation

**black´guard** *n.* a villain, scoundrel

**black´-heart´ed** *adj.* wicked, sinister **—black´-heart´ed·ly** *adv.* **—black´-heart´ed·ness** *n.*

**black hole** a collapsed star with a gravitational field so strong that no light or matter can escape it

**black light** infrared or ultraviolet light used for special effects, night vision, etc.

**black´list** *n.* a list of those to be excluded, as from working, trading, etc. *—vt.* to deliberately exclude

**black magic** sorcery, witchcraft

**black´mail´** *n.* extortion *—vt.* to extort payment by threat of disclosure

**black mar´ket** *n.* illegal trade in goods or currency **—black´-mar´ket** *adj.* **—black´-mar´ket·eer, black´-mar´ket·er** *n.*

**black´-mar´ket** *vt.* to trade on the black market

**black´out´** *n.* the extinguishing of all lights; a loss of electricity to an area; a temporary loss of consciousness or memory

**black sheep** a family or group member who is considered different, usually less reputable or successful

**black´smith** *n.* one who works in iron

**black tie** of a mode of dress that includes a black bow tie, tuxedo, etc.; formal; of an affair that requires formal dress

**black´top** *(US) n.* a material such as asphalt used to surface roads; a road so surfaced *–vt.* to suface a road with asphalt

**bladder** *n.* a pouch in animals to hold gas or liquid; anything resembling such a pouch

**blade** *n.* a plant leaf, such as grass; any broad, flat surface, as of an oar or certain bones; the cutting part of an instrument, as a knife or scissors

**blame** *n.* condemnation, denunciation; accountability for a wrong *–vt.* to charge with responsibility for a wrong; to condemn or rebuke **–blam´a·ble** *adj.* **–blam´a·bly** *adv.* **–blame´ful** *adj.* **–blame´ful·ly** *adv.* **–blame´ful·ness** *n.*

**blame´less** *adj.* innocent; irreproachable; free of blame **–blame´less·ly** *adv.* **–blame´less·ness** *n.*

**blanch** *vi.* to whiten *–vt.* to make white; to bleach; to immerse food briefly in boiling water prior to skinning, freezing, etc.

**bland** *adj.* soothing, mild; insipid, dull

**blan´dish** *vt.* to persuade by guile or flattery **–blan´dish·er** *n.* **–blan´dish·ment** *n.*

**blank** *adj.* empty, vacant, unadorned; not filled out, as of a form *–n.* a void; emptiness; a form or questionnaire **–draw a blank** unable to remember or accomplish something **blank´ly** *adv.* **–blank´ness** *n.*

**blan´ket** *adj.* of that encompassing a number of elements, as *blanket insurance coverage* *–n.* a bed covering; anything that covers like a blanket: *a blanket of flowers* *–vt.* to cover; to canvass: *blanket the area with pollsters*

**blank verse** poetry that does not rhyme

**blare** *n.* a harsh noise *–vi., vt.* to sound loudly

**blar´ney** *n.* flattering speech

**bla·sé´** *adj.* indifferent, unconcerned; bored

**blas´pheme´** *vt.* to speak or act in an irreverent manner *–vi.* to utter blasphemy **–blas´phem·er** *n.*

**blas´phe·my** *n.* a profane or irreverent act or expression, esp. toward something considered sacred **–blas´phe·mous** *adj.* **–blas´phe·mous·ly** *adv.*

**blast** *n.* sudden rush of air; a harsh sound; an explosion *–vi.* to make a harsh sound; to set off an explosive *–vt.* to explode; to denounce

**blast furnace** a furnace for separating impurities from metallic ore

**bla´tant** *adj.* offensively noisy; obvious, conspicuous **–bla´tan·cy** *n.* **–bla´tant·ly** *adv.*

**blaze** *n.* a burst of flame or light *–vi.* to burn brightly; to shine brightly

**bla´zer** *n.* a sports jacket

**bleach** *n.* a substance used to whiten *–vi.* to grow white *–vt.* to remove color; to make white **–bleach´er** *n.*

**bleach´ers** *pl. n.* the least expensive seating, often long benches, especially at sporting events

**bleak** *adj.* desolate; dreary; gloomy

**blear´y** *adj.* blurred or indistinct **–blear´i·ly** *adv.* **–blear´i·ness** *n.*

**bleat** *n.* the characteristic cry of an animal *–vi., vt.*

**bleed** *vi.* to lose vital fluid, as blood from a person or sap from a tree; to run together, as paints or dye; to be printed off the edge of a page *–vt.* to draw fluid or gas from; to print off the edge of a page; to impoverish

**blem´ish** *n.* a flaw or defect *–vt.* to deface

**blend** *n.* a mixture *–vi., vt.* to mix; to combine so as to make a gradual transition, as of colors

**bless** *vt.* to consecrate; to favor **–bless´ed·ness** *n.*

**bless´ed** *adj.* consecrated; blissfull; rewarded **–bless´ed·ly** *adv.*

**bless´ing** *n.* an invocation; grace before a meal; divine sanction; good fortune

**blight** *n.* a plant disease; anything that damages *–vt.* to destroy

**blimp** *n.* an airship

**blind** *adj.* sightless; unseen *–n.* anything that obscures or conceals *–vt.* to deprive of sight; to dazzle **–blind´er** *n.* **–blind´ly** *adv.* **–blind´ness** *n.*

**blind´fold** *n.* anything that restricts sight or comprehension *–vt.* to cover the eyes of; to mislead

**blind´ing** *adj.* with great speed; faster than the eye can follow **–blind´ing·ly** *adv.*

**blind spot** an area where vision or visual reception is restricted; a prejudice that distorts ones perception or thinking

**blink** *vi., vt.* to close and open the eyelids quickly; to flash on and off as a light

**blink´er** *n.* a flashing light, as on a vehicle or a stationary mounting; *(US)* an automobile turn signal

**blintz, blintze** *n.* a thin pancake rolled around a filling

**bliss** *n.* great happiness; ecstasy rapture **–bliss´ful** *adj.* **–bliss´ful·ly** *adv.* **–bliss´ful·ness** *n.*

**blis´ter** *n.* a bulging sac of matter on the skin; anything similar to a skin blister; a transparent covering for merchandise attached to a cardboard backing *–vi., vt.* to form a blister **–blis´ter·y** *adj.*

**blithe** *adj.* gay; lighthearted; vivacious **–blithe´ly** *adv.* **–blithe´ness** *n.* **–blithe´some** *adj.*

**bliz´zard** *n.* a violent snowstorm

**bloat** *vi. vt.* to swell

**blob** *n.* a clump of indefinite shape; a large person

**bloc** *n.* a political alliance

**block** *n.* a large chunk of material; a system of pulleys; a related or contiguous group; a barrier *—vt.* to hinder or restrict; to form a rough plan **—block´age** *n.*
**block´ade´** *n.* a barrier *—vt.* to set up a barrier **—block·ad´er** *n.*
**block´bust·er** *adj.* of that which is extravagant, as a movie, book, etc. *—n.* an extravagant or ostentatious work; an investor or real estate agent who creates the impression of a change in the ethnic makeup of a neighborhood so as to buy property at reduced prices
**block´head** *n.* a stupid person; **block´head·ed** *adj.*; **block´head·ed·ness** *n.*
**block letter** a plain alphanumeric character, without serifs or any embellishment
**blond** *adj.* of fair skin, hair, etc.; of a light wood finish
**blonde** *n.* a blond female
**blood** *n.* a vital body fluid; heritage; kinship **—new blood** a new member or members
**blood bank** a reserve of liquid or dried human blood
**blood bath** a massacre; wholesale replacement of a complany's executives
**blood brother** a male sibling; one bound by an oath or ceremony
**blood count** clinical analysis of the contents of a quantity of blood
**blood´curd·ling** *adj.* frightening; ghastly
**blood´ed** *adj.* pedigreed; of known stock
**blood´hound** *n.* a breed of dog used in tracking; a person who is relentless in pursuit
**blood´less** *adj.* lacking blood; without bloodshed, peaceful; lacking feeling, indifferent **—blood´less·ly** *adv.* **—blood´less·ness** *n.*
**blood´let·ting** *n.* bloodshed; figuratively, the replacement of a number of employees in a company or division
**blood money** payment for performance of that which is illegal or unethical; financial gain from the suffering of others
**blood pressure** a measure of the force of blood coursing through the arteries
**blood relation, blood relative** one related by birth
**blood´shed** *n.* carnage; slaughter
**blood´stained** *adj.* soiled by blood; guilty of shedding the blood of another
**blood´suck·er** *n.* a leech; one who takes as much as possible from another; a parasite **—blood´suck·ing** *adj.*
**blood´thirst·y** *adj.* barbarous; inclined to murder; of a ruthless nature **—blood´thirst·i·ly** *adv.* **—blood´thirst·i·ness** *n.*
**blood vessel** any of the arteries, veins or capillaries which carry blood throughout the body
**blood´y** *adj.* of the shedding of blood; bleeding or containing blood; bloodstained; murderous **—blood´i·ly** *adv.* **—blood´i·ness** *n.*
**bloom** *n.* a flower; a healthy glow *—vi.* to flower; to glow
**bloop´er** *n.* a mistake; a silly blunder
**blos´som** *n.* a flower; *vi.* to flower; to develop
**blot** *n.* a flaw; dishonor; a spot or stain *—vt.* to stain; to dishonor; to get rid of **—blot´ter** *n.*
**blotch** *n.* a stain or blemish *—vt.* to blemish
**blotch´y** *adj.* marked by discoloration; covered with blemishes **—blotch´i·ness** *n.*
**blouse** *n.* a loose shirt
**blow** *n.* a sharp rap; a setback; a blast of air; a windstorm *—vi.* to move air, as by the wind or the lungs; to be carried by moving air; to be stormy *—vt.* to expel air; to propel by moving air; to waste money; to fail; to leave **—blow up** to explode; to form by blowing, as a balloon; to enlarge a photograph
**blow´out** *n.* the bursting of a tire; a large party or celebration
**blow´torch** *n.* a tool that produces a flame for softening metal, removing paint, etc.
**blow·up** *n.* an explosion; an enlarged photograph
**blub´ber** *n.* whale fat; excess fat on humans *—vi.* to weep **—blub´ber·y** *adj.*
**bludg´eon** *n.* a heavy club *—vt.* to strike with a club; to bully
**blue** *adj.* bluish in color; despondent *—n.* anything the color or near the color of the clear sky *—vt.* to make blue in color
**blue baby** a child born with a heart or respiratory defect
**blue´bell** *n.* any of a variety of plants with blue bell-shaped flowers
**blue blood, blue´blood** *n.* one descended from aristocracy; high society, upper class **—blue´-blood·ed** *adj.*
**blue chip, blue´chip** *adj.* designating of a group of companies whose stocks are characterized by stability of price and earnings; of anything that is perceived as stable **—blue´-chip** *adj.*
**blue collar** a label applied to industrial workers
**blue´grass** *adj.* of a type of southern mountain music *—n.*
**blue jeans, blue·jeans** *n.* a type of trouser made from blue denim
**blue laws** any of the state laws or local ordinances that prohibit the transaction of business on Sunday
**blue´nose** *n.* one who attempts to impose his or her moral code on others
**blue-pen´cil** *vt.* to edit or correct
**blue´print** *n.* an architect or engineer's drawing; any detailed plan of action
**blue ribbon** first prize in a judged competition
**blue-sky´** *adj.* of no intrinsic value; a wish or dream
**blue streak** of anything fast, lively or animated

**bluff** *adj.* exhibiting an abrupt manner *–n.* a steep bank; an act of deception *–vt.* to mislead by feigning; to deceive

**blun´der** *n.* a foolish mistake *–vi.* to make a foolish error; to move clumsily **–blun´der·er** *n.* **–blun´der·ing·ly** *adv.*

**blunt** *adj.* not sharp; plain-spoken, curt; slow-witted, dull *–vt.* to dull; to reduce the effectiveness of **–blunt´ly** *adv.* **–blunt´ness** *n.*

**blur** *n.* anything indistinct *–vt., vi.* to make or become indistinct **–blur´ry** *adj.*

**blurb** *n.* a brief commercial or announcement; a brief comment or extract from a review on a book cover or jacket

**blurt** *vt.* to say without thinking

**blush** *n.* a sudden reddening of the face; a reddish color *–vi., vt.* to become red or reddish **–blush´er** *n.* **–blush´ing·ly** *adv.*

**blus´ter** *n.* arrogant speech, often empty threats *–vi.* to blow in violent gusts; to act in an arrogant, bullying manner **–blus´ter·ing·ly** *adv.* **–blus´ter·ous, blus´ter·y** *adj.*

**bo´a** *n.* a large snake; a long scarf made of soft material, as of fur or feathers

**boar** *n.* a mature male pig

**board** *n.* a thin plank; any of various flat panels fashioned for a special purpose; meals provided for pay; a group that controls or regulates *–vt.* to supply with meals; to get on a vessel *–vi.* to take meals at a boarding house

**board´er** *n.* a lodger; a paying guest who is provided room and meals

**board foot** a measure of lumber that equals one square foot, one inch thick

**boarding house** an establishment that provides rooms and meals for paying guests

**boarding school** a school that provides a residence and meals for the students

**board´walk** *n.* a wooden walkway built along a beach

**boast** *vi., vt.* to brag *–n.* pretension **–boast´er** *n.* **–boast´ful** *adj.* **–boast´ful·ly, boast´ing·ly** *adv.*

**boat** *n.* any vessel that plies the inland seas **–boat´er** *n.* **–boat´ing** *adj., n.*

**bob´bin** *n.* a spool for thread or yarn

**bobby pin** *(US)* a metal hair pin

**bob´sled** *n.* a long sled with two sets of runners and a steering mechanism

**bock beer** a dark German beer

**bod´ice** *n.* the upper part of a woman's dress

**bod´i·ly** *adj.* physical; of the body *–adv.* totally, entirely

**bod´y** *n.* physical structure; the main part of anything; a person; a group considered as a unit; characteristic density

**body politic** society; those who are united under a government

**bog** *n.* a small swamp or marsh

**bo´gus** *adj.* of doubtful authenticity

**bo·he´mi·an** *n.* one who is unconventional, as an artist, writer, etc.

**boil** *vi.* to bubble from heat; to cook in a boiling liquid; to churn; to seethe with rage *–vt.* to heat to the boiling point; to process in a boiling liquid

**boil´er** *n.* a tank for heating water to produce steam; a tank for heating and storing water

**boiling point** the temperature at which a liquid boils; conditions under which one is inclined to lose control

**bois´ter·ous** *adj.* noisy; rowdy **–bois´ter·ous·ly** *adv.* **–bois´ter·ous·ness** *n.*

**bold** *adj.* daring; forceful; impudent **–bold´ly** *adv.* **–bold´ness** *n.*

**bold´-faced, bold´faced** *adj.* impudent; brazen

**bo·le´ro** *n.* a Spanish dance; a short jacket

**bol´lix** *vt.* to bungle; to mismanage

**bol´ster** *n.* a long pillow *–vt.* to prop up; to reinforce **–bol´ster·er** *n.*

**bolt** *n.* a bar for securing an entrance; a threaded fastener; a roll of cloth; a sudden start *–vi.* to spring suddenly; to break away *–vt.* to secure with a bar or lock; to fasten with a bolt; to eat hurriedly; to break away, as from a group

**bomb** *n.* a casing filled with an explosive, compressed gas, etc.; a failure *–vi.* to fail utterly *–vt.* to attack with bombs

**bom·bas´tic** *adj.* high-sounding but meaningless **–bom´bast´** *n.* **–bom·bas´ti·cal·ly** *adv.*

**bomb´shell** *n.* a bomb; any sudden shock or surprise; a rude awakening

**bo´na fide** *adj.* genuine; sincere; in good faith

**bo·nan´za** *n.* a rich source of ore; any profitable venture

**bon´bon** *n.* a small candy

**bond** *n.* a formal obligation; a thing that binds *–vt.* to place or hold under bond; to place in a bonded warehouse; to tie or join together **–bond´a·ble** *adj.* **–bond´er** *n.*

**bond´age** *n.* servitude, enslavement

**bond´ed** *adj.* secured by a bond; in a bonded warehouse; bound by fetters

**bonds´man** *n.* one who furnishes a bond for another for a fee

**bone** *n.* hard issue forming the parts of a skeleton *–vt.* to remove bones from

**bon´er** *n.* a silly mistake; a blooper

**bon´fire´** *n.* a large outdoor fire

**bon´net** *n.* a females hat

**bo´nus** *n.* an extra payment, especially an incentive; any extra benefit

**bon´y** *adj.* of a bone or bones; skinny, emaciated; with many bones, as of a food fish **–bon´i·ness** *n.*

**boob** *n.* one who is foolish; an oaf **–boo´by** *n.*

**booby trap** a device designed to be set off by an unsuspecting victim

**book** *n.* a set of pages bound together with a protective cover; a division of a lengthly literary work; a body of information about a particular subject

**book´case** *n.* a freestanding set of shelves for holding books, artifacts, etc.

**book´end** *n.* a device to keep a row of books in place

**book´ie** *n.* a bookmaker: one who takes bets, as on horse races or athletic contests

**book´ish** *adj.* scholarly; given to studying **– book´ish·ly** *adv.* **–book´ish·ness** *n.*

**book´keep·ing** *n.* the recording of the financial transactions of an organization **–book´keep·er** *n.*

**book´let** *n.* a small book or pamphlet

**book´mak·er** *n.* one who accepts wagers on races, athletic contests, etc. **–book´mak·ing** *n.*

**book´mark** *n.* a device to keep the reader's place in a book

**book´mo·bile´** *n.* a vehicle that serves as a mobile library

**book´plate** *n.* a label in or on a book that identifies the owner

**book review** a verbal or written commentary about a book

**book´worm** *n.* one who spends considerable time reading or studying

**boom** *n.* a deep sound, as of thunder; an upturn in business activity *–vi.* to make a deep sound

**boo´me·rang** *n.* a flat, bent stick that, when thrown, returns to the thrower; anything that acts differently than planned, creating the opposite effect of that intended

**boon** *n.* good fortune

**boon´dog·gle** *n.* a pointless project, often undertaken with public funds; a no-win situation

**boor** *n.* one who is vulgar or unrefined **–boor´ish** *adj.* **–boor´ish·ly** *adv.* **–boor´ish·ness** *n.*

**boost** *n.* assistance; an increase *–vt.* to push upward; to increase; to support or promote **–boost´er** *n.*

**boot** *n.* a covering for the foot and lower leg *–vt.* to kick; to dismiss from a job

**booth** *n.* a stall for the display or sale of goods, as at a fair; partially isolated seating in a restaurant

**boot´leg´** *adj.* illegal *–vi., vt.* to transport or sell illegally **–boot´leg·ger** *n.*

**boo´ty** *n.* loot; spoils of war

**booze** *n.* any alcoholic beverage **–booz´er** *n.* **–booz´y** *adj.*

**bor´der** *n.* a boundary; margin *–vt.* to extend along the boundary

**bor´der·line** *adj.* marginal; of questionable value *–n.* an edge or line of demarcation

**bore** *n.* a round hole; a dull person or event *–vt.* to make a round hole; to make weary by being dull **–bor´er** *n.*

**bore´dom** *n.* lack of interest; listlessness

**bor´ing** *adj.* uninteresting, tiresome, or dull **– bor´ing·ly** *adv.* **–bor´ing·ness** *n.*

**bor´ough** *n.* in Britain and some US states, an incorporated town

**bor´row** *vi. vt.*, to take something with agreement to return or repay in kind or equivalent; to adopt, as an idea **–bor´row·er** *n.*

**bos´om** *n.* the human breast; closeness, likened to being clasped to ones breast **–bos´om·y** *adj.*

**boss** *n.* supervisor; a person in charge *–vi., vt.* to supervise

**boss´y** *adj.* acting like a boss; domineering **–boss´i·ness** *n.*

**boss´ism** *n.* control of a political district by an autocratic leader

**bot´a·ny** *n.* the study of plants **–bo·tan´i·cal** *adj.* **–bo·tan´i·cal·ly** *adv.* **–bot´a·nist** *n.*

**botch** *n.* a shoddy piece of work *–vt.* to bungle; to do a shoddy job **–botched** *adj.* **–botch´er** *n.* **–botch´y** *adj.*

**both´er** *n.* a cause of irritation; vexation *–vi.* to be concerned with; to fuss over *–vt.* to disturb or trouble; to inconvenience **–both´er·some** *adj.*

**bot´tle** *n.* a glass container with a narrow neck; the amount a bottle can hold *–vt.* to put into bottles **–bot´tler** *n.*

**bot´tle·neck´** *n.* a place where progress is obstructed

**bot´tom** *adj.* of the lowest point *–n.* the lowest part of anything; the seat of a chair

**bouf·fant´** *adj.* puffed out, as a hairdo

**bough** *n.* the branch of a tree

**boul´der** *n.* a large rock or stone worn smooth by weather or water

**bou´le·vard´** *n.* a broad paved street, often landscaped

**bounce** *n.* a rebound; the capacity to rebound; zest, spirit *–vi.* to rebound; to spring; to return a check for insufficient funds *–vt.* to throw so as to cause a rebound; to eject an undesirable person; to dismiss from employment **–bounc´er** *n.*

**bound** *adj.* obligated; determined; tied or restricted in some way *–n.* a leap *–vi.* to leap; to border on another area *–vt.* to cause to leap or bounce; to mark or provide with boundaries

**bound´a·ry** *n.* a border or limit

**bound´less** *adj.* without end; unlimited **–bound´less·ly** *adv.***–bound´less·ness** *n.*

**boun´te·ous** *adj.* plentiful **–boun´ti·ful** *adj.* **–boun´ti·ful·ly** *adv.* **–boun´ti·ful·ness** *n.*

**boun´ty** *n.* a profusion; a reward or inducement

**bou·quet´** *n.* a bundle of cut flowers; fragrance

**bour´bon** *n.* a whiskey distilled mainly from corn *—adj.* made from or with bourbon
**bour·geois** *adj.* of the middle class; conventional *—n.* a member of the middle class
**bour·geoi·sie´** *n.* the middle class as a whole
**bout** *n.* a struggle; an incident, as of an illness
**bou·tique´** *n.* a small specialty shop
**bou·ton·niere´** *n.* a flower worn in the buttonhole of a lapel
**bo´vine** *adj.* of oxen; exhibiting the qualities of an ox
**bow** *n.* a bending of the head or body; the front of a vessel; a curve; a device for shooting arrows; a decorative knot *—vi., vt.* to bend the body in greeting; to yield
**bow´el** *n.* an intestine *—pl.* **bow´els** the intestines collectively; the inside of anything perceived as deep and dark: *the bowels of the earth*
**bowl** *n.* a deep, rounded dish for food; anything similar in shape *—vt.* to participate in the game of bowling
**bow´leg·ged** *adj.* having legs that are bowed
**bowl´er** *n.* one who bowls; a derby
**bowl´ing** *n.* a game of tenpins
**box** *n.* a container made of cardboard, wood, etc.
**box´car** *(US) n.* a rail freight car
**box´er** *n.* a prizefighter
**box office** location where tickets are sold, as for a sporting event
**box score** detailed statistics of a sporting event
**box seat** premium seats at a theater, sports stadium, etc.
**boy** *n.* a male youth **—boy´hood** *n.* **—boy´ish** *adj.* **—boy´ish·ly** *adv.* **—boy´ish·ness** *n.*
**boy´cott´** *n.* a refusal to have dealings with *—vt.* to avoid dealings with
**bra** *n.* a brassière; the top part of a two-piece swimsuit
**brace** *n.* a support or fastener; a pair of marks {} to connect elements or lines; a pair of like things *—vt.* to support; to fit out with braces; to steady oneself for an impact **—brac´er** *n.*
**brace´let** *n.* a piece of jewelry worn on the wrist or ankle
**brack´et** *n.* a support projecting from a wall; an angled support; a pair of marks [] to enclose words; a group of associated elements within a larger array *—vt.* to support or enclose with brackets; to group associated elements
**brack´ish** *adj.* slightly salty; disagreeable in taste
**brad** *n.* a small finishing nail
**brag** *vi., vt.* to say boastfully *—n.* a boast; something boasted about; a boaster
**brag·ga·do´ci·o** *n.* bravado; a swaggering manner
**brag´gart, brag´ger** *n.* one who boasts; a blowhard **—brag´gart·ly** *adv.*
**braid** *(US) n.* a strip of interwoven hair; a band of woven decorative material *—vt.* to interweave; to trim with interwoven material **—braid´er** *n.* **—braid´ing** *n.*
**braille** *n.* a method of writing that the blind can read by touch
**brain** *n.* a mass of tissue in the skull; the center of thought; mental ability; an intelligent person
**brain´child** *n.* that produced by one's own creative powers
**brain´less** *adj.* lacking common sense; mindless
**brain´pow·er** *n.* the ability to think; intellect
**brain´storm** *n.* inspiration *—vi.* to take part in a freewheeling session designed to generate ideas **—brain´storm·er** *n.*
**brain´wash´** *vt.* to indoctrinate to a new set of beliefs
**brain´y** *adj.* extremely intelligent; quick-witted **—brain´i·ness** *n.*
**braise** *vt.* to simmer in liquid
**brake** *n.* any device for slowing or stopping motion *—vi., vt.* to slow or stop
**bran** *n.* the outer husk of grain
**branch** *n.* any extension from a main part or course *—vi.* to extend from the main part
**brand** *n.* a burning stick; a mark of ownership, stigma, etc.; a trademark *—vt.* to mark, as with a brand
**bran´dish** *vt.* to wave menacingly
**brand´-new** *adj.* recently introduced or acquired; not used
**bran´dy** *n.* an alcoholic beverage distilled from wine
**brash** *adj.* impetuous; insolent **—brash´ly** *adv.* **—brash´ness** *n.*
**brass** *n.* an alloy of copper and zinc; fittings, instruments, etc. made from the alloy; boldness, impudence; high-ranking officers, executives, etc. *—adj.* pertaining to or made from brass
**brass´y** *adj.* brazen; impudent **—brass´i·ly** *adv.* **—brass´i·ness** *n.*
**brat** *n.* a badly behaved child **—brat´ty** *adj.*
**bra·va´do** *n.* pretended courage; bluster
**brave** *adj.* courageous; bold *—vt.* to face courageously **—brave´ness** *n.* **—brave´ly** *adv.*
**brav´er·y** *n.* courage
**bra·vu´ra** *n.* a showy display; ostentation
**brawl** *n.* a noisy quarrel *—vt.* to quarrel noisily **—brawl´er** *n.*
**brawn** *n.* muscle; muscular strength **—brawn´i·ness** *n.* **—brawn´y** *adj.*
**bray** *n.* the harsh cry of a donkey; any similar noise
**bra´zen** *adj.* of or like brass; bold, impudent **—bra´zen·ly** *adv.* **—bra´zen·ness** *n.*
**bra´zier** *n.* a coal heater or cooker; a worker in brass
**breach** *n.* a break or opening; a violation of a contract; a disagreement *—vt.* to break through; to violate an agreement
**bread** *n.* a baked or fried food made from grain; food in general; money
**bread and butter** the essentials; primary, as of an

important or profitable product line of a company
**bread line** a place where free food is distributed; those waiting for free food
**breadth** *n.* width; the distance from one side to the other
**bread´win·ner** *n.* the one who works to support others in a family or group
**break** *n.* a breach or fracture; a stopping or pause; an interval of rest; luck or opportunity: *to get a break*; a sudden move *–vi.* to split, come apart; to become inoperable; to sever relations; to appear or happen suddenly; to run away *–vt.* to part by force; to ruin or cause to fail; to violate the terms of a contract **–break´a·ble** *adj.*
**break´age** *n.* things broken; an allowance for things broken
**break dance** a style of acrobatic dance **–break dancer, break dancing**
**break´down** *n.* a failure to work, as of a machine; a separation into parts for analysis
**break´er** *n.* a wave that strikes against the shore
**breakfast** *n.* the first meal of the day *–vi.* to eat breakfast
**break´-in** *adj.* of a period of trial, adjustment or training *–n.* unauthorized entry, as to rob
**breaking point** the maximum level of stress that can be tolerated by a person or object
**break´neck** *adj.* of travel at a high rate of speed; dangerous
**break´through´** *n.* an important finding
**break´up** *n.* a tearing down or disintegration; a separation
**break´wa·ter** *n.* a barrier outside a harbor to shield against the impact of waves
**breast** *n.* the front of the chest
**breast´plate** *n.* a piece of armor to protect the chest
**breath** *n.* air taken into and expelled from the lungs; the act of breathing; a light breeze; a whisper
**breathe** *vi., vt.* to take air into the lungs; to whisper **–not breathe a word** promise to keep a secret
**breath´er** *n.* a break; a brief rest period
**breath´tak·ing** *adj.* exciting; awe-inspiring
**breeches** *pl. n.* tapered trousers ending just below the knee; any trousers
**breed** *n.* a group descended from common ancestors; a particular type *–vi.* to originate; to reproduce *–vt.* to bring forth young; to raise, as by selection or training **–breed´er** *n.*
**breed´ing** *n.* the production of offspring; good manners, courtesy
**breeze** *n.* a gentle wind; something easy to do *–vi.* to move quickly **–breez´i·ly** *adv.* **–breez´i·ness** *n.* **–breez´y** *adj.*
**breeze´way** *n.* an enclosed passageway between buildings or parts of a building
**breth´ren** *pl. n.* brothers
**brev´i·ty** *n.* the quality of being brief
**brew** *vi., vt.* to make beer, coffee, etc; to formulate a plan **–brew´er** *n.*
**brew´age** *n.* the brewing process; something brewed
**brew´er·y** *n.* a place where beers are made
**bribe** *n.* a payment to influence another *–vi.* to influence with a payment **–brib´a·ble** *adj.* **–brib´er** *n.* **–brib´er·y** *n.*
**brick** *n.* a clay building block; anything shaped like a brick; a reliable person *–vt.* to build with brick **–hit the bricks** go on strike
**brick´bat** *n.* a harshly critical comment; an aspersion
**brid´al** *adj.* of a bride or wedding
**bride** *n.* a woman recently or about to be married
**bride´groom** *n.* a man recently or about to be married
**brides´maid** *n.* a bride's attendant
**bridge** *n.* a structure spanning an obstacle; any similar structure or link
**bridge´work** *n.* dentures
**bri´dle** *n.* a harness for guiding a horse; anything that restrains *–vi.* to take offense *–vt.* to control, as with a bridle
**brief** *adj.* momentary; concise *–n.* a summary **–brief´ly** *adv.* **–brief´ness** *n.*
**brief´case** *n.* a piece of hand luggage for carrying documents
**brief´ing** *n.* a short summary of a situation; a set of instructions
**brig** *n.* short for brigantine; a military guardhouse
**bri·gade´** *n.* a group organized for a common purpose
**brig´an·tine** *n.* a two-masted square-rigged vessel
**bright** *adj.* full of light or color; quick-witted; lively, animated; auspicious, encouraging **–bright´ly** *adv.* **–bright´ness** *n.*
**bright´en** *vi., vt.* to make bright, as by polishing **–bright´en·er** *n.*
**bril´liant** *adj.* full of light; dazzling ingenious; talented *–n.* a gem of fine cut **–bril´liance, bril´lian·cy** *n.* **–bril´liant·ly** *adv.*
**brim** *n.* the topmost edge of a container, a projecting rim, as of a hat *–vt., vi.* to fill or be full **–brim´ful** *adj.*
**brim´less** *adj.* without a projecting brim, especially of a hat
**brim´stone** *n.* sulphur
**brine** *n.* a salt solution; the sea or its water **–brin´i·ness** *n.* **–brin´y** *adj.*
**bring** *vt.* to convey to a designated place; to influence **–bring about** cause to happen
**brink** *n.* the edge, especially of a precipice
**bri´oche** *n.* a light, rich bread
**brisk** *adj.* quick; active; stimulating **–brisk´ly** *adv.* **–brisk´ness** *n.*
**bris´tle** *n.* short, stiff hair *–vi.* to become tense; to

make offense **–bris´tly** *adj.* **–bris´tli·ness** *n.*

**brittle** *adj.* easily broken; fragile; unbending **–brit´tle·ness** *n.*

**broach** *vt.* to bring up for discussion

**broad** *adj.* wide in scope; open, obvious; general **–broad´en** *vi., vt.* **–broad´ly** *adv.* **–broad´ness** *n.*

**broad´cast´** *adj.* of radio or television *–vi., vt.* to make known over a wide area

**broad´cloth´** *n.* a fine, smooth cloth

**broad´-mind´ed** *adj.* open to unconventional ideas or actions **broad´-mind·ed·ly** *adv.*; **broad´-mind·ed·ness** *n.*

**bro·cade´** *n.* a heavy fabric covered with a raised design

**bro·chure´** *n.* a small booklet or folder

**brogue** *n.* a type of accent

**broil** *n.* a thing cooked by broiling *–vt.* to cook by direct exposure to intense heat **–broil´er** *n.*

**bro´ken** *adj.* in pieces; out of order; imperfect; ill or dispirited

**bro´ker** *n.* one who trades as agent for another, as of stock

**bro´ker·age** *n.* the office of a broker; fees charged by a broker

**bron´co** *n.* a horse of the western plains, often wild

**bronze** *n.* an alloy of copper and tin

**brooch** *n.* a large decorative pin, usually worn on a woman's dress

**brood** *adj.* of an animal kept for breeding *–n.* all the offspring hatched at once; all of the children in a family *–vi., vt.* to sit on eggs; to meditate morbidly; to pine or grieve **–brood´er** *n.* **–brood´i·ness** *n.* **–brood´y** *adv.*

**brook** *n.* a small stream

**broom** *n.* a bundle of stiff fibers for sweeping

**broth** *n.* a clear, thin meat or vegetable soup

**broth´el** *n.* a place of prostitution

**broth´er** *n.* a male sibling; a close friend; a fellow member of a fraternity, etc. **–broth´er·hood** *n.*

**broth´er-in-law** *n.* a brother by marriage

**brow** *n.* the forehead; the projecting top of a steep bank

**brow´beat** *vt.* to intimidate; to harangue **–brow´beat·er** *n.*

**brown´-bag** *(US) vi., vt.* to bring one's own lunch; to bring liquor to a restaurant that is not licensed to sell it **–brown-bag´ger** *n.*

**brown´out** *n.* a dimming of lights during an electrical shortage

**brown´stone** *n.* a house with a front of brown stone, especially one in a row of like houses

**browse** *vi., vt.* to feed on young shoots or leaves; to examine casually **–brows´er** *n.*

**bruise** *n.* a slight injury *–vt.* to wound without breaking the skin; to damage one's ego, etc.

**bruis´er** *n.* a large, strong man, often a prize fighter

**brunch** *n.* a late, often elaborate, first meal of the day

**brunet, bru·nette´** *adj.* having dark hair or eyes *–n.* a person with dark hair or eyes

**brunt** *n.* the main shock or impact

**brush** *n.* bristles attached to a handle for cleaning, etc.; a dense growth of bushes, etc.; a light touch; a brief encounter *–vi., vt.* to use a brush; to touch lightly

**brusque** *adj.* abrupt in manner; discourteous; curt **–brusque´ly** *adv.* **–brusque´ness** *n.*

**bru´tal** *adj.* extremely cruel **–bru·tal´i·ty** *n.* **–bru´tal·ly** *adv.*

**bru´tal·ise** *(Brit.)*, **bru´tal·ize** *(US) vt.* to degrade or demean; to humiliate **–bru·tal·i·sa´tion, bru·tal·i·za´tion** *n.*

**brute** *adj.* unreasoning; savage; carnal *–n.* a beast; a barbarian; a monster

**brut´ish** *adj.* bestial; savage **–brut´ish·ly** *adv.* **–brut´ish·ness** *n.*

**bub´ble** *n.* a tiny ball of gas trapped in a liquid or a film of liquid; anything shaped like a bubble *–vi., vt.* to make or form bubbles **–bub´bly** *adj.*

**buc·ca·neer´** *n.* a pirate

**buck** *n.* a male animal *–vi., vt.* to move in an effort to throw a rider

**buck´et** *n.* a container for dipping or carrying water, coal, etc.; anything that looks or functions like a bucket

**buck´le** *n.* a device for connecting the ends of a strap; a decoration that looks like a buckle *–vi., vt.* to join with a buckle; to bend under heat or pressure

**buck´ram** *n.* a coarse cotton or linen cloth

**buck´shot** *n.* heavy shot for bringing down large game

**buck up** to encourage or cheer up

**bu·col´ic** *adj.* of a country or farm setting **–bu·col´i·cal·ly** *adv.*

**bud** *n.* a small growth on a plant that precedes a leaf or flower **–nip in the bud** to stop in the early stages **–bud´like** *adj.*

**bud´dy** *n.* a close friend; a comrade

**buddy system** a pairing of comrades for mutual protection

**budge** *vi.* to move a little

**budg´et** *n.* a projection of anticipated need or use, often financial *–vi., vt.* to plan future needs **–bud´get·ar·y** *adj.*; **bud´get·er** *n.*

**buff** *vt.* to shine, polish; to burnish **–in the buff** naked

**buf´fet** *n.* a blow *–vt.* to strike repeatedly

**buf·fet´** a sideboard for storing tableware and from which food is served; an informal meal at which guests serve themselves

**buff´er** *n.* a machine, person or device that polishes; padding or another device to lessen the shock of contact

**buf·foon´** *n.* a clown or jester; a fool, jerk **–buf·foon´er·y** *n.* **–buf·foon´ish** *adj.*

**bug** *n.* any insect or similar organism; a disease-causing microorganism; an annoying defect; a small microphone for eavesdropping *–vt.* to hide a microphone for eavesdropping; to annoy

**bug´a·boo** *n.* a gremlin; something that causes difficulty, fear, or anxiety

**bug´-eyed** *adj.* amazed; astonished

**bug´gy** *adj.* infested with bugs; ecocentric, crazy *–n.* a light, one-horse carriage

**bu´gle** *n.* a hunting or military horn *–vi., vt.* to signal with a bugle call **–bu´gler** *n.*

**build** *n.* the physical form of a person *–vi.* to put up a building; to increase in amount, intensity, etc. *–vt.* to construct; to cause to grow; to establish as a basis **–build´er** *n.*

**build´ing** *n.* a structure with sidewalls and a roof

**build´up** *n.* information designed to promote; puffery; a gradual increase: *an inventory buildup*

**built´-in** *adj.* installed as part of the structure, such as for cabinets or appliances

**built´-up** *adj.* of land covered by buildings in close proximity to each other

**bulb** *n.* the tuberous root of a plant; anything similar in shape

**bul´bous** *adj.* round; shaped like a bulb; rotund, corpulent

**bulge** *n.* an outward swelling; a projection *–vi., vt.* to swell out; to project **–bulg´i·ness** *n.*

**bulk** *adj.* of the aggregate; not broken down *–n.* the main part *–vi., vt.* to enlarge, expand; to buy in bulk; to purchase a large quantity, not broken down for resale

**bulk´head** *n.* a wall, as of a ship or airplane

**bulk´y** *adj.* of significant size; awkward or difficult to handle; more because of size than weight **–bulk·i·ness** *n.*

**bull** *n.* the adult male of certain large animals; a speculator who anticipates higher prices

**bull´doz´er** *n.* a powerful earthmoving machine; one who aggressively promotes an idea, cause, etc. **–bull´doze** *vt.*

**bul´le·tin** *n.* a brief statement; a timely report; a newsletter

**bul´let·proof** *adj.* unable to pierce with bullets; of an agreement or contract that cannot be broken

**bull´frog´** *n.* a large North American frog

**bull´head´ed** *adj.* stubborn; obstinate **–bull´head·ed·ly** *adv.* **–bull´head·ed·ness** *n.*

**bull´horn** *n.* a hand-held amplifier

**bul´lion** *n.* bulk gold or silver

**bull´ock** *n.* a steer; a castrated bull

**bull´pen** *n.* an area where the members of a baseball team wait when they are not playing; any waiting or holding area; those not participating who are available to be called on

**bull´s´eye** *n.* the center of a target; the achievement of a goal

**bul´ly** *n.* one who intimidates those who are smaller or weaker *–vi., vt.* to intimidate

**bul´wark** *n.* a fortification; the side of a ship above the deck

**bum** *adj.* of inferior quality; erroneous or worthless *–n.* a tramp or derelict; a loafer; one addicted to a pursuit to the neglect of all else *–vi.* to live as a vagrant or by begging *–vt.* to get by begging or free-loading

**bum´mer** *n.* a bad experience; a washout

**bump** *n.* a blow; a bulge or swelling *–vi., vt.* to hit or collide with

**bump´er** *adj.* remarkablv large: *a bumper crop –n.* a guard to absorb the shock of collision

**bump´kin** *n.* an unrefined person; a country boy

**bump´tious** *adj.* arrogantly conceited **–bump´tious·ly** *adv.* **–bump´tious·ness** *n.*

**bump´y** *adj.* marked by bulges; rough; irregular **–travel a bumpy road** undertake a difficult task **–bump´i·ness** *n.*

**bun** *n.* a small bread roll

**bunch** *n.* a cluster of like things attached or together *–vi., vt.* to gather together **–bunch´i·ness** *n.* **–bunch´y** *adj.*

**bun´dle** *n.* a number of things bound together *–vt.* to make into bundles; to dress warmly

**bung** *n.* a stopper in a barrel or cask

**bun´ga·low´** *n.* a small house

**bun´gee, bun´gee cord** *n.* an elastic cord used to secure cargo

**bungee jumping** the sport of leaping from a height with an elastic cord attached to one's ankles so as to break the fall before hitting the surface

**bun´gle** *vi., vt.* to make or work clumsily *–n.* an imperfect performance **–bun´gler** *n.* **–bun´gling·ly** *adv.*

**bun´ion** *n.* an inflammation on the big toe

**bunk** *n.* a bed attached to the wall; any sleeping place; meaningless or misleading information *–vi.* to sleep in a bunk or makeshift bed

**bunk´er** *n.* a fortified position

**bunk´house** *n.* sleeping quarters to accommodate a number of workers such as field hands

**bunk mate, bunk´mate** *n.* one who shares quarters or lives in the same bunkhouse

**bun´ny** *n.* a rabbit

**bunt** *vi., vt.* to hit a pitched baseball lightly so as to keep it in the infield *–n.* **–sacrifice bunt** a strategy that will likely result in an out for the batter with the intention of advancing another base runner **–bunt´er** *n.*

**bun´ting** *n.* cloth used to make flags, banners, etc.; a decorative banner; a baby's garment or wrapping

**buoy** *n.* a fixed float in water to mark a navigable channel, a hazard, etc. *—vt.* to keep afloat; to encourage **—buoy´an·cy** *n.* **—buoy´ant** *adj.*

**bur´den** *n.* a heavy or difficult load; a responsibility *—vt.* to weigh down **—bur´den·some** *adj.*

**bu´reau** *(US) n.* a chest of drawers; an office, department, or agency

**bu·reauc´ra·cy** *n.* governing through a number of departments or sections, each with limited jurisdiction or authority **—bu´reau·crat** *n.*

**bu·reau·crat´ic** *adj.* to act strictly according to the rules **—bu·reau·crat´i·cal·ly** *adv.*

**bu·reau´cra·tise** *(Brit.)*, **bu·reau´cra·tize** *(US) vi., vt.* to make into or develop into a bureaucrat or bureaucracy **—bu·reau·cra·ti·sa´tion, bu·reau·cra·ti·za´tion** *n.*

**burg** *n.* a small town or village, usually inferring one that is quiet or backward

**bur´geon** *vi.* to grow rapidly or profusely; to flourish

**burg´er** *n.* a ground meat, fish or vegetable patty; a sandwich made with such a patty

**bur´gla·ry** *n.* the act of breaking in to commit a crime **—bur´glar** *n.* **—bur´glar·ize** *vi.*

**bur´i·al** *n.* the act of burying

**bur´lap** *(US) n.* a coarse cloth used in the making of sacks and as a backing of upholstry or carpeting

**bur·lesque´** *n.* broad comedy; satire; a type of theatrical entertainment *—vt.* to imitate with mockery or satire

**bur´ly** *adj.* strong and muscular **—bur´li·ness** *n.*

**burn** *n.* an injury caused by fire *—vi.* to be on fire; to emit light or heat; to be injured by fire; to be heated, as with emotion *—vt.* to set on fire; to injure, change or consume by fire **—burn´er** *n.* **—burnt** *adj.*

**bur´nish** *n.* a smooth luster *—vt.* to polish **—bur´nish·er** *n.*

**bur·noose´, bur·nous´** *n.* a long hooded cloak

**burp** *n.* belch

**burp gun** an automatic weapon

**bur´ro** *n.* a donkey

**bur´row** *n.* a hole dug by an animal for shelter *—vi., vt.* to make or hide in a burrow **—bur´row·er** *n.*

**bur´sar** *n.* one dealing with money, especially the comptroller of a college or university

**bur´sa·ry** *n.* a treasury or repository for funds, especially for a college or university

**burst** *n.* a sudden action, as an explosion or eruption *—vi.* to break apart suddenly; to express sudden emotion or action *—vt.* to cause to break apart

**bur´y** *vt.* to place in the ground; to cover so as to hide; to remove from one's conscious mind; to completely absorb oneself

**burying ground** a cemetery, especially of ancient origin

**bus** *n.* a motor vehicle designed to carry a large number of passengers; an omnibus; *(Brit.)* a large, often double-decker, passenger vehicle that operates locally

**bus´boy** *n.* a restaurant worker whose duty it is to clear tables

**bush** *n.* a woody plant with a profusion of low branches; an area with many such plants; anything like such a plant **—beat around the bush** to talk around an issue without committing oneself **—bush´i·ness** *n.* **—bush´y** *adj.*

**bushed** *adj.* tired; fatigued

**bush´el** *n.* a dry measure of 4 pecks or 32 dry quarts

**bush´ing** *n.* a sleeve for reducing friction between machine parts

**bush´whack** *vi., vt.* to attack from ambush **—bush´whack·er** *n.*

**busi´ness** *n.* commerce; the buying and selling of goods and services; one's occupation; any activity or matter for concern: *the business of planning a party, mind your own business* **—got the business** subjected to rough treatment, hazing, teasing, etc. **—to mean business** to be sincere or resolute

**busi´ness·like** *adj.* of a professional; manner; systematic, orderly

**buss** *n.* a kiss; a smack on the lips *—vi., vt.* to kiss playfully

**bust** *n.* a sculpture of a person from head to the upper chest; the chest; an undertaking that is a failure; a severe economic downturn *—vi., vt.* to break; to make or become bankrupt

**bus´tle** *n.* brisk activity *—vi.* to move briskly **—bus´tling·ly** *adv.*

**bus´y** *adj.* active; occupied **—bus´i·ly** *adv.* **—bus´y·ness** *n.*

**bus´y·bod·y** *n.* one who is overly concerned with or meddles in the affairs of others

**bus´y·work** *n.* useless activity intended to appear worthwhile

**butch´er** *n.* one who processes and sells meat; a murderer *—vt.* to kill animals or process their meat; to massacre; to do sloppy work **—butch´er·y** *n.*

**but´ler** *n.* a manservant usually in charge of food service

**butler's pantry** a station between the kitchen and dining room where the table service is kept

**but´ter** *n.* edible fat obtained from churning cream; any spread used like butter **—but´ter·y** *adj.*

**but´ter·ball** *n.* affectionately, a chubby person

**but´ter·fat** *n.* the fat in milk that is churned into butter

**but´ter·fin·gered** *adj.* of one who is clumsy **—but´ter·fin·ger** *n.*

**but´ter·fly´** *adj.* of or like a butterfly *—n.* an insect noted for its colorful wings

**butterfly bandage** an adhesive plaster shaped like

a butterfly with wings extended, used to keep a wound tightly closed

**but´ter·milk´** *n.* the liquid remains left after churning butter

**but´ter·scotch** *adj.* of a flavoring of brown sugar and butter *—n.* the flavoring; a candy made with this flavor

**but´ton** *n.* a small device for fastening clothing; a thing resembling a button *—vi., vt.* to fasten with buttons **—button down** to finalize, take care of the last detail **—button up** don't speak; keep a secret **—on the button** on time, in place, etc.; precise

**but´ton-down** *adj.* of a shirt or jacket collar whose tips are buttoned to the garment; conservative

**but´ton·hole** *n.* an opening in clothing designed to receive a button *—vt.* to compel one to listen

**but´tress** *n.* a structure that extends out from a wall to reinforce it; reinforcement *—vt.* to reinforce, support **—flying buttress** a buttress built away from a wall and connected to it by an arch

**bux´om** *adj.* full-figured **—bux´om·ly** *adv.* **—bux´om·ness** *n.*

**buy** *n.* anything purchased; a bargain *—vt.* to obtain for money; accept as valid **—buy´a·ble** *adj.* **—buy´er** *n.*

**buy off** to bribe

**buy time** to stall

**buzz** *n.* a droning sound; a low murmur; a telephone call *—vi.* to make a droning sound, like that of a bee; to talk excitedly in a low tone *—vt.* to speak rapidly in a low tone; to make a telephone call; to signal with a buzzer

**buzz´er** *n.* a device that signals with a buzzling sound, as for a timer

**by** *prep.* proximity in space or time; at the hand of; through the medium of *—adv.* near

**by´-and-by´** *n.* at some time in the future

**bye law** *(Brit.)* the rules governing an association or organization

**by´gone** *adj.* past **—let bygones be bygones** forgive a past indiscretion

**by´law** *(US) n.* the rules governing an association or organization

**by´-line** *n.* an attribution; a naming of the author, as for a newspaper or magazine article **—by´-lin·er** *n.*

**by´pass´** *n.* an alternative or auxiliary route; that which provides an auxilliary route *—vt.* to detour; to circumvent

**by´-path** *n.* a route seldom taken

**by´-play** *n.* events taking place aside from the main activity, as in a play or office politics

**by´-prod´uct** *n.* material, often waste, accumulated as the result of processing; a secondary product, often from the waste created by primary manufacturing or processing

**by´stand·er** *n.* one who is present, but not involved

**byte** *n.* a set of binary digits that is transferred as a unit in a computer; a computer word

**by´way** *n.* a side road, often branching from a main road

**c, C** *n.* third letter of the English alphabet; third-rate; in Roman characters, the symbol for 100

**cab** *n.* a taxicab; a separate area for the operator of a vehicle or heavy machinery

**cab´driv·er, cab´by** *n.* one who operates a taxicab

**ca·bal´** *n.* a group of plotters; a secret plot

**cab´a·la, cab·ba´la** *n.* mystical teachings of Hebrew origin; any mystical or esoteric doctrine **—cab·a·lis´tic** *adj.*

**ca·ba´na** *n.* a shelter for changing at a beach or pool

**cab·a·ret´** *n.* a nightclub

**cab´in** *n.* a small house; a room on a boat, plane, etc.

**cabin boy** an apprentice seaman who performs menial tasks on board ship

**cab´i·net** *n.* an article of furniture used for storage; a body of advisors

**cab´i·net·mak·er** *n.* a craftsman in making wood articles **—cab´i·net·ry, cab´i·net·work** *n.*

**cabin fever** anxiety, agitation or boredom as the result of living in a confined space

**ca´ble** *n.* a heavy rope, often of metal; a bundle of insulated conductors; a cablegram; cable television *—vt.* to connect with cable; to send a cablegram

**cable car** a vehicle for the transport of passengers or freight, drawn by a cable up a sharp incline, across a ravine, etc.

**ca´ble·gram** *n.* a message carried by undersea cable

**cable television** a system that provides for the transmission of television signals to subscribers outside of a normal viewing area.

**ca´ble·vi·sion** *n.* cable television

**ca·boo´dle** *n.* a batch or group

**ca·boose´** *(US) n.* the last car on a freight train; the trainmen's car

**cab·ri·o·let´** *n.* a small horse-drawn carriage

**cab´stand** *n.* a place designated for taxicabs or carriages to wait for fares

**ca·ca´o** *n.* a tropical tree that bears the seeds for making chocolate; the seeds of the cacao tree

**cache** *n.* a place for storing food or supplies; the material thus stored; in a computer, a memory location set aside to store data for quick retrieval

**ca·chet´** *n.* a mark attesting to authenticity, quality, approval, etc.

**ca·coph´o·ny** *n.* dissonance; a harsh noise **—ca·coph´o·nous** *adj.* **—ca·coph´o·nous·ly** *adv.*

**cac´tus** *n., pl.* **cac´ti, cac´tus·es** a desert plant with spiney leaves

**cad** *n.* one who exhibits coarse or crude behavior; a nasty person; a rogue

**ca·dav´er** *(US) n.* a dead body
**ca·dav´er·ous** *adj.* pale, gaunt; like a corpse **—ca·dav´er·ous·ly** *adv.* **—ca·dav´er·ous·ness** *n.*
**ca´dence, ca´den·cy** *n.* a rhythmic flow of sound, as of poetry; a measured beat, as in marching **ca´denced, ca´dent** *adj.*
**ca·den´tial** *adj.* pertaining to a cadence or a cadenza
**ca·den´za** *n.* an intricate flourish in a musical solo
**ca·det´** *n.* a student in a military school
**cadge** *vi., vt.* to beg or acquire by begging; to freeload **—cadg´er** *n.*
**ca´dre** *n.* staff; key personnel charged with training or leading others
**ca·du´ce·us** *n.* a winged staff with coiled serpents that is the emblem of the medical profession **—ca·du´ce·an** *adj.*
**cae·sar´e·an, caesarean section** *n.* a technique for delivering a baby by surgery
**ca·fe´, ca·fé´** *n.* a coffee-house or restaurant
**café au lait** a beverage of equal parts dark coffee and scalded milk
**caf´e·te´ri·a** *n.* a self-service or limited service restaurant; *(US)* a facility where employee meals are served
**caf·feine´** *n.* a stimulant occurring naturally in coffee and tea, and that is added to some sodas, diet pills, medications, etc. **—caf´fein·at·ed** *adj.*
**caf´tan** *n.* a long-sleeved robe; a long, loose dress
**cage** *n.* a place of confinement *—vt.* to put in confinement
**ca´gey** *adj.* cunning; shrewd, clever **—ca´gi·ly** *adv.* **—cag´i·ness** *n.*
**cai´man, cay'man** *n.* a Central or South American reptile similar to the alligator
**cais´son** *n.* an ammunition chest; a wagon for transporting ammunition
**caisson disease** a painful condition caused by the formation of nitrogen bubbles in the bloodstream, such as for a deep sea diver who surfaces too quickly
**cai´tiff** *adj.* cowardly, despicable *—n.* one who is mean or vulgar
**ca·jole´** *vi., vt.* to press with repeated appeals; to wheedle by flattery **—ca·jole´ment, ca·jol´er·y** *n.* **—ca·jol´er** *n.* **ca·jol´ing·ly** *adv.*
**cake** *n.* a sweet, bread-like pastry; something molded into a patty, block, or brick *—vi., vt.* to harden or form a crust **—icing on the cake** something extra; an unexpected bonus **—piece of cake** easy to do
**cake´walk** *n.* a strutting dance; a thing easily accomplished
**ca·lam´i·ty** *n.* extreme misfortune; tragedy **—ca·lam´i·tous** *adj.* **— ca·lam´i·tous·ly** *adv.* **—ca·lam´i·tous·ness** *n.*
**cal´ci·fy** *vi., vt.* to turn to stone or a stone-like mass **—cal·cif´ic** *adj.* **—cal·ci·fi·ca´tion** *n.*
**cal´ci·mine** *n.* a white liquid used to cover plastered walls
**cal´ci·um** *n.* a mineral essential to the growth of bones, teeth, etc.
**cal´cu·late´** *vt.* to determine by using mathematics; to estimate; to intend: calculated to handle most of the traffic **—cal·cu·la´tion** *n.* **—cal´cu·la·tive** *adj.* **—cal´cu·la·tor** *n.*
**cal´cu·lat·ed** *adj.* arrived at by computation or reckoning; deliberate **—cal´cu·lat·ed·ly** *adv.* **—cal´cu·lat·ed·ness** *n.*
**cal´cu·lat·ing** *adj.* scheming; shrewd or crafty **—cal´cu·lat·ing·ly** *adv.*
**cal´cu·lous** *adj.* relating to or having a stony deposit
**cal´cu·lus** *n., pl.* **cal´cu·li, cal´cu·lus·es** a stone-like deposit, as in the kidney or gallbladder; a system of computation employing symbolic notation
**cal´dron, caul´dron** *n.* a large kettle
**cal´en·dar** *n.* a system for arranging the months, weeks, and days of the year; a list of appointments
**calf** *n., pl.* **calves** the young of certain animals; the cured hide of a young cow: calfskin; the fleshy back of the leg below the knee
**cal´i·ber** *n.* the diameter of a cylindrical object, as a gun; the quality of a person
**cal´i·brate** *vt.* to regulate or adjust a measuring instrument or device **—cal·i·bra´tion** *n.* **—cal´i·bra·tor** *n.*
**cal´i·co´** *n.* a printed cotton cloth
**cal´i·per** *n.* a device for measuring thickness or diameter
**ca´liph, ca´lif** *n.* an Islamic leader or ruler
**ca´liph·ate** *n.* land ruled by a caliph
**cal´is·then´ics** *pl. n.* exercises to develop the body
**cal·lig´ra·phy** *n.* handwriting as an art form; embellished handwriting **—cal·lig´ra·pher** *n.* **—cal·li·graph´ic** *adj.*
**call´ing** *n.* the act of one who calls; one's profession or vocation
**calling card** a small card containing one's name and other information appropriate to its use, such as address, profession, etc.; a business card
**cal·li´o·pe´** *n.* a keyboard instrument similar to the organ that uses steam whistles to create tones
**cal´lous** *adj.* heartless; indifferent **—cal´lous·ly** *adv.* **—cal´lous·ness** *n.*
**cal´low** *adj.* young and inexperienced; immature **—cal´low·ness** *n.*
**cal´lus** *n.* a thickened formation of skin
**call waiting** a feature of some telephone systems that alerts one who is on the phone of another incoming call
**calm** *adj.* still; tranquil; composed *—n.* stillness; tranquility *—vi., vt.* to soothe or pacify **—calm´ly** *adv.* **—calm´ness** *n.*
**calm´a·tive** *n.* a sedative

**cal´o•rie** *n.* one of two measures of heat, the small or *gram calorie* and the large or *kilogram calorie*; the large calorie, used to measure the energy produced by food –**ca•lor´ic** *adj.* –**ca•lor´i•cal•ly** *adv.*

**cal•o•rif´ic** *adj.* producing heat; of high calorie foods –**cal•o•rif´i•cal•ly** *adv.*

**cal•o•rim´e•ter** *n.* a device for measuring quantities of heat

**ca•lum´ni•ate** *vi., vt.* to spread slanderous rumors –**ca•lum•ni•a´tion** *n.* –**ca•lum´ni•a•tor** *n.*

**ca•lum´ni•ous** *adj.* slanderous –**ca•lum´ni•ous•ly** *adv.*

**cal´um•ny** *n.* slander; defamation

**calve** *vi., vt.* to give birth to a calf

**ca•lyp´so** *n.* the rhythmic music of Trinidad –*adj.*

**ca•ma•ra´de•rie** *n.* good fellowship

**cam´ber** *n.* arching; curvature

**cam´bist** *n.* one who deals in foreign exchange; a publication that lists rates of exchange –**cam´bist•ry** *n.*

**cam´bric** *n.* a fine linen fabric

**cam´cord•er** *n.* a portable video camera

**cam´el** *n.* a common beast of burden in the deserts of Asia and Africa –**cam´el•eer´** *n.*

**cam´e•o´** *n.* a shell or gem carved in relief; a brief appearance by a noted performer

**cam´er•a** *n.* a device for recording visual images –**cam´er•a•man** *n.*

**cam´er•a lu´ci•da** *n.* an optical device for projecting an image on a flat surface

**cam´ou•flage´** *n.* the art of protection through the deceptive use of color and form; any device employed to conceal or deceive

**camp** *n.* an area of temporary living, as for soldiers or vacationers; something flamboyant, outdated, artificial, etc. –*vi., vt.* to live temporarily ourdoors –**camp´er** *n.* –**camp´ground, camp´site** *n.*

**cam•paign´** *n.* an undertaking organized to achieve a specific objective –*vi.* to participate in such an undertaking –**cam•paign´er** *n.*

**cam•pa•ni´le** *n.* a bell tower

**cam•pa•nol´o•gy** *n.* the art of designing and making bells –**cam•pa•nol´o•gist** *n.*

**camp´fire** *n.* an outdoor fire for cooking, warmth, or as a gathering place for campers

**cam´pus** *adj.* of a school or its buildings, grounds, etc. –*n.* the grounds or buildings of a complex, such as for a school, hospital, etc.

**ca•nal´** *n.* an artificial waterway; a waterway improved so as to be navigable; a duct or channel –*vt.* to build a canal

**can´a•pé** *n.* an appetizer comprised of bread or crackers spread with meat, cheese, etc.

**ca•nard´** *n.* a misleading story; a hoax

**can´cel** *vt.* to invalidate; to rescind; to delete –**can´cel•a•ble** *adj.* –**can´cel•er** *n.* –**can•cel•la´tion** *n.*

**can´cer** *n.* a malignant growth; any infectious evil –**can´cer•ous** *adj.* –**can´cer•ous•ly** *adv.*

**can•de•la´brum** *n., pl.* **can•de•la´bra** a large, branching candle holder

**can´did** *adj.* straightforward, honest; impartial –**can´did•ly** *adv.* –**can´did•ness** *n.*

**can´di•date** *n.* a nominee for office, an award, etc.

**can´died** *adj.* cooked in or coated with sugar

**can´dle** *n.* a wax or tallow cylinder surrounding a wick that can be burned to give off light; anything similar in form or use –*vt.* to examine, as eggs, by placing in front of a bright light –**burn the candle at both ends** to work or play so hard as to burn up one's energy –**not hold a candle to** to be in some way inferior

**can´dle•light** *adj.* lighted by candles, as *a candlelight supper*, of the soft light of candles –*n.* subdued light

**can´dle•pow•er** *n.* an expression of the intensity of a light

**can´dle•stick** *n.* a candle; a candle holder; a candelabrum

**can´dor** *n.* frankness or honesty of expression; impartiality

**can´dy** *(US) n.* a confection made primarily from sugar and flavoring –*vt.* to glaze with a sugar syrup

**candy striper** a hospital volunteer worker

**cane** *n.* the stem of certain woody piants; the plants themselves; split rattan used in weaving; a walking stick; a rod used for flogging –*vt.* to beat, as with a cane –**can´er** *n.*

**cane´brake** *n.* a stand of sugar cane

**cane sugar** sugar obtained from cane

**ca´nine´** *adj.* of or like a dog –*n.* a dog; a sharp-pointed tooth

**can´is•ter** *n.* a small storage container; any similar container

**can´ker** *n.* an ulcerous sore; something that tends to corrupt –*vi., vt.* to infect or corrupt –**can´ker•ous** *adj.*

**canned** *adj.* of food that has been processed and sealed in metal containers; material recorded for later broadcast; prepared ahead; contrived

**can´ner** *n.* a person or company involved in the processing and packaging of food

**can´ner•y** *n.* an industrial plant where raw food is processed

**can´ni•bal** *n.* any creature that eats its own kind –**can´ni•bal•ism** *n.* –**can•ni•bal•is´tic** *adj.*

**can´ni•bal•ise** *(Brit.),* **can´ni•bal•ize** *(US) vi., vt.* to devour one's own kind; to take parts from to use in repairing or building another

**can´ny** *adj.* cautious, watchful; shrewd –**can´ni•ly** *adv.* –**can´ni•ness** *n.*

**ca•noe´** *n.* a light, narrow boat –*vi., vt.* to travel or carry by canoe

**can´on** *n.* the laws of a church; an established principle, a standard

**ca·non´ic, ca·non´i·cal** *adj.* according to church law; accepted as a standard **—ca·non´i·cal·ly** *adv.* **—can·on·ic´i·ty** *n.*

**can´on·ist** *n.* an authority in canon law **—can·on·is´tic** *adj.*

**can´on·ize** *vt.* to sanctify or consecrate; to glorify, venerate **—can·on·i·za´tion** *n.* **—can´on·ry** *n.*

**canon law** the precepts that govern a church

**can´o·py** *n.* a protective, roof-like covering; anything similar in form or function *—vt.* to create an overhead covering

**cant** *n.* a sloping surface; the terminology peculiar to a particular group; insincere speech *—vi., vt.* to slope or cause to slope; to speak in a particular jargon

**can´ta·loupe´** *n.* a variety of melon

**can·tan´ker·ous** *adj.* quarrelsome, disagreeable

**caf´e·te´ri·a** *n.* a self-service or limited service restaurant; *(US)* a facility where employee meals are served

**can·teen´**[1] *n.* a small sealed container for drinking water; a place where food is served to workers

**can·teen´**[2] *(Brit.)* a collection of cutlery

**can´ti·cle** *n.* a hymn

**can´ti·lev·er** *n.* a projection anchored only by the wall from which it emerges

**can´tor** *n.* a choir leader; a leader in prayer or scripture reading

**can´vas** *n.* a heavy cloth used for sails, tents, oil paintings, etc.; an oil painting

**can´vass** *vi., vt.* to blanket an area for opinions, votes, etc. **—can´vass·er** *n.*

**can´yon** *n.* a narrow gorge

**cap** *n.* a tight-fitting covering for the head; any cover, as for a bottle, jar, etc. *—vt.* to place a top on; to cover

**ca´pa·ble** *adj.* having the necessary skill **—ca·pa·bil´i·ty, ca´pa·ble·ness** *n.* **—ca´pa·bly** *adv.*

**ca·pa´cious** *adj.* spacious; massive; having the space to hold much **—ca·pa´cious·ly** *adv.* **—ca·pa´cious·ness** *n.*

**ca·pac´i·ty** *n.* the ability to hold; having the necessary aptitude; properly qualified or authorized

**cape** *n.* a sleeveless outer garment, a cloak; a point of land extending into a body of water

**caper** *n.* a playful leap; a silly action or prank *—vi.* to leap in a playful manner: frolic

**cap´il·lar´y** *adj.* like a hair; of the hair-like blood vessels of the body *—n.* any of the tiny blood vessels of the body **—cap·il·la´ceous** *adj.*

**cap·il·lar´i·ty** *n.* the interaction between contacting surfaces of a liquid and a solid that encloses it

**cap´i·tal** *adj.* punishable by death; most significant; first-rate *—n.* the center of an industry, government, etc.; assets, as money or property; an uppercase letter; the top of a column

**cap´i·tal·ism** *n.* an economic system in which most means for the production of goods and services are privately owned **—cap´i·tal·ist** *n.* **—cap·i·tal·is´tic** *adj.* **—cap·i·tal·is´ti·cal·ly** *adv*

**cap´i·tal·ise** *(Brit.)*, **cap´i·tal·ize** *(US) vt.* to write the first letter or all of the letters of a word in uppercase; to finance; to exploit or turn to a profit **—cap·i·tal·i·sa´tion, cap·i·tal·i·za´tion** *n.*

**capital punishment** a penalty of death

**Capitol** the building in which the US Congress meets **—capitol** the building housing a state legislature in the US

**ca·pit´u·late´** *vi.* to surrender, often condition- ally **—ca·pit·u·la´tion** *n.*

**ca·pote´** *n.* a long, hooded cloak

**ca·price´** *n.* a sudden impetuous action; a tendency to unpredictable change **—ca·pri´cious** *adj.* **—ca·pri´cious·ly** *adv.* **—ca·pri´cious·ness** *n.*

**cap´size** *vt.* to upend **—cap´siz·a·ble** *adj.*

**cap´stan** *n.* a shipboard apparatus for hoisting an anchor; a spindle that drives magnetic tape

**cap´sule´** *n.* a small container, such as a seed pod or that used to hold a single dose of medicine; a closed compartment, as for personnel and instruments in a spacecraft **—cap´su·lar, cap´su·late, cap´su·lat·ed** *adj.*

**cap´sul·ize** *vt.* to summarize; to furnish in an abbreviated form

**cap´tain** *n.* an officer in a military or quasi-military hierarchy; a group leader in some enterprise, as *captain of the team*

**cap´tion** *n.* a heading or title, as of a legal document or a composition; descriptive matter

**cap´tious** *adj.* intended to be critical; fond of finding fault **—cap´tious·ly** *adv.* **—cap´tious·ness** *n.*

**cap´ti·vate´** *vt.* to attract, as by charm; to fascinate or bewitch **—cap´ti·vat·ing·ly** *adv.* **—cap·ti·va´tion** *n.* **—cap´ti·va·tor** *n.*

**cap´tive** *adj.* held prisoner; restricted; fascinated *—n.* a prisoner **—cap´tiv´i·ty** *n.* **—cap´tor** *n.*

**captive audience** an audience held by one's charm or charisma; an audience that cannot leave, as at a bussiness meeting

**cap´ture** *n.* the act of taking or being taken prisoner; that taken *—vt.* to take and hold; to captivate, as by charm **—cap´tor, cap´tur·er** *n.*

**car** *n.* an automobile; a space or area for passengers, as on an elevator; *(US)* a railway passenger vehicle

**ca·rafe´** *n.* a container for serving beverages

**car´a·mel** *n.* burnt sugar used as a flavoring; a candy of this flavor; the color of burnt sugar **—car´a·mel·ize** *vi., vt.*

**car´at** *n.* a unit of weight for gems

**car´a·van**[1] *n.* a company of travelers; a file of vehicles or pack animals **—car´a·van·er, car´a·van·ner** *n.*

**car´a·van²** *n. (Brit.)* a mobile home

**car·a·van´sa·ry** *n.* an inn with a large center courtyard; a haven for caravans

**car´a·vel** *n.* a small, 15th century sailing ship

**car´a·way** *n.* a seed used for flavoring; the herb that produces such seeds

**car´bine** *n.* a light rifle

**car´bo·hy´drate** *n.* an organic compound composed of carbon, hydrogen, and oxygen

**car´bon** *n.* a nonmetallic chemical element present in all organic compounds –**car·bo·na´ceous, car·bon´ic, car·bon·if´er·ous** *adj.*

**car´bo·nate** *vt.* to infuse with carbon dioxide, as *carbonated water* –**car·bon·a´tion** *n.*

**carbon dating** determination of the age of a relic by measurement of the amount of carbon 14 remaining in it –**car´bon-date** *vt.*

**car·bon di·ox·ide** *n.* a colorless, odorless gas released by respiration and absorbed by plants

**carbon 14** a radioactive isotope of carbon used to date relics

**car´bon·ize** *vt.* to convert to carbon; to coat or combine with carbon

**car·bon mon·ox·ide** *n.* a colorless, odorless, poisonous gas

**carbon paper** a thin paper placed between sheets of writing paper to transfer an image from the top sheet to the sheet below

**carbon copy** an exact duplicate

**car·bon tet·ra·chlo·ride** *n.* a colorless liquid solvent commonly used as a cleaning fluid

**car´bun·cle** *n.* a deep red gemstone; a large painful skin eruption similar to a boil –**car·bun´cu·lar** *adj.*

**car´bu·re·tor** *n.* a device for mixing air and gas to feed an internal combustion engine –**car´bu· ret** *vt.* **car·bu·ri·za´tion** *n.*

**car´cass** *n.* a dead animal; the human body

**car·cin´o·gen** *n.* a cancer-causing substance –**car·ci·no·gen´e·sis** *n.* –**car·cin·o·gen´ic** *adj.*

**car·ci·no´ma** *n.* a cancerous growth –**car·ci·nom´a·tous** *adj.*

**car·ci·no·ma·to´sis** *n.* the spread of a carcinoma throughout the body

**card** *n.* a small, stiff sheet of paper, plastic, etc.; a witty or amusing person –**business card** a card that identifies one in business, especially a salesperson –**credit card** identification signifying that the bearer is authorized to purchase on credit –**playing card** a set of cards containing numbers, pictures, etc. used as elements in a game –**trading card** any of a series of cards depicting noted personalities, events, etc.

**car´da·mom** *n.* a spice

**card´board** *n.* a stiff paper-like material –*adj.* of or like cardboard

**card-carrying** *adj.* of one who is a member; of one who espouses a cause, as a *card-carrying environmentalist*

**car´di·ac´** *adj.* of the heart

**car´di·gan** a long-sleeved sweater that buttons down the front

**car´di·nal** *adj.* primary; foremost –**car´di·nal·ly** *adv.*

**cardinal number** a number that designates quantity, in contrast to an *ordinal number* that denotes relative position

**car·di·ol´o·gy** *n.* the branch of medicine that deals with the heart, its function, and diseases –**car·di·o·log´ic, car·di·o·log´i·cal** *adj.*

**car·di·ol´o·gist** *n.* one who specializes in diseases of the heart

**card shark** an expert player at cards, often, one who cheats

**card table** a felt-topped table designed for card playing; a utility table with folding legs

**care** *n.* having concern; acting with caution; having responsibility –*vi., vt.* to feel concern –**couldn´t care less** of no concern

**ca·reen´** *vi., vt.* to lean sideways; to swerve

**ca·reer´** *n.* one's progress through life; a line of work –**ca·reer´ism** *n.* –**ca·reer´ist** *n.*

**care´free** *adj.* without concern or worry; lighthearted

**care´ful** *adj.* cautious; attentive to detail; frugal –**care´ful·ly** *adv.* –**care´ful·ness** *n.*

**care´giv·er** *n.* an individual or organization charged with the health and well-being of another

**care´less** *adj.* reckless, lacking reasonable caution; inattentive to detail –**care´less·ly** *adv.* –**care´less·ness** *n.*

**ca·ress´** *vt.* to touch lightly, as by a breeze; to stroke lovingly –*n.* an expression of affection; a gentle touching –**ca·ress´ing·ly** *adv.* –**ca·ress´ive** *adj.*

**car´et** *n.* a mark (^) used to show where something is to be inserted

**care´tak·er** *n.* one hired to maintain or preserve, as of a house or grounds; one temporarily filling a position pending a permanent appointment

**care´worn** *adj.* weary; showing the effects of a burden

**car´fare** *n.* the price of a ride, as on a public conveyance

**car´go** *n.* freight

**car´i·ca·ture** *n.* an exaggerated likeness; something so inferior as to be absurd –*vt.* to ridicule; to create a distorted likeness –**car´i·ca·tur·ist** *n.*

**car´ies** *n.* the decay of teeth

**car´il·lon** *n.* an instrument that sounds musical passages with the use of bells –**car·il·lon·neur´** *n.*

**car´load** *n.* the amount that can be carried by a freight or passenger vehicle

**car´mine** *n.* deep red

**car´nage** *n.* a massacre; the remains of a slaughter

**car´nal** *adj.* of the flesh; of worldly pleasures; temporal –**car·nal´i·ty** *n.* –**car´nal·ly** *adv.*

**car´ni•val** *n.* a time of merrymaking; a local festival, as *a summer carnival;* *(US)* a traveling show

**car´ni•vore** *n.* any creature that consumes the flesh of another

**car•niv´o•rous** *adj.* flesh-eating

**car´ol** *n.* a song of joy *—vi.* to sing **—car´ol•er, car´ol•ler** *n.*

**car´o•tene, car´o•tin** *n.* a food substance that is converted to vitamin A in the liver

**ca•rot´e•noid** *adj.* of a pigment in the yellow to red range *—n.*

**ca•rot´id** *adj.* of the two main arteries of the neck *—n.*

**ca•rouse´** *n.* drunken revelry *—vi.* to engage in drunken revelry **—ca•rous´al** *n.* **—ca•rous´er** *n.*

**car•ou•sel´, car•rou•sel´** *n.* a merry-go-round; a revolving device that feeds in a continuous stream, as for viewing slides or in a baggage claim area

**carp** *vi.* to find fault; to complain regularly of petty grievances

**car´pen•ter** *n.* a worker in wood *—vi.* to work with wood as a builder or fabricator **—car´pen•try** *n.*

**car´pet** *n.* a thick covering for a floor **—car´pet•ing** *n.*

**car´pet•bag** *n.* a type of luggage made from carpeting

**carpetbagger** a derogatory term for politicians, swindlers, etc. from northern states who migrated south to take advantage of conditions following the Civil War

**car pool** a group of individuals who share driving, as to work, school, etc. **—car´pool** *vi.*

**car´port** *n.* a permanent structure, usually beside a house, for protecting an automobile

**car** *n.* an automobile; a space or area for passengers, as on an elevator

**car´riage** *n.* one's bearing; a horsedrawn vehicle **—baby carriage** a small vehicle for transporting the very young

**car´riage** *n.* *(Brit.)* a railway passenger vehicle

**car´ri•er** *n.* a person or vehicle that transports; one infected by a disease without exhibiting symptoms **—common carrier** an individual or company that contracts for the transfer of goods

**car´ri•on** *n.* decaying flesh

**car´ry** *vt.* to convey from one place to another; to support or sustain

**carried away** caught up in events, emotion, etc.

**carry on** to operate or manage, as a business; to remain firm in the face of adversity; to behave childishly

**car´ry•o•ver** *n.* something left from a previous time, as a staff member from a previous administration

**car´ry-out, car´ry•out** *adj.* of restaurant food that is to be eaten off the premises

**cart** *n.* a small wheeled conveyance that is pulled or pushed *—vt.* to transport by cart **—cart´er** *n.*

**cart off** to take away

**cart´age** *n.* the act of transporting, usually for a fee; a charge for transporting, as freight

**carte blanche** full authority to do as one wishes

**car´tel´** *n.* an alliance of individual businesses, formed to fix prices and production; any coalition for a common cause

**car•tog´ra•phy** *n.* the art of making maps **—car•tog´ra•pher** *n.* **—car•to•graph´ic, car•to•graph´i•cal** *adj.*

**car´ton** *n.* a cardboard box

**car´toon´** *n.* a caricature; a line drawing *—vi., vt.* to make or draw cartoons **—animated cartoon** a series of drawings that can be viewed quickly to create the impression of movement **—car•toon´ist** *n.*

**car´tridge´** *n.* a small carrier for material to be inserted into a larger device, as for film, tape, etc.

**cart´wheel** *n.* an acrobatic maneuver that involves supporting the body by each hand and foot in quick succession while remaining perpendicular to the surface so as to create the impression of a turning wheel

**carve** *vt.* to shape or fashion by cutting; to divide by cutting or as if by cutting **—carve up** to divide into portions; to share **—carv´er** *n.*

**carv´ing** *n.* a figure or design, often in wood, formed by cutting

**cas•cade´** *n.* a succession of steep waterfalls; a number of devices connected in series *—vi., vt.*

**case** *n.* an instance or occurrence; a legal action; a container **—just in case** in reserve for a contingency **—on his/her case** critical, faultfinding

**case book** a reference work

**case study** an analysis of a specific unit, as the progression of a disease in particular individuals

**case´work•er** *n.* a social worker who is charged with the investigation and oversight of specific clients **—case´work** *n.*

**cash** *n.* money in hand; currency; liquid assets *—vt.* to convert into cash, as *to cash in stocks and bonds* **—petty cash** a small amount of money kept in an office for incidental purchases **—cash´a•ble** *adj.*

**cash-and-carry** terms of a sale: no credit and no delivery

**cash bar** a facility where beverages may be purchased, such as at a reception, banquet, etc.

**cash´book** *n.* a record of cash transactions; a cash journal

**cash box** storage for cash receipts, petty cash, etc.

**cash crop** produce, etc. grown to sell in contrast to that grown for feed

**cash discount** a rebate for paying cash

**cash´ew** *n.* a type of edible nut; the tree on which it grows

**cash•ier´** *n.* one who handles cash transactions; one responsible for the receipt and disbursement of cash in a business

**cash´mere** *n.* a type of fine wool; cloth made from the

wool

**cash reg·is·ter** *n.* a machine for recording sales and storing cash, checks, etc. received

**cas´ing** *n.* framework, as for a tire, door, etc.; the outer covering of sausage

**cask** *n.* a barrel

**cas´ket** *n.* a small chest; a coffin

**cas´se·role** *n.* an earthenware pot with bulging sides and a tight-fitting lid; the slow baking of food in such a pot; a combination of foods cooked and served in a single dish

**cas·sette** *n.* a small case for film, magnetic tape, etc.

**cas´sock** *n.* a clergyman's robe

**cast** *n.* the act or technique of throwing or projecting, as an object or a glance; a thing formed, as in a mold; all of the actors in a theatrical production; the appearance of a thing *–vi., vt.* to throw with vigor; to select performers for roles

**cast´a·way** *n.* one who is shipwrecked; a thing that has been relinquished or abandoned

**caste** *n.* social position or status based on wealth, birth, etc.

**cas´tel·lat·ed** *adj.* built like a castle **–cas·tel·la´tion** *n.*

**cas´ti·gate´** *vt.* to criticize severely **–cas´ti·ga´tion** *n.* **–cas´ti·ga·tor** *n.*

**cast´ing** *n.* that formed in a mold

**cast iron** an alloy of iron

**cas´tle** *n.* a fortification

**cast´off** *adj.* discarded *–n.* discarded material, a remnant

**castor oil** an oil extracted from castor beans, used for lubrication and as a medication

**cas´trate** *vt.* to remove the testicles from; to spay; to make ineffectual, as by depriving of authority **–cas·tra´tion** *n.*

**cas´u·al** *adj.* without plan; haphazard; careless or unconcerned **–cas´u·al·ly** *adv.* **–cas´u·al·ness** *n.*

**cas´u·al·ty** *n.* a serious accident; anyone harmed as the result of an accident or incident

**cat·a·bol´ic** *adj.* of the conversion of living tissue to energy **–cat·a·bol´i·cal·ly** *adv.* **–ca·tab´o·lism** *n.*

**cat´a·clysm** *n.* a major disturbance **–cat·a·clys´mal, cat·a·clys´mic** *adj.* **–cat·a·clys´mi·cal·ly** *adv.*

**cat´a·comb´** *n.* an underground cemetery

**cat´a·lep·sy** *n.* an abnormal condition characterized by muscular rigidity and a trancelike state **–cat·a·lep´tic** *adj.*

**cat´a·log´, cat´a·logue´** *n.* a book advertising merchandise for sale; any extensive listing of related material *–vi., vt.* to list or classify **–cat´a·log·er, cat´a·log·ist** *n.*

**ca·tal´y·sis** *n.* the changing of the rate of a chemical reaction by the addition of another substance

**cat´a·lyst** *n.* a substance that changes the rate of a chemical reaction; a person or thing that serves to bring about a conclusion or resolution **–cat·a·lyt´ic** *adj.* **–cat·a·lyt´i·cal·ly** *adv.*

**catalytic converter** a device that acts on automobile exhaust fumes so as to reduce pollution

**cat´a·lyze** *vt.* to bring about with the use of a catalyst **–cat´a·lyz·er** *n.*

**cat´a·ma·ran´** *n.* a sailboat with twin hulls

**cat´a·mount** *n.* a wildcat

**cat´a·pult** *n.* an ancient seige weapon; a device for launching airplanes from the deck of a ship *–vi., vt.*

**cat´a·ract´** *n.* a large waterfall; a disease of the eye

**ca·tarrh´** *n.* inflammation of a mucous membrane **–ca·tarrh´al** *adj.* **–ca·tarrh´al·ly** *adv.*

**ca·tas´tro·phe** *n.* any great or sudden disaster; a complete failure **–cat·a·stroph´ic, cat·a·stroph´i·cal** *adj.* **–cat·a·stroph´i·cal·ly** *adv.*

**cat burglar** a thief who enters through the upper stories of a building

**cat´call** *n.* a sound of disapproval, directed at a speaker, actor, etc. *–vi., vt.* to utter or jeer with catcalls

**catch** *n.* a prize; that captured; a drawback; a fastener *–vi.* to take hold *–vt.* to take hold; to deceive; to take unawares; to overtake

**catch´all** *n.* a place where a variety of things are kept or left; a useless item

**catchall phrase** meaningless drivel

**catch´ing** *adj.* contagious

**catch on** to understand, comprehend; to become popular

**catch phrase** a slogan or motto designed to capture the attention of the listener

**catch´y** *adj.* attention-getting; easily remembered **–catch´i·ness** *n.*

**cat´e·chise** *(Brit.)*, **cat´e·chize** *(US)* *vt.* to teach, especially religion, by the use of questions and answers **–cat·e·chi·sa´tion, cat·e·chi·za´tion** *n.*

**cat´e·chism** *n.* a set of questions and answers for teaching fundamentals, as of a religion **–cat·e·chis´mal** *adj.*

**cat´e·chist** *n.* one who teaches using questions and answers **–cat·e·chis´tic, cat·e·chis´ti·cal** *adj.*

**cat·e·chu´men** *n.* one being instructed in fundamentals

**cat´e·gor´i·cal** *adj.* without qualification; absolute **–cat·e·gor´i·cal·ly** *adv.*

**cat´e·go·rize** *vt.* to classify or type; to arrange **–cat·e·go·ri·za´tion** *n.*

**cat´e·go´ry** *n.* a classification

**cat·e·na´tion** *n.* formed in succession; a continuity **–cat´e·nate** *vt.*

**ca´ter** *vi.* to provide food or entertainment; to indulge the wishes of another **–ca´ter·er** *n.*

**cat´er·waul** *n.* a wail, as of a rutting cat; discordant screeching *–vi.*

**cat´gut** *n.* a tough line used for stringing musical

instruments, tennis rackets, etc.

**ca·thar´sis** *n.* a cleansing or purgation **–ca·thar´tic, ca·thar´ti·cal** *adj.*

**ca·the´dral** *n.* a large church

**cathedral ceiling** a vaulted dome

**cath´e·ter** *n.* a slender tube passed through a body opening for examination, passing fluid, etc. **–cath´e·ter·ize** *vt.*

**cath´ode-ray tube** a vacuum tube that displays images by the projection of electrons on its surface

**cath´o·lic** *adj.* broad in scope or taste **–ca·thol´i·cal·ly** *adv.* **–cath·o·lic´i·ty** *n.* **–ca·thol´i·cise** *(Brit.)*, **ca·thol´i·cize** *(US) vi., vt.*

**cat´nap** *n.* a light sleep *–vi.* to doze

**cat´nip** *n.* a type of mint

**cat-o´-nine´tails** *n.* a whip comprised of nine knotted cords

**cat´tle** *n.* livestock

**cat´ty** *adj.* catlike, cunning; malicious, vindictive, spiteful

**catty-corner, catty-cornered** *adj.* diagonal *–adv.* at a diagonal

**cat´walk** *n.* a narrow walkway allowing access to remote parts of equipment, buildings, etc. for the purpose of monitoring or maintenance

**cau´cus** *n.* a closed conference; a faction within a political party

**cau´dal** *adj.* of or like a tail; near the tail **–cau´dal·ly** *adv.*

**cau´date** *adj.* having a tail

**caul** *n.* the membrane surrounding a fetus

**caul´dron** *n.* a large kettle

**caulk** *n.* a malleable sealer for seams in wood, tile, etc. *–vt.* to apply a sealer

**caulking compound** a sealant for wood, tile, etc.

**caus´al** *adj.* of, or relating to, cause and effect **–caus´al·ly** *adv.* **–cau·sal´i·ty** *n.*

**cau·sa´tion** *n.* the act of causing **–caus´a·tive** *adj.*

**cause** *n.* any source or agent of change; an objective or goal *–vt.* to make something happen **–caus´er** *n.*

**cause´way** *n.* an elevated road, as across water or a swamp

**caus´tic** *adj.* corrosive; biting or sarcastic **–caus´ti·cal·ly** *adv.*

**cau´ter·ise** *(Brit.)*, **cau´ter·ize** *(US) vt.* to destroy unwanted tissue or seal a wound by burning

**cau´tion** *n.* discretion; prudence; a warning *–vt.* to warn; to admonish **–cau´tion·ar·y** *adj.* **–cau´tious** *adj.* **–cau´tious·ly** *adv.* **–cau´tious· ness** *n.*

**cav´al·cade´** *n.* a procession; a series of events

**cav´a·lier´** *adj.* casual; carefree or nonchalant; hauty or arrogant *–n.* an armed horseman; a gentleman **–cav·a·lier´ly** *adv.* **–cav·a·lier´ness** *n.*

**cav´al·ry** *n.* mounted soldiers **–cav´al·ry·man** *n.*

**cave** *n.* a hollow area under the earth

**ca´ve·at** *n.* a formal notice or warning

**cave´-in** a place where the surface gives way, as over a cave or sink hole

**cave man** prehistoric man; a rough or crude individual

**cav´ern** *n.* a hollow place in the earth, a large cave **–cav´ern·ous** *adj.*

**cav´i·ar** *n.* the eggs of a fish: roe

**cav´il** *n.* a trivial objection *–vi.* to quibble or make trivial objections **–cav´il·er** *n.*

**cav´i·ty** *n.* a hole or hollow place

**ca·vort´** *vi.* to frolic; to prance

**caw** *n.* the call of a crow *–vi.*

**cay** *n.* an offshore island, reef, etc.

**cay·enne´** *n.* a hot red pepper

**CD** *n.* a compact disc

**cease** *vi., vt.* to shop **–ces·sa´tion** *n.*

**cease-fire** agreement to a temporary cessation of hostilities

**cease´less** *adj.* without end; never stopping; constant **–cease´less·ly** *adv.*

**cede** *vt.* to surrender, as one's rights or the possession of something

**ce·dil´la** *n.* a mark under the letter *c* (ç) to indicate that it is to be pronounced like an *s*

**ceil´ing** *n.* the top of a room; an upper limit **–hit the ceiling** to grow excited; to lose one's temper

**cel´e·brant** *n.* one who celebrates **–cel´e·bra·tor** *n.*

**cel´e·brate´** *vt.* to commemorate with ceremony or rejoicing; to praise publicly; to make widely known **–cel·e·bra´tion** *n.* **–cel´e·bra·tive** *adj.* **–cel·e·bra·to·ry** *adj.*

**cel´e·brat·ed** *adj.* widely known and praised

**ce·leb´ri·ty** *n.* one who is famous

**ce´ler´i·ty** *n.* quickness of action; dispatch

**ce·les´tial** *adj.* of the sky or the bodies seen in the sky, as the sun, moon, etc. **–ce·les´tial·ly** *adv.*

**celestial navigation** laying a course by sighting on the stars

**cel´i·ba·cy** *n.* abstinence from sexual intercourse; the state of being unmarried

**cel´i·bate** *adj.* unmarried; abstaining from sexual intercourse *–n.* one who abstains from sexual intercourse; one unmarried, esp. to comply with religious vows

**cell** *n.* a small plain room; the fundamental component of all organisms; a basic unit of a storage battery **–celled, cel´lu·lar** *adj.*

**cel´lar** *n.* an underground area, often used for storage **–in the cellar** the lowest possible standing, as of an athletic team

**cell division** the means by which cells reproduce

**cel´lo** *n.* a stringed instrument of the violin family **–cel´list** *n.*

**cel´lo·phane´** *n.* a thin, transparent material made from cellulose

**cell phone, cellular phone** *(US)* a mobile telephone

**cel´lu·lar** *adj.* like a cell; consisting of cells —**cel·lu·lar´i·ty** *n.*

**cel´lule** *n.* a small cell

**cel´lu·lite** *n.* fatty deposits, esp. around the thighs

**cel´lu·lose** *n.* a complex carbohydrate found in the cell walls of plants and used in the manufacture of a number of products

**Cel´si·us** *adj.* of a thermometer on which the freezing point of water is 0° and the boiling point is 100°

**ce·ment´** *n.* a building material used as a solid section or as mortar to bind other materials; an adhesive —*vt.* to join with cement; to unite firmly —**ce·men·ta´tion** *n.* —**ce·ment´er** *n.*

**cem´e·ter´y** *n.* a place set aside for burial of the dead

**ce´no·bite** *n.* a member of a religious order living communally, as in a monastery or nunnery —**cen´o·bit´ic, cen´o·bit´i·cal** *adj.*

**cen´o·taph** *n.* a monument to a dead person whose remains are elsewhere; an empty tomb

**cen´ser** *n.* an incense holder

**cen´sor** *n.* one authorized to examine printed matter, sound or motion picture recordings, etc. for objectionable material —*vt.* to review so as to ban that found objectionable —**cen´sor·a·ble** *adj.* —**cen·so´ri·al** *adj.* —**cen´sor·ship** *n.*

**cen·so´ri·ous** *adj.* expressing censure; faultfinding; tending to be critical —**cen·so´ri·ous·ly** *adv.* —**cen·so´ri·ous·ness** *n.*

**cen´sur·a·ble** *adj.* subject to reprimand; at fault, blameful —**cen´sur·a·bly** *adv.*

**cen´sure** *n.* disapproval; an official rebuke —*vt.* to express disapproval —**cen´sur·er** *n.*

**cen´sus** *n.* a count of the population

**cen´taur** *n.* a mythical creature, half man and half horse

**cen·te·nar´i·an** *n.* one who has lived to the age of 100 years

**cen·ten´a·ry** *adj.* a period of 100 years; a one-hundredth anniversary

**cen·ten´ni·al** *adj.* of a hundred —*n.* a one-hundredth anniversary

**cen´ter** *(US) n.* a point equally distant from all others; the middle point or part of anything; a hub of activity, influence, etc. —*vi.* to focus or concentrate —*vt.* to place on or at a point of focus

**cen´ter·board** *n.* a sheet of wood or steel that descends below the keel of a sailing vessel —**retractable centerboard** a centerboard that can be raised for traversing shallow water

**centered** *(US) adj.* focused or concentrated; self-confident; being at the center

**center of gravity** *(US)* the point at which the weight of a thing is concentrated

**cen´ter·piece** *n.* the dominating decoration or display on a buffet or dining table

**cen·tes´i·mal** *adj.* of a hundredth part —**cen·tes´i·mal·ly** *adv.*

**cen´ti·grade´** *adj.* divided into one hundred degrees; of the Celsius thermometer

**cen´ti·gram** *n.* one hundredth part of a gram

**cen´ti·me´ter** *n.* one hundredth part of a meter

**cen´tral** *adj.* at or near the center; of basic or significant importance; of a single source of control —**cen·tral´i·ty** *n.* —**cen´tral·ly** *adv.*

**central heating** a single, centralized heating plant that serves an entire building or group of buildings

**cen´tral·ism** *n.* a system in which all power and authority is concentrated at or near one place —**cen´tral·ise** *(Brit.),* **cen´tral·ize** *(US) vi., vt.* —**cen·tral·i·sa´tion, cen·tral·i·za´tion** *n.*

**central nervous system** the brain and spinal cord of the body

**central processing unit** (CPU) the primary chip that controls a computer

**cen´tre** *(Brit.) n.* a point equally distant from all others; the middle point or part of anything; a hub of activity, influence, etc. —*vi.* to focus or concentrate —*vt.* to place on or at a point of focus

**centred** *(Brit.) adj.* focused or concentrated; self-confident; being at the centre

**centre of gravity** *(Brit.)* the point at which the weight of a thing is concentrated

**cen´trif´u·gal** *adj.* moving away from a center —**cen·trif´u·gal·ly** *adv.*

**centrifugal force** the tendency of anything revolving around a center to move outward, away from the center

**cen´tri·fuge** *n.* a device that pushes matter outward by revolving at a high rate of speed, as a laboratory machine that separates particles of varying density

**cen·trip´e·tal** *adj.* moving toward a center —**cen·trip´e·tal·ly** *adv.*

**cen·tu´ri·on** *n.* a soldier in ancient Rome who commanded one hundred men

**cen´tu·ry** *n.* a period of one hundred years; a group of one hundred

**ce·phal´ic** *adj.* of the head

**ce·ram´ic** *adj.* of objects made from baked clay, such as pottery —**ce·ram´ist** *n.*

**ce·ram´ics** *n.* the art of making objects from baked clay; ceramic products

**ce´re·al** *n.* a grain used as food; a food prepared from grain —*adj.*

**cer´e·bral** *adj.* of the brain or the intellect —**cer·e´bral·ly** *adv.*

**cerebral palsy** a disorder resulting from damage to the central nervous system

**cer´e·brum** *n.* the front part of the brain

**cer´e·ment** *n.* a shroud; a burial garment

**cer·e·mo´ni·al** *adj.* of a ritual; stately or solemn *—n.* a formal system of ritual associated with a particular event **—cer·e·mo´ni·al·ism** *n.* **—cer·e·mo´ni·al·ist** *n.* **—cer·e·mo´ni·al·ly** *adv.*

**cer·e·mo´ni·ous** *adj.* with great formality; devoted to ritual or ceremony **—cer·e·mo´ni·ous·ly** *adv.* **—cer·e·mo´ni·ous·ness** *n.*

**cer´e·mo´ny** *n.* a formal rite or ritual; a formality

**ce·rise´** *adj.* bright red

**cer´tain** *adj.* definite; reliable; inevitable; of an indefinite quality, as *a certain something* **—cer´tain·ly** *adv.*

**cer·tain·ty** *n.* without doubt

**cer·tif´i·cate** *n.* an official document attesting to something, as of birth or completion of a course of study **—cer´ti·fi·a·ble** *adj.* **—cer´ti·fi·a·bly** *adv.*

**certificate of deposit** a document confirming the deposit of funds with a bank or other financial institution, usually to earn interest for a fixed period

**cer´ti·fi·ca´tion** *n.* affirmation, acceptance

**cer´ti·fied** *adj.* authorized; approved; vouched for

**certified check** an instrument for the transfer of funds that confirms the existence of those funds

**certified mail** mail that is confirmed as to time deposited and delivered

**certified public accountant** an accountant recognized as having complied with the laws of the state as to knowledge of his trade

**cer´ti·fy** *vt.* to make known as certain; to declare in writing **—cer´ti·fi·er** *n.*

**cer´ti·tude** *n.* conviction; with absolute confidence

**ce·ru´le·an** *adj.* azure blue in color

**cer´vi·cal** *adj.* of the cervix

**cer´vix** *n.* the neck or a neck-like part of the body

**ces·sa´tion** *n.* an ending or stopping

**ces´sion** *n.* a surrender or renunciation; a waiver

**cess´pool** *n.* a large receptical for receiving effluence from a household; a place that is corrupted

**chad** *n.* bits of paper removed from perforated tape or punch cards used in computer processing

**chafe** *n.* tenderness or wear from friction *—vi.* to rub; to become irritated *—vt.* to irritate by rubbing; to annoy **—chafe at the bit** to show impatience **—chaf´er** *n.*

**chaff** *n.* the waste from threshing; anything worthless

**chaf´ing dish´** *n.* a serving dish with a heat source for cooking or keeping food warm

**cha·grin´** *n.* embarrassment *—vt.* to embarrass

**chain** *n.* a flexible series of links; any series of logically connected elements; a thing that binds *—vt.* to bind or restrain, as with a chain

**chain gang** a prison work party

**chain letter** a letter containing a request, and asking that the same request be passed on to others

**chain lightning** a stroke of lightning seen as having many branches; of a person who seems to move quickly in many directions at once

**chain reaction** a series of events in which each incident influences the next

**chain saw** a portable power saw with teeth attached to a chain

**chain-smoke** to smoke cigarettes continuously, one after another **—chain smoker**

**chain store** a retail outlet that is one of many operating under the same name

**chair** *n.* a place for sitting; a position of authority *—vt.* to preside over, as a meeting

**chair´lift** *n.* a type of conveyance for transporting skiers up a hill

**chair´man** *n.* one who officiates, as over a committee or a meeting **—chair´man·ship** *n.*

**chair´person** *n.* one who officiates; often used to avoid the gender connotation of *chairman*

**chaise longue, chaise lounge** *n.* a long chair with support for the legs and back

**cha·let´** *n.* a style of Swiss house

**chal´ice** *n.* a goblet

**chalk** *n.* a type of limestone; a marker for writing on a blackboard, etc. *—vt.* to write with chalk **—chalk´i·ness** *n.* **—chalk´y** *adj.*

**chalk´board** *n.* a blackboard or slate; a surface for writing with chalk

**chal´lenge** *n.* a difficult task; an invitation to compete; a calling into question *—vt.* to invite one to compete; to call into question **—chal´lenge·a·ble** *adj.* **—chal´leng·er** *n.*

**chal´leng·ing** *adj.* difficult, formidable; intriguing, fascinating

**cham´ber** *n.* a room, bedroom; a meeting room; a board or council; any enclosed space or compartment

**cham´ber·maid** *n.* one who cleans rooms, as in a hotel

**chamber music** light music for performance by a small musical group

**chamber of commerce** an organization dedicated to the promotion of business

**champ** *n.* a champion *—vt.* to chew **—champ at the bit** be impatient

**cham·pagne´** *n.* a sparkling wine from the Champagne region of France; commonly, a wide variety of light, sparkling wines; the yellowish color of the wine

**cham´pi·on** *n.* one who supports a cause; one with the attributes of a winner *—vt.* to fight for; to support **—cham´pi·on·ship** *n.*

**chance** *adj.* fortuitous, unplanned *—n.* a happening without discernible cause; an unexpected occurrence; a wager; an opportunity *—vi.* to occur accidentally *—vt.* to risk **—chanc´i·ness** *n.* **—chanc´y** *adj.*

**chance´ful** adj. full of outstanding events; momentous

**chan´cel·ler·y** *n.* the office of chancellor

**chan´cel·lor** *n.* president of a university; in some countries, the prime minister **–chan´cel·lor·ship** *n.*

**chan´de·lier´** *n.* an elaborate hanging light fixture

**change** *n.* the process of altering; a substitution; a transformation; coins *–vi., vt.* to make or become different; to exchange; to transform

**change´a·ble** *adj.* able to be altered; temporary; adaptable or flexible; unstable, flighty, or fickle **–change·a·bil´i·ty, change´a·ble·ness** *n.* **–change´a·bly** *adv.*

**change´ful** *adj.* unstable; likely to change; variable; **change´ful·ly** *adv.*; **change´ful·ness** *n.*

**change´less** *adj.* constant; permanent **–change´less·ly** *adv.* **–change´less·ness** *n.*

**change of heart** a shift in thinking or attitude

**change of pace** something dissimilar; a difference or respite from the usual

**change´o·ver** *n.* passing from one to another; a transformation; an altering of configuration, as of industrial equipment altered to manufacture a different product

**chang´er** *n.* one who changes; that which changes records, disks, etc.

**chan´nel** *n.* the bed of a flowing body of water; a passageway for liquid; a band or route for communications *–vt.* to wear into grooves or ruts; to send through a channel; to direct **–chan´nel·ize** *vt.* **–chan·nel·i·za´tion** *n.*

**chan´nel·ing** *n.* the concept that one may be a conduit for another, such as for spiritual force **–chan´nel·er** *n.*

**chant** *n.* a primitive musical form; a rhythmic recitation as of a slogan *–vi., vt.* **–chant´er** *n.*

**cha´os** *n.* extreme confusion or disorder **–cha´ot´ic** *adj.* **–cha·ot´i·cal·ly** *adv.*

**chap** *n.* a male, man or boy *–vi., vt.* to roughen the skin, as from the wind

**cha·pa·re´jos** *n.* leather leg protectors worn by cowboys; chaps

**chap·ar·ral** *n.* a thicket

**cha·pa´ti** *n.* a skillet bread indigenous to India

**cha·peau´** *n., pl.* **cha·peaus´, cha·peaux´** a hat

**chap´el** *n.* a small room set aside for worship; a small church

**chap´er·on´** *n.* one who escorts or oversees, especially the activities of a young unmarried female *–vt.* to overseer or supervise **–chap´er·on·age** *n.*

**chap´lain** *n.* a clergyman, especially one appointed to service in an institution, organization, etc. **–chap´lain·cy, chap´lain·ship** *n.*

**chap´let** *n.* prayer beads

**chaps** *n.* leather leg protectors worn by cowboys; chaparejos

**chap´ter** *n.* a main division of a book; a distinct period; a branch of an organization

**char** *vi., vt.* to scorch; to reduce to charcoal

**char´ac·ter** *n.* any mark or symbol used in writing or printing; a distinctive quality; moral or ethical strength; a particular person in a book, play, history, etc.; an odd person

**character actor** an actor or actress who specializes in portraying unusual individuals

**character assassination** slander with intent to destroy credibility

**char·ac·ter·is´tic** *adj.* typical; distinguishing *–n.* a distinctive attribute or style **–char·ac·ter·is´ti·cal·ly** *adv.*

**char´ac·ter·ize** *vt.* to depict, typify **–char·ac·ter·i·za´tion** *n.*

**cha·rade´** *n.* a game in which common sayings, titles, etc. are acted out; a thinly disguised deception; a sham

**char´broil** *vt.* to broil over charcoal; to barbecue **–char´broiled** *adj.*

**char´coal´** *n.* charred wood used as fuel; a stick for sketching *–vt.* to charbroil; to sketch with charcoal

**charge** *n.* asking price; a financial obligation; an assigned duty; one given into the care of another; a call to attack; mild excitement *–vt.* to set a price; to incur a financial obligation; to command; to hold liable; to accuse; to attack *–vi.* to set a price **–charge´a·ble** *adj.*

**charge account** an agreement with a merchant or financial institution that allows one to purchase on credit

**charge card** identification for one who has a charge account

**char·gé d´af·faires´** *n.* a diplomatic officer

**char´i·ot** *n.* a two-wheeled, horse-drawn vehicle; the family car *–vi., vt.* to convey, ride or drive in a chariot **–char´i·o·teer´** *n.*

**cha·ris´ma** *n.* leadership quality; charm, appeal

**char´is·mat´ic** *adj.* having charisma; of certain religious groups *–n.* one reputed to have divine powers

**char´i·ta·ble** *adj.* generous; forgiving **–char´i·ta·ble·ness** *n.* **–char´i·ta·bly** *adv.*

**char´i·ty** *n.* almsgiving; an institution for providing aid to those in need

**char´la·tan** *n.* a fake; one who falsely claims to have certain knowledge or skill **–char´la·tan·ism, char´la·tan·ry** *n.*

**charley horse** a muscle cramp

**charm** *n.* something assumed to have magical power; a quality that attracts or pleases *–vt.* to attract or please **–charm´er** *n.*

**charmed** fortunate, lucky **–live a charmed life** protected from misfortune

**charm´ing** *adj.* captivating; appealing or attractive **–charm´ing·ly** *adv.*

**chart** *n.* a map, as for navigation; a graphic representation of data *–vt.* to make a map or graph **–chart´er** *n.* **–char´tist** *n.*

**char´ter** *n.* a document that attests to or authorizes formation, sets forth aims, grants specific rights, etc., as a *corporate* or *city charter*; to lease, as a boat or plane *—vt.* to establish by charter; to lease

**charter member** one who joins an organization at the time of its inception

**char·treuse´** *n.* a pale green color; a type of liqueur *—adj.*

**char´y** *adj.* cautious

**chase** *n.* pursuit *—vt.* to pursue; to drive away *—vi.* to follow in pursuit **—chas´er** *n.*

**chasm** *n.* a narrow gorge or ravine; any sharp division **—chas´mal** *adj.*

**chaste** *adj.* virtuous, pure in thought or conduct **—chaste´ly** *adv.* **—chaste´ness, chas´ti·ty** *n.*

**chas´ten** *n.* to correct by punishing **—chas´ten·er**

**chas´tise´** *vt.* to punish; to scold sharply **—chas´tise´ment** *n.* **—chas·tis´er** *n.*

**chas´ti·ty** *n.* purity; innocence

**chat** *n.* casual conversation *—vi.* to converse in a easy-going manner **—chat´ti·ly** *adv.* **—chat´ti·ness** *n.* **—chat´ty** *adj.*

**cha·teau´** *n.* a country house

**chat´tel** *n.* moveable personal property

**chat´ter** *n.* foolish talk *—vi.* to speak rapidly and foolishly; to click rapidly or rattle

**chat´ter·box** *n.* one who talks constantly

**chauf´feur** *n.* a hired driver; anyone who drives for another *—vt.* to drive for another

**chau´vin·ism** *n.* fanatical patriotism; irrational belief in the superiority of one's sex, race, etc. **—chau´vin·ist** *n.* **—chau·vin·is´tic** *adj.* **—chau·vin·is´ti·cal·ly** *adv.*

**cheap** *adj.* inexpensive; of little value **—cheap´ly** *adv.* **—cheap´ness** *n.*

**cheap´en** *vt.* to depreciate; to debase or degrade

**cheap shot** an underhanded remark

**cheap·skate** *n.* one unwilling to spend money

**cheat** *n.* a swindle; one who defrauds *—vi., vt.* to defraud; to be dishonest **—cheat´er** *n.*

**check** *n.* a stop or slowing; an examination for quality, etc.; a bill, as at a restaurant; a negotiable instrument for the transfer of money; a pattern made up of squares *—vt.* to slow or stop, as forward progress; to examine for errors, etc. **—check´er** *n.*

**check´er·board** *adj.* of a pattern of squares *—n.* a game board consisting of alternating dark and light squares used to play checkers and chess

**checking account** *(US)* a monetary deposit that permits the transfer of funds by writing checks

**check´list** *n.* a reference list for checking tasks, names, etc.

**check´mate** *n.* a winning move in chess; any action that frustrates the aims of another

**check´off** *n.* a system for the collection of union dues through payroll deduction

**check´-out, check´out** *n.* the tallying of purchases; a time by which a hotel room must be vacated without penalty; examination or verification

**check´point** *n.* a location for inspection or verification, as in a roadrace or at a border

**check´room** *n.* a place for hanging coats, storing luggage, etc.

**check´up** *n.* an examination, as by a doctor

**ched´dar** *n.* a type of cheese

**cheek** *n.* the side of the face; impertinence, rudeness

**cheek´bone** *n.* a bone at the side of the face near the top of the cheek

**cheek´y** *adj.* brazen, bold; impertinent **—cheek´i·ly** *adv.* **—cheek´i·ness** *n.*

**cheer** *n.* a pleasant mood; a source of pleasure; a shout of approval or encouragement *—vi., vt.* to gladden; to sound approval **—cheer´ful** *adj.* **—cheer´ful·ly** *adv.* **—cheer´ful·ness** *n.*

**cheer´lead·er** *n.* one of a group who leads cheering for an athletic team; one who is seen as overzealous in promoting a person, company, cause, etc.

**cheer´less** *adj.* dreary; dismal; barren **—cheer´less·ly** *adv.* **—cheer´less·ness** *n.*

**cheer´y** *adj.* happy; light-hearted; jaunty **—cheer´i·ly** *adv.* **—cheer´i·ness** *n.*

**cheese** *n.* a food made from the pressed curds of soured milk

**cheese´cake** *n.* a pie-like dessert based on creamed cottage or ricotta cheese; a picture of a scantily clad man or woman

**cheese´cloth** *n.* a loosely woven cotton cloth used for cleaning, straining, etc.

**chees´y** *adj.* of or like cheese in texture, taste, etc; lacking in quality **—chees´i·ness** *n.*

**chef** *n.* a cook; one in charge of a kitchen

**chem´i·cal** *adj.* of chemistry, made from chemicals *—n.* a substance used in or made by a chemical process **—chem´i·cal·ly** *adv.*

**chemical warfare** the use of chemicals, such as poison gas, to defeat an enemy

**che·mise´** *n.* a type of dress or an undergarment for women

**chem´is·try** *n.* the study of the properties of matter **—chem´ist** *n.*

**chem·o·ther´a·py** *n.* the treatment of illness or disease by the use of chemicals **—chem·o·ther´a·pist** *n.*

**cheque** *n.* *(Brit.)* a bill, as at a restaurant; a negotiable instrument for the transfer of money; a pattern made up of squares

**cher´ish** *vt.* to hold dear; to protect; to harbor, as an idea **—cher´ish·er** *n.* **—cher´ish·ing·ly** *adv.*

**che·root´** *n.* a type of cigar

**cher·vil** *n.* an herb used for flavoring

**chess** *n.* a board game for two players **—chess´board, chess´man, chess´men** *n.*

**chest** *n.* the front of the body between the neck and the abdomen; a box for storage; a cabinet
**chest´nut** *n.* a type of edible nut or the tree on which it grows; a reddish-brown horse *–adj.* the brown color of the nut –pull chestnuts out of the fire to recover from a potentially difficult situation
**chest of drawers** a piece of furniture containing several drawers for storage, as for clothing
**chest´y** *adj.* having a large chest; buxom
**chev´ron** *n.* a uniform insignia worn on the sleeve to denote rank
**chew** *vt., vi.* to grind with the teeth; to consider **–chew out** to scold; upbraid **–chew the fat, chew the rag** to talk; converse **–chew´a·ble** *adj.* **–chew´er** *n.*
**chew´y** *adj.* of food, such as meat, that is tough or difficult to chew **–chew´i·ness** *n.*
**chic** *adj.* stylish; smartly dressed *–n.* refinement in style or manner
**chi·can´er·y** *n.* deception by means of crafty speech or action; trickery
**chi´chi** *adj.* elegant in style or manner; of a style that is overdone; of one haughty in manner
**chick** *n.* a young bird; a young woman
**chick´en** *n.* a common domestic fowl; a coward *–adj.* fearful, timid; overly strict or severe **–chicken out** to back down **–no spring chicken** no longer young
**chicken feed** an inconsequential amount, usually of money; insignificant
**chick´en-heart´ed** *adj.* fearful; fainthearted
**chicken pox** a childhood disease
**chicken wire** a light fencing made of wire intertwined to form geometric patterns
**chic´le** *n.* substance use in the making of chewing gum
**chic´o·ry** *n.* a type of flowering plant; its leaves, used in salad; its root, used to flavor coffee
**chide** *vi., vt.* to scold quietly **–chid´ing·ly** *adv.*
**chief** *adj.* most significant, as *the chief ingredient* *–n.* a leader
**Chief Executive** President of the United States
**chief executive, chief executive officer** the highest ranking administrator of an organization
**chief justice** the official head of a judicial body
**chief´ly** *adj.* of or like a chief *–adv.* especially, mainly, primarily
**chief of staff** the leading director of an organization
**chief of state** a head of government
**chief´tain** *n.* a chief
**chif·fon´** *n.* a lightweight cloth
**chif·fo·nier´** *n.* a chest of drawers
**child** *n., pl.* **chil´dren** an infant; offspring **–child´s play** easy
**child´bear·ing** *n.* the process of carrying an unborn child and giving birth *–adj.*
**child´birth** *n.* the act of bringing forth a baby
**child´hood** *n.* the years from infancy to puberty; a time of growth and development
**child´ish** *adj.* acting like a child; immature; silly **–child´ish·ly** *adv.* **–child´ish·ness** *n.*
**child´less** *adj.* having no offspring
**child´like** *adj.* exhibiting the attributes or temperament of a child; innocent; adolescent
**chil´i** *n.* a type of pepper; a dried red pepper used for seasoning
**chill** *adj.* slightly cold *–n.* coldness; shivering caused by a disease *–vt.* to make cold **–chill´ness** *n.*
**chill´er** *n.* that shocks or frightens, as a book, movie, etc.
**chill´y** *adj.* of a discernibly cold, uncomfortable environment; uncomfortable from the cold; of discourteous, unfriendly behavior, as *a chilly reception* **–chill´i·ness** *n.*
**chill´ing** *adj.* frightening; causing concern **–chill´ing·ly** *adv.*
**chime** *n.* a bell; the sound of bells tuned to a musical scale *–vi., vt.* to sound in harmony **–chime in** to interrupt or take part in **–chim´er** *n.*
**chi·me´ra** *n.* an imaginary monster; a wild fancy **–chi·mer´ic, chi·mer´i·cal** *adj.* **–chi·mer´i·cal·ly** *adv.*
**chim´ney** *n.* a channel for smoke to escape
**chimney sweep** one whose profession is cleaning chimneys
**chin** *n.* the front of the lower jaw *–vi.* to idly chat or gossip
**chi´na** *n.* porcelain or a similar material, originally made in China; fine dinnerware **–chi´na·ware** *n.*
**china cabinet, china closet** a cupboard for storing and displaying fine dinnerware
**chine** *n.* a backbone or spine
**chink** *n.* a crack or slit *–vt.* to fill in a crack **–a chink in one's armor** a weakness
**chi´no** *n.* a cotton cloth **–chinos casual slacks** made from the cloth
**chi·noi·se·rie´** *n.* an oriental style of decoration, as for furniture, textiles, etc.
**chintz´y** *adj.* cheap; gawdy, vulgar; of poor quality
**chip** *n.* a small piece; a thin slice; a spot where a small piece has been removed; a marker or token used as a game piece *–vi., vt.* to break off a small piece **–a chip off the old block** a son who is much like his father **–chip in** to contribute **–have a chip on one's shoulder** to be testy or quarrelsome **–in the chips** wealthy
**chipped beef** dried beef, sliced very thin; thinly sliced dried beef served in a sauce
**chip´per** *adj.* light-hearted; cheerful *–n.* a tool for chipping
**chi´rop´o·dist** *n.* a podiatrist; a specialist in disorders of the foot **–chi·rop´o·dy** *n.*
**chi´ro·prac´tor** *n.* one who treats disorders of the body

by manipulating the joints –**chi´ro·prac´tic** *adj., n.*

**chis´el** *n.* a tool for cutting and shaping wood –*vt.* to cut with a chisel; to cheat; to obtain by deception –**chis´el·er** *n.*

**chit** *n.* a bill, usually for a small amount; a marker

**chit´chat** *n.* idle, often meaningless, talk

**chiv´al·ry** *n.* the qualities attributed to knighthood, such as fine manners, bravery, etc. –**chiv´al·rous** *adj.* –**chiv´al·rous·ly** *adv.* –**chiv´al·rous·ness** *n.*

**chive** *n.* an herb used for flavoring

**chlo´ri·nate** *vt.* to treat with chlorine, as water for purification –**chlo·rin·a´tion** *n.*

**chlo´rine** *n.* a chemical used for water purification, as a cleaning and bleaching agent, etc.

**chock** *n.* a block used as a stopper or wedge, as to keep a wheeled vehicle from rolling; a device on the deck of a ship through which rope is guided

**chock-full** *adj.* filled to the brim

**choc´o·hol·ic** *n.* one who is extremely fond of chocolate

**choc´o·late** *n.* a flavoring made from cacao beans –*adj.* flavored with chocolate –**choc´o·lat·ey** *adj.*

**choice** *adj.* preferred; superior –*n.* the act or right of choosing; a thing chosen; an alternative; a favored part; the finest part

**choir** *n.* an organized group of singers; a part of a church set aside for singers: *a choir loft*

**choir´boy** *n.* one who sings in the choir; one who cultivates the image of being well-behaved

**choke** *n.* the sounds made by one choking; a device that alters the flow of air to an engine –*vi.* to have difficulty breathing; to have difficulty performing, as *to choke under pressure* –*vt.* to throttle or strangle; to obstruct or restrict, as the flow of air to a combustion engine

**choke back** to suppress, as tears

**choke´ber·ry** *n.* a fruit reputed to cause choking if eaten; the bush on which the berries grow

**choke´bore** *n.* a shotgun bore configuration that maintains a tight pattern of shot

**choke´cher·ry** *n.* a fruit reputed to cause choking if eaten; the tree or bush on which the berries grow

**choke collar** a collar, as for a dog, that tightens as strain is put on the leash; a tight leather collar with metal studs

**choke chain** a leash that is part of a choke collar

**choke down** to eat with difficulty, as of a food that is not to one's liking

**chok´er** *n.* one who throttles another; jewelry or furs that fit closely around the neck

**choke up** to block or clog; to be overcome by emotion

**chol´er** *n.* a state of irritation; anger or rage –**chol´er·ic** *adj.*

**cho´line** *n.* a B vitamin

**choose** *vi., vt.* to select; to prefer as an option

**choos´y** *adj.* selective; fastidious

**chop** *n.* a cut of meat that includes the rib; a sharp blow –*vt.* to cut with a sharp blow; to cut into small pieces

**chop´per** *n.* a helicopter

**chop´py** *adj.* characterized by quick starts and stops or direction changes; discordant –**chop´pi·ly** *adv.* –**chop´pi·ness** *n.*

**chop´sticks** *n.* a pair of relatively small straight rods used in the orient to manipulate food in cooking, eating, etc.

**chop su´ey** a quasi-oriental dish of meat and vegetables in a sauce, usually served over rice

**cho´ral** *adj.* of a performance by a choir or chorus; of the work performed –**cho´ral·ly** *adv.*

**cho·rale´** *n.* a choir or chorus; a musical work performed by a choir or chorus

**chord** *n.* a set of musical tones sounded together; anything harmonious, as of thought or emotion; a straight line joining two points of an arc

**chore** *n.* a small task; a difficult or unpleasant job

**cho·re´a** *n.* a nervous disorder characterized by spastic motions

**cho´re·o·graph** *vi., vt.* to create and direct a dance; to carefully plan and direct the execution of any activity

**cho´re·og´ra·phy** *n.* creation and direction of dances –**cho·re·og´ra·pher** *n.* –**cho·re·o·graph´ic** *adj.* –**cho·re·o·graph´i·cal·ly** *adv.*

**chor´tle** *n.* a quiet laugh; a chuckling sound –*vi., vt.* to chuckle or snicker

**chorus** *n.* a group that performs as a unit, as singers or dancers; the part performed by a chorus; a group or action that is in accord, as *a chorus of dissension*; the refrain of a song –*vi., vt.* to perform in unison –**cho´ris·ter** *n.*

**chos´en** *adj.* of one selected, often for a special honor; favored, as by good fortune

**chow** *n.* a breed of dog, short for *chow chow*; food –**chow time meal time**

**chow´der** *n.* a type of soup; a hodgepodge –**chowder-head** one whose thinking is muddled

**chow mein´** a quasi-oriental stew of meat and vegetables, served with fried noodles and rice

**chris´ten** *vt.* to baptize or name; to bring into service; to use for the first time –**chris´ten·ing** *n.*

**chris´ten·dom** *n.* the time of Christianity; that portion of the earth populated by Christians; all of the known or inhabited world

**Christian** *adj.* of those who follow the teachings of Christ –*n.* a follower of Christ

**Chris·ti·an´i·ty** *n.* the Christian religion; Christians generally

**Christian name** one's given name as distinguished from a family name

**Christian Science** of those who believe in the healing power of the teachings of Christianity

**chro´mat´ic** *adj.* of colors; progressing by semitones in music –*n.* a modified musical tone –**chro·mat´i·cal·ly** *adv.*

**chro´ma·tin** *n.* the substance in cells that forms chromosomes

**chrome** *n.* chromium used for plating –*vt.* to plate with chromium

**chro´mi·um** *n.* a metallic element that resists corrosion

**chro´mo·some´** *n.* a strand of DNA that carries hereditary information

**chron´ic** *adj.* continuous or recurring often; habitual, as *a chronic eater* –**chron´i·cal·ly** *adv.*

**chron´i·cle** *n.* an ordered record of events; a detailed report –*vt.* to record or narrate events –**chron´i·cler** *n.*

**chro·nol´o·gy** *n.* the study of the fixing of dates and the order of events; an ordered record of events –**chron·o·log´ic, chron·o·log´i·cal** *adj.* –**chron·o·log´i·cal·ly** *adv.* –**chro·nol´o·gist** *n.*

**chro·nom´e·ter** *n.* a device for measuring time with great precision –**chron·o·met´ric, chron·o·met´ri·cal** *adj.* –**chron·o·met´ri·cal·ly** *adv.*

**chro·nom´e·try** *n.* the study and implementation of methods for the extremely accurate measuring of time

**chub´by** *adj.* round and plump

**chuck** *n.* an adjustable device for securing a tool, as a drill in a bit; a shim –*vt.* to throw; to throw away or discard

**chuck´le** *n.* a quiet laugh –*vi.* to laugh quietly-chuck´ler *n.*

**chuck´le·head** *n.* a silly or foolish person

**chum** *n.* a friend or associate; bits of fish or fish entrails used as bait –*vi.* to hang about together; to scatter fish parts on the water in an effort to attract game fish –**chum´mi·ly** *adv.* –**chum´mi·ness** *n.* –**chum´my** *adj.*

**chump** *n.* one who is gullible; the victim of a con game; a stupid or foolish person

**chunk** *n.* a lump; a substantial amount –*vt.* to cut or form into lumps

**chunk´y** *adj.* stocky, especially of a person; containing solid bits, as *chunky peanut butter* –**chunk´i·ness** *n.*

**church** *n.* a place set apart for worship; a group of worshippers who ascribe to similar beliefs –**church´go·er** *n.*

**church´ly** *adj.* of one who is pious, worshipful; of a church or its offices

throw away or discard

**chuck´le** *n.* a quiet laugh *vi.* to laugh quietly –**chuck´ler** *n.*

**chuck´le·head** *n.* a silly or foolish person

**chum** *n.* a friend or associate; bits of fish or fish entrails used as bait –*vi.* to hang about together; to scatter fish parts on the water in an effort to attract game fish –**chum´mi·ly** *adv.* –**chum´mi·ness** *n.* –**chum´my** *adj.*

**chump** *n.* one who is gullible; the victim of a con game; a stupid or foolish person

**chunk** *n.* a lump; a substantial amount –*vt.* to cut or form into lumps

**chunk´y** *adj.* stocky, especially of a person; containing solid bits, as *chunky peanut butter* –**chunk´i·ness** *n.*

**church** *n.* a place set apart for worship; a group of worshippers who ascribe to similar beliefs –**church´go·er** *n.*

**church´ly** *adj.* of one who is pious, worshipful; of a church or its offices

**church´war·den** *n.* a long clay pipe

**church´y** *adj.* of one who is unusually preoccupied with religion or the affairs of a church

**church´yard** *n.* the grounds about a church, often serving as a burial plot for its members

**churl** *n.* a bumpkin; a grouch or curmudgeon

**churl´ish** *adj.* crude, vulgar; grouchy, surly –**churl´ish·ly** *adv.* –**churl´ish·ness** *n.*

**churn** *n.* a container in which cream is made into butter –*vi., vt.* to make butter in a churn; to agitate violently –**churn´er** *n.*

**chute** *n.* an inclined trough

**chut´ney** *n.* a relish of fruit and spices

**chutz´pah, chutz´pa** *n.* brazenness; audacity; insolence

**cic´a·trix** *n., pl.* **cic´a·tri·ces, cic´a·trix·es** fibrous tissue that forms at the healing of a wound; a scar

**cic´a·trise** *(Brit.)*, **cic´a·trize** *(US) vi., vt.* to heal by forming a scar –**cic·a·tri·sa´tion, cic·a·tri·za´tion** *n.*

**ci´der** *n.* a juice from apples

**ci·gar´** *n.* a roll of cured tobacco for smoking

**cig´a·ret´, cig´a·rette´** *n.* finely cut cured tobacco rolled in paper for smoking

**cil´i·a** *n. pl., sing.* **cil´i·um** small hair or hair-like projections in or on a life form –**cil´i·ar·y** *adj.* –**cil´i·ate** *adj.*

**cinch** *n.* a wide belt used to secure a saddle or pack; a task that is easy to do –*vt.* to secure a saddle or pack with a cinch; to make certain

**cinc´ture** *n.* a belt or sash; something that encircles –*vt.* to bind or encircle

**cin´der** *n.* a rough, rock-like material formed by exposure to great heat, as lava or slag; material that has been burned, but not turned to ash

**cinder block** a concrete block for building

**cin´e·ma** *n.* a movie theater; the making of films; the motion-picture industry

**cin·e·ma·tog´ra·pher** *n.* one who operates a motion-picture camera; one who produces or directs the making of films

**cin·e·ma·tog´ra·phy** *n.* the art of motion picture photography **–cin·e·mat·o·graph´ic** *adj.* **–cin·e·mat·o·graph´i·cal·ly** *adv.*

**cin·e·rar´i·um** *n.* a place where the ashes of cremated bodies are kept **–cin´er·ar·y** *adj.*

**cin´na·bar** *n.* mercuric sulphide, the source of mercury; bright red

**ci´pher** *n.* the character zero; a thing of no value; a system for coding messages; an encoded message

**cir´ca** *prep.* about, esp. of an approximate date, as *circa 1500*

**cir·ca·di´an** *adj.* of the biological rhythms associated with the twenty-four hour day

**cir´cle** *n.* a round figure, ring, or orb; a group of people; an extent, as of influence; a revolution or cycle *–vi.* to revolve; to move in a circle *–vt.* to move around; to encircle, surround

**cir´clet** *n.* a small circle

**cir´cuit** *n.* a somewhat circular or continuous route; a journey over such a route made in the exercise of a calling, as for a judge or preacher; the course of an electric current **–cir´cuit·ry** *n.*

**circuit board** an insulated board to which the elements of a circuit are affixed and connected

**circuit breaker** a safety device that interrupts an electrical circuit in the event of an overload

**circuit court** a judicial forum that sits periodically in various places throughout an area

**cir·cu´i·tous** *adj.* roundabout or devious **–cir·cu´i·tous·ly** *adv.*

**cir´cu·lar** *adj.* round; of that which is moving in a circle; circuitous *–n.* a printed advertisement that is widely distributed **–cir·cu·lar´i·ty, cir´cu·lar·ness** *n.* **–cir´cu·lar·ly** *adv.*

**cir´cu·late´** *vi., vt.* to move about freely, as a guest at a party; to move on a predetermined course, as blood through the body **–cir´cu·la´tion** *n.* **–cir´cu·la·tor** *n.* **–cir´cu·la·to·ry** *adv.*

**cir·cum´fer·ence** *n.* the boundary of a circle or an area **–cir·cum·fer·en´tial** *adj.* **–cir·cum·fer·en´tial·ly** *adv.*

**cir´cum·lo·cu´tion** *n.* an evasive, lengthly means of expression **–cir·cum·loc´u·to·ry** *adj.*

**cir´cum·nav´i·gate** *vt.* to travel completely around **–cir·cum·nav·i·ga´tion** *n.*

**cir´cum·scribe** *vt.* draw a line around; to define the limits of **–cir·cum·scrib´a·ble** *adj.* **–cir·cum·scrip·tion** *n.*

**cir´cum·spect´** *adj.* cautious; prudent **–cir·cum·spec´tion, cir´cum·spect·ness** *n.* **–cir·cum·spec´tive** *adj.* **–cir·cum·spect´ly** *adv.*

**cir´cum·stance´** *n.* a related fact or condition; a happening; a ceremonial display

**cir´cum·stan´tial** *adj.* based on circumstances; of little importance; inconclusive **–cir·cum·stan·ti·al´i·ty** *n.* **–cir´cum·stan´tial·ly** *adv.*

**circumstantial evidence** in a court of law, information that is not conclusive, but that may infer proof

**cir·cum·stan´ti·ate** *vt.* to verify **–cir·cum·stan·ti·a´tion** *n.*

**cir´cum·vent** *vt.* to go around, or bypass; to avoid by craft **–cir´cum·vent·er** *n.* **–cir·cum·ven´tion** *n.* **–cir·cum·ven´tive** *adj.*

**cir´cus** *n.* a traveling show featuring trained animals, clowns, acrobats, etc.; frantic activity or disorder

**cis´tern** *n.* a storage tank for water; a container for catching rain water; a reservoir

**cit´a·del** *n.* a fortress or stronghold; a place of refuge

**ci·ta´tion** *n.* a quotation or reference; a summons to appear in court; formal acknowledgment; a commendation

**cite** *vt.* to quote; to summon before a court of law **–cit´a·ble** *adj.*

**cit´ied** *adj.* of an area having cities; of or like a city

**cit´i·fy** *vt.* to build up and make like a city; to become like a city person in manner, dress, etc; **–cit´i·fied** *adj.*

**cit´i·zen** *n.* one who is entitled to the full protection of the state; an inhabitant of any place; **cit´i·zen·ship** *n.*

**cit´i·zen·ry** *n.* citizens collectively

**citizen´s arrest** apprehension or citation by one who is not an officer of the law

**cit´ric** *adj.* pertaining to citrus fruit; the acid of such fruit; citric acid

**cit·ron·el´la** *n.* a pungent oil used in the making of perfumes, insect repellent, etc.

**cit´rus** *n.* trees that bear fruit such as oranges, lemons, limes, etc.; the fruit of these trees *–adj.*

**citrus fruit** oranges, lemons, limes, grapefruit, etc.

**cit´y** *(US) n.* an incorporated area that is self-governing according to the laws of its state

**cit´y** *(Brit.) n.* an urban area with a cathedral or that has been designated a city by royal warrant

**city council** elected members of the governing body of a city

**city father** anyone who wields power in the running of a city

**city hall** the seat of government in a city **–can´t fight city hall** expressing the futility of opposing established authority or dogma

**city manager** a professional administrator hired by a city to oversee the operation of its departments

**city planning** the science and process of regulating growth and change in a city

**cit´y·scape** *n.* a view of a city, its skyline, etc.

**city slicker** one who is perceived as being too suave or urbane

**civ´ic** *adj.* of a city or its citizens **–civ´i·cal·ly** *adv.*

**civ´ic-mind´ed** *adj.* inclined to act in the best interests of a city or its citizens **–civ´ic-mind´ed·ly** *adv.* **–civ´ic-mind´ed·ness** *n.*

**civics** *n.* the study of the rights and duties of citizenship

**civ´il** *adj.* of citizens; civilized in manner; formally polite; of matters that pertain to the rights of individuals **–ci·vil´ian** *n.* **–civ´il·ly** *adv.*

**civil defense** a program for recruiting, organizing, and training a group of volunteers to be called on for the protection of and to civilians in the event of enemy attack or natural disaster

**civil disobedience** a tactic for opposing government action or policy through noncompliance

**civil engineer** an engineer who specializes in the concept and development of construction projects for a community, such as roads, bridges, etc.

**ci·vil´ian** *n.* persons not associated with the military, law enforcement, etc. *–adj.* of civilians or civil life

**ci·vil´ian·ize** *vt.* to revert or place under civilian control **–ci·vil·ian·i·za´tion** *n.*

**ci·vil´i·ty** *n.* good breeding; courteous behavior

**civ·i·li·sa´tion** *(Brit.)*, **civ·i·li·za´tion** *(US) n.* the state of being or becoming civilized; the aggregate culture of a people; the comforts and protection of a civilized state

**civ´i·lise** *(Brit.)*, **civ´i·lize** *(US) vi., vt.* to convert from a savage state **–civ´i·lis·a·ble, civ´i·liz·a·ble** *adj.* **–civ´i·lised, civ´i·lized** *adj.*

**civil law** the law that pertains to the rights of individuals

**civil liberty** the right of an individual to act without interference from the government except as required for public safety

**civil rights** rights granted by the Constitution

**civil service** of those employed by the government, excepting the military or elected officials

**civil war** war between opposing factions within a nation

**clab´ber** *n.* thick sour milk *–vi., vt.* to curdle

**clad** *adj.* clothed; covered, as by a layer of metal

**clad´ding** *n.* a layer of metal covering another; the procedure for affixing one layer of metal to another

**claim** *vt.* to request or demand as a right; to state as fact *–n.* a demand; the basis for a demand; a thing demanded; an assertion **–claim´a·ble** *adj.* **–claim´ant, claim´er** *n.*

**claiming race** a horse race in which the participating horses are made available for sale

**clair·voy´ant** *adj.* of the ability to sense or perceive that which is not apparent *–n.* one with such ability **–clair·voy´ance** *n.* **–clair·voy´ant·ly** *adv.*

**cla´mant** *adj.* crying out noisily; insistent **–cla´mant·ly** *adv.*

**clam´bake** *n.* an outing featuring raw, steamed, or baked clams

**clam´ber** *vi.* to climb with much action of the hands and feet

**clam´my** *adj.* unpleasantly cold and damp **–clam´mi·ly** *adv.* **–clam´mi·ness** *n.*

**clam´or** *n.* a loud, sustained outcry *–vi.* to make insistent demands **–clam´or·er** *n.* **–clam´or·ous** *adj.* **–clam´or·ous·ly** *adv.* **–clam´or·ous·ness** *n.*

**clamp** *n.* a device used to join or hold *–vt.* to join with a clamp

**clamp´down** *n.* the imposition of restrictions or regulations **–clamp down** to grow more restrictive; to forbid or prohibit

**clan** *n.* a family, group of families, or tribe; a group with common interests **–clan´nish** *adj.* **–clan´nish·ly** *adv.* **–clan´nish·ness** *n.* **–clans´man** *n.*

**clan·des´tine** *adj.* kept secret or hidden **–clan·des´tine·ly** *adv.* **–clan·des´tine·ness** *n.*

**clang** *n.* a loud, harsh, metallic sound *–vi.* to make such a sound

**clang´or** *n.* a repeated or persisting clanging sound *–vi.* to make such a noise **–clang´or·ous** *adj.* **–clang´or·ous·ly** *adv.*

**clap** *n.* a sudden sharp sound; a blow *–vi., vt.* make a sharp sound; to applaud **–clap´per** *n.*

**clap´board** *n.* wood siding *–vt.* to apply wood siding

**clap´trap** *n.* idle words

**clar´et** *n.* a dry red wine

**clar´i·fy** *vi., vt.* to make or become clear, as a liquid; to make or become easier to understand **–clar·i·fi·ca´tion** *n.*

**clar´i·net´** *n.* a single-reed woodwind instrument **–clar·i·net´ist** *n.*

**clar´i·on** *adj.* clear, sharp, distinct *–n.* a medieval trumpet; the sound made by a clarion *–vt.* to proclaim clearly and distinctly

**clar´i·ty** *n.* the quality of being clear

**clash** *n.* a harsh clanging noise; a conflict between hostile forces or ideas *–vi.* to collide with a harsh noise; to come into conflict

**clasp** *n.* a fastener; an embrace *–vt.* to fasten as with a clasp; to embrace

**class** *n.* a distinct type or category; social rank; quality, especially of manners or dress *–vt.* to grade or rank

**class action,** class action suit a legal action on behalf of a large group of people, such as against the manufacturer of a defective product

**clas´sic** *adj.* of the highest order; famous; traditional; uncomplicated *–n.* a work of the highest order; a thing, that is famous or traditional **–clas´si·cal** *adj.* **–clas´si·cal·ly** *adj.* **–clas´si·cal·ness** *n.*

**clas´si·cism** *n.* the qualities associated with the art of ancient Greece or Rome; classical scholarship **–clas´si·cist** *n.* **–clas´si·cize** *vi., vt.*

**clas´si·fied** *adj.* arranged in suitable categories; secret

**classified ad, classified advertisement** small advertisements in a periodical, usually arranged according to subject matter

**clas´si·fy** *vt.* to arrange according to a system of categories; to restrict the use or distribution of **–clas´si·fi·a·ble** *adj.* **–clas´si·fi·ca´tion** *n.* **–clas´si·fi·er** *n.*

**class´ism** *n.* consciousness of the differences in station between persons; discrimination based on social standing **–class´ist** *adj., n.*

**class´mate** *n.* one who is in the same class in school; one who graduates in the same year as another, whether or not attending the same classes

**class´room** *n.* any room where classes are taught

**class´y** *adj.* of one with fine manners or style; elegant; splendid **–class´i·ness** *n.*

**clat´ter** *n.* noise; a racket or hubbub *–vi.* to rattle or reverberate **–clat´ter·er** *n.* **–clat´ter·ing·ly** *adv.* **–clat´ter·y** *adj.*

**clause** *n.* a part of a sentence; a section of a legal document **–claus´al** *adj.*

**claus·tro·pho´bi·a** *n.* a fear of confined or restricted spaces **–claus·tro·pho´bic** *adj.*

**cla´vier, cla·vier´** *n.* any stringed instrument that has a keyboard; the keyboard of such an instrument

**claw** *n.* a curved appendage, often sharp-pointed, used for grasping; anything that resembles a claw

**clay** *n.* a type of earth that becomes malleable when moistened; a material used in the making of pottery, models, etc. **–clay´ey** *adj.*

**clay´more** *n.* a broadsword

**clay pigeon** a clay disk used as a target in skeet shooting; one who is unknowingly open to attack, especially in office politics

**clean** *adj.* free of contamination; pure, undefiled; distinct, readable; smooth or well proportioned; flawless *–adv.* neatly; entirely *–vi.* to be cleansed *–vt.* to wash or scrub; to disinfect; to prepare food for cooking or eating **–clean´a·ble** *adj.* **–clean´er** *n.* **–clean´ness** *n.*

**clean´-cut** *adj.* clear, precise; of a pleasing appearance

**clean´ly** *adj.* kept clean *–adv.* in a clean manner **–clean´li·ness** *n.*

**cleanse** *vt.* to make clean; to absolve; to free from sin **–cleans´er** *n.* **–cleans´ing** *adn., n.*

**clean-shaven** without facial hair

**clean´up** *n.* the process of cleaning; the ridding of corruption, vice, etc.

**clear** *adj.* bright, unclouded; distinct, unmistakable; calm, untroubled, as *a clear conscience*; unencumbered, as from debt or lien *–adv.* obviously, completely *–vi.* to become clear; to be absolved *–vt.* to set or make free, unblock; to wipe clean; to absolve; to jump over **–clear the air** to discuss freely, as a difference of opinion **–clear up** to explain **–in the clear** absolved of guilt or suspicion **–clear´ly** *adv.* **–clear´ness** *n.*

**clear´ance** *n.* exoneration; permission, official sanction; the space between two objects in close proximity

**clear´-cut** *adj.* without ambiguity; denuded of trees *–vt.* to cut down all of the trees in an area

**clear headed** *adj.* discerning; reasonable, sensible **–clear´head·ed·ly** *adv.* **–clear´head·ed·ness** *n.*

**clear´ing** *n.* an area devoid of trees

**clear´ing·house** *n.* a facility for collection, processing, etc., of information or negotiable instruments such as bank drafts

**clear´-sight·ed** *adj.* shrewd; keenly perceptive **–clear´-sight·ed·ly** *adv.* **–clear´-sight·ed·ness** *n.*

**cleat** *n.* a small projection on furniture, footwear, etc.; a device on the deck or gunnel of a ship for securing lines

**cleave** *vi., vt.* to split; to separate **–cleav´a·ble** *adj.*

**clem´en·cy** *n.* leniency, mercy

**clench** *n.* a rigid hold *–vt.* to make a fist; to grit one's teeth

**cler´gy** *n.* collectively, those ordained for religious service

**cler´i·cal** *adj.* of a clerk in an office or a member of the clergy **–cler´i·cal·ly** *adv.*

**clerical collar** a stiff white collar worn by certain members of the clergy as a sign of office

**clerk** *n.* an office worker or official in charge of records; a counter person, as a hotel or sales clerk

**clev´er** *adj.* skillful; intelligent; witty **–clev´er·ly** *adv.* **–clev´er·ness** *n.*

**cli·ché´** *n.* a trite phrase **–cli·ched´** *adj.*

**cli´ent** *n.* a customer; one who is dependent on or served by another **–cli·en´tal** *adj.*

**cli·en·tele´** *n.* all the clients of a business as a group

**cliff** *n.* a high, steep face of rock

**cliff´-hang·er, cliff´hang·er** *n.* a story that is full of suspense

**cli´mate** *n.* the prevailing weather conditions of an area; any condition that may influence, as *the climate for change* **–cli·mat´ic** *adj.*

**cli·ma·tol´o·gy** *n.* the study of climate **–cli·ma·to·log´i·cal** *adj.* **–cli·ma·tol´o·gist** *n.*

**cli´max´** *n.* the final, forceful, or significant element in a series; a turning point or crisis

**climb** *n.* the act of scaling, as a mountain; advancement or improvement, as *the climb up the corporate ladder* *–vi., vt.* to mount by use of the hands and feet; any ascension, as through the offices of a company **–climb´a·ble** *adj.* **–climb´er** *n.*

**clinch** *n.* a fastening; a hug *–vt.* to fasten; to conclude **–clinch´er** *n.*

**cling** *vi.* to hold fast, adhere; to remain near, be emotionally attached **–cling´er** *n.* **–cling´i·ness** *n.* **–cling´ing·ly** *adv.* **–cling´y** *adj.*

**clinging vine** one who is inclined to great dependence on others

**cling´stone** *adj.* of a fruit with pulp firmly attached to the pit *–n.*

**clin´ic** *n.* a place for the medical treatment of ambulatory patients; an infirmary or dispensary; an intensive learning session, as *a sales clinic*

**clin´i•cal** *adj.* of a clinic; of an atmosphere like a clinic: sterile; scientific or objective **–clin´i•cal•ly** *adv.*

**clinical thermometer** a thermometer used to measure body temperature

**clip** *n.* a thing cut, as hair or a piece of film; a fast pace; a sharp blow; a fastener *–vi.* to cut off; to move rapidly *–vt.* to cut or cut off; to shorten by cutting, as vowels or syllables from a word, when speaking; to strike with a sharp blow; to cheat; to fasten

**clip´board** *n.* a writing surface of pressed board or plastic with a clamp at the top to hold papers

**clip joint** an establishment that regularly overcharges

**clip´-on** *adj.* having a fastener for attaching as *a clip-on tie*

**clip´per** *n.* a person who cuts or trims; a tool for such cutting, as *hedge clippers*; a type of sailing ship

**clip´ping** *n.* the act of cutting off; that cut off, as trimmings; an item cut from a periodical

**clique** *n.* a small exclusive group **–cli´quey, cli´quish** *adj.* **–cli´quish•ly** *adv.* **–cli´quish•ness** *n.*

**cloak** *n.* a long cape; that which covers or conceals *–vt.* to cover or conceal; to camouflage

**cloak´-and-dag´ger** *adj.* of the activities of secret agents, spies, etc.

**cloak´room** *n.* a place for the safekeeping of coats, hats, etc.

**clob´ber** *vt.* to hit forcefully; to win by a wide margin

**clock** *n.* a mechanism for calibrating and marking time; any device similar to a clock in function *–vt.* to measure the time taken to perform a task; to measure output, distance, etc. **–time clock** a device that records the arrival and departure of employees

**clock´wise** *adj., adv.* in the direction of the hands of a clock

**clock´work** *n.* the moving parts of a clock; any mechanism that is similar to that of a clock like clockwork precise; according to plan

**clod** *n.* a lump of earth; a dull or stupid person **–clod´dish** *adj.* **–clod´dish•ly** *adv.* **–clod´dish•ness** *n.*

**clod´hop•per** *n.* an unrefined person: a country bumpkin; a heavy shoe, as worn by a farmer

**clog** *vi.* to become obstructed *–vt.* to obstruct or impede *–n.* an obstruction; a shoe with a wooden sole **–clog´gi•ness** *n.* **–clog´gy** *adv.*

**clois´ter** *n.* a covered walk around a courtyard; a place of seclusion *–vt.* to seclude or protect **–clois´tered** *adj.* **–clois´tral** *adj.*

**close** *adj.* nearby; like in form, thought, emotion, etc.; confining; restrictive; limited **–close´ly** *adv.* **–close´ness** *n.*

**close** *n.* an ending, conclusion *–vi., vt.* to conclude; to shut; to connect **–clos´a•ble** *adj.*

**close by** near; beside

**close call, close shave** a near miss; a narrow escape

**closed captioned** of a television broadcast that displays printed dialogue for the benefit of the hearing impaired

**closed shop** designating of an employer who agrees to hire only those who belong to or agree to join a particular union or unions

**close´fist•ed** *adj.* stingy, miserly **–close´fist•ed•ness** *n.*

**close´out** *n.* the selling of goods at a discount, to dispose of discontinued items or to liquidate the business *–vi., vt.* to close or sell out a business interest

**close quarters** a crowded space

**clos´et** *(US) n.* a small room for storage *–vt.* to consult privately in a closed room: *closeted with one's attorney*

**close´up** an intimate or near view to show detail, emphasis, etc.

**clos´ing** *adj.* of the final stages, as *closing arguments in a trial* *–n.* the ending or finalization, as of a speech, letter, etc.

**closing costs** monies exchanged as agreed at the finalizing of a contract, esp. for the purchase of property

**clo´sure** *n.* a conclusion; anything that closes

**clot** *n.* a soft mass *–vi.* to thicken or coagulate

**cloth** *n.* a fabric

**clothe** *vt.* to cover, as with clothing, to furnish with clothing **–clothes** *n. pl.* wearing apparel

**clothes´horse** *n.* one who is inordinately fond of clothes

**clothes´line** *n.* a cord, rope, etc. on which clothing is hung out to dry

**clothes peg** *n. (Brit.)* a device for securing clothing to a line for drying

**clothes´pin** *(US) n.* a device for securing clothing to a line for drying

**clothes tree** an upright post with hooks near the top for hanging hats and coats

**cloth´ier** *n.* one who manufactures or sells clothes

**cloth´ing** *n.* all of one's garments; wearing apparel in general

**clo´ture** *n.* a parliamentary maneuver for closing debate and putting the matter to an immediate vote

**cloud** *n.* a mist of water droplets suspended in the atmosphere; a cloud-like mass of smoke, dust, etc.; anything in the air that resembles a cloud, as *a cloud of locusts*; anything that casts a shadow or gloom *–vi., vt.* to obscure or overshadow **–have one's head in the clouds daydream –living under a cloud** under suspicion; depressed **–cloud´i•ness** *n.* **–cloud´y** *adj.*

**cloud´burst** a sudden heavy rain
**cloud´less** *adj.* without clouds; clear, sunny –**cloud´less·ly** *adv.* –**cloud´less·ness** *n.*
**cloud nine** a state of bliss
**clout** *n.* a blow; power or influence –*vt.* to strike
**clove** *n.* a fragrant spice; a segment of a bulb, as of garlic
**clo´ven** *adj.* split; cleft
**clo´ver·leaf** *n.* a complex highway interchange
**clown** *n.* a performer who entertains with broad humor; one who acts like a fool; one clumsy or incompetent –*vi.* to perform or act like a fool –**clown´ish** *adj.* –**clown´ish·ly** *adv.* –**clown´ish·ly** *adv.* –**clown´ish·ness** *n.*
**cloy** *vi., vt.* to make unpleasant by excess, esp. of something very rich or sweet –**cloy´ing·ly** *adv.*
**club** *n.* a heavy stick used as a weapon; a group of persons organized for a common purpose –*vt.* to strike with a club
**club´foot´** *n.* a congenital deformity of the foot
**club´house** *n.* the meeting place or facilities used by the members of an organization
**cluck** *n.* the sound of a hen; a foolish person
**clue** *n.* information that may help to solve a puzzle –**clue in** to inform or provide with information
**clum´sy** *adj.* awkward; poorly fashioned –**clum´si·ly** *adv.* –**clum´si·ness** *n.*
**clus´ter** *n.* a group of similar or like things gathered together –*vi., vt.* to grow or come together –**clus´ter·y** *adj.*
**clutch** *n.* a grasping, as with a hand or claw; a mechanical device that grabs and holds –*vt.* to grasp and hold closely
**clut´ter** *n.* a number of items scattered in disarray –*vt.* to scatter, litter
**coach** *(US)* *n.* the main passenger compartment of a train or plane; an instructor or trainer –*vt.* to teach or train
**coach** *(Brit.)* *n.* a large motor vehicle designed to carry passengers between cities or towns; an instructor or trainer –*vt.* to teach or train
**co·ag´u·late** *vi., vt.* to change from a liquid state to a thick, soft mass –**co·ag·u·la´tion** *n.* –**co·ag´u·la·tive** *adj.* –**co·ag´u·la·tor** *n.*
**coal** *n.* a combustible mineral; an ember
**co´a·lesce´** *vi.* to unite or merge into a single unit –**co·a·les´cence** *n.* –**co·a·les´cent** *adj.*
**co·a·li´tion** *n.* a temporary union of persons, groups, etc. for some special purpose –**co·a·li´tion·al** *adj.* –**co·a·li´tion·ist** *n.*
**co-an´chor** *n.* one who shares the duties of anchorperson on a news program –*vi., vt.*
**coarse** *adj.* of a rough surface, manner, etc.; of a person or thing that is vulgar or obscene –**coarse´ly** *adv.* –**coarse´ness** *n.*
**coarse´-grained´** *adj.* having a rough texture
**coars´en** *vi., vt.* to make rough
**coast** *n.* land near the sea –*vi.* to move pulled by the force of gravity or momentum; to slack off or proceed with little effort, relying on past success –**coast´al** *adj.* –**coast´al·ly** *adv.*
**coast´er** *n.* a flat bottomed conveyance for sliding down hill, usually on snow or ice; a sled; a mat, etc. placed under a container to protect the surface beneath it
**coast guard** a naval force charged with the protection of a nation's coast
**coast´line** *n.* a strip of land where a body of water touches the shore
**coat** *n.* an outer garment; protective covering; a layer, as *a coat of paint*
**coat´dress** *n.* a long frock that buttons down the front similar to a coat
**coat´ing** *n.* a layer, as *a coating of wax*; material for making coats
**coat of arms** an insignia or emblem that identifies a family, clan, nation, etc.; armorial bearings
**coat of mail** a medieval garment intended to protect the upper body
**coat´rack** *n.* an upright post with hooks near the top for hanging hats and coats; a series of hooks for hanging coats, hats, etc., attached to a wall
**coat´room** *n.* a place for safekeeping coats, hats, etc.
**coat´tail** *n.* the bottom of a coat at the back –**on someone´s coattails** to attain success by identifying with someone who is successful
**co-au´thor** *n.* one who writes or creates in collaboration with another
**coax** *vi.* to cajole –*vt.* to persuade by cajolery or wheedling –**coax´er** *n.* –**coax´ing·ly** *adv.*
**co·ax´i·al** *adj.* having a common axis; of a transmission line that has a central conductor insulated from a surrounding conductor
**coaxial cable** *n.* cable used to transmit telephone, television, etc. signals
**cob** *n.* the cylindrical core from which the kernels of corn grow; a male swan
**co´balt** *n.* a metallic chemical element
**cobalt blue** dark blue
**cob´ble** *vt.* to repair shoes
**cob´bler** *n.* one who makes or repairs shoes; a fruit pie
**cob´ble-stone** *n.* rounded stone used for paving
**COBOL** *n.* COmmon Business Oriented Language; a computer programming language with vocabulary and syntax similar to everyday English
**cob´web´** *n.* a spider web; something similar to a spider web
**co´ca** *n.* a family of tropical plants, the dried leaves of which are the source for cocaine
**co´caine´** *n.* a narcotic made from dried coca leaves

**co·cain´ism** *n.* addiction to cocaine
**co·cain´ize** *vt.* to treat with cocaine —**co·cain·i·za´tion** *n.*
**coc´cyx** *n.* a small bone at the lower end of the spine
**co·chair´** *n.* one who shares the duties of a chairperson —*vi.*
**cock** *n.* the male of certain birds; a device for regulating the flow of liquid or gas; the striking part of the lock of a gun; small pile of hay; a jaunty angle —*vt.* to set for release, as of a fist, a gun, a camera, etc.; to set at a jaunty angle
**cock-a-leek´ie** *n.* a Scottish soup based on chicken and leeks
**cock´a·ma·mie** *adj.* fictional; fabricated; ridiculous
**cock-and-bull story** a fabrication
**cocked hat** a three-cornered hat knock into a cocked hat to spoil; to reveal as false
**cock´eyed** *adj.* out of alignment; ridiculous; of a concept or reasoning that is awry
**cock´ney** *n.* a rhyming dialect from the East End of London; a native speaker of the dialect —*adj.* of the dialect or those who speak it
**cock´sure** *adj.* arrogantly self-confident
**cock´tail´** *n.* a beverage or food served before or at the start of a meal
**cock´y** *adj.* overconfident; flamboyant
**co´coa´** *n.* a powder made from processed cacao beans; a beverage made from this powder; a brown color
**cocoa** butter a fat derived from cacao seeds
**co´co·nut** *n.* the fruit of the coconut palm
**coconut milk** the thin liquid from the center of the coconut
**coconut oil** an oil obtained from coconut meat
**coconut palm** a tropical tree that produces coconuts
**co·coon´** *n.* a protective cover spun by certain insect larvae; any similar cover
**cod** *n.* a type of food fish that is also the source of cod-liver oil
**co´da** *n.* a phrase or section added to a musical composition to signal its end
**cod´dle** *vt.* to overindulge; to pamper or treat gently; to cook by poaching in water that is kept just below the boiling point
**code** *n.* a systematic arrangement of a body of law, regulations, etc.; a system of symbols or signs for sending messages —*vt.* to translate into representative symbols, as *to code a computer program* —**cod´er** *n.*
**co·de·fend´ant** *n.* one who, with another or others, is accused of a crime or wrongdoing
**co´deine** *n.* a narcotic derivative of opium
**codg´er** *n.* an old man, often eccentric or senile
**cod´i·cil** *n.* an addendum, as to a contract or a will
**cod´i·fy** *vt.* to arrange according to an established system **cod´i·fi·ca´tion** *n.* —**cod´i·fi·er** *n.*
**cod´-liv·er oil** *n.* oil from the liver of codfish, rich in vitamins A and D
**co´ed´** *adj.* coeducational —*n.* a female student
**co·ed´it** *vt.* to work with another in preparing a book, journal, etc. for publication —**co·ed´i·tor** *n.*
**co·ed·u·ca´tion·al** *adj.* of an institution of learning that caters to both male and female students —**co·ed·u·ca´tion** *n.* —**co·ed·u·ca´tion·al·ly** *adv.*
**co·erce´** *vt.* to bring about by force; to compel under duress —**co·erc´i·ble** *adj.*
**co·er´cion** *n.* the use of threats or force to compel —**co·er´cive** *adj.* —**co·er´cive·ly** *adv.* —**co·er´cive·ness** *n.*
**co·ex·ist´** *vi.* to exist at the same time, place, etc.; to live side by side in harmony —**co·ex·is´tence** *n.* —**co·ex·is´tent** *adj.*
**cof´fee** *n.* a beverage made from the ground seeds of a tropical plant; the plant or its seeds; an informal gathering; a light brown color
**coffee beans** the seeds of the coffee plant
**coffee break** a brief rest period for workers
**cof´fee·cake** *n.* a bread-like pastry usually served as a light repast with coffee
**cof´fee·house** *n.* a café that serves coffee and light refreshments
**coffee maker** an appliance, often electric, for making coffee; a coffee pot
**cof´fee·pot** *n.* a utensil of metal, glass, etc. for the making and serving of coffee
**coffee shop** a coffeehouse; a retail shop that sells exotic coffee and utensils for making and serving coffee
**coffee table** a low table, usually part of a living room set
**cof´fer** *n.* a strongbox; a reinforced shelter; a cofferdam
**cof´fer·dam** *n.* a barrier to hold back water for construction or repairs taking place below water level
**cof´fin** *n.* a box for burial
**cog** *n.* any of the teeth on a gear; a minor, but necessary, functionary
**co´gent** *adj.* forceful or compelling, as of an argument —**co´gen·cy** *n.*
**cog´i·tate´** *vi.* to consider carefully —**cog´i·ta´tion** *n.* —**cog´i·ta·tive** *adj.* —**cog´i·ta·tor** *n.* —**cog´i·ta·tive·ly** *adv.*
**cog´nac** *n.* a brandy produced in the Cognac region of France, distilled from wine
**cog´nate´** *adj.* of common ancestry —**cog·na´tion** *n.*
**cog·ni´tion** *n.* the mental processes generally, such as perception, reasoning and judgement —**cog·ni´tion·al** *adj.* —**cog´ni·tive** *adj.*
**cog´ni·zance** *n.* knowledge, especially that gained through observation; awareness —**cog´ni·za·ble** *adj.* —**cog´ni·zant** *adj.*
**cog´no´men** *n.* a family name; any name

**cog´wheel** *n.* a wheel with teeth around the rim

**co·hab´it** *vi.* to live together in a sexual relationship —**co·hab´i·tant** *n.* —**co·hab·i·ta´tion** *n.*

**co´here´** *vi.* to hold together naturally or logically —**co´her´ence** *n.*

**co·her´ent** *adj.* congruous; logically connected; understandable —**co·her´ent·ly** *adv.*

**co·he´sive** *adj.* adhesive; sticking together; **co·he´sion** *n.*; **co·he´sive·ly** *adv.* **co·he´sive·ness** *n.*

**co´hort** *n.* a colleague or friend; a contemporary

**cóif** *vt.* to style hair —*n.* coiffure

**coif·fure´** *n.* a hair style

**coin** *n.* a metal piece of fixed monetary value —*vt.* to mint coins; to make or invent, as *to coin a phrase* —**coin´er** *n.*

**coin´age** *n.* the process of minting coins; the money system of a country

**co´in·cide´** *vi.* to correspond exactly, as in form, space, time, etc.; to be in accord

**co·in´ci·dence** *n.* the condition of coinciding; a series of chance events that seem to have been planned —**co·in´ci·dent** *adj.*

**co·in·ci·den´tal** *adj.* of that which coincides; accidental; characterized by chance —**co·in·ci·den´tal·ly** *adv.*

**coin-op´er·at·ed** *adj.* of a device that is made to function by inserting coins, as *a coin-operated game*

**co·i´tus, co·i´tion** *n.* sexual intercourse; **co´i·tal** *adj.*

**col´an·der** *n.* a perforated container used in cooking for draining off liquid

**cold** *adj.* of a low temperature; lacking heat or warmth; unfeeling or unfriendly —*n.* the absence of heat; a viral infection of the respiratory tract —**go in cold** without preparation —**have cold feet** to be reticent, afraid —**have down cold** know thoroughly —**in the cold** left out or ignored —**turn a cold shoulder** to scorn or ignore

**cold´blood´ed** *adj.* of a creature with a low body temperature; unfeeling, callous —**cold´blood´ed·ly** *adv.* —**cold´blood´ed·ness** *n.*

**cold chisel** a hardened steel tool for cutting or breaking metal

**cold cream** a cosmetic skin cleanser

**cold cuts** any of a variety of processed meats, usually served cold

**cold front** the leading edge of a cold air mass that influences the weather in the areas it approaches

**cold´heart´ed** *adj.* unresponsive to affection; lacking compassion —**cold´heart´ed·ly** *adv.* —**cold´heart´ed·ness** *n.*

**cold´ly** *adv.* in a cool fashion: *coldly polite* —**cold´ness** *n.*

**cold pack** a cool, wet compress applied to an injury, such as a sprain; a chemical ice pack used in first aid

**cold snap** a sudden bout of cold weather

**cold sore** a viral infection of small blisters about the mouth, usually following a cold, fever, etc.

**cold storage** a storage area for refrigerating food, safekeeping of furs during the off-season, etc.

**cold turkey** suddenly, without preparation, often of quitting a habit, as smoking

**cold war** a state of unfriendly relations between countries without actual fighting

**cole´slaw** *n.* a salad of shredded cabbage and dressing

**col´ic** *n.* persistent discomfort experienced by an infant, characterized by constant crying —**col´ick·y** *adj.*

**col´i·se´um** *n.* a building for sporting events, shows, etc.

**co·li´tis** *n.* an inflammation of the large intestine

**col·lab´o·rate´** *vi.* to work together; to cooperate in an undertaking —**col·lab·o·ra´tion** *n.* —**col·lab´o·ra·tive** *adj.* —**col·lab´o·ra·tive·ly** *adv.* —**col·lab´o·ra´tor** *n.*

**col·lage´** *n.* an artistic composition constructed of odd bits of material —**col·lag´ist** *n.*

**col·lapse´** *vi.* to fall or break down suddenly; to fold into a compact unit —**col·laps·i·bil´i·ty** *adv.* —**col·laps´i·ble** *adj.*

**col´lar** *n.* the part of a garment that rests on or near the neck; a decorative or functional band worn around the neck

**col´lards, col´lard greens** *n.* a green leafy vegetable

**col´late** *vt.* to gather together in order, as typed pages or sections of a book —**col·la´tor** *n.*

**col·lat´er·al** *adj.* similar; of a thing pledged as a guarantee for fulfillment of an obligation —*n.* that pledged as a guarantee —**col·lat´er·al·ly** *adv.*

**col·lat´er·al·ize** *vt.* to pledge as security; to guarantee by pledging security

**col´league´** *n.* an associate, usually in business

**col·lect´** *vi., vt.* to gather together; to secure payment —**col·lect´a·ble, col·lect´i·ble** *adj.* —**col·lec´tion** *n.* —**col·lec´tor** *n.*

**col·lect´ed** *adj.* gathered together, accumulated; self-possessed: calm and composed

**col·lect´ive** *adj.* as a group; consolidated; of a venture characterized by people working together as a group —*n.* a cooperative organization —**col·lec´tive·ly** *adv.*

**collective bargaining** negotiations between employees as a group and their employer

**col´lege** *n.* an institution of learning; an association of individuals for a special purpose: *electoral college*

**col·le´gi·an** *n.* a student at a college —**col·le´gi·ate** *adj.*

**col·lide´** *vi.* to come together violently

**col·li´sion** *n.* a coming together violently; a clash of opinions, etc.

**col´lo·cate** *vt.* to arrange; categorize

**col·lo´qui·al** *adj.* conversational; of a word or phrase used informally —**col·lo´qui·al·ly** *adv.*

**col·lo´qui·al·ism** *n.* a word or phrase used informally

**col´lo·quy** *n.* a formal discussion

**col·lu´sion** *n.* a conspiracy; a plot to act, especially for some illegal purpose **–col·lu´sive** *adj.* **–col·lu´sive·ly** *adv.*

**co´lon** *n.* a punctuation mark (:); the large intestine from the cecum to the rectum

**colo´nel** *n.* a military officer **–col´o·nel·cy** *n.*

**co·lo´ni·al** *adj.* of an outpost of a government or society

**co·lo´ni·al·ism** *n.* a government policy of settling new lands, especially for exploitation **–co·lo´ni·al·ist** *adj., n.*

**col´o·nist** *n.* one who establishes or lives in a colony **–col´o·nise´** *(Brit.),* **col´o·nize´** *(US) vt.* **–col´o·ni·sa´tion, col´o·ni·za´tion** *n.*

**col·on·nade´** *n.* a series of upright columns

**col´o·phon** *n.* a printed emblem, as of a publisher or trade union

**col´or** *(US) n.* the separation of white light into varying wavelengths; the sensation created in the eye by light waves of varying lengths; any substance used to dye, tint, etc. *–vi., vt.* to give or change color

**col·or·a´tion** *n.* the shades and tones that make up the color of a thing

**col´or·blind** *(US) adj.* incapable of distinguishing between certain colors; without racial prejudice **–col´or·blind·ness** *n.*

**col´ored** *(US) adj.* having color; of a non-caucasian race; biased, as *colored by one's belief*

**col´or·fast** *(US) adj.* of a garment or material that will not bleed color or fade when washed

**col´or·ful** *(US) adj.* bright; picturesque; quaint or unusual **–col´or·ful·ly** *adv.* **–col´or·ful·ness** *n.*

**color guard** *(US)* those who carry and accompany the flag or flags

**col´or·ing** *(US) n.* the process of applying color; the color applied

**col´or·ist** *(US) n.* one who applies color, especially to black and white drawings or motion pictures

**col´or·ize** *(US) vt.* to add color to a photograph or motion picture that was shot in black and white **–col·or·i·za´tion** *n.*

**col´or·less** *(US) adj.* bland; uninteresting

**col´ors** *(US) n.* a banner or flag that identifies a nation, clan, fighting unit, etc.

**co·los´sal** *adj.* amazingly large **–co·los´sal·ly** *adv.*

**co·los´sus** *n.* an extremely large structure, statue, etc.; one who is bigger than life

**co·los´to·my** *n.* surgery that creates an opening in the colon for disposal of body waste

**col´our** *(Brit.) n.* the separation of white light into varying wavelengths; the sensation created in the eye by light waves of varying lengths; any substance used to dye, tint, etc. *–vi., vt.* to give or change color

**col´our·blind** *(Brit.) adj.* incapable of distinguishing between certain colors; without racial prejudice **–col´our·blind·ness** *n.*

**col´oured** *adj. (Brit.)* having color; of a non-caucasian race; biased, as *colored by one's belief*

**col´our·ful** *adj. (Brit.)* bright; picturesque; quaint or unusual **–col´our·ful·ly** *adv.* **–col´our·ful·ness** *n.*

**col´our·ing** *n. (Brit.)* the process of applying color; the color applied

**col´our·ist** *n. (Brit.)* one who applies color, especially to black and white drawings or motion pictures

**col´our·ise** *vt. (Brit.)* to add color to a photograph or motion picture that was shot in black and white **–col·our·i·sa´tion** *n.*

**col´our·less** *adj. (Brit.)* bland; uninteresting

**col´ours** *(Brit.) n.* a banner or flag that identifies a nation, clan, fighting unit, etc.

**colt** *n.* a young horse, donkey, etc.

**col´umn´** *n.* a slender support; any similar formation; a vertical strip on a written or printed page made up of horizontal lines **–col·um´nar** *adj.*

**co·lum·ni·a´tion** *n.* the use of columns in architecture

**col´um·nist** *n.* a writer of commentary in a magazine or newspaper

**co´ma** *n.* a state of deep sleep caused by illness or injury

**com´bat** *n.* armed conflict, a battle; a struggle **–com·bat´** *vt.* to fight against; to contend

**com·bat´ant** *n.* one who takes part in a war or struggle

**combat fatigue** mental illness brought on by prolonged exposure to combat conditions

**com·ba´tive** *adj.* inclined to fight **–com·bat´ive·ly** *adv.* **–com·bat´ive·ness** *n.*

**com´bi·na·tion** *n.* a union created by the blending or merging of divers things **–com·bi·na´tion·al** *adj.*

**com´bine** *n.* a machine for harvesting grain; an association, as of businesses, for a common purpose **–com·bine´** *vi., vt.* to join forces; unite **–com·bin´a·ble** *adj.* **–com·bin·a·bil´i·ty** *n.*

**com´bo** *n.* a small instrumental ensemble

**com·bus´ti·ble** *adj.* easily ignited and burned; excitable *–n.* a material that is easily ignited **–com·bus·ti·bil´i·ty** *n.* **–com·bus´ti·bly** *adv.*

**com·bus´tion** *n.* the process of burning

**come´back** *n.* a return or attempt to return to a previous state, as in politics or show business; a sharp retort

**co·me´di·an** *n.* one who writes or performs comedy

**co·me´dic** *adj.* pertaining to comedy **–co·me´di·cal·ly** *adv.*

**come´down** *n.* a reversal of fortune

**com´e·dy** *n.* any writing, acting, etc. designed to make others laugh

**comedy of errors** a series of mistakes that are more humorous than tragic

**come´ly** *adj.* attractive; pleasing in appearance —**come´li·ness** *n.*

**come´on** *n.* an enticement; something offered as an incentive

**co·mes´ti·ble** *n.* food

**come·up´pance** *n.* a humbling penalty that is deserved; retaliation

**com´fort** *n.* a feeling of contentment; any attempt to relieve pain or stress; one who provides relief —*vt.* to relieve from pain or stress; to aid or assist

**com´fort·a·ble** *adj.* at ease; free from pain or stress; adequate, as *a comfortable living* —**com´fort·a·ble·ness** *n.* —**com´fort·a·bly** *adv.*

**com´fort·er** *n.* one who consoles; *(US)* a heavy bed covering

**com´ic** *adj.* funny, silly, or humorous —*n.* a comedian

**com´i·cal** *adj.* amusing, humorous; facetious —**com´i·cal·ly** *adv.* —**com´i·cal·ness** *n.*

**comic book** a book of stories illustrated with cartoon characters

**comic opera** a humorous work in the style of grand opera

**comic relief** a humorous incident that punctuates an otherwise serious situation in life or the theater

**comic strip** a series of cartoons that tell a story

**com´ing** *adj.* drawing near; full of promise —**have it coming** deserve, as punishment

**com´ing-out´** *n.* a debut, often as one comes of age for courting

**com´ma** *n.* a punctuation mark(,)

**com·mand´** *n.* the authority to lead or direct; an order, the ability to use well, as *command of the language* —*vt.* to direct or order —**com·mand´a·ble** *adj.*

**com´man·dant** *n.* a commanding officer

**com·man·deer´** *vt.* to take without permission, especially to take for official use

**com·mand´er** *n.* one who is in charge; a leader

**commander in chief** the senior commanding officer

**com·mand´ing** *adj.* having power or authority; impressive; compelling —**com·mand´ing·ly** *adv.*

**commanding officer** one who is in charge of a military unit or post

**com·mand´ment** *n.* a rule or regulation

**com·man´do** *n.* a warrior trained to operate inside enemy territory

**command post** temporary headquarters for one directing a military operation

**com·mem´o·rate´** *vt.* to honor the memory of, as by a memorial —**com·mem·o·ra´tion** *n.* —**com·mem´o·ra·tive** *adj., n.* —**com·mem´o·ra·to·ry** *adj.*

**com·mence´** *vi., vt.* to begin

**com·mence´ment** *n.* an induction or beginning; a school graduation ceremony

**com·mend´** *vt.* to praise; to entrust, as *commend to one's care* —**com·men´da·to·ry** *adj.*

**com·mend´a·ble** *adj.* worthy of praise; admirable —**com·mend´a·bly** *adv.*

**com·men·da´tion** *n.* a medal, plaque, etc. that designates one as worthy of praise

**com·men´su·ra·ble** *adj.* to the same degree; proportionate —**com·men´su·ra·bly** *adv.*

**com·men´su·rate** *adj.* equivalent or comparable; corresponding in size or degree —**com·men´su·rate·ly** *adv.* —**com·men´su·rate·ness** *n.*

**com·men·su·ra´tion** *n.* the consideration of things by resemblance to one another

**com´ment** *n.* a note or remark of explanation, observation, criticism, etc. —*vi.* to speak or write about —**com´men·tar´y** *n.* —**com·men·tar´i·al** *adj.*

**com´men·ta·tor** *n.* one who reports on and expresses an opinion of current events —**com´men·tate** *vi., vt.*

**com´merce** *n.* the buying and selling of goods and services

**com·mer´cial**[1] *adj.* of commerce; undertaken for profit —*n.* paid advertising, as on television, radio, etc. —**com·mer´cial·ly** *adv.*

**com·mer´cial**[2] *(Brit.) n.* a traveling salesman

**commercial art advertising art** and design as distinguished from art that is purely decorative

**com·mer´cial·ism** *n.* operating mainly for profit

**com·mer´cial·ize** *vt.* to operate for profit or in the manner of a commercial venture, often of something that heretofore was operated for the public good —**com·mer·cial·i·za´tion** *n.*

**commercial traveler** a traveler on business, as a salesman

**com·min´gle** *vi., vt.* to mix together; to combine

**com·mis´er·ate** *vi., vt.* to feel or express sorrow or pity —**com·mis·er·a´tion** *n.* —**com·mis´er·a·tive** *adj.* —**com·mis´er·a·tive·ly** *adv.* —**com·mis´er·a·tor** *n.*

**com´mis·sar·y** *n.* a store or cafeteria

**com·mis´sion** *n.* the authority to carry out certain duties; the duties so authorized; a group given such authority —*vt.* to grant authority to perform some function or duty

**com·mis´sion·er** *n.* one given authority by a commission to act; the head of a government department

**com·mis´sion·a·ble** *adj.* of sales for which a fee is to be paid, as to a salesman, stock broker, etc.

**com·mit´** *vt.* to do; to give, as for safekeeping or confinement;, tobind or obligate —**com·mit´tal** *n.*

**com·mit´ment** *n.* a pledge or promise; dedication

**com·mit´tee** *n.* a group appointed for a special purpose

**com·mo´di·ous** *adj.* spacious —**com·mo´di·ous·ly** *adv.* —**com·mo´di·ous·ness** *n.*

**com·mod´i·ty** *n.* anything useful that can be traded

**com´mon** *adj.* ordinary; basic; widespread; shared by many —*n.* a public square —**com·mon·al´i·ty, com´mon·al·ty** *n.* —**com´mon·ly** *adv.* —**com´mon·**

ness n.

**common carrier** a company or person that transports passengers or freight

**common denominator** a multiple that is common to the denominators of all of the fractions in a set of two or more; a feature that is shared by two or more things under consideration

**com´mon·er** n. one who is not of noble blood

**common ground** an area of agreement

**common law** the law based on tradition or usage

**common law marriage** a marriage without legal sanction

**com´mon·place** *adj.* ordinary —n. anything that is ordinary or trite

**com´mon·sense** *adj.* sound, rational, as *a commonsense decision*

**common sense** reasonable judgement

**common touch** having empathy for the average citizen

**com´mon·wealth** n. the welfare of the general public

**com´mon·wealth** n. the people of a state, nation, etc.; a government so designated

**com·mo´tion** n. a disturbance; confusion

**com·mu´nal·ize** *vt.* to make into a commune; to transfer or add property to a commune

**com´mune** n. a group of people banded together for a common purpose, to share labor and its rewards, etc.; a cooperative **—com·mu´nal** *adj.* **—com·mu´nal·ly** *adv.* **—com·mu´nal·ism** n. **—com·mu´nal·ist** n. **—com·mu·nal·is´tic** *adj.*

**com·mune´** *vi.* to converse with; be in harmony with, as *to commune with nature*

**com·mu´ni·ca·ble** *adj.* able to be passed on; infectious or contagious, as a disease **—com·mu·ni·ca·bil´i·ty, com·mu´ni·ca·ble·ness** n. **—com·mu´ni·ca·bly** *adv.*

**com·mu´ni·cate´** *vi.* to share information; be understood —*vt.* to convey information; to make known; to transmit, as an illness

**com·mu´ni·ca´tion** n. a letter, news; the act of communicating

**com·mun´ion** n. a close fellowship; an intimate association; a group who comprise such a fellowship, as of a Christian denomination **—com·mu´ni·cant** n.

**com´mu·nism** n. the concept of a classless society with common ownership of property **—com´mu·nist** n. **—com´mu·nis´tic** *adj.* **—com´mu·nis´ti·cal·ly** *adv.*

**com·mu´ni·ty** n. society in general; the members of a political unit; collectively, those who share a common interest, as *the community of artists*

**community college** an educational institution, often providing vocational training or the first two years of a liberal arts education

**community property** property held in common by a married couple or by a community at large

**community service** voluntary work for a charitable or government organization; work in the community assigned as punishment for wrongdoing

**com´mu·nize** *vt.* to place in ownership and control of the community at large

**com·mu·ta´tion** n. a substitution or exchange; the act of traveling to and from work, often on public transportation

**com·mute´** *vi.* to travel to and from work; to make an exchange —*vt.* to substitute or replace **—com·mut´er** n.

**com´pact´** *adj.* requiring little space, small or light —n. a covenant; a small automobile

**com·pact´** *adj.* tightly packed —*vt.* to pack tightly **—com·pact´ly** *adv.* **—com·pact´ness** n. **—com·pac·tor** n.

**compact disk** n. device for storing data, as to create sound or for computer files

**com·pan´ion** n. one who accompanies another; a thing that is a part of a set **—com·pan´ion·ship** n.

**com·pan´ion·a·ble** *adj.* cordial, congenial; having the qualities of a good companion **—com·pan´ion·a·ble·ness** n. **—com·pan´ion·a·bly** *adv.*

**companion piece** an item of furniture, decor, etc. that fits with others to make a set

**com·pan´ion·way** n. a hall or stairway aboard ship

**com´pa·ny** n. an assembly or association of persons for some purpose; a guest; companionship **—ship´s company** the crew of a ship

**company store** a retail establishment operated by a company for its employees

**company union** an employee bargaining unit that is not affiliated with any other union; often describing a bargaining unit that is controlled by the employer

**com´pa·ra·ble** *adj.* able to be compared; similar **—com·pa·ra·bil´i·ty, com´pa·ra·ble·ness** n. **—com´pa·ra·bly** *adv.*

**com·par´a·tive** *adj.* relative to another or others, as *comparative philosophy*; corresponding **—com·par´a·tive·ly** *adv.*

**com·pare´** *vt.* to examine for similarities or differences **—com·par´i·son** n.

**com·part´ment** n. a section into which a larger space is divided **—com·part·men´tal** *adj.* **—com·part·men·tal·i·za´tion** n. **—com·part·men´tal·ize** *vt.*

**com·pas´sion** n. concern for the troubles of another; pity; sympathy **—com·pas´sion·ate** *adj.* **—com·pas´sion·ate·ly** *adv.*

**com·pas´sion·less** *adj.* without pity; unfeeling

**com·pat´i·ble** *adj.* capable of existing or working well together **—com·pat·i·bil´i·ty, com·pat´i·ble·ness** n. **—com·pat´i·bly** *adv.*

**com·pa´tri·ot** n. a colleague or associate

**com·peer´** n. a comrade or friend; a peer; one's equal

**com·pel´** *vt.* to force or bring about by force **—com·pel´lent** *adj.*

**com·pel´ling** *adj.* forceful; impressive –**com·pel´ling·ly** *adv.*

**com·pen´di·ous** *adj.* of that summarized briefly

**com·pen´di·um** *n.* a synopsis; an abridgement

**com´pen·sate´** *vt.* to offset; to pay, as for services or for damages –**com·pen´sa·ble** *adj.* –**com´pen·sa·tive, com·pen´sa·to·ry** *adj.*

**com´pen·sa´tion** *n.* payment, as restitution for a wrong or remuneration for services rendered –**com·pen·sa´tion·al** *adj.*

**com·pete´** *vi.* to work against; to contend

**com´pe·tence, com´pe·ten·cy** *n.* adequate qualification; fitness

**com´pe·tent** *adj.* qualified; suitable; adequate –**com´pe·tent·ly** *adv.*

**com´pe·ti´tion** *n.* rivalry in business, sports, etc.; a rival

**com·pet´i·tive** *adj.* inclined to rivalry –**com·pet´i·tive·ly** *adv.* –**com·pet´i·tive·ness** *n.*

**com·pet´i·tor** *n.* a rival, as an individual or team; one who competes

**com·pile´** *vt.* to gather and arrange in some order, as of data or a series of literary works –**com´pi·la´tion** *n.*

**com·pil´er** *n.* one who compiles; a computer program that translates high-level program instructions into machine language

**com·pla´cence, com·pla´cen·cy** *n.* contentment; self-satisfaction; apathy –**com·pla´cent** *adj.* –**com·pla´cent·ly** *adv.*

**com·plain´** *vi.* to express dissatisfaction –**com·plain´er** *n.* –**com·plain´ing·ly** *adv.*

**com·plain´ant** *n.* in law, one who files a complaint

**com·plaint´** *n.* an expression of dissatisfaction

**com·plai´sant** *adj.* striving to please; accommodating; obliging –**com·plai´sance** *n.* –**com·plai´sant·ly** *adv.*

**com·plect´ed** *adj.* of skin coloring, as *light complected*

**com´ple·ment** *n.* that which completes –*vt.* to make complete

**com·ple·men´ta·ry** *adj.* of a part that completes; corresponding –**com·ple·men´tal** *adj.*

**complementary angle** an angle that, when added to its complement, equals 90°

**com´plete´** *adj.* lacking nothing –*vt.* to conclude; to accomplish successfully –**com·ple´tion** *n.* –**com·plete´ly** *adv.* --**com·plete´ness** *n.*

**com·plex´** *adj.* complicated –**com´plex** *n.* a group of related elements taken as a single entity, as *an apartment complex* –**com·plex´i·ty** *n.* –**com·plex´ness** *n.*

**com·plex´ion** *n.* appearance of the skin; the general nature of a thing –**com·plex´ioned** *adj.*

**com·pli´ance** *n.* a tendency to yield; conformity –**com·pli´a·ble, com·pli´ant** *adj.* –**com·pli´ant·ly** *adv.*

**com´pli·cate´** *vt., vi.* to make or grow difficult

**com´pli·cat·ed** *adj.*; made up of many parts; intricate, tangled; difficult to understand –**com´pli·cat·ed·ly** *adv.* –**com´pli·cat·ed·ness** *n.* –**com·pli·ca´tion** *n.*

**com·plic´i·ty** *n.* involvement in wrongdoing

**com´pli·ment** *n.* a statement of praise; an act of courtesy –*vt.* to praise or congratulate –**com´pli·men´ta·ry** *adj.*; **com·pli·men´ta·ri·ly** *adv.*

**com·ply´** *vi.* to act on another's request

**com·po´nent** *n.* an integral part

**com·port´** *vt.* to conduct oneself in a particular manner –**com·port´ment** *n.*

**com·pose´** *vt.* to form by combining; to put in order; to create, as of music; to calm oneself; to arrange elements on a page for printing

**com·posed´** *adj.* calm, deliberate

**com·pos´er** *n.* one who creates, especially of music

**com·pos´ite** *adj.* made up of several parts –*n.* a material made from a joining of several materials –**com·pos´ite·ly** *adv.*

**com´po·si´tion** *n.* the act of forming or combining; the placement of combined elements; a thing formed or composed

**com·pos´i·tor** *n.* one who sets type for printing

**com´post** *n.* decomposed organic matter used as potting soil –*vt.* to transform into compost

**com·po´sure** *n.* tranquillity, selfcontrol

**com´pote** *n.* a dessert of fruit marinated in syrup; a stemmed serving dish

**com´pound´** *adj.* made up of two or more elements –*n.* a mixture

**com·pound´** *vt.* to combine; to increase or intensify by adding to, as *compound interest, compounding a problem*

**compound fracture** a broken bone that pierces the skin

**compound interest** interest on a loan that is calculated on the principal plus accrued interest

**com´pre·hend´** *vt.* to understand; to take in, include –**com·pre·hend´i·ble, com·pre·hen´si·ble** *adj.* –**com·pre·hend´ing·ly** *adv.* –**com´pre·hen´sion** *n.*

**com´pre·hen´sive** *adj.* taking in much; broad in scope –*n.* a detailed layout, as for an advertisement –**com´pre·hen´sive·ly** *adv.* –**com·pre·hen´sive·ness** *n.*

**com´press** *n.* a pad of cloth or gauze used medically to apply heat, cold, pressure, etc. to a wound or injury –**com·press´** *vt.* to press together; to squeeze; to make compact –**com·press´i·ble** *adj.* –**com·pres´sor** *n.* –**com·pres´sion** *n.*

**com·prise´** *vt.* to include; to consist of

**com´pro·mise** *n.* a settlement resulting from concessions –*vt.* to settle by concession; to expose to danger or difficulty, as by carelessness: *his actions have compromised our position*

**comp·trol´ler** *n.* one who oversees the financial affairs of an organization

**com·pul´sion** *n.* a driving force; an irrational impulse –**com·pul´sive** *adj.* –**com·pul´sive·ly** *adv.*

**com·pul´so·ry** *adj.* required; obligatory

**com·punc´tion** *n.* uneasiness or doubt aroused by the prospect of wrongdoing

**com·pute´** *vt.* to calculate **–com·put´a·ble** *adj.* **–com´pu·ta´tion** *n.*

**com·put´er** *n.* an electronic device for processing data **–computer literate** familiar with the operation of a computer

**com·put·er·ese´** *n.* terminology used by those involved with computers or computer programs

**computer graphics** artwork produced with the aid of a computer

**com·put´er·ise** *(Brit.)*, **com·put´er·ize** *(US) vt.* to operate or enable to operate with the aid of or under the control of a computer **–com·put·er·i·sa´tion** *(Brit.)*, **com·put·er·i·za´tion** *(US) n.*

**computer virus** a program that causes malfunction in a computer or computer program

**com´rade´** *n.* a friend or companion **–com´rade·ly** *adj.* **–com´rade·ship** *n.*

**con** *adv.* against; of an opposing view *–n.* an opposing position; a swindle; a convict *–vt.* to swindle; to trick, especially by lies or smooth talk

**con·cat´e·nate** *vt.* to join; to link together **–con·cat·e·na´tion** *n.*

**con´cave´** *adj.* curved like the inner surface of a sphere *–n.* **–con·cave´ly** *adv.*

**con·ceal´** *vt.* to cover; to keep secret **–con·ceal´a·ble** *adj.* **–con·ceal´er** *n.* **–con·ceal´ment** *n.*

**con·cede´** *vt.* to acknowledge reluctantly, to grant, as a privilege

**con·ceit´** *n.* an overly high opinion of oneself **–con·ceit´ed** *adj.* **–con·ceit´ed·ly** *adv.* **–con·ceit´ed·ness** *n.*

**con·ceiv·a·ble** *adj.* able to be believed or understood **–con·ceiv´a·ble** *adv.*

**con·ceive´** *vt.* to imagine; to understand

**con´cen·trate´** *n.* a substance that has been made more dense or intense, often by the removal of water *–vi., vt.* to increase in density or intensity **–con´cen·tra´tion** *n.*

**concentration camp** a place for the internment of prisoners of war, political prisoners, etc.

**con·cen´tric, con·cen´tri·cal** *adj.* having a common center **–con·cen´tri·cal·ly** *adv.* **–con·cen·tric´i·ty** *n.*

**con´cept´** *n.* a theory, a broad understanding

**con·cep´tion** *n.* a beginning; an impression or understanding **–con·cep´tion·al** *adj.*

**con·cep´tu·al** *adj.* theoretical or abstract; ideal **–con·cep´tu·al·ly** *adv.*

**con·cep´tu·al·ize** *vt.* to form a theory or opinion **–con·cep·tu·al·i·za´tion** *n.*

**con·cern´** *n.* a matter of interest; a feeling of anxiety, a business firm *–vt.* to show interest; to cause anxiety **–con·cerned´** *adj.*

**con´cert** *n.* mutual understanding; a program of music **–con·cert´** *vt.* to arrange or resolve by mutual understanding

**con·cert´ed** *adj.* harmoniously; unified, as *a concerted effort* **–con·cert´ed·ly** *adv.*

**concert grand** a large piano intended for a concert hall

**con·cer·ti´na** *n.* a small musical instrument with a bellows and keys to change pitch

**con·cer´to** *n.* a musical composition arranged for an orchestra and a solo instrument

**con·ces´sion** *n.* the act of conceding; a thing conceded; space leased for a business venture on the land of another, as *a food concession*

**con·ces´sion·aire´** *n.* one who operates a business on the property of another for some consideration

**conch** *n.* a large marine mollusk with a spiral shell

**con·cil´i·ate´** *vt.* to appease, placate **–con·cil´i·a´tion** *n.* **–con·cil´i·a·tor** *n.* **–con·cil´i·a·to·ry** *adj.*

**con·cise´** *adj.* succinct; brief and to the point **–con·cise´ly** *adv.* **–con·cise´ness** *n.*

**con´clave** *n.* a large gathering; a secret meeting

**con·clude´** *vt.* to bring to a close; to deduce by reasoning **–con·clu´sion** *n.*

**con·clu´sive** *adj.* final; convincing **–con·clu´sive·ly** *adv.* **–con·clu´sive·ness** *n.*

**con·coct´** *vt.* to make or devise from a variety of elements **–con·coc´tion** *n.*

**con·com´i·tant** *adj.* associated with; connected **–con·com´i·tance, con·com´i·tan·cy** *n.*

**con´cord** *n.* harmony or agreement; a treaty to establish peaceful relations

**con·cord´ance** *n.* an agreement; an index of leading words in a text

**con·cor´dant** *adj.* agreeing; harmonious

**con´course´** *n.* a broad walkway; an open area from passing or congregating as at an airline terminal

**con´crete´** *adj.* formed into a solid mass; precise *–n.* a building material formed of cement, sand, and gravel *–vi., vt.* to solidify **–con·crete´ly** *adv.* **–con·crete´ness** *n.*

**con·cre´tion** *n.* a hardened mass

**con·cu´pis·cence** *n.* intense desire; lustfulness **–con·cu´pis·cent** *adj.*

**con·cur´** *vi.* to correspond or coincide; to agree **–con·cur´rence, con·cur´ren·cy** *n.*

**con·cur´rent** *adj.* in agreement; occurring or existing together; convergent **–con·cur´rent·ly** *adv.*

**con·cus´sion** *n.* a shock, as from an impact; an injury caused by an impact

**con·demn´** *vt.* to disapprove; to find one guilty; to impose punishment; to declare unfit for use **–con·dem´na·ble** *adj.* **–con´dem·na´tion** *n.* **–con·demn´er** *n.*

**con´den·sa´tion** *n.* compression or compaction; an

abridgement

**con·dense´** *vt.* to make dense; to compress; to abridge or summarize —**con·den·sa·bil´i·ty** *n.* —**con·dens´a·ble** *adj.*

**condensed milk** a thick, sweet milk processed from fresh cow's milk

**con´de·scend´** *vi.* to do that considered beneath one's dignity or station —**con·de·scend´ence, con´de·scen´sion** *n.*

**con·de·scend´ing** *adj.* patronizing; disdainful; smug —**con·de·scend´ing·ly** *adv.*

**con·dign´** *adj.* suitable, especially of punishment

**con´di·ment** *n.* a seasoning or relish for food

**con·di´tion** *n.* a requirement; a circumstance; anything that modifies something else —*vt.* to modify or influence

**con·di´tion·al** *adj.* contingent on circumstances; true only if certain requirements are satisfied —**con·di´tion·al·ly** *adv.*

**con·di´tioned** *adj.* in a proper or desired state of being

**con·dole´** *vi.* to sympathize; to console; to comfort

**con·do´lence** *n.* an expression of sympathy

**con´do·min´i·um**[1] *(Brit.)* *n.* a territory governed by two or more nations

**con´do·min´i·um**[2] *(US)* *n.* an apartment owned by the tenant; a building in which such an apartment is located

**con·done´** *vt.* to forgive; to disregard without protest —**con·don´a·ble** *adj.*

**con´dor** *n.* a large vulture

**con·duce´** *vi.* to assist or contribute

**con·du´cive** *adj.* contributing or leading to —**con·du´cive·ness** *n.*

**con´duct** *n.* the way one acts —**con·duct´** *vt.* to lead; to behave in a certain manner; to convey

**con·duc´tor** *n.* a leader; a guide; a person in charge; material which transmits heat or electricity

**con·duct´ance** *n.* the ability to transmit electricity —**con·duc´tive** *adj.* —**con·duc·tiv´i·ty** *n.* —**con·duc´tor** *n.*

**con·duc´tion** *n.* conveyance, as of electricity through a wire

**con´duit** *n.* a channel, as to carry water, electric lines, etc.

**cone** *n.* a geometric solid created by a circle and a surface that runs from the diameter of the circle to the end of the line extending from the center of the circle and perpendicular to its base

**con´fab** *n.* a discussion; confabulation —*vi.*

**con·fab·u·la´tion** *n.* a conversation or informal discussion —**con·fab´u·late** *vi.* —**con·fab´u·la·tor** *n.* —**con·fab´u·la·to·ry** *adj.*

**con·fec´tion** *n.* any sweet edibles, such as candied fruit, cookies, etc. —**con·fec´tion·ar·y** *adj.* —**con·fec´tion·er** *n.*

**confectioners´ sugar** finely ground sugar

**con·fec´tion·er·y** *n.* a shop where confections are made or sold

**con·fed´er·a·cy** *n.* an alliance of people, states, etc. joined for a common purpose —**con·fed´er·a´tion** *n.*

**con·fed´er·ate** *n.* an associate or accomplice —*vt.* to unite

**con·fer´** *vi.* to meet for discussion —*vt.* to grant, as an honorary degree —**con´fer·ee´** *n.*

**con´fer·ence** *n.* a formal meeting for discussion

**conference call** a telephone connection for more than two persons

**con·fess´** *vt.* to acknowledged

**con·fes´sion** *n.* an admission of guilt

**con·fes´sion·al** *n.* a small enclosure in a church where parishioners confess their sins to a priest

**con·fes´sor** *n.* one who confesses; a priest who hears confessions

**con·fet´ti** *n.* small bits of colored paper tossed in the air during festivities

**con´fi·dant** *n.* a trusted friend

**con·fide´** *vi., vt.* to share a secret

**con´fi·dence** *n.* trust or faith in anything; self-assurance; that confided as a secret

**confidence game** a swindle

**confidence man** a swindler

**con´fi·dent** *adj.* self-assured —**con´fi·dent·ly** *adv.*

**con´fi·den´tial** *adj.* secret —**con·fi·den·ti·al´i·ty** *n.* —**con·fi·den´tial·ly** *adv.*

**con·fid´ing** *adj.* trusting —**con·fid´ing·ly** *adv.*

**con·fig´ure** *vt.* to set up or arrange in a particular way

**con·fig´u·ra´tion** *n.* arrangement of the parts that make up a thing; the structure of a thing based on the arrangement of its parts —**con·fig´u·ra´tion·al·ly** *adv.* —**con·fig´u·ra´tion·al** *adj.*

**con´fine** *n.* an enclosure —**con·fine´** *vt.* to restrict; to shut in —**con·fin´a·ble** *adj.* —**con·fine´ment** *n.*

**con·firm´** *vt.* to prove; to validate, as by formal approval —**con´fir·ma´tion** *n.*

**con·firmed´** *adj.* resolved; proved

**con´fis·cate** *vt.* to seize, usually by authority —**con·fis·ca´tion** *n.* —**con·fis´ca·to·ry** *adj.*

**con´fla·gra´tion** *n.* a large destructive fire

**con´flict** *n.* a clash of ideas, interests, etc.; open warfare —**con·flict´** *vi.* to clash

**conflict of interest** a situation that occurs when one is in a position of moral obligation that is at variance with personal interest

**con´flu·ence** *n.* a flowing together, as of two rivers or a crowd of people —**con´flu´ent** *adj.*

**con·form´** *vi.* to adapt; to follow custom or tradition —**con·form´er, con·form´ist** *n.* —**con·form´i·ty** *n.*

**con·for·ma´tion** *n.* the symmetry or form of a structure

**con·found´** *vt.* to confuse, bewilder —**con·found´ed**

*adj.*

**con·fra·ter´ni·ty** *n.* a brotherhood; a group associated for a common purpose, as religious or charitable **–con·fra·ter´nal** *adj.*

**con·front´** *vt.* to come or bring face to face **–con·fron·ta´tion** *n.* **–con·fron·ta´tion·al** *adj.*

**con·fuse´** *vt.* to bewilder; to mistake, as one thing for another; to mingle indiscriminately **–con·fus´ing** *adj.* **–con·fus´ing·ly** *adv.*

**con·fu´sion** *n.* bewilderment; a state of chaos or disorder

**con·fute´** *vt.* to prove in error **–con´fu·ta´tion** *n.*

**con´ga** *n.* a Latin American dance or its music

**con·geal´** *vi., vt.* to thicken or solidify by cooling **–con·geal´a·ble** *adj.* **–con·geal´ment** *n.*

**con·gen´ial** *adj.* friendly; compatible **–con·ge·ni·al´i·ty** *n.* **–con·ge´nial·ly** *adv.*

**con·gen´i·tal** *adj.* existing at birth; hereditary **–con·gen´i·tal·ly** *adv.*

**con·gest´** *vt.* to clog or obstruct, as nasal passages; to overcrowd, as a highway **–con·ges´tive** *adj.*

**con·ges´ted** *adj.* overcrowded **–con·ges´tion** *n.*

**con·glom´er·ate** *adj.* gathered together in a mass or group –*n.* an agglomeration; a corporation made up of a number of smaller diversified companies –*vi., vt.* to form or cause to form in a mass **–con·glom·er·a´tion** *n.*

**con·grat´u·late** *vt.* to compliment; to express joy **–con·grat´u·la·tor** *n.* **–con·grat´u·la·to·ry** *adv.*

**con·grat·u·la´tions** *n.* an expression of pleasure at the good fortune of another

**con´gre·gate** *vi.* to gather; to assemble **–con´gre·ga´tion** *n.* **–con·gre·ga´tion·al** *adj.*

**con·gre·ga´tion·al·ism** *n.* a church society in which local assemblies are autonomous **–con·gre·ga´tion·al·ist** *n.*

**con´gress** *n.* a coming together; a formal assembly **–Congress** the federal legislature of the U.S. **–con·gres´sion·al** *adj.*

**con·gru´ence, con·gru´en·cy** *n.* a state of agreement; harmony, accord **–con´gru·ent** *adj.* **–con·gru´ent·ly** *adv.* **–con·gru´i·ty** *n.*

**con´gru·ous** *adj.* appropriate, seemly, suitable or fitting to the circumstances **–con´gru·ous·ly** *adv.* **–con´gru·ous·ness** *n.*

**con´i·cal** *adj.* shaped like a cone **–con´i·cal·ly** *adv.*

**co´ni·fer** *n.* an evergreen tree or shrub **–co·nif´er·ous** *adj.*

**con·jec´tur·al** *adj.* based on speculation **–con·jec´tur·al·ly** *adv.*

**con·jec´ture** *n.* speculation; a judgement based on incomplete information –*vt.* to speculate

**con·join´** *vi., vt.* to unite or connect

**con´ju·gal** *adj.* of or pertaining to marriage **–con·ju·gal´i·ty** *n.* **–con´ju·gal·ly** *adv.*

**con´ju·gate** *adj.* joined together –*vt.* join; to give the inflections of a verb **–con´ju·ga´tion** *n.* **–con·ju·ga´tion·al, con´ju·ga·tive** *adj.* **–con·ju·ga´tion·al·ly** *adv.* **–con´ju·ga·tor** *n.*

**con·junct´** *adj.* collective –*n.* that joined with another

**con·junc´tion** *n.* a joining together; a word that connects other words, phrases, or clauses **–con·junc´tion·al** *adj.*

**con·junc´tive** *adj.* connective; serving as a conjunction –*n.* a conjunction

**con·junc·ti·vi´tis** *n.* an inflammation of the eyelid

**con´jure** *vi., vt.* to summon a spirit, as by magic **–con·jur·a´tion** *n.* **–con´jur·er, con´ju·ror** *n.*

**conk** *n.* a blow –*vt.* to strike **–conk out** to suddenly fail or quit, as a machine or a person

**con man** a confidence man; swindler

**con·nect´** *vi.* to become linked –*vt.* to link together **–con·nect´er, con·nec´tor** *n.*

**con·nect´a·ble** *adj.* able to be connected **–con·nect·a·bil´i·ty** *adv.*

**con·nect´ed** *adj.* linked; joined in order; having important social or business contacts **–con·nect´ed·ly** *adv.* **–con·nect´ed·ness** *n.*

**con·nec´tive** *adj.* serving to join or link –*n.* a bond; anything that joins or links **–con·nec´tive·ly** *adv.* **–con·nec·tiv´i·ty** *n.*

**con·nec´tion** *n.* a joining; a part that joins; a relationship; an important contact

**con·nip´tion** *n.* a fit; a frenzy; excitement or rage

**con·niv´ance** *n.* secret involvement; wrongdoing

**con·nive´** *vi.* to cooperate secretly in wrongdoing **–con·niv´er** *n.*

**con´nois·seur´** *n.* one with expert knowledge, especially of the arts; a person of discriminating taste

**con·no·ta´tion** *n.* an implied meaning; an insinuation **–con´no·ta·tive** *adj.* **–con´no·ta·tive·ly** *adv.*

**con·note´** *vt.* to suggest or imply

**con·nu´bi·al** *adj.* of marriage

**con´quer** *vi., vt.* to overcome **–con´quer·a·ble** *adj.* **–con´quer·or** *n.* **–con´quest** *n.*

**con·san´guine, con·san·guin´e·ous** *adj.* of common ancestry **–con·san·guin´e·ous·ly** *adv.*

**con´san·guin´i·ty** *n.* related through a common ancestor; a close association

**con´science** *n.* a sense of right and wrong

**conscience-stricken** *adj.* feeling remorse for wrongdoing

**con´sci·en´tious** *adj.* guided by conscience; thorough **–con·sci·en´tious·ly** *adv.* **–con·sci·en´tious·ness** *n.*

**conscientious objector** one who, because of religious or moral beliefs, refuses to serve in combat

**con´scious** *adj.* awake; aware of one's own and other's existence, actions, etc. **–con´scious·ly** *adv.* **–con´scious·ness** *n.*

**con´script** *n.* one drafted into the military

**con·script´** *vt.* to draft into military service
**con´se·crate´** *vt.* to set apart as sacred; to dedicate to a worthy cause —**con´se·cra´tion** *n.*
**con·sec´u·tive** *adj.* proceeding in logical order —**con·sec´u·tive·ly** *adv.* —**con·sec´u·tive·ness** *n.*
**con·sen´su·al** *adj.* mutually consenting —**con·sen´su·al·ly** *adv.*
**con·sen´sus** *n.* general agreement
**con·sent´** *n.* permission —*vi.* to grant permission —**con·sent´er** *n.*
**con´se·quence** *n.* something that logically follows an action; relative significance, as *of little or no consequence*
**con´se·quent** *adj.* following as a result —*n.* anything that follows
**con·se·quen´tial** *adj.* having significance; that creates an effect or is an effect —**con·se·quen´tial·ly** *adv.* —**con·se·quen´tial·ness** *n.*
**con´se·quent·ly** *adv.* as a result
**con·serv´an·cy** *n.* a group or society devoted to the preservation of natural resources
**con·ser·va´tion** *n.* the protection of natural resources
**conservation of energy** the scientific principal that in a closed system energy may be converted to another form, but is never diminished
**con·serv´a·tism** *n.* a policy that advocates moderation, or opposition to change
**con·serv´a·tive** *adj.* typified by a lack of flamboyance; cautious; reserved or moderate —*n.* one who is reserved or moderate in manner —**con·serv´a·tive·ly** *adv.*
**con·serv´a·to·ry** *n.* a greenhouse for the display of plants; a school of music or drama
**con·serve** *n.* a type of fruit preserve —*vt.* to guard against damage or waste; to make a fruit preserve
**con·sid´er** *vt.* to carefully contemplate; to bear in mind; to be respectful of; to deem, believe
**con·sid´er·a·ble** *adj.* large, extensive; substantial —**con·sid´er·a·bly** *adv.*
**con·sid´er·ate** *adj.* having regard for others; **con·sid´er·ate·ly** *adv.* —**con·sid´er·ate·ness** *n.*
**con·sid´er·a´tion** *n.* careful contemplation; payment for services
**con·sid´ered** *adj.* given careful thought
**con·sid´er·ing** *adv., prep.* taking into account
**con·sign´** *vt.* to give over to another
**con´sign·ee´** *n.* one to whom goods are transferred
**con·sign´ment** *n.* goods transferred to another for sale or safekeeping —**con·sign´or** *n.*
**con·sist´** *vi.* to be made up of
**con·sist´ence, con·sist´en·cy** *n.* uniformity; texture
**con·sist´ent** *adj.* constant; unwavering; harmonious —**con·sist´ent·ly** *adv.*
**con·sis´to·ry** *n.* a church council
**consolation prize** a reward for one who participates in a contest, but does not win
**con·sole´** *vt.* to comfort —**con·sol´a·ble** *adj.* —**con´so·la´tion** *n.*
**con·sol´i·date´** *vi., vt.* to combine; to strengthen by combining or compacting —**con·sol·i·da´tion** *n.*
**con·som·mé´** *n.* a clear broth
**con´so·nance, con´so·nan·cy** *n.* harmony; a pleasant blending of a combination of sounds
**con´sort** *n.* a spouse or associate —**con·sort´** *vi., vt.* to associate with
**con·sor´ti·um** *n.* an alliance, as of business firms, to promote a common interest
**con·spic´u·ous** *adj.* obvious; apparent; notable; *conspicuous bravery* —**con·spic´u·ous·ly** *adv.* —**con·spic´u·ous·ness** *n.*
**conspicuous consumption** extravagance in acquiring goods and wastefulness in their use
**con·spir´a·cy** *n.* a secret plan; those involved in carrying out such a plan —**con·spir´a·tor** *n.*
**con·spir´a·to´ri·al** *adj.* of or inclined to scheming or collusion; conspiring —**con·spir´a·to´ri·al·ly** *adv.*
**con·spire´** *vi.* to plot secretly; to work together, as of circumstances
**con´sta·ble** *n.* an officer of the law
**con·stab´u·lar·y** *n.* the jurisdiction of a peace officer; law officers collectively
**con´stant** *adj.* unchanging; continual; steadfast —*n.* that which is unchanging —**con´stan·cy** *n.* —**con´stant·ly** *adv.*
**con·ster·na´tion** *n.* a state of confusion and distress
**con·stit´u·en·cy** *n.* a district or the persons in the district that an elected official represents; generally, the body of one's supporters —**con·stit´u·ent** *adj.*
**con´sti·tute´** *vt.* to found, establish; to make up, be the parts of
**con´sti·tu´tion** *n.* the fundamental structure of a thing —**con·sti·tu´tion·al** *adj.* —**con·sti·tu·tion·al´i·ty** *n.* —**con·sti·tu´·tion·al·ly** *adv.*
**con·strain´** *vt.* to confine; to restrain; to compel —**con·straint´** *n.*
**con·strict´** *vt.* to make smaller by squeezing or contracting —**con·stric´tion** *n.*
**con·strict´tor** *n.* a thing that constricts; a snake that kills its prey by squeezing
**con·struct´** *vt.* to build; to piece together —**con·struc´tion** *n.* —**con·struc´tor** *n.*
**con·struc´tive** *adj.* of that which is helpful or useful: *constructive criticism*; affirmative; instructive —**con·struc´tive·ly** *adv.* —**con·struc´tive·ness** *n.*
**con·strue´** *vt.* to interpret or deduce; to understand —**con·stru´a·ble** *adj.*
**con´sul** *n.* an official appointed to serve a government or its citizens on foreign soil —**con´su·lar** *adj.*
**con´su·late** *n.* the offices of a consul; the authority of a consul

**con·sult´** *vi.* to meet to exchange views –*vt.* to refer to for advice or information

**con·sult´ant** *n.* a professional who is hired to analyze and advise, as *a management consultant*

**con·sul·ta´tion** *n.* a meeting to share knowledge and plan a course of action –**con·sul´ta·tive** *adj.* –**con·sul´ta·tive·ly** *adv.*

**con·sult´ing** *adj.* one who acts in an advisory capacity, as *a consulting physician*

**con·sum´a·ble** *adj.* subject to being expended or dissipated, as *a consumable resource* –*n.* any material that is used up or spent in the course of its use

**con·sume´** *vt.* to make use of; to deplete, devour, or destroy –**con·sum´er** *n.*

**consumer credit** a loan or line of credit provided for the purchase of consumer goods

**consumer goods** possessions that satisfy the needs of individuals in contrast to those used in the production of goods and services

**con·sum´er·ism** *n.* a passion for acquisition of personal property; the concept that a healthy economy requires a strong consumer market; advocacy to protect consumers from false advertising, shoddy merchandise, etc.

**con´sum·mate** *adj.* complete or perfect; skillful *vt.* to complete or perfect –**con·sum´mate·ly** *adv.*

**con·sump´tion** *n.* the using of goods or services; the amount used; a wasting of the body by disease –**con·sump´tive** *adj.* –**con·sump´tive·ly** *adv.*

**con´tact** *n.* the condition of touching; a communication, as by telephone or letter; one connected in some way, as *a business contact* –*vt.* to touch; to communicate with

**contact lens** a corrective lens worn directly over the eyeball

**con·ta´gion** *n.* the spread of disease by contact; the disease itself

**con·ta´gious** *adj.* spread by contact –**con·ta´gious·ly** *adv.* –**con·ta´gious·ness** *n.*

**con·tain´** *vt.* to hold or have the capacity to hold; to keep within fixed limits –**con·tain´a·ble** *adj.* –**con·tain´er** *n.*

**con·tain´er·ize** *vt.* to place in a large container, often of standardized containers that ease handling in transshipment

**con·tain´ment** *n.* a limiting or confinement, as of the spread of a conflict, political system, etc.

**con·tam´i·nate´** *vt.* to pollute; to make impure –**con·tam´i·nant, con·tam´i·na·tor** *n.* –**con·tam´i·na´tion** *n.*

**con·temn´** *vt.* to view with contempt; to despise –**con·temn´er, con·tem´nor** *n.*

**con´tem·plate** *vt.* to study or ponder intently; to consider as a possible course of action –**con´tem·pla´tion** *n.*

**con·tem´pla·tive** *adj.* inclined to be reflective or thoughtful –**con·tem´pla·tive·ly** *adv.* –**con·tem´pla·tive·ness** *n.*

**con·tem´po·ra´ne·ous** *adj.* contemporary

**con·tem´po·rar´y** *adj.* of or related to the same time; current, as in style –*n.* one living at the same time or in the present time

**con·tem´po·rize** *vi., vt.* to make suitable to the time

**con·tempt´** *n.* disdain; a show of disrespect, as for a court or legislative body –**con·tempt´i·ble** *adj.* –**con·tempt·i·bil´i·ty, con·tempt´i·ble·ness** *n.* –**con·tempt´i·bly** *adv.*

**con·temp´tu·ous** *adj.* disdainful –**con·temp´tu·ous·ly** *adv.* –**con·temp´tu·ous·ness** *n.*

**con·tend´** *vi.* to compete; to argue or dispute –*vt.* to claim to be true –**con·tend´er** *n.*

**con·tent´** *adj.* satisfied –*n.* satisfaction –**con´tent** *n.* all that is contained within

**con·tent´ed** *adj.* satisfied –**con·tent´ed·ly** *adv.* –**con·tent´ed·ness** *n.*

**con·ten´tion** *n.* an argument or dispute; an assertion

**con·ten´tious** *adj.* quarrelsome –**con·ten´tious·ly** *adv.* –**con·ten´tious·ness** *n.*

**con·ter´mi·nous** *adj.* within the same boundary –**con·ter´mi·nous·ly** *adv.*

**con´test** *n.* a competition or competing –**con·test´** *vt.* to dispute or challenge; to compete –**con·test´a·ble** *adj.* –**con·test´a·bly** *adv.*

**con·tes´tant** *n.* one who disputes, as a will; one who competes

**con´text´** *n.* the setting in which a thing appears or occurs –**con·tex´tu·al** *adj*

**con·tig´u·ous** *adj.* touching; adjacent –**con·tig´u·ous·ly** *adv.* –**con·tig´u·ous·ness** *n.*

**con´ti·nence** *n.* moderation; selfrestraint –**con´ti·nent** *adj.* –**con´ti·nent·ly** *adv.*

**con´ti·nent** *n.* any of the great land masses of the earth –**con·ti·nen´tal** *adj.* –**con·ti·nen´tal·ly** *adv.*

**continental breakfast** a light breakfast of juice, coffee, and sweet rolls

**continental drift** the gradual shifting of land mass on the earth's surface

**continental shelf** the land mass under shallow coastal waters

**con·tin´gence** *n.* contact; adjacency; a contingency

**con·tin´gen·cy** *n.* a possibility or likelihood; something that happens by chance

**con·tin´gent** *adj.* happening by chance; unpredictable –*n.* a contingency; a representative group

**con·tin´u·al** *adj.* repeated without interruption –**con·tin´u·al·ly** *adv.*

**con·tin´u·a´tion** *n.* restarting after a pause; a thing added, an extension

**con·tin´ue** *vi.* to endure, to remain in effect –*vt.* to persist; to remain; to resume after interruption

—**con·tin´u·ance** *n.*
**con´tin·u´i·ty** *n.* the quality of being continuous
**con·tin´u·ous** *adj.* unbroken; connected; without interruption —**con·tin´u·ous·ly** *adv.* —**con·tin´u·ous·ness** *n.*
**con·tort´** *vt.* to twist out of shape; to distort
**con·tort´ed** *adj.* twisted; misshapen; deformed —**con·tort´ed·ly** *adv.*
**con·tor´tion** *n.* an abnormal twisting, as of the body —**con·tor´tion·ist** *n.*
**con´tra·band´** *adj.* of goods prohibited by law from import or export —*n.* illegal merchandise
**con´tra·cep´tion** *n.* the prevention of pregnancy
**con·tra·cep´tive** *n.* a device or chemical used to prevent pregnancy —*adj.* pertaining to contraception; used to prevent pregnancy
**con´tract** *n.* a binding agreement, usually in writing, between two or more parties who each agree to do something —*vi., vt.* to enter into a formal agreement —**con·tract´** *vt.* to acquire, as a disease; to shorten or reduce in size
**con·trac´tion** *n.* something shortened, as a word; the shortening of a muscle under stress —**con·trac´tion·al** *adj.*
**con·trac´tu·al** *adj.* pertaining to or implying a formal agreement —**con·trac´tu·al·ly** *adv.*
**con·trac´tor** *n.* any of the parties to a contract —**con´trac·tor** *n.* one who agrees to perform a service for a stipulated price
**contract bridge** a card game in which the winning bidders establish the number of tricks to be taken
**con·tra·dict´** *vt.* to claim the opposite of; to be inconsistent with —**con·tra·dic´tion** *n.*
**con·tra·dic´tive, con·tra·dic´to·ry** *adj.* tending to refute; inconsistent —**con·tra·dic´tive·ly, con·tra·dic´to·ri·ly** *adv.* —**con·tra·dic´tive·ness** *n.*
**con´trail** *n.* a condensed vapor trail, as from an airplane or rocket
**con·trap´tion** *n.* a contrivance or apparatus considered strange; a makeshift device
**con·tra·pun´tal** *adj.* of counterpoint or its characteristic style —**con·tra·pun´tal·ly** *adv.*
**con·tra·ri´e·ty** *n.* dissension or opposition; an indication of inconsistency
**con´trar·y** *adj.* in opposition; disagreeable —*n.* a thing that is opposite —**con´trar·i·ness** *n.*
**con´trast** *n.* a significant difference —**con·trast´** *vi.* show difference when compared —*vt.* to set off so as to show difference
**con·tra·vene´** *vt.* to oppose; to contradict; to interfere or infringe on —**con·tra·ven´tion** *n.*
**con·tri´bute** *vi., vt.* to give in common with others; to submit for publication —**con´tri·bu´tion** *n.* —**con·trib´u·tor** *n.* —**con·trib´u·to·ry** *adj.*
**con·trite´** *adj.* feeling or expressing regret for an offense —**con·trite´ly** *adv.* —**con·trite´ness, con·tri´tion** *n.*
**con·triv´ance** *n.* a thing created, as a device or plan
**con·trive´** *vt.* to create, devise or scheme —**con·trived´** *adj.* —**con·triv´er** *n.*
**con·trol´** *n.* the power or authority to regulate or restrain; a device that regulates —*vt.* to regulate or restrain —**con·trol·la·bil´i·ty** *n.* —**con·trol´la·ble** *adj.*
**controlled** *adj.* kept in bounds
**controlled experiment** a test in which all known variables are carefully monitored
**controlled substance** a drug regulated by law or at the direction of a government agency
**con·trol´ler** *n.* a comptroller, the executive in an organization who is responsible for financial control; a device that regulates the operation of another
**controlling interest** the amount of investment in a company that allows unchallenged authority in directing its operation
**control tower** the site at an airport from which air traffic is directed
**con·tro·ver´sial** *adj.* subject to debate or disagreement —**con·tro·ver´sial·ly** *adv.*
**con´tro·ver·sy** *n.* a dispute between those holding opposite views
**con´tro·vert** *vt.* to dispute; to contradict —**con·tro·vert´i·ble** *adj.* —**con·tro·vert´i·bly** *adv.*
**con´tu·ma´cious** *adj.* obstinately disobedient
**con´tu·me·ly** *n.* arrogant rudeness; insolence —**con·tu·me´li·ous** *adj.* —**con·tu·me´li·ous·ly** *adv.*
**con·tuse´** *vt.* to injure without breaking the skin; to bruise
**con·tu´sion** *n.* a bruise
**co·nun´drum** *n.* an enigma; a puzzle
**con·va·lesce´** *vi.* to recover gradually from an illness; to regain health —**con·va·les´cence** *n.*
**con·va·les´cent** *adj.* regaining health after illness —*n.* one who is recovering
**con·vene´** *vi., vt.* to assemble, especially for a particular purpose
**con·ven´ient** *adj.* accessible; suited to one's purpose —**con·ven´ience** *n.* —**con·ven´ient·ly** *adv.*
**convenience store** a neighborhood shop or grocery offering a limited assortment of merchandise, often open around the clock
**con´vent** *n.* a religious community
**con·ven´tion** *n.* a gathering of members, delegates, etc.; practices generally accepted as by custom or formal agreement
**con·ven´tion·al** *adj.* customary; adhering to tradition; not unusual —**con·ven´tion·al´i·ty** *n.* —**con·ven´tion·al·ly** *adv.*
**con·ven·tion·eer´** *n.* one who attends a convention
**con·verge´** *vi.* to approach a common point; to grow closer —**con·ver´gence, con·ver´gen·cy** *n.* —**con·ver´gent** *adj.*

**con·ver´sant** *adj.* familiar or knowledgeable, especially by experience or study –**con·ver´sance** *n.*

**con·ver·sa´tion** *n.* an informal verbal exchange –**con·ver·sa´tion·al** *adj.* –**con·ver·sa´tion·al·ly** *adv.* –**con·ver·sa´tion·al·ist** *n.*

**conversation piece** a unique work of art, article of furniture, etc. that is inclined to attract comment

**con·verse´** *vi.* to speak familiarly –**con´verse** *adj.* reversed; transposed –*n.* interchanged; opposite

**con·ver´sion** *n.* a change from one form, use, etc. to another –**con·vert´** *vt.* –**con·vert´er** *n.*

**con·vert´i·ble** *adj.* able to be converted –*n.* anything designed to be converted; an automobile that can be changed to an open car –**con·vert´i·bil´i·ty** *n.* –**con·vert´i·bly** *adv.*

**con·vex´** *adj.* curved, like the outer surface of a sphere

**con·vey´** *vt.* to transport or transfer; to make known –**con·vey´er, con·vey´or** *n.*

**con·vey´ance** *n.* a means for transporting passengers or freight; the transfer of property, as by sale; the instrument of such a property transfer: a deed

**conveyor belt** a belt, chain, series of chains, etc. that transfers goods, as from one work station to another in a manufacturing plant

**con·vey´or·ize** *vt.* to install conveyor belt for the transfer of goods

**con´vict´** *n.* one found guilty of a crime; one serving a prison sentence –**con·vict´** *vt.* to find guilty; to condemn –**con·vic´tion** *n.*

**con·vince´** *vt.* to persuade; to argue into –**con·vinc´ing** *adj.* –**con·vinc´ing·ly** *adv.*

**con·viv´i·al** *adj.* congenial; gregarious –**con·viv·i·al´i·ty** *n.* –**con·viv´i·al·ly** *adv.*

**con·vo·ca´tion** *n.* a congregation; a formal gathering –**con·vo·ca´tion·al** *adj* –**con·vo·ca´tion·al·ly** *adv.*

**con·voke´** *vt.* to convene a meeting

**con·vo·lute´** *vt.* to form in a spiral; to twist or intertwine –**con·vo·lu´tion** *n.*

**con´vo·lut´ed** *adj.* complicated; intricate or twisted, as *convoluted logic* –**con´vo·lut·ed·ly** *adv.* –**con´vo·lut·ed·ness** *n.*

**con´voy** *n. (Brit.)* a company of travelers; a file of vehicles or pack animals

**con·vulse´** *vt.* to shake violently

**con·vul´sion** *n.* uncontrollable muscle spasms; any severe disturbance –**con·vul´sive** *adj.* –**con·vul´sive·ly** *adv.* –**con·vul´sive·ness** *n.*

**cook** *n.* one who prepares food –*vi.* to act as a cook; to be changed by exposure to intense heat –*vt.* to prepare food for eating, as by dressing, subjecting to heat, etc. –**cook the books** to prepare a false set of financial records –**cook up** to devise or concoct, as a plan

**cook´book** *n.* a book containing instructions for the preparation of food

**cook´er** *n.* any of a variety of devices designed for a particular type of cooking –**pressure cooker** a tightly lidded pot that cooks using steam pressure; a job where one works under extreme pressure

**cook´e·ry** *n.* the art of food preparation

**cook´ie** *(US) n.* a small cake-like confection

**cookie cutter** a device for shaping cookies –**cookie-cutter** a project that has been precisely planned

**cook´stove** *n.* a kitchen appliance for cooking food

**cook´ware** *n.* containers for holding food and implements for manipulating food while it is being cooked or otherwise processed

**cool** *adj.* more cold than hot; calm, collected; indifferent; in a discourteous manner –**cool´ly** *adv.* –**cool´ness** *n.*

**cool´ant** *n.* a substance that resists heat, as in an automobile engine, a refrigerator, etc.

**cool box** *(Brit.) n.* a storage unit where things are made or kept cool

**cool´er**[1] *(Brit.) n.* a detention cell

**cool´er**[2] *(US) n.* a storage space or unit where thing are made or kept cool; a wine cocktail

**cool-head´ed** *adj.* disposed to remain calm or composed

**coop** *n.* a small cage –*vt.* to confine –**flew the coop** escaped

**coop´er** *n.* one who makes barrels

**coop´er·age** *n.* the business of making barrels; barrels and casks collectively; the charge for making barrels

**co·op´er·ate´** *vi.* to work together; to comply –**co·op´er·a´tion** *n.*

**co·op´er·a·tive** *adj.* tending to work well with others; pertaining to a communal organization –*n.* an organization owned by and operated for the benefit to its members –**co·op´er·a·tive·ly** *adv.* –**co·op´er·a·tive·ness** *n.* –**co·op´er·a·tor** *n.*

**cop** *n.* a law officer –*vt.* to seize; to steal –**cop out** to give up

**co·pa·cet´ic** *adj.* fine, acceptable; peaceful

**cope** *vi.* to face and deal with, as a trying situation

**cop´i·er** *n.* one who imitates; a duplicating machine

**coping saw** a hand saw with a very thin blade used to cut decorative pieces

**co´pi·ous** *adj.* abundant; abounding in thoughts or words –**co´pi·ous·ly** *adv.* –**co´pi·ous·ness** *n.*

**cop´y** *n.* a reproduction; a manuscript; the text of a book, letter, etc. –*vt.* imitate; to reproduce

**cop´y·cat** *n.* one who imitates another

**copy machine** an office machine for making copies of documents

**cord** *n.* a light rope; *(US)* anything resembling a light rope, as *an electrical cord*; a measure of the volume of cut firewood

**cord´age** *n.* the amount of wood in a particular area

**cor´date´** *adj.* heart-shaped

**cor´dial** *adj.* friendly –**cor·dial´i·ty, cor´dial·ness** *n.* –**cor´dial·ly** *adv.*

**cord´ite** *n.* an explosive

**cord´less** *adj.* battery-operated; having no cord

**core** *n.* the innermost part of a thing –*vt.* to remove the inner part, especially of fruit

**cork** *n.* the outer bark of the cork tree; anything made of cork or like cork –*vt.* to stop a bottle, as with a cork

**cork´age** *n.* a charge for serving a bottle of wine, liquor, etc.

**cork´board** *n.* a decorative wall panel made from cork

**cork´screw** *n.* a device for removing a cork from a wine bottle

**corn** *n.* *(Brit.)* wheat or oats; *(US)* a cereal plant with seeds growing from a center stalk and covered by an outer husk; the edible seed of the corn plant; any of a variety of hard seeds, as *a peppercorn*; trite humor; a painful growth of thick skin on the foot –*vt.* to preserve with salt, as *corned beef*

**corn bread** a bread made with cornmeal

**corn´cob** *n.* the stalk on which kernels of corn grow

**cor´ner** *n.* the angle formed by the junction of two lines or surfaces –*adj.* located at or near a corner –*vt.* to trap in an awkward position –**around the corner** in the near future –**cut corners** cut back, as on materials, quality, proper procedure, etc., often with negative impact –**turn the corner** survive a crisis

**cor´ner·stone** *n.* a basic or essential element; one of the foundation stones at the corner of the building often inscribed with the construction date

**cor·net´** *n.* a brass wind instrument similar to a trumpet; a piece of paper or pastry formed into a cone and filled with a confection

**corn flour** *(Brit.)* *n.* a starch extracted from corn, used in cooking as a thickener

**cor´nice** *n.* a projected molding along the top of a building or above a window

**corn meal** ground meal made from corn

**corn´row** *n.* a hairstyle pattern of small tight braids

**corn´starch** *(US)* *n.* a starch extracted from corn, used in cooking as a thickener

**cor´nu·co´pi·a** *n.* a representation of a goat's horn overflowing with fruits, flowers, etc.; a conical container

**corn whiskey** an alcoholic beverage distilled from corn mash

**corn´y** *adj.* trite; hackneyed

**cor´ol·lar·y** *n.* an inference that naturally follows, as a mathematical proof stemming from a concept already proven

**cor´o·nar·y** *adj.* regarding the arteries that supply blood directly to the heart muscle; pertaining to the heart –*n.* a coronary artery; coronary thrombosis

**coronary bypass** an operation that shunts the flow of blood around a damaged artery in the heart

**coronary occlusion** coronary thrombosis

**coronary thrombosis** the obstruction of a coronary artery by a blood clot

**cor´o·na´tion** *n.* a ceremony for the crowning of a monarch

**cor´o·ner** *n.* a public official whose main duty is to inquire into any death that may not be due to natural cause

**cor·o·net´** *n.* a small crown

**cor´po·ral** *adj.* of the body –*n.* a non-commissioned officer

**cor´po·rate** *adj.* of a corporation

**corporate raider** an individual, consortium, corporation, etc. that attempts to gain control of a corporation by buying up its stock

**cor´po·ra´tion** *n.* a legal entity authorized to act as one individual

**cor·po´re·al** *adj.* of a material nature; tangible

**corps** *pl. n.* a body of people acting together under common direction

**corpse** *(Brit.)* *n.* a dead body

**cor´pu·lent** *adj.* excessively fat –**cor´pu·lence** *n.*

**cor´pus** *n., pl.* **cor´por·a** the main part or substance of a fleshly structure; a comprehensive collection of a specific type of writing

**cor´pus de·lic´ti** substantial proof that a crime has been committed; the body of a murder victim

**cor·ral´** *n.* an enclosure for livestock –*vt.* to surround and capture

**cor·rect´** *adj.* accurate; proper, suitable –*vt.* to make right; to adjust –**cor·rect´a·ble** *adj.* –**cor·rec´tive** *adj.* –**cor·rect´ly** *adv.* –**cor·rect´ness** *n.* –**cor·rec´tor** *n.*

**cor·rec´tion** *n.* the process of making right; an amount adjusted

**cor´re·late´** *vt.* to discover or establish a relationship –**cor´re·la´tion** *n.* –**cor·re·la´tion·al** *adj.*

**cor·rel´a·tive** *adj.* related, corresponding

**cor´re·spond´** *vi.* to be similar; to conform; to communicate by letter –**cor·re·spon´dence** *n.* –**cor·re·spond´en·cy** *adv.* –**cor·re·spond´ent** *n.*

**correspondence school** an institution that offers instruction by mail or computer

**cor´ri·dor** *n.* a long passageway

**cor´ri·gi·ble** *adj.* able to be reformed –**cor·ri·gi·bil´i·ty** *n.* –**cor´ri·gi·bly** *adv.*

**cor·rob´o·rate´** *vt.* to support or strengthen, as testimony –**cor·rob´o·ra´tion** *n.* –**cor·rob´o·ra·tive** *adj.* –**cor·rob´o·ra·tor** *n.*

**cor·rode´** *vt.* destroy gradually, as by rust or chemicals –**cor·rod´i·ble** *adj.* –**cor·ro´sion** *n.*

**cor·ro´sive** *adj.* tending to corrode –*n.* a substance that causes corroding –**cor·ro´sive·ly** *adv.* –**cor·ro´sive·ness** *n.*

**cor·rupt´** *adj.* marked by immorality; altered –*vt.* to pervert, debase; to alter, contaminate **–cor·rupt´er** *n.* **–cor·rupt´i·ble** *adj.* **–cor·rup´tion** *n.* **–cor·rupt´ly** *adv.* **–cor·rupt´ness** *n.*

**cor·rup´tive** *adj.* tending to make immoral or impure **–cor·rup´tive·ly** *adv.*

**cor·sage´** *n.* a small flower arrangement worn on a dress or the wrist

**cor´sair** *n.* a buccaneer, a pirate

**cor·tege´, cor·tège´** *n.* a group of attendants

**cor´tex** *n.* the outer layer of an internal organ

**cor´us·cate´** *vi.* to give off flashes of light; to sparkle, glitter **–cor·us·ca´tion** *n.*

**co´sign** *vi., vt.* to share responsibility for the obligation of another **–co·sig´na·to·ry** *adj.* **–co´sign·er** *n.*

**cos·met´ic** *adj.* tending to improve the appearance; superficial improvement *–n.* any of a variety of preparations for improving one's appearance **–cos·met´i·cal·ly** *adv.* **–cos·me·ti´cian** *n.*

**cos·me·tol´o·gy** *n.* the art of selecting and applying cosmetics

**cos´mic** *adj.* of the universe; of immense proportions

**cosmic dust** minute particles floating in space

**cosmic ray** a stream of charged particles from outer space

**cos·mog´o·ny** *n.* the study of the theories of creation

**cos·mog´ra·phy** *n.* collectively, the sciences that deal with the configuration of the universe **–cos·mog´ra·pher** *n.* **–cos·mo·graph´ic, cos·mo·graph´i·cal** *adj.* **–cos·mo·graph´i·cal·ly** *adv.*

**cos·mol´o·gy** *n.* the study of the formation and nature of the universe **–cos·mol´o·ger** *n.* **–cos·mo·log´ic, cos·mo·log´i·cal** *adj.* **–cos·mo·log´i·cal·ly** *adv.*

**cos´mo·naut** *n.* an astronaut

**cos´mo·pol´i·tan** *adj.* of that common to the entire world; worldly *–n.* an urbane or sophisticated person **–cos·mop´o·lite** *n.*

**cos´mos** *n.* universal order

**cost** *n.* price; the value of a thing; the expense of producing or obtaining something

**cost accounting** a system by which a company accounts for the expense of production

**cost´-ef·fec´tive** *adj.* considered worth the expenditure **–cost´-ef·fic´tive·ness** *n.*

**cost´ly** *adj.* expensive; splendid **–cost´li·ness** *n.*

**cost of living** expenditures for necessities

**cos´tume** *n.* the mode of dress typical to a time, place, etc.; clothing appropriate to a season, occasion, etc. **–cos´tum·er** *n.*

**costume jewelry** fake jewelry

**cot** *n.* a small, folding bed

**co´te·rie** *n.* a close circle of friends

**co·til´lion** *n.* a formal dance

**cot´tage** *n.* a simple house

**cottage cheese** a soft cheese of curds

**cottage industry** a small business, often conducted from a home

**cotter pin** a split pin used to fasten machine parts

**cot´ton** *n.* a tropical plant that produces soft hairs used in the making of thread for cloth; the soft hairs of the cotton plant; the thread or cloth produced

**cotton candy** *(US)* a confection made up of fibers of spun sugar

**cotton floss** *(Brit.)* a confection made up of fibers of spun sugar

**cotton gin** a device for separating the seeds from raw cotton

**cot´ton·seed** *n.* the seed from the cotton plant, a source of cooking oil

**cottonseed oil** oil from the seed of the cotton plant

**cot´ton·tail** *n.* a rabbit

**couch** *n.* *(US)* a sofa *–vt.* to cause to recline; to say or express in a particular way: *couched in terms of endearment* *–vi.* to recline

**cough** *n.* illness marked by frequent clearing of the lungs *–vi.* to expel air from the lungs suddenly and noisily

**cough drop** a small hard candy-like tablet, medicated to relieve coughing, sore throat, etc.

**cough syrup** a liquid patent medicine for the relief of coughing and other cold symptoms

**coun´cil** *n.* a group elected or appointed for some task, esp. for government administration **–coun´ci·lor** *n.*

**coun´sel** *n.* advice or guidance; a legal adviser *–vi., vt.* to give advice **–coun´se·lor** *n.*

**count** *vi., vt.* to number in order

**count´down** *n.* the final check or preparation before an event

**coun´te·nance** *n.* appearance *–vt.* to express approval

**coun´ter** *adj.* opposing *–adv.* in an opposing manner *–vi., vt.* to react or respond

**count´er** *n.* a device for counting; any flat working surface as in a store, a kitchen, etc.

**coun´ter·act** *vt.* to mitigate by opposing action **–coun·ter·ac´tion** *n.* **–coun·ter·ac´tive** *adj.*

**coun´ter·at·tack** *n.* a strategic move to blunt an attack *–vi., vt.* to attack in retaliation

**coun·ter·bal´ance** *n.* an element that counteracts another

**coun´ter·claim** *n.* an opposing claim, as in a lawsuit

**coun´ter·cul·ture** *n.* a lifestyle that opposes traditional values

**coun´ter·feit** *adj.* forged; fraudulent *–n.* an imitation *–vt.* to make a copy with intent to defraud; to fake *–vi.* to practice deception **–coun´ter·feit·er** *n.*

**coun·ter·in·tel´li·gence** *n.* techniques designed to thwart the activity of enemy agents; those employing such techniques

**coun´ter·mand** *vt.* to cancel or reverse, as a previous order

**coun´ter·meas·ure** *n.* an action in opposition to

another

**coun·ter·of·fen´sive** *n.* a counterattack

**coun´ter·pane** *n.* a bedspread

**coun´ter·part** *n.* an opposite number; anything with the same characteristics or function as another

**coun´ter·point** *n.* a thing that interacts with another; a musical form that features two simultaneous melodic lines

**coun·ter·pro·duc´tive** *adj.* serving to promote an effect opposite of that intended; detrimental

**coun´ter·rev·o·lu´tion** *n.* action against a revolutionary government; opposition to reform **—coun´ter·rev·o·lu´tion·ar·y** *adj.*

**coun´ter·sign´** *n.* a signature added to a signed document to authenticate or confirm the first signature; a secret sign or signal given as a required response *—vt.* to authenticate by signing

**coun´ter·sink** *vt.* to set the head of a screw in wood so that it is flush with the surface *—n.* a bit for widening the top of a hole to accept a screw head

**coun´ter·weight** *n.* a weight that balances another

**coun´tess** *n.* a woman of noble birth equal in rank to a count or earl

**count´less** *adj.* innumerable; a quantity that cannot be numbered

**coun´tri·fied** *adj.* having the characteristics of a farmer or smalltown dweller

**coun´try** *n.* the area claimed by a particular nation or state; a rural area *—adj.* of a rural area

**country club** a facility that serves the needs of its members for socializing, sports, etc.

**coun´try·man** *n.* another citizen of one's own country

**country music** a musical style indigenous to the southern U.S.

**country rock** a musical style that combines the style of country music with rock and roll

**coun´try·side** *n.* the view of a rural area

**coun´ty** *n.* an administrative subdivision in some nations, territories, and states

**county fair** an annual festival featuring exhibits of farm and commercial products from a county

**county seat** the location of the government of a county

**coup** *n.* a successful feat; a splendid achievement

**coup d´etat** the overthrow of a government

**cou·pé´** *n.* *(Brit.)* a half compartment at the end of a railway car

**coupe** *n.* a closed, two-door automobile

**cou´ple** *n.* a pair; two people united socially; something that links two things *—vt.* to link **—coup´ler** *n.* **—coup´ling** *n.*

**cou´pon** *n.* a printed paper entitling the bearer to a benefit, as an interest payment for a bond or a discount on merchandise; a form of transmittal, as for ordering goods or payment on an installment loan

**cour´age** *n.* the quality that allows one to face danger or adversity with confidence

**cou·ra´geous** *adj.* brave; fearless **—cou·ra´geous·ly** *adv.* **—cou·ra´geous·ness** *n.*

**cour´i·er** *n.* a messenger

**course** *n.* the direction or route moved; a method or sequence of action; a program of study *—vi., vt.* to race; to move swiftly; to dash

**court** *n.* an open area, as a square or short street surrounded by buildings; a closed play area for certain games; a forum of justice or the building in which it sits; royal persons or their households *—vt.* to supplicate or flatter to obtain some benefit

**cour´te·ous** *adj.* considerate; wellmannered **—cour´te·ous·ly** *adv.* **—cour´te·ous·ness** *n.*

**cour´te·san** *n.* a prostitute; the mistress of a man of importance

**cour´te·sy** *n.* politeness; an act of consideration; furnished without charge

**court´house** *n.* a building that houses a court of law

**court´ly** *adj.* dignified; elegant **—court´li·ness** *n.*

**court of appeals** a state or federal court to which may be appealed the decisions of a lower court

**court of law** a judicial forum

**court´room** *n.* the room in which legal proceedings are conducted before a judge

**court´ship** *n.* the process by which a person seeks to gain the approval of another; a wooing

**court´yard** *n.* an open space in the center of a large building

**cous´in** *n.* a relative of the same generation who is not a sibling

**cou·ture´** *n.* the business of designing women's clothing; high-fashion clothing **—cou·tu´rier** *n.*

**co·va´lence** *n.* the pairs of electrons that an atom can share **—co·va´lent** *n.*

**cove** *n.* a small sheltered bay along a shore or in the side of a mountain; the architectural equivalent, as a recess in a wall

**cov´en** *n.* an assembly of witches

**cov´e·nant** *n.* a binding agreement; a formal contract

**cov´er** *n.* a thing that shields, shelters, protects, etc. *—vt.* to place something over so as to hide, shelter, etc.

**cov´er·age** *n.* the amount and type of information, protection, etc. offered

**cov´er·all** *n.* a loose outer garment that covers the entire body except for the hands, feet and head

**cover charge** a fixed charge at a restaurant or night club, usually for entertainment

**cov´er·ing** *n.* a thing used to protect or shield

**cov´er·let** *n.* a light bed covering

**cov´ert** *adj.* hidden; disguised **—co´vert·ly** *adv.* **—co´vert·ness** *n.*

**cov´er-up** *n.* actions designed to hide the truth

**cov´et** *vi., vt.* to desire longingly –**cov´et·ous** *adj.* –**cov´e·tous·ly** *adv.* –**cov´e·tous·ness** *n.*
**cov´ey** *n.* a small flock of birds
**cow** *n.* the adult female of certain mammals; often, any domestic cattle
**cow´ard** *n.* one who lacks courage –**cow´ard·ice, cow´ard·li·ness** *n.* –**cow´ard·ly** *adv.*
**cow´bell** *n.* a bell hung around a cow's neck
**cow´boy** *n.* a worker on a cattle ranch
**cow´catch·er** *n.* a sloping bumper on the front of a locomotive designed to fend off obstacles on a railroad track
**cow college** a college of agriculture
**cow´er** *vi.* to shrink back or huddle, as from fear or cold
**cow´hand** *n.* a cowboy
**cow´hide´** *n.* leather made from the hide of a cow; a leather whip
**cowl** *n.* a hood or hooded garment; any similar covering, as for a chimney or engine
**cow´lick** *n.* an unruly shock of hair
**cowl´ing** *n.* a metal covering for an engine
**cow´punch·er** *n.* a cowboy
**co·work´er, co-work´er** *n.* an associate at work
**cox´swain** *n.* the helmsman of a small boat or racing shell
**coy** *adj.* shy, demur; affecting shyness; evasive –**coy´ly** *adv.*
**coz´en** *vi., vt.* to deceive; to obtain by deceit
**coz´y** *adj.* comfortable –*n.* a cover for a teapot –**cozy up** attempt to get in the good graces of another –**play it cozy** act cautiously or secretively –**co´zi·ly** *adv.* –**co´zi·ness** *n.*
**crab** *n.* a crustacean having eight legs and pincers; an ill-tempered person –*vi.* to fish for crabs; to complain
**crab´by** *adj.* grouchy; ill-humored –**crab´bi·ly** *adv.* –**crab´bi·ness** *n.*
**crack** *adj.* excelling, first-rate –*n.* a sharp sound; a fracture or narrow opening; a sharp blow; a type of cocaine –*vi., vt.* to produce a sharp sound; to strike; to split; to break down mentally –**crack the whip** to press workers for greater output; to demand strict adherence to rules
**crack´down** *n.* a strict enforcement or meting out of punishment –*vi.* to enforce strictly or punish more severely
**crack´er** *n.* a thin crisp wafer; *(US)* a country boy –**crack´ers** *(Brit.)* mentally deranged
**crack´er·jack** *adj.* outstanding; proficient
**crack´head** *n.* one who uses crack cocaine
**crack´house** *n.* a place where crack cocaine is processed and distributed
**crack´le** *n.* the finely cracked surface of some pottery –*vi.* to make a series of snapping or cracking noises, as of a fire –*vt.* to produce fine cracks on the surface of pottery
**crack´pot** *adj.* insane; offbeat, eccentric –*n.* a person who acts strange or eccentric
**crack´-up** *n.* an accident involving a moving vehicle; a mental breakdown
**cra´dle** *n.* a baby's bed; a place of early development, as *the cradle of civilization*; a device for supporting a heavy object
**craft** *n.* one's art or trade; skill in deception; ships of the sea or air –*vt.* to form with skill
**crafts´man** *n.* a skilled worker; an artisan –**crafts´man·ship** *n.*
**craft´y** *adj.* clever; scheming; deceitful –**craft´i·ly** *adv.* –**craft´i·ness** *n.*
**crag** *n.* a rough, steep projecting rock
**crag´gy** *adj.* rough and steep; irregular –**crag´gi·ness** *n.*
**cram** *vt.* to compress or compact; to fill beyond normal capacity
**cramp** *n.* a sudden involuntary muscular contraction –*vt.* to restrict
**cramped** *adj.* confined; restraining
**crane** *n.* a large wading bird; a machine for raising heavy objects
**cra´ni·al** *adj.* of the cranium
**cranial nerve** *n.* any of a number of nerves attached to the stem of the brain
**cra´ni·um** *n.* the skull
**crank** *n.* an arm attached to a shaft for transferring motion; an eccentric or complaining person –*vi., vt.* to turn a handle, as to start or operate
**crank´case** *n.* the oil reservoir that encloses a crankshaft
**crank´shaft** *n.* a rod that drives a crank for transferring movement
**crank´y** *adj.* irritable; ill-tempered; testy –**crank´i·ness** *n.*
**cran´ny** *n.* a small opening
**crap** *n.* excrement; junk, trash; foolishness; anything useless
**crap out** to lose at craps; to drop out due to exhaustion, fear, etc.
**crap´py** *adj.* of inferior quality
**craps** *pl. n.* a game of dice
**crap´shoot** *n.* a venture that carries risk or that cannot be controlled
**crap´u·lence** *n.* excessive eating or drinking –**crap´u·lent** *adj.*
**crap´u·lous** *adj.* inclined to excessive eating or drinking; suffering from such excess –**crap´u·lous·ly** *adv.*
**crash** *n.* a sudden loud noise; a collision; a sudden financial collapse –*vi.* to make a loud noise; to collide; to fail suddenly, as of a computer; to bed down in temporary quarters –*vt.* to cause a noise or

collision; to attend without an invitation
**crash helmet** *n.* headgear designed to protect the wearer from injury
**crash´-land** *vi., vt.* to set down an aircraft in an unconventional manner, as with malfunctioning equipment, etc.
**crash pad** temporary living quarters
**crass** *adj.* crude; vulgar; tasteless **–crass´ly** *adv.* **–crass´ness** *n.*
**crate** *n.* a box made of wood *–vt.* to pack in a wooden box **–crat´er** *n.*
**cra´ter** *n.* a bowl-shaped depression
**cra•vat´** *n.* a scarf worn at the neck
**crave** *vi., vt.* to long for **–crav´ing** *n.*
**cra´ven** *adj.* cowardly
**craw** *n.* the crop of a bird; an animal's stomach **–stick in one´s craw** to displease; irritate
**craw´dad** *n.* crayfish
**craw´fish** *n.* crayfish
**crawl** *n.* slow movement; a swimming stroke *–vi.* to move on hands and knees or by dragging the body along the ground; to move slowly or feebly
**crawl space** *(US)* a low space, as under a house, that allows access to wiring, plumbing, etc.
**cray´fish** *n.* a fresh-water crustacean similar to a lobster, but much smaller and without claws
**cray´on** *n.* a stick of colored wax for drawing, coloring, etc.
**craze** *n.* a current fad *–vi., vt.* to anger; to enrage
**cra´zy** *adj.* insane; foolish; overly enthusiastic *–n.* one who acts as though mentally unstable **–cra´zi•ly** *adv.* **–cra´zi•ness** *n.*
**creak** *n.* a squeaking sound *–vi.* to make such a sound
**creak´y** *adj.* squeaky **–creak´i•ly** *adv.* **–creak´i•ness** *n.*
**cream** *n.* a derivative of milk, rich in butterfat; a product made from cream; the color of cream; a cosmetic, medication, etc. that is the consistency of whipped cream.; the best part, as *cream of the crop* *–adj.* containing or like cream *–vt.* to remove the cream from milk; to blend to a smooth consistency
**cream cheese** a soft cheese made from cream
**cream´er** *n.* a pitcher for holding and serving cream; a nondairy product used to lighten and flavor coffee
**cream´er•y** *n.* adjunct to a dairy farm where milk is processed
**cream puff** a light pastry filled with whipped cream
**cream sauce** a smooth sauce made with milk or cream
**cream soda** a vanilla flavored soft drink
**cream´y** *adj.* containing cream; smooth, of the consistency of heavy cream **–cream´i•ness** *n.*
**crease** *n.* a line or mark made by folding, wrinkling, etc *–vt.* to make or form creases in
**cre•ate´** *vt.* to originate; to bring about; to produce through artistic endeavor
**cre•a´tion** *n.* the act of creating; that which is created **–cre•a´tor** *n.*
**cre•a´tion•ism** *n.* the belief that the account of the creation in the Bible is literally correct
**cre•a´tive** *adj.* displaying or rousing imagination or inventiveness **–cre•a´tive•ly** *adv.* **–cre•a´tive•ness** *n.*
**cre•a•tiv´i•ty** *n.* inventiveness
**crea´ture** *n.* a living being
**creature comforts** those things that provide contentment for the body
**cre´dence** *n.* acceptance as true
**cre•den´tial** *n.* anything that serves to identify or attest to one's knowledge or authority
**cre•den´za** *n.* a sideboard
**credibility gap** incongruity between what is said and what is done or appears to be true
**cred´i•ble** *adj.* plausible; believable **–cred•i•bil´i•ty** *n.*
**cred´it** *n.* trust; a favorable reputation; approval or praise *–vt.* to believe in; to assign, as an attribute **–cred´i•tor** *n.*
**credit card** a card attesting to the bearer's line of credit for the purchase of goods or services
**credit line** the amount of credit one is allowed
**credit rating** an assessment of one's ability and prospect for repaying obligations
**cre´do** *n.* a creed
**cre•du´li•ty** *n.* an inclination to believe without good cause
**cred´u•lous** *adj.* inclined to believe readily **–cred´u•lous•ly** *adv.* **–cred´u•lous•ness** *n.*
**creed** *n.* a statement of beliefs
**creek** *n.* *(US)* a stream; *(Brit.)* a small inlet of the sea **–up the creek** in a difficult predicament
**creel** *n.* a fisherman's bag
**creep** *vi.* to move with the body close to the ground; to move slowly, with great stealth **–creep´er** *n.*
**creep´y** *adj.* apprehensive; uneasy **–creep´i•ly** *adv.* **–creep´i•ness** *n.*
**cre´mate´** *vt.* to incinerate, esp. a dead body **–cre•ma´tion** *n.*
**cre•ma•to´ri•um, cre´ma•to•ry** *n.* a place where dead bodies are cremated
**cre´o•sote** *n.* a wood preservative
**crêpe** *n.* a thin crinkled cloth; a thin pancake, often wrapped around a filling
**crepe paper** a thin crinkled paper used for decoration
**cres•cen´do** *adj., adv.* gradually increasing *–n.* a gradual increase, as in loudness or intensity *–vi.*
**crest** *n.* a decorative plume, as on a helmet or the head of a bird; a device placed over a coat of arms; the highest point, as of a hill or wave **–crest´ed** *adj.*
**crest´fall•en** *adj.* saddened; shamed; disheartened
**cre•ta´ceous** *adj.* of chalk or a chalk-like substance
**cre´tin** *n.* a buffoon; one suffering from cretinism
**cre´tin•ism** *n.* a congenital disease marked by physical deformity and mental retardation

**cre·vasse´** *n.* a deep fissure; a chasm
**crev´ice** *n.* a narrow crack or opening
**crew** *n.* a group of people working together
**crew cut** a close-cropped hair style
**crew´el** *n.* a type of embroidery; the thread used
**crib** *n.* a bed with high sides for a small child; a small building or bin for storing grain *–vi., vt.* to cheat or steal
**crib´bage** *n.* a card game for two to four players in which score is kept on a pegboard
**crick** *n.* a stiffness of the back, neck, etc.
**crime** *n.* an act in violation of the law; a disgraceful act
**crim´i·nal** *adj.* relating to or in the nature of a crime *–n.* one convicted of a crime **–crim·i·nal´i·ty** *n.* **–crim´i·nal·ly** *adv.*
**criminal code** the body of law that deals with criminal offenses
**criminal court** a court that tries criminal cases
**criminal law** the branch of law that deals with crime and the punishment for commission of a crime
**crim·i·nol´o·gist** *n.* one who engages in the study and methodical investigation of crime **–crim·i·nol´o·gy** *n.*
**crimp** *n.* a pleat or fold *–vt.* to crumple or crinkle; to form into wrinkles
**crim´son** *adj., n.* deep red
**cringe** *vi.* to cower or shrink, as in fear
**crin´kle** *vi., vt.* to form in wrinkles; to rustle, as paper **–crin´kly** *adj.*
**crin´o·line** *n.* a petticoat; a stiff cloth used as a lining or undergarment
**crip´ple** *n.* one who is deprived of normal use of a limb *–vt.* to cause to lose the use of a limb; to impair, as a device or plan **–crip´pler** *n.*
**cri´sis** *n., pl.* **cri´ses** a decisive or turning point; a traumatic event
**crisp** *adj.* brittle; clean and fresh; invigorating *–vi., vt.* to make crisp **–burned to a crisp** blackened so as to be inedible or unusable; severely sunburned **–crisp´ly** *adv.* **–crisp´ness** *n.*
**crisp´y** *adj.* brittle **–crisp´i·ness** *n.*
**cri·te´ri·on** *n.* a basis for judging
**crit´ic** *n.* one who reviews movies, art, etc.; one who tends to faultfinding
**crit´i·cal** *adj.* tending to find fault; marked by careful analysis; dangerous; decisive **–crit´i·cal·ly** *adv.*
**crit´i·cise´** *(Brit.)*, **crit´i·cize´** *(US) vi., vt.* to evaluate; to find fault **–crit´i·cism** *n.*
**cri·tique´** *n.* a careful analysis
**crit´ter** *n.* a creature; a small animal
**croak** *n.* a deep, rough voice, as that of a frog *–vi., vt.* to utter a deep, rough sound; to die or cause to die
**crock** *n.* an earthenware pot; information deemed to be misleading or incorrect
**crock´er·y** *n.* pottery
**croc´o·dile** *n.* a large amphibious reptile
**crocodile tears** figurative tears shed in an insincere display of grief
**croc´o·dil´i·an** *adj.* like a crocodile
**crois·sant** *n.* a light breakfast roll shaped in a crescent
**crone** *n.* an old woman; a hag
**cro´ny** *n.* a close friend
**cro´ny·ism** *n.* the practice of appointing one's friends to key positions, especially in politics
**crook** *n.* an implement with a curved or bent part; one who lives by dishonest means *–vi., vt.* to bend
**crook´ed** *adj.* bent; dishonest
**croon** *vi., vt.* to sing in a low, soft tone, especially a romantic or sentimental ballad **–croon´er** *n.*
**crop** *n.* agricultural products; the amount of products harvested; a thing similar to a harvest, as *a crop of students*; things cut short, as a type of haircut, a riding whip, etc. *–vt.* to trim; to cut short or clip **–crop up** to appear suddenly or unexpectedly
**crop duster** a small airplane that flies low over a cultivated field to discharge insecticide or fungicide; the pilot of the aircraft; a business that provides such a service **–crop-dusting** *n.*
**crop´land** *n.* land where produce is grown
**crop´per** *n.* one who farms on shares, a sharecropper; a bad experience; a failed venture
**crop rotation** the practice of changing crops from year to year so as to avoid depleting the soil
**cro·quet´** *n.* a lawn game in which wooden balls are driven by mallets through a course of wickets
**cro·quette´** *n.* a deep-fried cake of chopped meat or seafood
**cross** *adj.* angry; cranky *–n.* a symbol composed of a horizontal and vertical line intersecting at or near their centers; a burden, affliction; a mixture, as a hybrid plant *–vt.* to intersect; to travel or reach over; to oppose **–cross a palm** to pay, as a bribe
**cross´beam** *n.* a structural member
**cross´bow** *n.* a medieval weapon of war
**cross´breed** *n.* a hybrid *–vi., vt.* to produce a hybrid as by pairing different lines of animals or plants **–cross´bred** *adj.*
**cross´check** *vi., vt.* to verify
**cross´-coun·try** *adj., adv.* across a land, as *a cross-country tour*, through rugged country, as *a cross-country race*
**cross´cur·rent** *n.* a flow of water, as in the ocean, that runs across the main current; any influence that is contrary to the main thrust, as *a crosscurrent of ideas*
**cross-ex·am·i·na´tion** *n.* a careful questioning, especially in court to refute earlier testimony **–cross´-ex·am´ine** *vi., vt.*
**cross´-eyed** *adj.* of a condition in which the movements of eyes are not properly coordinated
**cross´-fer·ti·li·za´tion** *n.* the process of breeding with a

plant or animal of a different line

**cross´hatch·ing** *n.* a drawing technique that creates shading with sets of crossing parallel lines —**cross´hatch** *vi., vt.*

**cross´ing** *n.* a place for moving from one side to the other, as of a street, river, etc.; a place where two ways cross, as of a road: an intersection

**cross´ly** *adv.* in a cantankerous manner

**cross´-pol´li·nate** *vi., vt.* to transfer pollen from a plant of one species to that of another —**cross´-pol·li·na´tion** *n.*

**cross´-ref´er·ence** *n.* a notation that refers to another source of information about a subject or to mention of the subject elsewhere —*vt.* to refer to another mention; to prepare a reference to other sources

**cross´road** *n.* an intersection of two roads; an important time or incident

**crossword, crossword puzzle** a word puzzle

**crotch** *n.* an intersection, as by the branches of a tree; the area where the legs meet at the trunk

**crotch´et** *n.* an odd or whimsical notion

**crouch** *vi.* to bend low with limbs drawn close, as though ready to spring; to cower in fear

**crou´pi·er** *n.* one who operates a casino gambling table

**crou´ton** *n.* a small piece of crisp bread garnish for soup or salad

**crow´bar** *n.* a metal bar designed as a prying tool

**crowd** *n.* a group of people gathered in one place; a number of people with something in common, as *the college crowd* —*vi., vt.* to squeeze or push —**city hall crowd** local politicians or bureaucrats

**crown** *n.* a head covering worn as a symbol of sovereignty; the power or office of a monarch; a symbol of distinction, as in sports —*vt.* to confer with a crown or the power, honor, etc. that it symbolizes; to be, or form, the highest part; to bring to successful completion

**crows´-feet** *n.* a pattern of lines around the corner of the eyes

**crow´s´-nest** *n.* a high platform used as a lookout, as on the mast of a sailing ship

**cru´cial** *adj.* extremely significant; decisive —**cru´cial·ly** *adv.*

**cru´ci·fy´** *vt.* to put to death by binding or nailing to a cross; to treat cruelly, especially verbally

**crud** *n.* gunk; a worthless or nasty thing

**crude** *adj.* in an unrefined or raw state; lacking manners or tact —**crude´ly** *adv.* —**crude´ness, cru´di·ty** *n.*

**cru´el** *adj.* inclined to purposely inflict misery; barbarous; pleasure taken in the suffering of others; heartless —**cru´el·ly** *adv.* —**cru´el·ness, cru´el·ty** *n.*

**cru´et** *n.* a narrow mouth jar

**cruise** *n.* a pleasure voyage —*vi.* to travel about, as for pleasure —**cruis´er** *n.*

**cruise control** a device for automatically maintaining constant speed in an automobile

**crul´ler** *n.* a cake fried in melted fat; an unraised doughnut

**crumb** *n.* a piece or fragment

**crum´ble** *vi., vt.* to break into small fragments; to collapse or disintegrate

**crum´bly** *adj.* tending to be easily broken into small pieces; consisting of fragments; dilapidated, fallen in —**crum´bli·ness** *n.*

**crum´my** *adj.* cheap; shoddy; shabby

**crum´pet** *n.* a small batter cake baked on a griddle, similar to an English muffin in the US

**crum´ple** *vi., vt.* to crush; to collapse

**crunch** *n.* a difficult economic situation —*vi., vt.* to grind with a crackling sound

**cru·sade´** *n.* a broad campaign for a good cause —*vi.* to participate in such a campaign —**cru·sad´er** *n.*

**crush** *n.* a crowding together; a passing infatuation; a fruit drink —*vt.* to press so as to bruise or break into smaller pieces; to press or crowd upon; to subdue —**crush´a·ble** *adj.*

**crust** *n.* a hard outer surface; insolence —*vi., vt.* to cover with a crisp or hard surface

**crust´y** *adj.* displaying a brusque, uncivil manner —**crust´i·ly** *adv.* —**crust´i·ness** *n.*

**crutch** *n.* any device used as an aid or support

**crux** *n.* a decisive factor; the heart of a matter

**cry** *n.* a scream or shout; weeping —*vi.* to scream or shout; to weep —*vt.* to plead or beg for —**a far cry** very different than expected

**cry´ba·by** *n.* one who complains excessively

**cry·o·gen´ics** *pl. n.* the science that deals with the creation and effects of low temperature —**cry·o·gen´ic** *adj.* —**cry·o·gen´i·cal·ly** *adv.*

**crypt** *n.* an underground chamber used as a burial place

**crypt·a·nal´y·sis** *n.* the science of deciphering codes

**cryp´tic** *adj.* enigmatic; having hidden meaning

**cryp´to·gram** *n.* a coded message

**cryp´to·graph** *n.* a means for the writing or deciphering of coded messages —**cryp·tog´ra·pher** *n.* —**cryp·tog´ra·phy** *n.*

**crys´tal** *adj.* of or like a high-quality glass or certain minerals; transparent —*n.* a high-quality glass or a thing made of the glass; geometrically shaped particles of a mineral; the glass covering a watch face

**crystal-clear** without flaw, like a crystal; easily seen or understood

**crys´tal·line** *adj.* like or made of crystal

**crys´tal·lize** *vi., vt.* to form or cause to form a crystal; to assume or bring to permanent form —**crys·tal·li·za´tion** *n.*

**cub´by·hole** *n.* a small compartment

**cube** *n.* a solid form having six square faces; the third power of any number —*vt.* to raise to the third power —**cu´bic** *adj.*

**cube steak** a piece of beef that has been tenderized by a pattern of cross cuts on the surface

**cu´bi·cle** *n.* a small enclosure, as for a single worker in an office

**cub´ism** *n.* an abstract syle of art using geometric patterns for representation —**cub´ist** *n.*

**cuck´old** *n.* a man whose wife has been unfaithful —**cuck´old·ry** *n.*

**cud** *n.* food regurgitated from the first stomach of a ruminating animal

**cud´dle** *n.* an embrace —*vi., vt.* to embrace

**cud´dly** *adj.* affectionate; lovable; appealing —**cud´dle·some** *adj.*

**cudg´el** *n.* a short heavy stick; a club

**cue** *n.* a signal or hint to prompt an action —*vt.* to signal

**cue ball** an unmarked ball struck with the cue in pool or billiards

**cuff** *n.* a slap with the open hand; a fold at the end of a shirt sleeve; *(US)* turned up material at the end of a trouser leg —*vt.* to slap with the open hand

**cui·sine´** *n.* a particular style of food preparation

**cul´-de-sac´** *n.* a street with a single outlet and a turnabout at the closed end

**cu´li·nar´y** *adj.* of the kitchen or cooking

**cull** *n.* something selected for removal, especially for poor quality —*vt.* to select

**cul´mi·nate´** *vi., vt.* to come or bring to completion —**cul·mi·na´tion** *n.*

**cul´pa·ble** *adj.* deserving blame —**cul·pa·bil´i·ty** *n.* —**cul´pa·bly** *adv.*

**cul´prit** *n.* one accused or guilty

**cult** *n.* a group considered to be extremist or obsessive in their beliefs

**cul´ti·vate´** *vt.* to tend crops; to promote or nurture, as an interest in learning —**cul´ti·vat·ed** *adj.* —**cul´ti·va´tion** *n.*

**cul´tur·al** *adj.* of a particular culture —**cul´tur·al·ly** *adv.*

**cul´ture** *n.* the characteristics of a society; enlightenment, refinement

**cultured pearl** a pearl grown from an implanted irritant

**culture shock** disorientation experienced by exposure to an unfamiliar environment

**cul´vert** *n.* a conduit or drain passing under a road, path, etc.

**cum´ber·some** *adj.* unwieldy; difficult to maneuver because of size or shape; bulky; awkward

**cu´mu·late** *vi., vt.* to collect; to accumulate —**cu´mu·la´tion** *n.* —**cu´mu·la·tive** *adj.*

**cu·mu·lo·nim´bus** *n.* a cloud structure associated with thunder and lightning storms

**cu´mu·lus** *n.* a tall cloud structure with a dark, flat, moisture-laden base —**cu´mu·lous** *adj.*

**cu·ne´i·form** *adj.* wedge-shaped, as the strokes or characters in certain ancient writing —*n.*

**cun´ning** *adj.* sly; crafty —*n.* skillful at deceiving

**cup** *n.* an open container for serving a beverage, broth, etc.; a standard measure of 8 ounces

**cup´board** *n.* a storage place for dinnerware

**cup´cake** *(US)* *n.* a small cake appropriate for a single serving

**cup´ful** *adj.* the amount a cup can hold; a cup measure of 8 ounces

**cu·pid´i·ty** *n.* avarice; greed

**cu´po·la** *n.* a domed ceiling; a small domed structure on a roof

**cur** *n.* a dog, usually a mongrel; a vile person

**cu´rate** *n.* a clergyman who assists a rector or vicar

**cu´ra·tor** *n.* a custodian

**curb** *n.* a checking or hindrance; a curbstone —*vt.* to subdue; to check

**curb service** service offered to patrons in their cars, as at a fast food restaurant

**curd** *n.* coagulated milk

**cur´dle** *vi., vt.* to turn into curd; to coagulate

**cu´ra·tor** *n.* an overseer, as of a museum

**cure** *n.* a method or agent that restores health or corrects an unpleasant condition —*vt.* to effect a recovery or remedy; to preserve, as food by smoking —**cur´a·ble** *adj.* —**cur´a·tive** *adj., n.*

**cure´-all** *n.* a remedy for all ills or troubles

**cur´few** *n.* a regulation specifying a time for citizens to be off the street; the time specified; a time set for a young person to be home

**cu´ri·os´i·ty** *n.* a desire to learn; a rare or unusual artifact

**cu´ri·ous** *adj.* eager to learn; very inquisitive; unusual —**cu´ri·ous·ly** *adv.* —**cu´ri·ous·ness** *n.*

**cur´li·cue** *n.* an ornate curve, as in caligraphy

**curling iron** a device for making curls in the hair

**curl´y** *adj.* having waves or ringlets; inclined to curl —**curl´i·ness** *n.*

**cur´mudg´eon** *n.* an ill-tempered or disparaging person

**cur´ren·cy** *n.* the money in use in a country or territory

**cur´rent** *adj.* of the present —*n.* a general tendency or movement —**cur´rent·ly** *adv.*

**current account** *(Brit.)* a monetary deposit that permits the transfer of funds by writing cheques

**cur·ric´u·lum** *n.* an established course of study; collectively, the studies offered by a particular school

**cur´ry** *n.* a piquant blend of spices; a dish or sauce prepared with curry —*vt.* to groom a horse

**cur´sive** *adj.* of handwriting in which all characters in a word are connected

**cur´so·ry** *adj.* hastily done; casual, as *a cursory glance*

**curt** *adj.* short, concise; brusque **–curt´ly** *adv.* **–curt´ness** *n.*

**cur´tail´** *vt.* to cut short; to reduce; to lessen **–cur·tail´ment** *n.*

**cur´tain** *n.* material hung as a decoration or barrier; something that covers or obscures, as *a curtain of fog* *–vt.* to cover, as with a curtain

**curtain call** a performer's return to the stage to acknowledge applause

**curtain raiser** a brief entertainment before the main show

**curt´sy** *n.* a polite bow *–vi.* to make a bow

**cur·va´ceous** *adj.* of a women with an attractive figure **–cur·va´ceous·ness** *n.*

**cur´va·ture´** *n.* a curve or curved part

**curve** *n.* a line or surface that deviates in a relatively smooth fashion *–vi., vt.* to deviate from a straight line or surface

**cush´y** *adj.* easy, as *a cushy job*

**cusp** *n.* a point or projection; an intersection of two lines **–cus´pi·date, cus´pi·dat·ed** *adj.*

**cus´pid** *n.* a tooth characterized by a single projection

**cuss** *n.* a person or animal, often used affectionately *–vi., vt.* to curse

**cus´tard** *n.* a thick, creamy dessert

**cus·to´di·an** *n.* a caretaker, as of an art collection, a building, etc. **–cus·to´di·al** *adj.*

**cus´to·dy** *n.* the act of caring for and protecting

**cus´tom** *adj.* made to order *–n.* common practice; tradition

**cus´tom·ar·y** *adj.* usual; according to custom **–cus´tom·ar´i·ly** *adv.*

**cus´tom-built´** *adj.* made to the buyer's specifications

**cus´tom·er** *n.* one who patronizes a business

**cus´tom·house** *n.* a clearing house at a port of entry for imports and exports

**cus´tom·ize** *vt.* to make or alter to suit the buyer's specifications

**cus´tom-made** *adj.* custom-built

**cut** *n.* an incision; a reduction; a sharp, derogatory comment *–vi.* to use a sharp instrument; to cause discomfort, as *a cutting remark*; to move quickly *–vt.* to penetrate with a sharp instrument; to reduce or trim, as *a cut in staff*; to offend with a sharp remark; to pass across or through; to discontinue or stop **–a cut above** significantly better **–cut and dried** a foregone conclusion; routine **–cut loose** to act with abandon **–cut no ice** of no influence **–cut out for** suited to **–cut through** get to the point

**cu·ta´ne·ous** *adj.* relating to the skin

**cut´back´** *n.* a reduction in production, personnel, expenses, etc.

**cu´ti·cle** *n.* the outer layer of skin: the epidermis; the hardened skin around the nails

**cut´ler·y** *n.* utensils for cutting

**cut´let** *n.* a slice of meat from the rib or leg; a chopped meat patty

**cut´off** *adj.* of an established limit *–n.* a shortcut; a valve or other device for shutting off flow

**cut´-rate** *adj.* of that offered for a reduced price; of questionable quality

**cut´throat** *adj.* murderous; unmerciful, relentless *–n.* a murderer

**cutting** *adj.* of a sharp instrument; sharp or piercing, as *a cutting wit* *–n.* the act of slicing, piercing, etc.; anything cut off

**cutting board** a wood, plastic, etc. surface used for cutting

**cutting edge** the latest innovation

**cut´up** *n.* a joker

**cu·vée´** *n.* a particular blend of wine

**cy´cle** *n.* the time during which an event or series of events occurs; a bicycle or motorcycle *–vi.* to occur in cycles; to pass through one occurrence; to ride a bicycle, etc.

**cy´clic, cy´cli·cal** *adj.* occurring in cycles **–cy´cli·cal·ly** *adv.*

**cy´clist** *n.* one who rides a bicycle or motorcycle

**cy´clone** *n.* a violent, rotating windstorm; a device used to separate materials by centrifugal force

**cyclone cellar** an underground shelter for safety from windstorms

**cy´clo·tron´** *n.* a particle accelerator

**cyn´ic** *n.* one who suspects or denies the sincerity of others **–cyn´i·cal** *adj.* **–cyn´i·cism** *n.*

**cy´no·sure** *n.* well-known personality

**cy·tol´o·gy** *n.* the science dealing with the study of cells

**czar** *n.* formerly, a male monarch; one having great power

**d, D** fourth letter of the English alphabet; in Roman characters, the symbol for 500

**dab** *n.* a small quantity *–vi., vt.* to pat lightly

**dab´ble** *vi.* to engage in superficially

**daf´fy** *adj.* silly, ridiculous

**daft** *adj.* insane; foolish

**dai´ly** *adj.* taking place each day *–adv.* every day

**daily double** a wager to choose winners in two specified events from a series of events

**dain´ty** *adj.* delicate; fragile **–dain´ti·ly** *adv.* **–dain´ti·ness** *n.*

**dair´y** *n.* a place for the processing or sale of milk and milk products

**dairy cattle** cows cultivated for their milk

**dairy farm** a farm that raises cattle for the production of milk products

**daisy chain** a connected series

**dal´li·ance** *n.* flirtation

**dal´ly** *vi.* to flirt or trifle with; to waste time
**dam** *n.* a barrier to hold back the flow, as of liquid; an obstruction *–vt.* to hold back as with a dam; obstruct
**dam´age** *n.* breakage; injury causing a loss of value *–vt.* to mar or injure **–dam´age·a·ble** *adj.*
**dam´ages** *n.* compensation ordered or paid for damage or injury
**dam´ask** *n.* a linen fabric; a rose color *–adj.* of damask linen; rose colored
**dame** *n.* a matron
**damp** *adj.* slightly moist *–n.* humidity; moisture *–vt.* to moisten; to slow a fire by reducing the air supply; to check, as sound waves **–damp´ish** *adj.* **–damp´ly** *adv.* **–damp´ness** *n.*
**damp´en** *vt.* to moisten; to check or deaden, as sound; to lessen, as enthusiasm *–vi.* to become moist **–damp´en·er** *n.*
**damp´er** *n.* a valve for controlling air flow in a line; a device that deadens, as the vibration of strings on a piano
**dance** *n.* graceful, rhythmic movement in time to music *–vi., vt.* to move in rhythm to music **–danc´er** *n.*
**danc´er·cise** *n.* rhythmic exercise set to music
**dan´der** *n.* temper; anger
**dan´di·fy** *vt.* to dress like a dude
**dan´dy** *adj.* first-rate *–n.* a man who is overly attentive to his appearance **–dan´dy·ish** *adj.* **–dan´dy·ism** *n.* **–dan´di·ly** *adv.*
**dan´ger** *n.* that liable to cause injury or pain
**dan´ger·ous** *adj.* perilous; liable or able to cause injury or harm **–dan´ger·ous·ly** *adv.* **–dan´ger·ous·ness** *n.*
**dan´gle** *vi., vt.* to hang loosely
**dank** *adj.* disagreeably damp; clammy **–dank´ly** *adv.* **–dank´ness** *n.*
**dap´per** *adj.* stylish; neatly and smartly dressed; alert, active **–dap´per·ly** *adv.* **–dap´per·ness** *n.*
**dare** *n.* a challenge *–vi.* to be sufficiently bold *–vt.* to have the necessary courage; to challenge **–dar´ing** *adj.* **–dar´ing·ly** *adv.* **–dar´ing·ness** *n.*
**dare´dev·il** *adj.* bold and adventurous *–n.* one who is willing to take chances; one who performs hazardous acts, esp. as part of a public performance **–dare´dev·il·ry, dare dev·il·try** *n.*
**dark** *adj.* lacking light; gloomy, dismal; sinister; unenlightened: *kept in the dark* *–n.* a lack of light; night **–dark´ish** *adj.* **–dark´ly** *adv.* **–dark´ness** *n.*
**dark´en** *vi.* to become dark or darker *–vt.* to make dark or darker; to cause to become obscure or confusing **–dark´en·er** *n.*
**dark horse** one who is unexpectedly successful, as in a horse race or political contest
**dark´room** *n.* a room for processing photographic film
**dart** *n.* a pointed missile used as a weapon or for games; a sudden rapid movement *–vi., vt.* to move suddenly and rapidly
**dash** *n.* a hasty move; a mark (-)of punctuation; a small amount *–vi.* to rush; to smash *–vt.* to thrust or smash violently; to act hastily
**dash´board** *n.* the panel of controls and gauges at the front of the passenger compartment of an automobile
**dash´ing** *adj.* adventurous, gallant; jaunty; stylishly elegant or splendid **–dash´ing·ly** *adv.*
**das´tard** *n.* a malicious or cowardly person **–das´tard·li·ness** *n.* **–das´tard·ly** *adv.*
**da´ta** *n. pl., sing.* **dat´um** information; facts or figures used in analysis
**da´ta·base** *n.* an orderly collection of related data, especially as stored in a computer
**data processing** *n.* the manipulation of data, especially by a computer
**date** *n.* a point in time, stated as a day, month and year; an appointment; a companion at a social function; a palm tree or its fruit *–vi.* to originate or exist from a particular time; to become obsolete: *the work rules have become dated*; to accompany socially *–vt.* to mark with or determine the date of; to arrange a meeting with
**date´book** *n.* an appointment book
**dat´ed** *adj.* marked with a date; from a previous time; out of style
**daub** *vi., vt.* to apply crudely, as paint, plaster, etc.
**daugh´ter** *n.* a female offspring
**daugh´ter-in-law** *n.* a son's wife
**daunt** *vt.* to discourage
**daunt´less** *adj.* daring; heroic; not to be discouraged **–daunt´less·ly** *adv.* **–daunt´less·ness** *n.*
**dav´en·port** *n.* *(Brit.)* a type of desk; *(US)* a sofa
**daw´dle** *vi., vt.* to waste time
**dawn** *n.* the start of daylight; a beginning *–vi.* to begin, as light in the morning sky
**day** *n.* the daylight hours, between sunrise and sunset; a 24-hour period; an era, as *olden days*
**day´bed** *n.* a lounge that can be used for a bed
**day´book** *n.* a daily journal
**day´break** *n.* dawn
**day camp** a camp program that does not provide overnight accommodations
**day care** the tending of children during the day or after school hours; a facility where children are cared for
**day´dream** *n.* a fantasy or dreamlike thoughts experienced while awake *–vi.* to be lost in reverie
**day laborer** a worker who is hired and paid daily as needed
**day´light** *n.* sunlight
**day nursery** a day care facility
**day one** the start of a venture or project
**day room** a recreation room

**day school** a private school that does not provide overnight accommodations
**day shift** the working hours from early morning until late afternoon
**day´time** *n.* the hours between sunrise and sunset
**day´-to-day´** *adj.* regular; routine
**daze** *n.* a stupor; bewilderment *–vt.* to stun; to bewilder **–daz´ed·ly** *adv.*
**daz´zle** *vi., vt.* to blind temporarily with bright light; to amaze, as by something exceptional **–daz´zler** *n.* **–daz´zling·ly** *adv.*
**dea´con, dea´con·ess** *n.* a man or woman who is a lay officer in a church; a minister's assistant
**de·ac´ti·vate** *vt.* to make a thing inoperable or ineffective; to release something or someone from military service **–de·ac·ti·va´tion** *n.* **–de·ac·ti·va´tor** *n.*
**dead** *adj.* lacking life; lacking vitality or brilliance, as *dead sound* or *a dead color*, dispassionate: *dead to emotion*; numb: *my arm feels dead*; ancient or out of date: *a dead language*; no longer productive or useful; absolute: *his assessment was dead on*; exhausted **–dead´ness** *n.*
**dead´beat** *adj.* an idler; one who doesn't repay debts
**dead´bolt** *n.* a latch that secures a door with a heavy bolt that can only be operated with a key
**dead center** at the exact center
**dead´en** *vt.* to anesthetize; to reduce, as the brilliance of color or the loudness of sound
**dead end** a street or road without an outlet; an unprofitable venture, course, etc. **–dead´-end´** *adj.* offering no means for continuation or advancement: *a dead-end job*
**dead´fall** *n.* a snare designed to drop a heavy object on its victim; a fallen tree and the debris it carries
**dead´head** *n.* a commercial vehicle running without paying cargo or passengers; a dull or stupid person *–vi.* to travel without cargo
**dead heat** a race that ends in a tie
**dead letter** a piece of mail that cannot be delivered or returned
**dead´line** *n.* a date or time established for the completion of something, as a task or a payment
**dead´lock** *n.* a stalemate
**dead´ly** *adj.* apt to cause serious injury or death; lethal; extremely accurate or effective: *deadly aim, deadly satire* **–dead´li·ness** *n.*
**dead´pan** *adj., adv.* without expression *–n.* a blank look
**dead reckoning** estimating position based on speed, travel time, and experience
**dead ringer** a precise match
**dead´wood** *n.* something useless
**deaf** *adj.* unable to hear; unwilling to listen or be persuaded **–deaf´ly** *adv.* **–deaf´ness** *n.*
**deaf´en** *vt.* to make deaf; to overwhelm with sound **–deaf´en·ing** *adj.* **–deaf´en·ing·ly** *adv.*
**deaf´-mute** *n.* one who is unable to hear or speak
**deal** *n.* an agreement; a business transaction; a distribution *–vi.* to take action; to do business *–vt.* to distribute, as playing cards **–deal´er** *n.*
**deal´er·ship** *n.* a business authorized by a manufacturer or distributor to market their product in a particular area
**dean** *n.* an officer in a school or college having jurisdiction over a particular group: *dean of men, dean of faculty*; one who is senior or preeminent: *the dean of country music*
**dear** *adj.* cherished; expensive *–n.* a loved one *–adv.* with affection; at great cost **–dear´ly** *adv.* **–dear´ness** *n.*
**dearth** *n.* a lack or scarcity
**death** *n.* the termination of life
**death´bed** *n.* the final hours of a person's life; the bed or place where one dies
**death benefit** an insurance payment to a beneficiary on the death of the policyholder
**death´blow** *n.* an event that causes death
**death certificate** the official record of a person's death
**death´less** *adj.* undying; enduring **–death´less·ly** *adv.* **–death´less·ness** *n.*
**death´like** *adj.* gaunt; pale
**death´ly** *adj.* ghastly; deathlike *–adv.* to a deadly extent **–death´li·ness** *n.*
**death rate** a ratio of the number of deaths per thousand persons for a particular area over a specified period of time
**death´trap** *n.* an unsafe place, predicament, etc.
**death warrant** official authorization to put a person to death
**death´watch** *n.* attendance at the bedside of a dying person
**death wish** a desire for one's own death
**de·ba´cle** *n.* the total dissolution of order; a rout
**de·bar´** *vt.* to exclude from a right or privilege; to prohibit or restrict **–de·bar´ment** *n.*
**de·bark´** *vi., vt.* to leave a ship or aircraft; disembark **–de·bar·ka´tion** *n.*
**de·base´** *vt.* to lower in worth or purity; to adulterate **–de·base´ment** *n.*
**de·bate´** *n.* an airing of opposing views; a formal argument *–vi., vt.* to discuss openly; to engage in formal argumentation; to consider or contemplate **–de·bat´a·ble** *adj.* **–de·bat´er** *n.*
**de·bauch´** *vt.* to corrupt or debase **–de·bauch´ed·ly** *adv.* **–de·bauch´ed·ness** *n.* **–de·bauch´er** *n.*
**de·bauch´er·y, de·bauch´ment** *n.* revelry; intemperance; excessive indulgence in sensual gratification
**de·ben´ture** *n.* a promissory note
**de·bil´i·tate´** *vt.* to drain of strength or energy **–de·bil·**

i·ta´tion *n.* –de·bil´i·ta·tive *adj.*

**de·bil´i·ty** *n.* weakness; an infirmity

**deb·o·nair´, deb·o·naire´** *adj.* sophisticated, urbane; nonchalant; carefree –**deb·o·nair´ly** *adv.* –**deb·o·nair´ness** *n.*

**de·brief´** *vt.* to examine and instruct, as for a returning agent, emissary, or ambassador

**de·bris´** *n.* scattered remains; rubble

**debt** *n.* something owed; an obligation

**debt´or** *n.* one who owes

**de·bug´** *vt.* to seek out and correct errors or malfunctions, as in a computer program

**de·bunk´** *vt.* to expose as false; demystify

**de·but´** *n.* a first public appearance; a beginning

**deb´u·tante** *n.* a young woman making her first formal appearance in society

**dec´ade** *n.* a group of ten; ten years

**dec´a·dence, dec´a·den·cy** *n.* a deterioration or decline, as in moral standards; a time of decline as in art or literature –**dec´a·dent** *adj.* –**dec´a·dent·ly** *adv.*

**de·caf´fein·ate** *vt.* to remove the caffeine, as from coffee or soft drinks –**de·caf´fein·at·ed** *adj.*

**dec´a·gon** *n.* a geometric form with ten sides

**dec·a·he´dron** *n.* a solid with ten surfaces

**de´cal** *n.* a decorative design for transferring to glass, wood, etc.

**de·cal´ci·fy** *vt.* to remove or reduce calcium, as from bones or teeth –*vi.* to lose calcium

**de·cant´** *vt.* to pour off a liquid, as wine, to eliminate sediment; to pour from one container to another –**de·can´ta·tion** *n.* –**de·cant´er** *n.*

**de·cap´i·tate** *vt.* to behead –**de·cap·i·ta´tion** *n.* –**de·cap´i·ta·tor** *n.*

**de·cath´lon** *n.* an athletic competition comprising ten events

**de·cay´** *n.* the decomposition of organic matter; a slow deterioration –*vi.* to decompose; to deteriorate slowly –*vt.* to cause decomposition or deterioration

**de·cease´** *vi.* to die –**de·ceased´** *adj.* –**de·ce´dent** *n.*

**de·ceit´** *n.* a misrepresentation; a dishonest action; trickery

**de·ceit´ful** *adj.* marked by deception; fraudulent –**de·ceit´ful·ly** *adv.* –**de·ceit´ful·ness** *n.*

**de·ceive´** *vt.* to mislead, as by lying or trickery –*vi.* to practice deceit –**de·ceiv´a·ble** *adj.* –**de·ceiv´er** *n.* –**de·ceiv´ing·ly** *adv.*

**de·cel´er·ate** *vi., vt.* to slow; to reduce speed –**de·cel·er·a´tion** *n.* –**de·cel´er·a·tor** *n.*

**de´cent** *adj.* proper; respectable; conforming to accepted standards; moderately good: *a decent performance* –**de´cen·cy, de´cent·ness** *n.* –**de´cent·ly** *adv.*

**de·cen´tral·ize** *vt.* to disperse personnel and authority, as for a corporation or government entity –**de·cen·tral·i·za´tion** *n.*

**de·cep´tion** *n.* practicing deceit; being deceived; a dishonest act or misrepresentation

**de·cep´tive** *adj.* misleading; designed to mislead or misrepresent –**de·cep´tive·ly** *adv.* –**de·cep´tive·ness** *n.*

**de·cer´ti·fy** *vt.* to revoke a license, endorsement, or authorization –**de·cer´ti·fi·ca´tion** *n.*

**de·cide´** *vt.* to settle, as a dispute; to bring to a decision –*vi.* to make a decision –**de·cid·a·bil´i·ty** *n.* –**de·cid´a·ble** *adj.* –**de·cid´er** *n.*

**de·cid´ed** *adj.* certain, clear-cut; without reservation; determined, resolute –**de·cid´ed·ly** *adv.* –**de·cid´ed·ness** *n.*

**de·cid´u·ous** *adj.* falling off or shed at specific seasons, as leaves or antlers; temporary, ephemeral –**de·cid´u·ous·ly** *adv.* –**de·cid´u·ous·ness** *n.*

**dec´i·mal** *adj.* based on the number 10 –*n.* a decimal fraction

**decimal point** the dot between a whole number and its fraction in base ten

**decimal system** a number system in base 10

**dec´i·mate** *vt.* to select by lot and kill one in ten; to destroy or slaughter a large part of –**dec·i·ma´tion** *n.*

**de·ci´pher** *vt.* to interpret, as that which is obscure, poorly written or encoded –**de·ci´pher·a·ble** *adj.* –**de·ci´pher·er** *n.* –**de·ci´pher·ment** *n.*

**de·ci´sion** *n.* a conclusion or judgment made on a matter under consideration

**de·ci´sive** *adj.* conclusive; resolving uncertainty; determined, positive; extremely important –**de·ci´sive·ly** *adv.* –**de·ci´sive·ness** *n.*

**de·claim´** *vi., vt.* to recite dramatically; proclaim; to vehemently speak out –*vi.* to recite eloquently –**dec·la·ma´tion** *n.* –**de·clam´a·to·ry** *adj.*

**de·clar´a·tive** *adj.* effecting to inform; making an assertion –**de·clar´a·tive·ly** *adv.*

**de·clare´** *vt.* to announce formally; to state positively or emphatically; to reveal or name –*vi.* to make a positive statement –**de·clar´a·ble** *adj.* –**dec´la·ra´tion** *n.* –**de·clar´er** *n.*

**de·clen´sion** *n.* a declining; a slope or descent; a deviation –**de·clen´sion·al** *adj.*

**dec·li·na´tion** *n.* a slope or descent; deviation, as from a standard; a courteous refusal –**dec·li·na´tion·al** *adj.*

**de·cline´** *n.* a downward slope or trend; deterioration or decay –*vi.* to gradually deteriorate; to refuse politely; to slope downward –*vt.* to refuse to accept; to cause to incline or slope

**de·cliv´i·ty** *n.* a sloping on a downward course –**de·cliv´i·tous, de·cliv´ous** *adj.*

**de·code´** *vt.* to translate a coded message

**de·com·mis´sion** *vt.* to take out of service

**de´com·pose´** *vt.* to break down into basic elements –*vi.* to disintegrate or decay –**de·com·pos·a·bil´i·ty**

*n.* –**de·com·pos´a·ble** *adj.* –**de·com´po·si´tion** *n.*

**de·com·press´** *vt.* to reduce pressure on, as for a deep-sea diver; to permit expansion by reducing pressure –**de·com·pres´sion** *n.*

**decompression chamber** an area with controlled air pressure to gradually acclimate to normal air pressure, as a deep-sea diver

**decompression sickness** a painful, potentially fatal condition caused by the formation of nitrogen bubbles in the blood due to a rapid reduction in pressure, as of a deep-sea diver who returns to the surface too quickly

**de·con·tam´i·nate** *vt.* to free from harmful matter; to make safe –**de·con·tam´·i·nant** *n.* –**de·con·tam·i·na´tion** *n.* –**de·con·tam´i·na·tor** *n.*

**de·cor´** *n.* a style of adornment, furnishings, etc. in an interior area

**dec´o·rate´** *vt.* to adorn or beautify; to paint and refurnish a home, office, etc.; to plan and direct a refurbishing; to honor, as with a medal –**dec´o·ra´tion** *n.* –**dec´o·ra·tor** *n.*

**dec´o·ra·tive** *adj.* ornamental; aesthetic; artistic –**dec´o·ra·tive·ly** *adv.* –**dec´o·ra·tive·ness** *n.*

**dec´o·rous** *adj.* characterized by decorum –**dec´o·rous·ly** *adv.* –**dec´o·rous·ness** *n.*

**de·cor´ti·cate** *vt.* to peel; to remove the outer layer from –**de·cor·ti·ca´tion** *n.*

**de·co´rum** *n.* fine manners; propriety

**de·cou·page´** *n.* a style of decoration characterized by designs or illustrations affixed to a surface and coated with varnish or laquer –*vt.*

**de´coy** *n.* a thing used to mislead or lure –*vi.*, *vt.* to lure, as into a trap **decrease** *vi.vt.* to become or cause to become gradually less or smaller –**de´crease** *n.* the process or lessening; the amount of reduction –**de·creas´ing·ly** *adv.*

**de·cree´** *n.* an official proclamation or order –*vt.* to order in an official capacity –*vi.* to issue a decree

**de·crep´it** *adj.* worn out, as by age or use –**de·crep´it·ness** *n.* –**de·crep´i·tude´** *n.*

**de·cry´** *vt.* to denounce; to criticize or condemn –**de·cri´al** *n.* –**de·cri´er** *n.*

**ded´i·cate** *vt.* to set apart for a special purpose; to devote oneself to a cause, course of action, etc.; to open with a ceremony, as of a building or park; to pay homage by dedicating, as of a book –**ded·i·ca´tion** *n.* –**ded´i·ca·tive** *adj.* –**ded´i·ca·tor** *n.*

**ded´i·cat·ed** *adj.* given over totally to a cause, a course of action, etc.; designed for a specific use: *a dedicated telephone line linking us to the Internet* –**ded´i·cat·ed·ly** *adv.*

**de·duce´** *vt.* to conclude or infer by reasoning –**de·duc·i·bil´i·ty** *n.* –**de·duc´i·ble** *adj.*

**de·duct´** *vt.* to take away: to subtract; to conclude by reasoning: to deduce –**de·duct·i·bil·i·ty** *n.* –**deduct´i·ble** *adj.*

**de·duc´tion** *n.* a subtraction or the amount subtracted: the process of reasoning to reach a conclusion; the conclusion reached –**de·duc´tive** *adj.* –**deduc´tive·ly** *adv.*

**deed** *n.* an act; a notable achievement; a legal document used to convey interest in property –*vt.* to transfer by means of a legal document

**deem** *vi.*, *vt.* to believe; to judge; to have as an opinion

**de·em´pha·size** *vt.* to reduce the importance of –**de-em´pha·sis** *n.*

**deep** *adj.* extending or located far from a reference point; of a specific extent: *ten inches deep*; penetrating; low in tone or pitch; abstract, difficult to comprehend; serious, earnest: *deep sorrow*; –**deep´ly** *adv.* –**deep´ness** *n.*

**deep´en** *vi.*, *vt.* to become or make deeper

**deep´freeze´** *vt.* to freeze food quickly to very low temperature

**deep´-fry** *vt.* to cook in a vat of hot grease

**deep´-root·ed** *adj.* having deep roots; firmly established

**deep´-seat·ed** *adj.* firmly established; difficult to change or overcome, as *deep-seated prejudice*

**deep space** outer space beyond the solar system

**de·face´** *vt.* to disfigure or mar; to damage in appearance, value, etc. –**de·face´a·ble** *adj.* –**de·face´ment** *n.* –**de·fac´er** *n.*

**de fac´ to** *Latin* existing in fact

**de·fame´** *vt.* to damage one's reputation by slander or libel –**def´a·ma´tion** *n.* –**de·fam´a·to·ry** *adj.* –**de·fam´er** *n.*

**de·fault´** *n.* a failure to fulfill an obligation or duty; a failure to appear, as for a competition –*vi.*, *vt.* to fail in fulfilling a duty or obligation –**de·fault´er** *n.*

**de·feat´** *n.* the act of conquering or the state of being conquered –*vt.* to overpower or conquer; to frustrate another's efforts

**de·feat´ist** *n.* one who expects or readily accepts defeat –*adj.* marked by an expectation or willingness to accept misfortune –**de·feat´ism** *n.*

**def´e·cate** *vi.* to eliminate waste matter from the body –*vt.* to clear of impurities –**def·e·ca´tion** *n.* –**def·e·ca´tor** *n.*

**de´fect, de·fect´** *n.* an imperfection or fault; a deficiency –**de·fect´** *vi.* to abandon a cause, one's country, etc., esp. to join the opposition –**de·fec´tion** *n.* –**de·fec´tor** *n.*

**de·fec´tive** *adj.* imperfect or deficient in some way –**de·fec´tive·ly** *adv.* –**de·fec´tive·ness** *n.*

**de·fence´** (*Brit.*) *n.* protection from harm; a means of protection; justification for an action; in law, a defendant and his or her solicitor or the arguments they present

**de·fend´** *vt.* to protect, as from danger; to justify, on one's actions; to contest, as a charge or suit *–vt.* to make a defense **–de·fend´a·ble** *adj.* **–de·fend´er** *n.*

**de·fend´ant** *n.* in law, one against whom an action is brought

**de·fen·es·tra´tion** *n.* the act of throwing out of a window

**de·fense´** *(US) n.* protection from harm; a means of protection; justification for an action; in law, a defendant and his or her lawyer or the arguments they present

**de·fense´less** *adj.* without protection; unable to defend onself; helpless **–de·fense´less·ly** *adv.* **–de·fense´less·ness** *n.*

**de·fen´si·ble** *adj.* capable of being justified or defended **–de·fen·si·bil·i·ty, de·fen´si·ble·ness** *n.* **–de·fen´si·bly** *adv.*

**de·fen´sive** *adj.* resistant to criticism; recalcitrant; tending to deny or justify, as one's actions *–n.* prepared to resist **–de·fen´sive·ly** *adv.* **–de·fen´sive·ness** *n.*

**de·fer´** *vi., vt.* to postpone; to procrastinate; to yield in deference to the wishes or judgment of another **–de·fer´ra·ble** *adj.* **–de·fer´rer** *n.* **–de·ferred´** *adj.*

**def´er·ence** *n.* courteous regard

**def´er·ent, def´er·en´tial** *adj.* respectful; polite; obedient **–def´er·en´tial·ly** *adv.*

**de·fi´ance** *n.* bold resistance or opposition; a disposition to challenge **–de·fi´ant** *adj.* **–de·fi´ant·ly** *adv.*

**de·fi´cience, de·fi´cien·cy** *n.* a lack of something; the nature of a thing that is lacking

**de·fi´cient** *adj.* lacking in something; defective in some way **–de·fi´cient·ly** *adv.*

**def´i·cit** *n.* a shortage; the amount of a shortage

**deficit financing** borrowing to cover the excess of expenditures over income

**deficit spending** a condition characterized by expenditures that exceed income

**de·file´** *vt.* to corrupt or debase; to pollute; to profane, as a reputation **–de·file´ment** *n.* **–de·fil´er** *n.* **–de·fil´ing·ly** *adv.*

**de·fine´** *vt.* to give precise value or meaning, as of a word; to describe; to specify a limit or boundary **–de·fin´a·ble** *adj.* **–de·fin´a·bly** *adv.* **–de·fin´er** *n.*

**def´i·nite** *adj.* having exact limits; clear in meaning; certain or positive **–def´i·nite·ly** *adv.* **–def´i·nite·ness** *n.*

**def·i·ni´tion** *n.* a statement of limits or meaning; the condition of being clearly outlined

**de·fin´i·tive** *adj.* conclusive; precise; being the most authoritative or accurate **–de·fin´i·tive·ly** *adv.* **–de·fin´i·tive·ness** *n.*

**de·flate´** *vi., vt.* to collapse or cause to collapse by the release of gas; to make smaller or less in value; to dishearten: *to deflate one's hopes* **–de·fla´tion** *n.* **–de·fla´tion·ar·y** *adj.*

**de·flect´** *vi., vt.* turn aside or cause to turn aside **–de·flect´a·ble** *adj.* **–de·flec´tion** *n.* **–de·flec´tive** *adj.* **–de·flec´tor** *n.*

**de·fo´li·ant** *n.* a chemical that causes a living plant to shed its leaves **–de·fo´li·ate** *vt.* **de·fo´li·a´tion** *n.* **–de·fo´li·a·tor** *n.*

**de·for´est** *vt.* to clear an area of trees **–de·for·est·a´tion** *n.* **–de·for´est·er** *n.*

**de·form´** *vt.* to damage the natural form or appearance of; to disfigure *–vi.* to become disfigured **–de·form·a·bil´i·ty** *n.* **–de·form´a·ble** *adj.* **–de·for·ma´tion** *n.*

**de·formed´** *adj.* misshapen or disfigured **–de·for´mi·ty** *n.*

**de·fraud´** *vt.* to take or withhold by deceit; to swindle **–de·fraud·a´tion** *n.* **–de·fraud´er** *n.*

**de·fray´** *vt.* to provide for payment or bear the expense of **–de·fray´a·ble** *adj.* **–de·fray´er, de·fray´ment** *n.* **–de·fray´er** *n.*

**de·frost´** *vt.* to remove frost for ice; to thaw **–de·frost´er** *n.*

**deft** *adj.* skillful; dexterous **–deft´ly** *adv.* **–deft´ness** *n.*

**de·funct´** *adj.* no longer existing; dead **–de·func´tive** *adj.* **–de·funct´ness** *n.*

**de·fy´** *vt.* to openly resist or oppose; to challenge; to baffle: *to defy understanding*

**de·gen´er·ate** *adj.* morally depraved: corrupted; having become deteriorated *–n.* one who is depraved or corrupted *–vi.* to decline in quality **–de·gen´er·a·cy, de·gen´er·ate·ness** *n.* **–de·gen´er·ate·ly** *adv.* **–de·gen´er·a·tive** *adj.*

**de·gen·er·a´tion** *n.* the process of becoming worse; the progressive deterioration of an organ or tissue

**de·grad´a·ble** *adj.* that can be reduced chemically **–de·grad·a·bil´i·ty** *n.*

**de·grade´** *vt.* to disgrace or debase; to reduce in value, quality, rank, etc.; to reduce by erosion *–vi.* to degenerate **–deg´ra·da´tion** *n.*

**de·grad´ed** *adj.* reduced in rank, quality, etc.; corrupted or debased **–de·grad´ed·ly** *adv.* **–de·grad´ed·ness** *n.*

**de·grad´ing** *adj.* debasing; humiliating **–de·grad´ing·ly** *adv.*

**de·grease´** *vt.* to cleanse or improve by removing grease: *degrease a fitting, degrease the soup* **–de·greas·er** *n.*

**de·gree´** *n.* a relative ranking, as of position, intensity, etc.; a unit on a scale, as for temperature, angles, arcs, etc. **–by degrees** little by little **–to a degree** somewhat

**de·hu´man·ize** *vt.* to strip of emotion or other human attributes; to make mechanical **– de·hu·man·i·za´tion** *n.*

**de·hu·mid´i·fi·er** *n.* a device that removes moisture from the air **–de·hu·mid·i·fi·ca´tion** *n.* **–de·hu·mid´i·fy** *vt.*

**de·hy´drate´** *vi.* to lose water *–vt.* to remove or deprive of water **de·hy·dra´tion** *n.* **–de·hy·dra´tor** *n.*

**de·ice´** *vt., vi.* to remove ice or prevent ice from forming

**de´i·fy** *vt.* to exalt, idealize; to look upon or worship as a god –**de·if´ic** *adj.* –**de·i·fi·ca´tion** *n.* –**de´i·fi·er** *n.*

**de´ism** *n.* the belief in creation by a supreme being who abstains from involvement in the world or its inhabitants –**de´ist** *n.* –**de·is´tic, de·is´ti·cal** *adj.* –**de·is´ti·cal·ly** *adv.*

**de´i·ty** *n.* a god; a divinity

**de·ject´** *vt.* to make unhappy; to depress –**de·jec´tion** *n.*

**de·ject´ed** *adj.* dispirited; depressed –**de·ject´ed·ly** *adv.* –**de·ject´ed·ness** *n.*

**de·lay´** *vt.* to postpone; to slow or detain –*vi.* to linger –*n.* that which causes lateness; the length of a postponement –**de·lay´er** *n.*

**de´le** *vt.* to take out; delete

**de·lec´ta·ble** *adj.* pleasing; delightful –**de·lec·ta·bil´i·ty, de·lec´ta·ble·ness** *n.* –**de·lec´ta·bly** *adv.*

**de´lec·ta´tion** *n.* delight; entertainment

**del´e·gate´** *n.* one authorized to speak or act for others –*vt.* to authorize or entrust another to act; to send as a representative –**del´e·ga´tion** *n.*

**de·lete´** *vt.* to eliminate, cross out, or erase

**del´e·te´ri·ous** *adj.* harmful; injurious –**del·e·te´ri·ous·ly** *adv.* –**del·e·te´ri·ous·ness** *n.*

**de·lib´er·ate** *adj.* intentional; carefully planned; unhurried –*vi., vt.* to think about and consider carefully –**de·lib´er·ate·ly** *adv.* –**de·lib´er·ate·ness** *n.*

**de·lib´er·a´tion** *n.* careful consideration; discussion and consideration of all sides of an issue, as by a panel of judges

**de·lib´er·a·tive** *adj.* contemplative; attributable to deliberation –**de·lib´er·a·tive·ly** *adv.* **de·lib´er·a·tive·ness** *n.*

**del´i·ca·cy** *n.* the quality of being beautiful or refined; frailty; requiring sensitivity: *a matter of some delicacy*; a special food

**del´i·cate** *adj.* fine or dainty; fragile; subtle; requiring or displaying remarkable tact –**del´i·cate·ly** *adv.* –**del´i·cate·ness** *n.*

**del·i·ca·tes´sen** *n.* a store where ready-to-eat foods are sold; the food sold in such a store

**de·li´cious** *adj.* pleasing to the senses –**de·li´cious·ly** *adv.* –**de·li´cious·ness** *n.*

**de´light** *n.* a thing that gives great pleasure; a quality that pleases: charm –*vi.* to give or take great pleasure –*vt.* to please or gratify –**de·light´ful** *adj.* –**de·light´ful·ly** *adv.* –**de·light´ful·ness** *n.*

**de·lin´e·ate** *vt.* to depict or describe with drawings or words –**de·lin·e·a´tion** *n.* –**de·lin´e·a·tive** *adj.* –**de·lin´e·a·tor** *n.*

**de·lin´quen·cy** *n.* failure to perform as required by duty or law; a fault or misdeed

**de·lin´quent** *adj.* of that contrary to what duty or the law requires; overdue, as an obligation –*n.* one who acts contrary to what duty or the law requires –**de·lin´quent·ly** *adv.*

**de·lir´i·ous** *adj.* marked by delirium; extemely pleased or excited –**de·lir´i·ous·ly** *adv.* –**de·lir´i·ous·ness** *n.*

**de·lir´i·um** *n.* a state of altered consciousness marked by anxiety, confused speech, hallucinations, confusion, etc. –**de·lir´i·um tre´ mens** an extreme case of delirium brought on by withdrawal from or excessive ingestion of alcoholic beverages

**de·liv´er** *vt.* to carry to or give over to another; to say: *deliver a speech or lecture*; to bring forth or produce, as a baby; to rescue: *deliver from the enemy* –*vi.* to fulfill a promise; to perform well –**de·liv·er·a·bil´i·ty** *n.* –**de·liv´er·a·ble** *adj.* –**de·liv´er·er** *n.*

**de·liv´er·ance** *n.* the condition of being set free; a pardon; redemption

**de·liv´er·y** *n.* a setting free; liberation; the conveyance or transference of goods; childbirth; one's speaking ability

**dell** *n.* a small grove; a shady retreat

**de·louse´** *vt.* to free of lice

**del´ta** *n.* the name or symbol (Δ) for the fourth letter of the Greek alphabet; something shaped like a triangle; an alluvial deposit at the mouth of a river

**del´toid** *adj.* triangular –*n.* a triangular muscle that covers the shoulder

**de·lude´** *vt.* to mislead or deceive –**de·lud´er** *n.*

**del´uge** *n.* a great flood; heavy rainfall; a thing that overwhelms –*vt.* to flood; to overwhelm

**de·lu´sion** *n.* a false or irrational belief –**de·lu´sion·al, de·lu´sion·ar·y** *adj.*

**de·lu´sive, de·lu´so·ry** *adj.* misleading; deceitful –**de·lu´sive·ly** *adv.*–**de·lu´sive·ness** *n.*

**de·luxe´** *adj.* luxurious; elegant

**delve** *vi.* to search resolutely

**de·mag´net·ize** *vt.* to cancel or neutralize magnetic properties

**dem´a·gogue** *n.* a revolutionary; one who arouses followers by appeals to emotion or prejudice –**dem´a·gog´ic** *adj.* –**dem·a·gog´i·cal·ly** *adv.* –**dem´a·gogu·er·y, dem´a·gog·y** *n.*

**de·mand´** *n.* an urgent or bold request: a thing requested; a formal request: a claim; a need –*vt.* to request boldly; to claim as due; to inquire formally; to require: *the job demands all of his time* –*vi.* to make a demand –**de·mand´a·ble** *adj.* –**de·mand´er** *n.*

**de·mand´ing** *adj.* difficult, challenging; hard to please –**de·mand´ing·ly** *adv.*

**de·mar·ca´tion** *n.* a separation or boundary; the fixing of boundaries or limits –**de·mar´cate** *vt.* –**de·mar´ca·tor** *n.*

**de·mean´** *vt.* to debase or humble

**de·mean´or** *n.* one's behavior or appearance

**de·ment´ed** *adj.* mentally ill –**de·ment´ed·ly** *adv.*

—**de·ment´ed·ness** *n.*
**de·men´tia** *n.* impairment of mental faculties; mental illness —**de·men´tial** *adj.*
**de·men´tia prae´cox´** *n.* schizophrenia
**dem´i·god** *n.* one who is godlike
**de·mise´** *n.* a termination of existence; death; a transfer of rights or authority —*vt.*, *vi.* to transfer or be transferred as by will or abdication
**dem´i·tasse** *n.* literally, half a cup; strong black coffee served after a meal or the small cup in which it is served
**dem´o** *n.* a demonstration, such as an audio or video tape showcasing an artist, a piece of music, etc.
**de·mo´bi·lize** *vt.* to disband, as troops; to discharge from military service —**de·mo·bi·li·za´tion** *n.*
**de·moc´ra·cy** *n.* the principle of the equality of rights, opportunity, etc. for all people; political control shared by the populace
**dem´o·crat´** *n.* one who advocates government by the people —**dem´o·crat´ic** *adj.* —**dem´o·crat´i·cal·ly** *n.*
**de·moc´ra·tize** *vt.*, *vi.* to make or become democratic —**de·moc´ra·ti·za´tion** *n.*
**dem·o·graph´ics** *n.* the classification of a population by age, sex, etc., especially for the marketing of consumer products —**dem·o·graph´ic, dem·o·graph´i·cal** *adj.* —**dem·o·graph´i·cal·ly** *adv.*
**de·mog´ra·phy** *n.* the study of the vital and social statistics within a population —**de·mog´ra·pher, de·mog´ra·phist** *n.*
**de·mol´ish** *vt.* to tear down, as a building; to destroy completely; to severely damage, as a person's reputation —**de·mol´ish·er** *n.*—**de·mol´ish·ment**
**dem´o·li´tion** *n.* the process of tearing down or destroying —**dem´o·li´tions** *n.* explosives —**dem´o·li´tion·ist** *n.*
**de´mon** *n.* an evil being; one who shows great energy or enthusiasm —**de·mon´ic** *adj.* —**de·mon´i·cal·ly** *adv.*
**de·mo´ni·ac, de´mo·ni´a·cal** *adj.* demon-possessed; fiendish; furious; frenzied —**de·mo·ni´a·cal·ly** *adv.*
**de´mon·ism** *n.* a belief in demons
**de·mon·ol´a·try** *n.* demon worship
**de·mon·ol´o·gy** *n.* the study of demons and demonolatry
**de·mon´stra·ble** *adj.* able to be shown or verified —**de·mon·stra·bil´i·ty** *n.* —**de·mon´stra·ble·ness** *n.* —**de·mon´stra·bly** *adv.*
**dem´on·strate´** *vt.* to prove by reasoning; to illustrate by showing in operation; to make evident, as an emotion —*vi.* to take part in a protest, as by congregating or marching —**dem´on·stra´tion** *n.* —**dem´on·stra·tor** *n.*
**de·mon´stra·tive** *adj.* able to be proved or verified; open and outgoing; openly affectionate —**de·mon´stra·tive·ly** *adv.* —**de·mon´stra·tive·ness** *n.*
**de·mor´al·ize´** *vt.* to dishearten; to cause confusion —**de·mor´al·i·za´tion** *n.*
**de·mote´** *vt.* to lessen in status or rank —**de·mo´tion** *n.*
**de·mount´** *vt.* to take down; to remove from a mounting —**de·mount´a·ble** *adj.*
**de·mur´** *n.* a delay or objection based on doubt —*vi.* to voice an objection
**de·mure´** *adj.* modest, reserved; affecting modesty —**de·mure´ly** *adv.* —**de·mure´ness** *n.*
**de·mur´rage** *n.* compensation paid to a freight company for delaying equipment, as by failure to load or unload in a timely fashion
**de·mys´ti·fy** *vt.* to take the mystery from; to expose, explain —**de·mys·ti·fi·ca´tion** *n.* —**de·mys´ti·fi·er** *n.*
**de·my·thol´o·gize** *vt.* to explain away or remove elements considered mythical, as from a creed, belief, etc. —**de·my·thol´o·gi·za·tion** *n.* —**de·my·thol´o·giz·er** *n.*
**den** *n.* the lair of an animal; a gathering place, as *a den of thieves*; a room in a house that serves as a study or retreat
**de·nat´u·ral·ize** *vt.* to revoke one's citizenship
**de·na´ture** *vt.* to change the nature or properties of, as through chemical action —**de·na´tur·ant** *n.* —**de·na·tur·a´tion** *n.*
**de·ni´a·ble** *adj.* possible to be disputed; that can be withheld or disowned —**de·ni·a·bil´i·ty** *n.* —**de·ni´a·bly** *adv.*
**de·ni´al** *n.* a refusal, as to honor a request; a disavowal; an unwillingness to believe or acknowledge
**de·ni´er** *n.* one who denies
**de·nier´** *n.* a measure of the fineness of thread
**den´i·grate** *vt.* to cast aspersions on one's character, reputation, etc. —**den·i·gra´tion** *n.* —**den´i·gra·tor** *n.* —**den´i·gra·to·ry** *adj.*
**den´im** *n.* a stout cloth used for work clothes
**den´i·zen** *n.* an inhabitant; one who frequents a particular place —**den·i·zen·a´tion** *n.*
**de·nom·i·na´tion** *n.* a name or designation; a specific unit of value; a religious group or sect within a larger group —**de·nom·i·na´tion·al** *adj.* —**de·nom·i·na´tion·al·ly** *adv.*
**de·nom·i·na´tion·al·ism** *n.* a system of separation by classification —**de·nom·i·na´tion·al·ist** *n.*
**de·nom´i·na·tor** *n.* one that names; an attribute common to the members of a group; the designation in a fraction that expresses the number of parts into which the whole is divided
**de·note´** *vt.* to signify or indicate; to serve as a symbol for —**de·not´a·ble** *adj.* —**de·no·ta´tive, de·no´tive** *adj.* —**de·no´ta·tive·ly** *adv.*
**de·nounce´** *vt.* to openly condemn or accuse —**de·nounce´ment** *n.* —**de·nounc´er** *n.*
**dense** *adj.* compact; thick; opaque; slow to compre-

hend **–dense´ly** *adv.* **–dense´ness** *n.*

**den´si·ty** *n.* a relative concentration of mass

**dent** *n.* an indentation in an otherwise smooth surface; an accomplishment, as *to put a dent in a list of tasks* *–vi.* to get a dent *–vt.* to cause a dent

**den´tal** *adj.* of the teeth **–den´tal·ly** *adv.*

**den´tate** *adj.* having teeth

**den´ti·frice** *n.* any of various products for cleaning the teeth

**den´tist** *n.* one who specializes in the care and treatment of the teeth **–den´tis·try** *n.*

**den·ti´tion** *n.* the process or time of teething; the types and arrangement of the teeth

**de´nu·date** *adj.* naked; stripped of foliage *–vt.* to denude **–de·nu·da´tion** *n.*

**de·nude´** *vt.* to strip bare, as of foliage

**de·nun´ci·ate** *vt.* to denounce **–de·nun´ci·a·tor** *n.* **de·nun´ci·a´tory** *adj.*

**de·nun·ci·a´tion** *n.* public condemnation **–de·nun´ci·a·tive** *adj.* **–de·nun´ci·a·tive·ly** *adv.*

**de·ny´** *vt.* refuse to acknowledge, believe, or allow

**de·o´dor·ant** *adj.* able to mask or destroy unpleasant odors *–n.* a substance applied to the body or released into the air that masks or destroys odors **–de·o´dor·i·za´tion** *n.* **de·o´dor·ize´** *vt.* **–de·o´dor·iz·er** *n.*

**de·ox·y·ri´bo·nu·cle·ic ac´id** DNA, that carries the genetic code within cells

**de·part´** *vi., vt.* to leave **–depart from** to deviate, as from a usual course **–de·par´ture** *n.*

**de·part´ment** *n.* a separate operating division, as in a business, government, or school; a field of study or knowledge; a regular section in a periodical **–de·part·men´tal** *adj.* **–de·part·men´tal·ly** *adv.* **–de·part·men´tal·ism** *n.*

**de·part·men´tal·ize** *vt.* to organize into separate operating units or subdivisions **–de·part·men·tal·i·za´tion** *n.*

**department store** a retail establishment that sells a wide variety of merchandise from various departments or sections

**de·par´ture** *n.* a setting out or leaving; a change or divergence from a standard course of action

**de·pend´** *vi.* to rely on; to place trust or confidence in; to be contingent upon

**de·pend´a·ble** *adj.* reliable; trustworthy **–de·pend·a·bil´i·ty** *n.* **–de·pend´a·ble·ness** *n.* **–de·pend´a·bly** *adv.*

**de·pen´dence, de·pen´dance** *n.* reliance on another, as for subsistence; faith or trust in another; an addiction **–de·pend´en·cy, de·pend´an·cy** *n.*

**de·pend´ent** *adj.* relying on something or someone else; contingent; subordinate; helpless **–de·pend´ent, de·pen´dant** *n.* one who relies on another, as for moral or financial support **–de·pend´ent·ly** *adv.*

**de·per´son·al·ize** *vt.* to consider or act objectively, removing personal considerations; to cause the loss of a sense of distinctiveness **–de·per·son·a·li·za´tion** *n.*

**de·pict´** *vt.* to portray by drawing, sculpting, etc.; to represent or describe in words or pictures **–de·pic´tion** *n.*

**dep´i·late** *vt.* to eliminate hair **–dep·i·la´tion** *n.* **–dep´i·la·tor** *n.* **–de·pil´a·to·ry** *adj., n.*

**de·plete´** *vt.* to use completely; to lessen gradually, as by use **–de·plet´a·ble** *adj.* **–de·ple´tion** *n.* **–de·ple´tive** *adj.*

**de·plor´a·ble** *adj.* tragic; distressing; unfortunate **–de·plor·a·bil´i·ty** *n.* **–de·plor´a·bly** *adv.*

**de·plore´** *vt.* to condemn as wrong or unjust; to regret

**de·ploy´** *vt.* to position according to a plan, as personnel or equipment *–vi.* to be positioned **–de·ploy·a·bil´i·ty** *n.* **–de·ploy´a·ble** *adj.* **–de·ploy´er** *n.* **de·ploy´ment** *n.*

**de·pop·u·la´tion** *n.* a sharp reduction in the number of inhabitants of an area, such as caused by disease or war **–de·pop´u·late** *vt.* **–de·pop´u·la·tor** *n.*

**de·port´** *vt.* to expel from a country; to conduct oneself in a particular manner

**de´por·ta´tion** *n.* banishment from a country **–de·port´a·ble** *adj.* **–de·port·ee´** *n.*

**de·port´ment** *n.* one's behavior

**de·pos´it** *n.* something of value placed with another for safekeeping or as security; something left behind, as silt by a flood *–vt.* to place or leave behind **–de·pos´i·tor** *n.* **–de·pos´i·to´ry** *n.*

**dep·o·si´tion** *n.* removal from power; the act of depositing; testimony taken under oath outside the court **–dep·o·si´tion·al** *adj.*

**de´pot´** *n.* a railway or bus station; a storehouse

**de·prave´** *vt.* to corrupt or pervert **–dep·ra·va´tion** *n.* **–de·praved´** *adj.* **–de·prav´ed·ly** *adv.* **–de·prav´i·ty** *n.*

**dep´re·cate** *vt.* to express disapproval; to belittle **–dep´re·cat·ing·ly** *adv.* **–dep·re·ca´tion** *n.* **–dep´re·ca·tor** *n.*

**dep´re·ca·tive, dep´re·ca·to·ry** *adj.* tending to express disapproval; belittling; apologetic **–dep·re·ca·to´ri·ly** *adv.*

**de·pre´ci·ate´** *vi.* to fall in value *–vt.* to lessen in value; to consider of little value **–de·pre´ci·a·ble** *adj.* **–de·pre·ci·a´tion** *n.* **–de·pre´ci·a·to·ry** *adj.*

**de·press´** *vt.* to lower, as one's spirit; to lessen, as the value of a thing; to push or press down **–de·press´ing** *adj.* **–de·press´ing·ly** *adv.* **–de·pres´sor** *n.*

**de·pres´sant** *n.* an agent that slows the vital functions; a sedative

**de·pressed´** *adj.* pressed down; downhearted, despondent; reduced in amount, value etc.

**de·pres´sion** *n.* despondency; a period of economic stagnation; a sunken or indented place in a surface

**de·pres´sive** *adj.* inclined to despondency; tending to cause a slowing of business activity **–de·pres´sive·ly** *adv.* **–de·pres´sive·ness** *n.*

**de·prive´** *vt.* to take from: dispossess; to keep from acquiring or enjoying: *to deprive of a normal home life* **–de·priv´al, dep·ri·va´tion·al** *adj.* **–dep·ri·va´tion** *n.* **–de·priv´a·ble** *adj.*

**de·prived´** *adj.* lacking the necessities of life; lacking opportunity; underprivileged

**dep´u·ty** *n.* one acting in the place of another; an aide or assistant; in some countries, a member of the legislature **–dep·u·ta´tion** *n.* **–dep´u·tize** *vi., vt.*

**de·rail´** *vi., vt.* to go or cause to go off the rails, as a train; to stop or cause to stop, as *a program derailed by a lack of interest* **–de·rail´ment** *n.*

**de·rail´leur** *n.* a device for shifting gears on a bicycle

**de·range´** *vt.* to disorder or disturb the arrangement of; to make insane

**de·range´ment** *n.* being out of the usual order; mental illness

**der´by** *n.* a contest or race; a type of felt hat

**de·reg´u·late** *vt.* to void or suspend the rules; to free from government control **–de·reg·u·la´tion** *n.* **–de·reg´u·la·tor** *n.*

**der´e·lict** *adj.* abandoned; negligent or delinquent as in carrying out a duty *–n.* property that has been abandoned; a social outcast; a loiterer **–der·e·lic´tion** *n.*

**de·ride´** *vt.* to mock or ridicule **–de·rid´er** *n.* **–de·rid´ing·ly** *adv.*

**de·ri´sion** *n.* the state of being mocked or ridiculed; a display of scorn or contempt

**de·ri´sive, de·ri´so·ry** *adj.* characterized by derision **–de·ri´sive·ly** *adv.* **–de·ri´sive·ness** *n.*

**der´i·va´tion** *n.* something derived: a derivative; the source from which something derives; the formation of a word from another word, as by adding a prefix or suffix **–der·i·va´tion·al** *adj.*

**de·riv´a·tive** *adj.* borrowed or learned, not original *–n.* something produced from another source **–de·riv´a·tive·ly** *adv.* **–de·riv´a·tive·ness** *n.*

**de·rive´** *vt.* to obtain from a source; to arrive at by reasoning; to trace a word to its origin

**der´ma** *n.* the dermis **–der´mal** *adj.*

**der·ma·ti´tis** *n.* an irritation of the skin

**der·ma·tol´o·gy** *n.* the scientific study of the skin, its diseases, and their treatment **–der·ma·to·log´ic, der·ma·to·log´i·cal** *adj.* **–der·ma·tol´o·gist** *n.*

**der´mis** *n.* the layer of skin below the epidermis

**de·rog´a·to´ry, de·rog´a·tive** *adj.* disparaging; tending to belittle **–de·rog·a·to´ri·ly** *adv.*

**der´rick** *n.* a machine for hoisting and moving heavy objects

**der´rin·ger** *n.* a small pistol

**der´vish** *n.* a member of a Muslim sect

**de·scend´** *vi., vt.* to progress downward; to move from a higher to lower level; to derive from a source, as an ancestor

**de·scend´ant, de·scend´ent** *n.* one who is of a particular lineage; anything traced back to an earlier form

**de·scend´er** *n.* the part of a typeset character that falls below the baseline

**de·scent´** *n.* a downward motion; an inclined surface; a lowering, as of status; a sudden onset

**de·scribe´** *vt.* to relay an account or impression; to represent in speech or writing; to draw or trace **–de·scrib´a·ble** *adj.* **–de·scrib´er** *n.*

**de·scrip´tion** *n.* an account or report that describes; a drawing or tracing

**de·scrip´tive** *adj.* serving to describe; illustrative **–de·scrip´tive·ly** *adv.* **–de·scrip´tive·ness** *n.*

**de·scrip´tor** *n.* an identifying emblem

**des´e·crate** *vt.* to violate that which is considered sacred; to profane **–des´e·crat·er, des´e·cra·tor** *n.* **–des·e·cra´tion** *n.*

**de·sen´si·tize** *vt.* to deaden or benumb; to make insensible, as by repeated exposure or shock; protect from extreme reaction to an antigen **–de·sen·si·ti·za´tion** *n.* **–de·sen´si·tiz·er** *n.*

**des´ert** *n.* a dry, often sandy, barren region

**des·ert´** *vi., vt.* to abandon **–de·ser´tion** *n.* **–de·sert´er** *n.*

**de·serve´** *vi., vt.* be worthy of

**de·served´** *adj.* honestly earned justified or suitable **–de·serv´ed·ly** *adv.* **–de·serv´ed·ness** *n.*

**de·serv´ing** *adj.* worthy of assistance, praise etc.: *a subject deserving of further study* **–de·serv´ing·ly** *adv.*

**des´ic·cate** *vt.* to dry thoroughly; to preserve food by drying *–vi.* to become dry **–des·ic·ca·tion** *n.* **–des´ic·ca·tor** *n.* **–des´ic·ca·tive** *adj.*

**de·sign´** *n.* a detailed plan or schematic; a bringing together of elements so as to present a congruous whole; an artistic rendering *–vt.* to invent or devise; to make a graphic representation; to have as a purpose or goal **–de·sign´ a·ble** *adj.* **–design´er** *n.*

**des´ig·nate** *vt.* to specify or appoint; to set aside, as for a specific purpose **–des·ig·na´tion** *n.* **–des´ig·na·tive, des´ig·na·tory** *adj.* **–des´ig·na·tor** *n.*

**designated driver** a group member who forgoes alcoholic beverages in order to chauffer those who are drinking

**designated hitter** in baseball, one who hits in place of the pitcher

**de·sign´ed·ly** *adv.* intentionally; deliberately

**des´ig·nee´** *n.* one named or set apart

**designer drug** a synthetic drug formulated to produce certain desired effects

**de·sign´ing** *adj.* scheming, crafty, or treacherous; of the making of designs or patterns *–n.* the art or business of making designs or patterns **–de·sign´ing·ly** *adv.*

**de·sir´a·ble** *adj.* worth seeking or having; beneficial: *a desirable change*; pleasing or attractive **–de·sir·a·bil´i·ty, de·sir´a·ble·ness** *n.* **–de·sir´a·bly** *adv.*

**de·sire´** *n.* a longing or craving; lust *–vt.* to want or express a wish for **–de·sire´er** *n.* **–de·sir´ous** *adj.* **–de·sir´ous·ly** *adv.* **–de·sir´ous·ness** *n.*

**de·sist´** *vi.* to cease; to abstain from **–de·sis´tance** *n.*

**desk** *n.* an executive work station; a table for writing or studying with drawers for storage

**desk´top** *n.* the working surface of a desk *–adj.* designed for use on a desk: *a desktop computer*

**desktop publishing** the use of a computer for the preparation of copy for printing

**des´o·late** *adj.* forsaken; dismal, dreary; disconsolate or forlorn *–vt.* to lay waste; to devastate **–des´o·late·ly** *adv.* **–des´o·late·ness** *n.* **–des´o·lat·er, des´o·la·tor** *n.* **–des´o·la´tion** *n.*

**de·spair´** *n.* a loss of hope *–vi.* to lose all hope **–de·spair´ing** *adj.* **–de·spair´ing·ly** *adv.*

**des´per·ate** *adj.* hopeless; dangerous; frantic; seeming so hopeless as to cause one to be reckless or foolhardy **–des´per·ate·ly** *adv.* **–des´per·ate·ness** *n.* **–des·per·a´tion** *n.*

**des·pic´a·ble** *adj.* detestable; deserving of contempt; mean or vile **–des·pic´a·bil·i·ty, de·spic´a·ble·ness** *n.* **–de·spic´a·bly** *adv.*

**de·spise´** *vt.* to regard with disdain or scorn; to look down on **–de·spis´a·ble** *adj.* **–de·spis´al** *n.* **–de·spis´er** *n.*

**de·spite´** *n.* an insult; an act of spite *–prep.* notwithstanding

**de·spond´** *vi.* to lose hope; to become depressed or discouraged **–de·spond´ing·ly** *adv.*

**de·spon´dent** *adj.* suffering a loss of courage or hope; dejected **–de·spon´dence, de·spon´den·cy** *n.* **–de·spon´dent·ly** *adv.*

**des´pot** *n.* an absolute ruler; a tyrant **–des·pot´ic, des·pot´i·cal** *adj.* **–des·pot´i·cal·ly** *adv.* **–des´pot·ism** *n.*

**des·sert´** *n.* the final course of a meal, usually something sweet

**des´ti·na´tion** *n.* the place to which someone or something is going or being sent

**des´tine** *vt.* to be determined or seem to be determined for a special goal or purpose

**des´ti·ny** *n.* the seeming inevitable course of events

**des´ti·tute´** *adj.* completely lacking or impoverished; without means of survival **–des´ti·tu´tion** *n.*

**de·stroy´** *vt.* to ruin utterly; to make useless; to tear down or demolish **–de·stroy´er** *n.*

**de·struct´** *n.* the demolition of a defective missile *–vt.* to destroy after launch *–vi.* to undergo deliberate destruction

**de·struc´ti·ble** *adj.* capable of being destroyed; easily broken **–de·struc·ti·bil´i·ty, de·struc´ti·ble·ness** *n.*

**de·struc´tion** *n.* the process or condition of being demolished or brought to ruin

**de·struc´tive** *adj.* producing or likely to produce destruction; tending to discourage or make ineffective: *destructive criticism* **–de·struc´tive·ly** *adv.* **–de·struc´tive·ness, de·struc·tiv´i·ty** *n.*

**des´ul·to·ry** *adj.* lacking direction or focus; random **–des´ul·to·ri·ly** *adv.* **–des´ul·to·ri·ness** *n.*

**de·tach´** *vt.* to disconnect; remove from attachment to **–de·tach·a·bil´i·ty** *adv.* **–de·tach´a·ble** *adj.* **–de·tach´a·bly** *adv.*

**de·tached´** *adj.* aloof, impartial; separated, cut off **–de·tach´ed·ly** *adv.* **–de·tach´ed·ness** *n.*

**de·tach´ment** *n.* the condition of being separated; impartiality or indifference; a military unit organized and trained, or sent off, for some special purpose

**de´tail** *n.* any of the minute parts that make up something; a precise account; a detachment of military personnel designated for a special mission *–vt.* to report in precise terms; to select or dispatch for a special purpose

**detail person** a company representative who visits distributors to tout the company's products, supervise promotions, etc.

**de·tain´** *vt.* to restrain or delay; to hold in custody **–de·tain´er** *n.* **–de·tain´ment** *n.*

**de·tect´** *vt.* to become aware of or search out something not readily apparent or that is hidden **–de·tect´a·ble, de·tect´i·ble** *adj.* **–de·tect´er** *n.* **–de·tec´tion** *n.*

**de·tec´tive** *n.* one who investigates crimes; anyone who painstakingly analyzes anything

**de·tec´tor** *n.* a device for discovering or disclosing the presence of something, as *a metal detector or smoke detector*

**détente´** *n.* a relaxing of tension between opposing groups

**de·ten´tion** *n.* a period of temporary custody or enforced delay **–de·ten´tive** *adj.*

**de·ter´** *vt.* to prevent or discourage by instilling doubt or fear **–de·ter´ment** *n.* **–de·ter´ra·ble** *adj.* **–de·ter´rer** *n.*

**de·ter´gent** *adj.* cleansing *–n.* a substance for cleansing **–de·ter´gence, de·ter´gen·cy** *n.*

**de·te´ri·o·rate´** *vi., vt.* to become or make worse **–de·te·ri·o·ra´tion** *n.* **–de·te·ri·o·ra´tive** *adj.*

**de·ter´min·a·ble** *adj.* able to be ascertained or established **–de·ter´mi·na·bil´i·ty** *n.* **–de·ter´min·a·bly** *adv.*

**de·ter´mi·nant** *n.* a factor that fixes or limits

**de·ter´mi·nate** *adj.* exactly fixed or limited; conclusive **–de·ter´mi·nate·ly** *adv.* **–de·ter´mi·nate·ness** *n.*

**de·ter´mi·na·tive** *adj.* tending to influence in deciding or settling *–n.* that which determines **–de·ter´mi·na·tive·ly** *adv.* **–de·ter´mi·na·tive·ness** *n.*

**de·ter´mine** *vt.* to set bounds; to render a decision; to reach a conclusion after study and consideration

–de·ter´mi·na´tion *n.* –de·ter´min·er *n.*

**de·ter´mined** *adj.* characterized by determination; resolved; steadfast in purpose **–de·ter´mined·ly** *adv.* **–de·ter´mined·ness** *n.*

**de·ter´min·ism** *n.* the belief that everything is predetermined by other events **–de·ter´min·ist** *n.* **–de·ter·min·is´tic** *adj.* **–de·ter·min·is´ti·cal·ly** *adv.*

**de·ter´rent** *adj.* tending to cause restraint *–n.* a thing that hinders; an obstacle **–de·ter´rence** *n.*

**de·test´** *vt.* to dislike intensely; to despise; loathe **–de·tes·ta´tion** *n.* **–de·test´er** *n.*

**de·test´a·ble** *adj.* disgusting; abhorrent; despicable **–de·test·a·bil´i·ty, de·test´a·ble·ness** *n.* **–de·test´a·bly** *adv.*

**de·throne** *vt.* to remove from power **–de·throne·ment** *n.*

**det´o·nate´** *vi., vt.* to explode or cause to explode **–det·o·na´tion** *n.* **–det´o·na·tor** *n.*

**de·tox´i·fy** *vt.* to counteract or remove poisonous properties from; to rid of the effects of poison; to treat so as to rid of dependence on alcohol or narcotics **–de·tox´i·fi·ca´tion** *n.*

**de·tract´** *vt.* to take away or withdraw *–vi.* to undergo removal of a valued quality or part **–de·trac´tion** *n.* **–de·trac´tive** *adj.* **–de·trac´tive·ly** *adv.* **–de·trac´tor** *n.*

**det´ri·ment** *n.* damage or loss; anything that causes damage **–det´ri·ment´al** *adj.* **–det´ri·ment´al·ly** *adv.*

**de·tri´tus** *n.* loose particles or fragments of rock created and deposited by natural forces; disintegrated matter: debris **–de·tri´tal** *adj.* **–de·tri´tion** *n.*

**deuce** *n.* a playing card or die with two spots

**de·val´u·ate, de·val´ue** *vt.* to reduce in value or significance

**de·val´u·a´tion** *n.* a reducing or reduction in value, especially of the exchange rate of a currency

**dev´as·tate** *vt.* to lay waste, as by war, storm, or fire; to overwhelm or stun, as by harsh criticism **–dev´as·tat·ing·ly** *adv.* **–dev·as·ta´tion** *n.* **–dev´as·ta·tor** *n.*

**de·vel´op** *vt.* to improve by realizing potential or capability; to expand or enlarge on; to increase effectiveness *–vi.* to grow or evolve: to advance from a lower to a higher state; to become revealed **–de·vel·op·a·bil´i·ty** *n.* **–de·vel´op·a·ble** *adj.*

**de·vel´oped** *adj.* technologically advanced; of an area or nation seen as highly evolved in terms of industry, finance, standard of living, etc.; of land cleared of natural growth and used for farming, industry, residents, etc.

**de·vel´op·er** *n.* a builder or contractor; one who oversees and finances or arranges financing for construction; a chemical used in the processing of photographic film

**de·vel´op·ing** *adj.* of an area or nation in the process of developing its industrial and economic capabilities

**de·vel´op·ment** *n.* a community where numerous dwellings are located or are under construction; an occurrence, often an outgrowth of an earlier action **–de·vel·op·men´tal** *adj.* **–de·vel·op·men´tal·ly** *adv.*

**de´vi·ant** *adj.* contrasting with the usual or normal *–n.* one whose behavior does not conform to accepted social standards **–de´vi·ance, de´vi·an·cy** *n.*

**de´vi·ate** *vi.* to depart from a normal or standard course **–de´vi·a´tion** *n.* **–de´vi·a·tor** *n.* **–de´vi·a·to·ry** *adj.*

**de·vice´** *n.* anything contrived, as a technique, a mechanical apparatus, etc; an ornamental embellishment

**dev´il** *n.* an evil spirit; a wicked person; one, often a child, who is mischievous **–poor devil** an unlucky person **–dev´il·ish** *adj.* **–dev´il·ish·ly** *adv.* **–dev´il·ish·ness** *n.*

**dev´il·ment** *n.* mischief

**dev´il·ry, dev´il·try** *n.* wickedness, sinfulness; mischief, impishness

**devil´s advocate** a church official assigned to find fault with those selected for beatification; anyone who explores the negative side of a proposition

**de´vi·ous** *adj.* deceptive; crafty; not direct, roundabout **–de´vi·ous·ly** *adv.* **–de´vi·ous·ness** *n.*

**de·vise´** *n.* a dividing, or giving of real property by will; the property given; a will or clause in a will that bequeaths real property *–vi., vt.* to create or contrive; to bequeath real property **–de·vis´a·ble** *adj.* **–de·vis´er** *n.*

**dev·i·see´** *n.* one to whom real property is given in a will

**de·vis´er** *n.* one who contrives or plots

**dev·i´sor** *n.* one who bequeaths real property

**de·vi´tal·ize** *vt.* to weaken or enfeeble; to deprive of life **–de·vi·tal·i·za´tion** *n.*

**de·void´** *adj.* lacking entirely; empty

**de·volve´** *vt., vi.* to pass or cause to be passed on to another, as accountability or an obligation **–dev·o·lu´tion, de·volve´ment** *n.*

**de·vote´** *vt.* to dedicate or assign for a specific purpose; to give, as time or effort

**de·vot´ed** *adj.* dedicated; loving and faithful; thoughtful, solicitous **–de·vot´ed·ly** *adv.* **–de·vot´ed·ness** *n.* **–dev´o·tee´** *n.*

**de·vo´tion** *n.* strong affection or dedication; piety **–de·vo´tion·al** *adj.* **–de·vo´tion·al·ly** *adv.*

**de·vour´** *vt.* to eat or absorb completely

**de·vout´** *adj.* very religious; expressing devotion; sincere **–de·vout´ly** *adv.* **–de·vout´ness** *n.*

**dew** *n.* drops of moisture formed by warm air contacting a cool surface **–dew´drop** *n.*

**dew´lap** *n.* a loose fold of skin hanging from the neck of certain animals

**dew point** the temperature at which moisture in the air condenses into liquid

**dew´y** *adj.* moist; like dew; brisk or exhilarating; innocence –**dew´i·ly** *adv.* –**dew´i·ness** *n.*

**dew´y-eyed** *adj.* displaying innocence or trust

**dex·ter´i·ty** *n.* skill with the hands or mind –**dex´ter·ous, dex´trous** *adj.* –**dex´ter·ous·ly, dex´trous·ly** *adv.* –**dex´ter·ous·ness, dex´trous·ness** *n.*

**dex´trose** *n.* sugar formed from starch; corn sugar

**di·a·be´tes** *n.* any of several diseases characterized by excessive thirst and frequent urination

**di´a·bet´ic** *n.* one who has diabetes

**di´a·bol´ic, di·a·bol´i·cal** *adj.* satanic; fiendish, wicked –**di·a·bol´i·cal·ly** *adv.* –**di·a·bol´i·cal·ness** *n.*

**di·ab´o·lism** *n.* devil or demon worship; fiendish or wicked deeds –**di·ab´o·list** *n.*

**di´a·crit´ic** *n.* any of the marks over or under a letter (ñ, ç, é, ü) that distinguish a change in pronunciation

**di·a·crit´i·cal** *adj.* helping to distinguish; marking a difference –**di·a·crit´i·cal·ly** *adv.*

**di´a·dem** *n.* a crown

**di´ag·nose** *vi., vt.* to make a critical analysis –**di·ag·nos´a·ble** *adj.*

**di´ag·no´sis** *n.* a critical analysis to determine the nature of a thing –**di·ag·nos´tic** *adj.* –**di·ag·nos´ti·cal·ly** *adv.*

**di´ag·nos·tics** *n.* the study or application of diagnosis –**di·ag·nos·ti´cian** *n.*

**di´a·gram** *n.* a sketch or drawing that explains or clarifies; a chart or graph –**di´a·gram·mat´ic, di´a·gram·mat´i·cal** *adj.* –**di´a·gram·mat´i·cal·ly** *adv.*

**di´al** *n.* the face of a watch or clock; a rotating disk, as on a telephone; a gauge or indicator; a knob used to indicate or adjust; *a radio dial*

**dialling code** *(Brit.)* a prefix to a telephone number that identifies the locality to which a call is being placed

**di´a·lect** *n.* the language variations commonly spoken in a particular place or by a particular group; speech characteristic of a class, trade, or profession –**di·a·lec´tal** *adj.* –**di·a·lec´tal·ly** *adv.*

**di·a·lec´tic** *n.* the examining of ideas through systematic argumentation or deduction –**di·a·lec´ti·cal** *adj.* –**di·a·lec´ti·cal·ly** *adv.*

**di·a·lec·tol´o·gy** *n.* the study of variations in a spoken language –**di·a·lec´ti·cian** *n.*

**di´a·logue´** *n.* conversation; an exchange of ideas; spoken lines in a play; a dissertation written in the form of a conversation

**di·al´y·sis** *n.* the means by which impurities are remove from the blood of patients suffering kidney failure

**di·am´e·ter** *n.* a line passing from one side to the other through the center of a circle or sphere; the length of such a line

**di·a·met´ric, di·a·met´ri·cal** *adj.* pertaining to a diameter; totally different, contrary, etc. –**di·a·met´ri·cal·ly** *adv.*

**diametrically opposed** completely different or incompatible, as at the opposite ends of a diameter

**di´a·mond** *n.* an extremely hard crystal of nearly pure carbon; a geometric figure of four equal sides that is not a square

**di·aph´a·nous** *adj.* extremely fine so as to be transparent; thin and airy –**di·aph´a·nous·ly** *adv.* –**di·aph´a·nous·ness** *n.*

**di´a·phragm´** *n.* a membrane that serves to separate

**di´a·rist** *n.* one who keeps a diary

**di´ar·rhe´a** *n.* morbid looseness of the bowels

**di´a·ry** *n.* a daily journal of events and observations

**di´a·tribe** *n.* a harsh tirade; a denunciation

**dice** *n. pl., sing.* **die** small gaming cubes marked with spots to indicate the value of a throw –*vt.* to cut, as vegetables, into small cubes

**dic´ey** *adj.* chancy; speculative

**di·chot´o·my** *n.* division into two, usually opposing, parts or viewpoint; in biology, a forking in pairs –**di·chot´o·mous** *adj.* –**di·chot´o·mous·ly** *adv.* –**di·chot´o·mous·ness** *n.*

**dick´er** *vi.* to barter; to bargain

**dic·tate´** *n.* a command; a guiding principle –*vi., vt.* to command with authority; to speak for another to record –**dic·ta´tion** *n.* –**dic·ta´tion·al** *adj.*

**dic´ta´tor** *n.* a ruler with unlimited power –**dic´ta·to´ri·al** *adj.*

**dic·ta´tor·ship** *n.* government by a dictator

**dic´tion** *n.* the choice of words and clarity of enunciation in speech

**dic´tion·ar´y** *n.* a list of words or references arranged alphabetically to provide a definition, translation to another language, etc.

**dic´tum** *n., pl.* **dic´tums, dic´ta** a pronouncement

**di·dac´tic, di·dac´ti·cal** *adj.* instructive; inclined to sermonizing –**di·dac´ti·cal·ly** *adv.* –**di·dac´ti·cism** *n.*

**die** *vi.* to stop living; to stop working, as of a motor or machine –*n.* a metal stamp

**die´-hard** *adj.* stubborn –*n.* one firmly committed to a fundamental principle, concept, etc.

**di´et** *n.* the food and drink normally consumed; special food as required for health, religious belief, etc. –*vi,* to limit one's intake of food for some reason –**di´e·tar·y, di·e·tet´ic** *adj.* –**di´et·er** *n.* –**di·e·ti´cian** *n.*

**di·e·tet´ics** *n.* the study of diet and its effects on physical health and development

**dif´fer** *vi.* to disagree; to be different

**dif´fer·ence** *n.* a distinctive mark or characteristic; anything that differentiates one thing from another; a variance in quantity, quality, etc.; a disagreement

**dif´fer·ent** *adj.* unlike; changed; diverse –**dif´fer·ent·ly** *adv.* –**dif´fer·ent·ness** *n.*

**dif·fer·en´tial** *adj.* of a difference; able to cause varied results *—n.* a difference; a gear that alters the output of an engine **—dif·fer·en´tial·ly** *adv.*

**dif·fer·en´ti·ate** *vi.* to become different *—vt.* to make different; to recognize a difference; to display a difference **—dif·fer·en·ti·a´tion** *n.*

**dif´fi·cult´** *adj.* requiring considerable effort; hard to accomplish, endure, please, understand, etc.; hard to deal with or satisfy **—dif´fi·cult´ly** *adv.* **—dif´fi·cul´ty** *n.*

**dif´fi·dence** *n.* a lack of self-confidence

**dif´fi·dent** *adj.* lacking confidence; shy; insecure **—dif´fi·dent·ly** *adv.*

**dif·fuse´** *adj.* widely spread or dispersed; of rambling or excessively wordy speech *—vi., vt.* to spread in all directions; to disperse widely **—dif·fuse´ly** *adv.* **—dif·fuse´ness** *n.*

**dif·fus´er, dif·fus´or** *n.* a device that diffuses, such as frosted glass covering a light bulb, or a baffle mounted in front of a loudspeaker

**dif·fus´i·ble** *adj.* suitable for effecting diffusion; able to be diffused **—dif·fus´i·bly** *adv.*

**dif·fu´sion** *n.* the dissemination of light or sound so as to create a soft, even impression over a wide area **—dif·fu´sion·al** *adj.*

**dif·fu´sive** *adj.* circulating; spread about **—dif·fu´sive·ly** *adv.* **—dif·fu´sive·ness** *n.*

**dig** *vt.* to make a hole; to uncover, as by removing protection or by careful study *—n.* a sarcastic remark **—dig in** get to work **—digs** living quarters **—dig´ger** *n.*

**di´gest** *n.* a condensation of a previously published literary work; a collection of works **—di·gest´** *vt.* to condense or summarize a literary work; to convert food for absorption by the body; to study and absorb information **—di·ges´tion** *n.*

**di·gest´i·ble** *adj.* able or fit to be digested **—di·gest·i·bil´i·ty** *n.* **—di·gest´i·bly** *adv.*

**di·ges´tive** *adj.* pertaining to or conducive to the digestion of food *—n.* anything that aids digestion **—di·ges´tive·ly** *adv.* **—di·ges´tive·ness** *n.*

**digestive system** the chain of body organs that ingest food, process and use part for energy, then discard waste matter

**dig´gings** *pl. n.* material unearthed; a place where digging takes place, as a mine

**dig´it** *n.* a finger or toe; one of the units of a numbering system, as 0 to 9 in base 10

**dig´i·tal** *adj.* discrete, having specific value; expressed in the units of a particular numbering system **—dig´i·tal·ly** *adv.*

**digital computer** a computer that manipulates digital data

**digital data** data represented in discrete values, in contrast to *analog*

**dig·i·tal´is** *n.* a medicine used by heart patients

**dig´ni·fied** *adj.* characterized by or displaying dignity; courtly or reserved **—dig´ni·fied·ly** *adv.*

**dig´ni·fy´** *vt.* to honor; to make someone or something seem more worthy than it is: *dignify a retreat by calling it an advance to the rear*

**dig´ni·tar´y** *n.* one of high rank or position

**dig´ni·ty** *n.* a presence that commands respect; poise; stateliness

**di·gress´** *vi.* to stray; as from the subject in speaking or writing **—di·gres´sion** *n.* **—di·gres´sion·al** *adj.*

**di·gres´sive** *adj.* distinguished by rambling or a departure from the main subject **—di·gres´sive·ly** *adv.* **—di·gres´sive·ness** *n.*

**dike** *n.* an embankment constructed to prevent flooding

**di·lap´i·date** *vi., vt.* to fall or cause to fall into disrepair or ruin **—di·lap·i·da´tion** *n.*

**di·lap´i·dat·ed** *adj.* broken down; fallen into disrepair

**di´late** *vi., vt.* to make or become larger; to expand **—di·lat·a·bil´i·ty** *n.* **—di·lat´a·ble** *adj.* **—di·lat´a·bly** *adv.* **—di·la´tive** *adj.*

**di´lat·ed** *adj.* expanded or distended **—di·lat´ed·ness** *n.*

**di·la´tion** *n.* a widening or expansion; the process of dilating

**di·la´tor** *n.* something that causes dilation, such as a muscle in the eye that dilates the pupil or a surgical instrument for spreading an opening

**dil´a·to·ry** *adj.* intended to delay; inclined to delay **—dil·a·to´ri·ly** *adv.* **—dil´a·to·ri·ness** *n.*

**di·lem´ma** *n.* a situation that calls for a choice between equally unpleasant options; any serious predicament **—on the horns of a dilemma** a choice between equally undesirable options

**dil´et·tan·te** *n.* one who dabbles in something for personal amusement; a lover of the arts *—adj.* characteristic of a dilettante **—dil´et·tan·tish** *adj.* **—dil´et·tan·te·ism, dil´et·tan·tism** *n.*

**dil´i·gent** *adj.* industrious; showing painstaking effort **—dil´i·gence** *n.* **—dil´i·gent·ly** *adv.*

**dill** *n.* an herb whose seeds or leaves are used to flavor foods

**dil´ly·dal·ly** *vi.* to waste time

**di·lute´** *adj.* thinned or weakened *—vt.* to make thinner or weaker by adding something **—di·lute´ness, di·lu´tion** *n.*

**dim** *adj.* faint, murky; ill defined; indistinct, as a sound; not encouraging: *dim prospects* *—vi., vt.* to grow or make faint or indistinct **—dim´ly** *adv.* **—dim´ness** *n.*

**di·men´sion** *n.* the measure of a thing, as its length, width or depth **—di·men´sion·al** *adj.* **—di·men·sion·al´i·ty** *n.* **—di·men´sion·al·ly** *adv.*

**di·min´ish** *vt., vi.* to make or become reduced in size, importance, etc. **—di·min´ish·a·ble** *adj.* **—di·min´ish·ment** *n.*

**diminishing returns** a lessening proportional increase, as in productivity or profitability, as more improvements or incentives are introduced

**dim·i·nu´tion** *n.* a lessening or reduction; something reduced **—dim·i·nu´tion·al** *adj.*

**di·min´u·tive** *adj.* very small; of a word or suffix expressing diminished size *—n.* something small; a word form expressing diminished size or station, as piglet for a small pig or sonny for a young son **—di·min´u·tive·ly** *adv.* **—di·min´u·tive·ness** *n.*

**dim´mer** *n.* a device for reducing the brightness of a lamp or light

**dim´ple** *n.* an indentation on the body, often on the cheek or chin; any small indentation, as a dent on a car body *—vt., vi.* to mark with or form dimples **—dim´ply** *adj.*

**din** *n.* a loud clamor

**dine** *vi.* to eat, often of a formal affair in the company of others *—vt.* to entertain at dinner

**din´er** *n.* one who is eating; in the US, a small informal restaurant

**di·nette´** *n.* a small dining area; tables and chairs for a dining area

**din´ghy** *n.* a small boat, often a tender to a larger boat or ship

**din´gy** *adj.* drab or dirty; grimy **—din´gi·ly** *adv.* **—din´gi·ness** *n.*

**dining room** living space set aside for taking meals

**dink´y** *adj.* diminutive; small

**din´ner** *n.* the main meal of the day; a social event featuring a large meal

**dinner jacket** a man's jacket worn on formal occasions; a tuxedo jacket

**dinner theater** a restaurant in which theatrical entertainment accompanies or follows dinner

**diph´thong´** *n.* a complex vowel sound made by sliding from one vowel to another in the same syllable

**di·plo´ma** *n.* a document testifying to completion of a course of study

**di·plo´ma·cy** *n.* the art of managing affairs between political entities; the ability to act with finesse and tact **—dip´lo·mat´** *n.* **—dip´lo·mat´ic** *adj.* **—dip·lo·mat´i·cal·ly** *adv.*

**diplomatic corps** collectively, those who staff a legation

**diplomatic immunity** exemption for members of the diplomatic corps from the taxes, court suits, etc. in the country to which they are posted

**dip´stick** *n.* a rod for measuring the level of liquid in a container; a stupid or silly person

**dire** *adj.* serious; extremely desperate; urgent; requiring immediate action: dire necessity **—dire´ly** *adv.* **—dire´ness** *n.*

**di·rect´** *adj.* straight; being the straightest course; uninterrupted in line of descent; immediate; absolute: *a direct opposite*; straight-forward or sincere *—vt.* to control or manage; to point out or guide; to instruct or order; to aim: *direct one's gaze* **—di·rect·ly** *adv.* **—di·rect´ness** *n.*

**direct current** electricity that flows in one direction

**direct deposit** a system whereby all or part of one's wages are credited to a bank account

**direct election** the selection of candidates for office by voters directly rather than through delegates

**di·rec´tion** *n.* instruction; supervision; a command; the point toward which a thing is facing or moving — **di·rec´tion·al** *adj.* **—di·rec·tion·al´i·ty** *n.* **di·rec´tion·al·ly** *adv.*

**di·rec´tive** *n.* an official order *—adj.* serving to rule or govern

**direct mail** advertising or sales material posted directly to specific individuals or households

**direct marketing** the sale or attempted sale of goods or services to specific persons or households, as by mail, telephone, etc.

**di·rec´tor** *n.* one who supervises or manages

**di·rec´to·rate** *n.* the board of directors of an organization; the office and trappings of a company or corporate director **—di·rec·to´ri·al** *adj.* **—di·rec´tor·ship** *n.*

**di·rec´to·ry** *n.* an alphabetical reference, as of individuals, companies, products, etc.; a directorate

**direct tax** a tax assessed on the person who pays it, such as an income or sales tax, in contrast to taxes paid by others and passed on through higher prices

**dirge** *n.* a mournful musical or literary work

**dir´i·gi·ble** *n.* an airship

**dirk** *n.* a dagger

**dirt** *adj.* surfaced with earth, as **a dirt road** or **a dirt floor** *—n.* soil or earth; anything unclean; gossip or scandal; pornography

**dirt-cheap** extremely inexpensive

**dirt´y** *adj.* soiled or having a soiled appearance; vulgar, lewd; contaminated *—vi., vt.* to soil or stain **—dirty linen** information that could prove embarrassing if generally known **—dirty pool** unfair tactics **—dirt´i·ly** *adv.* **—dirt´i·ness** *n.*

**dis·a´ble** *vt.* to make unfit for use; to incapacitate **—dis·a·bil´i·ty** *n.* **—dis·a´ble·ment** *n.* **—dis·a´bling** *adj.* **—dis·a´bling·ly** *adv.*

**dis·a´bled** *adj.* inoperative, as of a motor vehicle; incapacitated, as of a physical impairment *—n.* those who are physically incapacitated, considered as a group

**dis·a·buse´** *vt.* to rid of a false notion; to clarify

**dis´ad·van´tage** *n.* a handicap; unfavorable circumstances *—vt.* to hinder **—dis´ad·van´taged** *adj.* **—dis´ad·van·ta´geous** *adj.* **—dis´ad·van·ta´geous·ly** *adv.* **—dis´ad·van·ta´geous·ness** *n.*

**dis·af·fect´** *vt.* to cause estrangement; to alienate **—dis·**

**af·fect´ed** *adj.* **–dis·af·fect´ed·ly** *adv.* **–dis·af·fec´tion** *n.*

**dis´a·gree´** *vi.* to differ; to quarrel; to produce discomfort, as by eating certain foods **–dis·a·gree´ment** *n.*

**dis·a·gree´a·ble** *adj.* unpleasant; quarrelsome **–dis·a·gree´a·ble·ness** *n.* **–dis·a·gree´a·bly** *adv.*

**dis·al·low´** *vt.* to refuse to permit; to reject **–dis·al·low´a·ble** *adj.* **–dis·al·low´ance** *n.*

**dis´ap·pear´** *vi.* to pass from sight; to become extinct **–dis´ap·pear´ance** *n.*

**dis·ap·point´** *vt.* to fail to satisfy; to prevent fulfillment of the expectation of **–dis´ap·point´ment** *n.*

**dis·ap·point´ed** *adj.* frustrated in a desire or expectation **–dis·ap·point´ed·ly** *adv.*

**dis·ap·point´ing** *adj.* frustrating; not meeting expectation **–dis·ap·point´ing·ly** *adv.*

**dis·ap·prove´** *vi., vt.* to frown upon; to condemn **–dis·ap·prov´al** *n.* **–dis·ap·prov´er** *n.* **–dis·ap·prov´ing·ly** *adv.*

**dis´arm´** *vt.* to take weapons from; to weaken, render powerless; to win over by charm *–vi.* to relinquishment arms **–dis´arm´ing** *adj.* **–dis´arm´ing·ly** *adv.*

**dis´ar´ma·ment** *n.* the relinquishing of arms; the reduction or limitation of military forces or weapons

**dis·ar·ray´** *n.* a state of confusion or disorder *–vi.* to throw into confusion

**dis·as·sem´ble** *vt.* to tear down or dismantle **–dis·as·sem´bly** *n.*

**dis·as·so´ci·ate** *vt.* to separate; to cease to consider as allied; to withdraw from an alliance or relationship **–dis·as·so·ci·a´tion** *n.*

**dis·as´ter** *n.* an incidence of great harm or distress **–dis·as´trous** *adj.* **–dis·as´trous·ly** *adv.* **–dis·as´trous·ness** *n.*

**disaster area** a region officially recognized as a victim of disaster, such as a flood or hurricane, and often eligible for government aid

**dis·a·vow´** *vt.* to deny, as knowledge of or responsibility for **–dis·a·vow´a·ble** *adj.* **–dis·a·vow´al** *adj.* **–dis·a·vow´er** *n.*

**dis·band´** *vi.* to cease to function as a group *–vt.* to dissolve a group or organization; to release from military service **–dis·band´ment** *n.*

**dis·bar´** *vt.* to withdraw a lawyer's right to practice **–dis·bar´ment** *n.*

**dis´be·lieve´** *vi., vt.* to refuse to believe; to consider as false **–dis´be·lief´** *n.* **–dis·be·liev´er** *n.*

**dis·burse´** *vt.* to pay out **–dis·burs´a·ble** *adj.* **–dis·burse´ment** *n.* **–dis·burs´er** *n.*

**dis´card** *n.* something cast off or abandoned **–dis·card´** *vt.* to throw away; to cast aside or reject **–dis·card´a·ble** *adj.* **–dis·card´er** *n.*

**dis·cern´** *vt.* to perceive with the sight or in the mind; to recognize, especially as being different *–vi.* to recognize a difference **–dis·cern´i·ble** *adj.* **–dis·cern´i·bly** *adv.* **–dis·cern´ment** *n.*

**dis·cern´ing** *adj.* having good judgment; discriminating **–dis·cern´ing·ly** *adv.*

**dis·charge´** *vt.* to unload, as passengers or freight; to release, as from confinement or duty; to fulfill an obligation; to fire a weapon **–dis·charge´, dis´charge** *n.* the act of unloading, dismissing, etc.; that which is discharged **–dis·charge´a·ble** *adj.* **–dis·charge´er** *n.*

**dis·ci´ple** *n.* an active follower or adherent of a teacher or concept **–dis·ci´ple·ship** *n.*

**dis´ci·pline** *n.* a branch of knowledge or learning; formal training; self-control; acceptance of authority; punishment *–vt.* to train or control; to punish

**dis·ci·pli·nar´i·an** *n.* one who maintains or upholds strict discipline

**dis´ci·pli·nar·y** *adj.* relating to a branch of knowledge; punitive, as punishment for wrongdoing **–dis´ci·plin·er** *n.*

**dis·claim´** *vt.* to give up or deny a claim or connection **–dis·clam´a·to·ry** *adj.*

**dis·claim´er** *n.* a denial of responsibility; a relinquishing of a right or claim **–dis·cla·ma´tion** *n.*

**dis·close´** *vt.* to reveal or make known **–dis·clos´er** *n.* **–dis·clo´sure** *n.*

**dis·col´or** *vt.* to alter color, as by fading, soiling, etc. *–vi.* to become faded or soiled **–dis·col·or·a´tion, dis·col´or·ment** *n.*

**dis·com·bob´u·late** *vt.* to embarrass; to confuse **–dis·com·bob·u·la´tion** *n.*

**dis·com´fit** *vt.* to frustrate the plans or aspirations of; to make uncomfortable **–dis·com´fi·ture** *n.*

**dis·com´fort** *n.* physical or mental distress; uneasiness *–vt.* to make uneasy **–dis·com´fort·a·ble** *adj.* **–dis·com´fort·ing·ly** *adv.*

**dis·com·mode´** *vt.* to cause inconvenience **–dis·com·mo´di·ous** *adj.* **–dis·com·mo´di·ous·ly** *adv.* **–dis·com·mo´di·ous·ness** *n.*

**dis´con·cert´** *vt.* to confuse or embarrass **–dis·con·cert´ment** *n.*

**dis´con·cert´ed** *adj.* characterized by confusion or embarrassment **–dis´con·cert´ed·ly** *adv.* **–dis´con·cert´ed·ness** *n.*

**dis·con·cert´ing** *adj.* tending to cause confusion or embarrassment **–dis·con·cert´ing·ly** *adv.* **–dis´con·cert´ing·ness** *n.*

**dis´con·nect´** *vt.* to detach **–dis·con·nec´tion** *n.*

**dis·con·nect´ed** *adj.* separated; cut off; disjointed or incoherent, as a narrative **–dis·con·nect´ed·ly** *adv.* **–dis·con·nect´ed·ness** *n.*

**dis´con´so·late** *adj.* dejected, gloomy; inconsolable **–dis·con´so·late·ly** *adv.* **–dis·con´so·late·ness, dis·con·so·la´tion** *n.*

**dis´con·tent´** *adj.* displeased with present circumstances —*n.* a lack of satisfaction with present circumstances —*vt.* to make displeased or dissatisfied —**dis·con·tent´ed** *adj.* —**dis·con·tent´ed·ly** *adv.* —**dis·con·tent´ed·ness, dis·con·tent´ment** *n.*

**dis·con·tin´u·ance** *n.* a temporary cessation or termination; a suspension of legal action —**dis·con·tin·u·a´tion** *n.*

**dis´con·tin´ue** *vi., vt.* to stop or end

**dis·con·tin´u·ous** *adj.* disordered; disconnected; irrational —**dis·con·tin´u·ous·ly** *adv.* —**dis·con·ti·nu´i·ty** *n.*

**dis´cord´** *n.* a lack of harmony, disagreement; harsh sounds —**dis·cor´dance** *n.* —**dis´cord´ant** *adj.* —**dis·cor´dant·ly** *adv.*

**dis´count** *n.* a reduction or rebate from a standard price —**dis·count´** *vt.* to rebate or sell at a reduced price; to tender the proceeds of a loan after deducting interest; to minimize or reject as untrue or of little importance —**dis·count´a·ble** *adj.* —**dis´count·er** *n.*

**discount store** a shop or outlet specializing in merchandise sold at less than the usual price

**dis·cour´age** *vt.* to advise against; to attempt to dissuade; to dishearten —**dis·cour´age·ment** *n.* —**dis·cour´ag·ing** *adj.* —**dis·cour´ag·ing·ly** *adv.*

**dis´course´** *n.* to exchange ideas in conversation; a lengthly treatment of a subject in writing or speech —**dis·course´** *vi.* to converse; to write or speak at length —**dis´course´er** *n.*

**dis·cour´te·ous** *adj.* impolite; rude —**dis·cour´te·ous·ly** *adv.* —**dis·cour´te·ous·ness** *n.*

**dis·cour´te·sy** *n.* bad manners; an impolite manner, attitude, etc.

**dis·cov´er** *vt.* to obtain knowledge; to detect or make known, esp. for the first time —**dis·cov´er·a·ble** *adj.* —**dis·cov´er·er** *n.*

**dis·cov´er·y** *n.* detection or disclosure; findings, a thing discovered

**dis·cred´it** *n.* damage to one's reputation; anything causing such damage —*vt.* to cast doubt upon; to damage the reputation of another —**dis·cred´it·a·ble** *adj.* —**dis·cred´it·a·bly** *adv.*

**dis·creet´** *adj.* prudent; exercising caution, especially concerning the privacy and personal affairs of others —**dis·creet´ly** *adv.* —**dis·creet´ness** *n.*

**dis·crep´an·cy** *n.* a variance or inconsistency —**dis·crep´ant** *adj.* —**dis·crep'ant·ly** *adv.*

**dis·crete'** *adj.* comprised of unconnected, distinct parts —**dis·crete´ly** *adv.* —**dis·crete´ness** *n.*

**dis·cre´tion** *n.* the quality of being discreet; the ability or freedom to make decisions on one's own —**dis·cre´tion·ar·i·ly** *adv.* —**dis·cre´tion·ar·y** *adj.*

**dis·crim´i·nate´** *vi., vt.* to make distinction; to differentiate —**dis·crim´i·nate·ly** *adv.* —**dis·crim´i·na´tion** *n.*

**dis·crim´i·nat·ing** *adj.* able to differentiate; discerning —**dis·crim´i·nat·ing·ly** *adv.*

**dis·crim´i·na·tive** *adj.* having or forming distinctions —**dis·crim´i·na·tive·ly** *adv.*

**dis·crim´i·na·to·ry** *adj.* judgmental; discriminating

**dis·cur´sive** *adj.* rambling; wandering from one subject to another —**dis·cur´sive·ly** *adv.* —**dis·cur´sive·ness** *n.*

**dis·cuss´** *vt.* to talk or write about —**dis·cuss´a·ble, dis·cuss´i·ble** *adj.* —**dis·cuss´er** *n.* —**dis·cus´sion** *n.*

**dis·dain´** *n.* a show of contempt —*vt.* to treat with contempt; to deem unsuited to one's position

**dis·dain´ful** *adj.* showing contempt —**dis·dain´ful·ly** *adv.* —**dis·dain´ful·ness** *n.*

**dis·ease´** *n.* an illness of the body; any unsound or harmful condition —**dis·eased´** *n.*

**dis´em·bark´** *vi., vt.* to leave or be taken from a conveyance —**dis·em·bar·ka´tion, dis·em·bark´ment** *n.*

**dis´em·bod´y** *vt.* to separate from physical existence —**dis·em·bod´ied** *adj.* —**dis·em·bod´i·ment** *n.*

**dis·en·chant´** *vt.* to free from delusion —**dis·en·chant´er** *n.* —**dis´en·chant´ing·ly** *adv.* —**dis·en·chant´ment** *n.*

**dis·en·cum´ber** *vt.* to relieve of a burden or difficulty —**dis·en·cum´ber·ment** *n.*

**dis·en·fran´chise** *vt.* to deprive of a right or privilege; to deprive of the right to vote —**dis·en·fran´chise·ment** *n.*

**dis·en·tan´gle** *vt.* to unsnarl; to extricate; to free from confusion —**dis·en·tan´gle·ment** *n.*

**dis·fa´vor** *n.* disapproval —*vt.* to look upon with disapproval

**dis·fig´ure** *vt.* to spoil the appearance of —**dis·fig·u·ra´tion, dis·fig´ure·ment** *n.*

**dis·fran´chise** *vt.* disenfranchise

**dis·gorge´** *vi, vt.* to discharge the contents of

**dis·grace'** *n.* a loss of respect or honor; a thing that brings dishonor —*vt.* to bring dishonor upon; to dishonor by chastising publicly —**dis·grace´ful** *adj.* **dis·grace´ful·ly** *adv.* —**dis·grace´ful·ness** *n.*

**dis·grun´tle** *vt.* to make unhappy; to dissatisfy

**dis·guise´** *n.* that used to conceal the identity of a person or thing —*vt.* to alter or conceal the identity of; to misrepresent —**dis·guis´a·ble** *adj.* —**dis·guised´** *adj.*

**dis·gust´** *n.* a deep dislike; an aversion —*vt.* to arouse dislike; to offend —**dis·gust´ed** *adj.* —**dis·gust´ed·ly** *adv.* —**dis·gust´ed·ness** *n.*

**dis·gust´ing** *adj.* provoking disgust; nasty; distasteful, nauseating —**dis·gust´ing·ly** *adv.*

**dish** *n.* a container for food; food prepared in a particular way —*vt.* to serve up, as food

**dis·ha·bille´** *n.* a condition of partial, uncoordinated, or incongruous dress

**dis·har´mo·ny** *n.* a lack of harmony; dissonance; discord, as between persons, colors, etc. —**dis·har·**

**mo´ni·ous** *adj.* **—dis·har·mo´ni·ous·ly** *adv.* **—dis·har´mo·nize** *vi., vt.*

**dis·heart´en** *vt.* to lessen the courage, resolve, enthusiasm, etc. of

**dis·heart´en·ing** *adj.* tending to cause a loss of courage, enthusiasm, optimism, etc. **—dis·heart´en·ing·ly** *adv.* **—dis·heart´en·ment** *n.*

**di·shev´eled, di·shev´elled** *adj.* untidy; rumpled; disorderly **—di·shev´el** *vt.* **—di·shev´el·ment** *n.*

**dis·hon´est** *adj.* lacking honesty; deceitful; untrustworthy **—dis·hon´est·ly** *adv.* **—dis·hon´es·ty** *n.*

**dis·hon´or** *n.* a loss of honor, respect, etc.; something causing a loss of respect *—vt.* to cause a loss of honor; to treat with disrespect; to refuse to honor or pay, as an invoice **—dis·hon´or·a·ble** *adj.* **—dis·hon´or·a·ble·ness** *n.* **—dis·hon´or·a·bly** *adv.*

**dis´il·lu´sion** *vt.* to free from a false sentiment; to disappoint or disenchant **—dis·il·lu´sion·ment** *n.*

**dis·in·clined´** *adj.* hesitant; reluctant **—dis·in·cli·na´tion** *n.* **—dis·in·cline´** *vt., vi.*

**dis´in·fect´** *vt.* to sanitize; to sterilize **—dis·in·fec´tion** *n.*

**dis·in·fec´tant** *adj.* serving to sanitize *—n.* any substance used to sanitize

**dis·in·fec´tive** *adj.* disinfectant

**dis´in·gen´u·ous** *adj.* deceitful; insincere; crafty **—dis·in·gen´u·ous·ly** *adv.* **—dis·in·gen´u·ous·ness** *n.*

**dis´in·her´it** *vt.* to deprive of a right or privilege, especially the right of inheritance **—dis·in·her´i·tance** *n.*

**dis·in´te·grate** *vi., vt.* to break into fragments **—dis·in´te·grative** *adj.* **—dis´in·te·gra´tion** *n.* **—dis·in´te·gra·tor** *n.*

**dis·in·ter´** *vt.* to dig up from a grave **—dis·in·ter´ment** *n.*

**dis·in´ter·est** *n.* a lack of concern

**dis´in´ter·est·ed** *adj.* free of bias; impartial; indifferent **—dis´in´ter·est·ed·ly** *adv.* **—dis´in´ter·est·ed·ness** *n.*

**dis·join´** *vt.* to detach or separate *—vi* to become separated

**dis·joint´** *vt.* to dismember; to cut or take apart; to separate

**dis·joint´ed** *adj.* disconnected; lacking unity; incoherent; rambling **—dis·joint´ed·ly** *adv.* **—dis·joint´ed·ness** *n.*

**dis·junc´tive** *adj.* separating; causing sharp divisions **—dis·junc´tion, dis·junc´ture** *n.* **—dis·junc´tive·ly** *adv.*

**disk** *n.* a thin flat circular object; anything similar in form

**disk drive** the mechanism that spins a computer storage disk

**disk·ette´** *n.* a removable disk for computer data storage

**dis·like´** *n.* a feeling of distaste or aversion *—vt.* to look upon with distaste **—dis·lik´a·ble, dis·like´a·ble** *adj.*

**dis·lo´cate´** *vt.* to put out of proper place or position, esp. of a bone **—dis´lo·ca´tion** *n.*

**dis·lodge´** *vt.* to force from a position **—dis·lodge´ment** *n.*

**dis·loy´al** *adj.* unfaithful **—dis·loy´al·ly** *adv.* **—dis·loy´al·ty** *n.*

**dis´mal** *adj.* dreary, bleak **—dis´mal·ly** *adv.* **—dis´mal·ness** *n.*

**dis·man´tle** *vt.* to take apart systematically; to strip of furniture, equipment, etc. **—dis.man´tle·ment** *n.*

**dis·may´** *n.* a loss of resolve in the face of difficulty *—vt.* to cause alarm or loss of courage by describing impending danger or difficulty

**dis·mem´ber** *vt.* to cut up; to mutilate **—dis·mem´ber·ment** *n.*

**dis·miss´** *vt.* to send away; to release from employment; to put out of mind **—dis·mis´sal** *n.* **—dis·miss´i·ble** *adj.*

**dis·mis´sive** *adj.* displaying a lack of concern

**dis´o·be´di·ent** *adj.* refusing to obey; insubordinate **—dis´o·be´di·ence** *n.* **—dis·o·be´di·ent·ly** *adv.*

**dis´o·bey´** *vi., vt.* to fail or refuse to obey

**dis·or´der** *n.* a state of confusion or disarray; a public disturbance; an illness *—vt.* to throw into confusion or disarray **—dis·or´dered** *adj.* **—dis·or´dered·ly** *adv.* **—dis·or´dered·ness** *n.*

**dis·or´der·ly** *adj.* untidy, lacking order; rowdy, creating a disturbance **—dis·or´der·li·ness** *n.*

**dis·or´gan·ize** *vt.* to cause or create disorder; to eradicate the unity of **—dis·or·gan·i·za´tion** *n.*

**dis·o´ri·ent, dis·o´ri·en·tate** *vt.* to confuse, bewilder **—dis·o´ri·en·ta´tion** *n.*

**dis·own´** *vt.* to refuse to acknowledge or accept; to disinherit

**dis·par´age** *vt.* to discredit; to belittle **—dis·par´age·ment** *n.* **—dis·par´ag·ing** *adj.* **—dis·par´ag·ing·ly** *adv.*

**dis´pa·rate** *adj.* dissimilar; diversified **—dis·par´ate·ly** *adv.* **—dis·par´ate·ness** *n.*

**dis·par´i·ty** *n.* a difference, as in quality or quantity

**dis·pas´sion** *n.* a lack of emotional involvement; freedom from passion

**dis·pas´sion·ate** *adj.* free from emotional involvement; detached **—dis·pas´sion·ate·ly** *adv.* **—dis·pas´sion·ate·ness** *n.*

**dis·patch´** *n.* a sending out; a message sent; promptness in action *—vt.* to send out, usually with haste; to act quickly; to kill **—dis·patch´er** *n.*

**dis·pel´** *vt.* to drive away; to eliminate, as a rumor

**dis·pen´sa·ble** *adj.* not essential; unnecessary; that can be distributed **—dis·pens·a·bil´i·ty** *n.* **—dis·pen´sa·ble·ness** *n.*

**dis·pen´sa·ry** *n.* a place for obtaining medicines and medical aid

**dis·pen·sa´tion** *n.* a distribution; something distributed; a release or exemption, as from an obligation

–dis·pen·sa´tion·al *adj.* –dis´pen·sa·tor *n.*
**dis·pense´** *vt.* to distribute; give out; to administer, as justice; to absolve –**dispense with** to do without –dis·pens´er *n.*
**dis·perse´** *vt.* to cause to scatter widely; to drive off; to cause to disappear or dissipate, as mist; to separate light into its component colors –*vi.* to scatter in various directions; to disappear –**dis·per´sal, dis·per´sion** *n.* –**dis·pers´er** *n.* –**dis·pers´i·ble** *adj.* –**dis·per´sive** *adj.*
**dis·place´** *vt.* to move from a proper or usual place; to take the place of; to remove from office –**dis·plac´a·ble** *adj.* –**dis·place´ment** *n.* –**dis·plac´er** *n.*
**dis·play´** *n.* a public showing –*vt.* to show publicly
**dis·please´** *vi., vt.* to dissatisfy or annoy; to offend –**dis·pleas´ing·ly** *adv.* –**dis·pleas´ure** *n.*
**dis·pos´a·ble** *adj.* designed to be discarded after a single use –**dis·pos´a·bil·i·ty** *n.*
**disposable income** income that remains after taxes
**dis·pose´** *vt.* to place in proper order or form; to settle; to adjust mentally so as to be amenable or receptive –**dis·pos´al** *n.* –**dis·pos´er** *n.*
**dis·po·si´tion** *n.* one's usual temperament or inclination; a final settlement or solution
**dis·pos·sess´** *vt.* to deprive of a possession –**dis·pos·sessed´** *adj.* –**dis·pos·ses´sion** *n.* –**dis·pos·ses´sor** *n.*
**dis·pro·por´tion** *n.* a lack of harmony or symmetry –*vt.* to make disproportionate –**dis·pro·por´tion·al** *adj.* –**dis·pro·por´tion·al·ly** *adv.*
**dis·pro·por´tion·ate** *adj.* out of proportion; uneven –**dis·pro·por´tion·ate·ly** *adv.* –**dis·pro·por´tion·ate·ness** *n.*
**dis·prove´** *vt.* to expose as false; to refute –**dis·prov´a·ble** *adj.*
**dis·pu´ta·ble** *adj.* questionable; uncertain –**dis·put·a·bil´i·ty** *n.* –**dis·put´a·bly** *adv.*
**dis·pu´tant** *n.* one who quarrels or disagrees –*adj.* involving dispute
**dis´pu·ta´tion** *n.* a controversy; the act of disagreeing; a formal debate –**dis·pu·ta´tious, dis·pu´ta·tive** *adj.* –**dis·pu·ta´tious·ly** *adv.* –**dis·pu·ta´tious·ness** *n.*
**dis·pute´** *n.* a quarrel or argument; a disagreement –*vi.* to argue –*vt.* to argue about; to doubt the truth of –**dis·put´er** *n.*
**dis·qual´i·fy** *vt.* to declare ineligible –**dis·qual·i·fi·ca´tion** *n.*
**dis·qui´et** *n.* anxiety –*vt.* to make anxious
**dis·re·gard´** *n.* a lack of regard or respect –*vt.* to ignore or neglect
**dis·re·pair´** *n.* in need of repair; a product of neglect
**dis·rep´u·ta·ble** *adj.* lacking in character or respectability –**dis·rep´u·ta·ble·ness** *n.* –**dis·rep´u·ta·bly** *adv.*
**dis·re·pute´** *n.* a lack or loss of reputation
**dis·re·spect´** *n.* discourtesy; insolence –*vt.* to treat discourteously –**dis´re·spect´ful** *adj.* –**dis´re·spect´ful·ly** *adv.* –**dis´re·spect´ful·ness** *n.*
**dis·robe´** *vi., vt.* to undress –**dis·robe´ment** *n.*
**dis·rupt´** *vt.* to intrude; to upset an orderly process –**dis·rupt´er, dis·rupt´or** *n.* –**dis·rup´tion** *n.*
**dis·rup´tive** *adj.* rebellious; unruly; intruding –**dis·rup´tive·ly** *adv.* –**dis·rup´tive·ness** *n.*
**dis·sat·is·fac´to·ry** *adj.* not acceptable
**dis·sat´is·fy** *vt.* to fail to please –**dis·sat·is·fac´tion** *n.* –**dis·sat´is·fied** *adj.*
**dis·sect´** *vt.* to separate into parts; to examine closely –**dis·sect´ed** *adj.* –**dis·sec´tion** *n.* –**dis·sec´tor** *n.*
**dis·sem´ble** *vt.* to conceal so as to deceive –*vi.* to conceal one's true nature –**dis·sem´blance** *n.* –**dis·sem´bler** *n.*
**dis·sem´i·nate´** *vt.* to scatter; to spread widely –**dis·sem´i·na´tion** *n.* –**dis·sem´i·na´tor** *n.*
**dis·sen´sion** *n.* a disagreeing; a difference of opinion
**dis·sent´** *n.* a difference of opinion –*vi.* to express disagreement –**dis·sent´er** *n.* –**dis·sent´ing** *adj.* –**dis·sent´ing·ly** *adv.*
**dis·sen´tience** *n.* disagreement; opposition
**dis·sen´tient** *adj.* disagreeing –*n.* a dissenter
**dis·sen´tious** *adj.* opposing; disagreeing –**dis·sen´tious·ly** *adv.*
**dis´ser·tate** *vi.* speak at length
**dis´ser·ta´tion** *n.* a lengthly discourse –**dis·ser·ta´tion·al** *adj.*
**dis·serve** *vt.* to harm; treat badly
**dis·serv´ice** *n.* a harmful or thoughtless deed
**dis´si·dent** *adj.* hostile; opposed; of those opposing or disagreeing –*n.* one who opposes –**dis´si·dence** *n.* –**dis´si·dent·ly** *adv.*
**dis´sim´i·lar** *adj.* different –**dis·sim´i·lar·ly** *adv.*
**dis·sim´i·lar´i·ty** *n.* a difference; an instance of divergence or deviation
**dis·sim´i·late** *vt., vi.* to make or become different –**dis·sim´i·la·tive** *adj.*
**dis·sim·i·la´tion** *n.* making different
**dis·si·mil´i·tude** *n.* difference
**dis·sim´u·late** *vi., vt.* to conceal or disguise one's feelings by pretense –**dis·sim·u·la´tion** *n.* –**dis·sim´u·la·tive** *adj.* –**dis·sim´u·la·tor** *n.*
**dis´si·pate** *vi.* to waste one's life in debauchery; to vanish by dispersion –*vt.* to scatter, dispel, or disperse; to use recklessly, waste –**dis´si·pa´tion** *n.*
**dis´si·pat·ed** *adj.* scattered; depleted or destroyed; exhibiting the injurious effects of self-indulgence –**dis´si·pat·ed·ly** *adv.* –**dis´si·pat·ed·ness** *n.*
**dis·so´ci·ate** *vi., vt.* to separate; to sever ties –**dis·so´ci·at·ed** *adj.* –**dis·so·ci·a´tion** *n.*
**dis·so´ci·a·tive** *adj.* tending to produce separation
**dis·sol´u·ble** *adj.* able to be dissolved –**dis·sol·u·bil´i·ty, dis·sol´u·ble·ness** *n.*
**dis´so·lute** *adj.* lacking restraint; immoral –**dis´so·lute·ly** *adv.* –**dis´so·lute·ness** *n.*

**dis´so·lu´tion** *n.* a dissolving or termination, as of a meeting, a business, etc.

**dis·solve´** *vi., vt.* to change or cause to change into a liquid; to pass or make pass into solution: *dissolve the cocoa in hot water*; to disintegrate or disappear; to end, as a marriage **–dis·solv·a·bil´i·ty** *adv.* **–dis·solv´a·ble** *adj.* **–dis·solv´ent** *n.*

**dis´so·nance, dis´so·nan·cy** *n.* a disagreeable combination of sound; a lack of agreement or harmony **–dis´so·nant** *adj.* **–dis´so·nant·ly** *adv.*

**dis·suad´a·ble** *adj.* able to be persuaded against

**dis·suade´** *vt.* to persuade from a course of action **–dis·suad´er** *n.* **–dis·sua´sion** *n.*

**dis·sua´sive** *adj.* intended to discourage or prevent **–dis·sua´sive·ly** *adv.* **–dis·sua´sive·ness** *n.*

**dis´tal** *adj.* remote; far from origin or attachment **–dis´tal·ly** *adv.*

**dis´tance** *n.* the time or space between two points; reserve, remoteness *–vt.* to keep away; to act aloof

**dis´tant** *adj.* remote; far apart in time or space; reserved, aloof **–dis´tant·ly** *adv.*

**dis·taste´** *n.* repugnance

**dis·taste´ful** *adj.* offensive; unpleasant **–dis·taste´ful·ly** *adv.* **–dis·taste´ful·ness** *n.*

**dis·tem´per** *n.* an affliction or disease; an infectious disease of animals

**dis·tend´** *vi., vt.* to inflate; to stretch **–dis·ten´si·ble** *adj.* **–dis·ten´sion, dis·ten´tion** *n.*

**dis·til´, dis·till´** *vt.* to extract or concentrate by distillation **–dis·til´la·ble** *adj.*

**dis´til·late** *n.* the result of distillation

**dis·til·la´tion** *n.* the process of refining by heating a substance, then cooling and collecting the condensation; something produced by distilling **–dis·till´er** *n.* **–dis·till´er·y** *n.*

**dis·tinct´** *adj.* undeniably different; definite, unmistakable; clearly perceptible **–dis·tinct´ly** *adv.* **–dis·tinct´ness** *n.*

**dis·tinc´tion** *n.* a specific difference; a distinguishing characteristic or quality; eminence or prestige

**dis·tinc´tive** *adj.* characteristic; having a unique or uncommon quality **–dis·tinc´tive·ly** *adv.* **–dis·tinc´tive·ness** *n.*

**dis·tin´guish** *vi., vt.* to set apart; to recognize clearly; to bring prestige to: *distinguished in literary circles*

**dis·tin´guish·a·ble** *adj.* able to be discerned; perceptible; seen to be unique or different **–dis·tin·guish·a·bil´i·ty, dis·tin´guish·a·ble·ness** *n.* **–dis·tin´guish·a·bly** *adv.*

**dis·tin´guished** *adj.* celebrated, well-known; refined; extraordinary

**dis·tort´** *vt.* to bend out of shape; to misrepresent; to alter so as to spoil: *poor acoustics distorted the sound of the music* **–dis·tort´ed·ness, dis·tor´tion** *n.*

**dis·tor´tive** *adj.* causing distortion

**dis·tract´** *vt.* to divert attention away; to create confusion **–dis·tract´ing** *adj.* **–dis·tract´ing·ly** *adv.*

**dis·tract´ed** *adj.* diverted; confused; **–dis·tract´ed·ly** *adv.* **–dis·tract´ed·ness** *n.*

**dis·trac´tion** *n.* something that diverts one's attention, or that confuses or distresses; a drawing away on one's attention or concentration

**dis·tract´i·ble** *adj.* easily diverted or confused; **–dis·tract´i·bil·i·ty** *n.*

**dis·traught´** *adj.* deeply troubled; severely distressed

**dis·tress´** *n.* suffering, such as pain, anxiety, discomfort, etc.; a condition requiring immediate help: *a ship in distress* *–vt.* to cause pain, anxiety, etc.; to inflict suffering upon **–dis·tressed** *adj.* **–dis·tress´ing·ly** *adv.*

**dis·tress´ful** *adj.* causing worry or torment **–dis·tress´ful·ly** *adv.* **–dis·tress´ful·ness** *n.*

**dis·trib´u·tar·y** *n.* a channel or line of distribution flowing away from a main channel or line

**dis·trib´ute** *vt.* to disburse in more or less equal amounts, or according to a plan **–dis·trib´ut·a·ble** *adj.* **–dis´tri·bu´tion** *n.*

**distribution curve** a graphic representation of the concentration of elements in an array

**dis·trib´u·tive** *adj.* serving to disseminate or classify; pertaining to distribution **–dis·trib´u·tive·ly** *adv.* **–dis·trib´u·tive·ness** *n.*

**dis·trib´u·tor** *n.* one who is authorized to merchandise a particular product or brand; any merchant; a device that dispenses a measured quantity in a timely manner, as the device in an engine that feeds power to the spark plugs

**dis´trict** *n.* an area specially defined or distinguished by some characteristic

**district attorney** in the US, a prosecutor for the government

**dis·trust´** *n.* a lack of trust or confidence *–vt.* to lack confidence in **–dis·trust´ful** *adj.* **–dis·trust´ful·ly** *adv.* **–dis·trust´ful·ness** *n.*

**dis·turb´** *vt.* to upset the serenity or order of; to interrupt; to make uneasy

**dis·tur´bance** *n.* a commotion; disorder; a deviation from the usual

**dis·turbed´** *adj.* distressed, troubled; mentally or emotionally unstable

**dis·u·nite´** *vi., vt.* to divide or separate **–dis·un·ion** *n.*

**dis·use´** *n.* a state of neglect *–vt.* to take out of service; to abandon or discard

**ditch** *n.* a trench or channel used for carrying water or forming a barrier *–vt.* to make a ditch; to get rid of something; to deliberately leave behind

**di´the·ism** *n.* a belief in two supreme beings **–di·the·is´tic, di·the·is´ti·cal** *adj.*

**dith´er** *n.* a nervous or excited condition *–vi.* to act in a nervous or excited manner; to babble **–dith´er·**

y *adj.*
**dit´to** *n.* the same as previous; a repetition *—vt.* to duplicate; make a copy; to repeat **—ditto mark** a symbol ( " ) used in a list to indicate a repeat of the item above it
**dit´ty** *n.* a simple song
**ditty bag** a small bag or pouch for holding personal gear
**di·u·re´sis** *n.* excessive excretion of urine
**di´u·ret´ic** *adj.* tending to increase the output of urine *—n.* a substance that tends to increase the output of urine
**di·ur´nal** *adj.* happening each day; in the daytime **—di·ur´nal·ly** *adv.*
**di·van** *n.* a davenport or sofa
**dive** *n.* a headlong leap, as into water; a sudden dropping, as of prices; the descent of an airplane *—vi., vt.* to plunge or drop
**div´er** *n.* one who dives, esp. an underwater worker or explorer
**di·verge´** *vi.* to move in different directions from a common point **—di·ver´gence** *n.* **—di·ver´gent** *adj.* **—di·ver´gent·ly** *adv.*
**di´vers** *adj.* several
**div´ers** *n. pl.* those who dive
**di·verse´** *adj.* dissimilar; assorted **—di·verse´ly** *adv.* **—di·verse´ness** *n.*
**di·ver´si·fied** *adj.* disparate; dissimilar; sundry **—di·ver´si·ty** *n.*
**di·ver´si·fy´** *vt.* to add variety; to branch out into new fields **—di·ver´si·fi·ca´tion** *n.*
**di·ver´sion** *n.* a turning aside; a distraction **—di·ver´sion·ar·y** *adj.*
**di·vert´** *vt.* to turn aside; to distract
**di·vert´ing** *adj.* engaging; pleasing; entertaining **—di·vert´ing·ly** *adv.*
**di·ver´tisse·ment** *n.* an amusement or distraction, especially during an interlude in a theater performance
**di·vest´** *vt.* to get rid of; to deprive of, as of an office **—di·vest´i·ture, di·vest´ment** *n.*
**di·vide´** *vt.* to separate, as into parts or categories; to distribute in portions; to cause disagreement: *political beliefs divided them* *—vi.* to become separated; to share
**di·vid´ed** *adj.* separated; in disagreement **—di·vid´ed·ly** *adv.* **—di·vid´ed·ness** *n.*
**divided highway** *(US)* a road with a center strip that separates vehicles traveling in opposite directions
**di·vid´er** *n.* anything that serves to separate **—room divider** an article of furniture with open shelves, or a screen used to separate parts of a room
**div´i·dend** *n.* a bonus, often a share of profits divided among stockholders; an unexpected benefit
**div·i·na´tion** *n.* the art of prediction **—di·vin´a·to·ry** *adj.*
**di·vine´** *adj.* of the nature of a diety; godlike; pleasing *—vt.* to predict **—di·vine´ly** *adv.* **—di·vine´ness** *n.*
**di·vin´er** *n.* one who foretells the future; one who determines the presence of that not apparent, such as the location of water underground
**diving bell** a device used for exploring under water, supplied with air from a host vessel
**diving board** a springboard from which one can dive into a swimming pool
**diving suit** a heavy garment worn by a deep sea diver
**divining rod** a forked branch used by a diviner in locating water underground
**di·vin´i·ty** *n.* a divine nature; the study of theology; a type of candy
**di·vis´i·ble** *adj.* able to be separated into smaller parts; capable of being evenly divided by a particular number, leaving no remainder **—di·vis·i·bil´i·ty** *n.* **—di·vis´i·ble·ness** *n.*
**di·vi´sion** *n.* a partition; a portioning or the resulting portion; a rift or disagreement **—di·vi´sional, di·vi´sion·ar·y** *adj.* **—di·vi´sion·al·ly** *adv.*
**di·vi´sive** *adj.* provoking disagreement **—di·vi´sive·ly** *adv.* **—di·vi´sive·ness** *n.*
**di·vi´sor** *n.* the value by which a number is divided
**di·vorce´** *n.* the legal dissolution of a marriage; any radical separation, as of operations within a company or the association of concepts *—vt.* to dissolve a marriage; to entirely separate two or more entities or concepts from association or influence **—di·vorce´ment** *n.*
**di·vulge´** *vt.* to make known; reveal **—di·vulge´ment, di·vul´gence** *n.* **—di·vulg´er** *n.*
**di·vulse´** *vt.* to tear apart **—di·vul´sion** *n.* **—di·vul´sive** *adj.*
**diz´zy** *adj.* light-headed; dazed; silly; flighty **—diz´zi·ly** *adv.* **—diz´zi·ness** *n.*
**DNA** *n.* deoxyribonucleic acid, that carries the genetic code within cells
**do** *vi., vt.* to perform; to cause; to behave **—do in** to murder **—done in** tired; murdered **—do well** to prosper
**dó·a·ble** *adj.* able to be accomplished; profitable or expedient
**do´cent** *n.* a teacher or lecturer; *(US)* a tour guide **—do´cent·ship** *n.*
**doc´ile** *adj.* mild-mannered; submissive **—doc´ile·ly** *adv.* **—do·cil´i·ty** *n.*
**dock** *n.* a pier or wharf *—vt.* to bring a boat or ship into dock; to cut short; to deduct: *dock his wages for arriving late*
**dock´et** *n.* a court calendar
**doc´tor** *n.* one licensed to practice medicine; the highest degree awarded by a college or university *—vt.* to treat an illness or injury; to repair, especially in a makeshift fashion; to alter for some purpose

–**doc´tor·al** *adj.*
**doc´tor·ate** *n.* a doctor's degree
**doc´tri·naire´** *adj.* theoretical –*n.* one favoring theory over fact
**doc´trine** *n.* a statement of principals or policy –**doc´tri·nal** *adj.* –**doc´tri·nal·ly** *adv.*
**doc´u·ment** *n.* a written record of information or evidence –*vt.* to furnish supporting information or evidence –**doc´u·ment·a·ble** *adj.* –**doc·u·men·ta´tion** *n.*
**doc·u·ment´ary** *adj.* regarding a document or documents; of a factual report; based on documents –*n.* a book, movie etc. that presents a purportedly factual report –**doc·u·men·tar´i·an** *n.*
**dod´der** *vt.* to totter, as from age –**dod´der·ing** *adj.* –**dod´der·ing·ly** *adv.*
**dodge** *vt.* to sidestep; to avoid or evade by trickery –*vi.* to move suddenly; to employ trickery –*n.* a deception or ruse –**dodg´er** *n.*
**do´er** *n.* one who achieves
**doff** *vt.* to remove; to discard
**dog** *n.* a domesticated animal related to the wolf
**dog´-ear** *vt.* to turn down the corner of a page –*n.* a folded corner of a page –**dog´-eared** *adj.*
**dog´ged** *adj.* persistent –**dog´ged·ly** *adv.* –**dog´ged·ness** *n.*
**dog´ma** *n.* an authoritative statement of doctrine
**dog·mat´ic, dog·mat´i·cal** *adj.* adhering strictly to doctrine; dictatorial –**dog·mat´i·cal·ly** *adv.* –**dog´ma·tism** *n.* –**dog´ma·tist** *n.*
**doi´ly** *n.* a mat or runner used as a table decoration
**dol´drums** *n.* a depressed state of mind
**dole** *n.* a charitable gift; a thing portioned out carefully –*vt.* to give charitably; to portion out
**dole´ful** *adj.* mournful; full of sadness –**dole´ful·ly** *adv.* –**dole´ful·ness** *n.*
**do´lor** *n.* sorrow; anguish –**dol´or·ous** *adj.* –**do´lo·rous·ly** *adv.* –**do´lo·rous·ness** *n.*
**dolt** *n.* one who is slow-witted –**dolt´ish** *adj.* –**dolt´ish·ly** *adv.* –**dolt´ish·ness** *n.*
**do·main´** *n.* one's sphere of influence or control; territory controlled by a person, government, etc.
**do·mes´tic** *adj.* of a household; fond of caring for a home or family; pertaining to a country; of a tamed animal –*n.* a servant in the home –**do·mes´ti·cal·ly** *adv.*
**do·mes´ti·cate´** *vt.* to bring under control, as a wild plant or animal; to bring and adapt to a new region or country –**do·mes·ti·ca´tion** *n.*
**do·mes·tic´i·ty** *n.* a fondness for home and family
**dom´i·cile** *n.* a place of residence; a home
**dom´i·nate** *vt.* to control; to have preeminence –**dom´i·nance, dom·i·na´tion** *n.* –**dom´i·nant** *adj.* –**dom´i·nant·ly** *adv.*
**dom·i·neer´** *vi., vt.* to tyrannize or bully
**dom·ineer´ing** *adj.* assertive; overbearing –**dom´i·neer´ing·ly** *adv.* –**dom´i·neer´ing·ness**
**do·min´ion** *n.* sovereignty
**do´nate** *vt.* to contribute, especially to a worthy cause –**do·na´tion** *n.*
**done** *adj.* completed
**do´nor** *n.* a contributor
**doom** *n.* inevitable ruin; condemnation –*vt.* to destine for ruination; to condemn
**dooms´day** *n.* a time of final judgment
**door** *n.* an entryway
**dope** *n.* a drug; information
**dor´mant** *adj.* temporarily inactive –**dor´man·cy** *n.*
**dor´mi·to´ry** *n.* a building providing living quarters, esp. at a college or university; a large room providing sleeping accommodations for many people
**dor´y** *n.* a small rowboat
**dose** *n.* an amount to be given or taken at one time, as of a medicine –*vt.* to give in measured amounts –**dos´age** *n.*
**dos´si·er** *n.* information relating to a particular matter or person
**dot´age** *n.* childish behavior caused by old age: senility; extravagant affection
**do´tard** *n.* a senile old person
**dote** *vi.* to be excessively attentive to –**dot·er** *n.* –**dot´ing·ly** *adv.*
**dou´ble** *adj.* twofold; duplicated; paired; made for two –*n.* anything twice as much; a look-alike –*vt.* to make twice as much; to fold and make two layers –*vi.* to increase twofold; to reverse course; to serve in more than one capacity –**dou´bly** *adv.*
**dou´ble-deal´ing** *adj.* treacherous –**dou´ble-deal´er** *n.*
**dou´ble-deck´er** *n.* a bus with two levels, a sandwich or ice cream cone made in two layers, etc.
**dou´ble-en·ten´dre** *n.* a word or phrase having a double meaning, often risqué
**double helix** the coiled structure of DNA
**double standard** a code that is unevenly applied
**dou´blet** *n.* a pair; a short, close-fitting outer garment
**double take** an amusing delayed reaction
**doubt** *n.* uncertainty; a lack of trust; skepticism –*vi., vt.* to be uncertain or skeptical –**doubt´ful** *adj.* –**doubt´ful·ly** *adv.* –**doubt´ful·ness** *n.*
**doubt´less** *adj.* without question –**doubt´less·ly** *adv.* –**doubt´less·ness** *n.*
**dough´ty** *adj.* valiant –**dough´ti·ly** *adv.* –**dough´ti·ness** *n.*
**dour** *adj.* dreary; gloomy –**dour´ly** *adv.* –**dour´ness** *n.*
**douse** *vt.* to immerse in liquid; to wet thoroughly
**dove´tail´** *n.* a cutout, usually at the end of the strip of wood, shaped like the tail of a dove, that fits into a cutout in another piece to join the two –*vi., vt.* to connect with a dovetail joint; to fit closely; to

connect, as data, so as to form a logical sequence
**dov´ish** *adj.* peaceful –**dov´ish·ness**
**dow´a·ger** *n.* a dignified elderly lady
**dow´dy** *adj.* shabby –**dow´di·ly** *adv.* –**dow´di·ness** *n.*
**dow´el** *n.* a round piece of wood or metal, often used to join wooden parts
**dow´er** *n.* an endowment, esp. a widow's portion –*vt.* to furnish with a dower
**down** *adv.* from higher to lower; from a former or earlier time; to a diminished volume or bulk: *to boil down*; to a less active state; to greater intensity: *get down to work* –*adj.* toward a lower position; in a lower place; dejected –*vt.* to subdue; to swallow –*n.* a descent; a reversal of fortune
**down-and-out´** destitute
**down´cast** *adj.* dejected; despondent
**down´fall** *n.* a failure; disgrace
**down´grade** *vt.* to reduce or lower in status, earnings, etc.
**down´heart·ed** *adj.* dejected; discouraged –**down´heart·ed·ly** *adv.*
**down´pour** *n.* a heavy rain
**down´right** *adj.* absolute; straight forward –*adv.* utterly
**down´trod·den** *adj.* oppressed
**down´turn** *n.* an economic decline
**down´ward** *adj.*, *adv.* toward a lower point –**down´ward·ly, down´wards** *adv.*
**dow´ry** *n.* property brought by a bride to her husband at the time of marriage
**doze** *n.* a brief, light sleep –*vi.* to sleep lightly or briefly
**doz´en** *n.* a set of twelve
**drab** *adj.* dull; colorless –**drab´ly** *adv.* –**drab´ness** *n.*
**draft** *(US) adj.* drawn from a keg –*n.* a drawing or writing, often preliminary; a current of air; an order directing the payment of money; that drawn from a keg; the selection of a person or persons for some purpose; the depth of a vessel below the water line –*vt.* to make a layout; to sketch or write; to select for service –**draft·ee´** *n.*
**drafts´man** *n.* one who draws, especially designs or plans requiring precision
**drag** *n.* the act of pulling; any of a number of devices that are normally pulled or that check motion by weight, friction, etc.; an impedence or a measure of impedence; slow laborious movement; a thing that is tiresome; influence –*vi.* to be pulled or lag behind; to move slowly –*vt.* to pull; to draw out slowly or with difficulty –**main drag** a main road
**drag´on** *n.* a legendary beast
**dra·goon´** *n.* a cavalryman
**drain** *n.* a duct for carrying waste water, etc.; that which gradually draws off –*vi.*, *vt.* to draw off, as to remove water, etc.; to cause a depletion of energy, resources, etc. –**drain´age** *n.*
**drake** *n.* a male duck
**dram** *n.* a unit of weight; a small portion
**dra´ma** *n.* a play, or plays collectively; a serious play or actual events that emulate such a play –**dra·mat´ic** *adj.* –**dra·mat´i·cal·ly** *adv.* –**dram´a·tist** *n.*
**dra´ma·tis per·so´nae** *n.* a cast of characters
**dra·mat´ics** *n.* the art of staging drama; histrionics
**dram´a·tize´** *vt.* to adapt to use in a play; to present events in an exaggerated fashion –**dram´a·tiz·a·ble** *adj.* –**dram·a·ti·za´tion** *n.* –**dram´a·tiz·er** *n.*
**drape** *n.* a cloth hanging in folds; the way in which cloth hangs –*vt.* to cover or decorate with cloth; to arrange cloth; to hang loosely –**dra´per·y** *n.*
**dras´tic** *adj.* extreme; strong and rapid –**dras´ti·cal·ly** *adv.*
**draught** *(Brit.) adj.* drawn from a keg –*n.* a drawing or writing, often preliminary; a current of air; an order directing the payment of money; that drawn from a keg; the depth of a vessel below the water line –*vt.* to make a layout; to sketch or write
**draughts** *n. (Brit.)* a board game similar to checkers in the US
**draw** *n.* something that attracts or entices; a conflict ending in a tie –*vi.*, *vt.* to pull or drag; to suck; to entice; to compose or portray; to pull out –**draw the line** to set a limit
**draw´back´** *n.* a disadvantage or shortcoming
**draw´er** *n.* one who draws; a sliding container in furniture
**drawl** *n.* a manner of speaking characterized by drawn out vowels –*vi.*, *vt.* to speak slowly, drawing out vowels –**drawl´er** *n.* –**drawl´ing** *adj.* –**drawl´ing·ly** *adv.*
**dray** *n.* a low, heavy cart –**dray´man** *n.*
**dray´age** *n.* a fee for hauling
**dread** *n.* fearful anticipation –*vt.* to anticipate with fear or reluctance
**dread´ful** *adj.* inspiring dread; unpleasant, distasteful –**dread´ful·ly** *adv.* –**dread´ful·ness** *n.*
**dread´nought** *n.* a battleship
**dream** *n.* images occurring during sleep; a visionary concept; something extremely pleasant –*vi.* to experience in a dream; to deem practical –*vt.* to envision in a dream or as in a dream; to waste time –**dream´er** *n.* –**dream´ful** *adj.* –**dream´ful·ly** *adv.*
**dream´y** *adj.* pleasant; soothing –**dream´i·ly** *adv.* –**dream´i·ness** *n.*
**drear´y** *adj.* bleak, dismal; dull –**drear´i·ly** *adv.* –**drear´i·ness** *n.* –**drear´i·some** *adj.*
**dredge** *n.* a machine for clearing waterways –*vt.*, *vi.* to dig with or as with a dredge –**dredg´er** *n.*
**dregs** *pl. n.* residue; something that is worthless, as *the dregs of humanity*
**drench** *vt.* to saturate; to wet thoroughly

**dress** *vt.* to clothe; to trim, or adorn *–vi* to don or wear clothing *–n.* apparel **–dress up** to improve the appearance of; to don one's best clothing **–dress´mak·er** *n.* **–dress´mak·ing** *adj., n.*

**dress´er** *n.* a decorator, as *window dresser*; one who dresses well; *(US)* a chest of drawers

**dressing gown** *(Brit.)* a loose, casual garment, usually closed at the front with a belt

**drib´ble** *n.* a small amount *–vi., vt.* to trickle; to flow a little at a time

**drift** *n.* something carried, as by wind or water; gradual change in position; a trend *–vi.* to be carried by wind or water; to wander casually or aimlessly; to stray from a set course or position

**drift´er** *n.* a homeless person

**drill** *n.* practice exercises; a boring tool *–vi.* to use a drill *–vt.* to bore a hole; to train with the use of methodical exercises

**drink** *n.* a beverage *–vi., vt.* to ingest or absorb a liquid **–drink´a·ble** *adj.* **–drink´er** *n.*

**drip** *n.* a falling in drops; a drop of liquid; the sound of a falling drop of liquid *–vi., vt.* to fall or cause to fall in drops

**drive** *n.* the act of operating or propelling a motor vehicle; a trip by auto; a path for an auto; a sharp blow, as of a ball with a club, bat, etc.; an organized effort for some purpose; enthusiasm or vigor *–vi., vt.* to operate or propel; to hit a ball; to press toward a goal **–driv·a·bil´i·ty** *n.* **–driv´a·ble** *adj.* **–driv´er** *n.*

**driv´el** *n.* foolish talk *–vi., vt.* to utter foolishly **–driv´el·er, driv´el·ler** *n.*

**drive´way** *n.* a private access road

**driz´zle** *n.* a light rain *–vi., vt.* to fall in small or light drops; to lightly moisten **–driz´zly** *adj.*

**droll** *adj.* quaintly humorous **–droll´er·y** *n.* **–drol´ly** *adv.*

**drone** *n.* a loafer; a dull humming sound *–vi.* to speak monotonously

**droop** *vi.* to hang down; to become dejected **–droop´i·ness** *n.* **–droop´ing** *adj.* **–droop´ing·ly** *adv.* **–droop´y** *adj.*

**drop** *n.* the quantity of a liquid that can fall in one spherical mass; a small piece or amount; a sharp decline; the vertical distance between two levels; a location for depositing material for distribution; the material deposited *–vi., vt.* to fall or cause to fall or decline; to deposit at a specified location

**drop´let** *n.* small drop

**drop´out´** *n.* one who abandons an undertaking

**dross** *n.* waste matter

**drought** *n.* a long period of dry weather; any prolonged shortage **–drought´y** *adj.*

**drove** *n.* a large number moving together, as of people or cattle **–dro´ver** *n.*

**drown** *vi.* to die by suffocation in liquid *–vt.* to kill by suffocation in liquid; to overwhelm

**drowse** *vt., vi.* to make or become sleepy

**drow´sy** *adj.* sleepy; sluggish **–drows´i·ly** *adv.* **–drows´i·ness** *n.*

**drub** *vt.* to beat with a stick; to vanquish *–n.* a heavy blow

**drub´bing** *n.* a one-sided defeat

**drudge** *n.* one engaged in menial or dull work *–vi.* to labor at a menial or dull task

**drudg´er·y** *n.* work that is menial or tiresome

**drug** *n.* any substance that alters a body function *–vt.* to give an altering substance to; to add a narcotic to food or drink

**dru´id** *n.* a priest or sorcerer in ancient Gaul **–dru·id´ic, dru·id´ic·cal** *adj.* **–dru´id·ism** *n.*

**drum** *n.* a percussion instrument; a cylindrical receptacle; constant repetition *–vi., vt.* to beat constantly, as on a drum **–drum out** to expel **–drum up** to summon or seek by persistence: *drum up customers* **–drum´mer** *n.*

**drunk** *adj.* affected by alcoholic drink to the point of impairment; overcome by emotion *–n.* one who is legally or noticeable overcome by drink **–drunk´en** *adj.* **–drunk´en·ly** *adv.* **–drunk´en·ness** *n.* **–drunk´ard** *n.*

**dry** *adj.* lacking or freed of moisture; of any non-liquid substance; not sweet, as of a wine; plain, as of food served without butter or sauce; not marked by emotion; boring; unproductive *–vi., vt.* to become or make dry **–dri´ly, dry´ly** *adv.* **–dry´ness** *n.*

**dry´ad** *n.* a mythical wood nymph

**dry cell** *n.* a sealed battery

**dry´dock** *n.* a mooring that can be pumped free of water for the repair of ships *–vi., vt.* to go or be put into drydock

**dry goods** textile, fabrics

**dry rot** *n.* a fungal disease of wood or growing plants

**dry run** *n.* a rehearsal

**dual** *adj.* comprised of two parts **–du´al·ism** *n.* **–du·al·is´tic** *adj.* **–du·al·is´ti·cal·ly** *adv.* **–du·al´i·ty** *n.* **–du´al·ly** *adv.*

**dual carriageway** *(Brit.)* a road with a center strip that separates vehicles traveling in opposite directions

**dub** *vt.* to bestow knighthood; to confer with a title, nickname, etc.; to add music, subtitles, etc. to a film or recording

**du·bi´e·ty** *n.* doubt; uncertainty

**du´bi·ous** *adj.* questionable; suspect; causing or feeling doubt or uncertainty **–du´bi·ous·ly** *adv.* **–du´bi·ous·ness** *n.*

**du´bi·ta·ble** *adj.* uncertain **–du´bi·ta·bly** *adv.*

**du´cal** *adj.* of a duke or duchy

**duch´ess** *n.* the wife or widow of a duke

**duch´y** *n.* the realm of a duke

**duck** *n.* a web-footed water bird *–vi., vt.* to plunge into

water; to dodge; to evade or avoid
**duck´ling** *n.* a small or baby duck
**duct** *n.* a tubular channel **–duct´work** *n.*
**duc´tile** *adj.* able to be hammered thin; easily led **–duc´tile·ness, duc´til´i·ty** *n.*
**dude** *n.* a dandy **–dud´ish** *adj.*
**dud´geon** *n.* sullen displeasure
**due** *adj.* scheduled or expected, as for arrival or payment; fitting or deserved, as *due respect* –*n.* anything owed or deserved
**du´el** *n.* formal combat between two persons –*vi., vt.* to fight a duel **–du´el·er, du´el·ist** *n.*
**du·et´** *n.* a musical composition for two voices or instruments
**dug´out** *n.* a canoe; an underground shelter
**duke** *n.* an English peer below a prince or archbishop
**duke´dom** *n.* a duchy
**dul´cet** *adj.* pleasing to the ear; soothing **–dul´cet·ly** *adv.*
**dul´ci·mer** *n.* a stringed musical instrument
**dull** *adj.* mentally or physically slow; lacking spirit; boring; blunt, as of a knife; lacking brightness, as of color –*vt., vi.* to make or become dull **–dull´ish** *adj.* **–dull´ness, dul´ness** *n.* **–dul´ly** *adv.*
**dul´lard** *n.* a dull person
**duly** *adv.* in a proper manner
**dumb** *adj.* unable or unwilling to speak, as from shock or emotion; lacking intelligence **–dumb´ly** *adv.* **–dumb´ness** *n.*
**dumb´found, dum´found** *vt.* to astonish; to make speechless from shock
**dumb´struck** *adj.* shocked speechless
**dum´my** *n.* a stupid or foolish person; a representation of a person: *a ventriloquist's dummy, a store dummy*; a silent player, as in bridge –*adj.* fake or counterfeit; representational
**dump** *vt., vi.* to empty or unload; to get rid of –*n.* a place for refuse; a distribution point: *fuel dump*
**dump´ling** *n.* a filled pastry; dough dropped into soup or stew
**dump´ster** *n.* (*US*) a large metal container for trash
**dump´y** *adj.* short and thick
**dun** *vt., vi.* to press for payment
**dunce** *n.* an ignorant person
**dune** *n.* a hill or ridge of sand
**dung** *n.* animal excrement
**dun·ga·ree´** *n.* a sturdy cotton cloth **–dun·ga·rees´** work clothes
**dun´geon** *n.* an underground cell or vault
**dunk** *vi., vt.* to dip into liquid
**du·o·de´num** *n.* the section of the small intestine nearest to the stomach
**dupe** *n.* one easily deceived; a person deceived or used by another –*vt.* to deceive **–dup·a·bil·i·ty** *n.* **–dup´a·ble** *adj.* **–dup´er** *n.* **–dup·er·y** *n.*
**du´plex** *adj.* double –*n.* (*US*) two housing units that share a common wall
**du´pli·cate** *adj.* copied –*n.* an exact copy –*vt.* to make a copy; to repeat **–du·pli·ca´tion** *n.* **–du´pli·ca·tive** *adj.* **–du´pli·ca·tor** *n.*
**du·plic´i·ty** *n.* deception **–du·plic´i·tous** *adj.* **–du·plic´i·tous·ly** *adv.*
**du´ra·ble** *adj.* able to withstand heavy use **–du´ra·bil´i·ty, du´ra·ble·ness** *n.* **–du´ra·bly** *adv.*
**durable goods** products that have a relatively long life, such as automobiles or household appliances
**du·ra´tion** *n.* an interval of time
**du·ress´** *n.* threat or coercion
**dur´ing** *prep.* throughout; in the course of
**dusk** *adj.* dark in tone –*n.* the early evening darkness **–dusk´i·ly** *adv.* **–dusk´i·ness** *n.* **–dusk´y** *adj.*
**dust** *n.* a substance reduced to powder –*vt.* to remove dust from; to sprinkle with or cover lightly: *dust the fish with flour* **–dust´y** *adj.*
**dust´er** *n.* a device for removing dust; a protective garment
**du´te·ous** *adj.* obedient; attentive to duty **–du´te·ous·ly** *adv.* **–du´te·ous·ness** *n.*
**du´ti·ful** *adj.* having a sense of duty; obedient **–du´ti·ful·ly** *adv.* **–du´ti·ful·ness** *n.*
**duty** *n.* that required by custom, law, etc.; any task assigned or required by one's work; a tax on imported goods
**dwarf** *n.* any animal or plant notably smaller than most of its species –*vt.* to curb the natural growth of **–dwarf´ish** *adj.* **–dwarf´ish·ness** *n.* **–dwarf´ism** *n.*
**dwell** *vi.* to reside; to linger **–dwell´er** *n.* **–dwell´ing** *n.*
**dwin´dle** *vi.* to lessen gradually
**dye** *n.* coloring matter –*vt., vi.* to stain with liquid coloring
**dy·nam´ic, dy·nam´i·cal** *adj.* relating to force or to the study of force; marked by frequent change; forceful, intense **–dy·nam´i·cal·ly** *adv.* **–dy´na·mism** *n.*
**dy·nam´ics** *n.* the study of force; the forces that make up or cause changes in a system
**dy´na·mite** *n.* an explosive –*vt.* to destroy with an explosive
**dy´na·mo´** *n.* a machine for converting mechanical energy to electrical energy
**dy´nas·ty** *n.* a succession of rulers from the same family **–dy·nas´tic, dy·nas´ti·cal** *adj.* **–dy·nas´ti·cal·ly** *adv.*
**dyne** *n.* a unit of force
**dys´en·ter·y** *n.* an inflammation of the large intestine
**dys·func´tion** *n.* abnormal or impaired function **–dys·func´tion·al** *adj.*
**dys·lex´i·a** *n.* avisual impairment **–dys·lex´ic** *adj.*
**dys´pep´si·a** *n.* distressed digestion **–dys´pep´tic** *adj.*
**dys·pha´gia** *n.* difficulty in swallowing **–dys·phag´ic** *adj.*

**dys·pha´sia** *n.* difficulty with speech –**dys·pha´sic** *adj.*
**dys´tro·phy** *n.* a disorder caused by faulty nutrition –**dys·troph´ic** *adj.*

**e, E** fifth letter of the English alphabet
**each** *adj.* one of two or more –*adv.*
**ea´ger** *adj.* impatient or anxious –**ea´ger·ly** *adv.* –**ea´ger·ness** *n.*
**ea´gle-eyed** *adj.* having keen sight
**ear** *n.* the organ and sense of hearing; heed
**ear´ful** *n.* gossip
**ear´ly** *adj.* near the beginning; before the usual or expected time –**ear´li·ness** *n.*
**ear´mark** *vt.* to mark for identification; to set aside for a special purpose –*n.* an owner's mark
**earn** *vt.* to receive as payment for labor; to deserve for one's efforts; to yield, as a profit –**earn´er** *n.*
**earnings** *pl. n.* salary or wages; profit
**ear´nest** *adj.* serious; intense; important –**earnest money** a payment made in advance to seal a bargain –**ear´nest·ly** *adv.* –**ear´nest·ness** *n.*
**ear´shot** *n.* hearing distance
**earth** *n.* dry land or the soil on dry land; a place of being as contrasted to the spirit world –**Earth** the planet that supports human life; –**earth´ling** *n.* –**earth´ly** *adj.* –**earth´li·ness** *n.*
**earth´en** *n.* made of earth or baked clay –**earth´en·ware** *n.*
**earth´quake´** *n.* a tremor caused by disturbance of the earth's surface
**earth´work** *n.* a fortification
**earth´y** *adj.* crude, unrefined; natural –**earth´i·ness** *n.*
**ease** *n.* comfort; a state of rest; freedom from difficulty –*vi., vt.* to lessen or free from, as difficulty or pain; to move slowly and carefully –**ease´ful** *adj.* –**ease´ful·ly** *adv.* –**ease´ful·ness** *n.*
**ea´sel** *n.* a stand for displaying pictures, paintings, etc.
**ease´ment** *n.* relief, as from pain; something that provides relief; the right to limited use of property
**east** *n.* the general direction from which the sun rises –**the East** an eastern region; Asia –**east´er·ly** *adj., adv.* –**east´ward, east´ward·ly** *adj., adv.*
**east´ern** *adj.* pertaining to the east –**east´ern·er** *n.*
**eas´y** *adj.* done without difficulty; unhurried, relaxing –**eas´i·ly** *adv.* –**eas´i·ness** *n.*
**eas´y·go·ing** *adj.* relaxed; unhurried
**eat** *vi., vt.* to take in food; to consume or destroy: *eaten by rust*; to annoy –**eat´a·ble** *adj.* –**eat´er** *n.*
**eat´er·y** *n.* a restaurant
**eaves** *pl. n.* the projecting edge of a roof
**eaves´drop** *vi.* to listen secretly –**eaves´drop·per** *n.* –**eaves´drop·ing** *n.*
**ebb** *n.* a decline; a receding of tide waters (also **ebb tide**) –*vi.* to decline; to recede
**eb´on·ite** *n.* hard rubber
**eb´on·y** *n.* a hard wood, usually black –*adj.* made from ebony; black
**e·bul´lient** *adj.* exuberant; full of enthusiasm –**e·bul´lience, e·bul´lien·cy** *n.* –**e·bul´lient·ly** *adv.*
**ec·cen´tric** *adj.* off center; having different centers; unconventional –*n.* a device for transferring reciprocating motion; an odd or unconventional person –**ec·cen´tri·cal·ly** *adv.* –**ec·cen·tric´i·ty** *n.*
**ec·cle´si·as´tic** *n.* a cleric –**ec·cle´si·as´tic ec·cle·si·as´ti·cal** *adj.* pertaining to the church –**ec·cle·si·as´ti·cal·ly** *adv.*
**ec·cle·si·ol´o·gy** *n.* the study of church function, or of church architecture and ornamentation
**ec·dys´i·ast** *n.* a stripteaser
**ech´e·lon** *n.* a military formation; a level of responsibility or function
**e·chid´na** *n.* a spiny anteater
**echo** *n.* reflected sound –*vi.* to resound; to be repeated –*vt.* to repeat –**ech´o·er** *n.*
**ech·o·lo´cate** *vt.* to position by means of sound waves –**ech·o·lo·ca´tion** *n.* –**ech·o·lo´ca·tor** *n.*
**é´clair, e·clair´** *n.* a filled pastry
**e·clat´** *n.* a dazzling display; celebrity or renown
**ec·lec´tic** *adj.* from a variety of sources –*n.* one who utilizes material from a variety of sources –**ec·lec´ti·cal·ly** *adv.* –**ec·lec´ti·cism** *n.*
**e·clipse´** *n.* the obscuring of one celestial body by another; any dimming or diminishing –*vt.* to darken or diminish; to overshadow
**e·clip´tic** *n.* the plane that intersects the sun and the earth's orbit –**e·clip´tic, e·clip´ti·cal** *adj.* –**e·clip´ti·cal·ly** *adv.*
**e·col´o·gy** *n.* the study of the effects of a changing environment on organisms –**ec·o·log´ic, ec·o·log´i·cal** *adj.* –**ec·o·log´i·cal·ly** *adv.* –**e·col´o·gist** *n.*
**e·co·nom´ic** *adj.* of the production and management of wealth
**e·co·nom´i·cal** *adj.* done or intended to be done without waste; economic; pertaining to economics –**ec·o·nom´i·cal·ly** *adv.*
**e·co·nom´ics** *n.* the study of the production and management of wealth –**e·con´o·mist** *n.*
**e·con´o·my** *n.* the management of finances; care in the use of resources; a system for producing or managing resources
**e·con´o·mize** *vi.* to use carefully, especially by avoiding waste –**e·con´o·miz·er** *n.*
**ec´o·sys·tem** *n.* a community of organisms and their environment
**ec´ru** *adj.* light brown
**ec´sta·sy** *n.* emotional rapture or delight –**ec·stat´ic** *adj.* –**ec·stat´i·cal·ly** *adv.*
**ec·u·men´ic, ec·u·men´i·cal** *adj.* general or universal; promoting unity, esp. among religions –**ec·u·men´i·**

cal·ly *adv.* **—ec·u·me·nic´i·ty** *n.* **—ec´u·me·nism** *n.* **—ec´u·me·nist** *n.*

**ec´ze·ma** *n.* a skin inflammation

**e·da´cious** *adj.* voracious **—e·dac´i·ty** *n.*

**ed´dy** *n.* a circling current *—vi., vt.* to move or cause to move in circles

**e·de´ma** *n.* morbid accumulation of fluid

**e·den´tate** *adj.* toothless

**edge** *n.* a border or margin; the cutting part of a blade; a dividing line *—vt.* to create a border; to sharpen; to advance gradually

**edg´y** *adj.* irritable; nervous **—edg´i·ly** *adv.* **—edg´i·ness** *n.*

**ed´i·ble** *adj.* fit to be eaten **—ed·i·bil´i·ty, ed´i·ble·ness** *n.*

**e´dict** *n.* a formal decree; a strict order

**ed´i·fice** *n.* an imposing building

**ed´i·fy´** *vt.* to instruct or enlighten **—ed´i·fi·ca´tion** *n.* **—ed´i·fi·er** *n.* **—ed´i·fy·ing·ly** *adv.*

**ed´it** *vt.* to prepare a written work for publication; to correct or alter, as a motion picture, sound track, computer file, etc. **—ed´i·tor** *n.* **—ed´it·a·ble** *adj.*

**e·di´tion** *n.* the form of a published work; the number of copies issued at one time

**ed´i·to´ri·al** *adj.* of an editor *—n.* an article or essay expressing opinion **—ed·i·to´ri·al·ize** *vi.* **—ed·i·to´ri·al·ly** *adv.*

**ed´u·cate** *vt.* to teach or train, especially by formal study; to inform; to refine, as one's taste

**ed´u·cat·ed** *adj.* well-schooled; cultivated in speech, manner, etc.

**ed·u·ca´tion** *n.* the training of one's mind; knowledge attained by instruction; the art of teaching **—ed·u·ca´tion·al** *adj.* **—ed·u·ca´tion·al·ly** *adv.* **—ed´u·ca·tor** *n.*

**ed´u·cat·ive** *adj.* instructive

**e·duce´** *vt.* to draw out; to formulate **—e·duc´i·ble** *adj.* **—e·duc´tion** *n.* **—e·duc´tor** *n.*

**ee´rie, ee´ry** *adj.* weird; awesome; strange **—ee´ri·ly** *adv.* **—ee´ri·ness** *n.*

**ef·face´** *vt.* to obliterate; to make oneself insignificant **—ef·face´a·ble** *adj.* **—ef·face´ment** *n.* **—ef·fac´er** *n.*

**ef·fect´** *n.* something brought about; the power to influence *—vt.* to produce or cause **—ef·fec´tive** *adj.* **—ef·fec´tive·ly** *adv.* **—ef·fec´tive·ness** *n.*

**ef·fec´tu·al** *adj.* possessing power; in force, legal **—ef·fec·tu·al´i·ty** *n.* **—ef·fec´tu·al·ly** *adv.*

**ef·fec´tu·ate** *vt.* to bring about **—ef·fec·tu·a´tion** *n.*

**ef·fem´i·nate** *adj.* having female traits; characterized by weakness and overrefinement **—ef·fem´i·na·cy** *n.* **—ef·fem´i·nate·ly** *adv.*

**ef·fer·ves´cent** *adj.* emitting tiny bubbles, like champagne or soda; lively or vivacious **—ef·fer·vesce´** *vi.* **—ef·fer·ves´cence, ef·fer·ves´cen·cy** *n.* **—ef·fer·ves´cent·ly** *adv.*

**ef·fete´** *adj.* unproductive; burned out by self-indulgence **—ef·fete´ly** *adv.* **—ef·fete´ness** *n.*

**ef´fi·ca´cious** *adj.* capable of producing a desired effect **—ef·fi·ca´cious·ly** *adv.* **ef·fi·ca´cious·ness** *n.* **—ef´fi·ca·cy** *n.*

**ef·fi´cient** *adj.* producing a desired effect with a minimum of effort, waste, etc. **—ef·fi´cien·cy** *n.* **—ef·fi´cient·ly** *adv.*

**ef´fi·gy** *n.* a representative figure

**ef·flo·resce´** *vi.* to bear flowers **—ef·flo·res´cence** *n.* **—ef·flo·res´cent** *adj.*

**ef´flu·ence** *n.* that flowing out, especially of liquid waste

**ef·flu´vi·um** *n.* an invisible emanation; noxious fumes or vapor **—ef·flu´vi·al, ef·flu´vi·ous** *adj.*

**ef´fort** *n.* the energy expended or required to accomplish a task; an attempt; that attempted or accomplished

**ef´fort·less** *adj.* requiring little or no effort **—ef´fort·less·ly** *adv.* **—ef´fort·less·ness** *n.*

**ef·fron´ter·y** *n.* boldness; insolence

**ef·ful´gence** *n.* a shining forth; radiance **—ef·ful´gent** *adj.* **—ef·ful´gent·ly** *adv.*

**ef·fuse´** *vt., vi.* to pour forth or emanate **—ef·fu´sion** *n.*

**ef·fu´sive** *adj.* overly demonstrative; gushing **—ef·fu´sive·ly** *adv.* **—ef·fu´sive·ness** *n.*

**e·gal·i·tar´i·an** *adj.* of political and social equality **—e·gal·i·tar´i·an·ism** *n.*

**egg** *n.* a reproductive body; a female gamete **—lay an egg** to fail **—egg on** to incite

**egg´head´** *n.* an intellectual

**e´go** *n.* the conscious self

**e·go·cen´tric** *adj.* self-centered; caring only for one's own interests **—e·go·cen·tric´i·ty, e·go·cen´trism** *n.*

**e´go·ism** *n.* excessive concern with one's self; conceit; the belief that self-interest should be the primary goal of human conduct **—e´go·ist** *n.* **—e´go·is´tic, e´go·is´ti·cal** *adj.* **—e´go·is´ti·cal·ly** *adv.*

**e·go·ma´ni·a** *n.* excessive concentration on one's self and one's own concerns **—e·go·ma´ni·ac** *n.* **—e·go·ma·ni´a·cal** *adj.*

**e´go·tist** *n.* one with an overblown sense of self-importance **—e´go·tism** *n.* **—e´go·tis´tic, e´go·tis´ti·cal** *adj.* **—e´go·tis´ti·cal·ly** *adv.*

**e·gre´gious** *adj.* exceptionally bad **—e·gre´gious·ly** *adv.* **—e·gre´gious·ness** *n.*

**e´gress** *n.* a going out; an exit **—e·gres´sion** *n.*

**ei´der** *n.* a large sea duck

**ei´ther** *adj.* one of two

**e·jac´u·late´** *vt.* to utter or eject suddenly **—e·jac·u·la´tion** *n.* **—e·jac´u·la·tor** *n.*

**e·ject´** *vt.* to cast or drive out **—e·jec´tion** *n.* **—e·jec´tive** *adj.* **—e·jec´tive·ly** *adv.* **—e·jec´tor** *n.*

**eke** *vt.* to supplement; to produce with difficulty

**e·lab´o·rate** *adj.* developed with great attention to

detail; intricate *—vi., vt.* to work out or present in great detail **—e·lab´o·rate·ly** *adv.* **—e·lab´o·rate·ness, e·lab·o·ra´tion** *n.* **—e·lab´o·ra·tive** *adj.*

**é·lan´** *n.* dash; vivacity

**e·lapse´** *vi.* to pass by

**e·las´tic** *adj.* capable of quick recovery; easily adapting *—n.* a stretchable fabric **—e·las·tic´i·ty** *n.* **—e·las´ti·cal·ly** *adv.*

**e·late´** *vt.* raise the spirits of **—e·lat´ed** *adj.* **—e·lat´ed·ly** *adv.* **—e·lat´ed·ness** *n.*

**e·la´tion** *n.* exultation

**el´bow** *n.* the joint at the bend of the arm; any angular joint or fitting

**el´der** *adj.* older; superior in rank *—n.* an older person

**el´der·ly** *adj.* somewhat old

**el´dest** *adj.* first-born

**e·lect´** *adj.* chosen; singled out, exclusive *—n.* one chosen or singled out *—vt.* to choose or vote for **—the elect** a favored group

**e·lect´a·ble** *adj.* able or likely to be elected **—e·lect·a·bil´i·ty** *n.*

**e·lec´tion** *n.* the process of selecting for office

**e·lec·tion·eer´** *vi.* to seek election; to canvass for votes

**e·lec´tive** *adj.* chosen by votes; open to choice: optional

**e·lec´tor** *n.* a voter; a member of the electoral college **—e·lec´tor·al** *adj.*

**electoral college** the people chosen by the voters of a state to formally elect the president and vice president of the U.S.

**e·lec´tor·ate** *n.* a body of voters

**e·lec´tric, e·lec´tri·cal** *adj.* of or operated by electricity; emotionally charged **—e·lec´tri·cal·ly** *adv.* **—e·lec·tri´cian** *n.*

**e·lec´tric´i·ty** *n.* a flow of atomic particles used as a source of energy

**e·lec´tri·fy** *n.* to equip for operation by electricity; to startle or thrill **—e·lec·tri·fi·ca´tion** *n.*

**e·lec·tro·car´di·o·gram** *n.* a graph showing heart activity

**e·lec´tro·car´di·o·graph´** *n.* an instrument for recording activity of the heart **—e·lec·tro·car·di·og´ra·phy** *n.*

**e·lec´tro·cute´** *vt.* to execute by electricity **—e·lec·tro·cu´tion** *n.*

**e·lec´trode** *n.* a conducting element for an electric charge

**e·lec·tro·dy·nam´ics** *n.* the study of the interaction of electric currents and magnetic fields

**e·lec·tro·en·ceph´a·lo·gram** *n.* a record of the brain's electrical activity

**e·lec´tro·en·ceph´a·lo·graph** *n.* a device for recording electrical activity in the brain

**e·lec·trol´y·sis** *n.* a means to destroy unwanted body hair

**e·lec´tro·lyte** *n.* a chemical compound that becomes a conductor when dissolved or molten **—e·lec·tro·lyt´ic, e·lec·tro·lyt´i·cal** *adj.* **—e·lec·tro·lyt´i·cal·ly** *adv.*

**e·lec·tro·mag´net** *n.* a magnet produced by the flow of electricity through an outer coil **—e·lec´tro·mag·net´ic** *adj.* **—e·lec´tro·mag·net´i·cal·ly** *adv.* **—e·lec·tro·mag´net·ism** *n.*

**e·lec´tron** *n.* a negatively charged atomic particle

**e·lec´tron´ics** *n.* the study of carriers of electric charge

**e·lec·tro·stat´ic** *adj.* of electric charges at rest **—e·lec·tro·stat´i·cal·ly** *adv.*

**el·ee·mos´y·nar·y** *adj.* charity; nonprofit

**el´e·gance, el´e·gan·cy** *n.* a sense of propriety, grace, or beauty; tasteful luxury; cleverly simple, as of a solution **—el´e·gant** *adj.* **—el´e·gant·ly** *adv.*

**el´e·gy** *n.* a classical poem with a sorrowful theme **—el´e·gi´ac** *adj.* **—el´e·gize** *vt., vi.*

**el´e·ment** *n.* a basic substance or component; one's natural environment **—el´e·men´tal, el´e·men´tary** *adj.* **—el·e·men´tal·ly, el·e·men·tar´i·ly** *adv.*

**el´e·phant** *n.* a huge mammal with a flexible trunk and tusks **—el´e·phan´tine** *adj.*

**el´e·vate´** *vt.* to raise or lift to a higher level; to improve one's moral or intellectual awareness; to improve the spirits of **—el´e·vat·ed** *adj.* **—el´e·va´tion** *n.*

**elf** *n.* a mischievous sprite **—elf´in, elf´ish** *adj.*

**e·lic´it** *vt.* to draw out from, as for information; to bring out, as a reaction

**e·lide´** *vt.* to omit; to ignore **—e·lid´i·ble** *adj.*

**el´i·gi·ble** *adj.* qualified or suitable to participate **—el·i·gi·bil´i·ty** *n.* **—el´i·gi·bly** *adv.*

**e·lim´i·nate** *vt.* to remove or reject **—e·lim´i·na´tion** *n.* **—e·lim´i·na·tive** *adj.* **—e·lim´i·na·tor** *n.*

**e·lite´** *n.* the aristocracy; a small powerful group **—e·lit´ism** *n.* **—e·lit´ist** *n.*

**e·lix´ir** *n.* a medicinal preparation; a cure-all

**elk** *n.* a large deer with broad antlers

**el·lipse´** *n.* an oval geometric form **—el·lip´tic, el·lip´ti·cal** *adj.* **—el·lip´ti·cal·ly** *adv.*

**el·lip´sis** *n., pl.* **el·lip´ses** the omission of a word or phrase to complete a thought; marks that indicate omission as ... or ***

**elo·cu´tion** *n.* the art of public speaking **—el·o·cu´tion·ar·y** *adj.* **—el·o·cu´tion·ist** *n.*

**e·lon´gate** *vt., vi.* to make or grow longer **—e·lon´gate, e·lon´ga·ted** *adj.* made longer; slender **—e´lon·ga´tion** *n.*

**e·lope´** *vi.* to run away, esp. to marry **—e·lope´ment** *n.* **—e·lop´er** *n.*

**el´o·quence** *n.* expressive and compelling speech or writing **—el´o·quent** *adj.* **—el´o·quent·ly** *adv.*

**else** *adj.* different or other; more: *we need something else* *—adv.*

**e·lu´ci·date** *vt.* to clarify; to explain **—e·lu·ci·da´tion** *n.* **—e·lu´ci·da·tive** *adj.*
**e·lude´** *vt.* to evade or escape by cunning; to slip from memory **—e·lu´sion** *n.* **—e·lu´sive, e·lu´so·ry** *adj.* **—e·lu´sive·ly** *adv.* **—e·lu´sive·ness** *n.*
**e·ma´ci·ate´** *vt.* to make abnormally thin, as by disease or starvation **—e·ma´ci·a´tion** *n.* **—e·ma´ci·at·ed** *adj.*
**em´a·nate´** *vi.* to come forth, as from a source **—em´a·na´tion** *n.*
**e·man´ci·pate´** *vt.* to release from bondage or restraint **—e·man´ci·pa´tion** *n.* **—e·man´ci·pa·tor** *n.*
**e·mas´cu·late** *vt.* to deprive of force **—e·mas·cu·la´tion** *n.* **—e·mas´cu·la·tive, e·mas´cu·la·to·ry** *adj.* **—e·mas´cu·la·tor** *n.*
**em·balm´** *vt.* to treat a dead body so as to preserve it; to preserve in the memory **—em·balm´er** *n.* **em·balm´ment** *n.*
**em·bank´ment** *n.* a protective mound of earth or stone **—em·bank´** *vt.*
**em·bar´go** *n.* an order restricting or prohibiting trade in certain goods, to certain ports, etc. *—vt.* to place a restriction on trade
**em·bark´** *vi., vt.* to take or go aboard as for a journey **—em´bar·ka´tion** *n.* **—em·bark´ment** *n.*
**em·bar´rass** *vt.* to make ill at ease or self-conscious; to involve or be involved in financial difficulties **—em·bar´rassed·ly, em·bar´rass·ing·ly** *adv.* **—em·bar´rass·ing** *adj.* **—em·bar´rass·ment** *n.*
**em´bas·sy** *n.* the post, trappings, staff, buildings, etc. of an ambassador
**em·bat´tle** *vt.* to equip for battle; to fortify **—em·bat´tled** *adj.*
**em·bed´** *vt.* to set firmly
**em·bel´lish** *vt.* to add detail or adornment to: to decorate; to add particulars, often fictitious, to an account **—em·bel´lish·er** *n.* **—em·bel´lish·ment** *n.*
**em´ber** *n.* a live coal **—embers** *n.* a dying fire
**em·bez´zle** *vt.* to take illegally in violation of a trust **—em·bez´zle·ment** *n.* **—em·bez´zler** *n.*
**em·bit´ter** *vt.* to give rise to unhappiness or displeasure **—em·bit´ter·ment** *n.*
**em·bla´zon** *vt.* to adorn or decorate **—em·bla´zon·er** *n.* **—em·bla´zon·ment, em·bla´zon·ry** *n.*
**em´blem** *n.* a symbol or badge; an object representative of something else: *a cross is the emblem of the Christian church* **—em´blem·at´ic, em·blem·at´i·cal** *adj.* **—em·blem·at´i·cal·ly** *adv.*
**em·bod´y** *vt.* to collect into a whole; to include or incorporate into **—em·bod´i·ment** *n.*
**em·bold´en** *vt.* to give courage to
**em´bo·lism** *n.* stoppage in a blood vessel
**em´bo·lus** *n.* an object capable of obstructing a blood vessel
**em·bos´om** *vt.* to take in; shelter
**em·boss** *vt.* to adorn with a raised design **—em·boss´a·ble** *adj.* **—em·boss´er** *n.* **—em·boss´ment** *n.*
**em·brace´** *n.* a hug; acceptance *—vi.* to join in a hug *—vt.* to hug by holding close; to accept; to surround or include **—em·brace´a·ble** *adj.* **—em·brac´er** *n.*
**em·broi´der·y** *n.* ornamental needlework **—em·broi´der** *vt.* **—em·broi´der·er** *n.*
**em·broil´** *vt.* to draw into, as a conflict **—em·broil´ment** *n.*
**em´bry·o** *n.* the early developmental stage of an animal or plant; anything in the early stages of development **—em´bry·al, em´bry·on´ic** *adj.*
**em·bry·ol´o·gy** *n.* the study of embryos **—em·bry·ol´o·gist** *n.*
**e·mend´, e´men·date** *vt.* to correct a literary work **—e·mend´a·ble** *adj.* **—e´men·da´tion** *n.* **—e´men·da·tor** *n.* **—e·men´da·to·ry** *adj.*
**em´er·ald** *n.* a bright green precious stone
**e·merge´** *vi.* to come forth; to come into view; to form or evolve **—e·mer´gence** *n.* **—e·mer´gent** *adj.* **—e·merg´ing** *adj.*
**e·mer´gen·cy** *n.* a situation requiring immediate action
**e·mer´i·tus** *adj.* retired, but retained in a honorary position
**em´er·y** *n.* a very hard mineral used as an abrasive
**e·met´ic** *n.* a medicine used to induce vomiting *—adj.* causing vomiting
**em´i·grate´** *vi.* to leave a country or region to settle in another **—em´i·grant** *adj., n.* **—em´i·gra´tion** *n.* **—e´mi·gre´** *n.*
**em´i·nent** *adj.* renowned, exalted; rising high above others **—em´i·nence** *n.* **—em´i·nen·cy** *n.* **—em´i·nent·ly** *adv.*
**eminent domain** the right to take or purchase private property for public use
**em´is·sar´y** *n.* one sent on a special mission
**e·mis´sion** *n.* something omitted
**e·mit´** *vt.* to give out or discharge
**e·mol´u·ment** *n.* compensation for office or employment
**e·mote´** *vi.* to act melodramatically
**e·mo´tion** *n.* strong feeling; a state of mental agitation **—e·mo´tion·al** *adj.* **—e·mo´tion·al·ism** *n.* **—e·mo´tion·al·ly** *adv.*
**e·mo´tion·a·lize** *vt.* to make emotional **—e·mo·tion·al·i·za´tion** *n.*
**e·mo´tive** *adj.* tending to arouse emotion **—e·mo´tive·ly** *adv.* **—e·mo´tive·ness** *n.*
**em´pa·thy** *n.* identification with the emotions, thoughts, etc. of another **—em·pa·thet´ic, em·path´ic** *adj.* **—em·pa·thet´i·cal·ly** *adv.* **—em´pa·thize** *vi., vt.*
**em´per·or** *n.* ruler of an empire
**em´pha·sis** *n.* forcefulness; special attention or importance **—em´pha·size´** *vt.*

**em·phat´ic** *adj.* expressed with force; definite —**em·phat´i·cal·ly** *adv.*
**em·phy·se´ma** *n.* a lung condition marked by shortness of breath
**em´pire´** *n.* a vast organization under unified control
**em·pir´ic, em·pir´i·cist** *n.* one who seeks knowledge through experience —*adj.* empirical
**em·pir´i·cal** *adj.* based on experience and observation —**em·pir´i·cal·ly** *adv.* —**em·pir´i·cism** *n.*
**em·ploy´** *vt.* to engage the services of; to use —**em·ploy´ee** *n.* —**em·ploy´er** *n.* —**em·ploy´ment** *n.*
**em·ploy´a·ble** *adj.* capable of being employed or put to use —**em·ploy·a·bil´i·ty** *n.*
**em·po´ri·um** *n.* a marketplace
**em·pow´er** *vt.* to enable or permit —**em·pow´er·ment** *n.*
**emp´ty** *adj.* having nothing within; insincere; frivolous —*vt., vi.* to make or become empty; to transfer the contents of —**emp´ti·ly** *adv.* —**emp´ti·ness** *n.*
**e´mu** *n.* a flightless bird of Australia related to the ostrich
**em´u·late´** *vt.* to imitate; to strive to equal or surpass, esp. by imitation —**em´u·la´tion** *n.* —**em´u·la·tive** *adj.* —**em´u·la·tive·ly** *adv.* —**em´u·la·tor** *n.*
**e·mul´sion** *n.* a mixture in which small particles are suspended in a liquid —**e·mul´sive** *adj.*
**e·mul´si·fy** *vt.* to mix or whip so as to make into an emulsion —**e·mul·si·fi·ca´tion** *n.* —**e·mul´si·fi·er** *n.*
**en·a´ble** *vt.* to make possible
**en·act´** *vt.* to make into law —**en·act´ment** *n.*
**en·am´el** *n.* a glossy protective or decorative coating —*vt.* to surface with a hard protective coating
**en·am´or** *vt.* to inspire love
**en·cap´su·late** *vt.* to summarize —**en·cap·su·la´tion** *n.*
**en·ceph·a·li´tis** *n.* an inflammation of the brain —**en·ceph´a·lit´ic** *adj.*
**en·ceph´a·lon** *n.* the brain
**en·chant´** *vt.* to delight or charm as if by a magic spell —**en·chant´er** *n.* —**en·chant´ing** *adj.* —**en·chant´ing·ly** *adv.* —**en·chant´ment** *n.*
**en·ci´pher** *vt.* to translate into a secret code
**en·cir´cle** *vt.* to surround —**en·cir´cle·ment** *n.*
**en´clave** *n.* a distinct geographical or political area enclosed within a larger area
**en·close** *vt.* to surround or contain —**en·clo·sure** *n.*
**en·co´mi·um** *n.* a eulogy
**en·com´pass** *vt.* to include; to encircle or surround —**en·com´pass·ment** *n.*
**en´core** *n.* a repeat performance
**en·coun´ter** *n.* a meeting —*vi., vt.* to meet, especially unexpectedly or in conflict
**en·cour´age** *vt.* to support; to inspire with courage —**en·cour´age·ment** *n.* —**en·cour´ag·ing** *adj.* —**en·cour´ag·ing·ly** *adv.*
**en·croach´** *vi.* to intrude on the possessions or rights of another —**en·croach´ment** *n.*
**en·crust´** *vt.* to cover with a hard coating; to decorate, as with jewels —**en·crus·ta´tion** *n.*
**en·cum´ber** *vi.* to obstruct or weigh down so as to hinder —**en·cum´brance** *n.*
**en·cy´clo·pae´di·a, en·cy´clo·pe´di·a** *n.* an authoritative reference
**end** *n.* a terminal point
**en·dan´ger** *vt.* to imperil —**en·dan´ger·ment** *n.*
**en·dear´** *vt.* to make beloved —**en·dear´ing** *adj.* —**en·dear´ing·ly** *adv.*
**en·dear´ment** *n.* an expression of affection
**en·deav´or** *n.* a sincere effort; any undertaking —*vi., vt.* to make a sincere effort
**en·dem´ic** *adj.* occurring in or peculiar to a particular area or people, as an *endemic disease*
**end´less** *adj.* boundless; without end; forming a closed loop —**end´less·ly** *adv.* —**end´less·ness** *n.*
**en·dorse´** *vt.* to approve, support, or acknowledge —**en·dors´a·ble** *adj.* —**en·dors·ee´** *n.* —**en·dorse´ment** *n.* —**en·dors´er** *n.*
**en·dow´** *vt.* to provide with income; to furnish or equip —**en·dow´ment** *n.*
**en·dure´** *vi., vt.* to continue; to bear up, as under pain —**en·dur´a·ble** *adj.* —**en·dur´a·bly** *adv.* —**en·dur´ance** *n.*
**en´e·my** *n.* one hostile to another
**en·er·get´ic** *adj.* displaying energy —**en·er·get´i·cal·ly** *adv.*
**en´er·gize** *vt.* to bring to action —**en´er·giz·er** *n.*
**en´er·gy** *n.* the power to act effectively; power derived from natural sources, as oil, water, etc. —*adj.* pertaining or relating to power
**en´er·vate** *vt.* to deprive of energy; weaken —**en·er·va´tion** *n.* —**en´er·va·tor** *n.*
**en·fee´ble** *vt.* to weaken; to render helpless —**en·fee´ble·ment** *n.* —**en·fee´bler** *n.*
**en·fold´** *vt.* to embrace; to wrap
**en·force´** *vt.* to compel obedience —**en·force·a·bil´i·ty** *n.* —**en·force´a·ble** *adj.* —**en·force´ment** *n.* —**en·forc´er** *n.*
**en·fran´chise** *vt.* to endow with rights; to free from bondage —**en·fran´chise·ment** *n.*
**en·gage´** *vi., vt.* to hire; to promise to marry; to occupy oneself with —**en·gaged´** *adj.* —**en·gage´ment** *n.*
**en·gag´ing** *adj.* charming —**en·gag´ing·ly** *adv.*
**en·gen´der** *vt.* to bring about; to produce
**en´gine** *n.* a machine that converts energy into force
**en´gi·neer´** *n.* one who plans and manages scientifically —*vt.* to contrive; to plan and supervise
**en´gi·neer´ing** *n.* the application of scientific knowledge to the solving of practical problems
**en·grave´** *vt.* to carve or etch into a surface —**en·grav´er** *n.* —**en·grav´ing** *n.*
**en·gross´** *vt.* to absorb entirely —**en·gross´ing** *adj.*

—en·gross´ing·ly *adv.* —en·gross´ment *n.*

**en·gulf´** *vt.* to swallow up; to overwhelm

**en·hance´** *vt.* to embellish so as to improve quality or value **—en·hance´ment** *n.*

**e·nig´ma** *n.* something ambiguous or perplexing **—en´ig·mat´ic, e·nig·mat´i·cal** *adj.* **—e·nig·mat´i·cal·ly** *adv.*

**en·join´** *vt.* to forbid or prohibit

**en·joy´** *vt.* to find pleasure in; to have the use of **—en·joy´a·ble** *adj.* **—en·joy´a·ble·ness** *n.* **—en·joy´a·bly** *adv.* **—en·joy´ment** *n.*

**en·kin´dle** *vt.* to set on fire; to excite

**en·large´** *vt., vi.* to make or become larger **—en·large·ment** *n.*

**en·light´en** *vt.* to inform or impart special knowledge to **—en·light´en·ment** *n.*

**en·liv´en** *vt.* to stimulate

**en·mesh´** *vt.* to entangle

**en´mi·ty** *n.* hostility

**en·no´ble** *vt.* to confer nobility; to honor or venerate **—en·no´ble·ment** *n.* **—en·no´bler** *n.*

**en´nui** *n.* listlessness or indifference caused by boredom

**e·nor´mous** *adj.* of great size **—e·nor´mi·ty** *n.* **—enor´mous·ly** *adv.* **—e·nor´mous·ness** *n.*

**e·nough´** *adj.* adequate; sufficient *—adv.* sufficiently *—n.* an adequate supply *—interj.*

**en·rage´** *vt.* to make angry; to infuriate **—en·rage´ment** *n.*

**en·rap´ture** *vt.* to delight

**en·rich´** *vt.* to increase the wealth or quality of **—en·rich´ment** *n.*

**en·rol, en·roll´** *vt.* to register or place on record; to enlist **—en·rol´ment, en·roll´ment** *n.*

**en·sconce´** *vt.* to settle snuggly

**en·sem´ble** *n.* a suitable or pleasing combination, as of attire; a group of performers

**en·shrine´** *vt.* to hold sacred **—en·shrine´ment** *n.*

**en·shroud´** *vt.* to cover or conceal

**en´sign** *n.* a flag, banner, or symbol; a naval officer

**en´si·lage** *n.* stored fodder

**en·slave´** *vt.* to place in bondage; to dominate **—en·slave´ment** *n.* **—en·slav´er** *n.*

**en·snare´** *vt.* to trap

**en·sue´** *vi.* to result; to follow after

**en·sure´** *vt.* to make safe or secure; to make certain; to guarantee

**en·tail´** *vt.* to impose as a consequence **—en·tail´ment** *n.*

**en·tan´gle** *vt.* to complicate; to involve in difficulties **—en·tan´gle·ment** *n.* **—en·tan´gler** *n.*

**en·tente´** *n.* an understanding between nations

**en´ter** *vt.* to gain admission; to become a member; to begin; to record, as on a list

**en´ter·pris´ing** *adj.* displaying initiative **—en´ter·prise´** *n.* **—en´ter·pris·ing·ly** *adv.*

**en´ter·tain´** *vt.* to amuse; to offer hospitality to; to consider, as an idea or proposal **—en·ter·tain´er** *n.* **—en·ter·tain´ing** *adj.* **—en·ter·tain´ing·ly** *adv.* **—en·ter·tain´ment** *n.*

**en·thral´, en·thrall´** *vt.* to charm or fascinate **—en·thrall´ment, en·thral´ment** *n.*

**en·thu´si·asm** *n.* great excitement or interest **—en·thu´si·ast** *n.* **—en´thu·si·as´tic** *adj.* **—en·thu·si·as´ti·cal·ly** *adv.*

**en·tice´** *vt.* to attract with promises **—en·tice´ment** *n.* **—en·tic´ing** *adj.* **—en·tic´ing·ly** *adv.*

**en·tire** *adj.* complete; undivided **—en·tire´ly** *adv.* **—en·tire´ness, en·tire´ty** *n.*

**en·ti´tle** *vt.* to give right to; to authorize **—en·ti´tle·ment** *n.*

**en´ti·ty** *n.* any being; anything that exists

**en·tomb´** *vt.* to place for burial **—en·tomb´ment** *n.*

**en´to·mol´o·gy** *n.* the study of insects **—en·to·mo·log´ic, en·to·mo·log´i·cal** *adj.* **—en·to·mo·log´i·cal·ly** *adv.* **—en´to·mol´o·gist** *n.*

**en·tou·rage´** *n.* companions and attendants

**en´trance[1]** *n.* the act or means of entering **—en´trance·way** *n.*

**en·trance[2]** *vt.* to fill with delight or enchantment **—en·trance´ment** *n.* **—en·tranc´ing** *adj.* **—en·tranc´ing·ly** *adv.*

**en´trant** *n.* one who enters or takes part in, as a contest

**en·trap´** *vt.* to catch or ensnare; to trick or lure into danger or difficulty; to lay a trap for **—en·trap´ment** *n.*

**en·treat´** *vt., vi.* to plead or implore **—en·treat´ment** *n.* **—en·treat´y** *n.*

**en·trench´** *vt.* to fortify; to establish firmly **—en·trench´ment** *n.*

**en·tre·pre·neur´** *n.* one who undertakes a business venture, taking both control and risk **—en·tre·pre·neur´i·al** *adj.* **—en·tre·pre·neur´ship** *n.*

**en·trust´** *vt.* to give over for safekeeping

**en´try** *n.* a means or place of access; the act of entering; an item entered, as on a list; an entrant

**en·twine´** *vt. vi.*, to twist together

**e·nu´mer·ate** *vt.* to name one by one; to count **—e·nu´mer·a´tion** *n.* **—e·nu´mer·a·tive** *adj.* **—e·nu´mer·a·tor** *n.*

**e·nun´ci·ate** *vt.* to pronounce distinctly; to state precisely; to proclaim **—e·nun·ci·a´tion** *n.* **—e·nun´ci·a·tive** *adj.* **—e·nun´ci·a·tor** *n.*

**en·vel´op** *vt.* to surround completely with or as with a covering: *enveloped in mist* **—en·vel´op·ment** *n.* **—en·vel´op·er** *n.*

**en´ve·lope´** *n.* that which envelops or wraps around; a paper wrapper, as for a letter, documents, etc.

**en´vi·a·ble** *adj.* sufficiently desirable so as to provoke envy or admiration —**en´vi·a·bly** *adv.*

**en´vi·ous** *adj.* experiencing or expressing envy —**en´vi·ous·ly** *adv.* —**en´vi·ous·ness** *n.*

**en·vi´ron·ment** *n.* the combination of conditions that affect the growth and development of an organism; one's surroundings or circumstances —**en·vi´ron·men´tal** *adj.* —**en·vi´ron·men´tal·ly** *adv.*

**en·vi´ron·men´tal·ist** *n.* an advocate for environment preservation —**en·vi´ron·men´tal·ism** *n.*

**en·vi´rons** *pl. n.* the surrounding area; the environment

**en·vis´age** *vt.* to visualize; to form a mental image of —**en·vis´age·ment** *n.*

**en·vi´sion** *vt.* to imagine; to foresee

**en´voy** *n.* a diplomatic agent

**en´vy** *n.* resentment aroused by jealousy —*vt.* to regard jealously —**en´vi·er** *n.* —**en´vy·ing·ly** *adv.*

**e´on** *n.* an incalculable time

**ep´au·let´** *n.* a shoulder ornament on a uniform

**e·phem´er·al** *adj.* short-lived; transitory —**e·phem´er·al·ly** *adv.* —**e·phem´er·al·ness** *n.*

**ep´ic** *n.* a literary or dramatic work having a heroic theme —**ep´ic, ep´i·cal** *adj.* on a grand scale; heroic or legendary

**ep´i·cen·ter** *n.* the point on the earth's surface above the source of an earthquake; a central point

**ep´i·cure** *n.* a person of discriminating taste, especially for food and drink —**ep´i·cu´re·an** *adj.*, *n.* —**ep´i·cur·ism** *n.*

**ep´i·dem´ic** *n.* a widespread condition, situation, disease, etc. —**ep´i·dem´ic, ep·i·dem´i·cal** *adj.* affecting many in an area at once —**ep·i·dem´i·cal·ly** *adv.*

**ep·i·de·mi·ol´o·gy** *n.* the study of epidemics, their causes, and control —**ep·i·de·mi·o·log´i·cal** *adj.* —**ep·i·de·mi·o·log´i·cal·ly** *adv.* —**ep·i·de·mi·ol´o·gist** *n.*

**ep´i·der´mis** *n.* the outer layer of the skin —**ep´i·der´mal, ep´i·der´mic** *adj.*

**ep´i·gram´** *n.* a thought-provoking saying

**ep´i·lep·sy** *n.* a nervous disorder marked by loss of consciousness and sometimes convulsions

**ep´i·logue** *n.* a concluding section, as of a book or play

**e·pis´co·pa·cy** *n.* government of a church by bishops —**e·pis´co·pal** *adj.* —**e·pis´co·pa´li·an** *n.*, *adj.*

**e·pis´co·pate** *n.* the office of a bishop

**ep´i·sode´** *n.* one event in a series of related events; a notable incident —**ep·i·sod´ic, ep·i·sod´i·cal** *adj.* —**ep·i·sod´i·cal·ly** *adv.*

**e·pis·te·mol´o·gy** *n.* the philosophical study of human knowledge —**e·pis´te·mo·log´i·cal** *adj.* —**e·pis·te·mo·log´i·cal·ly** *adv.* —**e·pis·te·mol´o·gist** *n.*

**e·pis´tle** *n.* a letter, especially one of instruction

**ep´i·taph´** *n.* inscription on a tomb

**ep´i·thet´** *n.* a word or phrase used to characterize a person or thing, as *Lion-Hearted* in *Richard the Lion-Hearted* —**ep·i·thet´ic, ep·i·thet´i·cal** *adj.*

**e·pit´o·me** *n.* a typical example; a brief summary

**e·pit´o·mize** *vt.* to abridge; to be typical of

**ep´och** *n.* a period characterized by extraordinary events —**ep´och·al** *adj.*

**eq´ua·ble** *adj.* of uniform condition; not easily disturbed

**e´qual** *adj.* of the same value; fair and impartial; balanced —*vt.* to be or become equivalent —*n.* a person or thing that closely matches another —**e´qual·ly** *adv.*

**e·qual´i·ty** *n.* the condition of being equal —**e´qual·i·za´tion** *n.* —**e´qual·ize** *vt.* —**e´qual·iz·er** *n.*

**e´qua·nim´i·ty** *n.* calmness; composure

**e·quate´** *vt.* to make equal; to compare

**e·qua´tion** *n.* a complex array of elements, as *the human equation*; a mathematical statement expressing equality

**e·qua´tor** *n.* a circle around the earth equidistant from the poles —**e´qua·to´ri·al** *adj.*

**e·ques´tri·an** *adj.* of horses or horsemanship

**e´qui·lat´er·al** *adj.* having all sides equal —**e·qui·lat´er·al·ly** *adv.*

**e·qui´li·brate** *vi.*, *vt.* to balance; to be or bring to a state of equilibrium

**e·qui·lib´ri·um** *n.* a condition in which all factors are equal or balanced

**e´quine** *adj.* of horses —*n.* a horse

**e´qui·nox** *n.* one of two times each year when day and night are of equal length throughout the earth

**e·quip´** *vt.* to prepare as by outfitting with supplies or training —**e·quip´ment** *n.*

**eq´ui·ta·ble** *adj.* fair; impartial —**eq´ui·ta·ble·ness** *n.* —**eq´ui·ta·bly** *adv.*

**eq´ui·ty** *n.* fairness; impartiality; net assets

**e·quiv´a·lent** *adj.* equal or corresponding in value —*n.* that corresponds in value —**e·quiv´a·lence, e·quiv´a·len·cy** *adj.* —**e·quiv´a·lent·ly** *adv.*

**e·quiv´o·cate´** *vi.* speak with intent to deceive —**e·quiv´o·cal** *adj.* —**e·quiv´o·ca´tion** *n.*

**e´ra** *n.* a period encompassing important dates, events, etc.

**e·rad´i·cate´** *vt.* to destroy utterly —**e·rad´i·ca·ble** *adj.* —**e·rad·i·ca´tion** *n.*

**e·rase´** *vt.* to wipe out; to remove —**e·ra´sure** *n.* —**e·ras´er** *n.*

**e·rect´** *adj.* upright or vertical; standing —*vt.* to construct; to set in an upright or vertical position —**e·rec´tion** *n.* —**e·rect´ly** *adv.*

**e·rec´tile** *adj.* capable or becoming erect or being raised to an upright position —**e·rec·til´i·ty** *n.*

**erg** *n.* a unit of work or energy

**er·go·nom´ics** *n.* the science of designing equipment

or a workplace with intent to minimize operator fatigue **–er·go·nom´ic** *adj.* **–er·go·nom´i·cal·ly** *adv.*
**e·rode** *vt., vi.* to wear or become worn away **–e·ro´sion** *n.*
**e·rog´e·nous** *adj.* exciting sexually
**e·rot´ic** *adj.* tending to arouse sexually **–e·rot´i·cal·ly** *adv.* **–e·rot´i·cism** *n.*
**e·rot´i·ca** *n.* erotic materials, as books, pictures, etc.
**err** *vi.* to make a mistake; to sin **–er´ran·cy** *n.*
**er´rand** *n.* a short trip; to tend to a task, often for another
**er´rant** *adj.* wandering; straying from a proper course **–er´rant·ly** *adv.*
**er·rat´ic** *adj.* deviating from the customary or expected; lacking consistency **–er·rat´i·cal·ly** *adv.*
**er·ro´ne·ous** *adj.* inaccurate, incorrect **–er·ro´ne·ous·ly** *adv.* **–er·ro´ne·ous·ness** *n.*
**er´ror** *n.* something done wrongly; an inaccuracy
**er´satz´** *n.* an inferior substitute *–adj.* substitute
**erst´while** *adj.* former
**er´u·dite** *adj.* scholarly; learned **–er·u·di´tion** *n.*
**e·rupt´** *vi., vt.* to burst forth **–e·rupt´i·ble** *adj.* **e·rup´tion** *n.* **–e·rup´tive** *adj.* **–e·rup´tive·ly** *adv.* **–e·rup´tive·ness** *n.*
**es´ca·late´** *vi., vt.* to increase; to ascend or carry up
**es´ca·la´tor** *n.* a moving staircase
**es´ca·pade´** *n.* prank
**es·cape´** *n.* the act of breaking free; a means of breaking free *–vi., vt.* to elude, avoid, or break free
**es·ca´pism** *n.* a turning from unpleasant reality, as by daydreaming, etc. **–es·cap´ist** *adj., n.*
**es·carp´ment** *n.* a steep slope
**es·cha·tol´o·gy** *n.* the theological study of the destiny of man **–es·cha·to·log´i·cal** *adj.* **–es·cha·to·log´i·cal·ly** *adv.* **–es·cha·tol´o·gist** *n.*
**es·cheat´** *n.* reversion of property to the state in the absence of heirs *–vi., vt.* to revert or cause to revert to the state **–es·cheat´a·ble** *adj.*
**es·chew´** *vt.* to shun, as something injurious
**es´cort** *n.* one accompanying
**es·cort´** *vt.* to accompany
**es·crow** *n.* a thing of value held in the care of a third party until certain conditions are satisfied
**es·cutch´eon** *n.* a heraldic shield
**e·soph´a·gus** *n.* the tube that connects the mouth to the stomach
**es·o·ter´ic** *adj.* intended to be understood by a limited group; confidential **–es·o·ter´i·cal·ly** *adv.*
**es·pe´cial** *adj.* exceptional **–es·pe´cial·ly** *adv.*
**es´pi·o·nage** *n.* spying
**es·pla·nade´** *n.* a level public space
**es·pouse´** *vt.* to give or take in marriage; to take up, as a cause **–es·pous´al** *n.*
**es·pres´so** *n.* coffee made from beans that have been darkly roasted and finely ground
**es·py´** *vt.* to catch sight of
**es·quire´** *n.* a title of courtesy; a candidate for knighthood
**es´say** *n.* a brief written work; a testing of the nature of a thing *–vt.* to test, as ore
**es´sence** *n.* the basic nature or quality of a thing
**es·sen´tial** *adj.* fundamental; necessary *–n.* something fundamental or required **–es·sen´tial·ly** *adv.*
**es·tab´lish** *vt.* to create or install; to authenticate **–es·tab´lish·er** *n.* **–es·tab´lish·ment** *n.*
**es·tate´** *n.* one's entire wealth; landed property
**es·teem´** *n.* respect; reverence *–vt.* to value; to regard as: *esteem the recognition as an honor*
**es´ti·ma·ble** *adj.* deserving of esteem **–es´ti·ma·ble·ness** *n.* **–es´ti·ma·bly** *adv.*
**es´ti·mate´** *vt.* to approximate; to form an opinion *–n.* an appraisal or evaluation; an opinion **–es´ti·ma´tion** *n.*
**es·top´** *vt.* to prevent
**estrange´** *vt.* to alienate **–es·trange´ment** *n.*
**es´tu·ar´y** *n.* the mouth of a river where it meets the sea
**etch** *vi., vt.* to engrave with acid; to make a clear impression **–etch´ing** *n.* **–etch´er** *n.*
**e·ter´nal** *adj.* without end; perpetual **–e·ter´nal·ly** *adv.* **–e·ter´ni·ty** *n.*
**e·the´re·al** *adj.* light, airy **–e·the´re·al·ly** *adv.*
**eth´ic** *n.* a set of principles
**eth´i·cal** *adj.* morally right **–eth·i·cal´i·ty, eth´i·cal·ness** *n.* **–eth´i·cal·ly** *adv.*
**eth´ics** *n.* the accepted standard of morality
**eth´nic, eth´ni·cal** *adj.* of the customs, food, etc. characteristic to a group or culture **–eth´ni·cal·ly** *adv.* **–eth·nic´i·ty** *n.*
**eth´nol´o·gy** *n.* the study of human cultures
**e·ti·ol´o·gy** *n.* the study of origins, esp. of disease **–e·ti·o·log´i·cal** *adj.* **–e·ti·o·log´i·cal·ly** *adv.* **–e·ti·ol´o·gist** *n.*
**et´i·quette´** *n.* the rules for socially acceptable behavior
**e´tude** *n.* a musical exercise
**et´y·mol´o·gy** *n.* the origin and development of words **–et´y·mo·log´i·cal** *adj.*
**eu·gen´ic, eu·gen´i·cal** *adj.* of or relating to eugenics **–eu·gen´i·cal·ly** *adv.*
**eu´gen´ics** *n.* the study of improvements to the human race by selective breeding **–eu·gen´i·cist** *n.*
**eu´lo·gy** *n.* a tribute, especially for one who has died **–eu´lo·gize** *vt.*
**eu´phe·mism** *n.* a word or phrase substituted for one that may be offensive **–eu´phe·mis´tic, eu´phe·mis´ti·cal** *adj.* **–eu´phe·mis´ti·cal·ly** *adv.*
**eu·phon´ic, eu·pho´ni·ous** *adj.* pleasant or agreeable sounding **–eu·pho´ni·ous·ly** *adv.* **–eu·pho´ni·ous·ness** *n.*

**eu·pho´ni·um** *n.* a brass instrument similar to the baritone horn
**eu´pho·ny** *n.* a pleasant sounding word combination
**eu·pho´ri·a** *n.* a feeling of well-being **eu·phor´ic** *adj.* **–eu·phor´i·cal·ly** *adv.*
**eu·ryth´mics** *pl. n.* musical interpretation through rhythmic body movements **–eu·ryth´mic** *adj.*
**eu´tha·na´sia** *n.* ending the life of a suffering person painlessly and peacefully **–eu´tha·nize** *vt.*
**e·vac´u·ate´** *vt.* to depart from; to withdraw **–e·vac´u·a´tion** *n.*
**e·vade´** *vi., vt.* to avoid by cleverness or deceit
**e·val´u·ate** *vt.* to determine the worth of; to appraise **–e·val·u·a´tion** *n.*
**ev´a·nesce´** *vt.* to vanish slowly **–ev·a·nes´cence** *n.* **–ev´a·nes´cent** *adj.* **–ev´a·nes´cent·ly** *adv.*
**e´van·gel´ic, e´van·gel´i·cal** *adj.* believing in and adhering closely to Christian scripture; marked by enthusiasm or ardor **–e´van·gel´i·cal·ly** *adv.* **–e·van´ge·lism** *n.* **–e·van´ge·list** *n.*
**e·van·gel·is´tic** *adj.* of the crusading nature of one who has taken up a cause **–e·van·gel·is´ti·cal·ly** *adv.*
**e·van´gel·ize** *vi., vt.* to preach the gospel **–e·van·gel·i·za´tion** *n.* **–e·van´gel·iz·er** *n.*
**e·vap´o·rate** *vi., vt.* to become or convert into vapor **–e·vap·o·ra´tion** *n.* **–e·vap´o·ra·tive** *adj.* **–e·vap´o·ra·tor** *n.*
**e·va´sive** *adj.* deliberately vague, as *an evasive answer*, intended to avoid **–e·va´sion** *n.* **–e·va´sive·ly** *adv.* **–e·va´sive·ness** *n.*
**eve** *n.* the night before a special event
**e´ven** *adj.* smooth, level; unchanging, constant; calm, tranquil; balanced *–vt., vi.* to make or become smooth, level, etc. *–adv.* **–e´ven·ly** *adv.* **–e´ven·ness** *n.*
**eve´ning** *n.* the close of the day; nightfall
**e·vent´** *n.* an important occasion; an incident; an activity or one of a series of activities
**e·vent´ful** *adj.* momentous **–e·vent´ful·ly** *adv.* **–e·vent´ful·ness** *n.*
**e·ven´tu·al** *adj.* occurring in the future **–e·ven·tu·al´i·ty** *n.* **–e·ven´tu·al·ly** *adv.*
**ev´er** *adv.* at any time; in any way; always
**e·vert´** *vt.* to turn inside out **–e·ver´sion** *n.*
**eve´ry** *adj.* all, taken singly
**e·vict´** *vt.* to turn out legally; to dispossess **–e·vic´tion** *n.* **–e·vic´tor** *n.*
**ev´i·dence** *n.* that which serves to make clear or prove *–vt.* to make plain; to attest **–ev·i·den´tial** *adj.* **–ev·i·den´tial·ly** *adv.* **–ev·i·den´ti·ar·y** *adj.*
**ev´i·dent** *adj.* clear; obvious **–ev´i·dent·ly** *adv.*
**e´vil** *adj.* wicked or depraved; harmful *–n.* sinfulness; that which can harm **–e´vil·ly** *adv.* **–e´vil·ness** *n*
**e·vince´** *vt.* to demonstrate clearly **–e·vinc´i·ble** *adj.* **–e·vinc´i·bly** *adj.*
**e·vis´cer·ate** *vt.* to disembowel **–e·vis·cer·a´tion** *n.*
**e·voke´** *vt.* to call forth or summon **–ev´o·ca·ble** *adj.* **–e·vo·ca´tion** *n.* **–e·voc´a·tive** *adj.*
**ev·o·lu´tion** *n.* the process of evolving; gradual development or growth **–ev·o·lu´tion·al, ev·o·lu´tion·ar·y** *adj.* **–ev·o·lu´tion·al·ly, ev·o·lu´tion·ar·i·ly** *adv.*
**ev·o·lu´tion·ism** *n.* a theory of gradual biological change over time; a belief in biological evolution **–ev·o·lu´tion·ist** *n.*
**e·volve´** *vi., vt.* to progress or develop gradually **–e·volv´a·ble** *adj.* **–e·volve´ment** *n.*
**ew´er** *n.* a large pitcher
**ex·ac´er·bate´** *vt.* make more intense **–ex·ac·er·ba´tion** *n.*
**ex·act´** *adj.* very accurate; precise *–vt.* to obtain by force or authority **–ex·act´ing** *adj.* **–ex·act´ing·ly** *adv.* **–ex·act´ly** *adv.* **–ex·act´ness, ex·ac´ti·tude** *n.*
**ex·ac´tion** *n.* extortion
**ex·ag´ger·ate** *vi., vt.* to describe something as greater than it actually is **–ex·ag´ger·at·ed·ly** *adv.* **–ex·ag´ger·a´tion** *n.*
**ex·alt´** *vt.* to glorify or praise **–ex´al·ta´tion** *n.* **–ex·alt´er**
**ex·am´i·ne** *vt.* to inspect or test **–ex·am´in·a·ble** *adj.* **ex·am·i·na´tion** *n.* **–ex·am´in·er** *n.*
**ex·am´ple** *n.* that which typifies or serves as a model: *set a good example for the others*
**ex·as´per·ate** *vt.* to annoy or irritate **–ex·as´per·at·ing** *adj.* **–ex·as´per·at·ing·ly** *adv.* **–ex·as´per·a´tion** *n.*
**ex´ca·vate** *vt.* to make a hole or cavity; to uncover by digging **–ex´ca·va´tion** *n.*
**ex·ceed´** *vt.* to go beyond
**ex·ceed´ing** *adj.* surpassing **–ex´ceed´ing·ly** *adv.*
**ex·cel´** *vi., vt.* to be better or superior; to surpass
**ex´cel·lent** *adj.* outstanding; of exceptional quality **–ex´cel·lence** *n.* **–ex´cel·lent·ly** *adv.*
**ex·cel´si·or** *n.* packing material
**ex·cept´** *vt.* to exclude *–vi.* to object *–prep.* with the exception of **–ex·cept´ing** *prep.*
**ex·cep´tion** *n.* that which is different; that which is excluded; an objection **–ex·cep´tion·a·ble** *adj.* **–ex·cep´tion·al** *adj.* **–ex·cep´tion·al·ly** *adv.*
**ex´cerpt** *n.* an extract from a book or manuscript **–ex·cerpt´** *vt.* to remove or extract; to quote
**ex·cess´** *n.* an amount greater than needed; the amount by which one is greater than another; overindulgence **–ex´cess** *adj.* surplus **–ex·ces´sive** *adj.* **–ex·ces´sive·ly** *adv.* **–ex·ces´sive·ness** *n.*
**ex·change´** *vt.* to trade for something of equal value; to reciprocate; to replace *–vi.* to make a trade *–n.* an act of trading or reciprocating; a substitution; a place where something is traded, such as stocks **–ex·change·a·bil´i·ty** *n.* **–ex·change´a·ble** *adj.*
**ex´cise** *n.* an indirect tax or fee **–ex·cise´** *vt.* to remove, often by cutting **–ex·ci´sion** *n.*

**ex·cit´a·ble** *adj.* high-strung; emotional; easily excited **—ex·cit·a·bil´i·ty** *n.* **—ex·cit´a·ble·ness** *n.* **—ex·cit´a·bly** *adv.*
**ex·cite´** *vt.* to stir the emotions; to provoke **—ex·cit´ed** *adj.* **—ex·cit´ed·ly** *adv.* **—ex·cit´ed·ness** *n.*
**ex·cite´ment** *n.* a state of high emotion; something that thrills
**ex·cit´ing** *adj.* exhilarating; intensely emotional **—ex·cit´ing·ly** *adv.*
**ex·claim´** *vi., vt.* to cry out suddenly **—ex´cla·ma´tion** *n.* **—ex·clam´a·to·ry** *adj.*
**ex·clude´** *vt.* to put out or leave out; to except **—ex·clud´a·ble** *adj.* **—ex·clu´sion** *n.* **—ex·clu´sion·ar·y** *adj.*
**ex·clu´sive** *adj.* limited to a certain person or group; regarded as incompatible; restricted **—ex·clu´sive·ly** *adv.* **—ex·clu´sive·ness** *n.*
**ex´com·mu´ni·cate´** *vt.* to expel in disgrace *—adj.* expelled or excluded **—ex´com·mu´ni·ca´tion** *n.*
**ex·co´ri·ate** *vt.* to abrade the skin; to denounce
**ex´cre·ment** *n.* refuse matter; feces
**ex·cre´ta** *n.* waste matter eliminated from the body **—ex·crete´** *vt.* **—ex·cre´tion** *n.* **—ex´cre·to·ry** *adj.*
**ex·cru´ci·at·ing** *adj.* causing severe mental or physical pain; intense **—ex·cru´ci·ate** *vt.* **ex·cru´ci·at·ing·ly** *adv.*
**ex´cul·pate´** *vt.* to prove innocent **—ex·cul·pa´tion** *n.* **—ex·cul´pa·to·ry** *adj.*
**ex·cur´sion** *n.* a short journey; a group tour
**ex·cuse´** *vt.* to overlook; to free from blame; to offer a reason or apology; to free from an obligation *—n.* justification for an offense; that which relieves of obligation **—ex·cus´a·ble** *adj.* **—ex·cus´a·bly** *adv.* **—ex·cus´er** *n.*
**ex´e·cra·ble** *adj.* appallingly bad **—ex´e·cra·bly** *adv.* **—ex´e·cra·ble·ness** *n.*
**ex´e·crate** *vt.* to denounce; to loathe **—ex·e·cra´tion** *n.*
**ex´e·cute´** *vt.* to perform; to put into effect; to validate; to put to death **—ex´e·cut·a·ble** *adj.* **—ex´e·cu´tion** *n.*
**ex·ec´u·tive** *n.* an official exercising administrative control over a governmental or private concern *—adj.* administrative; having the ability to direct or control
**ex·em´plar** *n.* a typical example
**ex·em´pla·ry** *adj.* worthy of imitation; commendable **—ex·em´pla·ri·ly** *adv.* **—ex·em´pla·ri·ness** *n.*
**ex·em´pli·fy** *vt.* to show by example **—ex·em´pli·fi·ca´tion** *n.*
**ex·empt´** *adj.* freed from, as an obligation *—vt.* to free from a duty or obligation **—ex·emp´tion** *n.*
**ex´er·cise** *n.* activity designed to improve strength or endurance; something practiced to develop a skill; a ceremony *—vt.* to train; to make use of, as authority
**ex·ert´** *vt.* to put forth; bring to bear **—ex·er´tion** *n.*
**ex·fo´li·ate** *vt., vi.* to peel off; to remove or come off in flakes, layers, etc. **—ex·fo·li·a´tion** *n.* **—ex·fo´li·a·tive** *adj.*
**ex´hale´** *vi.* to breathe out **—ex·ha·la´tion** *n.*
**ex·haust´** *vt.* to use up; to drain of resources, energy, etc. **—ex·haust·i·bil´i·ty** *n.* **—ex·haust´i·ble** *adj.*
**ex·haust´ed** *adj.* used up; consumed; extremely tired **—ex·haust´ed·ly** *adv.*
**ex·haust´ing** *adj.* producing exhaustion; tiring
**ex·haus´tion** *n.* extreme fatigue
**ex·haus´tive** *adj.* extensive or complete: *exhaustive research* **—ex·haus´tive·ly** *adv.* **—ex·haus´tive·ness** *n.*
**ex·hib´it** *vt.* to display; to present for inspection *—vi.* to place on display *—n.* a display; something displayed **—ex·hi·bi´tion** *n.*
**ex·hi·bi´tion·ist** *n.* one who behaves so as to attract attention; one driven to indecent exposure **—ex·hi·bi´tion·ism** *n.*
**ex·hil´a·rate** *vt.* to cheer; to stimulate or enliven **—ex·hil´a·rat·ing** *adj.* **—ex·hil´a·rat·ing·ly** *adv.*
**ex·hil·a·ra´tion** *n.* elation; excitement **—ex·hil´a·ra·tive** *adj.*
**ex·hort´** *vt.* to advise strongly; to entreat **—ex·hor·ta´tion** *n.*
**ex·hume´** *vt.* to disinter; to dig up or disclose **—ex·hu·ma´tion** *n.*
**ex·i´gen·cy** *n.* a condition that requires immediate action; an emergency; a pressing need **—ex´i·gent** *adj.* **—ex´i·gent·ly** *adv.*
**ex·ig´u·ous** *adj.* meager, sparse
**ex´ile** *n.* expulsion, banishment; one who has been banished *—vt.* to expel or banish, as from a country
**ex·ist´** *vi.* to have reality; to be present; to continue to be **—ex·ist´ence** *n.* **—ex·ist´ent** *adj.*
**ex·is·ten´tial·ism** *n.* a philosophy or religion that stresses free will and the responsibility of humanity for its actions **—ex·is·ten´tial·ist** *n.* **—ex·is·ten´tial** *adj.* **—ex·is·ten´tial·ly** *adv.*
**ex´it** *n.* a going out or departure; a way out
**ex´o·dus** *n.* a departure or leaving, especially by a large group
**ex·og´a·my** *n.* the custom of marrying outside one's social unit **—ex·og´e·mous** *adj.*
**ex·on´er·ate** *vt.* to clear of an accusation; to prove blameless **—ex·on·er·a´tion** *n.*
**ex·or´bi·tant** *adj.* excessive, as of a price **—ex·or´bi·tance** *n.* **—ex·or´bi·tant·ly** *adv.*
**ex´or·cise´, ex´or·cize´** *vt.* to drive out an evil spirit by ritual incantations; to free from evil influence **—ex´or·cism** *n.* **—ex´or·cist** *n.*
**ex·ot´ic** *adj.* foreign; strange or unusual; alluring **—ex·ot´i·cal·ly** *adv.*
**ex·pand´** *vi., vt.* to make or become greater in size or scope; to spread or extend **—ex·pand´a·ble** *adj.* **—ex·pan´sion** *n.* **—ex·pan´sive** *adj.*
**ex·panse´** *n.* unbroken space; wide extent **—ex·pan´sion**

n.

**ex·pan´sive** *adj.* extensive; amiable or outgoing –**ex·pan´sive·ly** *adv.* –**ex·pan´sive·ness** *n.*

**ex·pa´ti·ate** *vi.* to speak at length and in great detail; to elaborate –**ex·pa·tri·a´tion** *n.*

**ex·pect´** *vt.* to anticipate as likely or deserving –**ex·pect´a·ble** *adj.* –**ex·pect´a·bly** *adv.* –**ex·pect´an·cy** *n.* –**ex·pect´ant** *adj.* –**ex·pect´ant·ly** *adv.*

**ex·pec·ta´tion** *n.* something expected; the hope for good to come

**ex·pec´to·rant** *n.* medication to help clear mucus from the lungs

**ex·pec´to·rate** *vi., vt.* to spit –**ex·pec·to·ra´tion** *n.*

**ex·pe´di·ent** *adj.* appropriate; convenient; useful –*n.* something suited to a pressing need –**ex·pe´di·ence, ex·pe´di·en·cy** *n.* –**ex·pe´di·ent·ly** *adv.*

**ex´pe·dite** *vt.* to hasten; to speed the progress of –**ex´pe·dit·er** *n.*

**ex·pe·di´tion** *n.* a voyage taken for some purpose; collectively, those who journey and their equipment –**ex·pe·di´tion·ar·y** *adj.*

**ex·pe·di´tious** *adj.* rapid, speedy –**ex·pe·di´tious·ly** *adv.* –**ex·pe·di´tious·ness** *n.*

**ex·pel´** *vt.* to drive out by force; to eject by authority –**ex·pel´la·ble** *adj.*

**ex·pend´** *vt.* to spend or use up –**ex·pend·a·bil´i·ty** *n.* –**ex·pend´a·ble** *adj.*

**ex·pend´i·ture** *n.* an expense; a disbursement

**ex·pense´** *n.* an outlay in money, time, etc.; a cost

**ex·pen´sive** *adj.* costly

**ex·pe´ri·ence** *n.* that learned from personal observation or involvement –*vt.* to live through –**ex·pe·ri·en´tial** *adj.* –**ex·pe´ri·en´tial·ly** *adv.*

**ex·per´i·ment** *n.* a test to learn about the unknown or verify that which is known –*vi.* to try or test –**ex·per´i·ment·er** *n.*

**ex·per´i·men´tal** *adj.* in a developmental state –**ex·per´i·men´tal·ism** *n.* –**ex·per´i·men´tal·ist** *n.* –**ex·per´i·men´tal·ly** *adv.*

**ex·per·i·men·ta´tion** *n.* the process of testing and recording results

**ex·pert´** *adj.* having great skill or knowledge –*n.* one knowledgeable or skilled in a particular field –**ex´pert·ly** *adv.* –**ex´pert·ness** *n.*

**ex·per·tise´** *n.* the skill, knowledge, etc. of an expert

**ex´pi·ate´** *vt.* make amends; to atone –**ex´pi·a´tion** *n.*

**ex·pire´** *vi.* to die; to come to an end, as an offer –**ex´pi·ra´tion** *n.*

**ex·plain´** *vi., vt.* make clear or understandable –**ex·plain´a·ble** *adj.* –**ex´pla·na´tion** *n.*

**ex´ple·tive** *n.* an exclamation; a word or phrase that does not add meaning –**ex´ple·to·ry** *adj.*

**ex´pli·ca·ble** *adj.* explainable –**ex´pli´ca·bly** *adv.*

**ex´pli·cate** *vt.* to explain

**ex·plic´it** *adj.* distinct; clearly stated; clearly established –**ex·plic´it·ly** *adv.* –**ex·plic´it·ness** *n.*

**ex·plode´** *vi., vt.* to blow up; to burst with a loud sound

**ex´ploit, ex·ploit´** *n.* a remarkable or daring feat –**ex·ploit'** *vt.* to use to one's advantage and, often, to the disadvantage of another; to take unfair advantage of –**ex·ploit´a·ble** *adj.* –**ex·ploi·ta´tion** *n.* –**ex·ploit´a·tive, ex·ploit´ive** *adj.* –**ex·ploit´er** *n.*

**ex·plore´** *vi., vt.* to investigate or examine exhaustively –**ex´plo·ra´tion** *n.* –**ex·plor´a·tive, ex·plor´a·to·ry** *adj.* –**ex·plor´er** *n.*

**ex·plor´a·ble** *adj.* able to be explored

**ex·plo´sion** *n.* a sudden, loud blowing up or bursting; a sudden outburst; a sudden increase

**ex·plo´sive** *adj.* pertaining to an explosion; liable to cause violence or an outburst –*n.* a substance, such as dynamite, that can explode –**ex·plo´sive·ly** *adv.* –**ex·plo´sive·ness** *n.*

**ex·po´nent** *n.* one who promotes a cause; a symbol used in mathematics to indicate the number of times a value is multiplied by itself, as in $2^3 = 2 \times 2 \times 2$ where $^3$ is the exponent

**ex´port** *n.* goods, ideas, etc. that are sent out of a country or area –**ex·port´** *vt.* to send out of a country or area

**ex·po·sé´** *n.* a description or airing, as of a scandal or an illegal act

**ex·pose´** *vt.* to lay open or leave unprotected

**ex·po·si´tion** *n.* a public exhibition; a detailed explanation

**ex·po´sure** *n.* a revealing, as of an illegal act; the condition of being open to the elements

**ex·pos´tu·late´** *vi.* to argue against –**ex·pos·tu·la´tion** *n.*

**ex·press´** *vt.* to convey in words; to represent by symbols, as in mathematics; to press or force out, as by pressure –*adj.* deliberate, definite; high speed or non-stop, as of a train –*adv.* by fast delivery –*n.* a system for transporting rapidly

**ex·pres´sion** *n.* a means of conveying: *an expression of good will*; something conveyed; a saying

**ex·pres´sive** *adj.* demonstrative; meaningful –**ex·pres´sive·ly** *adv.* –**ex·pres´sive·ness** *n.*

**ex·pul´sion** *n.* the condition of being forced out or expelled –**ex·pul´sive** *adj.*

**ex·punge´** *vt.* to erase or delete

**ex´qui·site** *adj.* beautiful; delicately crafted –**ex·quis´ite·ly** *adv.* –**ex·quis´ite·ness** *n.*

**ex´tant** *adj.* still existing

**ex·tem´po·ra´ne·ous, ex·tem´po·rar´y** *adj.* improvised; speaking without notes –**ex·tem·po·ra´ne·ous·ly** *adv.*

**ex·tend´** *vi., vt.* to enlarge; to stretch out –**ex·tend´ed** *adj.* –**ex·ten´sion** *n.*

**ex·ten´sive** *adj.* great in amount, extent, etc. –

**ex·ten´sive·ly** *adv.* **–ex·ten´sive·ness** *n.*
**ex·tent´** *n.* the scope or range of a thing
**ex·ten´u·ate** *vt.* to diminish the seriousness, as of an offense, by offering an excuse for the action – **ex·tenu·a´tion** *n.* **–ex·ten´u·a·tive, ex·ten´u·a·to·ry** *adj.* **–ex·ten´u·a·tor** *n.*
**ex·te´ri·or** *adj.* outermost; of the outside *–n.* the outside; an outer surface
**ex·ter´mi·nate** *vt.* to destroy; to eradicate completely **–ex·termi·na´tion** *n.* **–ex·ter´mi·na·tive, ex·ter´mi·na·to·ry** *adj.* **–ex·ter´mi·na·tor** *n.*
**ex·ter´nal** *adj.* on or of the outside
**ex·tinct´** *adj.* no longer in existence **–ex·tinc´tion** *n.*
**ex·tin´guish** *vt.* to put out or quench; to destroy – **ex·tin´guish·a·ble** *adj.* **–ex·tin´guish·er** *n.*
**ex´tir·pate** *vt.* to uproot; to destroy completely, exterminate **–ex·tir´pa·tion** *n.*
**ex·tol´, ex·toll´** *vt.* to praise; exalt
**ex·tort´** *vt.* to obtain by violence or threats **–ex·tor´tion** *n.* **–ex·tor´tion·ist** *n.*
**ex´tra** *adj.* being more than required; additional *–n.* something special or additional *–adv.* unusually
**ex´tract** *n.* a thing drawn out by distillation, etc.; a quote taken from an article, book, etc. **–ex·tract´** *vt.* to draw out, as by distillation; to quote a selection
**ex·tra·cur·ric´u·lar** *adj.* outside the regular course of studies or work
**ex´tra·dite** *vt.* to give over a person accused of a crime to another jurisdiction
**ex·tra´ne·ous** *adj.* not belonging; unrelated **–ex·tra´ne·ous·ly** *adv.*
**ex·tra·or´di·nar·y** *adj.* unusual; out of the ordinary; exceptional **–ex·tra·or·di·nar´i·ly** *adv.*
**ex·trap´o·late** *vt.* to project a value outside the range of available data based on what is known about that data **–ex·trap·o·la´tion** *n.*
**ex·tra·sen´so·ry** *adj.* outside the range of normal senses, as *extrasensory perception*
**ex·trav´a·gance** *n.* excess spending; immoderation in anything **–ex·trav´a·gant** *adj.* **–ex·trav´a·gant·ly** *adv.*
**ex´tra·vert, ex´tro·vert** *n.* one who is active and aggressive **–ex·tro·ver´sion** *n.*
**ex·treme´** *adj.* most remote; utmost; to the greatest degree *–n.* a limit; a thing that is as far from another in distance, character, etc. as possible **–ex·treme´ly** *adv.* **–ex·trem´i·ty** *n.*
**ex´tri·cate** *vt.* to release, as from difficulty; to disentangle **–ex´tri·ca·ble** *adj.* **–ex´tri·ca·bly** *adv.* **–ex·tri·ca´tion** *n.*
**ex·u´ber·ant** *adj.* high spirited; enthusiastic **–ex·u´ber·ance** *n.* **–ex·u´ber·ant·ly** *adv.*
**ex·ult´** *vi.* to rejoice, celebrate
**ex·ur´ban·ite** *n.* one who lives in the suburbs of a city, often commuting to the city for work

**f, F** sixth letter of the English alphabet
**fa´ble** *n.* a fictitious story designed to teach a lesson
**fab´ric** *n.* cloth; the structure of a thing
**fab´ri·cate´** *vt.* to manufacture or assemble; to invent a story; to lie **–fab´ri·ca´tion** *n.*
**fab´u·lous** *adj.* imaginary; fictitious; incredible, astonishing
**fac´et** *n.* the small plane surface of a gem; any aspect of a thing
**fa·ce´tious** *adj.* amusing; whimsical
**fac´ile** *adj.* easy; accomplished with little effort **fac´ile·ly** *adv.* **–fac´ile·ness** *n.*
**fa·cil´i·tate´** *vt.* to make convenient or easier
**fa·cil´i·ty** *n.* the absence of difficulty; skill; a building or equipment set aside for a particular purpose
**fac·sim´i·le** *n.* a reproduction
**facsimile, fax** *n.* a device for transmitting documents over telephone lines; a copy of the document transmitted
**fact** *n.* the truth; reliable information; anything that happens
**fac´tion** *n.* a group within an organization, united against others in the organization **–fac´tion·al** *adj.* **–fac´tion·al·ism** *n.*
**fac´tious** *adj.* tending to cause dissension **–fac´tious·ly** *adv.* **–fac´tious·ness** *n.*
**fac·ti´tious** *adj.* forced or artificial; not genuine **–fac·ti´tious·ly** *adv.* **–fac·ti´tious·ness** *n.*
**fac´tor** *n.* one who conducts business as agent for another; any cause or condition that effects a result
**fac´to·ry** *n.* a building used for the manufacture or assembling of goods
**fac´ul·ty** *n.* the ability to act; any mental or physical ability; a body of teachers
**fade** *vi.* to lose color or distinction; to diminish in some way **–fad´ed·ness** *n.*
**fail** *vi., vt.* to fall short of need; to cease to function properly; to be unsuccessful, as in business **–fail´ure** *n.*
**faint** *adj.* lacking in strength; indistinct *–vi.* to swoon **–faint´ly** *adv.* **–faint´ness** *n.*
**faith** *n.* unflagging trust; belief without firm proof; belief in a supreme being: a religion; fidelity – **faith´ful** *adj.* **–faith´ful·ly** *adv.* **–faith´ful·ness** *n.*
**fal´con** *n.* a bird of prey, often one trained to hunt small game
**fall** *vi.* to descend; to decline; to tumble down or collapse *–n.* the act of falling; *(US)* autumn
**fal´la·cy** *n.* illogical reasoning **–fal·la´cious** *adj.* **–fal·la´cious·ly** *adv.* **–fal·la´cious·ness** *n.*
**fal'li·ble** *adj.* questionable; liable to err **–fal·li·bil´i·ty, fal´li·ble·ness** *n.* **–fal´li·bly** *adv.*
**false** *adj.* deceitful; unfaithful; artificial **–false´ly** *adv.*
**fal´si·fy** *vt.* to misrepresent; to alter a document with fraudulent intent **–fal´si·fi·ca´tion** *n.*

**fa·mil´iar** *adj.* intimate, informal; common; presumptuous **–fa·mil·i·ar´i·ty** *n.* **–fa·mil´iar·ize** *vt.* **–fa·mil·iar·i·za´tion** *n.*

**fam´i·ly** *n.* the members of one's household; close relatives; a social unit, such as a tribe; a related group, as of certain plants or animals

**fam´ine** *n.* a critical shortage of food

**fam´ish** *vi., vt.* to be or cause to be hungry; to starve or cause to starve

**fa´mous** *adj.* very well known; renowned **–fa´mous·ly** *adv.*

**fa·nat´ic, fa·nat´i·cal** *adj.* overly enthusiastic *–n.* one who is unreasonably zealous **–fa·nat´i·cal·ly** *adv.* **–fa·nat´i·cism** *n.*

**fan´cy** *adj.* elaborate; intricate *–n.* a whim; a delusion *–vt.* to imagine; to be fond of **–fan´ci·ful** *adj.* **–fan´ci·ful·ly** *adv.*

**fang** *n.* a long, pointed tooth

**fan·tas´tic** *adj.* imaginary; strange, odd; fanciful

**farce** *n.* a broad comedy or satire; empty actions or ceremony **–far´ci·cal** *adj.*

**fare** *n.* the price for transport; one being transported: a passenger; food *–vi.* to prosper; to turn out

**far´ther** *adj.* more distant *–adv.* more remote in time or place

**fas´ci·nate** *vt.* to charm, bewitch; to captivate **fas´ci·nat·ing** *adj.* **–fas´ci·nat·ing·ly** *adv.* **–fas´ci·na´tion** *n.*

**fash´ion** *n.* a popular style of dress *–vt.* to make or adapt **–fash´ion·a·ble** *adj.* **–fash´ion·a·ble·ness** *n.* **–fash´ion·a·bly** *adv.*

**fas´ten** *vi.* to become attached *–vt.* to attach or secure **–fas´ten·er** *n.*

**fas·tid´i·ous** *adj.* particular; difficult to satisfy; oversensitive **–fas·tid´i·ous·ly** *adv.* **–fas·tid´i·ous·ness** *n.*

**fa´tal** *adj.* deadly; decisive; fateful **–fa´tal·ist** *n.* **–fa·tal·is´tic** *adj.* **–fa·tal·is´ti·cal·ly** *adv.*

**fate** *n.* the inescapable future; destiny *–vt.* to predestine **–fat´ed** *adj.* **–fate´ful** *adj.* **–fate´ful·ly** *adv.*

**fath´om** *n.* a measure for testing the depth of water, equal to 6 feet *–vt.* to comprehend

**fa·tigue´** *n.* weariness, exhaustion *–vi., vt.* to make or grow exhausted

**fat´u·ous** *adj.* silly, foolish; dim-witted **–fat´u·ous·ly** *adv.* **–fat´u·ous·ness** *n.*

**fau´cet** *(US) n.* a device for regulating the flow of a liquid

**fault** *n.* a flaw in appearance or structure; a mistake; a liability **–fault´i·ness** *n.* **–fault´y** *adj.*

**faux pas´** *n.* a socially unacceptable error; a tactless deed

**fa´vour** *(Brit.)*, **fa´vor** *(US)* *n.* approval; a generous act; preferential treatment; a small gift *–vt.* to approve; to assist **–fa´vour·a·ble, fa´vor·a·ble** *adj.* **–fa´vour·a·ble·ness, fa´vor·a·ble·ness** *n.* **–fa´vour·a·bly, fa´vor·a·bly** *adv.*

**fa´vour·ite** *(Brit.)*, **fa´vor·ite** *(US)* *n.* something regarded with fondness; one liked and granted special privileges; one considered most likely to win a contest *–adj.* especially liked; preferred

**fawn** *vi.* to dote on; to curry favor **–fawn´er** *n.* **–fawn´ing·ly** *adv.*

**faze** *vt.* to disturb; to confuse

**fear** *n.* a state of anxiety or dread; uneasiness or concern *–vi.* to be afraid *–vt.* to dread; to regard with awe **–fear´ful** *adj.* **–fear´ful·ly** *adv.* **–fear´ful·ness** *n.*

**fea´si·ble** *adj.* within reason; possible to be carried out **–fea·si·bil´i·ty** *n.* **–fea´si·bly** *adv.*

**feast** *n.* a festivity; a banquet *–vi.* to dine extravagantly *–vt.* to entertain

**feat** *n.* an extraordinary deed

**fea´ture** *n.* a property or cast of a thing; a characteristic quality; a prominent article, as in a newspaper or periodical

**fe´ces´** *n. pl.* waste matter expelled by the body; excrement

**fed´er·al** *adj.* of a coalition of states, groups, etc.; of the government of the U.S. **–fed´er·al·ize** *vt.* **–fed´er·al·ly** *adv.*

**fed´er·ate** *vi., vt.* to unite under a common authority **–fed·er·a´tion** *n.* **–fed´er·a·tive** *adj.* **–fed´er·a·tive·ly** *adv.*

**fee** *n.* a charge or payment for a service, license, etc.

**fee´ble** *adj.* weak, infirm **–fee´ble·ness** *n.*

**feed** *vi.* to eat; to flow steadily *–vt.* to furnish with food; to supply with material, as for processing *–n.* food for animals

**feel** *n.* the sense of touch; emotional or intuitive perception *–vi., vt.* to sense by touch; to believe, based on emotion or intuition **–feel´ing** *adj.* **–feel´ing·ly** *adv.*

**feign** *vi., vt.* to pretend **–feign´ed·ly, feign´ing·ly** *adv.* **–feign´er** *n.*

**feint** *n.* a deceptive move to throw an opponent off guard *–vi., vt.* to make a deceptive move

**feis´ty** *adj.* lively or flamboyant; spirited **–feis´ti·ness** *n.*

**fe·lic´i·tate** *vt.* to congratulate; to wish one well; to make happy **–fe·lic´i·ta´tion** *n.* **–fe·lic´i·tous** *adj.* **–fe·lic´i·tous·ly** *adv.* **–fe·lic´i·tous·ness** *n.*

**fe·lic´i·ty** *n.* happiness; light-heartedness; a pleasing quality

**fe´line** *adj.* of or like a cat *–n.* a cat

**fel´low** *n.* an associate or colleague; a scholar

**fel´on** *n.* one guilty of a serious crime

**fel´o·ny** *n.* a serious crime **–fe·lo´ni·ous** *adj.* **–fe·lo´ni·ous·ly** *adv.* **–fe·lo´ni·ous·ness** *n.*

**fe´male** *adj.* of the sex that bears offspring; of a mechanical part designed to receive a projecting connector –*n.* a female animal or plant

**fem´i·nine** *adj.* having the qualities of a female –**fem´i·nine·ly** *adv.* –**fem·i·nin´i·ty** *n.*

**fem´i·nist** *n.* one who advocates equal rights for women –**fem´i·nism** *n.*

**fence** *n.* a barrier that divides property or affords protection; one who deals in stolen goods –*vi.* to be evasive; to deal in stolen goods –*vt.* to restrict, as by a barrier; to sell to a dealer in stolen goods

**fenc´ing** *n.* the art of combat with a foil, saber, etc.

**fend** *vi.* to provide for oneself –*vt.* to ward off; to defend

**fend´er** *(US) n.* a guard or cushion that protects from damage by contact, as on an automobile or boat

**fer·ment´** *n.* any substance that causes fermentation; a state of agitation –*vi.* to undergo fermentation; to be in an agitated state –*vt.* to cause fermentation; to agitate

**fer·men·ta´tion** *n.* a chemical conversion brought on by a ferment; agitation

**fe·ro´cious** *adj.* savage; unmerciful; ravenous –**fe·ro´cious·ly** *adv.* –**fe·ro´cious·ness, fe·roc´i·ty** *n.*

**fer´ry** *vt.* to convey passengers or freight by boat or aircraft –*n.* a vehicle used for such conveyance

**fer´tile** *adj.* productive; teeming; rich in natural resources –**fer·til´i·ty** *n.*

**fer´vid** *adj.* impassioned; zealous –**fer´vid·ly** *adv.*

**fer´vour** *(Brit.)*, **fer´vor** *(US) n.* ardor; zeal; enthusiasm

**fes´ter** *vi., vt.* to form pus; to rankle or embitter

**fes´ti·val** *n.* a celebration

**fes´tive** *adj.* joyous, lighthearted –**fes´tive·ly** *adv.* –**fes´tive·ness** *n.*

**fes·tiv´i·ty** *n.* a festival or celebration

**fes·toon´** *n.* a hanging garland; a decorative molding –*vt.* to decorate with garlands

**fete, fête** *n.* a festival –*vt.* to honor with a festival or celebration

**fe´tish** *n.* an object regarded as having magical powers; an object of inordinate devotion –**fe´tish·ism** *n.*

**fet´id** *adj.* having an offensive smell; stinking **fet´id·ly** *adv.* –**fet´id·ness** *n.*

**fe·tol´o·gy** *n.* the medical discipline that deals with the study and care of a fetus

**fet´ter** *n.* a chain or shackle for the feet; a restraint –*vt.* to constrain with shackles; to restrain

**fe´tus** *n.* an unborn young in the uterus or egg

**feud** *n.* a bitter, long-lasting quarrel, especially between families, clans, etc. –*vi.* to sustain a long-standing quarrel

**fe´ver** *n.* a condition characterized by increased body temperature; a state of exceptional excitement

**fi·an·cé´** *n.* a man who is engaged to be married

**fi·an·ceé´** *n.* a woman who is engaged to be married

**fi·as´co** *n.* a complete and utter failure; a debacle

**fi´at** *n.* a legal order; a decree

**fi´ber** *(US)*, **fi´bre** *(Brit.) n.* a threadlike structure –**fi´bered, fi´ber·less** *adj.* –**fi'brous** *adj.*

**fick´le** *adj.* flighty or unstable in attention, affection, etc. –**fick´le·ness** *n.*

**fic´tion** *n.* an imaginary story; a narrative portraying imaginary characters and events –**fic´tion·al** *adj.* –**fic´tion·al·ly** *adv.* –**fic´tion·al·ize** *vt.*

**fic´ti´tious** *adj.* pretended; made up, imaginary –**fic·ti´tious·ly** *adv.* –**fic·ti´tious·ness** *n.*

**fi·del´i·ty** *n.* loyalty; devotion to duty or obligation; accuracy in description, reproduction, etc.

**fi·du´ci·ar´y** *adj.* of one who holds something in trust for another; of that held in trust –*n.* one who holds in trust

**field** *n.* open land; a plot of ground set aside for crops or pasture; any unbroken expanse; an area of endeavor or knowledge, as *the computer field*

**fiend** *n.* an evil spirit, a demon; one who is exceptionally cruel; one addicted to a drug or activity –**fiend´ish** *adj.* –**fiend´ish·ly** *adv.* –**fiend´ish·ness** *n.*

**fie·rce** *adj.* savagely cruel; violent; passionate or intense, as *a fierce longing* –**fierce´ly** *adv.* –**fierce´ness** *n.*

**fi´er·y** *adj.* containing or like fire; impetuous or emotional –**fier´i·ly** *adv.* –**fi´er·i·ness** *n.*

**fight** *vi., vt.* to take part in a conflict or battle –*n.* any conflict or struggle; a quality of boldness; readiness to struggle –**fight´er** *n.*

**fig´ur·a·tive** *adj.* symbolic; not to be taken in the literal sense –**fig´u·ra·tive·ly** *adv.* –**fig´ur·a·tive·ness** *n.*

**fig´ure** *n.* a form or likeness; a diagram; a character that represents a value –*vi., vt.* to calculate; to consider

**fil´a·ment** *n.* a thin threadlike component

**file** *n.* a storage cabinet, folder, etc. for keeping papers; a collection of related data stored together; a line of people or things, one behind the other; a tool for smoothing, scraping, etc. –*vi.* to march in line; to formally petition or register, as to a court –*vt.* to place in order and store documents, data, etc.; to place on public record; to smooth or scrape with a tool

**fil´i·al** *adj.* of that expected or due of a son or daughter

**fil´i·gree´** *n.* delicate ornamental work of intertwined gold or silver wire

**fill** *n.* anything used to take up space or make full; a section of land which has been built up; a satisfactory amount –*vt.* to bring to a desired level; to make full; to occupy; to furnish what is needed; to satisfy one's hunger

**fil´ly** *n.* a young mare

**film** *n.* a thin layer or coating; sensitized material used in photography; a motion picture –*vi., vt.* to cover with a thin layer; to shoot a motion picture

**fil´ter** *n.* a porous substance used for straining and separating materials –*vi., vt.* to pass through a filter

–**fil´ter·er** *n.*

**filth** *n.* offensive dirt; grime; contamination; lewd material; an obscenity

**filth´y** *adj.* dirty; obscene –**filth´i·ly** *adv.* –**filth´i·ness** *n.*

**fil´trate** *vt.* to strain or separate –*n.* a substance that has been filtered –**fil·tra·tion** *n.*

**fi´nal** *adj.* at the end; conclusive –*n.* the last of a series

**fi´nance, fi·nance´** *n.* the management of money –*vt.* to furnish or obtain money or credit –**fi·nan´cial** *adj.* –**fi·nan´cial·ly** *adv.*

**finances** the resources of a person, company, etc.

**fin·an·cier´** *n.* one specializing in financial operations

**find** *n.* an amazing discovery; something discovered –*vt.* to discover or perceive; to experience, as *to find pleasing*

**fine** *adj.* of exceptional quality; small, thin, or keen –*n.* money payment imposed as a penalty –*vt.* to impose a fine

**fin´ger** *n.* one of the digits projecting from the hand; anything resembling a finger –*vt.* to touch with the fingers; to point out

**fi´nis** *n.* finish

**fin´ish** *n.* the end or conclusion; completion, perfection; the surface of an object; fineness of manner and speech –*vt.* bring to an end or complete; to use up; to sand, rub, or apply a final coat of paint, varnish, etc.

**fi´nite** *adj.* having limits that are clearly defined

**fir** *n.* a cone-bearing evergreen tree

**fire** *n.* burning; combustion; strong feeling, ardor; a discharge of firearms –*vi.* to start burning; to become excited; to discharge from a firearm –*vt.* to set afire; to bake in a kiln; to excite, inspire; to discharge a firearm; to dismiss an employee

**fire´proof** *adj.* not easily burned –*vt.* to treat so as to be less combustible

**firm** *adj.* that is solid or dense; not yielding to pressure; secure, immovable; settled, as the terms of a contract; determined –*n.* a business

**fir´ma·ment** *n.* the dome or arch of the heavens

**first** *adj.* preceding all others –*n.* one who or that which is above all others in rank, position, etc.; the beginning –*adv.*

**first aid** emergency treatment, esp. while awaiting professional medical attention

**first´-class´, first´-rate´** *adj.* of the best quality –*adv.*

**fis´cal** *adj.* of taxation or public finances; of financial policy in general –**fis´cal·ly** *adv.*

**fish** *n.* an aquatic animal with gills –*vi., vt.* to try to catch fish –*adj.* pertaining to or made from fish

**fis´sion** *n.* a splitting apart –**nuclear fission** the splitting of atoms to release energy –**fis´sion·a·ble** *adj.*

**fis´sure** *n.* a long, narrow crack

**fist** *n.* a hand with fingers pressed into the palm

**fit** *adj.* able, competent; appropriate, suitable; trim, healthy –*n.* the state of being appropriate or of the proper size; a seizure –*vi.* to be suited –*vt.* to be appropriate; to alter so as to make suitable; to insert in position –**fit´ness** *n.*

**fit´ting** *adj.* appropriate; suitable –*n.* the process of testing or altering for a proper fit; a part that serves to connect –**fit´ting·ly** *adv.* –**fit´ting·ness** *n.*

**fix** *n.* an awkward situation –*vt.* to fasten firmly; to establish with certainty; to repair –**fix´a·ble** *adj.* –**fix´er** *n.*

**fix·a´tion** *n.* a preoccupation; an obsession –**fix´ate** *vi., vt.*

**fix´ture** *n.* anything firmly fastened, such as electrical fittings in a building; anything that has been in place so long as to seem permanently attached

**flab´by** *adj.* soft, weak; lacking good physical form –**flab´bi·ness** *n.*

**flac´cid** *adj.* weak, feeble, soft –**flac·cid´i·ty, flac´cid·ness** *n.* –**flac´cid·ly** *adv.*

**flag** *n.* a cloth banner decorated with colors or symbols –*vi.* to grow weak; to tire –*vt.* to signal with a flag or by waving as with a flag

**flag´el·late** *vt.* to whip –**flag·el·la´tion** *n.*

**fla´grant** *adj.* outrageous; openly disgraceful –**fla´gran·cy** *n.* –**fla´grant·ly** *adv.* –**fla´grant·ness** *n.*

**flake** *n.* a small, thin piece; one who is flightly or fickle –*vi., vt.* to form or chip off into flakes –**flak´i·ly** *adv.* –**flak´i·ness** *n.* –**flak´y** *adj.*

**flame** *n.* light from a fire –*vi.* to burn with a bright light; to become excited; to show the flush of excitement –**flam´ing** *adj.* –**flam´ing·ly** *adv.*

**flange** *n.* a projection at the edge of a wheel, track, etc. that serves to connect, guide, strengthen, etc.

**flank** *n.* the side –*vt.* to be positioned at the side of

**flap** *n.* a flat, broad piece connected at one end that hangs loose; a slapping sound made as if by a flap; a state of excitement –*vi., vt.* to move back and forth; to flutter

**flare** *n.* a bright light used as a signal; a sudden burst of light –*vi.* to emit a sudden burst of light; to spread out at one end

**flash** *adj.* happening suddenly or quickly –*n.* a brief gleam of light; anything that comes and goes in a brief span; ostentation –*vi.* to emit a sudden blaze of light; to pass by swiftly –*vt.* to send out or display briefly –**flash´i·ly** *adv.* –**flash´i·ness** *n.* –**flash´y** *adj.*

**flash´back´** *n.* a memory or reminiscence; an interruption in the action of a story, play, etc. to portray an earlier event

**flask** *n.* a small bottle

**flat[1]** *adj.* having a relatively even surface; showing little or no variation; lying prone; bland; lacking finances –*n.* a level surface; a musical note lowered by a half step or the symbol to indicate this —*adv.* —**flat´ly** *adv.* —**flat´ness** *n.* —**flat´ten** *vi., vt.*

**flat²** *n. (Brit.)* a room or rooms serving as living quarters

**flat´ter** *vt.* to compliment excessively or disingenuously —**flat´ter·er** *n.* —**flat´ter·ing** *adj.* —**flat´ter·ing·ly** *adv.* —**flat´ter·y** *n.*

**flaunt** *vi., vt.* to make an ostentatious or impudent display —**flaunt´ing·ly** *adv.*

**fla´vor** *(US) n.* a quality that affects taste; anything added to impart a particular taste; a distinctive quality, as of a place —*vt.* to impart flavor to —**fla´vor·er** *n.* —**fla´vor·ous, fla´vor·y** *adj.* —**fla´vor·ous·ly** *adv.*

**fla´vor·ful** *(US) adj.* full of flavor; delectable —**fla´vor·ful·ly** *adv.*

**fla´vor·ing** *(US) n.* a substance, such as an extract, that imparts flavor

**fla´vor·less** *(US) adj.* lacking flavor; flat or insipid

**fla´vour** *(Brit.) n.* a quality that affects taste; anything added to impart a particular taste; a distinctive quality, as of a place —*vt.* to impart flavor to —**fla´vour·er** *n.*

**fla´vour·ful** *(Brit.) adj.* full of flavor; delectable

**fla´vour·ing** *(Brit.) n.* a substance, such as an extract, that imparts flavor

**fla´vour·less** *(Brit.) adj.* lacking flavor; flat or insipid

**flaw** *n.* a defect —*vt., vi.* to make or become defective

**flay** *vt.* to strip the skin from, as by whipping; to criticize harshly

**fleck** *n.* a small particle —*vt.* to cover with specks

**flee** *vi., vt.* to run away or escape

**fleece** *n.* the coat of wool that covers a sheep —*vt.* to clip the wool from a sheep; to defraud

**fleet** *adj.* swift; temporary —*vi.* to proceed swiftly fleet'ly *adv.* —**fleet´ness** *n.*

**fleet** *n.* the ships, planes, trucks, etc., operating under a single authority, as a military command or a company

**fleet´ing** *adj.* passing quickly; transitory —**fleet´ing·ly** *adv.* —**fleet´ing·ness** *n.*

**flesh** *n.* the meat of the body of an animal; the edible portion of fruits and vegetables; the human body; human desires, in contrast to the spiritual

**flesh´ly** *adj.* pertaining to the body; sensual, not spiritual: *fleshly desires*; plump —**flesh´li·ness** *n.*

**flex´i·ble** *adj.* able to be bent without breaking; amenable to change —**flex´i·bil´i·ty** *n.* —**flex´i·bly** *adv.*

**flex´time** *n.* a system that allows employees to vary their working hours, usually to accommodate those with small children or to relieve traffic congestion

**flight** *n.* travel by air; fleeing, running away; a set of steps

**flight´y** *adj.* frivolous; whimsical —**flight´i·ly** *adv.* —**flight´i·ness** *n.*

**flim´sy** *adj.* easily damaged; fragile; poorly fashioned —**flim´si·ly** *adv.* —**flim´si·ness** *n.*

**flinch** *vi.* to wince or shrink back, as from a blow or pain

**fling** *vt.* to throw forcefully or violently; to act with spontaneity, as *to fling oneself into a project* —*n.* the act of throwing violently; a time of wild abandon

**flint** *n.* a very hard stone

**flint´y** *adj.* like flint; unyielding —**flint´i·ly** *adv.* —**flint´i·ness** *n.*

**flip´pant** *adj.* frivolous; marked by a lack of reverence; impertinent —**flip´pan·cy** *n.* —**flip´pant·ly** *adv.*

**flirt** *n.* a trifler; a coquette —*vi.* to trifle with the affections of another; to consider briefly —**flir´ta´tion** *n.* —**flir·ta´tious** *adj.* —**flir·ta´tious·ly** *adv.* —**flir ta´tious·ness** *n.*

**float** *n.* anything that rests on the surface of a liquid; a decorated platform in a parade —*vi.* to rest on the surface of a liquid; to drift on the air —*vt.* to cause to come to rest on the surface of a liquid —**float´a·ble** *adj.*

**flock** *n.* a group of animals; any group or congregation —*vi.* to assemble in a group

**flog** *vt.* to beat with a whip

**flood** *n.* the covering of normally dry land with water; a deluge or glut, as of mail —*vt.* to overflow, inundate, or glut

**flood control** measures taken, such as the building of dams, to prevent flooding

**floor** *n.* the surface of a room on which one walks or stands; any bottom surface, as *the floor of a canyon*; a level of a building; recognition to speak at a formal gathering —*vt.* to build or refinish a walking surface; to defeat or astound

**flo´ra** *n.* the plants of a particular region

**flo´ral** *adj.* of or like flowers —**flo´ral·ly** *adv.*

**flor´id** *adj.* gaudy, ornate; of a rosy complexion —**flo·rid´i·ty, flor´id·ness** *n.* —**flor´id·ly** *adv.*

**flor´ist** *n.* one who cultivates or sells flowers

**flo·til´la** *n.* a fleet of boats or small ships

**floun´der** *n.* any of a variety of flatfishes —*vi.* to have difficulty; to struggle —**floun´der·ing·ly** *adv.*

**flour** *n.* a fine meal ground from grain —*vt.* to make into flour; to sprinkle with flour

**flour´ish** *n.* anything showy, as decoration or adornment; a sweeping motion of the arms; an elaborate sounding of brass, a fanfare —*vi.* to prosper —*vt.* to decorate in an ornate fashion; to wave with a sweep of the arm —**flour´ish·er** *n.*

**flout** *vi., vt.* to mock; to regard contemptuously —*n.* a mocking insult —**flout´ing·ly** *adv.*

**flow** *n.* an emanation; the amount or rate of discharge; the current or course of a river, stream, etc.; a continuous stream, as of thoughts or ideas —*vi.* to move in a stream; to progress smoothly —**flow´ing·ly** *adv.* —**flow´ing·ness** *n.*

**flow´er** *n.* a bloom; a plant cultivated for its blossoms; the best part or time: *the flower of youth* –*vi.* to bloom; to attain the best level –*vt.* to decorate with blossoms –**flow´ered** *adj.* –**flow´er·i·ly** *adv.* –**flow´er·i·ness** *n.* –**flow´er·ing** *adj.* –**flow´er·y** *adj.*
**fluc´tu·ate´** *vi.* to vary continuously; to waver –*vt.* to cause to waver –**fluc´tu·a´tion** *n.*
**flue** *n.* a passage for exhausting smoke, hot air, etc.
**flu´ent** *adj.* smooth flowing; able to speak or write well –**flu´en·cy** *n.* –**flu´ent·ly** *adv.*
**flu´id** *adj.* flowing or able to flow; marked by graceful movement; readily changed: *a fluid policy* –*n.* a substance that can flow –**flu·id´i·ty, flu´id·ness** *n.* –**flu´id·ly** *adv.*
**fluke** *n.* that brought about by chance
**flunk** *vi., vt.* to fail in school
**flunk´y** *n.* a servant; one engaged for menial tasks
**flush** *adj.* well supplied; even –*n.* a rapid flow; a warm glow; sudden exhilaration –*vi., vt.* to flow rapidly; to clean with a rapid flow of liquid; to blush
**flus´ter** *vi., vt.* to make or become nervous or confused
**flut´ter** *n.* rapid waving or fluctuation; a commotion –*vi., vt.* to wave or fluctuate rapidly; to move restlessly –**flut´ter·y** *adj.*
**flux** *n.* a flowing; a state of constant change
**fly** *n.* a flap over an opening in clothing, a tent, etc.; an insect –*vi., vt.* to travel by air; to operate an aircraft; to flee
**fo´cus** *n.* the point where rays of light, etc. converge; any point of concentration, activity, etc. –*vi., vt.* to adjust to produce a clear image –**fo´cal** *adj.*
**foe** *n.* an adversary, enemy
**fog** *n.* a dense mist –*vt.* to obscure –**fog´gi·ness** *n.* **fog´gy** *adj.*
**foi´ble** *n.* a minor weakness
**foil** *n.* a thin sheet of metal; a fencing sword –*vt.* to frustrate
**foist** *vt.* to pass off by trickery
**fold** *n.* a mark made by doubling; a pen for sheep –*vi.* to close, as a business –*vt.* to double by placing one part over another; to envelop
**fo´li·age** *n.* a mass of plant leaves
**folk** *adj.* of the common people –*n.* the people generally; a tribe, family, nation, etc. –**folks·y** *adj.*
**folk´lore´** *n.* the traditions of a culture
**fol´low** *vi.* to come next; to result –*vt.* to come next; to conform; to happen as a result; to trail or pursue –**follow through** to complete –**follow up** to study more closely –**fol´low·er** *n.* –**fol´low·ing** *adj.*
**fol´low·ing** *adj.* ensuing –*n.* a group of supporters; a calling
**fol´ly** *n.* foolishness; a frivolous act or undertaking
**fo·ment´** *vt.* to advocate; to incite, as rebellion
**fond** *adj.* cherished: *fond memories*; doting or indulgent –**fond´ly** *adv.* –**fond´ness** *n.*
**fon´dle** *vt.* to caress or stroke
**font** *n.* one size and style of type; a water basin or fountain; a place of origin
**food** *n.* any substance that nourishes; something that stimulates, as *food for thought*
**fool** *n.* one lacking common sense; a silly person –*vi.* to act silly –*vt.* to mislead or cheat –**fool´ish** *adj.* –**fool´ish·ly** *adv.* –**fool´ish·ness** *n.*
**fop** *n.* one overly devoted to personal appearance
**for´age** *n.* food for animals, fodder; a search for food –*vi., vt.* search for food or supplies
**for´ay** *n.* a raid –*vt.* to raid or venture
**for·bear´** *vi., vt.* to abstain; to restrain oneself –**for·bear´ance** *n.* –**for·bear´ing·ly** *adv.*
**for·bid´** *vt.* to prohibit; to order against; to prevent –**for·bid´dance** *n.* –**for·bid´den** *adj.*
**for·bid´ding** *adj.* frightening; unpleasant –**for·bid´ding·ly** *adv.*
**force** *n.* potency, might; the power to compel; a group organized for a purpose –*vt.* to overpower; to compel by might –**force´ful** *adj.* –**force´ful·ly** *adv.*
**fore´bear** *n.* an ancestor
**fore·bode´** *vi., vt.* to predict; to anticipate the unpleasant –**fore·bod´ing** *n.*
**fore´cast** *n.* a prediction –*vi., vt.* to anticipate
**fore·close´** *vi., vt.* to take away the right to redeem mortgaged property –**fore´clo´sure** *n.*
**fore´fa·ther** *n.* an ancestor
**fore·go´** *vt.* to go before
**for´eign** *adj.* from another country; unfamiliar; exotic
**fore´man** *n.* one in charge of a group
**fo·ren´sic** *adj.* pertaining to legal or formal argumentation –**fo·ren´si·cal·ly** *adv.*
**fore´run´ner** *n.* one sent or coming before; an ancester; a sign of something to follow
**fore·see´** *vt.* to predict; to foretell –**fore·see´a·ble** *adj.*
**fore´sight´** *n.* the ability to anticipate
**for´est** *n.* an extensive growth of trees
**fore·tell´** *vi., vt.* to predict
**for·ev´er** *adv.* for all time
**for´feit** *n.* that lost by neglect, etc. –*vt.* to give up –**for´fei·ture** *n.*
**fore·warn´** *vt.* to warn beforehand
**forge** *n.* a furnace for heating metal –*vi., vt.* to form laboriously, as metal; to falsify in order to deceive
**for´ger·y** *n.* an illegal making or altering, as of money or a signature; an imitation or fake
**for·get´** *vi., vt.* to lose from memory; to overlook or neglect –**for·get´a·ble, for·get´ta·ble** *adj.*
**for·get´ful** *adj.* losing or having lost the ability to remember; careless or neglectful –**for·get´ful·ly** *adv.* –**for·get´ful·ness** *n.*
**for·give´** *vt.* to pardon; to overlook
**fork** *n.* a device with prongs at one end, used to hold

or move something: *salad fork, pitchfork*; a dividing —*vi.* to branch —*vt.* to split into branches; to use a fork, as for eating —**forked** *adj.*

**for·lorn´** *adj.* abandoned; wretched, without hope

**form** *n.* configuration; a mold; type; convention; method —*vi.* to take shape —*vt.* to mold or shape; to conceive in the mind

**for'mal** *adj.* according to custom; correct or suitable, as *formal dress*; precise in manner; stodgy —**for´mal·ly** *adv.*

**for·mal´ity** *n.* careful adherence to custom; an official act

**for·ma´tion** *n.* a thing formed; arrangement or configuration

**for´mer** *adj.* coming before; preceding; the first of two

**for´mi·da·ble** *adj.* awesome; threatening; overwhelming —**for´mi·da·bly** *adv.*

**for´mu·la** *n.* a representation using logic symbols; a precise method or specification

**for´mu·late** *vt.* to conceive or develop; to express as a formula —**for·mu·la´tion** *n.*

**for·ni·ca´tion** *n.* sexual intercourse between unmarried persons —**for´ni·cate** *vi.*

**for·sake´** *vt.* to forgo; to leave or abandon

**forte** *n.* one's special ability

**for´ti·fy** *vt.* to make stronger

**for´ti·tude** *n.* strength of character; determination

**fort´night** *n.* two weeks time

**for·tu´i·tous** *adj.* occurring by chance; fortunate —**for·tu´i·tous·ly** *adv.* —**for·tu´i·tous·ness, for·tu´i·ty** *n.*

**for´tu·nate** *adj.* lucky; auspicious —**for´tu·nate·ly**

**for´tune** *n.* luck; fate; riches

**fo´rum** *n.* a gathering for discussion

**fos´sil** *n.* preserved remains —**fos´sil·ize** *vt.*

**fos´ter** *vt.* to promote; to nurture

**foul** *adj.* offensive; profane; underhanded; entangled; unpleasant, as weather —*vi., vt.* to soil; to entangle —**foul´ly** *adv.*

**found** *adj.* discovered —*vt.* to establish or bring into being; to cast metal

**foun·da´tion** *n.* a fundamental principle; an endowment for financing charitable works

**foun´dry** *n.* the process of casting metal; a place where metal is cast

**foun´tain** *n.* a natural or artificial spring; a reservoir

**fox´y** *adj.* crafty, cunning; attractive, seductive —**fox´i·ness** *n.*

**fra´cas** *n.* a brawl

**fraction** *n.* a small part; a value expressed as a numerator and denominator, as ½

**frac´tious** *adj.* unruly; difficult to manage; irritable or testy

**fracture** *n.* a crack or break —*vi., vt.* to crack or break

**frag´ile** *adj.* easily damaged; delicate —**frag´ile·ly** *adv.* —**frag´ile·ness, fra·gil´i·ty** *n.*

**frag´ment** *n.* a part or piece, often detached —**frag´men·tar´y** *adj.*

**fra´grance, fra´gran·cy** *n.* a pleasant odor —**fra´grant** *adj.* —**fra´grant·ly** *adv.*

**frail** *adj.* easily damaged; delicate; feeble or weak —**frail´ly** *adv.* **frail´ness** *n.* —**frail´ty** *n.*

**frame** *n.* a skeletal structure; a general form; a field of view —*vt.* to shape or form; to provide a border for —**frame´a·ble** *adj.*

**frame of reference** a point or aspect from which something is viewed

**fran´chise´** *n.* any right or privilege granted by a government, organization, etc.

**fran´gi·ble** *adj.* fragile; brittle

**frank** *adj.* open and honest

**frantic** *adj.* distraught by anger, worry, etc.; highly emotional —**fran´ti·cal·ly** *adv.*

**fra·ter´nal** *adj.* brotherly

**frat´er·nize** *vi.* to be friendly; to have friendly relations with, esp. of those in an occupied or conquered territory —**frat·er·ni·za´tion** *n.* —**frat´er·niz·er** *n.*

**fraud** *n.* deception; a swindle; a faker

**fraud´u·lent** *adj.* deceitful; marked by fraud —**fraud´u·lence** *n.* —**fraud´u·lent·ly** *adv.*

**fray** *n.* a brawl —*vi., vt.* to become tattered or worn

**freak** *adj.* abnormal; bizarre —*n.* an abnormality —**freak´ish** *adj.*

**free** *adj.* not busy or in use; independent; unrestrained; unencumbered: without debt or obligation; without cost —*vt.* to release or make available —**free´ly** *adv.*

**fren´zy** *n.* a sudden burst of agitation or activity —**fren´zied** *adj.*

**fre´quent** *adj.* happening often —**fre·quent´** *vt.* to stop by often

**fres´co** *n.* a watercolor painting on wet plaster

**fresh** *adj.* newly made or obtained; natural; naive or uninitiated; impertinent or impudent —**fresh´ly** *adv.* —**fresh´ness** *n.*

**fret** *vt., vi.* to make or be irritated or annoyed —**fret´ful** *adj.* —**fret´ful·ly** *adv.* —**fret´ful·ness** *n.*

**fri´a·ble** *adj.* easily crumbled

**fric´tion** *n.* a rubbing or abrasion; discord caused by differences

**friend** *n.* one who is known, liked, trusted, etc.; an ally or supporter

**fright** *n.* sudden alarm or terror; a startling sight

**fright´en** *vt.* to cause alarm or terror

**frill** *n.* gathered or pleated edging; an unnecessary adjunct —**fril´li·ness** *n.* —**frill´y** *adj.*

**fringe** *adj.* at the outer edge; minor or peripheral —*n.* ornamental edging; an outer edge or periphery —*vt.* to decorate with a fringe

**fringe benefit** indirect compensation to an employee in the form of insurance, paid leave, etc.

**frisky** *adj.* energetic; playful

**frit´ter** *n.* deep-fried fruit or vegetables coated with batter *–vt.* to waste a little at a time
**friv´o·lous** *adj.* trivial; not serious or sensible **–fri·vol´i·ty** *n.* **–friv´o·lous·ly** *adj.*
**frol´ic** *n.* merriment, play *–vi.* to play **–frol´ic·some** *adj.*
**front** *n.* the forward part or position; appearance or demeanor; an area of activity **–fron´tal** *adj.*
**fron·tier´** *n.* the border of a country; an unexplored area
**frost** *n.* ice crystals; coldness of air, manner, etc. *–vt.* to coat with frost or anything resembling frost, as icing for a cake **–frost´i·ly** *adv.* **–frost´i·ness** *n.* **–frost´y** *adj.*
**froth** *n.* foam; something trivial *–vi., vt.* to foam
**frown** *n.* a stern look denoting disapproval or deep thought *–vi., vt.* to scowl; to show disapproval
**frugal** *adj.* thrifty; inexpensive **–fru´gal´i·ty** *n.*
**fruit** *n.* the edible portion of a plant; a consequence **–fruit´ful** *adj.*
**fru·i´tion** *n.* the yielding of results; fulfillment
**frus´trate´** *vt.* to nullify, as the efforts of another **frus´tra´tion** *n.*
**fu´el** *n.* anything consumed to produce energy
**fu´gi·tive** *n.* one who flees; something elusive
**ful´crum** *n.* the support on which a lever pivots
**ful·fill´** *vt.* to perform or accomplish
**full** *adj.* containing all, or nearly all, that is possible; of the highest degree; puffed out **–full´ness** *n.* **–ful´ly** *adv.*
**ful´mi·nate´** *n.* an explosive salt *–vi., vt.* to denounce loudly; to explode **–ful´mi·na´tion** *n.*
**ful´some** *adj.* obsequious or fawning; abundant
**fum´ble** *vi., vt.* to grope awkwardly; to blunder
**fume** *n.* vapor *–vi.* to give off vapor; to show anger
**fu´mi·gate´** *vt.* to disinfect with gas **–fu´mi·ga´tion** *n.*
**func´tion** *n.* normal use or purpose; a ceremony or event *–vi.* to perform as designed
**fund** *n.* assets designated for some purpose; an institution charged with management of such assets *–vt.* to finance
**fun´da·men´tal** *adj.* essential; basic *–n.* a principle; an essential part
**fu´ner·al** *n.* a ceremony or procession concerned with the burial of the dead
**fu·ne´re·al** *adj.* solemn
**fur´bish** *vt.* to restore; to polish
**fu´ri·ous** *adj.* enraged; frenzied
**fur´nace** *(US) n.* an appliance for producing heat, as for warming a home or firing metal or glass
**fur´nish** *vt.* to supply; to provide
**fur´nish·ings** *pl. n.* furniture, drapes, carpets, etc. for the home; clothing and accessories
**fur´ni·ture** *n.* household goods such as tables, chairs, and beds
**fu´ror** *n.* a state of excitement
**fur´row** *n.* a rut, as made by a plow or a wheeled vehicle; a deep wrinkle *–vt.* to make a furrow *–vt.* to become furrowed or wrinkled
**fur´ther** *adj.* additional; more distant *–adv.* farther; to a greater extent; moreover *–vt.* to aid or promote **–fur´ther·more** *adv.*
**fur´tive** *adj.* stealthy, sneaky
**fu´ry** *n.* violent anger; violence
**fuse** *n.* a device for setting off an explosive; a device that prevents the overloading of an electrical circuit *–vi., vt.* to unite or blend
**fu´sion** *n.* a melting or joining by heat; a nuclear reaction
**fuss** *n.* a quarrel; a commotion; needless concern or attention *–vi.* to complain; to make a bother over trifles *–vt.* to worry needlessly
**fu´tile** *adj.* hopeless; trivial **–fu´tile·ness, fu´til´i·ty** *n.*
**fu´ture** *adj.* that is to come or happen; expected *–n.* a time or event to come; outlook
**fuzz´y** *adj.* indistinct

**g, G** seventh letter of the English alphabet; a slang term for 1000 dollars
**gab** *n.* idle talk *–vi.* to gossip
**gabble** *n.* meaningless chatter *–vi., vt.* to jabber or chatter
**gadg´et** *n.* any implement; a device of limited utility
**gag** *n.* a joke or hoax; something placed over or in the mouth to prevent speech; anything that restricts free speech *–vi.* to choke or retch *–vt.* to silence by force, threat, etc.
**gai´e·ty** *n.* mirth; festivity; gaudiness
**gain** *n.* an increase; an advantage *–vi., vt.* to acquire; to reach
**gala** *adj.* joyful *–n.* a joyful celebration
**gal´ax·y** *n.* a star system; any gathering of distinctive persons or things
**gale** *n.* a strong wind
**gall** *n.* bile; impertinence
**gal´lant** *adj.* chivalrous; noble, dashing **–gal·lant´** *n.* a lover; one who is chivalrous **–gal´lant·ly** *adv.*
**gal´lon** *n.* a liquid measure equal to four quarts
**gam´bit** *n.* a strategy designed to gain an advantage
**gam´ble** *n.* a risk *–vi., vt.* to take a risk
**gam´bol** *vi.* to jump about; to frolic
**gan´der** *n.* a male goose **–take a gander** have a look
**gang** *n.* a group associated in some way
**gang´ster** *n.* one belonging to a group of criminals
**gaol** *(Brit.),* **jail** *(US) n.* a place of confinement for one awaiting trial or guilty of a minor offense *–vt.* to confine in a jail
**gaol´er** *(Brit.),* **jail´er** *(US) n.* one charged with the upkeep of a jail
**gape** *n.* a large opening; an open-mouthed stare *–vi.* to

yawn or stare in amazement with the mouth open; to open wide
**ga·rage´** *n.* a building for storing or repairing an automobile
**garb** *n.* clothing *–vt.* to clothe
**gar´ble** *vt.* to confuse or distort
**gar´bage** *(US) n.* waste, trash
**gar´den** *n.* a plot of cultivated land *–vi., vt.* to cultivate a plot of land **–gar´den·er** *n.*
**gar´gle** *n.* a solution for medicating or cleansing the throat *–vi., vt.* to cleanse or medicate the throat
**gar´ish** *adj.* overly ornate, gaudy **–gar´ish·ly** *adv.*
**gar´ment** *n.* an item of clothing
**gar´ner** *vt.* to collect and store; to acquire
**gar´nish** *n.* a decoration *–vt.* to decorate
**gar´ret** *n.* an attic room
**gar´ru·lous** *adj.* chattering; wordy **–gar´ru·lous·ness** *n.*
**gas** *n.* vapor; a mixture of gasses as used for anes- thesia, fuel, etc.; something enjoyable; *(US)* gasoline
**gash** *n.* a deep cut *–vt.* to make a deep cut
**gasket** *n.* a washer; a seal to prevent leakage
**gas·o·line´** *n.* a flammable liquid fuel distilled from petroleum
**gasp** *n.* a difficult catching of the breath *–vi.* to inhale sharply or with difficulty
**gas´tric** *adj.* pertaining to the stomach
**gath´er** *vi.*, to assemble; to accumulate *–vt.* to convene or assemble; to accumulate; to draw together; to infer or conclude
**gaud´y** *adj.* garish; vulgar
**gauge** *n.* a standard measure or means of estimating; a measuring device *–vt.* to measure or estimate
**gaunt** *adj.* thin and bony; drawn; dreary, barren
**gay** *adj.* lively, merry; bright **–gai´ly** *adv.*
**gaze** *n.* a steady look *–vi.* to look intently; to stare
**gaz´et·teer´** *n.* a geographical dictionary or index
**gear** *n.* personal property; equipment; a device used to transmit energy in a machine
**gem** *n.* a precious stone; anything prized for its value
**gene** *n.* any of the units in a chromosome that transmits hereditary characteristics
**gen´e·al´o·gy** *n.* a record of one's lineage; the study of lineage
**gen´er·al** *adj.* extensive and diversified; non-exclusive; imprecise **–gen·er·al´i·ty** *n.* **–gen´er·al·ly** *adv.* **–gen´er·al·ize** *vt.* **–gen·er·al·i·za´tion** *n.*
**gen´er·ate´** *vt.* to originate or bring into being; produce
**gen´er·a´tion** *n.* the process of producing; a single stage of descent or development
**ge·ner´ic** *adj.* of a class or group; lacking a brand name
**gen´er·ous** *adj.* gracious, unselfish; ample **–gen·er·os´i·ty** *n.* **–gen´er·ous·ly** *adv.*
**gen´e·sis** *n.* origin
**ge·net´ic,** *ge.net'i.cal adj.* of origin or ancestry **–ge·net´i·cal·ly** *adv.*
**ge·net´ics** *n.* the study of ancestry **–ge·net´i·cist** *n.*
**gen´ial** *adj.* pleasant; amiable **–ge·ni·al´i·ty** *n.*
**gen´ius** *n.* exceptional natural ability or mental capacity
**gen´o·cide´** *n.* the systematic extermination of a people
**gen´tle** *adj.* kindly; temperate; courtly; tame
**gen´u·ine** *adj.* authentic; sincere and honest
**ge·og´ra·phy** *n.* the study of the earth and its inhabitants; the physical nature of an area **–ge´o·graph´ic,ge´o·graph´ic·al** *adj.*
**ge·ol´o·gy** *n.* the study of the earth's structure and its development **–ge´o·log´ic, ge´o·log´ic·al** *adj.* **–ge·ol´o·gist** *n.*
**germ** *n.* the basic form from which an organism sprouts; any microorganism, especially one that is harmful; a basic concept
**ger´mi·nate´** *vi., vt.* to sprout; to begin growth **–ger·mi·na´tion** *n.*
**ges·tic´u·late´** *vi., vt.* to gesture
**ges´ture** *n.* a move that emphasizes; something done for effect
**get** *vt.* to receive or acquire in some way; to understand
**ghast´ly** *adj.* shocking; terrifying; ghostlike; offensive
**ghet´to** *n.* a district to which a minority group is restricted
**ghost** *n.* a disembodied spirit; a faint suggestion
**gi´ant** *adj.* of great size *–n.* anything of exceptional size
**gibe** *n.* a taunting remark *–vi., vt.* to taunt or ridicule
**gift** *n.* something freely given; a natural ability: *the gift of gab*
**gi·gan´tic** *adj.* enormous
**gig´gle** *n.* a silly nervous laugh *–vi.* to laugh nervously
**gild** *vt.* to coat with gold; to make attractive; to make seem attractive
**gilt** *adj.* gilded *–n.* gilding
**gim´mick** *n.* a thing designed to deceive; a device to gain attention **–gim´mick·ry** *n.*
**gird** *vt.* to encircle with a belt or band
**gird´er** *n.* a large supporting beam
**gist** *n.* the primary concept
**give** *vi., vt.* to contribute; to impart; to yield to pressure
**glad** *adj.* happy; pleased **–glad´den** *vt.* **–glad´ly** *adv.*
**glade** *n.* an open space in a wooded area
**glance** *n.* a brief look; a deflecting *–vi.* to strike and fly off at an angle; to look briefly
**glare** *n.* an intense light; a fixed stare *–vi.* to shine intensely; to stare **–glar´ing** *adj.*
**glaze** *n.* a glassy finish *–vt.* to give a glassy coating or finish; to fit with glass

**gleam** *n.* a flash of light; a faint display *—vi.* to appear briefly
**glean** *vt.* to collect grain left by reapers; to obtain piecemeal, as information **—glean´ings** *n.*
**glee** *n.* gaiety, merriment
**glib** *adj.* fluency that often implies insincerity **—glib´ly** *adv.*
**glide** *n.* a smooth, flowing movement *—vi.* to move in a smooth, flowing manner
**glim´mer** *n.* a faint light; a trace *—vi.* to appear faintly
**glimpse** *n.* a quick view *—vi.* to glance *—vt.* to view briefly
**glis´ten** *vi.* to sparkle or shine
**glit´ter** *n.* a sparkling light; bits of decorative material *—vi.* to sparkle; to be brilliant **—glit´ter´y** *adj.*
**gloat** *vi.* to view with malicious pleasure
**glob´al** *adj.* world-wide; comprehensive
**globe** *n.* a sphere; the earth
**glob´ule** *n.* a tiny globe; a drop
**gloom** *n.* dimness or darkness; despondency –gloom'y *adj.*
**glo´ri·ous** *adj.* splendid; pleasant; famed **—glo´ri·ous·ly** *adv.*
**glo´ry** *n.* splendor; fame; a state of well-being *—vi.* to be proud of or rejoice in –glorify *vt.* **—glo´ri·ous** *adj.* **—glo´ri·ous·ly** *adv.*
**gloss** *n.* shine or luster; a superficial image *—vt.* to make shiny; to pass over or cover up, as a fault or error **—gloss´i·ness** *n.* **—gloss´y** *adj.*
**glos´sa·ry** *n.* a list of terms with definitions
**glow** *n.* light produced by heat; a feeling of warmth *—vi.* to give off light; to be flushed from emotion, good health, etc.
**glow´er** *n.* a scowl *–vi.* to scowl
**glue** *n.* an adhesive *—vt.* to affix, as with an adhesive
**glum** *adj.* sullen, dejected
**glut** *n.* an oversupply *—vt.* to oversupply; to overburden
**glut´ton** *n.* an overeater; one with unusual capacity
**gnaw** *vi., vt.* to wear away, as with the teeth; to worry
**goad** *vt.* to prod or urge; to provoke
**goal** *n.* an objective toward which one strives
**gob´ble·dy·gook** *n.* wordy and ambiguous language
**gob´let** *n.* a stemmed drinking glass
**gob´lin** *n.* a mischievous elf
**gone** *adj.* departed; used up
**gon´er** *n.* a person or thing that is beyond help
**gore** *n.* blood from a wound *—vi.* to wound with a horn
**gorge** *n.* a ravine; the throat or gullet *—vi., vt.* to devour
**gor´geous** *adj.* exceptionally beautiful; delightful
**gos´sip** *n.* idle chatter; a rumor; one who gossips *—vi.* to engage in idle chatter
**gouge** *n.* a type of chisel; an overcharging *—vt.* to cut into; to cheat by overcharging
**gour´mand** *n.* one fond of good food; a glutton
**gour´met** *n.* a good judge of fine food and drink
**gov´ern** *vi., vt.* to control or influence; to regulate or restrain
**gov´ern·ment** *n.* a system of administration, its personnel and agencies
**gown** *n.* a long flowing garment
**grab** *vt.* to seize roughly; to take by deceit; to attract one's attention; to impress
**grace** *n.* an attractive or pleasing quality; good will; the temporary extension of a due date; a blessing *—vt.* to adorn; to dignify
**grace´ful** *adj.* having elegance of form or movement **—grace´ful·ly** *adv.* **—grace´ful·ness** *n.*
**gra´cious** *adj.* courteous and affable; compassionate; comfortable or luxurious: *gracious living* **—gra´cious·ly** *adv.* **—gra´cious·ness** *n.*
**gra·da´tion** *n.* a gradual progression
**grade** *n.* any of the levels in a progression; a rating; a degree of slope *—vt.* to rate or classify according to level; to change the level or slope of
**gradient** *adj.* sloping *—n.* a slope, or degree of slope
**grad´u·al** *adj.* progressing in slow or regular steps **—grad´u·al·ly** *adv.* **—grad´u·al·ness** *n.*
**grad´u·ate´** *n.* one who has completed a course of study; a container for measuring *—vi.* to complete a course of study *—vt.* to award a diploma; to mark a container for measuring **—grad·u·a´tion** *n.*
**graf·fi´to** *n., pl.* **graf·fi´ti** a crudely-drawn inscription
**graft** *n.* the joining of living tissue; the tissue so joined; profit gained by extortion *—vi., vt.* to join tissue; to obtain by extortion
**gram´mar** *n.* the structure of a language; the rules for use of a language **—gram·mar´i·an** *n.* **—gram·mat´i·cal** *adj.*
**grand** *adj.* higher in rank; imposing; luxurious; noble **—grandeur** *n.*
**gran´dil´o·quent** *adj.* spoken pretentiously **—gran´dil´o·quence** *n.*
**gran´di·ose** *adj.* pompous
**grant** *n.* something given, as a favor or privilege *—vt.* to give
**gran´u·lar** *adj.* grainy
**gran´ule** *n.* a small particle
**graph´ic, graph´i·cal** *adj.* explicit; described clearly; regarding anything written or pictorial
**grap´ple** *vi.* to struggle with *—vt.* to seize
**grasp** *n.* a firm hold; the ability to hold or comprehend *—vt.* to take hold; to comprehend
**grasp´ing** *adj.* greedy
**grate** *n.* a framework of metal bars *—vt.* to make a harsh sound by scraping; to irritate; to shred, as cheese *–vi.* to make a harsh sound; to irritate
**grate´ful** *adj.* appreciative **—grate´ful·ly** *adv.*

**grat´i·fy´** *vt.* to afford pleasure; to indulge **–grat´i·fi·ca´tion** *n.*
**grat´i·tude´** *n.* appreciation
**gra·tu´i·tous** *adj.* given freely; without cause: *gratuitous violence* **–gra·tu´i·tous·ly** *adv.*
**gra·tu´i·ty** *n.* a gift for services
**grave** *adj.* serious; somber *–n.* a place for burial
**grav´el** *n.* crushed rock
**grav´i·tate´** *vi.* to be inclined or attracted towards **–grav´i·ta´tion** *n.*
**grav´i·ty** *n.* seriousness; the attraction between celestial bodies
**graze** *vi., vt.* to feed on; to touch lightly in passing
**grease** *n.* melted animal fat; a lubricant *–vt.* to lubricate or coat with a lubricant **–greas´y** *adj.*
**great** *adj.* large; extensive; important; skillful
**greed** *n.* excessive desire **–greed´i·ness** *n.* **–greed´y** *adj.*
**greet** *vt.* to welcome; to acknowledge in a particular way **–greet´ing** *n.*
**gre·gar´i·ous** *adj.* sociable; tending to join or associate in groups
**grid** *n.* a network of horizontal and vertical parallel lines, bars, etc.
**gri´dle** *n.* a flat iron pan for baking or frying
**grief** *n.* sadness, sorrow; a difficulty, or its cause
**griev´ance** *n.* a wrong; a complaint based on a wrong
**grieve** *vt., vi.* to cause or express grief
**grim** *adj.* stern; forbidding
**grime** *n.* dirt; filth **–grim´y** *adj.*
**grin** *n.* a broad smile *–vi.* to smile broadly
**grind** *vt.* to crush; to shape by rubbing; to oppress
**grip** *n.* a tight hold; a device for grasping; a small suitcase *–vi., vt.* to hold
**gripe** *n.* a complaint *–vi.* to complain
**gris´ly** *adj.* horrible, ghastly
**grit** *n.* small, hard particles; determination or pluck *–vt.* to clench or grind the teeth **–grit´ty** *adj.*
**groan** *n.* a deep sound expressing pain or distress; a moan *–vi.* to make a low moaning sound
**grog´gy** *adj.* sluggish or dazed
**grom´met** *n.* reinforcement for a hole punched in cloth or other light material
**groom** *n.* a bridegroom; one who tends horses *–vt.* to make attractive; to train for a purpose
**groove** *n.* a channel; a settled pattern *–vt.* to cut a channel
**grope** *vi.* to feel around or search uncertainly *–vt.* to fondle **–grop´er** *n.* **–grop´ing** *adj.*
**gross** *adj.* coarse, unrefined; offensive; flagrant; total, as *gross income* *–n.* total; twelve dozen *–vi., vt.* to earn in total
**gro·tesque´** *adj.* bizarre; distorted; hideous **–gro·tesque´ly** *adv.* **–gro·tesque´ness** *n.*
**grot´to** *n.* a cavern
**grouch** *n.* one prone to complaining; a discontented person *–vi.* to grumble or comjplain; to sulk **–grouch´i·ly** *adv.* **–grouch´i·ness** *n.* **–grouch´y** *adj.*
**ground** *n.* the surface, as of the earth, floor, etc.; soil; an area set aside for a special use: *playground, burial ground*; a basis or foundation *–vt.* to place on the surface; to provide a basis
**grounds** *pl. n.* land around an estate
**ground´less** *adj.* without cause
**group** *n.* a number of persons or things taken together *–vi., vt.* to form or arrange together
**group´ie** *n.* an avid fan
**grouse** *n.* a game bird; a complaint *–vi.* to complain
**grove** *n.* a stand of trees without undergrowth
**grov´el** *vi.* to cower; to fawn over; to humble oneself
**grow** *vi.* to come to be; to increase *–vt.* to cultivate **–growth** *n.*
**grown** *adj.* mature; cultivated in a certain way
**grub´by** *adj.* filthy; wretched
**grudge** *n.* ongoing resentment for a real or imagined wrong
**gru´el·ing** *adj.* extremely demanding; exhausting
**grue´some** *adj.* frightful; hideous; grotesque
**gruff** *adj.* brusque; surly **–gruff´ly** *adv.*
**grum´ble** *vi.* complain; rumble
**grump´y** *adj.* grouchy
**grun´gy** *adj.* filthy; shabby
**guar´an·tee´** *n.* assurance; surety *–vt.* to assure **–guar´an·tor** *n.*
**guard** *n.* any person or thing that protects against loss or harm *–vt.* to keep watch; to protect
**guard´ed** *adj.* protected; cautious: *guarded optimism* **–guard´ed·ly** *adv.* **–guard´ed·ness** *n.*
**gu´ber·na·to´ri·al** *adj.* relating to the office of governor
**guess** *n.* an estimate *–vi., vt.* to estimate; to presume
**guest** *n.* a visitor; one receiving hospitality; a visiting artist
**guide** *n.* that leads or directs *–vt.* to lead or direct **–guid´ance** *n.*
**guild** *n.* an association formed for the mutual aid and benefit of its members
**guile** *n.* craftiness, cunning
**guilt** *n.* liability for a wrong **–guilt´y** *adj.*
**guise** *n.* outward appearance; pretense
**gulch** *n.* a ravine
**gulf** *n.* a large inlet partially hemmed in by land; a wide gap or expanse
**gul´li·ble** *adj.* easily deceived **–gul·li·bil´i·ty** *n.* **–gul´li·bly** *adv.*
**gul´ly** *n.* a small ravine worn by erosion *–vt.* to form a gully
**gump´tion** *n.* initiative; nerve
**gu´ru** *n.* a spiritual advisor; a prominent leader
**gush** *n.* a strong flow *–vi.* to surge forth; to be overly

enthused –**gush´y** *adj.*
**gust** *n.* a sudden burst or rush, as of wind –**gust´y** *adj.*
**gus´ta·to´ry** *adj.* pertaining to the sense of taste
**gus´to** *n.* enthusiasm, ardor
**gut´tur·al** *adj.* of a harsh or throaty sound
**guz´zle** *vi., vt.* to drink greedily
**gyp** *n.* a swindle or swindler –*vi., vt.* to swindle or cheat
**gy´rate´** *vi.* to revolve in a circle or spiral –**gy´ra´tion** *n.*

**h, H** eighth letter of the English alphabet
**hab´er·dash·er** *n. (Brit.)* a seller of cloth and sewing needs; one who sells men's clothing –**hab´er·dash·er·y** *n.*
**hab´it** *n.* a customary behavior pattern; an addiction; a special manner of dress –**ha·bit´u·al** *adj.* –**ha·bit´u·al·ly** *adv.* –**ha·bit´u·al·ness** *n.*
**hab´i·tat** *n.* a creature's native environment
**hab·i·ta´tion** *n.* a dwelling
**ha·bit´u·é** *n.* a habitual visitor or frequenter of a place
**hack´neyed** *adj.* commonplace; made trite by overuse
**hag** *n.* an ugly old woman; a witch
**hag´gard** *adj.* drawn or gaunt –**hag´gard·ly** *adv.* –**hag´gard·ness** *n.*
**hag´gle** *vi.* to bargain
**hail** *n.* frozen rain; a shout of greeting; a barrage –*vi.* to fall as frozen rain –*vt.* to greet with cheers; to call out; to pour
**hair grip** *(Brit.)* a metal hair pin
**hair slide** *(Brit.)* a small appliance for keeping hair in place
**hal´cy·on** *adj.* tranquil
**hale** *adj.* healthy
**half** *adj.* being one of two equal or nearly equal parts; partial –*adv.* partly –*n.* one of two equal or nearly equal parts
**half´heart´ed** *adj.* lacking enthusiasm –**half´heart´ed·ly** *adv.*
**hal´i·to´sis** *n.* stale breath
**hall** *n.* a large room, as *a dance hall*; a passageway –**hall´way** *n.*
**hall´mark** *n.* a mark indicating quality; a distinctive feature
**hal´low** *vt.* to make or regard as holy
**hal·lu´ci·nate** *vi., vt.* to see or sense that which is not real; to fantasize –**hal·lu´ci·na´tion** *n.* –**hal·lu´ci·na´to·ry** *adj.*
**hal·lu´ci·no·gen** *n.* a substance that causes one to hallucinate
**halt** *n.* a stop, often temporary –*vi.* to stop; to hesitate or be uncertain –*vt.* to cause to stop
**halve** *vt.* to divide; to reduce by half
**ham´let** *n.* a small village
**ham´per** *n.* a large basket –*vt.* to prevent from moving freely
**hand** *n.* the part of the body at the end of the arm; anything designating of the hand's function, as gripping, fashioning, etc. –*vt.* to offer or provide
**hand´book** *n.* a manual
**hand´ful** *n.* all the hand can hold; a small amount; something or someone difficult to manage
**hand´i·cap´** *n.* a hindrance –*vt.* to hinder
**hand´i·work´** *n.* that done by one's own efforts
**han´dle** *n.* that part of an object designed for gripping –*vt.* to touch, hold, use, etc.; to manage or deal with; to trade in
**hand´out** *n.* a charitable gift; a promotional flyer
**hand´pick´** *vt.* to choose with care –**hand´picked´** *adj.*
**hand´some** *adj.* attractive; impressive –**hand´some·ly** *adv.* –**hand´some·ness** *n.*
**hand-to-mouth** *adj.* barely subsisting
**hand´y** *adj.* easily accessible; useful; skillful –**hand´i·ly** *adv.*
**hang** *vi., vt.* to suspend or be suspended
**hang´ing** *adj.* suspended –*n.* a decorative device for a wall
**hang-up** *n.* a difficulty or inhibition
**hap´haz´ard** *adj.* random –*adv.* by chance
**hap´less** *adj.* unlucky
**hap´pen** *vi.* to occur
**hap´pen·ing** *n.* an important event
**hap´py** *adj.* fortunate; pleased –**hap´pi·ly** *adv.* –**hap´pi·ness** *n.*
**ha·rangue´** *n.* a bombastic lecture –*vi., vt.* to lecture in a harsh and severe manner
**har´ass** *vt.* to pester or worry
**har´bin·ger** *n.* a precursor –*vt.* to herald
**har´bor** *n.* a place of refuge –*vt.* to provide shelter; to entertain or cling to, as an idea or impression
**hard** *adj.* physically or mentally inflexible; intense; unyielding; difficult –*adv.* with difficulty; diligently; with force; to a solid state
**hard-bitten** *adj.* tough
**hard´en** *vi.* to toughen –*vt.* to make tough or tougher
**hard´head´ed** *adj.* practical; obstinate
**hard´ly** *adv.* barely; probably not
**hard´-nosed´** *adj.* stubborn; practical
**hard´ship** *n.* any difficulty
**har´dy** *adj.* strong; resolute
**harm** *n.* damage –*vt.* to cause damage to –**harm´ful** *adj.*
**harm´less** *adj.* not likely to cause damage or distress –**harm´less·ly** *adv.* –**harm´less·ness** *n.*
**har´mo·ny** *n.* agreement; a pleasing combination –**har´mo´ni·ous** *adj.* –**har·mo´ni·ous·ly** *adv.* –**har·mo´ni·ous·ness** *n.*
**har´row·ing** *adj.* distressing
**har´ry** *vt.* to raid or harass

**harsh** *adj.* disagreeably coarse or rough; stern **–harsh´ly** *adv.* **–harsh´ness** *n.*

**har´vest** *n.* a season's crop; the gathering of a crop; the time for gathering; the outcome of any action *–vi., vt.* to get as the result of effort

**has´-been** *n.* one no longer famous, productive, etc.

**has´sle** *n.* a quarrel; difficulty *–vi.* to quarrel *–vt.* to annoy

**haste** *n.* quickness; fast action, often implying carelessness

**has´ten** *vi.* to be quick; to accelerate

**hast´y** *adj.* overly quick; done or made in a hurry; impetuous **–hast´i·ly** *adv.*

**hate** *n.* intense dislike *–vi., vt.* to dislike intensely **–hate´ful** *adj.* **–ha´tred** *n.*

**haugh´ty** *adj.* proud, arrogant; contemptuous of others

**haul** *n.* the act of pulling or carrying; that carried; the distance traveled *–vi., vt.* to pull or carry

**haunt** *n.* a place often visited *–vt.* to visit often; to pervade

**have** *vt.* to possess; to gain; to control or be controlled by

**ha´ven** *n.* a shelter; a refuge

**hav´oc** *n.* chaos or destruction

**haz´ard** *n.* an uncertainty, a danger *–vt.* to endanger; to venture **–haz´ard·ous** *adj.* **–haz´ard·ous·ly** *adv.* **–haz´ard·ous·ness** *n.*

**haze** *n.* a light mist or smog; a vagueness of mind **–haz´i·ly** *adv.* **–haz´i·ness** *n.* **–haz´y** *adj.*

**head** *n.* the part of the body that contains sensory organs for sight, smell, taste, and hearing, and through which an animal feeds; intellect or aptitude; the foremost part; a leader *–vt.* to lead or direct

**head´ing** *n.* forming a head; direction of motion

**head´long** *adj.* uncontrollable; reckless *–adv.* recklessly

**head´-on´** *adj.* direct *–adv.* directly

**heal** *vi., vt.* to become or make healthy

**health** *n.* soundness of body or mind **–health´y** *adj.*

**heap** *n.* an accumulation; a mound; a large amount *–vt.* to amass in one place; to give in large amounts: *heap compliments on*

**hear** *vi.* be able to sense sound; to be informed *–vt.* to sense sound; to be informed of; to heed; to consider formally

**hear´say** *n.* rumor

**heart** *n.* the body organ that pumps blood; the essence or core of anything

**heart´en** *vt.* to encourage

**heart´felt** *adj.* sincere

**heart´less** *adj.* insensitive

**heart´rend·ing** *adj.* distressing

**heart´y** *adj.* enthusiastic; robust; unreserved **–heart´i·ly** *adv.* **–heart´i·ness** *n.*

**heat** *n.* warmth; warming *–vi., vt.* to become or make hot; to become or cause to become aroused

**heat´ed** *adj.* intense

**heav´y** *adj.* weighty; over-weight; serious or intense; greater than normal **–heav´i·ly** *adv.* **–heav´i·ness** *n.*

**heav´y-hand´ed** *adj.* tactless

**heav´y-heart´ed** *adj.* sad

**heck´le** *vt.* to taunt **–heck´ler** *n.*

**hec´tic** *adj.* frenzied

**hedge** *n.* a boundary of bushes or trees *–vi.* to be evasive; to make compensating investments in order to lessen risk *–vt.* to sit a border of bushes; to surround, as with restrictions; to lessen a risk

**heed** *n.* close attention *–vi., vt.* to pay attention

**heft´y** *adj.* large; weighty

**height** *n.* extreme: *the height of indecency*; an elevation; the distance from bottom to top

**height´en** *vi., vt.* to become or make higher or more intense

**hein´ous** *adj.* atrocious

**help** *n.* aid; a remedy; employees *–vi., vt.* to assist; to remedy or improve **–help´ful** *adj.* **–help´ful·ly** *adv.* **–help´ful·ness** *n.*

**help´less** *adj.* powerless to help oneself; incapable of aiding another **–help´less·ly** *adv.* **–help´less·ness** *n.*

**hence** *adv.* from this place or time; therefore

**hence´forth´** *adv.* from now on

**her´ald** *n.* a harbinger *–vt.* to foretell or publicize

**her´biv·ore** *n.* an animal that feeds mainly on plants **–her·biv´o·rous** *adj.*

**herd** *n.* a large group *–vi., vt.* to gather or move a large group; to tend a group of animals

**he·red´i·tar·y** *adj.* inherited

**he·red´i·ty** *n.* inherited characteristics

**her´e·sy** *n.* rejection of an accepted or established concept or belief

**her´e·tic** *n.* one who rejects an established belief **–he·ret´i·cal** *adj.*

**her´it·age** *n.* that is or can be inherited; culture, tradition, etc. that is handed down

**her´mit** *n.* a recluse

**he´ro** *n.* one noted for courage, greatness, etc.; the central figure in a story **–he·ro´ic, he·ro´i·cal** *adj.* **–he·ro´i·cal·ly** *adv.*

**hes´i·tant** *adj.* uncertain, doubtful **–hes´i·tan·cy** *n.*

**hes´i·tate´** *vi.* to pause or waver; to be uncertain **–hes´i·ta´tion** *n.*

**hes´si·an** *n.* *(Brit.)* a coarse cloth used in the making of sacks and as a backing for upholstry or carpeting

**hew** *vt.* to chop or hack

**hex** *(US)* *n.* a spell *–vt.* to cast a spell

**hi·a´tus** *n.* a break in continuity; an interruption

**hic´cup, hic´cough** *n.* an involuntary sound made by a sudden closing of the respiratory tract

**hid´den** *adj.* concealed; secret

**hide** *vi., vt.* to conceal
**hide´bound** *adj.* opinionated
**hid´e·ous** *adj.* repulsive; terrifying
**high** *adj.* elevated; prominent; greater than normal, as in size, intensity, importance, etc. **–high and mighty** haughty; snobbish
**high´er-up** *n.* one superior in rank or position
**high´hand·ed** *adj.* haughty
**high´-spir·it·ed** *adj.* lively
**high´-strung´** *adj.* nervous
**high´way** *(US) n.* a main road
**hi´jack** *vt.* to take by force
**hike** *n.* a long walk; a rise, as in prices *–vi.* to walk *–vt.* to raise; to pull up
**hi·lar´i·ous** *adj.* very funny
**hill** *n.* a plot of ground higher than its surroundings; a pile or mound
**hill´ock** *n.* a small hill
**hin´der** *vi., vt.* to delay or obstruct
**hin´drance** *n.* an obstacle
**hinge** *n.* a flexible joint *–vi. vt.* to be or to make contingent on something else
**hint** *n.* a slight indication *–vi., vt.* to intimate
**hire** *vt.* to employ for payment
**hir´sute** *adj.* hairy
**his·tor´ic, his·tor´i·cal** *adj.* relating to the past; notable **–his·tor´i·cal·ly** *adv.* **–his·tor´i·cal·ness** *n.*
**his´to·ry** *n.* an account of the past **–his´to´ri·an** *n.*
**hit** *n.* a blow; a success *–vi., vt.* to strike; to discover
**hoard** *n.* a hidden supply *–vt.* to obtain and store in reserve
**hoarse** *adj.* harsh sounding
**hoar´y** *adj.* grayish-white; old
**hoax** *n.* a deception
**hob´by** *n.* a favored pastime
**hob´nob** *vi.* to socialize
**ho´bo** *(US) n.* a vagrant
**hod** *n.* a V-shaped trough for hauling bricks or mortar; a coal scuttle
**hog´wash** *n.* nonsense
**hoist** *n.* the act of lifting; a device for raising heavy loads *–vt.* to lift or pull up
**ho´kum** *n.* nonsense
**hold** *n.* the act of grasping; an influence or controlling force *–vi.* to maintain a grasp; to remain in a particular state *–vt.* to grasp; to sustain; to contain
**hole** *n.* an opening; a hollow; a crude or squalid shelter
**hol´i·day´** *adj.* festive: *a holiday mood –n.* a day of rest, commemoration, etc.
**hol´ler** *n.* a yell *–vi., vt.* to call out
**hol´low** *adj.* empty inside, not solid; sunken or indented *–n.* a recess *–vi., vt.* to become or make hollow
**hol´o·caust´** *n.* great destruction
**hom´age** *n.* a profession of fealty or loyalty; worship
**home** *n.* the place where one lives; one's native state, country, or land *–adj.* of or relating to a place of residence or origin *–adv.* at or in the direction of home; toward the point directed
**home´ly** *adj.* plain; simple; unpretentious
**home´stead´** *n.* buildings and land that constitute a home
**home´y** *adj.* simple; comfortable
**hom´i·cide** *n.* the killing of one person by another; one who kills another **–hom´i·ci´dal** *adj.*
**hom·i·let´ics** *n.* the art of sermonizing
**hom´i·ly** *n.* a sermon or lecture, often to teach a practical lesson
**hom´i·ny** *n.* hulled and dried corn
**ho·mo·ge´ne·ous** *adj.* of a similar kind or type; uniform throughout
**ho·mog´e·nize** *vt.* to make homogeneous; to disperse particles evenly throughout a liquid
**homogenized milk** milk that has been processed to break up fat globules and distribute them evenly throughout
**ho·mol´o·gous** *adj.* corresponding or similar in many aspects
**hom´o·nym** *n.* a word that sounds like another, but that differs in meaning and often in spelling
**Ho´mo sa´pi·ens** *n.* the human race
**ho´mo·sex´u·al** *n.* one attracted to persons of the same sex
**hone** *vt.* to sharpen *–n.* a stone for sharpening
**hon´est** *adj.* free from deceit; marked by integrity; respectable; trustworthy; fair **–hon´es·ty** *n.* **–hon´est·ly** *adv.*
**hon´ey** *n.* a thick, sweet liquid produced from nectar for food by bees and certain other insects; something good *–vt.* to sweeten with honey
**hon´ey·comb** *n.* a network of wax cells made by bees; any similar structure *–vt.* to permeate with small holes
**hon´ey·moon** *n.* a wedding trip; any brief period of accord
**honk** *n.* the call of a wild goose; any similar sound *–vi., vt.*
**hon´or** *n.* great respect; a mark of special recognition; reputation; an exalted rank *–vt.* to esteem or respect; to afford special recognition; to recognize or pay as a due debt **–hon´or·a·ble** *adj.* **–hon´or·a·bly** *adv.* **–hon´or·a·ble·ness** *n.*
**hon·o·rar´i·um** *n.* a fee paid to a speaker or lecturer
**hon´or·ar·y** *adj.* conferred without duties or pay
**hon·or·if´ic** *adj.* that which confers or shows respect *–n.* an honorary title
**hon´our** *(Brit.) n.* great respect; a mark of special recognition; reputation; an exalted rank *–vt.* to esteem or respect; to afford special recognition; to recognize or pay as a due debt

**hood** *n.* a covering, as for the head, an engine, or a stove; a hoodlum *—vt.* to cover with a hood
**hood´lum** *n.* a young rowdy; a gangster
**hood´wink** *vt.* to deceive
**hoof** *n.* a horny substance that covers the feet of certain mammals *—vi., vt.* to walk or dance
**hoof´er** *n.* one who dances for a living
**hook** *n.* a bent device used to snag or hang; a fishhook; a means of attracting or snaring *—vt.* to catch, connect, or suspend by means of a hook; to steal
**hoo´li·gan** *n.* a hoodlum
**hoop** *n.* a band of metal or wood as used to secure the staves of a cask or to hold embroidery; anything similar in the form of a hoop, as earrings or a plaything *—vt.* to secure with a band
**hoot´e·nan´y** *n.* an informal gathering of folk musicians
**hop** *vi.* to jump on one foot; to move quickly *—n.* a short distance; a quick trip
**hope** *vi.* to desire or anticipate with expectation of fulfillment *—n.* confident expectation **—hope´ful** *adj.* **—hope´ful·ly** *adv.* **—hope´ful·ness** *n.*
**hop´per** *n.* a container, especially one emptied through a gate at the bottom; a person or insect that hops
**horde** *n.* a great crowd; a throng
**ho·ri´zon** *n.* a line where earth and sky appear to converge; the extent of one's perception or interest
**hor´i·zon´tal** *adj.* level with or parallel to the horizon
**hor´mone** *n.* any of a number of substances produced in the body to regulate physiological activity
**horn** *n.* a hard projection that grows from the head of certain animals; material which coats the surface of an animal horn; something having the shape of a horn; a wind instrument made from a horn; a brass wind instrument
**hor´net** *n.* a type of wasp
**ho·rol´o·gy** *n.* the study of time; the art of creating timepieces
**hor´o·scope** *n.* an aspect of the heavens by which astrologers attempt to foretell the future
**hor·ren´dous** *adj.* dreadful
**hor´ri·ble** *adj.* inspiring horror; dreadful
**hor´rid** *adj.* hideous; shocking
**hor´ri·fy´** *vt.* to overwhelm with terror **—hor·ri·fi·ca´tion** *n.*
**hor´ror** *n.* great revulsion or fear
**hors d´oeu·vre** *pl., n.* appetizers, usually served before a meal
**horse** *n.* a hoofed mammal domesticated for riding or hauling; a carpenter's frame for holding wood; cavalry: *horse soldiers —adj.* of or relating to a horse *—vt.* to provide with a horse
**horse´play** *n.* rough boisterous play
**horse´pow·er** *n.* a unit used to express the power of an engine
**hor´ta·to·ry** *adj.* expressing encouragement
**hor´ti·cul´ture** *n.* the science of cultivating plants **—hor´ti·cul´tur·ist** *n.*
**hose** *n.* socks or stockings: hosiery; a flexible pipe for conveying fluids *—vt.* to wet down or wash with a hose; to deceive
**ho´sier·y** *n.* socks and stockings
**hos´pice** *n.* a lodging or shelter
**hos´pi·ta·ble** *adj.* cordial, helpful, or generous; suitable or favorable for habitation **—hos´pi·ta·ble·ness** *n.* **—hos´pi·ta·bly** *adv.* **—hos´pi·tal´i·ty** *n.*
**hos´pi·tal** *n.* a building or location for the care of the sick and injured **—hos·pit·tal·i·za´tion** *n.* **—hos´pit·tal·ize** *vt.*
**host** *n.* one who receives guests, either socially or as an employee of a business; a master of ceremonies; a throng or multitude; an organism on which another lives
**hos´tage** *n.* one held as security for the fulfillment of a pledge or against the threat of harm
**hos´tel** *n.* lodging, esp. for hikers
**host´ess** *n.* a female host; a greeter at a restaurant or club
**hos´tile** *adj.* feeling or displaying ill will; threatening; antagonistic; detrimental to health or well-being *—n.* an enemy **—hos´til´i·ty** *n.*
**hot** *adj.* of a relatively high temperature; burning to the taste or touch; marked by passion; angry *—adv.* in a hot manner **—hot´ly** *adv.*
**hot´-blood´ed** *adj.* passionate
**hot´dog´** *n.* a frankfurter; a frankfurter served on a long roll; a daredevil or showoff
**ho·tel´** *n.* an establishment that offers lodging and often meals to paying guests
**hot´house** *n.* a greenhouse with heat and humidity controlled for the cultivation of plants
**hot´line** *n.* a direct channel of communication for handling crises or problems
**hot´-rod´** *n.* a car that has been modified to increase acceleration or running speed
**hound** *n.* a dog commonly used in hunting; one diligent in the pursuit of an interest *—vt.* to badger or annoy
**hour** *n.* a period of time equal to sixty minutes; the customary or set period for an activity; a significant time: *the hour of reckoning* **—hour´ly** *adv.*
**house** *n.* a building that serves as a dwelling or shelter; a family or lineage; a business establishment; a branch of the legislature *—vt.* to provide living space; to shelter or store
**house´hold** *n.* all of the persons who share a dwelling *—adj.* pertaining to or used in a dwelling; common place
**hov´el** *n.* a wretched dwelling
**hov´er** *vi.* to remain over, in, or near

**how** *adv.* in what manner; by what means; to what extent
**how·ev´er** *adv.* by whatever means
**howl** *n.* the plaintive wail of a beast; something very funny *—vi., vt.* to utter a plaintive wail
**hoy´den** *n.* a boisterous woman
**hub** *n.* the center of a wheel or similar rotating object; a center of interest or activity
**hub´bub´** *n.* uproar, bustle
**hub´cap´** *n.* the covering for a hub
**huck´ster** *n.* a peddler or pitchman; one who sells or promotes with overblown claims
**hud´dle** *vi., vt.* to crowd together; to crouch *—n.* a dense crowd; a quick, informal meeting
**hue** *n.* a gradation of color; a color or tint
**huff** *vt.* to offend *—vi.* to be indignant or offended *—n.* a feeling of anger or annoyance
**huff´y** *adj.* easily offended
**hug** *vt.* to embrace or hold close; to keep close to: *the boat hugged the shore*; to hold fast *—n.* an embrace
**huge** *adj.* exceedingly large; of great extent
**hulk** *n.* an old unwieldy or unseaworthy ship; an abandoned hull; anything bulky or unwieldy
**hull** *n.* a husk: the outer covering of a seed or fruit; the body of a ship *—vt.* to remove the husk from, as of peas
**hum** *vi., vt.* to make a low, droning sound, as that made by a bee; to sing without voicing words *—n.* a low, droning sound
**hu´man** *adj.* of, relating to, or having the form or characteristics of a human being; of human attributes as distinguished from those of the animals *—n.* a human being **—hu´man·ly** *adv.* **—hu´man·ness** *n.*
**hu·mane´** *adj.* characterized by compassion; pertaining to human values
**hu·man´i·tar´i·an** *n.* one concerned with the welfare of others
**hu´man´i·ty** *n.* the human race; the quality of being human or humane
**hu´man·ize** *vt., vi.* to make or become human or humane
**hum´ble** *adj.* meek; submissive; unpretentious *—vt.* to humiliate; to abase
**hum´bug** *n.* foolish talk; something intended to deceive
**hu´mid** *adj.* moist or damp
**hu´mid´i·fi·er** *n.* a device for adding moisture to the air
**hu´mid´i·ty** *n.* dampness; a measure of the amount of moisture in the surrounding air
**hu´mi·dor** *n.* a tobacco container that retains moisture
**hu·mil´i·ate´** *vt.* to embarrass or shame **—hu·mil·i·a´tion** *n.*
**hu´mil´i·ty** *n.* the quality of being humble; modesty
**hum´ming·bird´** *n.* a very small bird with brilliant plumage, notable for very rapid wing movement that allows the bird to hover and dart
**hu´mor** *(US) n.* an amusing quality; that intended to incite laughter; one's disposition *—vt.* to indulge the whims of another
**hu´mor·ist** *n.* an entertainer or writer who specializes in relating amusing stories
**hu´mor·ous** *adj.* expressing humor; amusing **—hu´mor·ous·ly** *adv.* **—hu´mor·ous·ness** *n.*
**hu´mour** *(Brit.) n.* an amusing quality; that intended to incite laughter; one's disposition *—vt.* to indulge the whims of another
**hu´mus** *n.* organic matter in soil
**hun´ger** *n.* a desire or craving *—vi.* to have a strong desire, especially for food **—hun´gry** *adj.* **—hun´gri·ly** *adv.* **—hun´gri·ness** *n.*
**hunk** *n.* a large piece of something
**hunt** *vi., vt.* to seek or search *—n.* the act of seeking wild game; a hunting expedition; a diligent search
**hur´dle** *n.* a barrier over which competitors leap; any obstacle to a goal *—vt., vi.* to surmount an obstacle or obstacles
**hurl** *vt.* to throw violently; to utter vehemently; to vomit
**hur´ri·cane** *n.* a violent storm accompanied by high winds
**hur´ry** *vi., vt.* to move or cause to move with haste *—n.* haste
**hurt** *vt.* to injure physically or mentally; to impair or lessen: *hurt one's chances* *—n.* something painful or that causes suffering **—hurt´ful** *adj.* **—hurt´ful·ly** *adv.* **—hurt´ful·ness** *n.*
**hur´tle** *vt., vi.* to throw or move violently
**hus´band** *n.* a married man *—vt.* to conserve or use economically: *to husband one's resources*
**hus´band·ry** *n.* the study of agriculture or livestock breeding; careful management
**husk** *n.* the outer covering of some seeds, fruits, or vegetables *—vt.* to remove the covering from
**husk´y** *adj.* of a voice with a hoarse or rough quality; sturdily built
**hus´sy** *n.* a saucy female
**hus´tle** *vi., vt.* to move or cause to move energetically or roughly; to shove or jostle; to convince by questionable means
**hut** *n.* a crude dwelling
**hy´brid** *n.* a thing produced by combining dissimilar species or elements *—adj.* pertaining to a hybrid **—hy´brid·ize** *vt., vi.* **—hy·brid·i·za´tion** *n.*
**hy´dra** *n.* a freshwater polyp; persistent evil
**hy´drant** *n.* an outlet from a water main, used to draw water for fighting fires, cleaning streets, etc.
**hy´drate** *n.* a compound of water and other molecules or atoms *—vt.*

**hy´drau´lic** *adj.* operated by fluid under pressure

**hy´drau´lics** *n.* the science of the dynamics of fluid in motion

**hy´dro·e·lec´tric** *adj.* of electricity generated by water power

**hy´dro·foil** *n.* a structure that holds the hull of a boat out of the water when it is in motion; a boat equipped with hydrofoils, also called a *hydroplane*

**hy´dro·gen** *n.* a flammable gas, lightest of all the elements

**hydrogen bomb** a powerful explosive device activated by the fusion of hydrogen isotopes

**hy·drom´e·ter** *n.* a device to measure the specific gravity of a liquid

**hy´dro·pho´bi·a** *n.* rabies

**hy´dro·plane** *n.* a seaplane; a small boat that skims the surface of water; a hydrofoil *—vt.* to skim the surface of water

**hy·dro·pon´ics** *n.* the cultivation of plants without soil

**hy·e´na** *n.* a scavenging carnivorous mammal of Africa and Asia

**hy´giene** *n.* the science of the preservation of health; any practice that serves to promote good health **—hy·gi·en´ic** *adj.* **—hy·gi·en´i·cal·ly** *adv.*

**hymn** *n.* a song of praise

**hym´nal** *n.* a book or collection of hymns

**hy·per´bo·la** *n.* a type of geometric curve

**hy·per´bo·le** *n.* a figure of speech in which exaggeration is used for emphasis: *I could eat a horse*

**hy·per·bol´ic** *adj.* representing or shaped like a hyperbola; exaggerated: containing hyperbole

**hy·per·crit´i·cal** *adj.* excessively exacting

**hy·per·sen´si·tive** *adj.* excessively tense or delicate

**hy´per·son´ic** *adj.* moving, or capable of moving, at several times the speed of sound

**hy´per·ten´sion** *n.* high blood pressure

**hy·per·thy´roid·ism** *n.* a disorder caused by an overly active thyroid gland

**hy´phen** *n.* a punctuation mark (-) used to separate syllables, parts of a compound word, or phrases **—hy·phen´ate** *vt.*

**hyp·no´sis** *n.* a sleep-like state that may open one's mind to suppressed memories

**hyp·not´ic** *adj.* of hypnosis; spellbinding

**hyp´no·tism** *n.* the act of inducing hypnosis **—hyp´no·tize´** *vt.*

**hy·po·chon´dri·a** *n.* excessive anxiety about one's health **—hy·po·chon´dri·ac** *n.*

**hy·poc´ri·sy** *n.* pretending to a belief that one does not hold **—hyp´o·crite** *n.* **—hyp·o·crit´i·cal** *adj.* **—hyp·o·crit´i·cal·ly** *adv.*

**hy´po·der´mic** *adj.* of the layer of tissue beneath the skin; of injection beneath the skin *—n.* a hypodermic injection, needle, or syringe

**hy´po·ten´sion** *n.* low blood pressure

**hy·pot´e·nuse´** *n.* the side that is opposite the right angle of a right triangle

**hy´poth´e·sis** *n., pl.* **hy´poth´e·ses** a theory based on fact, put forth for further testing **—hy´po·thet´ic, hy·po·thet´i·cal** *adj.* **—hy·po·thet´i·cal·ly** *adv.*

**hys·ter·ec´to·my** *n.* surgical excision of part or all of the uterus

**hys·te´ri·a** *n.* excessive, uncontrollable emotion; a neurosis marked by physical ailment without apparent cause

**hys·ter´ic, hys·ter´ic·al** *adj.* characterized by hysteria

**hys·ter´ics** *n.* an attack of hysteria

**i, I** ninth letter of the English alphabet; in Roman characters, the symbol for one

**ice** *n.* frozen water; a dessert comprised of crushed or shaved ice and a sweet flavoring *—vt.* to cool, as with ice; to cover and decorate a cake with a sugar mixture

**ice´berg´** *n.* a huge mound of floating ice

**ice´box** *n.* a refrigerator; an insulated cabinet used to cool food

**ice´cap** *n.* a mass of ice covering a large tract of land

**ice sheet** *n.* a large continental glacier

**ich·thy·ol´o·gy** *n.* the study of fishes

**i´ci·cle** *n.* a hanging taper of ice formed by dripping water

**i´ci·ly** *adv.* in a cold or haughty manner

**ic´ing** *n.* a sugar mixture used to coat and decorate a cake

**i´con** *n.* an image; a sacred picture; one who is revered; a small image on a computer screen that represents a command, data type, etc.

**i´con´o·clast** *n.* a destroyer of sacred images; one who attacks traditional institutions

**i´cy** *adj.* covered with ice; cold or slippery; cold and unfriendly **—ic´i·ness** *n.*

**id** *n.* that part of the subconscious concerned with instinctive or primitive impulses

**i·de´a** *n.* a mental image; a scheme; a concept or opinion

**i·de´al** *adj.* perfect or excellent; typical; existing in theory or in the mind *—n.* a thing considered a model for perfection **—i·de´al·ly** *adv.*

**i·de´al·ism** *n.* the practice of seeking the best in everything; the belief that all is for good

**i·de´al·ist** *n.* a visionary; one inspired by that which is ideal **—i·de·al·is´tic, i·de·al·is´ti·cal** *adj.* **—i·de·al·is´ti·cal·ly** *adv.*

**i·de´al·ize´** *vt.* to envision as ideal

**i·den´ti·cal** *adj.* alike in every way

**i·den´ti·fi·ca´tion** *n.* the act of recognition or classification; credentials that establish one's identity

**i·den´ti·fy** *vt.* to establish the identity of *—vi.* to establish a unity with certain others **–i·den´ti·fi·a·ble** *adj.*

**i·den´ti·ty** *n.* characteristics by which a person or thing is recognized or defined

**id´e·ol´o·gy** *n.* a set of beliefs or doctrines **–i·de·ol´o·gist** *n.*

**id´i·o·cy** *n.* folly; mental retardation

**id´i·om** *n.* an expression or usage peculiar to a particular language or region **–id´i·o·mat´ic, id´i·o·mat´i·cal** *adj.* **–id´i·o·mat´i·cal·ly** *adv.*

**id·i·o·syn´cra·sy** *n.* a characteristic peculiar to a person or group

**id´i·ot** *n.* one who is foolish or stupid; formerly, a classification for mental retardation, now considered offensive in that context

**id·i·ot´ic** *adj.* foolish or stupid

**i´dle** *adj.* not busy or in use; tending to avoid work *–vt.* to waste time **–i´dly** *adv.*

**i´dol** *n.* an image; an object of worship; one who is revered or adored

**i´dol´a·try** *n.* the worship of idols; excessive devotion **–i´dol´a·ter** *n.* **–i´dol´a·trous** *adj.*

**i´dol·ize´** *vt.* to make the object of excessive devotion

**i´dyl, i´dyll** *n.* a short narrative or poem describing a pastoral or romantic scene

**if** *conj.* on condition that; whether or not *–n.* a supposition or condition

**ig´ne·ous** *adj.* pertaining to fire; formed by fire

**ig´nite´** *vt.* to set afire; to arouse passion *–vi.* to burn

**ig·ni´tion** *n.* the act of setting or being set on fire; a system for igniting the fuel in an internal-combustion engine

**ig·no´ble** *adj.* base; vulgar; of low birth

**ig´no·min·y** *n.* disgrace; shame **–ig·no·min´i·ous** *adj.* **–ig·no·min´i·ous·ly** *adv.* **–ig·no·min´i·ous·ness** *n.*

**ig´no·ra´mus** *n.* an ignorant person

**ig´no·rance** *n.* a lack of experience or knowledge; the state of being uninformed

**ig´no·rant** *adj.* lacking knowledge; uninformed

**ig·nore´** *vt.* to disregard

**ilk** *n.* type or kind

**ill** *adj.* sick; harmful; of a hostile nature *–n.* harmful; the cause of suffering or misfortune

**ill-ad·vised´** *adj.* unwise; evidencing a lack of careful thought

**ill´-bred´** *adj.* crude or impolite

**il·le´gal** *adj.* prohibited by law *–n.* one who enters the country illegally **–il´le·gal´i·ty** *n.*

**il·leg´i·ble** *adj.* difficult or impossible to decipher; unreadable **–il·leg·i·bil´i·ty** *n.*

**il·le·git´i·mate** *adj.* contrary to law; illegal; born out of wedlock **–il·le·git´i·ma·cy** *n.* **–il·le·git´i·mate·ly** *adv.*

**ill´-fat´ed** *adj.* likely to end badly

**ill´-got´ten** *adj.* obtained dishonestly

**il·lib´er·al** *adj.* selfish; bigoted; vulgar, ill-bred

**il·lic´it** *adj.* unlawful; prohibited

**il·lit´er·a·cy** *n.* the state of being unable to read or write

**il·lit´er·ate** *adj.* lacking formal education; lacking comprehension of a particular branch of art or knowledge *–n.* one who is unable to read and write

**ill´ness** *n.* a sickness or disease

**il·log´i·cal** *adj.* contrary to reason; unreasonable or unreasoning

**ill´-tem´pered** *adj.* querulous; irritable **–ill´-tem´pered·ly** *adv.* **–ill´-tem´pered·ness** *n.*

**il·lum´i·nate, il·lu´mine** *vi., vt.* to light or make brighter; to clarify, as by example or illustration; to decorate a printed page

**il·lu·mi·na´tion** *n.* lighting; clarification or instruction

**il·lu´sion** *n.* an erroneous or deceptive impression

**il·lu´so·ry** *adj.* based on illusion; deceptive; not real

**il´lus·trate** *vt.* to clarify or explain, as by example; to decorate with pictures

**il·lus·tra´tion** *n.* an example or explanation; a picture

**il·lus´tra·tive** *adj.* serving to illustrate or explain; symbolic

**il·lus´tri·ous** *adj.* distinguished; eminent

**ill will** *n.* malevolence; hostility

**im´age** *n.* a likeness; something that closely resembles another; a concept or mental picture; the way in which one is perceived

**im´a·ge·ry** *n.* a mental image; the use of imaginative language to describe

**im·ag´i·na·ble** *adj.* that can be imagined; conceivable; plausible

**im·ag´i·na·ry** *adj.* fanciful; theoretical; nonexistent

**im·ag´i·na´tion** *n.* the ability to hypothesize; creativity; the formation of mental images

**im·ag´i·na·tive** *adj.* inventive; creative **–im·ag´i·na·tive·ly** *adv.* **–im·ag´i·na·tive·ness** *n.*

**im·ag´ine** *vi., vt.* to picture or create in the mind

**im·bal´ance** *n.* a state of unevenness

**im´be·cile, im·be·cil´ic** *adj.* silly; foolish

**im´be·cile** *n.* a foolish person; one lacking intellect; formerly, a classification for mental retardation, now considered offensive **–im´be·cil´i·ty** *n.*

**im·bibe´** *vt.* to drink *–vi.* to consume an alcoholic beverage

**im·bro´glio** *n.* an entanglement; confusion

**im·bue´** *vt.* to permeate

**im´i·tate** *vt.* to copy or impersonate, as in appearance or style, generally in a flattering way; to mimic, often with exaggeration and in an unflattering manner

**im·i·ta´tion** *n.* the act of imitating; a copy or likeness; a substitute of lesser quality

**im´i·ta·tive** *adj.* involving imitation; not original or genuine, deceptive

**im·mac´u·late** *adj.* absolutely pure or clean; without blemish
**im´ma·nent** *adj.* existing within; deep-seated —**im´ma·nence** *n.*
**im·ma·te´ri·al** *adj.* lacking importance; not significant; lacking substance
**im·ma·ture´** *adj.* not yet ripe; not fully grown; childish: wanting of adult qualities
**im·meas´ur·a·ble** *adj.* boundless; incapable of being measured
**im·me´diate** *adj.* at this instant; near the present time; near at hand —**im·me´di·a·cy** *n.*
**im·me·mo´ri·al** *adj.* before memory or recorded history
**im·mense´** *adj.* extremely large; seeming boundless
**im·merse´** *vt.* to submerge in liquid; to become deeply involved; to baptize by submersing the body completely in water —**im·mer´sion** *n.*
**im´mi·grant** *n.* one newly-arrived in a country with intent to settle
**im´mi·grate** *vi.* to newly enter a country with intent to settle
**im·mi·gra´tion** *n.* settlement in a land to which one is not native
**im´mi·nent** *adj.* impending; about to occur
**im·mo·bil´i·ty** *n.* the state of being motionless or unable to move —**im·mo´bile** *adj.*
**im·mod´er·ate** *adj.* excessive
**im·mod´est** *adj.* bold; egotistical; lacking modesty
**im´mo·late** *vt.* to sacrifice —**im·mo·la´tion** *n.*
**im·mor´al** *adj.* characterized by a lack of virtue; contrary to accepted standards of morality
**im·mo·ral´i·ty** *n.* a lack of virtue; an immoral act
**im·mor´tal** *adj.* of that which cannot die; everlasting; enduring —*n.* a god; a person worth remembering
**im·mor·tal´i·ty** *n.* the condition of living or being remembered forever
**im·mov´a·ble** *adj.* fixed in place; unable to be moved
**im·mune´** *adj.* not subject to or affected by; exempt
**im·mu´ni·ty** *n.* exemption or freedom from certain restrictions; protection from disease
**im´mu·nize** *vt.* to protect, as from disease, prosecution, etc.
**im·mu·nol´o·gy** *n.* the science dealing with the immune system and means of preventing disease
**im·mure´** *vt.* to confine within a wall; to protect or imprison
**im·mu´ta·ble** *adj.* not subject to change
**imp** *n.* a small demon; a mischievous child
**im´pact** *n.* a collision; the force of a collision; an effect: *the negative impact of television on book sales* —**im·pact´** *vt.* to strike with force; to pack firmly; to have effect on —**im·pact´ed** *adj.*
**im·pair´** *vt.* to cause to diminish, as in quantity or value—*poor materials impair our ability to create a quality product*
**im·pale´** *vt.* to thrust a pale or sharp stake through the body; to render helpless
**im·pal´pa·ble** *adj.* not perceived by touch; not easily grasped by the mind
**im·pan´el** *vt.* to prepare a list, as for jury duty
**im·part´** *vt.* to give or confer; to convey, as knowledge
**im·par´tial** *adj.* not biased; without prejudice —**im·par´tial·ly** *adv.* —**im·par´tial·ness** *n.*
**im·par´ti·al´i·ty** *n.* objectivity; not partial or biased
**im·pass´a·ble** *adj.* unable to be travelled over or through —**im·pass·a·bil´i·ty, im·pas´si·ble·ness** *n.* —**im·pass·a·bly** *adv.*
**im´passe** *n.* a situation that leaves no room for compromise; a stalemate
**im·pas´si·ble** *adj.* apathetic; not easily aroused emotionally —**im·pas·si·bil´i·ty, im·pas´si·ble·ness** *n.* —**im·pas´si·bly** *adv.*
**im·pas´sioned** *adj.* ardent; designed to arouse passion
**im·pas´sive** *adj.* insensible to pain; showing no emotion —**im·pas´sive·ly** *adv.* —**im·pas´sive·ness** *n.*
**im·pa´tience** *n.* restlessness, intolerance
**im·pa´tient** *adj.* unable to wait; restless; anxious; intolerant —**im·pa´tient·ly** *adv.* —**im·pa´tient·ness** *n.*
**im·peach´** *vt.* to accuse or charge with misconduct in office; to attempt to discredit
**im·pec´ca·ble** *adj.* nattily attired; without flaw or imperfection —**im·pec´ca·bly** *adv.*
**im·pe·cu´ni·ous** *adj.* lacking means; penniless —**im·pe·cu´ni·ous·ly** *adv.* —**im·pe·cu´ni·ous·ness** *n.*
**im·pede´** *vt.* to slow the progress of; to obstruct
**im·ped´i·ment** *n.* an obstruction; a condition that prevents clear articulation, as *a speech impediment*; in law, an obstacle that bars the making of legal contract
**im·pel´** *vt.* to drive or urge forward; to spur to action
**im·pend´** *vi.* to be about to happen; to approach and threaten, as *an impending storm*
**im·pen´e·tra·ble** *adj.* unable to be penetrated; incomprehensible —**im·pen´e·tra·ble·ness** *n.* —**im·pen´e·tra·bly** *adv.*
**im·pen´i·tent** *adj.* without regret or remorse —**im·pen´i·tence** *n.* —**im·pen´i·tent·ly** *adv.*
**im·per´a·tive** *adj.* pressing; obligatory —*n.* an order or obligation —**im·per´a·tive·ly** *adv.* —**im·per´a·tive·ness** *n.*
**im·per·cep´ti·ble** *adj.* that cannot be perceived —**im·per·cep´ti·ble·ness** *n.* —**im·per·cep´ti·bly** *adv.*
**im·per´fect** *adj.* deficient; flawed —**im·per´fect·ly** *adv.* —**im·per´fect·ness** *n.*
**im·per·fec´tion** *n.* a flaw
**im·pe´ri·al** *adj.* of a ruler or empire; majestic; of great size —**im·pe´ri·al·ly** *adv.*
**im·pe´ri·al·ism** *n.* the policy of extending an empire by acquiring new territory or establishing dominance

over other nations

**im·per´il** *vt.* to endanger

**im·pe´ri·ous** *adj.* arrogant; overbearing –**im·pe´ri·ous·ly** *adv.* –**im·pe´ri·ous·ness** *n.*

**im·per´ma·nent** *adj.* not lasting; transient –**im·per´ma·nence** *n.* –**im·per´ma·nent·ly** *adv.*

**im·per´me·a·ble** *adj.* not subject to penetration, as by moisture –**im·per·me·a·bil´i·ty** *n.* –**im·per´me·a·bly** *adv.*

**im·per´son·al** *adj.* not referring or relating to a particular person or thing: *an impersonal view*; cold or indifferent –**im·per´son·al·ly** *adj.*

**im·per´son·ate´** *vt.* to fraudulently pretend to be another; to mimic another for the purpose of entertaining –**im·per´son·a´tion** *n.*

**im·per´ti·nent** *adj.* disrespectful or insolent –**im·per´ti·nence** *n.* –**im·per´ti·nent·ly** *adv.*

**im·per·turb´a·ble** *adj.* calm; not disposed to becoming disturbed or agitated

**im·per´vi·ous** *adj.* impenetrable; not influenced, as by emotion, fear, flattery, etc. –**im·per´vi·ous·ly** *adv.* –**im·per´vi·ous·ness** *n.*

**im·pet´u·ous** *adj.* marked by sudden impulse or passion; spontaneous –**im·pet´u·ous·ly** *adv.* –**im·pet´u·ous·ness** *n.*

**im´pe·tus** *n.* a stimulus; action associated with or caused by a stimulus; momentum

**im·pinge´** *vi., vt.* to touch or encroach upon

**im´pi·ous** *adj.* lacking piety; blasphemous –**im´pi·ous·ly** *adv.* –**im´pi·ous·ness** *n.*

**im·pla´ca·ble** *adj.* unable to be placated; unbending –**im·pla´ca·bly** *adv.* –**im·pla´ca·ble·ness** *n.*

**im·plant´** *vt.* to establish or instill; to plant surgically –*n.* a thing inserted by surgery

**im·plau´si·ble** *adj.* not believable –**im·plau´si·bly** *adv.*

**im´ple·ment** *n.* a tool or device –*vt.* to use or put into force

**im´pli·cate´** *vt.* to incriminate; to imply; to entangle or involve

**im´pli·ca´tion** *n.* something implied; a link or involvement

**im·plic´it** *adj.* understood or implied; absolute –**im·plic´it·ly** *adv.* –**im·plic´it·ness** *n.*

**im·plode´** *vt., vi.* to burst inward

**im·plore´** *vt.* to beg or plead

**im·ply´** *vt.* to infer by logic; to signify indirectly

**im·po·lite´** *adj.* rude; discourteous –**im·po·lite´ly** *adv.* –**im·po·lite´ness** *n.*

**im·pol´i·tic** *adj.* imprudent or unwise

**im·pon´der·a·ble** *adj.* impossible to evaluate –**im·pon·der·a·bil´i·ty** *n.* –**im·pon´der·a·bly** *adv.*

**im·port´** *vt.* to bring in from another country; to transfer computer data between applications or platforms –*vi.* to be of significance –**im´port** *n.* a thing brought in; meaning or significance –**im´por·ta´tion** *n.*

**im·port´ed** *adj.* foreign; brought from elsewhere

**im·por´tance** *n.* significance; personal distinction or standing

**im·por´tant** *adj.* significant –**im·por´tant·ly** *adv.*

**im·por´tu·nate** *adj.* persistently pleading; urgently requesting –**im·por´tu·nate·ly** *adv.* –**im·por´tu·nate·ness** *n.*

**im´por·tune´** *vi., vt.* to plead persistently

**im·pose´** *vt.* to apply with authority or as if by authority; to force on others; to lay out a publication for printing –*vi.* to take advantage of

**im·pos´ing** *adj.* impressive by virtue of size or power

**im´po·si´tion** *n.* something burdensome or that has been forced upon; advantage taken; a graphic representation of the layout of a publication

**im·pos´si·bil´i·ty** *n.* that which is unattainable or likely to end in failure

**im·pos´si·ble** *adj.* unattainable or impractical to accomplish; not believable of existing; difficult to cope with; unacceptable, as *impossible manners* –**im·pos·si·bil´i·ty** *n.* –**im·pos´si·bly** *adv.*

**im·pos´tor** *n.* one who assumes a false identity

**im·pos´ture** *n.* deception using an assumed identity

**im´po·tence** *n.* a condition marked by weakness; the inability to have sexual intercourse

**im´po·tent** *adj.* lacking strength or power; ineffective; unable to have sexual intercourse –**im´po·tence, im´po·ten·cy** *n.* –**im´po·tent·ly** *adv.*

**im·pound´** *vt.* to legally seize and hold

**im·pov´er·ish** *vt.* to deprive of, as wealth or resources

**im·pov´er·ished** *n.* devoid of wealth or resources; poverty-stricken

**im·prac´ti·cal** *adj.* not effective, prudent, or economical; unable to function in an orderly or efficient manner –**im·prac·ti·cal´i·ty** *n.*

**im´pre·cate´** *vt.* to call evil down upon; to curse –**im´pre·ca´tion** *n.*

**im·preg´na·ble** *adj.* impossible to take by assault; impossible or nearly impossible to contest or challenge, as an assertion –**im·preg·na·bil´i·ty** *n.* –**im·preg´na·bly** *adv.*

**im·preg´nate´** *vt.* to saturate; to make pregnant

**im·pre·sa´ri·o** *n.* an organizer or manager of musical entertainment

**im·press´** *vt.* to find favor; to attract notice; to plant in the mind; to mark, as if by pressure; to force into service

**im·pres´sion** *n.* a firm image in the mind; a vague notion; a mark or image on a surface made by or as if by pressure; a printed image; all of the copies of a publication printed at one time

**im·pres´sion·a·ble** *adj.* receptive to outside influence

**im·pres´sion·ism** *n.* a school of art and literature that focuses on quick concept or perception of the

subject
**im·pres´sive** *adj.* stirring; tending to impress
**im·pri·ma´tur** *n.* approval; sanction
**im´print** *n.* a distinguishing mark or emblem – **im·print´** *vt.* to produce a mark or sensory impression on
**im·pris´on** *vt.* to confine
**im·prob´a·ble** *adj.* unlikely or doubtful **–im·prob·a·bil´i·ty** *n.* **–im·prob´a·bly** *adv.*
**im·promp´tu** *adj.* spontaneous; unrehearsed *–adv.* extemporaneously
**im·prop´er** *adj.* unsuitable or inappropriate to a particular need or use; not in compliance with standards of common decency or accepted mores **–im·prop´er·ly** *adv.* **–im´pro·pri´e·ty** *n.*
**im·prove´** *vt., vi.* to make or become more useful or valuable
**im·prove´ment** *n.* something that has been enhanced or added to; an enhanced condition
**im·prov´i·dent** *adj.* not exercising due caution; rash **–im·prov´i·dence** *n.* **–im·prov´i·dent·ly** *adv.*
**im´pro·vise´** *vt.* to perform without advance preparation; to create from materials at hand **–im·prov·i·sa´tion** *n.* **–im·prov·i·sa´tion·al** *adj.*
**im·pru´dent** *adj.* unwise **–im·pru´dence** *n.* **–im·pru´dent·ly** *adv.*
**im´pu·dent** *adj.* marked by audacity; impertinent; bold **–im´pu·dence** *n.* **–im´pu·dent·ly** *adv.*
**im·pugn´** *vt.* to challenge as false
**im´pulse´** *n.* a surge; a sudden urge that leads to action; a stimulus
**im·pul´sive** *adj.* tending to act on a whim; characterized by impulsive action **–im·pul´sive·ly** *adv.* **–im·pul´sive·ness** *n.*
**im·pun´i·ty** *n.* immunity or deliverance from punishment or loss
**im·pure´** *adj.* contaminated; adulterated; lewd or obscene **–im·pure´ly** *adv.* **–im·pure´ness** *n.*
**im´pu·ta´tion** *n.* an insinuation
**im·pute´** *vt.* to assign, as a quality or blame
**in´a·bil´i·ty** *n.* a lack of power or capability
**in·ac·ces´si·ble** *adj.* not approachable; remote; unattainable **–in·ac·ces´si·bly** *adv.* **–in·ac·ces´si·ble·ness** *n.*
**in·ac´cu·ra·cy** *n.* an instance of being incorrect or inexact
**in·ac´cu·rate** *adj.* incorrect; not exact; misleading **–in·ac´cu·rate·ly** *adv.* **–in·ac´cu·rate·ness** *n.*
**in·ac´tion** *n.* a state of immobility or idleness
**in·ac´tive** *adj.* immobile or idle; not currently in use; retired from service **–in·ac´tiv·ly** *adv.* **–in´ac·tiv´i·ty** *n.*
**in·ad´e·qua·cy** *n.* a weakness; ineptitude
**in·ad´e·quate** *adj.* not sufficient for the intended purpose **–in·ad´e·quate·ly** *adv.*
**in·ad·mis´si·ble** *adj.* not allowing **–in·ad·mis·si·bil´i·ty** *n.*
**in´ad·vert´ent** *adj.* careless or thoughtless; not intentional **–in´ad·vert´ent·ly** *adv.*
**in·al´ien·a·ble** *adj.* not allowing of change or transfer **–in·al·ien·a·bil´i·ty** *n.* **–in·al´ien·a·bly** *adv.*
**in·am·o·ra´ta** *n.* a woman whom one loves
**in·ane´** *adj.* pointless; lacking substance; empty of meaning **–in·ane´ly** *adv.* **–in·an´i·ty** *n.*
**in·an´i·mate** *adj.* lacking the qualities associated with a living organism; lacking spirit or energy **–in·an´i·mate·ly** *adv.* **–in·an´i·mate·ness** *n.*
**in·ap·pro´pri·ate** *adj.* unsuitable **–in·ap·pro´pri·ate·ly** *adv.* **–in·ap·pro´pri·ate·ness** *n.*
**in·apt´** *adj.* inept; inappropriate **–in·apt´ly** *adv.* **–in·apt´ness** *n.*
**in·ar·tic´u·late** *adj.* unable to speak or express in words; unable to speak distinctly; incomprehensible **–in·ar·tic´u·late·ly** *adv.* **–in·ar·tic´u·late·ness** *n.*
**in·at·ten´tive** *adj.* indifferent; preoccupied **–in·at·ten´tive·ly** *adv.* **–in·at·ten´tion** *n.*
**in·au´gu·rate´** *vt.* to begin or bring into use with ceremony, as an induction into office or the dedication of a facility; to cause to begin
**in·au´gu·ra´tion** *n.* a ceremony of installation or induction **–in·au´gu·ral** *n.*
**in·aus·pi´cious** *adj.* unfavorable **–in·aus·pi´cious·ly** *adv.* **–in·aus·pi´cious·ness** *n.*
**in´born** *adj.* present at birth; innate
**in´bred** *adj.* inborn
**in·cal´cu·la·ble** *adj.* that cannot be calculated or assessed; unpredictable
**in·can·des´cent** *adj.* glowing as a direct result of being heated; shining brilliantly **–in·can·des´cence** *n.* **–in·can·des´cent·ly** *adv.*
**in·can·ta´tion** *n.* a chant or recitation reputed to invoke magic; a ritual supplication or prayer
**in·ca´pa·ble** *adj.* lacking qualification or competence **–in·ca·pa·bil´i·ty, in·ca´pa·ble·ness** *n.* **–in·ca´pa·bly** *adv.*
**in·ca·pac´i·tate´** *vt.* to deprive of potential or capability; to invalidate or disqualify
**in·ca·pac´i·ty** *n.* a lack of potential or ability; something that disqualifies
**in·car´cer·ate´** *vt.* to imprison; to confine **–in·car´cer·a´tion** *n.*
**in·car´nate** *adj.* manifest; especially in human form; personified *–vt.* to manifest or personify **–in´car·na´tion** *n.*
**in·cen´di·ar´y** *adj.* capable of causing fire; inclined to inflame, as emotions *–n.* a device intended to cause fire; one who starts a fire with malicious intent; one who stirs emotion to incite rebellion
**in´cense** *n.* a substance burned to create a pleasing aroma **–in·cense´** *vt.* to excite to anger

**in·cen´tive** *n.* something that serves to encourage or inspire; the prospect of penalty or reward that spurs to action

**in·cep´tion** *n.* a beginning –**in·cep´tive** *adj.*

**in·ces´sant** *adj.* continuous; without interruption –**in·ces´sant·ly** *adv.*

**in´cest** *n.* sexual intercourse between closely related persons

**in´ci·dence** *n.* the act of occurring; a rate of occurrence

**in´ci·dent** *n.* a single event or occurrence; a relatively minor occurrence

**in·ci·den´tal** *adj.* occurring as a minor adjunct; accidental, unplanned –*n.* a minor item of expense –**in·ci·den´tal·ly** *adv.*

**in·cin´er·ate´** *vi., vt.* to burn or cause to burn entirely –**in·cin´er·a´tor** *n.*

**in·cip´i·ent** *adj.* starting to come into being –**in·cip´i·ence** *n.* –**in·cip´i·ent·ly** *adv.*

**in·cise´** *vt.* to cut into or carve, as with a sharp implement; to engrave

**in·ci´sion** *n.* a cut, especially into tissue during surgery; a mark or scar left by surgery

**in·ci´sive** *adj.* keen or sharp, as in thought or language –**in·ci´sive·ly** *adv.* –**in·ci´sive·ness** *n.*

**in·ci´sor** *n.* a front cutting tooth

**in·cite´** *vt.* to provoke to action; to instigate

**in·clem´ent** *adj.* stormy; cruel or merciless –**in·clem´en·cy** *n.* –**in·clem´ent·ly** *adv.*

**in·cli·na´tion** *n.* a disposition or preference of one thing over another; an inclined surface

**in·cline´** *vt.* to slope or lean; to tend toward or show a preference; to deviate –*vt.* to cause to slope or lean –*n.* a slope

**in·clined´** *adj.* sloping or leaning; tending toward as a preference

**in·clude´** *vt.* to take in, embrace, or contain as a part –**in·clu´sion** *n.*

**in·clu´sive** *adj.* incorporating most or all; including all in the range specified –**in·clu´sive·ly** *adv.* –**in·clu´sive·ness** *n.*

**in·cog·ni´to** *adj., adv.* with identity hidden or obscured

**in·co·her´ence** *n.* a lack of order: the inability to communicate clearly

**in·co·her´ent** *adj.* lacking order or agreement; disjointed; unable to communicate in a distinct or organized manner; inarticulate –**in·co·her´ent·ly** *adv.*

**in´come** *n.* something of value received in exchange, such as for goods or labor; earnings

**in´com·ing** *adj.* coming in; about to come in

**in·com·men´su·ra·ble** *adj.* not to be measured or compared –**in·com·men·su·ra·bil´i·ty, in·com·men´su·ra·ble·ness** *n.* –**in·com·men´su·ra·bly** *adv.*

**in·com·men´su·rate** *adj.* disproportionate; inadequate –**in·com·men´su·rate·ly** *adv.* –**in·com·men´su·rate·ness** *n.*

**in·com·mo´dious** *adj.* inconvenient or uncomfortable –**in·com·mo´dious·ly** *adv.* –**in·com·mo´dious·ness** *n.*

**in·com´pa·ra·ble** *adj.* exceptional; so remarkable or unusual as to be beyond comparing –**in·com·pa·ra·bil´i·ty, in·com´pa·ra·ble·ness** *n.* –**in·com´pa·ra·bly** *adv.*

**in·com·pat´i·bil´i·ty** *n.* the inability to exist harmoniously

**in·com·pat´i·ble** *adj.* unsuited for affiliating or blending; contradictory; mutually exclusive; irreconcilable; mutually repelling; incongruous –**in·com·pat·i·bil´i·ty** *n.* –**in·com·pat´i·bly** *adv.*

**in·com´pe·tence** *n.* a lack of ability

**in·com´pe·tent** *adj.* inadequate or unsuited, as by lack of certain qualities or abilities; not legally qualified, such as by mentality –*n.* one who is unable to function in certain circumstances –**in·com´pe·tence, in·com´pe·ten·cy** *n.* –**in·com´pe·tent·ly** *adv.*

**in·com·plete´** *adj.* not finished; missing an integral part; designation in lieu of a grade for failure to complete the requirements of a course of study –**in·com·plete´ly** *adv.* –**in·com·plete´ness** *n.*

**in·com·pre·hen´si·ble** *adj.* difficult or impossible to understand or accept –**in·com·pre·hen·si·bil´i·ty, in·com·pre·hen´si·ble·ness** *n.* –**in·com·pre·hen´si·bly** *adv.*

**in·con·ceiv´a·ble** *adj.* impossible to grasp or accept; so improbable as to be considered impossible –**in·con·ceiv´a·bly** *adv.*

**in·con·gru´i·ty** *n.* inconsistency; something inconsistent

**in·con´gru·ous** *adj.* inappropriate or incompatible; inconsistent –**in·con´gru·ous·ly** *adv.* –**in·con´gru·ous·ness** *n.*

**in·con·se·quen´tial** *adj.* of little importance –**in·con·se·quen´tial·ly** *adv.*

**in·con·sid´er·a·ble** *adj.* trivial –**in·con·sid´er·a·ble·ness** *n.* –**in·con·sid´er·a·bly** *adv.*

**in·con·sid´er·ate** *adj.* thoughtless of others; insensitive; lacking consideration –**in·con·sid´er·ate·ly** *adv.* –**in·con·sid´er·ate·ness** *n.*

**in·con·sist´en·cy** *n.* a discrepancy

**in·con·sis´tent** *adj.* lacking agreement or harmony; not logical; erratic or unpredicable –**in·con·sis´tent·ly** *adv.*

**in·con·spic´u·ous** *adj.* not easily seen; hardly noticeable –**in·con·spic´u·ous·ly** *adv.* –**in·con·spic´u·ous·ness** *n.*

**in·con´stant** *adj.* fickle –**in·con´stan·cy** *n.* –**in·con´stant·ly** *adv.*

**in·con·test´a·ble** *adj.* unquestionable –**in·con·test´a·bly** *adv.*

**in·con´ti·nent** *adj.* lacking selfcontrol; unable to control bodily discharges —**in·con´ti·nence, in·con´ti·nen·cy** *n.* —**in·con´ti·nent·ly** *adv.*

**in·con·tro·vert´i·ble** *adj.* not subject to question; not able to deny or disprove —**in·con·tro·vert·i·bil´i·ty, in·con·tro·vert´i·ble·ness** *n.* —**in·con·tro·vert´i·bly** *adv.*

**in·con·ven´ience** *n.* that which is not convenient; a source of bother —*vt.* to cause difficulty or annoyance

**in·con·ven´ient** *adj.* unsuited to one's comfort or needs; difficult to use; poorly timed —**in·con·ven´ient·ly** *adv.*

**in·cor´po·rate** *vi., vt.* to become or cause to become united or combined; *(US)* to form or cause to form a legal corporation

**in·cor·po·ra´tion** *n.* a thing added; the act of including; *(US)* legally incorporating

**in·cor·po´re·al** *adj.* lacking physical or material form; spiritual —**in·cor·po´re·al·ly** *adv.*

**in·cor·rect´** *adj.* inaccurate; unsuitable or improper —**in·cor·rect´ly** *adv.* —**in·cor·rect´ness** *n.*

**in·cor´ri·gi·ble** *adj.* incapable of being changed or reformed; difficult to control or restrain: *an incorrigible liar* —*n.* one who cannot be changed or reformed —**in·cor·ri·gi·bil´i·ty, in·cor´ri·gi·ble·ness** *n.* —**in·cor´ri·gi·bly** *adv.*

**in·crease´** *vt., vi.* to make or become more or larger —**in´crease** *n.* the amount or rate by which something is augmented

**in·cred´i·ble** *adj.* so inconceivable or unlikely as to cause disbelief: *an incredible story*; amazing or startling: *an incredible performance* —**in·cred´i·bil´i·ty, in·cred´i·ble·ness** *n.* —**in·cred´i·bly** *adv.*

**in·cred´u·lous** *adj.* not inclined to believe; showing disbelief: *an incredulous look* —**in·cre·du´li·ty** *n.* —**in·cred´u·lous·ly** *adv.*

**in´cre·ment** *n.* a steady growth of or addition to; a slight increase; one of a series —**in·cre·men´tal** *adj.*

**in·crim´i·nate** *vt.* to accuse of involvement, especially in a wrongful act; to implicate by inference —**in·crim·i·na´tion** *n.*

**in´cu·bate** *vt.* to provide an environment suitable for growth and development, as of eggs or living tissue; to hatch —*vi.* to develop and hatch —**in·cu·ba´tion** *n.*

**in´cu·ba·tor** *n.* equipment that maintains a controlled environment, as for hatching eggs or as life support for a premature baby

**in´cu·bus** *n.* a nighmare; a male demon

**in·cul´cate** *vt.* to teach or indoctrinate by frequent or repeated instruction —**in´cul·ca´tion** *n.*

**in·cul´pate** *vt.* incriminate —**in´cul·pa´tion** *n.*

**in·cum´bent** *adj.* exacted as a duty; obligatory; lying or resting upon something else; presently in office —*n* one who presently holds an office —**in·cum´ben·cy** *n.*

**in·cur´** *vt.* to become liable or responsible for

**in·cur´a·ble** *adj.* incapable of being remedied or relieved —**in·cur´a·ble·ness** *n.* —**in·cur´a·bly** *adv.*

**in·cur´sion** *n.* an act of entering, usually into another's territory; an invasion

**in·debt´ed** *adj.* obligated —**in·debt´ed·ness** *n.*

**in·dec´ent** *adj.* contrary to the prevailing standard of good taste or modesty —**in·dec´ent·ly** *adv.*

**in·de´cen·cy** *n.* immodesty, lewdness

**in·de·ci´sion** *n.* the inability to make a determination

**in·de·ci´sive** *adj.* prone to doubt or uncertainty; inconclusive, as *an indecisive victory* —**in·de·ci´sive·ly** *adv.* —**in·de·ci´sive·ness** *n.*

**in·de·fat´i·ga·ble** *adj.* tireless

**in·de·fen´si·ble** *adj.* unable to be defended —**in·de·fen·si·bil´i·ty, in·de·fen´si·ble·ness** *n.* —**in·de·fen´si·bly** *adv.*

**in·def´i·nite** *adj.* lacking precise limits; uncertain or undecided; vague —**in·def´i·nite·ly** *adv.* —**in·def´i·nite·ness** *n.*

**in·del´i·ble** *adj.* impossible to remove, as certain inks or stains; unable to forget: *the horror left an indelible impression* —**in·del´i·bly** *adv.*

**in·dem´ni·fy** *vt.* to compensate for loss or damage

**in·dem´ni·ty** *n.* protection, exemption, or compensation from loss or injury

**in·dent´** *vt., vi.* to make or form a blank space between a margin and printed or written matter

**in·den·ta´tion** *n.* an indent; a dent, notch etc.

**in·den´ture** *n.* a contract; a legal instrument binding a servant to his master

**in·de·pend´ence** *n.* autonomy; freedom

**in·de·pend´ent** *adj.* free from the control of others; self-supporting —**in·de·pend´ent·ly** *adv.*

**in-depth´** *adj.* detailed

**in·de·struct´i·ble** *adj.* permanent; unable to be destroyed —**in·de·struct·i·bil´i·ty** *n.* —**in·de·struct´i·bly** *adv.*

**in·de·ter´mi·nate** *adj.* not precisely fixed; indefinite —**in·de·ter´mi·nate·ly** *adv.*

**in´dex** *n., pl.* **in´dex·es, in´di·ces** a list of material contained within a printed work; any list or directory; an indicator that characterizes a set of data, as *the Consumer Price Index* —*vt.* to provide with an index; to list, catalog, or otherwise arrange

**in´di·cate** *vt.* to point out or signify; to comment briefly

**in·di·ca´tion** *n.* a hint or suggestion; something suggested as necessary or practical for treatment of an illness or condition

**in·dic´a·tive** *adj.* serving to designate; characteristic

**in´di·ca·tor** *n.* any mechanism, index, etc. that serves to measure or quantify a value; *(Brit.)* a turn signal on a car

**in·dict´** *vt.* to accuse or charge with wrongdoing

**in·dict´ment** *n.* a formal accusation of offense as decided by a grand jury

**in·dif´fer·ence** *n.* unconcern or detachment; coldness, aloofness

**in·dif´fer·ent** *adj.* not involved; neutral or unconcerned; of little consequence or quality **—in·dif´fer·ent·ly** *adv.*

**in·dig´e·nous** *adj.* native; natural; inherent **—in·dig´e·nous·ly** *adv.* **—in·dig´e·nous·ness** *n.*

**in´di·gence** *n.* poverty

**in´di·gent** *adj.* impoverished *—n.* one who is poor or needy

**in·di·gest´i·ble** *adj.* impossible or difficult to digest

**in·di·ges´tion** *n.* discomfort caused by difficulty in digesting

**in·dig´nant** *adj.* angry over a wrong or injustice **—in·dig´nant·ly** *adv.*

**in·dig·na´tion** *n.* righteous anger

**in·dig´ni·ty** *n.* an affront; humiliation

**in´di·go´** *n.* a blue dye

**in·di·rect´** *adj.* in a roundabout manner; devious **—in·di·rect´ly** *adv.* **—in·di·rect´ness** *n.*

**in·dis·creet´** *adj.* tactless; imprudent; thoughtless **—in·dis·creet´ly** *adv.* **—in·dis·creet´ness** *n.*

**in·dis·crete´** *adj.* undivided; tightly bound; that can not be divided

**in·dis·cre´tion** *n.*tactlessness

**in·dis·crim´i·nate** *adj.* random; without order **—in·dis·crim´i·nate·ly** *adv.* **—in·dis·crim´i·na·tion** *n.*

**in·dis·pen´sa·ble** *adj.* essential; definitely needed **—in·dis·pen´sa·bly** *adv.*

**in·dis·posed´** *adj.* reluctant or unwilling, as to honor a request; ill or ailing **—in·dis·pose´** *vt.*

**in·dis·put´a·ble** *adj.* not to be denied; incontestable **—in·dis·put´a·bly** *adv.*

**in·dis·sol´u·ble** *adj.* that cannot be destroyed; perpetually binding

**in·dis·tinct´** *adj.* not clear; dim or faded; not easily understood **—in·dis·tinct´ly** *adv.* **—in·dis·tinct´ness** *n.*

**in·di·vid´u·al** *adj.* relating to one only; by or for one; distinctive *—n.* a lone person or thing considered apart from its group; one marked by a special quality **—in·di·vid´u·al·ism** *n.* **—in·di·vid´u·al·ly** *adv.*

**in·di·vid·u·al´i·ty** *n.* the qualities that make one distinctive; the quality of being unique **—in·di·vid´u·al·ize** *vt.*

**in·doc´tri·nate** *vt.* to instruct or propagandize, especially in a particular doctrine or ideology; to acquaint, as with a new employer's rules and policies

**in·doc·tri·na´tion** *n.* instruction or training

**in´do·lent** *adj.* habitually lazy; slothful **—in´do·lence** *n.* **—in´do·lent·ly** *adv.*

**in·dom´i·ta·ble** *adj.* unable to be subdued; unconquerable **—in·dom´i·ta·ble·ness** *n.* **—in·dom´i·ta·bly** *adv.*

**in·du´bi·ta·ble** *adj.* undeniable; too obvious to be doubted **—in·du´bi·ta·ble·ness** *n.* **—in·du´bi·ta·bly** *adv.*

**in·duce´** *vt.* to persuade to action; to cause or bring about

**in·duce´ment** *n.* an incentive; something that inspires or persuades

**in·duct´** *vt.* to formally place into office or a position; to acquaint with or instruct in, as to a new position

**in·duc´tion** *n.* entrance into office; a ceremony for inducting into office; the process of reasoning that draws broad conclusions from specific facts

**in·duc´tive** *adj.* relating to logical induction **—in·duc´tive·ly** *adv.* **—in·duc´tive·ness** *n.*

**in·dulge´** *vt.* to yield to desires, especially those that are unreasonable or outrageous *—vi.* to gratify one's desires; to take part in

**in·dul´gence** *n.* an act of gratification; intemperance

**in·dus´tri·al** *adj.* of or relating to manufacturing and trade **—in·dus´tri·al·ly** *adv.*

**in·dus´tri·al·ize** *vt.* to convert the economy of a country or area to one based on industry; to make into an industry **—in·dus·tri·al·i·za´tion** *n.*

**in·dus´tri·ous** *adj.* dedicated to a task or cause **—in·dus´tri·ous·ly** *adv.* **—in·dus´tri·ous·ness** *n.*

**in´dus·try** *n.* manufacture and trade in commercial goods; active dedication to a task

**in·e´bri·ate** *vt.* to intoxicate; to exhilarate as if intoxicated **—in·e´bri·ate, in·e´bri·a·ted** *adj.* intoxicated; drunk **—in·e´bri·a´tion** *n.*

**in·ef´fa·ble** *adj.* indescribable; taboo to utter **—in·ef´fa·bly** *adv.*

**in·ef·fec´tive** *adj.* not creating an intended effect; inadequate **—in·ef·fec´tive·ly** *adv.* **—in·ef·fec´tive·ness** *n.*

**in·ef·fec´tu·al** *adj.* fruitless **—in·ef·fec´tu·al·ly** *adv.*

**in·ef·fi´cient** *adj.* wasteful; incompetent **—in·ef·fi´cien·cy** *n.* **—in·ef·fi´cient·ly** *adv.*

**in·el´i·gi·ble** *adj.* precluded, as by restrictions or lack of ability **—in·el´i·gi·bil´i·ty** *n.* **—in·el´i·gi·bly** *adv.*

**in·ept´** *adj.* displaying a lack of ability; incompetent; clumsy **—in·ept´i·tude, in·ept´ness** *n.* **—in·ept´ly** *adv.*

**in·e·qual´i·ty** *n.* a difference or disparity

**in·eq´ui·ta·ble** *adj.* unfair **—in·eq´ui·ta·bly** *adv.*

**in·eq´ui·ty** *n.* an injustice

**in·ert´** *adj.* motionless; inactive; unable to move; lethargic **—in·ert´ly** *adv.* **—in·ert´ness** *n.*

**in·er´tia** *n.* in physics, the tendency of a body at rest to remain at rest and of one in motion to continue moving in the same direction; reluctance to move or change

**in·ev´i·ta·ble** *adj.* impossible to change or prevent;

unavoidable; inescapable **—in·ev·i·ta·bil´i·ty, in·ev´i·ta·ble·ness** *n.* **—in·ev´i·ta·bly** *adv.*

**in·ex´o·ra·ble** *adj.* unyielding; implacable; not to be persuaded to change **—in·ex·o·ra·bil´i·ty, in·ex´o·ra·ble·ness** *n.* **—in·ex´o·ra·bly** *adv.*

**in·ex·pe´ri·ence** *n.* a lack of skill

**in·ex·pe´ri·enced** *adj.* lacking the skill customarily gained from practical experience

**in·ex´pert** *adj.* unskilled **—in·ex´pert·ly** *adv.* **in·ex´pert·ness** *n.*

**in·ex´pi·a·ble** *adj.* that may not be atoned for

**in·ex´pli·ca·ble** *adj.* impossible to explain or understand **—in·ex·pli·ca·bil´i·ty, in·ex´pli·ca·ble·ness** *n.* **—in·ex´pli·ca·bly** *adv.*

**in·ex·press´i·ble** *adj.* that cannot be described **—in·ex·press·i·bil´i·ty** *n.* **—in·ex·press´i·bly** *adv.*

**in·ex´tri·ca·ble** *adj.* that cannot be disentangled or undone; impossible to resolve **—in·ex´tri·ca·bly** *adv.*

**in·fal´li·ble** *adj.* incapable of failure or error **—in·fal´li·bil´i·ty** *n.* **—in·fal´li·bly** *adv.*

**in´fa·mous** *adj.* having a bad reputation; deserving of low regard **—in´fa·mous·ly** *adv.* **—in´fa·mous·ness** *adv.*

**in´fa·my** *n.* disgrace

**in´fan·cy** *n.* childhood; the early stages of development

**in´fant** *n.* a young child; in law, a minor *—adj.* pertaining to a young or early state

**in´fan·tile** *adj.* relating to infancy; childlike

**in´fan·try** *n.* soldiers trained to fight on foot

**in·fat´u·ate** *vt.* to provoke unreasoning affection or passion; to incite foolish behavior **—in·fat·u·a´tion** *n.*

**in·fect´** *vt.* to contaminate or corrupt, especially with organisms that cause disease

**in·fec´tion** *n.* invasion of the body by disease-causing microorganisms; an infectious disease

**in·fec´tious** *adj.* caused by infection; tending to spread from one to another **—in·fec´tious·ly** *adv.* **—in·fec´tious·ness** *n.*

**in·fer´** *vt.* to presume or conclude from available evidence; to insinuate or hint

**in´fer·ence** *n.* the process of reaching a conclusion from information available **—in´fer·en´tial** *adj.* **—in´fer·en´tial·ly** *adv.*

**in·fe´ri·or** *adj.* of a lesser quality; lower in value; subordinate *—n.* one who is lower in rank or station

**in·fe·ri·or´i·ty** *n.* the state of being lower in quality, rank, etc.

**in·fer´nal** *adj.* fiendish

**in·fer´no** *n.* a place of fiery heat

**in·fest´** *vt.* to inhabit in overwhelming numbers

**in´fi·del** *n.* a non-believer

**in·fi·del´i·ty** *n.* sexual unfaithfulness; a lack of loyalty

**in´fight·ing** *n.* a bitter struggle or dissension, esp. between rivals in the same organization

**in´fil·trate** *vt.* to secretly enter and take up position; to permeate, as by a liquid

**in´fi·nite** *adj.* without limit **—in´fi·nite·ly** *adv.* **—in´fi·nite·ness** *n.*

**in´fin·i·tes´i·mal** *adj.* minuscule; immeasurably small **—in´fin·i·tes´i·mal·ly** *adv.*

**in·fin´i·ty** *n.* a limitless expanse, time, or quantity

**in·firm´** *adj.* feeble or weak, as from old age or disease; irresolute

**in·fir´ma·ry** *n.* a small clinic or dispensary

**in·fir´mi·ty** *n.* an ailment or weakness, as from old age

**in·flame´** *vi., vt.* to become or cause to become excited or aroused; to redden and swell as of a sore; to catch or set on fire

**in·flam´ma·ble** *adj.* combustible; easily excited **—in·flam·ma·bil´i·ty, in·flam´ma·ble·ness** *n.*

**in´flam·ma´tion** *n.* redness or swelling caused by irritation or infection

**in·flam´ma·to·ry** *adj.* intended to arouse passion, violence, etc.; causing inflammation

**in·flate´** *vt.* to fill with air and cause to swell; to enlarge or expand improperly: *to inflate the price of scarce goods* *—vi.* to become enlarged or swelled **—in·fla´tion** *n.*

**in·flect´** *vt.* to modify in tone or pitch **—in·flec´tion** *n.*

**in·flex´i·bil´i·ty** *n.* unwillingness or inability to change

**in·flex´i·ble** *adj.* not easily bent or changed; inelastic; rigid **—in·flex·i·bil´i·ty, in·flex´i·ble·ness** *n.* **in·flex´i·bly** *adv.*

**in·flict´** *vt.* to impose on, as punishment or hardship **—in·flic´tion** *n.*

**in´flu·ence** *n.* a power that effects; an effect shaped by control or persuasion *—vt.* to effect by persuasion

**in·flu·en´tial** *adj.* having the power to influence

**in·flu·en´za** *n.* a contagious viral disease marked by infection of the respiratory tract, fever and muscular ache

**in´flux** *n.* a flowing in

**in·form´** *vi., vt.* to to make known; to provide information; to reveal

**in·for´mal** *adj.* casual; unofficial **—in·for´mal·ly** *adv.*

**in´for·mal´ity** *n.* casualness; the absence of ceremony or formality

**in·form´ant** *n.* a person who testifies against others

**in·for·ma´tion** *n.* a body of knowledge or data

**in·for´ma·tive** *adj.* providing information; revealing **—in·for´ma·tive·ly** *adv.*

**in·frac´tion** *n.* violation of rules

**in·fran´gi·ble** *adj.* incapable of being smashed

**in·fra·red´** *adj.* pertaining to radiation between red and microwave on the spectrum

**in´fra·struc·ture** *n.* the elements of a structure, system, etc.

**in·fre´quent** *adj.* at large intervals of time or space

—**in·fre´quen·cy** *n.* —**in·fre´quent·ly** *adv.*

**in·fringe´** *vi., vt.* to intrude upon; to transgress —**in·fringe´ment** *n.*

**in·fu´ri·ate´** *vt.* to enrage

**in·fuse´** *vt.* to introduce into; to inspire; to steep without boiling in order to extract something, —**in·fu´sion** *n.*

**in·gen´ious** *adj.* resourceful, clever —**in·gen´ious·ly** *adv.* —**in·gen´ious·ness** *n.*

**in·ge·nu´i·ty** *n.* resourcefulness

**in·gen´u·ous** *adj.* innocent; lacking sophistication; straightforward —**in·gen´u·ous·ly** *adv.* —**in·gen´u·ous·ness** *n.*

**in·gest´** *vt.* take into the body for digestion; to eat

**in·glo´ri·ous** *adj.* marked by failure or disgrace —**in·glo´ri·ous·ly** *adv.* —**in·glo´ri·ous·ness** *n.*

**in´got** *n.* a lump of cast metal

**in·grain´** *vt.* to fix or instill, as in the mind —**in·grained´** *adj.*

**in´grate** *n.* one who is ungrateful

**in·gra´ti·ate** *vt.* to curry favor

**in·gre´di·ent** *n.* one of the elements in a mixture

**in·hab´it** *vt.* to occupy or reside in; to fill —**in·hab´it·ant** *n.*

**in·hal´ant** *n.* medicine inhaled as a vapor —**in´ha·la·tor** *n.*

**in·hale´** *vt.* to draw into the lungs; to take in quickly, as food —*vi.* to breathe in —**in·hal´er** *n.*

**in·her´ent** *adj.* inherited; intrinsic —**in·her´ent·ly** *adv.*

**in·her´it** *vt.* to receive, acquire, or take over from another —**in·her´it·ance** *n.*

**in·hib´it** *vt.* to hold back or restrain

**in·hi·bi´tion** *n.* a restraint; something that inhabits

**in·hos·pi´ta·ble** *adj.* unfriendly; barren: offering little to promote life or growth

**in·hu´man, in·hu·mane´** *adj.* lacking human qualities, as pity or compassion

**in·im´i·cal** *adj.* unfriendly

**in·im´i·ta·ble** *adj.* that cannot be imitated

**in·iq´ui·ty** *n.* wickedness; evil; a wicked or evil act —**in·iq´ui·tous** *adj.*

**in·i´tial** *adj.* the first instance of; appearing at the beginning —*n.* the first letter or letters of a proper name —*vt.* to sign with initials

**in·i´ti·ate** *vt.* to introduce; to start; to induct into, as a club —*n.* one newly allowed or soon to be allowed into membership; an inductee

**in·i·ti·a´tion** *n.* a ceremony or ritual for induction; the act of bringing into being

**in·i´ti·a·tive** *n.* the quality or motivation that drives one to begin or pursue an action; a first move; the power to originate, as legislation

**in·ject´** *vt.* to insert or introduce into

**in·ju·di´cious** *adj.* unwise; lacking judgement —**in·ju·di´cious·ly** *adv.* —**in·ju·di´cious·ness** *n.*

**in·junc´tion** *n.* a command or directive; a legal order prohibiting a course of action

**in´jure** *vt.* to cause harm to; to wound

**in·jur´i·ous** *adj.* harmful

**in´ju·ry** *n.* damage or harm; an injustice for which one may seek legal redress

**in·jus´tice** *n.* an instance of wrongdoing; a violatioin of rights

**ink** *n.* colored liquid used for writing or printing —*vt.* to mark with ink

**ink´ling** *n.* a hint, suggestion, or notion

**in´lay** *vt.* to set decorative material into —*n.* —**in´laid** *adj.*

**in´let** *n.* a recess along a coast; an access from the sea to inland waters

**in´mate** *n.* one confined to an institution

**in´most** *adj.* furthest from the exterior; secret or intimate

**inn** *n.* a lodging for travelers, usually serving food and drink, a tavern or restaurant

**in·nate´** *adj.* inborn

**in´ner** *adj.* further inside; private or secret

**in´ner·most** *adj.* most intimate

**inn´keep·er** *n.* one who operates a public hostelry

**in´no·cence** *n.* freedom from guilt; a lack of cunning or guile

**in´no·cent** *adj.* uncorrupted; blameless; unsophisticated; harmless —*n.* a guileless or unsophisticated person

**in·noc´u·ous** *adj.* inoffensive; unlikely to stimulate; having no harmful qualities —**in·noc´u·ous·ly** *adv.* —**in·noc´u·ous·ness** *n.*

**in´no·vate** *vi., vt.* to introduce or change

**in·no·va´tion** *n.* something new; the process of introducing something new

**in·nu·en´do** *n.* an insinuation, often derogatory

**in·nu´mer·a·ble** *adj.* incalculable; too many to count —**in·nu´mer·a·bly** *adv.*

**in·oc´u·late´** *vt.* to immunize, esp. by vaccination —**in·oc´u·la´tion** *n.*

**in·of·fen´sive** *adj.* harmless; without fault

**in·op´er·a·ble** *adj.* unable to be made to function; inappropriate for a surgical procedure

**in·op´er·a·tive** *adj.* not working; no longer in force

**in·op·por·tune´** *adj.* ill-timed —**in·op·por·tune´ly** *adj.* —**in·op·por·tune´ness** *n.*

**in·or´di·nate** *adj.* excessive; exceeding reasonable bounds —**in·or´di·nate·ly** *adv.* —**in·or´di·nate·ness** *n.*

**in´put** *n.* that directed into, as power or energy to drive a machine; data entered into a computer

**in´quest** *n.* an investigation or inquiry into a matter

**in·qui´e·tude** *n.* a state of unrest

**in·quire´** *vi., vt.* to investigate or ask about

**in´quir·y** *n.* an investigation in search of the truth; a question

**in·qui·si´tion** *n.* an investigation

**in·quis´i·tive** *adj.* overly curious; eager to learn —**in·quis´i·tive·ly** *adv.* —**in·quis´i·tive·ness** *n.*

**in·quis´i·tor** *n.* an examiner

**in´road** *n.* an encroachment or invasion

**in·sane´** *adj.* psychotic; characterized by immoderate or foolish action —**in·sane´ly** *adv.* —**in·sane´ness** *n.*

**in·san´i·ty** *n.* mental disorder; an extremely foolish action

**in·sa´ti·a·ble, in·sa´ti·ate** *adj.* unable to be satisfied —**in·sa´ti·a·bly** *adv.* —**in·sa´ti·a·ble·ness** *n.*

**in·scribe´** *vt.* to write or carve on a surface; to engrave; to dedicate a book, treatise, etc. to someone

**in·scrip´tion** *n.* words written or engraved, as on a plaque or the flyleaf of a book; a dedication

**in·scru´ta·ble** *adj.* incomprehensible

**in´sect** *n.* a usually small animal characterized by a segmented body and three pairs of legs

**in·sec´ti·cide** *n.* a chemical used to kill insects

**in·se·cure´** *adj.* uncertain; lacking stability —**in·se·cur´i·ty** *n.* —**in·se·cure´ly** *adv.*

**in·sem´i·nate** *vt.* to inpregnate by injecting semen —**in·sem·i·na´tion** *n.*

**in·sen´sate** *adj.* inanimate: incapable of sensation; lacking reason; hard-hearted

**in·sen´si·ble** *adj.* unconscious; indifferent

**in·sen´si·tive** *adj.* incapable of feeling; numb; unconcerned with the feelings of others —**in·sen·si·tiv´i·ty, in·sen´si·tive·ness** *n.* —**in·sen´si·tive·ly** *adv.*

**in·sen´ti·ent** *adj.* inanimate: totally lacking in life or consciousness —**in·sen´ti·ence** *n.*

**in·sep´a·ra·ble** *adj.* indivisible; closely associated: *inseparable playmates*

**in·sert´** *vt.* to place into or among —**in´sert** *n.* an enclosure, as a card or flyer placed in a magazine

**in·ser´tion** *n.* something added; the act of adding or inserting

**in·side´** *adj.* inner; select or confidential, as *inside information* —*adv.* into —*n.* an interior surface or part —**in·sid´er** *n.*

**in·sid´i·ous** *adj.* harmful and subtly conveyed or accumulated —**in·sid´i·ous·ly** *adv.* —**in·sid´i·ous·ness** *n.*

**in´sight** *n.* the ability to recognize the true nature of a situation

**in·sig´ni·a** *n.* a badge or emblem, as of office or rank

**in·sig·nif´i·cance** *n.* unimportance

**in·sig·nif´i·cant** *adj.* unimportant; having little force or value; of small size or quantity —**in·sig·nif´i·cant·ly** *adv.*

**in·sin·cere´** *adj.* pretentious; deceitful or hypocritical

**in´sin·cer´i·ty** *n.* deceit; hypocrisy

**in·sin´u·ate** *vt.* to convey, as a notion or opinion, in a subtle manner

**in·sin·u·a´tion** *n.* a subtle hint

**in·sip´id** *adj.* uninteresting; dull; lacking flavor —**in·sip´id·ly** *adv.* —**in·sip´id·ness** *n.*

**in·sist´** *vi.* to be firm or persistent —*vt.* to demand firmly or persistently

**in·so·bri´e·ty** *adj.* drunkenness

**in´so·lent** *adj.* rude or disrespectful; insulting —**in´so·lence** *n.*

**in·sol´u·ble** *adj.* not able to be dissolved; insolvable —**in·sol´u·bil´i·ty** *n.*

**in·solv´a·ble** *adj.* difficult or impossible to solve or explain

**in·sol´vent** *adj.* unable to pay one's debts; of or relating to bankruptcy —*n.* a person who is bankrupt

**in·som´ni·a** *n.* the persistent inability to sleep

**in·spect´** *vt.* to examine carefully or critically

**in·spec´tion** *n.* an examination

**in·spec´tor** *n.* one whose job it is to examine; a police officer

**in·spi·ra´tion** *n.* stimulation to a high level of creativity; a sudden creative idea

**in·spire´** *vt.* to invigorate or encourage

**in·spir´it** *vt.* to exhilarate; to instill with courage

**in·stall´** *vt.* to set up, attach, or build into; to admit into office

**in·stal·la´tion** *n.* the placement of fixtures or equipment; something installed

**in·stall´ment** *n.* one of a series, as of periodic payments

**in´stance** *n.* an occurrence; an example or illustration

**in´stant** *adj.* immediate; designed for easy or quick preparation —*n.* a particular point in time —**in·stan·ta´ne·ous** *adj.*

**in´stant·ly** *adv.* immediately

**in·stead´** *adv.* alternatively

**in´sti·gate** *vt.* to initiate, incite, or urge —**in·sti·ga´tion** *n.*

**in·still´** *vt.* to implant or infuse, as an idea; to teach or indoctrinate

**in´stinct** *n.* inborn or natural behavior

**in·stinc´tive** *adj.* intuitive; natural

**in´sti·tute** *n.* an established organization; buildings and land occupied by an organization —*vt.* to enact or establish

**in·sti·tu´tion** *n.* the act of founding or establishing; a custom or tradition; an established organization or the buildings and land it occupies —**in·sti·tu´tion·al** *adj.* —**in·sti·tu´tion·al·ly** *adv.*

**in·struct´** *vt.* to educate or edify; to order or direct firmly —*vi.* to discharge the duties of an instructor

**in·struc´tion** *n.* guidance; the imparting of knowledge; a direct order —**in·struc´tion·al, in·struc´tive** *adj.* —**in·struc´tive·ly** *adv.*

**in·struc´tor** *n.* a teacher; one who passes on knowledge

**in´stru·ment** *n.* an implement or tool; a device for

producing musical sounds; a legal contract —**in·stru·men´ta·list** *n.*
**in·stru·men´tal** *adj.* serving as an agency for; partly responsible; of music written for a particular instrument
**in·stru·men·tal´i·ty** *n.* agency
**in·stru·men·ta´tion** *n.* a musical arrangement; a group of instruments
**in·sub·or´di·nate** *adj.* rebellious; hesitant or unwilling to obey
**in´sub·or´di·na´tion** *n.* rebellion against authority
**in·suf´fer·a·ble** *adj.* intolerable; difficult to endure —**in·suf´fer·a·bly** *adv.* —**in·suf´fer·a·ble·ness** *n.*
**in·suf·fi´cient** *adj.* not enough; lacking —**in·suf·fi´cient·ly** *adv.*
**in´su·lar** *adj.* detached; isolated
**in´su·late** *vt.* to isolate; to separate or protect with a barrier
**in·su·la´tion** *n.* a protective covering; protection from external influence —**in´su·la·tor** *n.*
**in·sult´** *vi., vt.* to offend or treat offensively —**in´sult** *n.* an offensive act or utterance
**in·su´per·a·ble** *adj.* impossible to be overcome —**in·su´per·a·bly** *adv.*
**in·sup·port´a·ble** *adj.* intolerable; that cannot be justified
**in·sur´ance** *n.* protection against loss
**in·sure´** *vt.* to make certain; to protect with an insurance policy
**in·sur·ed´** *adj.* protected
**in·sur´gent** *n.* one who rebels against constituted authority —*adj.* rebellious
**in·sur·mount´a·ble** *adj.* that cannot be passed over or overcome —**in·sur·mount·a·bil´i·ty** *n.* —**in·sur·mount´a·bly** *adv.*
**in·sur·rec´tion** *n.* an act of open rebellion
**in·sus·cep´ti·ble** *adj.* not vulnerable
**in·tact´** *adj.* complete; not damaged or diminished in any way
**in·tan´gi·ble** *adj.* indefinable by the senses —**in·tan´gi·ble·ness** *n.* —**in·tan´gi·bly** *adv.*
**in´te·ger** *n.* a whole number
**in´te·gral** *adj.* necessary to make complete; essential
**in´te·grate** *vt.* to bring together; to unify
**in·te·gra´tion** *n.* a unifying or blending
**in·teg´ri·ty** *n.* strict compliance to an ethical standard; the state of being whole or sound
**in´tel·lect** *n.* the capacity for reason or understanding
**in·tel·lec´tu·al** *adj.* relating or appealing to the intellect; intelligent —*n.* one given to intellectual pursuits
**in·tel´li·gence** *n.* the capacity for knowledge; information or news, especially that which is secret
**in·tel´li·gent** *adj.* having knowledge or the ability to acquire knowledge —**in·tel´li·gent·ly** *adv.*
**in·tel·li·gent´si·a** *n.* the intellectual elite
**in·tel´li·gi·ble** *adj.* able to be understood
**in·tem´per·ance** *n.* excessive indulgence
**in·tend´** *vt.* to have in mind, as for a particular use or plan of action
**in·tend´ed** *adj.* intentional
**in·tense´** *adj.* extreme, as in force or magnitude; emotional —**in·tense´ly** *adv.* —**in·tense´ness, in·ten´si·ty** *n.*
**in·ten´si·fy** *vi., vt.* to grow or make stronger
**in·ten´sive** *adj.* characterized by a sense of vigor or concentration —**in·ten´sive·ly** *adv.* —**in·ten´sive·ness** *n.*
**in·tent´** *adj.* firmly fixed in the mind —*n.* something intended —**in·tent´ly** *adv.*
**in·ten´tion** *n.* aim; purpose
**in·ten´tion·al** *adj.* deliberate; planned —**in·ten´tion·al·ly** *adv.*
**in·ter´** *vt.* to bury or entomb
**in·ter·act´** *vi.* to relate or act mutually —**in·ter·ac´tion** *n.*
**in·ter·cede´** *vt.* to plead on behalf of another
**in·ter·cept´** *vt.* to interrupt the progress of —**in·ter·cep´tion** *n.*
**in·ter·ces´sion** *n.* a plea for another; mediation
**in·ter·change´** *vi., vt.* to change or cause to change successively, as the elements in a design —**in´ter·change** *n.* a system of ramps that allows access to intersecting highways
**in´ter·course** *n.* communication between persons; sexual relations
**in·ter·de·pen´dence, in·ter·de·pend´en·cy** *n.* mutually dependent —**in·ter·de·pen´dent** *adj.* —**in·ter·de·pen´dent·ly** *adv.*
**in·ter·dict´** *vt.* to prohibit by law or by order of the church —*n.* a legal prohibition; censure by the church —**in·ter·dic´tion** *n.*
**in´ter·est** *n.* curiosity about something in particular; the right to a share in something; a fee for the loan of money —*vt.* to hold one's attention
**in´ter·est·ed** *adj.* connected or affected in some way, as *an interested party*
**in´ter·est·ing** *adj.* inviting attention —**in´ter·est·ing·ly** *adv.*
**in·ter·fere´** *vt.* to intervene
**in·ter·fer´ence** *n.* something that obstructs; an act of interrupting or obstructing
**in·ter·ga·lac´tic** *adj.* existing between galaxies
**in´ter·im** *n.* a time between events —*adj.* effective for a time
**in·te´ri·or** *adj.* of the inside; situated away from the coast —*n.* the internal part; the internal affairs of a political entity
**in·ter·ject´** *vt.* to insert between other components —**in·ter·jec´tion** *n.*
**in·ter·lace´** *vt.* to weave or entwine; to unite

**in´ter·leaf** *n.* a blank sheet placed between pages in a book –**in·ter·leave´** *vt.*

**in´ter·lock** *vt., vi.* to join together; to link

**in´ter·lop·er** *n.* one who meddles in the affairs of others

**in´ter·lude** *n.* a lull or intervening time

**in·ter·me´di·ar·y** *n.* an agent or mediator

**in·ter·me´di·ate** *adj.* occurring between

**in·ter´ment** *n.* burial

**in·ter´mi·na·ble** *adj.* without terminus; endless; tiresome –**in·ter´mi·na·bly** *adv.*

**in·ter·min´gle** *vt., vi.* to combine or become mingled together

**in·ter·mis´sion** *(US) n.* a pause between events, as the acts of a play

**in·ter·mit´tent** *adj.* not continuous –**in·ter·mit´tent·ly** *adv.*

**in·ter·mix´** *vt., vi.* to mix or become mixed together

**in´tern** *n.* one who is apprenticed –**in·tern´** *vt.* to confine, as in prison –*vi.* to serve as an apprentice –**in·tern·ee´** *n.* –**in´tern·ship** *n.*

**in·ter´nal** *adj.* of the area inside or within borders –**in·ter´nal·ly** *adv.*

**in·ter·na´tion·al** *adj.* worldwide; between nations –**in·ter·na´tion·al·ism** *n.* –**in·ter·na´tion·al·ly** *adv.*

**in·ter·nec´ine** *adj.* of a struggle within an organization; mutually destructive

**in·tern´ment** *n.* confinement, as in prison

**in·ter´nist** *n.* a physician specializing in internal medicine

**in·ter·per´son·al** *adj.* between persons

**in´ter·play** *n.* interaction between parties

**in·ter´po·late** *vt.* to insert new material derived from that which precedes and that which follows it –**in·ter·po·la´tion** *n.*

**in·ter·pose´** *vt.* to inject into or between elements

**in·ter´pret** *vt.* to translate, explain, or illuminate

**in·ter·pre·ta´tion** *n.* an explanation; a presentation marked by a particular style or point of view

**in·ter´pret·er** *n.* one who translates or explains

**in·ter·re·late´** *vt., vi.* to bring or come into interdependent association –**in·ter·re·la´tion·ship** *n.*

**in·ter´ro·gate** *vt.* to cross-examine

**in·ter·ro·ga´tion** *n.* a formal questioning –**in·ter´ro·ga·tor** *n.* –**in·ter·rog´a·tive** *adj.*

**in·ter·rupt´** *vt.* to break in or interfere with the continuity of

**in·ter·rup´tion** *n.* a delay or intrusion

**in·ter·sect´** *vt., vi.* to cross or abut; to form an intersection

**in·ter·sec´tion** *n.* the point where two or more lines, streets, etc. abut or cross

**in·ter·sperse´** *vt.* to place at regular intervals throughout

**in´ter·twine** *vt., vi.* to unite by interlacing

**in´ter·val** *n.* space or time between

**in·ter·vene´** *vi.* to come between; to interfere

**in·ter·ven´tion** *n.* interference in the affairs of another, as a person or state

**interview** *n.* a meeting in which one person elicits information from another, as for publication, or in which information is exchanged, as in a *job interview*

**in·tes´tine** *n.* the long passage between the stomach and the anus that plays a major role in digestion and the subsequent evacuation of waste –**in·tes´ti·nal** *adj.*

**in´ti·ma·cy** *n.* closeness

**in´ti·mate** *adj.* marked by one's innermost thoughts, feelings, etc.; closely associated; of informality and privacy –*n.* a close associate –*vt.* to hint –**in´ti·mate·ly** *adv.*

**in·ti·ma´tion** *n.* information communicated subtly and indirectly; a hint

**in·tim´i·date** *vt.* to frighten; to pressure by threatening –**in·tim·i·da´tion** *n.*

**in·tol´er·a·ble** *adj.* unbearable; grossly offensive –**in·tol´er·a·bly** *adv.*

**in·tol´er·ant** *adj.* bigoted or prejudiced; unwilling to accept; *intolerant of evil* –**in·tol´er·ance** *n.* –**in·tol´er·ant·ly** *adv.*

**in·to·na´tion** *n.* modulation of the voice

**in·tone´** *vt., vi.* to recite or chant in a monotone

**in·tox´i·cant** *n.* a means of intoxication, as an alcoholic beverage or a narcotic

**in·tox´i·cate** *vt.* to inebriate or befuddle, as by strong drink; to stimulate, as by good news, beautiful scenery, etc.

**in·tox·i·ca´tion** *n.* drunkenness; stimulation

**in·trac´ta·ble** *adj.* obstinate or undisciplined; difficult to control, as *an intractable disease* –**in·trac·ta·bil´i·ty, in·trac´ta·ble·ness** *n.* –**in·trac´ta·bly** *adv.*

**in·tran´si·gence** *n.* a refusal to compromise, even from an untenable position; obstinacy; stubbornness

**in·tran´si·gent** *adj.* intolerant and uncompromising; obstinate

**in·tra·ve´nous** *adj.* injected into or situated within a vein –**in·tra·ve´nous·ly** *adv.*

**in·trep´id** *adj.* fearless –**in·trep´id·ly** *adv.* –**in·trep´id·ness** *n.*

**in´tri·ca·cy** *n.* something extremely complex

**in´tri·cate** *adj.* elaborately complex or involved –**in´tri·cate·ly** *adv.* –**in´tri·cate·ness** *n.*

**in·trigue´** *n.* a secret scheme or plot –*vi.* to plot secretly –*vt.* to arouse interest

**in·trin´sic** *adj.* of an inborn quality –**in·trin´si·cal·ly** *adv.*

**in·tro·duce´** *vt.* to present for consideration; to acquaint one person with another

**in·tro·duc´tion** *n.* the presentation of a person, idea, etc.; a time or ceremony of presentation

**in·tro·duc´to·ry** *adj.* of the presentation of something new

**in·tro·spec´tion** *n.* contemplation and self examination

**in´tro·vert** *n.* one whose interests are directed inward —**in·tro·ver´sion** *n.* —**in·tro·ver´sive** *adj.*

**in·trude´** *vi., vt.* to intervene or cause to intervene where one is not wanted

**in·trud´er** *n.* one who meddles or enters improperly

**in·tru´sion** *n.* an interruption; unwarranted meddling —**in·tru´sive** *adj.* —**in·tru´sive·ly** *adv.* —**in·tru´sive·ness** *n.*

**in·tu·i´tion** *n.* an instinctive feeling that something has happened or is about to happen

**in·tu´i·tive** *adj.* instinctive; perceived or concluded without the benefit of reason —**in·tu´i·tive·ly** *adv.* —**in·tu´i·tive·ness** *n.*

**in´un·date** *vt.* to overwhelm, especially with flood waters

**in·un·da´tion** *n.* a flooding or overflowing

**in·ure´** *vt.* to acclimate or accustom to something unpleasant

**in·vade´** *vt.* to attack, as of an act of war; to enter and remain, as of an infestation —**in·vad´er** *n.*

**in·val´id** *adj.* not legal; not legally binding; faulty —**in´va·lid** *n.* one who is disabled by illness or injury

**in·val´i·date** *vt.* to revoke or nullify

**in·val´u·a·ble** *adj.* priceless

**in·var´i·a·ble** *adj.* unchanging —**in·var´i·a·bly** *adv.*

**in·va´sion** *n.* an attack by a hostile force; an infestation

**in·va´sive** *adj.* tending to invade or intrude

**in·vec´tive** *adj.* characterized by abusive language —*n.* abusive language or discourse; a denunciation

**in·veigh´** *vt.* to protest vigorously

**in·vei´gle** *vt.* to entice or trick by coaxing or flattery

**in·vent´** *vt.* to create something new; to misrepresent, as by way of an excuse —**in·ven´tor** *n.*

**in·ven´tion** *n.* something newly created

**in·ven´tive** *adj.* clever; creative; resourceful —**in·ven´tive·ly** *adv.* —**in·ven´tive·ness** *n.*

**in´ven·to·ry** *n.* a list of goods in stock; an accounting —*vt.* to count and record goods on hand

**in·verse´** *adj.* reversed —**in·verse´ly** *adv.*

**in·vert´** *vt.* to reverse position, as to turn inside out or upside down

**in·ver´te·brate** *adj.* lacking a backbone —*n.* an animal that has no backbone

**in·vest´** *vt.* to buy in anticipation of future profit; to charge with authority; to formally install in office

**in·ves´ti·gate** *vi., vt.* to make careful inquiry

**in·ves·ti·ga´tion** *n.* a detailed inquiry

**in·vest´ment** *n.* the placing of resources in the hope of profit —**in·ves´tor** *n.*

**in·vet´er·ate** *adj.* well-established; persisting

**in·vid´i·ous** *adj.* expressing ill·will; malicious —**in·vid´i·ous·ly** *adv.* —**in·vid´i·ous·ness** *n.*

**in·vig´o·rate** *vt.* to enliven; to energize; —**in·vig·o·ra´tion** *n.*

**in·vig´o·rat·ing** *adj.* tending to entergize; refreshing or stimulating —**in·vig´o·rat·ing·ly** *adv.*

**in·vin·ci·bil´i·ty** *n.* the quality of being invulnerable

**in·vin´ci·ble** *adj.* unconquerable

**in·vi´o·la·ble** *adj.* that cannot be profaned; invincible —**in·vi·o·la·bil´i·ty** *n.* —**in·vi´o·la·bly** *adv.*

**in·vi´o·late** *adj.* not violated; pure

**in·vis´i·ble** *adj.* unseen; not open to view —**in·vis´i·bly** *adv.*

**in·vi·ta´tion** *n.* a formal request for one to be present; an allurement or temptation

**in·vi·ta´tion·al** *n.* an event limited to those invited, as a celebrity golf tournament —*adj.* restricted to invited participants

**in·vite´** *vt.* to formally request, as the presence of another; to tempt

**in·vit´ing** *adj.* attractive; enticing

**in·vo·ca´tion** *n.* an appeal; a prayer, especially at the start of a religious ceremony —**in´vo·ca·tor** *n.* —**in·voc´a·to·ry** *adj.*

**in´voice** *n.* a statement of charges for goods or services —*vt.* to tender a bill for goods or services

**invoke´** *vt.* to call up, as a spirit; to beseech or appeal earnestly

**in·vol´un·tar·y** *adj.* unintentional; instinctive —**in·vol·un·tar´i·ly** *adv.*

**in·vo·lu´tion** *n.* involvement; complexity

**in·volve´** *vt.* to include or connect to; to implicate or incriminate; to become engrossed in; to complicate

**in·volved´** *adj.* complicated; engrossed; emotionally committed

**in·volve´ment** *n.* participation; entanglement

**in·vul´ner·a·ble** *adj.* invincible; impossible to harm or damage —**in·vul·ner·a·bil´i·ty** *adv.*

**in´ward** *adj.* related to the inside —*adv.* toward the inside —**in´ward·ly** *adv.*

**i·o´ta** *n.* small amount

**i·ras´ci·ble** *adj.* irritable; quick to anger; marked by anger —**i·ras´ci·bly** *adv.*

**i´rate, i·rate´** *adj.* incensed; marked by anger: *an irate caller* —**i·rate´ly** *adv.*

**ire** *n.* anger

**irk** *vt.* to vex or annoy

**irk´some** *adj.* annoying; disturbing

**i´ron** *n.* a metallic element used extensively in structural materials; something made from iron; a symbol of unyielding strength —*vt., vi.* to smooth clothing —*adj.* made of or containing iron; strong and unyielding

**i·ron´ic, i·ron´i·cal** *adj.* paradoxical; mocking; displaying irony —**i·ron´i·cal·ly** *adv.*

**i´ro·ny** *n.* a paradox between what happens and wha

might be expected to happen; a literary style often used to mock or satirize convention

**ir·ra´di·ate** *vt.* to clarify or illuminate; to expose to radiation —**ir·ra·di·a´tion** *n.*

**ir·rad´i·ca·ble** *adj.* impossible to destroy —**ir·rad´i·ca·bly** *adv.*

**ir·re·deem'a·ble** *adj.* that cannot be redeemed; impossible to recover or reform —**ir·re·deem'a·bly** *adv.*

**ir·ra´tion·al** *adj.* not subject to reason; illogical; silly —**ir·ra·tion·al´i·ty** *n.* —**ir·ra´tion·al·ly** *adv.*

**ir·rec·on·cil´a·ble** *adj.* that cannot be reconciled or justified —**ir·rec·on·cil´a·ble·ness** *n.* —**ir·rec·on·cil´a·bly** *adv.*

**ir·re·deem´a·ble** *adj.* that cannot be redeemed; impossible to recover or reform —**ir·re·deem´a·bly** *adv.*

**ir·re·fut´a·ble** *adj.* indisputable; not subject to argument or dispute

**ir·reg´u·lar** *adj.* contrary to that which is normal or conventional; not symmetrical or uniform —**ir·reg´u·lar·ly** *adv.*

**ir·reg·u·lar´i·ty** *n.* an abnormality or oddity

**ir·rel´e·vance, ir·rel´e·van·cy** *n.* the quality of being trivial, unconnected, or not pertinent to the matter at hand

**ir·rel´e·vant** *adj.* not pertinent —**ir·rel´e·vant·ly** *adv.*

**ir·re·li´gious** *adj.* not religious: hostile to religion

**ir·re·mis´si·ble** *adj.* incurable; unpardonable

**ir·rep´a·ra·ble** *adj.* hopeless; impossible to mend or correct —**ir·rep´a·ra·bly** *adv.*

**ir·re·place´a·ble** *adj.* priceless; that cannot be replaced

**ir·re·press´i·ble** *adj.* that cannot be controlled; overly enthusiastic —**ir·re·press´i·ble·ness** *n.* —**ir·re·press´i·bly** *adv.*

**ir·re·proach´a·ble** *adj.* blameless

**ir·re·sist´i·ble** *adj.* overwhelming; compelling —**ir·re·sist´i·ble·ness** *n.* —**ir·re·sist´i·bly** *adv.*

**ir·res´o·lute** *adj.* lacking in purpose or resolution; wavering —**ir·res´o·lute·ly** *adv.* —**ir·res´o·lute·ness, ir·res·o·lu´tion** *n.*

**ir·re·spec´tive** *adj.* regardless —**ir·re·spec´tive·ly** *adv.*

**ir·re·spon'si·ble** *adj.* thoughtless; unpredictable; lacking a sense of duty —**ir·re·spon'si·ble·ness** *n.* —**ir·re·spon'si·ble** *adv.*

**ir·rev´er·ence** *n.* a lack of respect

**ir·rev´er·ent** *adj.* disrespectful of that which is considered proper —**ir·rev´er·ent·ly** *adv.*

**ir·rev´o·ca·ble** *adj.* that cannot be retracted or changed —**ir·rev´o·ca·bly** *adv.*

**ir´ri·gate** *vt.* to furnish water for growing plants; to cleanse, as a wound, with liquid —**ir´ri·ga·ble** *adj.*

**ir·ri·ga´tion** *n.* a system for supplying water; the process of providing water for plants or liquid for cleansing

**ir´ri·ta·ble** *adj.* ill-tempered; easily provoked or offended —**ir´ri·ta·ble·ness** *n.* —**ir´ri·ta·bly** *adv.*

**ir´ri·tant** *n.* something that annoys

**ir´ri·tate** *vt.* to provoke to anger; to chafe or abrade, as the skin —**ir´ri·tat·ing·ly** *adv.*

**ir´ri·tat·ed** *adj.* troubled or disturbed

**ir´ri·ta´tion** *n.* something that troubles or vexes; an irritant

**is´land** *n.* a body of land surrounded completely by water; a structure or area similarly isolated

**i´so·late** *vt.* to detach and set apart

**i·so·la´tion** *n.* separation; seclusion

**i·sola´tion·ist** *n.* one who believes in minimal involvement in the affairs of other nations

**is´sue** *n.* the act of flowing out; something published or distributed; an edition —*vi., vt.* to flow or cause to flow out; to originate from a source; to distribute

**itch** *n.* a skin irritation; a desire —*vi.* to sense an irritation or desire —**itch´i·ness** *n.* —**itch´y** *adj.*

**i´tem** *n.* a single element that is part of a whole, such as a clause in a document, an article in a book or newspaper, etc.

**i´tem·ize** *vt., vi.* to enumerate, one by one —**i´tem·i·za´tion** *n.*

**it´er·ance, it·er·a´tion** *n.* repetition

**it´er·ate** *vt.* to repeat

**i·tin´er·ant** *adj.* roving —*n.* a wanderer —**i·tin´er·ant·ly** *adv.*

**i·tin´er·ar·y** *n.* a travel plan

**i´vied** *adj.* coated with ivy

**i´vy** *n.* a climbing or trailing plant

**j, J** tenth letter of the English alphabet

**jab** *n.* a quick poke or punch —*vi., vt.* to poke, especially with a sharp instrument; to punch with a short, quick movement

**jab´ber** *vi., vt.* to speak rapidly or nonsensically —*n.* senseless talk —**jab´ber·er** *n.*

**ja·bot´** *n.* ornamental ruffles on the front of a shirt or blouse

**jack** *n.* a device for raising heavy objects; a type of food fish; (*US*) a plug for connecting electronic devices —*vt.* to raise with the aid of a jack; to raise, as prices

**jack´al** *n.* a wild dog

**jack´ass** *n.* the male ass; a stupid person

**jack´boot** *n.* a heavy boot reaching above the knee

**jack´daw** *n.* a small black bird related to the crow

**jack´et** *n.* a short coat; an outer covering or container —*vt.* to cover with a jacket

**jack´et·ed** *adj.* covered with a jacket

**jack´knife** *n.* a pocket knife designed in such a way that the blade folds into the handle

**jack´pot** *n.* a prize or pool of money; winnings; a bonanza or reward

**jack´rab·bit** *n.* a large American hare

**jade** *vt., vi.* to wear out or become worn by overindulgence —*n.* a shrewish woman; a gemstone, usually pale green

**jad´ed** *adj.* world-weary; pretentiously indifferent –**jad´ed·ly** *adv.* –**jad´ed·ness** *n.*

**jag´ged** *adj.* characterized by an irregular edge –**jag´ged·ly** *adv.* –**jag´ged·ness** *n.*

**jag´uar** *n.* a large spotted cat

**jail** *(US),* **gaol** *(Brit.) n.* a place of confinement for one awaiting trial or guilty of a minor offense –*vt.* to confine in a jail

**jail´er** *(US),* **gaol´er** *(Brit.) n.* one charged with the upkeep of a jail

**ja·la·pe´ño** *n.* a pungent tropical pepper having red or green fruit

**ja·lop´y** *n.* an old, broken-down car

**jal´ou·sie** *n.* a door or window covering having adjustable horizontal slats

**jam** *n.* a preserve of sugar and fruit; a crush of people; a difficult situation –*vt., vi.* to cram or become crammed in a tight space

**jamb** *n.* a vertical piece that forms the side of a door or window

**jam·ba·lay´a** *n.* a spicy Creole dish of rice with a variety of seafood or meat

**jam´bo·ree´** *n.* a large gathering; a festive celebration

**jam session** an unrehearsed gathering or meeting, especially of musicians

**jan´gle** *n.* a discordant metallic sound –*vi., vt.* to make or cause such a sound –**jan´gler** *n.*

**jan´i·tor** *(US) n.* one charged with the maintenance of a building –**jan·i·to´ri·al** *adj.*

**ja·pan´** *n.* a hard glossy coating; an item coated or decorated in the Japanese manner –*vt.* to coat with japan

**jape** *n.* a jest or prank –*vi.* to joke or jest –**jap´er** *n.* –**jap´er·y** *n.*

**jar** *n.* a small cylindrical container; a jolt or bump –*vi., vt.* to shake or cause to shake; to irritate or shock

**jar´di·niere´** *n.* an ornamental pot or stand for flowers

**jar´gon** *n.* a patois or dialect; the specialized terms of a profession or trade

**jar·gon·is´tic** *adj.* of the nature of a jargon

**jar´gon·ize** *vt., vi.* to translate into or speak in a dialect

**jas´mine** *n.* any of a species of flowering shrubs, some of which are used in making fragrances and tea; a fragrance or tea produced from the jasmine flower

**jas´per** *n.* a type of yellow, red, or brown quartz

**jaun´dice** *n.* abnormal yellowing of the skin, eyeballs, etc.; hostility, such as caused by envy or distrust –*vt.* to affect with jaundice; to be influenced by envy or distrust

**jaunt** *n.* an excursion; a short pleasure trip –*vi.* to make a short trip

**jaun´ty** *adj.* in a free and easy manner; buoyant; self-confident –**jaun´ti·ly** *adv.* –**jaun´ti·ness** *n.*

**jav´e·lin** *n.* a short light spear

**jaw** *n.* one of two bony structures forming the frame for the mouth; anything that grips like a jaw –*vi., vt.* to talk or scold

**jaw´bone** *n.* a bone of the jaw –*vt., vi.* to urge or argue vigorously

**jazz** *n.* an American musical form marked by syncopated rhythm, disonance, etc. –*adj.* pertaining to jazz –**jazz´man** *n.*

**jeal´ous** *adj.* envious; fearful of competition; protective, as *jealous of one's social standing* –**jeal´ous·ly** *adv.* –**jeal·ous·ness** *n.*

**jeal´ou·sy** *n.* possessive envy

**jeer** *n.* an abusive or mocking remark –*vi., vt.* to mock or ridicule –**jeer'ing·ly** *adv.*

**je·june´** *adj.* dull or lifeless; childlike –**je·june´ly** *adv.*

**jell** *vi., vt.* to become firm or cause to become firm; to take shape

**jel´ly** *n.* a sweet or savory gelatinous food

**jeop´ar·dize** *vt.* to expose to danger

**jeop´ar·dy** *n.* risk of loss; danger

**jerk** *n.* a sudden, quick action; a silly or foolish person –*vt.* to pull with a sudden snap –*vi.* to make a lurching or quivering move –**jerk´i·ly** *adv.* –**jerk´i·ness** *n.*

**jer´kin** *n.* a short jacket

**jerk´y** *adj.* marked by abrupt jolts or lurching, as *a jerky ride*; marked by short, abrupt movement, as *jerky handwriting*

**jer´ky** *n.* cured meat

**jer·o·bo´am** *n.* a wine bottle with a capacity of 3 liters

**jer´ry-built** *adj.* shoddily constructed; improvised

**jer´sey** *n.* a knitted fabric; clothing made from this fabric; a pullover shirt or sweater

**jest** *n.* a joke or prank –*vi.* to tease or mock; to speak in fun

**jest´er** *n.* a professional comedian; one given to light banter

**jet** *n.* a flow of fluid or gas forced through a small opening at high pressure; a device that creates such a flow; a vehicle propelled by this flow; a dense, black color –*vi.* to travel in a jet-propelled aircraft

**jet engine** *n.* an engine that develops thrust by forcing fluid exhaust through a nozzle

**jet´sam** *n.* material jettisoned by a ship in distress

**jet´ti·son** *vt.* to throw overboard, as from a ship; to discard

**jet´ty** *n.* a structure that extends out from shore to protect a harbor or shoreline

**jew´el** *n.* a precious stone; an ornament set with precious stones; something highly prized –**jew´el·er, jew´el·ler** *n.*

**jew´el·ler·y** *(Brit.)* **jew´el·ry** *(US) n.* ornaments made of precious metals and set with precious stones

**jif´fy** *n.* a brief span of time

**jig** *n.* a lively dance or its music; a device for holding or guiding a tool or material being worked *—vi.* to dance a jig

**jig´ger** *n.* a 1½ ounce measure; 1½ ounces

**jig´gle** *vi.* to bounce lightly up and down or from side to side **–jig´gly** *adj.*

**ji·had´** *n.* a holy war or pious quest

**jilt** *vi.* to reject suddenly, as a lover

**jim´my** *n.* a short crowbar *–vt.* to force, as with a crowbar

**jin´gle** *n.* a short rhyme or song; a light metallic tinkling sound *–vi., vt.* to make or cause to make such a sound **–jin´gly** *adj.*

**jin´go** *n.* one who aggressively supports his or her nation

**jin´go·ism** *n.* extreme nationalism

**jinx** *n.* a hex or spell; a person or thing that brings bad luck *–vt.* to bring bad luck

**jit´ney** *n.* a small passenger vehicle; a dilapi- dated vehicle

**jive** *n.* the jargon of jazz; nonsensical talk *–vt., vi.* to talk nonsensically

**job** *n.* work for pay; the type of work one does; a task or duty; something worked on or at

**job´ber** *n.* one who buys in large quantities from manufacturers or distributors and sells to retailers

**job´less** *adj.* out of work

**jock´ey** *n.* one who rides horses professionally; one associated with a particular vehicle, profession, etc., as *a jet jockey* or *a disc jockey –vi., vt.* to ride, as a horse; to maneuver: *jockey for position*

**jo·cose´** *adj.* given to humor **–jo·cose´ly** *adv.* **–jo·cose´ness, jo·cos´i·ty** *n.*

**joc´u·lar** *adj.* given to joking **–joc·u·lar´i·ty** *n.* **–joc´u·lar·ly** *adv.*

**joc´und** *adj.* lighthearted **–jo·cun´di·ty** *n.* **–joc´und·ly** *adv.*

**jodh´purs** *n.* riding pants, wide at the hips and closefitting below the knee

**jog** *n.* a slow, steady trot; a slight jostling or nudge *–vi., vt.* to move or cause to move at a slow run; to jostle or nudge

**jog´gle** *vt., vi.* to shake lightly

**join** *vt., vi.* to bring or come together; to connect

**join´er** *n.* a carpenter; a tool designed to fashion joints

**joint** *n.* a place where two pieces come together; a seedy establishment, such as a tavern; a marijuana cigarette *–adj.* shared **–joint´ed** *adj.* **–joint´ly** *adv.*

**joist** *n.* a horizontal beam

**joke** *n.* an amusing story or act *–vi.* to speak or act in fun **–jok´ing·ly** *adv.*

**jok´er** *n.* a jester or prankster

**jol´li·ty** *n.* merriment

**jo´ly** *adj.* cheerful, exhibiting good humor **–jol´li·ly** *adv.*

**jolt** *n.* a jarring bump; a shock or surprise *–vt.* to jar with or as if by a sharp blow; to shock **–jolt´y** *adj.*

**josh** *vi.* to joke; to tease playfully **–josh´er** *n.*

**jos´tle** *vt.* to push or bump while walking by **–jos´tler** *n.*

**jot** *n.* a small amount *–vt.* to write hastily

**jot´ted** *adj.* written hastily

**jot´ting** *n.* a short note

**jounce** *n.* a jolting movement *–vi., vt.* to move or cause to move with a jolt

**jour´nal** *n.* an account, as of one's finances or activities; a newspaper or periodical **–jour´nal·ize** *vt.*

**jour´nal·ism** *n.* the writing and editing of news items

**jour´nal·ist** *n.* one who writes for a newspaper or periodical **–jour·nal·is´tic** *adj.* **–jour·nal·is´ti·cal·ly** *adv.*

**jour´ney** *n.* the act of traveling or the distance traveled *–vi., vt.* to travel

**jour´ney·man** *n.* one who has completed an apprenticeship

**joust** *n.* medieval combat between mounted opponents; a competition; a confrontation suggestive of such rivalry *–vi.* to compete; to engage in a battle of words or wits **–joust´er** *n.*

**jo´vi·al** *adj.* extremely cordial and sociable **–jo´vi·al·ly** *adv.*

**jowl** *n.* the flesh of the cheek or jaw

**jowl´y** *adj.* having loose hanging flesh about the cheeks and jaws

**joy** *n.* intense happiness or pleasure; the cause of such pleasure

**joy´ful** *adj.* expressing or feeling joy **–joy´ful·ly** *adv.* **–joy´ful·ness** *n.*

**joy´less** *adj.* lacking joy; sad **–joy´less·ly** *adv.* **–joy´less·ness** *n.*

**joy´ous** *adj.* causing or expressing joy **–joy´ous·ly** *adv.* **–joy´ous·ness** *n.*

**joy´stick** *n.* a cursor control for playing computer games

**ju´bi·lant** *adj.* extremely happy; rapturous **–ju´bi·lance** *n.* **–ju´bi·lant·ly** *adv.*

**ju´bi·late** *vi.* to rejoice

**ju·bi·la´tion** *n.* rapture; a manifestation of joy

**ju´bi·lee** *n.* a celebration; an occasion for rejoicing

**judge** *n.* an officer of the court; one appointed to arbitrate or decide the relative worth of something *–vt.* to decide after argument, as in a court of law; to form an opinion, usually based on careful study

**judg·mat´ic, judg·mat´i·cal** *adj.* judicious **–judg·mat´i·cal·ly** *adv.*

**judge´ship** *n.* the office and authority of a judge

**judge´ment, judg´ment** *n.* the ability to discern; the process of forming an opinion based on observation and consideration; an opinion so formed

**judg·men´tal** *adj.* tending to judge; relating to judgment

**ju·di´cial** *adj.* relating to a court of law; pronouncing judgment **–ju·di´cial·ly** *adv.*

**ju·di´ciar·y** *n.* the court system; those who administer justice

**ju·di´cious** *adj.* marked by prudence; careful; discreet; sensible **–ju·di´cious·ly** *adv.* **–ju·di´cious·ness** *n.*

**ju´do** *n.* a form of hand-to-hand combat developed in Japan

**jug** *n.* a large, rounded container with a small mouth and a handle

**jug´ger·naut** *n.* an overwhelming force, esp. one that seems able to destroy everything in its path

**jug´gle** *vt.* to keep objects in the air by alternately tossing them up and catching them; to experience difficulty holding several objects or moving between activities; to alter so as to deceive, as *to juggle the books* **–jug´gler** *n.*

**jug´u·lar** *adj.* about the neck or throat

**juice** *n.* liquid derived from plant or animal tissue **–juic´er** *n.*

**juic´y** *adj.* full of juice; mouthwatering; having substance or special meaning, as *a juicy story* **–juic´i·ness** *n.*

**juke´box** *n.* a coin-operated phonograph

**ju·li·enne´** *n.* a broth containing strips of vegetable *–adj.* cut into long, thin strips

**jum´ble** *n.* a confusing mixture *–vt., vi.* to mix or be mixed in a haphazard fashion

**jum´bo** *adj.* large in size

**jump** *n.* a leap; the distance covered by a leap *–vi., vt.* to move or cause to move or change suddenly

**jump´er** *n.* one who jumps or is likely to jump; a cable used to shunt an electrical circuit; *(Brit.)* a sweater; *(US)* a loose sleeveless dress worn over a blouse

**jump´i·ness** *n.* nervousness

**jump´suit** *n.* a one-piece garment that covers the entire body

**jump´y** *adj.* nervous

**junc´tion** *n.* a place where two things meet or join, such as roads or power lines **–junc´tion·al** *adj.*

**junc´ture** *n.* a junction; a place where two things are joined

**jun´gle** *n.* a wilderness characterized by tangled undergrowth; a jumbled or confusing accumulation, as *a jungle of statutes*; an environment characterized by intense rivalry

**jun´ior** *adj.* younger in age; lower in rank *–n.* the younger of two; one lower in rank; a third year student

**junk** *n.* objects cast off; something of poor quality or meaningless *–vt.* to discard *–adj.* worthless

**junk bond** a high yield corporate bond that entails a high risk

**junk´er** *n.* an old, beat-up car

**jun´ket** *n.* an outing; a trip at public expense or to influence a potential benefactor **–jun´ke·teer´** *n.*

**junk food** snack food that lacks nutritional value

**jun´ta** *n.* a small group of legislators or rulers of a country, often after seizing power

**ju´ral** *adj.* relating to the law

**ju´rat** *n.* certification on an affidavit

**ju·rid´ic, ju·rid´i·cal** *adj.* relating to administration of the law **–ju·rid´i·cal·ly** *adv.*

**ju·ris·dic´tion** *n.* the range or extent of one's authority

**ju·ris·dic´tion·al** *adj.* relating to the limits of one's rights or authority **–ju·ris·dic´tion·al·ly** *adv.*

**ju·ris·pru´dence** *n.* the science of law **–ju·ris·pru´dent** *adj., n.* **–ju·ris·pru·den´tial** *adj.*

**ju´rist** *n.* one experienced in the law

**ju·ris´tic** *adj.* relating to a jurist or to matters of the law **–ju·ris´ti·cal·ly** *adv.*

**ju´ror** *n.* one serving on a jury

**ju´ry** *n.* a group of persons sworn to hear both sides of an issue and to pass judgment

**ju´ry-rig** *vt.* to rig for emergency use; to improvise

**just** *adj.* fair and fitting; conforming to what is right; impartial *–adv.* precisely; barely **–just´ly** *adv.* **–just´ness** *n.*

**jus´tice** *n.* adhering to what is right or just **–jus´tice·ship** *n.*

**jus´ti·fi·a·ble** *adj.* able to be proved correct; warranted **–jus·ti·fi·a·bil´i·ty, jus´ti·fi·a·ble·ness** *n.* **–jus´ti·fi·a·bly** *adv.*

**jus·ti·fi·ca´tion** *n.* defense; explanation **–jus´ti·fi·ca·tive** *adj.*

**jus´ti·fy** *vt.* to prove to be correct; to absolve of blame

**jut** *vi., vt.* to extend or cause to extend outward

**ju´ve·nile** *adj.* young; relating to young people; characterized by immature behavior **–ju´ve·nile·ly** *adv.* **–ju´ve·nile·ness** *n.*

**jux´ta·pose** *vt.* to place side by side, especially for comparison **–jux·ta·po·si´tion** *n.* **–jux·ta·po·si´tion·al** *adj.*

**k, K** eleventh letter of the English alphabet

**ka·lei´do·scope** *n.* an optical device that produces changing colored patterns by means of small bits of glass and mirrors; something that is constantly changing **–ka·lei·do·scop´ic, ka·lei·do·scop´i·cal** *adj.* **–ka·lei·do·scop´i·cal·ly** *adv.*

**kan´ga·roo´** *n.* an Australian leaping marsupial

**kan´ji** *n.* Japanese picture writing

**ka´pok** *n.* a cottonlike fiber used to stuff mattresses

**ka·put´** *adj.* not working; used up or gone bad

**ka·ra´te** *n.* a system of self-defense that originated in Japan

**kar´ma** *n.* one's destiny as determined by conduct

**katz´en·jam·mer** *n.* a hangover; a bewildered state

**kay´ak** *n.* an enclosed canoe with a small opening for its occupant who propels it with a double-ended paddle

**ka·zoo´** *n.* an instrument with a vibrating membrane that produces a humming sound

**ke·bob´** *n.* a bit of food that is broiled or barbequed on a skewer; a shish kebob

**kedge** *n.* a light anchor

**keel** *n.* the lowest point along the length of a vessel —*vi.* to roll over

**keen** *adj.* sharp, as a knife blade; intelligent and perceptive; sensitive, as *a keen eye*; eager for, as *keen on sailing* —**keen´ly** *adv.* —**keen´ness** *n.*

**keep** *vt.* to retain as a possession; to tend or care for; to cause to continue without change; to restrain or prevent —*vi.* to continue; to remain unchanged —*n.* care or support; a stronghold, as in a castle

**keep´er** *n.* an overseer

**keep´sake** *n.* a memento

**ke·fir´** *n.* a drink made from fermented cow's milk

**keg** *n.* a small barrel; a 100 pound measure, used for nails

**keg´ler** *n.* one who bowls

**kelp** *n.* a type of seaweed

**kempt** *adj.* neat; orderly

**ken´nel** *n.* an animal shelter; a business that boards or breeds dogs

**ker´a·tin** *n.* a tough protein that forms nails, horns, etc. —**ke·rat´i·nous** *adj.*

**ker´chief** *n.* large handkerchief worn on the head or tied around the neck; a bandanna

**kerf** *n.* a cut made by an axe or saw

**ker´nel** *n.* a grain or seed; the most significant or central part

**ker´o·sene** *(US) n.* a fuel distilled from petroleum

**ketch** *n.* a two-masted vessel

**ket´tle** *n.* a metal pot, often with a handle and a lid; a teakettle

**key** *n.* a notched device that fits into a hole for unlocking, winding, etc.; a critical element or clue; the pitch of a musical tone

**key´board** *n.* a set of keys as on a typewriter, piano, etc.

**key´board·ist** *n.* one who plays a piano, synthesizer, etc.

**keycard** *n.* a small rigid card that opens a lock by means of a coded electronic strip

**key club** a private club to which members gain entrance with a real or symbolic key

**keynote address** an opening speech that sets the theme for a meeting, conference, etc.

**key´pad** *n.* a device for inputting data as to a computer

**key´stone** *n.* the topmost stone in an arch; a fundamental element

**khak´i** *n.* a tannish brown color; a cloth of this color —*adj.*

**kib´itz** *vi.* to chat informally; to intrude; to offer unwanted advice —**kib´itz·er** *n.*

**kick** *n.* a sharp blow with the foot; a thrust of the foot, as in swimming or dancing; vigor or stimulation as though from a kick: *we get a kick from dancing* —*vi., vt.* to strike out with the foot

**kick´back** *n.* a payback for part of monies received: a bribe; a violent reaction; a backlash

**kick´er** *n.* one who kicks; an important contingency that may be a detraction or a benefit

**kick´off** *n.* a traditional or ceremonial beginning

**kid** *n.* the young of certain animals, especially the goat; the meat or hide of a young goat; a young person —*vi., vt.* to engage in goodnatured banter —**kid´der** *n.*

**kid´nap** *vt.* to abduct or hold illegally, esp. for ransom —**kid´nap·er, kid´nap·per** *n.*

**kid´ney** *n.* one of a pair of organs that filter body fluids

**kid´skin** *n.* leather from the skin of a young goat

**kill** *vt.* to put to death; to destroy, extinguish, exhaust, or end in some way; to overwhelm: *the pace is killing me, his act killed the crowd* —*n.* the act of killing or that which has been killed, as in hunting —**kill´er** *n.*

**kill´joy** *n.* one who undermines the pleasure of others

**kiln** *n.* an oven used for baking or drying, especially to fire ceramics

**kil´o·byte** *n.* a computer unit equal to 1,024 bytes

**kil´o·cal·o·rie** *n.* a unit of potential energy contained in food; a nutritionist's calorie, commonly called a large calorie

**kil´o·cy·cle** *n.* one thousand cycles

**ki·lom´e·ter** *n.* one thousand meters —**kil·o·met´ric** *adj.*

**ki·mo´no** *n.* a robe-like outer garment indigenous to Japan

**kin** *adj.* of the same ancestry —*n.* those to whom one is related

**kind** *adj.* benevolent, compassionate, and humane in nature —*n.* a class or type unified by common traits; something similar, as *a kind of colonial house*

**kin´der·gar·ten** *n.* school for young children —**kin´der·gart·ner** *n.*

**kind´heart·ed** *adj.* having a kind and sympathetic nature —**kind'heart·ed·ly** *adv.* —**kind´heart·ed·ness** *n.*

**kin´dle** *vt., vi.* to set or catch on fire; to stimulate, as emotion —**kin´dling** *n.*

**kind´ly** *adj.* of a kind disposition —*adv.* pleasantly or politely —**kind´li·ness** *n.*

**kind´ness** *n.* the state of being kind or acting in a kind manner; a courtesy or act of charity

**kin´dred** *adj.* of common origins or nature

**ki·net´ic** *adj.* depending on or producing motion

—**ki·net´i·cal·ly** *adv.*

**kinetic energy** the energy of a body attributable to its motion

**ki·net´ics** *n.* the study of the dynamics of material bodies

**king** *n.* a male sovereign; one superior in a particular field —*adj.* pre-eminent

**king´dom** *n.* the domain of a king; a broad domain, as *the animal kingdom*

**king´ly** *adj.* regal; in the manner of a king —*adv.* —**king´li·ness** *n.*

**king´pin** *n.* a leader; the most important person

**kink** *n.* a tight curl; a cramp; a quirk or impediment

**kink´y** *adj.* tightly curled; strange or quirky —**kink´i·ness** *n.*

**kin´ship** *n.* relationship by blood

**ki´osk** *n.* a small, free-standing structure, such as a gazebo or newsstand

**kip´per** *n.* a fish that has been cured by salting and smoking —*vt.* to cure by salting or smoking

**kir** *n.* dry white wine flavored with crème de cassis

**kirk** *n.* a Scottish church

**kirsch** *n.* a clear brandy made from fermented cherry juice

**kiss** *n.* an affectionate or respectful touching of the lips; a light, fleeting touch —*vi., vt.* to touch with the lips; to touch lightly —**kiss´a·ble** *adj.*

**kit** *n.* a collection of articles or equipment, as *a tool kit*; the container for such a collection

**kitch´en** *n.* an area where food is prepared; a staff or a collection of implements for preparing food

**kitch·en·ette´** *n.* a small kitchen, often an adjunct to a larger eating or living area

**kitch´en·ware** *n.* collectively, the implements used in the preparation of food

**kite** *n.* a type of hawk; a light frame covered with paper that is flown in the wind; a counterfeit negotiable instrument used to obtain funds —*vt., vi.* to issue or obtain money with a counterfeit instrument

**kit´ty** *n.* money that has been pooled for some purpose

**klep·to·ma´ni·ac** *n.* one with an obsessive urge to steal regardless of need —**klep·to·ma´ni·a** *n.*

**klutz** *n.* one who is clumsy or lacking in social grace —**klutz´i·ness** *n.* —**klutz´y** *adj.*

**knack** *n.* a special talent or skill

**knap´sack** *n.* a sturdy bag with shoulder straps, usually for carrying camping gear

**knave** *n.* one of humble birth; commonly, a rascal or rogue —**knav´ish** *adj.* —**knav´ish·ly** *adv.* —**knav´ish·ness** *n.*

**knav´er·y** *n.* deceitful or underhanded transactions

**knead** *vt.* to fold and press with the hands, as dough; to massage —**knead´er** *n.*

**knee** *n.* the joint between the thigh and lower leg; the part of a garment that covers the knee —*vt.* to strike with the knee

**knee´-jerk** *adj.* involuntary, as a reaction; unthinking acceptance

**kneel** *vi.* to rest on one or both knees —**kneel´er** *n.*

**knell** *n.* the slow, solemn tolling of a bell

**knick´er·bock·ers** *(US) n.* full trousers that are cut off and tied just below the knee

**knick´knack** *n.* a small curio or ornamental piece

**knife** *n.* a tool consisting of a thin blade attached to a handle, used for cutting or spreading

**knight** *n.* a medieval high-born mounted soldier; one who champions a cause —**knight´li·ness** *n.* —**knight´ly** *adj.*

**knight-er´rant** *n.* a knight who seeks adventure to prove himself; an adventure-seeker

**knight´hood** *n.* a rank conferred by a sovereign for outstanding service

**knish** *n.* a savory pastry filled with potato, meat, etc. and baked or fried

**knit** *vt., vi.* to make by intertwining strands of yarn; to join or become joined tightly, as a bone fracture; to draw or come together in wrinkles, as a furrowed brow —**knit´ter** *n.*

**knit´ting, knit´wear** *n.* garments made by knitting

**knob** *n.* a stubby projection; a rounded handle, as on a door or drawer

**knobbed** *adj.* having a knob

**knob´by** *adj.* have the appearance of a knob, as *knobby knees*

**knock** *vi., vt.* to strike solidly; to collide or cause to collide; to criticize —*n.* a sharp blow

**knock´off** *adj.* a cheap imitation

**knoll** *n.* a low, rounded hill; a hillock

**knot** *n.* a fastener or decoration made by tying; a tight group, as of people; a tight feeling; the joint of a tree trunk from which a branch grows; one nautical mile; a speed of one nautical mile per hour —*vt., vi.* to fasten with or form into a knot; to tangle or become entangled

**knot´ty** *adj.* snarled, as a rope; containing many knots, as a board; difficult to resolve, as a problem or puzzle

**know** *vt., vi.* to possess information and understanding; to comprehend —**know´a·ble** *adj.*

**know´-how** *n.* expertise

**know´ing** *adj.* knowledgeable; shrewd; secretly aware; deliberate or intentional —**know´ing·ly** *adv.* —**know´ing·ness** *n.*

**knowl´edge** *n.* information or awareness gained from study or experience

**knowl´edge·a·ble** *adj.* possessing learning or experience —**knowl´edge·a·bly** *adv.*

**knuck´le** *n.* a bulge formed by the bones in a joint

**knurl** *n.* a protuberance; small ridges employed as an

aid to gripping —**knurled, knurl´y** *adj.*
**ko·a´la** *n.* an Australian arborial marsupial
**ko´an** *n.* a Zen riddle in the form of a paradox
**kook** *n.* an unconventional person —**kook´y** *adj.*
**ko´sher** *adj.* conforming to Jewish dietary laws; broadly used to describe that which is valid or legitimate
**ko´to** *n.* a Japanese stringed instrument
**kraut** *n.* sauerkraut
**kris** *n.* a Malaysian dagger
**kryp´ton** *n.* an inert gas used in fluorescent bulbs
**ku´chen** *n.* yeast dough coffee cake
**ku´dos** *n.* acclaim for achievement
**küm´mel** *n.* caraway seed liqueur
**kum´quat** *n.* a small, orange-like fruit
**kung fu** *n.* Chinese martial art similar to karate

**l, L** twelfth letter of the English alphabet
**lab** *n.* laboratory
**la´bel** *n.* a tag or stamp that serves to identify, instruct, etc.; a distinguishing appellation —*vt.* to attach or ascribe with a label —**la´bel·er, la´bel·ler** *n.*
**la´bor** *(US) n.* physical or mental effort; workers collectively; the exertion of childbirth —*vi.* to expend energy; to toil conscientiously; to move with difficulty; to experience childbirth —**la´bor·er** *n.*
**lab´o·ra·to·ry** *n.* a place of research or learning
**la´bored** *(US) adj.* accomplished with great effort
**la´bor-inten·sive** *adj.* requiring a disproportionate amount of physical labor
**la·bo´ri·ous** *adj.* difficult or exhausting —**la·bo´ri·ous·ly** *adv.* —**la·bo´ri·ous·ness** *n.*
**la´bour** *(Brit.) n.* physical or mental effort; workers collectively; the exertion of childbirth —*vi.* to expend energy; to toil conscientiously; to move with difficulty; to experience childbirth —**la´bour·er** *n.*
**la´boured** *(Brit.) adj.* accomplished with great effort
**lab´y·rinth** *n.* a maze; something intricate —**lab·y·rin´thi·an, lab·y·rin´thine** *adj.*
**lace** *n.* a cord used to draw together or fasten; a delicate fabric —*vt.* to put in place by threading or intertwining; to spread throughout: *a soup laced with sherry, a speech laced with technical terms* —**lace into** to assail verbally —**lac´ing** *n.*
**lac´er·ate** *vt.* to cut or tear, as flesh —*adj.* torn
**lac·er·a´tion** *n.* a jagged wound
**lach´ry·mose** *adj.* tearful; tending to cause tears —**lach´ry·mal** *adj.* —**lach´ry·mose·ly** *adv.* —**lach·ry·mos´i·ty** *n.*
**lack** *n.* a deficiency, as in substance or quality —*vi., vt.* to have little; to be in need of something
**lack·a·dai´si·cal** *adj.* languid; lacking spirit —**lack·a·dai´si·cal·ly** *adv.* —**lack·a·dai´si·cal·ness** *n.*
**lack´ey** *n.* a menial; a fawning attendant
**lack´lus·ter** *adj.* wanting in vitality
**la·con´ic, la·con´i·cal** *adj.* not wordy; disinclined to converse —**la·con´i·cal·ly** *adv.*
**lac´quer** *n.* a clear, protective coating —*vt.* to coat with lacquer
**la·crosse´** *n.* a type of field hockey
**lac´tate** *vi.* to produce milk
**lac·ta´tion** *n.* the production of milk in the mammary glands; the period of such production —**lac·ta´tion·al** *adj.*
**lac´te·al** *adj.* relating to milk —**lac´te·al·ly** *adv.*
**lac´tic** *adj.* relating to or derived from milk
**lac·tif´er·ous** *adj.* producing milk —**lac·tif´er·ous·ness** *n.*
**lac´y** *adj.* resembling lace; flimsy —**lac´i·ly** *adv.* —**lac´i·ness** *n.*
**lad** *n.* a young man
**lad´der** *n.* a framework of parallel sides joined by rungs used for climbing; an analogous means of ascent or descent: *the corporate ladder*
**lade** *vt.* to load with cargo; to dip or ladle, as soup
**lad´en** *adj.* weighed down; oppressed
**lad´ing** *n.* cargo
**la´dle** *n.* a deep-bowled serving spoon —*vt.* to serve or apportion, as with a ladle —**la´dle·ful** *adj.* —**la´dler** *n.*
**la´dy** *n.* a well-mannered woman; the female head of a household
**la´dy·fin·ger** *n.* a small oval cake
**lady in waiting** a female attendant
**lady-killer** a man who is extremely attractive to women
**la´dy·like** *adj.* having the manners or bearing of a lady
**lady´s maid** a personal servant to a lady
**lag** *vi.* to fall behind; to falter
**la´ger** *n.* a type of beer
**lag´gard** *n.* one who falls behind; a straggler —*adj.* slow —**lag´gard·ly** *adv.* —**lag´gard·ness** *n.*
**la·goon´** *n.* a shallow body of water, especially near the sea
**la´ic, la´i·cal** *adj.* secular —*n.* a layperson
**laid´-back´** *adj.* serene or casual
**lair** *n.* an animal's den; one's habitat or domain
**lais´sez-faire** *n.* a policy of noninterference
**la´i·ty** *n.* those who are not members of the clergy
**lake** *n.* a large inland body of water
**lake´front, lake´shore, lake´side** *n.* land along the shore of a lake
**la´ma** *n.* a Tibetan or Mongolian Buddhist monk
**la´ma·ser·y** *n.* a monastery for lamas
**lam·baste´** *vt.* to rebuke sharply; to reprimand
**lame** *adj.* disabled; halting; weak or ineffective: *a lame excuse* —*vt.* to injure so as to disable —**lame´ly** *adv.* —**lame´ness** *n.*
**la·mé´** *n.* a fabric containing metallic thread
**lame´brain** *n.* a stupid or silly person
**lame duck** a person in office awaiting installation of

a successor

**la·ment´** *n.* an expression of sorrow or affliction *—vi., vt.* to express grief, sorrow, or remorse **—lam´en·ta·ble** *adj.* **—la·men´ta·ble·ness** *n.* **—lam´en·ta·bly** *adv.*

**lam·en·ta´tion** *n.* a lament

**lam´i·na** *n.* a thin sheet or layer **—lam´i·nal, lam´i·nar** *adj.*

**lam´i·nate** *n.* a thin material, often an outer covering for protection or embellishment *—vt.* to cover with a thin layer of material; to form from thin layers **—lam´i·na·tor** *n.*

**lam´i·nat·ed** *adj.* coated with or formed from thin layers

**lam·i·na´tion** *n.* the process of coating or joining; material formed from such process

**lamp** *n.* a device that provides light or heat

**lamp´black** *n.* fine carbon used as a pigment

**lam·poon´** *n.* a satirical work that ridicules convention *—vt.* to satirize **—lam·poon´er, lam·poon´ist** *n.* **—lam·poon´er·y** *n.*

**la·nai´** *n.* a roofed porch or patio, often enclosed

**lance** *n.* a weapon comprised of a long shaft with a pointed end *—vt.* to pierce, as with a pointed weapon or instrument **—lanc´er** *n.*

**lan´cet** *n.* a surgical knife

**land** *n.* a piece of property; real estate; a nation or country *—vi., vt.* to come or bring to a place **—land´less** *adj.* **—land´own·er** *n.*

**land bridge** dry ground that joins two land masses

**land´ed** *adj.* possessing property

**land´fall** *n.* the place where one alights after a journey by sea or air

**land´fill** *n.* property used for or created by depositing solid waste between layers of soil

**land grant** property deeded by a government, usually for a special purpose or requiring that certain conditions be met

**land´hold·er** *n.* a property owner

**land´ing** *n.* a termination, as of a sea or air voyage; a place for transferring cargo; the termination of a staircase

**land´la·dy, land´lord** *n.* one who owns or manages rental property

**land´locked** *adj.* without access to the sea

**land´mark** *n.* a boundary marker; a prominent feature that serves as a guide; an important building or area preserved for posterity

**land´scape** *n.* a scenic view *—vt.* to beautify property by contouring, planting, etc. *—vi.* to beautify property as a vocation **—land´scap·er, land´scap·ist** *n.*

**lands´man** *n.* one who works the land; one who is from the same area or country

**lane** *n.* a narrow byway; a specific channel defined for certain use: *a highway passing lane, a sea lane*

**lan´guage** *n.* a system of sounds, symbols, gestures, etc. by which humans and other creatures communicate

**lan´guid** *adj.* lacking vitality or force; sluggish **—lan´guid·ly** *adv.* **—lan´guid·ness** *n.*

**lan´guish** *vi.* to be or to become weak or neglected **—lan´guish·er** *n.* **—lan´guish·ing·ly** *adv.* **—lan´guish·ment** *n.*

**lan´guor** *n.* a lack of energy; a lethargic condition

**lan´guor·ous** *adj.* lacking energy; lethargic **—lan´guor·ous·ly** *adv.* **—lan´guor·ous·ness** *n.*

**lank** *adj.* lean and gaunt **—lank´ness** *n.* **—lank´ly** *adv.*

**lank´y** *adj.* tall and thin, often awkward **—lank´i·ness** *n.*

**lan´tern** *n.* a lamp with a protective, often decorative, case

**lantern jaw** a protruding lower jaw **—lantern-jawed** *adj.*

**lan´yard** *n.* a short rope, such as used for securing a ship's rigging or for firing a cannon; a decorative cord attached to a small utensil, such as a knife

**lap** *n.* the flat surface formed by the upper legs when a person is seated; the amount by which one piece lies over another; the act or sound of taking in liquid with the tongue *—vi., vt.* to lie or cause to lie over something; to overlap; to take in or make the sound of taking in liquid with the tongue

**lap belt** a safety harness worn across the lap

**la·pel´** *n.* an extended collar that folds back against the front of a garment

**lap´i·dar·y** *n.* one who finishes or deals in gems

**lapse** *n.* a minor, temporary fault or break; a deterioration; the termination of a right *—vi.* to deteriorate or deviate from an accepted course; to lose a right

**lap´top** *n.* a portable computer

**lar´ce·nous** *adj.* given to larceny **—lar´ce·nous·ly** *adv.*

**lar´ce·ny** *n.* the unlawful taking of another's property **—lar´ce·ner, lar´ce·nist** *n.*

**lard** *n.* rendered fat *—vt.* to prepare meat for cooking by injecting with strips of fat

**lar´der** *n.* a store of food; a pantry

**large** *adj.* of greater than average size or scope; extensive; important; significant **—large´ly** *adv.* **—large´ness** *n.*

**lar·gess´** *n.* generosity; gifts given generously

**lar´i·at** *n.* a lasso

**lark** *n.* a songbird; a spontaneous escapade **—lark´er** *n.*

**lark´y** *adj.* spontaneous; silly

**lar´va** *n., pl.* **larvae** the form of an insect before metamorphosis **—lar´val** *adj.*

**lar´vi·cide** *n.* a poison that destroys larvae **—lar´vi·cid·al** *adj.*

**la·sa´gna** *n.* a baked dish comprised of wide, flat pasta layered with sauce, meat, cheese, etc.

**las·civ´i·ous** *adj.* lewd; arousing sexual desire **—las·civ´i·ous·ly** *adv.* **—las·civ´i·ous·ness** *n.*

**lash** *n.* a whip; a sudden blow or impact; a stinging attack of words, as *a tongue-lashing*; an eyelash *—vi., vt.* to strike suddenly as if with a whip; to attack with words

**lash´ing** *n.* a ritualized beating; a flogging; a rope or cord used to bind or secure

**lass, las´sie** *n.* a young woman

**las´si·tude** *n.* lethargy; a feeling of apathy or fatigue

**las´so** *n.* a rope with a noose at one end used mainly to control livestock *—vt.* to catch with a noose or as if with a noose **—las´so·er** *n.*

**last** *n.* the end or one at the end *—adj., adv.* final: *last place*; the only one left: *the last honest man*; most recent but one: *last year —vi., vt.* to continue; to endure or persist **—last´ly** *adv.*

**last hurrah** a final effort

**last´ing** *adj.* permanent; enduring for a long time **—last´ing·ly** *adv.* **—last´ing·ness** *n.*

**last name** *(US)* a surname; a family name

**last word** the final say in a dispute; the latest or most modern

**latch** *n.* a catch or lock, as for a door *—vi., vt.* to close or lock as with a latch

**latch´key** *n.* a key for a latch or lock

**latchkey child** a child of working parents left at home unsupervised for at least part of the day

**late** *adj.* occurring after the usual or expected time; well on in time: *the late show, late in life*; recent: *latebreaking news*; former or deceased: *our late chairman, the late Mr. Jones —adv.* after the usual or expected time; recently **—late´ness** *n.*

**late´ly** *adv.* recently

**lat´en** *vi., vt.* to become or cause to become late

**la´tent** *adj.* potential, but not evident; undeveloped **—la´ten·cy** *n.* **—la´tent·ly** *adv.*

**lat´er·al** *adj.* to the side; sideways: *a lateral move* **—lat´er·al·ly** *adv.*

**lat´est** *n.* newest; most recent

**lath** *n.* a thin wood strip

**lathe** *n.* a machine for cutting and shaping wood or metal

**lath´er** *n.* foam *—vt., vi.* to coat or become coated with lather **—lath´er·er** *n.* **—lath´er·y** *adj.*

**lat´ish** *adj.* somewhat late

**lat´i·tude** *n.* an angular distance as from the earth's equator or a celestial body; a range in which to function, especially outside normal constraints: *a greater latitude of tolerance* **—lat·i·tu´di·nal** *adj.* **—lat·i·tu´di·nal·ly** *adv.*

**lat´ke** *n.* a potato pancake

**la·trine´** *n.* a communal toilet

**lat´ter** *adj.* the second of two; nearer the end **—lat´ter·ly** *adv.*

**lat´tice** *n.* an open panel of crisscrossed slats of wood, metal, etc. **—lat´ticed** *adj.* **—lat´tice·work** *n.*

**laud** *vt.* to praise **—laud´a·bil´i·ty, laud´a·ble·ness** *n.*

**laud´a·ble** *adj.* worthy of praise **—laud´a·bly** *adv.* **—lau·da´tion** *n.*

**laud´a·tive, lau´da·to·ry** *adj.* bestowing praise **—laud·a·to´ri·ly** *adv.*

**laugh** *vi.* to express amusement by making an impromptu, inarticulate sound; to mock with such sounds **—laugh´er** *n.*

**laugh´a·ble** *adj.* disdainful **—laugh´a·ble·ness** *n.* **—laugh´a·bly** *adv.*

**laugh´ing** *adj.* expressing amusement **—laugh´ing·ly** *adv.*

**laughing gas** nitrous oxide, used as an anesthetic

**laugh´ing·stock** *n.* something to be ridiculed

**laugh´ter** *n.* the sound of laughing; sounds indicating merriment or derision

**launch** *vt.* to set in motion *—vi.* to begin, as a new venture

**launch pad** a platform and scaffold for launching a spacecraft

**launch vehicle** a rocket for launching a spacecraft

**launch window** the space of time during which a spacecraft can be launched to achieve a desired trajectory

**laun´der** *vt.* to wash, as clothing; to conceal or obscure, as the origin of money or information **—laun´der·er** *n.*

**laun·der·ette´** *n.* a commercial selfservice laundry

**laun´dress, laun´dry·man** *n.* one who takes in laundry

**Laun´dro·mat®** a launderette

**laun´dry** *n.* clothes to be washed; a place for washing clothes

**lau´re·ate** *adj.* decked with laurel; distinguished *—n.* one deserving of special honor for achievement

**la´va** *n.* molten rock from a volcano; the rock formed when molten rock cools and hardens

**lav´a·liere´** *n.* jewelry consisting of a necklace and pendant

**lav´a·to·ry** *n.* a public bathroom; a washbasin with running water; a toilet

**lave** *vt.* to bathe

**lav´ish** *adj.* extravagant; profuse *—vt.* to furnish in abundance **—lav´ish·er** *n.* **—lav´ish·ly** *adv.* **—lav´ish·ness** *n.*

**law** *n.* a code or system of conduct established by custom or authority

**law´a·bid´ing** *adj.* faithful to the law

**law´break·er** *n.* one who violates the law

**law´ful** *adj.* sanctioned by law **—law´ful·ly** *adv.* **—law´ful·ness** *n.*

**law´less** *adj.* not founded in law; without sanction; disregarding the constraints of law **—law´less·ly** *adv.* **—law´less·ness** *n.*

**law´mak·er** *n.* a legislator
**law´man** *n.* an officer who enforces the law
**lawn** *n.* a tended tract of grass
**lawn tennis** the game of tennis played on a grassy surface
**law´suit** *n.* a court action
**law´yer** *n.* one who gives counsel and support in legal matters
**lax** *adj.* slack, indifferent; not exacting or demanding **–lax´i·ty** *n.*
**lax´a·tive** *n.* something that causes evacuation of the bowels
**lay** *vt.* to place or arrange in a particular way *–adj.* of the laity; not of a particular profession
**lay´a·bout** *n.* a loafer
**lay´er** *n.* a single thickness, as of material; a hen kept for egg production *–vi., vt.* to form in layers
**lay´man, lay´per·son, lay´wom·an** *n.* one who is not of the clergy; an outsider, not associated with a specified profession
**lay´off** *n.* a suspension for lack of work; a period of inactivity
**laze** *vi., vt.* to loaf
**la´zy** *adj.* inclined to inactivity; inviting idleness: *a lazy day* **–la´zi·ly** *adv.* **–la´zi·ness** *n.*
**la´zy·bones** *n.* a loafer
**lea** *n.* a meadow
**lead** *vt., vi.* to guide or direct; to go first *–n.* the first position; the amount by which one is ahead; a clue or suggestion
**lead´en** *adj.* heavy, as lead; dull or listless, as *a leaden color* **–lead´en·ly** *adv.* **–lead´en·ness** *n.*
**lead´er** *n.* one who guides or is in command; one in a position of influence or importance; a strip of material that precedes or joins, as on a film strip or fishing line
**lead´er** *(Brit.)* *n.* a newspaper or magazine article expressing editorial opinion
**lead´er·ship** *n.* guidance; the capacity to guide or command
**lead´-in** *n.* an introduction
**lead´ing** *adj.* most prominent; situated at the front; designed to elicit a particular response, as *a leading question*; directing or guiding
**leading edge** the foremost or latest trend
**leading lady, leading man** the principal character in a work of fiction
**lead´off** *n.* an opening move; one who starts first
**leaf** *n.* a usually flat appendage issuing from the stem of a plant; a thin sheet of material, as *gold leaf*; a page of a book *–vi., vt.* to browse through, as papers or the pages of a book
**leaf´age** *n.* foliage
**leaf´let** *n.* a pamphlet or flier
**leaf´y** *adj.* having or consisting of leaves; producing leaves **–leaf´i·ness** *n.*
**league** *n.* an association, joined to further a common interest *–vi., vt.* to come or bring together in association
**leak** *n.* a small opening that allows a substance such as gas or water to escape; the substance that has escaped *–vi., vt.* to allow a substance to escape; to become known or disclosed through unauthorized channels
**leak´age** *n.* a substance that has escaped through a leak; the amount lost through a leak
**leak´y** *adj.* inclined to leak **–leak´i·ness** *n.*
**lean** *adj.* having little fat, as meat; thin or spare, as in body build; without excess or waste, as in business or financial matters *–vi., vt.* to incline or cause to incline **–lean´ly** *adv.* **–lean´ness** *n.*
**lean´ing** *n.* a tendency or preference
**lean´-to** *n.* a makeshift shelter; a structure with a roof that slopes from a high point on one side to the ground on the opposite side
**leap** *vi., vt.* to jump or cause to jump or act abruptly
**learn** *vi., vt.* to acquire knowledge or understanding; to be informed or find out; to memorize **–learn´er** *n.*
**learn´ed** *adj.* scholarly **–learn´ed·ly** *adv.* **–learn´ed·ness** *n.*
**learn´ing** *n.* knowledge or understanding acquired by study
**learning curve** a representation of the time needed to acquire a skill
**lease** *n.* a contract that grants the use of property for a fee *–vt.* to use or grant the use of property by contract **–leas´a·ble** *adj.*
**lease´back** *n.* a contract for leasing sold property back to the seller
**lease´hold** *n.* property controlled by a lease
**leash** *n.* a length of chain, rope, etc. used as a restraint *–vt.* to restrain
**least** *adj.* lowest in rank, importance, or magnitude *–adv.*
**leath´er** *n.* the dressed hide of an animal; a thing made from leather
**leath´er·work** *n.* things made from leather; decorative work on leather **–leath´er·work·er** *n.* **–leath´er·work·ing** *n.*
**leath´er·y** *adj.* having the texture or consistency of leather; tough **–leath´er·i·ness** *n.*
**leave** *n.* consent; a departure *–vt.* to depart; to abandon or overlook, as *to leave behind* or *to leave something out*
**leav´en, leav´en·ing** *n.* a substance such as yeast that causes fermentation
**leav´ings** *n.* the remains or residue
**lech´er·y** *n.* a preoccupation with sex; lust **–lech´er** *n.* **–lech´er·ous** *adj.* **–lech´er·ous·ly** *adv.* **–lech´er·ous·ness** *n.*

**lec´tern** *n.* a stand with a sloping top for holding a speaker's notes

**lec´ture** *n.* an address to a group intended to enlighten; a reprimand *—vi., vt.* to expound on a subject; to deliver a series of talks; to admonish **—lec´tur·er** *n.*

**lec´tur·er** *(Brit.) n.* an educator; an instructor, especially at a college or university

**le´der·ho·sen** *n.* leather shorts

**ledge** *n.* a horizontal projection that forms a shelf

**ledg´er** *n.* a book for recording financial transactions

**lee** *n.* the side away from the wind

**leech** *n.* a worm that feeds on blood; a parasite *—vi.* to affix oneself like a parasite *—vt.* to draw off the resources of

**leer** *n.* a sly look expressing lust *—vi.* to view with lust or maliciousness **—leer´ing·ly** *adv.*

**leer´y** *adj.* wary; distrustful **—leer´i·ness** *n.*

**lee´way** *n.* a margin of space or latitude

**left** *adj.* of the left side of the body; at or toward the left

**left field** the left side of a baseball field as viewed from home plate; a radical view

**left´ist** *n.* a radical *—adj.* liberal or radical

**leg** *n.* a limb on a vertebrate that supports and propels; any similar appendage; the part of clothing that covers the leg; a segment, as of a journey or a contest

**leg´a·cy** *n.* something passed on from an ancestor or predecessor

**le´gal** *adj.* based on, established by, or in conformity with the law **—le´gal·ly** *adv.* **—le·gal´i·ty** *n.*

**le·gal·ese´** *n.* the jargon of the legal profession

**le´gal·ism** *n.* overly strict interpretation or adherence to the law **—le´gal·is´tic** *adj.* **—le·gal·is´ti·cal·ly** *adv.*

**le´gal·ize** *vt.* to make legal; to sanction by law **—le·gal·i·za´tion** *n.*

**legal pad** a writing tablet of ruled sheets, 8½ x 14 inches

**le´gal-size** *adj.* of paper that is 8½ x 14 inches; an envelope, folder, etc. sized to hold legal paper

**legal tender** currency authorized and that must be accepted for the payment of debts

**leg´end** *n.* a popular, often heroic, fable; a celebrated individual or deed; an inscription

**leg´end·ar·y** *adj.* of the nature of a legend; celebrated

**leg´er·de·main´** *n.* sleight of hand; trickery

**leg´gy** *adj.* having long legs

**leg´i·ble** *adj.* clear; able to be read **—leg·i·bil´i·ty, leg´i·ble·ness** *n.* **—leg´i·bly** *adv.*

**le´gion** *n.* a large number; a multitude

**leg´is·late** *vi., vt.* to write or enact laws **—leg´is·la·tor** *n.* **—leg·is·la·to´ri·al** *adj.*

**leg·is·la´tion** *n.* a law or set of laws

**leg´is·la·tive** *adj.* of a governing body; of the making of law **—leg´is·la·tive·ly** *adv.*

**leg´is·la·ture** *n.* a governing body charged with the making of laws

**le·git´** *adj.* legitimate

**le·git´i·mate** *adj.* complying with the law or recognized standards; reasonable or logical: *a legitimate objection, a legitimate conclusion* **—le·git´i·ma·cy** *n.* **—le·git´i·mate·ly** *adv.*

**leg´man** *n.* one whose job it is to gather information, run errands, etc. for others

**leg´room** *n.* space to stretch the legs; room in which to act or maneuver

**leg´ume** *n.* a pod, as of a bean, that splits to reveal seeds **—le·gu´mi·nous** *adj.*

**lei** *n.* a crown or wreath of flowers

**lei´sure** *n.* time free of pressing obligations

**lei´sure·ly** *adj.* characterized by an unhurried or deliberate pace *—adv.* in an unhurried way **—lei´sure·li·ness** *n.*

**lemon law** a law that provides for the repair or replacement of defective products, especially of motor vehicles

**lend** *vt.* to permit the temporary use of; to offer or impart, as *to lend a sense of security* **—lend´er** *n.*

**length** *n.* a measure of distance or duration from beginning to end **—go to great length** to make a significant effort; do all that is necessary

**length´en** *vi., vt.* to become or make longer

**length´y** *adj.* somewhat long in duration; longer than seems necessary **—length´i·ly** *adv.* **—length´i·ness** *n.*

**le´ni·ent** *adj.* indulgent; not strict **—le´nience, le´nien·cy** *n.* **—le´ni·ent·ly** *adv.*

**lens** *n.* transparent material that has been shaped to bend light rays so as to form an image

**le´o·nine** *adj.* having lion-like qualities

**le´o·tard** *n.* a close-fitting one-piece garment worn by gymnasts, dancers, etc.

**lep´er** *n.* one afflicted with leprosy; one shunned as though afflicted **—lep´er·ous** *adj.*

**lep´re·chaun** *n.* a fairy cobbler of Irish folklore

**lep´ro·sy** *n.* a mildly contagious tropical disease that can cause paralysis, numbness, and deformity **—lep·rot´ic** *adj.*

**lep´rous** *adj.* having leprosy **—lep´rous·ly** *adv.* **—lep´rous·ness** *n.*

**les´bi·an** *n.* a homosexual woman **—les´bi·an·ism** *n.*

**le´sion** *n.* a wound or abrasion

**less, less´er** *adj.* smaller or not as important

**les·see´** *n.* one who leases from another

**less´en** *vt., vi.* to make or become less

**les´son** *n.* something learned or to be learned; a formal course of instruction; a part of a course of instruction

**les´sor** *n.* one who leases to another

**let** *vt.* to permit or allow; to rent or lease *—vi.* to be rented or leased

**let´down** *n.* disappointment

**le´thal** *adj.* harmful; able to cause death **–le´thal·ly** *adv.*

**le·thar´gic, le·thar´gi·cal** *adj.* sluggish; listless; apathetic **–le·thar´gi·cal·ly** *adv.*

**leth´ar·gy** *n.* dullness; apathy

**let´ter** *n.* a written symbol; a written communication

**letter bomb** an explosive device sent through the mail

**let´tered** *adj.* learned; inscribed with letters

**let´up** *n.* a pause or lull

**leu·ke´mi·a** *n.* a disease of the blood

**lev´ee** *n.* an embankment along a river or around an irrigated field to prevent runoff

**lev´el** *n.* a relative ranking: *a level of understanding, the upper level of management*; a flat surface; any of a variety of devices for determining deviation from the horizontal *–adj.* having the same relative ranking; determined to be horizontal *–vt.* to make horizontal or flat; to measure deviation from the horizontal, as with a surveyor's instrument **–on the level honest**; fair **–lev´el·ly** *adv.*

**lev´el·head´ed** *adj.* having common sense **–lev´el·head´ed·ly** *adv.* **–lev´el·head´ed·ness** *n.*

**lev´er** *n.* a simple machine used to transfer energy, composed of a rigid rod pivoting on a fulcrum; a protruding handle

**lev´er·age** *n.* an advantage, as provided by a lever; political or financial prominence or power

**leveraged buyout** the use of a company's own assets to finance debt incurred in its acquisition

**le·vi´a·than** *n.* a monster; an exceptionally large specimen

**lev´i·tate** *vi., vt.* to float or cause to float in the air with no visible means of support **–lev·i·ta´tion** *n.* **–lev·i·ta´tion·al** *adj.* **–lev´i·ta·tor** *n.*

**lev´i·ty** *n.* frivolity; flippancy

**lev´y** *vt.* to assess and collect, as taxes or fines *–n.* monies collected

**lewd** *adj.* obscene; depraved **–lewd´ly** *adv.* **–lewd´ness** *n.*

**lex·i·cog´ra·phy** *n.* the work or method of compiling a dictionary **–lex·i·cog´ra·pher** *n.* **–lex´i·co·graph´ic, lex·i·co·graph´i·cal** *adj.* **–lex·i·co·graph´i·cal·ly** *adv.*

**lex´i·con** *n.* a dictionary; a collection of terms peculiar to a particular discipline

**li·a·bil´i·ty** *n.* a debt or obligation for which one is responsible

**li´a·ble** *adj.* legally responsible; at risk: *you are liable to get hurt*; extremely likely: *if I see it, I'm liable to eat it*

**li´ai·son** *n.* a connection or link, especially for communication between groups; one who serves as a link: *the company liaison with the press*; a clandestine affair

**li´ar** *n.* one who deceives by lying

**li·ba´tion** *n.* a beverage **–li·ba´tion·ar·y** *adj.*

**li´bel** *n.* in law, a malicious falsehood, written or printed, that defames *–vt.* **–li´bel·er** *n.*

**li´bel·ous, li´bel·lous** *adj.* based on libel **–li´bel·ous·ly, li´bel·lous·ly** *adv.*

**lib´er·al** *adj.* open to new ideas and concepts; not strict; lavish in giftgiving **–lib´er·al·ly** *adv.* **–lib´er·al·ness** *n.*

**lib´er·al·ize** *vi., vt.* to become or make more liberal: *we need to liberalize out trade policies* **–lib·er·al·i·za´tion** *n.*

**lib´er·ate** *vt.* to set free, as from bondage or onerous convention **–lib´er·a·tor** *n.*

**lib·er·a´tion** *n.* the act of freeing or being set free; the process of seeking equal rights or status **–lib·er·a´tion·ist** *n.*

**lib·er·tar´i·an** *n.* one who believes in freedom of the individual from government intervention

**lib´er·tine** *n.* one who lacks a sense of moral restraint; a reprobate **–lib´er·tin·ism** *n.*

**lib´er·ty** *n.* freedom from restraint or restriction; certain rights granted by custom or legislation

**li·bid´i·nous** *adj.* displaying lust; salacious **–li·bid´i·nous·ly** *adv.* **–li·bid´i·nous·ness** *n.*

**li·bi´do** *n.* the energy associated with inherent biological impulses; sexual appetite **–li·bid´i·nal** *adj.* **–li·bid´i·nal·ly** *adv.*

**li´brar·y** *n.* a collection, as of printed matter, sound or video recordings, computer programs, etc.; the place where such a collection is kept **–li·brar´i·an** *n.*

**li·bret´to** *n.* words set to music or a publication containing those words, such as for an opera **–li·bret´tist** *n.*

**li´cence** *(Brit.)* *n.* legal authorization or a document attesting to such authorization; lack of restraint or adherence to common practice **–li´cense** *vt.* to grant authorization to or for something; to formally permit

**li´cense** *(US)* *n.* legal authorization or a document attesting to such authorization; lack of restraint or adherence to common practice *–vt.* to grant authorization to or for something; to formally permit **–li´cens·a·ble** *adj.* **–li´cens·er, li´cen´sor** *n.* **–li´cens·ee´** *n.*

**li·cen´tious** *adj.* lacking restraint or regard for accepted morality **–li·cen´tious·ly** *adv.* **–li·cen´tious·ness** *n.*

**lic´it** *adj.* legal

**lick** *n.* the act of stroking or touching with, or as with, the tongue; a small amount: *he hasn't a lick of sense*; a blow: *get in your licks* *–vt.* to stroke with the tongue; to touch, as with the tongue: *flames licked the walls*; to overcome: *lick the problem*; to punish by striking

**lick´ing** *n.* a spanking; a hard loss: *the team took a licking*

**lid** *n.* a cover for a container

**lie** *n.* something meant to deceive; the manner in which something is positioned *–vi.* to pass on false information or create a false impression; to recline; to be in a certain place: *the river lies between two hills*

**lien** *n.* the right to property as security for a debt

**lieu·ten´ant** *n.* an officer in a military or quasi-military organization; a deputy or assistant who may act in place of a superior **—lieu·ten´an·cy** *n.*

**life** *n.* the condition of a functioning creature; the time, or any portion of the time, between birth and death; a group of living things, as *plant life*; a particular segment of one's existence, as *social life, artistic life*

**life´-and-death´** *adj.* critical

**life cycle** the stages of development of a living creature

**life expectancy** statistically, the length of time a creature can be expected to live

**life´less** *adj.* dead; inanimate; lacking spirit **—life´less·ly** *adv.* **—life´less·ness** *n.*

**life´like** *adj.* precisely imitating life: *a lifelike portrait*

**life´sav·er** *n.* a person or thing that serves in a crisis

**life style** a mode of living that reflects the values of an individual or group

**lift** *vi.* to rise; to disperse: *the ban was lifted* —*vt.* to raise; to give a ride to; to steal —*n.* an instance of rising; a ride offered to a pedestrian; a rise in condition or attitude

**lift** *(Brit.)* *n.* a structure for raising or lowering people or freight, as in a building; an elevator

**lig´a·ment** *n.* connective tissue of the body; any connective bond **—lig´a·men´ta·ry, lig´a·men´tous** *adj.*

**lig´a·ture** *n.* a cord, thread, bandage, etc. that serves to unite or bind; a symbol created from two or more characters, such as *æ*

**light** *n.* illumination, or its source; clarification: *shed new light*; a source of fire —*vi.* to give off illumination; to start to burn; to dismount, as from a vehicle —*vt.* to cause to give off light; to cause to start to burn —*adj.* illuminated; of color that is less dark; relatively little, as of weight: *a light load*, quantity: *light rain*, force: *a light slap*, etc.; insubstantial: *a light step, light armor* —*adv.*

**light´en** *vi., vt.* to become or make brighter; to become or make less heavy or oppressive

**light´-fin·gered** *adj.* inclined to steal; adept at petty theft

**light´head´ed** *adj.* giddy or faint **—light´head´ed·ly** *adv.* **—light´head´ed·ness** *n.*

**light´heart·ed** *adj.* free of care **—light´heart·ed·ly** *adv.* **—light´heart·ed·ness** *n.*

**light´ing** *n.* the style or fixtures for artificial illumination; the light provided

**light´ly** *adv.* with little exertion; delicately; in a free and easy way

**light´ning** *n.* a natural electric discharge or the flash it makes —*adj.* quick or abrupt

**light pen** an input device for a computer

**light show** a brilliant display of laser light

**light table** a glass-topped table illuminated from below, used to view and work with film, etc.

**light´weight** *n.* a weight class in sports, as boxing; a person lacking in knowledge, ability, etc. —*adj.* relatively light in substance or weight: *a lightweight sweater*

**light´-year** *n.* the distance traveled by light in one earth year

**lig´ne·ous** *adj.* resembling wood

**like** *vt.* to enjoy or be inclined toward —*vi.* to show preference for —*n.* a preference —*adj.* similar —*prep.* in the same or a similar manner **—lik´a·ble, like´a·ble** *adj.* **—lik´a·ble·ness, like´a·ble·ness** *n.*

**like´li·hood** *n.* probability

**like´ly** *adj.* possible or believable

**like´-mind´ed** *adj.* in agreement

**lik´en** *vt.* to compare

**like·ness** *n.* a representation, as a portrait or bust

**like´wise** *adj.* also: *we are likewise interested in the painting*

**lik´ing** *n.* a fondness or preference

**lilt** *n.* a light, cheerful style of speech or song; a jaunty walk —*vi., vt.* to speak or sing in a light, cheerful style

**limb** *n.* an appendage, as the branch of a tree or extremity of an animal

**lim´ber** *adj.* flexible; supple **—lim´ber·ly** *adv.* **—lim´ber·ness** *n.*

**limber up** to flex or make flexible, as a warm-up before heavy exercise

**lime´light** *n.* a center of attention (from an early stage light produced by heating lime)

**lim´er·ick** *n.* a light verse of five lines with the rhyming sequence *aabba*

**lim´it** *n.* the boundary of an area; a restriction or condition; an amount that may not be exceeded: *to the limit of our ability* —*vt.* to confine within a boundary; to firmly establish. as a requisite **—lim´it·a·ble** *adj.*

**lim·i·ta´tion** *n.* a restriction; a deficiency

**lim´it·ed** *adj.* restricted or deficient in some way: *a limited victory*; cramped or confined —*n.* a train that makes only express stops

**limited edition** a work of which only a specified number of copies are produced, as of literature or art, often signed by the maker

**limited war** a conflict to achieve a specific goal short of total conquest

**lim´it·ing** *adj.* serving to limit

**lim´it·less** *adj.* unbounded; without limit; infinite **—lim´it·less·ly** *adj.* **—lim´it·less·ness** *n.*

**lim´o, lim´ou·sine** *n.* a large, elegant automobile, usually chauffeur-driven

**limp** *n.* a hesitant or hobbling gait —*vi.* to move haltingly: *despite cutbacks, we limped along with the remain-*

*ing staff*; to hobble *—adj.* lacking rigidity; lacking strength or vigor: *a limp handshake* **—limp´ly** *adv.* **—limp´ness** *n.*

**lim´pid** *adj.* of a clear and serene liquid, as *a limpid pool*; logical and lucid, as *a limpid account* **—lim´pid·ly** *adv.* **—lim´pid·ness** *n.*

**line** *n.* a stripe made by a writing instrument; any similar mark; a real or imaginary stripe between fixed points: *a firing line*; things formed in a row or a series; a sequence; the material used to form a connection: *phone line, electric line*; a transportation system; an area of competence or employment: *a line of work*; a row of words or symbols; a brief note; a concept or notion: *thinking along another line* *—vt.* to cover the interior: *to line a jacket*

**lin´e·age** *n.* ancestry

**lin´e·al** *adj.* directly descended from an ancestor; relating to a particular lineage **—lin´e·al·ly** *adv.*

**lin´e·ar** *adj.* in a line; one-dimensional **—lin´e·ar·ly** *adv.*

**lin´en** *n.* cloth or articles made from flax thread *—adj.* made of or resembling linen

**linen closet** a storage area for bedding, tablecloths, etc.

**lin´er** *n.* material that covers the inside, as of a coat; a large passenger ship or airplane

**lines´man** *n.* a sports official who judges from the sideline

**line´up** *n.* persons assembled for identification; a group of people identified with a common purpose: *a lineup of backers, a lineup of players*

**lin´ger** *vi.* to remain longer than anticipated; to be slow to act **—lin´ger·er** *n.* **—lin´ger·ing·ly** *adv.*

**lin·ge·rie´** *n.* women's underclothing

**lin´go** *n.* an unfamiliar or specialized language or vocabulary

**lin´guist** *n.* one who speaks several languages; an authority in linguistics

**lin·guis´tics** *n.* the study of human speech **—lin·guis´tic** *adj.* **—lin·guis´ti·cal·ly** *adv.*

**lin´i·ment** *n.* a liquid rubbed on the skin to relieve pain or tension

**lin´ing** *n.* material that covers the inside, as of a coat

**link** *n.* one of a series: *a link in a chain*; a connector: *a communications link* *—vi., vt.* to connect

**linked** *adj.* connected in some way

**li·no´le·um** *n.* a durable floor covering

**lint** *n.* bits of fiber shed from woven material; downy fibers from linen, used to dress wounds **—lint´y** *adj.*

**lin´tel** *n.* the brace at the top of a window or door frame

**li´on** *n.* a large carniverous feline; a person distinguished for bravery; a celebrity

**li´on·heart´ed** *adj.* extremely brave **—li´on·heart·ed·ness** *n.*

**li´on·ize** *vt.* to treat as a celebrity **—li·on·i·za´tion** *n.*

**lip** *n.* the fleshy structure surrounding the mouth; a part that surrounds an opening; impertinent speech

**lip service** professed agreement without supporting action

**liq´ue·fy** *vi., vt.* to become or make liquid

**li·queur´** *n.* an alcoholic beverage, usually sweet and flavored with fruit, herbs, or spices

**liq´uid** *adj.* flowing or capable of flowing; of assets readily convertible into cash **—li·quid´i·ty** *n.*

**liq´ui·date** *vt.* to discharge, as an obligation; to convert into cash; to destroy *—vi.* to close out a business, etc. by disposing of its assets; **—liq´ui·da´tion** *n.* **—liq´ui·da·tor** *n.*

**li´quor** *(US)* *n.* a distilled alcoholic beverage; liquid obtained from cooking

**lisle** *n.* a fine cotton fabric

**lisp** *n.* a speech defect typified by difficulty in articulating the sounds of s and z *—vi., vt.* to speak with a lisp **—lisp´er** *n.*

**list** *n.* a catalog or roster of items, as for shopping, things to do, etc.; a tilting to one side *—vt.* to itemize; to cause to tilt *—vi.* to tilt to one side

**lis´ten** *n.* to be attentive; to heed **—lis´ten·er** *n.*

**lis´ten·a·ble** *adj.* reasonably pleasing to the ear: *despite its flaws the recording is listenable* **—lis·ten·a·bil´i·ty** *n.*

**list´less** *adj.* lacking vitality or spirit; apathetic, indifferent **—list´less·ly** *adv* **—list´less·ness** *n.*

**list price** the selling price of an item as recommended by the manufacturer

**lit´a·ny** *n.* a responsive prayer; something often repeated: *a litany of acclamation*

**li´ter** *(US)* *n.* a unit of volume equal to approximately 33.8 ounces

**lit´er·a·cy** *n.* education, as the ability to read and write

**lit´er·al** *adj.* precise in interpretation; verbatim **—lit´er·al·ness** *n.*

**lit´er·al·ly** *adv. precisely; word for word*

**lit´er·ar·y** *adj.* relating to or fond of literature **—lit´er·ar·i·ly** *adv.* **—lit´er·ar·i·ness** *n.*

**lit´er·ate** *adj.* educated; well-informed **—lit´er·ate·ly** *adv.* **—lit´er·ate·ness** *n.*

**lit·e·ra´ti** *n. pl.* cultivated or well educated people collectively

**lit´er·a·ture** *n.* printed matter; a collection of writings

**lithe, lithe´some** *adj.* supple or graceful **—lithe´ly, lithe´some·ly** *adv.* **—lithe´ness, lithe´some·ness** *n.*

**lith´o·graph** *n.* a print made by lithography *—vt.* to print by lithography **—lith´o·graph´ic, lith·o·graph´i·cal** *adj.* **—lith·o·graph´i·cal·ly** *adv.*

**li·thog´ra·phy** *n.* a process for printing fine reproductions **—li·thog´ra·pher** *n.*

**lit´i·gant** *n.* one involved in a lawsuit *—adj.* engaged in a lawsuit

**lit´i·gate** *vi., vt.* to take part in or bring about legal action **–lit´i·ga·ble** *adj.* **–lit·i·ga´tion** *n.* **–lit´i·ga·tor** *n.*

**li·ti´gious** *adj.* tending to be involved in legal action **–li·ti´gious·ly** *adv.* **–li·ti´gious·ness** *n.*

**litmus test** a chemical test using litmus to determine acidity; a test that uses a single determinant to reach a conclusion

**li´tre** *(Brit.) n.* a unit of volume equal to approximately 33.8 US ounces

**lit´ter** *n.* heedlessly discarded trash; the animal young from a single birth; material used to line the cage of an animal; a framework for transporting goods or a person *–vi., vt.* to scatter, as trash

**lit´tle** *n.* a small amount *–adj.* modest in size or amount; unimportant *–adv.* slightly; not at all **–lit´tle·ness** *n.*

**little theater** an experimental theater or community playhouse

**lit´ur·gy** *n.* a set form for worship or ritual **–li·tur´gi·cal** *adj.* **–li·tur´gi·cal·ly** *adv.*

**liv´a·ble, live´a·ble** *adj.* suitable for habitation; acceptable or tolerable **–liv´a·ble·ness, live´a·ble·ness** *n.*

**live** *vi.* to possess life; to exist *–adj.* having life; useable, having potential, as *live ammunition, live wires, live copy*; physically present, as *a live show, a live audience*

**live´-in** *adj.* having lodging in one's place of employment; living with another

**live´li·hood** *n.* one's means of support

**live´ly** *adj.* marked by energy and spirit; active: *a lively imagination –adv.* **–live´li·ness** *n.*

**liv´en** *vi., vt.* to become or make lively

**liv´er·ied** *adj.* uniformed

**liv´er·wurst** *n.* a sausage made of ground liver

**liv´er·y** *n.* a uniform; the care and boarding of horses; a service that rents out vehicles, such as boats or automobiles

**live´stock** *n.* domestic animals

**live wire** *n.* an electric wire attached to a power source; a person who is dynamic or energetic

**liv´id** *adj.* extremely angry **–li·vid´i·ty, liv´id·ness** *n.* **–liv´id·ly** *adv.*

**liv´ing** *adj.* having life or existence; pertaining to existence: *living conditions –n.* the condition of being alive; the means to support life

**living wage** earnings sufficient to provide the necessities of life

**living will** *n.* a will stipulating action to be taken if the maker is alive but unable to respond on his or her own behalf

**load** *n.* weight or volume that is carried, supported, etc.; a burden of work or responsibility *–vi., vt.* to put or place into or on

**load´ed** *adj.* having or carrying a full load; having a troublesome or hidden meaning

**loaf** *n.* an oblong mass, as *a loaf of bread* or *meat loaf*

**loaf´er** *n.* one who is frequently inactive or unemployed **–loaf** *vi.*

**loan** *n.* something given or received for temporary use **–loan´er** *n.*

**loan shark** one who lends money at a high rate of interest

**loath** *adj.* hesitant or reluctant

**loathe** *vt.* to despise **–loath´er** *n.* **–loath´ing·ly** *adv.*

**loath´ing** *n.* profound aversion

**loath´some** *adj.* arousing intense dislike **–loath´some·ly** *adv.* **–loath´some·ness** *n.*

**lob´by** *(US) n.* an entryway or waiting room; persons attempting to influence others to support a cause *–vi., vt.* to attempt to influence, as legislators **–lob´by·ist** *n.*

**lo´cal** *adj.* of a specific, relatively small area or political subdivision; contained, not widespread *–n.* a regional chapter of a lodge, labor union, etc.; a train that stops at every station **–lo´cal·ly** *adv.*

**lo·cale´** *n.* a location, as a site or setting for an event

**lo·cal´i·ty** *n.* a particular place

**lo´cal·ize** *vt.* to restrict to a particular area **–lo·cal·i·za´tion** *n.*

**local option** a provision of a law that permits a local jurisdiction to adopt or reject enforcement within its jurisdiction

**lo´cate** *vi.* to situate, as a home or business *–vt.* to learn the position of; to assign to a place **–lo·cat´a·ble** *adj.* **–lo·cat´er** *n.*

**lo·ca´tion** *n.* a place or position; a place designated for a specific use

**lock** *n.* a device or means of securing; a closed section of a channel where the water level can be raised or lowered to match the level of the next section; a piece of hair *–vi., vt.* to become or make secure, as with a lock; to become or make immobile; to link together

**lock´er** *n.* a storage compartment

**lock´et** *n.* a small hinged case hanging on a necklace

**lock´out** *n.* the closing of a workplace to striking employees

**lo·co·mo´tion** *n.* the act of moving from one place to another

**lo·co·mo´tive** *adj.* able to move from place to place *–n.* a self-propelled engine

**lo·cu´tion** *n.* a manner of speech

**lode** *n.* a mineral deposit; an abundant source

**lodge** *n.* a rustic dwelling; a meeting hall *–vi., vt.* to temporarily live in or provide living space; to place or plant, as for safekeeping

**lodg´ing** *n.* a place to live, usually temporary **–lodg´er** *n.*

**loft** *n.* a large, open storage area directly under the roof of a building; a gallery or alcove: *choir loft*

**loft´y** *adj.* tall or towering; arrogant or haughty —**loft´i·ly** *adv.* —**loft´i·ness** *n.*

**log** *n.* a roughly trimmed tree trunk or large branch; a record, as of performance or progress —*vt.* to set down in writing; to accumulate, as time or distance: *logged 2000 miles on the trip*

**log´book** *n.* a book for recording official data relating to the operation of a ship, aircraft, etc.

**loge** *n.* the front rows of the mezzanine or a box in a theater

**log´ic** *n.* the fundamentals of reasoning, without regard to content or effectiveness; sound reasoning; the comparable functions in a computer program

**log´i·cal** *adj.* capable of analytical thought; reasonable, based on the information available —**log·i·cal´i·ty, log´i·cal·ness** *n.* —**log´i·cal·ly** *adv.*

**lo·gis´tics** *n.* planning and managing the details of an operation

**lo´go, log´o·type** *n.* the symbol or trademark of a business or organization

**lo´gy** *adj.* lethargic; muddled, as though awakening from sleep

**loi´ter** *vi.* to loll or linger about; to waste time —**loi´ter·er** *n.* —**loi´ter·ing·ly** *adv.*

**loll** *vi.* to move or lie about in a relaxed fashion —**loll´ing·ly** *adv.*

**lone** *adj.* without anyone or anything else; lacking companionship

**lone´ly** *adj.* saddened by being alone; deserted: *a lonely wasteland* —**lone´li·ly** *adv.* —**lone´li·ness** *n.*

**lon´er** *n.* one who works alone or shuns the company of others

**lone´some** *adj.* lonely —**lone´some·ly** *adv.* —**lone´some·ness** *n.*

**lone wolf** one who works alone; one who avoids the company of others

**long** *vi.* to have a craving or desire —*adj.* relatively lengthy, as of distance, height, time, etc.; of specific length or duration: *six inches long, two hours long* —*adv.*

**lon·gev´i·ty** *n.* long life or duration —**lon·ge´vous** *adj.*

**long face** a gloomy expression

**long´hair** *n.* one with a refined taste in art, especially music —**long´hair, long´haired** *adj.*

**long´hand** *n.* cursive writing

**long haul** a significant length of time or distance —**long´-haul´** *adj.*

**long´ing** *n.* a craving or desire —**long´ing·ly** *adv.*

**lon´gi·tude** *n.* an angular distance, as from the prime meridian or a celestial body

**lon·gi·tu´di·nal** *adj.* of longitude; running lengthwise —**lon·gi·tu´di·nal·ly** *adv.*

**long´-last´ing, long´-lived´** *adj.* continuing a long time

**long´-range´** *adj.* of a long span of time or distance: *long-range planning*

**long´shore·man** *n.* a dock worker

**long shot** a venture that holds little prospect of success

**long´-stand´ing** *adj.* lasting; of long duration

**long´-suf´fer·ing** *adj.* uncomplaining; patiently enduring hardship —**long´-suf´fer·ing·ly** *adv.*

**long suit** one's greatest asset

**long´-term** *adj.* involving an extended span of time: *long-term planning*

**long´-wind·ed** *adj.* wordy or tiresome —**long´-wind·ed·ly** *adv.* —**long´-wind·ed·ness** *n.*

**loo´fa, loo´fah** *n.* the dried spongelike part of the fruit of a tropical vine, used for cleansing the skin

**look** *n.* a gaze, stare, glance, etc.; appearance or fashion —*vi.* to use eyesight; to occupy one's attention: *look after the dog*; to seek out or search; to appear to be: *look happy* —*vt.* to turn one's eyes to; to appear to be: *looks the part*

**loom** *vi.* to appear and hover over; to menace

**loon, loo´ny** *n.* a foolish or insane person

**loo´ny** *adj.* foolish or insane

**loop** *n.* a length of material formed into a circular pattern; the shape so described; a circle —*vi., vt.* to form or fasten into a circle; to move in a circular pattern —**looped** *adj.*

**loop´hole** *n.* an oversight, as in the law, that provides a means of escape or avoidance

**loose** *adj.* not attached or confined; poorly attached or fitted: *a loose screw, loose clothing*; lacking discipline: *loose morals*; vague: *a loose interpretation* —*vi., vt.* to become or make less restrained; to release —**loose´ly** *adv.* —**loose´ness** *n.*

**loose end** an unresolved detail

**loos´en** *vi., vt.* to become or make loose or looser

**loot** *n.* stolen goods —*vi., vt.* to plunder —**loot´er** *n.*

**lop** *vt.* to cut off or eliminate

**lope** *n.* a leisurely gait —*vi.*

**lop´sid·ed** *adj.* bulkier or heavier on one side; tipped to one side —**lop·sid·ed·ly** *adv.* —**lop´sid·ed·ness** *n.*

**lo·qua´cious** *adj.* talkative —**lo·qua´cious·ly** *adv.* —**lo·qua´cious·ness, lo·quac´i·ty** *n.*

**lord** *n.* one of high rank or power; a god —*vi.* to domineer

**lord´ly** *adj.* majestic or noble; pretentious or arrogant; domineering —**lord´li·ness** *n.*

**lore** *n.* collected traditions or wisdom, as of a culture; knowledge

**lor·gnette´** *n.* corrective lenses mounted on a short handle

**lose** *vt.* to be deprived of, as through carelessness, theft, or legal action; unable to keep: *lose one's life, lose respect*; to rid oneself of: *lose weight, lose a pursuer* —*vi.* to endure loss —**los´er** *n.*

**loss** *n.* deprivation; something taken away, misplaced,

wasted, etc.

**loss leader** something offered at a low price to attract customers

**lost** *adj.* no longer in one's possession; no longer in evidence

**lot** *n.* a group of associated things; a large amount; one of a quantity of tokens used for selecting at random; one's fate as though chosen by lot; a plot or parcel of land, especially one occupied by or intended for a residence

**lo´tion** *n.* a liquid applied externally as medication or cosmetic

**lot´ter•y** *n.* a selection made by lot

**loud** *adj.* designating of high amplification; of bright colors or glaringly bad design, as clothing **–loud´ly** *adv.* **–loud´ness** *n.*

**loud´en** *vi., vt.* to become or make louder

**loud´mouth** *n.* one who speaks loudly or thoughtlessly **–loud´mouthed** *adj.*

**lounge** *n.* a waiting room; a tavern or cafe attached to a hotel or restaurant; a type of couch with no back and a headrest at one end *–vi., vt.* to recline or pass time leisurely **–loung´er** *n.*

**loupe** *n.* a small, powerful magnifying glass used by printers, jewelers, etc.

**louse** *n.* a tiny, parasitic insect; a disreputable person *–vt.* to botch or fumble

**lous´y** *adj.* infested, as with lice; of poor quality or taste; unpleasant **–lous´i•ly** *adv.* **–lous´i•ness** *n.*

**lout** *n.* one regarded as ill-mannered or tiresome **–lout´ish** *adj.* **–lout´ish•ly** *adv.* **–lout´ish•ness** *n.*

**lou´ver** *n.* an opening for ventilation having angled slats to keep out rain

**lov´a•ble, love´a•ble** *adj.* having qualities that invite affection **–lov•a•bil´i•ty, lov´a•ble•ness** *n.* **–lov´a•bly** *adv.*

**love** *n.* a strong attraction brought about by affection or desire; an object of affection or desire; sexual intercourse *–vt.* to have an affection or desire for; to engage in sexual intercourse

**love affair** an intimate relationship; a strong attraction: *America's love affair with the automobile*

**love child** a child born out of wedlock

**love feast** a symbolic meal intended to promote friendship

**love´-in** *n.* a symbolic gathering intended to promote love and understanding

**love´lorn** *adj.* deprived of love or a lover

**love´ly** *adj.* beautiful and charming; something attractive or appealing *–adv.* **–love´li•ness** *n.*

**lov´er** *n.* one who is devoted to another person, activity, etc.; a sexual partner

**love seat** a seat for two people

**love´sick** *adj.* distracted by love **–love´sick•ness** *n.*

**lov´ing** *adj.* affectionate **–lov´ing•ly** *adv.*

**loving cup** a decorative urn, often one given as an award

**low** *adj.* of less than usual or acceptable height, amount, quality, etc. *–adv.*

**low´ball** *vi., vt.* to understate or underbid *–adj.*

**low blow** an unfair or unprincipled attack

**low´born** *adj.* of humble birth

**low´boy** *n.* a low chest of drawers

**low´bred** *adj.* unrefined

**low´brow** *n.* one having unrefined tastes *–adj.* suited to an unrefined person

**low´-budg´et** *adj.* produced at little cost; inferior, second-rate

**low´-cal´** *adj.* having less than the normal amount of calories

**low comedy** burlesque or slapstick comedy

**low´down** *n.* gossip; latest information

**low´-down** *adj.* base; contemptible

**low´-end** *adj.* among the lowest in price or quality

**low´er** *adj.* less in price, quality, position, etc. *–n.* a menacing look *–vi., vt.* to become or make less; to appear or look menacing **–low´er•ing•ly** *adv.*

**lowest common denominator** the lowest number evenly divisible by a group of fractions; that which is understood or accepted by most of the people in a population

**low´-grade´** *adj.* of poor quality

**low´-key´** *adj.* restrained; subdued

**low´-lev´el** *adj.* of little importance, intensity, etc.

**low´life** *n.* a disreputable person

**low´ly** *adj.* unpretentious; humble in nature or rank *–adv.* **–low´li•ness** *n.*

**low´-pres•sure** *adj.* relaxed; easygoing

**low´-pro´file** *adj.* of a deed or activity performed quietly so as to avoid undue attention

**low´-spir•it•ed** *adj.* depressed; lacking vitality **–low´-spir•it•ed•ly** *adv.* **–low´-spir•it•ed•ness** *n.*

**low-tech, low-technology** *adj.* of a device, system, etc. that does not employ or require a modern system or technique

**low´-tick´et** *adj.* relatively inexpensive

**lox** *n.* smoked salmon

**loy´al** *adj.* marked by allegiance to a person, organization, etc.; faithful **–loy´al•ist** *n.* **–loy´al•ly** *adv.* **–loy´al•ty** *n.*

**loz´enge** *n.* a medicated candy

**lu´au** *n.* a traditional Hawaiian feast

**lube** *vt.* to lubricate

**lu´bri•cate** *vt.* to apply a substance to moving parts to reduce friction **–lu´bri•cant** *n.* **–lu•bri•ca´tion** *n.*

**lu´cent** *adj.* clear or transparent; luminous **–lu´cen•cy** *n.* **–lu´cent•ly** *adv.*

**lu´cid** *adj.* clear; easily understood; sane or rational **–lu•cid´i•ty, lu´cid•ness** *n.* **–lu´cid•ly** *adv.*

**luck** *n.* the chance events that act upon one's life

**luck´i·ly** *adv.* by good fortune

**luck´y** *adj.* having or bringing good fortune —**luck´i·ness** *n.*

**lu´cra·tive** *adj.* profitable —**lu´cra·tive·ly** *adv.* —**lu´cra·tive·ness** *n.*

**lu´cre** *n.* money

**lu´di·crous** *adj.* incongruous; laughable —**lu´di·crous·ly** *adv.* —**lu´di·crous·ness** *n.*

**lug** *vi., vt.* to pull or carry with difficulty

**luge** *n.* a racing sled

**lug´gage** *n.* bags for carrying a traveler's personal effects; all of the effects carried by a traveler

**lu·gu´bri·ous** *adj.* extravagantly melancholy or somber; mournful —**lu·gu´bri·ous·ly** *adv.* —**lu·gu´bri·ous·ness** *n.*

**luke´warm** *adj.* slightly warm; lacking enthusiasm: *a lukewarm response* —**luke´warm·ly** *adv.* —**luke´warm·ness** *n.*

**lull** *n.* a period of relative quiet or calm —*vt.* to calm or quiet, as one's fears

**lull´a·by** *n.* a song that soothes or quiets, especially for a child

**lum´ber** *(Brit.) n.* unwanted items —*vi.* to move clumsily; to plod

**lum´ber** *(US) n.* wooden boards, molding, etc. used in construction —*vi.* to move clumsily; to plod

**lu´mi·nar·y** *n.* one who is distinguished; one who serves as a model for others

**lu·mi·nes´cence** *n.* light accompanied by relatively little heat —**lu·mi·nes´cent** *adj.*

**lu´mi·nous** *adj.* giving off light; brightly illuminated; easily understood —**lu·mi·nos´i·ty, lu´mi·nous·ness** *n.* —**lu´mi·nous·ly** *adv.*

**lump** *n.* a bulge or swelling; a clump or piece of something, often oddly shaped; a total amount —*adj.* complete: *a lump sum* —*vt.* to compile or consider as a whole: *they lump all expenses into a single category*

**lump´y** *adj.* not smooth, as of a sauce; not comfortably, as of a mattress —**lump´i·ness** *n.*

**lu´na·cy** *n.* madness; foolishness or silliness —**lu´na·tic** *n., adj.*

**lu´nar** *adj.* involving the moon

**lunar eclipse** an obscuring of the moon caused by the earth passing between the sun and the moon

**lunar month** the average time between new moons

**lunatic fringe** fanatical members of a group

**lunch** *n.* a midday meal —*vi.* to eat a midday meal —**lunch´er** *n.*

**lunch´eon** *n.* a midday gathering for a light meal

**lunch´eon·ette´** *n.* an eatery where light, simple meals are served

**luncheon meat, lunchmeat** processed meat served cold, usually on a sandwich

**lunge** *n.* a sudden thrust —*vi., vt.* to thrust or cause to thrust forward suddenly

**lunk´head** *n.* someone regarded as slow or stupid

**lurch** *n.* a sudden jerking movement; an unsteady gait —*vi.* to move jerkily; to walk with an unsteady gait —**lurch´ing·ly** *adv.*

**lure** *n.* an attraction or enticement —*vt.* to attract or entice, especially with an inducement

**lu´rid** *adj.* gruesome or ghastly; pale or sallow —**lu´rid·ly** *adv.* —**lu´rid·ness** *n.*

**lurk** *vi.* to prowl stealthily; to lie in wait unnoticed —**lurk´er** *n.* —**lurk´ing·ly** *adv.*

**lus´cious** *adj.* sweet and juicy; beautiful or sensuous —**lus´cious·ly** *adv.* —**lus´cious·ness** *n.*

**lush** *adj.* characterized by abundance, as of vegetation; luxurious or extravagant —**lush´ly** *adv.* —**lush´ness** *n.*

**lust** *n.* an intense craving —*vi.* to have an intense desire, especially sexual —**lust´ful** *adj.* —**lust´ful·ly** *adv.* —**lust´ful·ness** *n.*

**lus´ter** *(US),* **lus´tre** *(Brit.) n.* radiance; brilliance; the gloss on pottery achieved by glazing —*vt.* to apply a glaze —*vi.* to become glossy —**lus´trous** *adj.* —**lus´trous·ly** *adv.* —**lus´trous·ness** *n.*

**lust´y** *adj.* robust; boisterous —**lust´i·ly** *adj.* —**lust´i·ness** *n.*

**lux·u´ri·ant** *adj.* marked by abundant growth; characterized by extravagance —**lux·u´ri·ance** *n.* —**lux·u´ri·ant·ly** *adv.*

**lux·u´ri·ate** *vi.* to revel in pleasure or luxury

**lux·u´ri·ous** *adj.* characterized by extravagance or indulgence —**lux·u´ri·ous·ly** *adv.* —**lux·u´ri·ous·ness** *n.*

**lux´u·ry** *n.* something that is not a necessity, but that contributes to one's comfort and enjoyment

**lynch** *vt.* to execute by hanging without due process of law —**lynch´ing** *n.*

**lyr´ic** *adj.* of poetry or verse set to music that expresses deep emotion

**lyr´i·cal** *adj.* melodious or poetic —**lyr´i·cal·ly** *adv.* —**lyr´i·cal·ness** *n.*

**lyr´i·cist, lyr´ist** *n.* one who writes song lyrics

**m, M** thirteenth letter of the English alphabet; the symbol for 1000 in Roman characters

**ma·ca´bre** *adj.* gruesome; horrible; associated with death

**mac·ad´am** *n.* a type of road covering consisting of stones bound with asphalt —**mac·ad·am·i·za´tion** *n.* —**mac·ad´am·ize** *vt.*

**mac·a·ro´ni** *n.* a type of pasta formed into short, hollow tubes

**mac´a·roon´** *n.* a cookie flavored with almond or coconut

**mace** *n.* a medieval war club; a ceremonial scepter; an aromatic spice obtained from the outer shell of the nutmeg seed

**mac´er·ate** *vi., vt.* to become or make soft by soaking **—mac·er·a´tion** *n.* **—mac´er·a·tor** *n.*

**ma·chet´e** *n.* a large knife used mainly for cutting brush, etc.

**Mach·i·a·vel´li·an** *adj.* marked by cunning and duplicity

**mach´i·nate** *vt.* to plot **—mach·i·na´tion** *n.* **—mach´i·na·tor** *n.*

**ma·chine´** *n.* a mechanical device that modifies and transfers energy; broadly, any contrivance that aids in performing a task; anything or anyone that performs in a standardized or predictable manner *—adj.* of or like a mechanical device *—vi., vt.* to fashion or be fashioned by a mechanical device **—ma·chin´er·y** *n.* **—ma·chin´ist** *n.*

**machine language** basic computer instructions

**machine shop** a workshop for fashioning or repairing machines

**machine tool** a power-driven tool

**ma·chis´mo** *n.* an inflated notion or display of masculinity

**ma´cho** *adj.* characterized by excessively masculine behavior *—n.* a male overly impressed with displays of masculinity or virility

**mack´i·naw** *n.* a heavy woolen coat

**mack´in·tosh** *n.* a raincoat

**mac´ra·mé´** *n.* coarsely knotted thread or cord

**mac´ro** *n.* a macroinstruction: a single computer command that triggers a series of actions

**mac·ro·bi·ot´ics** *n.* the promotion of good health and well-being by regulation of the diet **—mac·ro·bi·ot´ic** *adj.* **—mac·ro·bi·ot´ic·al·ly** *adv.*

**mac´ro·cosm** *n.* the universe; any large, multifaceted aggregate **—mac´ro·cos´mic** *adj.*

**mac´ro·scop´ic, mac·ro·scop´i·cal** *adj.* large enough to be seen with the naked eye **—mac·ro·scop´i·cal·ly** *adv.*

**mad** *adj.* angry; insane or acting as though insane; lacking sound judgment; expressing strong emotion, especially anger

**mad´am** *n.* a polite form for addressing a woman

**mad´cap** *adj.* wild and reckless; uninhibited

**mad´den** *vi., vt.* to become or make angry

**mad´den·ing** *adj.* tending to cause anger **—mad´den·ing·ly** *adv.*

**made** *adj.* fashioned or produced, often in combined form: *American-made, handmade*

**made´-to-or´der** *adj.* fashioned according to furnished instructions or specifications; well-suited: *a made-to-order solution*

**made´-up´** *adj.* fictitious; complete

**mad´house** *n.* a place of disorganization and chaos

**mad´ly** *adj.* in a foolish or frenzied manner

**mad´man** *n.* one who acts in an insane manner

**mad´ness** *n.* insanity; excessive enthusiasm

**ma·dras´** *n.* a cotton cloth woven in a variety of colors and designs

**mad´ri·gal** *n.* a vocal composition for several voices **—mad´ri·gal·ist** *n.*

**mael´strom** *n.* a large whirlpool; a turbulent situation

**mae´stro** *n.* a master, especially a renowned musician

**mag´a·zine´** *n.* a printed periodical; a storehouse; a storage compartment, as for film or tape

**mag´got** *n.* an insect larva; a grub

**mag´ic** *n.* a display of supernatural power; sorcery; entertainment using sleight of hand, misdirection, illusion, etc.; a mystifying quality or ability: *the magic of her music —adj.* relating to the supernatural; mystical **—mag´i·cal** *adj.* **—mag´i·cal·ly** *—adv.* **ma·gi´cian** *n.*

**mag´is·trate** *n.* a local official such as a justice of the peace **—mag·is·te´ri·al** *adj.* **—mag·is·te´ri·al·ly** *adv.* **—mag´is·tral** *adj.*

**mag´is·tra·cy** *n.* the office of a magistrate; the area under the jurisdiction of a magistrate

**mag´ma** *n.* molten rock that forms part of the earth's core

**mag·na·nim´i·ty** *n.* an act of generosity or forgiveness

**mag·nan´i·mous** *adj.* generous and noble of spirit; inclined to forgive **—mag·nan´i·mous·ly** *adv.* **—mag·nan´i·mous·ness** *n.*

**mag´nate** *n.* a prominent industrialist

**mag´net** *n.* an object surrounded by a magnetic field; anything that tends to attract

**mag·net´ic** *adj.* having power to attract **—mag·net´i·cal·ly** *adv.*

**magnetic field** the area of force surrounding a magnet

**magnetic north** the direction of one of the earth's magnetic poles; the direction in which the arrow on a magnetic compass points

**magnetic pole** one of two areas on a magnet where the force is most concentrated

**mag´net·ism** *n.* the energy of a magnet; the power to attract

**mag´net·ize** *vt.* to make magnetic; to fascinate or attract, as if by a magnet: *magnetized by her beauty* **—mag´net·iz·a·ble** *adj.* **—mag·net·i·za´tion** *n.*

**mag·ne´to** *n.* a device that converts direct current to alternating current

**mag´ne·tron** *n.* a tube that produces microwave radiation, used in cooking

**mag·ni·fi·ca´tion** *n.* an enlarged image; the amount by which an image has been made larger

**mag·nif´i·cence** *n.* grandeur or luxuriousness

**mag·nif´i·cent** *adj.* majestic or noble, as in appearance, word, or deed; exceptionally good: *a magnificent day* **—mag·nif´i·cent·ly** *adv.*

**mag´ni·fy** *vt.* to make larger or make appear larger **—mag´ni·fi·er** *n.*

**mag´ni·tude** *n.* size or extent; importance

**mag´num** *n.* a wine bottle that holds 1.5 *liters*
**magnum opus** a masterpiece
**maid´en** *n.* an unmarried woman *—adj.* pertaining to or befitting a maiden; unmarried; original or beginning: *a maiden voyage* **—maid´en·ly** *adj.*
**mail** *(US) n.* letters, packages, etc. accepted for delivery by the postal system *—vi., vt.* to send via the postal system **—mail·a·bil´i·ty** *adv.* **—mail´a·ble** *adj.*
**mail drop** a place where mail is delivered and held for an addressee, usually referring to a place other than one's home or business
**mail´er** *n.* one who uses the mails, especially in large volume for advertising, solicitation, etc.; a person or company that prepares mail in volume for delivery to the postal service; a container for items to be mailed, as a tube, padded envelope, etc.; a piece or package of commercial mail
**mail´ing** *n.* a large volume of like pieces sent at one time
**mail order** the business of buying or selling by mail
**maim** *vt.* to mutilate or disable
**main** *adj.* most significant *—n.* the dominant part; a large pipe or conduit; the open sea **—might and main** physical strength
**main drag** *(US)* the principal street or road in an area
**main´frame** *n.* a large computer designed to serve numerous terminals
**main´land** *n.* a large body of land; a continent, as distinguished from an island **—main´land·er** *n.*
**main´ly** *adv.* largely; predominantly
**main´stream** *n.* the dominant or accepted views of a community or group *—adj.* conventional or traditional
**main·tain´** *vt.* to uphold; to preserve in an existing or desired state, as *to maintain order* **—main·tain´a·ble** *adj.*
**main´te·nance** *n.* the care required to preserve in good order
**maî´tre d´, maî´tre d´hô·tel´** *n.* a headwaiter
**ma·jes´tic, ma·jes´ti·cal** *adj.* stately or dignified in manner; magnificent **—ma·jes´ti·cal·ly** *adv.* **—ma·jes´ti·cal·ness** *n.*
**maj´es·ty** *n.* the grandeur and nobility of a sovereign; elegance or splendor; "*...purple mountains' majesty...*"
**ma·jol´i·ca** *n.* a type of Italian pottery
**ma´jor** *n.* a rank in a military or quasi-military organization *—adj.* among the most important: *a major talent*; of exceptional scope, size, etc.
**ma·jor·do´mo** *n.* the chief steward of a household; a butler
**ma·jor´i·ty** *n.* a number greater than half; a political group that controls more than half the votes on an issue; legally of age
**make** *vi., vt.* to assemble or fashion; to create or produce; to cause **—mak´er** *n.*
**make´-be·lieve** *n.* a flight of fancy *—adj.* fanciful
**make´-do, make´shift** *n.* a convenient substitute *—adj.* temporary; provisional
**make´up** *n.* the manner in which something is arranged or constituted; cosmetics; a school assignment or test that compensates for missing or unsatisfactory work
**make´-work** *n.* low priority tasks intended to fill a worker's idle time
**mal´ad·just´ed** *adj.* poorly adjusted, especially to the stresses of life **—mal´ad·just´ment** *n.*
**mal´a·droit´** *adj.* inept; unskilled **—mal·a·droit´ly** *adv.* **—mal·a·droit´ness** *n.*
**mal´a·dy** *n.* an ailment or affliction
**mal·aise´** *n.* a feeling of uneasiness or despondency
**mal´a·prop·ism** *n.* incorrect use of a word by mistaking it for another that sounds similar
**ma·lar´ia** *n.* an infectious disease characterized by alternating chills and fever **—ma·lar´i·al** *adj.*
**mal´con·tent** *n.* one who is habitually disgruntled; an agitator *—adj.* disgruntled; discontent
**male** *adj.* of the sex that fertilizes the eggs of the female; masculine; of a coupling device designed to fit into a recess or socket *—n.* a male person, animal, or plant
**mal·e·dic´tion** *n.* a curse **—mal·e·dic´to·ry** *adj.*
**mal´e·fac´tor** *n.* a criminal **—mal´e·fac´tion** *n.*
**ma·lef´ic** *adj.* evil
**ma·lef´i·cence** *n.* a hurtful or wicked quality; doing mischief
**ma·lef´i·cent** *adj.* harmful or hurtful; wicked
**ma·lev´o·lence** *n.* malicious or spiteful behavior
**ma·lev´o·lent** *adj.* malicious or spiteful; signifying or giving rise to evil: *a malevolent omen* **—ma·lev´o·lent·ly** *adv.*
**mal·fea´sance** *n.* misconduct or an impropriety, especially by a public official **—mal·fea´sant** *adj.*
**mal´for·ma´tion** *n.* a deformity **—mal·formed´** *adj.*
**mal·func´tion** *n.* a failure to function properly *—vi.* to perform poorly or not at all; break down
**mal´ice** *n.* a desire to deliberately harm; spite **—ma·li´cious** *adj.* **—ma·li´cious·ly** *adv.* **—ma·li´cious·ness** *n.*
**ma·lign´** *vt.* to speak ill of; to slander **—ma·lign´er** *n.* **—ma·lign´ly** *adv.*
**ma·lig´nant** *adj.* extremely harmful, as a disease; malevolent **—ma·lig´nance, ma·lig´nan·cy** *n.* **—ma·lig´nant·ly** *adv.*
**ma·lin´ger** *vi.* to avoid, work by feigning illness **—ma·lin´ger·er** *n.*
**mall** *(US) n.* a shaded walk, often lined with shops; a large enclosed shopping complex; a park-like public area
**mal´le·a·ble** *adj.* flexible or adaptable; able to be molded **—mal·le·a·bil´i·ty, mal´le·a·ble·ness** *n.* **—mal´le·**

**a·bly** *adv.*

**mal´let** *n.* a type of hammer, especially one with a soft head

**mal·nour´ished** *adj.* lacking proper food; showing signs of such lack **—mal·nu·tri´tion** *n.*

**mal·o´dor·ous** *adj.* foul smelling **—mal·o´dor·ous·ly** *adv.* **—mal·o´dor·ous·ness** *n.*

**mal·prac´tice** *n.* improper treatment by or conduct of a professional, as a doctor or lawyer

**malt** *n.* a grain that has germinated and dried for use in brewing or as a nutrient; a beverage brewed from or flavored with malt *—vi., vt.* to become or cause to become malt

**mal´treat´** *vt.* to abuse **—mal´treat´ment** *n.*

**mam´bo** *n.* a Latin American dance or music for the dance *—vi.* to dance the mambo

**mam´mal** *n.* any of a class of warmblooded vertebrates that suckle their young **—mam·ma´li·an** *adj.*

**mam·mal´o·gy** *n.* the study of mammals

**mam´mon** *n.* wealth deemed to exert a harmful influence

**mam´moth** *n.* a large elephant, now extinct; anything very large *—adj.* huge; enormous

**man** *n.* a an adult male human; humans in general; one endowed with qualities associated with maleness, as strength or stamina; a male underling or assistant *—vt.* to assign or take a position; to staff **—manned** *adj.*

**man´a·cle** *n.* a restraint, especially one attached at the wrists *—vt.* to constrain

**man´age** *vi., vt.* to direct or control; to administer; to bring about; to have charge of **—man´ag·er** *n.* **—man´a·ge´ri·al** *adj.*

**man´age·a·ble** *adj.* compliant; submissive; able to be controlled or accomplished: *a manageable task* **—man´age·a·bil´i·ty, man´age·a·ble·ness** *n.* **—man´age·a·bly** *adv.*

**man´age·ment** *n.* those who guide or direct a business

**man´date** *n.* an order or declaration; an assignment, as by the electorate: *the people's mandate*; a charge *—vt.* to assign or require **—man´da·tor** *n.*

**man´da·to·ry** *adj.* required; compulsory

**man´-day´** *n.* the work of one person for one day

**man´do·lin´** *n.* a small stringed instrument **—man´do·lin´ist** *n.*

**mane** *n.* long hair growing about the neck of some animals; long human hair

**man´-eat·er** *n.* an animal that feeds or is professed to feed on human flesh; a predatory woman **—man´-eat·ing** *adj.*

**ma·neu´ver** *(US) n.* a change in speed, direction, etc. as of an aircraft; a move or series of moves to fulfill a purpose *—vi., vt.* to change course; to perform moves that influence people or events **—ma·neu´ver·a·bil´i·ty** *n.* **—ma·neu´ver·a·ble** *adj.* **—ma·neu´ver·er** *n.*

**man´ful·ly** *adv.* in a manner characteristic of a man

**mange** *n.* a skin disease of domestic animals

**man´ger** *n.* a feeding trough for livestock

**man´gle** *vt.* to disfigure by cutting, pounding, etc.; to ruin through ignorance or ineptness: *he mangled the introductions* **—man´gler** *n.*

**man´gy** *adj.* shabby or rundown; affected with mange **—man´gi·ly** *adv.* **—man´gi·ness** *n.*

**man´han·dle** *vt.* to treat roughly

**man´-hour´** *n.* the work of one person for one hour

**man´hunt** *n.* an extensive search, as for a fugitive

**ma´nia** *n.* an obsession; irrational behavior **—man´ic** *adj.*

**ma´ni·ac** *n.* an insane person; one who acts in an irrational or capricious manner **—ma·ni´a·cal** *adj.* **—ma·ni´a·cal·ly** *adv.*

**man´i·cure** *n.* a trimming and polishing of the fingernails *—vt.* to care for the fingernails; to crop closely and evenly: *a manicured lawn* **—man´i·cur·ist** *n.*

**man´i·fest** *adj.* evident; obvious *—n.* a list of cargo, passengers, etc. *—vt.* to reveal or become evident **—man´i·fest·ly** *adv.*

**man·i·fes·ta´tion** *n.* evidence or proof of something; the embodiment of a spirit

**man·i·fes´to** *n.* a statement of beliefs or aims

**ma·nip´u·la·ble, ma·nip´u·lat·a·ble** *adj.* that can be manipulated **—ma·nip·u·la·bil´i·ty** *n.*

**ma·nip´u·late** *vt.* to control or shape; to persuade or alter by devious means **—ma·nip·u·la´tion** *n.* **—ma·nip´u·la·tor** *n.* **—ma·nip´u·la·to·ry** *adj.*

**ma·nip·u·la´tion** *n.* the controlling or altering of something; sly, often deceitful, persuasion

**ma·nip´u·la·tive** *adj.* tending to persuade or alter: *the use of manipulative reasoning* **—ma·nip´u·la·tive·ly** *adv.* **—ma·nip´u·la·tive·ness** *n.*

**man´kind´** *n.* humanity; the human race

**man´ly** *adj.* masculine **—man´li·ness** *n.*

**man´-made´** *adj.* manufactured; artificial

**man´ne·quin** *n.* a model of the human body used to display clothing

**man´ner** *n.* a style or mode, as of conduct or carriage **—man´nered** *adj.*

**man´ner·ism** *n.* a distinctive trait; an affectation; an artistic style marked by distortion **—man´ner·ist** *n.* **—man·ner·is´tic** *adj.*

**man´ner·ly** *adj.* having excellent manners *—adv.* politely **—man´ner·li·ness** *n.*

**man´nish** *adj.* affecting the style of a man **—man´nish·ly** *adv.* **—man´nish·ness** *n.*

**ma·noeu´vre** *(Brit.) n.* a change in speed, direction, etc. as of an aircraft; a move or series of moves to fulfill a purpose *—vi., vt.* to change course; to perform moves that influence people or events

**man of God, man of the cloth** a clergyman

**man´of letters** a scholar

**man of the world** a sophisticate
**man´or** *n.* a landed estate or the main house on an estate —**ma·no´ri·al** *adj.*
**man´pow·er** *n.* the laborers, soldiers, etc. that are available or required
**man´sard** *n.* a roof with a double pitch
**manse** *n.* a clergyman's house
**man´sion** *n.* a large house
**man´slaugh·ter** *n.* murder by accident
**man·teau´** *n.* a cloak
**man´tel, man´tel·piece** *n.* a shelf over a fireplace
**man·til´la** *n.* a light lace scarf or head-covering
**man´tle** *n.* a cloak; something that covers or conceals: *a mantle of fog* —*vt., vi.* to cover or be covered or concealed
**man´tra** *n.* a word or phrase chanted as an aid to meditation —**man´tric** *adj.*
**man´u·al** *adj.* referring to the hands or work performed by hand —*n.* a reference or instruction book —**man´u·al·ly** *adv.*
**manual training** training in practical arts such as woodworking
**man·u·fac´ture** *vi., vt.* to fashion, fabricate, or assemble, either by hand or with the aid of machinery; to create, a usually false, story or report —*n.* the production of goods —**man·u·fac´tur·a·ble** *adj.* —**man·u·fac´tur·er** *n.* —**man·u·fac´tur·ing** *n.*
**man·u·mit´** *vt.* to liberate, as a slave —**man·u·mis´sion** *n.*
**ma·nure´** *n.* dung or decaying matter used to fertilize crops —*vt.* to add fertilizer to, as crops —**ma·nur´er** *n.* —**ma·nu´ri·al** *adj.*
**man´u·script** *n.* text lettered by hand; an unpublished text
**man·y** *n., pron.* a large number —*adj.* numerous
**man´y·fold** *adv.* a large number of times
**man´y·sid´ed** *adj.* having many sides, perspectives, etc. —**man´y·sid´ed·ness** *n.*
**map** *n.* a depiction of an area, as of a city, the earth, etc. —*vt.* to survey and depict graphically; to set out in detail: *map a strategy for sales* —**map´mak·er, map´per** *n.* —**map´pa·ble** *adj.*
**mar** *vt.* to damage by marking; to deface
**mar·a·schi´no** *n.* a sweet liqueur made from cherries
**mar´a·thon** *n.* a competition requiring endurance, as a long-distance race —**mar´a·thon·er** *n.*
**ma·raud´** *vi., vt.* to attack and plunder —**ma·raud´er** *n.*
**mar´ble** *n.* a type of multicolored stone —**mar´ble, mar´ble·ize** *vt.* to streak with color, imitating marble —**mar´bled** *adj.* —**mar´bly** *adj.*
**marble cake** a cake streaked with batters of different colors
**mar´bling** *n.* a streaking resembling that of marble; the creation of marble-like streaks, as in a design
**march** *n.* an orderly forward movement; a gathering to protest or champion a cause —*vi., vt.* to move or cause to move forward in an orderly, methodical manner —**march´er** *n.*
**marching orders** instructions or permission to proceed, as with a business plan
**mar´ga·rine** *n.* a butter substitute
**mar´gin** *n.* a limit, as the blank space around a printed page; an allowance for variation
**mar´gin·al** *adj.* barely acceptable —**mar·gin·al´i·ty** *n.* —**mar´gin·al·ly** *adv.* —**mar´gin·al·ize** *vt.*
**ma·ri·a´chi** *n.* a Mexican street band
**ma·ri´na** *n.* a docking area for small boats
**mar´i·nade´** *n.* a seasoned liquid for steeping food before cooking
**mar´i·nate** *vi., vt.* to soak in a marinade —**mar·i·na´tion** *n.*
**ma·rine´** *adj.* relating to the sea or seamen —**mar´i·ner** *n.*
**mar´i·o·nette´** *n.* a puppet moved by strings or wires
**mar´i·tal** *adj.* relating to marriage —**mar´i·tal·ly** *adv.*
**mar´i·time** *adj.* at or near the sea; pertaining to the sea or seamen
**mark** *n.* a random impression, as a scratch, blotch, etc.; a representative symbol or sign; a rating; an objective —*vt.* to imprint; to scratch of blotch; to identify by or as if by a symbol; to label, as with a price; to notice —*vi.* to make a mark; to notice —**make a mark** to be successful or notable —**mark down** to lower the price of —**mark time** to pause or wait for a propitious moment —**mark up** to increase the price of —**wide of the mark** a failure
**mark´down** *n.* a discount
**marked** *adj.* noticeable; prominent —**mark´ed·ly** *adv.* —**mark´ed·ness** *n.*
**mark´er** *n.* something that serves to identify; an implement used to imprint or write; an IOU
**mar´ket** *n.* the business of buying and selling; a place where goods are available for sale; trading in a commodity —*vi., vt.* to buy or sell —**mar·ket·abil´i·ty** *n.* —**mar´ket·a·ble** *adj.*
**mar´ket·er** *n.* one who deals in a commodity
**mar´ket·place** *n.* a place where goods are bought and sold; a domain recognized as a distinct area of trade: *the literary marketplace*
**market research** the accumulation and analysis of consumer-related data
**market share** the portion of total trade in a particular commodity that a company controls or may expect to control
**market value** the price at which a commodity may reasonable be expected to be bought or sold
**mark´ing** *n.* a distinctive feature or pattern, as on an animal
**mark´up** *n.* the amount by which the cost of a market-

able product is increased to arrive at a selling price

**mar´ma·lade** *n.* a thick preserve made from fruit

**mar´riage** *n.* the uniting of a man and woman as husband and wife; the joining of two elements: *the marriage of flavors that make a food unique, the marriage of wit and beauty*

**mar´riage·a·ble** *adj.* suited or able to be married: *of marriageable age* **—mar·riage·a·bil´i·ty, mar´riage·a·ble·ness** *n.*

**marriage of convenience** a union arranged for practical reasons, such as for political or economic benefit

**mar´ry** *vt.* to join as husband and wife; to combine or closely unite two entities *—vi.* to take as a husband or wife **—mar´ried** *adj.*

**marsh** *n.* land that is wet and muddy **—marsh´land** *n.*

**mar´shal** *n.* an officer in a law enforcement or similar agency *—vt.* to gather or arrange: *marshal forces for an attack*

**marsh´mal·low** *n.* a soft, spongy confection **—marsh´mal·low·y** *adj.*

**marsh·y** *adj.* wet and muddy **—marsh´i·ness** *n.*

**mar·su´pi·al** *n.* a mammal that bears its young in an external pouch *—adj.* having a pouch

**mart** *n.* a market

**mar´tial** *adj.* referring to war or warriors **—mar´tial·ism** *n.* **—mar´tial·ist** *n.* **—mar´tial·ly** *adv.*

**martial art** any technique of combat or war

**martial law** government by military authority

**mar´ti·net´** *n.* a strict disciplinarian

**mar·ti´ni** *n.* a cocktail of gin or vodka and dry vermouth

**mar´tyr** *n.* one who endures suffering or death for a belief or cause; one who suffers without complaint; oen who exaggerates discomfort in order to elicit sympathy *—vt.* to persecute or put to death for devotion to a belief or cause **—mar´tyr·dom** *n.*

**mar´vel** *n.* something that fills with awe or wonder *—vi., vt.* to wonder at; to be amazed

**mar´vel·ous** *adj.* wonderous; impressive **—mar´vel·ous·ly** *adv.* **—mar´vel·ous·ness** *n.*

**mar´zi·pan** *n.* an almond-flavored confection

**mas·car´a** *n.* eye makeup

**mas´cot** *n.* a symbol, usually an animal, believed to bring good luck

**mas´cu·line** *n.* characteristic of a male; attributes associated with a male **—mas´cu·line·ly** *adv.* **—mas·cu·lin´i·ty** *n.*

**mash** *n.* a pulpy mass *—vt.* to reduce to a pulpy mass

**mash´er** *n.* a utensil for crushing or pulverizing; one who makes unwanted sexual advances

**mask** *n.* a covering for the face, as to conceal identity or for protection; a representation of a face hung as a wall ornament *—vi., vt.* to conceal or cover, esp. of the face **—masked** *adj.*

**mas´och·ist** *n.* one who derives pleasure from being abused **—mas´och·ism** *n.* **—mas´och·is´tic** *adj.* **—mas·och·is´ti·cal·ly** *adv.*

**ma´son** *n.* one who works with stone **—ma´son·ry** *n.*

**mas´quer·ade´** *n.* a costume party; a deception *—vi.* to wear or assume a disguise

**mass** *n.* a clump; physical bulk; an undetermined number or amount *—vi., vt.* to assemble or be assembled into a mass *—adj.* large in number or scale

**mas´sa·cre** *n.* indiscriminate slaughter *—vt.* to slaughter **—mas´sa·crer** *n.*

**mas·sage´** *n.* a rubdown *—vt.* to relax the muscles by rubbing or kneading; to manipulate, as data **—mas·sag´er** *n.*

**mas·seur´, mas·seuse´** *n.* a man or woman, respectively, trained in the art of massage

**mas´sive** *adj.* large or bulky; imposing; cumbersome **—mas´sive·ly** *adv.* **—mas´sive·ness** *n.*

**mass-market** *adj.* produced for general consumption

**mass media** collectively, those communication systems that attract a large audience

**mass´-pro·duce´** *vt.* to manufacture in large quantities using assembly-line techniques **—mass´-pro·duc´tion** *n.*

**mass transit** collectively, the transportation systems that carry large numbers of passengers on a regular basis

**mas´ter** *adj.* primary or controlling: *a master plan*; proficient or knowledgeable: *a master electrician* *—n.* one who owns or controls; a teacher; one proficient in a craft; one who possesses exceptional knowledge or ability in a particular field *—vt.* to control; to acquire knowledge or ability **—mas´tery** *n.*

**mas´ter·ful** *adj.* domineering; having or exhibiting skill: *a masterful painting* **—mas´ter·ful·ly** *adv.* **—mas´ter·ful·ness** *n.*

**master key** a passkey

**mas´ter·ly** *adj.* having or exhibiting the skill of a master *—adv.*

**mas´ter·mind** *n.* one with the ability to conceive or direct a complex operation *—vt.* to plan and direct skillfully

**master of ceremonies** one presiding over a banquet or entertainment, charged with introductions

**mas´ter·piece** *n.* an outstanding work, as of art

**mas´ter·stroke** *n.* a singular action or achievement

**mas´ter·work** *n.* a masterpiece

**mast´head** *n.* the name of a periodical or newspaper as it appears on a cover, a first, or a leading page; the listing in a publication of its ownership, staff, circulation, etc.

**mas´ti·cate** *vi., vt.* to chew food; to reduce to a pulp **—mas·ti·ca´tion** *n.* **—mas´ti·ca·tor** *n.*

**mas´to·don** *n.* an extinct elephantlike animal

**mas·tur·ba´tion** *n.* stimulation of the genitals to orgasm by means other than sexual intercourse

—**mas´tur·bate** *vi., vt.* —**mas·tur·ba´tion·al, mas´tur·ba·to·ry** *adj.* —**mas´tur·ba·tor** *n.*

**mat** *n.* a flat section of material used for a bed, a covering, protection, etc.; a protective border placed over a picture —*vi., vt.* to press or tangle into a mat

**mat´a·dor** *n.* a bullfighter

**match** *n.* a small strip of material used to produce fire; something that is exactly or nearly like another; something compatible or harmonious; a sporting contest —*vt.* to give or get something identical, comparable, or compatible —**match´able** *adj.*

**match´less** *adj.* without equal —**match´less·ly** *adv.* —**match´less·ness** *n.*

**match´mak·er** *n.* one who arranges marriages —**match´mak·ing** *n.*

**mate** *n.* one of a pair; a close friend or ally —*vi., vt.* to pair, as in marriage or for breeding

**ma·te´ri·al** *adj.* relevant; tangible —*n.* unprocessed matter, information, etc.: *building material, material for a book or play, material for a dress,* etc.

**ma·te´ri·al·ism** *n.* excessive concern for worldly matters or possessions —**ma·te´ri·al·ist** *n.* —**ma·te´ri·al·is´tic** *adj.* —**ma·te´ri·al·is´ti·cal·ly** *adv.*

**ma·te´ri·al·ize** *vi.* to appear suddenly —*vt.* to cause to come forth —**ma·te·ri·al·i·za´tion** *n.*

**ma·te´ri·al·ly** *adv.* to a meaningful extent

**ma·ter´nal** *adj.* of a mother or motherhood —**ma·ter´nal·ism** *n.* —**ma·ter·nal·is´tic** *adj.* —**ma·ter´nal·ly** *adv.*

**ma·ter´ni·ty** *n.* the emotions associated with motherhood —*adj.* relating to pregnancy or childbirth

**math, math·e·mat´ics** *n.* the science of numbers

**math·e·mat´i·cal** *adj.* pertaining to numbers —**math·e·mat´i·cal·ly** *adv.* —**math·e·ma·ti´cian** *n.*

**mat´i·nee´** *n.* an afternoon performance

**ma´tri·arch** *n.* a woman who heads a family; a respected woman —**ma´tri·ar´chal, ma·tri·ar´chic** *adj.* —**ma·tri·ar´chal·ism** *n.*

**ma´tri·ar·chy** *n.* a society that traces its lineage through women

**ma·tric´u·late** *vt., vi.* to permit or be permitted into, as a course of study —**ma·tric´u·lant** *n.* —**ma·tric·u·la´tion** *n.*

**ma·tri·lin´e·age** *n.* maternal lineage —**ma·tri·lin´e·al** *adj.* —**ma·tri·lin´e·al·ly** *adv.*

**mat´ri·mo·ny** *n.* the union of two persons in marriage; the state of being married —**mat´ri·mo´ni·al** *adj.* —**mat´ri·mo´ni·al·ly** *adv.*

**ma´trix** *n.* a mold or pattern

**ma´tron** *n.* a mature woman; a female supervisor —**ma´tron·li·ness** *n.* —**ma´tron·ly** *adj.*

**matte** *n.* a soft or dull finish —*adj.* having a soft or dull finish

**mat´ter** *n.* substance; something of interest or focus: *a financial matter* —*vi.* to be important

**mat´ter-of-fact´** *adj.* objective; unemotional; unimaginative —**mat´ter-of-fact´ly** *adv.* —**mat´ter-of-fact´ness** *n.*

**mat´ting** *n.* a rough fabric, as used for floor covering; an accumulation of material that forms a covering

**mat´tress** *n.* a pad or mat used for sleeping

**mat´u·rate** *vi.* to mature or ripen —**mat·u·ra´tion** *n.* —**mat·u·ra´tion·al, mat´u·ra·tive** *adj.*

**ma·ture´** *adj.* fully developed; characteristic of full development; ripe —*vi., vt.* to ripen or cause to ripen; to become due, as a debt —**ma·ture´ly** *adv.* —**ma·ture´ness, ma·tur´i·ty** *n.*

**mat´zo** *n.* unleavened bread

**maud´lin** *adj.* tearful; nauseatingly sentimental

**maul** *n.* a heavy hammer; a sledgehammer —*vt.* to beat or batter; to mangle by rough treatment —**maul´er** *n.*

**mau·so·le´um** *n.* a tomb; a tomblike room or building

**ma´ven** *n.* an expert

**mav´er·ick** *adj.* independent; radical —*n.* a nonconformist; one who acts independently

**mawk´ish** *adj.* overly sentimental —**mawk´ish·ly** *adv.* —**mawk´ish·ness** *n.*

**max´im** *n.* an adage or motto

**max´i·mal** *adj.* of a maximum; largest —**max´i·mal·ly** *adv.*

**max´i·mize** *vt.* to increase or emphasize as much as possible —**max·i·mi·za´tion** *n.* —**max´i·miz·er** *n.*

**max´i·mum** *adj.* of the largest possible or allowed —*n.* the largest amount or extent

**may´be** *adv.* possibly —*n.* a possibility

**may´hem** *n.* deliberate injury to a person; reckless damage or destruction; a state of turmoil

**may´o, may´on·naise** *n.* a thick, rich white sauce or dressing

**may´or** *n.* a municipal administrator —**may´or·al** *adj.* —**may´or·al·ty** *n.*

**maze** *n.* a complex pattern, as of paths or lines; a network of complicated or confusing elements: *an intricate maze of building codes* —**maz´i·ness** *n.* —**maze´like, maz´y** *adj.*

**mead´ow** *n.* an expanse of pasture or grassland —**mead´owy** *adj.*

**mea´ger** *(US)*, **mea´gre** *(Brit.)* *adj.* scant; lacking, as in quality —**mea´ger·ly, mea´gre·ly** *adv.* —**mea´ger·ness, mea´gre·ness** *n.*

**meal** *n.* edible grain, whole or ground; the food eaten at a sitting

**meal´y** *adj.* containing or resembling meal —**meal´i·ness** *n.*

**meal´y-mouthed** *adj.* tending to avoid direct and honest discourse

**mean** *adj.* cruel or malicious; low, as in quality or amount; selfish or miserly —*n.* midway between extremes –*vt.* to indicate or intend: *this means war, I mean to win*

**me·an´der** *vi.* to wander aimlessly; to travel a winding course –*n.* a winding course **–me·an´der·er** *n.* **–me·an´der·ing·ly** *adv.* **–me·an´drous** *adj.*

**mean´ing** *adj.* revealing; having purpose –*n.* significance or purpose; that which is understood – **mean´ing·ful** *adj.* **–mean´ing·ful·ly, mean´ing·ly** *adv.* **–mean´ing·ful·ness** *n.*

**mean´ing·less** *adj.* without purpose; insignificant **–mean´ing·less·ly** *adv.* **–mean´ing·less·ness** *n.*

**mean´ly** *adv.* in a shabby way

**mean´ness** *n.* cruelty or malice; a lack, as in quality or amount; selfishness

**mean´-spir´it·ed** *adj.* characterized by pettiness – **mean´-spir´it·ed·ly** *adv.* **–mean´-spir´it·ed·ness** *n.*

**mea´sur·a·ble** *adj.* that can be quantified; finite; significant **–mea·sur·a·bil´i·ty, mea´sur·a·ble·ness** *n.* **–mea´sur·a·bly** *adv.*

**mea´sure** *n.* a standard unit, such as an inch or a pound, used to express size, weight, etc.; a device calibrated to such a standard; an unspecified amount: *enjoying a measure of fame*; an unspecified action: *time to take corrective measures* –*vi., vt.* to express or gauge, as size or capacity, in terms of a standard unit **–beyond measure** incalculable **–in some measure** to an unspecified extent **–measure up** to fulfill expectations **–mea´sur·er** *n.*

**mea´sured** *adj.* steady and deliberate: *spoke in measured tones* **–mea´sured·ly** *adv.* **–mea´sured·ness** *n.*

**mea´sure·less** *adj.* without limit **–mea´sure·less·ly** *adv.* **–mea´sure·less·ness** *n.*

**mea´sure·ment** *n.* a determination of size, capacity, etc.; a system for such determination

**meat** *n.* the edible flesh of an animal or plant; a main idea: *the meat of the discussion*

**meat-and-potatoes** *adj.* basics

**meat´ball** *n.* ground meat formed into a sphere and baked or fried; a foolish person

**meat´y** *adj.* containing meat; important or significant **–meat´i·ness** *n.*

**me·chan´ic** *n.* one who repairs machines

**me·chan´i·cal** *adj.* relating to or driven by mechanical action or a machine; in a perfunctory manner **–me·chan´i·cal·ly** *adv.* **–me·chan´i·cal·ness** *n.*

**mechanical advantage** the ratio of the output of a mechanism to the input energy required or expended

**me·chan´ics** *n.* the study of force acting on a material body; the study of machinery

**mech´a·nism** *n.* the parts, action, or operation of a mechanical device

**mech´a·nize** *vt.* to equip with machines; to automate **–mech·a·ni·za´tion** *n.*

**med´al** *n.* a small, flat article of ornamented metal recognizing a person, event, etc. **–med´al·ist** *n.*

**me·dal´lion** *n.* a large medal or emblem that serves as an ornament, identification, etc.; food cut or formed in circles

**med´dle** *vi.* to interfere in the affairs of another **–med´dler** *n.*

**med´dle·some** *adj.* tending to interfere **–med´dle·some·ly** *adv.* **–med´dle·some·ness** *n.*

**med´e·vac** *n.* medical evacuation: the transporting of injured by air to a medical facility

**me´dia** *n.* plural of *medium*; the forms of mass communication collectively, as newspapers, television, etc.

**media event** an occurrence that prompts wide coverage by the news media

**me´di·al** *adj.* median **–me´di·al·ly** *adv.*

**me´di·an** *adj.* relating to the middle –*n.* a middle part **–me´di·an·ly** *adv.*

**me´di·ate** *vt.* to resolve a dispute between two or more parties –*vi.* to act as the agent of reconciliation **–me´di·ate·ly** *adv.* **–me·di·a´tion** *n.* **–me·di·a´tive** *adj.* **–me´di·a·tor** *n.*

**med´ic** *n.* a physician, especially in the military

**med´i·cal** *adj.* of the science of healing: *medical treatment* **–med´i·cal·ly** *adv.*

**me·dic´a·ment** *n.* a medicine

**med´i·cate** *vt.* to treat with medicine **–med·i·ca´tion** *n.* **–med´i·ca·tive** *adj.*

**me·dic´i·nal** *adj.* of or like medicine **–me·dic´i·nal·ly** *adv.*

**med´i·cine** *n.* the science or practice of healing; something prescribed to treat an illness

**medicine show** a sophisticated sales pitch reminiscent of traveling shows in the past that attracted audiences for the selling of patent, often ineffective, medicines

**me·di·e´val** *adj.* of the Middle Ages; antiquated; barbaric **–me·di·e´val·ly** *adv.*

**me·di·e´val·ism** *n.* the study of life in the Middle Ages; a custom or practice of the Middle Ages **–me·di·e´val·ist** *n.*

**me´di·o´cre** *adj.* unexceptional; barely acceptable; inferior **–medi·oc´ri·ty** *n.*

**med´i·tate** *vi., vt.* to deliberate or consider; to spend time in quiet contemplation **–med·i·ta´tion** *n.* **–med´i·tat·or** *n.*

**med´i·ta·tive** *adj.* characterized by quiet contemplation; thoughtful or reflective **–med´i·ta·tive·ly** *adv.* **–med´i·ta·tive·ness** *n.*

**me´di·um** *adj.* between extremes –*n.* something approximately midway between limits; a substance or means by which something is attained: *oil paint is the medium for this portrait, a credit card is the preferred medium for shoppers*

**medium of exchange** the accepted currency in a particular society or circumstance, as dollars, pounds, pesos, shells, etc.

**med´ley** *n.* an assortment; a conglomeration

**meek** *adj.* subdued or submissive; humble **–meek´ly** *adv.* **–meek´ness** *n.*

**meet** *vt.* to come upon or confront; to make the acquaintance of; to gather, as for discussion; to satisfy: *meet the requirements for a job* *–vi.* to come together; to assemble; to be introduced *–n.* a gathering, as for athletic competition

**meet´ing** *n.* an encounter or confrontation; a gathering; am intersecting, as of two roads

**meg´a·dose** *n.* a large measure, as of medicine

**meg´a·hertz** *n.* one million cycles per second, as of a radio frequency or computer speed

**meg´a·lith** *n.* a large stone monument **–meg´a·lith´ic** *adj.*

**meg·a·lo·ma´ni·a** *n.* obsession with wealth or power **–meg·a·lo·ma´ni·ac** *n.* **–meg·a·lo·ma·ni´a·cal, meg·a·lo·man´ic** *adj.*

**meg·a·lop´o·lis** *n.* an area of closely joined cities and their surrounding areas **–meg´a·lo·pol´i·tan** *adj.*

**meg´a·phone** *n.* a device that amplifies the voice **–meg·a·phon´ic** *adj.* **–meg·a·phon´i·cal·ly** *adv.*

**mel´a·mine** *n.* a type of plastic

**mel´an·cho´lia** *n.* a mental disorder marked by depression **–mel·an·cho´li·ac** *n.*

**mel´an·choly** *adj.* sadly quiet and contemplative *–n.* a condition marked by sadness or gloom and a quiet attitude, as though deep in thought **–mel´an·chol´ic** *adj.* **–mel´an·chol´i·cal·ly** *adv.*

**me·lagne´** *n.* a collection or jumble

**mel·a·no´ma** *n.* a darkly-colored growth, usually occurring on the skin and often malignant

**meld** *n.* a blending together *–vi., vt.* to become or cause to become mingled: *cook lightly so that the flavors can meld*

**me´lee** *n.* a violent clash or mingling

**mel´io·rate** *vi., vt.* to improve, as a condition **–mel´io·ra·ble** *adj.* **–me·lio·ra´tion** *n.* **–me´lio·ra·tive** *adj.* **–me·lio·ra´tor** *n.*

**mel·lif´lu·ent** *adj.* mellifluous **–mel·lif´lu·ence** *n.* **–mel·lif´lu·ent·ly** *adv.*

**mel·lif´lu·ous** *adj.* smooth and mellow, as of a voice or musical tone **–mel·lif´lu·ous·ly** *adv.* **–mel·lif´lu·ous·ness** *n.*

**mel´low** *adj.* soft and rich, as a flavor or sound; pleasant and unhurried, as of a conversation *–vi., vt.* **–mel´low·ly** *adv.* **–mel´low·ness** *n.*

**me·lod´ic** *adj.* tuneful **–me·lod´i·cal·ly** *adv.*

**me·lo´di·ous** *adj.* harmonious; pleasing to the ear **–me·lo´di·ous·ly** *adv.* **–me·lo´di·ous·ness** *n.*

**mel´o·dra·ma** *n.* a theatrical work characterized by overdrawn characterizations and exaggerated emotion **–mel´o·dra·mat´ic** *adj.* **–mel´o·dra·mat´i·cal·ly** *adv.*

**mel´o·dy** *n.* a musical strain; a series of tones comprising a tune that expresses the theme of a musical composition

**melt** *vi., vt.* to transform from a solid to a liquid state; to soften, dissolve, or disappear: *as we rode away, the scene melted in the distance* **–melt·a·bil´i·ty** *n.* **–melt´a·ble** *adj.* **–melt´er** *n.* **–melt´ing·ly** *adv.*

**mem´ber** *n.* one who belongs or is a part of: *a club member, a member of the band*; part of an organism, as a limb; a distinct part of something, as a structure

**mem´ber·ship** *n.* affiliation with an organization; collectively, those who are affiliated

**mem´brane** *n.* a thin sheet of tissue that serves as a cover or lining

**me·men´to** *n.* a keepsake

**mem´o, mem·o·ran´dum** *n.* a written communication

**mem´oir** *n.* an autobiography **–mem´oir·ist** *n.*

**mem·o·ra·bil´ia** *pl. n.* souvenirs or mementos associated with a person, place, event, etc.

**mem´o·ra·ble** *adj.* worth remembering; unusual **–mem·o·ra·bil´i·ty, mem´o·ra·ble·ness** *n.* **–mem´o·ra·bly** *adv.*

**me·mo´ri·al** *adj.* commemorative *–n.* a monument, ceremony, etc. that serves as a remembrance **–me·mo´ri·al·ly** *adv.*

**me·mo´ri·al·ize** *vt.* to commemorate **–me·mo·ri·al·i·za´tion** *n.*

**mem´o·rize** *vt.* to commit to memory **–mem´o·riz·a·ble** *adj.* **–mem·o·ti·za´tion** *n.* **–mem´o·riz·er** *n.*

**mem´o·ry** *n.* the ability to remember and recall; something remembered

**men´ace** *n.* a threat *–vt.* to threaten **–men´ac·ing·ly** *adv.*

**me·nag´er·ie** *n.* an assortment of animals; a place where animals are confined; a collection

**mend** *vi., vt.* to make or become better; to correct, repair, or heal **–mend´a·ble** *adj.* **–mend´er** *n.*

**men·da´cious** *adj.* lying or deceitful, as of a person, statement, etc. **–men·da´cious·ly** *adv.* **–men·da´cious·ness, men·dac´i·ty** *n.*

**men´di·cant** *adj.* pertaining to a beggar; depending on alms *–n.* a beggar **–men´di·can·cy, men·dic´i·ty** *n.*

**me´ni·al** *adj.* servile or humble; befitting a servant *–n.* a servant **–me´ni·al·ly** *adv.*

**men´su·ra·ble** *adj.* that can be measured **–men·su·ra·bil´i·ty, men´su·ra·ble·ness** *n.*

**men·su·ra´tion** *n.* the process of measuring **–men´su·ra·tive** *adj.*

**men´tal** *adj.* relating to the mind **–men´tal·ly** *adv.*

**men´tal·ism** *n.* the concept that some mental phenomena are beyond explanation; parapsychological events, such as telepathy **–men´tal·ist** *n.* **–men·tal·is´tic** *adj.*

**men·tal´i·ty** *n.* one's intellectual capacity; a manner of thinking: *an optimistic mentality*

**mental retardation** a deficiency in mental development

**men´tion** *n.* a casual reference; a tribute, *as honorable mention* —*vt.* to refer to —**men´tion·able** *adj.* —**men´tion·er** *n.*

**men´tor** *n.* a trusted advisor or teacher

**men´u** *n.* a list of available food items; any list of options

**me´nu-driv·en** *adj.* of a computer program that offers lists of options for the operator to select

**mer´can·tile** *adj.* relating to the marketing of goods; commercial —**mer´can·til·ism** *n.* —**mer·can·til·is´tic** *adj.*

**mer´ce·nar·y** *n.* a soldier in the pay of a foreign government; one motivated mainly by personal gain —*adj.* influenced by desire for gain —**mer·ce·nar´i·ly** *adv.* —**mer´ce·nar·i·ness** *n.*

**mer´chan·dise** *n.* goods that are bought and sold —*vi., vt.* to sell or promote the sale of —**mer´chan·dis·er** *n.* —**mer´chan·dis·ing** *n.*

**mer´chant** *adj.* pertaining to commercial trade —*n.* one who makes a business of selling for profit —**mer´chant·able** *adj.*

**merchant marine** merchant ships or their crews

**mer´ci·ful** *adj.* showing mercy —**mer´ci·ful·ly** *adv.* —**mer´ci·ful·ness** *n.*

**mer´ci·less** *adj.* showing no mercy; lacking compassion —**mer´ci·less·ly** *adv.* —**mer´ci·less·ness** *n.*

**mer·cu´ri·al** *adj.* volatile; fluctuating; likely to change abruptly —**mer·cu´ri·al·ly** *adv.* —**mer·cu´ri·al·ness** *n.*

**mer´cy** *n.* compassion; an act of forgiveness or compassion

**mere** *adj.* insignificant; inconsequential —**mere´ly** *adv.*

**mer·e·tri´cious** *adj.* gaudy; insincere —**mer·e·tri´cious·ly** *adv.* —**mer·e·tri´cious·ness** *n.*

**merge** *vt., vi.* to combine or become combined —**mer´gence** *n.*

**merg´er** *n.* a combining, as of companies or interests

**me·ringue´** *n.* egg whites, beaten until stiff and sometimes sweetened, then baked, usually used as a topping or dessert shell

**mer´it** *n.* a worthwhile quality —*vt.* to be worthy of; to deserve

**mer·i·toc´ra·cy** *n.* a hierarchy based on ability —**mer·i·to·crat´ic** *adj.*

**mer·i·to´ri·ous** *adj.* praiseworthy; commendable —**mer·i·to´ri·ous·ly** *adv.* —**mer·i·to´ri·ous·ness** *n.*

**mer´maid, mer´man** *n.* a mythical creature that is half fish and half human

**mer´ri·ment** *n.* lively fun; gaiety

**mer´ry** *adj.* joyous; happy; marked by laughter or mirth —**mer´ri·ly** *adv.* —**mer´ri·ness** *n.*

**mer´ry-go-round** *n.* a revolving platform ridden for pleasure

**mer´ry·mak·er** *n.* a participant in a festive event; a reveler —**mer´ry·mak·ing** *n.*

**me´sa** *n.* a broad plateau with steep sides

**mesh** *n.* a loose, open fabrication of thread, wire, etc; —*vi., vt.* to fit or make fit together: *meshing gears, meshing ideas* —**mesh´work** *n.*

**mes´mer·ize** *vt.* to fascinate; to hypnotize —**mes´mer·ism, mes·mer·i·za´tion** *n.*

**mess** *n.* disordered clutter; a jumble; a large quantity; *a mess of data* —*vi., vt.* to clutter; to make untidy

**mes´sage** *n.* a communication; the underlying lesson or guidance contained in a communication

**mes´sen·ger** *n.* one who carries or delivers messages or small packages; a courier —*vt.* to send by courier

**mess´y** *adj.* disorderly; unpleasant: *a messy divorce* —**mess´i·ly** *adv.* —**mess´i·ness** *n.*

**met´a·bol´ic** *adj.* pertaining to or relating to metabolism —**met·a·bol´i·cal·ly** *adv.*

**me·tab´o·lism** *n.* the process by which a living organism converts food into energy, synthesizes substances necessary to life, manufactures tissue, etc.

**me·tab´o·lize** *vt., vi.* to change or undergo change by metabolism —**me·tab´o·liz·able** *adj.*

**met´al** *n.* any of the elements or a combination of elements that are usually shiny, good conductors, and ductile —**me·tal´lic** *adj.* **me·tal´li·cal·ly** *adv.*

**met´al·lur·gy** *n.* the technique for extracting metals from ore or combining them to produce alloys —**met´al·lur´gic, met´al·lur´gi·cal** *adj.* —**met·al·lur´gi·cal·ly** *adv.* —**met´al·lur·gist** *n.*

**met·a·mor´pho·sis** *n.* a transformation, especially one that seems miraculous, as that of a caterpillar into a butterfly —**met·a·mor´phic** *adj.* —**met·a·mor´phism** *n.* —**met·a·mor´phose** *vi., vt.*

**met´a·phor** *n.* a figure of speech in which one thing is used to designate something different: *all the world's a stage* —**met·a·phor´ic, met·a·phor´i·cal** *adj.* —**met·a·phor´i·cal·ly** *adv.*

**met´a·phys´ics** *n.* the branch of philosophy that deals with the essential nature of reality —**met·a·phys´i·cal** *adj.* —**met·a·phys´i·cal·ly** *adv.*

**mete** *vt.* to measure and distribute

**me´te·or** *n.* a bright streak in the heaven produced when a meteoroid enters the earth's atmosphere

**me·te·or´ic** *adj.* pertaining to meteors; pertaining to atmospheric phenomenon; swift, as *a meteoric rise to power* —**me·te·or´i·cal·ly** *adv.*

**me´te·or·ite** *n.* an object from space that has fallen into the earth's atmosphere —**me·te·or·it´ic, me·te·or·it´i·cal** *adj.*

**me´te·or·oid** *n.* any of the small particles of matter moving through space

**me·te·o·rol´o·gy** *n.* the study of atmospheric phenomenon, esp. relating to weather —**me·te·or·o·log´ic, me·te·or·o·log´i·cal** *adj.* —**me·te·or·o·log´i·cal·ly**

*adv.* **—me·te·o·rol´o·gist** *n.*
**me´ter** *(Brit.) n.* a device for measuring
**me´ter** *(US) n.* a rhythmic pattern, as in poetry or music; a device for measuring; a unit of length in the metric system *—vt.* to measure with a meter; to provide in measured amounts
**meth´od** *n.* a systematic procedure; orderliness in manner or mode
**me·thod´i·cal** *adj.* in a systematic or orderly fashion **—me·thod´i·cal·ly** *adv.* **—me·thod´i·cal·ness** *n.*
**meth·od·ol´o·gy** *n.* the body of systematic procedures that characterize a particular area of study or investigation **—meth·od·o·log´i·cal** *adj.* **—meth·od·o·log´i·cal·ly** *adv.* **—meth·od·ol´o·gist** *n.*
**me·tic´u·lous** *adj.* precise; marked by unusual attention to detail **—me·tic´u·lous·ly** *adj.* **—me·tic´u·lous·ness** *n.*
**me´tre** *(Brit.) n.* a rhythmic pattern, as in poetry or music; a unit of length in the metric system *—vt.* to measure with a meter; to provide in measured amounts
**metric system** *n.* a decimal system of weights and measure **—met´ric** *adj.*
**met´ro** *adj.* metropolitan
**met´ro·nome** *n.* a device used to mark time in music **—met´ro·nom´ic** *adj.*
**me·trop´o·lis** *n.* a major urban area
**met´ro·pol´i·tan** *adj.* of a major urban area
**met´tle** *n.* courage; strength of character **—met´tle·some** *adj.*
**mez´za·nine´** *n.* a balcony; a landing or balcony between two main floors of a building
**mi·as´ma** *n.* foul air; a corrupting influence spread as though carried in the air **—mi·as´mal, mi·as·mat´ic, mi·as´mic** *adj.*
**mi´crobe** *n.* a microorganism **—mi·cro´bi·al, mi·cro´bic** *adj.*
**mi´cro·bi·ol´o·gy** *n.* the study of microorganisms **—mi´cro·bio·log´i·cal** *adj.* **—mi´cro·bi·ol´o·gist** *n.*
**mi´cro·com·put·er** *n.* a portable computer such as a laptop or notebook computer
**mi´cro·cosm** *n.* a small representation of a much larger system **—mi´cro·cos´mic, mi·cro·cos´mi·cal** *adj.*
**mi·crom´e·ter** *n.* a device for making small measurements
**mi·cro·min´i·a·tur·i·za´tion** *n.* reduction to extremely small size or scale **—mi·cro·min´i·a·ture** *adj.* **—mi·cro·min´i·a·tur·ize** *vt.*
**mi·cro·or´ga·nism** *n.* a microscopic creature
**mi´cro·phone** *n.* a device for converting sound waves into electronic impulses **—mi´cro·phon´ic** *adj.*
**mi´cro·proc·es·sor** *n.* an integrated circuit that comprises the central processing unit of a computer
**mi´cro·pro´gram** *n.* any of the individual computer instructions that together comprise a complete command
**mi´cro·scope** *n.* a device for magnifying objects that cannot be seen with the naked eye **—mi´cro·scop´ic** *adj.* **—mi·cro·scop´i·cal·ly** *adv.*
**mi´cro·wave** *n.* an electromagnetic energy wave; a microwave oven *—vt.* to cook in a microwave oven
**mid´dle** *adj.* positioned approximately midway between extremes *—n.* a center or midpoint
**mid´dle·man** *n.* a go-between; one who buys in large volume from a few sources and distributes in smaller quantities to retailers or consumers; a jobber
**middle management** administrators and supervisors who deal mainly with the day-to-day operation of a business
**mid´land** *n.* the central part of a country
**mid´riff** *n.* the part of the body between the chest and the abdomen
**midst** *n.* positioned in or among; located at or near the midpoint
**mid´way** *n.* an assortment of carnival sideshows, games, etc.; halfway
**mid´wife** *n.* one trained to assist in childbirth **—mid·wife´ry** *n.*
**mien** *n.* one's appearance or demeanor
**miff** *vi., vt.* to be or cause to be offended or annoyed
**might** *n.* strength or power
**might´y** *adj.* strong or powerful; imposing; impressive **—might´i·ly** *adv.* **—might´i·ness** *n.*
**mi´graine** *n.* a severe headache **—mi·grain´ous** *adj.*
**mi´grant** *adj.* migratory *—n.* one who moves frequently, often in search of work
**mi´grate** *vi.* to move frequently and often, regularly; to move from one area, country, etc. to another
**mi·gra´tion** *n.* a move, especially of a group moving together
**mi´gra·to·ry** *adj.* tending to move often, especially with the change of seasons
**mild** *adj.* gentle or moderate **—mild´ly** *adv.* **—mild´ness** *n.*
**mil´dew** *n.* a type of fungus; a coating caused by this fungus
**mile** *n.* a measure of distance
**mile´age** *n.* distance traveled; an amount paid or allowed for business travel
**mile´post, mile´stone** *n.* a distance marker set beside a road; anything that is a mark of progress: *graduation from college is a milepost on the way to a successful career*
**mi·lieu´** *n.* environment; surroundings
**mil´i·tant** *adj.* belligerent or aggressive in nature **—mil´i·tance, mil´i·tan·cy** *n.* **—mil´i·tant·ly** *adv.*
**mil´i·ta·rism** *n.* an emphasizing of the need for military preparedness; a philosophy that emphasizes military spirit or values **—mil´i·ta·rist** *n.* **—mil´i·ta·ris´tic** *adj.* **—mil·i·ta·ris´ti·cal·ly** *adv*

**mil´i·ta·rize** *vt.* to prepare for war or for use by armed forces —**mil·i·ta·ri·za´tion** *n.*

**mil´i·tar·y** *adj.* related to armed forces or to war —**mil·i·tar´i·ly** *adv.*

**mi·li´tia** *n.* a citizen army —**mi·li´tia·man** *n.*

**milk** *n.* fluid produced by mammals to feed their young; any similar fluid, as from a plant —*vt.* to draw off or extract milk from; to take advantage of —**milk´i·ness** *n.* —**milk´y** *adj.*

**mill** *n.* a place for grinding grain; a factory; a device or machine that transforms by grinding, shaping, etc.; something that functions or seems to function methodically: *the rumor mill* —*vt.* to transform by a machine or other device —*vi.* to move about in a disorderly fashion —**mill´er** *n.*

**mil·len´ni·um** *n.* a period of a thousand years; a thousand-year period of joy and plenty as foretold in the Christian Bible —**mil·len´ni·al** *adj.* —**mil·len´ni·al·ist** *n.* —**mil·len´ni·al·ly** *adv.*

**mil´li·ner** *n.* one who makes or sells women's hats —**mil´li·nery** *n.*

**mil´lion·aire´** *n.* a wealthy person; one who possesses over a million dollars worth of assets

**mill´stone** *n.* a large, heavy stone used in milling grain; a burden: *debt can be a millstone around one's neck*

**milque´toast** *n.* a timid person

**mime** *n.* one who performs without words; a pantomime —*vi., vt.* to communicate with gestures —**mim´er** *n.*

**mim´e·o·graph** *n.* a machine that duplicates or prints documents from a stencil; copies made with such a machine —*vi., vt.*

**mim´ic** *n.* one who portrays another, often with exaggeration —*vt.* to imitate closely —**mim´ick·er** *n.* —**mim´ic·ry** *n.*

**min´a·ret´** *n.* a tower on a mosque from which Muslims are summoned to prayer

**min´a·to·ry, min·a·to´ri·al** *adj.* threatening —**min·a·to´ri·al·ly, min´a·to·ri·ly** *adv.*

**mince** *vi.* to walk or speak in an affected manner —*vt.* to chop into small pieces; to lessen or cushion so as to be polite: *to mince words* —**minc´er** *n.*

**mince´meat** *n.* a thick, spicy concoction of fruit and meat used especially as a pie filling

**mind** *n.* consciousness or awareness of being; the intellect that comprises such elements as memory, original thought, and emotion; the ability to think —*vi., vt.* to behave; to notice or give heed to; to be concerned about

**mind´-al·ter·ing** *adj.* that distorts the consciousness or intellect

**mind´-bog·gling** *adj.* overwhelming; extremely impressive —**mind´-bog·gler** *n.*

**mind´-expand·ing** *adj.* creating greater awareness: *education is mind-expanding*; psychedelic: creating distorted perception

**mind´ful** *adj.* careful, attentive; maintaining awareness —**mind´ful·ly** *adv.* —**mind´ful·ness** *n.*

**mind´less** *adj.* without reason or purpose; lacking care or caution; indifferent —**mind´less·ly** *adv.* —**mind´less·ness** *n.*

**mind·set, mind´-set** *n.* a fixed attitude or response; a predilection

**mind´s eye** imagination or memory

**mine** *n.* a hole in the ground or a tunnel, especially to extract minerals; any source, as of material or information: *the library is a mine for knowledge*; an explosive device used in warfare —*vi., vt.* to dig a tunnel; to extract minerals from the earth; to set a hidden explosive device

**mine´field** *n.* an area seeded with explosive devices; something potentially dangerous or unpleasant: *the minefield of morality in politics*

**min´er·al** *n.* naturally occurring inorganic matter —*adj.* of or containing inorganic matter

**min·er·al´o·gy** *n.* the study of minerals —**min·er·al·og´ic, min´er·al·og´i·cal** *adj.* —**min·er·al·og´i·cal·ly** *adv.* —**min·er·al´o·gist** *n.*

**mineral oil** a colorless, tasteless oil derived from petroleum

**mineral water** water that contains mineral salts, produced naturally or artificially

**min·e·stro´ne** *n.* an Italian soup of beans, pasta, and vegetables

**min´gle** *vi., vt.* to combine or mix together

**min´i·a·ture** *adj.* small or smaller —*n.* something small for its type; a copy or model of something larger —**min´i·a·tur·ist** *n.*

**min´i·a·tur·ize** *vt.* to make smaller without loss of utility: *to miniaturize computer components*; to make a model or copy in miniature —**min·i·a·tur·i·za´tion** *n.*

**min´i·bus** *n.* a small bus; a public conveyance used especially on routes traveled by few passengers

**min´i·cam** *n.* a portable video camera

**min´i·com·put·er** *n.* a computer that is smaller than a mainframe, but not easily portable; a desktop computer

**min´i·mal** *adj.* the smallest possible; barely adequate —**min´i·mal·ly** *adv.*

**min´i·mal·ism** *n.* a style of art characterized by simplicity of form, color, etc. —**min´i·mal·ist** *n.*

**min´i·mize** *vt.* to make with the smallest practical investment of resources; to downplay: *they minimized the extent of the loss* —**min´i·miz·er** *n.*

**min´i·mum** *n.* the least possible or allowable —*adj.*

**min´ion** *n.* a subordinate; a toady

**min´i·se·ries** *n.* a television program aired in a specific number of episodes

**min´is·ter** *n.* a clergyman; a government official —*vi.*

to care for others

**min´is·te´ri·al** *adj.* of a clergyman or government official, or their offices —**min·is·te´ri·al·ly** *adv.*

**min·is·tra´tion** *n.* the act of caring for another —**min´is·tra´tive** *adj.*

**min´is·try** *n.* the office and duties of a minister; a department of government or the building in which it is housed; the care of others

**min´now** *n.* a type of small fish

**mi´nor** *adj.* of less significance —*n.* something less by comparison; one who is not of legal age

**mi·nor´i·ty** *n.* the smaller of two groups that comprise a whole; the time before one is of legal age

**min´strel** *n.* a wandering singer and poet; a minstrel show

**minstrel show** a variety show performed by singers, comics, etc. in blackface

**mint** *adj.* new in appearance, as if freshly made: *in mint condition* —*n.* a place where coins are struck; a plentiful amount —*vt.* to make or strike coins —**mint´er** *n.*

**min·u·et´** *n.* a type of formal dance

**min´us·cule** *adj.* tiny

**min´ute** *n.* a small span of time; 1/60th of an hour —**mi·nute´** *adj.* very small; detailed or exacting, as of an examination —**mi·nute´ly** *adv.* —**mi·nute´ness** *n.*

**mi·nu´ti·a** *n., pl.* **mi·nu´ti·ae** a small often insignificant detail

**minx** *n.* a flirtatious or defiant woman —**minx´ish** *adj.*

**mir´a·cle** *n.* an event that seems to be scientifically unexplainable; a supernatural occurrence

**miracle drug** a medicine that is unusually effective or that can be used to treat a variety of illnesses

**mi·rac´u·lous** *adj.* of the nature of a miracle —**mi·rac´u·lous·ly** *adv.* —**mi·rac´u·lous·ness** *n.*

**mi·rage´** *n.* an illusion, such as the sight of water in the desert when there is none; something flimsy or fanciful

**mire** *n.* an expanse of wet, muddy ground; a swamp; a difficult situation —*vi., vt.* to become stuck, as if in a mire: *they were mired in paperwork* —**mir´y** *adj.*

**mir´ror** *n.* a surface that reflects a visual image; something thought of as presenting an image: *auto sales mirror the strength of the economy*

**mirror image** a reverse image, as presented in a mirror

**mirth** *n.* lighthearted merriment

**mirth´ful** *adj.* expressing lighthearted gaiety —**mirth´ful·ly** *adv.*—**mirth´ful·ness** *n.*

**mirth´less** *adj.* lacking gaiety; somber —**mirth´less·ly** *adv.* —**mirth´less·ness** *n.*

**mis·ad·ven´ture** *n.* misfortune

**mis´an·thrope, mis·an´thro·pist** *n.* one who dislikes or distrusts people; a recluse —**mis´an·throp´ic, mis´an·throp´i·cal** *adj.* —**mis´an·throp´i·cal·ly** *adv.*

**mis·an´thro·py** *n.* hatred or distrust of people in general

**mis´ap·pre·hend´** *vt.* to misunderstand —**mis·ap·pre·hen´sion** *n.*

**mis·ap·pro´pri·ate** *vt.* to take or use improperly or illegally —**mis·ap·pro·pri·a´tion** *n.*

**mis·be·have´** *vt.* to conduct oneself badly or improperly —*vi.* to behave badly —**mis·be·hav´er** *n.* —**mis·be·hav´ior** *n.*

**mis·cal´cu·late** *vi., vt.* to plan, judge, or tally inaccurately —**mis·cal·cu·la´tion** *n.*

**mis·car´riage** *n.* the premature birth of a nonviable fetus; a spontaneous abortion; a failure or malfunction: *a miscarriage of justice* —**mis·car´ry** *vi.*

**mis´ceg·e·na´tion** *n.* a mixing of races, as by marriage

**mis·cel·la´ne·a** *pl. n.* a collection of written works or items

**mis·cel·la´ne·ous** *adj.* comprising a variety —**mis·cel·la´ne·ous·ly** *adv.* —**mis·cel·la´ne·ous·ness** *n.*

**mis´cel·la·ny** *n.* a collection

**mis·chance´** *n.* misfortune

**mis´chief** *n.* a deliberate act that causes damage or distress; a tendency to perform such acts; one who engages in such acts —**mis´chief-mak´er** *n.*

**mis´chie·vous** *adj.* inclined to playful action such as teasing, or bothersome behavior such as being destructive or spreading rumors —**mis´chie·vous·ly** *adv.* —**mis´chie·vous·ness** *n.*

**mis·con·cep´tion** *n.* a misunderstanding —**mis·con·ceive´** *vt.*

**mis·con´duct** *n.* action contrary to accepted standards; wrongdoing, especially by a public official or one charged with protecting the interests of another —**mis´con·duct´** *vt.* to behave improperly; to mismanage the assets of another

**mis´con·strue´** *vt.* to misinterpret

**mis´cre·ant** *n.* a villain; a criminal —*adj.* villainous

**mis·deed´** *n.* the violation of a rule or law

**mis´de·mean´or** *n.* a minor crime

**mis·di·rect´** *vt.* to improperly instruct or inform; to deliberately draw attention away from —**mis·di·rec´tion** *n.*

**mi´ser** *n.* one who hoards money

**mis´er·a·ble** *adj.* wretched; unpleasant —**mis´er·a·ble·ness** *n.* —**mis´er·a·bly** *adv.*

**mi´ser·ly** *adj.* stingy —**mi´ser·li·ness** *n.*

**mis´er·y** *n.* suffering or distress; anything that causes suffering

**mis´fit´** *n.* one who does not harmonize or conform; a maladjusted person

**mis·for´tune** *n.* bad luck; adversity or a condition brought on by adversity

**mis·giv´ing** *n.* a feeling of doubt or uncertainty

**mis·guide´** *vt.* to guide or direct improperly; to mislead; to lead astray —**mis·guid´ance** *n.* —**mis·**

**guid´er** *n.*
**mis·guid´ed** *adj.* improperly directed; based on improper information or logic: *misguided efforts* **—mis·guid´ed·ly** *adv.*
**mis·han´dle** *vt.* to mismanage; to treat roughly or clumsily
**mis´hap** *n.* an accident
**mish´mash** *n.* a jumble of miscellaneous things; a poorly assembled or organized collection: *a mishmash of information*
**mis·in·form´** *vt.* to advise inadequately or inaccurately; to mislead **—mis·in·form´ant, mis·in·form´er** *n.* **—mis·in·for·ma´tion** *n.*
**mis·in·ter´pret** *vt.* to misunderstand; to explain incorrectly **—mis´in·ter·pre·ta´tion** *n.* **—mis´in·ter´pret·er** *n.*
**mis·judge´** *vt.* to form an opinion wrongly or unfairly *—vi.* to err in judging **—mis·judg´ment** *n.*
**mis·lay´** *vt.* to place and forget
**mis·lead´** *vt.* to direct wrongly or improperly; to lead astray **—mis·lead´er** *n.*
**mis·lead´ing** *adj.* deceptive **—mis·lead´ing·ly** *adv.*
**mis·man´age** *vt.* to conduct or supervise carelessly or wrongfully **—mis·man´age·ment** *n.*
**mis·match´** *n.* an incompatible or unfit pairing *—vt.*
**mis·no´mer** *n.* an inappropriate name or designation
**mi´so** *n.* a thick fermented paste used especially in soup
**mis·og´a·mist** *n.* one who hates marriage **—mis·o·gam´ic** *adj.* **—mis·og´a·my** *n.*
**mis·og´y·nist** *n.* one who hates women **—mis·og·y·nis´tic, mi·sog´y·nous** *adj.* **—mi·sog´y·ny** *n.*
**mis·place´** *vt.* to mislay or lose; to put in the wrong place **—mis·place´ment** *n.*
**mis´print** *n.* a printing error *—vt.*
**mis·pri´sion** *n.* concealment of a crime
**mis·pro·nounce´** *vt.* to enunciate incorrectly **—mis·pro·nun·ci·a´tion** *n.*
**mis·quote´** *vt.* to cite incorrectly **—mis·quo·ta´tion** *n.*
**mis·read´** *vt.* to read or interpret incorrectly; to misunderstand
**mis·re·mem´ber** *vt.* to recall incorrectly; to fail to recall
**mis·rep·re·sen·ta´tion** *n.* a false or misleading depiction **—mis´rep·re·sent´** *vt.*
**miss** *n.* a failing; a form of address for an unmarried woman *—vi., vt.* to fail to make contact, as in hitting or catching a ball; to exclude or allow to pass: *miss an opportunity*; to discover or endure the loss of: *I miss my friends*
**mis´sal** *n.* a prayer book
**mis·shape´** *vt.* to fashion badly; to deform or distort **—mis·shap´en·ly** *adv.*
**mis´sile** *n.* a projectile
**miss´ing** *adj.* absent or lacking; gone
**missing link** something lacking in a sequence, as in the evolutionary chain of a creature
**mis´sion** *n.* a group or organization established for a special purpose, as of a diplomatic or religious nature; the function or task of such a group **—mis´sion·ar·y** *n., adj.*
**mis´sive** *n.* a letter or memo; any written message
**mis·speak´** *vi., vt.* to speak incorrectly or out of turn
**mis·spend** *vt.* to squander
**mis·step´** *n.* a slipping or stumbling; a mistake or blunder
**mist** *n.* minute droplets that form a haze; something that obscures *—vt., vi.* to make or become dim: *to mist over*; to rain in fine droplets **—mist´i·ly** *adv.* **—mist´i·ness** *n.* **—mist´y** *adj.*
**mis·tak´a·ble** *adj.* susceptible to misunderstanding **—mis·tak´a·bly** *adv.*
**mis·take´** *n.* an error; a misunderstanding *—vi.* to make a mistake *—vt.* to misinterpret; to wrongly identify a person
**mis·tak´en** *adj.* misinformed or misguided; wrong **—mis·tak´en·ly** *adv.*
**mis´ter** *n.* a form of address for a man
**mis·treat´** *vt.* to handle roughly or clumsily **—mis·treat´ment** *n.*
**mis´tress** *n.* a woman in authority; one who owns or controls; a teacher; one who possesses exceptional knowledge or ability in a particular field; a female who is companion to and supported by a man not her husband
**mis·tri´al** *n.* a trial in which a verdict is not rendered or that is declared invalid
**mis·trust´** *n.* uncertainty, doubt, or suspicion *—vi., vt.* to regard with doubt or suspicion **—mis·trust´ful** *adj.* **—mis·trust´ful·ly** *adv.* **mis·trust´ful·ness** *n.*
**mist´y-eyed** *adj.* sentimental; tearful
**mis·un·der·stand´** *vt.* to misinterpret
**mis·un·der·stand´ing** *n.* a calm disagreement or quarrel; a misinterpretation
**mis·un·der·stood´** *adj.* misinterpreted; misjudged; not appreciated
**mis·use´** *n.* an improper use; abuse *—vt.* to use wrongly or improperly; to abuse **—mis·us´age** *n.*
**mi´ter** *n.* a tall ornamental headdress worn by church leaders; the office of a bishop; one of the bevels that make up a miter joint *—vt.* to raise to the rank of bishop; to join with a miter
**miter box** a guide designed to assist in the cutting of a miter
**miter joint** a coupling of two angled pieces, as at the corner of a picture frame
**mit´i·gate** *vi., vt.* to become or make less intense or severe **—mit´i·ga·ble** *adj.* **—mit·i·ga´tion** *n.* **—mit´i·ga·tive, mit´i·ga·to·ry** *adj.* **—mit´i·ga·tor** *n.*
**mitt** *n.* a glove, especially one worn for protection:

*catcher's mitt, oven mitt*

**mit´ten** *n.* a glove with one pocket for the thumb and another for the four fingers

**mix** *n.* a combination of ingredients *—vi., vt.* to become or cause to become combined; to blend in; to confuse: *the waiter mixed up their orders* **—mix´a·ble** *adj.*

**mixed** *adj.* combined; consisting of differing elements: *of mixed blood*

**mixed´-up´** *adj.* confused or befuddled

**mix´er** *n.* a device that combines or blends; the non-alcoholic beverage in a cocktail; a type of gathering; one who meets easily with others

**mix´ture** *n.* a mix; anything that results from mixing or combining

**mix´-up** *n.* a state of turmoil or confusion

**mne·mon´ics** *n.* any formula or technique used as a memory aid **—mne·mon´i·cal·ly** *adv.* **—mne·mon´ic, mne·mon´i·cal** *adj.*

**moan** *n.* a low, doleful sound **—moan´er** *n.*

**moat** *n.* a protective ditch

**mob** *n.* a large crowd, often disorderly; a group of criminals *—vt.* to crowd or overwhelm

**mo´bile** *adj.* movable; easily moved *—n.* a piece of hanging art made up of balanced pieces that move freely

**mo·bil´i·ty** *n.* movement; the ability to move easily

**mo´bi·lize** *vt.* to make moveable; to organize and deploy, as for a cause **—mo·bi·li·za´tion** *n.*

**mob´ster** *n.* a criminal

**moc´ca·sin** *n.* footwear similar to a slipper, often of leather

**mo´cha** *n.* a rich coffee; a flavoring of coffee and chocolate

**mock** *adj.* imitation; false *—vi., vt.* to ridicule or imitate derisively **—mock´er** *n.* **—mock´ery** *n.* **—mock´ing·ly** *adv.*

**mock´-up** *n.* a scale model; a layout for a printed page

**mode** *n.* a particular manner or fashion **—mod´al** *adj.*

**mod´el** *n.* a copy or prototype; one who poses for an artist or displays clothing, etc.; an ideal: *a model of virtue —vi., vt.* to make a model; to pose; to display by wearing

**mod´el·ing** *n.* the art of sculpting; the act of posing, as for an artist

**mo´dem** *n.* a device that converts data from digital to analog and back

**mod´er·ate** *adj.* not extreme or excessive *—n.* one who is not inclined to extreme views, as in politics *—vi., vt.* to become or make less extreme; to preside as moderator **—mod´er·ate·ly** *adv.* **—mod´er·ate·ness** *n.* **—mod·er·a´tion** *n.*

**mod´er·a·tor** *n.* one who mediates or officiates, as at a meeting

**mod´ern** *adj.* of recent time or development **—mod´ern·ly** *adv.* **—mod´ern·ness** *n.*

**mod´ern·ize** *vi., vt.* to become or make contemporary **—mod·ern·i·za´tion** *n.*

**mod´est** *adj.* unpretentious; diffident; conforming to convention; not given to extremes: *a modest proposal* **—mod´est·ly** *adv.* **—mod´es·ty** *n.*

**mod´i·cum** *n.* a small amount

**mod·i·fi·ca´tion** *n.* a change or alteration; the result of such change **—mod´i·fi·ca·to·ry** *adj.*

**mod´i·fy** *vt.* to change or alter, especially to make less extreme **—mod·i·fi·a·bil´i·ty** *n.* **—mod´i·fi·a·ble** *adj.* **—mod´i·fi·er** *n.*

**mod´ish** *adj.* smart or trendy; in the current style **—mod´ish·ly** *adv.* **—mod´ish·ness** *n.*

**mod´u·lar** *adj.* of a module; based on the use of or made up of modules **—mod´u·lar·ize** *vt.* **—mod´u·lar·ized** *adj.*

**mod´ule** *n.* a self-contained component that may be attached as or where needed, such as a part of a furniture grouping, a sound system, or a computer program

**mo´dus ope·ran´di** *n.* a manner of operating

**mo´dus vi·ven´di** *n.* a manner of living

**mo´gul** *n.* one who is rich or powerful

**moi´e·ty** *n.* a half; a portion

**moist** *adj.* slightly wet; damp **—moist´ly** *—adv.* **—moist´ness** *n.*

**moist´en** *vi., vt.* to become or make slightly wet **—moist´en·er** *n.*

**mois´ture** *n.* slight wetness, as dampness in the air or condensation on a surface

**mois´tur·ize** *vt.* to add wetness to **—mois´tur·iz·er** *n.*

**mo´lar** *n.* a large tooth used to grind foods

**mo·las´ses** *n.* a thick, sweet syrup

**mold**[1] *(US) n.* a form for casting an image *—vi.* to be shaped in or as if in a form *—vt.* to form or shape **—mold´able** *adj.* **—mold´er** *n.*

**mold**[2] *(US) n.* a type of fungal growth *—vt.* to be marked or damaged by a fungal growth

**mold, mold´ing** *n.* a decorative strip used as trim, as around a door or window

**mold´er** *(US) vi.* to gradually decay

**mold´y** *(US) adj.* damaged or spoiled by a fungal growth; having a musty odor **—mold´i·ness** *n.*

**mol´e·cule** *n.* the smallest particle of matter having distinctive chemical and physical properties; a tiny particle **—mo·lec´u·lar** *adj.*

**mo·lest´** *vt.* to disturb or annoy; to accost improperly in a sexual manner **—mo·les·ta´tion** *n.* **—mo·lest´er** *n.*

**mol´li·fy** *vt.* to soothe or pacify; to soften **—mol·li·fi·ca´tion** *n.* **—mol´li·fy·ing·ly** *adv.*

**mol´lusk** *n.* a marine invertebrate with a soft body and a hard protective shell **—mol·lus´coid** *adj.*

**molt** *(US) vi., vt.* to shed, as feathers or an outer skin

—**molt´er** *n.*

**mol´ten** *adj.* extremely hot and melted or liquified

**mo´ment** *n.* a brief interval: *he'll be along in a moment;* importance: *a breakthrough of great moment*

**mo´men·tary** *adj.* existing for a brief time —**mo´men·tar´i·ly** *adv.* —**mo´men·tar·i·ness** *n.*

**mo·men´tous** *adj.* of great importance —**mo·men´tous·ly** *adv.* —**mo·men´tous·ness** *n.*

**mo·men´tum** *n.* a measure of the force of a body in motion; the force or energy generated by ideas or events

**mon´arch** *n.* an absolute ruler —**mo·nar´chal, mo·nar´chic, mo·nar´chi·cal** *adj.* —**mo·nar´chal·ly** *adv.*

**mon´ar·chism** *n.* advocacy of a monarchy —**mon´ar·chist** *n.* —**mon·ar·chist´ic** *adj.*

**mon´ar·chy** *n.* government by a sovereign, usually selected by hereditary succession and for life —**mo·nar´chi·al** *adj.*

**mon´as·ter·y** *n.* a religious community, often secluded —**mon´as·te´ri·al** *adj.*

**mo·nas´tic** *adj.* typical of a monastery, as an austere or disciplined environment —**mo·nas´ti·cal·ly** *adv.*

**mon·au´ral** *adj.* monophonic: of sound directed through a single channel —**mon·au´ral·ly** *adv.*

**mon´e·ta·rism** *n.* the management of an economy by adjustment of the domestic money supply —**mon´e·ta·rist** *n.*

**mon´e·tary** *adj.* regarding money or finances —**mon·e·tar´i·ly** *adv.*

**mon´ey** *n.* legal tender; the currency, notes, etc. issued by a government; an expression of wealth: *in the money*

**mon´ey·bags** *n.* a wealthy person; a spendthrift

**mon´eyed** *adj.* wealthy

**mon´ey·grub´ber** *n.* one intent on amassing wealth —**mon´ey·grub´ bing** *adj.*

**mon´ey·mak·ing** *adj.* profitable —**mon´ey·mak·er** *n.*

**mon´ger** *n.* a tradesman: *a fishmonger,* a promoter or advocate of something: *a peacemonger, a scandalmonger*

**mon´grel** *adj.* of mixed breed —*n.* a plant or animal that is the result of interbreeding —**mon·grel·i·za´tion** *n.* —**mon´grel·ize** *vt.*

**mon´i·tor** *n.* a device that controls or provides an overview of a system; an adviser or assistant; an overseer —*vt.* to oversee or regulate —**mon´i·to´ri·al** *adj.* —**mon·i·to´ri·al·ly** *adv.* —**mon´i´tor·ship** *n.*

**mon´i·to·ry** *adj.* admonishing; cautionary

**monk** *n.* a member of a religious order, residing in a monestary —**monk´hood** *n.*

**monk´ish** *adj.* characteristic of a monk or a monastic life; austere or disciplined —**monk´ish·ly** *adv.* —**monk´ish· ness** *n.*

**mon´o·chro·mat´ic** *adj.* having one color —**mon·o·chro·mat´i·cal·ly** *adv.* —**mon·o·chro·ma·tic´i·ty** *n.*

**mon´o·chrome** *n.* a picture or image in one color —*adj.* monochromatic —**mon·o·chro´mic** *adj.*

**mon´o·cle** *n.* a corrective lens for one eye —**mon´o·cled** *adj.*

**mo·noc´ra·cy** *n.* government by a single person —**mon´o·crat** *n.* —**mon·o·crat´ic** *adj.*

**mo·nog´a·my** *n.* the practice of having one spouse or mate at a time; the practice of taking one spouse or mate for a lifetime —**mo·nog´a·mist** *n.* —**mo·nog´a·mous** *adj.* —**mo·nog´a·mous·ly** *adv.*

**mon´o·gram** *n.* a letter or letters designed as a distinguishing emblem —*vt.* to adorn with a monogram —**mon´o·gram·mat´ic** *adj.*

**mon´o·graph** *n.* a scholarly dissertation —**mo·nog´ra·pher** *n.* —**mon´o·graph´ic** *adj.*

**mon´o·lith** *n.* a large block of stone that forms a column or monument; something massive and solid —**mon´o·lith´ic** *adj.* —**mon·o·lith´i·cal·ly** *adv.*

**mon´o·log, mon´o·logue** *n.* an informal discourse by a single person that may be dramatic or comedic —**mo·nol´o·gist** *n.*

**mon·o·pho´bi·a** *n.* fear of being alone

**mon·o·phon´ic** *adj.* monaural; of a musical composition that is mainly a single line of melody —**mon·o·phon´i·cal·ly** *adv.* —**mo·noph´o·ny** *n.*

**mo·nop´o·lize** *vt.* to dominate, as a conversation; to control, as the market in certain goods —**mo·nop·o·li·za´tion** *n.*

**mo·nop´o·ly** *n.* absolute control of a market by a limited number; those having control, or the commodity or service thereby controlled; any control, as if by a monopoly: *they act as if they have a monopoly on integrity* —**mo·nop´o·list** *n.* —**mo·nop´o·lis´tic** *adj.* —**mo·nop·o·lis´ti·cal·ly** *adv.*

**mon´o·rail** *n.* a train that travels on or is suspended from a single rail

**mon´o·syl·lab´ic** *adj.* pertaining to a word of one syllable —**mon·o·syl·lab´i·cal·ly** *adv.*

**mon´o·the·ism** *n.* belief in a single god —**mon´o·the·ist** *n.* —**mon´o·the·is´tic, mon·o·the·is´ti·cal** *adj.* —**mon·o·the·is´ti·cal·ly** *adv.*

**mon´o·tone** —*n.* an instrumentation or vocalization in a single tone; an illustration in a single color; a listless or boring delivery: *he droned on in a monotone* —**mon·o·ton´ic** *adj.* —**mon·o·ton´i·cal·ly** *adv.*

**mo·not´o·nous** *adj.* tedious or tiresome; spoken in a monotone —**mo·not´o·nous·ly** *adv.* —**mo·not´o·ny** *n.*

**mon´ster** *n.* a frightening creature; someone abnormally cruel; a deformed organism; something very large

**mon´strous** *adj.* frightening; abnormally cruel; deformed; huge —**mon·stros´i·ty** *n.* —**mon´strous·ly** *adv.* —**mon·strous·ness** *n.*

**mon·tage´** *n.* a work of art made up of a number of

separate designs or pictures
**month** *n.* a period approximating one cycle of the moon; one-twelfth of a year
**month´ly** *adj.* occurring every month –*n.* a periodical that is published every month
**mon´u·ment** *n.* a memorial, such as a structure or plaque; a structure or plate anchored in the ground as a boundry or survey marker; an outstanding example: *the decor is a monument to bad taste*
**mon·u·men´tal** *adj.* impressive, as in size or significance –**mon·u·men´tal·ly** *adv.*
**mooch** *vi., vt.* to freeload or get by begging –**mooch´er** *n.*
**mood** *n.* one's state of mind or attitude
**mood´y** *adj.* sullen; susceptible to depression; temperamental –**mood´i·ly** *adv.* –**mood´i·ness** *n.*
**moon** *n.* a satellite of a planet; the bared buttocks –*vi.* to languish about as though distracted –*vt.* to bare the buttocks in a playful manner
**moon´light** *n.* light reflected from the moon –*vi.* to work at a second job, often at night
**moon´shine** *n.* illegal whiskey –**moon´shin·er** *n.*
**moon´struck** *adj.* beguiled by romantic notions
**moor** *vi., vt.* to secure or anchor, as a boat or plane
**moor´age, moor´ing** *n.* a place where a boat or plane may be secured; the charge for use of such a place
**moot** *adj.* that can be disputed; of no significance
**mop** *n.* a clump or mass of soft material, usually attached to a handle and used for cleaning; something resembling a soft clump or mass: *a mop of hair* –*vi., vt.* to wash or wipe by rubbing; to make clean; to complete a task: *mop up the details of the contract* –**mop´-up** *n.*
**mope** *vi.* to act dejected; to sulk –**mop´er** *n.* –**mop´ey, mop´ish** *adj.* –**mop´ish·ly** *adv.*
**mop´pet** *n.* a child
**mo·raine´** *n.* debris deposited by a glacier, as rocks or boulders –**mo´rain´ic** *adj.*
**mor´al** *adj.* conforming to what is right or just –*n.* a truth or principle, as contained in a story or saying –**mor´al·ly** *adv.*
**mo·rale´** *n.* one's attitude or sense of enthusiasm, resolve, or confidence
**mor´al·ist** *n.* one overly concerned with morals; one inclined to impose his or her values on others –**mor´al·ism** *n.* –**mor´al·is´tic** *adj.*–**mor·al·is´ti·cal·ly** *adv.*
**mo·ral´i·ty** *n.* a system or sense of what is right or just; conduct that is true to such a system
**mor´al·ize** *vi., vt.* to pronounce judgement or lecture on morals –**mor·al·iz·a´tion** *n.*
**mo·rass´** *n.* a wetland; a marsh or bog; something that impedes: *a morass of regulations*
**mor·a·to´ri·um** *n.* a suspension or delay: *a moratorium on nuclear testing*–**mor´a·to·ry** *adj.*
**mor´bid** *adj.* diseased; caused by disease; gruesome; abnormally preoccupied by that which is gruesome –**mor´bid·ly** *adv.* –**mor´bid·ness** *n.*
**mor·da´cious** *adj.* sharp or caustic; sarcastic –**mor·da´cious·ly** *adv.* –**mor·dac´i·ty** *n.*
**mor´dant** *adj.* sharp or incisive; caustic –*n.* a corrosive substance used in etching –**mor´dan·cy** *n.*–**mor´dant·ly** *adv.*
**more** *adj.* greater, as in number or degree; enhanced or extended –*n.* an additional amount –*adv.*
**mo´res** *n.* the accepted standards of a society, as in customs, manners, or morals
**morgue** *n.* a place where dead bodies are kept awaiting identification, autopsy, burial, etc.; a library or reference file, especially in a news office
**mor´i·bund** *adj.* nearing death; outdated –**mor·i·bun´di·ty** *n.* –**mor´i·bund·ly** *adv.*
**morn** *n.* daybreak; the daylight hours of morning
**morn´ing** *n.* that part of the day from midnight to noon or from sunrise to noon; a beginning
**mo´ron** *n.* someone regarded as stupid or very foolish –**mo·ron´ic** *adj.* –**mo·ron´i·cal·ly** *adv.*
**mo·rose´** *adj.* surly or gloomy –**mo·rose´ly** *adv.* –**mo·rose´ness** *n.*
**mor·phol´o·gy** *n.* the scientific study of the form and structure of things, as of organisms or of words –**mor´pho·log´ic, mor·pho·log´i·cal** *adj.* –**mor·pho·log´i·cal·ly** *adv.* –**mor·phol´o·gist** *n.*
**mor´row** *n.* the next day
**mor´sel** *n.* a bit of food, especially a delicacy; a small amount: *a morsel of kindness*
**mor´tal** *adj.* of the physical person in contrast to the spiritual or supernatural; susceptible to death; deadly –*n.* a human being –**mor´tal·ly** *adv.*
**mor·tal´i·ty** *n.* the limits to being mortal; a rate of death or failure
**mor´tar** *n.* a bonding material used in construction; something that bonds: *the star is the mortar that holds the show together*, a type of cannon; a container in which material such as spice or chemicals are ground with a pestle
**mor´tar·board** *n.* a board used for carrying mortar; a flat-topped graduation cap
**mort´gage** *n.* the pledge of property as security for payment of a debt; a contract stipulating the terms of such a pledge –*vt.* to pledge property –**mort´gage·a·ble** *adj.*
**mort·ga·gee´** *n.* one who lends and holds a mortgage
**mort´ga·gor** *n.* one who borrows and mortgages
**mor·ti´cian** *n.* one who prepares the dead for burial; an undertaker
**mor·ti·fi·ca´tion** *n.* humiliation or shame; discipline or penance as by self-denial
**mor´ti·fy** *vi.* to undergo discipline through self-denial –*vt.* to humiliate or shame; to discipline oneself

through self-denial

**mor´tise** *n.* a slot designed to accept a tenon and form a joint in a piece of wood or other material

**mor´tu·ary** *n.* a place where dead bodies are kept in preparation for burial

**mo·sa´ic** *n.* a design made on a surface by joining small colored pieces, such as tiles; something resembling a mosaic –**mo·sa´i·cal·ly** *adj.*

**mosque** *n.* a Muslim house of worship

**most** *adj.* of the greatest number or amount –*n.* the larger part; the greatest amount –*adv.* to the greatest degree, extent, etc.

**mostl´y** *adv.* frequently; largely

**mot** *n.* a witty remark

**mote** *n.* a speck

**mo·tel´** *n.* a lodging for travelers

**moth´-eat·en** *adj.* passé; shabby, as though attacked by moths

**moth´er** *adj.* being of a source or derived from: *English is our mother tongue* –*n.* a female parent; one who gives birth –*vt.* to give birth; to rear

**moth´er·board** *n.* a panel that contains the primary circuitry for a computer

**moth´er-in-law** *n.* the mother of one's spouse

**mother lode** an abundant source

**moth´er·ly** *adj.* nurturing; having the qualities of a mother

**mother tongue** one's native language

**mo·tif´** *n.* a recurring theme, as in art or decorating

**mo´tile** *adj.* having the power of motion –**mo·til´i·ty** *n.*

**mo·tion** *n.* a movement; the act of moving; a proposal, as put before a court or in a formal meeting –*vi., vt.* to gesture or guide

**mo´tion·less** *adj.* immobile; still –**mo´tion·less·ly** *adv.* –**mo´tion·less·ness** *n.*

**mo´ti·vate** *vt.* to rouse to action –**mo´ti·va´tor** *n.*

**mo·ti·va´tion** *n.* an inducement –**mo·ti·va´tion·al** *adj.* –**mo·ti·va´tion·al·ly** *adv.*

**mo·tive** *n.* an urge that induces one to act

**mot´ley** *adj.* varied; marked by variety or incongruity; multicolored –*n.* a multi-colored garment as worn by court jesters of old; an incongruous mixture

**mo´tor** *adj.* of motion or things associated with motion –*n.* a device that produces mechanical energy –*vi., vt.* to travel or convey by motor vehicle

**mo´tor·cade** *n.* a parade of motor vehicles

**motor vehicle** a free-wheeling conveyance, such as a car or truck, powered by a built-in engine

**mot´tled** *adj.* spotted with a variety of colors or tints –**mot´tle** *vt.* –**mot´tling** *n.*

**mot´to** *n.* a word or phrase that expresses a worthwhile thought

**mould**[1] *(Brit.) n.* a form for casting an image –*vi.* to be shaped in or as if in a form –*vt.* to form or shape –**mould´er** *n.*

**mould**[2] *(Brit.) n.* a type of fungal growth– *vt.* to be marked or damaged by a fungal growth

**mould´er** *(Brit.) vi.* to gradually decay

**mould´y** *(Brit.) adj.* damaged or spoiled by a fungal growth; having a musty odor –**mould´i·ness** *n.*

**moult** *(Brit.) vi., vt.* to shed, as feathers or an outer skin –**moult´er** *n.*

**mound** *n.* a pile or heap; a knoll or small hill –*vt.* to make into a heap

**mount** *n.* a riding horse; a device that holds something, as for display –*vi., vt* to ascend, as stairs; to get onto, as a horse; to fix in place, as pictures in an album; to increase, as cost –**mount´a·ble** *adj.* –**mount´er** *n.*

**mount, moun´tain** *n.* elevated land of substantial height and mass; a large amount: *we faced a mountain of work*

**mountain dew** moonshine

**moun´tain·ous** *adj.* resembling a mountain: extremely large; full of mountains –**moun´tain·ous·ly** *adv.*

**mountain range** a string of connected mountains

**moun´te·bank** *n.* a charlatan; originally, a fast-talking seller of useless medicine or tonic

**mourn** *vi., vt.* to express grief or sorrow –**mourn´er** *n.*

**mourn´ful** *adj.* expressing or suggesting grief or sorrow: *a mournful sound* –**mourn´ful·ly** *adv.* –**mourn´ful·ness** *n.*

**mourn´ing** *n.* a period of grieving for the dead; the signs of grieving, as black clothing or arm band

**mouse** *n.* a small rodent; a timid person; a computer control device –**mous´ey, mous´y** *adj.*

**mousse** *n.* any of a number of light desserts or savory dishes bound by whipped cream and gelatin and served cold; a preparation used to style the hair

**mous´tache** *n.* hair grown on the upper lip

**mouth** *n.* the body opening for taking in food; any restricted opening, as of a river, a bottle, or a cave –*vi., vt.* to speak; to form words without sound

**mouth´y** *adj.* given to excessive or offensive speech; annoyingly talkative –**mouth´i·ly** *adv.* –**mouth´i·ness** *n.*

**move** *vi., vt.* to advance, or cause to advance from one place to another; to alter position; to act or be active; to be or cause to be emotionally aroused; to propose a course, as in court or a formal meeting –**mov·a·bil´i·ty, mov´a·ble·ness** *n.* –**mov´a·ble** *adj.* –**mov´a·bly** *adv.*

**move´ment** *n.* a change in position; a steady or gradual change

**mov´er** *n.* one who transports goods; one purposeful in seeking advancement

**mov´ing** *adj.* in motion; of the transfer of goods; tending to arouse an emotional response –**mov´ing·ly** *adv.*

**mow** *n.* a place in a barn for the storage of feed; the

feed stored *—vi., vt.* to cut down, as grain **—mow´er** *n*

**much** *adj.* considerable, as in quantity or extent *—n.* a considerable amount *—adv.* to a great degree; approximately

**mu´ci·lage** *n.* an adhesive **—mu´ci·lag´i·nous** *adj.*

**muck** *n.* a wet sticky mixture; filth; something offensive *—vt.* to soil; to botch: *he mucked up the deal* **—muck´y** *adj.*

**muck´rak·er** *n.* one who exposes the shortcomings of those in the public eye **—muck´rake** *vi.*

**mud** *n.* a mixture of soil and water; plaster or mortar; charges of wrongdoing or indiscretion

**mud´dle** *n.* confusion or disorder; a predicament *—vi., vt.* to be or make confused; to mismanage **—mud´dler** *n.* **—mud´dle-head·ed** *adj.*

**mud´dy** *adj.* stained with mud; murky or hazy: *muddy coffee, muddy thinking* **—mud´di·ly** *adv.* **—mud´di·ness** *n.*

**mud´sling·er** *n.* one who levels charges of wrongdoing or indiscretion, especially at a political opponent **—mud´sling·ing** *n.*

**muff** *vi., vt.* to perform badly; to bungle

**muf´fin** *n.* a type of quick bread

**muf´fle** *vt.* to suppress or deaden sound; to maintain secrecy, as if by covering

**muf´fler** *n.* a heavy scarf; *(US)* a device for deadening sound, as from an engine

**mug** *n.* a heavy cup; one's face or expression; a gangster *—vi.* to contort the face for comic effect *—vt.* to assault

**mug´ger** *n.* one who makes comical faces; one who assaults

**mug´gy** *adj.* warm and humid **—mug´gi·ness** *n.*

**mulch** *n.* ground cover placed around plants to protect them *—vt.* to distribute ground cover

**mul´ish** *adj.* obstinate **—mul´ish·ly** *adv.* **—mul´ish·ness** *n.*

**mull** *vi., vt.* to ponder

**mul´ti·col´ored** *adj.* made up of a variety of colors

**mul·ti·cul´tur·al** *adj.* involving a diversity of cultures **—mul·ti·cul´tur·al·ism** *n.*

**mul´ti·di·men´sion·al** *adj.* diverse; varied in proportions and scope **—mul´ti·di·men·sion·al´i·ty** *n.*

**mul·ti·fac´et·ed** *adj.* diverse; having many aspects; versatile

**mul´ti·far´i·ous** *adj.* having great variety, diverse **—mul·ti·far´i´ous·ly** *adv.* **—mul·ti·far´i·ous·ness** *n.*

**mul´ti·form** *adj.* having many forms **—mul´ti·form´i·ty** *n.*

**mul´ti·lat´er·al** *adj.* involving several groups or nations; having many sides **—mul·ti·lat´er·al·ly** *adv.*

**mul·ti·lin´gual** *adj.* proficient in several languages **—mul·ti·lin´gual·ism** *n.* **—mul·ti·lin´gual·ly** *adv.*

**mul´ti·me´di·a** *n.* the mingling of several means of communication, such as visual images and sound on the computer, or the use of newspapers, radio, and television for an advertising campaign *—adj.* of the combining of media: *a multimedia presentation*

**mul´ti·na´tion·al** *adj.* involving several nations, such as for a trade agreement *—n.* a company with operations in several countries

**mul´ti·ple** *adj.* relating to several

**mul´ti·plex** *n.* a single building that contains a number of similar units, such as movie theaters

**mul·ti·pli·ca´tion** *n.* the process of increasing a number by adding it to itself a given number of times; animal or plant reproduction **—mul·ti·pli·ca´tion·al** *adj.*

**mul·ti·plic´i·ty** *n.* a large or varied collection: *a multiplicity of styles*

**mul´ti·ply** *vi., vt.* to increase or grow in numbers **—mul´ti·pli·able, mul´ti·plic´a·ble** *adj.*

**mul·ti·task´ing** *adj.* of a computer or computer application capable of performing several tasks at the same time

**mul´ti·tude** *n.* a large number; the general public

**mul·ti·tu´di·nous** *adj.* of a large number **—mul·ti·tu´di·nous·ly** *adv.* **—mul·ti·tu´di·nous·ness** *n.*

**mum´ble** *n.* an indistinct articulation or utterance *—vi., vt.* to speak indistinctly **—mum´bler** *n.* **—mum´bling·ly** *adv.* **—mum´bly** *adj.*

**mum´bo jum´bo** *n.* gibberish

**mum´mer** *n.* one who masquerades, esp. for certain festivals; an actor **—mum´mery** *n.*

**mum·mi·fi·ca´tion** *n.* preparation of a body for burial in the manner of the ancient Egyptians; the drying and preservation of a cadaver by natural conditions **—mum´mi·fy** *vi., vt.* **—mum´my** *n.*

**mumps** *pl. n.* a viral disease manifested mainly in the swelling of the salivary glands

**munch** *vi., vt.* to chew food **—munch´a·ble** *adj.*

**munch´ies** *n.* snack food

**munch´kin** *n.* a small person, especially a child

**mun·dane´** *adj.* common or ordinary; not exceptional: *a mundane performance* **—mun·dane´ly** *adv.* **—mun·dane´ness** *n.*

**mu·nic´i·pal** *adj.* relating to a municipality or to local government **—mu·nic´i·pal·ly** *adv.*

**mu·nic·i·pal´i·ty** *n.* a local governmental unit, as for a city or town

**mu·nic´i·pal·ize** *vt.* to bring under municipal authority or ownership **—mu·nic·i·pal·i·za´tion** *n.*

**mu·nif´i·cent** *adj.* generous **—mu·nif´i·cence** *n.* **—mu·nif´i·cent·ly** *adv.*

**mu·ni´tions** *pl. n.* arms and ammunition

**mu´ral** *n.* a painting or photograph applied directly to a wall or ceiling **—mu´ral·ist** *n.*

**mur´der** *n.* an unlawful killing; something arduous or unpleasant: *this chemistry test is murder* *—vt.* to

kill or destroy; to corrupt: *he murders the language* **—mur´der·er** *n.*
**mur´der·ous** *adj.* capable of killing; menacing; unpleasant: *murderous weather* **—mur´der·ous·ly** *adv.* **—mur´der·ous·ness** *n.*
**murk´y** *adj.* dark or gloomy; hazy **—murk´i·ly** *adv.* **—murk´i·ness** *n.*
**mur´mur** *n.* a low-pitched, indistinct sound *—vi., vt.* to complain or utter in a low tone
**mus´cle** *n.* fibrous tissue that serves to achieve movement in the body; strength or force *—vi.* to crowd or intrude: *they muscled their way into our group*
**mus´cu·lar** *adj.* relating to the muscles; inferring power **—mus·cu·lar´i·ty** *n.* **—mus´cu·lar·ly** *adv.*
**muse** *n.* a spiritual or intellectual guide *—vi.* to ponder or meditate **—mus´ing** *n.* **—mus´ing·ly** *adv.*
**mu·se´um** *n.* a place dedicated to preservation, as of art or historical objects
**mush** *n.* porridge; a pasty mass; exaggerated affection **—mush´y** *adj.* **—mush´i·ly** *adv.* **—mush´i·ness** *n.*
**mush´room** *n.* a type of fungus, esp. those which are edible; something in the umbrella shape characteristic of mushrooms *—vi.* to grow rapidly or in the shape of a mushroom *—adj.* pertaining to or like a mushroom
**mu´sic** *n.* a contrived or natural sound that is pleasant to the ear; a musical score
**mu´si·cal** *adj.* relating to or resembling music; able to produce music; set to music *—n.* a musical comedy show **—mu´si·cal·ly** *adv.* **—mu·si·cal´i·ty** *n.*
**musical chairs** a game in which players are eliminated as they compete for a limited number of chairs; a reorganizing that is more of form than of substance, often in an attempt to confuse
**musical comedy** a theatrical work dominated by music and dance; a light opera
**mu·si´cian** *n.* one who composes or performs music
**music of the spheres** harmonious music in outer space, thought at one time to be produced by the motion of heavenly bodies
**mu·si·col´o·gy** *n.* the study of music **—mu·si·co·log´i·cal** *adj.* **—mu·si·co·log´i·cal·ly** *adv.* **—mu·si·col´o·gist** *n.*
**mus´lin** *n.* a type of fabric
**muss** *n.* a mess *—vt.* to make a mess; tousle: *don't muss my hair* **—muss´i·ly** *adv.* **—muss´i·ness** *n.***—muss´y** *adj.*
**mus´sel** *n.* a type of marine or freshwater mollusk
**must** *n.* something required *—aux. verb* a requirement: *you must be a member to attend*; a command: *you must leave now*; a likelihood: *they must have seen the notice*; a certainty: *all good things must end*; intention: *I must go now*
**mus´tache** *n.* a moustache
**mus´ter** *n.* a gathering *—vi.* to assemble *—vt.* to call together; to summon or marshal: *muster the courage to ask*
**must´y** *adj.* stale, as of a smell; old or out of date **—mus´ti·ly** *adv.* **—must´i·ness** *n.*
**mu´ta·ble** *adj.* changeable **—mu·ta·bil´i·ty, mu´ta·ble·ness** *n.* **—mu´ta·bly** *adv.*
**mu·ta´tion** *n.* a change or modification; the process of changing; something created by change, especially genetic **—mu´tant** *n.* **—mu´tate** *vi., vt.* **—mu·ta´tion·al** *adj.* **—mu·ta´tion·al·ly** *adv.*
**mute** *adj.* unable or unwilling to speak; expressed without sound: *mute admiration* *—n.* one who cannot speak **—mute´ly** *adv.* **—mute´ness** *n.*
**mut´ed** *adj.* indistinct; subdued
**mu´ti·late** *vt.* to maim or cripple; to disfigure **—mu·ti·la´tion** *n.* **—mu´ti·la·tor** *n.*
**mu´tiny** *n.* open rebellion against authority; revolt **—mu´ti·nous** *adj.* **—mu´ti·nous·ly** *adv.*
**mutt** *n.* a dog of mixed breed
**mut´ter** *n.* a low, mumbling utterance *—vi., vt.* to utter in a low voice; to quietly grumble or complain **—mut´ter·er** *n.* **—mut´ter·ing·ly** *adj.*
**mu´tu·al** *adj.* reciprocal or common: *mutual respect, mutual interest* **—mu·tu·al´i·ty** *n.* **—mu´tu·al·ly** *adv.*
**muu´muu** *n.* a long, loose dress
**muz´zle** *n.* the snout of an animal; a device that covers a snout; something that prevents free speech *—vt.* to restrain with a muzzle; to prevent from speaking
**my·o´pia** *n.* nearsightedness **—my·op´ic** *adj.* **—my·op´i·cal·ly** *adv.*
**myr´i·ad** *adj.* innumerable *—n.* a large number
**mys·te´ri·ous** *adj.* marked by mystery; puzzling or enigmatic **—mys·te´ri·ous·ly** *adv.* **—mys·te´ri·ous·ness** *n.*
**mys´ter·y** *n.* something not immediately or easily understood, or that is ultimately beyond comprehension; a work of fiction
**mys´tic** *n.* one involved in mysticism
**mys´tic, mys´ti·cal** *adj.* of mysticism; mysterious; incomprehensible to the senses **—mys´ti·cal·ly** *adv.* **—mys´ti·cal·ness** *n.*
**mys´ti·cism** *n.* a belief in a reality beyond the understanding or comprehension of the senses
**mys´ti·fy** *vt.* to puzzle or perplex **—mys´ti·fy·ing** *adj.* **—mys´ti·fy·ing·ly** *adj.*
**mys·tique´** *n.* a special quality attributed to someone or something
**myth** *n.* a legend or folk tale; a fictitious tale; something that is untrue or only partly true: *the myth of upward mobility* **—myth´ic, myth´i·cal** *adj.* **—myth´i·cal·ly** *adv.*
**myth´i·cize** *vt.* to fashion a myth about: *mythicizing the American dream*
**myth·o·log´i·cal** *adj.* of mythology; imaginary **—myth·o·log´i·cal·ly** *adv.*
**my·thol´o·gy** *n.* a collection of myths; the study of

myths —**my·thol´o·gist** *n.* —**my·thol´o·gize** *vi., vt.*

**n, N** fourteenth letter of the English alphabet; in mathematics, an indefinite number
**nab** *vt.* to snatch or seize; to arrest —**nab´ber** *n.*
**na´bob** *n.* a rich or distinguished person
**na´dir** *n.* the lowest point
**nag** *n.* one given to complaining or chastising; a horse, often, old or inferior —*vi., vt.* to scold or annoy by scolding; to torment or be a source of torment
**nail** *n.* metal fastener; a hard covering at the end of a finger or toe; to fasten or secure —**nail´er** *n.*
**na·ive´** *adj.* unsophisticated; guileless; gullible —**na·ive´ly** *adv.* —**na·ive´ness** *n.*
**na·ive·té´** *n.* inexperience; ingenuousness
**na´ked** *adj.* uncovered or unprotected —**na´ked·ly** *adv.* —**na´ked·ness** *n.*
**nam´by-pam´by** *adj.* sentimental or weak —*n.* one given to sentimentality or perceived as weak
**name** *n.* a word by which something is known; a designation or title; a disparaging epithet —*vt.* to give a distinctive designation to: *name the baby*; to appoint or assign, as to a rank or position —**name´able** *adj.* —**nam´er** *n.*
**name brand** a trademark or unique symbol that identifies a product —**name´-brand** *adj.*
**name´-drop·ping** *n.* an attempt to amplify one's importance by suggesting association with wellknown persons —**name´-drop** *vi.* —**name´-drop·per** *n.*
**name´less** *adj.* countless; unnamed; anonymous: *the nameless poor*; indescribably offensive: *the nameless horrors of war* —**name´less·ly** *adv.* —**name´less·ness** *n.*
**name´ly** *adv.* specifically
**nan´ny** *n.* a nursemaid
**nap** *n.* a brief sleep; a soft raised surface as on a carpet —*vi.* to sleep briefly
**nape** *n.* the back of the neck
**na´per·y** *pl. n.* household linens
**nap´kin** *n.* a cloth or paper towelette used when dining
**nar´cis·sism** *n.* excessive concern with or devotion to one's self or one's appearance —**nar´cis·sist** *n.* —**nar·cis·sis´tic** *adj.* —**nar·cis·sis´ti·cal·ly** *adv.*
**nar·co·lep´tic** *n.* one given to uncontrolled seizures of deep sleep —**nar´co·lep·sy** *n.*
**nar·co´sis** *n.* stupor produced by a narcotic
**nar·cot´ic** *adj.* soothing or addictive —*n.* an addictive drug; something soothing or seemingly addictive —**nar·cot´i·cal·ly** *adv.*
**nar´rate** *vi., vt.* to recite or describe; to give an account of; to provide commentary, as for a documentary —**nar·rat·a·bil´i·ty** *n.* —**nar´rat·a·ble** *adj.* —**nar´rat·er, nar´ra·tor** *n.*
**nar·ra´tion** *n.* an act or process of recounting events; that which is recounted —**nar·ra´tion·al** *adj.* —**nar·ra´tion·al·ly** *adv.*
**nar´ra·tive** *n.* a story; an account of an event or series of events —*adj.* having the qualities of a narration —**nar´ra·tive·ly** *adv.*
**nar´row** *adj.* small in width; confined or limited: *a narrow opening, a narrow margin*; extremely close: *a narrow margin* —*n.* a confined passage —*vi., vt.* to become or make confined or restricted —**nar´row·ly** *adv.* —**nar´row·ness** *n.*
**nar´row-mind´ed** *adj.* limited in belief or opinion; biased; prejudiced —**nar´row-mind´ed·ly** *adv.* —**nar´row-mind´ed·ness** *n.*
**na´sal** *adj.* of the nose —**na·sal´i·ty** *n.* —**na´sal·ly** *adv.*
**nas´cent** *adj.* beginning; emerging —**nas´cence, nas´cen·cy** *n.*
**nas´ty** *adj.* offensive; unpleasant —**nas´ti·ly** *adv.* —**nas´ti·ness** *n.*
**na´tal** *adj.* of birth
**na´tion** *n.* a group of people bound by a common government, heritage, etc.; the land occupied by such a group; a government —**na´tion·al** *adj.* —**na´tion·al·ly** *adv.*
**na´tion·al·ism** *n.* loyalty or devotion to one's government or heritage; patriotism; a movement for independence —**na´tion´al·ist** *n.* —**na·tion·al·is´tic** *adj.* —**na·tion·al·is´ti·cal·ly** *adv.*
**na·tion´al´i·ty** *n.* one's affiliation with a particular government or heritage
**na´tion·al·ize** *vt.* to convert to government ownership; to make nationwide in scope —**na·tion·al·i·za´tion** *n.*
**na´tion-wide´** *adj.* throughout the nation
**na´tive** *adj.* of or associated with a particular place; connected by birth; natural or inherited: *native talent* —*n.* one connected by birth —**na´tive·ly** *adj.* —**na´tive·ness** *n.*
**na·tiv´i·ty** *n.* birth
**nat´ter** *vi.* to chatter idly
**nat´ty** *adj.* dapper; smart or stylish in appearance —**nat´ti·ly** *adv.* —**nat´ti·ness** *n.*
**nat´u·ral** *adj.* occurring in nature; usual, typical, or characteristic; simple and unrehearsed —*n.* one who is well-suited —**nat´u·ral·ly** *adv.* —**nat´u·ral·ness** *n.*
**natural history** the study of things that exist in nature, especially regarding their development
**nat´u·ral·ist** *n.* one who studies natural history; one in harmony with nature —**nat·u·ral·is´tic** *adj.* —**nat·u·ral·is´ti·cal·ly** *adv.*
**nat·u·ral·iza´tion** *n.* the process of becoming accepted or acclimated —**nat´u·ral·ize** *vi., vt.*
**natural law** principles that derive from nature
**natural resource** wealth that occurs in nature
**natural science** the study and classification of things that exist in nature

**natural selection** the theory that organisms best adapted to an environment will survive and improve with succeeding generations

**na´ture** *n.* the realm of living things; the processes and power that control living organisms; the quality of something: *a quiet nature*

**naught** *n.* nothing

**naugh´ty** *adj.* disobedient; mischievous; playfully improper: *a naughty story* **–naugh´ti·ly** *adv.* **–naugh´ti·ness** *n.*

**nau´sea** *n.* illness marked by a queasy stomach; revulsion, as though to make one vomit

**nau´se·ate** *vi., vt.* to have or cause a queasy stomach; to disgust **–nau´se·at·ing** *adj.* **–nau´se·at·ing·ly** *adv.*

**nau´seous** *adj.* causing nausea; disgusting; affected by nausea **–nau´seous·ly** *adv.* **–nau´seous·ness** *n.*

**nau´ti·cal** *adj.* of ships or shipping **–nau´ti·cal·ly** *adv.*

**na´val** *adj.* applicable to a navy; of ships or shipping

**nave** *n.* the central aisle of a church

**na´vel** *n.* the process on a mammal left by removal of the umbilical cord

**nav´i·ga·ble** *adj.* suitable for passage through

**nav´i·ga·ble** *adj.* suitable for passage through or over **–nav·i·ga·bil´i·ty, nav´i·ga·ble·ness** *n.* **–nav´i·ga·bly** *adv.*

**nav´i·gate** *vi., vt.* to plot or direct the course of; to travel by means of ship or aircraft

**nav·i·ga´tion** *n.* the charting of a course; shipping or transport collectively **–nav·i·ga´tion·al** *adj.*

**nav´i·ga·tor** *n.* one skilled in navigation; one who plots or directs a course, as of a ship or aircraft

**na´vy** *n.* the branch of the military that operates on the sea

**nay** *adv.* no *–n.* a negative vote

**nay´say·er** *n.* one inclined to be negative; one who disagrees

**ne·an´der·thal** *n.* Neanderthal man, an extinct species; one exhibiting characteristics that might be attributable to a cave man: brutish or uncouth

**near** *adj., adv.* approaching or close to; almost: *a near miss –vi., vt.* to come or draw near **–near´ly** *adv.* **–near´ness** *n.*

**near´by´** *adj., adv.* not far from

**near´sight·ed** *adj.* unable to see clearly at a distance **–near´sight·ed·ly** *adv.* **–near´sight·ed·ness** *n.*

**neat** *adj.* orderly or tidy; clever or adroit; undiluted **–neat´ly** *adv.* **–neat´ness** *n.*

**neat´en** *vt.* to put in order or make tidy

**neb´bish** *n.* a timid person **–neb´bish·y** *adj.*

**neb´u·lous** *adj.* hazy or indistinct; vague or confused: *a nebulous promise* **–neb´u·lous·ly** *adv.* **–neb´u·lous·ness** *n.*

**nec´es·sar·y** *adj.* essential; required: *fill out the necessary paperwork* **–nec´es·sar´i·ly** *adv.*

**ne·ces´si·tate** *vt.* to require or make unavoidable; to make compulsory **–ne·ces·si·ta´tion** *n.* **–ne·ces´si·ta·tive** *adj.*

**ne·ces´si·ty** *n.* something essential or requiredneck *n.* a narrow body part that joins, as between the head and the trunk; a narrow section, *as a neck of land, neck of a bottle*, etc. *–vi., vt.* to kiss and caress

**neck´band** *n.* a strip of cloth sewn inside a collar; a type of necklace

**neck´er·chief** *n.* a kerchief designed to be worn around the neck

**neck´lace** *n.* an ornamental loop worn around the neck

**neck´line** *n.* the shape or form of that portion of a garment that goes around the neck

**neck´piece** *n.* an article of clothing worn loosely around the neck, as a strip of fur

**neck´tie** *n.* a strip of cloth worn around the neck, usually under the collar and tied in front

**neck´wear** *n.* any article of clothing or jewelry worn about the neck

**nec´ro·man·cy** *n.* communication with the dead; black magic **–nec´ro·man·cer** *n.* **–nec·ro·man´tic** *adj.*

**nec·ro·phil´i·a** *n.* obsession with death and dead bodies **–nec´ro·phile** *n.* **–nec·ro·phil´i·ac** *adj., n.* **–nec·ro·phil´ic** *adj.*

**nec·ro·pho´bi·a** *n.* an abnormal fear of death and dead bodies **–nec·ro·pho´bic** *adj.*

**ne·crop´o·lis** *n.* a place of burial, especially one that belongs to an ancient city

**nec´tar** *n.* a sweet liquid secreted by certain plants; an especially delicious drink **–nec·tar´e·an, nec´tar·ous** *adj.*

**need** *n.* a lack of something; a thing required or desired; a necessity; a state of poverty *–vt.* to have want of; to require *–vi.* to be in want; to be obliged or compelled: *I need to leave* **–need´er** *n.*

**need´ful** *adj.* needed or required; needy **–need´ful·ly** *adv.* **–need´ful·ness** *n.*

**nee´dle** *n.* a slender device, tapered to a point at one end: *sewing needle, hypodermic needle, knitting needle*

**nee´dle·craft** *n.* things made with the use of a needle, as for sewing or knitting; the art of creating with the use of a needle

**nee´dle·point** *n.* decorative needlework

**needless** *adj.* unnecessary; useless: *spent needless hours daydreaming* **–need´less·ly** *adv.* **–need´less·ness** *n.*

**nee´dle·work** *n.* needlecraft

**need´y** *adj.* poor; overly dependent on the support of others

**ne´er´-do-well** *n.* a capricious or unreliable person

**ne·far´i·ous** *adj.* extremely wicked **–ne·far´i·ous·ly** *adv.* **–ne·far´i·ous·ness** *n.*

**ne·gate´** *vt.* to nullify or retract **–ne·ga´tor, ne·gat´er** *n.* **–ne·ga´tion** *n.* **–ne·ga´tion·al** *adj.*

**neg´a·tive** *adj.* expressing opposition or denial; lacking any affirmative quality: *a negative philosophy* **—neg´a·tive·ly** *adv.* **—neg´a·tive·ness, neg·a·tiv´i·ty** *n.*

**neg´a·tiv·ism** *n.* a tendency to reject or ignore the suggestions of others **—neg´a·tiv·ist** *n.* **—neg´a·tiv·is´tic** *adj.*

**ne·glect** *n.* indifference or carelessness *—vt.* to disregard or be indifferent to; to be careless or irresponsible **—ne·glect´er** *n.*

**ne·glect´ful** *adj.* marked by carelessness or disregard **—ne·glect´ful·ly** *adv.* **—ne·glect´ful·ness** *n.*

**neg·li·gee´** *n.* a woman's dressing gown

**neg´li·gent** *adj.* tending to neglect; careless **neg´li·gence** *n.* **—neg´li·gent·ly** *adv.*

**neg´li·gi·ble** *adj.* insignificant; inconsequential **—neg·li·gi·bil´i·ty, neg´li·gi·ble·ness** *n.* **—neg´li·gi·bly** *adv.*

**ne·go´ti·a·ble** *adj.* that can be bargained for; transferable by delivery or endorsement, such as cash, a promissory note or a bond **—ne·go´ti·a·bly** *adv.* **—ne·go·ti·a·bil´i·ty** *n.*

**ne·go´ti·ate** *vi.* to confer in an attempt to reach agreement *—vt.* to compromise or agree, as to price, terms, etc.; to transfer ownership, as of a security **—ne·go·ti·a´tion** *n.* **—ne·go´ti·a·tor** *n.* **—ne·go´ti·a·to·ry** *adj.*

**neigh´bor** *(US) n.* one who lives near; anything near or adjacent *—vi., vt.* to live or be situated near *—adj.* near to; adjacent

**neigh´bor·hood** *(US) n.* collectively, those who live near one another or the area in which they live; a proximity: *it will cost in the neighborhood of ten dollars*

**neigh´bor·ly** *(US) adj.* friendly or helpful **—neigh´bor·li·ness** *adv.*

**neigh´bor** *(Brit.) n.* one who lives near; anything near or adjacent *—vi., vt.* to live or be situated near *—adj.* near to; adjacent

**neigh´bour·hood** *(Brit.) n.* collectively, those who live near one another or the area in which they live; a proximity: *it will cost in the neighborhood of ten pounds*

**neigh´bour·ly** *(Brit.) adj.* friendly or helpful **—neigh´bour·li·ness** *adv.*

**nei´ther** *adj.* not either; not one or the other

**nem´e·sis** *n.* an enemy, especially one seeking retribution or revenge; something harmful

**ne·o·clas´sic, ne´o·clas´si·cal** *adj.* pertaining to the revival of earlier forms, as in classical music or literature **—ne·o·clas´si·cism** *n.* **—ne·o·clas´si·cist** *n.*

**ne·o·con·serv´a·tism** *n.* a reactionary or traditionalist philosophy that arises in response to excessive liberalism of an earlier period **—ne·o·con·serv´a·tive** *n.*

**ne·ol´o·gism, ne·ol´o·gy** *n.* a new word; a new meaning for a word or expression; the creation of a new word, meaning, or expression **—ne·ol´o·gist** *n.* **—ne·ol·o·gis´tic, ne·ol·o·gis´ti·cal** *adj.*

**ne´o·phyte** *n.* a novice; a recent convert

**neph´ew** *n.* the son of one's sibling

**nep´o·tism** *n.* favoritism to a relation, as by granting employment **—nep´o·tist** *n.* **—nep·o·tis´tic, nep·o·tis´ti·cal** *adj.*

**nerd** *n.* one engrossed in scholarly pursuits to the exclusion of regard for personal appearance or the social graces **—nerd´y** *adj.*

**nerve** *n.* any of the fibers that transmit signals throughout the body; courage; impudence **—nerv´y** *adj.* **—nerv´i·ness** *n.*

**nerve center** a set of nerve cells that perform a specific function in the body; a control center: *the CPU is the nerve center of the computer*

**nerve´less** *adj.* lacking courage; cool in a crisis, as though not affected by natural fear or caution **—nerve´less·ly** *adv.* **—nerve´less·ness** *n.*

**nerve´-rack·ing** *adj.* irritating, difficult, or wearisome

**ner´vous** *adj.* of the nerve system; high-strung or excitable; agitated or apprehensive **—ner´vous·ly** *adv.* **—ner´vous·ness** *n.*

**ne´science** *n.* ignorance; a lack of knowledge or awareness **—ne´scient** *adj.*

**nest** *n.* a cozy shelter, especially for rearing young; a refuge; a group of objects that fit together: *a nest of boxes —vi., vt.* to fit or place together snugly **—nest´a·ble** *adj.*

**nest egg** money or investments set aside for future use

**nes´tle** *vi., vt.* to lie or place snugly or comfortably

**net** *adj.* remaining after deductions, as for waste or expenses: *net profit, net weight —n.* the amount remaining, as for profit or yield; a mesh of fabric or rope, usually to catch or hold something *—vt.* to produce, as profit; to catch, as in a net **—net´ta·ble** *adj.*

**net´tle** *n.* a prickly plant *—vt.* to annoy or irritate

**net´tle·some** *adj.* irritating

**net´work** *n.* a system or structure with interconnecting bonds: *communications network, old boy network*

**net´work·ing** *n.* the exchange of information or assistance among those having mutual interests

**neu´ral** *adj.* regarding the nerves or nervous system

**neu·ral´gia** *n.* pain associated with a nerve **—neu·ral´gic** *adj.*

**neu·ri´tis** *n.* inflammation of a nerve **—neu·rit´ic** *adj.*

**neu·rol´o·gy** *n.* the study of the workings and disorders of the nervous system **—neu·ro·log´ic, neu·ro·log´i·cal** *adj.* **—neu·ro·log´i·cal·ly** *adv.* **—neu·rol´o·gist** *n.*

**neu´ron** *n.* a nerve cell **—neu´ro·nal, neu·ron´ic** *adj.*

**neu·ro´sis** *n.* a mental or emotional disorder **—neu·rot´ic** *adj., n.* **—neu·rot´ic·al·ly** *adv.*

**neu´tral** *adj.* not supporting either position in a controversy; unbiased or disinterested; drab or colorless **—neu´tral·ism, neu·tral´i·ty** *n.* **—neu´tral·ist** *n.* **—neu·tral·is´tic** *adj.*

**neu´tral·ize** *vt.* to make neutral; to nullify or cancel out **—neu·tral·i·za´tion** *n.* **—neu´tral·iz·er** *n.*

**nev´er** *adv.* not ever

**nev´er·the·less´** *adv.* disregarding that: *he has failed twice, nevertheless he plans to try again*

**new** *adj.* recently formed or discovered; previously unused; different: *a new style*; inexperienced: *a new employee* —**new´ness** *n.*

**New Age** *adj.* characteristic of a less traditional approach to spirituality, healing, the arts, etc.

**new´found** *adj.* recently acquired or cognizant of : *newfound freedom*

**new´ish** *adj.* relatively new

**new´ly** *adv.* recently; freshly

**news** *pl. n.* new information, especially that reported by the print or electronic media; information of interest to the general public or to a particular group

**news´cast** *n.* a broadcasting of the news on radio or television —**news´cast·er** *n.*

**news´let·ter** *n.* a publication containing informatoin for a select audience

**news´mag·a·zine** *n.* a slick periodical, usually weekly, devoted to current events

**news´pa·per** *n.* a daily or weekly periodical that reports on current events; newsprint

**news´print** *n.* inexpensive paper used for short-lived publications such as newspapers

**news´wor·thy** *adj.* considered to be of interest to the readers of a publication —**news´wor·thi·ness** *n.*

**news´y** *adj.* containing fresh news or gossip —**news´i·ness** *n.*

**next** *adj.* following immediately in sequence: *the next minute*; close by: *the next room* —*n.* that which comes immediately after —*adv.*

**next of kin** one's closest relative or relatives

**nib´ble** *n.* a small bite —*vi., vt.* to take or eat in small bites —**nib´bler** *n.*

**nice** *adj.* pleasing; courteous or considerate; delicate or subtle: *a nice sense of tact* —**nice´ly** *adv.* —**nice´ness** *n.*

**ni´ce·ty** *n.* a precise, subtle, or refined quality

**niche** *n.* a recess or alcove; a special area, as of activity or interest

**nick** *n.* a small cut or indentation —*vt.* to make a small cut in

**nick´name** *n.* a familiar name, as a short form of a proper name or one that is descriptive

**niece** *n.* the daughter of one's sibling, or a wife or husband's sibling

**nif´ty** *adj.* very good; clever

**nig´gard·ly** *adj.* closefisted; reluctant to give or spend —**nig´gard** *n.* —**nig´gard·li·ness** *n.*

**nig´gle** *vi.* to constantly nag or complain over trifles —**nig´gling** *adj., n.* —**nig´gling·ly** *adv.*

**nigh** *adj., adv.* near; nearly

**night** *n.* the period between sunset and sunrise; the evening hours before midnight

**night´cap** *n.* a beverage taken at the end of an evening or just before going to bed

**night´club** *n.* an eating and drinking establishment that offers entertainment in the evening

**night´fall** *n.* dusk; the approaching darkness of night

**night´gown** *n.* a woman's frock worn for sleeping

**night´ly** *adj.* occurring every night; occurring during the night —*adv.* by night; every night

**night´mare** *n.* a frightening dream; a terrifying experience —**night´mar·ish** *adj.* —**night´mar·ish·ly** *adv.*

**night´spot** *n.* a nightclub

**night´stand** *n.* a small table situated at the side of a bed

**night´stick** *(US) n.* a staff carried by a uniformed police officer

**night table** a nightstand

**night´time** *adj.* during the night —*n.* the time from sunset to sunrise or from dark to dawn

**ni´hi·lism** *n.* a philosophy that denies all existence; the rejection of religion and morality; the concept that conditions can be improved only by destroying the existing political and social structure —**ni´hi·list** *n.* —**ni´hi·lis´tic** *adj.*

**ni·hil´i·ty** *n.* nothingness

**nil** *n.* nothing

**nim´ble** *adj.* quick and agile; sharp witted —**nim´ble·ness** *n.* —**nim´bly** *adv.*

**nim´bus** *n.* a halo or disk of light encircling the head

**nin´com·poop** *n.* a silly or foolish person

**nin´ja** *n.* a 14th century Japanese assassin

**nin´ny** *n.* a nincompoop

**nip** *n.* a sip, especially of liquor; a small bite or particle; a sharp or stinging quality, as of cold air or spicy food —*vt.* to sip; to bite or pinch off; to sting

**nip´per** *n.* a tool for grasping or for making small cuts, such as pliers

**nip´ping** *adj.* stinging, as from cold or spiced food —**nip´ping·ly** *adv.*

**nip´ple** *n.* a small projection on a mammary gland from which milk is released; any similar projection used to release or eject a liquid

**nip´py** *adj.* biting or sharp; somewhat chilly —**nip´pi·ly** *adv.* —**nip´pi·ness** *n.*

**nir·va´na** *n.* an ideal state —**nir·va´nic** *adj.*

**nit´pick** *vi.* to find fault or quarrel over trifles —**nit´pick·er** *n.* —**nit´pick·ing** *n.*

**nit´ty-grit´ty** *n.* the essence of something —*adj.* basic

**nit´wit** *n.* one regarded as silly or foolish

**nix** *vt.* to negate or put an end to

**no** *adj.* not any: *there is no time left*; absolutely not: *he's no leader* —*n.* a negative response

**no´-account** *adj.* valueless; useless

**no·bil´i·ty** *n.* the state of being exalted; a class of persons of high rank or status; noteworthy moral excellence

**no´ble** *adj.* pertaining to or having qualities attributable to nobility, as regal bearing, courage, generosity, etc. **—no´ble·ness** *n.* **—no´bly** *adv.*

**no·blesse´ oblige´** the obligation of high ranking persons to behave honorably and generously

**no´body** *n.* a person of no importance *—pron.* no one

**no´cent** *adj.* harmful

**noc·tur´nal** *adj.* occurring in the night **—noc·tur´nal·ly** *adv*

**noc´turne** *n.* a painting of a night scene; a gentle, dreamy musical composition

**noc´u·ous** *adj.* harmful or detrimental **—noc´u·ous·ly** *adv.*

**nod** *n.* assent or agreement *—vi., vt.* to move the head up and down, especially as an assent or acknowledgement; to briefly drift off to sleep

**nod´ule** *n.* a small lump **—nod´u·lar** *adj.*

**no´-fault** *adj.* of insurance or a legal action that honors a claim without assigning blame

**no´-frills´** *adj.* lacking any special features or amenities

**no´-go´** *n.* a termination

**no´-good´** *adj.* lacking value

**noise** *n.* a loud or unpleasant sound; a complaint; interference on a transmission line; unwanted or meaningless data *—vt.* to spread information, especially gossip or rumors

**noise´less** *adj.* silent **—noise´less·ly** *adv.* **—noise´less·ness** *n.*

**noise´mak·er** *n.* one who makes noise; a device for making raucous sound at a celebration **—noice´mak·ing** *n.*

**noi´some** *adj.* disgusting, especially of an odor; dangerous or deadly, as fumes **—noi´some·ly** *adv.* **—noi´some·ness** *n.*

**nois´y** *adj.* making or marked by noise **—nois´i·ly** *adv.* **—nois´i·ness** *n.*

**no´mad** *n.* a wanderer; one who lacks a permanent home **—no·mad´ic** *adj.* **—no·mad´i·cal·ly** *adv.*

**no man´s land** a strip of land marking a division between warring parties; land that is unclaimed or unexplored

**nom de guerre** an assumed name

**nom de plume** a pen name; a name assumed by a writer

**no´men·cla·ture** *n.* a name or designation; a system of names, as used in a scientific discipline

**nom´i·nal** *adj.* of a name or designation; of a small or token amount; of the face value of a security; existing in name only **—nom´i·nal·ly** *adv.*

**nom´i·nate** *vt.* to name as a candidate for office; to appoint to office **—nom´i·na´tion** *n.* **—nom´i·na·tor** *n.*

**nom´i·nee´** *n.* one named as a candidate

**non´age** *n.* the time during which one is legally underage

**non´cha·lant´** *adj.* seemingly casual or indifferent **—non´cha·lance´** *n.* **—non´cha·lant·ly** *adv.*

**non·com·mit´tal** *adj.* guarded about one's feelings or opinions **—non·com·mit´tal·ly** *adv.*

**non·com·pli´ance** *n.* a failure to conform or accede, as to a court order or ordinance **—non·com·pli´ant** *adj., n.*

**non com´pos men´tis** legally incompetent; not of sound mind

**non·con·form´ist** *n.* one in opposition to accepted customs or practices **—non·con·form´i·ty** *n.*

**non´de·script** *adj.* lacking any distinctive characteristics

**none** *adv.* not at all *—pron.* no one

**non·en´ti·ty** *n.* something of no importance; something that does not exist

**non·e·vent´** *n.* a minor function or gathering promoted out of proportion to its importance

**non·ex·is´tent** *adj.* not real; imaginary **—non·ex·is´tence** *n.*

**non·fea´sance** *n.* failure to discharge a duty or obligation

**non´fic´tion** *n.* writing that is factual or professed to be so **—non·fic´tion·al** *adj.*

**non´pa·reil´** *adj.* without equal

**non·par´ti·san** *adj.* neutral; not aligned with any particular group or cause *—n.* **—non·par´ti·san·ship** *n.*

**non´plus´** *vt.* to bewilder; to put at a loss for words

**non·pro·duc´tive** *adj.* not profitable or useful; not involved directly in producing, as of supervisory or management personnel

**non·prof´it** *adj.* of an organization that operates to serve, rather than for profit

**non·pro·lif·er·a´tion** *adj.* stemming growth or acquisition, as of nuclear weapons

**non pro·se´qui·tur** judgment against a plaintiff who fails to appear in court

**non´sense** *n.* something having no meaning or that is of no value; foolishness

**non·sen´si·cal** *adj.* unintelligible; without meaning; absurd **—non·sen·si·cal´i·ty, non·sen´si·cal·ness** *n.* **—non·sen´si·cal·ly** *adv.*

**non·vi´o·lence** *n.* reliance on peaceful means to achieve objectives

**nook** *n.* a cranny or compartment; a hiding place; a recess or corner of a room, often offering a measure of privacy

**noon** *n.* midday; the time when the sun is at or near its highest point

**no one** *pron.* nobody; not one person

**noose** *n.* a rope loop

**norm** *n.* a standard

**nor´mal** *adj.* typical, usual, or standard; sane **—nor´mal·cy, nor·mal´i·ty** *n.* **—nor´mal·ly** *adv.*

**nor´mal·ize** *vt.* to make normal **—nor·mal·i·za´tion** *n.*

–nor´mal·iz·er *n.*

**north** *n.* the direction to the left of the sunrise, roughly perpendicular to the path of the sun; an area located in that general direction

**nose** *n.* the organ at the front of the face for detecting odors; the sense of smell; an aroma, as of a wine; the ability to find, as if by smell: *a nose for news*; the front, as of an aircraft, rocket, etc.

**nose´-dive** *vi.* to suddenly plummet: *our sales took a nose-dive* **–nose´dive** *n.*

**nose job** rhinoplasty: plastic surgery on the nose

**nosh** *n.* a snack *–vi.*

**no´-show** *n.* one who does not arrive as promised

**nos·tal´gia** *n.* a sentimental longing for the past **–nos·tal´gic** *adj.* **–nos·tal´gi·cal·ly** *adv.*

**nos´tril** *n.* one of the openings in the nose

**nos´trum** *n.* an untested medicine or remedy

**nos´y** *adj.* curious or prying **–nos´i·ly** *adv.* **–nos´i·ness** *n.*

**not** *adv.* in no way

**no´ta·ble** *adj.* distinctive or remarkable, as of an event; important or distinguished, as of a person; deserving notice **–no·ta·bil´i·ty, no´ta·ble·ness** *n.* **–no´ta·bly** *adv.*

**no·ta·ri·za´tion** *n.* certification by a notary public, as of a signature **–no´ta·rize** *vt.*

**no´ta·ry, no´ta·ry pub´lic** *n.* one authorized to perform certain legal duties **–no·tar´i·al** *adj.* **–no·tar´i·al·ly** *adv.*

**no·ta´tion** *n.* a note or comment, often added to existing text; a system of symbols used for a particular purpose, as in mathematics or computer programming **–no·ta´tion·al** *adj.*

**notch** *n.* a small cut or nick

**note** *n.* a short, informal letter; a written record, as of the main points of a lecture, annotations in a publication, a reminder, etc.; currency or a document convertible to currency *–vt.* to make a written record of; to take notice of

**not´ed** *adj.* distinguished; famous **–not´ed·ly** *adv.*

**note´wor·thy** *adj.* deserving of notice **–note´wor·thi·ly** *adv.* **–note´wor·thi·ness** *n.*

**noth´ing** *adj.* meaningless: *a nothing day* *–n.* something of no value *–pron.* not anything

**noth´ing·ness** *n.* a void

**no´tice** *n.* an announcement or warning; observation or attention *–vt.* to observe or become aware of **–no·tice·a·bil´i·ty** *n.* **–no´tice·a·ble** *adj.* **–no´tice·a·bly** *adv.*

**no´ti·fy** *vt.* to serve notice; to inform or make known **–no´ti·fi·ca´tion** *n.* **–no´ti·fi·er** *n.*

**no´tion** *n.* an idea or opinion; a theory; a disposition toward **–no´tion·al** *adj.*

**no·to·ri´e·ty** *n.* fame; reputation

**no·to´ri·ous** *adj.* infamous; wellknown **–no·to´ri·ous·ly** *adv.* **–no·to´ri·ous·ness** *n.*

**not·with·stand´ing** *prep.* in spite of *–adv.*

**noun** *n.* a word that names a person, place, thing, etc.

**nour´ish** *vt.* to promote the development of; to provide with food or other necessities for life and growth **–nour´ish·ment** *n.*

**nou·veau´ riche** one who flaunts newly acquired wealth

**nou·velle´ cui·sine´** a style of cooking that stresses fresh ingredients and light sauces

**nov´el** *adj.* new and unusual **–nov´el·ly** *adj.*

**nov´el** *n.* a book-length, fictional story **–nov´el·ist** *n.* **–nov·el·is´tic** *adj.* **–nov·el·is´ti·cal·ly** *adv.*

**nov´el·ette´** *n.* a short novel

**nov´el·ize** *vt.* to write a fictional account based on a true story, a historical event, a play or movie, etc.

**no·vel´la** *n.* a short novel; a short story

**nov´el·ty** *n.* the quality of being original or fresh; something unique; a fad; a trinket

**nov´ice** *n.* one new to a trade or activity; an apprentice

**now** *adj.* at this time *–adv.* immediately; promptly

**no way** *interj.* absolutely not

**no´where** *adv.* not anywhere *–n.* remote

**no´-win´** *adj.* stalemated or deadlocked

**no´wise** *adv.* in no way

**nox´ious** *adj.* harmful **–nox´ious·ly** *adv.* **–nox´ious·ness** *n.*

**noz´zle** *n.* a spout or outlet for controlling the flow of a liquid

**nu´ance** *n.* a subtlety; a slight variation

**nub** *n.* a knob or protuberance; the gist or substance of something **–nub´bly, nub´by** *adj.*

**nu´bile** *adj.* of marriageable age; sexually mature **–nu·bil´i·ty** *n.*

**nu´cle·ar** *adj.* of a nucleus; atomic

**nuclear energy** energy created by nuclear reaction

**nuclear power** power such as electricity generated by nuclear fission or fusion

**nuclear reactor** a device for harnessing nuclear energy

**nu´cle·us** *n.* the center or essence of something

**nude** *adj.* unclothed or uncovered *–n.* a naked body, especially a statue or painting **–nude´ly** *adv.* **–nude´ness, nu´di·ty** *n.*

**nudge** *n.* a light push; one who persists in annoying or complaining *–vt.* to touch or push gently

**nud´ism** *n.* a belief in the practice of living in the nude to promote health and well-being **–nud´ist** *n., adj.*

**nug´get** *n.* a small lump or portion

**nui´sance** *n.* a bother or annoyance; an illegal action that interferes with the rights of others

**nuke** *vt.* to use a nuclear bomb; to microwave

**null** *adj.* nonexistent or insignificant; invalid

**nul´li·fy** *vt.* to invalidate or neutralize **–nul·li·fi·ca´tion** *n.* **–nul´li·fi·er** *n.*

**numb** *adj.* lacking physical or emotional feeling —*vt., vi.* to make or become numb —**numb´ly** *adv.* —**numb´ness** *n.*

**num´ber** *n.* an integer; one of a series in a normal progression; a set of numerals that represent something unique: *telephone number, house number* —*vt.* to assign a position in a series; to count or total —**num´ber·er** *n.*

**num´ber-crunch·ing** *n.* performing complex calculations —**num´ber-crunch·er** *n.*

**num´ber·less** *adj.* innumerable; limitless

**numb´skull** *n.* a numskull

**nu´mer·a·ble** *adj.* that can be enumerated

**nu´mer·al** *n.* a symbol representing a number

**nu·mer´ic, nu·mer´i·cal** *adj.* of a number or numbers —**nu·mer´i·cal·ly** *adv.*

**nu·mer·ol´o·gy** *n.* the belief that there is secret meaning associated with number values, as of a date or the number of letters in a name —**nu·mer·o·log´i·cal** *adj.* —**nu·mer·ol´o·gist** *n.*

**nu´mer·ous** *adj.* many; a large number —**nu´mer·ous·ly** *adv.* —**nu´mer·ous·ness** *n.*

**nu·mis·mat´ics** *n.* the collection or study of coinage —**nu·mis·mat´ic** *adj.* —**nu·mis·mat´i·cal·ly** *adv.* —**nu·mis´ma·tist** *n.*

**num´skull** *n.* a simpleton or fool

**nup´tial** *adj.* of marriage or a marriage ceremony —**nup´tial·ly** *adv.*

**nup´tials** *n.* a wedding ceremony

**nurse** *n.* one trained in ministering to the sick; one in charge of young children —*vt.* to tend or care for another; to sustain or conserve —**nurs·er** *n.*

**nur´ser·y** *n.* a place set aside for children; a place where plants are grown

**nurse´s aide** one who assists a registered or practical nurse

**nurs´ing** *n.* the profession of a nurse; the care of a nurse

**nursing home** a residence for the elderly or those very ill

**nur´ture** *vt.* to care for; to aid in growth and improvement —**nur´tur·ance** *n.* —**nur´tur·ant** *n.* —**nur´tur·ing** *adj.*

**nut** *n.* a seed contained in a hard shell; one considered to be insane or eccentric ; a fanatic

**nu´tri·ent** *adj.* providing nutrition; nourishing —*n.* a source of nourishment

**nu´tri·ment** *n.* food; anything that promotes growth and development —**nu·tri·men´tal** *adj.*

**nu·tri´tion** *n.* the study of food and nourishment; the process by which food is digested and used in the body —**nu·tri´tion·al** *adj.* —**nu·tri´tion·al·ly** *adv.* —**nu·tri´tion·ist** *n.*

**nu·tri´tious** *adj.* nourishing —**nu·tri´tious·ly** *adv.* —**nu·tri´tious·ness** *n.*

**nu´tri·tive** *adj.* nutritious; pertaining to nutrition —**nu´tri·tive·ly** *adv.* —**nu´tri·tive·ness** *n.*

**nut´ty** *adj.* nut-like; crazy; wild and foolish —**nut´ti·ly** *adv.* —**nut´ti·ness** *n.*

**nuz´zle** *vi., vt.* to nestle; to push gently with the nose

**o, O** fifteenth letter of the English alphabet

**oaf** *n.* one who is slow-witted or clumsy —**oaf´ish** *adj.* —**oaf´ish·ly** *adv.* —**oaf´ish·ness** *n.*

**oa´sis** *n., pl.* oa'ses a haven of greenery in the midst of a wasteland; a place of refuge or one that differs from its surroundings: *an oasis of excellence in the midst of mediocrity*

**oast** *n.* an oven for drying grain or tobacco

**oath** *n.* a solemn promise; an irreverent or blasphemous use of a sacred name

**ob´du·rate** *n.* hardhearted; stubborn —**ob´du·ra·cy** *n.* —**ob´du·rate·ly** *adj.* —**ob´du·rate·ness** *n.*

**o·be´di·ent** *adj.* deferential to authority; submissive —**o·be´di·ence** *n.* —**o·be´di·ent·ly** *adv.*

**o·bei´sant** *adj.* respectful —**o·bei´sance** *n.* —**o·bei´sant·ly** *adv.*

**ob´e·lisk** *n.* a tall stone shaft

**o·bese´** *adj.* extremely overweight —**o·bese´ly** *adv.* —**o·be´si·ty** *n.*

**o·bey´** *vi., vt.* to accept or comply with

**ob´fus´cate** *vt.* to make confused —**ob´fus·ca´tion** *n.* —**ob´fus·ca·tor** *n.* —**ob·fus´ca·to·ry** *adj.*

**o·bit´** *n.* an obituary

**o·bit´u·ar·y** *n.* a published account of a death, often including highlights of the person's life, information about family, etc.

**ob´ject** *n.* a thing that can be perceived by the senses; a goal or objective; a recipient: *the object of our attention* —**ob·ject´** *vi., vt.* to oppose or dissent —**ob·jec´tor** *n.*

**ob·jec´tion** *n.* the act of opposing; remarks made in opposition; a reason for opposing

**ob·jec´tion·a·ble** *adj.* offensive —**ob·jec´tion·a·bly** *adv.* —**ob·jec´tion·a·ble·ness** *n.*

**ob·jec´tive** *adj.* fair and unbiased —*n.* a tangible goal —**ob·jec´tive·ly** *adv.* —**ob·jec´tive·ness, ob·jec·tiv´i·ty** *n.*

**object lesson** a concrete example

**ob´jet d´art** an art object

**ob·la´tion** *n.* a solemn offering, especially as an act of worship —**ob·la´tion·al, ob´la·to·ry** *adj.*

**ob´li·gate** *adj.* essential —*vt.* to bind or compel as by indebtedness, a sense of morality, etc. —**ob´li·ga·tor** *n.*

**ob·li·ga´tion** *n.* a responsibility dictated by conscience or law; a debt —**ob·li·ga´tion·al** *adj.*

**o·blig´a·to·ry** *adj.* required; morally or legally binding —**o·blig´a·to´ri·ly** *adv.*

**o·blige´** *vt.* to require, as a legal or moral matter; to accommodate or assist

**o·blig´ing** *adj.* disposed to be accommodating —**o·blig´ing·ly** *adv.* —**o·blig´ing·ness** *n.*
**o·blique´** *adj.* inclined or slanting; angled; indirect, as *an oblique reference* —**o·blique´ly** *adv.* —**o·blique´ness** *n.*
**ob·liq´ui·ty** *n.* inclination or the amount of inclination from a horizontal or vertical —**ob·liq´ui·tous** *adj.*
**ob·lit´er·ate** *vt.* to remove completely —**ob·lit·er·a´tion** *n.* —**ob·lit´er·a·tive** *adj.* —**ob·lit´er·a·tor** *n.*
**ob·liv´i·on** *n.* obscurity; nonexistence; the condition of being completely forgotten
**ob·liv´i·ous** *adj.* preoccupied; lacking awareness —**ob·liv´i·ous·ly** *adv.* —**ob·liv´i·ous·ness** *n.*
**ob´long** *adj.* elongated
**ob´lo·quy** *n.* severe denunciation
**ob·nox´ious** *adj.* offensive or objectionable; impolite —**ob·nox´ious·ly** *adv.* —**ob·nox´ious·ness** *n.*
**o´boe** *n.* a double-reed wind instrument —**o´bo·ist** *n.*
**ob·scene´** *adj.* contrary to accepted morality or propriety —**ob·scene´ly** *adv. n.*
**ob·scen´i·ty, ob·scene´ness** *n.* something that is offensive or indecent; an obscene remark
**ob·scu´rant** *adj.* tending to make indistinct: *an obscurant mist*; marked by opposition to improvement or enlightenment —*n.* one who opposes education or enlightenment —**ob·scu´ran·tism** *n.* —**ob·scu´rant·ist** *n.*
**ob·scure´** *adj.* not clearly perceived; indistinct —*vt.* to conceal or make indistinct —**ob·scure´ly** *adv.* —**ob·scure´ness** *n.*
**ob·scu´ri·ty** *n.* the condition of being unknown or indistinct
**ob·se´qui·ous** *adj.* groveling or subservient; fawning —**ob·se´qui·ous·ly** *adv.* —**ob·se´qui·ous·ness** *n.*
**ob·serv´a·ble** *adj.* noticeable; that can be perceived by sight —**ob·serv´a·bly** *adv.*
**ob·serv´ance** *n.* a traditional rite or celebration; an act of compliance, as to custom or law
**ob·serv´ant** *adj.* quick to comprehend or obey; attentive; strict in complying, as to duty or the law —**ob·serv´ant·ly** *adv.*
**ob·ser·va´tion** *n.* the act of complying, as to custom or law; a record of careful study; a comment or mention —**ob·ser·va´tion·al** *adj.* —**ob·ser·va´tion·al·ly** *adv.*
**ob·serv´a·to·ry** *n.* a place with a commanding view, especially one equipped to study the heavens
**ob·serve´** *vt.* to notice or watch carefully; to celebrate a traditional rite; to abide by custom or law; to mention —*vi.* to make a casual remark; to take notice —**ob·serv´er** *n.* —**ob·serve´ing·ly** *adv.*
**ob·sess´** *vt.* to be totally preoccupied —**ob·sess´ing·ly** *adv.*
**ob·ses´sion** *n.* an unnatural or irrational fascination or compulsion; the focus or subject of this fascination —**ob·ses´sion·al** *adj.* —**ob·ses´sion·al·ly** *adv.*
**ob·ses´sive** *adj.* compulsive —**ob·ses´sive·ly** *adv.* —**ob·ses´sive·ness** *n.*
**ob·so·les´cence** *n.* the process of going out of use; the condition of being out-dated —**ob·so·lesce´** *vi.* —**ob·so·les´cent** *adj.* —**ob·so·les´cent·ly** *adv.*
**ob´so·lete´** *adj.* no longer in use or useful; out-of-date —**ob·so·lete´ly** *adv.* —**ob·so·lete´ness** *n.*
**ob´sta·cle** *n.* a hindrance; a barrier or obstruction
**ob·ste·tri´cian** *n.* a physician who specializes in obstetrics
**ob·stet´rics** *n.* the care of women during and immediately following pregnancy —**ob·stet´ri·cal** *adj.* —**ob·stet´ri·cal·ly** *adv.*
**ob´sti·nate** *adj.* stubborn; defying control or treatment, as an illness —**ob´sti·na·cy, ob´sti·nate·ness** *n.* —**ob´sti·nate·ly** *adv.*
**ob·strep´er·ous** *adj.* unruly; defiant **ob·strep´er·ous·ly** *adv.* —**ob·strep´er·ous·ness** *n.*
**ob·struct´** *vt.* to interfere or hinder; to block the view of —**ob·struct´er, ob·struc´tor** *n.* —**ob·struc´tive** *adj.* —**ob·struc´tive·ness** *n.*
**ob·struc´tion** *n.* an act, thing etc. that blocks or hinders —**ob·struc´tion·ism** *n.*
**ob·struc´tion·ist** *n.* one who delays or blocks, especially the introduction of new ideas
**ob·tain´** *vt.* to gain possession of —**ob·tain´a·ble** *adj.*
**ob·trude´** *vi., vt.* to attempt to press one's person or opinions on another —**ob·trud´er** *n.* —**ob·tru´sion** *n.*
**ob·tru´sive** *adj.* interfering; overly conspicuous —**ob·tru´sive·ly** *adv.* —**ob·tru´sive·ness** *n.*
**ob·tuse´** *adj.* dull or ignorant; lacking understanding —**ob·tuse´ly** *adv.* —**ob·tuse´ness** *n.*
**ob·vert´** *vt.* to turn over
**ob´vi·ate** *vt.* to make unnecessary: *the alarm system obviated the need for a guard* —**ob·vi·a´tion** *n.* —**ob´vi·a·tor** *n.*
**ob´vi·ous** *adj.* clearly seen or understood —**ob´vi·ous·ly** *adv.* —**ob´vi·ous·ness** *n.*
**oc·ca´sion** *n.* an event or opportunity —*vt.* to cause
**oc·ca´sion·al** *adj.* occurring infrequently —**oc·ca´sion·al·ly** *adv.*
**oc´ci·dent** *n.* the west; countries west of the orient —**oc´ci·den´tal** *adj.*
**oc·cult´** *adj.* obscured or hidden; mysterious; relating to the supernatural —**oc·cult´ly** *adv.* —**oc·cult´ness** *n.*
**oc·cult´ism** *n.* belief in the supernatural —**oc·cult´ist** *n.*
**oc´cu·pan·cy** *n.* the possession of an office, home, etc.; the period of such possession
**oc´cu·pant** *n.* one who fills a position or inhabits a place
**oc·cu·pa´tion** *n.* an activity, esp. as a means of livelihood; occupancy —**oc·cu·pa´tion·al** *adj.* —**oc·cu·**

**pa´tion·al·ly** *adv.*

**oc´cu·py** *vt.* to fill, as time or space; to hold one's attention; to control, as by conquest **—oc´cu·pi·er** *n.*

**oc·cur´** *vi.* to happen; to present itself, as an idea **—oc·cur´rence** *n.* **—oc·cur´rent** *adj.*

**o´cean** *n.* a large body of salt water; a large amount: *an ocean of paperwork* **—o·ce·an´ic** *adj.*

**o·cea·nog´ra·pher** *n.* one engaged in scientific study of the ocean and its phenomena **—o·cea·no·graph´ic, o·cea·no·graph´i·cal** *adj.* **—o·cea·no·graph´i·cal·ly** *adv.* **—o·cean·og´ra·phy** *n.*

**o·cea·nol´o·gist** *n.* an oceanographer **—o·cea·no·log´ic, o·cea·no·log´i·cal** *adj.* **—o·cea·nol´o·gy** *n.*

**oc´ta·gon** *n.* an eight-sided polygon **—oc·tag´o·nal** *adj.* **—oc·tag´o·nal·ly** *adv.*

**oc´tal** *adj.* a number system based on units of eight

**oc·tet´** *n.* a group of eight; music written for eight instruments

**oc´u·lar** *adj.* of the eye or the sense of sight

**oc´u·list** *n.* a physician who specializes in treating the eyes; an optomotrist or opthalmologist

**odd** *adj.* strange or different; unusual or unexpected: *taking place at an odd hour,* of a remainder or uneven amount **—odd´ly** *adv.* **—odd´ness** *n.*

**odd´ball** *n.* an eccentric

**odd´i·ty** *n.* something unusual

**odds** *n. pl.* a ratio or other expression of probability: *the odds are two-to-one he'll take the job*

**ode** *n.* a lyric poem **—od´ic** *adj.* **—od´ist** *n.*

**o´di·ous** *adj.* offensive; engendering aversion **—o´di·ous·ly** *adv.* **—o´di·ous·ness** *n.*

**o´di·um** *n.* hatred or aversion

**o·dom´e·ter** *n.* a device for measuring distance traveled

**o´dor** *(US) n.* something perceived by smell; an aroma

**o·dor·if´er·ous** *adj.* having an aroma **—o·dor·if´er·ous·ly** *adv.* **—o·dor·if´er·ous·ness** *n.*

**o´dor·less** *adj.* lacking aroma

**o´dor·ous** *adj.* having a distinctive aroma **—o´dor·ous·ly** *adv.* **—o´dor·ous·ness** *n.*

**o´dour** *(Brit.) n.* something perceived by smell; an aroma

**off** *adj., adv., prep.* away from; at a distance; removed

**of´fal** *n.* waste, especially the inedible parts of an animal

**off´beat** *adj.* unconventional

**off´-col´or** *adj.* in poor taste; obscene

**of·fence´** *(Brit.) n.* a violation, as of custom or law, that which arouses disapproval

**of·fend´** *vi., vt.* to effect or arouse disapproval **—of·fend´er** *n.*

**of·fense´** *(US) n.* a violation, as of custom or law; that which arouses disapproval

**of·fen´sive** *adj.* disagreeable; vulgar or insulting **—of·fen´sive·ly** *adv.* **—of·fen´sive·ness** *n.*

**of´fer** *n.* something submitted for consideration **—***vt.* to present or submit

**of´fer·ing** *n.* a gift; something presented, as for sale

**of´fice** *n.* a place for conducting business; a position of authority

**of´fi·cer** *n.* one in authority

**of·fi´cial** *adj.* relating to a particular office or position; authorized **—***n.* one who holds a position of authority **—of·fi´cial·dom** *n.* **—of·fi´cial·ly** *adv.*

**of·fi´ci·ar·y** *n.* officials, collectively

**of·fi´ci·ate** *vt.* to preside, as a chairperson; to perform the duties of an office **—of·fi´ci·a·tor** *n.*

**of·fi´cious** *adj.* overly eager to offer assistance or advice **—of·fi´cious·ly** *adv.* **—of·fi´cious·ness** *n.*

**off´shoot** *n.* anything that branches off from a main source

**off´spring** *n.* progeny, descendants

**oft** *adv.* often

**of´ten** *adv.* frequently

**of´ten·times** *adv.* frequently

**o´gle** *vi., vt.* to look or stare rudely **—o´gler** *n.*

**o´gre** *n.* a mythical monster; one deemed to be barbaric or terrifying **—o´gre·ish** *adj.*

**oil** *n.* a generally liquid or liquifiable substance used in cooking, as a lubricant, or for fuel **—oil´i·ness** *n.* **—oil´y** *adj.*

**oint´ment** *n.* a salve

**old** *adj.* aged or elderly; of a specific age: *ten years old;* showing signs of age or wear; seasoned or matured

**old´-fash´ioned** *adj.* out-of-date; tending to outdated styles or concepts

**old hat** commonplace or hackneyed

**old money** inherited wealth

**old school** a commitment to tradition

**old wives´ tale** superstition; a traditional belief

**o´leo** *n.* oleomargarine

**o´le·o·mar´ga·rine** *n.* margarine, a substitute for butter

**ol·fac´to·ry** *adj.* of the sense of smell

**ol´i·gar·chy** *n.* a governmental system controlled by a small group of people **—ol´i·gar´chic, ol·i·gar´chi·cal** *adj.*

**ol·i·gop´o·ly** *n.* a market dominated by few suppliers **—ol·i·gop´o·lis´tic** *adj.*

**ol·i·gop´so·ny** *n.* a market dominated by few buyers **—ol·i·gop·so·nis´tic** *adj.*

**o´li·o** *n.* a type of stew; a mixture or collection

**om´buds·man** *n.* an investigator and mediator, especially one who settles disputes between citizens and governmental or private organizations

**o´men** *n.* a sign or indication that supposedly predicts good or evil, or that is seen to predict the future

**om´i·nous** *adj.* threatening; inauspicious; characterized by an evil omen **—om´i·nous·ly** *adv.* **—om´i·nous·ness** *n.*

**o·mis´sion** *n.* something omitted or neglected
**omit´** *vt.* to leave out; to fail to include or perform
**om´ni·bus** *adj.* including many things: *an omnibus bill that provides for both taxes and welfare* —*n.* a large passenger vehicle: a bus
**om·nip´o·tent** *adj.* having unlimited power —**om·nip´o·tence** *n.* —**om·nip´o·tent·ly** *adv.*
**om·nis´cient** *adj.* having unlimited knowledge —**om·nis´cience** *n.* —**om·nis´cient·ly** *adv.*
**om·niv´o·rous** *adj.* taking both plants and animals for food —**om´ni·vore** *n.* —**om·niv´o·rous·ly** *adv.* —**om·niv´o·rous·ness** *n.*
**on´com·ing** *adj.* approaching
**on´er·ous** *adj.* difficult or troublesome —**on´er·ous·ly** *adv.* —**on´er·ous·ness** *n.*
**one´-sid´ed** *adj.* prejudiced; unfair; favoring one person, argument, etc. over another —**one´-sid´ed·ly** *adv.* —**one´-sid´ed·ness** *n.*
**one´-up´man·ship** *n.* an attempt to outdo another in the matter of possessions or accomplishments
**on´go·ing** *adj.* continuous; in progress
**on´set** *n.* a beginning
**on´slaught** *n.* an attack; an outpouring
**o´nus** *n.* responsibility; burden
**on´ward** *adj., adv.* forward
**ooze** *n.* something that leaks out; slimy mud —*vi.* to flow or leak out slowly; to give off, as a particular quality: *she oozes charisma* —*vt.* to give off
**o·pac´i·ty** *n.* a lack of clarity or transparency
**o·paque´** *adj.* not transparent; impervious to light; ambiguous or obscure: *opaque reasoning* —**o·paque´ly** *adv.* —**o·paque´ness** *n.*
**o´pen** *adj.* accessible; unlocked or unobstructed; unrestricted; available; candid and straightforward; lacking prejudice: *open-minded* —*vi., vt.* to become or make accessible; to begin, as of a meeting or a business —**o´pen·ly** *adv.* —**o´pen·ness** *n.*
**o´pen·ing** *n.* a clear passage or space; a beginning; an opportunity or vacancy
**o´pen-mind´ed** *adj.* receptive to new ideas; able to be reasoned with —**o´pen-mind´ed·ly** *adv.* —**o´pen-mind´ed·ness** *n.*
**op´er·a** *n.* a musical drama —**op·er·at´ic** *adj.* —**op·er·at´i·cal·ly** *adv.*
**op´er·a·ble** *adj.* able to be put to use; that can be corrected by surgery —**op·er·a·bil´i·ty** *n.* —**op´er·a·bly** *adv.*
**op´er·ate** *vi.* to function, as of a machine; to perform surgery —*vt.* to control or cause to function; to manage, as a business
**op·er·a´tion** *n.* the condition or an instance of functioning: *a manufacturing operation*; a procedure or method; surgery —**op·er·a´tion·al** *adj.* —**op·er·a´tion·al·ly** *adv.*
**op´er·a·tive** *adj.* functioning well —**op´er·a·tive·ly** *adv.*
**op´er·a·tor** *n.* one who controls or runs, as a machine or a business
**op·er·et´ta** *n.* a light opera
**oph·thal·mol´o·gy** *n.* the branch of medicine that deals with the study of the eye, its diseases, and treatment —**oph·thal´mo·log´ic, oph·thal·mo·log´i·cal** *adj.* —**oph·thal·mol´o·gist** *n.*
**o´pi·ate** *n.* a sedative; anything that dulls the senses
**o·pin´ion** *n.* a belief or judgment that may be based on knowledge or simple emotion
**o·pin´ion·at·ed** *adj.* having strong, often radical, beliefs —**o·pin´ion·at·ed·ly** *adv.* —**o·pin´ion·at·ed·ness** *n.*
**o´pi·um** *n.* a narcotic derived from the opium poppy
**op·po´nent** *adj.* acting in opposition —*n.* one who opposes
**op´por·tune´** *adj.* timely or suitable —**op´por·tune´ly** *adv.* —**op·por·tune´ness** *n.*
**op·por·tun´ist** *n.* one who makes the mostof an advantage, often unmindful of others —**op·por·tun·is´tic** *adj.* —**op·por·tun·is´ti·cal·ly** *adv.*
**op·por·tu´ni·ty** *n.* an advantageous occasion or time
**op·pos´a·ble** *adj.* capable of being opposite or reversed, esp. of the thumb; that can be confronted or countered —**op·pos·a·bil´i·ty** *n.* —**op·pos´a·bly** *adv.*
**op·pose´** *vt.* to act in conflict with; to place across from —**op·pos´er** *n.* —**op·pos´ing·ly** *adv.*
**op´po·site** *adj.* positioned or placed across from; facing or moving away; facing or moving the wrong way; contrary —**op´po·site·ly** *adv.* —**op´po·site·ness** *n.*
**op·po·si´tion** *n.* the state of conflicting; those in disagreement —**op·po·si´tion·al** *adj.*
**op·press´** *vt.* to suppress by maltreatment or abuse; to overburden; to depress mentally —**op·pres´sion** *n.* —**op·pres´sor** *n.*
**op·pres´sive** *adj.* marked by persecution, hardship, etc.; producing depression —**op·pres´sive·ly** *adv.* —**op·pres´sive·ness** *n.*
**op·pro´bri·ous** *adj.* contemptuous or reproachful; shameful —**op·pro´bri·ous·ly** *adv.* —**op·pro´bri·ous·ness** *n.*
**op·pro´bri·um** *n.* shameful conduct; a cause of shame or disgrace
**opt** *vi.* to choose
**op´tic** *adj.* relating to the eye —**op´ti·cal·ly** *adv.*
**op´ti·cal** *adj.* relating to vision
**optical illusion** a deceptive or misleading image
**op·ti´cian** *n.* one who makes or sells eyeglasses or other optical devices
**op´tics** *pl. n.* the branch of science dealing with vision and light
**op´ti·mal** *adj.* most favorable —**op´ti·mal·ly** *adv.*
**op´ti·mism** *n.* an
**op´ti·mism** *n.* an inclination to expect a favorable outcome —**op´ti·mist** *n.* —**op´ti·mis´tic** *adj.* —**op·ti·mis´ti·cal·ly** *adv.*

**op´ti·mize** *vt.* to maximize effectiveness **—op·ti·mi·za´tion** *n.*
**op´ti·mum** *adj.* most favorable
**op´tion** *n.* a choice; a right to choose or elect
**op´tion·al** *adj.* discretionary
**op·tom´e·try** *n.* the technology involved in examining, diagnosing problems, and prescribing treatment for the eyes **—op´to·met´ric, op·to·met´ri·cal** *adj.* **—op·tom´e·trist** *n.*
**op´u·lent** *adj.* marked by wealth or abundance; profuse **—op´u·lence, op´u·len·cy** *n.* **—op´u·lent·ly** *adv.*
**o´pus** *n.* a creative literary or musical composition
**or´a·cle** *n.* a prophet; a visionary; one considered a source of great wisdom
**o·rac´u·lar** *adj.* prophetic; obscure or ambiguous, as the prophesies of an oracle **—o·rac·u·lar´i·ty** *n.* **—o·rac´u·lar·ly** *adv.*
**o´ral** *adj.* spoken; relating to speech or the mouth **—o´ral·ly** *adv.*
**o·rate´** *vi.* to speak formally **—or·a´tion** *n.* **—or´a·tor** *n.*
**or·a·tor´i·cal** *adj.* pertaining to an orator or oratory **—or·a·tor´i·cal·ly** *adv.*
**or´a·to·ry** *n.* the art of public speaking
**orb** *n.* a sphere
**or´bit** *n.* the path traveled by one body around another, as of a satellite around the earth; a sphere of influence *—vi.* to travel in an orbit *—vt.* to place in an orbit **—or´bit·al** *adj.*
**or´chard** *n.* trees grown for their produce, such as fruit, nuts, etc.**or´ches·tra** *n.* a large group of musicians; the area of a theater directly in front of the stage **—or·ches´tral** *adj.* **—or·ches´tral·ly** *adv.*
**or´ches·trate** *vt.* to arrange music; to coordinate an activity: *orchestrate a corporate buyout* **—or·ches·tra´tion** *n.* **—or´ches·tra·tor** *n.*
**or·dain´** *vt.* to charge with holy orders; to decree or dictate **—or·dain´ment** *n.*
**or´deal** *n.* a trying experience
**or´der** *n.* a logical sequence or arrangement; a command or request; a group or organization *—vt.* to arrange; to instruct or direct **—or´der·er** *n.*
**or´der·ly** *adj.* neat; systematic or methodical; peaceful and lawabiding *—n.* a hospital attedant; a soldier assigned to attend an officer **—or´der·li·ness** *n.*
**or´di·nance** *n.* a law, especially a local regulation or statute
**or´di·nary** *adj.* common; unexceptional *—n.* that which is usual or normal **—or·di·nar´i·ly** *adv.* **—or·di·nar´i·ness** *n.*
**ord´nance** *n.* military arms and equipment
**ore** *n.* mineral rock from which a useful substance can be extracted
**or´gan** *n.* a musical instrument; a body part; a controlled-circulation publication
**or·gan´ic** *adj.* of or relating to living tissue or things **—or·gan´i·cal·ly** *adv.*
**or´ga·nism** *n.* a life form
**or´gan·ist** *n.* one who plays an organ
**or·ga·ni·za´tion** *n.* the process of bringing together or making functional; an entity so formed; an association of persons united for a common purpose **—or·ga·ni·za´tion·al** *adj.* **—or·ga·ni·za´tion·al·ly** *adv.*
**or´ga·nize** *vt.* to make orderly or functional; to bring together or establish **—or´ga·niz·er** *n.*
**or´ga·nized** *adj.* established; functional; orderly
**or´gasm** *n.* sexual climax **—or·gas´mic, or·gas´tic** *adj.*
**or´gy** *n.* revelry; uncontrolled indulgence **—or·gi·as´tic** *adj.* **—or·gi·as´ti·cal·ly** *adj.*
**o´ri·ent** *vt.* to position according to the points of the compass or some other point of reference; to familiarize, as with a company's policies and procedures
**o´ri·en·tate** *vt.* to orient **—o·ri·en·ta´tion** *n.*
**or´i·fice** *n.* an opening **—or´i·fi´cial** *adj.*
**or´i·gin** *n.* a beginning; a source
**o·rig´i·nal** *adj.* first or new; different or imaginative *—n.* a thing from which others are derived; a prototype
**o·rig·i·nal´i·ty** *n.* creativeness; innovation
**o·rig´i·nal·ly** *adv.* first; initially
**o·rig´i·nate** *vi., vt.* to come or bring into existence **—o·rig·i·na´tion** *n.* **—o·rig´i·na·tor** *n.*
**or´na·ment** *n.* a decoration or embellishment *—vt.* to decorate or embellish
**or´na·men´tal** *adj.* decorative **—or·na·men´tal·ly** *adv.* **—or·na·men·ta´tion** *n.*
**or·nate´** *adj.* elaborately styled or decorated **—or·nate´ly** *adv.* **—or·nate´ness** *n.*
**or´ner·y** *adj.* surly or irritable **—or´ner·i·ness** *n.*
**or·ni·thol´o·gy** *n.* the study of birds **—or·nith´o·log´ic, or·nith´o·log´i·cal** *adj.* **—or·ni·thol´o·gist** *n.*
**or´phan** *adj.* lacking parents; unsupported, as *the orphan concept of cold fusion* *—n.* a child without parents *—vt.* to deprive of one or both parents
**or´phic** *adj.* mystical
**ort** *n.* a scrap, especially of food left after a meal
**or·tho·don´tia, or·tho·don´tics** *n.* dentistry involved in the prevention and correction of irregularities in teeth **—or·tho·don´tic** *adj.* **—or·tho·don´tist** *n.*
**or´tho·dox** *adj.* adhering to traditional or established ways **—or´tho·dox·y** *n.*
**or·tho·pe´dics** *n.* the branch of medicine concerned with ailments of the skeletal system **—or·tho·pe´dic** *adj.* **—or·tho·pe´di·cal·ly** *adv.* **—or´tho·pe´dist** *n.*
**os´cil·late** *vi.* to move back and forth; to vibrate **—os·cil·la´tion** *n.*
**os´cu·late** *vi.* to come together *—vt.* to kiss **—os·cu·la´tion** *n.*
**os·mo´sis** *n.* the tendency of fluid to pass through a thin membrane until it is of equal density on both sides; a gradual, often unnoticed, process of absorb-

ing or learning —os´mose *vi., vt.* —os·mot´ic *adj.* —os·mot´i·cal·ly *adv.*

**os·si·fi·ca´tion** *n.* the process of forming bone; the process of becoming hardened or the material so formed —os·sif´ic *adj.* —os´si·fy *vi., vt.*

**os·ten´si·ble** *adj.* appearing as; professed or pretended: *his ostensible goal is progress, but he really means to sow dissent* —os·ten´si·bly *adv.*

**os·ten´sive** *adj.* apparent or seeming —os·ten´sive·ly *adv.*

**os·ten·ta´tion** *n.* a pretentious display intended to impress

**os·ten·ta´tious** *adj.* overly showy —os·ten·ta´tious·ly *adv.* —os·ten·ta´tious·ness *n.*

**os´tra·cize** *vt.* to isolate or banish, as from a group —os´tra·cism *n.*

**oth´er** *adj.* distinct from; remaining from those indicated

**oth´er·wise** *adv.* differently; in a different setting or circumstance

**oth´er·world´ly** *adj.* mystical; unconcerned with the present —oth´er·world´li·ness *n.*

**o´ti·ose** *adj.* idle, indolent —o´ti·ose·ly *adv.* —oti·os´i·ty *n.*

**oust** *vt.* to eject or force out —oust´er *n.*

**out** *adj., adv.* exterior; away or apart from; distinct from that which is usual or accepted

**out´age** *n.* a shortage or variance, a temporary interruption, as of electrical power

**out´break** *n.* an outset or beginning as of sudden violence or disease

**out´burst** *n.* an abrupt discharge or disturbance

**out´cast** *n.* one who has been expelled or rejected —*adj.* rejected

**out´come** *n.* a consequence or result

**out´cry** *n.* a protest or clamor

**out·dat´ed** *adj.* antiquated; no longer popular or stylish —out·dat´ed·ness *n.*

**out·do´** *vt.* to surpass

**out·doors´** *n.* outside; away from civilization —out´door´ *adj.*

**out´er** *adj.* external or exterior

**outer space** beyond the limits of a planet's atmosphere

**out´fit** *n.* a set of clothing or equipment —*vt.* to furnish with clothing or equipment —out´fit·ter *n.*

**out·fox´** *vt.* to outsmart

**out´go** *n.* expeditures

**out´go´ing** *adj.* sociable; leaving, as from a place or position

**out´grow´** *vt.* to become too large for, as clothing; to overcome or depart from, as immature habits

**out´growth** *n.* something produced as a result

**out·ing** *n.* an airing or excursion

**out·land´ish** *adj.* foreign or unconventional —out·land´ish·ly *adv.* —out·land´ish·ness *n.*

**out´law** *n.* a criminal: a rebel or radical —*vt.* to prohibit

**out´lay** *n.* an expenditure

**out´let** *n.* an opening, as for egress or escape; a shop that sells goods or services, especially a specific brand or at reduced prices; a connector, as for electricity or a telephone

**out´line** *n.* a plan or general description; a line drawing that defines the shape of an object —*vt.* to provide a general description; to create a line drawing

**out´look** *n.* a particular viewpoint; an assessment of future prospects

**out´ly·ing** *adj.* distant; far removed

**out´mod´ed** *adj.* no longer practical or fashionable

**out´-of-date´** *adj.* outmoded

**out´-of-doors´** *n.* outdoors

**out´-of-pock´et** *adj.* of a cash expenditure

**out´-of-the-way´** *adj.* remote

**out·pace´** *vt.* to exceed, as in growth or expectations: *the cost to operate the business could quickly outpace our income*

**out´pa·tient** *n.* one treated at a hospital or clinic without an overnight stay

**out·per·form´** *vt.* to achieve better results than another

**out´put** *n.* an amount produced; that which is produced

**out´rage** *n.* an offensive act; anger caused by such an act —*vt.* to make violently angry

**out·ra´geous** *adj.* extremely offensive; excessive or unconventional: *charged an outrageous price* —out·ra´geous·ly *adv.* —out·ra´geous·ness *n.*

**out´right** *adj., adv.* direct and without reservation; completely and entirely

**out´set** *n.* a beginning

**out·side´** *adj.* of the outer limit —*n.* the outer surface or limit —*adv.*

**out·sid´er** *n.* one who does not belong or fit in

**out·smart´** *vt.* to outwit or outmaneuver; to deceive

**out´spo´ken** *adj.* candid —out'spo'ken·ly *adv.* —out'spo'ken·ness *n.*

**out·stand´ing** *adj.* notable or exceptional; unsettled, as an unpaid debt —out·stand´ing·ly *adv.*

**out´strip´** *vt.* to outrun or exceed

**out´ward** *adj., adv.* toward the outside; external —out´ward´ly *adv.* —out´ward·ness *n.*

**out´wit´** *vt.* to trick or deceive

**o´val** *adj.* elliptical; egg-shaped —*n.* —o´val·ly *adv.* —o´val·ness *n.*

**o´vate** *adj.* oval, as of a leaf —o´vate·ly *adv.*

**o·va´tion** *n.* spirited applause —o·va´tion·al *adj.*

**ov´en** *n.* a closed compartment for baking or drying

**o´ver** *adj.* extreme; extra —*adv.* above; across: *he jumped over the puddle*; as far as: *move over to the table*; completed or done *—prep.*

**o·ver·a·chieve´** *vi.* to be more successful than anticipated; to accomplish more than expected **—o·ver·a·chieve´ment** *n.* **—o·ver·a·chieve´er** *n.*

**o·ver·act´** *vi., vt.* to overplay or exaggerate a role

**o·ver·ac´tive** *adj.* more active than normal or expected **—o·ver·ac·tiv´i·ty** *n.*

**o´ver·age** *n.* an excess

**o·ver·all´** *adj.* all-inclusive

**o´ver·alls** *n. (Brit.)* a one-piece garment customarily worn over street clothes to protect them; *(US)* loose trousers with a bib front and shoulder straps

**o·ver·awe´** *vt.* to inspire great wonderment or veneration

**o·ver·bear´** *vt.* to dominate

**o·ver·bear´ing** *adj.* domineering or arrogant **—o´ver·bear´ing·ly** *adv.*

**o·ver·blown´** *adj.* excessive

**o´ver·build´** *vi., vt.* to fill an area with more structures than necessary or practical

**o´ver·bur´den** *vt.* to overload or overwork

**o´ver·cast** *adj.* cloudy or misty; gloomy

**o·ver·charge´** *vt.* to request an excessive price for *—n.* an excessive charge

**o´ver·coat** *n.* a heavy coat that covers most of the body

**o·ver·come´** *vt.* to defeat or prevail over *—vi.* to win

**o·ver·com·mit´** *vt.* to obligate beyond one's abillity to perform **—o·ver·com·mit´ment** *n.*

**o·ver·com´pen·sate** *vt.* to react immoderately to a real or imagined error or shortcoming *—vi.* to make too great a compensation for **—o´ver·com·pen´sa·to·ry** *adj.* **—o´ver·com·pen·sa´tion** *n.*

**o·ver·crowd´** *vi., vt.* to crowd or cause to crowd excessively

**o·ver·de·vel´op** *vt.* to improve or expand excessively **—o·ver·de·vel´op·ment** *n.*

**o·ver·do´** *vi., vt.* to overreach or carry to extremes

**o´ver·dose** *n.* an excessive dosage or amount *—vt.* to take or administer an excessive dose

**o·ver·draft** *n.* an amount drawn from an account in excess of available funds

**o·ver·draw´** *vt.* to withdraw from an account in excess of available funds; to exaggerate

**o·ver·dress´** *vi., vt.* to wear attire that is too elaborate or out of place

**o´ver·due´** *adj.* being beyond the time when expected or due

**o·ver·es´ti·mate** *vt.* to esteem or appraise too highly

**o·ver·ex·pose´** *vt.* to exhibit or allow excessive access to

**o·ver·ex·tend´** *vt.* to obligate or use beyond a reasonable limit **—o·ver·ex·ten´sion** *n.*

**o´ver·flow** *n.* an excessive amount; a device that allows excess to escape *—vi., vt.* to spill over; to abound

**o´ver·growth** *n.* luxurious or excessive growth, especially of plants **—o·ver·grow´** *vi., vt.* **—o·ver·grown´** *adj.*

**o´ver·hang´** *vi., vt.* to extend beyond, as the edge of a roof over the walls below

**o´ver·haul´** *vt.* to renovate or make extensive repairs

**o´ver·head** *n.* the cost of operating a business such as the rent and utilities, excluding the cost of producing a product or service *—adj.* **—o·ver·head´** *adv.* above the level of the head

**o·ver·hear´** *vi., vt.* to hear without the speaker's knowledge

**o·ver·in·dulge´** *vt.* to partake excessively **—o´ver·in·dul´gence** *n.* **—o´ver·in·dul´gent** *adj.* **—o´ver·in·dul´gent·ly** *adv.*

**o´ver·joyed** *adj.* delighted **—o´ver·joy´** *vt.*

**o´ver·kill** *n.* an excess of that required

**o´ver·lay** *n.* something spread over to cover or embellish *—vt.*

**o´ver·look** *n.* a vantage point **—o´ver·look´** *vt.* to watch over or supervise; to disregard or omit

**o´ver·ly** *adv.* excessively

**o·ver·much´** *adj., adv.* excessive

**o·ver·night´** *adj.* extending over one night or throughout the night

**o·ver·night´er** *n.* a trip of more than a single day; one making an overnight stay; a suitcase

**overnight bag** a suitcase to carry clothing, etc. for a short trip

**o´ver·pass** *(US) n.* a passageway over a road, walkway, etc.

**o·ver·pay´** *vi.* to pay in excess of what is required or necessary **—o·ver·pay´ment** *n.*

**o·ver·play´** *vt.* to stress excessively

**o´ver·pop·u·la´tion** *n.* overcrowding that causes depletion of resources **—o·ver·pop´u·late** *vi., vt.*

**o·ver·pow´er** *vt.* to overwhelm

**o·ver·price´** *vt.* to price or value too highly

**o´ver·print** *n.* an image printed over an existing image **—o·ver·print´** *vt.*

**o·ver·pro·duce´** *vt.* to manufacture more than is required **—o·ver·pro·duc´tion** *n.*

**o·ver·qual´i·fied** *adj.* possessing education or experience beyond that required for a particular job

**o·ver·rate´** *vt.* to rank or appraise too highly

**o·ver·reach´** *vt.* to go beyond that which is right or prudent

**o·ver·re·act´** *vi.* to react excessively or inappropriately **—o·ver·re·ac´tion** *n.*

**o·ver·rule´** *vt.* to rule against an earlier decision

**o·ver·run´** *vi., vt.* to spread or extend over a reasonable or normal limit

**o·ver·seas´** *adj.* of places across the sea

**o·ver·see´** *vt.* to supervise **—o´ver·seer** *n.*

**o·ver·sell´** *vt.* to contract to sell more than is available

to praise or promote too highly
**o·ver·shad´ow** *vt.* dominate
**o·ver·shoot´** *vi., vt.* to exceed or go beyond
**o´ver·sight** *n.* supervision; an unintentional error
**o·ver·sim´pli·fy** *vi., vt.* to explain in terms so simple as to cause misunderstanding **–o·ver·sim´pli·fi·ca´tion** *n.*
**o´ver·size, o´ver·sized** *adj.* larger than usual or necessary
**o·ver·spend´** *vi., vt.* to spend in excess; to tire
**o·ver·state´** *vt.* to exaggerate **–o·ver·state´ment** *n.*
**o·vert´** *adj.* open and public; sanctioned: *an overt military operation* **–o·vert´ly** *adv.*
**o·ver·tax´** *vt.* to burden excessively
**o´ver-the-count´er** *adj.* of medicine that can be sold without a doctor's prescription
**o·ver·throw´** *vt.* to overturn, as a govenment; to throw, as a ball past its intended mark **–o·ver·throw´er** *n.*
**o´ver·time** *n.* time past an established norm, as work beyond a normal eight hour day
**o´ver·tone** *n.* an inference or hint: *an explanation with overtones of condescension*
**o´ver·ture** *n.* a musical introduction; an approach that signals readiness to negotiate
**o´ver·view** *n.* a general view; a summary
**o·ver·wea´ry** *adj.* exhausted
**o·ver·whelm´** *vt.* to defeat; to astonish; to inundate **–o·ver·whelm´ing** *adj.* **–o·ver·whelm´ing·ly** *adv.*
**o·ver·work´** *vi., vt.* to work or use too much
**o·ver·wrought´** *adj.* overexcited or agitated; overly ornate
**o´vine** *adj.* pertaining to sheep; sheeplike
**o´void** *adj.* shaped like an egg
**owe** *vi., vt.* to be indebted
**ow´ing** *adj.* unpaid
**own** *adj.* of one's possession *–vt.* to possess or control *–vi., vt.* to admit or acknowledge **–own´er** *n.* **–own´er·ship** *n.*
**ox·i·da´tion** *n.* the combining of oxygen with another substance
**ox´i·dize** *vt.* to combine with oxygen **–ox´i·diz´able** *adj.* **–ox´i·di·za´tion** *n.* **–ox´i·diz·er** *n.*
**ox´y·gen** *n.* a non-metallic element that mixes readily with most other elements, is necessary for plant and animal respiration, and is required for most combustion
**ox´y·gen·ate** *vt.* to combine with oxygen **–ox·y·gen·a´tion** *n.*
**ox·y·mo´ron** *n.* a descriptive phrase that incorporates seemingly contradictory terms, as *a sweet sadness* or *the silence was deafening* **–ox·y·mo·ron´ic** *adj.*

**p, P** sixteenth letter of the English alphabet
**pace** *n.* a manner of walking; the speed at which one walks or at which an event takes place; a stride of about 30 inches *–vt., vi.* to walk; to measure by paces
**pace´mak·er** *n.* a device used to regulate the heartbeat
**pach´y·derm** *n.* any of a variety of large animals with think hides such as the elephant or rhinoceros **–pach·y·der´mal, pach·y·der´ma·tous** *adj.*
**pa·cif´ic** *adj.* peaceful, tranquil **–pa·cif´i·cal·ly** *adv.*
**pac·i·fi·ca´tion** *n.* appeasement **–pac´i·fi·ca·tor** *n.* **–pa·cif´i·ca·to·ry** *adj.*
**pac´i·fism** *n.* the rejection of the use of violence in the settling of conflicts **–pac´i·fist** *n.* **–pac·i·fis´tic** *adj.* **–pac·i·fis´ti·cal·ly** *adv.*
**pac´i·fy** *vt.* to ease anger or conflict **–pac´i·fi·a·ble** *adj.*
**pack** *n.* a small package; a set of like items: *a pack of cards*; a closed bag with straps for carrying necessary items for hiking, camping etc.; a group, generally functioning as a unit *–vt., vi.* to place in a container or containers; to press together or compress **–pack´a·ble** *adj.*
**pack´age** *n.* a container holding items for storage or transport; a combination of elements taken together: *a package deal* *–vt.* to make into or offer as a combination **–pack´ag·er** *n.*
**pack´ag·ing** *n.* material used to form a package or to protect or cushion a packaged item; the way in which something is presented
**pack´et** *n.* a small package
**pack´ing** *n.* material used to protect or cushion a packaged item
**pact** *n.* an agreement; a contract
**pad** *n.* a thin protective cushion; sheets of writing paper glued together at one end *–vt.* to protect with soft material; to increase deceitfully: *pad a speech with irrelevant stories, pad an expense account* **–pad´ding** *n.*
**pad´dle** *n.* any of a variety of flattened implements used for such things as mixing, propelling a boat, spanking, etc. *–vi., vt.* to propel with a paddle; to spank **–pad´dler** *n.*
**pa´gan** *adj.* without religion; heathenish *–n.* a nonreligious person **–pa´gan·dom** *n.* **–pa´gan·ish** *adj.* **–pa´gan·ism** *n.*
**page** *n.* one side of a sheet of paper *–vt.* to summon by calling aloud or with a beeper
**pag´eant** *n.* an elaborate procession or celebration **–pag´eant·ry** *n.*
**pag´i·nate** *vt.* to number the pages of a publication **–pag·i·na´tion** *n.*
**pa·go´da** *n.* an ornate multi-storied tower that serves as a Buddhist shrine
**pail** *n.* a cylindrical container with a handle used for carrying liquids
**pain** *n.* a disagreeable sensation caused by injury, etc.; suffering *–vi., vt.* to cause pain **–take pains** to exercise great care **–pain´ful** *adj.* **–pain´ful´ly** *adv.*

–**pain´ful´ness** *n.*

**pain´kill·er** *n.* a medication that relieves pain –**pain´kill·ing** *adj.*

**pain´less** *adj.* free from pain; causing no pain –**pain´less·ly** *adj.* –**pain´less·ness** *n.*

**pains´tak·ing** *adj.* requiring great care; careful –*n.* very careful work –**pains´tak·ing·ly** *adv.*

**paint** *n.* liquid coloring used to decorate or protect; the coating formed when the liquid dries –*vi., vt.* to cover with paint; to create an image with paint or with words –**paint´a·ble** *adj.* –**paint´er** *n.*

**paint´ing** *n.* the process or business of covering surfaces with paint; a picture or design created with paint

**pair** *n.* two persons or things sharing something in common –*vi., vt.* to come or bring together in a pair

**pal** *n.* a friend

**pal´ace** *n.* a grand and sumptuous residence –**pa·la´tial** *adj.* –**pa·la´tial·ly** *adv.* –**pa·la´tial·ness** *n.*

**pal´at·a·ble** *adj.* edible; acceptable: *a palatable solution* –**pal´at·a·bil´i·ty** –**pal´at·a·ble·ness** *n.* –**pal´at·a·bly** *adv.*

**pal´ate** *n.* the roof of the mouth; the sense of taste

**pale** *adj.* light in color; pallid; dim –*vt., vi.* to make or become pale –**pale´ly** *adv.* –**pale´ness** *n.* –**pal´ish** *adj.*

**pal´ette** *n.* a flat panel for mixing artist's colors; the colors used by an artist

**pal´i·mo·ny** *n.* financial support for a former companion

**pal´in·drome** *n.* a word, phrase, etc. that can be read backward or forward, such as *a man, a plan, a canal, Panama* –**pal´in·drom´ic** *adj.*

**pal·i·sade´** *n.* a steep cliff, often overlooking a body of water

**pall** *n.* gloom; a dark cover, as of clouds or smoke

**pal´li·ate** *vt.* to excuse; to relieve or ease as symptoms of an illness –**pal·li·a´tion** *n.* –**pal´li·a·tor** *n.*

**pal´li·a·tive** *adj.* serving to relieve the symptoms of an illness –**pal´li·a·tive·ly** *adv.*

**pal´lid** *adj.* extremely pale; ashen –**pal´lid·ly** *adv.* –**pal´lid·ness, pal´lor** *n.*

**palm´is·try** *n.* the telling of fortunes from the patterns on the palm of the hands –**palm´ist** *n.*

**pal´pa·ble** *adj.* obvious; tangible –**pal·pa·bil´i·ty, pal´pa·ble·ness** *n.* –**pal´pa·bly** *adv.*

**pal´pi·tate** *vi.* to tremble or quiver; to pulsate –**pal´pi·tat·ing·ly** *adv.* –**pal´pi·ta´tion** *n.*

**pal´try** *adj.* trivial; insignificant; of little worth –**pal´tri·ly** *adv.* –**pal´tri·ness** *n.*

**pam´per** *vt.* to cater to excessively; to indulge –**pam´per·er** *n.*

**pamph´let** *n.* a leaflet or brochure –**pam´phlet·ar·y** *adj.* –**pam´phle·teer** *n.*

**pan** *n.* a shallow metal container used for cooking; any similar container such as a *dishpan*; harsh criticism –*vi., vt.* to seek out or separate by rinsing: *to pan for gold*; to criticize

**pan·a·ce´a** *adj.* a cure-all –**pan·a·ce´an** *adj.*

**pa·nache´** *n.* spirit or zest

**pan·chro·mat´ic** *adj.* sensitive to all colors: *panchromatic film* –**pan·chro´ma·tism** *n.*

**pan·dem´ic** *adj.* general; universal

**pan·de·mo´ni·um** *n.* noisy confusion

**pan´der** *vi.* to cater to or exploit the baser tastes of others; to procure for sexual affairs –*n.* a procurer or pimp

**pane** *n.* a panel of glass for a window; a flat piece or surface

**pan´el** *n.* a flat decorative section set off from the rest of the object of which it is a part: *a door panel*; any similar section: *an instrument panel*; a group formed for some specific purpose: *a panel of judges* –*vt.* to provide with panels

**pan´el·ing** *n.* a wall covering

**pan´el·ist** *n.* a member of a group formed for a specific purpose, as to judge a contest or discuss an issue

**pang** *n.* a sudden sharp pain or emotion: *a pang of guilt*

**pan´han·dle** *(US) vi.* to beg for food, etc. –**pan´han·dler** *n.*

**pan´ic** *n.* sudden fear; general hysteria –*vi., vt.* to become or cause to become fearful –**pan´ick·y** *adj.*

**pan´icked, pan´ick·ing** *adj.* driven by fear

**pan´ic-strick·en** *adj.* overcome by fear or dread

**pan´o·ply** *n.* an extensive or impressive display

**pan·o·ram´a** *n.* an extensive view –**pan´o·ram´ic** *adj.* –**pan·o·ram´i·cal·ly** *adv.*

**pant** *vi.* to take short rapid breaths

**pan´to·graph** *n.* a mechanical device used to make a copy of a drawing, diagram, etc. –**pan·tog´ra·pher** *n.* –**pan·to·graph´ic** *adj.*

**pan´to·mime** *n.* communication by means of gestures; a performance that expresses ideas without speech –*vt., vi.* to express in pantomime –**pan´to·mim´ic** *adj.* –**pan´to·mimist** *n.*

**pan´try** *n.* a closet for storing food and food service items; an area where foods are plated or otherwise prepared for serving

**pap** *n.* soft food, as for infants or the infirm; a thing of little significance

**pa´per** *adj.* formed of or resembling paper; lacking substance: *paper shuffling, paper profits* –*n.* a thin material made from wood or cloth pulp; a formal dissertation or document of value; a daily newspaper –*vt.* to cover with paper

**pa´per·back** *n.* a book with a thick paper cover –*adj.*

**pa´per·push·er** *n.* an inconsequential bureaucrat

**paper tiger** one who is weak or ineffectual while pretending to be strong and forceful

**pa·pier-mâ·ché´** *n.* paper pulp, easily shaped when wet, that dries to a hard surface

**par** *adj.* normal —*n.* an established standard or level for comparison; the face value of a negotiable instrument, such as a stock or bond

**par´a·ble** *n.* a story with a moral

**par´a·chute** *n.* a cloth canopy attached with cords to a person or object to slow the rate of descent from a high altitude —*vi., vt.* to descend or land by parachute —**par´a·chut·ist** *n.*

**pa·rade´** *n.* a procession, that can be formal such as a *Thanksgiving Day parade*, or informal as for *a parade of shoppers*; a series of things or events: *a parade of sitcoms on television* —**pa·rad´er** *n.*

**par´a·digm** *n.* an example or model —**par´a·dig·mat´ic** *adj.* —**par´a·dig·mat´i·cal·ly** *adv.*

**par´a·dise** *n.* a perfect place of peace and beauty —**par´a·di·sa´ic, par´a·di·sa´i·cal, par´a·di·si´a·cal** *adj.* —**par´a·di·sa´i·cal·ly, par´a·di·si´a·cal·ly** *adv.*

**par´a·dox** *n.* a statement that seems contradictory, but that may nevertheless be true *such as standing in one place is more tiring than walking*; an enigma, as a person or thing that possesses contradictory qualities —**par·a·dox´i·cal** *adj.* —**par·a·dox´i·cal·ly** *adv.* —**par·a·dox´i·cal·ness** *n.*

**par´a·gon** *n.* an example of perfection: *a paragon of virtue*

**par´a·graph** *n.* a section of prose that typically deals with a single topic or quotation —*vt.* to divide into paragraphs —**par´a·graph´ic, par´a·graph´i·cal** *adj.* —**par´a·graph´i·cal·ly** *adv.*

**par·a·jour´nal·ism** *n.* reporting that embodies some fictional license, as a study of student life that features a character who is a composite of several individuals —**par·a·jour´nal·ist** *n.* —**par·a·jour·nal·is´tic** *adj.*

**par·a·le´gal** *n.* one trained to assist an attorney

**par´al·lax** *n.* apparent displacement of an object caused by a change in the observer's position —**par·al·lac´tic** *adj.* —**par·al·lac´ti·cal·ly** *adv.*

**par´al·lel** *adj.* being of equal distance from each other at all points; being or moving in concert: *the story of parallel careers* —*n.* a resemblance or likeness; comparable —*vt.* to make parallel; to extend parallel to; to resemble or correlate —**par´al·lel·ism** *n.*

**par´a·lyse** *(Brit.) vt.* to render unable to move or function

**pa·ral´y·sis** *n.* a loss of ability to move or function

**par·a·lyt´ic** *adj.* paralyzed —**par·a·lyt´i·cal·ly** *adv.*

**par´a·lyze** *(US) vt.* to render unable to move or function —**par·a·ly·za´tion** *n.* —**par´a·lyz·ing·ly** *adv.*

**par·a·med´ic** *n.* one trained to provide emergency medical treatment and to assist a doctor —**par·a·med´i·cal** *adj.*

**pa·ram´e·ter** *n.* a boundary or limitation —**par´a·met´ric, par·a·met´ri·cal** *adj.*

**par´a·mount** *adj.* of primary importance; dominant —**par´a·mount·cy** *n.* —**par´a·mount·ly** *adv.*

**par´amour** *n.* a lover

**par·a·noi´a** *n.* irrational fear or distrust —**par´a·noi´ac, par´a·noid** *adj., n.*

**par´a·nor´mal** *adj.* outside the realm of normal knowledge or description —**par´a·nor´mal·ly** *adj.*

**par´a·pher·na´lia** *n.* the implements customarily used for a particular activity; equipment: *an artist's paraphernalia*

**par´a·phrase** *n.* a retelling in different words, usually to simplify or to clarify —*vi., vt.* to retell; restate —**par´a·phras·a·ble** *adj.* —**par´a·phras·er** *n.*

**para·ple´gia** *n.* paralysis of the lower part of the body —**par´a·ple´gic** *n., adj.*

**par´a·pro·fes´sion·al** *n.* one trained to assist another in a particular profession

**par´a·psy·chol´o·gy** *n.* the study of paranormal activity —**par´a·psy·cho·log´i·cal** *adj.* —**par´a·psy·chol´o·gist** *n.*

**par´a·site** *n.* an organism that is supported by another organism without providing anything to its host; one who relies on the generosity of others —**par´a·sit´ic, par´a·sit´i·cal** *adj.* —**par´a·sit´i·cal·ly** *adv.*

**par´a·sol** *n.* a small umbrella used as cover or protection from the sun

**par´boil** *vt.* to boil food briefly before cooking by some other method

**par´cel** *n.* a package; a section of land —*vt.* to divide and portion out

**parch** *vt., vi.* to make or become extremely dry or shriveled with heat; to make or become thirsty

**parch´ment** *n.* originally, animal skin used as a writing surface; paper made to resemble cured or treated animal skin

**par´don** *n.* forgiveness, as from punishment for a crime or for a social blunder —*vt.* to release from punishment; to forgive —**par´don·a·ble** *adj.* —**par´don·a·bly** *adv.* —**par´don·er** *n.*

**pare** *vt.* to remove the outer part by cutting; to trim

**par´ent** *n.* an ancestor; a mother or father: a source: *the automobile is parent to urban blight* —**pa·ren´tal** *adj.* —**pa·ren´tal·ly** *adv.* —**par´ent·hood** *n.*

**par´ent·age** *n.* one's lineage

**pa·ren´the·sis** *n., pl.* **pa·ren´the·ses** either of the curved symbols ( ) used to set apart a word or words as in a sentence or parts of a mathematical formula

**par´en·thet´ic, par´en·thet´i·cal** *adj.* an aside; a comment apart, as though set off by parenthesis —**par´en·thet´i·cal·ly** *adv.*

**par´ent·ing** *n.* performance of the duties of a parent

**par ex´cel·lence** *adj.* pre-eminent; beyond comparing

**pa·ri´ah** *n.* an outcast

**par´ish** *n.* a district in the charge of a clergyman; a

church congregation; a civil district that corresponds to a township or county **—pa·rish´ion·er** *n.*

**par´i·ty** *n.* equality or equivalence

**park** *n.* a section of land set aside usually for recreation or for its natural beauty; an area set aside for a particular purpose as *an industrial park* *—vt.* to place or leave temporarily, as a car

**park´way** *(US) n.* a wide landscaped road

**par´lance** *n.* a style of speech; jargon: *the parlance of a printer*

**par´ley** *n.* a conference, especially between adversaries *—vi.* to hold a conference

**par´lia·ment** *n.* a legislative body

**par´lia·men´ta·ry** *adj.* of a parliament, or its customs and rules **—par´lia·men·tar´i·an** *n.* **—par´lia·men´ta·ri·ly** *adv.*

**par´lor** *n.* a room set aside for a special purpose, as the entertainment of visitors

**pa·ro´chi·al** *adj.* relating to a local parish; local or conservative; provincial **—pa·ro´chi·al·ism** *n.* **—pa·ro´chi·al·ist** *n.* **—pa·ro´chi·al·ly** *adv.*

**par´o·dy** *n.* a comic work that ridicules the style of another; something so bad as to be a mockery *—vt.* to ridicule; to make a travesty of **—pa·rod´ic, pa·rod´i·cal, par´o·dis´tic** *adj.* **—par´o·dist** *n.*

**par´ox·ysm** *n.* a sudden emotional outburst, as of laughter or anger; a sudden attack or worsening of a disease **—par´ox·ys´mal** *adj.* **—par´ox·ys´mal·ly** *adv.*

**par·quet´** *n.* a floor of inlaid wood formed in geometric patterns

**par´ri·cide** *n.* the murdering of a close relative, especially of one´s parents **—par´ri·ci´dal** *adj.*

**parry** *n.* evasion, as of a blow or an embarrassing question *—vi., vt.* to ward off or avoid

**parse** *vt.* to examine in detail by separating into components

**par·si·mo´ni·ous** *adj.* extremely frugal **—par·si·mo´ni·ous·ly** *adv.* **—par·si·mo´ni·ous·ness, par´si·mo·ny** *n.*

**part** *adj.* incomplete; partial *—n.* a portion of a whole *—vt., vi.* to separate or become separated **—part´ly** *adv.*

**par·take´** *vt., vi.* to take or receive a share in **—par·tak´er** *n.*

**par´tial** *adj.* incomplete; involving a part only; prejudiced or biased **—par´tial·ness** *n.*

**par·tial´i·ty** *n.* fondness or preference; bias

**par´tial·ly** *adv.* not completely

**par·tic´i·pate** *vi.* to engage in; to share in **—par·tic´i·pant, par·tic´i·pa·tor** *n.* **—par·tic·i·pa´tion** *n.* **—par·tic´i·pa·tive** *adj.*

**par´ti·cle** *n.* a tiny piece; the least possible amount: *not a particle of decency in him*

**par·tic´u·lar** *adj.* fussy, attentive to detail; of a specific thing; noteworthy: *a gem of particular fineness* *—n.* a detail of specific: *fill me in on the particulars*

**par·tic·u·lar´i·ty** *n.* attention to detail; distinctiveness or individuality

**par·tic´u·lar·ly** *adv.* especially

**par´ti·san** *adj.* biased *—n.* an ardent supporter **—par´ti·san·ship** *n.*

**par´tite** *adj.* divided

**par·ti´tion** *n.* a separation; something that separates *—vt.* to divide or separate into parts **—par·ti´tion·er** *n.*

**part´ner** *n.* one allied with another, as in business or marriage; an associate **—part´ner·ship** *n.*

**par´ty** *adj.* of a group: *party politics*; of a social gathering: *a party mood* *—n.* a group or gathering: *a political party, a cocktail party*; a participant: *party to the action* *—vi.* to carouse **—party line** the standards or ideals of a particular group **—party pooper** one who shuns or avoids involvement **—par´ty·er** *n.*

**pass** *n.* a passageway; a ticket or permit; a kind of throw; a sexual overture *—vi., vt.* to move by or beyond; to transfer: *pass the salt*; to bandy: *words passed between them*; to be satisfactory: *he passed the exam*

**pass´a·ble** *adj.* accessible or navigable, as a road; generally acceptable; adequate **—pass´a·ble·ness** *n.* **pass´a·bly** *adv.*

**pas´sage** *n.* a journey; a path or road; movement, transition or progress: *the passage of time*; an excerpt from literature, music, etc.; enactment, as of a law

**pas´sage·way** *n.* a walkway; a corridor or hallway that permits movement between rooms, buildings, etc.

**pas·sé´** *adj.* no longer fashionable

**pas´sen·ger** *n.* a rider

**pas´ser·by´** *n., pl.* **pas´sers·by´** one who passes by chance

**pas´sion** *n.* intense emotion **—pas´sion·al, pas´sion·ate** *adj.* **—pas´sion·ate·ly** *adv.* **—pas´sion·ate·ness** *n.*

**pas´sion·less** *adj.* lacking emotion; detached **—pas´sion·less·ly** *adv.* **—pas´sion·less·ness** *n.*

**pas´sive** *adj.* accepted without reaction; complacent **—pas´sive·ly** *adv.* **—pas´sive·ness** *n.*

**pas´siv·ist** *n.* one who shuns violence as means to achieve an end **—pas´siv·ism** *n.* **—pas·siv´i·ty** *n.*

**past** *adj.* former or prior; gone by: *in years past* *—n.* a former time or event *—prep.* beyond: *they drove past their destination*

**paste** *n.* a thick smooth compound as of food: *tomato paste*; an adhesive *—vt.* to fasten with paste

**pas·tel´** *adj.* of a pale color *—n.* a pale color; a chalk-like artist´s medium for producing such colors **—pas·tel´ist** *n.*

**pas´teur·ize** *vt.* to process food so as to retard spoilage **—pas·teur·i·za´tion** *n.*

**pas´time** *n.* an amusement or diversion

**pas´to·ral** *adj.* of the country or country life; rustic *—n.* an artistic work that emulates country life, in music, called a *pas.to.rale´* **—pas´to·ral·ism** *n.* **—pas´to·ral·ist**

*n.* **—pas´to·ral·ly** *adv.*

**pas´ture** *n.* vegetation eaten by grazing animals; the land on which such vegetation grows; the grazing of animals *—vt.* to put an animal out to graze **—pas´tur·a·ble** *adj.* **—pas´tur·age** *n.*

**past´y** *adj.* appearing pale or sickly; the consistency of paste **—past´i·ness** *n.*

**pat** *adj.* to the point: *a pat answer —n.* a light tap or caress; a bit of food, a small piece: *a pat of butter —vt.* to lightly tap or caress; to flatten or compress by patting *—vi.* to tap lightly

**patch** *n.* a small piece or part: *an elbow patch, a patch of land —vt.* to apply a patch of material, as for mending or decoration **—patch´a·ble** *adj.* **—patch´er** *n.*

**patch´work** *n.* something, such as a quilt, made from patches

**patch´y** *adj.* described by patches; uneven or variable: *a patchy performance* **—patch´i·ly** *adv.* **—patch´i·ness** *n.*

**pate** *n.* the top of the head

**pat´ent[1]** *adj.* protected by patent or trademark *—n.* a right granted an inventor to alone profit from his or her work for a specified period *—vt.* to apply for or grant a patent **—pat·ent·a·bil´i·ty** *n.* **—pat´ent·a·ble** *adj.* **—pat´ent·ed** *adj.* **—pat´en·tee´** *n.* **—pat´en·tor** *n.*

**pat´ent[2]** *adj.* obvious or apparent **—pat´ent·ly** *adv.*

**pa·ter´nal** *adj.* relating to fatherhood **—pa·ter´nal·ly** *adv.*

**pa·ter´nal·ism** *n.* governing in a benevolent or fatherly fashion **—pa·ter´nal·is´tic** *adj.* **—pa·ter·nal·is´ti·cal·ly** *adv.*

**pa·ter´ni·ty** *adj.* of the verification of fatherhood and establishment of responsibility for support of offspring *—n.* fatherhood

**path** *n.* a route along which something travels or progresses **—path´way** *n.*

**pa·thet´ic, pa·thet´i·cal** *adj.* deserving of pity; inspiring contempt **—pa·thet´i·cal·ly** *adv.*

**path·o·log´i·cal** *adj.* relating to pathology; of behaviour that is habitual or obsessive **—path·o·log´i·cal·ly** *adv.*

**pa·thol´o·gy** *n.* the study of diseases **—pa·thol´o·gist** *n.*

**pa´thos** *n.* feelings of sympathy or sorrow

**pa´tience** *n.* the ability to accept without complaint, as inconvenience or delay

**pa´tient** *adj.* accepting of inconvenience or difficulty; tolerant *—n.* one under the care of a physician, dentist, chiropractor, etc. **—pa´tient·ly** *adv.*

**pat´i·na, pat·i´na** *n.* change brought about by age and exposure, as the greenish layer that forms on copper or the delicate luster of old wood **—pat´i·naed, pat·i´naed** *adj.* **—pat´i·nate** *vt., vi.*

**pat´io** *n.* outdoor living space adjacent to a dwelling

**pa·tis´se·rie** *n.* a French bakery

**pa´tois** *n.* a provincial dialect; the vernacular of a particular group

**pa´tri·arch** *n.* a man who heads a family or group, or considered its founder; an elder; the oldest member of a group **—pa´tri·ar´chal, pa´tri·ar´chic** *adj.* **—pa´tri·ar´chal·ly** *adv.*

**pa´tri·archy** *n.* a society that traces its lineage through men

**pa·tri´cian** *n.* an aristocrat; one of refined manners and taste *—adj.* aristocratic; pertaining to aristocracy **—pa·tri´cian·ly** *adj.*

**pat´ri·cide** *n.* the murdering of one's father **—pat´ri·cid´al** *adj.*

**pat·ri·lin´e·age** *n.* ancestry traced through men **—pat·ri·lin´e·al** *adj.* **—pat·ri·lin´e·al·ly** *adv.*

**pat´ri·mo·ny** *n.* inheritance from a father **—pat·ri·mo´ni·al** *adj.* **—pat·ri·mo´ni·al·ly** *adv.*

**pa´tri·ot** *n.* one who supports his or her country **—pa´tri·ot´ic** *adj.* **—pa´tri·ot´i·cal·ly** *adv.* **—pa´tri·ot·ism** *n.*

**pa·trol´** *n.* a person or persons who move about and monitor an area *—vt., vi.* to go about an area for the purpose of guarding or inspecting **—pa·trol´ler** *n.*

**pa´tron** *n.* a customer; one who supports an institution or cause **—pa´tron·age** *n.*

**pa´tron·ize** *vt.* to frequent, as of a customer; to support, as a cause; to treat condescendingly **—pa·tron·i·za´tion** *n.* **—pa´tron·iz·ing** *adj.* **—pa´tron·iz·ing·ly** *adv.*

**pat´ter** *n.* a prepared spiel, as of a salesperson or entertainer; meaningless chatter; a soft tapping sound *—vt., vi.* to speak glibly

**pat´tern** *n.* a model or drawing used as a guide in making something: *a dress pattern*; a reoccurring feature or characteristic: *a pattern of behavior —vt.* to make after a model or plan

**pat´ty** *n.* a flat round portion of food: *a hamburger patty*; a small pastry shell

**pau´ci·ty** *n.* a lack or scarcity

**paunch** *n.* a protruding abdomen **—paunch´i·ness** *n.* **—paunch´y** *adj.*

**pau´per** *n.* an impoverished person **—pau´per·ism** *n.* **—pau´per·ize** *vt.*

**pause** *n.* a temporary halt, as by indecision; a deliberate hesitation for effect: *a dramatic pause for emphasis —vi.* to temporarily cease speech or action

**pave´ment** *(US) n.* a durable surface as for covering a walkway or roadway **—pave** *vt.* **—pav´er** *n.* **—pav´ing** *n.*

**pa·vil´ion** *n.* a somewhat open, often temporary, shelter as at a picnic, campground, or fair

**pawn** *n.* something held as security against a loan; one held hostage *—vt.* to use or give as security **—pawn´a·ble** *adj.* **—pawn´bro·ker** *n.* **—pawn´er** *n.* **—pawn´shop** *n.*

**pay** *vt.* to give something of value in return for goods or services; to reward or punish: *they have to pay for* *disloyalty*; to render, as a compliment *—vi.* to make payment; to be profitable: *it pays to be ready —n.* compensation **—pay´a·ble** *adj.* **—pay·ee´** *n.* **—pay´er** *n.***—pay´ment** *n.*

**peace** *n.* freedom from hostility; serenity **—peace´ful** *adj.* **—peace´ful·ly** *adv.* **—peace´ful·ness** *n.*

**peace´a·ble** *adj.* disposed to peace; tranquil **—peace´a·ble·ness** *n.* **—peace´a·bly** *adv.*

**peace´keep·er** *n.* one who assures or maintains peace **—peace´keep·ing** *adj.*

**peace´mak·er** *n.* a settler of disputes **—peace´mak·ing** *adj.*

**peak** *adj.* at or near the upper limit *—n.* a pointed top; the height of development *—vi.* to bring to a climax or high level of development

**peaked** *adj.* pointed

**peak´ed** *adj.* appearing sickly **—peak´ed·ness** *n.*

**peal** *n.* a ringing *—vi., vt.* to sound or ring

**peas´ant** *n.* a rustic; an uncouth person **—peas´ant·ry** *n.*

**peb´ble** *n.* a small stone **—peb´bly** *adj.*

**pec´ca·ble** *adj.* likely to sin **—pec´ca·bil´i·ty** *adj.*

**pec·ca·dil´lo** *n.* a petty sin; a minor indiscretion

**pec´cant** *adj.* sinful **—pec´can·cy** *n.* **—pec´cant·ly** *adv.*

**peck** *vi.* to strike with a beak; to nibble; to kiss lightly *—n.*

**peck´ish** *adj.* irritable

**pec´u·late** *vt.* to wrongfully appropriate, as funds entrusted to one´s care; to embezzle **—pec·u·la´tion** *n.* **—pec´u·la·tor** *n.*

**pe·cu´liar** *adj.* odd or unusual; unique; characteristic of a particular person, group, etc. **—pe·cu·liar´i·ty** *n.* **—pe·cu´liar·ly** *adv.*

**pe·cu´ni·ar·y** *adj.* monetary **—pe·cu´ni·ar´i·ly** *adv.*

**ped·a·gog´ics, ped´a·go·gy** *n.* the teaching profession **—ped·a·gog´ic, ped·a·gog´i·cal** *adj.* **—ped·a·gog´i·cal·ly** *adv.*

**ped´a·gogue** *n.* an instructor; a narrow-minded teacher

**ped´al** *adj.* relating to the foot *—n.* a small pad for the foot that attaches to a device such as a bicycle or organ *—vt., vi.* to operate or propel by means of a pedal

**pe·dan´tic** *adj.* overly concerned with scholarship and formality **—ped´ant** *n.* **—pe·dan´ti·cal·ly** *adv.* **—ped´ant·ry** *n.*

**ped´dle** *vi.* to travel about selling *—vt.* to offer for sale; to promote or attempt to sell, an an idea **—ped´dler** *n.*

**ped´es·tal** *n.* a foundation or base, as for a statue

**pe·des´tri·an** *adj.* of travel by foot; ordinary or trite *—n.* one moving on foot **—pe·des´tri·an·ism** *n.*

**pe·des´tri·an·ize** *vt.* to convert to use for foot travel **—pe·des·tri·an·i·za´tion** *n.*

**pe·di·a·tri´cian** *n.* a physician who specializes in treating infants **—pe´di·at´ric** *adj.* **—pe·di·at´rics** *n.*

**ped´i·gree** *n.* a list of ancestors; lineage

**pe·do·phile, pe·do·phil´i·ac** *n.* an adult who is sexually attracted to children **—pe·do·phil´i·a** *n.* **—pe·do·phil´ic** *adj.*

**peek** *n.* a momentary view or glance *—vi.* to view quickly as from hiding; to emerge, as though hiding: *tips of flowers peek through the underbrush*

**peel** *n.* the outer covering of certain fruits and vegetables *—vi., vt.* to come off or strip off, as bark or skin **—peel´er** *n.*

**peep** *n.* a short high-pitched sound, as of a bird; a sly glance *—vi.* to utter a weak cry; to glance furtively **—peep´er** *n.*

**peer** *vi.* to stare *—n.* an equal before the law; a person of noble birth **—peer´age** *n.*

**peer´less** *adj.* unequaled; incomparable

**peeve** *vi., vt.* to become or cause to become annoyed *—n.* a complaint or grievance

**pee´vish** *adj.* disagreeable; fretful; showing discontent **—pee´vish·ly** *adv.* **—pee´vish·ness** *n.*

**peg** *n.* a wooden pin used to join two pieces; a marker *—vt.* to fasten or mark with pegs

**peign·oir´** *n.* a dressing gown

**pej·o·ra´tion** *n.* a process of degeneration; the course by which a word becomes degenerated, such as that of *silly* which once meant *blessed*

**pe·jo´ra·tive** *adj.* disparaging or derisive *—n.* a derisive word or phrase **—pe·jo´ra·tive·ly** *adv.*

**pelf** *n.* money or riches; ill-gotten gains or spoils

**pel´let** *n.* a small solid bit of matter, such as a pill

**pell´-mell´** *adv.* in disorderly manner; hurriedly; in confused haste; impetuously

**pelt** *n.* an animal skin *—vt.* to strike repeatedly

**pen** *n.* a writing instrument; a coop or similar enclosure *—vt.* to write; to confine or cage

**pe´nal** *adj.* relating to punishment **—pe´nal·ly** *adv.*

**pe´nal·ize** *vt.* to punish; to impose a penalty on **—pe·nal·iza´tion** *n.*

**pen´al·ty** *n.* a punishment dictated by law or rules; consequences: *they suffered the penalty of failure to plan properly*

**pen´ance** *n.* an action to show remorse for wrongdoing

**penchant** *n.* an inclination or tendency; a predisposition

**pen´cil** *n.* a writing instrument *—vt.* to write

**pencil pusher** *n.* a clerk

**pen´dant** *n.* a hanging ornament

**pen´dent** *adj.* hanging or projecting **—pend´ent·ly** *adv.*

**pend´ing** *adj.* awaiting settlement *—prep.*

**pen´du·lous** *adj.* hanging so as to swing freely; dangling **—pen´du·lous·ly** *adv.* **—pen´du·lous·ness** *n.*

**pen´du·lum** *n.* a hanging weight that swings cyclically

to control a device such as a clock

**pen´e·tra·ble** *adj.* accessible; able to penetrate **–pen·e·tra·bil´i·ty** *n.* **–pen´e·tra·bly** *adv.*

**pen´e·trate** *vt.* to gain entrance; to pierce; to affect profoundly **–pen·e·tra´tion** *n.* **–pen´e·tra·tor** *n.*

**pen´e·trat·ing** *adj.* piercing; perceptive or shrewd; intrusive **–pen´e·trat·ing·ly** *adv.*

**pen´e·tra·tive** *adj.* having power to penetrate **–pen´e·tra·tive·ly** *adv.*

**pe·nin´su·la** *n.* a point of land that projects into a body of water **–pe·nin´su·lar** *adj.*

**pen´i·tence** *n.* remorse for misdeeds

**pen´i·tent** *adj.* sorrowful or atoning for guilt *–n.* **–pen´i·tent·ly** *adv.*

**pen´i·ten´tial** *adj.* suffering remorse **–pen·i·ten´tial·ly** *adv.*

**pen·i·ten´tia·ry** *(US) n.* a prison

**pen´nant** *n.* a tapered streamer used for recognition or signaling

**pen´ni·less** *adj.* poverty-stricken **–pen´ni·less·ly** *adv.* **–pen´ni·less·ness** *n.*

**pen´ny** *(US) n.* a coin of small value; a cent

**penny ante** of little consequence; trivial

**pe·nol´o·gy** *n.* the study of prisons and rehabilitation **–pe´no·log´i·cal** *adj.* **–pe·nol´o·gist** *n.*

**pen´sion** *n.* money paid or to be paid regularly during retirement *–vt.* to grant a pension to **–pen´sion·a·ble** *adj.* **–pen´sion·er** *n.*

**pen´sive** *adj.* inclined to thought; thoughtful **–pen´sive·ly** *adv.* **–pen´sive·ness** *n.*

**pent´house** *n.* a residence on the roof or upper floors of a building

**pent´-up´** *adj.* held in or repressed: *pent-up anxiety*

**pe·nu´ri·ous** *adj.* frugal or miserly; unproductive or barren, as land **–pe·nu´ri·ous·ly** *adv.* **–pe·nu´ri·ous·ness** *n.*

**pen´u·ry** *n.* poverty; barrenness

**peo´ple** *n.* human beings in general; a group of persons with something in common: *people of Asian descent* *–vt.* to populate

**pep** *n.* energy *–vt.* to enervate

**pep´py** *adj.* full of energy **–pep´pi·ly** *adv.* **–pep´pi·ness** *n.*

**per** *adv., prep.* for each

**per cap´i·ta** *adv.* per person

**per·ceive´** *vt., vi.* to understand; to become aware of **–per·ceiv·a·bil´i·ty** *n.* **–per·ceiv´a·ble** *adj.* **–per·ceiv´a·bly** *adv.* **–per·ceiv´er** *n.*

**per·cent´** *n.* parts per hundred

**per·cep´ti·ble** *adj.* able to be perceived or discerned **–per·cep·ti·bil´i·ty** *n.* **–per·cep´ti·bly** *adv.*

**per·cep´tion** *n.* discernment or judgment; insight gained from observation **–per·cep´tion·al** *adj.* **–per·cep´tu·al** *adj.* **–per·cep´tu·al·ly** *adv.*

**per·cep´tive** *adj.* discerning; observant **–per·cep´tive·ly** *adv.* **–per·cep´tive·ness, per·cep·tiv´i·ty** *n.*

**perch** *n.* a roost for a bird; a lofty position ***–vi., vt.*** to alight or set on a perch **–perch´er** *n.*

**per·chance´** *adv.* possibly; conceivably

**per´co·late** *vi., vt.* to pass or cause to pass through a filter *–n.* a filtered liquid **–per·co·la´tion** *n.* **–per´co·la·tor** *n.*

**per·cus´sion** *n.* a striking together or colliding **–per·cus´sive** *adj.* **–per·cus´sive·ly** *adv.* **–per·cus´sive·ness** *n.*

**per·di´tion** *n.* damnation

**per´e·gri·nate** *vi.* to travel or roam, especially on foot *–vt.* to travel over or through **–per·e·gri·na´tion** *n.* **–per´e·gri·na·tor** *n.*

**pe·remp´to·ry** *adj.* decisive or final; dictatorial **–pe·remp´to·ri·ly** *adv.* **–pe·remp´to·ri·ness** *n.*

**pe·ren´ni·al** *adj.* long-lasting or enduring; recurring often **–per·en´ni·al·ly** *adv.*

**per´fect** *adj.* complete; free of faults; well-suited; capable **–per´fect·ly** *adv.* **–per´fect·ness** *n.*

**per·fect´** *vt.* to further develop or complete; to make flawless **–per·fect´er** *n.*

**per·fect´i·ble** *adj.* able to become or to be made flawless **–per·fect´i·bil´i·ty** *n.*

**per·fec´tion** *n.* the state of being perfect

**per·fec´tion·ism** *n.* an abnormal obsession with idealistic goals **–per·fec´tion·ist** *n.* **–per·fec·tion·is´tic** *adj.*

**per·fid´i·ous** *adj.* deliberately unfaithful or treacherous **–per·fid´i·ous·ly** *adv.* **–per´fid·y** *n.*

**per´fo·rate** *vt.* to pierce; to mark with rows of holes for ease of separating **–per´for·a·ble** *adj.* **–per´fo·rat·ed** *adj.* **–per·fo·ra´tion** *n.* **–per´fo·ra·tor** *n.*

**per·form** *vt., vi.* to act on and complete; to function; to present in public for entertainment **–per·form´able** *adj.* **–per·form´ance** *n.* **–per·form´er** *n.*

**per´fume** *n.* an ingredient that gives off a pleasant aroma; a pleasant aroma

**per·fum´er·y** *n.* a concern that makes or sells perfume; the art of making and marketing perfume **–per·fum´er** *n.*

**per·func´to·ry** *adj.* indifferent; done mechanically, casually, or carelessly **–per·func´to·ri·ly** *adv.* **–per·func´to·ri·ness** *n.*

**per·haps´** *adv.* conceivably; possibly

**per´il** *n.* exposure to danger *–vt.* to expose to danger **–per´il·ous** *adj.* **–per´il·ous·ly** *adv.* **–per´il·ous·ness** *n.*

**pe·rim´e·ter** *n.* the boundary or border of an area **–per·i·met´ric, per·i·met´ri·cal** *adj.* **–per·i·met´ri·cal·ly** *adv.*

**pe´ri·od** *n.* a span of time; *(US)* a punctuation mark that indicates the end of a sentence

**pe´ri·od´ic** *adj.* cyclical; recurring at regular intervals **–pe·ri·od´i·cal·ly** *adv.* **–pe·ri·o·dic´i·ty** *n.*

**pe·ri·od´i·cal** *n.* a publication issued at regular intervals

—*adj.* pertaining to a publication, such as a magazine or journal, that is published at regular intervals

**per·i·pa·tet´ic** *adj.* roaming about; itinerant —*n.* one given to roaming —**per·i·pa·tet´i·cal·ly** *adv.*

**pe·riph´er·al** *adj.* pertaining to an outer area; of minor significance —**pe·riph´er·al·ly** *adv.*

**pe·riph´ery** *n.* a line or area that forms a perimeter

**per´ish** *vi.* to decay or die; to pass from existence —**per·ish·a·bil´i·ty, per´ish·a·ble·ness** *n.* —**per´ish·a·ble** *adj.* —**per´ish·a·bly** *adv.*

**per´jure** *vt.* to testify falsely; to violate an oath or a promise —**per´jur·er** *n.* —**per·ju´ri·ous** *adj.* —**per·ju´ri·ous·ly** *adv.* —**per´jury** *n.*

**perk´y** *adj.* lively; proud or haughty —**perk´i·ly** *adv.* **perk´i·ness** *n.*

**per´ma·nent** *adj.* durable; enduring; unchanging —**per´ma·nence, per´ma·nen·cy, per´ma·nent·ness** *n.* —**per´ma·nent·ly** *adv.*

**per´me·a·ble** *adj.* pervious; that can be infiltrated or saturated —**per·me·a·bil´i·ty, per´me·a·ble·ness** *n.* **per´me·a·bly** *adv.*

**per´me·ate** *vt.* to spread completely throughout —*vi.* to penetrate and spread throughout —**per·me·a´tion** *n.* —**per´me·a·tive** *adj.*

**per·mis´si·ble** *adj.* that can be allowed —**per·mis·si·bil´i·ty, per·mis´si·ble·ness** *n.* —**per·mis´si·bly** *adv.*

**per·mis´sion** *n.* approval or authorization

**per·mis´sive** *adj.* that grants permission; likely to allow: lenient —**per·mis´sive·ly** *adv.* —**per·mis´sive·ness** *n.*

**per·mit´** *vt.* to allow or authorize —**per´mit** *n.* a document that grants permission, such as a license —**per´mit·tee** *n.*

**per·mu·ta´tion** *n.* an alteration or transformation —**per·mu·ta´tion·al** *adj.*

**per·ni´cious** *adj.* likely to be harmful or injurious —**per·ni´cious·ly** *adv.* —**per·ni´cious·ness** *n.*

**per´o·rate** *vi.* to speak at length: lecture; to summarize at the end of a speech —**per·o·ra´tion** *n.* —**per·o·ra´tion·al** *adj.*

**per·pen·dic´u·lar** *adj.* at right angles to the horizon —*n.* a line, plane, etc. that is at right angles to another —**per·pen·dic·u·lar´i·ty** *n.* —**per·pen·dic´u·lar·ly** *adv.*

**per´pe·trate** *vt.* to commit, as a crime —**per·pe·tra´tion** *n.* —**per´pe·tra·tor** *n.*

**per·pet´u·al** *adj.* continuing indefinitely; recurrent —**per·pet´u·al·ly** *adv.*

**per·pet´u·ate** *vt.* to endure indefinitely —**per·pet·u·a´tion** *n.* —**per·pet´u·a·tor** *n.*

**per·pe·tu´i·ty** *n.* endlessness; the quality of continuing indefinitely

**per·plex´** *vt.* to confound or confuse —**per·plexed´** *adj.* —**per·plex´ed·ly, per·plex´ing·ly** *adv.*

**per´qui·site** *n.* an allowance or benefit associated with position: *comfort is a perquisite of the moneyed class*

**per´se·cute** *vt.* to oppress or abuse, particularly because of race, religion, etc.; to harass —**per·se·cu´tion** *n.* —**per·se·cu´tion·al, per´se·cu·tive, per´se·cu·to·ry** *adj.* —**per´se·cu·tor** *n.*

**per·se·ver´ance** *n.* patience and persistence; determination —**per´se·vere´** *vi.* —**per·se·ver´ing·ly** *adv.*

**per´si·flage** *n.* good-natured banter

**per·sist´** *vi.* to persevere in spite of obstacles; to endure —**per·sist´ence, per·sist´en·cy** *n.* —**per·sist´ent** *adj.* —**per·sist´ent·ly** *adv.* —**per·sist´er** *n.*

**per´son** *n.* an individual; the character, appearance, or characteristics of an individual; a living human body

**per´son·a·ble** *adj.* agreeable or pleasant in appearance or manner —**per´son·a·ble·ness** *n.* —**per´son·a·bly** *adv.*

**per´son·age** *n.* an eminent person

**per´son·al** *adj.* relating to a particular person; done by or for a particular person; intimate —**per´son·al·ly** *adv.*

**per·son·al´i·ty** *n.* the character, characteristics, and other qualities of a particular person; distinctive attributes; a famous person —**per´son·al·ize** *vt.* —**per·son·al·i·za´tion** *n.*

**per·son´i·fy** *vt.* to represent by or endow with human qualities —**per·son·i·fi·ca´tion** *n.* —**per·son´i·fi·er** *n.*

**per´son·nel´** *n.* the employees of an organization; persons collectively

**per·spec´tive** *n.* a particular view or viewpoint; a panorama; a device that gives a flat rendering the impression of three dimensions —**per·spec´tiv·al** *adj.* —**per·spec´tive·ly** *adv.*

**per·spi·ca´cious** *adj.* demonstrating unusual insight —**per·spi·ca´cious·ly** *adj.* —**per·spi·ca´cious·ness, per·spi·cac´i·ty, per·spi·cu´ity** *n.*

**per·spire´** *vi., vt.* to expel through the pores —**per·spi·ra´tion** *n.* —**per·spir´a·to·ry** *adj.*

**per·suade´** *vt.* to convince by reason or pleas —**per·suad´a·ble, per·sua´si·ble** *adj.* —**per·suad´er** *n.*

**per·sua´sion** *n.* the power to convince another; a firm opinion or conviction —**per·sua´sive** *adj.* —**per·sua´sive·ly** *adv.* —**per·sua´sive·ness** *n.*

**pert** *adj.* vivacious; impudently saucy or forward —**pert´ly** *adv.* —**pert´ness** *n.*

**per·tain´** *vi.* to belong or relate to; to be pertinent to

**per´ti·na´cious** *adj.* persistent; obstinate —**per´ti·na´cious·ly** *adv.* —**per´ti·na´cious·ness, per·ti·nac´i·ty** *n.*

**per´ti·nent** *adj.* relevant; applicable —**per´ti·nence, per´ti·nen·cy** *n.* —**per´ti·nent·ly** *adv.*

**per·turb´** *vt.* to disquiet or worry —**per·turb´a·ble** *adj.* —**per·tur·ba´tion** *n.*

**pe·ruse´** *vt.* to study thoroughly; to scrutinize —**pe·rus´able** *adj.* —**pe·rus´al** *n.* —**pe·rus´er** *n.*

**per·vade´** *vt.* to penetrate or permeate **–per·va´sion** *n.* **–per·va´sive** *adj.* **–per·va´sive·ly** *adv.* **–per·va´sive·ness** *n.*

**per·verse´** *adj.* evil or wicked; contrary or obstinate **–per·verse´ly** *adv.* **–per·verse´ness, per·ver´sity** *n.*

**per·ver´sion** *n.* deviation from what is normal, especially of sexual desire or activity; something perverted **–per·ver´sive** *adj.*

**per·vert´** *vt.* to use improperly; to distort the meaning of; to corrupt or lead away from approved or accepted conduct **–per´vert** *n.* **–per·vert´er** *n.* **–per·vert´i·ble** *adj.*

**per·vert´ed** *adj.* characterized by perversion **–per·vert´ed·ly** *adv.* **–per·vert´ed·ness** *n.*

**per´vi·ous** *adj.* permeable; capable of being penetrated; open to argument **–per´vi·ous·ly** *adv.* **–per´vi·ous·ness** *n.*

**pes´ky** *adj.* annoying; troublesome **–pesk´i·ly** *adv.* **–pesk´i·ness** *n.*

**pes´si·mist** *n.* one who tends to a negative view **–pes´si·mism** *n.* **–pes·si·mis´tic** *adj.* **–pes·si·mis´ti·cal·ly** *adv.*

**pest** *n.* a nuisance; something that is harmful, as a virus

**pes´ter** *vt.* to harass or annoy **–pes´ter·er** *n.*

**pes´ti·cide** *n.* a chemical used to destroy weeds or insects **–pes´ti·ci·dal** *adj.*

**pes´ti·lence** *n.* a widespread disease: an epidemic; any dangerous or harmful agent **–pes´ti·lent, pes´ti·len´tial** *adj.* **–pes·ti·len´tial·ly** *adv.*

**pes´tle** *n.* a device used for crushing or blending, as in a mortar

**pet** *n.* a tame animal treated with affection; a person treated affectionately *–adj.* regarded as favored or a favorite *–vt.* to indulge; to caress

**pe·tite´** *n.* small

**pe·ti´tion** *n.* an appeal or request to a higher authority *–vi., vt.* to make an appeal **–pe·ti´tion·a·ble** *adj.* **–pe·ti´tion·ar·y** *adj.* **–pe·ti´tion·er** *n.*

**pet´ri·fy** *vt.* to fossilize; to paralyze with fright

**pet´rol** *(Brit.) n.* fuel for a motor vehicle

**pe·tro´le·um** *(US) n.* crude oil

**pet´ti·fog** *vi.* to quibble over trifles **–pet´ti·fog´ger** *n.* **–pet´ti·fog·ger·y** *n.*

**pet´tish** *adj.* irritable; peevish **–pet´tish·ly** *adv.* **–pet´tish·ness** *n.*

**pet´ty** *adj.* trivial or unimportant; mean or miserly; narrow-minded **–pet´ti·ly** *adv.* **–pet´ti·ness** *n.*

**pet´u·lant** *adj.* ill-tempered; irritable **–pet´u·lance, pet´u·lan·cy** *n.* **–pet´u·lant·ly** *adv.*

**phan´tasm** *n.* an apparition; an illusion **–phan·tas´mal, phan·tas´mic** *adj.*

**phan·tas·ma·go´ri·a** *n.* bizarre imagery as in artwork or as in a dream **–phan·tas·ma·gor´ic, phan·tas´ma·gor´i·cal** *adj.* **–phan·tas´ma·gor´i·cal·ly** *adv.*

**phan´tom** *adj.* illusory; imaginary *–n.* an apparition or ghost

**phar·ma·ceu´tic, phar·ma·ceu´ti·cal** *adj.* pertaining to pharmacy or pharmacists *–n.* a drug **–phar·ma·ceu´ti·cal·ly** *adv.*

**phar·ma·ceu´tics** *pl. n.* the science of preparing medicinal compounds; medicinal compounds collectively

**phar´ma·cist** *n.* a qualified druggist

**phar·ma·col´o·gy** *n.* the study of drugs and their uses; the properties of a drug **–phar·ma·co·log´ic, phar·ma·co·log´i·cal** *adj.* **–phar·ma·co·log´i·cal·ly** *adv.* **–phar·ma·col´o·gist** *n.*

**phar´ma·cy** *n.* a drugstore

**phase** *n.* a particular stage or state of progress **–pha´sic** *adj.*

**phe·nom´e·nal** *adj.* extraordinary or remarkable **–phe·nom´e·nal·ly** *adv.*

**phe·nom´e·non** *n.* an unusual or extraordinary person, thing, or event

**phi´al** *n.* a vial

**phi·lan´der** *vi.* to make love casually, without intent to marry **–phi·lan´der·er** *n.*

**phi·lan´thro·py** *n.* charity or benevolence for the good of others; a humanitarian endeavor **–phil·an·throp´ic, phil·an·throp´i·cal** *adj.* **–phil·an·throp´i·cal·ly** *adv.* **–phi·lan´thro·pist** *n.*

**phi·lat´e·ly** *n.* stamp collecting **–phil·a·tel´ic, phil·a·tel´i·cal** *adj.* **–phil·a·tel´i·cal·ly** *adv.* **–phi·lat´e·list** *n.*

**phi·lol´o·gy** *n.* classical studies, especially to ascertain meaning or certify the authenticity of literary works **–phil·o·log´ic, phil·o·log´i·cal** *adj.* **–phil·o·log´i·cal·ly** *adv.* **–phi·lol´o·gist** *n.*

**phi·los´o·phy** *n.* the study of knowledge; a fundamental principle; a system of beliefs **–phi·los´o·pher** *n.* **–phil´o·soph´ic, phil´o·soph´i·cal** *adj.* **–phil´o·soph´i·cal·ly** *adv.* **phi·los´o·phize** *vi.* **–phi·los´o·phiz·er** *n.*

**phil´ter** *n.* a magic potion

**phleg·mat´ic, phleg·mat´i·cal** *adj.* impassive; composed; unemotional **–phleg·mat´i·cal·ly** *adv.*

**pho´bia** *n.* an irrational fear or aversion **–pho´bic** *adj.*

**phone** *n.* a telephone

**pho·net´ics** *n.* the sounds of speech or of a specific language **–pho·net´ic, pho·net´i·cal** *adj.* **–pho·net´i·cal·ly** *adv.*

**phon´ics** *n.* the sounds of speech in relation to spelling; phonetics **–phon´ic** *adj.* **–phon´i·cal·ly** *adv.*

**pho´ny** *adj.* imitation or artificial; fake *–n.* an imitation; a fake

**pho´to·cop·y** *n.* a duplicate made by the use of photography *–vt.* to reproduce by means of a photocopy machine

**pho·tog´ra·phy** *n.* the art of reproducing images by means of photosensitive coatings **–pho·to·graph´ic,**

**pho·to·graph´i·cal** *adj.* **–pho·to·graph´i·cal·ly** *adv.*

**pho´to, pho´to·graph** *n.* an image captured by means of photography *–vt.* to capture by photography **–pho´to·graph·a·ble** *adj.* **–pho·tog´ra·pher** *n.*

**pho·to·sen´si·tive** *adj.* sensitive or reactive to light rays **–pho·to·sen·si·tiv´i·ty** *n.* **–pho·to·sen·si·ti·za´tion** *n.* **–pho·to·sen´si·tize** *vt.*

**pho·to·syn´the·sis** *n.* the process by which plants derive nourishment using light as an energy source **–pho·to·syn·thet´ic** *adj.* **–pho·to·syn·thet´i·cal·ly** *adv.*

**phrase** *n.* a group of words that express a thought, but that do not comprise a complete sentence *–vt., vi.* to express in a certain way, as *to phrase tactfully* **–phras´a·ble** *adj.* **–phras´al** *adj.* **–phras´al·ly** *adv.*

**phra·se·ol´o·gy** *n.* the way in which a thought or idea is expressed; one´s style of speaking or writing **–phra·se·o·log´ical** *adj.* **–phra·se·ol´o·gist** *n.*

**phre·nol´o·gy** *n.* the belief that character and intelligence can be determined by the configuration of the skull **–phre·nol´o·gist** *n.*

**phys´i·cal** *adj.* applicable to the body or to tangible matter as distinguished from the mental or spiritual **–phys·i·cal´i·ty** *n.* **–phys´i·cal·ly** *adv.*

**phy·si´cian** *n.* a doctor of medicine; one devoted to healing

**phys´ics** *n.* the study of matter and energy **–phys´i·cist** *n.*

**phys·i·ol´o·gy** *n.* the study of living organisms **–phys´i·o·log´i·cal** *adj.* **–phys´i·o·log´i·cal·ly** *adv.* **–phys·i·ol´o·gist** *n.*

**phy·sique´** *n.* the structure and appearance of the body

**pic·a·yune´** *adj.* of little value; trivial; unimportant

**pick** *vt.* to select or separate; to gather or pluck **–pick´er** *n.*

**picked** *adj.* chosen carefully

**pick´et** *n.* a protester, often with a sign stating a grievance; a pointed stake **–pick´et·er** *n.*

**pick´y** *adj.* extremely fussy **–pick´i·ness** *n.*

**pic´nic** *n.* an outing or an outdoor meal; something seen as easy to do; an enjoyable experience **–pic´nick·er** *n.*

**pic·to´ri·al** *adj.* pertaining to pictures; containing pictures *–n.* a publication containing mostly pictures **–pic·to´ri·al·ly** *adj.*

**pic·to´ri·al·ize** *vt.* to illustrate **–pic·to·ri·al·i·za´tion** *n.*

**pic´ture** *n.* an illustration; a visual or oral depiction; a mental image; a motion picture *–vt.* to visualize; to describe vividly

**pic·tur·esque´** *adj.* striking or impressive **–pic·tur·esque´ly** *adv.* **–pic´tur·esque´ness** *n.*

**pid´dling** *adj.* trivial

**piece** *n.* a part or portion; something of a type: *a piece of music, a piece of funiture* *–vt.* to join together

**pièce de ré´sis·tance´** *n.* a primary or outstanding element, especially of a meal

**piece´meal** *adj.* accomplished in stages *–adv.* gradually

**pierce** *vt.* to penetrate **–pierc´er** *n.* **–pierc´ing** *adj.* **–pierc´ing·ly** *adv.*

**pi´e·ty** *n.* devotion or reverence **–pi´etism** *n.* **–pi·etis´tic** *adj.*

**pig´head·ed** *adj.* stubborn; obstinate **–pig´head·ed·ly** *adv.* **–pig´head·ed·ness** *n.*

**pig´ment** *n.* a dye or coloring **–pig´men·tary** *adj.*

**pig·men·ta´tion** *n.* a characteristic color

**pik´er** *n.* a cheapskate

**pile** *n.* a heap; an accumulation, as of money *–vt., vi.* to make or form a heap

**pil´fer** *vt., vi.* to steal **–pil´fer·age** *n.*

**pil´grim** *n.* a traveler, especially one who is on a sacred journey **–pil´grim·age** *n.*

**pill** *n.* a capsule of medicine; someone who is annoying or disagreeable

**pil´lage** *vt.* to take by force; to plunder **–pil´lag·er** *n.*

**pil´lar** *n.* a supporting column; a responsible person: *a pillar of the community*

**pil´low** *n.* a cushion used for resting the head or for decoration **–pil´low·y** *adj.*

**pi´lot** *n.* one who operates or guides a craft; that which guides or directs on a course: *a pilot hole for a screw, a television pilot*

**pim´ple** *n.* a small swelling of the skin; a similar bulge on a hard surface **–pim´pled, pim´ply** *adj.*

**pin** *n.* a thin rod of metal, wood, etc. used for fastening; a decorative jewel attached with a pin; something that attaches in place, as a *hairpin* or *clothespin*; something long and slender, as a *rolling pin*; *(Brit.)* the contact points for an electrical connector *–vt.* to fasten, attach, or hold as with a pin; to fix; as for liability: *don´t pin the blame on me, pin him down to get a decision*

**pinch** *n.* a sprinkling or dash: *a pinch of salt*; a predicament *–vt.* to squeeze so as to cause discomfort; to arrest; to steal *–vi.* to squeeze; to be stingy; to become constricted **–pinch´a·ble** *adj.* **–pinch´er** *n.*

**pinch´pen·ny** *adj.* miserly *–n.* a penny pincher

**pin´na·cle** *n.* a crest or summit

**pi´o·neer´** *adj.* early or experimental; brave or adventurous *–n.* an explorer or settler of new territory *–vt., vi.* to take the lead; to prepare the way

**pi·os´i·ty** *n.* exaggerated piety

**pi´ous** *adj.* devout, reverent **–pi´ous·ly** *adv.* **–pi´ous·ness** *n.*

**pipe** *n.* a hollow tube used to convey liquid, etc.; a smoking implement *–vt.* to convey, as liquid, through a pipe

**pip´ing** *n.* a network of pipes; trimming, as on a uniform; decoration on a cake or pastry

**pi´quant** *adj.* spicy; interesting or charming **–pi´quan·cy, pi´quant·ness** *n.* **–pi´quant·ly** *adv.*

**pique** *n.* a sense of indignation or ire *—vt.* to irritate; to excite or arouse, as one's curiosity
**pi'ra·cy** *n.* robbery or blackmail; the illegal selling of protected material **—pi'rate** *n., vt., vi.* **—pi·rat'ic, pi·rat'i·cal** *adj.* **—pi·rat'i·cal·ly** *adv.*
**pis'tol** *n.* a handgun
**pit** *n.* a hole in the ground; a small indentation; an area set aside for a special purpose: *an orchestra pit —vt., vi.* to mark or become marked with indentations; to place in conflict: *an individual pitted against the system*
**pitch** *vt.* to throw; to set up: *pitch camp*; to set at an angle; to promote: *pitch the benefits, not the product —n.* a sales talk
**pitch'er** *n.* one who throws; *(US)* a container for liquids: a jug
**pitch'man** *n.* one who attempts to sell, especially aggressively
**pit'e·ous** *adj.* pitiful; stirring or deserving pity **—pit'e·ous·ly** *adv.* **—pit'e·ous·ness** *n.*
**pit'fall** *n.* a hazard
**pith** *n.* the core or essence
**pith'y** *adj.* meaningful; brief **—pith'i·ly** *adv.* **—pith'i·ness** *n.*
**pit'i·ful** *adj.* arousing pity or contempt; pathetic **—pit'i·ful·ly** *adv.* **—pit'i·ful·ness** *n.*
**pit'i·less** *adj.* unfeeling; having no mercy **—pit'i·less·ly** *adv.* **—pit'i·less·ness** *n.*
**pit'tance** *n.* a trifling sum
**pit'y** *n.* compassion or sympathy aroused by the suffering of another **—pit'i·a·ble** *adj.* **—pit'i·a·ble·ness** *n.* **—pit'i·a·bly** *adv.*
**piv'ot** *n.* the thing or point on which something turns *—vi.* to turn on a pivot **—piv'ot·al** *adj.* **—piv'ot·al·ly** *adv.*
**pix'i·lat·ed** *adj.* frivolous or whimsical **—pix·i·la'tion** *n.*
**plac'a·ble** *adj.* inclined to tolerance or acceptance **—placa·bil'i·ty, plac'a·ble·ness** *n.*
**pla'cate** *vt.* to appease or pacify **—pla'cat·er** *n.* **—pla·ca'tion** *n.* **—pla'ca·tive, pla'ca·to·ry** *adj.*
**place** *n.* a particular position, space, or locality; one's status, rank, or job *—vt.* to situate in a particular location; to appoint to a position; to find a home or job for **—place'ment** *n.*
**pla·ce'bo** *n.* a fake or phony medication; a sugar pill
**plac'id** *adj.* peaceful or calm **—pla·cid'i·ty, plac'id·ness** *n.* **—plac'id·ly** *adv.*
**pla'gia·rism** *n.* misappropriation of the works or ideas of another **—pla'gia·rist** *n.* **—pla'gia·ris'tic** *adj.* **—pla'gia·rize** *vi., vt.*
**plague** *n.* a sudden spread of disease; a disaster; a sudden outbreak; an annoyance *—vt.* to annoy; to afflict with disease or disaster
**plain** *adj.* unadorned; simple; open or obvious; ordinary **—plain'ly** *adv.* **—plain'ness** *n.*
**plaint** *n.* a complaint
**plain'tiff** *n.* one who accuses in a court of law
**plain'tive** *adj.* mournful; lamenting **—plain'tive·ly** *adv.* **—plain'tive·ness** *n.*
**plan** *n.* a strategy worked out in advance of an action; an outline or diagram *—vt.* to work out the means for doing something; to have as an intention **—plan'ner** *n.*
**plane** *adj.* level *—n.* a flat surface **—pla'nar** *adj.*
**plan'et** *n.* a heavenly body that revolves around a star **—plan'e·tar·y** *adj.*
**plan·e·tar'i·um** *n.* a room or building equipped for viewing images of the heavens
**plank** *n.* a piece of lumber; a component of a political platform **—plank'ing** *n.*
**plant** *n.* an organism that grows from the ground; etc.; a manufacturing facility *—vt.* to sow seeds; to set firmly in place **—plant'er** *n.*
**plan·ta'tion** *n.* land under cultivation; an estate
**plaque** *n.* a flat decorative panel or plate
**plas'ter** *n.* a compound used to coat or patch walls *—vt.* to cover with or as with plaster; to affix **—plas'ter·er** *n.*
**plas'tic** *adj.* malleable; artificial *—n.* a flexible synthetic material that can be hardened and adapted to a variety of uses **—plas'ti·cal·ly** *adj.* **—plas·tic'i·ty** *n.*
**plat** *n.* a plot of land; a map showing existing or planned building lots, streets, etc. *—vt.* to make an area map showing this detail
**plate** *n.* a flat piece of material, such as for holding food, for decoration, or as part of a machine; food service for one *—vt.* to overlay or coat **—plat'ed** *adj.*
**pla·teau'** *n.* a flat-topped hill
**plat'form** *n.* a raised landing such as a stage; a statement of beliefs or goals, especially political
**plat'i·tude** *n.* a trite expression; a cliché **—plat·i·tu'di·nal, plat·i·tu'di·nous** *adj.* **—plat·i·tu'di·nous·ly** *adv.*
**pla·ton'ic** *adj.* spiritual; ideal
**pla·toon'** *n.* a small group set on a common purpose
**plat'ter** *n.* a large plate
**plau'dit** *n.* acclamation; praise
**plau'si·ble** *adj.* probable; convincing; seeming to justify belief **—plau·si·bil'i·ty, plau'si·ble·ness** *n.* **—plau'si·bly** *adv.*
**play** *vi., vt.* to act out a role; to perform; to participate, as in a game *—n.* a dramatic performance; the looseness of a machine part **—play'er** *n.*
**play'ful** *adj.* frolicsome or mischievous **—play'ful·ly** *adv.* **—play'ful·ness** *n.*
**play'wright** *n.* a writer of plays
**plaz'a** *n.* a public square
**plea** *n.* a request or appeal
**plead** *vi., vt.* to beseech; to offer an excuse or justification **—plead'a·ble** *adj.* **—plead'er** *n.* **—plead'ing·**

ly *adv.*

**pleas´ant** *adj.* providing pleasure **–pleas´ant·ly** *adv.* **–pleas´ant·ness** *n.*

**pleas´ant·ry** *n.* a polite or humorous remark

**please** *vi., vt.* to give pleasure *–adv.* **–pleas´ing** *adj.* **–pleas´ing·ly** *adv.*

**plea´sur·a·ble** *adj.* enjoyable; pleasing **–plea´sur·a·ble·ness** *n.* **–plea´sur·a·bly** *adv.*

**plea´sure** *n.* a feeling of delight; that which brings happiness or enjoyment; a preference **–plea´sure·ful** *adj.*

**plea´sure·less** *adj.* devoid of humor or amusement **–plea´sure·less·ly** *adv.*

**ple·be´ian** *adj.* common; unrefined **–ple·be´ian·ism** *n.* **–ple·be´ian·ly** *adv.*

**pleb´i·scite** *n.* choosing by vote of the complete electorate **–ple·bis´ci·tar·y** *adj.*

**pledge** *n.* a binding promise; security for payment of a debt *–vt.* **–pledge´a·ble** *adj.* **–pledg·ee´** *n.* **–pledg´er** *n.*

**ple´na·ry** *adj.* complete and unrestricted **–ple´na·ri·ly** *adv.*

**plen´i·tude** *n.* an abundance **–plen´i·tu´di·nous** *adj.*

**plen´te·ous** *adj.* abundant; plentiful **–plen´te·ous·ly** *adv.* **–plen´te·ous·ness** *n.*

**plen´ti·ful** *adj.* abundant; bountiful **–plen´ti·ful·ly** *adv.* **–plen´ti·ful·ness** *n.*

**plen´ty** *adj.* abundant *–adv.* extremely *–n.* an adequate amount; an abundance

**pleth´o·ra** *n.* an excess **–ple·thor´ic** *adj.* **–ple·thor´i·cal·ly** *adv.*

**pli´a·ble** *adj.* flexible; readily shaped or influenced; impressionable **–pli·a·bil´i·ty, pli´a·ble·ness** *n.* **–pli´a·bly** *adv.*

**pli´ant** *adj.* yielding; docile; adaptable **–pli´an·cy, pli´ant·ness** *n.* **–pli´ant·ly** *adv.*

**pli´ers** *n.* a hand tool for grasping or turning

**plight** *n.* a predicament or difficulty; a condition or state; a promise *–vt.* to promise or pledge

**plod** *vi., vt.* to move or work steadily and painstakingly **–plod´der** *n.* **–plod´ding·ly** *adv.*

**plot** *n.* a parcel of land, especially one occupied by or intended for a residence; a story line; a plan or conspiracy *–vt.* to locate; as on a map or chart; to take part in a conspiracy *–vi.* to conspire **–plot´ter** *n.*

**plow** *n.* an implement for breaking ground, moving snow, etc. *–vi., vt.* to break up or move with a plow; to move forcefully, as with a plow **–plow´a·ble** *adj.* **–plow´er** *n.*

**pluck** *n.* boldness or determination *–vt.* to pull out; to remove brusquely **–pluck´er** *n.*

**pluck´y** *adj.* spirited; courageous **–pluck´i·ly** *adv.* **–pluck´i·ness** *n.*

**plug** *n.* material that closes or obstructs; an electrical connector; casual mention of a product *–vt.* to stop up or close off; to advertise a product *–vi.* to become stopped up or closed off

**plumb** *adj.* precisely vertical *–adv.* vertical; squarely *–n.* a weight attached to a line used to establish a precise vertical *–vt.* to make vertical; to check with a plumb

**plume** *n.* an ornamental feather or clump or feathers; a feather-like form **–plu´mage** *n.*

**plum´met** *vi.* to fall rapidly

**plump** *adj.* having a full rounded figure *–vt., vi.* to make or become plump

**plun´der** *n.* stolen property *–vt. vi.* to take by force **–plun´der·a·ble** *adj.* **–plun´der·er** *n.* **–plun´der·ous** *adj.*

**plunge** *vi., vt.* to fall or thrust vigorously

**plu´ral** *adj.* comprising more than one

**plu´ral·ism** *n.* the condition of a society made up of diverse groups **–plu·ral´i·ty** *n.*

**plus** *adj.* positive; added *–conj.* added to *–n.* something added

**plush** *adj.* sumptuous; opulent **–plush´i·ness plush´ness** *n.* **–plush´ly** *adv.* **–plush´y** *adj.*

**plu·toc´ra·cy** *n.* government by the wealthy **–plu´to·crat** *n.* **–plu·to·crat´ic** *adj.* **–plu·to·crat´i·cal·ly** *adv.*

**ply** *n.* one of two or more layers *–vt.* to regularly practice or provide, as a trade or service

**pneu·mat´ic** *adj.* relating to air; operated by the use of air **–pneu·mat´i·cal·ly** *adv.*

**poach** *vt.* to cook in boiling liquid; to trespass and take unlawfully, as fish or game *–vi.* to trespass **–poach´er** *n.*

**pock´et** *n.* a small pouch, such as attached to a garment; an opening or cavity *–adj.* pertaining to a pocket; small enough to fit a pocket, as *a pocket calculator* *–vt.* to take **–pock´et·a·ble** *adj.* **–pock´et·er** *n.*

**po·di´a·try** *n.* the branch of medicine dealing with the feet **–po·di´a·trist** *n.*

**po´di·um** *n.* a speaker's platform

**po´em** *n.* a literary work in verse **–po´e·sy** *n.* **–po´et** *n.*

**po·et´ic, po·et´i·cal** *adj.* typifying the traits of poetry as lyrical, romantic, or idyllic **–po·et´i·cal·ly** *adv.*

**po´et·ry** *n.* poetic works; the traits of a poem

**po·grom´** *n.* systematic persecution

**poi´gnant** *adj.* mentally intense; distressing or moving **–poi´gnance, poi´gnan·cy** *n.* **–poi´gnant·ly** *adv.*

**point** *n.* a sharp end; a projection: *a point of land*; a dot; a particular spot: *at some point in time*; a distinct element, quality, or condition: *the point of the discussion* *–vi., vt.* to direct attention to **–point´ed** *adj.* **–point´ed·ly** *adv.* **–point´y** *adj.*

**point´less** *adj.* without meaning; ineffective **–point´less·ly** *adv.* **–point´less·ness** *n.*

**poise** *n.* an attitude of grace, dignity, and composure *–vt., vi.* to balance or hover

**poi´son** *n.* a chemical that can cause illness or death; something similarly harmful *—vt.* to administer a harmful substance; to have a harmful effect *—adj.* lethal **—poi´son·er** *n.* **—poi´son·ous** *adj.* **—poi´son·ous·ly** *adv.* **—poi´son·ous·ness** *n.*

**poke** *n.* a punch or jab *—vt.* to thrust or jab; to punch *—vi.* to meddle; to pry; to putter or dawdle

**poke·y, pok´y** *adj.* slow; hesitant **—pok´i·ly** *adv.* **—pok´i·ness** *n.*

**po´lar·ize** *vt.* to consolidate according to differing views **—po´lar·iz·a·ble** *adj.* **—po·lar·iz·a´tion** *n.*

**po·lem´ic** *n.* a contentious view **—po·lem´ic, po·lem´i·cal** *adj.* **—po·lem´i·cal·ly** *adv.*

**po·lem´ics** *n.* the art of debate **—po·lem´i·cist** *n.*

**po·lem´i·cize** *vi.* to involve in debate or disputation

**po·lice´** *n.* a department or persons charged with enforcement of the laws of a community *—vt.*

**pol´i·cy** *n.* a plan or procedure; an insurance contract

**pol´ish** *n.* luster or sheen; refinement *—vt.* to make smooth and bright; to make refined or elegant **—pol´ish·er** *n.*

**po·lite´** *adj.* considerate and tactful; courteous or elegant **—po·lite´ly** *adv.* **—po·lite´ness** *n.*

**pol´i·tic** *adj.* discreet; shrewd or crafty **—pol´i·tic·ly** *adv.*

**po·lit´i·cal** *adj.* relating to government or politics, or to the tactics for gaining power **—po·lit·i·cal·i·za´tion** *n.* **—po·lit´i·cal·ize** *vt.* **—po·lit´i·cal·ly** *adv.*

**po·lit´i·cize** *vt.* to act in the interest of political gain

**pol´i·tics** *n.* the science of government; tactics for gaining and holding power **—pol·i·ti´cian** *n.*

**poll** *n.* voting; a survey of public opinion *—vt.* to cast or record votes; to question for a survey **—poll´er, poll´ster** *n.*

**pol·lute´** *vt.* to contaminate or make unfit to use **—pol·lu´tant** *n.* **—pol·lut´er** *n.* **—pol·lu´tion** *n.*

**pol´ter·geist** *n.* a supernatural being that creates noises and disorder

**po·lyg´a·mous** *adj.* relating to the circumstance of having more than one spouse at a time **—po·lyg´a·mist** *n.* **—po·lyg´a·mous·ly** *adv.* **—po·lyg´a·my** *n.*

**pol´y·the·ism** *n.* belief in more than one god **—pol´y·the·ist** *n.* **—pol·y·the·is´tic, pol·y·the·is´ti·cal** *adj.* **—pol·y·the·is´ti·cal·ly** *adv.*

**pomp** *n.* pageantry; a magnificent display

**pomp´ous** *adj.* pretentious; boastful and arrogant **—pom·pos´i·ty, pomp´ous·ness** *n.* **—pomp´ous·ly** *adv.*

**pond** *n.* a small body of water

**pon´der** *vt.* to consider carefully *—vi.* to meditate **—pon´der·a·ble** *adj.* **—pon´der·a·bil´i·ty** *n.*

**pon´der·ous** *adj.* weighty; dull or lifeless **—pon´der·ous·ly** *adv.* **—pon´der·ous·ness** *n.*

**pon·tif´i·cate** *vi.* to speak dogmatically **—pon·tif´i·ca·tor** *n.* **—pon·tif·i·ca´tion** *n.*

**pool** *n.* an accumulation of liquid; a small body of water; an assemblage of persons or resources *—vi., vt.* to merge resources

**poor** *adj.* lacking wealth; lacking basic needs; inferior in quality or quantity **—poor´ness** *n.*

**pop´u·lace** *n.* the general public

**pop´u·lar** *adj.* generally accepted; well-liked **—pop´u·lar·ly** *adv.*

**pop·u·lar´i·ty** *n.* general acceptance; the quality of being liked

**pop´u·lar·ize** *vt.* to make generally acceptable **—pop·u·lar·i·za´tion** *n.*

**pop´u·late** *vt.* to inhabit; to furnish with inhabitants

**pop·u·la´tion** *n.* the people of an area or of a particular grouping **—pop´u·list** *n.*

**pop´u·lous** *adj.* well-populated **—pop´u·lous·ly** *adv.* **—pop´u·lous·ness** *n.*

**por´ce·lain** *n.* a fine glazed ceramic; china

**porch** *n.* an open or partly open area connected to a building at an entryway

**por·nog´ra·phy** *n.* sexually explicit material **—por·nog´ra·pher** *n.* **—por·no·graph´ic** *adj.* **—por·no·graph´i·cal·ly** *adv.*

**po·ros´i·ty** *n.* the quality of being porous; a measure of the level of absorbency of a substance

**po´rous** *adj.* having pores; absorbent; penetrable **—po´rous·ly** *adv.* **—po´rous·ness** *n.*

**port** *n.* a place for docking ships; the left side of a ship; an opening; a fortified wine

**por´ta·ble** *adj.* designed to be easily carried or moved **—por·ta·bil´i·ty, por´ta·ble·ness** *n.* **—por´ta·bly** *adv.*

**por´tal** *n.* an entryway

**por·tend´** *vt.* to predict or foretell

**por´tent** *n.* a sign or omen

**por·ten´tous** *adj.* ominous or foreboding **—por·ten´tous·ly** *adv.* **—por·ten´tous·ness** *n.*

**port·fo´li·o** *n.* a briefcase or folder for holding papers; a collection of documents: *an artist's portfolio, a stock portfolio*

**por´ti·co** *n.* an open porch

**por´tion** *n.* a part or share; the amount of food served to one person *—vt.* to separate into parts; to distribute **—por´tion·a·ble** *adj.* **—por´tion·er** *n.*

**port´ly** *adj.* stout **—port´li·ness** *n.*

**por´trait** *n.* a formal painting or photograph of a person; a verbal picture **—por´trait·ist** *n.* **—por´trai·ture** *n.*

**por·tray´** *vt.* to represent in a picture, through words, or as an actor **—por·tray´a·ble** *adj.* **—por·tray´al** *n.* **—por·tray´er** *n.*

**pose** *n.* a feigned attitude; an affectation *—vi.* to assume or hold a position; to feign an attitude; to misrepresent: *to pose as an expert* *—vt.* to cause to sit, as for a portrait; to put forth, as a question or threat **—pos´er** *n.*

**posh** *adj.* comfortable

**po·si´tion** *n.* a specific place; a particular viewpoint; social or professional status *—vt.* to place especially or appropriately **—po·si´tion·al** *adj.* **—po·si´tion·er** *n.*

**pos´i·tive** *adj.* certain, absolutely sure; decisive; direct **—pos´i·tive·ly** *adv.* **—pos´i·tive·ness** *n.*

**pos·sess´** *vt.* to have, as goods, traits, or emotions; to dominate **—pos·ses´sor** *n.*

**pos·ses´sion** *n.* a thing owned or in one´s custody

**pos·ses´sive** *adj.* jealous; exhibiting a desire to control **—pos·ses´sive·ly** *adv.* **—pos·ses´sive·ness** *n.* **—pos·ses´so·ry** *n.*

**pos·si·bil´i·ty** *n.* something likely

**pos´si·ble** *adj.* likely or able to be **—pos´si·bly** *adv.*

**post** *n.* a shaft or rod of wood, metal, etc. used as a support or connection; a place of appointment or assignment; mail *—vt.* to announce publicly, as by hanging a sign; to appoint or assign; *(Brit.)* to send via the postal system **—post´al** *adj.*

**pos·te´ri·or** *adj.* situated behind *—n.* the buttocks **—pos·te·ri·or´i·ty** *n.* **—pos·te´ri·or·ly** *adv.*

**pos·ter´i·ty** *n.* succeeding generations

**post´hu·mous** *adj.* occurring after a person´s death **—post´hu·mous·ly** *adv.* **—post´hu·mous·ness** *n.*

**post´-mor´tem** *adj.* after death *—n.* an autopsy

**post·pone´** *vt.* put off to a future time **—post·pon´a·ble** *adj.* **—post·pone´ment** *n.*

**post´script** *n.* something added to a written or printed document

**pos´tu·late** *n.* a presumption or supposition *—vt.* to presume without proof or confirmation **—pos·tu·la´tion** *n.*

**pos´ture** *n.* characteristic bearing, manner, or attitude *—vi.* to affect an attitude **—pos´tur·al** *adj.*

**po´ta·ble** *adj.* suitable for drinking *—n.* a beverage **—po·ta·bil´i·ty, po´ta·ble·ness** *n.*

**po´tent** *adj.* strong; powerful **—po´ten·cy** *n.* **—po´tent·ly** *adv.*

**po´ten·tate** *n.* a sovereign; one who dominates

**po·ten´tial** *adj.* possible *—n.* an unrealized capacity or capability **—po·ten·ti·al´i·ty** *n.* **—po·ten´tial·ly** *adv.*

**poth´er** *n.* a disturbance *—vi., vt.* to be or cause to be concerned about inconsequential things

**po·tion** *n.* a medicine or drug

**pot´pour·ri´** *n.* a mixture or medley; a conglomeration

**pot´sherd** *n.* a fragment of pottery

**pot´tage** *n.* a thick soup or stew

**pot´ter·y** *n.* baked clay vessels

**pouch** *n.* a bag or recepticle for carrying: *tobacco pouch, mail pouch* **—pouch´y** *adj.*

**pounce** *vi.* to attack or seize suddenly **—pounc´er** *n.*

**pound** *n.* a unit of weight or currency; a place of confinement *—vt.* to strike repeatedly; to tread heavily; to confine

**pour** *vi., vt.* to flow or make to flow in a steady stream; to rain profusely **—pour´er** *n.*

**pout** *n.* a facial expression denoting displeasure *—vi.* to be sullen **—pout´er** *n.* **—pout´ing·ly** *adv.* **—pout´y** *adj.*

**pov´er·ty** *n.* a state of want; lacking means; inadequacy

**pow´der** *n.* material made up of fine particles *—vi., vt.* to become or cause to become granular or pulverized **—pow´der·er** *n.* **—pow´der·y** *adj.*

**pow´er** *n.* strength, energy; the energy or ability to act effectively; the authority to act *—vt.* to provide with a means of propulsion *—adj.* operated by a motor or by electricity **—pow´er·ful** *adj.* **—pow´er·ful·ly** *adv.* **—pow´er·ful·ness** *n.*

**pow´er·bro·ker** *n.* one who controls through political or financial connections

**pow´er·less** *adj.* helpless; lacking strength or authority **—pow´er·less·ly** *adv.* **—pow´er·less·ness** *n.*

**power of attorney** authority to act as agent for another

**prac´ti·ca·ble** *adj.* achievable; attainable **—prac·ti·ca·bil´i·ty** *n.* **—prac´ti·ca·bly** *adv.*

**prac´ti·cal** *adj.* useful or usable; workable or sensible **—prac·ti·cal´i·ty, prac´ti·cal·ness** *n.*

**prac´ti·cal·ly** *adv.* in a practical manner; almost

**prac´tice** *n.* repetition to improve competence; a usual mode or manner of functioning; a profession **—prac´tice** *(US)*, **prac´tise** *(Brit.) vt., vi.* to repeat an action in order to acquire skill; to perform according to custom; to work at a profession **—prac´ticed** *adj.* **—prac´tic·er** *n.*

**prac·ti´tion·er** *n.* one who follows a particular course, such as a profession or a lifestyle

**prag·mat´ic** *adj.* practical; concerned with facts and logic **—prag·mat´i·cal·ly** *adv.* **—prag·mat´i·cism** *n.* **—prag´ma·tism** *n.* **—prag´ma·tist** *n.* **—prag·ma·tis´tic** *adj.*

**praise** *n.* an expression of admiration or approval *—vt.* to express approval of; to honor or glorify, as of a god

**praise´wor·thy** *adj.* deserving praise; commendable **—praise´wor·thi·ly** *adv.* **—praise´wor·thi·ness** *n.*

**prance** *vi.* to strut and frolic in a spirited manner **—pranc´er** *n.* **—pranc´ing·ly** *adv.*

**prank** *n.* a practical joke; a playful escapade **—prank´ish** *adj.* **—prank´ish·ly** *adv.* **—prank´ish·ness** *n.* **—prank´ster** *n.*

**prate** *n.* idle chatter *—vi., vt.* to talk idly and frivolously **—prat´er** *n.* **—prat´ing·ly** *adv.*

**prat´tle** *n.* childlike or foolish talk *—vi., vt.* to speak in a childish manner **—prat´tler** *n.* **—prat´tling·ly** *adv.*

**prayer** *n.* an earnest appeal or supplication **—pray** *vi., vt.* **prayer´ful** *adj.* **prayer´ful·ly** *adv.* **prayer´ful·ness** *n.*

**pray´er** *n.* one who prays

**preach** *vi., vt.* to lecture or sermonize, especially in a dull and dogmatic fashion —**preach´er** *n.* —**preach´ing·ly** *adv.*

**preach´i·fy** *vi.* to lecture in a dull, didactic fashion —**preach·i·fi·ca´tion** *n.*

**preach´y** *adj.* overly given to preaching or moralizing

**pre´am·ble** *n.* a preface to a formal document

**pre´ar·range´** *vt.* to set up or organize in advance —**pre·ar·range´ment** *n.*

**pre·car´i·ous** *adj.* uncertain or unstable —**pre·car´i·ous·ly** *adv.* —**pre·car´i·ous·ness** *n.*

**pre·cau´tion** *n.* care taken to avoid hazards —**pre·cau´tion·ary** *adj.*

**pre·cede´** *vt., vi.* to come or go before

**prec´e·dence, prec´e·den·cy** *n.* priority; superiority

**prec´e·dent** *n.* an example or pattern

**pre´cept** *n.* a rule or principle that defines a policy; an instruction —**pre·cep´tive** *adj.* —**pre·cep´tive·ly** *adv.*

**pre´cinct** *n.* a minor territorial or jurisdictional district

**pre´cious** *adj.* valuable; cherished; overly refined or nice —*adv.* —**pre´cious·ly** *adv.* —**pre´cious·ness** *n.*

**prec´i·pice** *n.* a cliff´s edge; the edge or threshold of danger

**pre·cip´i·tant** *adj.* impulsive; sudden or rash —**pre·cip´i·tance, pre·cip´i·tan·cy** *n.* —**pre·cip´i·tant·ly** *adv.*

**pre·cip´i·tate** *adj.* hasty or rash —*vi., vt.* to fall or cause to fall, as rain; to hasten the occurrence of —**pre·cip´i·tate·ly** *adv.* —**pre·cip´i·tate·ness** *n.* —**pre·cip´i·ta·tive** *adj.* —**pre·cip´i·ta·tor** *n.*

**pre·cip·i·ta´tion** *n.* haste or rashness; falling moisture, such as rain, snow, or sleet

**pre·cip´i·tous** *adj.* steep —**pre·cip´i·tous·ly** *adv.* —**pre·cip´i·tous·ness** *n.*

**pré·cis´** *n.* a synopsis or summary of a text

**pre·cise´** *adj.* exact; well-defined —**pre·cise´ly** *adv.* —**pre·cise´ness** *n.* —**pre·ci´sion** *n., adj.*

**pre·clude´** *vt.* to exclude or prohibit —**pre·clu´sion** *n.* —**pre·clu´sive** *adj.* —**pre·clu´sive·ly** *adv.*

**pre·co´cious** *adj.* exhibiting early maturity; mature beyond what may be expected for the subject´s chronological age —**pre·co´cious·ly** *adv.* —**pre·co´cious·ness, pre·coc´i·ty** *n.*

**pre·cog·ni´tion** *n.* foresight; prescience —**pre·cog´ni·tive** *adj.*

**pre´con·ceive´** *vt.* to reach a conclusion without complete information —**pre·con·cep´tion** *n.*

**pre·con·di´tion** *n.* a requisite for further action

**pre·cur´sor** *n.* a forerunner or harbinger —**pre·cur´sive, pre·cur´so·ry** *adj.*

**pred´a·tor** *n.* one that preys on others —**pred·a·to´ri·ly** *adv.* —**pred´a·to·ri·ness** *n.* —**pred´a·to·ry** *adj.*

**pre·des·ti·na´tion** *n.* the belief that one´s destiny is determined in advance —**pre·des´ti·nate, pre·des´tine** *vt.*

**pre·des·ti·nar´i·an** *adj.* relating to or believing in predestination —*n.* one who believes in predestination —**per·des·ti·nar´i·an·ism** *n.*

**pre·de·ter´mine** *vt.* to ascertain an outcome in advance —**pre·de·ter´mi·nate** *adj.* —**pre·de·ter·mi·na´tion** *n.*

**pre·dic´a·ment** *n.* a difficult situation

**pred´i·cate** *vt., vi.* to assert or profess —**pred·i·ca´tion** *n.* —**pred·i·ca´tion·al** *adj.* —**pred´i·ca·tive** *adj.* —**pred´i·ca·tive·ly** *adv.*

**pre·dict´** *vt.* to assert in advance on the basis of theory or experience —*vi.* to foretell or prophesy —**pre·dict·a·bil´i·ty** *adv.* —**pre·dict´a·ble** *adj.* —**pre·dict´a·bly** *adv.* —**pre·dic´tive** *adj.* —**pre·dic´tive·ly** *adv.* —**pre·dic´tive·ness** *n.* —**pre·dic´tor** *n.*

**pre·dic´tion** *n.* a thing predicted

**pred´i·lec´tion** *n.* a tendency

**pre´dis·pose´** *vt.* to influence or make susceptible —**pre·dis·po·si´tion** *n.*

**pre·dom´i·nant** *adj.* most important or widespread —**pre·dom´i·nance** *n.* —**pre·dom´i·nant·ly** *adv.*

**pre·dom´i·nate** *vi.* to be superior to all others in some way —**pre·dom´i·nat·ing·ly** *adv.* —**pre·dom´i·nate·ly** *adv.* —**pre·dom·i·na´tion** *n.* —**pre·dom´i·na·tor** *n.*

**pre·em´i·nent** *adj.* distinguished; outstanding —**pre·em´i·nence** *n.* —**pre·em´i·nent·ly** *adv.*

**pre·empt´** *vt.* to usurp or confiscate; to take precedence, as in a right to purchase —**pre·emp´tor** *n.* —**pre·emp´to·ry** *adj.*

**pre·emp´tion** *n.* the right to purchase before others; seizure or appropriation —**pre·emp´tive** *adj.* —**pre·emp´tive·ly** *adv.*

**preen** *vt.* to groom carefully; to gloat —*vi.* to primp; to gloat

**pref´ace** *n.* an introduction or opening message, as in a book —*vt.* to furnish with an opening message; to serve as an introductory message

**pre·fer´** *vt.* to favor over another; to like better —**pref´er·ence** *n.*

**pref´er·a·ble** *adj.* more desirable —**pref´er·a·bil´i·ty, pref´er·a·ble·ness** *n.* —**pref´er·a·bly** *adv.*

**pref·er·en´tial** *adj.* favored; granting assistance —**pref·er·en´tial·ism** *n.* —**pref·er·en´tial·ly** *adv.*

**preg´na·ble** *adj.* pervious; vulnerable —**preg·na·bil´i·ty** *adv.*

**preg´nant** *adj.* carrying a developing offspring; significant or meaningful —**preg´nan·cy** *n.* —**preg´nant·ly** *adv.*

**pre·hen´sile** *adj.* adapted for grasping, as a monkey´s tail —**pre·hen·sil´i·ty** *adv.*

**pre·hen´sion** *n.* apprehension, understanding

**pre·his·tor´ic, pre´his·tor´i·cal** *adj.* belonging to the time before recorded history —**pre´his·tor´i·cal·ly** *adv.* —**pre·his´to·ry** *n.*

**prej´u·dice** *n.* prejudgment; opinion founded on bias –*vt.* to influence another to prejudge; to wrong by opinion or action **–prej´u·di´cial** *adj.* **–prej´u·di´cial·ly** *adv.*

**pre·lim´i·nar·y** *adj.* introductory or preceding –*n.* an introduction; something that precedes **–pre·lim·i·nar´i·ly** *adv.*

**pre·mar´i·tal** *adj.* before marriage **–pre·mar´i·tal·ly** *adv.*

**pre·ma·ture´** *adj.* before the correct or proper time **–pre·ma·ture´ly** *adv.* **–pre·ma·ture´ness** *n.* **–pre·ma·tur´i·ty** *n.*

**pre·med´i·tate** *vt. vi.* to plan or consider in advance **–pre·med´i·ta·tive** *adj.* **–pre·med´i·ta·tor** *n.*

**pre·med´i·tat·ed** *adj.* characterized by deliberate intention **–pre·med´i·tat·ed·ly** *adv.* **–pre·med·i·ta´tion** *n.*

**pre·mier´** *adj.* foremost –*n.* a chief administrative officer

**pre·miere´** *n.* an introductory public performance –*vt., vi.* to present publicly for the first time

**prem´ise** *n.* an assumption that is the basis for debate or resolution

**pre´mi·um** *adj.* excellent; superior; –*n.* a reward or bonus; an excess amount by which something is valued or paid

**pre·mo·ni´tion** *n.* foreboding; a sign or omen **–pre·mon·i·to´ri·ly** *adv.* **–pre·mon´i·to·ry** *adj.*

**pre·nup´tial** *adj.* before marriage

**pre·oc´cu·pied** *adj.* distracted; immersed in thought; troubled **–pre·oc·cu·pa´tion** *n.* **–pre·oc´cu·py** *vt.*

**pre·or·dain´** *vt.* to predetermine; to destine **–pre·or·di·na´tion** *n.*

**prep·a·ra´tion** *n.* arrangements made in advance; readiness; a mixture made for some purpose **–pre·par´a·tive** *adj. n.* **–pre·par´a·tive·ly** *adv.*

**pre·par´a·to·ry** *adj.* introductory or preliminary, as a course of study –*adv.* in making ready for **–pre·par·a·to´ri·ly** *adv.*

**pre·pare´** *vt.* to arrange in advance; to provide what is needed; to make complete **–pre·par´ed·ness** *n.* **–pre·par´er** *n.*

**pre·pay´** *vt.* to pay in advance **–pre·pay´ment** *n.*

**pre·pon´der·ant** *adj.* superior; dominant **–pre·pon´der·ance** *n.* **–pre·pon´der·ant·ly** *adv.*

**pre·pos´ter·ous** *adj.* absurd; irrational **–pre·pos´ter·ous·ly** *adv.* **–pre·pos´ter·ous·ness** *n.*

**pre´quel** *n.* a story recounting events that lead up to those in a work published earlier

**pre·req´ui·site** *n.* a requirement or condition for further action –*adj.* required or necessary

**pre·rog´a·tive** *n.* a right or privilege, such as granted by virtue of rank or birth

**pres´age** *n.* an omen or intuition –*vt., vi.* **pres´age·ful** *adj.*

**pre´sci·ence** *n.* foreknowledge of coming events **–pre´scient** *adj.* **–pre´scient·ly** *adv.*

**pre·scribe´** *vt.* to direct or order **–pre·scrib´er** *n.*

**pre·scrip´tion** *n.* directions or instructions; a formula, as for preparing a medicine

**pres´ence** *n.* attendance, proximity, or influence: *their presence at the meeting is vital*; one's appearance or bearing: *a commanding presence*

**pres´ent** *adj.* at this moment; current; existing; here; near at hand –*n.* now

**pres´ent** *n.* a gift **–pre·sent´** *vt.* to offer or give, as a gift

**pre·sent´a·ble** *adj.* suitable for offering or giving **–pre·sent·a·bil´i·ty, pre·sent´a·ble·ness** *n.* **–pre·sent´a·bly** *adv.*

**pre·sen·ta´tion** *n.* something offered or given **–pre·sen·ta´tion·al** *adj.*

**pres´ent·ly** *adv.* soon

**pres·er·va´tion·ist** *n.* one who supports the protection of natural areas **–pres·er·va´tion·ism** *n.*

**pre·serv´a·tive** *n.* a substance that keeps food from spoiling –*adj.*

**pre·serve´** *n.* an area set aside to be kept in its natural state –*vt.* to protect; to save in a natural state; to prepare food so as to prevent spoilage **–pre·serv´a·ble** *adj.* **–pres·er·va´tion** *n.* **–pre·serv´er** *n.*

**pre·side´** *vi.* to officiate, as at a meeting; to direct or control **–pre·sid´er** *n.*

**pres´i·dent** *n.* a chief officer or executive; one who presides **–pres´i·den·cy** *n.* **–pres·i·den´tial** *adj.* **–pres·i·den´tial·ly** *adv.*

**press** *n.* journalism or journalists; a machine for printing; any device used to apply pressure; urgency –*vt., vi.* to apply pressure

**pres´sure** *n.* the applying of constant physical or mental forces –*vt.* to persuade

**pres´sur·ise** (*Brit.*) *vt.* to apply mental pressure; to persuade

**pres·ti·dig·i·ta´tion** *n.* sleight-of-hand **–pres·ti·dig´i·ta·tor** *n.*

**pres·tige´** *n.* distinction or renown; esteem **–pres·tig´i·ous** *adj.* **–pres·tig´i·ous·ly** *adv.* **–pres·tig´i·ous·ness** *n.*

**pre·sume´** *vt.* to take for granted; to undertake without proper authorization –*vi.* to make excessive demands on **–pre·sum´a·bly, pre·sum´ed·ly** *adv.* **–pre·sum´er** *n.*

**pre·sump´tion** *n.* something taken for granted; arrogance

**pre·sump´tive** *adj.* based on probability; providing reasonable cause for belief **–pre·sump´tive·ly** *adv.*

**pre·sum´ing** *adj.* presumptuous **–pre·sum´ing·ly** *adv.*

**pre·sump´tu·ous** *adj.* impudent or rude; overly forward **–pre·sump´tu·ous·ly** *adv.* **–pre·sump´tu·ous·ness** *n.*

**pre·sup·pose´** *vt.* to take for granted **–pre·sup·po·si´tion** *n.*

**pre·tend´** *vt., vi.* to feign or mimic; to make believe; to be deceitful or attempt to deceive **–pre·tence´** *(Brit.),* **pre·tense´** *(US) n.*

**pre·tend´ed** *adj.* insincere; feigned or counterfeit **–pre·tend´ed·ly** *adv.*

**pre·ten´tious** *adj.* presumptuous or arrogant; pompous or showy **–pre·ten´sion, pre·ten´tious·ness** *n.* **–pre·ten´tious·ly** *adv.*

**pre´text** *n.* subterfuge; an alleged reason

**pret´ti·fy** *vt.* to make attractive

**pret´ty** *adj.* attractive; considerable: *a pretty mess;* insubstantial: *pretty words* *–adv.* quite; somewhat **–pret´ti·ly** *adv.* **–pret´ti·ness** *n.*

**pre·vail´** *vi.* to overcome; to influence or effect **–pre·vail´er** *n.*

**pre·vail´ing** *adj.* dominant; generally accepted **–pre·vail´ing·ly** *adv.*

**prev´a·lent** *adj.* common or widespread **–prev´a·lence** *n.* **–prev´a·lent·ly** *adv.*

**pre·var´i·cate** *vi.* to lie **–pre·var·i·ca´tion** *n.* **–pre·var´i·ca·tor** *n.*

**pre·vent´** *vt.* to keep from happening; to prohibit or hamper **–pre·vent´a·ble** *adj.* **–pre·vent´er** *n.* **–pre·ven´tion** *n.*

**pre·vent´a·tive, pre·ven´tive** *adj.* hindering; precautionary *–n.* something that prevents, as protection from disease **–pre·ven´tive·ly** *adv.* **–pre·ven´tive·ness** *n.*

**pre´view** *n.* an advance view; a survey or inspection *–vt.* to view in advance

**pre´vi·ous** *adj.* former; having occurred earlier **–pre´vi·ous·ly** *adv.*

**prey** *n.* one that is hunted; a victim *–vi.* to hunt; to victimize

**price** *n.* the cost or value of something *–vt.* to set a value for

**price´less** *adj.* of immeasurable value

**pric´ey** *adj.* expensive

**prick** *n.* a sharp pain; a puncture *–vt., vi.*

**pride** *n.* self-esteem; haughtiness or disdain **–pride´ful** *adj.* **–pride´ful·ly** *adv.* **–pride´ful·ness** *n.*

**prig** *n.* a prude; one who is overly correct or formal **–prig´ger·y** *n.* **–prig´gish** *adj.* **–prig´gish·ly** *adv.* **–prig´gish·ness** *n.*

**prim** *adj.* overly exacting or proper; demur; orderly **–prim·ly** *adv.* **–prim´ness** *n.* **–pri´ma·cy** *n.*

**pri´mal** *adj.* primitive; original; primary

**pri´mary** *adj.* first; earliest; fundamental; principal **–pri·mar´i·ly** *adv.*

**prime** *adj.* excellent; of the finest quality; original *–n.* the age of full perfection or vigor: *the prime of life;* the best of anything *–vt.* to prepare or make ready: *prime a pump;* to apply an initial coating **–prime´ly** *adv.* **–prime´ness** *n.*

**pri·me´val** *adj.* ancient; primitive **–pri·me´val·ly** *adv.*

**prim´i·tive** *adj.* simple; ancient; uncivilized **–prim´i·tive·ly** *adv.* **–prim´i·tive·ness** *n.*

**pri·mor´di·al** *adj.* primitive; original **–pri·mor´di·al·ly** *adv.*

**primp** *vt., vi.* to groom with care

**prince** *n.* a nobleman; one who is outstanding **–prince´li·ness** *n.* **–prince·ly** *adj.*

**prin´cess** *n.* a noblewoman

**prin´ci·pal** *adj.* first or leading *–n.* a person of importance **–prin´ci·pal·ly** *adv.*

**prin´ci·ple** *n.* a fundamantal rule or concept; an ideal **–prin´ci·pled** *adj.*

**print** *n.* duplicate made by transferring an image to a receptor such as paper; an indentation made by pressure *–vi., vt.* **–print´er** *n.* **–print´ing** *n.* **–print´mak·er** *n.*

**pri´or** *adj.* preceding

**pri·or´i·tize** *vt.* to organize in order of importance **–pri·or´i·ty** *n.* **–pri·or·i·ti·za´tion** *n.*

**pris´on** *n.* a place of confinement **–pris´on·er** *n.*

**pris´sy** *adj.* unduly proper **–pris´si·ly** *adv.* **–pris´si·ness** *n.*

**pris´tine** *adj.* unspoiled

**pri´vate** *adj.* not open to the public; not public: *private ownership;* secluded **–pri´va·cy** *n.* **–pri´vate·ly** *adv.* **–pri´vate·ness** *n.*

**pri·va´tion** *n.* abject poverty

**priv´i·lege** *n.* a special right

**priv´i·leged** *adj.* invested with a special right or advantage

**prize** *n.* an award; something desired *–adj.* greatly valued *–vt.* to value highly

**prob´a·ble** *adj.* likely; worth believing although unproven **–prob·a·bil´i·ty** *n.* **–prob´a·bly** *adv.*

**pro·ba´tion** *n.* a trial period **–pro·ba´tion·al** *adj.* **–pro·ba´tion·ary** *adj.* **–pro·ba´tion·er** *n.*

**pro´bi·ty** *n.* honesty; integrity

**prob´lem** *adj.* difficult to manage: *a problem child* *–n.* something to be considered; a puzzle or dilemma

**prob´lem·at´ic, prob´lem·at´i·cal** *adj.* difficult; doubtful **–prob´lem·at´i·cal·ly** *adv.*

**pro·ce´dure** *n.* a manner of doing something; a system for doing **–pro·ce´dur·al** *adj.* **–pro·ce´dur·al·ly** *adv.*

**pro·ceed´** *vi.* to move forward

**pro´ceeds** *n.* money received; yield

**pro·ceed´ing** *n.* a process or procedure

**proc´ess** *n.* a set of actions; a system

**pro·ces´sion** *n.* an orderly progression; a parade

**proc´es·sor** *n.* a device for manipulating: *a food processor, a data processor*

**pro·claim´** *vt.* to announce; to praise **–pro·claim´er** *n.* **–pro·clam´a·to·ry** *adj.*

**proc·la·ma´tion** *n.* a formal announcement or edict

**pro·cliv´i·ty** *n.* an inherent inclination or tendency
**pro·cras´ti·nate** *vi.* to put off taking action —*vt.* to postpone or delay —**pro·cras·ti·na´tion** *n.* —**pro·cras´ti·na·tor** *n.*
**pro·cure´** *vt.* to acquire —**pro·cur´a·ble** *adj.* —**pro·cure´ment** *n.* —**pro·cur´er** *n.*
**prod** *vt.* to goad or provoke —*n.* anything that incites to action
**prod´i·gal** *adj.* wasteful —**prod·i·gal´i·ty** *n.* —**prod´i·gal·ly** *adv.*
**pro·di´gious** *adj.* extraordinary or impressive —**pro·di´gious·ly** *adv.* —**pro·di´gious·ness** *n.*
**prod´i·gy** *n.* one with exceptional talent; a genius
**prod´uce** *n.* that which is made; farm products —**pro·duce´** *vt.* to make or manufacture; to create —**pro·duc´er** *n.* —**prod´uct** *n.*
**pro·duc´tion** *n.* output or yield
**pro·duc´tive** *adj.* fruitful or prolific; effective —**pro·duc´tive·ly** *adv.*
**pro·duc·tiv´i·ty** *n.* the speed or effectiveness for generating output
**pro·fane´** *adj.* sacrilegious or irreverent; vulgar or base —*vt.* to desecrate or debase —**prof·a·na´tion** *n.* —**pro·fan´a·to·ry** *adj.* —**pro·fane´ly** *adv.* —**pro·fan´er** *n.*
**pro·fane´ness, pro·fan´i·ty** *n.* irreverence; the use of abusive or vulgar language
**pro·fess´** *vt.* to claim or declare; to pretend or feign —**pro·fess´ed·ly** *adv.*
**pro·fes´sion** *n.* an occupation, especially one requiring special training; a declaration of faith
**pro·fes´sion·al** *adj.* skillful —*n.* one skilled or specially trained —**pro·fes´sion·al·ly** *adv.*
**pro·fes´sor** *n.* *(Brit.)* a distinguished teacher at a college or university; *(US)* an educator, especially at a college or university —**pro·fes·so´ri·al** *adj.* —**pro·fes·so´ri·al·ly** *adv.*
**prof´fer** *vt.* to offer
**pro·fi´cient** *adj.* competent or able —**pro·fi´cien·cy** *n.* —**pro·fi´cient·ly** *adv.*
**pro´file** *n.* a summary; a side view
**prof´it** *n.* gain from a business venture —*vt., vi.* to realize gain or benefit; to be of benefit to —**prof·it·a·bil´i·ty** *n.* —**prof´it·a·ble** *adj.* —**prof´it·a·bly** *adv.*
**prof´i·teer´** *vi.* to make an unreasonable profit —*n.*
**prof´li·gate** *adj.* extravagant or wasteful —**prof´li·ga·cy** *n.* —**prof´li·gate·ly** *adv.*
**pro·found´** *adj.* deep or penetrating; scholarly —**pro·found´ly** *adv.* —**pro·found´ness** *n.*
**pro·fun´di·ty** *n.* the quality of being profound; a scholarly paper, theory, etc.
**pro·fuse´** *adj.* abundant —**pro·fuse´ly** *adv.* —**pro·fuse´ness** *n.*
**pro·fu´sion** *n.* an abundance or outpouring
**prog´e·ny** *n.* an offspring; a descendant
**prog·no´sis** *n.* a forecast or prediction
**prog·nos´ti·cate** *vt.* to predict —**prog·nos·ti·ca´tion** *n.* —**prog·nos´ti·ca·tor** *n.*
**pro´gram** *(US)* *n.* a schedule or agenda; a radio or television broadcast; a set of computer instructions —*vt.* to prepare a schedule or agenda; to write computer instructions —**pro´gram·ma·ble** *adj.* —**pro´gram·mer** *n.*
**pro´gramme** *(Brit.)* *n.* a schedule or agenda; a radio or television broadcast —*vt.* to prepare a schedule or agenda
**prog´ress** *n.* a moving forward; advancement, development, or improvement —**pro·gress´** *vi.* to move forward; to advance; to grow or improve —**pro·gres´sion** *n.*
**pro·gres´sive** *adj.* receptive to fresh ideas or concepts —**pro·gres´sive·ly** *adv.* —**pro·gres´sive·ness** *n.*
**pro·hib´it** *vt.* to forbid or ban —**pro·hi·bi´tion** *n.*
**pro·hib´i·tive** *adj.* forbidding —**pro·hib´i·tive·ly** *adv.*
**proj´ect** *n.* a plan; a serious undertaking —**pro·ject´** *vt.* to extend or thrust forward —**pro·jec´tile** *n.*
**pro·jec´tion** *n.* a bulge or protuberance; an extended part; a forecast based on historical data
**pro·le·tar´i·at** *n.* the working class —**pro´le·tar´i·an** *adj.*
**pro·lif´er·ate** *vi., vt.* to increase rapidly —**pro·lif·er·a´tion** *n.*
**pro·lif´ic** *adj.* producing or capable of producing in abundance —**pro·lif´i·ca·cy** *n.* —**pro·lif´i·cal·ly** *adv.*
**pro·lix´** *adj.* excessively wordy
**pro´logue** *n.* an introductory text
**pro·long´** *vt.* to extend or lengthen
**prom´e·nade´** *n.* a public walkway —*vi., vt.* to take a leisurely walk
**prom´i·nent** *adj.* clearly discernable; well-known or celebrated —**prom´i·nence** *n.* —**prom´i·nent·ly** *adv.*
**pro·mis´cu·ous** *adj.* tending to casual relationships; indiscriminate; random —**prom·is·cu´i·ty** *n.* —**pro·mis´cu·ous·ly** *adv.* —**pro·mis´cu·ous·ness** *n.*
**prom´ise** *n.* a pledge or vow —*vt.* —**prom´is·er** *n.* —**prom´is·ing** *adj.* —**prom´is·so·ry** *adj.*
**pro´mo** *n.* a promotional message or campaign
**prom´on·to·ry** *n.* a high point of land extending out into a body of water
**pro·mote´** *vt.* to advance to a higher level; to attempt to make more popular or prominent —**pro·mot´a·ble** *adj.* —**pro·mot´er** *n.*
**pro·mo´tion** *n.* an elevation in status or position; a program to improve the perception of a person, product, or concept —**pro·mo´tion·al** *adj.*
**prompt** *adj.* punctual; timely —*vt.* to arouse or provoke; to remind —**prompt´er** *n.* —**prompt´ly** *adv.* —**prompt´ness** *n.*
**prom´ul·gate** *vt.* to announce publicly or officially —**prom·ul·ga´tion** *n.* —**prom´ul·ga·tor** *n.*
**prone** *adj.* lying face downward; disposed to or likely

–**prone´ly** *adv.*

**prong** *n.* a slender pointed extension; *(US)* the contact points for an electrical connection

**pro´noun** *n.* a designation that substitutes for a noun

**pro·nounce´** *vt., vi.* to utter or speak clearly; to announce officially –**pro·nounce´a·ble** *adj.* –**pro·nounce´ment** *n.*

**pro·nounced´** *adj.* distinctive; obvious –**pro·nounc´ed·ly** *adv.* –**pro·nounc´ed·ness** *n.*

**pro·nun·ci·a´tion** *n.* the generally accepted sound of a spoken word

**proof** *n.* evidence; a demonstration of authenticity; verification or validation

**proof´read** *vt., vi.* to review copy for errors –**proof´read·er** *n.*

**prop** *n.* a support –*vt.* to support or assist

**prop·a·gan´da** *n.* information designed to promote a cause or point of view –**prop·a·gan´dist** *n.* –**prop·a·gan·dis´tic** *adj.* –**prop·a·gan´dize** *vi., vt.*

**prop´a·gate** *vt.* to breed or multiply; to spread or extend –**prop·a·ga´tion** *n.* –**prop´a·ga·tor** *n.*

**pro·pel´** *vt.* to drive forward

**pro·pel´lant, pro·pel´lent** *n.* a substance that serves to push or thrust –*adj.* serving to propel

**pro·pen´si·ty** *n.* an inclination or tendency

**prop´er** *adj.* appropriate; fitting; according to convention –**prop´er·ly** *adv.* –**prop´er·ness** *n.*

**prop´er·tied** *adj.* having assets, especially land as a source of income

**prop´er·ty** *n.* one´s belongings or possessions; a section of land, a characteristic or quality

**proph´e·cy** *n.* a prediction or forecast

**proph´e·sy** *vt.* to predict or foretell

**proph´et** *n.* one who pronounces or interprets by divine inspiration; a spokesperson –**pro·phet´ic, pro·phet´i·cal** *adj.* –**pro·phet´i·cal·ly** *adv.*

**pro·phy·lac´tic** *adj.* protective, as against disease –*n.*

**pro·pin´qui·ty** *n.* nearness; similarity

**pro·pi´ti·ate** *vt.* to appease

**pro·pi´tious** *adj.* promising or favorable, as of circumstances; kindly disposed –**pro·pi´tious·ly** *adv.* –**pro·pi´tious·ness** *n.*

**pro·po´nent** *n.* an advocate or defender, a supporter

**pro·por´tion** *n.* a share; relative magnitude; symmetry –**pro·por´tion·al** *adj.* –**pro·por´tion·ate** *adj.*

**pro·pos´al** *n.* an offer or proposition; a plan or scheme

**pro·pose´** *vt.* to suggest; or recommend; to put forth for consideration; to intend –*vi.* to make an offer, as of marriage –**pro·pos´er** *n.*

**prop·o·si´tion** *n.* something offered for consideration –**prop·o·si´tion·al** *adj.*

**pro·pound´** *vt.* to put forth, as for consideration or solution –**pro·pound´er** *n.*

**pro·pri´e·tar·y** *adj.* pertaining to a proprietor; protected, as by copyright or patent –*n.* ownership –**pro·pri·e·tar´i·ly** *adv.*

**pro·pri´e·tor** *n.* an owner; one having exclusive right to –**pro·pri´e·tor·ship** *n.*

**pro·pri´e·ty** *n.* the mark of good breeding; conformity to society´s standards

**pro·rate´** *vt., vi.* to distribute or divide proportionally

**pro·sa´ic** *adj.* commonplace; mundane, humdrum, or dull –**pro·sa´i·cal·ly** *adv.* –**pro·sa´ic·ness** *n.*

**pro·scribe´** *vt.* to condemn or forbid –**pro·scrip´tion** *n.* –**pro·scrip´tive** *adj.* –**pro·scrip´tive·ly** *adv.*

**prose** *n.* the style of ordinary conversation, in contrast to poetry

**pros´e·cute** *vt.* to initiate legal proceedings; to pursue or carry on so as to complete –**pros´e·cut·a·ble** *adj.* –**pros·e·cu´tion** *n.* –**pros´e·cu·tor** *n.* –**pros·e·cu·to´ri·al** *adj.*

**pros´e·lyte** *n.* one who has been converted –*vt., vi.* to proselytize

**pros´e·lyt·ize** *vt., vi.* to convert, as to a religion, doctrine, or political view –**pros´e·lyt·iz·er** *n.*

**pros´pect** *n.* an expectation or possibility –*vt., vi.* to search or explore

**pro·spec´tive** *adj.* hoped for –**pro·spec´tive·ly** *adv.*

**pro·spec´tus** *n.* a summary, as of the details concerning a venture or investment

**pros´per** *vi.* to thrive; to be financially successful

**pros·per´i·ty** *n.* affluence or wellbeing

**pros´per·ous** *adj.* successful; flourishing –**pros´per·ous·ly** *adv.* –**pros´per·ous·ness** *n.*

**pros´the·sis** *n.* a device intended to replace a missing body part –**pros·thet´ic** *adj.* –**pros·thet´i·cal·ly** *adv.* –**pros·thet´ics** *n.*

**pros´ti·tute** *n.* one who accepts money or other consideration for sex or other base end –*vt.* to use or offer for base purposes –**pros·ti·tu´tion** *n.*

**pros´trate** *adj.* lying prone; submissive; overcome or exhausted –*vt.* to bow down or lie flat, as in submission; to overcome

**pros·tra´tion** *n.* a state of exhaustion or collapse

**pro·tag´o·nist** *n.* the principal or leading character in a story

**pro·tect´** *vt.* to safeguard against damage or harm –**pro·tect´ing·ly** *adv.* –**pro·tec´tion** *n.*

**pro·tec´tive** *adj.* suited to or intended to safeguard –*n.* something that protects –**pro·tec´tive·ly** *adv.* –**pro·tec´tive·ness** *n.*

**pro·tec´tion·ism** *n.* a system of tariffs or quotas designed to protect domestic business from an influx of imported goods; the advocacy of such a system –**pro·tec´tion·ist** *n.*

**pro·tec´tor** *n.* a person or thing that safeguards or protects

**pro´té·gé** *n.* one endorsed by a person of influence

**pro tem** *adv.* pro tempore

**pro tem´po·re** *adv.* temporarily; for the time being

**pro´test** *n.* a declaration or display of disapproval **–pro·test´** *vt.* to object strongly and solemnly **–prot´es·ta´tion** *n.* **–pro·test´er** *n.*

**pro´to·col** *n.* a code of conduct; proper etiquette; ceremony

**pro´to·type** *n.* a model **–pro·to·typ´ic, pro·to·typ´i·cal** *adj.*

**pro·tract´** *vt.* to draw out or prolong **–pro·tract´ed·ly** *adv.* **–pro·tract´ed·ness** *n.* **–pro·trac´tion** *n.* **–pro·trac´tive** *adj.*

**pro·trude´** *vt., vi.* to jut or thrust outward **–pro·trud´ent** *adj.* **–pro·tru´sion** *n.*

**pro·tu´ber·ance** *n.* something that protrudes, as a knob or a swelling **–pro·tu´ber·ant** *adj.* **–pro·tu´ber·ant·ly** *adv.*

**proud** *adj.* full of self-esteem; of vain or arrogant conceit; dignified **–proud´ly** *adv.* **–proud´ness** *n.*

**prove** *vt.* to establish by argument or evidence **–prov·a·bil´i·ty** *n.* **–prov´a·ble** *adj.* **–prov´a·bly** *adv.*

**prov´en** *adj.* verified

**prov´en·der** *n.* supplies or provisions

**prov´erb** *n.* a saying or adage

**pro·ver´bi·al** *adj.* widely alluded to or believed **–pro·ver´bi·al·ly** *adv.*

**pro·vide´** *vt.* to supply or furnish; to stipulate **–pro·vid´er** *n.*

**prov´i·dence** *n.* advance preparation; divine guidance **–prov´i·dent, prov·i·den´tial** *adj.* **–prov·i·den´tial·ly, prov´i·dent·ly** *adv.*

**prov´ince** *n.* an outlying area

**pro·vin´cial** *adj.* crude or unsophisticated **–pro·vin´cial·ism, pro·vin·ci·al´i·ty** *n.* **–pro·vin·cial·i·za´tion** *n.* **–pro·vin´cial·ly** *adv.*

**pro·vi´sion** *n.* an act of providing; supplies provided; a requirement *–vt.* to supply **–pro·vi´sion·er** *n.*

**pro·vi´sion·al** *adj.* temporary **–pro·vi´sion·al·ly** *adv.*

**pro·vi´so** *n.* a stipulation **–pro·vi´so·ry** *adj.*

**prov·o·ca´tion** *n.* something that provokes **–pro·voc´a·tive** *adj.* **–pro·voc´a·tive·ly** *adv.* **–pro·voc´a·tive·ness** *n.*

**pro·voke´** *vt.* to induce, as to action or anger

**pro·vok´ing** *adj.* troubling or vexing **–pro·vok´ing·ly** *adv.*

**prow´ess** *n.* notable skill or daring

**prowl** *vt., vi.* to move stealthily **–prowl´er** *n.*

**prox´i·mal** *adj.* adjacent; nearest **–prox´i·mal·ly** *adv.*

**prox´i·mate** *adj.* approximate **–prox´i·mate·ly** *adv.* **–prox´i·mate·ness** *n.*

**prox·im´i·ty** *n.* nearness

**prox´y** *n.* an agent; the authority to act as agent

**prude** *n.* one overly concerned with propriety **–prud´er·y** *n.* **–prud´ish** *adj.* **–prud´ish·ly** *adv.* **–prud´ish·ness** *n.*

**pru´dence** *n.* caution or good judgement in the conduct of one´s business **–pru´dent, pru·den´tial** *adj.* **–pru·den´tial·ly, pru´dent·ly** *adv.*

**prune** *n.* a partially dried plum *–vt., vi.* to trim or excise that which is superfluous or excessive **–prun´er** *n.*

**pru´ri·ent** *adj.* overly interested in or attracted by sexual matters **–pru´ri·ence, pru´ri·en·cy** *n.* **–pru´ri·ent·ly** *adv.*

**pry** *vi.* to snoop or meddle *–vt.* to force open *–n.* a lever or bar, as for prying open

**pseu´do·nym** *n.* an alias; an artist's fictitious name **–pseu·don´y·mous** *adj.* **–pseu·don´y·mous·ly** *adv.*

**psy´che** *n.* the subconscious mind; the soul

**psych·e·del´ic** *adj.* characterized by hallucination or distortion *n.* a substance that alters awareness **–psych·e·del´i·cal·ly** *adj.*

**psy·chi´a·try** *n.* the diagnosis and treatment of mental disorders **–psy·chi·at´ric** *adj.* **–psy·chi·at´ri·cal·ly** *adv.* **–psy·chi´a·trist** *n.*

**psy´chic** *adj.* mental; relating to exceptional mental processes such as ESP *–n.* a spiritualist **–psy´chi·cal·ly** *adv.*

**psy´cho** *adj.* mentally ill; deranged; psychopathic *–n.* a psychopath

**psy·cho·anal´y·sis** *n.* a type of treatment for mental or emotional disorders **–psy·cho·an´a·lyst** *n.* **–psy´cho·an·a·lyt´ic, psy·cho·an·a·lyt´i·cal** *adj.* **–psy·cho·an·a·lyt´i·cal·ly** *adv.* **–psy·cho·an´a·lyze** *vt.*

**psy´cho·bab·ble** *n.* psychological terminology, used especially in derogation

**psy·cho·log´i·cal** *adj.* touching on the mind or emotions **–psy·cho·log´i·cal·ly** *adv.* **–psy·chol´o·gist** *n.* **–psy·chol´o·gy** *n.*

**psy·cho·path´ic** *adj.* antisocial, aggressive, or perverted **–psy´cho·path** *n.* **–psy·cho·path´i·cal·ly** *adv.*

**psy·cho´sis** *n.* a mental disorder

**psy·cho·so·mat´ic** *adj.* of an illness caused by mental or emotional disorder **–psy·cho·so·mat´i·cal·ly** *adv.*

**psy·cho·ther´a·py** *n.* treatment for a mental or emotional disorder **–psy·cho·ther´a·pist** *n.*

**psy·chot´ic** *adj.* mentally deranged

**pub** *n.* a public house; a tavern

**pub´lic** *adj.* common or shared; of a community **–pub´lic·ly** *adv.*

**pub·li·ca´tion** *n.* printed material; the communication of information

**public house** *(Brit.)* a tavern

**pub·lic´i·ty** *n.* information distributed widely, usually of a promotional nature **–pub´li·cist** *n.* **–pub´li·cize** *vt.*

**pub´lish** *vt.* to promote or broadcast widely; to print and issue *–vi.* to engage in the business of publishing; to have one´s work published **–pub´lish·a·ble** *adj.* **–pub´lish·er** *n.*

**puck´er** *n.* a wrinkle *–vt., vi.* to gather or become gathered into small folds

**puck´ish** *adj.* impish **–puck´ish·ly** *adv.* **–puck´ish·ness** *n.*
**pud´dle** *n.* a small pool of liquid **–pud´dly** *adj.*
**pudg´y** *adj.* chubby; fat **–pudg´i·ness** *n.*
**pu´er·ile** *adj.* childish or juvenile **–pu´er·ile·ly** *adv.* **–pu·er·il´i·ty** *n.*
**puff** *n.* a short breath; a brief gust of air *–vi., vt.* **–puff´i·ly** *adv.* **–puff´i·ness** *n.* **–puff´y** *adj.*
**puff´er·y** *n.* exaggerated praise; promotion
**pu´gi·lism** *n.* the sport of boxing **–pu´gi·list** *n.* **–pu´gi·lis´tic** *adj.*
**pug·na´cious** *adj.* belligerent **–pug·na´cious·ly** *adv.* **–pug·na´cious·ness, pug·nac´i·ty** *n.*
**pul´chri·tude** *n.* great beauty **–pul·chri·tu´di·nous** *adj.*
**pule** *vi.* to whine or whimper
**pull** *n.* allure; influence *–vt.* to apply force to draw toward; to tug; to attract *–vi.* to use force in hauling, dragging, etc.
**pul´ley** *n.* a simple machine for multiplying effort
**pulp** *n.* soft, moist matter *–vt.* to reduce to pulp **–pulp´i·ness** *n.* **–pulp´y** *adj.*
**pul´pit** *n.* a lectern, especially for religious services
**pul´sate** *vi.* to vibrate rhythmically **–pul·sa´tion** *n.* **–pul·sa´tor** *n.* **–pul´sa·to·ry** *adj.*
**pulse** *n.* a rhythmic beating
**pul´ver·ize** *vt.* to crush; to reduce to powder **–pul´ver·iz·able** *adj.* **–pul´ver·i·za´tion** *n.* **–pul´ver·iz·er** *n.*
**pum´mel** *vt.* to beat, especially with the fists
**pump** *n.* a device for moving liquid *–vi., vt.* to pull or push as with a pump; to move up and down as though with a pump handle **–pump´er** *n.*
**pun** *n.* a play on words *–vi.* **–pun´ster** *n.*
**punch** *n.* a tool for piercing or stamping; a fruit beverage *–vt.* to strike, as with a fist
**punc·til´i·ous** *adj.* attentive to detail; precise **–punc·til´i·ous·ly** *adv.* **–punc·til´i·ous·ness** *n.*
**punc´tu·al** *adj.* on time; prompt **–punc·tu·al´i·ty, punc´tu·al·ness** *n.* **–punc´tu·al·ly** *adv.*
**punc·tu·a´tion** *n.* marks in writing to indicate pauses, separations, etc.; a pause or emphasis in speaking **–punc´tu·ate** *vi., vt.* **–punc´tu·a·tor** *n.*
**punc´ture** *vt.* to pierce *–n.* a hole made by piercing
**pun´dit** *n.* a critic or scholar **–pun´dit·ry** *n.*
**pun´gent** *adj.* sharp or biting **–pun´gen·cy** *n.* **–pun´gent·ly** *adv.*
**pun´ish** *vt.* to penalize for an offense **–pun·ish·a·bil´i·ty** *n.* **–pun´ish·a·ble** *adj.* **–pun´ish·er** *n.* **–pun´ish·ment** *n.*
**pu´ni·tive, pu´ni·to·ry** *adj.* inflicting or designed to inflict punishment **–pu´ni·tive·ly** *adv.* **–pu´ni·tive·ness** *n.*
**pu´ny** *adj.* weak or frail **–pu´ni·ness** *n.*
**pu´pil** *n.* a student
**pup´pet** *n.* a small figure with jointed parts moved by strings, the hands, etc.; one controlled by another **–pup´pe·teer´** *n.* **–pup´pet·ry** *n.*
**pup´py** *n.* a small dog
**pur´chase** *n.* a thing bought *–vt.* to buy through exchange **–pur´chas·a·ble** *adj.* **–pur´chas·er** *n.*
**pure** *adj.* free of dirt or pollutants; without fault **–pure´ly** *adv.* **–pure´ness** *n.* **–pu´ri·ty** *n.*
**pu·rée´** *n.* a smooth or blended food product *–vt.* to reduce to a thick smooth paste
**pur´ga·tive** *adj.* tending to cleanse *–n.* a medication used in purging the bowels: a laxative **–pur·ga´tion** *n.*
**pur´ga·to·ry** *n.* a place of banishment or suffering; in theology, a place where the soul is purged of sin **–pur´ga·to´ri·al** *adj.*
**purge** *vt.* to cleanse or purify; to rid of impurities or individuals considered undesirable; *–n.* an act of purification; an action to rid of undesirable elements, as in a government or private organization; to cause evacuation of the bowels
**pu·ri·fi·ca´tion** *n.* an act of cleansing
**pu´ri·fy** *vt.* to free of impurities or defilement **–pu´ri·fi·er** *n.*
**pur´ist** *n.* one committed to being exact or correct **–pu·ris´tic** *adj.*
**pu·ri·tan´i·cal** *adj.* marked by strict morality **–pu·ri·tan´i·cal·ly** *adv.* **–pu·ri·tan´i·cal·ness** *n.*
**pur·loin´** *vi., vt.* to steal
**pur·port´** *vt.* to claim or have intention **–pur·port´ed** *adj.* **–pur·port´ed·ly** *adv.*
**pur´pose** *n.* an aim or goal; an intention
**pur´pose·ful** *adj.* having intent **–pur´pose·ful·ly** *adv.* **–pur´pose·ful·ness** *n.*
**pur´pose·ly** *adv.* with specific intent
**pur´pos·ive** *adj.* serving a purpose **–pur´pos·ive·ly** *adv.* **–pur´pos·ive·ness** *n.*
**purse** *n.* *(Brit.)* a small receptacle used by women to carry currency, credit cards, etc.; *(US)* a woman´s handbag; an award of money *–vt.* to gather in small folds, as the lips to show disapproval
**purs´er** *n.* a ship´s officer responsible for accounts, tickets, freight, etc.
**pur·sue´** *vt.* to chase or hunt; to aspire or strive for **–pur·su´a·ble** *adj.* **–pur·su´er** *n.*
**pur·suit´** *n.* a hunt or chase; an activity, such as a hobby
**pu´ru·lent** *adj.* containing pus **–pu´ru·lence** *n.* **–pu´ru·lent·ly** *adv.*
**pur·vey´** *vt., vi.* to provide **–pur·vey´ance** *n.* **–pur·vey´or** *n.*
**pur´view** *n.* extent, as of capability or authority; range of view or understanding
**push** *vt., vi.* to apply force to; to press *–n.* energy; drive
**push´y** *adj.* aggressive
**pu·sil·lan´i·mous** *adj.* cowardly **–pu·sil·la·nim´i·ty** *n.*

—**pu·sil·lan´i·mous·ly** *adv.*

**put** *vt.* to place; to cause to be placed, as by propelling or thrusting: *put an arrow in the bull's-eye*; to cause or impose: *put them to work* —*vi.* to proceed: *put to sea*

**pu´ta·tive** *adj.* supposed —**pu´ta·tive·ly** *adv.*

**pu·tre·fac´tion** *n.* decomposed organic matter —**pu´tre·fac´tive** *adj.* —**pu´tre·fy** *vi., vt.*

**pu´trid** *adj.* decaying; corrupt; vile or offensive —**pu·trid´i·ty, pu´trid·ness** *n.* —**pu´trid·ly** *adv.*

**put´ter** *n.* a golf club —*vt.* to proceed or work in a dawdling or ineffective manner; to poke about —*vi.* to waste time —**put´ter·er** *n.*

**putz** *n.* a dolt —*vi.* to putter

**puz´zle** *n.* a mystery —*vt.* to baffle or bewilder —**puz´zler** *n.*

**pyre** *n.* a formation of material for burning a dead body

**q, Q** seventeenth letter of the English alphabet

**quack** *n.* the sound of a duck; a bogus or incompetent doctor —**quack´er·y** *n.*

**quad´ran·gle** *n.* a plane figure with four sides; an area enclosed by buildings —**quad·ran´gu·lar** *adj.*

**quad´rant** *n.* a 90° arc; one fourth of a circle

**quad·ra·phon´ic, quad·ri·phon´ic** *adj.* of a four channel sound system

**quad´ri·lat´er·al** *n.* a figure bounded by four sides —*adj.*

**quad·ri·ple´gi·a** *n.* paralysis of the body from the neck down —**quad·ri·ple´gic** *adj., n.*

**quad´ru·ped** *n.* a four-footed animal —**quad´ru·pe·dal** *adj.*

**quad·ru´ple** *adj.* involving four parts —*vt., vi.* to multiply by four —**quad·ru´ply** *adv.*

**quad·rup´let** *n.* one of four born at the same time

**quad´ru·plex** *n.* a dwelling made up of or divided into four living units

**quaff** *vt., vi.* to drink —**quaff´er** *n.*

**quag´mire** *n.* a slough or swamp; a difficult situation

**quaint** *adj.* curious or uncommon; picturesque —**quaint´ly** *adv.* —**quaint´ness** *n.*

**quake** *n.* an earthquake —*vi.* to tremble or shake —**quak´y** *adj.*

**qual´i·fied** *adj.* capable; with limitations, as *qualified approval* —**qual´i·fied·ly** *adv.*

**qual´i·fi·er** *n.* that which limits or modifies

**qual´i·fy** *vi., vt.* to be or make eligible; to describe; to limit —**qual·i·fi·ca´tion** *n.*

**qual´i·ty** *n.* a characteristic or trait; excellence —**qual´i·ta·tive** *adj.* —**qual´i·ta·tive·ly** *adv.*

**qualm** *n.* uneasiness or uncertainty —**qualm´ish** *adj.* —**qualm´ish·ly** *adv.* —**qualm´ish·ness** *n.*

**quan´da·ry** *n.* a dilemma; uncertainty

**quan´ti·fy** *vt.* to express in terms of quantity; to set or devise a limit —**quan·ti·fi´a·ble** *adj.* —**quan·ti·fi´a·bly** *adv.* —**quan·ti·fi·ca´tion** *n.* —**quan´ti·fi·er** *n.*

**quan´ti·tate** *vt.* to determine the quantity of

**quan´ti·ta·tive** *adj.* measurable —**quan´ti·ta·tive·ly** *adv.* —**quan´ti·ta·tive·ness** *n.*

**quan´ti·ty** *n.* an amount; a considerable volume

**quar´an·tine** *n.* a period of isolation, especially to prevent the spread of disease —*vt.* to place or order to be placed in isolation —**quar´an·tin·a·ble** *adj.*

**quar´rel** *n.* a disagreement; an argument —*vt.* —**quar´rel·er, quar´rel·ler** *n.* —**quar´rel·some** *adj.*

**quar´ry** *n.* something pursued; an excavation —*vt.* to dig up, as stone

**quart** *n.* a liquid measure equal to 32 ounces

**quar´ter** *n.* one-fourth; a U.S. or Canadian coin —*vt.* to divide into four parts; to furnish lodging

**quar´ter·ly** *adj.* occurring every three months

**quar·tet´** *n.* a group of four

**quar´to** *n.* a page or book size equal to one-quarter of a sheet

**quash** *vt.* to suppress

**qua´si** *adj.* resembling

**qua´train** *n.* a poem of four lines

**qua´ver** *vi.* to tremble —**qua´ver·ing·ly** *adv.* —**qua´ver·y** *adj.*

**quea´sy** *adj.* nauseated; uneasy or troubled —**quea´si·ly** *adv.* —**quea´si·ness** *n.*

**queen** *n.* a female ruler; wife of a king; the breeding member of a colony of ants, bees, etc. —**queen´ly** *adj., adv.*

**queer** *adj.* strange, unusual; unconventional —**queer´ly** *adv.* —**queer´ness** *n.*

**quell** *vt.* to suppress; to ease or calm

**quench** *vt.* to end or extinguish; to moisten or drench —**quench´a·ble** *adj.* —**quench´er** *n.*

**quer´u·lous** *adj.* complaining; peevish; disgruntled —**quer´u·lous·ly** *adv.* —**quer´u·lous·ness** *n.*

**que´ry** *n.* a question or inquiry —*vt.* to question —**que´ri·er, que´rist** *n.*

**quest** *n.* a search; a journey of exploration —*vi.* to go on a search —**quest´er** *n.*

**ques´tion** *n.* an inquiry; something open to discussion —*vt.* to interrogate; to doubt; to challenge —*vi.* to ask —**ques´tion·er** *n.* —**ques´tion·ing·ly** *adv.*

**ques´tion·a·ble** *adj.* open to question; suspect —**ques·tion·a·bil´i·ty, ques´tion·a·ble·ness** *n.* —**ques´tion·a·bly** *adv.*

**ques´tion·naire´** *n.* a list of questions, as for a survey

**queue** *n.* a waiting line, as of people

**quib´ble** *n.* a petty argument —*vi.* to fret over a trivial matter —**quib´bler** *n.*

**quick** *adj.* swift and abrupt; alert, intelligent —**quick´ly** *adv.* —**quick´ness** *n.*

**quick´en** *vt.* to stimulate; to hasten —*vi.* to move more briskly; to come to life —**quick´en·er** *n.*

**quick´-tem´pered** *adj.* easily angered

**quick´-wit´ted** *adj.* alert; quick to discern **–quick´-wit´ted·ly** *adv.* **–quick´-wit´ted·ness** *n.*
**quid pro quo** an equal exchange
**qui·es´cent** *adj.* still; inactive **–qui·es´cence** *n.* **–qui·es´cent·ly** *adv.*
**qui´et** *adj.* silent; calm; tranquil *–vt.* to still noise; to make serene *–vi.* to become still **–qui´et·ly** *adv.* **–qui´et·ness** *n.*
**qui´e·tude** *n.* a state of tranquillity **–qui·e´tus** *n.*
**quilt** *n.* a thick covering, especially one stuffed with cotton, down, etc. *–vi.* to make such a cover **–quilt´er** *n.*
**qui´nine** *n.* an alkaloid used to treat malaria
**quin·tes´sence** *n.* the essence of a thing **–quin·tes·sen´tial** *adj.* **–quin·tes·sen´tial·ly** *adv.*
**quin·tet´** *n.* a group of five
**quip** *n.* a witty remark, usually spontaneous **–quip´ster** *n.*
**quirk** *n.* an idiosyncrasy **–quirk´i·ly** *adv.* **–quirk´i·ness** *n.* **–quirk´y** *adj.*
**quit** *vi.* to resign; to cease; to leave *–vt.* to discontinue; to relinquish; to leave
**quite** *adv.* totally; absolutely; to a great extent, as *quite nice*
**quiv´er** *n.* vibration *–vi.* to shudder or tremble **–quiv´er·y** *adj.*
**quix·ot´ic** *adj.* idealistic **–quix·ot´i·cal·ly** *adv.*
**quiz** *n.* a short test *–vt.* to question
**quiz´zi·cal** *adj.* curious; puzzling **–quiz´zi·cal·ly** *adv.*
**quo·ta´tion** *n.* a citing of the words or work of another
**quote** *n.* a quotation *–vt.* to repeat the words of another; to cite; to state a price **–quot·a·bil´i·ty** *n.* **–quot´a·ble** *adj.* **–quot´er** *n.*
**quo·tid´i·an** *adj.* commonplace; daily
**quo´tient** *n.* the result of dividing one number by another

**r, R** eighteenth letter of the English alphabet
**rab´bet** *n.* a groove into which an opposing piece fits to form a joint
**rab´bi** *n.* a Jewish scholar **–rab·bin´ic, rab·bin´i·cal** *adj.*
**rab´bin·ate** *n.* the office or function of a rabbi
**rab´ble** *n.* an unruly mob; riffraff
**rab´ble-rous·er** *n.* a troublemaker
**rab´id** *adj.* fanatical; frenzied **–ra·bid´i·ty, rab´id·ness** *n.* **–rab´id·ly** *adv.*
**race[1]** *n.* a group of people linked by appearance, geographical location, etc. **–ra´cial** *adj.* **–ra´cial·ly** *adv.*
**race[2]** *n.* a sporting event decided by speed; any similar rivalry or motion toward an end *–vi.* to take part in a race; to proceed at great speed **–rac´er** *n.*
**rac´ism** *n.* discrimination based on race **–rac´ist** *n.*
**rack** *n.* a frame, stand, etc. to hold something; an instrument of torture; a cut of meat *–vt.* to cause severe distress: *racked by pain*
**rack´et** *n.* a disturbing noise; a criminal activity; an effortless task or job **–rack´ety** *adj.*
**rack´e·teer´** *n.* one operating an illegal business
**rac´on·teur** *n.* a skilled storyteller
**rac´y** *adj.* spirited; risqué or suggestive; lewd **–rac´i·ly** *adv.* **–rac´i·ness** *n.*
**ra´dar** *n.* a device that uses high frequency radio waves to determine the position, speed, etc. of a distant object
**ra´di·ant** *adj.* emitting heat or light; bright, glowing **–ra´di·ance** *n.* **–ra´di·ant·ly** *adv.*
**ra´di·ate** *vi., vt.* to extend from a central point; to emit **–ra'di·a'tion** *n.*
**rad´i·cal** *adj.* deviating from the usual; extreme *–n.* one who advocates extreme change **–rad´i·cal·ism** *n.* **–rad·i·cal·i·za´tion** *n.* **–rad´i·cal·ize** *vt.* **–rad´i·cal·ly** *adv.*
**ra´di·o·ac·tiv´i·ty** *n.* the presence or emission of radiation **–ra·di·o·ac´tive** *adj.*
**ra·di·ol´o·gy** *n.* the medical use of radioactive materials to diagnose and treat disease **–ra·di·o·log´i·cal** *adj.* **–ra·di·ol´o·gist** *n.*
**raff´ish** *adj.* jaunty, fun-loving **–raff´ish·ly** *adv.* **–raff´ish·ness** *n.*
**raft** *n.* a flat-bottomed float; a large number *–vi.* to travel by raft
**raft´er** *n.* one who travels by raft
**raf´ter** *n.* a beam that supports a roof or upper story of a building
**rag** *adj.* made from bits of cloth or a cloth pulp *–n.* a piece of cloth
**rag´a·muf·fin** *n.* a squalid or pitiful child
**rage** *n.* violent anger; passion *–vi.* to speak or act violently
**rag´ged** *adj.* tattered; worn or frayed; rough or uneven **–rag´ged·ly** *adv.* **–rag´ged·ness** *n.* **–rag´ged·y** *adj.*
**ra·gout´** *n.* a spicy stew
**rag´time** *n.* an American music form marked by syncopation
**raid** *n.* an unexpected assault as by an armed force or a business competitor *–vi., vt.* **–raid´er** *n.*
**rail** *n.* a horizontal bar
**rai´ment** *n.* clothing
**rain** *n.* drops of water condensed from the air; anything falling like rain *–vi.* to fall like rain; to furnish in profusion **–rain´y** *adj.*
**raise** *vt.* to move or make higher; to increase; to build **–rais´er** *n.*
**rai·son d´ê´tre** a reason for being
**rake[1]** *n.* a garden tool *–vt.* to scrape, smooth, etc. with a rake; to search carefully
**rake[2]** *n.* a womanizer; a lewd man **–rak´ish** *adj.* –

**rak´ish·ly** *adv.* **–rak´ish·ness** *n.*
**ral´ly** *n.* an assemblage *–vi.* to assemble; to recover from a difficulty
**ram** *n.* a device used to batter or crush *–vt.* to strike heavily; to force or cram into place
**ram´ble** *n.* a leisurely stroll *–vi.* to wander aimlessly **–ram´bler** *n.* **–ram´bling** *adj.* **–ram´bling·ly** *adv.*
**ram·bunc´tious** *adj.* restive; disorderly **–ram·bunc´tious·ly** *adv.* **–ram·bunc´tious·ness** *n.*
**ram·i·fi·ca´tion** *n.* a consequence of an action, problem, etc.
**ramp** *n.* a generally sloping surface that links two levels
**ram´page** *n.* savage or frenzied behavior *–vi.* to act violently **–ram´pag·er** *n.*
**ram´pant** *adj.* uncontrolled; without restraint **–ramp´an·cy** *n.* **–ram´pant·ly** *adv.*
**ram´part** *n.* a fortification or barricade
**ranch** *n.* a large farm for raising stock **–ranch´er** *n.*
**ran´cid** *adj.* of stale or tainted fats **–ran·cid´i·ty, ran´cid·ness** *n.*
**ran´cor** *n.* harsh resentment; animosity **–ran´cor·ous** *adj.* **–ran´cor·ous·ly** *adv.* **–ran´cor·ous·ness** *n.*
**ran´dom** *adj.* lacking order; haphazard **–ran´dom·ly** *adv.* **–ran´dom·ness** *n.*
**ran´dom·ize** *vt.* to arrange haphazardly **–ran·dom·i·za´tion** *n.* **–ran´dom·iz·er** *n.*
**rand´y** *adj.* lascivious; lecherous **–rand´i·ness** *n.*
**range** *n.* reach or scope; the area or extent of an activity, thing, etc.; limits of travel, variation, etc. *–vi.* to wander; to vary within limits
**rang´y** *adj.* tall and thin **–rang´i·ness** *n.*
**rank** *adj.* having an offensive odor; utter or complete as *a rank amateur* *–n.* one's station or position *–vt.* to arrange or place in position
**ran´kle** *vt.* to irritate
**ran´sack** *vt.* to search or seek aggressively
**ran´som** *n.* a payment for release *–vt.* **–ran´som·er** *n.*
**rant** *vi., vt.* to speak wildly, often incoherently **–rant´er** *n.*
**rap** *n.* a light blow, a tapping noise; informal dialogue *–vt.* to strike lightly; to discuss
**ra·pa´cious** *adj.* avaricious or greedy; ravenous **–ra·pa´cious´ly** *adv.* **–ra·pa´cious·ness, ra·pac´i·ty** *n.*
**rap´id** *adj.* swift; occurring with unusual speed **–ra·pid´i·ty** *n.* **–rap´id·ly** *adv.*
**rap·pel´** *vi.* to descend along a vertical surface by means of a rope
**rap·port´** *n.* understanding
**rap·proche·ment´** *n.* reconciliation; the establishing of harmonious relations
**rapt** *adj.* enthralled or engrossed; spellbound **–rapt´ly** *adv.*
**rap´ture** *n.* joy, ecstasy
**rap´tur·ous** *adj.* transported by emotion **–rap´tur·ous·ly** *adv.* **–rap´tur·ous·ness** *n.*
**rare** *adj.* uncommon, unusual; excellent, incomparable **–rare´ly** *adv.* **–rar´i·ty** *n.*
**rar´e·fy** *vi., vt.* to filter or purify; to make less dense
**ras´cal** *n.* a playful rogue; a scoundrel **–ras´cal·ly** *adj.*
**rash** *adj.* impulsive or impetuous; reckless **–rash´ly** *adv.* **–rash´ness** *n.*
**rasp** *n.* a coarse file; a harsh sound *–vt., vi.* to abrade; to speak in a hoarse voice **–rasp´er** *n.* **–rasp´i·ness** *n.* **–rasp´ing·ly** *adv.* **–rasp´ish, rasp´y** *adj.*
**ratch´et** *n.* a mechanism that limits movement of a wheel or bar to a single direction
**rate** *n.* a relative value, as *rate of speed, birth rate,* etc.; a charge or value per unit *–vt.* to place a value on **–rat·a·bil´i·ty, rat´a·ble·ness** *n.* **–rat´a·ble** *adj.* **–rat´a·bly** *adv.* **–rat´ing** *n.*
**rath´er** *adv.* preferably; to some extent; more accurately
**rat´i·fy** *vt.* to approve; to sanction **–rat·i·fi·ca´tion** *n.*
**ra´tio** *n.* a proportional relationship between two similar things
**ra´tion** *n.* an assigned measure, as of food or fuel for a particular undertaking *–vt.* to allot or distribute
**ra´tio·nal** *adj.* sane; able to reason **–ra´tion·al·ly** *adv.* **–ra·tio·nal´i·ty** *n.*
**ra´tio·nale´** *n.* grounds for reasoning; interpretation
**ra´tio·nal·ize** *vt.* to reason; to explain away **–ra·tio·nal·iza´tion** *n.*
**rat´tle** *n.* a chattering sound; a device that produces such a sound *–vi.* to make a chattering sound; to speak rapidly, often carelessly
**rat´ty** *adj.* squalid or shabby
**rau´cous** *adj.* loud and rowdy; boisterous **–rau´cous·ly** *adv.* **–rau´cous·ness** *n.*
**raun´chy** *adj.* sloppy; lewd or obscene **–raun´chi·ly** *adv.* **–raun´chi·ness** *n.*
**rav´age** *n.* devastation *–vi., vt.* to destroy **–rav´ag·er** *n.*
**rave** *vi., vt.* to babble incoherently; to praise
**rav´el** *vi.* to fray or unravel; to become tangled **–rav´el·er** *n.*
**rav´en·ous** *adj.* hungry; insatiable; greedy **–rav´en·ous·ly** *adv.* **–rav´en·ous·ness** *n.*
**raw** *adj.* uncooked; natural, not processed; inexperienced; exposed **–raw´ly** *adv.*
**ray** *n.* a beam or shaft, as of light
**reach** *n.* an extent or range *–vi., vt.* to extend to; to arrive at **–reach´a·ble** *adj.*
**re·act´** *vi.* to respond or reply **–re·ac´tion** *n.*
**re·ac´tion·ar·y** *adj.* in opposition to progress
**re·ac´tive** *adj.* readily responsive to stimulus, especially of chemistry or physics **–re·ac´tive·ly** *adv.* **–re·ac´tive·ness** *n.* **–re·ac´tor** *n.*
**read** *vi., vt.* to study and understand, as written characters or symbols **–read·a·bil´i·ty, read´a·ble´ness** *n.* **–read´a·ble** *adj.* **–read´a·bly** *adv.* **–read´er** *n.*

**read´er·ship** *n.* collectively, the subscribers to a publication

**read´y** *adj.* prepared and available; eager **–read´i·ly** *adv.* **–read´i·ness** *n.*

**re´al** *adj.* genuine; not imaginary. **–re´al·ism** *n.* **–re´al·ist** *n.*

**re´al·is´tic** *adj.* practical; truly representative **–re·al·is´ti·cal·ly** *adv.*

**re·al´i·ty** *n.* the state of being true; acceptance of that which is true

**re´al·ize** *vt.* to recognize as true; to make true: *to realize an objective* **–re·al·iza´tion** *n.*

**re´al·ly** *adv.* truly; exceptionally

**realm** *n.* one's sphere or domain

**re´al·ty** *n.* real estate

**reap** *vi., vt.* to harvest; to gain, as a reward for effort **–reap´er** *n.*

**rear** *n.* back; the position farthest from the front **–***vt.* to care for or raise, as a child

**rea´son** *n.* explanation, as for an action; intellect; a cause to believe **–***vi., vt.* to consider logically; to persuade by logic **–rea´son·er** *n.*

**rea´son·a·ble** *adj.* able to reason; governed by reason **–rea´son·a·ble´ness** *n.* **–rea´son·a·bly** *adv.*

**re´as·sure´** *vt.* to encourage; to restore confidence **–re·as·sur´ance** *n.* **–re·as·sur´ing·ly** *adv.*

**re´bate** *n.* a discount or deduction **–***vt.* **–re´bat·er** *n.*

**reb´el** *n.* one who defies authority **–re·bel´** *vt.* to resist authority or influence

**re·bel´lion** *n.* a show of defiance **–re·bel´lious** *adj.* **–re·bel´lious·ly** *adv.* **–re·bel´lious·ness** *n.*

**re·bound´** *vi.* to bounce back; to recover, as from illness or defeat

**re·buff´** *n.* a rejection or rebuke; a slight or snub **–***vt.*

**re·buke´** *n.* a reprimand **–***vt.*

**re·but´** *vt.* to answer by opposing **–re·but´tal** *n.* **–re·but´ter** *n.*

**re·cal´ci·trant** *adj.* stubbornly defiant **–re·cal´ci·trance, re·cal´ci·tran·cy** *n.*

**re·call´, re´call** *n.* the ability to remember; a calling back, as of workers or a defective product **–re·call´** *vt.* **–re·call´a·ble** *adj.*

**re·cant´** *vt.* to take back, as of a former belief

**re´cap** *n.* a summary **–***vt.* to recapitulate

**re·ca·pit´u·late** *vt.* to summarize **–re·ca·pit·u·la´tion** *n.*

**re·cede´** *vi.* to move back

**re·ceipt´** *n.* proof of payment; a receiving **–***vt., vi.*

**re·ceiv´a·ble** *adj.* awaiting payment; unpaid **–***n.* an outstanding account

**re·ceive´** *vt.* to get, take possession of; to experience or undergo; to make welcome, as a guest **–re·ceiv´er –re·ceiv´er·ship**

**re´cent** *adj.* at a time just earlier than now **–re´cen·cy, re´cent·ness** *n.* **–re´cent·ly** *adv.*

**re·cep´ta·cle** *n.* a container

**re·cep´tion** *n.* a greeting; a social gathering; acceptance

**re·cep´tive** *adj.* able or willing to receive; open-minded **–re·cep´tive·ly** *adv.* **–re·cep´tive·ness, re·cep·tiv´i·ty** *n.*

**re´cess** *n.* a hollow or nook, as in a wall; an intermission **–***vt.* to create a nook **–***vi.* to take a break

**re·ces´sion** *n.* a receding or withdrawal; an economic downturn **–re·ces´sion·ar·y** *adj.*

**re·cid´i·vism** *n.* a reversion to earlier conduct, especially of a criminal **–re·cid´i·vist** *n.* **–re·cid·i·vis´tic, re·cid´i·vous** *adj.*

**rec´i·pe** *n.* instructions, especially for the preparation of food or medication

**re·cip´i·ent** *n.* one who receives **–re·cip´i·ence** *n.*

**re·cip´ro·cal** *adj.* complementary; interdependent **–re·cip´ro·cal·ly** *adv.* **–re·cip´ro·cal·ness** *n.*

**re·cip´ro·cate** *vi., vt.* to give or take in return; to move back and forth **–re·cip·ro·ca´tion** *n.* **–re·cip´ro·ca·tive** *adj.* **–re·cip´ro·ca·tor** *n.*

**rec·i·proc´i·ty** *n.* a mutually beneficial interchange

**re·cit´al** *n.* a public performance, as of music or dance; a detailed chronicling **–re·cit´al·ist** *n.*

**re·cite´** *vt.* to repeat a memorized text; to recount in detail **–rec·i·ta´tion** *n.* **–re·cit´er** *n.*

**reck´less** *adj.* rash; heedless of consequences **–reck´less·ly** *adv.* **–reck´less·ness** *n.*

**reck´on** *vt.* to calculate or consider **–reck´on·er** *n.*

**re·claim** *vt.* to recover by returning to a prior condition, such as for land, or by processing, such as waste that is recycled for a new use **–re·claim´able** *adj.* **–rec·la·ma´tion** *n.*

**re·cline´** *vi.* to lean back or lie down

**rec´luse** *n.* one who lives in seclusion **–re·clu´sion** *n.* **–re·clu´sive** *adj.*

**rec´og·nize** *vt.* to distinguish or identify; to acknowledge, as a claim **–rec·og·ni´tion** *n.* **–rec´og·niz·a·ble** *adj.* **–rec´og·niz·a·bly** *adv.* **–rec´og·niz·er** *n.*

**re·coil´** *vi.* to draw back, as in alarm or fright

**rec·ol·lect´** *vi., vt.* to remember **–rec·ol·lec´tion** *n.*

**rec·om·mend´** *vt.* to advise or endorse **–rec·om·mend´a·ble** *adj.* **–rec·om·men·da´tion** *n.* **–rec·om·mend´er** *n.*

**rec´om·pense** *n.* compensation, as for services rendered or for damages **–***vt.* to repay, as for damages

**rec´on·cile** *vt.* to resolve differences, as between associates, accounts, one's own misgivings, etc. **–rec·on·cil·a·bil´i·ty, rec´on·cil·a·ble·ness** *n.* **–rec´on·cil·a·ble** *adj.***–rec´on·cil·a·bly** *adv.* **–rec´on·cil·er** *n.* **–rec·on·cil·i·a´tion** *n.*

**rec´ord** *n.* a document, registry, etc. used to retain information; the information so retained **–re·cord´** *vt.* to set down information by some permanent means

**re·coup´** *vt.* to regain, as to make up for a loss –**re·coup´a·ble** *adj.* –**re·coup´ment** *n.*
**re·cov´er** *vt.* to regain; to return to a former state –**re·cov´er·a·ble** *adj.*–**re·cov´ery** *n.*
**rec´re·ant** *adj.* disloyal; cowardly –**rec´re·ance, rec´re·an·cy** *n.* –**rec´re·ant·ly** *adv.*
**rec·re·a´tion** *n.* diversion or amusement –**rec·re·a´tion·al** *adj.*
**re·crim·i·na´tion** *n.* the countering of one charge with another –**re·crim´i·na·tive, re·crim´i·na·to·ry** *adj.* –**re·crim´i·na·tor** *n.*
**re·cruit´** *n.* a new member –*vt., vi.* to secure new members, as for the military or for volunteer work –**re·cruit´er** *n.* –**re·cruit´ment** *n.*
**rec´tan·gle** *n.* a plane figure of four sides at right angles to each other –**rec·tan´gu·lar** *adj.*
**rec´ti·fy** *vt.* to correct –**rec´ti·fi·a·ble** *adj.* –**rec·ti·fi·ca´tion** *n.*
**rec´ti·tude** *n.* righteousness
**rec´to** *n.* the right-hand page of a book
**re·cum´bent** *adj.* resting or reclining –**re·cum´bence, re·cum´ben·cy** *n.* –**re·cum´bent·ly** *adv.*
**re·cu´per·ate** *vt., vi.* to recover, as from illness or adversity; to recover after losing, as of money –**re·cu·per·a´tion** *n.* –**re·cu´per·a·tive** *adj.*
**re·cur´** *vi.* to occur again –**re·cur´rence** *n.* –**re·cur´rent** *adj.* –**re·cur´rent·ly** *adv.*
**re·cuse´** *vt.* to seek disqualification from judging or decision-making because of a perceived prejudice or the possibility of conflict of interest
**re·cy´cle** *vt.* to reuse or prepare for reuse –**re·cy´cla·ble** *adj.*
**re·deem´** *vt.* to reclaim or retrieve, as by fulfilling a pledge; to convert, as for stocks or bonds –**re·deem´a·ble** *adj.* –**re·demp´tion** *n.* –**re·demp´tion·al, re·demp´tive, re·demp´to·ry** *adj.*
**re·de·ploy´** *vt.* to move, as men and material, to improve efficacy –**re·de·ploy´ment** *n.*
**red´o·lent** *adj.* suggesting or reminiscent –**red´o·lence, red´o·len·cy** *n.* –**red´o·lent·ly** *adv.*
**re·doubt´a·ble** *adj.* formidable; awe-inspiring –**re·doubt´a·bly** *adv.*
**re·dress´** *n.* remedy for a wrong –*vt.* to set right, as by compensation or punishment –**re·dress´er** *n.*
**re·duce´** *vt.* to diminish or decrease, as in rank, size, strength, etc. –**re·duc´er** *n.* –**re·duc·i·bil´i·ty** *n.*–**re·duc´i·ble** *adj.* –**re·duc´i·bly** *adv.* –**re·duc´tion** *n.*
**re·dun´dant** *adj.* superfluous; unnecessary –**re·dun´dan·cy** *n.* –**re·dun´dant·ly** *adv.*
**reek** *vi.* to emit a stench; to be offensive: *testimony reeking of bias*
**reel** *n.* a device to hold flexible material such as tape or rope; *(Brit.)* a device to hold cotton or thread; a lively dance –*vt.* to wind around a reel –*vi.* to lurch or stagger
**re·fer´** *vt.* to direct to; to assign or attribute to –*vi.* to mention; to make reference to –**re·fer´a·ble** *adj.* –**re·fer´ral** *n.* –**ref´er·ence** *n.*
**ref·er·en´dum** *n.* submission of a public matter to popular vote
**re·fine´** *vt., vi.* to make or become pure, rid of unsuitable elements; to make or become more elegant or polished –**re·fined´** *adj.* –**re·fine·ment** *n.* –**re·fin´er** *n.*
**re·fin´er·y** *n.* an industrial installation for purifying sugar, coal, petroleum, etc.
**re·flect´** *vt.* to mirror; to cast back an image –*vi.* to ponder –**re·flec´tion** *n.* –**re·flec´tion·al** *adj.*
**re·flec´tive** *adj.* tending to cast back an image; given to deep thought –**re·flec´tive·ly** *adv.* –**re·flec´tive·ness** *n.*
**re´flex** *adj.* instinctive –*n.* an involuntary response
**re·form´** *adj.* advocating change: *a reform movement* –*n.* a correction or improvement –*vt.* to correct or improve –**re·form´a·ble** *adj.* –**ref·or·ma´tion** *n.* –**re·for´ma·tive** *adj.* –**re·form´er** *n.*
**re·frac´tion** *n.* the bending of a wave, such as light or sound, from its usual course –**re·fract´** *vt.* –**re·frac´tion·al, re·frac´tive** *adj.* –**re·frac´tive·ly** *adv.* –**re·frac´tive·ness** *n.*
**re·frain´** *n.* an oft repeated phrase or subject –*vi.* to abstain; to hold back from
**re·fresh´** *vt.* to revive or restore –**re·fresh´ing** *adj.* –**re·fresh´ing·ly** *adv.*
**re·fresh´ment** *n.* that refreshes, as food or drink
**re·frig´er·ant** *n.* that which serves to cool
**re·frig´er·ate** *vt.* to make cold; to preserve by cooling –**re·frig·er·a´tion** *n.*
**ref´uge** *n.* a place of safety or shelter –**ref´u·gee** *n.*
**re·ful´gent** *adj.* radiant; glorious –**re·ful´gence, re·ful´gen·cy** *n.* –**re·ful´gent·ly** *adv.*
**re´fund** *n.* a return or repayment –**re·fund´** *vt., vi.* to repay –**re·fund´a·ble** *adj.*
**re·fur´bish** *vt.* to restore or renovate –**re·fur´bish·ment** *n.*
**re·fuse´** *vt., vi.* to decline or deny –**ref´use** *n.* trash or waste –**re·fus´al** *n.*
**re·fute´** *vt.* to disprove; to contradict –**re·fut´a·ble** *adj.* –**re·fut´a·bly** *adv.* –**re·fut´al, ref·u·ta´tion** *n.* –**re·fut´er** *n.*
**re´gal** *adj.* befitting royalty; stately; splendid –**re·gal´i·ty** *n.* –**re´gal·ly** *adv.*
**re·gale´** *vt.* to entertain lavishly –**re·gale´ment** *n.*
**re·ga´lia** *n.* the trappings of royalty; an impressive array
**re·gard´** *n.* respect or admiration; deliberate heed –*vt.* to admire; to observe carefully; to deem to be –*vi.* to heed; to gaze
**re·gard´less** *adj.* disregarding –*adv.* despite
**re·gime´** *n.* a specific government, management,

order, etc.
**reg´i·men** *n.* a system, as of diet, exercise, etc.
**re´gion** *n.* an area with natural or appointed boundaries **–re´gion·al** *adj.* **–re´gion´al·ly** *adv.*
**reg´is·ter** *n.* a record of data; alignment of printed matter; a musical range *–vt., vi.* to record officially or formally; to show: *register disbelief*
**reg·is·tra´tion** *n.* an official recording **–reg´is·trant** *n.* **–reg´is·trar** *n.* **–reg´is·try** *n.*
**re·gress´** *vi.* to move backward; to degenerate **–re·gres´sion** *n.* **–re·gres´sive** *adj.* **–re·gres´sive·ly** *adv.* **–re·gres´sor** *n.*
**re·gret´** *n.* a feeling of sorrow or remorse about something past *–vt.* to feel remorse **–re·gret´ful** *adj.* **–re·gret´ful·ly** *adv.* **–re·gret´ful·ness** *n.*
**re·gret´ta·ble** *adj.* unfortunate **–re·gret´ta·bly** *adv.* **–re·gret´ter** *n.*
**reg´u·lar** *adj.* normal or usual; methodical; periodic; conforming to expectations **–reg·u·lar´i·ty** *n.* **–reg´u·lar·ly** *adv.*
**reg´u·late** *vt.* to control or direct; to adjust **–reg·u·la´tion** *n.* **–reg´u·la·tive, reg´u·la·to·ry.** *adj.* **–reg´u·la·tor** *n.*
**re·gur´gi·tate** *vt.* to disgorge; to throw up **–re·gur·gi·ta´tion** *n.*
**re·ha·bil´i·tate** *vt.* to restore to a former state; to restore to health **–re·ha·bil´i·tant** *n.* **–re·ha·bi´li·ta´tion** *n.*
**re·hearse´** *vt.* to practice **–re·hears´al** *n.*
**re·im·burse´** *vt.* to pay back, as for expense or loss **–re·im·burs´a·ble** *adj.* **–re·im·burse´ment** *n.*
**re·in·car·na´tion** *n.* the belief that after death the soul is reborn in another body
**re·in·force´** *vt.* to strengthen **–re·in·force´ment** *n.*
**re·in·state´** *vt.* to restore, as to use, a former state, etc.
**re·it´er·ate** *vt.* to repeat **–re·it·er·a´tion** *n.* **–re·it´er·a·tive** *adj.* **–re·it´er·a·tive·ly** *adv.*
**re´ject** *n.* one that has been discarded **–re·ject´** *vt.* to refuse; to discard **–re·ject´er, re·jec´tor** *n.* **–re·jec´tion** *n.*
**re·joice´** *vi., vt.* to feel or express joy
**re·join´der** *n.* a response, especially to a challenge
**re·ju´ve·nate** *vt.* to refresh and revitalize **–re·ju·ve·na´tion** *n.* **–re·ju´ve·na·tor** *n.*
**re·lapse´** *n.* regression to a former state, such as a recurrence of an illness during recuperation or after recovery *–vi.* to lapse back, as into illness or addiction
**re·late´** *vt.* to recount or describe; to connect or associate **–re·lat´a·ble** *adj.* **–re·lat´er, re·la´tor** *n.*
**re·lat´ed** *adj.* associated or connected
**re·la´tion** *n.* an association, or one associated, by birth or marriage; a connection, such as cause and effect **–re·la´tion·al** *adj.* **–re·la´tion·ship** *n.*
**rel´a·tive** *adj.* connected or affiliated; comparable *–n.* a family member **–rel´a·tive·ly** *adv.* **–rel·a·tiv´i·ty** *n.*
**re·lax´** *vi., vt.* to ease tension or stress; to be or make less stringent or intense **–re·lax·a´tion** *n.* **–re·lax´ed** *adj.*
**re´lay, re·lay´** *vt.* to transmit; to send forward
**re·lease´** *n.* liberation; a mechanical catch *–vt.* to set free; to issue for publication **–re·leas´er** *n.*
**rel´e·gate** *vt.* to assign, as a task or position, often in the sense of limiting or downgrading **–rel·e·ga´tion** *n.*
**re·lent´** *vi.* to surrender or soften, as a harsh attitude
**re·lent´less** *adj.* unyielding; persistent **–re·lent´less·ly** *adv.*
**rel´e·vant** *adj.* applicable to the matter at hand **–rel´e·vance, rel´e·van·cy** *n.* **–rel´e·vant·ly** *adv.*
**re·li´a·ble** *adj.* dependable **–re·li·a·bil´i·ty, re·li´a·ble·ness** *n.* **–re·li´a·bly** *adv.*
**re·li´ance** *n.* confidence or trust **–re·li´ant** *adj.* **–re·li´ant·ly** *adv.*
**rel´ic** *n.* an artifact; a thing of historical value
**re·lief´** *n.* aid or assistance; alleviation from distress, pain, etc. **–re·liev´a·ble** *adj.* **–re·lieve´** *vt.* **–re·liev´er** *n.*
**re·li´gion** *n.* the belief in a controlling power outside oneself; a system of belief; an order of worship; an obsessive pursuit or cause **–re·li´gious** *adj.* **–re·li´gious·ly** *adv.* **–re·li´gious·ness** *n.*
**re·lin´quish** *vt.* to give up or abandon **–re·lin´quish·er** *n.* **–re·lin´quish·ment** *n.*
**rel´ish** *n.* an appreciation or particular liking; a condiment *–vt.* to enjoy *–vi.* to gratify
**re·luc´tant** *adj.* hesitant or unwilling **–re·luc´tance** *n.* **–re·luc´tant·ly** *adv.*
**re·ly´** *vi.* to trust completely; to depend on, as for help or support **–re·li´er** *n.*
**re·main´** *vi.* to continue unchanged; to stay
**re·main´der** *n.* that left after part has been removed
**re·mark´** *n.* a comment *–vt.* to comment briefly; to notice
**re·mark´a·ble** *adj.* noteworthy; striking or exceptional **–re·mark´a·ble·ness** *n.* **–re·mark´a·bly** *adv.*
**re·me´di·a·ble** *adj.* that can be corrected **–re·me´di·a·ble·ness** *n.* **–re·me´di·a·bly** *adv.*
**re·me´di·al** *adj.* intended to correct **–re·me´di·al·ly** *adv.* **–re·me·di·a´tion** *n.*
**rem´e·dy** *n.* something that corrects *–vt.* to make right
**re·mem´ber** *vi.* to keep in the mind; to retain *–vt.* to recall to mind
**re·mem´brance** *n.* recollection or reminiscence; something that serves to commemorate
**re·mind´** *vt.* to prompt recall **–re·mind´er** *n.*
**rem·i·nisce´** *vi.* to dwell on the past **–rem·i·nis´cence** *n.* **–rem·i·nis´cent** *adj.* **–rem·i·nis´cent·ly** *adv.*–**rem·i·nis´cer** *n.*
**re·miss´** *adj.* negligent or careless in attention to duty **–re·miss´ly** *n.* **–re·miss´ness** *n.*
**re·mis´sion** *n.* a lessening or relief as from pain, etc.

**re·mit´** *vt.* to transfer, as money, for deposit or payment **—re·mit´ta·ble** *adj.* **—re·mit´tance** *n.* **—re·mit´ter** *n.*

**re·mit´tent** *adj.* having temporary relief, as of a disease **—re·mit´tence, re·mit´ten·cy** *n.* **—re·mit´ tent·ly** *adv.*

**rem´nant** *n.* a scrap or piece, especially of fabric; a remaining trace or indication

**re·mon´strate** *vi.* to protest *—vt.* to argue against **—re·mon´strance, re·mon·stra´tion** *n.* **—re·mon´stra·tive** *adj.* **—re·mon´stra·tive·ly** *adv.* **—re·mon´stra·tor** *n.*

**re·morse´** *n.* repentance; sorrow for misconduct **—re·morse´ful** *adj.* **—re·morse´ful·ly** *adv.*

**re·morse´less** *adj.* lacking pity **—re·morse´less·ly** *adv.*

**re·mote´** *adj.* distant; secluded **—re·mote´ly** *adv.* **—re·mote´ness** *n.*

**re·move´** *vt.* to take away *—vi.* to relocate **—re·mov´a·ble** *adj.* **—re·mov´al** *n.* **—re·moved´** *adj.* **—re·mov´er** *n.*

**re·mu´ner·ate** *vt.* to compensate or make payment, as for goods or services **—re·mu´ner·a·ble** *adj.* **—re·mu·ner·a´tion** *n.* **—re·mu´ner·a·tive** *adj.* **—re·mu´ner·a·tive·ly** *adv.* **—re·mu´ner·a·tor** *n.*

**ren´ais·sance´** *n.* a revival or rebirth

**rend** *vt.* to tear apart

**ren´der** *vt.* to give or provide, as for payment or approval; to depict, as by drawing; to express, as by performing; to melt down fat **—ren´der·able** *adj.* **—ren´der·ing** *n.*

**ren´dez·vous** *n.* an arranged meeting; a meeting place *—vi., vt.* to meet or cause to meet at a specific place and time

**ren·di´tion** *n.* performance or interpretation, as of a piece of music

**ren´e·gade** *n.* a rebel or traitor; a defector

**re·nege´** *vi.* to fail to live up to a commitment **—re·neg´er** *n.*

**re·new´** *vt.* to restore; to make new again; to reaffirm or extend, as a license, a contract, etc. **—re·new´a·ble** *adj.* **—re·new´al** *n.*

**re·nounce´** *vt.* to repudiate or deny; to forsake, as a right **—re·nounce´ment, re·nun·ci·a´tion** *n.*

**ren´o·vate** *vt.* to restore or redecorate **—ren·o·va´tion** *n.* **—ren´o·va·tor** *n.*

**re·nowned´** *adj.* celebrated; distinguished **—re·nown´** *n.*

**rent** *n.* payment for occupancy or use *—vi.* to hire out *—vt.* to grant or obtain temporary use for payment **—rent·a·bil´i·ty** *n.* **—rent´a·ble** *adj.* **—rent´al** *n.* **—rent´er** *n.*

**re·nun·ci·a´tion** *n.* a renouncing **—re·nun´ci·a·tive, re·nun´ci·a·to·ry** *adj.*

**re·pair´** *vt.* to restore to good or useable condition; to rectify or make up for *—n.* an assessment of condition: *the house seems to be in good repair* **—re·pair´a·ble** *adj.* **—re·pair´er** *n.*

**rep´a·ra·ble** *adj.* repairable; worthwhile to repair **—rep´a·ra·bly** *adv.*

**rep·a·ra´tion** *n.* compensation for a loss; atonement

**rep´ar·tee´** *n.* witty conversation

**re·past´** *n.* food; a meal

**re·pa´tri·ate** *n.* one returned or reconciled to citizenship, a country, etc. *—vt., vi.* to return or be returned to one's country **—re·pa·tri·a´tion** *n.*

**re·pay´** *vt.* to reimburse or pay back; to refund **—re·pay´a·ble** *adj.* **—re·pay´ment** *n.*

**re·peal´** *vt.* to revoke, as a law **—re·peal´a·ble** *adj.* **—re·peal´er** *n.*

**re·peat´** *vt., vi.* to say or do again **—re·peat´a·ble** *adj.* **—re·peat´ed** *adj.* **—re·peat´ed·ly** *adv.* **—re·peat´er** *n.*

**re·pel´** *vt.* to repulse or ward off; to disgust or offend **—re·pel´lent** *adj.*

**re·pent´** *vi., vt.* to feel remorse or regret; to change one's feelings about **—re·pent´ance** *n.* **—re·pent´ant** *adj.* **—re·pent´ant·ly** *adv.*

**re·per·cus´sion** *n.* backlash; an unexpected consequence of an action **—re·per·cus´sive** *adj.*

**rep´er·toire** *n.* a list of works adopted by a performer or group of performers

**rep·e·ti´tion** *n.* reiteration; the process of repeating **—rep´e·ti´tious, re·pet´i·tive** *adj.* **—rep·e·ti´tious·ly, re·pet´i·tive·ly** *adv.* **—rep´e·ti´tious·ness, re·pet´i·tive·ness** *n.*

**re·place´** *vt.* to put back in place; to substitute or supplant; to return or restore **—re·place´a·ble** *adj.* **—re·place´ment** *n.*

**re·plen´ish** *vt.* to refill **—re·plen´ish·er** *n.* **—re·plen´ish·ment** *n.*

**re·plete´** *adj.* abundant; lavish **—re·plete´ness** *n.* **—re·ple´tion** *n.*

**rep´li·ca** *n.* a copy, often on a reduced scale

**rep´li·cate** *vt.* to repeat or duplicate, as. an experiment; to make copies of **—rep·li·ca´tion** *n.* **—rep´li·ca·tive** *adj.*

**re·ply´** *n.* a response *—vi.* to give an answer; to respond **—re·pli´er** *n.*

**re·port´** *n.* a precise account; a rumor *—vt.* to inform; to present an account of **—re·port´a·ble** *adj.* **—re·port´age** *n.* **—re·port´er** *n.* **—rep·or·to´ri·al** *adj.* **—rep·or·to´ri·al·ly** *adv.*

**re·port´ed·ly** *adv.* according to rumor or hearsay

**re·pose´** *n.* sleep; calm; peacefulness *—vi.* to lie prone **—re·pos´er** *n.* **—re·pose´ful** *adj.* **—re·pose´ful·ly** *adv.*

**re·pos´i·to·ry** *n.* a place for safekeeping; a container

**re·pos·sess´** *vt.* to reclaim, as for nonpayment **—re·pos·ses´sion** *n.*

**rep·re·hen´si·ble** *adj.* deserving blame; wicked **—rep·re·hen·si·bil´i·ty, rep·re·hen´si·ble·ness** *n.* **—rep·re·hen´si·bly** *adv.*

**rep·re·sent´** *vt.* to present a likeness of, to stand in place of, as an agent –**rep·re·sent·a·bil´i·ty** *n.* –**rep·re·sent´a·ble** *adj.* –**rep·re·sen·ta´tion** *n.* –**rep·re·sen·ta´tion·al** *adj.*

**rep·re·sent´a·tive** *adj.* typical; characteristic –*n.* an example; an agent or delegate –**rep·re·sent´a·tive·ly** *adv.*

**re·press´** *vt.* to restrain or control; to quell or curb –**re·press´er, re·pres´sor** *n.* –**re·press´i·ble** *adj.* –**re·pres´sion** *n.*

**re·pres´sive** *adj.* tending to restrain or control excessively, such as by a dictator or government –**re·pres´sive·ly** *adv.* –**re·pres´sive·ness** *n.*

**re·prieve´** *n.* relief; deferment or repeal, as from punishment –*vt.* to suspend temporarily

**rep´ri·mand** *n.* censure; condemnation –*vt.* to admonish or censure

**re·pri´sal** *n.* retaliation

**re·proach´** *n.* condemnation; disgrace –*vt.* to criticize or rebuke –**re·proach´a·ble** *adj.* –**re·proach´a·bly** *adv.* –**re·proach´ful** *adj.* –**re·proach´ful·ly** *adv.* –**re·proach´ful·ness** *n.*

**rep´ro·bate** *adj.* perverted –*n.* an immoral person –**rep·ro·ba´tion** *n.* –**rep´ro·ba·tive** *adj.*

**re´pro·duce´** *vt.* to copy or duplicate; to propagate –**re·pro·duc´tion** *n.*–**re·pro·duc´tive** *adj.*

**re·proof´** *n.* disapproval

**re·prove´** *vt.* to criticize; to admonish –**re·prov´al** *n.* –**re·prov´ing** *adj.* –**re·prov´ing·ly** *adv.*

**re·pub´lic** *n.* a government controlled by the people or their representatives –**re·pub´li·can** *adj., n.* –**re·pub´li·can·ism** *n.*

**re·pu´di·ate** *vt.* to reject or disavow; to disown –**re·pu·di·a´tion** *n.* –**re·pu´di·a·tive** *adj.* –**re·pu´di·a·tor** *n.*

**re·pug´nance, re·pug´nan·cy** *n.* a feeling of dislike or repulsion

**re·pug´nant** *adj.* offensive; revolting –**re·pug´nant·ly** *adv.*

**re·pulse´** *vt.* to fend off or repel, as an attack; to spurn by insolence or indifference –**re·pul´sion** *n.*

**re·pul´sive** *adj.* offensive; repugnant –**re·pul´sive·ly** *adv.* –**re·pul´sive·ness** *n.*

**rep´u·ta·ble** *adj.* of good reputation –**rep·u·ta·bil´i·ty** *n.* –**rep´u·ta·bly** *adv.*

**rep·u·ta´tion** *n.* one's standing; the way in which one is regarded by others; prominence or notoriety

**re·pute´** *n.* reputation –*vt.* to deem or consider as –**re·put´ed** *adj.* –**re·put´ed·ly** *adv.*

**re·quest´** *n.* an entreaty; something asked for –*vt.* to express a desire for –**re·quest´er** *n.*

**re·quire´** *vt.* to need; to demand or oblige: *we require a deposit* –**re·quire´ment** *n.* –**re·quir´er** *n.*

**req´ui·site** *adj.* required –*n.* that which is necessary or obligatory –**req´ui·site·ly** *adv.*

**req·ui·si´tion** *n.* a formal request –**req·ui·si´tion·er** *n.*

**re·quite´** *vt.* to repay or compensate; to return in kind –**re·quit´a·ble** *adj.* –**re·quit´al** *n.*

**re·scind´** *vt.* to repeal; to nullify –**re·scind´a·ble** *adj.* –**re·scind´ment** *n.*

**res´cue** *vt.* to liberate; to set free –**res´cu·a·ble** *adj.* –**res´cu·er** *n.*

**re·search´** *n.* scientific examination; deliberate study –**re·search´a·ble** *adj.* –**re·search´er** *n.*

**re·sem´blance** *n.* similarity to –**re·sem´ble** *vt.*

**re·sent´** *vt.* to take offense, as at an insult or slight –**re·sent´ful** *adj.*–**re·sent´ful·ly** *adv.* –**re·sent´ful·ness** *n.* –**re·sent´ment** *n.*

**res·er·va´tion** *n.* something withheld; an agreement to hold, as a table at a restaurant; something set aside, as land for special use; hesitance or misgivings

**re·serve´** *n.* restraint; caution; something set aside –*vt.* to set aside –**re·serv´a·ble** *adj.* –**re·serv´ed** *adj.*–**re·serv´ed·ly** *adv.* –**re·serv´ed·ness** *n.*

**res´er·voir** *n.* a reserve supply, as of water or oil

**re·side´** *vi.* to inhabit; to live in

**res´i·dence** *n.* one's home –**res´i·den·cy** *n.* –**res´i·dent** *adj., n.* –**res´i·den´tial** *adj.*

**res´i·due** *n.* a remainder –**re·sid´u·al** *adj., n.* –**re·sid´u·al·ly** *adv.*

**re·sign´** *vt.* to renounce or give up; to accept as unavoidable –**res·ig·na´tion** *n.*

**re·sign´ed** *adj.* complacent; submissive –**re·sign´ed·ly** *adv.* –**re·sign´ed·ness** *n.*

**re·sil´ience, re·sil´ien·cy** *n.* flexibility –**re·sil´ient** *adj.* –**re·sil´ient·ly** *adv.*

**re·sist´** *vt.* to defy or oppose; to withstand –**re·sist´er** *n.* –**re·sist´i·ble** *adj.* –**re·sist´i·bly** *adv.*

**re·sis´tive** *adj.* tending to or marked by resistance: *plants resistive to drought* –**re·sis´tive·ly** *adv.* –**re·sis´tive·ness** *n.*

**re·sist´ance** *n.* any force tending to hinder or oppose; the capacity of an organism to ward off harmful substances –**re·sist´ant** *adj.*

**res´o·lute** *adj.* determined –**res´o·lute·ly** *adv.* –**res´o·lute·ness** *n.*

**res·o·lu´tion** *n.* determination; an outcome; a formal pronouncement; visual clarity

**re·solve´** *n.* a sense of purpose; determination –*vt.* to decide: *resolve to be neater,* to solve; to end successfully –**re·solv·a·bil´i·ty** *n.*–**re·solv´a·ble** *adj.* –**re·solv´ed·ly** *adv.* –**re·solv´er** *n.*

**res´o·nant** *adj.* sonorous; resounding –**res´o·nance** *n.* –**res´o·nant·ly** *adv.* –**res´o·nate** *vi.*–**res·o·na´tion** *n.*

**re·sort´** *n.* a vacation retreat; a resource –*vt.* to fall back on

**re·sound´** *vi.* to echo; to reverberate –**re·sound´ing** *adj.* –**re·sound´ing·ly** *adv.*

**re´source** *n.* that available for use, as means for production, inner strength, property, etc.

**re·source´ful** *adj.* clever or imaginative –**re·source´ful·ly** *adv.* –**re·source´ful·ness** *n.*

**re·spect´** *n.* esteem or admiration; consideration: *a respect for power*; a feature or detail: *alike in many respects* —*vt.* to admire or esteem; to consider —**re·spect´er** *n.* —**re·spect´ful** *adj.* —**re·spect´ful·ly** *adv.* —**re·spect´ful·ness** *n.*

**re·spect´a·ble** *adj.* worthy of esteem; conventional —**re·spect·a·bil´i·ty, re·spect´a·ble·ness** *n.* —**re·spect´a·bly** *adv.*

**re·spec´tive** *adj.* specific or distinct —**re·spec´tive·ly** *adv.*

**res·pi·ra´tion** *n.* the process of breathing —**res´pi·ra·to·ry** *adj.*

**res´pite** *n.* a short rest

**re·splen´dent** *adj.* brilliant, sparkling —**re·splen´dence, re·splen´den·cy** *n.* —**re·splen´dent·ly** *adv.*

**re·spond´** *vi.* to answer; to react: *respond to treatment* —**re·spon´dence, re·spon´den·cy** *n.* —**re·spon´dent** *adj.*

**re·sponse´** *n.* a reply or reaction

**re·spon´si·ble** *adj.* accountable for one's actions; capable of acting alone —**re·spon·si·bil´i·ty** *n.* —**re·spon´si·ble·ness** *n.* —**re·spon´si·bly** *adv.*

**re·spon´sive** *adj.* tending to respond or react, as to advice, learning, etc. —**re·spon´sive·ly** *adv.* —**re·spon´sive·ness** *n.*

**rest** *n.* relaxation; a pause; a remainder —*vi., vt.* to relax; to lie against or on —**rest´ful** *adj.* —**rest´ful·ly** *adv.* —**rest´ful·ness** *n.*

**res´tau·rant** *n.* a public eating place —**res´tau·ra·teur´** *n.*

**res·ti·tu´tion** *n.* restoration; compensation

**res´tive** *adj.* impatient —**res´tive·ly** *adv.* —**res´tive·ness** *n.*

**rest´less** *adj.* uneasy; impatient; unable or unwilling to rest —**rest´less·ly** *adv.* —**rest´less·ness** *n.*

**re·stor´a·tive** *adj.* having power to restore; corrective —*n.* a substance that restores health or well-being: a tonic —**re·stor´a·tive·ly** *adv.* —**re·stor´a·tive·ness** *n.*

**re·store´** *vt.* to return to a former condition, position, etc.; to make amends —**res·to·ra´tion** *n.* —**re·stor´er** *n.*

**re·strain´** *vt.* to check or hold back; to confine —**re·strain´a·ble** *adj.*

**re·straint´** *n.* control or restriction

**re·strict´** *vt.* to limit —**re·strict´ed** *adj.* —**re·stric´tion** *n.*

**re·stric´tive** *adj.* serving to restrict or limit —**re·stric´tive·ly** *adv.* —**re·stric´tive·ness** *n.*

**re·sult´** *n.* an effect, as of an action —*vi.* to follow as an outcome of —**re·sult´ant** *adj.*

**re·sume´** *vt.* to begin again after an interruption —**re·sum´a·ble** *adj.* —**re·sump´tion** *n.*

**ré´su·mé** *n.* *(Brit.)* a summary or summing up; *(US)* a description of one's qualifications for employment

**re·sur´gence** *n.* a renewal or reawakening —**re·sur´gent** *adj.*

**res·ur·rect´** *vt.* to restore or revive, as a past strategy or custom —**res·ur·rec´tion** *n.* —**res·ur·rec´tion·al** *adj.* —**res·ur·rec´tor** *n.*

**re·sus´ci·tate** *vt., vi.* to revive —**re·sus´ci·ta·ble** *adj.* —**re·sus·ci·ta´tion** *n.*

**re´tail** *n.* the sale of goods directly to consumers —*vt.* to sell in small quantity, direct to the consumer —*adj., adv.* —**re´tail·er** *n.*

**re·tain´** *vt.* to keep in one's possession; to remember; to hire, as an attorney, by paying a fee —**re·tain´a·ble** *adj.*

**re·tain´er** *n.* a fee paid to engage or reserve services; a servant

**re·tal´i·ate** *vi., vt.* to repay in kind; to avenge —**re·tal·i·a´tion** *n.* —**re·tal´i·a·tive, re·tal´i·a·to·ry** *adj.* —**re·tal´i·a·tor** *n.*

**re·tard´** *n.* a slowing —*vt.* to impede the course of —**re·tard´er** *n.*

**re·ten´tion** *n.* memory; the ability to keep and hold —**re·ten´tive** *adj.* —**re·ten´tive·ly** *adv.* —**re·ten´tive·ness** *n.*

**ret´i·cent** *adj.* restrained or reserved; hesitant —**ret´i·cence** *n.* —**ret´i·cent·ly** *adv.*

**ret´i·nue** *n.* a group of followers

**re·tire´** *vi., vt.* to withdraw or be removed, as from a field of battle, from an occupation, or at the end of a day —**re·tired´** *adj.* —**re·tir·ee´** *n.* —**re·tire´ment** *n.*

**re·tir´ing** *adj.* withdrawn

**re·tort´** *n.* a sharp reply —*vt., vi.* to respond —**re·tort´er** *n.*

**re·tract´** *vt., vi.* to take back, as an accusation —**re·tract·a·bil´i·ty, re·tract·i·bil´i·ty** *n.* —**re·tract´a·ble, re·tract´i·ble** *adj.* —**re·trac´tion** *n.*

**ret·ri·bu´tion** *n.* compensation; reward or punishment

**re·trieve´** *vt.* to regain —**re·triev·a·bil´i·ty** *n.* —**re·triev´a·ble** *adj.* —**re·triev´al** *n.* —**re·triev´er** *n.*

**ret´ro** *adj.* of things past; retroactive

**ret·ro·ac´tive** *adj.* applying to a prior period —**ret´ro·ac´tion** *n.* —**ret·ro·ac´tive·ly** *adv.*

**ret´ro·grade** *adj.* opposite; regressing to a prior state

**ret´ro·gress** *vi.* to revert to an earlier state —**ret·ro·gres´sion** *n.* —**ret·ro·gres´sive** *adj.* —**ret·ro·gres´sive·ly** *adv.*

**ret´ro·spect** *n.* a reflection of things past; a look back —**ret·ro·spec´tion** *n.* —**ret·ro·spec´tive** *adj.* —**ret·ro·spec´tive·ly** *adv.*

**re·turn´** *adj.* of a coming back or reciprocating —*n.* a thing brought or sent back; a profit —*vi., vt.* to go or send back; to yield, as a profit; to revert to a former owner —**re·turn´a·ble** *adj.* —**re·turn·ee´** *n.*

**re·un´ion** *n.* a gathering of former members: *a class reunion*

**re·vamp´** *vt.* to reorganize or renovate

**re·veal´** *vt.* to expose or disclose

**rev´el** *vi.* to delight in; to carouse *–n.* a celebration **–rev´el·er, rev´el·ler** *n.* **–rev´el·ry** *n.*

**rev·e·la´tion** *n.* something revealed; sudden inspiration or understanding

**re·venge´** *n.* reprisal or retribution *–vt.* to retaliate **–re·venge´ful** *adj.* **–re·venge´ful·ly** *adv.*

**rev´e·nue** *n.* income; gross receipts

**re·ver´ber·ant** *adj.* tending to or characterized by reverberation **–re·ver´ber·ant·ly** *adv.*

**re·ver´ber·ate** *vt.* to resound or echo repeatedly **–re·ver·ber·a´tion** *n.* **–re·ver´ber·a·tive** *adj.* **–re·ver´ber·a·tor** *n.*

**re·vere´** *vt.* to regard with awe; to venerate **–rev´er·ence** *n.* **–rev´er·ent** *adj.* **–rev´er·en´tial** *adj.* **–rev´er·ent·ly** *adv.*

**rev´er·ie** *n.* idle contemplation; daydreaming

**re·verse´** *adj.* backward; opposite *–n.* an opposite side, condition, etc.; misfortune *–vt.* to change to the opposite, as of a movement, a decision, etc. **–re·ver´sal** *n.* **–re·vers·i·bil´i·ty, re·vers´i·ble·ness** *n.* **–re·vers´i·ble** *adj.* **–re·vers´i·bly** *adv.*

**re·vert´** *vi.* to return to previous condition **–re·ver´sion** *n.* **–re·vert´er** *n.* **–re·vert´i·ble** *adj.*

**re·view´** *n.* a reexamination; a critique or criticism *–vt.* to reconsider or restudy **–re·view´a·ble** *adj.* **–re·view´er** *n.*

**re·vile´** *vt.* to berate verbally **–re·vile´ment** *n.* **–re·vil´er** *n.* **–re·vil´ing·ly** *adv.*

**re·vise´** *vt.* to change or modify **–re·vis´a·ble** *adj.* **–re·vis´al** *n.* **–re·vis´er** *n.* **–re·vi´sion** *n.* **–re·vi´sion·ar·y** *adj.*

**re·vive´** *vt., vi.* to restore to consciousness or life; to bring or come back into use **–re·viv´al** *n.*

**re·voke´** *vt.* to nullify or repeal **–rev´o·ca·ble, re·vok´a·ble** *adj.* **–rev·o·ca´tion** *n.* **–rev´o·ca·to·ry** *adj.* **–re·vok´er** *n.*

**re·volt´** *n.* a rebellion *–vi.* to oppose or rebel; to disgust **–re·volt´er** *n.***–re·volt´ing** *adj.* **–re·volt´ing·ly** *adv.*

**rev·o·lu´tion** *n.* rotation; an abrupt, radical change **–rev·o·lu·tion·ar´i·ly** *adv.* **–rev´o·lu´tion·ar·y** *adj.* **–rev·o·lu´tion·ist** *n., adj.* **–rev·o·lu´tion·ize** *vt.*

**re·volve´** *vi.* to rotate; to turn on an axis

**re·vue´** *n.* a musical comedy show

**re·vul´sion** *n.* a sudden aversion or abhorrence **–re·vulsed´** *adj.* **–re·vul´sive** *adj.*

**re·ward´** *n.* compensation, as for a commendable act – *vt.* to recompense **–re·ward´a·ble** *adj.* **–re·ward´ing** *adj.*

**rhap´so·dy** *n.* a state of ecstasy; excessive enthusiasm; an elegant literary or musical work **–rhap·sod´ic, rhap·sod´i·cal** *adj.* **–rhap·sod´i·cal·ly** *adv.* **–rhap´so·dist** *n.***–rhap´so·dize** *vt., vi.*

**rhet´o·ric** *n.* the art of effective speaking or writing; pretentious, vacuous speech **–rhe·tor´i·cal** *adj.* **–rhe·tor´i·cal·ly** *adv.* **–rhet·o·ri´cian** *n.*

**rhyme** *n.* a similarity in the sounds of words; verse with lines ending in words that sound similar *–vi., vt.* **–rhym´er** *n.*

**rhythm** *n.* regular cadence or accent; the harmonious pattern of a work **–rhyth´mic, rhyth´mi·cal** *adj.* **–rhyth´mi·cal·ly** *adv.*

**rib´ald** *adj.* marked by vulgar humor **–rib´al·dry** *n.*

**rib´bon** *n.* a thin strip of material used for tying, for decoration, etc. **–rib´boned** *adj.* **–rib´bon·y** *adj.*

**rich** *adj.* wealthy; plentiful; elegant or lavish **–rich´es** *n.* **–rich´ly** *adv.* **–rich´ness** *n.*

**rick´et·y** *adj.* wobbly

**rid** *vt.* to release or free from **–rid´dance** *n.* **–rid´der** *n.*

**rid´dle** *n.* a puzzle *–vt.* to perforate

**ride** *vi.* to be conveyed; seeming to be conveyed: *riding on a cloud* **–rid´er** *n.* **–rid´ing** *n.*

**rid´i·cule** *n.* words or action intended to mock; derision *–vt.* to make fun of

**ri·dic´u·lous** *adj.* absurd; deserving of ridicule – **ri·dic´u·lous·ly** *adv.***–ri·dic´u·lous·ness** *n.*

**rife** *adj.* abundant

**ri´fle** *n.* a firearm *–vt.* to search through or plunder

**rift** *n.* a fracture or tear

**right** *adj.* fitting and proper; equitable; accurate; lawful *–adv.* exactly; quite *–n.* that which is proper; privilege *–vt.* to correct **–right´ful** *adj.* **–right´ful·ly** *adv.* **–right´ful·ness** *n.* **–right´ly** *adv.*

**right´eous** *adj.* moral; virtuous **–righ´teous·ly** *adv.* **–righ´teous·ness** *n.*

**rig´id** *adj.* stiff; inflexible **–ri·gid´i·ty** *n.* **–rig´id·ly** *adv.* **–rig´id·ness** *n.*

**rig´or** *(US)* *n.* harshness; hardship **–rig´or·ous** *adj.* **–rig´or·ous·ly** *adv.* **–rig´or·ous·ness** *n.*

**rig´our** *(Brit.)* *n.* harshness; hardship **–rig´or·ous** *adj.* **–rig´or·ous·ly** *adv.* **–rig´or·ous·ness** *n.*

**rile** *vt.* to anger; to irritate or vex

**rim** *n.* a border or edge

**rind** *n.* a firm covering, as on fruit or bacon

**ring** *n.* a circular object, area, shape, etc.; a group or gang: *an extortion ring*

**ring´let** *n.* a lock of hair

**rinse** *n.* a liquid used in washing, to remove soap, to color the hair, etc. *–vt.* **–rins´a·ble, rins´i·ble** *adj.* **–rins´er** *n.*

**ri´ot** *n.* a public disturbance involving a large group of people; an eruption, as of merriment or revelry *–vi.* **–ri´ot·er** *n.* **–ri´ot·ous** *adj.* **–ri´ot·ous·ly** *adv.* **–ri´ot·ous·ness** *n.*

**rip** *n.* a tear or split *–vt.*

**ripe** *adj.* mature; fully developed **–ripe´ly** *adv.* **–rip´en** *vt., vi.* **–ripe´ness** *n.*

**rip´ple** *n.* a small wave or wave-like motion *–vi.* – **rip´ply** *adj.*

**rise** *vi.* to move or proceed upward; to increase, as in price, intensity, etc.; to get up, as from a chair or bed; to emerge or originate **–ris´er** *n.* **–ris´ing** *adj.*

**risk** *n.* possible hazard or danger; the probability for loss, as by an investor, a lender, an insurer, etc. **–risk´i·ness** *n.* **–risk´y** *adj.*

**ris·qué´** *adj.* lewd or suggestive

**rite** *n.* a ritual or ceremony

**rit´u·al** *n.* an observance; a formality; an orderly procedure *–adj.* **–rit´u·al·ism** *n.* **–rit´u·al·ist** *n.* **–rit´u·al·is´tic** *adj.* **–rit´u·al·is´ti·cal·ly, rit´u·al·ly** *adv.* **–rit´u·al·ize** *vt.* **–rit·u·al·i·za´tion** *n.*

**ri´val** *n.* one in competition with another *–vt.* to equal or exceed *–adj.* competing **–ri´val·rous** *adj.* **–ri´val·ry** *n.*

**rive** *vt.* to split or tear apart

**riv´er** *n.* a large body of naturally flowing water; an abundant flow **–sell down the river** to betray

**riv´et** *n.* a fastener used to join metal plates *–vt.* to join with a rivet; to fasten firmly; to attract and hold the attention of **–riv´et·er** *n.*

**road** *n.* a course for the passage of vehicles, etc.; any real or imagined course: *the road to ruin* **–road´way** *n.*

**roam** *vt., vi.* to wander or move about **–roam´er** *n.*

**roar** *n.* a deep, prolonged cry; a burst of laughter *–vi., vt.*

**roar´ing** *adj.* flourishing or robust **–roar´ing·ly** *adv.*

**roast** *vt.* to cook with dry heat; to subject to excessive heat; to deride *–n. (US)* a cut of meat; a gathering; derision *–adj.* **–roast´er** *n.*

**rob** *vt.* to take or withhold unjustly **–rob´ber** *n.* **–rob´ber·y** *n.*

**robe** *n.* a loose flowing garment; a dressing gown

**ro´bot** *n.* a device that can be programmed to perform a variety of tasks; one who functions mechanically **–ro·bot´ic** *adj.*

**ro·bot´ics** *n.* the scientific study of robots; the creation of robots

**ro·bust´** *adj.* strong and healthy **–ro·bust´ly** *adv.* **–ro·bust´ness** *n.*

**rock** *n.* a hard natural formation; a firm support: *he's been a rock in these difficult times* *–vi., vt.* to wobble or sway

**rock´y** *adj.* containing or suggesting rock; unsteady; difficult or discouraging, as though moving over rocks **–rock´i·ness** *n.*

**ro·co´co** *n.* an ornate style of architecture, music, etc.

**rod** *n.* a thin straight shaft

**rogue** *n.* a scoundrel; a mischievous person; an abnormal plant or animal **–rogu´er·y** *n.* **–rogu´ish** *adj.* **–rogu´ish·ly** *adv.* **–rogu´ish·ness** *n.*

**roil** *vt.* to disturb or stir up **–roil´y** *adj.*

**role** *n.* a part for an actor; the behavior or attention to duty expected of a person

**roll** *n.* a cylinder, as of film, tape, etc.; a small piece of baked bread; a registry; a rocking motion *–vi., vt.* to move or cause to move by turning; anything that suggests such movement: *get the program rolling, the clouds rolled by* **–roll´er** *n.*

**rol´lick·ing** *adj.* playful; boisterous **–rol´lick·ing·ly** *adv.* **–rol´lick.some, rol´lick·y** *adj.*

**ro·mance´** *n.* a passionate fondness, such as infatuation or love; a fascination; a fantasy or fictional account *–vi., vt.* **–ro·manc´er** *n.*

**ro·man´tic** *adj.* characterized by thoughts or feelings of infatuation, idealism, etc.; visionary; impractical *–n.* **–ro·man´ti·cal·ly** *adv.*

**ro·man´ti·cize** *vt.* to regard as romantic **–ro·man·ti·ci·za´tion** *n.*

**romp** *vi.* to frolic or play *–n.* noisy frolic; an easy victory **–romp´er** *n.*

**roof** *n.* a top covering; an upper surface *–vt.* **–roof´er** *n.*

**room** *n.* adequate space; a divided area within a structure *–vi.* to occupy a room **–room´er** *n.*

**room´y** *adj.* spacious; having adequate space **–room´i·ness** *n.*

**root** *n.* the base of a plant that usually grows underground; a base, source, or core; a mental or emotional attachment *–vi., vt.* **–root´er** *n.*

**ros´ter** *n.* a list

**ros´trum** *n.* a speaker's platform

**ros´y** *adj.* bright and flushed, as a rose; optimistic

**rot** *n.* decomposition; silliness *–vi.* to decay or disintegrate **–rot´ten** *adj., adv.* **–rot´ten·ly** *adv.* **–rot´ten·ness** *n.*

**ro´tate** *vt., vi.* to revolve; to proceed by turns **–ro´tat·a·ble** *adj.* **–ro·ta´tion** *n.* **–ro·ta´tion·al** *adj.*

**rote** *n.* a method for learning by repetition

**ro·tund´** *adj.* round; plump **–ro·tun´di·ty** *n.*

**rough** *adj.* of a coarse or irregular surface; crude or impolite; difficult; disorderly **–rough´en** *vt.* **–rough´en·er** *n.* **–rough´ly** *adv.* **–rough´ness** *n.*

**round** *adj.* curved; of a curved shape, as a circle, globe, cylinder, etc.; full-toned; approximate: *a round number* *–n.* an accumulation, as *a round of drinks, a round of activities,* etc. **–round´ed** *adj.* **–round´ed·ness, round´ness** *n.*

**round´a·bout** *adj.* circuitous or indirect: *a roundabout answer*

**rouse** *vi., vt.* to awaken or cause to wake; to excite to action **–rous´er** *n.* **–rous´ing** *adj.* **–rous´ing·ly** *adv.*

**rout** *n.* a defeat; disorderly flight *–vt.* to defeat or put to flight

**route** *n.* a road or course; an itinerary *–vt.* to send or direct by a certain course **–rout´er** *n.*

**rou·tine´** *adj.* usual or customary *–n.* a regular procedure **–rou·tine´ly** *adv.* **–rou·tin´ize** *vt.*

**rove** *vi., vt.* to wander **–rov´er** *n.*

**row** *n.* a continuous line; a disturbance *–vt.*
**row´dy** *adj.* clamorous; disorderly *–n.* a ruffian – **row´di·ly** *adv.* **–row´di·ness** *n.* **–row´dy·ism** *n.*
**rub** *vi., vt.* to stroke using pressure *–n.* a pitfall
**rub´bish** *n.* trash; nonsense **–rub´bish·y** *adj.*
**rub´ble** *n.* stone fragments **–rub´bly** *adj.*
**rub´down** *n.* a massage
**rude** *adj.* ill-mannered; unrefined; crude, primitive **–rude´ly** *adv.* **–rude´ness** *n.*
**ru´di·ment** *n.* a basic component **–ru·di·men´tal** *adj.*
**ru·di·men´ta·ry** *adj.* fundamental; embryonic **–ru·di·men·ta´ri·ly** *adv.* **–ru·di·men´ta·ri·ness** *n.*
**rue** *vi., vt.* to regret **–rue´ful** *adj.* **–rue´ful·ly** *adv.* **–rue´ful·ness** *n.*
**ruf´fi·an** *n.* a hoodlum or tough
**ruf´fle** *n.* a frilled trim *–vi.* to rumple or wrinkle; to irritate or annoy
**rug´ged** *adj.* sturdy; strong; tempestuous **–rug´ged·ly** *adv.* **–rug´ged·ness** *n.*
**ru´in** *n.* total destruction *–vt.* to destroy utterly **–ru´in·ous** *adj.* **–ru´in·ous·ly** *adv.*
**rule** *n.* a governing authority; regulation; a generally accepted condition or course of action *–vi., vt.* to direct and control; to judge or decree **–rul´a·ble** *adj.* **–rul´er** *n.*
**rum´ble** *n.* a deep undulating sound *–vi.* **–rum´bler** *n.* **–rum´bling·ly** *adv.* **–rum´bly** *adj.*
**ru´mi·nate** *vi., vt.* to ponder; consider intensely **–ru·mi·na´tion** *n.* **–ru´mi·na·tive** *adj.* **–ru´mi·na·tive·ly** *adv.* **–ru´mi·na·tor** *n.*
**rum´mage** *vt.* to search thoroughly; to disorganize while inspecting **–rum´mag·er** *n.*
**ru´mor** *n.* gossip; unconfirmed news **–ru´mor·mon·ger** *n.*
**rum´ple** *vt.* to wrinkle **–rum´ply** *adj.*
**run** *n.* an indefinite period: *for the run of the play*; ordinary: *run of the mill –vi.* to move swiftly; to move or operate: *the motor runs smoothly*; to flow, as liquid from a container; to extend: *the road runs up to the house, the trees run along the road*, etc. **–run´ner** *n.* **–run´ning** *adj., n.*
**rup´ture** *n.* a break *–vt., vi.* to break apart
**ru´ral** *adj.* of the country **–ru´ral·ly** *adv.*
**ruse** *n.* a ploy or stratagem
**rush** *n.* abrupt motion; haste; a swell of emotion *–vi.* to move quickly
**rus´tic** *adj.* rural; unsophisticated **–rus´ti·cal·ly** *adv.*
**rus´tle** *vt., vi.* to make a soft crackling sound
**rut** *n.* a groove worn into a path or roadway **–rut´ty** *adj.*
**ruth´less** *adj.* lacking pity or compassion **–ruth´less·ly** *adv.* **–ruth´less·ness** *n.*

**s, S nineteenth letter of the English alphabet**
**sab·bat´i·cal** *n.* a leave of absence, often a paid leave for travel and research
**sa´ber** *n.* a curved sword
**sa·bot´** *n.* a wooden shoe
**sab´o·tage** *n.* destructive action to obstruct or defeat an enemy *–vi., vt.* **–sab´o·teur´** *n.*
**sa´chem** *n.* a Native American chieftain
**sa·chet´** *n.* a small perfumed parcel used to freshen the clothing in drawers or closets
**sack** *n.* a bag for holding loose articles; dismissal from a job *–vt.* to plunder; to dismiss
**sac´ra·ment** *n.* a traditional religious rite **–sac·ra·men´tal** *adj.* **–sac·ra·men´tal·ly** *adv.*
**sa´cred** *adj.* deserving of reverence or respect **–sa´cred·ly** *adv.***–sa´cred·ness** *n.*
**sac´ri·fice** *n.* an offering *–vt.* to give something valued for a thing considered more valuable: *she sacrificed her career to raise a family* **–sac´ri·fi·cer** *n.* **–sac·ri·fi´cial** *adj.* **–sac·ri·fi´cial·ly** *adv.* **–sac´ri·fic·ing·ly** *adv.*
**sac´ri·lege** *n.* desecration or disrespect of that considered sacred **–sac·ri·le´gious** *adj.* **–sac·ri·le´gious·ly** *adv.* **–sac·ri·le´gious·ness** *n.*
**sac´ro·sanct** *adj.* sacred or hallowed **–sac´ro·sanc´ti·ty** *n.*
**sad** *adj.* unhappy; sorrowful or downhearted; somber; dire or unfortunate: *a sad state of affairs* **–sad´den** *vi., vt.* **–sad´ly** *adv.* **–sad´ness** *n.*
**sa´dism** *n.* the achieving of satisfaction by inflicting pain on others; a psychological disorder **–sa´dist** *n.* **–sa·dis´tic** *adj.* **–sa·dis´ti·cal·ly** *adv.*
**sa·fa´ri** *n.* a journey, especially for hunting
**safe** *adj.* free from risk or danger *–n.* a repository for protecting property **–safe´ly** *adv.* **–safe´ty** *n.*
**safe´guard** *n.* something that protects, as a mechanism, a preventive measure, a clause in a contract, etc. *–vt.* to protect
**sag** *vi.* to droop or slump
**sa·ga´cious** *adj.* discerning; wise **–sa·ga´cious·ly** *adv.* **–sa·ga´cious·ness** *n.* **–sa·gac´i·ty** *n.*
**sage** *adj.* wise and discerning **–sage´ly** *adv.* **–sage´ness** *n.*
**saint** *n.* one recognized as being extremely virtuous **–saint´ed** *adj.* **–saint´li·ness** *n.* **–saint´ly** *adj.*
**sake** *n.* reason or purpose: *for the sake of argument*; self-interest; *for the sake of his career*
**sal´a·ble, sale´a·ble** *adj.* marketable
**sa·la´cious** *adj.* arousing sexual desire; lascivious – **sa·la´cious·ly** *adv.* **–sa·la´cious·ness, sa·lac´i·ty** *n.*
**sal´a·ry** *n.* fixed wages **–sal´a·ried** *adj.*
**sale** *n.* the exchange of goods or services for money **–sales´man, sales´per·son, sales´wom·an** *n.*
**sa´li·ent** *adj.* important or conspicuous; protruding **–sa´lience** *n.* **–sa´li·ent·ly** *adv.*
**sa´line** *adj.* consisting of or characteristic of salt; salty **–sa·lin´i·ty** *n.*
**sal´low** *adj.* of a sickly or pasty complexion **–sal´low·**

**ness** *n.*
**sal´ly** *n.* a sudden assault; an excursion; a witty remark —*vi.* to rush out suddenly or energetically
**sa·lon´** *n.* a large room or gallery for receiving guests; a fashionable social or intellectual gathering
**sal´sa** *n.* a spicy sauce
**salt** *n.* a crystalline substance used to season or preserve food, or as medication; table salt —*vt.* to add salt; to treat with a salt; to disperse throughout: *salted the report with statistics*
**salt´y** *adj.* containing too much salt; spirited or risqué, as *salty language* —**salt´i·ly** *adv.* —**salt´i·ness** *n.*
**sa·lu´bri·ous** *adj.* healthy or wholesome —**sa·lu´bri·ous·ly** *adv.* —**sa·lu´bri·ous·ness, sa·lu´bri·ty** *n.*
**sal´u·tar·y** *adj.* beneficial —**sal·u·tar´i·ly** *adv.* —**sal´u·tar·i·ness** *n.*
**sal·u·ta´tion** *n.* a greeting —**sal·u·ta´tion·al** *adj.*
**sa·lute´** —*n.* an act or form of greeting; a gesture of welcome or honor: *a salute to a great poet* —*vt.* to greet; to honor, as with a gesture of respect
**sal´vage** *n.* property saved from destruction —*vt.* to retrieve for future use —**sal´va·ble, sal´vage·a·ble** *adj.* —**sal·vage·a·bil´i·ty** *n.* —**sal´vag·er** *n.*
**salve** *n.* an ointment —*vt.* to alleviate or remedy, as by soft words or apology
**same** *adj.* identical
**same´ness** *n.* monotony; a lack of diversity
**sam´ple** *n.* a representative part; an example —*vt.* to test by tasting
**sa´mu·rai** *n.* a Japanese warrior class
**san·a·tar´i·um, san·a·to´ri·um** *n.* a hospital or retreat for therapy or fitness
**sanc·ti·mo´ni·ous** *adj.* pretentiously pious —**sanc·ti·mo´ni·ous·ly** *adv.* —**sanc·ti·mo´ni·ous·ness** *n.* **sanc´ti·mo·ny** *n.*
**sanc´tion** *n.* authorization or permission; a penalty for nonconformity —*vt.* to approve; to punish for transgression
**sanc´tu·ar·y** *n.* a sacred place; an asylum
**san´dal** *n.* an open shoe held on with straps
**sane** *adj.* having a sound mind —**sane´ly** *adv.* **sane´ness** *n.*
**san´guine** *adj.* optimistic; confident; of a red or ruddy color —**san´guine·ly** *adv.* —**san´guine·ness** *n.*
**san´i·tar´i·um** *n.* a sanatorium
**san´i·tar·y** *adj.* uncontaminated; free of germs
**san·i·ta´tion** *n.* the process of maintaining sanitary conditions; a local agency responsible for the removal of garbage
**san´i·tize** *vt.* to make sanitary
**san´i·ty** *n.* soundness of mind
**sans** *prep.* without
**sap´i·ent** *adj.* wise —**sap´i·ence** *n.* —**sap´i·ent·ly** *adv.*
**sar´casm** *n.* a caustic rejoinder intended to ridicule —**sar·cas´tic** *adj.* —**sar·cas´ti·cal·ly** *adv.*
**sar·coph´a·gus** *n.* a stone coffin
**sar·don´ic** *adj.* sarcastic —**sar·don´i·cal·ly** *adv.*
**sar·to´ri·al** *adj.* of a clothier or clothing —**sar·to´ri·al·ly** *adv.*
**sash** *n.* a band of cloth worn as a belt or a mark of rank; a frame for a window pane
**sa·shay´** *n.* an overly casual or showy style of movement —*vi.*
**sas´sy** *adj.* insolent, disrespectful; spirited, jaunty —**sass** *n., vt.*
**sa·tan´ic, sa·tan´i·cal** *adj.* wicked; diabolic —**sa·tan´i·cal·ly** *adv.*
**sate** *vt.* satiate
**sat´el·lite** *n.* a celestial body that orbits a planet; a dependency, as a community or nation that is dominated or dependent on another
**sa´ti·a·ble** *adj.* that can be satisfied —**sa·ti·a·bil´i·ty** *n.* —**sa´ti·a·bly** *adv.*
**sa´ti·ate** *vt.* to satisfy completely —**sa·ti·a´tion** *n.*
**sat´ire** *n.* a literary work that uses mockery or ridicule to expose human frailty —**sa·tir´ic, sa·tir´i·cal** *adj.* —**sa·tir´i·cal·ly** *adv.* —**sat´i·rist** *n.*—**sat´i·rize** *vt.*
**sat·is·fac´tion** *n.* gratification; fulfillment, as of an obligation —**sat·is·fac´to·ri·ly** *adv.* —**sat´is·fac´to·ry** *adj.*
**sat´is·fy** *vt.* to fulfill, as a desire or promise; to convince or persuade; to pacify —*vi.* to be sufficient —**sat´is·fied** *adj.* —**sat´is·fi·er** *n.* —**sat´is·fy·ing·ly** *adv.*
**sa´trap** *n.* a petty official
**sat´u·rate** *vt.* to soak or fill completely —**sat´u·rant** *n.* —**sat´u·rat·ed** *adj.* —**sat·u·ra´tion** *n.* —**sat´u·ra·tor** *n.*
**sa´tyr** *n.* a mythical creature, part man and part goat —**sa·tyr´ic, sa·tyr´i·cal** *adj.*
**sauce** *n.* a seasoned liquid or condiment served with food; a gravy
**sau´cy** *adj.* impudent; pert —**sau´ci·ly** *adv.* —**sau´ci·ness** *n.*
**saun´ter** *vi.* to stroll leisurely —**saun´ter·er** *n.*
**sau·té´** *vt.* to fry lightly
**sav´age** *adj.* uncivilized; vicious, ferocious —*n.* a rude or unruly person —*vt.* to attack —**sav´age·ly** *adv.* —**sav´age·ness** *n.* —**sav´age·ry** *n.*
**save** *vt.* to rescue from danger or destruction; to set aside for the future; to conserve —**sav´able** *adj.* —**sav´er** *n.*
**sa´vor** *n.* a characteristic flavor or quality —*vt.* to season; to taste; ro relish, enjoy —**sa´vor·er** *n.* —**sa´vor·y** *adj.*
**say** *vt.* to speak; to express in words; to allege —*vi.* to speak
**saying** *n.* a maxim or axiom
**scab´bard** *n.* a sheath for a weapon
**scab´rous** *adj.* roughened; difficult to handle tactfully; salacious —**scab´rous·ly** *adv.* —**scab´rous·ness** *n.*
**scaf´fold** *n.* a raised platform; a temporary structure for workmen —**scaf´fold·ing** *n.*
**scal´a·wag** *n.* a worthless person; a rascal

**scald** *vt., vi.* to burn or become burned or cleaned with hot liquid or steam –*n.*

**scale**[1] *n.* a protective plate covering certain fish, reptiles, etc. –*vt., vi.* to strip of scales; to form scales **–scal´y** *adj.* **–scal´i·ness** *n.*

**scale**[2] *vt., vi.* to ascend; to climb **–scal´er** *n.* **–scal´a·ble** *adj.*

**scal´lop** *n.* any of various hinged shell mollusks; an ornamental edging **–scal´loped** *adj.* **–scal´lop·er** *n.*

**scalp** *n.* the skin at the top and back of the head –*vt.* to buy and resell tickets for a profit **–scalp´er** *n.*

**scal´pel** *n.* a surgical knife

**scamp** *n.* a rogue or rascal; a scalawag; an impish child **–scamp´ish** *adj.* **–scamp´ish·ness** *n.*

**scam´per** *vi.* to run quickly

**scan** *vt.* to examine closely; to glance at **–scan´ner** *n.*

**scan´dal** *n.* injury to one's reputation; malicious gossip **–scan´dal·ous** *adj.* **–scan´dal·ous·ly** *adv.* **–scan´dal·ous·ness** *n.*

**scan´dal·ize** *vt.* to shock; to outrage morally **–scan·dal´i·za´tion** *n.*

**scant** *adj.* meager; a bit less than **–scant´ly** *adv.* **–scant´ness** *n.*

**scant´y** *adj.* too little; insufficient; less than necessary **–scant´i·ly** *adv.* **–scant´i·ness** *n.*

**scar** *n.* a mark left after healing

**scarce** *adj.* rare; unusual; insufficient **–scar´ci·ty, scarce´ness** *n.* **–scarce´ly** *adv.*

**scare** *vt.* to frighten –*vi.* to take fright **–scar´i·ly** *adv.* **–scar´y** *adj.*

**scarf** *n.* a cloth band worn as a garment; a table runner

**scarp** *n.* a steep slope

**scathe** *vt.* to criticize severely; to denounce **–scath´ing** *adj.* **–scath´ing·ly** *adv.*

**sca·tol´o·gy** *n.* the study of excrement **–scat·o·log´ic, scat·o·log´i·cal** *adj.*

**scat´ter** *vt.* to throw about; to disperse –*vi.* to separate and depart **–scat´tered** *adj.* **–scat´ter·er** *n.*

**scav´enge** *vt.* to forage; to scrounge **–scav´eng·er** *n.*

**sce·nar´io** *n.* an outline of a dramatic work

**scene** *n.* a locality or area; a setting for a drama

**sce´ner·y** *n.* landscape; a theater backdrop

**sce´nic** *adj.* of a beautiful natural vista **–sce´ni·cal·ly** *adv.*

**scent** *n.* an odor or aroma; a fragrance **–scent´ed** *adj.*

**scep´ter** *n.* a wand or staff denoting authority

**sched´ule** *n.* *(US)* a timetable; *(Brit.)* a plan or list of appointments, social activities, etc.; a detailed plan –*vt.* to plan to take place at a specified time

**sche´ma** *n.* a summary or diagram

**sche·mat´ic** *adj.* relating to a scheme –*n.* a diagram **–sche·mat´i·cal·ly** *adv.*

**scheme** *n.* a plan or program; a plot –*vt., vi.* to plan or plot **–schem´er** *n.*

**schism** *n.* a division into factious groups **–schis·mat´ic** *adj.* **–schis·mat´i·cal·ly** *adv.*

**schol´ar** *n.* a learned person; an authority **–schol´ar·ly** *adj.*

**schol´ar·ship** *n.* learning; financial or other aid to a student

**scho·las´tic, scho·las´ti·cal** *adj.* pertaining to education **–scho·las´ti·cal·ly** *adv.*

**school** *n.* an educational institution; a congregation of fish –*vi.* to come together in a school

**school'ing** *n.* formal instruction; classroom instruction

**sci´ence** *n.* knowledge gained by observation and experiment **–sci·en·tif´ic** *adj.* **–sci·en·tif´i·cal·ly** *adv.* **–sci´en·tist** *n.*

**scim´i·tar** *n.* a curved saber

**scin·til´la** *n.* a trace

**scin´til·late** *vi.* to be witty; to sparkle **–scin´til·lat·ing** *adj.* **–scin´til·lat·ing·ly** *adv.* **–scin·til·la´tion** *n.*

**sci'on** *n.* a descendant

**scoff** *vi.* to address scornfully **–scoff´er** *n.*

**scold** *vt., vi.* to find fault –*n.* a nag **–scold´er** *n.*

**sconce** *n.* an ornamental bracket

**scoop** *n.* an implement for measuring or dipping; a ladle –*vt.* to dip with a scoop

**scope** *n.* a range of view or action

**scorch** *vt.* to burn slightly –*n.* the mark of a burn

**score** *n.* points in a game or test; written music; a group of 20

**scorn** *n.* a feeling of contempt –*vt.* to treat with contempt **–scorn´ful** *adj.* **–scorn´ful·ly** *adv.* **–scorn´ful·ness** *n.*

**scotch** *vt.* to wound; to suppress

**scoun´drel** *n.* an unscrupulous person; a villain

**scour** *vt.* to clean thoroughly; to brighten by rubbing

**scourge** *n.* a whip; severe punishment; anything causing suffering –*vt.* to flog or otherwise punish **–scourg´er** *n.*

**scout** *n.* one sent out to get information –*vt.* to spy upon

**scowl** *n.* an angry or gloomy aspect –*vi.* to wrinkle the brow; to look threatening or angry –*vt.* to express by scowling **–scowl´er** *n.* **–scowl´ing·ly** *adv.*

**scrag´gly** *adj.* uneven, irregular

**scram´ble** *vi.* to move in a disorderly manner –*vt.* to mix hurriedly or haphazardly –*n.* a struggle **–scram´bler** *n.*

**scrap** *n.* a fragment; a quarrel –*vt.* to discard –*vi.* to quarrel –*adj.* waste; fragmentary

**scrape** *vt.* to rub so as to abrade; to gather with effort –*n.* the act, effect, or noise of scraping; a difficult situation; a fight **–scrap´er** *n.*

**scrap´py** *adj.* very competitive; tough **–scrap´pi·ly** *adv.* **–scrap´pi·ness** *n.*

**scratch** *vt.* to mark with something sharp; to scrape lightly as to relieve itching; to write hurriedly; to cancel or withdraw *–vi.* to manage with difficulty *–n.* a mark or sound of scratching *–adj.* hasty or haphazard **–scratch´er** *n.* **–scratch´i·ly** *adv.* **–scratch´i·ness** *n.* **–scratch´y** *adj.*

**scrawl** *n.* irregular or illegible writing *–vt., vi.* to write hastily **–scrawl´er** *n.*

**scrawn´y** *adj.* lean and bony **–scrawn´i·ness** *n.*

**scream** *n.* a piercing cry *–vt., vi.* to cry out, as in pain or terror **–scream´er** *n.* **–scream´ing·ly** *adv.*

**screech** *n.* a shrill cry; any similar sound: the screech of brakes **–screech´er** *n.* **–screech´i·ness** *n.* **–screech´y** *adj.*

**screed** *n.* a prolonged tirade; a harangue

**screen** *n.* a light partition; a fine mesh; something that conceals or protects; a curtain for projecting images *–vt.* to conceal; to sift; to classify **–screen´er** *n.*

**screw** *n.* a threaded mechanical device for joining or affixing *–vt., vi.* to tighten or fasten

**scrib´ble** *vt.* to write hastily *–n.* **–scrib´bler** *n.*

**scribe** *n.* a clerk or public writer

**scrim** *n.* a lightweight fabric

**scrimp** *vt., vi.* to be economical; to skimp

**scrip** *n.* writing; an instrument of entitlement, as to stock, property or money

**script** *n.* cursive writing; the text of a play **–script´er** *n.*

**scrip´ture** *n.* sacred writings **–scrip´tur·al** *adj.* **–scrip´tur·al·ly** *adv.*

**scriv´en·er** *n.* a scribe or notary

**scroll** *n.* a parchment roll

**scrounge** *vt., vi.* to scavenge; to forage **–scroung´er** *n.*

**scrub** *vt., vi.* to rub vigorously *–n.* stunted growth **–scrub´bi·ness** *n.* **–scrub´by** *adj.*

**scruff** *n.* the nape of the neck

**scruff'y** *adj.* shabby, seedy

**scrump´tious** *adj.* delicious; elegant **–scrump´tious·ly** *adj.* **–scrump´tious·ness** *n.*

**scru´ple** *n.* reluctance fostered by disapproval **–scru´pu·lous** *adj.* **–scru´pu·lous·ly** *adv.* **–scru´pu·lous·ness** *n.*

**scru´ti·nize** *vt.* to examine carefully; to observe **–scru´ti·niz·er** *n.* **–scru´ti·ny** *n.*

**scuf´fle** *n.* a disorderly struggle *–vi.* to struggle; to drag one's feet

**sculp´ture** *n.* a three-dimensional work of art *–vt.* to fashion or manufacture such a work **–sculp´tor** *n.*

**scum** *n.* impure matter on the surface of a liquid; a low contemptible person **–scum´mi·ness** *n.* **scum´my** *adj.*

**scur´ril·ous** *adj.* grossly offensive; abusive: *a scurrilous attack* **–scur´ril·ous·ly** *adv.* **–scur´ril·ous·ness** *n.*

**scur´ry** *vi.* to move hurriedly; to scamper

**scut´tle** *n.* a small covered opening or hatchway *–vt.* to wreck or destroy; to sink a ship; to move like a crab

**sea** *n.* a great body of salt water; the ocean; anything vast

**seal** *n.* an impression made on a document attesting to its authenticity; a decorative stamp *–vt.* to close securely or permanently **–seal´able** *adj.* **–seal´er** *n.*

**seam** *n.* a visible junction between parts

**seam´y** *adj.* unpleasant; depraved or base; squalid **–seam´i·ness** *n.*

**sé´ance** *n.* a sitting; a meeting to seek communication from the spirit of the dead

**sear** *vt.* to dry up or wither; to scorch *–adj.* withered

**search** *vt.* to look through thoroughly; to seek out *–n.* **–search´a·ble** *adj.* **–search´er** *n.*

**search´ing** *adj.* examining thoroughly: *a searching investigation*; observant or penetrating: *a searching look* **–search´ing·ly** *adj.* **–search´ing·ness** *n.*

**sea´son**[1] *n.* a division of the year; a time of special activity, as *baseball season* **–sea´son·al** *adj.* **–sea´son·al·ly** *adv.*

**sea´son**[2] *vt.* to add spices, etc. to food; to improve or make fit by aging **–sea´son·ing** *n.*

**sea´son·a·ble** *adj.* in keeping with or usual for the season or time; practical for the season **–sea´son·a·ble·ness** *n.* **–sea´son·a·bly** *adv.*

**seat** *n.* something to sit on; the place where a thing is situated: *the seat of government* *–vt.* to put in a sitting position or on a seat; to accommodate: *the room will seat 30 people*; to set firmly or establish in a place

**seat´ing** *n.* the seats available: *seating for fifty*; the arrangement of seats, as in a theater: *balcony seating* **–seat´er** *n.*

**sea´wor·thy** *adj.* of a boat that is in fit condition and ready for use **–sea´wor·thi·ness** *n.*

**se·cede´** *vt.* to formally withdraw **–se·ced´er** *n.*

**se·ces´sion** *n.* the act of seceding **–se·ces´sion·al** *adj.* **–se·ces´sion·ism** *n.* **–se·ces´sion·ist** *n.*

**se·clude´** *vt.* to set or keep apart; to isolate

**se·clud´ed** *adj.* separated; protected **–se·clud´ed·ly** *adv.* **–se·clud´ed·ness** *n.*

**se·clu´sion** *n.* solitude; retirement **–se·clu´sive** *adj.* **–se·clu´sive·ly** *adv.* **–se·clu´sive·ness** *n.*

**sec´ond** *n.* a unit of time; an angular measure; a formal attendant, as in a duel; something of inferior quality *–adj.* of a brief time; next in order; of lesser value *–vt.* to formally support

**sec´ond·ar·y** *adj.* of second rank **–sec´on·dar·ily**

**se´cret** *adj.* kept hidden; esoteric; not revealed, as *a secret partner*; mysterious *–n.* a mystery; something known to only a few **–se´cre·cy, se´cret·ness** *n.* **–se´cret·ly** *adv.*

**sec´re·tary** *n.* one who deals with correspondence and clerical business; an official responsible for record keeping in a business or other organization; the head of a government department; a type of writing desk **–sec´re·tar´i·al** *adj.*

**se·crete´** *vt.* to conceal; to hide away; to form and

release, as digestive fluids **—se·cre´tion** *n.*

**se´cre·tive** *adj.* disposed to secrecy **—se´cre·tive·ly** *adv.* **—se´cre·tive·ness** *n.*

**sect** *n.* a separate group, especially a religious or philosophical faction broken away from a larger order **—sec·tar´i·an** *adj.* **—sec·tar´i·an·ism** *n.*

**sec´tion** *n.* a separate part; the act of separating by cutting *—vt.* to divide into parts **—sec´tion·al** *adj.*

**sec´tor** *n.* a section, especially of a military position

**sec´u·lar** *adj.* worldly; temporal; not controlled by or concerned with religion **—sec´u·lar·ism** *n.* **—sec´u·lar·ist** *n.* **—sec·u·lar·is´tic** *adj.*

**sec´u·lar·ize** *vt.* to convert from sacred to secular use

**se·cure´** *adj.* unlikely to the threatened or overcome; confident *—vt.* to protect; to make certain; to obtain **—se·cur´a·ble** *adj.* **—se·cur´er** *n.* **—se·cure´ly** *adv.* **—se·cure´ness** *n.*

**se·cur´i·ty** *n.* the state of being secure; persons responsible for the protection of others, as in a building, shopping mall, etc.; measures calculated to provide for protection; something pledged for payment of a debt

**se·dan´** *n.* a closed automobile **—sedan chair** a closed chair with poles at the side for carrying

**se·date´** *adj.* composed; dignified *—vt.* to calm with medication **—se·date´ly** *adv.* **—se·date´ness** *n.*

**sed´a·tive** *adj.* tending to calm *—n.* a medicine that serves to calm **—se·da´tion** *n.*

**sed´en·tary** *adj.* inactive; characterized by sitting **—sed´en·tar´i·ly** *adv.* **—sed´en·tar´i·ness** *n.*

**sed´i·ment** *n.* matter that settles to the bottom of a liquid; fragmentary material deposited by water, ice, etc. **—sed´i·men´ta·ry** *adj.* **—sed·i·men·ta´tion** *n.*

**se·di´tion** *n.* resistance or action against lawful authority **—se·di´tious** *adj.* **—se·di´tious·ly** *adv.* **—se·di´tious·ness**

**se·duce´** *vt.* to lead astray: *seduced by quick profit*; to tempt or entice into a wrong **—se·duc´er** *n.* **—se·duce´a·ble, se·duc´i·ble** *adj.* **—se·duc´tion** *n.*

**se·duc´tive** *adj.* tending to seduce **—se·duc´tive·ly** *adv.* **—se·duc´tive·ness** *n.*

**sed´u·lous** *adj.* diligent; industrious **—sed´u·lous·ly** *adv.* **—sed´u·lous·ness** *n.*

**see** *vt.* to view with the eyes; to perceive with the mind; to encounter: *I often see her*; to be certain: *see that you go* *—vi.* to exercise the power of sight; to comprehend; to be attentive

**seed** *n.* the ovule that produces a plant; the origin of anything; any small granular fruit *—vt.* to plant; to spread, as with seeds; to remove the seeds from **—seed´er** *n.*

**seed´y** *adj.* overflowing with seeds; gone to seed; shabby **—seed´i·ly** *adv.* **—seed´i·ness**

**seek** *vt.* to go in search of; to strive for **—seek´er** *n.*

**seem** *vi.* to appear to be

**seem´ing** *adj.* projecting a false appearance: *her seeming indifference hides her pain* *—n.* outward appearance **—seem·ing·ly** *adj.* **—seem´ing·ness** *n.*

**seem´ly** *adj.* proper; decorous **—seem´li·ness** *adv.*

**seep** *vi.* to gradually diffuse; to penetrate through small openings **—seep´age** *n.*

**se´er** *n.* a prophet; one who foretells the future

**seethe** *vi.* to boil; to be agitated, as by rage

**seg´ment** *n.* a distinct part; a part cut off *—vt., vi.* to cut or separate into parts **—seg·men´tal** *adj.* **—seg·men´tal·ly** *adv.* **—seg´men·tar·y** *adj.*

**seg´re·ga·ble** *adj.* that can be separated: *segregable expenses*

**seg´re·gate** *vt.* to isolate or separate from a larger group *—adj.* separated or set apart **—seg·re·ga´tion** *n.* **—seg´re·ga·tive** *adj.*

**seg·re·ga´tion·ist** *n.* one who believes in the separation of races, as in housing, schools, and work

**se´gue** *vi.* to move smoothly from one element to another, as *the segue from daylight to dusk*

**seis´mic, seis´mi·cal** *adj.* pertaining to earthquakes

**seis´mo·graph** *n.* an instrument for recording movements in the earth's crust **—seis´mo·graph´ic** *adj.* **—seis·mog´ra·pher** *n.* **—seis·mog´ra·phy** *n.*

**seis·mol´o·gy** *n.* the study of earthquakes and related phenomena **—seis·mo·log´ic, seis·mo·log´i·cal** *adj.* **—seis·mo·log´i·cal·ly** *adv.* **—seis·mol´o·gist** *n.*

**seize** *vt.* to grasp suddenly and forcefully; to understand; to take possession by force; to take immediate advantage **—seiz´a·ble** *adj.* **—seiz´er** *n.*

**sei´zure** *n.* the act of seizing; a sudden attack or incapacitation, as by an illness

**sel´dom** *adv.* infrequently; at widely spaced intervals *—adj.* infrequent or rare **—sel´dom·ness** *n.*

**se·lect´** *vt., vi.* to choose *—adj.* superior to others of its type; particular in choosing **—se·lec´tion** *n.*

**se·lec´tive** *adj.* very particular; choosy **—se·lec´tive·ly** *adv.* **—se·lec´tive·ness, se·lec·tiv´i·ty** *n.* **—se·lec´tor** *n.*

**self** *n.* the distinct identity and individuality of a person or thing; personal advantage *—adj.* of the same quality or kind

**self´-cen´tered** *adj.* concerned exclusively with one's own needs and desires **—self´-cen´tered·ly** *adv.* **—self´-cen´tered·ness** *n.*

**self-con´fi·dence** *n.* belief in one's own ability, judgement, etc. **—self-con´fi·dent** *adj.* **—self-con´fi·dent·ly** *adv.*

**self-con´scious** *adj.* uncomfortable under the scrutiny of another; ill at ease in a particular situation **—self-con´scious·ly** *adv.* **—self-con´scious·ness** *n.*

**self-con·trol´** *n.* command of one's impulses, emotions, etc.

**self-dis´ci·pline** *n.* control of oneself, especially for personal betterment

**self-es·teem´** *n.* a just opinion of oneself; an overestimate of oneself; conceit

**self-im·por´tance** *n.* an overestimation of one's prominence; conceit –**self-im·por´tant** *adj.* –**self-im·por´tant·ly** *adv.*

**self´-in·dul´gence** *n.* excessive gratification of one's desires –**self´-in·dul´gent** *adj.* –**self´-in·dul´gent·ly** *adv.*

**self´ish** *adj.* motivated by personal desires while disregarding the feelings of others –**self´ish·ly** *adv.* –**self´ish·ness** *n.*

**self´less** *adj.* having little concern for oneself; unselfish –**self´less·ly** *adv.* –**self´less·ness** *n.*

**self-pos·ses´sion** *n.* complete control to one's powers or faculties –**self-pos·sessed´** *adj.*

**self-pres·er·va´tion** *n.* the instinctive drive to avoid harm

**self-re·li´ance** *n.* dependence on one's own ability, resources, etc. –**self-re·li´ant** *adj.* –**self-re·li´ant·ly** *adv.*

**self-right´eous** *adj.* confident of one's own moral superiority –**self-right´eous·ly** *adv.* –**self-right´eous·ness** *n.*

**self-suf·fi´cien·cy** *n.* the ability to maintain oneself without the assistance of others –**self-suf·fi´cient** *adj.* –**self-suf·fi´cient·ly** *adv.*

**sell** *vt.* to transfer property for a consideration; to offer for sale –*vi.* to work in sales –**sell´er** *n.*

**sel´vage** *n.* the edge of a fabric finished so as not to ravel

**se·man´tics** *pl. n.* the study of the structure, meaning, changes, etc. of speech forms; a deliberate distortion of meaning –**se·man´tic** *adj.* –**se·man´ti·cal·ly** *adv.* –**se·man´ti·cist** *n.*

**sem´blance** *n.* a likeness or resemblance; the barest trace

**sem´i-** *prefix* partly: *semiautomatic*; exactly half: *semicircle*; occurring twice in the period: *semiannual*

**sem´i·nar** *n.* an informal meeting to address a particular topic

**sem´i·nary** *n.* a school of theology –**sem·i·nar´i·an** *n.*

**sen´ate** *n.* a legislative body –**sen´a·tor** *n.* –**sen·a·to´ri·al** *adj.* **sen´a·tor·ship** *n.*

**send** *vt.* to transmit; to cause or enable to go: *send to school*; to drive or impel –**send´er** *n.*

**se´nile** *adj.* of old age, especially when accompanied by mental infirmity –**se´nile·ly** *adv.* **se·nil´i·ty** *n.*

**sen´ior** *adj.* older in years or time of service –*n.* any elderly person; one more advanced in rank, dignity, etc; a member of a graduating class –**se·nior´i·ty** *n.*

**sen´sate** *adj.* having physical sensation; perceived by the senses –**sen´sate·ly** *adv.*

**sen·sa´tion** *n.* stimulation of a sense organ, as hearing or taste; the capacity to respond to such stimulation; a state of mind induced by indeterminate stimuli, as *a sensation of fear*

**sen·sa´tion·al** *adj.* of the senses or sensation; causing excitement –**sen·sa´tion·al·ly**

**sen·sa´tion·al·ism** *n.* the theory that all knowledge has a sensory basis; techniques intended to shock or startle –**sen·sa´tion·al·ist** *n.* –**sen·sa·tion·al·is´tic** *adj.* –**sen·sa´tion·al·ize** *vt.*

**sense** *n.* any of the faculties of a sentient being to respond to stimuli, as sound, hunger, etc.; a special capacity to appreciate, as *a sense of humor*; a vague perception, as *a sense of danger*; the power of reason –*vt.* to perceive; to become aware

**sense´less** *adj.* unconscious; incapable of feeling; lacking good sense; without apparent reason: *a senseless crime* –**sense´less·ly** *adv.* –**sense´less·ness** *n.*

**sen´si·ble** *adj.* possessing good mental perception; perceptible through the senses or to mind –**sen·si·bil´i·ty** *n.* –**sen´si·ble·ness** *n.* –**sen´si·bly** *adv.*

**sen´si·tive** *adj.* acutely responsive to certain sensation; responsive to the feelings and attitudes of others; appreciative of aesthetic or intellectual qualities; easily irritated or offended –**sen´si·tive·ly** *adv.* –**sen´si·tive·ness, sen·si·tiv´i·ty** *n.*

**sen´si·tize** *vt.* to make sensitive

**sen´sor** *n.* a device that responds to stimuli, as an electric eye

**sen·so´ri·al, sen´so·ry** *adj.* of the senses or sensation

**sen´su·al** *adj.* unduly indulgent to the appetites or senses –**sen´su·al·ly** *adv.* –**sen´su·al·ize** *vt.* –**sen·su·al·i·za´tion** *n.*

**sen´su·al·ism** *n.* excessive indulgence in sensual pleasures; the philosophical concept that sensual pleasures represent the highest good –**sen´su·al·ist** *n.* –**sen·su·al·is´tic** *adj.*

**sen´su·al´i·ty** *n.* the state of being sensual; lewdness; lasciviousness

**sen´su·ous** *adj.* appealing to the senses –**sen´su·ous·ly** *adv.* –**sen´su·ous·ness** *n.*

**sen'tence** *n.* a determination or judgment; a penalty pronounced in court; in grammar, a group of words that express a thought

**sen´tient** *adj.* possessing powers of perception –**sen´tience** *n.* –**sen´tient·ly** *adv.*

**sen´ti·ment** *n.* delicate sensibility; a complex of feelings used as a basis for judgment –**sen·ti·men´tal** *adj.* –**sen·ti·men´tal·ism** *n.* –**sen·ti·men´tal·ist** *n.* –**sen·ti·men´tal·ly** *adv.*

**sen·ti·men·tal´i·ty** *n.* the quality of being overly sentimental

**sen´ti·nel** *n.* a guard

**sen´try** *n.* a guard, especially a soldier

**sep´a·ra·ble** *adj.* capable of being divided –**sep´a·ra·ble·ly** *adv.* –**sep´a·ra·ble·ness** *n.*

**sep´a·rate** *vt.* to set apart or divide; to isolate –*vt.* to become divided; to draw apart –*adj.* distinct; apart from others; detached; existing independently

**—sep´a·rate·ly** *adv.* **—sep´a·rate·ness** *n.* **—sep´a·ra·tive** *adj.* **—sep´a·ra·tor** *n.*

**sep·a·ra´tion** *n.* the state of being apart; a gap or dividing line

**sep´a·rat·ist** *n.* one who advocates separation, as of races or religions, or by political boundaries **—sep´a·rat·ism** *n.*

**sep´ul·cher** *n.* a burial place; a tomb or vault

**se·pul´chral** *adj.* of a sepulcher; dismal in aspect **—se·pul´chral·ly** *adv.*

**se´quel** *n.* something that follows; a narrative that develops from a previous one; a consequence

**se´quence** *n.* the process of following in order **—se·quen´tial** *adj.* **—se·quen·ti·al´i·ty** *n.* **—se·quen´tial·ly** *adv.*

**se·ques´ter** *vt.* to place apart; to seclude, as a jury during the course of a trial; property taken into custody pending settlement of a claim **—se·ques´tered** *adj.*

**ser´e·nade´** *n.* a love song *—vi., vt.* to sing, especially to one's love **—ser´e·nad´er** *n.*

**ser·en·dip´i·ty** *n.* the faculty of making fortunate discoveries by accident **—ser·en·dip´i·tous** *adj.* **—ser·en·dip´i·tous·ly** *adv.*

**se·rene´** *adj.* untroubled; tranquil **—se·rene´ly** *adv.* **—se·rene´ness, se·ren´i·ty** *n.*

**se´ri·al** *adj.* arranged in a series; presented at regular intervals *—n.* a story presented in regular installments, as in a periodical or on television **—se´ri·al·ize** *vt.* **—se´ri·al·ly** *adv.*

**se´ries** *n.* an arrangement or succession of related things

**ser´if** *n.* a light stroke crossing or projecting from the main stroke in a letter

**se´ri·ous** *adj.* thoughtful; sober; involving much work or difficulty; of grave importance; grim or critical, as *a serious accident* **—se´ri·ous·ly** *adv.* **—se´ri·ous·ness** *n.*

**ser´mon** *n.* a lecture; a serious talk; a discourse, especially on a text from the Bible **—ser·mon´ic** *adj.* **—ser´mon·ize** *vt., vi.*

**ser´pent** *n.* a snake

**ser´pen·tine** *adj.* winding, like a serpent

**ser´rate, ser´rat·ed** *adj.* having sawlike teeth, as the edge of certain leaves **—ser·ra´tion** *n.*

**se´rum** *n.* the fluid constituent of blood; a fluid that confers immunity

**ser´vant** *n.* one employed to assist in domestic matters

**serve** *vt.* to work as a servant; to be of service to; to satisfy the requirements of; to perform the duties of an office; to satisfy, as a term of enlistment or incarceration *—vi.* to be a servant; to perform the duties of employment, office, etc.; to wait on others; be useful or suitable **—serv´er** *n.*

**serv´ice** *n.* the act of serving; the manner in which one is served; a business or occupational category, as *a delivery service*; maintenance and repair; an act of public worship *—vt.* to maintain or repair *—adj.* pertaining to the act of serving; designated for those who serve or supply: *service entrance*

**serv´ice·a·ble** *adj.* useful; beneficial; durable **—serv·ice·a·bil´i·ty, serv´ice·a·ble·ness** *n.* **—serv´ice·a·bly** *adv.*

**ser´vile** *adj.* submissive; befitting a servant; abject **—ser´vile·ly** *adv.* **—ser´vile·ness, ser·vil´i·ty** *n.*

**ses´sion** *n.* the meeting of a legislative assembly, court, etc.; a time of specified activity: *a bull session*

**set** *vt.* to place; to fix in place; to bring to a specified condition: *set a fire, set at ease*; to restore: *set a broken bone*; to establish: *set boundaries*; to mount, as a gem; to value: *set a price —vi.* to wane, as *the setting sun*; to solidify; to begin: *set out, set to work —n.* a group regarded as associated: *the jet set*; a number of things belonging together

**set´tle** *vt.* to put in order; to set to rights; to establish in place: *settle in*; to calm or quiet; to sink to the bottom; to decide or determine finally; to pay, as a debt *—vi.* to come to rest; to sink gradually; to become established; to pay a bill

**set´tle·ment** *n.* the condition of being settled; an area newly colonized; an agreement or adjustment **—set´tler** *n.*

**sev´er** *vt.* to separate; to cut or break into parts; to break off, as a relationship *—vi.* to break or come apart **—sev´er·a·ble** *adj.* **—sev´er·ance** *n.*

**sev´er·al** *adj.* more than two, but not a large number; individually different, diverse **—sev´er·al·ly** *adv.*

**se·vere´** *adj.* harsh; extremely strict; austere in disposition or manner; plain and simple **—se·vere´ly** *adv.* **—se·vere´ness** *n.* **—se·ver´i·ty** *n.*

**sew** *vt.* to make, mend, or fasten with needle and thread *—vi.* to work with needle and thread

**sex** *n.* the division, male or female, by which organisms are distinguished with reference to the reproductive functions; activity concerned with sexual desire or reproduction

**sex´ism** *n.* discrimination against one of the opposite sex **—sex´ist** *n., adj.*

**sex´less** *adj.* having no sex; without sexual interest or distinction **—sex´less·ly** *adv.* **—sex´less·ness** *n.*

**sex´ton** *n.* a church officer responsible for maintenance

**sex´u·al** *adj.* pertaining to sex and its functions; characterized by or having sex **—sex·u·al´i·ty** *n.* **sex´u·al·ly** *adv.*

**sex´y** *adj.* provocative; stimulating **—sex´i·ly** *adv.* **—sex´i·ness** *n.*

**shab´by** *adj.* threadbare; characterized by worn or ragged garments; paltry **—shab´bi·ly** *adv.* **—shab´bi·ness** *n.*

**shack** *n.* a crudely built dwelling **—shack up** *(US)* to live somewhere temporarily; to live together as husband and wife without benefit or matrimony

**shade** *vt.* to screen from light or heat; to represent by gradation of color *–n.* relative darkness caused by interruption of light; a darkened gradation of color; a minute variation: *shade of meaning*; a screen that partly obscures light: *a lamp shade*

**shad´ow** *n.* comparative darkness caused by interruption of light; the image produced by that which interrupts light; the shaded portion of a picture; a trace: *not a shadow of evidence –vt.* to cast a shadow; to follow **–shad´ow·y** *adj.*

**shad´y** *adj.* shaded or sheltered; morally or legally suspect: *a shady deal* **–shad´i·ly** *adv.* **–shad´i·ness** *n.*

**shaft** *n.* a long narrow rod; a long handle; a beam of light; any long, narrow, relatively straight structure or opening as *an elevator shaft* or *an air shaft*

**shag** *n.* a coarse cloth or coat; a once popular dance *–vt., vi.* to make or become coarse or rough

**shag´gy** *adj.* resembling rough hair or wool; unkempt **–shaggy-dog story** a long involved story with a meaningless punch line **–shag´gi·ly** *adv.* **–shag´gi·ness** *n.*

**shake** *vt., vi.* to vibrate with short, rapid movements; to agitate or rouse **–shak´a·ble** *adj.*

**shak´y** *adj.* not solid or well founded; not reliable; marked by weakness or shaking **–shak´i·ly** *adv.* **–shak´i·ness** *n.*

**shal´low** *adj.* lacking depth or extent: *a shallow closet*; superficial or unintelligent, especially of a person **–shal´low·ly** *adv.* **–shal´low·ness** *n.*

**sham** *adj.* false; pretended *–n.* a hoax; a counterfeit; artificiality or pretension

**sham´ble** *vi.* to walk with shuffling or unsteady gait

**shame** *n.* a sense of guilt or unworthiness; disgrace or humiliation; a disappointment: *it's shame they can't go –vt.* to cause to feel shame; to bring shame upon; to impel through a sense of shame

**shame´ful** *adj.* disgraceful; scandalous; indecent **–shame´ful·ly** *adv.* **–shame´ful·ness** *n.*

**shame´less** *adj.* brazen; immodest; done without shame **–shame´less·ly** *adv.* **–shame´less·ness** *n.*

**shan´ty** *n.* a small, poorly built dwelling; a shack

**shape** *n.* outward form; final form: *put into shape –vt.* to give form to; to adapt or modify; to put in final form *–vi.* to develop or take shape **–shap´a·ble** *adj.* **–shaped** *adj.* **–shap´er** *n.*

**shape´less** *adj.* lacking form or symmetry **–shape´less·ly** *adv.* **–shape´less·ness**

**shape´ly** *adj.* having a pleasing form **–shape´li·ness** *adv.*

**shard** *n.* a broken piece, as of pottery

**share** *n.* a portion due or contributed; stock in a company *–vt., vi.* to participate in; to divide into equal parts **–shar´er** *n.*

**sharp** *adj.* having a keen edge; capable of cutting or piercing; abrupt: *a sharp curve*; well-defined: *sharp contrast*; quick to perceive; shrewd; intense: *a sharp wit, a sharp temper –adv.* **–sharp´ly** *adv.* **–sharp´ness** *n.*.

**sharp´en** *vt., vi.* to make or become sharp **–sharp´en·er** *n.*

**shat´ter** *vt.* to break into pieces suddenly; to damage or demolish: *the loss shattered her hopes –vi.* to burst **–shat´ter·ing·ly** *adv.*

**shave** *vt.* to remove hair with a razor; to trim closely; to slice thinly; to graze or come close *–n.* the act of cutting with a razor; a thin slice **–shav´en** *adj.* **–shav´er** *n.*

**shawl** *n.* a cloth wrap worn over the head or shoulders

**sheaf** *n.* bound stalks of cut grain; a collection of things banded or tied; a quantity: *a sheaf of papers*

**sheath** *n.* a case, as for a sword or knife *–vt.* to place or enclose in or as in a sheath or covering

**sheathe** *vt.* put into a sheath; to protect or conceal, as by covering **–sheath´ing** *n.*

**shed** *vt.* to pour forth, as tears; to radiate: the *sun shed its rays*; to repel, as rain; to cast off by natural process, as a snake's skin; to get rid of: *he shed 10 pounds just by exercising –vi.* to cast off by natural process *–n.* a small storage building **–shed light on** to explain or make clear

**sheen** *vi.* to glisten *–n.* a glossy finish; luster

**sheep** *n.* a wooly ruminant, especially those domesticated for their fleece, flesh, and hide

**sheep´ish** *adj.* embarrassed; meek or timid **–sheep´ish·ly** *adv.* **–sheep´ish·ness**

**sheet** *n.* a thin, broad piece of material; a broad, flat expanse; cloth used as bedding; a piece of paper *–vt.* to form or cut into sheets *–adj.* formed or cut into sheets

**shelf** *n.* a platform or ledge designed to hold articles; a projecting rock ledge **–shelv´ing** *n.*

**shell** *n.* a hard outer covering; anything like a shell, as the framework of a building, a hollow pastry, etc.; a projectile containing explosives, etc.; a psychological barrier: *come out of one's shell –vt.* to remove the outer covering from; to bombard

**shel´ter** *n.* that which covers or protects *–vt.* to provide cover **–shel´ter·er** *n.*

**shib´bo·leth** *n.* a test word; a watchword

**shield** *n.* a relatively flat plate of defensive armor, usually carried on the arm; anything that protects; a shield-like badge or emblem; a heraldic escutcheon *–vt.* to guard or protect; to hide from view

**shift** *vt., vi.* to change position *–n.* a change in attitude, position, loyalty, etc.; a dress that is unbelted or fitted at the waist

**shift´less** *adj.* unwilling to work; lazy; incompetent **–shift´less·ly** *adv.* **–shift´less·ness** *n.*

**shift´y** *adj.* characterized by deceit or trickery; resourceful **–shift´i·ly** *adv.* **–shift´i·ness**

**shim´mer** *vi.* to shine faintly; to glimmer –*n.* a gleaming –**shim´mer·y** *adj.*

**shim´my** *n.* a jazz dance; an undesirable vibration

**shine** *vi.* to emit light; to glow; to excel –*vt.* to brighten by rubbing –*n.* radiance; sheen; a liking or fancy –**shin´er** *n.*

**shin´gle** *n.* a thin tapering piece used in courses to cover a roof; a sign outside the office of a doctor, lawyer, etc. –*vt.*

**shin´y** *adj.* glistening; polished –**shin´i·ness** *n.*

**ship** *n.* a deep-water vessel; an aircraft or spacecraft –*vt.* to transport

**ship´ment** *n.* goods transported –**ship´per** *n.*

**shirk** *vt., vi.* to avoid work or obligation –**shirk´er** *n.*

**shirt** *n.* a garment for the upper part of the body

**shirt´ing** *n.* material used for making shirts, blouses etc.

**shiv´er** *vi.* tremble, as with cold or fear –**shiv´er·y** *adj.*

**shoal** *n.* a shallow place in a body of water

**shock** *n.* a violent blow; a jolt to the mind or emotions; trauma associated with injury –*vt.* to horrify or disgust –**shock´er** *n.*

**shock´ing** *adj.* causing sudden surprise or horror –**shock´ing·ly** *adv.*

**shod´dy** *adj.* poorly made –**shod´di·ly** *adv.* –**shod´di·ness** *n.*

**sho´gun** *n.* former hereditary leader of the Japanese militia

**shoot** *vt.* to wound with a projectile from a weapon; to fire a weapon; to send forth, as a glance; to pass over swiftly, as rapids; to photograph –*vi.* to discharge; to move swiftly; to put forth buds –*n.* the act of shooting; early growth –**shoot´er** *n.*

**shop** *n.* a place where goods and services are sold, manufactured, or repaired –*vi.* to inspect and purchase goods –**shop assistant** *(Brit.)* one who works in a retail shop –**shop´per** *n.*

**shore** *n.* land adjacent to a body of water

**short** *adj.* of less than average or usual length, height, or extent; of brief duration; of a limited distance; less than required: *short of the mark* –**short´ness** *n.*

**short´age** *n.* an inadequate supply; the amount of a deficiency or shortfall

**short´com·ing** *n.* a defect

**short´en** *vt., vi.* to make or become reduced in length

**short´ly** *adv.* soon

**shout** *n.* a sudden, loud outcry –*vt., vi.* to utter loudly –**shout´er** *n.*

**shove** *vt., vi.* to push; to press forcibly against –**shov´er** *n.*

**shov´el** *n.* a flattened scoop with a handle –*vt., vi.* to take up with a shovel; to toss hastily –**shov´el·er** *n.* –**shov´el·ful** *n.*

**show** *vt.* to present to view; to explain or prove; to lead: *show them in*; to enter in a show or exhibition –*vi.* to become visible; to appear –*n.* a production, as a movie or live performance; an exhibition; a competition for displaying and judging; ostentation: *mere show*

**show´er** *n.* one who exhibits at a show: a brief rain; a sudden or liberal outpouring: *a shower of accolades*; a party honoring an event as *a bridal shower* or *baby shower*; a means for cleansing the body with a fine spray of water or the bathroom appliance used for such cleansing –*vt., vi.* to make wet or bathe, as in a shower

**show´man** *n.* one skilled in the art of performing or of managing performances –**show´man·ship** *n.*

**show´place** *n.* an extremely attractive or well-ordered site

**show´y** *adj.* flamboyant; ostentatious –**show´i·ness** *n.*

**shred** *n.* a fragment –*vt.* to cut or tear into fragments –**shred´der** *n.*

**shrew** *n.* a tiny mouselike creature; a vexatious or nagging woman –**shrew´ish** *adj.* –**shrew´ish·ly** *adv.* –**shrew´ish·ness** *n.*

**shrewd** *adj.* having keen insight; calculating –**shrewd´ly** *adv.* –**shrewd´ness** *n.*

**shriek** *n.* a shrill cry –*vi.*

**shrill** *adj.* high-pitched and piercing –*vi., vt.* to make or cause to make a piercing sound –**shrill´ness** *n.* –**shril´ly** *adv.*

**shrine** *n.* a sacred place; a place of worship; a site or structure respected for its importance; a memorial dedicated to a person, event, etc.

**shrink** *vi.* to contract; diminish; to recoil, as in disgust –*vt.* to cause to shrink –**shrink´a·ble** *adj.* –**shrink´age** *n.*

**shriv´el** *vt., vi.* to contract into wrinkles; to make or become helpless

**shroud** *n.* cloth used to wrap a corpse; something that covers or conceals –*vt.* to cover or conceal

**shrug** *vt., vi.* to draw up the shoulders, as in doubt or indifference

**shuck** *n.* a covering, such as a husk, shell, or pod –*vt.* to remove an outer covering, as *to shuck peas* or *shuck one's garments*

**shud´der** *vi.* to tremble, as from fright or cold

**shuf´fle** *vt., vi.* to move with a dragging gait; to mix, as a deck of playing cards; to move, change, or rearrange –*n.* a trick or deception

**shunt** *vt., vi.* to turn aside; to divert –*n.* a railroad switch; a connector that diverts power, etc.

**shut** *vt.* to close, as a door or window; to collapse after use, as an umbrella; to exclude: *they shut out the riff-raff*

**shut´-in** *n.* an invalid; one who is unable to leave –*adj.*

**shy** *adj.* uneasy in the company of others; timid; easily startled; expressing reserve, as *a shy look* –*vt.* draw back, as *to shy away* –**shy´ly** *adv.* –**shy´ness** *n.*

**shy´ster** *n.* an unscrupulous businessman

**sib´i·lant** *adj.* hissing; in grammar, expressing a consonant, as *s, z, sh,* and *zh,* uttered with a hissing sound **–sib´i·lance** *n.* **–sib´i·lant·ly** *adv.*

**sib´ling** *n.* a brother or sister

**sick** *adj.* ill; affected by disease; weak; nauseated; emotionally upset; *sick with grief*; monotonous: *sick of dining alone* **–sick´ness** *n.*

**sick´en** *vt., vi.* to make or become sick or repelled **–sick´en·ing** *adj.* **–sick´en·ing·ly** *adv.*

**sick´le** *n.* a cutting implement with a long, curved blade mounted on a short handle

**sick´ly** *adj.* habitually ailing; characterized by sickness; weak or unconvincing; *a sickly excuse* –*adv.* **–sick´li·ness** *n.*

**side** *n.* the boundry of a surface or an object; the lateral half of a surface or object; an aspect or point of view; a group competing together

**si·de´re·al** *adj.* relating to the stars

**si´dle** *vi.* to move sideways –*n.* a sideways movement

**siege** *n.* the surrounding of a place so as to seize it; a prolonged bout, as *a siege of illness* –*vt.* to besiege or assault

**sieve** *n.* a utensil such as a wire mesh attached to a rigid frame for separating out coarse particles –*vt., vi.* to force or pass through a sieve; to sift

**sift** *vt.* to examine carefully; to separate out; to filter; as *to sift fact from fiction* **–sift´er** *n.*

**sigh** *n.* a deep audible breath –*vi.* to make a sound to express sorrow, weariness, etc.; to make a sound suggestive of a sigh –*vt.* to express with a sigh

**sight** *n.* vision; an image perceived by the eye; mental perception: *don't lose sight of our objective*; a device for aiming; observation with a telescope –*vt.* to catch sight of; to observe through a telescope or similar device –*vi.* to take aim; to make an observation –*adj.* performed without previous preparation: *sight reading*; due when presented: *a sight draft* **–sight´ed** *adj.*

**sight´less** *adj.* blind; invisible **–sight´less·ly** *adv.* **–sight´less·ness** *n.*

**sign** *n.* a telltale mark or indication: *a sign of aging, the first sign of spring*; an action used to communicate; a symbol: *black armbands are a sign of grief*; a structure containing advertising, directions, etc. –*vt., vi.* to write one's signature; to indicate or signal **–sign´er** *n.*

**sig´nal** *n.* an agreed upon sign or event; that used to convey information –*adj.* out of the ordinary; notable –*vt.* to convey or communicate by a sign

**sig´na·to·ry** *n.* one bound by a signed document –*adj.* being a signer

**sig´na·ture** *n.* the name of a person written by himself; any identifying mark or sign; a folded sheet that constitutes a part of a book; symbols at the beginning of a piece of music that indicate time and key

**sig·nif´i·cant** *adj.* rich in meaning; important **–sig·nif´i·cance, sig·nif´i·can·cy** *n.* **–sig·nif´i·cant·ly** *adv.*

**sig´ni·fy** *vt.* to represent; to make known by signs or words –*vi.* to have meaning or importance

**si´lent** *adj.* not making any sound; mute; taciturn, disinclined to talk; not audible; free from disturbance; the absence of comment: *he was silent on the issues* **–si´lence** *n.* **–si´lent·ly** *adv.*

**sil·hou·ette´** *n.* a profile drawing or portrait filled in with uniform color

**sil´ly** *adj.* foolish; frivolous –*adv.* **–sil´li·ness** *n.*

**silt** *n.* extremely fine particles carried by water; a deposit of such particles **–silt´y** *adj.*

**sim´i·an** *n.* an ape or monkey –*adj.*

**sim´i·lar** *adj.* bearing resemblance; having like characteristics **–sim·i·lar´i·ty** *n.* **–sim´i·lar·ly** *adv.*

**sim´i·le** *n.* a figure of speech expressing likeness

**si·mil´i·tude** *n.* similarity

**sim´mer** *vi.* to boil gently; to be near to showing emotion –*vt.* to cook by boiling gently –*n.*

**si´mo·ny** *n.* the buying or selling of that which is sacred

**sim´per** *vi.* to smirk –*vt.* to say with a smirk –*n.* a silly, self-conscious smile

**sim´ple** *adj.* easy to understand or do; plain and unadorned, as clothing or food; having nothing added: *the simple truth*; free from affectation; silly or foolish; ordinary **–sim´ple·ness** *n.*

**sim·plic´i·ty** *n.* the state of being simple

**sim´pli·fy** *vt.* to make easy to understand or do **–sim·pli·fi·ca´tion** *n.* **–sim´pli·fi·er** *n.*

**sim·plis´tic** *adj.* overly simple; tending to overlook potential complications **–sim·plis´ti·cal·ly** *adv.*

**sim´ply** *adv.* in a simple manner; really: *simply adorable*

**sim´u·late** *vt.* to make a pretense of; to assume the appearance of **–sim·u·la´tion** *n.* **–sim´u·la·tive** *adj.* **–sim´u·la·tive·ly** *adv.* **–sim´u·la·tor** *n.*

**si·mul·ta´ne·ous** *adj.* occurring or existing at the same time **–si·mul·ta´ne·ous·ly** *adv.* **–si·mul·ta´ne·ous·ness** *n.*

**sin** *n.* a transgression against moral or religious law –*vi.* to do wrong **–sin´ful** *adj.* **–sin´ful·ly** *adv.* **–sin´ful·ness** *n.*

**since** *adv.* from a past time to the present; at some time before the present: *he has since recovered* –*prep.* from a time in the past: *since you left* –*conj.* inasmuch as

**sin·cere´** *adj.* genuine; free from hypocrisy or deceit **–sin·cere´ly** *adv.* **–sin·cer´i·ty** *n.*

**sin´e·cure** *n.* a position that provides compensation with little or no effort

**sing** *vi.* to produce musical sounds with the voice or as with the voice –*vt.* to perform vocally; to chant **–sing´a·ble** *adj.* **sing´er** *n.*

**singe** *vt.* to burn slightly *–n.* a superficial burn
**sin´gle** *adj.* consisting of one; solitary; unmarried **–sin´gle•ness** *n.* **–sin´gly** *adv.*
**sin´gu•lar** *adj.* unique; remarkable; uncommon **–sin•gu•lar´i•ty** *n.* **–sin´gu•lar•ly** *adv.* **–sin´gu•lar•ness** *n.*
**sin´is•ter** *adj.* of the left side; evil; ominous; threatening misfortune **–sin´is•ter•ly** *adv.* **–sin´is•ter•ness** *n.*
**sin´is•tral** *adj.* of or facing the left **–sin´is•tral•ly** *adv.*
**sink** *vi.* to go beneath the surface; to descend slowly; to slope gradually; to approach death; to lessen: *his voice sank* *–vt.* to cause to go beneath the surface; to cause to drop or lessen; to defeat *–n.* a basin with running water and a drain; a depression in a land surface; a device that absorbs or dissipates energy: *a heat sink* **–sink´a•ble** *adj.* **–sink´er** *n.*
**sen´u•ous** *adj.* winding or undulating; devious **–sin´u•ous•ly** *adv.* **–sin´u•ous•ness** *n.*
**sip** *vt., vi.* to drink in small quantities *–n.* a small drink **–sip´per** *n.*
**si´phon** *n.* a tube or device for transferring liquid *–vt.* to draw off
**sir** *n.* respectful address to a man; a title for barons or knights
**sire** *n.* the male parent of an animal
**si´ren** *n.* an enticing woman; a device that warns by producing a loud distinctive sound *–adj.* seductive
**sis´sy** *n.* an effeminate man; a weakling
**sis´ter** *n.* a female sibling
**sit** *vi.* to rest on the buttocks or haunches; to perch or roost; to pose; to meet or hold a session; to be situated or located *–vt.* to seat oneself
**si•tar´** *n.* a long-necked stringed instrument similar to a lute, used for Hindu music **–si•tar´ist** *n.*
**site** *n.* a specific place or location
**sit´u•ate** *vt.* to place or locate
**sit•u•a´tion** *n.* the way in which a thing rests; a condition as modified or determined by circumstance; a salaried post; a state of affairs, especially one that is difficult or significant **–sit•u•a´tion•al** *adj.* **–sit•u•a´tion•al•ly** *adv.*
**siz´a•ble** *adj.* comparatively large **–siz´a•ble•ness** *n.* **–siz´a•bly** *adv.*
**size** *n.* the dimensions of a thing; one of a series of standard measures, as for shoes, hats, etc.
**siz´zle** *vi.* to emit a hissing sound *–n.* a hissing sound caused by heat
**skate** *n.* a runner or wheels attached to a shoe for gliding over ice, pavement, etc. *–vi.* to glide over a smooth surface **–skat´er** *n.*
**skel´e•ton** *n.* the supporting framework of a vertebrate; the main supporting parts of a structure; mere sketch or outline **–skel´e•tal** *adj.* **–skel´e•tal•ly** *adv.*
**skep´ti•cal** *adj.* doubtful or suspicious **–skep´ti•cal•ly** *adv.* **–skep´ti•cal•ness** *n.*
**skep´ti•cism** *n.* the belief that absolute knowledge is unattainable; a doubting or incredulous state; doubt about basic religious doctrines **–skep´tic** *n.*
**sketch** *n.* a rough drawing; a preliminary study; a brief description; a short play **–sketch´er** *n.*
**sketch´y** *adj.* lacking detail; superficial **–sketch´i•ly** *adv.* **–sketch´i•ness** *n.*
**skew´er** *n.* a long rod for holding food while roasting *–vt.* to run through or fasten as with a skewer
**skiff** *n.* a light rowboat or sailing vessel
**skill** *n.* proficiency; a specific craft or trade **–skilled, skill´ful** *adj.* **–skill´ful•ly** *adv.* **–skill´ful•ness** *n.*
**skil´let** *n.* a frying pan
**skim** *vt.* to remove matter from the surface of a liquid; to move lightly over a surface; to cover with a thin film; to read over hastily *–vi.* to move lightly over a surface; to glance over; to become covered with a thin film *–n.* a thin coating **–skim´mer** *n.*
**skimp** *vi,. vt.* to do poorly or carelessly; to provide too little **–skimp´ing•ly** *adv.*
**skimp´y** *adj.* scanty; barely enough; insufficient **–skimp´i•ly** *adv.* **–skimp´i•ness** *n.*
**skin** *n.* the outer covering of an animal body; a container made from the skin of an animal; any outer layer, as the rind of fruit
**skin´flint** *n.* one obsessed with saving money
**skin´ny** *adj.* overly thin **–skin´ni•ness** *n.*
**skip** *vi.* to move by a series of light hops; to ricochet *–vt.* to leap over or bypass; to fail to attend *–n.*
**skir´mish** *n.* a minor encounter; an unimportant dispute *–vi.* to battle **–skir´mish•er** *n.*
**skirt** *n.* a woman's garment or that part of a garment that hangs from the waist; anything that hangs or covers like a skirt; the border of an area: *outskirts* *–vt.* to form the border of; to avoid: *skirt the town* *–vi.* to pass along the border
**skit** *n.* a short play
**skit´tish** *adj.* easily frightened, as a horse; playful **–skit´tish•ly** *adv.* **–skit´tish•ness** *n.*
**skulk** *vi.* to move about furtively **–skulk´er** *n.*
**sky** *n.* heaven; the upper atmosphere
**slab** *n.* a thick, flat slice
**slack** *adj.* hanging loosely; listless; careless; lacking activity **–slack´en** *vi., vt.* **–slack´ness** *n.*
**slack´er** *n.* idler; one who shirks
**slake** *vt.* to quench: *slake one's thirst*
**slam** *vt.* to shut violently; to dash; to criticize *–vi.* to shut with force *–n.* severe criticism
**slan´der** *vt., vi.* to utter false statements; to defame *–n.* a false statement **–slan´der•er** *n.* **–slan´der•ous** *adj.* **–slan´der•ous•ly** *adv.* **–slan´der•ous•ness**
**slang** *n.* the special language of a particular group; words or phrases derived from unconventional use of standard vocabulary **–slang´i•ly** *adv.* **–slang´i•ness** *n.* **–slang´y** *adj.*
**slant** *vt.* to cause to slope; to write from a biased point

of view —*adj.* sloping —*n.* an incline; an opinionated view —**slant´ing** *adj.* —**slant´ing·ly** *adv.*

**slap** *vt.* to strike with the open hand; to insult —*n.* a blow; an insult —**slap´per** *n.*

**slash** *vt.* to cut violently; to strike with a whip; to reduce sharply —*vi.* to make a long sweeping stroke —*n.* a cut or gash; an ornamental slit in a garment; a forest clearing covered with debris —**slash´er** *n.*

**slat** *n.* a thin strip of wood

**slaugh´ter** *vt.* to kill for food; to murder savagely —*n.* a savage killing —**slaugh´ter·er**

**slave** *n.* one owned by another; one completely subject to another or to some habit or influence; a device controlled by another device —*vi.* to toil ceaselessly

**slav´er** *n.* a person or vessel engaged in slave trade

**slav´ery** *n.* the holding of persons as property; submission to a habit or influence; constant toil

**slay** *vt.* to kill violently —**slay´er** *n.*

**slea´zy** *adj.* shoddy or shabby; vulgar or tawdry —**slea´zi·ness**

**sled** *(US)* *n.* a vehicle with runners designed to carry loads over snow and ice —*vt., vi.* to convey or ride on a sled —**sled´der** *n.*

**sledge** *(Brit.)* *n.* a vehicle mounted on low runners to carry loads over frozen or rough terrain, especially one pulled by draft animals *vt., vi.* to transport or travel by sledge

**sleek** *adj.* smooth and glossy; well-groomed; slick —**sleek´ly** *adv.* —**sleek´ness** *n.*

**sleep** *n.* a period of rest characterized by cessation of voluntary movement and indifference to external stimuli —*vt., vi.* to rest or fall asleep

**sleep´er** *n.* one who sleeps; a railway sleeper car; something or someone that unexpectedly excels; *(Brit.)* a section of concrete or timber that separates and supports railway tracks

**sleep´less** *adj.* unable to sleep; always active —**sleep´less·ly** *adv.* —**sleep´less·ness** *n.*

**sleep´y** *adj.* drowsy; lethargic or sluggish —**sleep´i·ly** *adv.* —**sleep´i·ness** *n.*

**sleet** *n.* partly frozen rain —*vi.* to fall as frozen rain —**sleet´y** *adj.*

**sleeve** *n.* the part of a garment that covers the arm; a covering or wrapper

**sleigh** *n.* a horse-drawn vehicle with runners for transporting people or goods over snow or ice —*vi.* to ride in a sleigh

**sleight** *n.* dexterity; a deception —**sleight of hand** trickery or deception performed by deft manipulation of small objects

**slen´der** *adj.* long and thin; attractively slim —**slen´der·ly** *adv.* —**slen´der·ness** *n.*

**slen´der·ize** *vt., vi.* to make or become slender

**sleuth** *n.* a detective —*vi.* to work as a detective

**slice** *n.* a thin piece cut from a larger one; a portion —*vt.* to cut from a larger piece; to divide into parts —*vi.* to cut, as with a knife —**slice´a·ble** *adj.* —**slic´er** *n.*

**slick** *adj.* smooth or sleek; deceptively clever —*n.* a film of oil

**slide** *vi.* to move smoothly over a surface; to slip from a position —*n.* an inclined plane for moving persons or material; a glass plate for mounting microscope specimens; a transparency; a part or mechanism that slides; the slipping of a mass of earth or snow —**slid´er** *n.*

**slight** *adj.* of small importance; slender in build; frail —*vt.* to do carelessly or thoughtlessly; to treat as trival —*n.* an act of disrespect —**slight´ly** *adv.* —**slight´ness** *n.*

**slim** *adj.* lacking girth; meager: *a slim chance* —*vt., vi.* to make or become slimmer —**slim´ly** *adv.* —**slim´ness** *n.*

**slime** *n.* moist, adhesive mud or earth; a mucous discharge from certain organisms —*vt.* to smear with slime

**slim´y** *adj.* covered with slime; filthy or foul —**slim´i·ly** *adv.* —**slim´i·ness** *n.*

**sling** *n.* a strap for hurling a stone; a device for holding an injured arm; a strap for lifting heavy objects —*vt.* to throw or fling

**slink** *vi.* to move furtively

**slink´y** *adj.* stealthy; graceful, serpentine: *a slinky dress* —**slink´i·ly** *adv.* —**slink´i·ness** *n.*

**slip** *vt.* to put on or off easily; to convey slyly; to pass unobserved —*vi.* to slide so as to lose one's footing; to fall into error; to escape; to move stealthily; to overlook —*n.* a sudden slide; an error; a woman's undergarment; a pillowcase; undesired motion: *the problem is caused by slip in the gears*

**slip´per** *n.* a light, casual shoe

**slip´per·y** *adj.* being so smooth as to make sliding likely; elusive; unreliable —**slip´per·i·ness** *n.*

**slit** *n.* a long, narrow opening —*vt.* to cut lengthwise

**slith´er** *vi.* to glide like a snake —*n.* a sinuous gliding movement —**slith´er·y** *adj.*

**slob** *n.* a careless or ill-kempt person

**slob´ber** *vt.* to ooze from the mouth; to shed or spill from the mouth, as in eating —*vi.* to slaver; to talk or act gushingly —*n.* sentimental talk

**slog** *vt., vi.* to plod

**slo´gan** *n.* a catchword or motto

**slo·gan·eer´** *vi.* to coin or use slogans —*n.* one who creates or uses slogans

**sloop** *n.* a small sailboat

**slop** *vi., vt.* to splash or cause to splash or spill —*n.* waste food; swill

**slope** *vi.* to slant —*n.* a slanting surface; the degree of inclination of a line or surface

**slop´py** *adj.* watery or pulpy; messy; marked by carelessness: *a sloppy job*; overly sentimental —**slop´pi·ly** *adv.*

**–slop´pi·ness** *n.*

**slosh** *vi.* to splash; to flounder **–slosh´y** *adj.*

**slot** *n.* a narrow groove or opening: *a coin slot, mail slot;* a narrow cut designed to receive a corresponding part; an opening, as for a job or an event *–vt.* to cut a slot; to assign: *slot a job interview*

**sloth** *n.* a slow-moving mammal; laziness

**sloth´ful** *adj.* inclined to idleness or inactivity **–sloth´ful·ly** *adv.* **–sloth´ful·ness** *n.*

**slouch** *n.* a drooping movement or appearance; an incompetent person *–vi.* to sit or move in an ungraceful, drooping manner **–slouch´i·ly** *adv.* **–slouch´i·ness** *n.* **–slouch´y** *adj.*

**slough** *n.* a stagnant swamp or backwater **–slough´y** *adj.*

**slov´en·ly** *adj.* untidy and careless in appearance *–adv.* **–slov´en·li·ness** *n.*

**slow** *adj.* taking a long time; not hasty; dull in comprehending; tedious; not brisk *–vt., vi.* to make or become slow or slower; to delay *–adv.* at less than normal speed **–slow´ly** *adv.* **–slow´ness** *n.*

**sludge** *n.* soft mud or slush **–sludg´y** *adj.*

**slug´gard** *n.* a slow or lazy person; an idler **–slug´gard·ly** *adv.* **–slug´gard·ness** *n.*

**slug´gish** *adj.* inactive; habitually slow and lazy **–slug´gish·ly** *adv.* **–slug´gish·ness** *n.*

**sluice** *n.* an artificial channel for conducting water; a device for controlling flow

**slum** *n.* a squalid street or section of the city

**slum´ber** *vi.* to sleep lightly *–n.* quiet sleep **–slum´ber·ous** *adj.*

**slump** *vi.* to fall or fail suddenly; to stand or walk in a stooped manner; to slouch *–n.* a collapse or decline, as in business activity

**slur** *vt.* to slight or disparage; to pronounce indistinctly *–n.* a disparaging remark

**slush** *n.* soft, sloppy material; sentimental words **–slush´i·ness** *n.* **–slush´y** *adj.*

**slut** *n.* a slatternly woman; a promiscuous woman **–slut´tish** *adj.* **–slut´tish·ly** *adv.* **–slut´tish·ness** *n.*

**sly** *adj.* stealthily clever; roguish **–sly´ly** *adv.* **–sly´ness** *n.*

**smack** *n.* a quick, sharp sound; a noisy kiss; a slap

**small** *adj.* not as large as others of its kind; little; unimportant; having little body or volume; meanspirited: *a small person –n.* a petite or slender part: *the small of the back –adv.* **–small´ish** *adj.* **–small´ness** *n.*

**smart** *n.* a stinging sensation *–vi.* to cause or experience a stinging sensation; to experience remorse *–vt.* to cause a stinging pain; to feel such a pain; to feel anguish: *their cruel remarks smart –adj.* intelligent; clever or shrewd; impertinent; brisk: *a smart pace;* fashionable **–smart´ly** *adv.*

**smart´en** *vt., vi.* to improve one's appearance; to make or become more knowledgeable

**smash** *vt.* to break into pieces; to crush; to strike *–n.* an outstanding success **–smash´er** *n.*

**smat´ter·ing** *n.* a little bit; superficial knowledge

**smear** *vt.* to soil; to apply in a thick coat; to slander

**smell** *vt.* to perceive through the nose; to examine or discover by odor *–n.* an unpleasant odor; a faint suggestion **–smell´i·ness** *n.* **–smell´y** *adj.*

**smile** *n.* a pleased expression *–vi.* to appear cheerful; to show approval **–smil´ing·ly** *adv.*

**smirch** *vt.* to soil; to defame or dishonor *–n.* a smear

**smirk** *n.* a sarcastic or derisive grin *–vi.* to grin **–smirk´er** *n.*

**smite** *vt.* to strike hard; to afflict or kill with a sudden blow

**smock** *n.* a loose outer garment

**smog** *n.* a noxious mist caused by the action of sunlight on atmospheric pollutants **–smog´gy** *adj.*

**smoke** *n.* the vaporous byproduct of combustion; something resembling this; something to smoke: a tobacco product *–vi.* to give off smoke; to make use of tobacco products *–vt.* to flavor food by treating with smoke; to force out as with smoke **–smok´er** *n.*

**smok´y** *adj.* containing or emitting smoke; discolored by smoke; being the gray color of smoke **–smok´i·ly** *adv.* **–smok´i·ness** *n.*

**smol´der** *vi.* to burn slowly; to have suppressed feelings or emotions

**smooth** *adj.* of an even surface; without lumps; suave and flattering, especially deceitfully *–vt., vi.* to make or become even; to make free of lumps **–smooth´ly** *adv.* **–smooth´ness** *n.*

**smoth´er** *vt.* to prevent from breathing; to suffocate; to stifle or overwhelm: *smother with kindness*

**smudge** *vt., vi.* to smear or become smeared *–n.* a stain; heavy smoke designed to drive away insects or protect plants from frost **–smudg´i·ness** *n.* **–smudg´y** *adj.*

**smug** *adj.* self-satisfied; complacent **–smug´ly** *adj.* **–smug´ness** *n.*

**smug´gle** *vt.* to take in or out of a country illegally **–smug´gler** *n.*

**smut** *n.* blackening made by soot or smoke; something obscene; a fungal disease of plants

**smut´ty** *adj.* stained with soot; obscene **–smut´ti·ly** *adv.* **–smut´ti·ness** *n.*

**snack** *n.* a light meal; a small amount of food *–vi.* to eat a small amount

**snag** *n.* a jagged bulge; an obstacle or difficulty *–vt.* to catch, as clothing, on something jagged or protruding

**snap** *n.* a sharp sound; a quick, sharp closing of the jaws; a sudden breaking or release; a fastener; brisk energy; an easy task *–adj.* done suddenly: *made a snap judgement;* that fastens with a snap *–vi., vt.* to grasp suddenly; to speak sharply; to move quickly and smartly

**snap´pish** *adj.* apt to speak crossly; disposed to snap or bite, as a dog –**snap´pish·ly** *adv.* –**snap´pish·ness** *n.*

**snap´py** *adj.* smart or stylish; snappish –**snap´pi·ly** *adv.* –**snap´pi·ness** *n.*

**snare** *n.* a trap for catching animals, something that misleads –*vt.* to trap; to entrap by trickery

**snarl** *n.* a growl; a tangle, as of hair –*vi.* to growl; to speak harshly; to become entangled –**snarl´er** *n.* **snarl´y** *adj.*

**snatch** *vt.* to seize suddenly or eagerly; to obtain as opportunity allows: *snatch a little sleep between calls* –**snatch´er** *n.*

**sneak** *vi., vt.* to move or act in a stealthy manner –*n.* a stealthy movement; a dishonest person –*adj.* stealthy –**sneak´i·ly, sneak´ing·ly** *adv* –**sneak´i·ness** *n.* –**sneak´y** *adj.*

**sneak´er** *(US) n.* a flexible sports shoe with a soft rubber sole

**sneer** *n.* a scornful grimace –*vi.* to show or express contempt –**sneer´ing·ly** *adv.*

**snick´er** *n.* a smothered laugh –*vi., vt.* to laugh derisively

**sniff** *vi.* to breath audibly in short bursts through the nose –*vt.* to inhale; to smell –*n.*

**snif´fle** *vi.* to breathe with difficulty; to snivel –*n.* –**snif´fler** *n.*

**snif´ter** *n.* a roundish goblet for serving brandy

**snip** *vt., vi.* to cut with short, quick strokes –*n.* a small cut

**snip´pet** *n.* a small clipping

**snip´py** *adj.* abrupt; insolent; rude –**snip´pi·ly** *adv.* –**snip´pi·ness** *n.*

**snitch** *vt.* to steal –*vi.* to inform on

**sniv´el** *vi.* to whine tearfully –*n.* –**sniv´el·er** *n.*

**snob** *n.* one preoccupied with wealth and station; one who affects to be superior –**snob´ber·y, snob´bish·ness** *n.* –**snob´bish·ly** *adv.*

**snood** *n.* a hairnet

**snoop** *vi.* to pry –*n.* –**snoop´er** *n.* –**snoop´y** *adj.*

**snoot´y** *adj.* haughty; snobbish –**snoot´i·ly** *adv.* –**snoot´i·ness** *n.*

**snooze** *vi.* to sleep lightly –*n.* a brief, light sleep

**snore** *vi.* to breathe with snorting noises while sleeping –*n.* –**snor´er** *n.*

**snow** *n.* precipitation in the form of ice crystals –*vi., vt.* to fall or cause to fall as snow

**snub** *vt.* to treat with disdain –*n.* a deliberate slight –**snub´ber** *n.*

**snug** *adj.* cozy; close-fitting –**snug, snug´ly** *adv.* –**snug´ness** *n.*

**snug´gle** *vt., vi.* to nestle or cuddle

**soak** *vt.* to saturate; to drench

**soap** *n.* a sudsy cleansing agent –**soap opera** an ongoing, usually daytime, radio or television drama, originally sponsored by companies that made and sold soap –**soap´i·ness** *n.* –**soap´y** *adj.*

**soar** *vi.* to float aloft; to glide through the air –**soar´er** *n.* –**soar´ing·ly** *adv.*

**sob** *vi., vt.* to weep audibly

**so´ber** *adj.* unaffected by an alcoholic beverage; temperate or rational; solemn or serious –*vt., vi.* to make or become sober –**so´ber·ly** *adv.* –**so´ber·ness** *n.*

**so·bri´e·ty** *n.* the state of being unaffected by drink, composure or seriousness

**so´bri·quet** *n.* a nickname

**so´cia·ble** *adj.* inclined to prefer company; friendly; characterized by friendly conversation –**so·cia·bil´i·ty, so´cia·ble·ness** *n.* –**so´cia·bly** *adv.*

**so´cial** *adj.* of society or its mores; friendly; pertaining to public welfare; existing in communities –*n.* an informal gathering

**so´cial·ite** *n.* one prominent in fashionable society

**so´cial·ize** *vi.* take part in social activities –*vt.* to control or adapt for the needs of society –**so·cial·i·za´tion** *n.* –**so´cial·iz·er** *n.*

**so´cial·ly** *adv.* with regard to society; *socially acceptable*

**so·ci´e·tal** *adj.* of the function, structure, etc. of society –**so·ci´e·tal·ly** *adv.*

**so·ci´e·ty** *n.* a group of people sharing certain characteristics, as language, customs, etc.; the fashionable members of a community; an association joined for a common purpose, shared interest, etc.

**so·ci·ol´o·gy** *n.* the study of the origin, evolution etc. of human society –**so´ci·o·log´ic, so´ci·o·log´i·cal** *adj.* –**so´ci·o·log´i·cal·ly** *adv.* –**so·ci·ol´o·gist** *n.*

**so´ci·o·path** *n.* one who is antisocial or hostile to society –**so·ci·o·path´ic** *adj.*

**sock´et** *n.* a depression into which a corresponding part fits, as a light socket that holds a bulb; *(Brit.)* a connector for electricity or a telephone

**sod** *n.* grassy surfaced soil –*vt.* to cover with sod

**sodden** *adj.* saturated; drenched; dull, as from drink –**sod´den·ly** *adv.* –**sod´den·ness** *n.*

**soft** *adj.* easily changed by pressure; easily worked; less hard than others of the same kind; smooth and delicate; expressing mildness or sympathy –**soft, soft´ly** *adv.* –**soft´ness** *n.*

**soft´en** *vt., vi.* to make or become soft –**soft´en·er** *n.*

**sog´gy** *adj.* soaked with moisture; heavy and wet –**sog´gi·ly** *adv.* –**sog´gi·ness** *n.*

**soil** *n.* a layer of rock particles mixed with decaying matter that forms the outer crust of the earth; a spot or stain –*vt., vi.* to make or become dirty

**soi·rée´** *n.* an evening reception

**so´journ** *vi.* to stay temporarily –*n.* a short stay –**so´journ·er** *n.*

**sol´ace** *vt.* to comfort; to alleviate or soothe –*n.* that which furnishes comfort in grief –**sol´ac·er** *n.*

**so´lar** *adj.* pertaining to the sun, as *solar energy*

**so·lar´i·um** *n.* a place, often glassed in, where one can sit in the sun

**sole** *adj.* only; being the only one, as *the sole survivor* —*n.* the bottom surface of the foot or a shoe; a flat fish

**sol´e·cism** *n.* a grammatical error; any incongruity —**sol´e·cist** *n.* —**sol´e·cis´tic** *adv.*

**sole´ly** *adj.* by oneself alone; entirely

**sol´emn** *adj.* sacred; marked by ceremonial observance, majesty, or power —**sol´emn·ly** *adv.* —**sol´emn·ness** *n.*

**so·lem´ni·ty** *n.* a solemn rite

**sol´em·nize** *vt.* to perform according to ritual, as *to solemnize a marriage* —**sol·em·ni·za´tion** *n.*

**so·lic´it** *vt.* to ask for earnestly; to entice to an immoral act —**so·lic·i·ta´tion** *n.*

**so·lic´i·tor** *n.* one who seeks money for charity, merchandise, etc.; the chief law officer of a municipality

**so·lic´i·tous** *adj.* full of concern —**so·lic´i·tous·ly** *adv.* —**so·lic´i·tous·ness** *n.*

**so·lic´i·tude** *n.* care or concern, as for another; that which makes one concerned or anxious

**sol´id** *adj.* having shape and volume; resistant to pressure; filling a space; of the same substance throughout: *solid gold*; well-built; financially sound; reliable, as *a solid citizen* —*n.* a three-dimensional object —**sol´id·ly** *adv.* —**so·lid´i·ty, sol´id·ness** *n.*

**so´li·dar´i·ty** *n.* unity of purpose

**so·lid´i·fy** *vt., vi.* to make or become solid —**so·lid·i·fi·ca´tion** *n.* —**so·lid´i·fi·er** *n.*

**so·lil´o·quy** *n.* a speech by which a lone actor reveals his thoughts to an audience —**so·lil´o·quist, so·lil´o·quiz·er** *n.* —**so·lil´o·quize** *vi.*

**sol´ip·sism** *n.* the philosophy that only knowledge of the self is verifiable and is therefore the only reality —**sol´ip·sist** *n.* —**sol·ip·sis´tic** *adj.*

**sol´i·taire** *n.* a gem set alone; a card game for one

**sol´i·tar·y** *adj.* alone; remote or excluded —**sol´i·tar·i·ly** *adv.* —**sol´i·tar·i·ness** *n.*

**sol´i·tude** *n.* seclusion; loneliness

**so´lo** *n.* anything accomplished without assistance, especially of a performance —*adj.* performed alone —*vi.* to perform alone; to pilot an aircraft for the first time without an instructor on board —**so´lo·ist** *n.*

**sol´stice** *n.* either of the times each year when the sun is farthest from the celestial equator

**sol´u·ble** *adj.* capable of being solved or explained; capable of being dissolved —**sol´u·ble·ness** *n.* —**sol´u·bly** *adv.*

**so·lu´tion** *n.* a mixture of varying proportions; the answer to or resolution of a problem

**solve** *vt.* to work out a correct solution or answer —**solv·a·bil´i·ty** *n.* —**solv´a·ble** *adj.* —**sol´ver** *n.*

**sol´vent** *adj.* financially sound; capable of dissolving —*n.* a substance capable of dissolving other substances —**sol´ven·cy** *n.*

**som´ber** *adj.* dark, gloomy; melancholy —**som´ber·ly** *adv.* —**som´ber·ness** *n.*

**some** *adj.* of an indeterminate number —*pron.* a certain undetermined number: *take some, some prefer it* —*adv.*

**some´body** *pron.* an unknown or unnamed person —*n.* a person of importance

**some´day** *adv.* at some future time

**some´how** *adv.* in some unspecified way

**some´one** *pron.* some unspecified person

**song** *n.* a short musical composition for voice; any melodic utterance

**son´ic** *adj.* relating to sound

**son´net** *n.* a poem of 14 lines —**son´ne·teer´** *n.*

**so·no´rous** *adj.* of a deep rich sound; lofty sounding —**so·no´rous·ly** *adv.* —**so·no´rous·ness** *n.*

**soon** *adv.* in the near future; early: *it came too soon*; willingly: *I would as soon go as not*

**soot** *n.* a fine black deposit from incomplete combustion —**soot´i·ness** *n.* —**soot´y** *adj.*

**soothe** *vt.* to calm; to relieve, as pain —*vi.* to afford relief —**sooth´er** *n.* —**sooth´ing** *adj.* —**sooth´ing·ly** *adv.*

**sooth´say·er** *n.* one who claims to be able to foretell the future —**sooth´say·ing** *n.*

**soph´ism** *n.* misleading argument; a fallacy —**soph´is·try** *n.*

**soph´ist** *n.* a learned person; one who argues deviously

**so·phis´ti·cate** *n.* one presumed to be worldlywise

**so·phis´ti·cat·ed** *adj.* cultured; refined; complex —**so·phis·ti·ca´tion** *n.*

**soph´o·more** *(US) n.* a second-year student —*adj.* of a second-year student or the second year of school

**soph·o·mor´ic** *(US) adj.* of a sophomore; shallow, pretentious; immature —**soph·o·mor´i·cally** *adv.*

**sop·o·rif´ic** *adj.* tending to cause sleep; sleepy

**sop´ping** *adj.* drenched

**so·pra´no** *n.* a voice or music of the highest range; one who sings such music —*adj.*

**sor´cer·er** *n.* a wizard or magician

**sor´cer·ess** *n.* a female wizard; a witch

**sor´cer·y** *n.* magic; witchcraft —**sor´cer·ous** *adj.* —**sor´cer·ous·ly** *adv.*

**sor´did** *adj.* degrading; vile; squalid —**sor´did·ly** *adv.* —**sor´did·ness** *n.*

**sore** *n.* a place on the body that is bruised, inflamed, etc.; anything causing pain or trouble —*adj.* tender; pained or distressed —**sore´ness** *n.*

**sore´ly** *adv.* distressingly; extremely: *sorely needed*

**so·ror´i·ty** *n.* a woman's organization

**sor´row** *n.* pain or sadness because of loss, etc.; an event that causes distress; the expression of grief —**sor´row·ful** *adj.* —**sor´row·ful·ly** *adv.* —**sor´row·ful·ness** *n.*

**sor´ry** *adj.* feeling regret or remorse; affected by sorrow; paltry or worthless: *a sorry piece of work* —**sor´ri·ly** *adv.*

–**sor´ri·ness** *n.*

**sort** *vt.* to arrange by kind, size, etc. –*n.* a collection characterized by similar qualities; a particular kind: *that sort of person* –**sort´a·ble** *adj.* –**sor´ter** *n.*

**soul** *n.* the moral or spiritual part of man; emotional or spiritual depth or vitality; the essence of something; embodiment: *the soul of generosity*; the disembodied spirit of one who has died

**soul´ful** *adj.* full of emotion –**soul´ful·ly** *adv.* –**soul´ful·ness** *n.*

**sound** *n.* energy perceptible by the hearing; noise of a particular quality: *the sound of a door slamming*; significance: *a sinister sound* –*vi., vt.* to give forth or cause to give forth a sound –*adj.* healthy; free from flaw, decay, etc.; correct or logical: *sound advice*; financially solvent; thorough: *a sound thrashing* –**sound´ly** *adv.* –**sound´ness** *n.*

**sound´less** *adj.* silent; noiseless –**sound´less·ly** *adv.* –**sound´less·ness** *n.*

**soup** *n.* food cooked and served in a liquid

**soup·çon´** *n.* a small quantity; a taste

**sour** *adj.* sharp, acid, or tart to the taste; pertaining to fermentation –**sour´ly** *adv.* –**sour´ness** *n.*

**source** *n.* that from which something originates or is derived

**souse** *vt., vi.* to dip or steep in a liquid; to pickle –*n.* pickled meat; a drunkard

**south** *n.* the general direction to the right of sunrise –*adj.* in a southerly direction –**south´ern** *adj.*

**sou·ve·nir´** *n.* a memento

**sov´er·eign** *adj.* exercizing supreme jurisdiction; autonomous: *a sovereign state* –*n.* one who possesses supreme authority –**sov´er·eign·ty** *n.*

**sow** *vt., vi.* to scatter, as seed

**space** *n.* the expanse considered to be an integral part of the universe; a specific distance or area; an area designated for a particular use: *living space* –*adj.*

**spa´cial** *adj.* spatial

**spa´cious** *adj.* roomy; containing more than adequate space –**spa´cious·ly** *adv.* –**spa´cious·ness** *n.*

**span** *vt.* to measure; to extend across or over –*n.* the distance between two points; a part that extends between two points

**span´gle** *n.* a small bit of brilliant decoration –*vi., vt.* to glitter or cause to glitter –**span´gly** *adj.*

**spank** *vt.* to strike as punishment –**spank´er** *n.*

**spar** *n.* a pole supporting a sail –*vi.* to box; to bandy words

**spare** *vt.* to treat mercifully; to relieve from, as pain or expense; to use frugally –*adj.* over and above what is needed; held in reserve; lean; scanty –*n.* something saved for future use –**spare´ness** *n.*

**spar´ing** *adj.* scanty; frugal or stingy –**spar´ing·ly** *adv.*

**spark** *n.* a glistening or brilliant point or particle; a trace: *a spark of wit* –*vi.* to give off sparks –*vt.* to activate: *spark a revolution*

**spar´kle** *vi.* to glitter; to emit sparks; to effervesce, as certain wines; to be brilliant or vivacious –*n.* brilliance, vivacity –**spar´kler** *n.*

**sparse** *adj.* scattered; not dense –**sparse´ly** *adv.* –**sparse´ness, spar´si·ty** *n.*

**spasm** *n.* a sudden, involuntary muscular contraction; a sudden action or effort

**spas·mod´ic, spas·mod´i·cal** *adj.* temporary; transitory –**spas·mod´i·cal·ly** *adv.*

**spas´tic** *adj.* characterized by spasms –*n.* a person afflicted with a disability that causes spasms –**spas´ti·cal·ly** *adv.*

**spate** *n.* overflow; a sudden outpouring, as of words

**spa´tial** *adj.* relating to space –**spa´tial·ly** *adv.*

**spat´ter** *vi., vt.* to throw off or scatter in drops –*n.* a mark caused by spattering

**speak** *vi.* to utter; to express or convey, as in speech; to deliver an address; to converse –*vt.* to make known, as in speech; to utter in speech; to be capable of conversing, especially in a foreign language –**speak´a·ble** *adj.* –**speak´er** *n.*

**spear** *n.* a weapon consisting of a pointed head on a long shaft; a slender stalk

**spe´cial** *adj.* out of the ordinary; uncommon; designed for a specific purpose: *a special permit*; notable: *a special occasion* –*n.* something designated for a specific service, occasion, etc. –**spe´ci·al·ly** *adv.*

**spe´cial·ist** *n.* one devoted to a particular discipline

**spe·ci·al´i·ty, spe´ci·al·ty** *n.* something in which one specializes

**spe´ci·al·ize** *vt.* to concentrate on one particular activity, branch of learning; etc. –*vt.* to adapt for a particular use or purpose –**spe·ci·al·i·za´tion** *n.*

**spe´cie** *n.* coined money

**spe´cies** *n.* a category of animals or plants

**spe·cif´ic** *adj.* distinctly set forth; explicit –*n.* a medicine affecting a specific condition; a particular item or detail –**spe·cif´i·cal·ly** *adv.* –**spec·i·fic´i·ty**

**spec·i·fi·ca´tion** *n.* a detailed description of a device, part, project, etc.

**spec´i·fy** *vt.* to state in full and explicit detail –**spec´i·fi·a·ble** *adj.* –**spec´i·fi·er** *n.*

**spec´i·men** *n.* a person or thing regarded as representative of a class or type; a sample for laboratory analysis

**spe´cious** *adj.* apparently plausible, but actually without merit: *specious reasoning* –**spe´cious·ly** *adv.* –**spe´cious·ness** *n.*

**speck** *n.* a small spot or stain; a tiny particle or trace

**speck´le** *vt.* to mark with specks –*n.* a speck

**spec´ta·cle** *n.* a grand display, as a pageant, natural phenomenon, etc.; a deplorable exhibition

**spec·tac´u·lar** *adj.* wonderfully exciting –*n.* something lavish –**spec·tac·u·lar´i·ty** *n.* –**spec·tac´u·lar·ly** *adv.*

**spec´ta·tor** *n.* one who views; an eyewitness

**spec´ter** *n.* an apparition **–spec´tral** *adj.* **–spec´tral·ly** *adv.*

**spec´trum** *n.* the band of colors observed when a beam of white light is diffracted; a band of wave frequencies; a range: *a wide spectrum of activities*

**spec´u·late** *vi.* to ponder or theorize; to involve in an endeavor or make an investment that involves risk **–spec·u·la´tion** *n.* **–spec´u·la·tor** *n.* **–spec´u·la·to·ry** *adj.*

**spec´u·la·tive** *adj.* pertaining to conjecture; strictly theoretical; relating to financial risk; risky or doubtful **–spec´u·la·tive·ly** *adv.* **–spec´u·la·tive·ness** *n.*

**speech** *n.* the faculty of expressing with the spoken word; the power to speak; that which is spoken; a public address or lecture; a characteristic manner of speaking **–speech´i·fi·er** *n.* **–speech´i·fy** *vi.*

**speech´less** *adj.* mute; temporarily mute due to a physical disorder, emotion, etc.; inexpressible in words: *speechless wonder* **–speech´less·ly** *adv.* **–speech´less·ness** *n.*

**speed** *n.* rapidity of motion; the rate of movement *–vi.* to move or go rapidly *–vt.* to promote the forward progress of **–speed´er** *n.*

**speed´y** *adj.* characterized by speed; without delay **–speed´i·ly** *adv.* **–speed´i·ness** *n.*

**spells** *vt.* to pronounce or write the letters of a word; to relieve temporarily, as from work *–n.* a period of time; a turn of duty in relief of another; an incantation; a state of enchantment

**spell´bind** *vt.* to enthrall, as if by a spell **–spell´bind·ing·ly** *adv.* **–spell´bound** *adj.*

**spell´er** *n.* one who spells; a spelling book

**spe·lunk´er** *n.* one who explores and studies caves

**spend** *vt.* to pay out or disburse; to use up; to use wastefully or squander **–spend´a·ble** *adj.* **–spend´er** *n.*

**spend´thrift** *n.* one who is wasteful of money *–adj.* excessively lavish

**spent** *adj.* worn out or exhausted

**sperm** *n.* the male fertilizing fluid: semen; a male reproductive cell: spermatozoan

**spew** *vi.* to come or issue forth *–vt.* to eject or send forth

**sphere** *n.* a round body in which every point on the surface is equidistant from the center; a field of activity, influence, etc. **–spher´ic, spher´i·cal** *adj.* **–spher´i·cal·ly** *adv.*

**sphe´roid** *n.* a body approximating the form of a sphere

**sphinx** *n.* a mythical monster; a mysterious person

**spice** *n.* an aromatic substance used to flavor; that which gives zest or adds interest *–vi.* to season with spice; to add zest to **–spic´er** *n.*

**spic´y** *adj.* flavored or fragrant with spice; full of spirit; somewhat improper or risqué **–spic´i·ly** *adv.* **–spic´i·ness** *n.*

**spig´ot** *n.* a plug for a cask; a faucet or the valve by which it functions

**spike** *n.* a large, thick nail; a pointed projection, as on an iron fence or on the soles of shoes; a high slender heel of a woman's shoe; an ear of grain *–vt.* to fasten with a spike; to pierce with a spike

**spill** *vi., vt.* to run over or cause to run over *–n.* that which is spilled **–spill´age** *n.* **–spill´er**

**spill´way** *n.* a passage by which excess water escapes or is released

**spin** *vt.* to draw out and twist fiber into thread, yarn, etc.; to produce a web; to tell, as a story or yarn *–vi.* to make thread or yarn; to whirl rapidly *–n.* a ride, as in an automobile; the uncontrolled spiral descent of an airplane

**spin´dly** *adj.* of a slender, lanky form, suggesting weakness

**spine** *n.* the spinal column of a vertebrate; a hard, pointed outgrowth on the bodies of certain animals; a thorny projection on the stem of a plant; the back of a bound book **–spin´y** *adj.*

**spine´less** *adj.* lacking courage; weak or irresolute; having no backbone; having a flexible backbone **–spine´less·ly** *adv.* **–spine´less·ness** *n.*

**spin´et** *n.* a small harpsichord or upright piano

**spin´ster** *n.* a woman who has never married **–spin´ster·hood** *n.* **–spin´ster·ish** *adj.*

**spi´ral** *n.* a curve that winds like a screw thread; a continuously developing increase or decrease: *a price spiral* *–vi., vt.* to take or cause to take a spiral form or course *–adj.*

**spire** *n.* the tapering roof of a tower or steeple; a slender stalk

**spir´it** *n.* the animating principle of like and energy in man and animals; that part of human characterized by intelligence, emotion, etc.; a supernatural being; mood or disposition; vivacity or energy; unspecified intent: *the spirit of the law* *–vt.* to carry off mysteriously *–adj.* of ghosts or disembodied entities

**spir´it·ed** *adj.* lively, animated; having a specific characteristic: *mean-spirited* **–spir´it·ed·ly** *adv.* **–spir´it·ed·ness** *n.*

**spir´it·less** *adj.* lacking enthusiasm or courage **–spir´it·less·ly** *adv.* **–spir´it·less·ness** *n.*

**spir´i·tu·al** *adj.* pertaining to the highest moral or intellectual qualities of man; sacred or religious; supernatural **–spir·i·tu·al´i·ty, spir´i·tu·al·ness** *n.* **–spir´i·tu·al·ly** *adv.*

**spir´i·tu·al·ism** *n.* the belief that the spirits of the dead can communicate with the living; a philosophy that identifies the ultimate reality as basically spiritual **–spir´i·tu·al·ist** *n.* **–spir·i·tu·al·is´tic** *adj.*

**spite** *n.* malicious bitterness or resentment *–vt.* to vex maliciously **–spite´ful** *adj.* **–spite´ful·ly** *adv.*

**–spite´ful·ness** *n.*

**splash** *vt.* to spatter a liquid about; to display prominently: *splashed over the front page* –*n.* the act or noise of spattering; a small amount: *a splash of bitters*; a brilliant or ostentatious display **–splash´i·ly** *adv.* **–splash´i·ness** *n.* **–splash´y** *adj.*

**splat´ter** *vt., vi.* to spatter or splash in small drops: *a spatter of grease* –*n.* the mark or stain of a spatter; a small amount

**splay** *vt., vi.* to spread or extend outward –*adj.* spread or turned outward

**spleen** *n.* an organ of most vertebrates which modifies, filters, and stores blood; ill temper or spitefulness

**splen´did** *adj.* magnificent, imposing; conspicuously great or illustrious **–splen´did·ly** *adv.* **–splen´did·ness** *n.*

**splen´dor** *n.* magnificence; grandeur **–splen´dor·ous, splen´drous** *adj.*

**splice** *vt.* to unite, as two pieces of rope to form a continuous piece; to connect, as timbers, by beveling, scarfing, or overlapping –*n.* a joint made by splicing **–splic´er** *n.*

**splint** *n.* a thin, flexible strip used for basket weaving, chair bottoms, etc; an appliance to support or immobilize a part of the body –*vt.* to apply a splint

**splin´ter** *n.* a thin, sharp piece split or torn off; a sliver; a faction that has broken away from a larger group –*vt., vi.* to break into fragments; to separate into a smaller group **–splin´ter·y** *adj.*

**split** *vt.* to separate into two or more parts; to divide and distribute –*vi.* to break or divide lengthwise; become divided by disagreement; share with others –*n.* the act or result of splitting; a separation into factions; a share or portion –*adj.* divided or separated

**splurge** *vi.* to spend money lavishly or wastefully –*n.* a showy or extravagant display

**spoil** *vt.* to damage or destroy; to overindulge another –*vi.* to become tainted or decayed, as food

**spoil´age** *n.* that which is spoiled; the extent of waste or loss

**spoils** *n.* plunder seized by violence; government jobs awarded to the faithful supporters of a party

**spoke** *n.* one of the members of a wheel that connect it to the hub

**spo´ken** *adj.* uttered aloud; of a specific kind of speech: *soft-spoken*

**spokes·man** *n.* one who speaks on behalf of another

**sponge** *n.* an underwater; plantlike animal having a fibrous skeleton; the light, absorbent skeleton of such animals used for bathing, cleaning etc.; any absorbent substance used to clean, soak up liquids, etc.; leavened dough –*vt.* to wipe with a sponge; to impose on another **–spon´gi·ness** *n.* **–spong´y** *adj.*

**spong´er** *n.* one who uses a sponge; one who gathers sponges from the sea; one who takes advantage of the generosity of others

**spon´sor** *n.* one who acts as surety for another; a person or group who establishes or finances something –*vt.* to act as a sponsor **–spon·so´ri·al** *adj.* **–spon´sor·ship** *n.*

**spon·ta´ne·ous** *adj.* arising naturally and without constraint or prompting; produced without human involvement **–spon·ta·ne´i·ty** *n.* **–spon·ta´ne·ous·ly** *adv.* **–spon·ta´ne·ous·ness** *n.*

**spoof** *vt., vi.* to deceive; to satirize in a good- natured manner –*n.* a hoax; a playful parody

**spook** *vt.* to haunt; to frighten or disturb; to startle or frighten, as an animal, into flight

**spook´y** *adj.* ghostly, eerie; frightened, nervous **–spook´i·ly** *adv.* **–spook´i·ness** *n.*

**spool** *(US)* *n.* a cylinder for holding thread, wire, etc.

**spoon** *n.* an eating or serving utensil having a shallow oval bowl and a handle –*vt.* to lift up or out with a spoon

**spoon´ful** *n.* as much as a spoon will hold

**spoor** *n.* footprints or other traces of a wild animal

**spo·rad´ic, spo·rad´i·cal** *adj.* occurring infrequently; not widely diffused **–spo·rad´i·cal·ly** *adv.*

**spore** *n.* the reproductive body in plants that have no seeds; any minute organism

**sport** *n.* a diversion; a particular game or activity pursued for diversion; a spirit of raillery; a laughingstock –*vi.* to participate in games; to jest –*adj.* pertaining to sports; of casual wear

**sport´ing** *adj.* conforming to the spirit of sportsmanship

**spor´tive** *adj.* playful; interested in athletic games **–spor´tive·ly** *adv.* **–spor´tive·ness** *n.*

**sport´y** *adj.* colorful, as in dress **–sport´i·ly** *adv.* **–sport´i·ness** *n.*

**spot** *n.* a particular place; a mark, blot, stain, etc.; a mark on a playing card –*vt.* to mark or stain; to see and identify –*adj.* available once: *spot cash*

**spot´less** *adj.* free from dirt, etc.; unblemished as *a spotless reputation* **–spot´less·ly** *adv.* **–spot´less·ness** *n.*

**spot´ty** *adj.* having many spots; uneven, as in quality or performance **–spot´ti·ness** *n.*

**spouse** *n.* a partner in marriage

**spout** *vi., vt.* to pour out or cause to pour out, as a liquid under pressure; to utter angrily or at length

**sprawl** *vi.* to sit or lie ungracefully; to spread out, as vines, etc. **–sprawl´er** *n.*

**spray** *n.* a device for dispersing liquid in fine particles or the liquid dispelled; any similar dispersal, as a cluster of flowers –*vt., vi.* to disperse or send forth in fine particles **–spray´er** *n.*

**spread** *vt.* to open or unfold; to force apart; to distribute over a surface; to distribute over time or among a group; to disperse widely: *spread a rumor* –*vi.* to be extended or expanded; to be spread apart; to be dispersed —**spread´er** *n.*

**spread´sheet** *n.* a document with information arranged in rows and columns, often a computer program for processing numerical data

**spree** *n.* a period of heavy drinking; any boisterous fun

**sprig** *n.* a shoot or sprout of a plant

**spring** *vi.* to move or jump suddenly; to occur suddenly; to proceed as from a source —*vt.* to cause to move or occur suddenly —*n.* a device that yields under stress and returns to normal when the stress is removed; a flow of water; the season that precedes summer —*adj.* resilient —**spring´er** *n.*

**spring´y** *adj.* elastic; resilient

**sprin´kle** *vt.* to scatter in drops or small particles —*vi.* to fall in scattered drops —*n.* a small quantity; a light rain —**sprin´kler** *n.*

**sprint** *n.* a short race —*vi.* to run fast, especially for a short distance —**sprint´er** *n.*

**sprite** *n.* a fairy; a small elflike person

**sprout** *vi.* to put forth shoots; to begin to grow; to develop or grow rapidly —*n.* a new shoot on a plant

**spruce** *adj.* smart and neat in appearance —*n.* a type of pine tree or its wood —**spruce up** make neat and trim

**spry** *adj.* quick; agile —**spry´ly** *adv.* —**spry´ness** *n.*

**spume** *n.* froth or foam —*vi.* to foam

**spunk** *n.* slow-burning tinder; courage, pluck

**spunk´y** *adj.* spirited; daring —**spunk´i·ly** *adv.* —**spunk´i·ness** *n.*

**spur** *n.* a pointed device worn on a horseman's boot; any similar device, as climbing irons used by linemen; anything that incites or urges; a ridge extending laterally from a mountain; a railroad branch —*vt.* to prick or urge, as with spurs

**spu´ri·ous** *adj.* not genuine; illegitimate, as of birth —**spu´ri·ous·ly** *adv.* —**spu´ri·ous·ness** *n.*

**spurn** *vt., vi.* to reject with disdain

**spurt** *n.* a sudden gush or outbreak, as of liquid or energy —*vi.* to gush forth; to make a sudden, forceful effort

**sput´ter** *vi.* to make crackling or popping sounds while throwing off small particles, like burning wood or frying fat —*vi., vt.* to speak excitedly and incoherently —**sput´ter·er** *n.*

**spy** *n.* one hired to get secret information; one who watches secretly —*vi.* to watch closely or secretly; to examine carefully or pry into —*vt.* to observe stealthily; to catch sight of

**squab´ble** *vi.* to engage in a petty quarrel —*n.* a petty argument —**squab´bler** *n.*

**squad** *n.* a small group organized for a special purpose

**squal´id** *adj.* dirty, neglected, or poverty-stricken —**squal´id·ly** *adv.* —**squal´id·ness, squal´or** *n.*

**squall** *n.* a screaming outcry; a brief commotion; a sudden burst of wind, often accompanied by rain or snow —*vi.*

**squan´der** *vt.* to spend wastefully, as money or time —*n.* wastefulness —**squan´der·er** *n.* —**squan´der·ing·ly** *adv.*

**square** *n.* a plane figure having four equal sides and four right angles; a device used to test or lay out right angles; an open area bordered by intersecting streets —*adj.* of or like a square; perfectly adjusted; honest, fair —*vt.* to make square; to test for squareness; to adjust or make satisfactory: *to square accounts*; to reconcile or set right —*vi.* to be right angles; to conform or harmonize —**square´ness** *n.* —**squar´er** *n.*

**square, square´ly** *adv.* honestly, fairly; direct; at right angles

**squash** *vt.* to crush; to suppress —*vi.* to be smashed or crushed; to make a sucking sound —*n.* the sudden fall or sound made by a bursting body; the sound made by walking through ooze or muck; an indoor game played with rackets and ball; an edible gourd

**squat** *vi.* to crouch or cower; to settle on land illegally; to settle on government land in accordance with regulations —*adj.* short and thick —*n.* a crouching position —**squat´er** *n.*

**squat´ty** *adj.* short and thickset

**squeak** *n.* a thin penetrating sound —*vi., vt.* —**squeek through** narrowly avert failure —**squeak´i·ly** *adv.* —**squeak´i·ness** *n.* —**squeak´y** *adj.*

**squeal** *vi.* to utter a sharp, shrill cry; to betray an accomplice or a plot —*n.* a shrill cry, as of a pig —**squeal´er** *n.*

**squeam´ish** *adj.* easily shocked or nauseated; overly scrupulous —**squeam´ish·ly** *adv.* —**squeam´ish·ness** *n.*

**squeeze** *vt.* to extract by pressure; to embrace —*vi.* to apply pressure; to yield to pressure —*n.* pressure; an embrace; a time of difficulty; pressure exerted for extortion —**squeeze by** avoid failure by the narrowest of margins —**squeez´a·ble** *adj.* —**squeez´a·bly** *adv.* —**squeez´er** *n.*

**squelch** *vt.* to squash; to silence, as with a crushing retort —*vi.* to make or move with a sucking noise —*n.* a noise as made by wet boots; a crushing reply —**squelch´er** *n.*

**squint** *vi.* to peer with half-closed eyes —*vt.* to hold the eyes half shut as in glaring light —*n.* —**squint´er** *n.* —**squint´y** *adj.*

**squire** *n.* a knight's attendant; in England a prominent landowner; in the U.S. a village lawyer or justice of the peace; a gentleman escort or suitor

**squirm** *vi.* to bend and twist the body; wriggle; show signs of distress —*n.* a twisting motion

**squirt** *vi., vt.* to come forth or eject in a thin stream —*n.* a jet of liquid

**stab** *vt., vi.* to thrust or wound, as with a pointed weapon —*n.* a wound; a sharp pain; an effort

**sta·bil´i·ty** *n.* the condition of being stable; steadfastness of purpose

**sta´bi·lize** *vt.* to make stable; to keep from fluctuating —*vi.* to become stable —**sta·bi·li·za´tion** *n.* —**sta´bi·liz·er** *n.*

**sta´ble** *adj.* standing firmly in place; not easily moved or changed; having permanence; resistant to chemical change —*n.* a building for lodging horses or cattle; the racehorses of a particular owner; performers, writers, etc. under the same agency —**sta´ble·ness** *n.* —**sta´bly** *adv.*

**stack** *n.* a pile arranged in a somewhat orderly fashion; a large amount —*vt.* to gather into a pile; to arrange dishonestly so as to assure a certain result —**stack´a·ble** *adj.* —**stack´er** *n.*

**sta´di·um** *n.* a large structure for sporting events

**staff** *n.* a stick or rod carried as a cane; a cudgel; an emblem of authority; a pole that supports, as *a flagstaff*; a group of assistants or advisors; a group working together, as *a hospital staff* —**staff´er** *n.*

**stag** *n.* a male deer; an unaccompanied male; a gathering for men only —*adj.* for men only

**stage** *n.* a platform or area from which performances are given; a distinct step or level in a process; a portion of a journey —*vt.* to exhibit on the stage; to plan and carry out, as *to stage a protest*; to simulate: *stage for publicity* —**the stage** the acting profession; any activity or profession associated with theater or drama

**stag´ger** *vi.* to move unsteadily as if carrying something heavy —*vt.* to cause to stagger; to overwhelm, as with surprise or grief; to place in alternating positions —*n.* an unsteady walk —**stag´ger·er** *n.* —**stag´ger·ing·ly** *adj.*

**stag´nant** *adj.* not flowing; foul from standing; sluggish —**stag´nant·cy** *n.* —**stag´nant·ly** *adv.*

**stag´nate** *vi.* to become stagnant —**stag·na´tion** *n.*

**staid** *adj.* sedate; serious —**staid´ly** *adv.* —**staid´ness** *n.*

**stain** *n.* discoloration from foreign matter; a dye or pigment; a moral blemish —*vt.* to discolor; to color with a dye; to blemish —*vi.* to take or impart a stain —**stain´a·ble** *adj.* —**stain´er** *n.*

**stair** *n.* one of a set of steps for ascending or descending

**stake** *n.* a sharpened stick or post; something wagered, as betting money; an interest or share, as in an enterprise —*vt.* to mark a boundary with stakes; to wager; to back with money, equipment, etc.

**stale** *adj.* having lost freshness; deteriorated; lacking effectiveness, spontaneity, etc. —**stale´ness** *n.*

**stale´mate** *n.* a tie or deadlock —*vt.* bring to standstill

**stalk** *n.* a supporting part, as the stem of a plant —*vi., vt.* to approach stealthily —**stalk´er** *n.*

**stall** *n.* a compartment for the confinement of an animal; any small compartment; a delaying action; a condition in which an engine stops functioning —*vt.* to place or keep in a stall; to halt the progress of —*vi.* to come to a standstill; to make delays

**stal´wart** *adj.* strong and robust; determined; courageous —*n.* an uncompromising partisan —**stal´wart·ly** *adv.* —**stal´wart·ness** *n.*

**stam´i·na** *n.* endurance, as in withstanding hardship or difficulty

**stam´mer** *vt., vi.* to speak or utter with nervous repetitions, involuntary pauses, etc. —**stam´mer·er** *n.*

**stamp** *vt.* to strike heavily and noisily with the sole of the foot; to affect as by crushing with the foot: *stamp out opposition*; to cut or imprint with a die; to affix or impress with a die or as with a die —*vi.* to strike the foot heavily on the ground; to walk heavily and noisily —*n.* a machine or tool that cuts or shapes; an implement for imprinting or the imprint; printed proof that a tax or fee has been paid: *a postage stamp*; a specific quality: *the stamp of genius* —**stamp´er** *n.*

**stam·pede´** *n.* a sudden, impulsive rush, as of a herd of cattle or a crowd of people; a spontaneous trend, as to support a political candidate —*vt., vi.* to cause or participate in a sudden rush

**stance** *n.* a mode of standing; a point of view

**stanch** *vt.* to stop or check; to put an end to

**stand** *vi.* to maintain an upright position; to take a position: *stand aside*; to have position: *it stands on a hill*; to assume or maintain an attitude: *stand and fight*; to leave unchanged: *use the letter as it stands* —*vt* to place upright; to endure —*n.* a designated place or position: *a taxi stand*; an opinion or attitude; a structure upon which persons may sit or stand; a stall, etc. where merchandise is traded; a vertical growth of trees —**stand for** to represent; symbolize

**stan´dard** *n.* a flag or banner; an emblem or symbol; that generally accepted as a model; an established reference for weight, quality, value, etc. —*adj.* serving as a criterion or gauge; of recognized excellence, popularity etc.; not special in any way; typical

**stan´dard·ise** *(Brit.),* **stan´dard·ize** *(US)* *vt.* to make conform to, regulate, or test by a standard —**stan·dard·i·za´tion** *n.*

**stand´off** *n.* a draw or tie

**stand·off´ish** *adj.* aloof; cool —**stand·off´ish·ly** *adv.* —**stand·off´ish·ness** *n.*

**sta´ple** *n.* a principal commodity or product of a country or region; a product universally traded or used —*adj.* regularly traded, consumed, etc.

**star** *n.* a celestial object that emits radiant light; a conventional figure having radiating points; a person of outstanding accomplishment; the lead performer in a play, motion picture, etc. —*vi.* to be prominent or brilliant; to play a leading role —*adj.*

exceptional or outstanding: *the star player on our team*; of the stars: *a star-gazer*

**star´dom** *n.* the status of an outstanding performer

**stare** *vi., vt.* to gaze fixedly *—n.* a steady, fixed gaze

**stark** *adj.* barren, bleak; severe; lacking ornamentation, color, etc.; grim, pitiless: *stark reality —adv.* utterly: *stark naked* **—stark´ly** *adv.* **—stark´ness** *n.*

**star´ry** *adj.* marked with or abounding in stars; shining like a star **—star´ri·ness** *n.*

**start** *vi.* to make a quick, involuntary movement; to begin an action, undertaking etc.; to become active, operative, etc. *—vt.* to set in motion; to begin or commence; to set up or establish *—n.* a quick, startled movement; a beginning or commencement; a time or place of beginning

**start´er** *n.* a member at the beginning; one giving the signal to begin, as a race; one who sends out at intervals or at particular times, as trains or buses; a mechanical device, as for an engine; a substance that initiates a chemical reaction

**star´tle** *vt., vi.* to arouse or be aroused or excited suddenly **—star´tling** *adj.*

**star·va´tion** *adj.* insufficient to sustain life *—n.* the act of starving

**starve** *vi.* to perish from lack of food; to suffer extreme hunger; to suffer from lack: *starved for friendship —vt.* to cause to die of hunger; to deprive of something

**stash** *vt.* to hide or conceal for future use *—n.* a place where things are hidden; things hidden

**state** *n.* a mode or condition of existence: *a state of war*; an extreme mental condition; social status or position; a grand, ceremonious, or luxurious style: *to arrive in state*; a sovereign political unit *—adj.* of a government; intended for ceremonial use *—vt.* to set forth in speech or writing

**state´ly** *adj.* dignified; majestic *—adv.* loftily **—state´li·ness** *n.*

**stat´ic** *adj.* pertaining to bodies at rest or forces in equilibrium; at rest; not active *—n.* electrical noise, especially that which interferes with radio communication

**sta´tion** *n.* an assigned place, as of a guard; a headquarters; a place for accommodating passengers or freight on a bus or train line; social rank or standing *—vt.* to assign to a place; to set in position

**sta´tion·ar·y** *adj.* remaining in one place; fixed

**sta´tio·ner** *n.* a dealer in office supplies

**sta´tion·er·y** *n.* office supplies, as pens, papers etc.

**sta·tis´tic** *n.* a number or value based on a representative sampling, as of opinion, income, preference, etc. **—sta·tis´tic, sta·tis´ti·cal** *adj.* **—sta·tis´ti·cal·ly** *adv.*

**stat·is·ti´cian** *n.* one skilled in collecting, tabulating, and analyzing data

**sta·tis´tics** *n.* the collection and analysis of quantitative data

**stat´u·ary** *n.* statues collectively *—adj.* of statues

**stat´ue** *n.* a three-dimensional representation

**stat·u·esque´** *adj.* resembling a statue, as in proportion or dignity; attractive **—stat·u·esque´ly** *adv.* **—stat·u·esque´ness** *n.*

**stat·u·ette´** *n.* a small statue

**stat´ure** *n.* natural height; status or reputation

**sta´tus** *n.* state or condition; relative position or rank

**stat´ute** *n.* an established law or regulation

**stat´u·to·ry** *adj.* pertaining to a statute; based on legislative enactment **—stat´u·to·ri·ly** *adv.*

**staunch** *adj.* firm in principle; constant **—staunch´ly** *adv.* **—staunch´ness** *n.*

**stay** *vi.* to stop, halt; to remain: *stay at home, stay healthy —vt.* to bring to a halt; to hinder; to postpone *—n.* an act or time of staying; a suspension, as of judicial proceedings

**stead** *n.* the place of another as assumed by a substitute

**stead´fast** *adj.* firmly fixed, as in faith or devotion to duty **—stead´fast·ly** *adv.* **—stead´fast·ness** *n.*

**stead´y** *adj.* stable; not likely to shake or totter; unfaltering, constant; regular, as *a steady customer —vt., vi.* to make or become steady **—stead´i·ly** *adv.* **—stead´i·ness** *n.*

**steal** *vt.* to take unlawfully; to obtain subtly: *he has stolen her heart —vi.* to move quietly and stealthily; to commit theft *—n.* a bargain

**stealth** *n.* secret or furtive movement or behavior

**stealth´y** *adj.* marked by stealth; intended to avoid notice **—stealth´i·ly** *adv.* **—stealth´i·ness** *n.*

**steam** *n.* water vapor; the visible mist formed by the sudden cooling of hot steam *—vi.* to emit vapor; to move by the power of steam *—vt.* to treat with steam, as of cooking *—adj.* of, driven, or operated by steam; producing of containing steam **—steam´i·ness** *n.* **—steam´y** *adv.*

**steam´er** *n.* a steamship or steamboat; utensil for steaming food

**steed** *n.* a spirited horse

**steel** *n.* any of various alloys of iron; hardness of character *—adj.* made of steel; firm, unyielding **—steel´i·ness** *n.* **—steel´y** *adj.*

**steep**[1] *adj.* sloping sharply; precipitous; costly **—steep´ly** *adv.* **—steep´ness** *n.*

**steep**[2] *vt.* to soak in a liquid; to infuse, as with liquid for cooking

**stee´ple** *n.* the lofty structure above the roof of a church

**steer** *vt., vi.* to direct the course of

**steer´age** *n.* that part of an ocean vessel allotted to passengers paying the lowest fares

**stem** *n.* the main axis or a subsidiary stalk of a plant; the slender upright support of a goblet, vase, etc.; the rod used for winding a watch; the bow of a boat

—*vt.* to stop or hold back

**stench** *n.* an offensive odor

**sten´cil** *n.* an openwork pattern through which paint, etc. can penetrate to create a design on the surface beneath

**step** *n.* a move accomplished by lifting the foot and putting it down in a different place; the distance moved; a stair or ladder rung; one of a series of moves toward accomplishing something; the sound of a footfall —*vi.*, *vt.*

**stere** *n.* a cubic meter

**ster´e·o** *n.* a stereophonic sound system

**ster´e·o·type** *n.* a hackneyed expression, custom, or mode of thought; a metal printing plate —**ster´e·o·typed** *adj.* —**ste´reo·typ·er** *n.*

**ster´ile** *adj.* having no reproductive power; lacking productiveness; containing no microorganisms; lacking vigor: *sterile prose* —**ste·ril´i·ty** *n.*

**ster´i·lize** *vt.* to render incapable of reproduction; to destroy microorganisms —**ster·i·liza´tion** *n.* —**ster´i·liz·er** *n.*

**stern** *adj.* marked by severity or harshness; having an austere disposition; resolute: *showing stern resolve* —**stern´ly** *adv.* —**stern´ness** *n.*

**ste´ve·dore** *n.* one who loads or unloads ships —*vt.*, *vi.*

**stew´ard** *n.* one entrusted with the management of the affairs of others; one in charge of services for a club, ship, etc. —**stew´ard·ship** *n.*

**stick** *n.* a rigid shoot or branch from a tree or bush; any relatively long and thin piece of wood —*vt.* to pierce with a pointed object; to fasten, as with an adhesive —*vi.* to be or become fixed in place; to persevere or remain faithful

**stick´er** *n.* a gummed label; a prickly stem or bur

**stick´ler** *n.* one with exacting standards; a baffling problem

**stick´y** *adj.* tending to adhere; covered with adhesive; warm and humid; difficult: *a sticky situation* —**stick´i·ness** *n.*

**stiff** *adj.* rigid; resistant to bending; not easily moved: *a stiff bolt*; not natural or graceful: *a stuff bow*; strong and steady: *a stiff breeze*; thick, viscous: *a stiff batter*; harsh: *a stiff penalty*; stubborn, unyielding; difficult, arduous —*n.* an awkward or unresponsive person —**stiff´ly** *adv.* —**stiff´ness** *n.*

**stiff´en** *vt.*, *vi.* to make or become stiff or stiffer —**stiff´en·er** *n.*

**sti´fle** *vt.* to kill by stopping respiration; to hold back or suppress, as sobs —*vi.* to die of suffocation; to have difficulty breathing, as in a stuffy room —**sti´fler** *n.* —**sti´fling·ly** *adv.*

**stig´ma** *n.* a mark of disgrace; a spot or scar on the skin —**stig·mat´ic** *adj.* —**stig´ma·tize** *vt.*

**stile** *n.* a set of steps that span a fence or wall

**sti·let´to** *n.* a small dagger with a slender blade

**still** *adj.* motionless; free from disturbance or agitation; silent; hushed; soft or subdued —*n.* the absence of sound or noise —*adv.* up to this time; in spite of; in increasing degree —*conj.* nevertheless —*vt.* to silence or hush; to allay as fears —*vi.* to become still —**still´ness** *n.*

**stim´u·lant** *n.* a drug that stimulates; anything that rouses one to activity

**stim´u·late** *vt.* to rouse to activity; to affect by intoxicants —*vi.* to act as a stimulus or stimulant —**stim´u·lat·er, stim´u·la·tor** *n.* —**stim·u·la´tion** *n.*

**stim´u·lus** *n.*, *pl.* **stim´u·li** anything that rouses to activity

**sting** *vt.* to pierce or prick painfully; to cause to suffer sharp, smarting pain; to cause to suffer mentally —*vi.* to suffer a sharp, smarting pain; to suffer mental distress —*n.*

**sting´y** *adj.* extremely miserly; meager: *a stingy portion* —**stin´gi·ly** *adv.* —**stin´gi·ness** *n.*

**stink** *n.* a strong foul odor —*vi.*, *vt.* to give forth or cause to give forth a foul odor —**stink´er** *n.* —**stink´y** *adj.*

**stint** *vt.* to limit, as in amount —*vi.* to be frugal or sparing —*n.* a restriction or limit; a specific task or time: *a weekly stint* —**stint´er** *n.* —**sting´ing·ly** *adv.*

**sti´pend** *n.* a regular, fixed allowance

**stip´ple** *vt.* to depict an image with dots —*n.* a method of representing light and shadow using dots; stipled work

**stip´u·late** *vt.* to specify as the terms or requirements for an agreement —*vi.* to demand something as a requirement —**stip·u·la´tion** *n.* —**stip´u·la·tor** *n.*

**stir** *vt.* to mix thoroughly by a circular motion; to cause to move; to rouse, as from sleep or inactivity; to provoke —*vi.* to move; to be active —*n.* movement; public interest or excitement

**stitch** *n.* a single link of thread, yarn, etc. in a line of sewn material; a specific arrangement of thread, etc. as *a chain stitch*; a sudden sharp pain —*vi.* to sew —*vt.* to join or ornament with stitches —**stitch´er** *n.*

**sto·chas´tic** *adj.* characterized by conjecture; involving probability —**sto·chas´ti·cal·ly** *adv.*

**stock** *n.* the goods a merchant has on hand; the original from which others are descended or derived; the trunk or main stem of a plant; shares in a corporation; raw material; the broth from boiled vegetables, meat, etc. —*vt.* to supply with cattle, as for a farm; to supply with merchandise; to keep on hand; to sell; to supply with wildlife: *stock a pond*; to put aside for future use —*adj.* commonplace: *a stock item*; employed in tending to merchandise: *a stock clerk*

**stock·ade´** *n.* a defensive barrier or the area it encloses; an area used to confine prisoners —*vi.* to fortify with a stockade

**stock´y** *adj.* short and stout —**stock´i·ness** *n.*

**stodg´y** *adj.* dull or boring; heavy, as a feeling —**stodg´i·**

ly *adv.* –**stodg´i·ness** *n.*

**sto´ic** *n.* one apparently unaffected by emotion, such as pleasure or pain –**sto´ic, sto´i·cal** *adj.* impassive or indifferent to pain or suffering –**sto´i·cal·ly** *adv.* –**sto´i·cism** *n.*

**stoke** *vt.* to supply a furnace with fuel; to stir up –*vi.* to tend a fire –**stok´er** *n.*

**stol´id** *adj.* without feeling; impassive –**stol´id·ly** *adv.* –**stol´id·ness** *n.*

**stom´ach** *n.* a pouchlike dilation of the alimentary canal that serves as one of the principal organs of digestion; the abdomen; a desire –*vt.* to put up with; to endure

**stomp** *vt., vi.* to tread heavily upon –*n.* a jazz dance

**stone** *n.* a small piece of rock; a shaped rock, as *a gravestone*; something small and hard; the pit of a fruit –*adj.* made of stone –*vt.* to hurl stones at; to remove pits from

**ston´y** *adj.* abounding in stone; unfeeling: *hard as stone* –**ston´i·ly** *adv.* –**ston´i·ness** *n.*

**stooge** *n.* one who acts as or is the dupe of another

**stool** *n.* a backless and armless seat; a low bench for the feet or for kneeling; feces

**stoop** *vi.* to lean the body forward and down; to walk with the upper body bent forward; to lower or degrade oneself –*vt.* to bend forward –*n.* a habitual forward inclination of the head and shoulders; a small porch

**stop** *vt.* to bring to a halt; to prevent the completion of; to withhold or cut off; to cease doing; to check or stanch; to fill in or close, as with a cork –*vi.* to come to a halt –*n.* the act of stopping; an obstruction

**stop´per, stop´ple** *n.* a cork, plug, etc. –*vt.* to close with a cork, etc.

**stor´age** *n.* the placing of articles for safekeeping; a space or a charge for storing

**store** *vt.* to put away for safekeeping or future use –*n.* that which is put away; a place where merchandise is kept for sale –**set store by** to value or esteem; to believe –**store´house** *n.* –**store´keep·er** *n.*

**sto´rey** *(Brit.)* *n.* one level of a building

**sto´ried** *adj.* having a notable history

**storm** *n.* an atmospheric disturbance marked by strong winds, precipitation, etc.; heavy prolonged winds and precipitation; a violent emotional outburst; political or social disturbance: *a storm of protest* –*vi.* to blow or rage like a storm –*vt.* to attack

**storm´y** *adj.* characterized by storms; turbulent; violent –**storm´i·ly** *adv.* –**storm´i·ness** *n.*

**sto´ry** *n.* a narrative of an event, either true or invented; an account of facts; an anecdote; the plot of a fictional account; a falsehood; *(US)* one level of a building

**stout** *adj.* thick-set; firmly built; courageous –*n.* a strong dark beer –**stout´ly** *adv.* –**stout´ness** *n.*

**stout´-heart´ed** *adj.* brave, courageous –**stout·heart´ed·ly** *adv.* –**stout´-heart´ed·ness** *n.*

**stove** *n.* an appliance for heating or cooking

**stow** *vt.* to pack; to store –**stow away to** hide for safekeeping; to hide so as not to pay passage

**stow´age** *n.* the space or charge for stowing goods; goods stowed

**strad´dle** *vt.* to stand, sit, etc. with legs on either side of; to spread the legs wide apart; to appear to favor both sides of an issue –*n.* the act of straddling; a position of non-committal –**strad´dler** *n.* –**strad´dling·ly** *adv.*

**strag´gle** *vi.* to stray or wander; to fall behind; to occur at irregular intervals –**strag´gler** *n.* –**strag´gling·ly** *adv.* –**strag´gly** *adj.*

**straight** *adj.* extending without curve or bend; erect; fair and honest; correctly arranged; conforming to what is accepted as normal or conventional –*n.* an unbent piece or section –*adv.* in a direct course; at once, directly; without qualification –**straight´ness** *n.*

**straight´en** *vt., vi.* to make or become straight –**straight´en·er** *n.*

**strain** *vt.* to exert to the utmost; to injure by overexertion; to pass through a filter; to remove with a filter –*vi.* to make a violent effort; to become wrenched or twisted; to filter –*n.* any taxing demand on resources; any violent effort; an injury caused by excessive effort

**strain´er** *n.* a device that filters or sifts

**strait** *n.* a narrow passage of water that connects two larger bodies of water

**strand** *n.* fibers, wires, etc., singly or twisted together to form a rope, cable, etc.; a ropelike object –*vt., vi.* to leave or be left in a difficult or helpless situation

**strange** *adj.* unfamiliar; peculiar, out of the ordinary; out of place –**strange´ly** *adv.* –**strange´ness** *n.*

**stran´ger** *n.* an unfamiliar person; one who is ignorant of or oblivious to something: *a stranger to good manners*

**stran´gle** *vt.* to choke to death; to suppress –*vi.* to suffer or die from choking –**stran´gler** *n.*

**stran´gu·late** *vt.* to constrict so as to cut off circulation of the blood –**stran·gu·la´tion** *n.*

**strap** *n.* a long, narrow, flexible strip of a material such as leather –*vt.* to fasten, as with a strap; to beat, as with a strap

**strap´ping** *adj.* large and muscular; robust

**stra·te´gic, stra·te´gi·cal** *adj.* based on strategy; of that which is vital or essential –**stra·te´gi·cal·ly** *adv.*

**strat´e·gy** *n.* a broad-based plan; the use of artifice in striving for an objective –**strat´e·gist** *n.*

**strat´i·fy** *vt., vi.* to arrange or be formed in layers –**strat´i·fi·ca´tion** *n.*

**stray** *vi.* to wander from a proper course; to deviate

from right or goodness *–adj.* wandering: *a stray dog*; out of place: *a stray hair* *–n.* a domestic animal that has wandered **–stray´er** *n.*

**streak** *n.* a long, narrow strip; a contrasting mark or characteristic: *a steak of kindness* *–vi., vt.* to form a streak or streaks; to move at great speed; to run by naked, as for a thrill **–streak´er** *n.* **–streak´y** *adj.* **–streak´i·ly** *adv.* **–streak´i·ness** *n.*

**stream** *n.* a flow of water; any uninterrupted flow: *a stream of laughter* *–vi.* to pour forth or issue; to proceed without interruption

**street** *n.* a public walkway or road *–adj.* taking place on the street: *a street musician*

**strength** *n.* the quality of being physically strong; the capacity to apply or withstand force; intensity, as of light, sound, medication, etc.

**strength´en** *vt., vi.* to make or become strong or stronger **–strength´en·er** *n.*

**stren´u·ous** *adj.* marked by great effort or exertion **–stren´u·ous·ly** *adv.* **–stren´u·ous·ness** *n.*

**stress** *n.* physical or emotional tension; emphasis; pressure *–vt.* to subject to stress; to give emphasis or accent, as in speech **–stress´ful** *adj.* **–stress´ful·ly** *adv.*

**stretch** *vt.* to extend or draw out; to strain to the utmost; to adapt to circumstances: *stretch the truth* *–vi.* to extend from one place to another; to be extended beyond normal limits; to extend one's limbs *–n.* a continuous extend of space or time *–adj.* capable of being easily distended, as *stretch socks* – **stretch´a·ble** *adj.* **–stretch´a·bil´i·ty, stretch´i·ness** *n.* **–stretch´y** *adv.*

**strew** *vt.* so spread about at random; to be scattered over

**stri´ate** *vt.* to mark with grooves; stripes, etc. **–stri´ate, stri´at´ed** *adj.* **–stri·a´tion** *n.*

**strick´en** *adj.* affected by injury, disease, sorrow, etc.

**strict** *adj.* containing or enforcing severe rules or provisions; harsh, stern, exacting; absolute: *in strict confidence* **–strict´ly** *adv.* **–strict´ness** *n.*

**stric´ture** *n.* something that restricts; a narrowing or closure of a dust of the body

**stride** *n.* a long, often measured, step *–vi., vt.* to walk with long steps **–strid´er** *n.*

**stri´dent** *adj.* loud and harsh sounding **–stri´dence, stri´den·cy** *n.* **–stri´dent·ly** *adv.*

**strife** *n.* angry contention; a rivalry

**strike** *vt.* to hit; to crash into; to affect suddenly or in a specified manner; to cease work or interfere with the work of others as a protest: *a sit-down strike*; to make and confirm, as a bargain *–vi.* to come into violent contact; to sound from a blow; to cease work *–n.* a blow; a sudden success: *a lucky strike*; a work stoppage by employees **–strik´er** *n.*

**string** *n.* a slender line for tying parcels, etc.; a cord or wire for a musical instrument, tennis racket, etc.; a connected series of things on a cord or as on a cord *–vt.* to thread, as beads; to replace a cord, as on a musical instrument, racket, etc. *–vi.* to extend, proceed, or form in a series

**strin´gent** *adj.* rigid or severe, as regulations; convincing **–strin´gen·cy, strin´gent·ness** *n.* **–strin´gent·ly** *adv.*

**string´y** *adj.* like string, as of hair; forming or formed in strings; tall and wiry **–string´i·ness** *n.*

**strip** *n.* a narrow piece, often long; a set of cartoon drawings *–vt.* to lay bare; to deprive of something; to damage, as of gears or a bolt *–vi.* to undress

**stripe** *n.* a band that differs in color, texture, etc. from its surroundings; a distinctive quality; a blow struck with a whip or rod *–vt.* to mark with a contrasting band

**strip´ling** *n.* a lad

**strive** *vi.* to make an effort; to fight **–striv´er** *n.*

**stroll** *vi.* to walk in a casual manner *–n.* a leisurely walk **–stroll´er** *n.*

**strong** *adj.* physically powerful; healthy, robust; especially competent or able; firm, tenacious *–adv.* in a firm manner **–strong´ly** *adv.*

**struc´tur·al** *adj.* of or pertaining to construction **–struc´tur·al·ly** *adv.*

**struc´ture** *n.* that which is constructed; something based on a plan or design; a manner of design: *a wood frame structure*; the arrangement and relationship of the parts of a whole: *hierarchical structure* *–vt.* to build; to conceive as a structural whole

**strug´gle** *n.* an arduous effort; a war *–vt.* to contend with an adversary; to strive **–strug´gler** *n.* – **strug´gling·ly** *adv.*

**strut** *n.* a pompous walk; a supporting member of a framework *–vi.* to walk pompously *–vt.* to support or separate with a brace **–strut´ter** *n.* **–strut´ting·ly** *adv.*

**stub** *n.* a short remnant, as of a pencil, candle, etc. *–vt.* to strike; as the toe, against an obstacle accidently

**stub´ble** *n.* the remnants of plants in the ground after reaping; a short, bristly beard **–stub´bly** *adj.*

**stub´born** *adj.* inflexible; determined to have one's own way; not easily overcome **–stub´born·ly** *adv.* **–stub´born·ness** *n.*

**stub´by** *adj.* short and thick **–stub´bi·ness** *n.*

**stud** *n.* a short, ornamental knob or button; an upright member of a building frame *–vt.* to set thickly with ornamental buttons; to scatter over: *flowers stud the valley*

**stu´dent** *n.* one engaged in a course of study; a careful observer

**stu´dio** *n.* a working area for an artist, photographer, etc.

**stu´di·ous** *adj.* devoted to study; careful or attentive

—**stu´di·ous·ly** *adv.* —**stu´di·ous·ness** *n.*

**stud´y** *n.* the process of acquiring knowledge; a branch of knowledge; a room set aside for reading or studying —*vt.* to acquire knowledge of; to examine thoroughly —*vi.* to apply the mind to learning; to be a student

**stuff** *vt.* to fill completely; to plug or stop up —*n.* a fundamental element: *the stuff of genius*; personal possessions generally; unspecified matter; a miscellaneous collection

**stuff´y** *adj.* poorly ventilated; filled up so as to impede respiration; strait-laced, stodgy —**stuff´i·ly** *adv.* —**stuff´i·ness** *n.*

**stul´ti·fy** *vt.* to cause to appear absurd; to make useless or futile —**stul·ti·fi·ca´tion** *n.* —**stul´ti·fi·er** *n.*

**stum´ble** *vi.* to miss one's step and almost fall; to speak in a halting manner; to happen upon by chance; to do wrong —*vt.* to cause to stumble —*n.* the act of stumbling —**stum´bler** *n.* —**stum´bling·ly** *adv.*

**stump** *n.* that portion left when a part is cut off, as of a limb; a place where a political speech is made —*adj.* pertaining to political campaigning —*vt.* to make a political speech

**stun** *vt.* to render incapable of action; to astound, daze, or overwhelm

**stun´ning** *adj.* impressive; beautiful —**stun´ning·ly** *adv.*

**stunt** *vt.* to check the natural development of —*n.* a check in growth or development

**stu´pe·fa´cient** *adj.* stupefying —*n.* a drug that induces stupor

**stu´pe·fy** *vt.* to dull the senses or faculties; to amaze or astound —**stu·pe·fac´tion** *n.* —**stu´pe·fi·er** *n.*

**stu·pe·fac´tive** *adj., n.* stupefacient

**stu·pen´dous** *adj.* astonishing; of immense size, breadth, etc. —**stu·pen´dous·ly** *adv.* —**stu·pen´dous·ness** *n.*

**stu´pid** *adj.* lacking intelligence; dull-witted; tiresome or annoying —**stu·pid´i·ty, stu´pid·ness** *n.* —**stu´pid·ly** *adv.*

**stu´por** *n.* abnormal lethargy or intellectual dullness

**stur´dy** *adj.* robust and powerful; firm and resolute —**stur´di·ly** *adv.* —**stur´di·ness** *n.*

**stut´ter** *vt., vi.* to speak with spasmodic repetition —*n.* halting or repetitious speech —**stut´ter·er** *n.* —**stut´ter·ing·ly** *adv.*

**sty** *n.* a pen for swine; any filthy habitation; a pustule on the edge of an eyelid

**style** *n.* a fashionable appearance; a particular or distinctive fashion, form, or manner —*vt.* to give a name or title: *Richard I, styled "the Lion-Hearted"*; to cause to conform to a specific form

**styl´ish** *adj.* fashionable —**styl´ish·ly** *adv.* —**styl·ish·ness** *n.*

**styl´ist** *n.* a matter of style; a creator of style —**sty·lis´tic** *adj.* —**sty·lis´ti·cal·ly** *adv.*

**styp´tic** *adj.* tending to halt bleeding —*n.* an astringent —**styp´ti·cal** *adj.*

**sua´sion** *n.* persuasion —**sua´sive** *adj.* —**sua´sive·ly** *adv.* —**sua´sive·ness** *n.*

**suave** *adj.* smoothly pleasant and courteous —**suave´ly** *adv.* —**suave´ness, suav´i·ty** *n.*

**sub·con´scious** *adj.* not attended by full awareness —*n.* mental activity not in the focus of consciousness —**sub·con´scious·ly** *adv.* —**sub·con´scious·ness** *n.*

**sub´cul·ture** *n.* a group with behavioral characteristics that set it off from others within a culture —**sub·cul´tur·al** *adj.*

**sub´di·vide** *vt., vi.* to separate into smaller pieces; to divide a parcel of land into lots for individual sale

**sub´di·vi·sion** *n.* a tract of land made up of subdivided lots; a group of usually similar houses in an area

**sub·due´** *vt.* to gain dominion over; to repress —**sub·du´a·ble** *adj.* —**sub·du´er** *n.*

**sub´ject** *adj.* under the power of; having a tendency —*n.* one under the power of another; one employed or treated in a specified way; a theme or topic; a branch of learning —**sub·ject´** *vt.* to bring under control; to make liable or responsible for

**sub·jec´tive** *adj.* relating to personal feeling or opinion; influenced by emotion or prejudice —**sub·jec´tive·ly** *adv.* —**sub·jec´tive·ness, sub·jec·tiv´i·ty** *n.*

**sub·join´** *vt.* to add at the end —**sub·join´der** *n.*

**sub´ju·gate** *vt.* to conquer; to make subservient —**sub·ju·ga´tion** *n.* —**sub´ju·ga·tor** *n.*

**sub´li·mate** *vt.* to convert inappropriate behavior to that which is socially acceptable —**sub·li·ma´tion** *n.*

**sub·lime´** *adj.* characterized by grandeur —**sub·lime·ly** *adv.* —**sub·lime´ness** *n.*

**sub·lim´in·al** *adj.* below the threshold of consciousness; too slight to be perceived —**sub·lim´in·al·ly** *adv.*

**sub·merge´** *vt.* to place under water —*vi.* to sink beneath the surface —**sub·mer´gence** *n.*

**sub·merse´** *vt.* submerge —**sub·mer´sion** *n.*

**sub·mers´i·ble** *adj.* that may be submerged —*n.* a warship designed to operate both on the surface and under water; a small underwater craft used for observation, rescue, etc. —**sub·mers·i·bil´i·ty** *adv.*

**sub·mis´sion** *n.* yielding to another; the act of presenting for consideration, arbitration, etc.; something submitted, as a manuscript

**sub·mis´sive** *adj.* inclined to submit —**sub·mis´sive·ly** *adv.* —**sub·mis´sive·ness** *n.*

**sub·mit´** *vt.* to yield to another; to present for consideration —*vi.* to surrender; obey

**sub·or´di·nate** *adj.* lower in rank; secondary —*n.* a person of lower rank; a helper or assistant —*vt.* to assign a lower rank; to make subservient —**sub·or´di·nate·ly** *adv.* —**sub·or·di·na´tion** *n.*

**sub·orn´** *vt.* to bribe someone to commit perjury; to

incite to commit an unlawful act **–sub·or·na´tion** *n.*

**sub·poe´na** *n.* a writ requiring a court appearance

**sub´ro·gate** *vt.* to substitute one for another, especially of a creditor **–sub·ro·ga´tion** *n.*

**sub·scribe´** *vt.* to sign one's name to as an expression of assent; to promise to pay or contribute; to give approval; to agree; to promise to contribute money; to pay in advance, as for a periodical, tickets, etc. **–sub·scrib´er** *n.* **–sub·scrip´tion** *n.*

**sub´se·quent** *adj.* following in time, order, etc. **–sub´se·quence** *n.* **–sub´se·quent·ly** *adv.*

**sub·ser´vi·ent** *adj.* servile or obsequious **–sub·ser´vi·ence, sub·ser´vi·en·cy** *n.* **–sub·ser´vi·ent·ly** *adv.*

**sub·side´** *vi.* to sink to a lower level; to become calm or quiet **–sub·sid´ence** *n.*

**sub·sid´i·ar·y** *adj.* supplementary or auxiliary; pertaining to a subsidy *–n.* a business with over half its assets owned by another **–sub·sid´i·ar·i·ly** *adv.*

**sub´si·dize** *vt.* to furnish with financial aid **–sub´si·diz·er** *n.*

**sub´si·dy** *n.* a financial grant given by one person or government to another

**sub·sist´** *vi.* to continue to exist; to maintain life

**sub·sist´ence** *n.* that by which one subsists, as for food or earnings **–sub·sist´ent** *adj.*

**sub´stance** *n.* the material of which something is made; the essential component of anything; wealth or property; the quality of being constant or solid

**sub·stan´tial** *adj.* firm and solid; tangible; of significant worth or importance **–sub·stan´tial·ly** *adv.* **–sub·stan´tial·ness** *n.*

**sub·stan´ti·ate** *vt.* to verify by evidence; to prove **–sub·stan·ti·a´tion** *n.*

**sub´stan·tive** *n.* a noun or pronoun; a verbal form, phrase, etc. used in place of a noun *–adj.* that can be used as a noun; denoting existence; having substance **–sub´stan·tive·ly** *adv.* **–sub´stan·tive·ness** *n.*

**sub´sti·tute** *vt.* to put in place of another; to take the place of *–vi.* to act as a substitute *–n.* an alternate or replacement *–adj.* alternative; temporary: *a substitute teacher* **–sub·sti·tut·a·bil´i·ty** *n.* **–sub´sti·tut·a·ble** *adj.*

**sub·sti·tu´tion** *n.* the act of replacing; the state of being a replacement; a substitute **–sub·sti·tu´tion·al** *adj.* **–sub·sti·tu´tion·al·ly** *adv.*

**sub´ter·fuge** *n.* a deception

**sub·ter·ra´ne·an** *adj.* below the surface of the earth

**sub´til·ize** *vt., vi.* to make or become subtle; to argue with careful differentiation **–sub·til·i·za´tion** *n.*

**sub´tle** *adj.* not easily detected, as *a subtle aroma*; not obvious; skillful or ingenious **–sub´tle·ness** *n.* **–sub´tly** *adv.*

**sub´tle·ty** *n.* the quality of being subtle; a small differentiation

**sub·tract´** *vt., vi.* to take away or deduct **–sub·trac´tion** *n.* **–sub·trac´tive** *adj.*

**sub´urb** *n.* an area adjacent to a city; an outlying district **–sub·ur´ban** *adj.*

**sub·ur´ban·ite** *n.* a resident of a suburb

**sub·ur´bi·a** *n.* the suburbs or suburbanites collectively; the cultural world of suburbanites

**sub·ver´sive** *n.* one desiring to weaken or overthrow, as a government *–adj.* tending to undermine or weaken **–sub·ver´sion** *n.* **–sub·ver´sive·ly** *adv.*

**sub·vert´** *vt.* to corrupt; to destroy utterly

**sub´way** *n.* an underpass; an underground railway

**suc·ceed´** *vi.* to accomplish what is intended; to turn out as intended: *the plan succeeded*; to come next in a sequence *–vt.* to come after in time or order

**suc·cess´** *n.* a favorable process or termination; the gaining of fame, wealth, etc.; the scale or level of gain

**suc·cess´ful** *adj.* ending in success **–suc·cess´ful·ly** *adv.*

**suc·ces´sion** *n.* the act of following in order; the right to a predecessor's office, possessions, etc. **–suc·ces´sor** *n.*

**suc·ces´sive** *adj.* following in order **–suc·ces´sive·ly** *adv.*

**suc·cinct´** *adj.* presented clearly and concisely; marked by brevity **–suc·cinct´ly** *adv.* **–suc·cinct´ness** *n.*

**suc´cu·lent** *adj.* juicy; having thick fleshy leaves; interesting *–n.* a succulent plant **–suc´cu·lence** *n.* **–suc´cu·lent·ly** *adv.*

**suc·cumb´** *vi.* to yield, as to force or persuasion; to die

**such** *adj.* being the same or similar: *times such as these*; extreme: *such an uproar* *–pron.* the same as implied or indicated *–adv.* especially: *in such good spirits*

**suck** *vt.* to draw in by a partial vacuum; to pull or draw in as if by suction: *the lure of profit sucked him in* *–vi.* to draw in by suction; to suckle; to make a suckling sound

**suc´tion** *n.* the production of a partial vacuum *–adj.* creating or operating by suction

**sud´den** *adj.* happening quickly without warning; hasty, rash **–sud´den·ly** *adv.* **–sud´den·ness** *n.*

**suds** *pl. n.* froth, foam **–suds·y** *adj.*

**sue** *vt.* to take legal action in order to redress a wrong; to prosecute *–vi.* to institute legal proceedings; to seek to persuade by entreaty: *to sue for peace* **–su·a·bil´i·ty** *n.* **–su´a·ble** *adj.* **–su´er** *n.*

**suede** *n.* hide or fabric having a napped surface

**suf´fer** *vi.* to feel pain or distress; to sustain loss or injury; to undergo punishment *–vt.* to sustain or have inflicted on one; to endure; to allow **–suf´fer·a·ble** *adj.* **–suf´fer·a·bly** *adv.* **–suf´fer·er** *n.* **–suf´fer·ing** *adj.* **–suf´fer·ing·ly** *adv.*

**suf´fer·ance** *n.* permission granted or implied by failure to permit; the capacity for suffering

**suf·fice´** *vi.* to be sufficient or adequate

**suf·fi´cien·cy** *n.* that which is sufficient

**suf·fi´cient** *adj.* being all that is needed; enough **–suf·fi´cient·ly** *adv.*

**suf´fix** *n.* an addition to a word that modifies it or forms a new word *–vt.* to add as a suffix

**suf´fo·cate** *vt.* to kill by obstructing respiration; to cause distress by depriving of adequate oxygen; to smother, as a fire; to stifle: *suffocated by affection –vi.* to be distressed or to die by deprivation of oxygen; to become or feel stifled **–suf´fo·cat´ing·ly** *adv.* **–suf·fo·ca´tion** *n.* **–suf´fo·ca·tive** *adj.*

**suf´frage** *n.* the privilege of voting; a vote **–suf´frag·ist** *n.*

**suf´frag·ette´** *n.* a female advocate of women's right to vote

**suf·fuse´** *vt.* to spread over, as with a liquid, light, etc. **–suf·fu´sion** *n.* **–suf·fu´sive** *adj.*

**sug·gest´** *vt.* to present for consideration; to associate: *gold suggests wealth*; to imply: *her gesture suggests indifference*

**sug·gest´i·ble** *adj.* that can be recommended; easily lead **–sug·gest´i·bil´i·ty** *n.*

**sug·ges´tion** *n.* something offered for consideration; a small amount, a trace

**sug·ges´tive** *adj.* that stimulating thought or reflection; hinting at something improper **–sug·ges´tive·ly** *adv.* **–sug·ges´tive·ness** *n.*

**su´i·cide** *n.* the taking of one's own life; ruin brought on by one's own actions **–su´i·ci´dal** *adj.* **–su´i·ci´dal·ly** *adv.*

**suit** *n.* a garment or set of garments; a grouping or set of compatible things: *a bedroom suit*; a court proceeding; the courting of a woman *–vt.* to meet the requirements of; to satisfy; to adapt; to furnish with clothes *–vi.* to prove satisfactory **–suit´or** *n.*

**suit´a·ble** *adj.* appropriate or fitting **–suit·a·bil´i·ty, suit´a·ble·ness** *n.* **–suit´a·bly** *adv.*

**suite** *n.* a set of things intended for use together, as connecting rooms in a hotel; a set of matched furniture, a *suit*

**sulk** *vi.* to be sullen and withdrawn *–n.* a sullen mood

**sulk´y** *n.* a light, horse-drawn vehicle for one *–adj.* sullen and withdrawn **–sulk´i·ly** *adv.* **sulk´i·ness** *n.*

**sul´len** *adj.* ill-homored; glum; depressing; slow or sluggish **–sul´len·ly** *adv.* **–sul´len·ness** *n.*

**sul´ly** *vt.* to soil; to shame or defile

**sul´try** *adj.* hot and humid; arousing passion; sensual **–sul´tri·ly** *adv.* **–sul´tri·ness** *n.*

**sum** *n.* the entire amount; a summary

**sum´ma·rize** *vt.* to prepare or present as an outline or summary **–sum´ma·ri·za´tion** *n.* **–sum´ma·ri·zer** *n.*

**sum´ma·ry** *n.* a brief account *–adj.* containing the essential details; performed without ceremony or delay **–sum·mar´i·ly** *adv.*

**sum·ma´tion** *n.* the act of adding numbers; a final review of the main points of an argument

**sum´mit** *n.* the highest point or part; the highest level or office

**sum´mon** *vt.* to send for; to call together; to rouse to action **–sum´mon·er** *n.*

**sum´mons** *n.* a notice to appear in court; any call to appear

**sump´tu·ous** *adj.* lavish; luxurious **–sump´tu·ous·ly** *adv.* **–sump´tu·ous·ness** *n.*

**sunk´en** *adj.* lying at the bottom; lower than the surrounding area: *a sunken garden*

**sun** *n.* the star at the center of the solar system; any star *–vt.* to expose to the sun *–vi.* to bask in the sun

**sun´ny** *adj.* filled with sunlight; bright, cheerful **–sun´ni·ly** *adv.*

**sun´set** *n.* the time at which the sun falls below the horizon; a final period or decline

**sup** *vi.* to eat

**su´per** *adj.* surpassing others of its kind; outstanding *–n.* a superintendent

**su´per·a·ble** *adj.* that can be overcome **–su´per·a·bil´i·ty, su´per·a·ble·ness** *n.* **–su´per·a·bly** *adv.*

**su·perb´** *adj.* extraordinarily good **–su·perb´ly** *adv.* **–su·perb´ness** *n.*

**su·per·cil´i·ous** *adj.* haughtily disdainful; arrogant **–su·per·cil´i·ous·ly** *adv.* **–su·per·cil´i·ous·ness** *n.*

**su·per·fi´cial** *adj.* on or near the surface: *a superficial wound*; trivial, not profound; hasty: *a superficial examination*; apparent rather than real: *a superficial resemblance* **–su´per·fi·ci·al´i·ty** *n.* **–su·per·fi´cial·ly** *adv.*

**su·per´flu·ous** *adj.* surplus; exceeding what is needed; unnecessary or irrelevant: *a superfluous comment* **–su·per·flu´i·ty** *n.* **–su·per´flu·ous·ly** *adv.*

**su·per·in·tend´** *vt.* to direct or supervise **–su·per·in·tend´ence, su·per·in·tend´en·cy** *n.*

**su·per·in·tend´ent** *n.* one who has charge; one responsible for maintenance and repair

**su·pe´ri·or** *adj.* higher in rank, quality, etc.; affecting an attitude of indifference or disdain *–n.* one who is higher in rank **–su·pe·ri·or´i·ty** *n.* **–su·pe´ri·or·ly** *adv.*

**su·per´la·tive** *adj.* of the highest degree; most excellent; exaggerated *–n.* something of the highest grade **–su·per´la·tive·ly** *adv.* **–su·per´la·tive·ness** *n.*

**su·per·nat´u·ral** *adj.* existing outside the forces of nature; miraculous or divine; ghosts, demons, etc. *–n.* unnatural phenomena **–su·per·nat´u·ral·ly** *adv.* **–su·per·nat´u·ral·ness** *n.*

**su·per·nat´u·ral·ism** *n.* a belief in the supernatural; belief in a divine force that directs the universe **–su·per·nat´u·ral·ist** *adj., n.* **–su·per·nat´u·ral·is´tic** *adj.*

**su·per·sede´** *vt.* to set aside and replace with something newer or better; to take the place of **–su·per·sed´er** *n.*

**su·per·son´ic** *adj.* moving faster than the speed of sound

**su·per·sti´tion** *n.* an irrational belief; any practice inspired by such belief

**su·per·sti´tious** *adj.* influenced by superstition; based on superstition **–su·per·sti´tious·ly** *adv.* **–su·per·sti´tious·ness** *n.*

**su´per·vise** *vt.* to have charge of; to oversee or manage **–su·per·vi´sion** *n.* **–su´per·vi·sor** *n.* **–su´per·vi´so·ry** *adj.*

**su·pine´** *adj.* lying face up **–su·pine´ly** *adv.* **–su·pine´ness** *n.*

**sup´per** *n.* the evening meal; the last meal of the day

**sup·plant´** *vt.* to displace, as of something outdated; to displace by treachery **–sup·plant´er** *n.*

**sup´ple** *adj.* flexible; agile or graceful; yielding readily, compliant; adaptable *–vt., vi.* to make or become supple **–sup´ple·ness** *n.*

**sup´ple·ment** *n.* something added to correct or argument *–vt.* to make an addition to **–sup·ple·men´tal, sup´ple·men´ta·ry** *adj.* **–sup·ple·men´tal·ly** *adv.*

**sup´pli·cate** *vt.* to ask for humbly or by earnest prayer *–vi.* to make an earnest request **–sup´pli·cant** *n.* **–sup·pli·ca´tion** *n.*

**sup·ply´** *vt.* to make available or furnish; to provide for adequately *–vi.* to take the place of another temporarily *–n.* a quantity on hand; the amount available **–sup·pli´er** *n.*

**sup·port´** *vt.* to bear the weight of; to hold in position; to provide with necessities; to substantiate or defend; to provide with the means to endure *–n.* someone or something that supports

**sup·port´er** *n.* one who provides with necessities; a device that braces

**sup·port´ive** *adj.* contributing significantly to one's physical or emotional health **–sup·por´tive·ly** *adv.* **–sup·port´ive·ness** *n.*

**sup·pose´** *vt.* to believe to be possible; to expect; to imply **–sup·pos´a·ble** *adj.* **–sup·pos´a·bly** *adv.* **–sup·pos´er** *n.*

**sup·posed´** *adj.* accepted as genuine; imagined **–sup·pos·ed´ly** *adv.*

**sup·po·si´tion** *n.* a conjecture or assumption **–sup´po·si´tion·al** *adj.* **–sup´po·si´tion·al·ly** *adv.*

**sup·press´** *vt.* to end or stop; to hold back or repress; to check **–sup·pres´sant** *n.* **–sup·press´er, sup·pres´sor** *n.* **–sup·press´i·ble, sup·pres´sive** *adj.*

**sup·pres´sion** *n.* an instance of suppressing; the exclusion of unpleasant ideas, memories, etc. from consciousness

**su·prem´a·cy** *n.* supreme power or authority

**su·preme´** *adj.* dominant; highest in degree, etc.; ultimate **–su·preme´ly** *adv.*

**sur·cease´** *n.* a cessation *–vt., vi.* to end

**sure** *adj.* without doubt; positive **–sure´ly** *adv.* **–sure´ness** *n.*

**sur´e·ty** *n.* security against loss or damage

**surf** *n.* the swelling of the sea as it breaks on the shore *–vi.* to ride a surfboard **–surf´er** *n.*

**sur´face** *n.* the exterior; a superficial aspect *–vt.* to apply or improve an exterior; to cause to rise *–vi.* to rise; to come to public notice **–sur´fac·er** *n.*

**sur´feit** *vt.* to supply to excess *–vi.* to overindulge in food or drink *–n.* any excessive amount

**surge** *vi.* to roll with a swelling motion, as waves; to move in a wavelike motion; to increase or vary suddenly *–n.* a great swelling or rolling motion; any sudden increase

**sur´ger·y** *n.* medical treatment by manual and operative means; the branch of medicine concerned with treatment by surgery; an operating room **–sur´geon** *n.* **–sur´gi·cal** *adj.* **–sur´gi·cal·ly** *adv.*

**sur´ly** *adj.* ill-humored; gruff or insolent **–sur´li·ness** *n.*

**sur·mise´** *vt., vi.* to infer on slight evidence *–n.* a supposition

**sur·mount´** *vt.* to overcome; to mount or pass over, as an obstacle; to place above **–sur·mount´a·ble** *adj.*

**sur´name** *n.* a family name; a cognomen or nickname *–vt.* to furnish with a nickname

**sur·pass´** *vt.* to go beyond or past in degree or amount **–sur·pass´a·ble** *adj.* **–sur·pass´er** *n.*

**sur´plus** *n.* that over what is used or required *–adj.* an excess

**sur·prise´** *vt.* to cause to feel wonder or astonishment; to take unawares *–n.* astonishment; something that caused astonishment **–sur·pris´ing** *adj.* **–sur·pris´ing·ly** *adv.*

**sur·re´al** *adj.* having a dreamlike quality **–sur·re´al·ly** *adv.*

**sur·re´al·ism** *n.* an art movement characterized by the incorporation of dreamlike elements **–sur·re´al·ist** *adj., n.* **–sur·re·al·is´tic** *adj.* **–sur·re·al·is´ti·cal·ly** *adv.*

**sur·ren´der** *vt.* to yield; to give up in favor of another; to give oneself over to, as passion *–vi.* to give oneself up, as to an enemy *–n.* the act of surrendering **–sur·ren´der·er** *n.*

**sur·rep·ti´tious** *adj.* accomplished by secret means; acting with stealth **–sur·rep·ti´tious·ly** *adv.* **–sur·rep´ti´tious·ness** *n.*

**sur´ro·gate** *n.* someone taking the place of another; a probate court judge *–vt.* to deputize or substitute **–sur´ro·ga·cy** *n.*

**sur·round´** *vt.* to encircle or enclose

**sur·round´ings** *n.* that which constitutes one's environment

**sur·veil´lance** *n.* discreet observation of someone or

something

**sur·vey´, sur´vey** *vt.* to look at carefully; to scrutinize; to conduct a land survey so as to determine accurately the area, boundaries, etc. *—vi.* to survey land *—n.* the process of surveying land; the systematic collection and analysis of data; a general or overall view **—sur·vey´or** *n.*

**sur·viv´a·ble** *adj.* that can be survived **—sur·viv·a·bil´i·ty** *adv.*

**sur·vive´** *vi.* to remain alive or in existence; to live past the death of another *—vt.* to outlast; to go on living in spite of **—sur·viv´al** *n.* **—sur·vi´vor** *n.*

**sus·cep´ti·ble** *adj.* readily affected; vulnerable; capable of being influenced **—sus·cep·ti·bil´i·ty, sus·cep´ti·ble·ness** *n.* **—sus·cep´ti·bly** *adv.*

**sus·pect´** *vt.* to think guilty without proof; to distrust or doubt *—vi.* to have suspicions **—sus·pect´, sus´pect** *adj.* inspiring suspicion **—sus´pect** *n.* one who may be guilty of a crime

**sus·pend´** *vt.* to bar for a time as punishment; to cease or interrupt for a time; to defer action on; to move freely while hanging from a support or in the air

**sus·pense´** *n.* anxiety caused by uncertainty **—sus·pense´ful** *adj.*

**sus·pen´sion** *n.* a temporary removal from office, withholding of privilege, etc.; an interruption or cessation; a deferment; hanging freely; dispersion in a liquid or gas

**sus·pi´cion** *n.* an uncertain belief in the likelihood of another's guilt, wrongdoing etc.; a slight amount

**sus·pi´cious** *adj.* questionable; disposed to doubt **—sus·pi´cious·ly** *adv.* **—sus·pi´cious·ness** *n.*

**sus·tain´** *vt.* to keep up or maintain; to maintain by providing with necessities; to endure or withstand; to suffer or undergo; to uphold or prove as being true or just **—sus·tain´a·ble** *adj.*

**sus´te·nance** *n.* maintenance of life or health; that which sustains, as food

**svelte** *adj.* slender; smart or chic **—svelte´ly** *adv.* **—svelte´ness** *n.*

**swab** *n.* a soft, absorbent substance on the end of a short stick, used to apply medication, cleanse, etc.; a specimen taken for medical examination; a mop for cleaning floors, etc. *—vt.* to clean or apply medication with a swab **—swab´ber** *n.*

**swad´dle** *vt.* to wrap a newborn in strips of cloth; to wrap, as with a bandage *—n.* a band or cloth used as swaddling

**swag** *n.* a decorative hanging, such as a curtain or drape covering the top of a window and gathered in sections; a similar carved motif; stolen property; *(Austral.)* a bundle of personal belongings

**swag´ger** *vi.* to walk with an air of self-confidence; to behave or boast in a self-satisfied manner *—n.* a self-confident gait *—adj.* showy **—swag´ger·ing·ly** *adv.*

**swal´low** *vt.* to cause to pass from the mouth into the stomach; to take in or engulf; to submit to, as insults; to suppress: *swallow one's pride* *—n.* the amount taken in at one time; a mouthful; a small bird **—swal´low·er** *n.*

**swamp** *n.* a tract of low land saturated with water *—vt.* to drench with water; to overwhelm, as with work *—vi.* to sink in water **—swamp´land** *n.* **—swamp´y** *adj.*

**swank** *n.* an ostentatious display; stylishness *—adj.* stylish or smart

**swank´y** an ostentatiously fashionable **—swank´i·ly** *adv.* **—swank´i·ness** *n.*

**swap** *vt., vi.* to exchange or trade *—n.* something traded **—swap meet** a gathering in which goods are traded

**swarm** *n.* a large crowd or mass, especially one moving together *—vi.* to come together or move in great numbers; to be overrun: *swarming with tourists* *—vt.* to fill with a crowd

**swarth´y** *adj.* dark complexioned **—swarth´i·ness** *n.*

**swat** *vt.* to strike with a quick blow *—n.* **—swat´ter** *n.*

**swath** *n.* a strip or row, as of cut grain

**swathe** *vt.* to bind or wrap, as with bandages *—n.* a bandage

**sway** *vi.* to swing from side to side; to incline, as in opinion, sympathies etc.; to control *—vt.* to cause to swing or lean; to influence *—n.* power or influence; a turning from side to side

**swear** *vi.* to make a solemn affirmation; to make a vow; to use profanity *—vt.* to assert solemnly; to vow; to declare emphatically

**sweat** *vi.* to exude salty moisture from the pores; to condense moisture in drops on a surface; to work hard; to suffer, as from anxiety *—vt.* to exude or condense drops of moisture; to cause to sweat; to force to work for low wages, etc.; to join metal with solder; to subject to rigorous interrogation *—n.* **—sweat´i·ness** *n.* **—sweat´y** *adj.*

**sweep** *vt.* to clear or clean away, as with a broom, brush etc.; to pass over swiftly; to win overwhelmingly *—vi.* to clean a surface with a broom, etc.; to move quickly; to extend: *the road sweeps along the lake* *—n.* a long stroke or movement; the act of clearing; an unbroken stretch; an overwhelming victory; one who cleans chimneys, streets, etc.; a flowing contour **—sweep´er** *n.*

**sweet** *adj.* having a flavor like that of sugar; pleasing to the senses *—n.* someone or something agreeable or pleasing **—sweet´ly** *adv.* **—sweet´ness** *n.*

**sweet´en** *vt.* to make agreeable or pleasing **—sweet´en·er** *n.*

**swell** *vi.* to increase in size or volume, as by inflation or absorption; to increase in amount, etc.; to arise in waves, as the sea; to bulge *—vt.* to cause to increase, as in size, volume, amount, etc.; to cause to bulge; to puff with pride *—n.* an expansion; a rise or undulation; a bulge; a long continuous wave *–adj.* fashionable, elegant **–swell´ing** *n., adj.*

**swel´ter** *vi., vt.* to suffer or cause to suffer from oppressive heat *–n.* oppressive heat **–swel´ter·ing** *adj.* **–swel´ter·ing·ly** *adv.*

**swerve** *vi., vt.* to turn or cause to turn aside *–n.* a sudden turning

**swift** *adj.* moving or capable of moving with great speed; happening without delay **–swift´ly** *adv.* **–swift´ness** *n.*

**swill** *vt., vi.* to drink greedily or to excess *–n.* semiliquid food for animals; unappetizing food; garbage

**swim** *vi.* to move through water by moving the limbs; to move with a flowing motion; to be flooded *–vt.* to traverse by swimming; to cause to swim *–n.* the action or pastime of swimming; the distance swum **–swim´mer** *n.*

**swin´dle** *vt.* to cheat or defraud; to obtain by fraud *–vi.* to practice fraud *–n.* the act of defrauding **–swin´dler** *n.*

**swing** *vi.* to move to and fro rhythmically; to pivot; to be suspended; to be contemporary and sophisticated *–vt.* to cause to move to and fro; to brandish; to lift, hoist, or hang; to bring to a successful conclusion: *swing a deal* *–n.* a free swaying motion; a hanging seat; a trip or tour: *a swing through the low country*; a type of jazz music **–swing´er** *n.*

**swirl** *vi., vt.* to move or cause to move with a whirling motion *–n.*

**switch** *n.* a small flexible rod or whip; an act or mechanism for shifting or changing *–vt.* to whip or lash; to turn aside or divert; to exchange *–vi.* to turn aside; to change **–switch´er** *n.*

**swiv´el** *n.* a pivot that permits parts to rotate independently; anything that turns on a pivot *–vt., vi.* to turn, as on a swivel

**swoon** *vi.* to faint *–n.* a fainting spell

**swoop** *vi.* to descend suddenly; to pounce *–vt.* to seize suddenly *–n.* a sudden violent descent

**sword** *n.* a weapon consisting of a long blade fixed in a hilt

**syc´o·phant** *n.* a servile flatterer **–syc´o·phan·cy** *n.* **–syc´o·phan´tic, syc´o·phan´ti·cal** *adj.* **syc´o·phan´ti·cal·ly** *adv.*

**syl·lab´ic** *adj.* pertaining to syllables; having every syllable distinctly pronounced **–syl·lab´i·cal·ly** *adv.*

**syl·lab´i·cate, syl·lab´i·fy** *vt.* to form or divide into syllables **–syl·lab·i·ca´tion** *n.*

**syl´la·ble** *n.* a word or part of a word uttered in a single vocal impulse

**syl´la·bus** *n.* a concise description, as of a course of study

**syl´lo·gism** *n.* a form of reasoning in which a conclusion is derived from a commonality within two premises **–syl·lo·gis´tic, syl·lo·gis´ti·cal** *adj.* **–syl·lo·gis´ti·cal·ly** *adv.* **–syl´lo·gize** *vi., vt.*

**syl´van** *adj.* of a forest or wooded area; of a creature that lives in the woods; wooded

**sym·bi·o´sis** *n.* a mutually advantageous relationship between dissimilar organisms **–sym·bi·ot´ic, sym·bi·ot´i·cal** *adj.* **–sym·bi·ot´i·cal·ly** *adv.*

**sym´bol** *n.* a mark, character, emblem, etc. chosen to represent something else **–sym·bol´ic, sym·bol´i·cal** *adj.* **–sym·bol´i·cal·ly** *adv.*

**sym´bol·ism** *n.* the art of investing with symbolic meaning; a system of symbolic representation; symbolic meaning or character **–sym´bol·ist** *n.* **–sym·bol·is´tic** *adj.* **–sym·bol·is´ti·cal·ly** *adv.*

**sym´bol·ize** *vt.* to represent symbolically; to represent by a symbol; to use symbols

**sym´me·try** *n.* a balancing of parts or elements; the beauty and harmony that results from balance **–sym·met´ric, sym·met´ri·cal** *adj.* **–sym·met´ri·cal·ly** *adv.* **–sym·met´ri·cal·ness** *n.*

**sym·pa·thet´ic, sym·pa·thet´i·cal** *adj.* pertaining to sympathy; having compassion for others; being in accord or harmony; relating to sounds produced by responsive vibrations **–sym·pa·thet´i·cal·ly** *adv.*

**sym´pa·thize** *vi.* to understand the sentiments of another; to feel or express compassion; to be in harmony or agreement **–sym´pa·thiz·er** *n.* **–sym´pa·thiz´ing·ly** *adv.*

**sym´pa·thy** *n.* an agreement of feeling; compassion for another's suffering; agreement or accord; support or approval

**sym·pho´ni·ous** *adj.* in a state of accord; harmonious **–sym·pho´ni·ous·ly** *adv.*

**sym´pho·ny** *n.* an agreeable mingling of sounds; any agreeable blending, as of color; a composition for orchestra **–sym·phon´ic** *adj.* **–sym·phon´i·cal´ly** *adv.*

**sym·po´si·um** *n.* a meeting for discussion of a particular subject; a collection of writing on a particular subject

**symp´tom** *n.* a condition indicating the presence of disease; an indication that serves to point out something else: *a symptom of civil unrest* **–symp·to·mat´ic, symp·to·mat´i·cal** *adj.* **–symp·to·mat´i·cal·ly** *adv.*

**syn´a·gogue** *n.* a place of meeting for Jewish worship and religious instruction; a Jewish congregation

**syn´apse** *n.* the junction of two neurons across which a nerve impulse passes **–syn·ap´tic** *adj.* **syn·ap´ti·cal·ly** *adv.*

**syn·chron´ic** *adj.* synchronous; pertaining to the study of events of a particular time **–syn·chron´i·cal·ly** *adv.*

**syn´chro·nism** *n.* concurrence; a grouping of historic persons or events according to their dates **–syn·chro·nic´i·ty** *n.* **–syn·chro·nis´tic, syn·chro·nis´ti·cal** *adj.* **–syn·chro·nis´ti·cal·ly** *adv.*

**syn´chro·nize** *vi.* to occur at the same time; to operate in unison *—vt.* to cause to operate together; to assign the same date or period **—syn·chro·ni·za´tion** *n.*

**syn´chro·nous** *adj.* occurring at the same time **—syn´chro·nous·ly** *adv.* **—syn´chro·nous·ness** *n.*

**syn´co·pate** *vt.* to modify by syncopation

**syn·co·pa´tion** *n.* the suppression of an expected rhythmic accent in music

**syn´di·cate** *n.* an association united to engage in an enterprise *—vt.* to combine into a syndicate **—syn·di·ca´tion** *n.* **—syn´di·ca·tor** *n.*

**syn´drome** *n.* the combined symptoms characteristic of a specific disease; traits regarded as being characteristic of a condition, etc. **—syn´drom·ic** *adj.*

**syn´er·gism** *n.* the reinforcing action of separate organs, agents, etc. which produce a greater effect than any acting singly **—syn·er·gis´tic, syn·er·gis´ti·cal** *adj.*

**syn´er·gy** *n.* synergism

**syn´od** *n.* an ecclesiastical council

**syn´o·nym** *n.* a word having the same or almost the same meaning as another

**syn·on´y·mous** *adj.* being equivalent or smilar in meaning **—syn·on´y·mous·ly** *adv.*

**syn·op´sis** *n.* a condensation, as of a story, book etc.; a summary

**syn·op´tic** *adj.* giving a general view; offering a similar point of view

**syn´tax** *n.* the arrangement of words in grammatical construction **—syn·tac´tic, syn·tac´ti·cal** *adj.* **—syn·tac´ti·cal·ly** *adv.*

**syn´the·sis** *n., pl.* **syn´the·ses** the assembling of subordinate parts into a new form; the resulting complex form created

**syn´the·size** *vt.* to produce by synthesis

**syn´the·siz·er** *n.* an electronic device used to create musical tones

**syn·thet´ic, syn·thet´i·cal** *adj.* produced artificially, as by chemical synthesis; artificial **—syn·thet´i·cal·ly** *adv.*

**sy·ringe´** *n.* a device used to remove or inject fluids *—vt.* to cleanse or inject with a syringe

**syr´up** *n.* a thick, sweet liquid **—syr´up·y** *adj.*

**sys´tem** *n.* a group or arrangement of parts, facts, etc. that relate to or interact with each other; a group of logically related facts, beliefs, etc.; a method of classification, arrangement, etc. **—sys·tem·at´ic, sys·tem·at´i·cal** *adj.* **—sys·tem·at´i·cal·ly** *adv.*

**sys´tem·a·tize** *vt.* to organize, methodically **—sys·tem·a·ti·za´tion** *n.* **—sys´tem·a·tiz·er** *n.*

**sys·tem´ic** *adj.* of or pertaining to a system; affecting the body as a whole: *a systemic poison* **—sys·tem´i·cal·ly** *adv.*

**sys´tem·ize** *vt.* systematize **—sys·tem·i·za´tion** *n.*

**t, T** *n.* 20th letter of the English alphabet **—to a T** perfectly, precisely

**tab** *n.* a flap, projection, etc. as on a garment or file card *—vt.* to provide with a tab

**tab´er·na·cle** *n.* a house of worship; the ornamental receptacle for the eucharistic elements; formerly, the portable sanctuary used by the Israelites **—tab´er·nac´u·lar** *adj.*

**ta´ble** *n.* an article of furniture with a flat top and legs; the surface on which food is served, or the food served; an array of elements arranged in rows and columns for easy reference; a listing: *table of contents*; a tablet or slab *—vt.* to postpone discussion

**tab´leau** *n., pl.* **tab´leaux or tab´leaus** a picturesque representation

**table d´hôte** a complete meal served at a fixed price

**ta´ble·spoon** *n.* a measure equal to three teaspoons; a tablespoonful

**ta´ble·spoon·ful** *n.* the amount a tablespoon will hold; ½ fluid ounce

**tab´let** *n.* a pill; a pad of paper; a flat surface intended for an inscription or design

**ta´ble·ware** *n.* dishes and implements for dining

**tab´loid** *n.* a newspaper in which news is presented concisely and often sensationally

**ta·boo´, ta·bu´** *n.* a restriction or ban based on religious belief, custom, or convention *—adj.* restricted or prohibited *—vt.* to place under taboo

**tab´u·lar** *adj.* arranged in a table or list **—tab´u·lar·ly** *adv.*

**tab´u·late** *vt.* to arrange in a table or list **—tab·u·la´tion** *n.* **—tab´u·la·tor** *n.*

**ta·chom´e·ter** *n.* a device for indicating speed of rotation, as for an engine

**tach´y·car´di·a** *n.* an abnormally rapid heartbeat

**tac´it** *adj.* not spoken; inferred or implied without being directly stated **—tac´it·ly** *adv.*

**tac´i·turn** *adj.* habitually reserved **—tac·i·tur´ni·ty** *n.* **—tac´i·turn·ly** *adv.*

**tack** *n.* a small nail or pin with a broad flat head; a policy or course of action; a temporary fastening *—vt.* to fasten with a tack or tacks; to secure temporarily *—vi.* to change one's course of action: *take a different tack*

**tack´le** *n.* a combination of ropes and pulleys used for hoisting or moving objects; the rigging of a ship; sport or work gear *—vt.* to undertake, as *to tackle a problem*; to seize suddenly and forcefully **—tack´ler** *n.*

**tack´y** *adj.* slightly sticky; in poor taste **—tack´i·ness** *n.*

**ta´co** *n.* a fried tortilla folded around a filling

**tact** *n.* the ability to say or do the proper thing **—tact´ful** *adj.* **—tact´ful·ly** *adv.* **—tact´ful·ness** *n.*

**tac´ti·cal** *adj.* pertaining to tactics; adept at planning and maneuvering **—tac´ti·cal·ly** *adv.* **—tac·ti´cian** *n.*

**tac´tics** *n.* strategy; the art of maneuvering to gain an end

**tac´tile** *adj.* relating to the sense of touch; that may be touched or perceived by touch **–tac·til´i·ty** *n.*

**tact´less** *adj.* characterized by a lack of tact **–tact´less·ly** *adv.* **–tact´less·ness** *n.*

**taf´fe·ta** *n.* a fine, somewhat stiff fabric used for women's garments *–adj.* made of taffeta

**taf´fy** *n.* a chewy confection of brown sugar or molasses

**tag** *n.* an attachment that identifies, shows price, etc.; a children's game *–vt.* to fit with a tag; to follow closely; to touch, as in the game of tag

**Ta·ga´log** *n.* a Philippine native; the official language of the Philippines

**ta·hi´ni** *n.* sesame seed butter

**tail** *n.* flexible appendage at the hind end of an animal; anything resembling a tail, as the luminous cloud extending from a comet; the hind or back portion *–vt.* to be at the end of; to follow stealthily *–vi.* to follow closely; to diminish gradually *–adj.* rearmost; coming from behind

**tail´gate** *n.* a hinged gate at the back of a motor vehicle *–vt., vi.* to follow too closely for safety

**tai´lor** *n.* one who makes or repairs garments *–vi.* to do a tailor's work *–vt.* to fit with garments; to adapt to meet a need **–tai´lor·ing** *n.*

**tai´lored** *adj.* custom-made; severe or tight-fitting

**tai´lor-made´** *adj.* made by a tailor; perfectly suited to fill a need

**taint** *vt., vi.* to affect or be affected by contamination or corruption *–n.* a cause or result of contamination

**take** *vt.* to lay hold of or gain possession of; to choose; to steal; to undergo or submit to: *take a beating*; to accept; to charm or captivate; *take advantage of*; to perform, as an action; to feel *–vi.* to gain possession; to acquire; to be captivated: *taken with her beauty*; to require: *the cake takes two eggs*; to enter upon: *take a job*; to assume: *take the blame*; to have an intended effect *–n.* something taken; something received or the amount received: *the day's take for ticket sales* **–tak´a·ble** *adj.* **–tak´er** *n.*

**tale** *n.* a story; a narrative of events; idle or malicious gossip; a lie

**tale´bear·er** *n.* one who gossips or spreads rumors **–tale´bear·ing** *adj.*

**tal´ent** *n.* natural ability; a particular aptitude; collectively, those with special abilities **–tal´ent·ed** *adj.*

**tal´is·man** *n.* an object supposed to ward off evil or bring good luck; anything with seeming magical power **–tal·is·man´ic, tal·is·man´i·cal** *adj.*

**talk** *vi.* to express audibly; to communicate by means other than voice: *money talks*; to make sounds suggestive of speech *–vt.* to express in words *–n.* conversation or speech; a conference or discussion; sounds suggesting speech **–talk´er** *n.*

**talk´a·thon** *n.* a prolonged discussion, debate, etc.

**talk´a·tive** *adj.* given to much talk **–talk´a·tive·ly** *adj.* **–talk´a·tive·ness** *n.*

**talk´y** *adj.* talkative; given overly to talk: *a talky movie* **–talk'i·ness** *n.*

**tall** *adj.* of more than average height; of a specified height; exaggerated, as *a tall story*; extensive, as *a tall order* *–adv.* proudly: *to walk tall* **–tall´ish** *adj.* **–tall´ness** *n.*

**tal´low** *n.* rendered animal fat

**tal´ly** *n.* a score or mark; a reckoning; a mark indicating a number *–vt.* to score; to reckon; to cause to correspond *–vi.* to make a tally; to keep score; to agree precisely

**tal´on** *n.* the claw of an animal

**ta·ma´le** *n.* a Mexican food of seasoned ground beef rolled in corn meal, then wrapped in leaves and steamed

**tame** *adj.* domesticated; docile, subdued; lacking spirit, uninteresting *–vt.* to domesticate; to tone down **–tam´a·ble, tame´a·ble** *adj.* **–tame´ly** *adv.* **–tame´ness** *n.* **–tam´er** *n.*

**tamp** *vt.* to pack down

**tam´per** *vi.* to meddle in or interfere with; to make potentially harmful changes; to use improper measures, as bribery**–tam´per·er** *n.*

**tan** *vt.* to convert into leather; to darken by exposure to sunlight *–vi.* to become tanned *–n.* a yellow brown color; a dark coloring of the skin **–tan´ner** *n.*

**tan´dem** *adv.* one behind the other *–n.* a team of horses harnessed one behind the other or the carriage they pull; a bicycle with two or more seats *–adj.*

**tang** *n.* a sharp, penetrating taste or odor **–tang´i·ness** *n.* **–tang´y** *adj.*

**tan´gent** *adj.* touching without intersecting **–tan´gen·cy** *n.*

**tan·gen´tial** *adj.* pertaining to a tangent; touching lightly **–tan·gen·ti·al´i·ty** *n.* **–tan·gen´tial·ly** *adv.*

**tan´ger·ine´** *n.* a variety of orange

**tan´gi·ble** *adj.* perceptible by touch; real or concrete *–n.* assets having value that can be appraised **–tan·gi·bil´i·ty, tan´gi·ble·ness** *n.* **--tan´gi·bly** *adv.*

**tan´gle** *vt.* to twist into a mass; to ensnare or enmesh; to involve in such a way as to confuse *–vi.* to be or become tangled *–n.* a confused intertwining **–tan´gler** *n.***–tan´gly** *adj.*

**tan´go** *n.* a Latin American dance; the music for such a dance *–vi.*

**tank** *n.* a large receptacle for fluid; an armored combat vehicle *–vt.* to store in a tank

**tan´kard** *n.* a large, handled drinking cup, often with a cover

**tan´ner·y** *n.* a place where leather is tanned

**tan´ta·lize** *vt.* to torment by promising something,

then withholding it —**tan·ta·li·za´tion** *n.* —**tan´ta·liz·er** *n.* —**tan´ta·liz·ing·ly** *adv.*

**tan´ta·mount** *adj.* equivalent to

**tan´trum** *n.* a fit of temper

**tap** *n.* the act or sound of striking gently; a spout through which liquid is drawn; a plug or stopper —*vt.* to touch or strike gently; to provide with a spigot; to open so as to draw liquid; to draw upon

**tape** *n.* a long narrow strip —*vt.* to secure with tape —**tap´er** *n.*

**ta´per** *n.* a slender candle; a wick used to light candles; a cone; a gradual decrease —*vt., vi.* to make or become thin toward one end; to lessen gradually —*adj.*

**tap´es·try** *n.* a heavy woven textile with a pictorial design —*vt.* to adorn with tapestry

**tape´worm** *n.* a parasitic worm

**tap·i·o´ca** *n.* a starchy food obtained from cassava

**tar·an·tel´la** *n.* a lively Neopolitan dance

**ta·ran´tu·la** *n.* a large hairy spider

**tar´dy** *adj.* not coming or happening as anticipated; moving ahead slowly —**tar´di·ly** *adv.* —**tar´di·ness** *n.*

**tar´get** *n.* something shot at; the object of an action, as ridicule, criticism, etc. —*vt.* to establish as a goal —**tar´get·a·ble** *adj.*

**tar´iff** *n.* a schedule of duties to be paid, or those imposed, on imports and exports; a price schedule —*vt.* to fix a price on

**tarn** *n.* a small mountain lake

**tar´nish** *vt.* to dim the luster of; to sully or debase —*vi.* to become tarnished —**tar´nish·a·ble** *adj.*

**ta´ro** *n.* a tropical plant having a starchy edible rootstock

**ta´rot** *n.* a set of cards used mainly for fortunetelling

**tar·pau´lin** *n.* a waterproof material used as a protective covering

**tar´pon** *n.* a large game fish

**tar´ra·gon** *n.* a European plant with leaves used for seasoning

**tar´ry** *vi.* to put off going; to linger; to remain temporarily

**tar´sal** *adj.* pertaining to the ankle

**tar´sus** *n.* the ankle

**tart** *n.* a small filled pastry —*adj.* having a sharp sour taste; caustic; as a remark —**tart´ly** *adv.* —**tart´ness** *n.*

**tar´tan** *n.* a woollen fabric, especially one with a pattern distinctive to a particular Scottish clan

**task** *n.* a designated job, especially one required; a difficult assignment —*vi.* to assign a task; to overburden

**task´mas·ter** *n.* one who assigns tasks, especially burdensome ones

**tas´sel** *n.* a tuft of loose hanging cords such as used to ornament cushions, etc. —*vt.* to adorn with tassels —*vi.* to put forth tassels, as on corn

**taste** *vt.* to perceive the flavor of; to eat or drink a little; to experience —*vi.* to recognize a flavor; to take a small amount; to experience: *taste the fruits of victory;* to have a specific flavor —*n.* the sensation associated with stimulation of the taste buds; a small quantity or sample; a special fondness or appreciation: *a taste for music;* a respect for propriety and refinement —**taste´a·ble** *adj.*

**taste buds** receptors on the tongue stimulated by sweet, salt, sour, or bitter substances

**taste´ful** *adj.* conforming to good taste —**taste´ful·ly** *adv.* —**taste´ful·ness** *n.*

**taste´less** *adj.* without flavor; lacking tact or decorum —**taste´less·ly** *adv.* —**taste´less·ness** *n.*

**tast´y** *adj.* having a fine flavor —**tast´i·ly** *adv.* —**tast´i·ness** *n.*

**tat´ter** *n.* a torn shred —*vt., vi.* to make or become ragged —**tat´ters** ragged clothing

**tat·ter·de·ma´lion** *n.* one wearing ragged clothing; a ragamuffin —*adj.*

**tat´ter·sall** *n.* a pattern of intersecting dark lines on a light background; cloth of this design —*adj.*

**tat´tle** *vi., vt.* to gossip or reveal by gossiping —*n.* idle chatter —**tat´tler** *n.* —**tat´tling·ly** *adv.*

**tat´tle·tale** *n.* one who tattles —*adj.* revealing: *tattletale signs*

**tat·too´** *vt.* to mark the skin with patterns —*n.* a pattern or design on the skin; a continuous drumbeat; the sounding of a drum or bugle to signal a return to quarters —**tat·too´er, tat·too´ist** *n.*

**tat´ty** *adj.* somewhat worn or shabby

**taunt** *n.* a sarcastic remark; a jibe —*vt.* to provoke with derision or insults —**taunt´er** *n.* —**taunt´ing·ly** *adv.*

**taupe** *n.* a brownish gray color

**taut** *adj.* stretched tight; tidy —**taut´ly** *adv.* —**taut´ness** *n.*

**tau·tol´o·gy** *n.* the unnecessary repetition of the same concept in different words —**tau·to·log´ic, tau·to·log´i·cal** *adj.* —**tau·to·log´i·cal·ly** *adv.* —**tau·tol´o·gize** *vi.* —**tau·tol´o·gist** *n.*

**tav´ern** *n.* an inn; a place licensed to sell alcoholic beverages

**taw´dry** *adj.* cheap and showy; lacking taste or quality —**taw´dri·ly** *adv.* —**taw´dri·ness** *n.*

**tawn´y** *adj.* tan-colored —*n.* tan —**taw´ni·ness** *n.*

**tax** *n.* a charge levied for the support of government; a heavy demand, as on one's powers or resources —*vt.* to levy a tax on; to impose a burden on —**tax shelter** a financial manipulation designed to reduce tax liability —**tax·a·bil´i·ty** *n.* —**tax´a·ble** *adj.*

**tax·a´tion** *n.* the process of taxing; the amount levied; revenue raised from taxes

**tax´i** *n.* a taxicab —*vi.* to ride in a taxicab; to move along the surface, as of an airplane preparing to take off

**tax´i·cab** *n.* a passenger vehicle for hire

**tax´i·der·my** *n.* the art of stuffing and mounting animals —**tax·i·der´mal, tax·i·der´mic** *adj.* —**tax´i·**

**der·mist** *n.*
**tax´ing** *adj.* difficult, trying –**tax´ing·ly** *adv.*
**tax·on´o·my** *n.* the laws and principles of classification, as of plant and animal life into successive subgroups –**tax·o·nom´ic, tax·o·nom´i·cal** *adj.* –**tax·o·nom´i·cal·ly** *adv.* –**tax·on´o·mist** *n.*
**T cell** *n.* a type of white blood cell that performs various functions in the immune system
**tea** *n.* an Asian plant or its leaves, used in preparing a beverage; a beverage prepared from leaves, an animal extract, etc.; a social gathering –**tea service** a set of matching cups and saucers, a creamer, etc. used for serving tea
**teach** *vt.* to provide instruction to; to instruct in: *teach French*; to train –*vi.* to act as teacher –**teach·a·bil´i·ty, teach´a·ble·ness** *n.* –**teach´a·ble** *adj.* –**teach´a·bly** *adv.* –**teach´er** *n.*
**teaching machine** an interactive computer that presents material to a student and provides corrective feedback
**teak** *n.* an extremely durable wood or the tree from which it comes
**team** *n.* a group working together as a unit –*vi.* to work as a team –**team player** one who identifies with and cooperates in a team –**team´work** harmony of action among the members of a group
**team´ster** *n.* one who drives a team of horses or a motor vehicle
**tear** *n.* a drop of fluid from the eye; a break or rip, as in a fabric; a violent outburst –*vt.* to pull apart; to wound or lacerate; to distress or disrupt: *torn by dissension* –*vi.* to become torn; to move with haste or energy
**tear´ful** *adj.* causing tears; accompanied by tears –**tear´ful·ly** *adv.* –**tear´ful·ness** *n.*
**tear´ing** *adj.* with great haste
**tear´jerk·er** *n.* a book, play, etc. designed to evoke tears
**tear´y** *adj.* filled or wet with tears; sentimental; overemotional –**tear´i·ly** *adv.* –**tear´i·ness** *n.*
**tease** *vt.* to annoy or vex; to coax or beg; to comb –*vi.* to annoy in a petty way –*n.* one who teases –**teas´er** *n.* –**teas´ing·ly** *adv.*
**tea´spoon** *n.* a small spoon for measuring, stirring, etc. –**tea´spoon, tea´spoon·ful** *n.* the amount a teaspoon will hold
**tech´ni·cal** *adj.* pertaining to or characteristic of a particular art, trade, etc.; exhibiting teachnique; according to an accepted body of rules –**tech´ni·cal·ly** *adv.*
**technical foul** a violation of a rule that does not necessarily involve physical contact
**tech·ni·cal´i·ty** *n.* a technique or approach peculiar to an art, trade, etc.; a petty detail
**tech·ni´cian** *n.* one skilled in a particular field
**tech´nics** *n.* the study or principles of an art, trade, etc.
**tech·nique´** *n.* the way in which one works; the degree of skill one exhibits; any method of accomplishing something
**tech·noc´ra·cy** *n.* a government dominated by technicians –**tech´no·crat** *n.* –**tech´no·crat´ic** *adj.*
**tech·nol´o·gy** *n.* the technical means employed to meet the needs of a society; technical terms –**tech·no·log´ic, tech·no·log´i·cal** *adj.* –**tech·no·log´i·cal·ly** *adv.* –**tech·nol´o·gist** *n.*
**tec·ton´ics** *n.* the science or art of construction; the study of the movements of the earth's crust –**tec·ton´ic** *adj.* –**tec·ton´i·cal·ly** *adv.*
**te´di·ous** *adj.* boring or repetitious –**te´di·ous·ly** *adv.* –**te´di·ous·ness** *n.*
**te´di·um** *n.* the quality of being boring, monotonous, etc.
**teem** *vi.* to be full or overflowing –**teem´ing·ly** *adv.*
**teen´age, teen´-age, teen´aged, teen´-aged** *adj.* of the ages from 13 to 19 –**teen, teen´ager, teen´-ag´er** *n.*
**tee´ter** *vi.* to walk unsteadily; to vacillate or waver
**teethe** *vi.* to develop teeth
**tee·to´tal** *adj.* advocating abstention from the consumption of alcoholic beverages –**tee´to´tal·er** *n.* –**tee·to´tal·ism** *n.*
**tel´e·cast** *vt., vi.* to broadcast by television –*n.* –**tel´e·cast·er** *n.*
**tel·e·com·mu·ni·ca´tion** *n.* the technology of communicating at a distance as by radio, television, telephone, etc. –**tel·e·com·mu´ni·cate** *vt., vi.* –**tel·e·com·mu´ni·ca·tor** *n.*
**tel´e·com·mut·ing** *n.* the practice of working from home through a computer link –**tel´e·com·mute´** *vi.* –**tel´e·com·mut·er** *n.*
**tel´e·con´fer·ence** *n.* a meeting of people located at a distance by means of a telephone hookup or closed circuit television –*vi.* to participate in a teleconference –**tel´e·con´fer·enc·ing** *n.*
**tel´e·graph** *n.* a system for transmitting messages over a distance –**tel´e·gram** *n.* –**te·leg´ra·pher** *n.* –**te·leg´ra·phy** *n.*
**tel·e·ki·ne´sis** *n.* the unexplained movement of objects, as by occult power –**tel·e·ki·net´ic** *adj.*
**tel´e·mar·ket·ing** *n.* the selling of products by telephone or television –**tel´e·mar·ket·er** *n.*
**te·lem´e·try** *n.* the automatic measurement and transmission of data from a distance –**tel´e·me·ter** *n., vt.* –**tel·e·met´ric, tel·e·met´ri·cal** *adj.* –**tel·e·met´ri·cal·ly** *adv.*
**tel·e·ol´o·gy** *n.* the study of final causes; the explanation of natural phenomenon in terms of design and purpose –**tel·e·o·log´ic, tel·e·o·log´i·cal** *adj.* –**tel·e·o·log´i·cal·ly** - *adv.* –**tel·e·ol´o·gist** *n.*
**te·lep´a·thy** *n.* communication by other than normal

sensory means —tel·e·path´ic *adj.* —tel·e·path´i·cal·ly *adv.* —te·lep´a·thist *n.*

**tel´e·phone** *n.* a device for transmitting sound or speech over a distance —*vt., vi.* to communicate by telephone —**tel·e·phon´ic** *adj.* —**tel·e·phon´i·cal·ly** *adv.*

**te·leph´o·ny** *n.* the technology of telephone communication

**tel´e·pho´to** *adj.* of a system of lenses which produces a near view of a distant object

**tel·e·pho·tog´ra·phy** *n.* the technique for producing magnified photographs of distant objects —**tel e·pho·to·graph´ic** *adj.*

**tel´e·scope** *n.* an instrument for viewing distant objects —**tel´e·scop´ic** *adj.* —**tel´e·scop´i·cal·ly** *adv.*

**tel´e·thon** *n.* a television show intended to raise funds for charity

**tel·e·van´ge·lism** *n.* the broadcasting of religious shows intended to attract new adherents —**tel·e·van´ge·list** *n.*

**tel´e·vise** *vt., vi.* to transmit a television signal

**tel´e·vi·sion** *n.* a system, industry, etc. involved with the transmission of visual images and sound; a device for receiving such transmissions

**tell** *vt.* to narrate or relate in detail; to express in words; to ascertain or distinguish, as *to tell who is at fault* —*vi.* to give an account; to serve as an indication: *their rags told of their poverty* —**tell´a·ble** *adj.*

**tell´er** *n.* one who narrates, as a story; *(US)* a bank employee

**tell´ing** *adj.* producing a marked effect —**tell´ing·ly** *adv.*

**tell´tale** *adj.* revealing —*n.* one who tells on others, a tattler; an outward sign or indication

**tem·er·ar´i·ous** *adj.* daring or reckless —**tem·er·ar´i·ous·ly** *adv.* —**tem·er·ar´i·ous·ness** *n.*

**te·mer´i·ty** *n.* foolish disregard for danger

**tem´peh** *n.* a high-protein food made from fermented soybeans

**tem´per** *n.* a fit of anger; a tendency to quick anger; temperament; the hardness of a metal —*vt.* to moderate, as by adding something; to toughen, as by hardship —*vi.* to be or become tempered —**tem·per·a·bil´i·ty** *n.* —**tem´per·a·ble** *adj.*

**tem´per·a** *n.* a type of paint; a method of painting

**tem´per·a·ment** *n.* the nature or disposition of a person; an overly dramatic or moody disposition

**tem´per·a·men´tal** *adj.* pertaining to temperament; overly excitable, capricious, etc.; unpredictable —**tem´per·a·men´tal·ly** *adv.*

**tem´per·ance** *n.* moderation and self-control, especially in the indulgence of an appetite —*adj.* restraint

**tem´per·ate** *adj.* characterized by moderation or the absence of extremes; calm, restrained; practicing moderation in all things; of a climate that is not extreme: not overly hot or cold —**tem´per·ate·ly** *adv.* —**tem´per·ate·ness** *n.*

**tem´per·a·ture** *n.* a measure of the relative heat or cold as in the atmosphere, the body, etc.; an excess of heat in a body

**tem´pered** *adj.* of a particular temperament, as *even-tempered* or *quick-tempered*; modified by the addition of something else: *discipline tempered with love*; having a desired quality: *tempered steel*

**tem´pest** *n.* a violent wind; a violent disturbance

**tem·pes´tu·ous** *adj.* stormy, turbulent —**tem·pes´tu·ous·ly** *adv.* —**tem·pes´tu·ous·ness** *n.*

**tem´plate** *n.* a pattern used in the making or design of something

**tem´ple** *n.* a place dedicated to worship; an imposing structure dedicated to a special purpose, as *a temple of learning*

**tem´po** *n.* relative speed and rhythm, as of music

**tem´po·ral** *adj.* worldly; material as contrasted to spiritual; transitory; of or related to time —**tem·po·ral´i·ty, tem´po·ral·ness** *n.* —**tem´po·ral·ly** *adv.*

**tem´po·rar·y** *adj.* lasting for a time only; not permanent —*n.* a worker hired as seasonal help, to fill in for a permanent employee who is ill or on vacation, etc. —**tem·po·rar´i·ly** *adv.* —**tem´po·rar´i·ness** *n.*

**tem´po·rize** *vi.* to act evasively so as to gain time or defer commitment; to give in to the situation, circumstances, etc.; to compromise —**tem·po·ri·za´tion** *n.* —**tem´po·riz·er** *n.* —**tem´po·riz·ing·ly** *adv.*

**tempt** *vt.* to try to persuade to do, as by promises; to risk provoking: *to tempt fate*; to influence: *they were tempted by the promise of profit* —**tempt´a·ble** *adj.* —**tempt´er, tempt´ress** *n.*

**temp·ta´tion** *n.* that which tempts; the state of being tempted

**tempt´ing** *adj.* attractive; seductive —**tempt´ing·ly** *adv.* —**tempt´ing·ness** *n.*

**tem´pu´ra** *n.* a Japanese dish of vegetables or seafood fried in a light batter

**ten´a·ble** *adj.* capable of being maintained or defended, as a concept, position, etc. —**ten·a·bil´i·ty, ten´a·ble·ness** *n.* —**ten´a·bly** *adv.*

**te·na´cious** *adj.* obstinate or persistent, as in a belief; adhesive or sticky; strongly retentive, as of memory —**te·na´cious·ly** *adv.* —**te·na´cious·ness, te·nac´i·ty** *n.*

**ten´an·cy** *n.* the holding of property by any form of title; the period of tenancy

**ten´ant** *n.* one who rents or has title to property belonging to another; an occupant —*vt., vi.* to hold as, or to be, a tenant —**ten´ant·a·ble** *adj.* —**ten´ant·ry** *n.*

**tend** *vi.* to have an aptitude or inclination; to be in attendance, to serve; to give attention or care —*vt.* to take care of; to watch over

**tend´en·cy** *n.* an inclination; movement, as toward some end or result

**ten·den´tious, ten·den´cious** *adj.* disposed to a particular view **–ten·den´tious·ly** *adv.* **–ten·den´tious·ness** *n.*

**ten´der**[1] *adj.* delicate or fragile; youthful: *of a tender age*; marked by gentleness and consideration; expressing affection: *a tender look*; emotionally sensitive **–ten´der·ly** *adv.* **–ten´der·ness** *n.*

**tend´er**[2] *vt.* to present for acceptance, as an invitation or offer, the payment of a debt, etc. *–n.* an offer; that which is offered, especially money; a boat that services a larger vessel, as by ferrying passengers or supplies; a railway car attached to a steam locomotive to carry fuel and water; a person who tends or ministers

**ten´der·foot** *n.* a newcomer or beginner *–adj.* inexperienced

**ten´der·heart·ed** *adj.* responsive to another's troubles; compassionate; sympathetic **–ten´ der·heart·ed·ly** *adv.* **–ten´der·heart·ed·ness** *n.*

**ten´der·ize** *vt.* to make meat tender **–ten·der·i·za´tion** *n.* **–ten´der·iz·er** *n.*

**ten´der·loin** *n.* a tender cut of meat; a city district known for crime and corruption

**ten·di·ni´tis, ten·do·ni´tis** *n.* inflammation of a tendon

**ten´don** *n.* a band of tough, fibrous tissue that attaches muscle to bone **–ten´di·nous** *adj.*

**ten´dril** *n.* a delicate, curling extension by which certain plants attach themselves **–ten´dril·ed, ten´drill·ed, ten´dril·ous** *adj.*

**ten´e·ment** *n.* a rented room or set of rooms; commonly, a low-rent run-down apartment building; property held by a renter **–ten·e·men´tal, ten·e·men´ta·ry** *adj.*

**ten´et** *n.* a principle, doctrine, etc. held by a group or profession

**ten´on** *n.* a projection on the end of a timber for inserting into a mortise to form a joint

**ten´or** *n.* general character or nature; a general course or tendency; a male voice or singing part higher than a baritone *–adj.* of a voice, singing part, or musical instrument in the tenor range

**tense** *adj.* stretched tight; undermental stress; providing suspense *–vt., vi.* to make or become tense *–n.* the quality of a verb that denotes time or state of being: *past tense, present tense,* etc. **–tense´ly** *adv.* **–tense´ness** *n.*

**ten´sile** *adj.* pertaining to tension; capable of being stretched **–ten´sile·ly** *adv.* **–ten´sile·ness** *n.*

**tensile strength** resistance of a material to any force that may tend to rupture it

**ten´sion** *n.* the act of stretching or the condition of being stretched; mental strain or anxiety; a device on a machine that regulates stress **–ten´sion·al** *adj.*

**ten´sor** *n.* a muscle that tenses or stretches **–ten·so´ri·al** *adj.*

**tent** *n.* a portable shelter of canvas or similar mater al *–vi.* to pitch a tent; to camp

**ten´ta·cle** *n.* a long, flexible appendage of certain animals that function as the organ of touch or for grasping; a similar organ on the leaves of certain plants, such as for trapping insects **–ten´ta·cled, ten·tac´u·lar** *adj.*

**ten´ta·tive** *adj.* not finalized, subject to change; somewhat uncertain **–ten´ta·tive·ly** *adv.* **–ten´ta·tive·ness** *n.*

**ten´ter** *n.* a frame for stretching cloth to dry

**ten´ter·hook** *n.* a sharp pin for holding cloth on a tenter **–be on tenterhooks** to be in a state of anxiety

**ten´u·ous** *adj.* weak, lacking substance, as of an argument or reasoning; thin: lacking density, such as air at high altitudes **–ten´u·ous·ly** *adv.* **–ten´u·ous·ness** *n.*

**ten´ure** *n.* the right, condition, etc. of holding something, as property, office, or a position **–ten´ured, ten·u´ri·al** *adj.* **–ten·u´ri·al·ly** *adv.*

**tep´id** *adj.* moderately warm; unenthusiastic **–te·pid´i·ty, tep´id·ness** *n.* **–tep´id·ly** *adv.*

**te·qui´la** *n.* an alcoholic beverage of Mexican origin

**te·rat´o·gen** *n.* an agent that causes malformation, as in a developing fetus **–te·rat·o·gen´e·sis** *n.* **–te·rat·o·gen´ic** *adj.*

**ter´i·ya´ki** *n.* a Japanese dish of broiled marinated fish or meat

**term** *n.* a word or expression used to name something, convey a concept, etc.; the conditions of an agreement; a fixed period; a prescribed period *–vt.* to designate by means of a name

**term insurance** life insurance that is active for a specific period, as five years or ten years after which it can be renewed at a revised rate

**ter´ma·gant** *n.* a scolding woman *–adj.* abusive or quarrelsome

**ter´mi·na·ble** *adj.* that may be terminated **–ter·mi·na·bil´i·ty, ter´mi·na·ble·ness** *n.* **–ter´mi·na·bly** *adv.*

**ter´mi·nal** *adj.* pertaining to an end, as of an action, life, etc.; situated at or forming an end or limit *–n.* an intermediate or terminating point, as of a passenger station; an electrical junction; a station from which one communicates to or through a computer **–ter´mi·nal·ly** *adv.*

**ter´mi·nate** *vt.* to put an end to; to bound or limit *–vi.* to come to an end **–ter´mi·na·tive** *adj.* **–ter´mi·na·tive·ly** *adv.*

**ter·mi·na´tion** *n.* an ending, outcome, or conclusion; the condition of being terminated; that which bounds or limits **–ter·mi·na´tion·al** *adj.*

**ter´mi·na·tor** *n.* one who or that which terminates

**ter·mi·nol´o·gy** *n.* the terms relating to a particular

discipline, as in art, science, etc. **–ter·mi·no·log´i·cal** *adj.* **–ter·mi·no·log´i·cal·ly** *adv.* **–ter·mi·nol´o·gist** *n.*

**ter´mi·nus** *n.* the final point or end; a terminal

**ter·mi·tar´i·um** *n.* a termite nest

**ter´mite** *n.* an insect resembling the ant, noted for boring into wood

**terp´si·cho·re´an** *adj.* of or relating to dancing

**ter´race** *n.* a raised level space with sloping sides; a raised street supporting a row of houses; an open paved area connected to a house *–vt.* to form into or provide with a terrace **–terrace house** *(Brit.)* a house, usually of more than one storey, situated in a row of dwellings that share a common wall with one or more adjoining houses

**ter´ra cot´ta** reddish-brown clay pottery; a reddish-brown color **–ter´ra-cot´ta** *adj.*

**ter´ra fir´ma** solid ground

**ter·rain´** *n.* a land area described by a particular characteristic

**ter·rane´** *n.* a series of similar rock formations

**ter´ra·pin** *n.* a type of tortoise

**ter·rar´i·um** *n.* a glass enclosure for growing small plants

**ter·raz´zo** *n.* a flooring of stone chips set in mortar

**ter·res´tri·al** *adj.* belonging to the planet Earth; pertaining to earth; of land as distinct from water **–ter·res´tri·al·ly** *adv.*

**ter´ri·ble** *adj.* causing fear or dread; severe or extreme, as *a terrible headache*; dreadful, as *a terrible meal* **–ter´ri·ble·ness** *n.* **–ter´ri·bly** *adv.*

**ter´ri·er** *n.* a breed of small energetic dogs

**ter·rif´ic** *adj.* arousing fear or terror; unusually good **–ter·rif´i·cal·ly** *adv.*

**ter´ri·fy** *vt.* to fill with terror

**ter·rine´** *n.* a dish for cooking and serving food

**ter·ri·to´ri·al** *adj.* of a territory; restricted to a particular territory **–ter·ri·to´ri·al·ly** *adv.*

**territorial waters** coastal waters under the jurisdiction of a particular government

**ter·ri·to´ri·al·ize** *vt.* to organize as a territory; to create or extend a territory **–ter·ri·to·ri·al·i·za´tion** *n.*

**ter´ri·to·ry** *n.* the domain over which a government exercises jurisdiction; a distinctive area, as *a sales territory*; a region self-governed but lacking the status of a state or province

**ter´ror** *n.* great fear or something that causes such fear; a difficult child

**ter´ror·ism** *n.* violence committed to achieve a political end **–ter´ror·ist** *n.* **–ter·ror·is´tic** *adj.*

**ter´ror·ize** *vt.* to terrify, especially by acts of violence; to intimidate through terrorism **–ter·ror·i·za´tion** *n.* **–ter´ror·iz·er** *n.*

**ter´ry, ter´ry·cloth** *n.* an absorbent pile fabric

**terse** *adj.* short and to the point **–terse´ly** *adv.* **–terse´ness** *n.*

**ter´ti·ar·y** *adj.* third in importance, rank, etc.

**test** *vt.* to subject to examination *–vi.* to undergo or give an examination *–n.* an examination; a criterion or standard **–test·a·bil´i·ty** *n.* **–test´a·ble** *adj.*

**tes´ta·ment** *n.* the written statement of one's last will; a statement testifying to some belief; proof **–tes´ta·men´ta·ry** *adj.*

**tes´tate** *adj.* having a will **–tes´ta·cy** *n.* **–tes´ ta·tor** *n.*

**tes´ter** *n.* one who administers tests; a canopy, as over a bed

**tes´ti·cle** *n.* one of the two sex glands of the male **–tes·tic´u·lar** *adj.*

**tes´ti·fy** *vi.* to make a solemn declaration; to bear witness; to serve as evidence **–tes·ti·fi·ca´tion** *n.* **–tes´ti·fi·er** *n.*

**tes·ti·mo´ni·al** *n.* a statement endorsing character, value, etc.; public acknowledgment to show respect or appreciation

**tes´ti·mo·ny** *n.* a statement of a witness under oath; any public acknowledgment; any evidence or proof: *the dinner bore testimony to her skill as a cook*

**tes´ty** *adj.* irritable **–tes´ti·ly** *adv.* **–tes´ti·ness** *n.*

**tet´a·nus** *n.* an often fatal bacterial disease marked by spasmodic muscular contractions **–te·tan´ic** *adj.*

**tête´-à-tête´** *adj.* confidential *–n.* a private conversation

**teth´er** *n.* a line for restricting the movements of an animal; the limit of one's power, etc.

**te·tral´o·gy** *n.* a series of four novels, plays, etc.

**text** *n.* the words of an author or speaker; the main body of matter in a book; any of the written or printed versions of a piece of writing; the words of a song, opera, etc.

**text´book** *n.* a book used as a standard or basis of instructiontex'tile *n.* a fabric *–adj.* of weaving, woven fabric, or that which may be woven

**tex´tu·al** *adj.* of or relating to a text **–tex´tu·al·ly** *adv.*

**tex´tu·al·ism** *n.* the strict interpretation of a text, especially religious **–tex´tu·al·ist** *n.*

**tex´ture** *n.* the surface characteristic of a fabric; the characteristic of anything, especially in regard to appearance or tactile qualities: *the texture of bread*; the structure, form, etc. of a work of art, as *the tightly-knit texture of his prose*; the basic nature of something **–tex´tur·al** *adj.* **–tex´tur·al·ly** *adv.* **–tex´tured** *adj.*

**thal´a·mus** *n.* matter at the base of the brain involved in sensory transmission **–tha·lam´ic** *adj.*

**than·a·tol´o·gy** *n.* the study of death and dying **–than·a·tog´i·cal** *adj.* **–than·a·tol´o·gist** *n.*

**thane** *n.* in Anglo-Saxon England, one granted the land of a king or noble in exchange for military service; the chief of a Scottish clan

**thank** *vt.* to express gratitude

**thank´ful** *adj.* feeling or expressing gratitude –

**thank´ful·ly** *adv.* —**thank´ful·ness** *n.*

**thank´less** *adj.* unlikely to elicit approval; unappreciated —**thank´less·ly** *adv.* —**thank´less·ness** *n.*

**thanks´giv´ing** *n.* the act of giving thanks; a means of expressing thanks, as by prayer or celebration

**that** *adj.* pertaining to something previously mentioned, understood, or pointed out; denoting something more remote than the one with which it is being compared —*pron.* something mentioned, understood, etc.; the thing more remote —*adv.* to the extent required: *I can't see that far* —*conj.*

**thatch** *n.* a covering of leaves, reeds, etc. arranged so as to shed water; material used for such a covering —*vt.* to cover with a thatch —**thatch´er** *n.* —**thatch´y** *adj.*

**thaw** *vi.* to melt, as ice or snow; to rise in temperature so as to melt ice; to become less aloof —*vt.* to cause to thaw —*n.* the act of melting; warmth of temperature; progression toward sociability

**the´a·ter** *n.* a structure or area for the presentation of plays, operas, etc.; a similar place used for lectures, demonstrations, etc.; the world of the legitimate stage; a place that is the scene of action: *a theater of war*

**the·at´ric, the·at´ri·cal** *adj.* pertaining to any aspect of the theater, as script, actors, costumes, etc.; dramatically compelling; pretentious —**the·at´ri·cal·ism, the·at·ri·cal´i·ty** *n.* —**the·at´ri·cal·ly** *adv.*

**the·at´rics** *n.* undue dramatization

**theft** *n.* an act of stealing; that which is stolen

**the´ism** *n.* belief in a god or gods —**the´ist** *n.* —**the·is´tic, the·is´ti·cal** *adj.* —**the·is´ti·cal·ly** *adv.*

**theme** *n.* a main subject or topic, as of a work of art, speech, etc.; a short essay —**the·mat´ic, the·mat´i·cal** *adj.* —**the·mat´i·cal·ly** *adv.*

**the·oc´ra·cy** *n.* government by religious authority —**the·o·crat´ic, the·o·crat´i·cal** *adj.* —**the·o·crat´i·cal·ly** *adv.*

**the·od´o·lite** *n.* a surveying instrument

**the·og´o·ny** *n.* a chronicle of the geneology of gods —**the·o·gon´ic** *adj.*

**the·o·lo´gi·an** *n.* one trained in or engaged in the study of religious belief

**the·o·log´ic, the·o·log´i·cal** *adj.* relating to religious matters —**the·o·log´i·cal·ly** *adv.*

**the·ol´o·gy** *n.* the study of religion and religious doctrine

**the´o·rem** *n.* a proposition or theory that is demonstrably true or generally considered to be true

**the·o·ret´ic, the·o·ret´i·cal** *adj.* relating to theory; existing in theory only; disposed to speculation —**the·o·ret´i·cal·ly** *adv.*

**the´o·rize** *vi.* to speculate; to put forth as a theory —**the·o·ri·za´tion** *n.* —**the´o·riz·er** *n.* —**the´o·rist** *n.*

**the´o·ry** *n.* conjecture or speculation; a body of fundamental or abstract principles underlying an art, science, etc.; a proposed explanation

**the·os´o·phy** *n.* religious philosophy based on mystical insight —**the·o·soph´ic, the·o·soph´i·cal** *adj.* —**the·o·soph´i·cal·ly** *adv.* —**the·os´o·phist** *n.*

**ther´a·peu´tic, ther´a·peu´ti·cal** *adj.* having curative powers —**ther´a·peu´ti·cal·ly** *adv.*

**ther·a·peu´tics** *n.* the study of medical treatment and cures for illness and disease

**ther´a·py** *n.* the treatment of illness and disease; a type of treatment, as *physical therapy* or *psychotherapy* —**ther´a·pist** *n.*

**there** *adv.* in or at that place; yonder; in that respect —*n.* a position removed from that of the speaker

**there´a·bout, there´a·bouts** *adv.* approximately

**there´af´ter** *adv.* from that time on

**there´by´** *adv.* through the agency of

**there´fore´** *adv., conj.* for that reason; consequently

**there·in´** *adv.* in that respect

**there·in·af´ter** *adv.* in a subsequent part

**ther´e·min** *n.* an electronic instrument for producing musical tones

**there´upon´** *adv.* following or in consequence of

**there·with´** *adv.* thereupon

**ther´mal, ther´mic** *adj.* relating to or caused by heat; warm —*n.* a rising current of warm air

**ther·mo·dy·nam´ics** *n.* the study of the relationship between heat and other sources of energy —**ther·mo·dy·nam´ic, ther·mo·dy·nam´i·cal** *adj.* —**ther·mo·dy·nam´i·cal·ly** *adv.* —**ther·mo·dy·nam´i·cist** *n.*

**ther·mo·e·lec·tric´i·ty** *n.* electricity generated by heat —**ther·mo·e·lec´tric, ther·mo·e·lec´tri·cal** *adj.* —**ther·mo·e·lec´tri·cal·ly** *adv.*

**ther´mo·gram** *n.* the record made by a thermograph

**ther´mo·graph** *n.* a device for recording temperature as it is registered

**ther·mog´ra·phy** *n.* a process for producing raised letters on paper, such as business cards or stationery; the process of recording temperature variations with a thermograph —**ther·mo·graph´ic** *adj.* —**ther·mo·graph´i·cal·ly** *adv.*

**ther·mom´e·ter** *n.* a device for measuring temperature —**ther·mo·met´ric, ther·mo·met´ri·cal** *adj.* —**ther·mo·met´ri·cal·ly** *adv.*

**ther´mo·nu´cle·ar** *adj.* pertaining to the fusion of atomic particles at high temperatures

**ther·mo·plas´tic** *adj.* becoming soft when heated —*n.* a thermoplastic resin —**ther·mo·plas·tic´i·ty** *n.*

**ther´mo·stat** *n.* a device used to maintain a desired temperature range —**ther´mo·stat´ic** *adj.* —**ther´mo·stat´i·cal·ly** *adv.*

**ther·mo·trop´ic** *adj.* tending to grow or move toward a heat source, as of certain plants —**ther·mot´ro·pism** *n.*

**the·sau´rus** *n.* a collection of words with their synonyms; a collection of words or concepts relating

to a specific subject
**the´sis** *n., pl.* **the´ses** a proposition advanced and defended by argumentation; an unproved premise; a formal treatise on a specific subject
**thes´pi·an** *adj.* relating to drama —*n.* an actor or actress
**they** *pron.* persons or things previously mentioned; people in general: *you know what they say*
**thi·am´in, thi·am´ine** *n.* vitamin $B_1$
**thick** *adj.* relatively large in depth or extent; being of a specified dimension; having constituent elements closely packed: *a field thick with flowers*; viscous: *a thick sauce*; dense: *a thick fog*; very noticeable: *a thick accent* —*n.* the most dense or intense part: *the thick of battle* —*adv.* —**thick´ish** *adj.* —**thick´ly** *adj.* —**thick´ness** *n.*
**thick´en** *vt., vi.* to make or become thick or thicker —**thick´en·ing** *n.*
**thick´et** *n.* a dense growth, as of underbrush
**thick´-head·ed** *adj.* slow to learn or react; dumb —**thick´-head·ed·ness** *n.*
**thick´set´** *adj.* short and stocky; closely planted
**thick´-skinned´** *adj.* slow to anger; indifferent to insults
**thief** *n.* one who takes something belonging to another without permission
**thieve** *vt.* to steal —*vi.* to be a thief
**thiev´er·y** *n.* the act of stealing —**thiev´ish** *adj.* —**thiev´ish·ly** —*adv.* —**thiev´ish·ness** *n.*
**thigh** *n.* the part of the leg between the hip and the knee
**thin** *adj.* of little depth or width; lean and slender; lacking density: *a thin sauce* —*vt., vi.* to make or become thin or thinner —*adv.* —**thin´ly** *adv.*
**thing** *n.* that which exists as a separate entity; a matter or circumstance: *things have changed*; an act or event: *the right thing to do*; an idea or notion: *don't put things in her head*; an unexplainable or mysterious quality or attraction: *he has a thing for tall women*
**think** *vt.* to conceive mentally; to determine by reasoning; to believe to be true; to remember or recall; to intend —*vi.* to engage in rational thought; to weigh in the mind; to have a particular opinion, feeling etc.; to recall —**think better of** to reconsider —**think little of** consider to be inconsequential —**think the world of** to venerate or admire —**think´er** *n.*
**think´a·ble** *adj.* possible; worth considering —**think´a·bly** *adv.*
**think´ing** *adj.* intellectually active —*n.* a result of thought; one's opinion or bias
**think tank** *n.* a group, as of scientists, business executives, etc., organized for the study of a particular problem
**thin´-skinned´** *adj.* easily offended
**third** *adj., adv.* next in order after the second; being one of three equal parts —*n.*
**third´-rate´** *adj.* of poor quality
**third world** an underdeveloped nation
**thirst** *n.* a need for water; any craving, as *a thirst for alcohol* or *a thirst for glory* —*vi.* to have a desire or craving
**thirst´y** *adj.* lacking moisture; parched; eagerly desirous —**thirst´i·ly** *adv.* —**thirst´i·ness** *n.*
**this** *adj.* that near or present, understood, or just mentioned —*pron.* a person or thing near or present, etc. —*adv.*
**this´tle** *n.* a prickly plant —**this´tly** *adj.*
**thong** *n.* a narrow strip, as for fastening; a lash of a whip; a type of sandal; a type of beach wear
**tho·rac´ic** *adj.* relating to the thorax
**tho´rax** *n.* the part of the body between the neck and the abdomen, enclosed by the ribs; the middle segment of an insect
**thorn** *n.* a sharp outgrowth from a plant; a source of discomfort or annoyance
**thorn´y** *adj.* full of thorns; difficult or perplexing, as a problem —**thorn´i·ly** *adv.* —**thorn´i·ness** *n.*
**thor´ough** *adj.* attentive to details; complete or exhaustive, as *a thorough search* —**thor´ough·ly** *adv.* —**thor´ough·ness** *n.*
**thor´ough·bred** *adj.* bred from pure stock; possessing excellence —*n.* a horse bred for racing
**thor´ough·fare** *(US) n.* a main road
**thor´ough·go·ing** *adj.* characterized by thoroughness
**though** *conj.* notwithstanding; even if; and yet —*adv.*
**thought** *n.* the process or product of thinking; the concepts identified with a particular time, place, discipline, etc.: *modern political thought*; consideration or attention; preoccupation
**thought´ful** *adj.* contemplative or reflective; attentive or considerate; preoccupied —**thought´ful·ly** *adv.* —**thought´ful·ness** *n.*
**thought´less** *adj.* marked by a lack of care or regard; inconsiderate; flighty —**thought´less·ly** *adv.* —**thought´less·ness** *n.*
**thrall** *n.* a person or idea in bondage —**thrall´dom** *n.*
**thrash** *vt.* to thresh, as grain; to beat, as with a flail; to defeat utterly —*vi.* to move about with violent motions —**thrash´er** *n.*
**thread** *n.* a slender cord or line; a filament; something that runs through —*vt., vi.*
**thread´bare** *adj.* worn; commonplace —**thread´bare·ness** *n.*
**threat** *n.* a declaration of intent to inflict harm; a danger
**threat´en** *vt., vi.* to utter threats; to be or appear to be menacing —**threat´en·er** *n.* —**threat´en·ing·ly** *adv.*
**thresh** *vt.* to beat so as to separate grain from the husks —*vi.* to thrash about —**thresh´er** *n.*
**thresh´old** *n.* a doorsill; an entering point or beginning
**thrift** *n.* care in the management of one's resources

**–thrift´less** *adj.* **–thrift´less·ly** *adv.* **–thrift´less·ness** *n.*

**thrift´y** *adj.* practicing good management; prosperous **–thrift´i·ly** *adv.* **–thrift´i·ness** *n.*

**thrift´shop** a shop that deals in used articles

**thrill** *vi., vt.* to feel or cause to feel excitement *–n.* a feeling of excitement **–thrill´ing·ly** *adv.*

**thrill´er** *n.* an exciting book, play, movie, etc.

**thrive** *vi.* to be successful; to prosper; to flourish **–thriv´er** *n.* **–thriv´ing·ly** *adv.*

**throat** *n.* the front part of the neck; the passage extending from the back of the mouth; any narrow passage

**throat´y** *adj.* guttural or husky, as of a voice **–throat´i·ly** *adv.* **–throat´i·ness** *n.*

**throb** *vi.* to pulsate rhythmically; to show emotion by trembling *–n.* a pulsation **–throb´bing·ly** *adv.*

**throe** *n.* a violent pain, as in death or childbirth

**throm·bo´sis** *n.* the formation of a blood clot, as in the heart or an artery **–throm·bot´ic** *adj.*

**throm´bus** *n.* a clot formed in the heart or an artery

**throne** *n.* the authority of a ruler; a chair symbolizing authority

**throng** *n.* a closely crowded group of people *–vi., vt.* to gather or crowd together in large numbers

**throt´tle** *n.* a valve controlled the flow of fuel to an engine *–vt.* to choke or strangle; to silence or suppress; to change speed by means of a throttle **–throt´tler** *n.*

**through** *prep.* from end to end, side to side, etc.; permeating; by way of *–adv.*

**through·out´** *adv.* in every part *–prep.* all through

**throw** *vt.* to propel or hurl; to place carelessly; to direct or project *–vi.* to cast or fling something *–n.* an act of casting or flinging; the distance flung; a scarf or other light covering

**thrust** *vt.* to push or shove with force; to price *–vi.* to make a sudden push; to force oneself through *–n.* a sudden forceful push; a vigorous attack; a force that drive or propels; salient force: *the thrust of his remarks* **–thrust´er** *n.*

**thud** *n.* a dull, heavy sound; a blow or fall *–vi.*

**thug** *n.* a hoodlum or ruffian; formerly, a professional assassin in India **–thug´ger·y** *n.* **–thug´gish** *adj.*

**thumb** *n.* the short, thick digit of the human hand or a similar part of some animals

**thumb index** a series of indentations along the edge of a book to indicate its sections

**thumb´screw** *n.* a screw that can be turned with the fingers; an instrument of torture

**thumb´tack** *n.* a broad-handed tack

**thump** *n.* a blow made with a blunt object; the sound of such a blow *–vt., vi.* to beat or strike **–thump´er** *n.*

**thun´der** *n.* the sound that accompanies lightning; any similar noise *–vi., vt.* to make a noise reminiscent of thunder **–thun´der·er** *n.*

**thun´der·bolt** *n.* a lightning flash accompanied by thunder; a forceful person

**thun´der·clap** *n.* the sharp sound of thunder

**thun´der·cloud** *n.* a large, dark cloud

**thun´der·ous** *adj.* of a loud sound **–thun´der·ous·ly** *adv.*

**thun´der·show·er** *n.* rain accompanied by thunder and lightning

**thun´der·storm** *n.* a heavy blowing rain accompanied by thunder

**thun´der·strick·en, thun´der·struck** *adj.* astonished, amazed

**thwack** *vt.* to strike heavily with something flat *–n.*

**thwart** *vt.* to frustrate or foil by some means, as of a plan or scheme; to extend across *–n.* a seat or brace extending across a small boat or canoe *–adj.* extending or passing across **–thwart´er** *n.*

**thyme** *n.* a small plant of the mint family; the leaves of the plant, used for seasoning **–thy´mic, thym´y** *adj.*

**thy´mus** *n.* a ductless glandlike structure at the base of the neck

**thy´roid** *n.* cartilage of the larynx which form the Adam's apple; a large, ductless gland located near the larynx *–adj.*

**ti·ar´a** *n.* a jeweled head ornament or crown

**tib´ia** *n.* the larger of two leg bones extending below the knee; the shinbone **–tib´i·al** *adj.*

**tic** *n.* an habitual involuntary muscular spasm

**tick´et** *n.* a printed paper showing entitlement, as to transportation, entrance to a show, etc.; a tag or label; a list of candidates on a ballot; a court summons, as for a traffic violation *–vt.* to attach a label to; to furnish with a ticket

**tick´le** *vt.* to cause to laugh, especially by touching; to amuse or entertain *–vi.* to have or cause a tingling sensation *–n.*

**tick´ler** *n.* one who tickles; a book, file, etc. that serves as a reminder of things to be done at a certain time in the future

**tick´lish** *adj.* responsive to tickling; easily offended; requiring tact or delicate handling **–tick´lish·ly** *adv.* **–tick´lish·ness** *n.*

**tid´al** *adj.* pertaining to or influenced by the tide; dependent on the tide

**tidal wave** a great incoming rise of water; a surge, as of public opinion

**tid´bit** *n.* a delicacy

**tide** *n.* the periodic rise and fall of the ocean corresponding to the phases of the moon

**tide´land** *n.* land periodically covered by a rising tide

**tide´wa·ter** *n.* water near the coast that is affected by the movements of the tide

**ti´dings** *n.* news

**ti´dy** *adj.* neat and orderly *–vt., vi.* to put in order **–ti´di·ly** *adv.* **–ti´di·ness** *n.*

**tie** *vt.* to draw together or fasten with a cord, rope, etc.; to make a knot; to fasten or join; to equal another in score or achievement *–vi.* to make a connection; to make the same score *–n.* a fastener; any bond or connection; *(US)* a timber that supports railroad tracks

**tie´-in** *n.* something that connects or associates *–adj.*

**tier** *n.* one of a series arranged one above another, such as rows of seats in a sports arena

**tiff** *n.* a spat; a small argument *–vi.* to take part in a spat

**ti´ger** *n.* a large striped carnivorous feline; a fiercely determined or energetic person **–ti´ger·ish** *adj.*

**ti´ger-eye** *n.* a yellow and brown semiprecious stone

**tight** *adj.* firmly fixed or secure; fully stretched; difficult or demanding; *a tight schedule, a tight spot*; closely fitted; scarce; stingy; intoxicated *adv.* securely **–tight´ly** *adv.* **–tight´ness** *n.*

**tight´en** *vt., vi.* to make or become tight or tighter **–tight´en·er** *n.*

**tight´-fist´ed** *adj.* stingy **–tight´-fist´ed·ness** *n.*

**tight´-lipped** *adj.* uncommunicative; secretive

**tights** *n.* a close-fitting garment, worn by dancers, gymnasts, etc.

**tight´wad** *n.* a miser

**til´de** *n.* a diacritical mark (˜) used in Spanish and Portuguese to indicate a change in the pronunciation of certain letters

**tile** *n.* a thin piece used as an ornament and for covering roofs, floors, walls, etc. *–vt.* to cover with tiles **–til´er** *n.* **–til´ing** *n.*

**till** *vt., vi.* to work soil for the cultivation of crops *–n.* a money drawer; available cash

**till´age** *n.* the cultivation of land **–till´a·ble** *adj.*

**tilt** *vi., vt.* to incline or cause to incline at an angle

**tim´bal** *n.* a kettledrum

**tim´bale** *n.* a custard containing cheese, fish, vegetables, etc. and backed in a pastry mold

**tim´ber** *n.* *(Brit.)* wood dressed for use in construction; standing trees

**tim´ber·land** *n.* land covered with trees

**tim´ber·line** *n.* the imaginary line beyond which trees do not grow, as on a mountainside or the northern and southern tips of the planet

**tim´bre** *n.* the distinctive quality of a sound

**time** *n.* the concept of continuous existence: the past, present, and future; a distinct moment or period; a period considered as having distinct quality: *times are hard, have a good time*; a system for measuring duration; musical tempo *–adj.* relating to time; payable at a future date; designed to be active at a specified time *–vt.* to record the speed or duration of; to mark the rhythm of

**time´-hon´ored** *adj.* accepted as customary or traditional

**time´less** *adj.* eternal; not limited to a specific time **–time´less·ly** *adv.* **–time´less·ness** *n.*

**time´ly** *adj.* occurring at the proper or a convenient time **–time´li·ness** *n.*

**time´ous** *adj.* timely **–time´ous·ly** *adv.*

**time´-shar·ing** *n.* access to a large central computer by many users; the user of vacation property by several owners in turn based on an arranged schedule **–time´-share** *vt., vi.*

**time´ta·ble** *n.* a schedule showing the arrival and departure time of buses, trains, etc.; a plan for the completion of the parts of a project

**time´worn** *adj.* made ineffective by time or overuse, as a motto or maxim

**tim´id** *adj.* fearful; lacking self-confidence **–ti·mid´i·ty, tim´id·ness** *n.* **–tim´id·ly** *adv.*

**tim´ing** *n.* the art of regulating occurrence to insure maximum effect

**tim´o·rous** *adj.* fearful; anxious **–tim´o·rous·ly** *adv.* **–tim´o·rous·ness** *n.*

**tim´o·thy** *n.* a perennial grass grown mainly for cattle feed

**tim´pa·ni** *n.* kettledrums **–tim´pa·nist** *n.*

**tin** *n.* a metallic element used in making alloys

**tinc´ture** *n.* a medicinal solution; a coloring substance; a slight trace

**tin´der** *n.* any dry substance that ignites easily **–tin´der·y** *adj.*

**tin´der·box** *n.* a container of material for starting a fire; highly flammable material; an extremely excitable person

**tine** *n.* a prong, as on a fork

**tinge** *n.* a faint trace, as of color *–vt.* to tint or color lightly

**tin´gle** *vi., vt.* to experience or cause to experience a prickly, stinging sensation *–n.* a stinging sensation **–tin´gler** *n.* **–tin´gly** *adv.*

**tin´kle** *vi., vt.* to produce or cause to produce light metallic sounds, as of a bell **–tin´kly** *adj.*

**tin·ni´tus** *n.* a ringing or buzzing sound in the ears

**tin´ny** *adj.* made of or containing tin; flimsy; of a flat sound **–tin´ni·ly** *adv.* **–tin´ni·ness** *n.*

**tin´sel** *n.* thin glittering bits used for ornamentation; something that is showy, but of little value *–adj.* decorated with tinsel; gaudy or showy *–vt.* to decorate with tinsel **–tin´sel·ly** *adv.* **–tin´sel·ry** *n.*

**tin´smith** *n.* one who works with tin or tin plate

**tint** *n.* a pale color; a shading or gradation of color *–vt.* to apply color **–tint´er** *n.*

**tin·tin·nab·u·la´tion** *n.* the ringing of bells **–tin·tin·nab´u·lar, tin·tin·nab´u·lous** *adj.*

**ti´ny** *adj.* very small **–ti´ni·ness** *n.*

**tip** *n.* a light tap; a gift of money for service; a helpful hint; confidential information; an extremity; a piece made to cap an extremity *—vt.* to cause to lean; to overturn; to strike lightly; to adorn the tip of *—vi.* to become tilted; to overturn

**tip´off** *n.* a warning

**tip´ple** *vt., vi.* to drink frequently and habitually

**tip´sy** *adj.* unsteady; intoxicated **—tip´si·ly** *adv.* **—tip´si·ness** *n.*

**ti·rade´** *n.* a prolonged denunciation

**tire** *vt.* to reduce the strength of, as by exertion; to make weary or impatient *—vi.* to become weary; to lose patience *—n. (US)* a flexible covering for a wheel

**tired** *adj.* weary; fatigued **—tired´ness** *n.*

**tire´less** *adj.* not easily fatigued; energetic **—tire´less·ly** *adv.* **—tire´less·ness** *n.*

**tire´some** *adj.* tedious or boring; mundane **—tire´some·ly** *adv.* **—tire´some·ness** *n.*

**tis´sue** *n.* an aggregate of organic cells and associated matter having a particular function; a light fabric, as gauze; tissue paper; a light disposable sheet of paper used as a wipe

**tissue culture** tissue kept alive and growing in a culture medium

**tissue paper** thin paper for wrapping or protecting

**ti´tan** *n.* a giant

**tithe** *n.* one tenth; a tax or contribution for the support of the clergy and the church; any tax or levy *—vt.* to give or pay a tithe **—tith´a·ble** *adj.* **—tith´er** *n.*

**tit´il·late** *vt.* to cause a tickling sensation; to stimulate or excite, often erotically **—tit´il·lat·er** *n.* **—tit´il·lat·ing·ly** *adv.* **—tit·il·la´tion** *n.* **—tit´il·la·tive** *adj.*

**ti´tle** *n.* a descriptive name; the name of a book, song, etc.; a designation, as of rank, profession, etc.; the legal right to property *—vt.* to give a name or designation; to entitle to

**ti´tled** *adj.* having a title, especially one denoting nobility

**tit´ter** *n.* a suppressed laugh *—vi.* **—tit´ter·er** *n.* **—tit´ter·ing·ly** *adv.*

**tit´tle** *n.* the tiniest amount

**tit´u·lar** *adj.* existing in name or title only **—tit´u·lar·ly** *adv.*

**tiz´zy** *n.* a bewildered state of mind

**toad** *n.* a jumping amphibian resembling the frog; a loathsome person

**toad´y** *adj.* an obsequious flatterer; one who acts without scruples in order to gain favor *—vt., vi.* to flatter or serve without question **—toad´y·ism** *n.*

**toast** *vt., vi.* to make or become warm or browned; to drink to the health of another *—n.* a tribute of words followed by a drink; one who is well-known and greatly admired: *the toast of the town*

**toast´mas·ter** *n.* one who presides at a public banquet, calling the toasts, announcing speakers, etc.

**toast´y** *adj.* comfortably warm

**to·bog´gan** *n.* a long sledlike vehicle without runners for traveling over snow or ice *—vi.* to ride on a toboggan **—to·bog´gan·er, to·bog´gan·ist** *n.*

**tod´dle** *vi.* to walk unsteadily *—n.* a shaky walk **—tod´dler** *n.*

**tod´dy** *n.* whiskey, rum, or other spirits mixed with hot water, spices, and sugar

**to-do´** *n.* a fuss

**toe** *n.* a digit of the foot; the forward part of the foot; part of a covering for the foot

**to´fu** *n.* a cheese-like food made from soybeans

**to´ga** *n.* a loose flowing robe **—to´gaed** *adj.*

**to·geth´er** *adv.* in the company of others; collectively, as one unit: spent more money that all the others together **—to·geth´er·ness** *n.*

**tog´ger·y** *n.* clothing

**toil** *n.* strenuous labor *—vi.* to work hard *—vt.* to accomplish with great effort **—toil´er** *n.*

**toi´let** *n.* a bathroom fixture for disposing of body waste; the process of grooming *—adj.* used in grooming, as *toilet articles*

**toi´let·ry** *n.* something such as soap, cologne, etc. used in personal grooming

**toil´some** *adj.* involving hard work; difficult **—toil´some·ly** *adv.* **—toil´some·ness** *n.*

**to´ken** *n.* tangible evidence, as of affection, authority, etc.; a metal piece issued in place of currency *—adj.* nominal or minimal; partial

**to´ken·ism** *n.* an attempt to meet an obligation or condition with a symbolic gesture

**tol´er·a·ble** *adj.* endurable; barely satisfactory **—tol·er·a·bil´ity, tol´er·a·ble·ness** *n.* **—tol´er·a·bly** *adv.*

**tol´er·ance** *n.* freedom from prejudice; the ability to bear hardship; an allowance for variation; resistance to the effects of a substance

**tol´er·ant** *adj.* long-suffering; indulgent **—tol´er·ant·ly** *adv.*

**tol´er·ate** *vt.* to allow or concede; to bear **—tol·er·a´tion** *n.* **—tol´er·a·tive** *adj.* **tol´er·a·tor** *n.*

**toll** *n.* a tax or charge, as for passage; a charge for a special service; the sound of a bell rung slowly and regularly *—vi., vt.* to take or exact a charge; to sound or cause to sound, as a bell

**tomb** *n.* a burial place *—vt.* to entomb or bury

**tom´boy** *n.* a very active young girl **—tom´boy·ish** *adj.* **—tom´boy·ish·ly** *adv.* **—tom´boy·ish·ness** *n.*

**tomb´stone** *n.* a stone that marks a place of burial

**tome** *n.* a large heavy book

**tom·fool´er·y** *adj.* nonsensical behavior; foolishness

**to·mor´row** *n.* the next day after today *—adv.*

**ton** *n.* a measure of weight, such as: **—short ton** 2000 pounds **—long ton** 2240 pounds **—metric ton** 1000 kilograms

**to´nal** *adj.* pertaining to tone or tonality **–to´nal·ly** *adv.*

**to·nal´i·ty** *n.* a system or scheme of tones as in music or visual art

**tone** *n.* a musical sound or its quality; a characteristic tendency or quality: mode of one's writing or speech; style or elegance; the effect of light and color *–vt.* to impart a desired tone, as of sound or color **–tone down** to quiet or soften

**tone´less** *adj.* lifeless or flat **–tone´less·ly** *adv.* **–tone´less·ness** *n.*

**tongue** *n.* a muscular organ attached to the floor of the mouth; a manner of speaking; a language or dialect; something resembling a tongue **–tongue twister** a phrase difficult to repeat quickly

**tongue´-in-cheek** *adj.* said jokingly

**tongue´-lashing** *n.* a scolding

**tongue´-tied** *adj.* speechless

**ton´ic** *n.* something that promotes health or well-being; quinine water *–adj.* pertaining to tone; tending to stimulate or refresh

**ton´nage** *n.* weight expressed in tons; capacity

**ton´sil** *n.* either of two lymphoid masses located in the opening between the mouth and larynx

**ton·sil·lec´to·my** *n.* surgical removal of the tonsils

**ton·sil·li´tis** *n.* inflammation of the tonsils

**ton·so´ri·al** *adj.* of a barber or barbering

**ton´sure** *n.* shaving of the head, like that of a monk *–vt.* to shave part or all of the hair on the head

**ton´tine** *n.* an agreement by which an investment held in trust reverts to the survivor or survivors

**too** *adv.* also; excessive; extremely

**tool** *n.* any implement used in work or the performance of a task: *books are the tools of learning*; a person used to carry out the designs of another *–vt.* to form or shape with a tool; to scribe a motif or design on leather

**tool´ing** *n.* ornamental work, especially on leather

**tool´mak·er** *n.* a machinist who makes or repairs tools

**tooth** *n.* a hard structure in the mouth used for seizing and chewing food; a small projection, as on a saw or gear; a rough surface, as of paper; an appetite or taste for something

**tooth´ache** *n.* pain in or near a tooth

**tooth´less** *adj.* lacking teeth; lacking effectiveness **–tooth´less·ly** *adv.* **–tooth´less·ness** *n.*

**tooth´some** *adj.* pleasant tasting **–tooth´some·ly** *adv.* **–tooth´some·ness** *n.*

**tooth´y** *adj.* showing the teeth; having prominent or projecting teeth **–tooth´i·ly** *adv.* **–tooth´i·ness** *n.*

**top** *n.* the uppermost or highest part; an upper surface; a lid; the highest degree; the best *–adj.* relating to the top; most important or best *–vt.* to remove the uppermost part; to form or provide a top; to surmount or surpass

**top´coat** *n.* a light overcoat

**top´-heavy** *adj.* unstable due to excessive weight at the top; of an organization with an overly large executive staff **–top´-heav·i·ly** *adv.* **–top´-heav·iness** *n.*

**to´pi·ar·y** *n.* live bushes or trees trimmed or formed in decorative shapes *–adj.* pertaining to the art of topiary

**top´ic** *n.* the subject matter or substance, as for a speech, discussion, etc.

**top´i·cal** *adj.* relating to matters of local or current interest; pertaining to a topic **–top·i·cal´i·ty** *n.* **–top´i·cal·ly** *adv.*

**top´knot** *n.* a tuft or knot of hair or feathers at the top of the head; an ornament worn as a headdress

**top´less** *adj.* lacking a top; nude above the waist **–top´less·ness** *n.*

**top´-lev´el** *adj.* of the highest rank or importance

**to·pog´ra·phy** *n.* the physical features of a region or a representation of them; topographic surveying **–to·pog´ra·pher** *n.* **–top·o·graph´ic, top·o·graph´i·cal** *adj.* **–top·o·graph´i·cal·ly** *adv.*

**top´o·nym** *n.* a place name **–top·o·nym´ic, top·o·nym´i·cal** *adj.*

**to·pon´y·my** *n.* the study of the place names of a region or of a language

**top´ple** *vi.* to fall, as by its own weight *–vt.* to cause to fall; to overthrow

**top´soil** *n.* the surface soil of land

**top´sy-tur´vy** *adj., adv.* upside down; in utter disarray *–n.* a state of disorder **–top´sy-tur´vi·ly** *adv.* **–top´sy-tur´vi·ness** *n.*

**tor** *n.* a rocky peak

**torch** *n.* a flame at the end of a stick or rod; anything that brightens; a device producing an intense flame as for welding, removing paint, etc.

**torch´bear·er** *n.* one who carries a torch; one who conveys truth or knowledge, etc.; leader of a cause

**to´re·a·dor** *n.* a bullfighter

**tor´ment** *n.* intense pain or anguish; a source of pain or anguish **–tor·ment´** *vt.* to subject to torture; to harass **–tor·men´ter, tor·men´tor** *n.* **–tor·ment´ing·ly** *adv.*

**tor·na´do** *n.* a whirling wind of exceptional force

**tor·pe´do** *n.* a self-propelled underwater missile *–vt.* to damage or sink with a torpedo; to sabotage or destroy utterly

**tor´pid** *adj.* dormant; sluggish; apathetic **–tor·pid´i·ty, tor´pid·ness** *n.* **–tor´pid·ly** *adv.*

**tor´por** *n.* loss of sensibility or power of motion; apathy, listlessness **–tor´por·if´ic** *adj.*

**torque** *n.* a turning or twisting force; a measure of the tendency to cause rotation

**tor´rent** *n.* a rapid, turbulent stream of liquid; any violent flow: *a torrent of abuse* **–tor·ren´tial** *adj.* **–tor·ren´tial·ly** *adv.*

**tor´rid** *adj.* intensely hot and dry; passionate —**tor´rid·ly** *adv.* —**tor´rid·ness** *n.*
**tor´so** *n.* the trunk of the human body
**tort** *n.* a civil wrong not involving breach of contract —**tor´tious** *adj.*
**tor´te** *n.* a rich cake
**tor·tel·li´ni** *n.* small ring-shaped pasta stuffed with cheese, spinach, meat, etc.
**tor·ti´lla** *n.* a small, flat bread made of corn meal and baked on a skillet
**tor´toise** *n.* a land turtle
**tor´tu·ous** *adj.* twisting, as a road; devious, as *tortuous logic* —**tor´tu·ous·ly** *adv.* —**tor´tu·ous·ness** *n.*
**tor´ture** *n.* intense physical or mental suffering; something that causes pain —*vi.* to inflict pain upon; to cause to suffer —**tor´tur·er** *n.*
**tor´tur·ous** *adj.* pertaining to torture —**tor´tur·ous·ly** *adv.*
**toss** *vt.* to throw or cast; to pitch or fling about; to interject casually; to turn over and mix —*vi.* to be thrown about, as by the sea; to roll about restlessly, as in sleep —*n.* a throw; a quick movement; *a toss of the head* —**toss´er** *n.*
**toss´pot** *n.* a drunkard
**tos·ta´da** *n.* a crisp tortilla
**tot** *n.* a small child
**to´tal** *n.* the entire amount —*adj.* complete —*vt.* to ascertain the full amount —**to´tal·ly** *adv.*
**to·tal´i·tar´i·an** *adj.* of an oppressive government with absolute power —*n.* —**to·tal·i·tar´i·an·ism** *n.*
**to·tal´i·ty** *n.* a total amount; the state of being whole
**tote** *vt.* to carry —*n.* something carried —**tot´a·ble** *adj.* —**tot´er** *n.*
**to´tem** *n.* a natural object or representation believed to be ancestrally related and that serves as an emblem for a group, tribe, etc. —**to·tem´ic** *adj.* —**to´tem·ism** *n.*
**tot´ter** *vi.* to tremble or waver as if about to fall; to seem near to collapse; to walk unsteadily —*n.* an unsteady or wobbly manner of walking —**tot´ter·er** *n.* —**tot´ter·ing·ly** *adv.* —**tot´ter·y** *adj.*
**tou´can** *n.* a tropical bird with colorful plumage and a very large beak
**touch** *vt.* to perceive by feeling; to be in or come into contact with; to affect; to impress emotionally —*vi.* to come into or be in contact —*n.* a coming into contact; a sensation conveyed by contact; a distinctive manner or style: *the master's touch*; a trace or hint; the manner in which something is fingered, as piano keys —**touch on** to concern or relate to —**touch up** to add final corrections —**touch´a·ble** *adj.* —**touch´a·ble·ness** *n.*
**touched** *adj.* effected emotionally; mentally unbalanced; peculiar or eccentric
**touch´ing** *adj.* appealing to emotion —*prep.* with regard to; concerning —**touch´ing·ly** *adv.* —**touch´ing·ness** *n.*
**touch´y** *adj.* apt to take offense; liable to cause offense or contention —**touch·i·ly** *adv.* —**touch´i·ness** *n.*
**tough** *adj.* capable of bearing stress or strain; difficult to cut or chew; requiring intense effort; unyielding; severe or harsh —*n.* a rowdy —**tough´ly** *adv.* —**tough´ness** *n.*
**tough´en** *vt., vi.* to make or become tough or tougher —**tough´en·er** *n.*
**tough´-mind´ed** *adj.* facing difficulty with strength and resolve; unsentimental —**tough´-mind´ed·ly** *adv.* —**tough´-mind´ed·ness** *n.*
**tou·pee´** *n.* a small wig
**tour** *n.* a journey or excursion; a fixed period of service —*vt.* to make a trip; to take a show on the road —*vi.* to go on a trip
**tour´ism** *n.* recreational travel; the travel industry
**tour´ist** *n.* one who travels for pleasure —*adj.* relating to or suitable for recreational travelers —**tour·is´tic** *adj.* —**tour´ist·y** *adj.*
**tour´na·ment** *n.* a series of competitive events
**tour´ni·quet** *n.* a device to control severe external bleeding, as from a wound
**tou´sle** *vt.* to dishevel, as hair —*n.* mussed hair
**tout** *vt.* to solicit; to praise highly; to sell information about —*vi.* to solicit customers, patronage, etc.; to sell information —*n.* one who sells information —**tout´er** *n.*
**tow** *vt.* to pull or drag, as by rope, etc. —*n.* something being towed —**in tow** drawn or brought along: *she arrived with friends in tow* —**tow´a·ble** *adj.* —**tow´age** *n.*
**to´ward** *prep.* in the direction of; for the purpose of; near, approaching
**tow´el** *n.* cloth, paper, etc. used for wiping or polishing
**tow´el·ing** *n.* material used to make towels
**tow´er** *n.* a tall structure or part of a structure; a place of security —*vi.* to extend to a great height
**tow´er·ing** *adj.* very tall: *a towering figure*; very great: *a towering rage*
**town** *(US)* *n.* an incorporated populated area larger than a village and smaller than a city; a city; collectively, the inhabitants or government of a town —*adj.* pertaining to or characteristic of a town or its population
**town house** *(US)* a house, usually of more than one story, situated in a row of dwellings that share a common wall with one or more adjoining houses
**tow´path** *n.* a narrow road along a waterway, used by men or animals towing boats
**tox·e´mi·a** *n.* the presence of toxins in the blood —**tox·e´mic** *adj.*
**tox´ic** *adj.* poisonous; caused by poison or a toxin

—tox´i·cal·ly *adv.* —tox·ic´i·ty *n.*
**tox´i·cant** *n.* a poison —*adj.* poisonous
**tox·i·col´o·gy** *n.* the study of poisons, their detection, antidotes, etc. —**tox·i·co·log´ic, tox·i·co·log´i·cal** *adj.* —**tox·i·co·log´i·cal·ly** *adv.* —**tox·i·col´o·gist** *n.*
**tox´in** *n.* a poisonous substance
**toy** *n.* something designed for or serving as a plaything; something trifling or ineffectual —*vi.* to consider without conviction: *toy with an idea*; to use someone or something for one's own amusement —*adj.* designed as a toy; resembling a toy, as of a miniature
**trace** *n.* a vestige or mark left by someone or something no longer present; a barely detectable quality, characteristic, etc. —*vt.* to find or find out by investigation; to copy onto an overlay —*vi.* to follow a track, course of development, etc. —**trace·a·bil´i·ty, trace´a·ble·ness** *n.* —**trace´a·ble** *adj.* —**trace´a·bly** *adv.*
**trac´er·y** *n.* delicate ornamentation
**tra´chea** *n.* the windpipe; an air passage —**tra´che·al** *adj.*
**tra·che·ot´o·my· tra·che·os´to·my** *n.* a surgical incision into the trachea
**tra·cho´ma** *n.* a contagious viral disease of the eye —**tra·chom´a·tous** *adj.*
**track** *n.* a mark left by the passage of anything; a path beaten down by repeated use; any path, especially one describing movement; a trail or roadway; the act of following or tracing, as *keeping track of expenses*; a continuous belt by which some vehicles are moved; metal rails that control the course of a train or trolley car —*vt.* to follow the course of; to trail; to make tracks —*vi.* to leave tracks; to be in agreement: *thinking along the same track* —**track´a·ble** *adj.* —**track´er** *n.*
**track record** a history of achievement
**tract** *n.* an extended area; a short discourse or pamphlet
**trac´ta·ble** *adj.* easily led; malleable —**trac·ta·bil´i·ty, trac´ta·ble·ness** *n.* —**trac´ta·bly** *adv.*
**trac´tion** *n.* the act of pulling; the state of being pulled or drawn; pulling power; rolling friction, as of tires on the road —**trac´tion·al, trac´tive** *adj.*
**trac´tor** *n.* a vehicle used to pull farm machinery; a motor vehicle used to haul trailers, etc.
**trade** *n.* a business or craft; the people or companies engaged in a particular business; the buying and selling, or exchange of commodities; a firm's customers; an exchange of one thing for another —*vt.* to give in exchange; to barter —*vi.* to engage in commerce —*adj.* —**trad´a·ble** *adj.* —**trad´er** *n.*
**trade´mark** *n.* a name, symbol, etc. used to distinguish a product from all others; any distinctive feature —*vt.* to legally protect, as a name, symbol etc.
**tra·di´tion** *n.* the body of knowledge, customs, etc. transmitted down through generations —**tra·di´tion·al** *adj.* —**tra·di´tion·al·ly** *adv.*
**tra·di´tion·al·ism** *n.* adherence to tradition —**tra·di´tion·al·ist** *n.* —**tra·di·tion·al·is´tic** *adj.*
**tra·duce´** *vt.* to willfully harm through misrepresentation; to defame or slander —**tra·duce´ment** *n.* —**tra·duc´er** *n.* —**tra·duc´ing·ly** *adv.*
**traf´fic** *n.* the passing of people, vehicles, messages, etc. through a limited space or between certain points; those which are moving; the business of buying and selling: *to traffic in household items*; the business of transportation —**traf´fick·er** *n.*
**tra·ge´di·an** *n.* an actor or writer of tragedies
**trag´e·dy** *n.* drama in which the protagonist comes to an unhappy end; a tragic incident
**trag´ic** *adj.* of the nature of a tragedy; causing or likely to cause suffering —**trag´i·cal·ly** *adv.*
**trag·i·com´e·dy** *n.* drama having characteristics of both comedy and tragedy; an incident of this nature —**trag·i·com´ic, trag·i·com´i·cal** *adj.* —**trag·i·com´i·cal·ly** *adv.*
**trail** *vt.* to draw or drag lightly over a surface; to follow the track of; to be behind; to follow behind —*vi.* to hang or extend loosely so as to drag; to grow along the ground; to be behind; to lag behind —*n.* the track or traces left by something that has passed; something that follows, as vapor from a jet plane; *(US)* a worn path, such as one through a wilderness area
**trail´blaz·er** *n.* one that breaks a new trail; an innovator or pioneer
**trail´er** *(US) n.* a drawn vehicle equipped as living quarters or used to haul freight
**train** *n.* a series of connected rail cars; anything drawn along or following behind: *the train of a dress*; a set of connected things: *a train of thought* —*vt.* to make skillful or proficient; to teach; to point in an exact position: *train your eyes on the action* —*vi.* to undergo a course of instruction or preparation —**train·a·bil´i·ty** *adv.* —**train´a·ble** *adj.* —**train·ee´** *n.*
**train´er** *n.* one who trains or coaches, as an athlete or show animal; a device used to improve physical fitness or skill; *(Brit.)* a flexible sports shoe with a soft rubber sole: a sneaker
**train´ing** *n.* systematic instruction
**traipse** *vi.* to walk or wander about
**trait** *n.* a distinguishing quality
**trai´tor** *n.* one who betrays a trust; a person found guilty of treason
**trai´tor·ous** *adj.* constituting or resembling treason; characteristic of a traitor —**trai´tor·ous·ly** *adv.* —**trai´tor·ous·ness** *n.*
**tra·jec´to·ry** *n.* the path described by a body moving in space
**tramp** *vi.*, *vt.* to wander; to walk heavily —*n.* one who wanders, living by odd jobs or charity; a long walk; the sound of a heavy tread —**tramp´er** *n.*

**tram´ple** *vi.* to tread heavily; to injure or crush, as by treading heavily on *—vt.* to tread heavily or ruthlessly on **—tram´pler** *n.*

**trance** *n.* a dreamlike state as induced by hypnosis or a supernatural force; profound concentration **—trance´like** *adj.*

**tran´quil** *adj.* calm; quiet and motionless **—tran´quil·ly** *adv.* **—tran´quil·ness** *n.*

**tran´quil·ize** *vt., vi.* to make or become tranquil

**tran´quil·iz·er** *n.* a drug that calms without impairing consciousness

**tran·quil´li·ty** *n.* the state of being tranquil

**trans·act´** *vt.* to accomplish *—vi.* to carry on or conduct business **—trans·ac´tion** *n.* **—trans·ac´tion·al** *adj.* **—trans·ac´tor** *n.*

**tran·scend´** *vt.* to go beyond the limits of: *knowledge that transcends reason*; to rise above *—vi.* to excel

**tran·scen´dent** *adj.* transcendental; existing apart from the material universe **—tran·scen´dence, tran·scen´den·cy** *adj.* **—tran·scen´dent·ly** *adv.*

**tran·scen·den´tal** *adj.* beyond ordinary limits; supernatural; pertaining to transcendentalism **—tran·scen·den´tal·ly** *adv.*

**tran·scen·den´tal·ism** *n.* the philosophy that one can attain knowledge that transcends sensory phenomena **—tran·scen·den´tal·ist** *n.*

**tran·scribe´** *vt.* to copy or make a record of **—tran·scrib´er** *n.*

**tran´script** *n.* a copy; something recorded, as from a stenographer's notes **—tran·scrip´tion** *n.* **—tran·scrip´tion·al** *adj.*

**tran·sect´** *vt.* to divide by cutting across **—tran·sec´tion** *n.*

**trans´fer, trans·fer´** *vt.* to convey from one person or place to another **—trans´fer** *n.* that which is transferred, as a design; assignment of title or property **—trans·fer·a·bil´i·ty** *n.* **—trans·fer´a·ble** *adj.* **—trans·fer´al** *n.*

**trans·fig·u·ra´tion** *n.* a change in appearance

**trans·fig´ure** *vt.* to change the appearance of; to make splendid **—trans·fig´ure·ment** *n.*

**trans·fix´** *vt.* to pierce through; to impale; to render motionless, as with amazement

**trans·form´** *vt.* to change the form or appearance of; to change the nature or character of *—vi.* to be or become changed **—trans·form´a·ble** *adj.* **—trans·for·ma´tion** *n.*

**trans·fuse´** *vt.* to cause to flow from one person or thing to another; to pass into, permeate **—trans·fus´i·ble** *adj.* **—trans·fu´sion** *n.*

**trans·gress´** *vt.* to overstep the bounds of, as propriety or good taste *—vi.* to break a law; to sin **—trans·gress´i·ble** *adj.* **—trans·gres´sion** *n.* **—trans·gres´sive** *adj.* **—trans·gres´sive·ly** *adv.* **—trans·gres´sor** *n.*

**tran´sient** *adj.* not permanent; transitory: *a transient thought*; residing temporarily *—n.* a temporary resident, as at a hotel; a visitor; a tramp **—tran´sience, tran´sien·cy** *n.* **—tran´sient·ly** *adv.*

**tran´sit** *n.* the act of passing over or through; the process of change; the act of carrying across or through; transportation; a surveying instrument

**tran·si´tion** *n.* passage from one place, condition, etc. to another **—tran·si´tion·al, tran·si´tion·a·ry** *adj.* **—tran·si´tion·al·ly** *adv.*

**tran´si·to·ry** *adj.* existing only briefly; ephemeral **—tran·si·to´ri·ly** *adv.* **—tran´si·to·ri·ness** *n.*

**trans·late´** *vt.* to change into another language; to explain in other words **—trans·lat´a·ble** *adj.* **—trans·lat´a·ble·ness** *n.* **—trans·la´tion** *n.* **—trans·la´tor** *n.*

**trans·lu´cent** *adj.* allowing the passage of light, but not transparent **—trans·lu´cence, trans·lu´cen·cy** *n.* **—trans·lu´cent·ly** *adv.*

**trans·mi´grate** *vi.* to move, as from one country to another; to pass into another body, as of the soul at death **—trans·mi·gra´tion** *n.* **—trans·mi´gra·tor** *n.* **—trans·mi´gra·to·ry** *adj.*

**trans·mis´si·ble** *adj.* capable of being transmitted **—trans·mis´si·bil´i·ty** *n.*

**trans·mit´** *vt.* to send or pass on from one place, person, etc. to another; to serve as a medium of passage **—trans·mis´sion** *n.* **—trans·mit´ta·ble** *adj.* **—trans·mit´tal, trans·mit´tance** *n.* **—trans·mit´ter** *n.*

**trans·mog´ri·fy** *vt.* to transform radically; to make into something completely different **—trans·mog·ri·fi·ca´tion** *n.*

**tran´som** *n.* a horizontal piece over an opening: a lintel; a small window over a door

**trans·par´en·cy** *n.* the quality of being transparent; a section of photographic film

**trans·par´ent** *adj.* that can be seen through; easy to understand; obvious **—trans·par´ent·ly** *adv.* **—trans·par´ent·ness** *n.*

**trans·plant´** *vt.* to uproot a plant in order to replant it in another place; to move people or animals from one place to be resettled in another; to implant living tissue from one person or part of the body to another *—n.* that which is relocated **—trans·plant´a·ble** *adj.* **—trans·plant·ta´tion** *n.* **—trans·plant´er** *n.*

**trans·port´** *vt.* to carry or convey; to carry away with emotion **—trans´port** *n.* a means or system of conveyance; a state of emotional bliss **—trans·port·a·bil´i·ty** *n.* **—trans·port´a·ble** *adj.*

**trans·por·ta´tion** *n.* a means of transporting or traveling; the conveyance of passengers or freight

**trans·pose´** *vt.* to reverse in order **—trans·pos´a·ble** *adj.* **—trans·pos´er** *n.* **—trans·po·si´tion** *n.* **—trans·po·si´tion·al** *adj.*

**trans·sex´u·al** *n.* a person psychologically disposed to identify with the opposite sex **—trans·sex´u·al·ism** *n* **—trans·sex·u·al´i·ty** *n.*

**tran·sub·stan´ti·ate** *vt.* to transform from one substance into another —**tran·sub·stan·ti·a´tion** *n.*

**trans·verse´** *adj.* lying across —*n.* something that lies across, from side to side, as a beam —**trans·ver´sal** *adj.* —**trans·verse´ly** *adv.*

**trans·ves´tite** *n.* one who wears the clothes of the opposite sex

**trap** *n.* a device for catching animals; a devious plan by which a person may be caught unawares; a device that collects residue or prevents a return flow —*vt.* to catch —*vi.* to set traps for game —**trap´per** *n.*

**tra·peze´** *n.* a suspended bar for exercise or acrobatics

**trap´e·zoid** *n.* a four-sided plane figure with two parallel sides —**trap´e·zoi´dal** *adj.*

**trap´pings** *n.* adornment or ornamentation; goods or privileges associated with something: *the trappings of wealth*

**trash** *n.* (*US*) waste material; foolish talk; anything worthless —**trash´i·ness** *n.* —**trash´y** *adj.*

**trat·to·ri´a** *n.* an informal Italian restaurant

**trau´ma** *n.* physical injury or emotional shock —**trau·mat´ic** *adj.* —**trau·mat´i·cal·ly** *adv.* —**trau´ma·tize** *vt.*

**travail´** *n.* pain or anguish encountered in the course of effort; labor in childbirth —*vi.* to suffer the pangs of childbirth; to toil

**trav´el** *vi.* to make a journey; to proceed; to go from place to place —*vt.* to move or journey across or through —*n.* passage to or over a certain place; distance moved, as by a machine part —**trav´el·er** *n.*

**trav´eled** *adj.* having made many journeys; frequented by travelers: *a well-traveled path*

**trav´el·og, trav´el·ogue** *n.* a film documenting a traveled place; an illustrated lecture on travel

**tra·verse´** *vt.* to pass over, across, or through —*vi.* to move across; to move back and forth —**trav´erse** *n.* a crosspiece; a screen or barrier —*adj.* lying across —**tra·vers´a·ble** *adj.* —**tra·vers´al** *n.*

**trav´es·ty** *n.* an absurd rendering, as if in mockery: *the judge's decision was a travesty of justice* —*vt.* to parody

**trawl** *n.* a large fishing net; an anchored line from which many lines are strung —*vi.* to fish with a trawl —*vt.* to drag, as a net or line, to catch fish —**trawl´er** *n.*

**treach´er·ous** *adj.* likely to betray; potentially dangerous or unreliable, as *treacherous footing* —**treach´er·ous·ly** *adv.* —**treach´er·ous·ness** *n.*

**treach´er·y** *n.* violation of confidence; treason

**trea´cle** *n.* molasses; overly sentimental speech —**trea´cly** *adj.*

**tread** *vt.* to step or walk; to trample; to oppress harshly —*vi.* to walk; to press beneath the feet —*n.* the act or sound of treading or trampling; the part of a wheel that comes in contact with the surface; the impression made by a tire, foot, etc.; the length of a step

**trea´dle** *n.* a foot-operated lever —*vi.*

**tread´mill** *n.* a mechanism rotated by a walking animal; a monotonous routine

**trea´son** *n.* betrayal; a breach of faith —**trea´son·ous** *adj.* —**trea´son·ous·ly** *adv.*

**trea´son·a·ble** *adj.* involving or characteristic of treason —**trea´son·a·bly** *adv.*

**trea´sure** *n.* accumulated riches; something very precious —*vt.* to set a high value on

**trea´sur·er** *n.* one responsible for the receipt, care, and disbursement of revenues

**trea´sure-trove** *n.* hidden treasure; a rich or rewarding discovery

**trea´sur·y** *n.* a government department concerned with finances; a place where funds are received and disbursed —**Treasury** a government department in charge of collecting and managing revenues of the state; a security issued by the US Treasury

**treat** *vt.* to look upon or regard in a particular manner; to provide medical attention; to deal with in writing or speaking; to buy for another —*vi.* to deal with in writing or speaking; to pay for another, as the cost of dinner —**treat´er** *n.*

**treat´a·ble** *adj.* responsive to treatment

**trea´tise** *n.* a formal critique of a serious subject

**treat´ment** *n.* the act, manner, or process of dealing with something; a measure or measures designed to heal or alleviate

**trea´ty** *n.* a formal agreement between nations

**treb´u·chet** *n.* a medieval catapult

**tree** *n.* a woody perennial having a distinct trunk with branches and foliage well above the ground; something resembling a tree as a diagram, certain shrubs, etc. —*vt.* to force to take refuge in a tree

**trek** *vi.* to move along slowly or with effort; to journey —*n.* a journey —**trek´ker** *n.*

**trel´lis** *n.* a lattice used to support plants, etc.

**trem´ble** *vi.* to shake involuntarily; to vibrate —*n.* a perceptible shaking of a part of the body —**trem´bler** *n.* —**trem´bling·ly** *adv.* —**trem´bly** *adj.*

**tre·men´dous** *adj.* extraordinarily large; awe-inspiring; marvelous —**tre·men´dous·ly** *adv.* —**tre·men´dous·ness** *n.*

**trem´or** *n.* a sudden shaking or vibration; a state of agitation or excitement

**trem´u·lant** *adj.* tremulous; trembling

**trem´u·lous** *adj.* characterized by trembling; showing timidity —**trem´u·lous·ly** *adv.* —**trem´u·lous·ness** *n.*

**trench** *n.* a long, narrow ditch; a long, narrow area much deeper than that which surrounds it, as on the ocean floor —*vt., vi.* to dig a ditch

**tren´chant** *adj.* clear and effective; cutting or caustic —**tren´chan·cy** *n.* —**trench´ant·ly** *adv.*

**trench´er** *n.* a wooden board for cutting or serving food

**trench´er·man** *n.* a hearty eater
**trend** *n.* a prevailing tendency; a probable course; a popular preference *–vi.* to follow a general course; to exhibit a tendency
**trend´y** *adj.* of the latest styles; fashionable; inclined to adopt the current fashion **–trend´i·ly** *adv.* **–trend´i·ness** *n.*
**trep´id** *adj.* timid; timorous; trembling **–trep´id·ly** *adv.*
**trep·i·da´tion** *n.* agitation caused by fear or apprehension
**tres´pass** *vt.* to violate the rights of another; to go beyond the bounds of what is right or proper *–n.* a transgression of law or moral duty; an intrusion **–tres´pass·er** *n.*
**tress** *n.* a lock of hair **–tressed** *adj.*
**tres´tle** *n.* a framework used to support a table, platform, etc.; a framework bridge supporting a road or railway
**tri´ad** *n.* a group of three **–tri·ad´ic** *adj.*
**tri·age´** *n.* a system used to allocate a scarce commodity; the selection of persons for medical treatment based on immediate need
**tri´al** *n.* examination in a court of law; the process of testing; hardship *–adj.*
**tri´an·gle** *n.* a three-sided figure; something involving three persons **–tri·an´gu·lar** *adj.* **–tri·an·gu·lar´i·ty** *n.* **–tri·an´gu·lar·ly** *adv.*
**tri·an·gu·la´tion** *n.* a technique for surveying an area by dividing it into triangles and, working from a known baseline, determining its dimensions using trigonometry **–tri·an´gu·late** *vt.*
**tri·ath´lon** *n.* an athletic contest comprising three events
**tribe** *n.* a group of people united by ancestry, language, or culture **–trib´al** *adj.* **–trib´al·ism** *n.* **–trib´al·ly** *adv.*
**trib·u·la´tion** *n.* distress or suffering; a cause for distress
**tri·bu´nal** *n.* a court of justice or other judicial body; the seat set apart for judges, magistrates, etc.
**trib´u·tar·y** *adj.* flowing into or feeding a larger body; owing tribute*–n.*
**trib´ute** *n.* that paid to another for peace or protection; any obligatory payment
**tri·chi´na** *n.* a roundworm whose larvae cause trichinosis
**trich·i·no´sis** *n.* an affliction caused by eating undercooked meat **–trich´i·nous** *adj.*
**trick** *n.* a deception or practical joke; a malicious act; a peculiar trait or skill *–vt., vi.* to deceive or practice deceit **–trick´er, trick´ster** *n.* **–trick´er·y** *n.*
**trick´le** *vi.* to flow or move in a thin stream *–vt.* to cause to trickle *–n.* a thin stream
**trick´y** *adj.* deceitful; requiring adroitness or skill **–trick´i·ly** *adv.* **–trick´i·ness** *n.*
**tri·cus´pid, tri·cus´pi·dal** *adj.* having three points, as a molar; having three segments, as a heart valve
**tri´dent** *n.* a three-pronged spear used as a weapon or for fishing *–adj.* three-pronged **–tri·den´tate** *adj.*
**tried** *adj.* tested; freed of impurities
**tri·en´nial** *adj.* taking place every third year; lasting three years **–tri·en´nial·ly** *adv.*
**tri´fle** *vi.* to treat as of no value or importance; to toy with *–vt.* to spend idly and purposelessly *–n.* a thing of little value or importance; a small amount **–tri´fler** *n.*
**tri´fling** *adj.* frivolous; insignificant **–tri´fling·ly** *adv.*
**tri·fo´li·ate** *adj.* having three leaves
**tri·fur´cate, tri·fur´cat·ed** *adj.* having three forks or branches **–tri·fur·ca´tion** *n.*
**trig´ger** *n.* any of various devices designed to activate
**trig·o·nom´e·try** *n.* the branch of mathematics dealing with the relationships between the sides and angles of a triangle **–trig·o·no·met´ric, trig·o·no·met´ri·cal** *adj.* **–trig·o·no·met´ri·cal·ly** *adv.*
**tri·lat´er·al** *adj.* having three sides **–tri·lat´er·al·ly** *adv.*
**trill** *vt.* to sing or play in a quavering tone *–n.* an utterance of successive quavering tones; a warble
**tril´o·gy** *n.* a literary work made up of three parts, each complete by itself
**trim** *vt.* to remove by cutting; to ornament; to smooth or make neat *–n.* good physical condition; the molding or ornamentation of a building **–trim´ly** *adv.* **–trim´ness** *n.*
**tri·mes´ter** *n.* a three-month period **–tri·mes´tral, tri·mes´tri·al** *adj.*
**trin´ket** *n.* a small ornament; a trifle
**tri´o** *n.* a group of three
**trip** *n.* a journey; a misstep; a nimble step; a blunder *–vi.* to stumble; to move quickly and lightly; to make an error *–vt.* to cause to stumble or make a mistake
**tri´ple** *vt., vi.* to make or become three times as many or as large
**trip´let** *n.* any of three children from one birth
**trip´li·cate** *n.* one of three similar things *–vt.* **–trip´li·cate·ly** *adv.* **–trip·li·ca´tion** *n.*
**tri´pod** *n.* a three-legged stand **–trip´o·dal, tri·pod´ic** *adj.*
**trip´ping** *adj.* light, nimble **–trip´ping·ly** *adv.*
**trip´tych** *n.* a work of art on three adjacent panels
**tri´reme** *n.* an ancient warship with three banks of oars
**tri·sect´** *vt.* to divide into three equal parts **–tri·sec´tion** *n.* **–tri·sec´tor** *n.*
**trite** *adj.* made commonplace or hackneyed by frequent use **–trite´ly** *adv.* **–trite´ness** *n.*
**trit´u·rate** *vt.* to reduce to a fine powder; to pulverize *–n.* a pulverized pharmaceutical **–trit´u·ra·ble** *adj.* **–trit·u·ra´tion** *n.* **–trit´u·ra·tor** *n.*

**tri´umph** *vi.* to win a victory; to be successful *–n.* an important success **–tri·um´phal** *adj.* **–tri·um´phal·ly** *adv.*

**tri·um´phant** *adj.* victorious; exultant, as in victory **–tri·um´phant·ly** *adv.*

**tri·um´vi·rate** *n.* a coalition of three

**triv´et** *n.* a three-legged stand for holding a cooking vessel in a fireplace or a heated container on a tabletop

**triv´ia** *n.* insignificant matters

**triv´i·al** *adj.* of little importance; insignificant **–triv´i·al·ism** *n.* **–triv·i·al´i·ty** *n.* **–triv´i·al·ly** *adv.*

**triv´i·al·ize** *vt.* to regard as unimportant; to make trivial **–triv´i·al·i·za·tion** *n.*

**tro´che** *n.* a medicated lozenge

**trog´lo·dyte** *n.* a prehistoric man; a person considered to be primitive **–trog·lo·dyt´ic, trog·lo·dyt´i·cal** *adj.*

**trol´lop** *n.* an untidy woman

**troop** *n.* a gathering; a flock or herd; a unit of cavalry *–vi.* to move as a group **–troop´er** *n.*

**trope** *n.* a figure of speech

**tro´phy** *n.* something displayed as proof of victory

**trot** *n.* a slow running gait *–vi., vt.* to go or cause to go at a trot **–trot´ter** *n.*

**trou´ba·dour** *n.* a wandering minstrel

**trou´ble** *n.* distress or worry; something that causes difficulty; a difficult situation; a disease or ailment; effort; general unrest *–vt.* to distress or worry; to inconvenience or annoy; to cause physical pain or discomfort *–vi.* to take pains **–trou´bler** *n.*

**trou´ble·mak·er** *n.* one who habitually causes distress to others

**trou´ble·shoot·er** *n.* one adept at analyzing problems and devising solutions; one assigned to resolve problems, mediate disputes, etc.

**trou´ble·some** *adj.* difficult or trying; pertaining to a source of difficulty **–trou´ble·some·ly** *adv.* **–trou´ble·some·ness** *n.*

**trough** *n.* a container for food or water for animals; a long, narrow depression, as between waves

**trounce** *vt.* to beat or thrash severely

**troupe** *n.* a company of performers *–vi.* to travel as a performer **–troup´er** *n.*

**trous´seau** *n.* clothing and linens assembled by a bride

**trove** *n.* a collection of valuable items

**trow´el** *n.* an implement for digging, applying or smoothing plaster, etc. *–vt.* to dig or smooth with a trowel **–trow´el·er, trow´el·ler** *n.*

**tru´ant** *n.* a pupil who is absent without permission; one who shirks a responsibility *–adj.* a juvenile offender; a loafer *–vi.* to shirk responsibility **–tru´an·cy** *n.*

**truce** *n.* an agreement to suspend hostilities; a respite, as from pain

**truck** *n. (US)* a vehicle designed to transport heavy loads; a two-wheeled vehicle for moving loads a short distance: *a hand truck* *–vi.* to carry goods; to drive a truck **–truck´er** *n.*

**truck´age** *(US) n.* the conveyance of goods by truck; the charge for moving goods

**truck´ing** *(US) n.* the business of operating trucks

**truck´le** *vi.* to yield or submit weakly; to move on rollers or casters *–vt.* to cause to move on rollers or casters *–n.* a small wheel **–truck´ler** *n.*

**truc´u·lent** *adj.* of savage character; inclined to ferocity **–truc´u·lence, truc´u·len·cy** *n.* **–truc´u·lent·ly** *adv.*

**trudge** *vi.* to walk wearily or laboriously *–n.* a tiresome walk **–trudg´er** *n.*

**true** *adj.* faithful to reality; real or genuine; faithful or dependable, as to friends, promises, etc. *–vt.* to bring to conformity with a standard *–adv.* in truth, truly; within tolerance **–true´ness** *n.*

**truf´fle** *n.* an edible fungus, similar to a mushroom, regarded as a delicacy; a chocolate confection

**tru´ly** *adv.* conforming to fact; with accuracy; with loyalty

**trump** *n.* in card games, a card or suit selected to rank above all others; a hidden advantage *–vt.* to take with a trump; to surpass or beat; to outdo or outmaneuver *–vi.* to play a trump **–trump up** to invent for fraudulent purposes

**trump´er·y** *n.* worthless finery; nonsense

**trum´pet** *n.* a brass wind instrument of the upper register; something resembling the flaring bell of a trumpet; a loud penetrating sound *–vt.* to sound or publish abroad *–vi.* to blow a trumpet; to sound forth, like an elephant **–trum´pet·er** *n.*

**trun´cate** *vt.* to cut the top from *–adj.* ending abruptly, as though cut off **–trun´cate·ly** *adv.* **–trun·ca´tion** *n.*

**trun´cheon** *n.* a short, thick stick or club; a mark of office or authority; *(Brit.)* a policeman's nightstick *–vt.* to beat; to cudgel

**trunk** *n.* the main stem of a tree; the central part of an animal or human body; a main passage, as for blood, transportation, communication, etc.; a large container

**truss** *n.* a supporting framework, as for a roof or bridge *–vt.* to support or brace; to tie or bind

**trust** *n.* reliance on the integrity of a person or thing; something committed to one's care: *to hold funds in trust*; confident expectation; an affiliation of business firms to control output, prices, etc. *–vt.* to rely on; to commit to the care of another; to expect or believe *–vi.* to place confidence in *–adj.* held in trust

**trust·ee´** *n.* one entrusted with the management of property or affairs of another **–trust·ee´ship** *n.*

**trust´ful** *adj.* inclined to believe; showing trust **–trust´ful·ly** *adv.* **–trust´ful·ness** *n.*

**trust fund** assets held in trust

**trust´ing** *adj.* having or showing trust —**trust´ing·ly** *adv.* —**trust´ing·ness** *n.*

**trust´wor·thy** *adj.* deserving of confidence; reliable —**trust´wor·thi·ly** *adv.* —**trust´wor·thi·ness** *n.*

**trust´y** *adj.* faithful to duty —**trust´i·ly** *adv.* —**trust´i·ness** *n.*

**truth** *n.* conformity to fact; that which is true

**truth´ful** *adj.* conforming to fact; telling the truth —**truth´ful·ly** *adv.* —**truth´ful·ness** *n.*

**try** *vt.* to make an attempt; to make experimental use of; to subject to a test; to put severe strain on; to subject to stress; to extract by rendering —*vi.* to make an attempt; to put forth effort; to make a test —*n.* an attempt; a test

**try´ing** *adj.* difficult to endure —**try´ing·ly** *adv.* —**try´ing·ness** *n.*

**tryst** *n.* an appointment to meet; a meeting —*vi.*

**tsu·nam´i** *n.* an immense wave generated by an earthquake under the ocean

**tub** *n.* a large round flat-bottomed vessel, such as for washing or storage; *(US)* a bath or bathtub

**tu´ba** *n.* a large brass instrument of the lower register

**tub´by** *adj.* round and fat; resembling a tub

**tube** *n.* a long, hollow cylinder

**tu´ber** *n.* a short, thickened portion of an underground stem, as a potato; a tubercle

**tu´ber·cle** *n.* a small rounded eminence

**tu·ber´cu·lar** *adj.* affected with tubercles; tuberculosis

**tu·ber·cu·lo´sis** *n.* a communicable disease marked by tubercles in the lungs —**tu·ber´cu·lous** *adj.*

**tu´ber·ous** *adj.* bearing projections or prominences

**tub´ing** *n.* tubes collectively; a piece of tube or material for tubes

**tu´bu·lar** *adj.* having the form of a tube; consisting of tubes —**tu·bu·lar´i·ty** *n.* —**tu´bu·lar·ly** *adv.*

**tuck** *vt.* to press in the edges of; to wrap or cover snugly; to make folds by gathering or stitching —*vi.* to draw together; to make tucks —*n.* a fold sewn into a garment; something inserted or folded —**tuck´er** *n.*

**tuft** *n.* a clump, as of hair, feathers, etc. —*vt.* to provide with tightly drawn buttons, as on upholstery or pillows; to cover or adorn with tufts —*vi.* to form or grow in tufts —**tuft´ed** *adj.* —**tuft´er** *n.*

**tug** *vt., vi.* to pull with effort —*n.* a violent pull; a strenuous effort

**tu·i´tion** *n.* a charge or payment for instruction; the business of teaching —**tu·i´tion·al, tu·i´tion·ar·y** *adj.*

**tum´ble** *vi.* to toss about; to perform acrobatics —*vt.* to cause to fall

**tum´bler** *n.* a drinking glass; an acrobat; a revolving cage or cylinder for tossing like the tumbler on a clothes dryer

**tum´brel** *n.* a rude cart

**tu´me·fy** *vi., vt.* to swell or cause to swell —**tu´me·fa´cient** *adj.* —**tu·me·fac´tion** *n.*

**tu·mes´cent** *adj.* swelling; somewhat timid — **tu·mes´cence** *n.*

**tu´mor** *n.* a local swelling on or in the body —**tu´mor·ous** *adj.*

**tu´mult** *n.* a commotion or disturbance by a multitude; any violent commotion; mental or emotional agitation

**tu·mul´tu·ous** *adj.* characterized by tumult; greatly disturbed; stormy, tempestuous — **tu·mul´tu·ous·ly** *adv.* —**tu·mul´tu·ous·ness** *n.*

**tun** *n.* a large cask —*vt.* to put into a cask

**tu´na** *n.* a large food or game fish

**tun´a·ble, tune´a·ble** *adj.* that can be tuned, as a musical instrument —**tun·a·bil´i·ty, tun´a·ble·ness** *n.* —**tun´a·bly** *adv.*

**tun´dra** *n.* a rolling treeless plain

**tune** *n.* a coherent succession of musical tones; correct musical pitch; harmony; fine adjustment —*vt.* to adjust —**tun´er** *n.*

**tune´ful** *adj.* melodic —**tune´ful·ly** *adv.* —**tune´ful·ness** *n.*

**tune´less** *adj.* not in tune; lacking a melody —**tune´less·ly** *adv.* —**tune´less·ness** *n.*

**tu´nic** *n.* a loose outer garment gathered at the waist; a short coat

**tun´nel** *n.* an underground passageway —*vt.* to dig; to make a passageway through or under —**tun´nel·er, tun´nel·ler** *n.*

**tun´ny** *n.* tuna

**tur´ban** *n.* a head covering —**tur´baned** *adj.*

**tur´bid** *adj.* muddy; dense or opaque; confused —**tur·bid´i·ty, tur´bid·ness** *n.* —**tur´bid·ly** *adv.*

**tur´bine** *n.* a rotary engine

**tur´bot** *n.* a large European flatfish

**tur´bu·lent** *adj.* violently disturbed or agitated; tending to disturb —**tur´bu·lence, tur´bu·len·cy** *n.* —**tur´bu·lent·ly** *adv.*

**tu·reen´** *n.* a large covered bowl, as used for serving soup

**turf** *n.* a section or plot of grass; an area regarded possessively —*vt.* to cover with sod

**tur·ges´cent** *adj.* being or becoming swollen —**tur·ges´cence, tur·ges´cen·cy** *n.* —**tur·ges´cent·ly** *adv.*

**tur´gid** *adj.* unnaturally distended; swollen —**tur·gid´i·ty, tur´gid·ness** *n.* —**tur´gid·ly** *adv.*

**tur´key** *n.* a large North American bird; something lacking quality

**tur´moil** *n.* disturbance; tumult

**turn** *vi., vt.* to revolve or cause to revolve or rotate; to change the direction of; to give finished form; to bend, curve, twist, etc.; to transform; to translate; to change —*n.* the act of turning or being turned; a change of direction —**turn´er** *n.*

**turn´ing** *n.* the art of shaping on a lathe
**turn´pike** *n.* a toll road
**tur´pi·tude** *n.* depravity
**tur´ret** *n.* a small projecting tower **–tur´ret·ed** *adj.*
**tur´tle** *n.* a four-limbed reptile with a soft body encased in a shell
**tusk** *n.* a long projecting tooth *–vt.* to gore, root, etc. with a tusk
**tus´sle** *vt., vi.* to scuffle or struggle *–n.* a scuffle
**tu´te·lage** *n.* being under the care of a tutor or guardian; the office of a guardian; the act of tutoring
**tu´te·lar, tu´te·lar·y** *adj.* watching over; protecting
**tu´tor** *n.* a private teacher *–vt., vi.* to act as a tutor **–tu·to´ri·al** *adj.*
**tu´tu** *n.* a ballet skirt
**tux·e´do** *n.* formal dinner or evening attire
**twad´dle** *n.* pretentious, silly talk *–vt., vi.* **–twad´dler** *n.*
**twang** *vt., vi.* to make or cause to make a sharp, vibrant sound; to speak with a nasal sound *– n.* a sharp vibrating or nasal sound **–twang´y** *adj.*
**tweak** *vt.* to pinch or twist sharply; to fine-tune *–n.* a pinch
**tweed** *n.* a woolen fabric
**tweet** *vi.* to utter a thin, chirping note *–n.*
**tweez´ers** *n.* small pincers **–tweeze** *vt.*
**twid´dle** *vt.* to twirl idly *–vi.* to be busy about trifles
; *n.* a small shoot or branch
**´light** *n.* the period after sunset and before sunrise; ıny faint light; a period of waning glory, decline in achievements, etc.
**twin** *n.* either of two young from the same birth; one greatly similar to another
**twine** *vt.* to twist together; to coil about something *–vi.* to interlace; to proceed on a winding course *–n.* string; the act of entwining
**twinge** *n.* a sudden sharp pain; a mental pang *–vi., vt.* to feel or cause to feel a sudden pain
**twin´kle** *vi.* to shine intermittently; to sparkle; to move lightly and rapidly; to wink or blink *–vt.* to cause to flicker; a quick movement of the eyelids *–n.* a glimmer **–twin´kler** *n.*
**twin´kling** *n.* the act of something that twinkles; an instant, a moment; a wink
**twirl** *vt., vi.* to whirl or rotate rapidly; to twist or curl *–n.* a whirling motion; a curl or twist
**twist** *vt.* to wind around each other; to form by winding; to deform or distort *–vi.* to become twisted; to move in a winding course; to squirm or writhe *–n.* a curve or bend; a strain, as of a joint; an unnatural inclination; an unexpected turn or development **–twist´able** *adj.* **–twist´ing·ly** *adv.* **–twist´y** *adj.*
**twist´er** *n.* one or that which twists; a tornado or cyclone
**twit** *vt.* to taunt *–n.* a reproach or taunt; a foolish person
**twitch** *vt., vi.* to pull or move with a quick spasmodic jerk *–n.* a sudden involuntary muscle contraction
**two´-faced** *adj.* double-dealing; insincere **–two´-fac·ed·ly** *adv.* **–two´-fac·ed·ness** *n.*
**tycoon´** *n.* a wealthy, powerful businessman or financier
**tyke** *n.* a small child
**type´** *n.* a group having traits in common; a standard or model; a block of raised characters or other medium used for printing *–vt.* to represent; to typify; to classify
**type´set** *vt.* to make written material ready for printing **–type´set·ter** *n.***–type´set·ting** *n.*
**type´writ·er** *n.* a machine for producing characters on paper; a typist **–type´write** *vi., vt.*
**ty·phoi´dal** *adj.* pertaining to typhoid fever
**typhoid fever** a serious infectious disease contracted from contaminated water or food
**ty·phoon´** *n.* a violent tropical storm
**ty´phus** *n.* a contagious disease spread by fleas, lice, etc. **–ty´phous** *adj.*
**typ´i·cal** *adj.* characteristic of a group or type **–typ´i·cal·ly** *adv.* **–typ´i·cal·ness** *n.*
**typ´i·fy** *vt.* to represent by a type; to serve as an example **–typ·i·fi·ca´tion** *n.*
**typ´ist** *n.* one who operates a keyboard, as on a typewriter, typesetting machine, or computer word processor
**ty´po** *n.* an error in typing or printing
**ty·pog´ra·pher** *n.* one who sets written material into type suitable for printing
**ty·po·graph´ic, ty·po·graph´i·cal** *adj.* relating to typesetting or printing **–ty·pog´ra·phy** *n.*
**ty·ran´nic, ty·ran´ni·cal** *adj.* of or like a tyrant; despotic or arbitrary **–ty·ran´ni·cal·ly** *adv.*
**tyr´an·nize** *vi.* to exercise power cruelly; to rule as a tyrant *–vt.* to treat cruelly; to domineer **–tyr´an·niz·er** *n.*
**tyr´an·nous** *adj.* despotic; cruel **–tyr´an·nous·ly** *adv.* **–tyr´an·nous·ness** *n.*
**ty´rant** *n.* one who rules oppressively or cruelly; one who exercises power or authority in a harsh, cruel manner **–tyr´an·ny** *n.*
**tyre** *(Brit.) n.* a flexible covering for a wheel
**ty´ro** *n.* a novice or beginner

**u, U** twenty-first letter of the English alphabet
**u·biq´ui·tous** *adj.* seeming to be everywhere at once; omnipresent **–ubiq´ui·tous·ly** *adv.* **–ubiq´ui·tous·ness, ubi´qui·ty** *n.*
**ud´der** *n.* a pendulous, milk-secreting gland of a mammal for the feeding of offspring
**ug´ly** *adj.* distasteful to the senses; repulsive; morally revolting **–ug´li·ness**

**uku·le´le** *n.* a small guitar-like instrument having four strings

**ul´cer** *n.* an open sore on the skin or internally; a corrupt condition **–ul´cer·ate** *vi., vt.* **ul·cer·a´tion** *n.* **–ul´cer·a·tive** *adj.* **–ul´cer·ous** *adj.*

**ul´na** *n.* the larger of the two bones of the forearm **–ul´nar** *adj.*

**ul´ster** *n.* a long, loose overcoat

**ul·te´ri·or** *adj.* intentionally unrevealed; secondary in importance **–ul·te´ri·or·ly** *adv.*

**ul´ti·ma** *n.* the last syllable of a word

**ul´ti·mate** *adj.* last or final; beyond all others, as in size, quality, etc.; fundamental *–n.* the best, latest, most fundamental, etc. **–ul´ti·mate·ness** *n.*

**ul´ti·mate·ly** *adv.* in the end; finally

**ul·ti·ma´tum** *n.* final terms for settlement accompanied by a threat

**ul´tra** *adj.* extreme

**ul´tra·light** *n.* a lightweight airplane

**ul·tra·mod´ern** *adj.* extremely fresh and new **–ul·tra·mod´ern·ism** *n.* **–ul·tra·mod´ern·ist** *n.*

**ul·tra·son´ic** *adj.* pertaining to inaudible sound waves **–ul·tra·son´i·cal·ly** *adv.*

**ul·tra·sound´** *n.* the use of ultrasonic waves for medical diagnosis

**ul·tra·vi´o·let** *adj.* having a wavelength between visible violet and those of X-rays

**ul´u·late** *vi.* to howl or wail **–ul´u·lant** *adj.* **–ul´u·la´tion** *n.*

**um´ber** *n.* a brown iron oxide used as a pigment; a color made from umber *–adj.* pertaining to umber or its color

**um·bil´i·cal** *adj.* pertaining to or situated near the naval *–n.* a tube that serves as a connecting device for an astronaut or aquanaut outside the craft

**umbilical cord** the structure connecting a fetus with the placenta

**um·bil´i·cus** *n.* the naval

**um´brage** *n.* a feeling of anger or resentment; shade or shadow **–um·bra´geous** *adj.* **–um·bra´geous·ly** *adv.* **–um·bra´geous·ness** *n.*

**um·brel´la** *n.* a portable canopy on a folding frame that protects from sun or rain; something serving as a cover or shield

**um´laut** *n.* an altered vowel sound; two dots over a vowel, as ä, ë, etc., used to mark the change in sound

**um´pire** *n.* a person called on to settle a disagreement or dispute; one chosen to enforce the rules of certain games

**un·a·bat´ed** *adj.* maintaining original force or intensity: *the storm continued unabated for two hours*

**un·a´ble** *adj.* incompetent; ineffectual

**un·a·bridged´** *adj.* containing all of the original text; complete

**un·ac·cept´a·ble** *adj.* not satisfactory **–un·ac·cept·a·bil´i·ty** *n.* **–un·ac·cept´a·bly** *adv.*

**un·ac·count´a·ble** *adj.* impossible to explain **–un·ac·count·a·bil´i·ty, un·ac·count´a·ble·ness** *n.* **–un·ac·count´a·bly** *adv.*

**un·ac·cus´tomed** *n.* not familiar with; uncommon, strange **–un·ac·cus´tomed·ly** *adv.* **–un·ac·cus´tomed·ness** *n.*

**un·a·chiev´a·ble** *adj.* impossible or unlikely to attain

**un·ac·quaint´ed** *adj.* not having met; not informed: *unacquainted with the situation*

**un·a·dorned´** *adj.* plain; lacking embellishment

**un·a·dul´ter·at·ed** *adj.* pure; not dilute; complete, utter: *the unadulterated truth*

**un·ad·vised´** *adj.* rash or imprudent; uninformed **–un·ad·vis´ed·ly** *adv.* **–un·ad·vis´ed·ness** *n.*

**un·af·fect´ed** *adj.* natural or sincere; not influenced or changed **–un·af·fect´ed·ly** *adv.* **–un·af·fect´ed·ness** *n.*

**un·a·fraid´** *adj.* showing no fear

**un·aid´ed** *adj.* without assistance: *he prepared the dinner unaided*

**un·al·loyed´** *adj.* pure, not mixed; complete, unqualified **–un·al·loy´ed·ly** *adv.*

**un·al´ter·a·ble** *adj.* that connot be changed: *the unalterable onset of winter* **–un·al´ter·a·ble·ness** *n.* **–un·al´ter·a·bly** *adv.*

**u·nan´i·mous** *adj.* being in complete agreement; without dissent **–u·na·nim´i·ty, u·nan´i·mous·ness** *n.* **–u·nan´i·mous·ly** *adv.*

**un·ap·peal´ing** *adj.* lacking attraction; not inviting or tempting

**un·ap·proach´a·ble** *adj.* aloof; reserved; inaccessible **–un·ap·proach·a·bil´i·ty, un·ap·proach´a·ble·ness** *n.* **–un·ap·proach´a·bly** *adv.*

**un·a·shamed´** *adj.* feeling or showing no embarrassment: *unashamed to show emotion*

**un·asked´** *adj.* not asked, invited, or requested

**un·as·sail´a·ble** *adj.* not possible to contest or disprove; resistant to attack **–un·as·sail·a·bil´i·ty, un·as·sail´a·ble·ness** *n.* **–un·as·sail´a·bly** *adv.*

**un·as·sum´ing** *adj.* modest; unpretentious **–un·as·sum´ing·ly** *adv.* **–un·as·sum´ing·ness** *n.*

**un·at·tached´** *adj.* independent; not affiliated with any group; unmarried

**un·at·tain´a·ble** *adj.* impossible or unlikely to be accomplished **–un·at·tain·a·bil´i·ty, un·at·tain´a·ble·ness** *n.* **–un·at·tain´a·bly** *adv.*

**un·a·vail´a·ble** *adj.* not obtainable; not accessible **–un·a·vail·a·bil´i·ty** *n.*

**un·a·vail´ing** *adj.* ineffective; futile **–un·a·vail´ing·ly** *adv.*

**un·avoid´a·ble** *adj.* inevitable **–un·avoid·a·bil´i·ty, un·avoid´a·ble·ness** *n.* **–un·avoid´a·bly** *adv.*

**un·a·ware´** *adj.* carelessly unmindful; inattentive;

not informed *–adv.* unawares **–un·a·ware´ly** *adv.* **–un·a·ware´ness** *n.*

**un·a·wares´** *adv.* unexpectedly; without premeditation

**un·bal´ance** *vt.* to disturb or derange mentally

**un·bal´anced** *adj.* lacking mental stability; unequal; wobbly

**un·bear´a·ble** *adj.* intolerable; insufferable **–un·bear´a·ble·ness** *n.* **–un·bear´a·bly** *adv.*

**un·beat´a·ble** *adj.* not to be defeated; first-rate **–un·beat´a·bly** *adv.*

**un·be·com´ing** *adj.* inappropriate; not decorous, improper **–un·be·com´ing·ly** *adv.* **–un·be·com´ing·ness** *n.*

**un·be·liev´a·ble** *adj.* incredible; too astonishing to be believed **–un·be·liev´a·bly** *adv.*

**un·be·liev´er** *n.* a doubter or skeptic; one without religious faith **–un·be·liev´ing** *adj.* **–un·be·liev´ing·ly** *adv.* **–un·be·liev´ing·ness** *n.*

**un·bend´** *vt.* to relax, as from exertion; to dispense with formality *–vi.* to become free of restraint, formality, etc.

**un·bend´ing** *adj.* resolute; firm; not relaxed or able to relax **–un·bend´ing·ly** *adv.* **–un·bend´ing·ness** *n.*

**un·bi´ased** *adj.* impartial; not prejudiced **–un·bi´ased·ly** *adv.*

**un·bid´den** *adj.* spontaneous, done without asking; not commanded or invited

**un·blem´ished** *adj.* lacking fault: *an unblemished record*

**un·blink´ing** *adj.* without emotion; fearless **–un·blink´ing·ly** *adv.*

**un·bound´ed** *adj.* having no limits; unrestrained **–un·bound´ed·ly** *adv.* **–un·bound´ed·ness** *n.*

**un·bowed´** *adj.* not broken or subdued by adversity

**un·break´a·ble** *adj.* impossible or extremely difficult to break **–un·break´a·ble·ness** *n.* **–un·break´a·bly** *adv.*

**un·bri´dled** *adj.* unrestrained; uncontrolled

**un·bro´ken** *adj.* uninterrupted; continuous; not tamed **–un·bro´ken·ly** *adv.* **–un·bro´ken·ness** *n.*

**un·bur´den** *vt.* to relieve from cares or worries; to make known so as to gain relief

**un·can´ny** *adj.* unnatural; weird; seeming to be almost supernatural **–un·can´ni·ly** *adv.* **–un·can´ni·ness** *n.*

**un·car´ing** *adj.* lacking concern or sympathy

**un·ceas´ing** *adj.* without stopping; continuous; eternal **–un·ceas´ing·ly** *adv.* **–un·ceas´ing·ness** *n.*

**un·cen´sored** *adj.* not reviewed or examined for the purging of inappropriate material; complete, with nothing removed or struck out

**un·cer·e·mo´ni·ous** *adj.* casual, informal; without preamble; rude or discourteous **–un·cer·e·mo´ni·ous·ly** *adv.* **–un·cer·e·mo´ni·ous·ness** *n.*

**un·cer´tain** *adj.* not yet determined; unpredictable; doubtful or dubious; tenuous **–un·cer´tain·ly** *adv.* **–un·cer´tain·ty** *n.*

**un·change´a·ble** *adj.* that cannot be altered or modified **–un·change·a·bil´i·ty, un·change´a·ble·ness** *n.* **–un·change´a·bly** *adv.*

**un·chang´ing** *adj.* constant; enduring **–un·chang´ing·ly** *adv.* **–un·chang´ing·ness** *n.*

**un·char·ac·ter·is´tic** *adj.* unusual; strange or exceptional: *we were surprised by his uncharacteristic generosity* **–un·char·ac·ter·is´ti·cal·ly** *adv.*

**un·char´i·ta·ble** *adj.* not forgiving; unkind; lacking generosity **–un·char´i·ta·ble·ness** *n.* **–un·char´i·ta·bly** *adv.*

**un·chart´ed** *adj.* unknown; unexplored

**un·civ´il** *adj.* discourteous; ill-bred **–un·civ´il·ly** *adv.* **–un·civ´il·ness** *n.*

**un·civ´il·ized** *adj.* barbarous; rude and uncouth; remote from civilization **–un·civ´il·iz·ed·ly** *adv.*

**un·clad´** *adj.* without clothes; naked

**un·clean´** *adj.* soiled, squalid; morally or ceremonially impure **–un·clean´li·ness** *n.* **–un·clean´ly** *adv.*

**un·com´fort·a·ble** *adj.* ill at ease; causing uneasiness **–un·com´fort·a·ble·ness** *n.* **–un·com´fort·a·bly**

**un·com´mon** *adj.* remarkable; strange **–un·com´mon·ly** *adv.* **–un·com´mon·ness** *n.*

**un·com·mu´ni·ca·tive** *adj.* not disposed to talking; reserved **–un·com·mu´ni·ca·tive·ly** *adv.* **–un·com·mu´ni·ca·tive·ness** *n.*

**un·com´pli·cat·ed** *adj.* relatively simple or easy; fundamental or basic

**un·com´pro·mis·ing** *adj.* inflexible; strict **–un·com´pro·mis·ing·ly** *adv.*

**un·con·ceiv´a·ble** *adj.* that cannot be imagined or understood; unbelievable **–un·con·ceiv´a·ble·ness** *n.* **–un·con·ceiv´a·bly** *adv.*

**un·con·cerned´** *adj.* lacking interest; indifferent; not worried **–un·con·cern´** *n.* **–un·con·cern´ed·ly** *adv.* **–un·con·cern´ed·ness** *n.*

**un·con·di´tion·al** *adj.* absolute; without prerequisite or provision **–un·con·di´tion·al·ly** *adv.* **–un·con·di´tion·al·ness** *n.*

**un·con·di´tioned** *adj.* not restricted

**un·con´quer·a·ble** *adj.* that cannot be overcome or defeated **–un·con´quer·a·bly** *adv.*

**un·con´scion·a·ble** *adj.* unscrupulous; unbelievably bad or wrong **–un·con´scion·a·ble·ness** *n.* **–un·con´scion·a·bly** *adv.*

**un·con´scious** *adj.* lacking consciousness; not produced by conscious effort *–n.* that part of the mind that retains memories, compulsions, etc. not readily accessible to one´s consciousness **–un·con´scious·ly** *adv.* **–un·con´scious·ness** *n.*

**un·con·sti·tu´tion·al** *adj.* violating the precepts of a constitution **–un·con·sti·tu·tion·al´i·ty** *n.* **un·con·sti·tu´tion·al·ly** *adv.*

**un·con·trol´la·ble** *adj.* that cannot be governed or restrained; unmanageable **–un·con·trol·la·bil´i·ty, un·con·trol´la·ble·ness** *n.* **–un·con·trol´la·bly** *adv.*

**un·con·ven´tion·al** *adj.* not adhering to traditional rules, practices, etc. **–un·con·ven·tion·al´i·ty** *n.* **–un·con·ven´tion·al·ly** *adv.*

**un·co·or´di·nat·ed** *adj.* lacking muscular coordination; lacking planning or organization **–un·co·or´di·nat·ed·ly** *adv.*

**un·count´ed** *adj.* beyond counting; innumerable

**un·cou´ple** *vt.* to disconnect or unfasten

**un·couth´** *adj.* coarse, boorish, or unrefined **–un·couth´ly** *adv.* **–un·couth´ness** *n.*

**un·cov´er** *vt.* to remove a covering from; to make known; to discover or disclose *–vi.* to remove a covering

**unc´tion** *n.* the act of anointing; a substance, as oil, used for anointing; something that soothes; excessive or affected sincerity

**unc´tu·ous** *adj.* greasy or soapy to the touch; marked by excessive or affected sincerity; overly smooth or suave **–unc´tu·ous·ly** *adv.* **–unc´tu·ous·ness** *n.*

**un·daunt´ed** *adj.* fearless; intrepid **–un·daunt´ed·ly** *adv.* **–un·daunt´ed·ness** *n.*

**un·de·cid´ed** *adj.* uncertain; unsettled **–un·de·cid´ed·ly** *adv.* **–un·de·cid´ed·ness** *n.*

**un·de·ni´a·ble** *adj.* indisputable; unquestionable **–un·de·ni´a·ble·ness** *n.* **–un·de·ni´a·bly** *adv.*

**un´der** *prep.* beneath; covered by; lower than; less in value, amount, etc.; inferior to; subordinate to; being the subject of; by virtue of; having regard to *–adv.* underneath; in an inferior position; less in amount, value, etc. *–adj.*

**un·der·a·chieve´** *vi.* to perform below one´s capability **–un·der·a·chieve´ment** *n.* **–un·der·a·chiev´er** *n.*

**un·der·age´** *adj.* not of a requisite legal age

**un´der·brush** *n.* a small trees, shrubs, etc. growing beneath forest trees

**un´der·car·riage** *n.* the framework supporting the body of a structure

**un·der·class´man** *n.* a freshman or sophomore

**un´der·coat, un´der·coat·ing** *n.* a protective coating, as a primer, applied over bare wood or metal *–vt.* to apply a protective coating

**un´der·cov´er** *adj.* secret; engaged in spying

**un·der·cur·rent** *n.* a flowing layer of air or water beneath another layer or beneath the surface; a concealed or secret force or tendency

**un´der·done** *n.* not completely cooked

**un·der·es´ti·mate** *vt.* to place too low a value on; to misjudge or underrate **–un·der·es·ti·ma´tion** *n.*

**un´der·foot´** *adv.* beneath the feet; in the way

**un·der·go´** *vt.* to be subject to; to bear up under; to endure

**un·der·grad´u·ate** *n.* a college or university student who has not yet earned a degree

**un´der·ground** *adj.* situated or operating beneath the surface; done in secret *–n.* that which is beneath the surface; organized resistance against leadership, convention, etc. *–adv.*

**underground railway** *(Brit.)* a rapid transit system of trains running underground; a subway; *(US)* before 1861, a system for assisting fugitive slaves in the U.S.

**un´der·growth** *n.* underbrush

**un´der·hand·ed** *adj., adv.* done in a sly or treacherous manner **–un´der·hand·ed·ly** *adv.* **–un´der·hand·ed·ness** *n.*

**un´der·ly·ing** *adj.* positioned under; basic or fundamental, as *underlying principles*; not obvious, but implied

**un·der·mine´** *vt.* to excavate beneath; to weaken or impair secretly or insidiously

**un·der·nour´ish** *vt.* to provide food in insufficient quantity or quality to sustain health **–un·der·nour´ished** *adj.* **–un·der·nour´ish·ment** *n.*

**un´der·pass** *n.* a road, walkway, etc. that runs beneath another road, track, etc.

**un´der·pin·ning** *n.* material or framework supporting a structure from below; something seen as a basis or foundation: *the underpinnings of guilt in our society*

**un´der·priv´i·leged** *adj.* deprived socially and economically

**un·der·rate´** *vt.* to underestimate

**un´der·score** *vt.* to underline; to emphasize *–n.* a line drawn under type for emphasis

**un´der·signed** *n.* one who signs or attests to a document

**un·der·stand´** *vt.* to come to know the meaning or import of; to perceive the nature or character of; to have comprehension of; to suppose or believe; to accept as a condition *–vi.* to comprehend; to believe to be the case; to have sympathy or tolerance for **–un·der·stand·a·bil´i·ty** *n.* **–un·der·stand´a·ble** *adj.* **–un·der·stand´a·bly** *adv.*

**un·der·stand´ing** *n.* comprehension; the capacity to think, retain knowledge, etc.; an agreement; a viewpoint, interpretation, or opinion; sympathy or tolerance for others *–adj.* characterized by comprehension, sympathy, tolerance, etc. **–un·der·stand´ing·ly** *adv.*

**un·der·state´** *vt.* to relate or describe in a deliberately restrained manner **–un´der·state·ment** *n.*

**un·der·stat´ed** *adj.* marked by restraint; showing good taste: *understated elegance* **–un·der·stat´ed·ly** *adv.*

**un·der·stood´** *adj.* comprehended; taken for granted without utterance; agreed upon by all

**un´der·study** *n.* one prepared to fill in for another in an emergency, such as an actor *–vt., vi.* to learn, practice, etc. so as to be able to stand in for another

**un´der·take** *vt.* to agree to attempt; to contract to do

**un´der·tak·er** *n.* one who sets out to do something; one who prepares the dead for burial

**un der·tak´ing** *n.* an effort or endeavor; the business of preparing the dead for burial

**un´der·tone** *n.* a subdued sound, color, etc.; a meaning, quality, etc. implied but not expressed

**un·der·val´ue** *vt.* to rate something below its real worth; to regard as being of little value **—un·der·val·u·a´tion** *n.*

**un´der·world** *n.* the mythical abode of the dead; the realm of organized crime and vice

**un´der·write** *vt.* to sign; to assume liability; to guarantee, as of the shares in a new company *—vi.* to act as a guarantor, especially of insurance **—un´der·writ·er** *n.*

**un·de·served´** *adj.* not earned or deserved: *an undeserved honor*; unwarranted or unfair: an *undeserved punishment* **—un·de·serv´ed·ly** *adv.*

**un·de·sir´a·ble** *adj.* objectionable; not wanted *—n.* an objectionable person **—un·de·sir·a·bil´i·ty** *n.* **—un·de·sir´a·bly** *adv.*

**un·do´** *vt.* to cause to be as if never done; to loosen; to bring to ruin; to disturb emotionally **—un·do´ing** *n.* **—un·done´** *adj.*

**un·doubt´ed** *adj.* assured or certain; unsuspected **—un·doubt´ed·ly** *adv.*

**un·dress´** *vt.* to strip or disrobe; to remove the dressing from, as of a wound *—vi.* to remove one´s clothing *—n.* the state of being nude or only partially attired

**un´du·lant** *adj.* moving like a wave; fluctuating

**un´du·late** *vi., vt.* to move or cause to move like a wave **—un´du·late, un´du·lat·ed** *adj.* having a wavelike appearance

**un·du·la´tion** *n.* a waving or sinuous motion **—un´du·la·to·ry** *adj.*

**un·du´ly** *adv.* excessively; improperly or unjustly

**un·dy´ing** *adj.* immortal; eternal

**un·earned´** *adj.* not earned through one´s efforts; undeserved

**un·earth´** *vt.* to dig up; to discover

**un·earth´ly** *adj.* seemingly not of this world; supernatural; terrifying **—un·earth´li·ness** *n.*

**un·eas´y** *adj.* disturbed; disquieted; causing discomfort; not stable or secure, as *an uneasy peace* **—un·eas´i·ly** *adv.* **—un·eas´i·ness** *n.*

**un·em·ploy´a·ble** *adj.* not useful; unable to keep a job, as by lack of skills, illness, etc. *—n.* an unskilled or disabled person

**un·em·ployed´** *adj.* not having work; not put to use; idle **—un´em·ploy´ment** *n.*

**un·e´qual** *adj.* not alike, as in size or ability; inadequate; not uniform **—un·e´qual·ly** *adv.*

**un·e´qualed, un·e´qualled** *adj.* not to be matched or compared; without rivals

**un·e·quiv´o·cal** *adj.* understandable in only one way; not ambiguous **—un·e·quiv´o·cal·ly** *adv.* **—un·e·quiv´o·cal·ness** *n.*

**un·err´ing** *adj.* making no mistakes; certain **—un·err´ing·ly** *adv.*

**un·es·sen´tial** *adj.* not important; not required

**un·e´ven** *adj.* not smooth or level; rough; not balanced or matched; not uniform **—un·e´ven·ly** *adv.* **—un·e´ven·ness** *n.*

**un·e·vent´ful** *adj.* quiet; lacking unusual activity **—un·e·vent´ful·ly** *adv.* **—un·e·vent´ful·ness** *n.*

**un·ex·cep´tion·a·ble** *adj.* not open to question or objection; irreproachable **—un·ex·cep´tion·a·ble·ness —un·ex·cep´tion·a·bly**

**un·ex·cep´tion·al** *adj.* ordinary; not unusual **—un·ex·cep´tion·al·ly** *adv.*

**un·ex·pect´ed** *adj.* coming without warning; not foreseen **—un·ex·pect´ed·ly** *adv.* **—un·ex·pect´ed·ness** *n.*

**un·fail´ing** *adj.* fulfilling requirements or expectations; sure, infallible **—un·fail´ing·ly** *adv.* **—un·fail´ing·ness** *n.*

**un·fair´** *adj.* marked by injustice; biased; not honest or ethical **—un·fair´ly** *adv.* **—un·fair´ness** *n.*

**un·faith´ful** *adj.* disloyal; not abiding by a vow, duty, etc.; unreliable; adulterous **—un·faith´ful·ly** *adv.* **—un·faith´ful·ness** *n.*

**un·fa·mil´iar** *adj.* not versant in; outside the sphere of one´s knowledge; not previously known or seen, as *an unfamiliar face* **—un·fa·mil·i·ar´i·ty** *n.* **—un·fa·mil´iar·ly** *adv.*

**un·fath´om·a·ble** *adj.* incomprehensible; difficult or impossible to understand

**un·fa´vor·a·ble** *adj.* not propitious; detrimental **—un·fa´vor·a·ble·ness** *n.* **—un·fa´vor·a·bly** *adv.*

**un·feel´ing** *adj.* not sympathetic; showing no emotion **—un·feel´ing·ly** *adv.* **—un·feel´ing·ness** *n.*

**un·feigned´** *adj.* sincere **—un·feign´ed·ly** *adv.*

**un·fit´** *adj.* unsuitable for a given purpose; not physically or mentally sound **—un·fit´ly** *adv.* **—un·fit´ness** *n.*

**un·flag´ging** *adj.* not diminishing; tireless **—un·flag´ging·ly** *adv.*

**un·flap´pa·ble** *adj.* impassive; imperturbable **—un·flap·pa·bil´i·ty** *n.* **—un·flap´pa·bly** *adv.*

**un·fledged´** *adj.* inexperienced or immature

**un·flinch´ing** *adj.* steadfast; resolute **—un·flinch´ing·ly** *adv.*

**un·fold´** *vt.* to open or spread; to disclose gradually; to develop *—vi.* to expand; to develop fully

**un·fore·seen´** *adj.* unexpected; unpredicted; without warning

**un·for·get´ta·ble** *adj.* memorable; not likely to be forgotten **—un·for·get´ta·ble·ness** *n.* **—un·for·get´ta·bly** *adv.*

**unforgiving** *adj.* not willing to excuse or absolve; having little tolerance for error: *sailing over an unforgiving sea*

**un·for´tu·nate** *adj.* unlucky; resulting from misfortune; regrettable *—n.* a victim **—un·for´tu·nate·ly** *adv.*

**—un·for´tu·nate·ness** *n.*

**un·found´ed** *adj.* not based on fact; not established **—un·found´ed·ly** *adv.* **—un·found´ed·ness** *n.*

**un·fre´quent·ed** *adj.* rarely visited

**un·friend´ly** *adj.* not amiable or sympathetic; not favorable or propitious **—un·friend´li·ness** *n.*

**un·furl´** *vt., vi.* to unroll or spread out **—un·furled´** *adj.*

**un·gain´ly** *adj.* awkward; clumsy; poorly proportioned **—un·gain´li·ness** *n.*

**un·god´ly** *adj.* lacking reverence; sinful; outrageous *—adv.* outrageously **—un·god´li·ness** *n.*

**un·gov´ern·a·ble** *adj.* that cannot be governed or controlled **—un·gov´ern·a·ble·ness** *n.* **—un·gov´ern·a·bly** *adv.*

**un·gra´cious** *adj.* lacking manners; offensive **—un·gra´cious·ly** *adv.* **—un·gra´cious·ness** *n.*

**un·grate´ful** *adj.* lacking gratitude; disagreeable **—un·grate´ful·ly** *adv.* **—un·grate´ful·ness** *n.*

**un·guard´ed** *adj.* unprotected; thoughtless or careless; without guile **—un·guard´ed·ly** *adv.* **—un·guard´ed·ness** *n.*

**un´guent** *n.* an ointment or salve **—un´guen·tar·y** *adj.*

**un´gu·late** *adj.* having hoofs *—n.* a hoofed animal

**un·hand´** *vt.* to remove one´s hand from; to release

**un·hand´y** *adj.* inconvenient; lacking manual skill **—un·hand´i·ly** *adv.* **—un·hand´i·ness** *n.*

**un·hap´py** *adj.* sad or depressed; unfortunate; inappropriate; displeased **—un·hap´pi·ly** *adv.* **un·hap´pi·ness** *n.*

**un·health´y** *adj.* sickly; injurious to health; dangerous or risky **—un·health´i·ly** *adv.* **—un·health´i·ness** *n.*

**un·heard´-of** *adj.* unprecedented; outrageous

**un·hinge´** *vt.* to detach, as from hinges; to throw into confusion or derange

**un·ho´ly** *adj.* wicked; sinful

**u·ni·cel´lu·lar** *adj.* consisting of a single cell, as a protozoan **—u·ni·cel·lu·lar´i·ty** *n.*

**u´ni·corn** *n.* a mythical creature resembling a horse with a single horn growing from its head

**u´ni·form** *adj.* being always alike; consistent *—n.* similar clothing worn by members of an organization, service, etc *—vt.* to make comparable; to clothe with a uniform **—u·ni·form´i·ty, u´ni·form·ness** *n.* **—u´ni·form·ly** *adv.*

**u´ni·fy** *vt.* to bring together or unite; to make alike **—u´ni·fi·a·ble** *adj.* **—u·ni·fi·ca´tion** *n.* **—u´ni·fi·er** *n.*

**u·ni·lat´er·al** *adj.* relating to or affecting one side only; undertaken or obligating only one of two or more parties involved; having only one side; recognizing only one aspect as of an argument or discussion **—u·ni·lat´er·al·ly** *adv.*

**un·im·peach´a·ble** *adj.* beyond question; blameless **—un·im·peach´a·bly** *adv.*

**un·im·proved´** *adj.* having no improvement or progress made, as *an unimproved road*; not cleared or cultivated; unused

**un·in·spired´** *adj.* dull or boring; indifferent

**un·in·tel´li·gi·ble** *adj.* incomprehensible **—un·in·tel·li·gi·bil´i·ty, un·in·tel´li·gi·ble·ness** *n.* **—un·in·tel´li·gi·bly** *adv.*

**un·in·ten´tion·al** *n.* not deliberate or planned; inadvertent **—un·in·ten´tion·al·ly** *adv.*

**un·in´ter·est·ed** *adj.* indifferent; unconcerned **—un·in´ter·est·ed·ly** *adv.* **—un·in´ter·est·ed·ness** *n.*

**un´ion** *n.* a joining of two or more things; something formed by joining or combining; a device for joining mechanical parts *—adj.* pertaining to or involving a union

**un´ion·ism** *n.* labor unions collectively, their principles and practices **—un´ion·ist** *n.*

**un´ion·ize** *vi., vt.* to join or cause to join a labor union; to organize a union

**u·nique´** *adj.* being the only one of its kind; without equal; very unusual or remarkable **—u·nique´ly** *adv.* **—u·nique´ness** *n.*

**u´ni·sex** *adj.* appropriate to or characteristic of either sex *—n.* the integration of clothing, hair style, etc. so as to be appropriate for either sex

**u·ni·sex´u·al** *adj.* of only one sex; having to do with unisex **—u·ni·sex·u·al´i·ty** *n.* **—u·ni·sex´u·al·ly** *adv.*

**u´ni·son** *n.* a condition of perfect agreement; speaking or singing together as one

**u´nit** *n.* a value used as a standard of comparison or measurement; a measure of requirements for a scholastic degree; the quantity required to produce a desired effect; persons or things considered as constituent parts of a whole *—adj.* being a distinct part **—u´ni·tar·y** *adj.*

**u·nite´** *vt.* to join together; to bring into close connection; to possess in combination; to combine *—vi.* to be merged into one; to join together **—u·nit´ed** *adj.*

**u´ni·ty** *n.* the state or quality of being united; singleness of purpose; mutual understanding

**u·ni·ver´sal** *adj.* common everywhere; including all things, persons, etc. without exception; adapted to a variety of uses *—n.* any general notion or idea; a trait common to all men or cultures **—u·ni·ver´sal·ism** *n.* **—u·ni·ver´sal·ly** *adv.* **—u·ni·ver´sal·ness** *n.*

**u·ni·ver´sal·ize** *vt.* to make universal; to generalize **—u·ni·ver·sal·i·za´tion** *n.*

**u´ni·verse** *n.* the aggregate of all existing things; something extensive, as in a field of thought or activity

**u·ni·ver´si·ty** *n.* an institute of higher learning including its buildings, grounds, students, faculty, etc.

**un·just´** *adj.* not fair; wrongful **—un·just´ly** *adv.* **—un·just´ness** *n.*

**un·kempt´** *adj.* not neat or tidy

**un·kind´**, *adj.* lacking sympathy; harsh or cruel **—un·kind´li·ness, un·kind´ness** *n.* **—un·kind´ly** *adv.*

**un·known´** *adj.* not apprehended; not recognized or identified *–n.* an unfamiliar person or thing

**un·law´ful** *adj.* illegal; not moral or ethical – **un·law´ful·ly** *adv.* **–un·law´ful·ness** *n.*

**un·learned´** *adj.* illiterate; marked by lack of knowledge; acquired by means other than training **–un·learn´ed·ly** *adv.*

**un·leash´** *vt.* to set free from or as from leash

**un·less´** *conj.* except that *–prep.* excepting

**un·like´** *adj.* having little or no similarity *–prep.* different from; not characteristic of **–un·like´ness** *n.*

**un·like´ly** *adj.* improbable; contrary to expectation; not promising *–adv.* improbably **–un·like´li·hood, un·like´li·ness** *n.*

**un·lim´it·ed** *adj.* not restricted; having no boundaries

**un·load´** *vt.* to discharge, as cargo; to unburden; to dispose of by selling *–vi.* to discharge freight

**un·loose´** *vt.* to set free

**un·loos´en** *vt.* to undo or release

**un·luck´y** *adj.* not favored or favorable; unfortunate; likely to prove unfortunate **–un·luck´i·ly** *adv.* **–un·luck´i·ness** *n.*

**un·make´** *vt.* to restore to a previous condition; to ruin; to deprive of rank, power, etc.

**un·mask´** *vt.* to expose the true nature of *–vi.* to remove one´s disguise

**un·men´tion·a·ble** *adj.* not fit for discussion; too embarrassing to mention or discuss **–un·men´tion·a·ble·ness** *n.* **–un·men´tion·a·bly** *adv.*

**un·mer´ci·ful** *adj.* showing no mercy; cruel or pitiless; extreme or exorbitant **–un·mer´ci·ful·ly** *adv.* **–un·mer´ci·ful·ness** *n.*

**un·mis·tak´a·ble** *adj.* evident; obvious **–un·mis·tak´a·bly** *adv.*

**un·mit´i·gat·ed** *adj.* not relieved or lessened; absolute or thoroughgoing **–un·mit´i·gat·ed·ly** *adv.* **–un·mit´i·gat·ed·ness** *n.*

**un·nat´u·ral** *adj.* contrary to accepted standards of morality and decency; contrived or artificial **–un·nat´u·ral·ly** *adv.* **–un·nat´u·ral·ness** *n.*

**un·nec´es·sar·y** *adj.* not required **–un·nec·es·sar´i·ly** *adv.* **–un·nec·es·sar´i·ness** *n.*

**un·nerve´** *vt.* to deprive of resolve, courage, etc.; to make nervous **–un·nerve´ing·ly** *adv.*

**un·oc´cu·pied** *adj.* empty, uninhabited; idle, unemployed

**un·of·fi´cial** *adj.* not authorized or sanctioned; acting without authority **–un·of·fi´cial·ly** *adv.*

**un·op·posed´** *adj.* without opposition; not challenged: *the candidate for major ran unopposed*

**un·or´ga·nized** *adj.* without form or structure; not unionized

**un·or´tho·dox** *adj.* contrary to convention or tradition **–un·or´tho·dox·ly** *adv.* **–un·or´tho·dox·y** *n.*

**un·pal´at·a·ble** *adj.* not pleasing to the taste: *unpalatable food*; disagreeable or difficult to accept: *unpalatable criticism* **–un·pal·at·a·bil´i·ty** *n.* **–un·pal´at·a·bly** *adv.*

**un·par´al·leled** *adj.* unmatched; unprecedented

**un·pleas´ant** *adj.* disagreeable **–un·pleas´ant·ly** *adv.* **–un·pleas´ant·ness** *n.*

**un·plumbed´** *adj.* not fully measured or explored

**un·pop´u·lar** *adj.* generally disliked **–un·pop·u·lar´i·ty** *n.* **–un·pop´u·lar·ly** *adv.*

**un·prac´ticed** *adj.* not experienced; not used or tried

**un·prec´e·dent·ed** *adj.* being without precedent; new or novel

**un·pre·dict´a·ble** *adj.* unforeseen; that cannot be anticipated; tending to rash or unexpected action **–un·pre·dict·a·bil´i·ty, un·pre·dict´a·ble·ness** *n.* **–un·pre·dict´a·bly** *adv.*

**un·prej´u·diced** *adj.* free from bias; impartial

**un·prin´ci·pled** *adj.* unscrupulous; lacking a standard of morality

**un·print´a·ble** *adj.* profane or obscene

**un·pro·fes´sion·al** *adj.* violating the code, standards, etc. of a profession **–un·pro·fes´sion·al·ly** *adv.*

**un·prof´it·a·ble** *adj.* contributing nothing; lessening the profits of a business; serving no useful purpose **–unprof·it·a·bil´i·ty –un·prof´it·a·ble·ness** *n.* **–un·prof´it·a·bly** *adv.*

**un·qual´i·fied** *adj.* lacking qualifications; without limitation or restriction **–un·qual´i·fied·ly** *adv.*

**un·ques´tion·a·ble** *adj.* beyond doubt; indisputable – **un·ques´tion·a·ble·ness** *n.* **–un·ques´tion·a·bly** *adv.*

**un·rav´el** *vt.* to separate, as something tangled; to unfold or explain, as a plot *–vi.* to become untangled; to grow apparent

**un·read** *adj.* uninformed; unlearned; not yet examined

**un·read´a·ble** *adj.* illegible; poorly written

**un·read´y** *adj.* not prepared; illprepared

**un·re´al** *adj.* having no substance; fanciful, imaginary; not true or sincere **–un·re·al´i·ty** *n.*

**un·rea´son·a·ble** *adj.* acting contrary to reason; immoderate, exorbitant **–un·rea´son·a·ble·ness** *n.* **–un·rea´son·a·bly** *adv.*

**un·rea´son·ing** *adj.* irrational **–un·rea´son·ing·ly** *adv.*

**un·re·gen´er·ate** *adj.* not changed spiritually; sinful; stubbornly recalcitrant **–un·re·gen´er·a·cy** *n.* – **un·re·gen´er·ate·ly** *adv.*

**un·re·lent´ing** *adj.* determined; unyielding; not diminishing in pace, effort, etc. **–un·re·lent´ing·ly** *adv.*

**un·re·li´a·ble** *adj.* not dependable **–un·re·li·a·bil´i·ty, un·re·li´a·ble·ness** *n.* **–un·re·li´a·bly** *adv.*

**un·re·mit´ting** *adj.* not stopping or relaxing; incessant **–un·re·mit´ting·ly** *adv.*

**un·re·quit´ed** *adj.* not returned in kind

**un·re·served´** *adj.* without qualification; informal **–un·re·serv´ed·ly** *adv.* **–un·re·serv´ed·ness** *n.*

**un·rest´** *n.* restlessness; dissatisfaction bordering on revolt
**un·right´eous** *adj.* wicked, sinful, inequitable –**un·right´eous·ly** *adv.* –**un·right´eous·ness** *n.*
**un·ri´valed** *adj.* having no equal
**un·ruf´fled** *adj.* calm; undisturbed
**un·ru´ly** *adj.* tending to resist regulation; difficult to control –**un·ru´li·ness** *n.*
**un·sa´vor·y** *adj.* having a disagreeable taste or odor; lacking flavor; morally distasteful or offensive –**un·sa´vor·i·ly** *adv.* –**un·sa´vor·i·ness** *n.*
**un·scathed´** *adj.* not injured
**un·scru´pu·lous** *adj.* lacking restraint; unprincipled –**un·scru´pu·lous·ly** *adv.* –**un·scru´pu·lous·ness** *n.*
**un·sea´son·a·ble** *adj.* not suited or customary for the time of year; untimely –**un·sea´son·a·ble·ness** *n.* –**un·sea´son·a·bly** *adv.*
**un·seat´** *vt.* to depose or vote out
**un·seem´ly** *adj.* unbecoming; inappropriate –**un·seem´li·ness** *n.*
**un·set´tle** *vt.* to confuse, upset, or disturb –*vi.* to become unsettled
**un·shak´a·ble** *adj.* unable to be disturbed or agitated
**un·sight´ly** *adj.* offensive to the eyes; ugly
**un·skilled´** *adj.* lacking training or experience; requiring no special skill or training
**un·skill´ful** *adj.* awkward; incompetent –**un·skill´ful·ly** *adv.* –**un·skill´ful·ness** *n.*
**un·snarl´** *vt.* to disentangle
**un·so´cia·ble** *adj.* not inclined to the company of others; not conducive to friendly interchange or association –**un·so´cia·ble·ness** *n.* –**un·so´cia·bly** *adv.*
**un·so·phis´ti·cat·ed** *adj.* inexperienced, artless; genuine; not complicated –**un·so·phis´ti·cat·ed·ly** *adv.* –**un·so·phis´ti·cat·ed·ness, un·so·phis·ti·ca´tion** *n.*
**un·sound´** *adj.* not strong or solid; unhealthy; faulty or unfounded, as of reasoning –**un·sound´ly** *adv.* –**un·sound´ness** *n.*
**un·spar´ing** *adj.* generous or lavish; showing no mercy –**un·spar´ing·ly** *adv.* –**un·spar´ing·ness** *n.*
**un·speak´a·ble** *adj.* that cannot be expressed, as of something very good or very bad –**un·speak´a·ble·ness** *n.* –**un·speak´a·bly** *adv.*
**un·spoiled´** *adj.* not changed, as *an unspoiled wilderness*
**un·sta´ble** *adj.* lacking firmness or durability; easily influenced; emotionally unsettled; liable to change –**un·sta´ble·ness** *n.* –**un·sta´bly** *adv.*
**un·stead´y** *adj.* not steady; liable to move or sway; fluctuating; unreliable –**un·stead´i·ly** *adv.* –**un·stead´i·ness** *n.*
**un·struc´tured** *adj.* loosely organized
**un·strung´** *adj.* having string removed, as of beads, etc.; emotionally upset
**un·sub·stan´tial** *adj.* lacking substance or strength; having no valid basis in fact; fanciful –**un·sub·stan·ti·al´i·ty** *n.* –**un·sub·stan´tial·ly** *adv.*
**un·suit´a·ble** *adj.* inappropriate; unfitting –**un·suit·a·bil´i·ty, un·suit´a·ble·ness** *n.* –**un·suit´a·bly** *adv.*
**un·sung´** *adj.* not honored or celebrated; overlooked, as *an unsung hero*
**un·tan´gle** *vt.* to free from snarls; to clear up, as a confusing situation
**un·taught´** *adj.* lacking instruction or knowledge; learned or known without instruction
**un·ten´a·ble** *adj.* impossible to defend, save, preserve, etc. –**un·ten·a·bil´i·ty, un·ten´a·ble·ness** *n.*
**un·think´ing** *adj.* lacking thoughtfulness, care, or attention –**un·think´ing·ly** *adv.* –**un·think´ing·ness** *n.*
**un·ti´dy** *adj.* messy; disorderly –**un·ti´di·ly** *adv.* –**un·ti´di·ness** *n.*
**un·tie´** *vt.* to free from that which binds or restrains –*vi.* to loosen or undo
**un·til´** *prep.* up to the time of –*conj.* to the time when; to the place or degree that
**un·time´ly** *adj.* coming before; not at the proper time; premature or inopportune –*adv.* before time; inopportunely –**un·time´li·ness** *n.*
**un·told´** *adj.* not revealed; too great to be counted or measured
**un·touch´a·ble** *adj.* out of reach; beyond culpability or blame; forbidden; unpleasant or dangerous to touch –**un·touch·a·bil´i·ty** *n.* –**un·touch´a·bly** *adv.*
**un·true´** *adj.* false or incorrect; disloyal; not conforming to standard: not even, level, etc.
**un·truth´ful** *adj.* not telling the truth; inconsistent with the truth –**un·truth´ful·ly** *adv.* –**un·truth´ful·ness** *n.*
**un·tu´tored** *adj.* not educated
**un·u´su·al** *adj.* odd, rare, or extraordinary –**un·u´su·al·ly** *adv.* –**un·u´su·al·ness** *n.*
**un·ut´ter·a·ble** *adj.* too great, profound, etc, to be expressed in words –**un·ut´ter·a·ble·ness** *n.* –**un·ut´ter·a·bly** *adv.*
**un·var´nished** *adj.* not coated with varnish; not embellished or adorned: *the unvarnished truth*
**un·veil´** *vt.* to remove the covering from; to disclose to view; to reveal –*vi.* to remove one´s veil
**un·war´rant·a·ble** *adj.* that cannot be justified or excused; indefensible –**un·war´rant·a·bly** *adv.*
**un·war´rant·ed** *adj.* without justification
**un·war´y** *adj.* careless or incautious –**un·war´i·ly** *adv.* –**un·war´i·ness** *n.*
**un·whole´some** *adj.* detrimental to physical or mental health; unhealthy in appearance –**un·whole´some·ly** *adv.* –**un·whole´some·ness** *n.*
**un·wield´y** *adj.* difficult to move or control –**un·wield´i·ness** *n.*
**un·will´ing** *adj.* reluctant; done, said, granted, etc.

with reluctance **–un·will´ing·ly** *adv.* **–un·will´ing·ness** *n.*

**un·wind´** *vt.* to disentangle *–vi.* to become disentangled; to relax

**un·wise´** *adj.* showing a lack of wisdom or good sense **–un·wise´ly** *adv.*

**un·wit´ting** *adj.* having no knowledge; not intentional **–un·wit´ting·ly** *adv.*

**un·wor´thy** *adj.* not deserving; not befitting or becoming **–un·wor´thi·ly** *adv.* **–un·wor´thi·ness** *n.*

**un·writ´ten** *adj.* based on tradition, as *an unwritten law*; understood, as an agreement or arrangement between friends

**up** *adv.* toward a higher place; in or on a higher place; to or at that which is or is deemed to be higher *–adj.* moving or directed upward; at or to a high level, condition, etc. *–prep.* toward or at a higher point; to or at a point farther above or along *–n.* an ascent; a state of prosperity

**up´beat** *n.* an unaccented beat in music *–adj.* optimistic; confident

**up´braid´** *vt.* to reproach

**up´end´** *vt., vi.* to stand on end; to overturn

**up´grade** *n.* an upward slope *–vt.* to modernize or improve as in value, performance, etc.

**up·heav´al** *n.* a violent change, as in the established social order

**up·hold´** *vt.* to keep from falling or sinking; to aid, encourage, etc.

**up·hol´ster** *vt.* to fit with coverings, cushions, etc. **–up·hol´ster·er** *n.*

**up·hol´ster·y** *n.* the covering or repairing of furniture; material for covering furniture

**up´keep** *n.* the act, state, or cost of maintaining in good condition

**up·lift´** *vt.* to elevate; to put on a higher plane mentally, morally, culturally, etc. **–up´lift** *n.* the act of raising; elevation to a higher plane; a social movement aiming to improve

**up´per** *adj.* higher, as in position, rank, authority, etc. *–n.* something that is above another

**upper hand** an advantage

**up´per·most** *adj.* highest in rank, authority, etc.; foremost *–adv.*

**up´right** *adj.* erect; righteous *–n.* the state of being erect; something erect *–adv.* in an upright or vertical position **–up´right·ly** *adv.* **–up´right·ness** *n.*

**up´ris·ing** *n.* a revolt or insurrection; an upward slope

**up´roar** *n.* a state of confusion, disturbance, excitement, etc.

**up·roar´i·ous** *adj.* accompanied by a commotion; tumultuous; loud and boisterous; provoking laughter **–up·roar´i·ous·ly** *adv.* **–up·roar´i·ous·ness** *n.*

**up´root** *vt.* to tear up by the roots; to destroy utterly; to leave

**up·set´** *vt.* to overturn; to throw into confusion or disorder; to disconcert or disquiet; to defeat, especially to best a favored opponent **–up·set´, up´set** *adj.* overturned; disturbed **–up´set** *n.* the act of overturning; a physical or emotional disorder; defeat of a favored opponent **–up·set´ter** *n.* **–up·set´ting·ly** *adv.*

**up´shot** *n.* outcome or result

**up´side** *n.* the upper part; an advantage; an upward trend, as in business

**up·stand´ing** *adj.* honest or straightforward; upright; placed erect **–up·stand´ing·ness** *n.*

**up´start** *n.* one who attains sudden power, importance, etc.

**up´swing** *n.* a swinging upward; an increase or improvement, as in business climate

**up´tight´** *adj.* anxious or nervous; angry; conventional or conservative **–up´tight´ness** *n.*

**up´ward** *adv.* in or toward a higher place; in the upper parts; toward a better condition *–adj.* directed toward or located in a higher place **–upward mobility** the opportunity or ability to improve one´s income, status, etc. **–up´ward·ly** *adv.* **–up´wards** *adv.*

**ur´ban** *adj.* pertaining to a city or city life; living or located in a city **–ur´ban·ite** *n.*

**ur·bane´** *adj.* refined; suave **–ur·bane´ly** *adv.* **–ur·bane´ness** *n.* **–ur·ban´i·ty** *n.*

**ur´ban·ism** *n.* life in a city; the study of city life **–ur´ban·ist** *n.* **–ur´ban·is´tic** *adj.*

**ur´ban·ize** *vt.* to cause to assume the characteristics of a city; to cause to adopt an urban life style

**ur·ban·ol´o·gy** *n.* the study of cities and their problems **–ur·ban·ol´o·gist** *n.*

**urban renewal** a program for revitalizing cities

**urban sprawl** the spread of population, shopping centers, etc. into rural or undeveloped areas

**u·re´mi·a** *n.* a toxic condition caused by the presence in the blood of substance ordinarily excreted by the kidneys **–u·re´mic** *adj.*

**urge** *vt.* to drive or force forward; to entreat earnestly *–vi.* to present arguments, claims, etc. *–n.* a strong impulse; the act of urging

**ur´gent** *adj.* requiring prompt action; insistent **–ur´gen·cy** *n.* **–ur´gent·ly** *adv.*

**u·ri·nal´y·sis** *n.* chemical analysis of the urine

**u´ri·nate** *vi.* to pass urine **–u·ri·na´tion** *n.*

**u´rine** *n.* fluid filtered by the kidneys and passed off as waste **–u´ri·nar·y** *adj.*

**urn** *n.* a footed receptacle

**u·rol´o·gy** *n.* the study of the diseases, treatment, etc. of the urinary system **–u·ro·log´ic, u·ro·log´i·cal** *adj.* **–urol´o·gist** *n.*

**us´a·ble, use´a·ble** *adj.* that can be used; that may be useful **–us´a·ble·ness** *n.* **–us´a·bly** *adv.*

**us´age** *n.* the act or manner of using; customary or

habitual practice; the accepted manner of using words

**use** *vt.* to put into service; to take advantage of *–n.* the act of using or the state of being used; function; advantage or usefulness; the purpose for which something is used **–us´er** *n.*

**use´ful** *adj.* serviceable; helpful **–use´ful·ly** *adv.* **–use´ful·ness** *n.*

**use´less** *adj.* having no use; serving no function **–use´less·ly** *adv.* **–use´less·ness** *n.*

**ush´er** *n.* one who escorts theater patrons to their seats; an official doorkeeper; a male attendant in a wedding party *–vi., vt.* to serve as an usher

**u´su·al** *adj.* customary or common **–u´su·al·ly** *adv.* **–u´su·al·ness** *n.*

**u·su´ri·ous** *adj.* practicing usury; of the nature of or pertaining to usury **–u·su´ri·ous·ly** *adv.* **–u·su´ri·ous·ness** *n.*

**u·surp´** *vt.* to seize without authority; to take possession by force **–u·sur·pa´tion** *n.* **–u·surp´er** *n.*

**u´su·ry** *n.* lending money at excessive or unlawful interest rates; excessive or unlawful interest **–u´su·rer** *n.*

**uten´sil** *n.* an implement that serves a useful purpose

**u´tile** *adj.* useful

**u·til´i·ty** *n.* fitness for a practical purpose

**u´ti·lize** *vt.* to make use of **–u´ti·li·za´tion** *n.* **–u´ti·liz·er** *n.*

**ut´most** *adj.* of the highest or greatest degree; being at the furthest limit; extreme *–n.* the most or best possible

**ut´ter** *vt.* to say, express, give out, or send forth; to put in circulation *–adj.* complete; unqualified **–ut´ter·er** *n.* **–ut´ter·ly** *adv.*

**ut´ter·ance** *n.* a manner of speaking; a thing uttered

**ut´ter·most** *adj., n.* utmost

**v, V** twenty-second letter of the English alphabet; in Roman characters, the symbol for 5

**va´cant** *adj.* containing nothing; empty; not being used; having no incumbent, officer, etc., as of a post or office **–va´can·cy** *n.* **–va´cant·ly** *adv.* **–va´cant·ness** *n.*

**va´cate** *vt.* to make vacant; to set aside, as a ruling *–vi.* to leave an office, dwelling, etc.

**va·ca´tion** *(US) n.* time away from work for recreation or rest; a holiday *–vi.* to take a holiday **–va·ca´tion·er, va·ca´tion·ist** *n.*

**vac´ci·nate** *vt.* to innoculate as a preventive measure **–vac·ci·na´tion** *n.* **–vac´ci·na·tor** *n.*

**vac·cine´** *n.* a preparation used to provide immunity

**vac´il·late** *vt.* to waver; to be irresolute **–vac·il·la´tion** *n.* **–vac´il·la·tor** *n.* **–vac´il·la·to·ry** *adj.*

**va·cu´i·ty** *n.* emptiness; vacant space; a lack of intelligence; something inane or stupid

**vac´u·ous** *adj.* empty; lacking intelligence; lacking substance; devoid of meaning or expression: *a vacuous stare* **–vac´u·ous·ly** *adv.* **–vac´u·ous·ness** *n.*

**vac´u·um** *n.* a space nearly devoid of matter; a reduction of pressure below that of the surrounding atmosphere

**vag´a·bond** *n.* one who wanders without visible means of support; a shiftless, irresponsible person *–adj.* wandering; aimless; irresponsible **–vag´a·bond·age** *n.*

**va´gar·y** *n.* a wild fancy or extravagant notion

**va´grant** *n.* one without an established home or job; a tramp *–adj.* wandering aimlessly; wayward **–va´gran·cy** *n.* **–va´grant·ly** *adv.*

**vague** *n.* lacking definition; indistinct; not clearly stated **–vague´ly** *adv.* **–vague·ness** *n.*

**vain** *adj.* showing excessive pride in oneself; unproductive or useless **–in vain** to no purpose **–vain´ly** *adv.* **–vain´ness** *n.*

**vain´glo·ry** *n.* excessive vanity; ostentation **–vain·glo´ri·ous** *adj.* **–vain·glo´ri·ous·ly** *adv.* **–vain·glo´ri·ous·ness** *n.*

**val´ance** *(US) n.* decorative drapery hanging from the tester of a bedstead or across the top of a window; a decorative panel hat serves to cover the fixtures along the top of a window

**vale** *n.* a valley

**val·e·dic´tion** *n.* a farewell

**val·e·dic·to´ri·an** *n.* a student selected to give the farewell address at a graduation ceremony

**val´e·dic´to·ry** *adj.* of a leave-taking *–n.* a parting address

**va´lence** *n.* in chemistry, the capacity of an atom or radical to combine with another atom or radical

**val´et** *n.* a man´s personal servant; a hotel employee who performs personal services for guests, such as cleaning and pressing clothes *–vt., vi.* to serve as a valet

**val·e·tu·di·nar´i·an** *n.* a chronic invalid *–adj.* infirm or ailing; overly concerned about one´s health **–val·e·tu·di·nar´i·an·ism** *n.* **–val·e·tu´di·nar·y** *adj.*

**val´iant** *adj.* strong and courageous; performed with valor **–val´iance, val´ian·cy** *n.* **–val´iant·ly** *adv.*

**val´id** *adj.* based on facts or evidence; well founded; effective: *a valid system*; legally binding **–va·lid´i·ty, val´id·ness** *n.* **–val´id·ly** *adv.*

**val´i·date** *vt.* to confirm as true; to declare to be legally binding; to mark or stamp so as to give sanction or make official **–val·i·da´tion** *n.*

**va·lise´** *n.* a traveling bag

**val´ley** *n.* an area drained by a river; low land lying between mountains or hills; a hollow

**val´or** *n.* remarkable courage; bravery **–val´or·ous** *adj.* **–val´or·ous·ly** *adv.*

**val´u·a·ble** *adj.* having significant worth or value; costly

**—val´u·a·bles** *n.* expensive or treasured articles, such as jewelry **—val´u·a·ble·ness** *n.* **—val´u·a·bly** *adv.*

**val·u·a´tion** *n.* an estimate of worth; an estimated value **—val·u·a´tion·al** *adj.* **—val´u·a·tor** *n.*

**val´ue** *n.* the worth of a thing; something regarded as desirable or worthy; market price; a bargain; a number represented by a symbol; the relative lightness or darkness of a color *—vt.* to assess or appraise; to regard highly; to consider relatively important: *the value of good health* **—val´u·er** *n.*

**val´ued** *adj.* highly esteemed, as *a valued friend*; having a specific worth: *valued at ten dollars*

**val´ue·less** *adj.* worthless

**valve** *n.* a device that controls the movement or flow of a fluid **—val´vu·lar** *adj.*

**vam´pire** *n.* in folklore, a reanimated corpse that feeds on human blood; a person who preys on those of the opposite sex; a bat that feeds on the blood of mammals, also called *a vampire bat* **—vam´pir´ic, vam´pir·ish** *adj.* **—vam´pir·ism** *n.*

**van** *n.* a large, enclosed wagon or truck used to transport goods; *(Brit.)* a railroad car used to transport freight or baggage; *(Brit.)* a caravan; *(US)* a motor vehicle somewhat like a small bus, designed to transport passengers

**van´dal·ism** *n.* the willful defacement or destruction of property **—van´dal** *n.* **—van·dal·is´tic** *adj.*

**van´dal·ize** *vt.* to willfully deface or destroy the property of others **—van·dal·i·za´tion** *n.*

**vane** *n.* a thin plate, pivoted on a rod, to indicate wind direction; an arm or plate, as of a windmill, propeller, etc.

**van´guard** *n.* the forward part of an advancing army; the foremost position; leaders of a movement, trend, etc.

**va·nil´la** *n.* a climbing orchid of tropical America; flavoring extracted from the seed capsule of the orchid; a vanilla flavoring made synthetically **—va·nil´lic** *adj.*

**van´ish** *vi.* to disappear; to pass out of existence **—van´ish·ing·ly** *adv.* **—van´ish·ment** *n.*

**van´i·ty** *n.* excessive pride in one´s talents, looks, etc.; something worthless or futile; a dressing table **—vanity case** a traveling case for cosmetics, etc.

**van´quish** *vt.* to defeat in battle; to suppress, or overcome, as fear **—van´quish·a·ble** *adv.* **—van´quish·er** *n.* **—van´quish·ment** *n.*

**van´tage** *n.* superiority or advantage; a position or condition that offers an advantage; a position that affords an overall view

**vap´id** *adj.* flat or dull; lacking flavor or attraction **—va·pid´i·ty, vap´id·ness** *n.* **—vap´id·ly** *adv.*

**va´por** *n.* moisture in the air; any cloudy substance; something insubstantial and fleeting *—vt.* to vaporize *—vi.* to emit or pass off in vapor

**va´por·ize** *vt., vi.* to convert or be converted into vapor **—va´por·iz·a·ble** *n.* **—va·por·iza´tion** *n.*

**va´por·ous** *adj.* misty, like a vapor; emitting or forming vapor; whimsical **—va´por·ous·ly** *adv.* **—va´por·ous·ness** *n.*

**va´por·ware** *n.* computer software that is marketed before it is complete or ready for sale

**var´i·a·ble** *adj.* having the capacity to change; tending or likely to change; of no fixed size, amount, etc. *—n.* something liable or able to change **—var·i·a·bil´i·ty, var´i·a·ble·ness** *n.* **—var´i·a·bly** *adv.*

**var´i·ance** *n.* a discrepancy or difference; license or permission to do something contrary to local custom or ordinance

**va´i·ant** *adj.* differing, as from a standard or type *—n.* something that differs in form, as an alternate spelling or pronunciation

**var·i·a´tion** *n.* a difference or modification; the extent to which a thing differs; something that differs from others of the same type **—var·i·a´tion·al** *adj.*

**var´ied** *adj.* consisting of diverse sorts; modified or altered **—var´ied·ly** *adv.*

**var´i·e·gat·ed** *adj.* varied in color

**va·ri´e·tal** *adj.* describing a variety *—n.* a wine named for the variety of grape from which it is made **—va·ri´e·tal·ly** *adv.*

**va·ri´e·ty** *n.* diversity or difference; sort or kind: *a variety of mustard*; a collection or assortment

**var´i·ous** *adj.* different from one another; several; separate, identifiable; multifaceted **—var´i·ous·ly** *adv.* **—var´i·ous·ness** *n.*

**var´nish** *n.* a finish for furniture, etc.; outward show *—vt.* to coat with varnish; to hide or gloss over: *varnish the truth* **—var´nish·er** *n.*

**var´y** *vt.* to change or modify; to diversify *—vi.* to become changed; to deviate **—var´y·ing·ly** *adv.*

**vas´cu·lar** *adj.* pertaining to body vessels or ducts

**vast** *adj.* immense; great in quantity, importance, etc.; extensive **—vast´ly** *adv.* **—vast´ness** *n.*

**vat** *n.* a large open vessel or tub

**vaude´ville** *n.* theatrical entertainment consisting of short sketches, songs, dances, etc.; a variety show **—vaude·vil´lian** *n.*

**vault** *n.* an arched roof or ceiling; a room or compartment for storage or safekeeping; a burial chamber *—vi., vt.* to leap

**vault´ing** *n.* the construction that forms a vault

**vaunt** *vi., vt.* to boast *—n.* a brag or boast **—vaunt´ing·ly** *adv.*

**veer** *vi.* to turn; to shift as from an opinion, belief, etc. *—vt.* to change the direction of

**veg´an** *n.* a vegetarian whose diet is limited to food derived from plants

**veg´e·ta·ble** *n.* a plant cultivated for food; the edible part of a plant *—adj.* relating to or derived from plants: *vegetable oil*; made from edible plants: *vegetable soup*

**veg´e·tal** *adj.* pertaining to plants or vegetables

**veg·e·tar´i·an** *n.* one who does not eat meat; one who subscribes to any of a variety of diets that exclude meat and sometimes seafood or animal products such as eggs and milk *–adj.* relating to vegetarians or vegetarianism; consisting only of vegetables, grains, fruit, nuts, and seeds **–veg·e·tar´i·an·ism** *n.*

**veg´e·tate** *vi.* grow, as a plant; to exist in a monotonous, passive state

**veg·e·ta´tion** *n.* plant life **–veg´e·ta·tive** *adj.*

**ve´he·ment** *adj.* marked by strong feeling or passion; acting with great force **–ve´he·mence** *n.* **–ve´he·ment·ly** *adv.*

**ve´hi·cle** *n.* any conveyance for transporting people or freight **–ve·hic´u·lar** *adj.*

**veil** *n.* a thin fabric for covering the face; anything that conceals or covers *–vt.* to cover, conceal, disguise, etc.

**veil´ing** *n.* a covering, such as a veil; material for making a veil

**vein** *n.* a tubular vessel that conveys blood; a branching structure such as the ribs in a leaf or the wing of an insect; a colored streak as in wood, stone, etc.; a distinctive tendency or disposition *–vt.* to extend or mark throughout like veins **–veined** *adj.*

**veld, veldt** *n.* a South African plain

**vel´lum** *n.* fine parchment

**ve·loc´i·pede** *n.* an early form of the bicycle with pedals attached to a large front wheel

**ve·loc´i·ty** *n.* speed; quickness of motion

**ve·lour´** *n.* a soft fabric having a short, thick pile

**vel´vet** *n.* a fabric with a short, smooth pile on one side and a plain underside *–adj.* made of velvet; smooth and soft to the touch **–vel´vet·y** *adj.*

**ve´nal** *adj.* open to or characterized by corruption or bribery **–ve·nal´i·ty** *n.* **–ve´nal·ly** *adv.*

**vend** *vt.* to sell as an occupation; to sell through a vending machine *–vi.* to be employed in selling **–vend´er, ven´dor** *n.*

**ven·det´ta** *n.* a private feud in which the relatives of a slain or wronged person seek revenge; any bitter quarrel

**vend´i·ble, vend´a·ble** *adj.* salable; marketable *–n.* something for sale **–vend·i·bil´i·ty** *n.* **–vend´i·bly** *adv.*

**ve·neer´** *n.* a thin layer; surface or show, as *a veneer of civility* *–vt.* to cover with veneer; to conceal, as something disagreeable or coarse **–ve·neer´er** *n.*

**ven´er·a·ble** *adj.* worthy of respect because of dignity, age, etc **–ven·er·a·bil´i·ty, ven´er·a·ble·ness** *n.* **–ven´er·a·bly** *adv.*

**ven´er·ate** *vt.* to regard with respect or awe **–ven·er·a´tion** *n.* **–ven´er·a·tor** *n.*

**ve·ne´re·al** *adj.* pertaining to or proceeding from sexual intercourse

**ve·ne·re·ol´o·gy** *n.* the study of sexually transmitted disease **–ve·ne·re·o·log´i·cal** *adj.* **–ve·ne·re·ol´o·gist** *n.*

**ven´geance** *n.* infliction of a deserved penalty; retribution **–with a vengeance** with remarkable intensity or force; in the extreme

**venge´ful** *adj.* seeking revenge; unforgiving **–venge´ful·ly** *adv.* **–venge´ful·ness** *n.*

**ve´ni·al** *adj.* slight or trivial, as a fault **–ve·ni·al´i·ty** *n.* **–ve´ni·al·ly** *adv.*

**ven´i·son** *n.* the flesh of a wild animal, especially of a deer, used for food

**ven´om** *n.* poison secreted by certain reptiles, insects, etc.; ill will **–ven´om·ous** *adj.* **–ven´om·ous·ly** *adv.* **–ven´om·ous·ness** *n.*

**ve´nous** *adj.* pertaining to or carried by veins; designating blood returning to the heart and lungs; having veins **–ve´nous·ly** *adv.* **–ve´nous·ness** *n.*

**vent** *n.* an outlet or opening; a slit in a garment *–vt.* to give expression to; to permit escape, as a gas; to make a vent in

**ven·ti·la´tion** *n.* the free circulation of air; exposure to examination and discussion; oxygenation, as of blood **–ven´ti·late** *vt.* **–ven´ti·la·tive** *adj.*

**ven´tral** *adj.* toward or at the abdomen; situated near the abdomen **–ven´tral·ly** *adv.*

**ven´tri·cle** *n.* a small cavity in the body, such as the lower chambers of the heart or interconnecting cavities in the brain **–ven·tric´u·lar** *adj.*

**ven·tril´o·quism, ven·tril´o·quy** *n.* the art of speaking so that the sound seems to come from another source **–ven·tri·lo´qui·al, ven·tril´o·quis´tic** *adj.* **–ven·tri·lo´qui·al·ly** *adv.* **–ven·tril´o·quist** *n.* **–ven·tril´o·quize** *vi., vt.*

**ven´ture** *vt.* to expose to risk *–vi.* to take risk *–n.* an undertaking marked by risk; that which is risked, as *venture capital* **–ven´tur·er** *n.*

**venture capital** investment in a new, untried business; an investment that is at risk

**ven´ture·some** *adj.* bold or daring; involving risk **–ven´ture·some·ly** *adv.* **–ven´ture·some·ness** *n.*

**ven´tur·ous** *adj.* adventurous; risky **–ven´tur·ous·ly** *adv.* **–ven´tur·ous·ness** *n.*

**ven´ue** *n.* the place or setting of an action or event; in law, a place where a crime has been committed, where a cause of action arises, or where a trial must be held

**ve·ra´cious** *adj.* truthful; accurate **–ve·ra´cious·ly** *adv.* **–ve·ra´cious·ness** *n.*

**ve·rac´i·ty** *n.* honesty; accuracy

**ve·ran´da** *n.* an open porch along the side of a building

**verb** *n.* a word that expresses action, existence or occurrence

**ver´bal** *adj.* pertaining to words: *a verbal image*; concerned with words rather than ideas; literal *–n.* in grammar, a noun directly derived from a verb **–ver´bal·ly** *adv.*

**ver´bal·ist** *n.* one skilled in the use of words; one more concerned with words than with facts or ideas **–ver·bal·is´tic** *adj.*

**ver´bal·ize** *vt.* to express in words *–vi.* to speak or write in a wordy fashion **–ver·bal·i·za´tion** *n.* **–ver´bal·iz·er** *n.*

**ver·ba´tim** *adj., adv.* exactly, word for word

**ver´bi·age** *n.* the use of too many words; a manner of verbal expression

**ver·bose´** *adj.* overly wordy; repetitive or redundant; containing too many or unnecessary words **–ver·bose´ly** *adv.* **–ver·bose´ness, ver·bos´i·ty** *n.*

**ver´dant** *adj.* covered with green vegetation: *the verdant country-side*; inexperienced **–ver´dan·cy** *n.* **–ver´dant·ly** *adv.*

**ver´dict** *n.* the decision of a jury; a conclusion or opinion

**ver´dure** *n.* the fresh greenness of growing vegetation; lush vegetation **–ver´dur·ous** *adj.* **–ver´dur·ous·ness** *n.*

**verge** *n.* the extreme edge; a boundary *–vi.* to be contiguous or adjacent; to approach: *familiarity verging on insolence* *–vt.* to be in the process of change: *wilderness verging into farmland*

**ver·i·fi·ca´tion** *n.* a proof or confirmation

**ver´i·fi·a·ble** *adj.* that can be confirmed or proven **–ver·i·fi·a·bil´i·ty** *n.* **–ver´i·fi·a·bly** *adv.*

**ver´i·fy** *vt.* to prove; to test the accuracy or truth of

**ver·i·si·mil´i·tude** *n.* the appearance of truth or reality; that which has only the appearance of truth or reality: a likeness

**ver´i·ta·ble** *adj.* genuine or real; actual **–ver´i·ta·ble·ness** *n.* **–ver´i·ta·bly** *adv.*

**ver´i·ty** *n.* truth; the quality of being true or real

**ver·mi·cel´li** *n.* a slender, wormlike pasta

**ver´mi·form** *adj.* shaped like a worm

**ver´min** *n.* destructive small animals or parasitic insects; a repulsive person **–ver´min·ous** *adj.* **–ver´min·ous·ly** *adv.*

**ver·mouth´** *n.* a fortified wine

**ver·nac´u·lar** *n.* the language peculiar to a locality; common daily speech; the specialized vocabulary of a trade or profession *–adj.* of a native tongue; spoken or written in a particular language or argot; relating to a locality **–ver·nac´u·lar·ism** *n.* **–ver·nac´u·lar·ly** *adv.*

**ver´nal** *adj.* appropriate to spring; fresh or youthful **–ver´nal·ly** *adv.*

**ver´sa·tile** *adj.* having many talents; having many uses **–ver´sa·tile·ly** *adv.* **–ver·sa·til´i·ty** *n.*

**verse** *n.* poetry, as distinguished from prose; a line or group of lines, as of poetry, scripture, etc.

**versed** *adj.* skilled; knowledgeable

**ver´si·fy** *vt.* to turn into poetry *–vi.* to write poetry **–ver·si·fi·ca´tion** *n.* **–ver´si·fi·er** *n.*

**ver´sion** *n.* a translation or rendition; an adaptation, as *the film version of a novel*; a personal account or view **–ver´sion·al** *adj.*

**ver´so** *n.* a left-handed page; the reverse of a coin or medallion

**ver´sus** *prep.* against; considered as the alternative of

**ver´te·bra** *n., pl.* **ver´te·brae** a bone of the spinal column **–ver´te·bral** *adj.*

**ver´te·brate** *adj.* having a backbone; pertaining to or characteristic of creatures that have a backbone

**ver´ti·cal** *adj.* upright or erect; directly overhead; situated at right angles to the horizon *–n.* something upright **–vertical integration** a business structure that develops or grows by adding to its level of processing from a raw material to a finished product **–ver·ti·cal´i·ty, ver´ti·cal·ness** *n.* **–ver´ti·cal·ly** *adv.*

**ver·tig´i·nous** *adj.* affected by vertigo; spinning **–ver·tig´i·nous·ly** *adv.* **–ver·tig´i·nous·ness** *n.*

**ver´ti·go** *n.* dizziness; disorientation; a disorder in which, subject to certain stimuli, a person or his surroundings seem to whirl about

**verve** *n.* energy; enthusiasm

**ver´y** *adv.* to a high degree; exactly *–adj.* suitable; identical; the thing itself: *the very point I wanted to make*

**ves´i·cle** *n.* a small cavity or cyst; a blister **–ve·sic´u·lar** *adj.* **–ve·sic´u·late** *vi., vt.* **–ve·sic·u·la´tion** *n.*

**ves´pers** *n.* evening worship service

**ves´sel** *n.* an open container capable of holding liquid; a physical process that holds or carries a fluid: *a blood vessel*; a ship or aircraft

**vest** *n. (Brit.)* an undergarment worn under a shirt; *(US)* a short, sleeveless outer garment *–vt.* to confer, as ownership or authority *–vi.* to become legally vested

**vest´ed** *adj.* inalienable or absolute, as *a vested right*

**ves´ti·bule** *n.* a small entryway or antechamber; an enclosed passageway between cars of a passenger train **–ves·tib´u·lar** *adj.*

**ves´tige** *n.* a discernible trace; a remnant of an organ that is no longer functional **–ves·tig´ial** *adj.* **–ves·tig´ial·ly** *adv.*

**vest´ment** *n.* an article of clothing; a ritual garment

**ves´try** *n.* a room in a church used for storing vestments, conducting meetings, etc.; a church´s administrative body

**ves´try·man** *n.* a member of a church vestry

**vet´er·an** *n.* someone long experienced, as in the military or an occupation

**vet´er·i·nar·y** *adj.* of the prevention and treatment of diseases and injuries of animals: *veterinary medicine* **–vet·er·i·nar´i·an** *n.*

**ve´to** *vt.* to refuse, as approval or consent *—n.* the right to cancel, prohibit, or postpone; the exercising of such a right **—ve´to·er** *n.*
**vex** *vt.* to annoy; to trouble or afflict; to baffle or confuse **—vex·a´tion** *n.* **—vex´ed·ly** *adv.* **—vex´ed·ness** *n.*
**vexed** *adj.* annoyed or disturbed; baffled
**vex·a´tious** *adj.* annoying; disturbing **—vex·a´tious·ly** *adv.* **—vex·a´tious·ness** *n.*
**vi´a** *prep.* by way of; by means of
**vi´a·ble** *adj.* capable of living and developing normally; workable or practicable, as a plan **—vi·a·bil´i·ty** *n.* **—vi´a·bly** *adv.*
**vi´a·duct** *n.* a bridgelike structure of arched masonry that carries a road, pipeline, etc.
**vi´al** *n.* a small bottle
**vi´and** *n.* an article of food
**vi´brant** *adj.* vigorous or enthusiastic: *a vibrant personality*; energetic, powerful: *vibrant color* **—vi´bran·cy** *n.* **—vi´brant·ly** *adv.*
**vi´brate** *vi., vt.* to move or cause to move back and forth rapidly **—vi·bra´tion** *n.* **—vi·bra´tion·al, vi´bra·to·ry** *adj.* **—vi´bra·tor** *n.*
**vi·bra´to** *n.* a cyclical variation in the pitch of a musical tone
**vic´ar** *n.* one authorized to perform in the stead of another; a church representative
**vic´ar·age** *n.* the office of a vicar; a vicar´s residence
**vi·car´i·ous** *adj.* suffered or done in place of another; identifying with the experience of another; delegated **—vi·car´i·ous·ly** *adv.* **—vi·car´i·ous·ness** *n.*
**vice** *n.* moral depravity; an immoral action, trait, etc.; a habitual failing or shortcoming; *(Brit.)* a clamping device, as used to hold material for woodworking
**vice´roy** *n.* one who rules by the authority of a sovereign
**vi·chys·soise´** *n.* a cream soup of potato and leeks, usually served cold
**vi·cin´i·ty** *n.* nearness; proximity; a nearby area, region, etc.
**vi´cious** *adj.* dangerous; marked by evil intent: *a vicious rumor*; depraved or immoral forceful or immoral **—vi´cious·ly** *adv.* **—vi´cious·ness** *n.*
**vi·cis´si·tude** *n.* a change or alteration **—vi·cis´si·tudes** *pl. n.* irregular changes, as of conditions or fortune **—vi·cis·si·tu´di·nar·y, vi·cis·si·tu´di·nous** *adj.*
**vic´tim** *n.* one harmed in some way, as by injury, disease, fraud, trickery, etc.
**vic´tim·ize** *vt.* to cause to suffer; to cheat or dupe **—vic·tim·i·za´tion** *n.* **—vic´tim·iz·er** *n.*
**vic´tor** *n.* one who wins a struggle or contest **—vic´tor, vic·to´ri·ous** *adj.* **—vic´to·ry** *n.*
**vict´uals** *pl. n.* food prepared for consumption
**vid´e·o** *adj.* pertaining to television; producing a signal convertible into a television picture *—n.* a television image
**vid´e·o·con·fer·ence** *n.* a meeting between participants at a distance from each other via closed-circuit television
**vie** *vi.* to put forth effort; to compete in an athletic contest; to contend for superiority: *to vie for position*
**view** *n.* the act of seeing or examining; range of vision; something seen; one´s opinion or belief *—vt.* to look at; to examine; to consider; to regard in a certain way **—view´a·ble** *adj.* **—view´er** *n.*
**vig´il** *n.* the act or period of keeping watch
**vig´i·lant** *adj.* alert to danger; wary **—vig´i·lance** *n.* **—vig´i·lant·ly** *adv.*
**vig·i·lan´te** *n.* a member of a vigilance committee; one who advocates preempting the law **—vig·i·lan´tism** *n.*
**vi·gnette´** *n.* a picture that shades off gradually into the background; a brief literary sketch; a decorative design, as at the beginning of a book, chapter of a book, etc.
**vig´or** *n.* energy; vital or natural growth; intensity **—vig´or·ous** *adj.* **—vig´or·ous·ly** *adv.* **—vig´or·ous·ness** *n.*
**vile** *adj.* morally base; corrupt; loathsome; very bad, as *vile tasting* **—vile´ly** *adv.* **—vile´ness** *n.*
**vil´i·fy** *vt.* to speak of abusively; to defame **—vil·i·fi·ca´tion** *n.* **—vil´i·fi·er** *n.*
**vil´lage** *n.* in the US, a residential area smaller than a town but larger than a hamlet; the inhabitants of a village collectively **—vil´lag·er** *n.*
**vil´lain** *n.* a scoundrel
**vil´lain·ous** *adj.* wicked; evil **—vil´lain·ous·ly** *adv.* **—vil´lain·y** *n.*
**vim** *n.* force or vigor; energy
**vin´ci·ble** *adj.* easily overcome; that can be conquered or defeated **—vin·ci·bil´i·ty** *n.* **—vin´ci·bly** *adv.*
**vin´di·cate** *vt.* to clear of suspicion; to maintain, as a right or claim; to justify **—vin·di·ca´tion** *n.* **—vin´di·ca·tive, vin´di·ca·to·ry** *adj.* **—vin´di·ca·tor** *n.*
**vin·dic´tive** *adj.* having a vengeful spirit **—vin·dic´tive·ly** *adv.* **—vin·dic´tive·ness** *n.*
**vine** *n.* a climbing plant
**vin´e·gar** *n.* a variously flavored condiment and preservative; ascerbity, as of speech **—vin´e·gar·y** *adj.*
**vine´yard** *n.* an area devoted to the cultivation of grapes
**vin´i·cul·ture** *n.* the cultivation of grapes for wine **—vin´i·cul´tur·al** *adj.* **—vin´i·cul´tur·ist** *n.*
**vin´i·fy** *vt.* to convert into wine **—vin·i·fi·ca´tion** *n.*
**vi´nous** *adj.* pertaining to or characteristic of wine
**vin´tage** m. the yield of grapes or wine for one season; the region and year in which a wine is produced *—adj.* of a fine wine; of a good year for wine
**vint´ner** *n.* a wine maker; a wine merchant
**vi´nyl** *n.* a type of plastic

**vi·o´la** *n.* a musical instrument similar to a violin, slightly larger and with a deeper tone

**vi´ol·a·ble** *adj.* that can be or is likely to be violated **—vi·o·la·bil´i·ty, vi´ol·a·ble·ness** *n.* **—vi´ol·a·bly** *adv.*

**vi´o·late** *vt.* to break, as a law, agreement, etc.; to ravish or rape; to offend **—vi·o·la´tion** *n.* **—vi´o·la·tive** *adj.* **—vi´o·la·tor** *n.*

**vi´o·lence** *n.* physical force used to injure, damage, or destroy; intensity, severity; injury or damage, as by distortion or alteration

**vi´o·lent** *adj.* marked by great physical force or intense emotional excitement; characterized by intensity of any kind **—vi´o·lent·ly** *adv.*

**vi´o·let** *n.* a bluish-purple color; a plant or herb bearing violet-colored flowers

**vi·o·lin´** *n.* a stringed instrument of the highest register, usually played with a bow; a violinist

**vi·o·lin´ist** *n.* one who plays the violin

**vi´ol·ist** *n.* one who plays the viola

**vi·o·lon·cel´lo** *n.* a cello **—vi·o·lon·cel´list** *n.*

**vi´per** *n.* a kind of snake; a treacherous or spiteful person **—vi´per·ine** *adj.*

**vi´per·ish** *adj.* malicious or spiteful

**vi´per·ous** *adj.* pertaining to vipers or snakes; treacherous or spiteful **—vi´per·ous·ly** *adv.*

**vi·ra´go** *n.* an ill-tempered woman; a shrew

**vi´ral** *adj.* pertaining to or caused by a virus **—vi´ral·ly** *adv.*

**vi·res´cent** *adj.* greenish **—vi·res´cence** *n.*

**vir´gin** *n.* one who has never had sexual intercourse; an unmarried woman *—adj.* being a virgin; pertaining or suited to a virgin; uncorrupted, pure; not hitherto used or processed, as *virgin wool, virgin forest* **—vir´gin·al** *adj.* **—vir´gin·al·ly** *adv.* **—vir·gin´i·ty** *n.*

**vir´gule** *n.* a diagonal mark (/)

**vir·i·des´cent** *adj.* greenish; turning green **—vir·i·des´cence** *n.*

**vir´ile** *adj.* having the vigor or strength of manhood; able to procreate **—vi·ril´i·ty** *n.*

**vi·rol´o·gy** *n.* the study of viruses **—vi·rol´o·gist** *n.*

**vir´tu·al** *adj.* existing in essence or effect, but not in actual form **—vir·tu·al´i·ty** *n.* **—vir´tu·al·ly** *adv.*

**vir´tue** *n.* moral excellence; any admirable quality

**vir·tu·os´i·ty** *n.* technical mastery, as of a musical instrument

**vir·tu·o´so** *n.* a master of technique, especially in the arts *—adj.* capable of or displaying extraordinary skill: *a virtuoso violinist*

**vir´tu·ous** *adj.* righteous; pure and chaste **—vir´tu·ous·ly** *adv.* **—vir´tu·ous·ness** *n.*

**vir´u·lent** *adj.* extremely harmful; very infectious; full of hatred **—vir´u·lence** *n.* **—vir´u·lent·ly** *adv.*

**vi´rus** *n.* a parasite capable of reproduction only within living cells; a disease caused by a parasite; any evil influence

**vi´sa** *n.* official endorsement on a passport that permits the bearer to enter a country

**vis´age** *n.* appearance; aspect **—vis´aged** *adj.*

**vis´cer·a** *n.* the internal organs of the body

**vis´cer·al** *adj.* pertaining to the viscera; instinctive or emotional **—vis´cer·al·ly** *adv.*

**vis·cos´i·ty** *n.* a property of fluids by which they offer resistance to flow or change

**vis´cous** *adj.* resistant to flow; of high viscosity **—vis´cous·ly** *adv.* **—vis´cous·ness** *n.*

**vise** *(US) n.* a clamping device, as used to hold material for woodworking *—vt.* to hold or squeeze, as in a vise

**vis´i·ble** *adj.* capable of being seen; that can be perceived **—vis·i·bil´i·ty, vis´i·ble·ness** *n.* **—vis´i·bly** *adv.*

**vi´sion** *n.* the sense of sight; that which is seen; something beautiful; a mental image; foresight; imagination **—vi´sion·al** *adv.*

**vi´sion·ar·y** *adj.* existing in the imagination; affected by fantasies; speculative; impractical *—n.* one who has visions; one who plans or projects are impractical or unrealistic **—vi´sion·ar·i·ness** *n.*

**vis´it** *vt.* to look in on a person out of friendship, to meet in order to conduct business; to go or come to a place; to be a guest of; to inflict upon *—vi.* to pay a call; to stay with temporarily *—n.* a social call; a short stay **—vis´i·tor** *n.*

**vis´i·tant** *n.* a visitor; a migratory bird

**vis·it·a´tion** *n.* the act of visiting; an official inspection or examination **—vis·it·a´tion·al** *adj.*

**vi´sor** *n.* a projection, as on a hat, to shield the eyes

**vis´ta** *n.* a view; a mental image

**vi´su·al** *adj.* pertaining to the sense of sight; perceptible by sight; done or perceived only by sight *—n.* pictures, charts, etc. used to enhance a presentation **—vis´u·al·ly** *adv.* **—vis·u·al´i·ty** *n.*

**vis´u·al·ize** *vt., vi.* to form a mental image; to picture in the mind **—vis·u·al·i·za´tion** *n.* **—vis´u·al·iz·er** *n.*

**vi´tal** *adj.* pertaining to life; essential to or supporting life; of the utmost importance; dynamic and full of life **—vi´tal·ly** *adv.* **—vi´tal·ness** *n.*

**vi´tal·ism** *n.* the belief that a living organism is sustained by a vital force independent of all chemical and physical processes **—vi´tal·ist** *n.* **—vi·tal·is´tic** *adj.*

**vi·tal´i·ty** *n.* the power to live and develop; physical or mental energy

**vi´tal·ize** *vt.* to endow with life or energy; to make more spirited or energetic **—vi·tal·i·za´tion** *n.*

**vi´ta·min** *n.* any of a group of naturally occurring organic substances essential to the body´s normal health and growth

**vi´ti·ate** *vt.* to impair the use or value of; to render weak or ineffective; to make legally invalid **—vi·ti·**

**a´tion** *n.* **–vi´ti·a·tor** *n.*

**vit´i·cul·ture** *n.* the cultivation of grapes **–vit·i·cul´tur·al** *adj.* **–vit´i·cul·tur·ist** *n.*

**vit´re·ous** *adj.* glassy; obtained from glass; of the vitreous humor *–n.* the vitreous humor **–vit·re·os´i·ty, vit´re·ous·ness** *n.*

**vitreous humor** the clear jelly-like substance that fills the eyeball

**vit´ri·fy** *vt., vi.* to change or become changed into a glass or glass-like substance **–vit·ri·fi·a·bil´i·ty** *n.* **–vit´ri·fi·a·ble** *adj.* **–vit·ri·fi·ca´tion** *n.*

**vit´ri·ol** *n.* a sulfate of metal; sulfuric acid; harshness or bitterness of thought or expression; reproach

**vit·ri·ol´ic** *adj.* acrimonious; harsh or bitter, as *a vitriolic critique*

**vi·tu´per·ate** *vt.* to fault abusively; to berate or scold **–vi·tu´per·a·tive** *adj.* **–vi·tu´per·a·tive·ly** *adv.*

**vi·tu·per·a´tion** *n.* harsh or abusive language; the use of such language **–vi·tu´per·a·tor** *n.*

**vi·va´cious** *adj.* full of life and spirit **–vi·va´cious·ly** *adv.* **–vi·va´cious·ness, vi·vac´i·ty** *n.*

**viv´id** *adj.* strong or intense, as of color; suggesting life-like images; producing a sharp impression on the senses **–viv´id·ly** *adv.* **–viv´id·ness** *n.*

**viv´i·fy** *vt.* to give life to; to animate; to make more vivid or striking **–viv·i·fi·ca´tion** *n.* **–viv´i·fi·er** *n.*

**vi·vip´a·rous** *adj.* bringing forth live young that have developed within the mother's body **–viv·i·par´i·ty, vi·vip´a·rous·ness** *n.* **–vi·vip´a·rous·ly** *adv.*

**viv·i·sec´tion** *n.* cutting or dissection on a living animal **–viv´i·sect** *vt.* **–viv·i·sec´tion·al** *adj.* **–viv·i·sec´tion·ist** *n.*

**vix´en** *n.* a female fox; a quarrelsome or malevolent woman **–vix´en·ish** *adj.* **–vix´en·ly** *adj., adv.*

**vo·cab´u·lar·y** *n.* all the words of a language; all the words understood by an individual

**vo´cal** *adj.* pertaining to the voice; able to speak or utter sounds; speaking freely **–vo´cal·ly** *adv.* **–vo´cal·ness** *n.*

**vo´cal·ise** *(Brit.) vt.* to voice or make vocal *–vi.* to speak or sing

**vo´cal·ism** *n.* the use of the voice; a particular singing style

**vo´cal·ist** *n.* a singer; one who sings as a profession **–vo·cal·is´tic** *adj.*

**vo´cal·ize** *(US) vt.* to voice or make vocal *–vi.* to speak or sing **–vo·cal·i·za´tion** *n.* **–vo´cal·iz·er** *n.*

**vo·ca´tion** *n.* a regular job or profession; a career

**vo·ca´tion·al** *adj.* pertaining to a job or profession; of training designed to provide specific useful skills or those being trained: *vocational school* **–vo·ca´tion·al·ly** *adv.*

**vo·cif´er·ant** *adj.* vociferous

**vo·cif´er·ate** *vt., vi.* to cry out with a loud voice; to protest boisterously **–vo·cif·er·a´tion** *n.* **–vo·cif´er·a·tor** *n.*

**vo·cif´er·ous** *adj.* characterized by a loud outcry; noisy; clamorous **–vo·cif´er·ous·ly** *adv.* **–vo·cif´er·ous·ness** *n.*

**vogue** *n.* a fashion or style; popularity **–vogu´ish** *adj.* **–vogu´ish·ly** *adv.* **–vogu´ish·ness** *n.*

**voice** *n.* sound produced by the vocal organs; the quality of a sound; the right to expression, as of opinion, choice, etc.; the agency by which something is expressed: *our newspaper is the voice of the community* *–vt.* to put into speech; to give expression to **–voiced** *adj.* **–voiced´ness** *n.*

**voice´less** *adj.* having no voice or vote; having no means of expression **–voice´less·ly** *adv.* **–voice´less·ness** *n.*

**void** *adj.* containing nothing; completely lacking; having no legal force; useless **–void´a·ble** *adj.* **–void´ance** *n.*

**voile** *n.* a fine, sheer fabric

**vol´a·tile** *adj.* evaporating rapidly; prone to change suddenly and sharply; fleeting **–vol´la·tile·ness, vo·la·til´i·ty** *n.*

**vol´a·til·ize** *vi., vt.* to pass off or cause to pass off as vapor; to become or make volatile **–vol´a·til·iz·a·ble** *adj.* **–vo·la·til·i·za´tion** *n.* **–vol´a·til·iz´er** *n.*

**vol·can´ic** *adj.* pertaining to or produced by a volcano or volcanoes; like a volcano; explosive or violent **–vol·can´i·cal·ly** *adv.* **–vol·can·ic´i·ty** *n.*

**vol·ca´no** *n.* an opening in the earth from which hot matter is or has been ejected; a mound or mountain formed by ejected material

**vol·can·ol´o·gy** *n.* the study of volcanoes **–vol·can·o·log´ic, vol·can·o·log´i·cal** *adj.* **–vol·can·ol´o·gist** *n.*

**vo·li´tion** *n.* exercise of the will; willpower; the power to make a choice **–vo·li´tion·al, vo·li´tion·ar·y, vol´i·tive** *adj.* **–vo·li´tion·al·ly** *adv.*

**vol´ley** *n.* a simultaneous discharge; a discharge of many things, as bullets, stones, etc. *–vt., vi.* to discharge or be discharged in large numbers

**volt** *n.* a unit of electric and electromotive potential

**volt´age** *n.* electromotive force expressed in volts

**volt´me·ter** *n.* an instrument for measuring differences of electric potential

**vol´u·ble** *adj.* having fluency in speaking; talkative **–vo´lu·bil´i·ty, vol´u·ble·ness** *n.* **–vol´u·bly** *adv.*

**vol´ume** *n.* a book, especially one that is part of a set; a bound set of periodicals; an amount, as of number, space, sound, etc.; a capacity or space occupied, as of a container or area

**vo·lu´mi·nous** *adj.* sufficient to fill volumes; large or extensive **–vo·lu·mi·nos´i·ty, vo·lu´mi·nous·ness** *n.* **–vo·lu´mi·nous·ly** *adv.*

**vol´un·ta·rism** *n.* the use of volunteer labor to achieve an end, such as for staffing phones or raising funds;

willing participation; the philosophy that free will is fundamental to individual action or experience **–vol´un·ta·rist** *n.* **–vol·un·ta·ris´tic** *adj.*

**vol´un·tar·y** *adj.* done of one´s own free will; acting without constraint; intentional; able to choose or elect: optional; supported by charitable donations of money or time **–vol´un·tar´i·ly** *adv.* **–vol´un·tar·i·ness** *n.*

**vol·un·teer´** *n.* an unpaid worker; one who enters into or performs of his own free will *–adj.* pertaining to or composed of volunteers *–vt.* to offer or give voluntarily *–vi.* to enter or offer to enter into a service without pay

**vol·un·teer´ism** *n.* the practice of being a volunteer or using unpaid volunteer workers, such as in a charitable organization

**vo·lup´tu·ar·y** *n.* one addicted to luxury and indulgence *–adj.* pertaining to or marked by luxury and extravagance

**vo·lup´tu·ous** *adj.* pertaining to sensuous or sensual gratification; suggesting the satisfaction of sensual desire **–vo·lup´tu·ous·ly** *adv.* **–vo·lup´tu·ous·ness** *n.*

**vom´it** *vi., vt.* to disgorge the contents of the stomach *–n.* matter ejected in vomiting **–vom´it·er** *n.*

**voo´doo** *n.* a religion characterized by belief in sorcery and the use of charms, etc.; a charm or spell believed to have magical powers *–vt.* to bewitch *–adj.* – **voo´doo·ism** *n.* **–voo´doo·ist** *n.* **–voo·doo·is´tic** *adj.*

**vo·ra´cious** *n.* eager, insatiable; eating greedily – **vo·ra´cious·ly** *adv.* **–vo·ra´cious·ness, vo·rac´i·ty** *n.*

**vor´tex** *n., pl.* **vor´tex·es, vor´ti·ces** a mass of rotating or whirling fluid; something resembling a vortex, as a situation difficult to escape **–vor´ti·cal** *adj.* **–vor´ti·cal·ly** *adv.*

**vo´ta·rist, vo´ta·ry** *n.* one bound by vows, as a nun or priest; one who is intensely devoted, as a believer or ardent disciple; one devoted to a particular pursuit or study

**vote** *n.* a formal expression of choice; a ballot or other means of expressing choice; the number of ballots cast; the right to vote; a voter *–vt.* to determine by vote; to cast one´s vote for *–vi.* to cast one´s vote

**vo´tive** *adj.* performed in fulfillment of a vow **–vo´tive·ly** *adv.* **–vo´tive·ness** *n.*

**vouch** *vi.* to give assurance or guarantee; to support or justify *–vt.* to bear witness to; to declare; to provide or disclose as support or justification

**vouch´er** *n.* a document that serves to authorize or attest; one who vouches for another

**vouch·safe´** *vt.* to permit or grant *–vi.* to condescend or deign

**vow** *n.* a solemn promise; an emphatic affirmation *–vt.* to promise solemnly; to make a solemn promise or threat *–vi.* to make a vow

**voy´age** *n.* a long journey *–vi.* to make a voyage – **voy´ag·er** *n.*

**vo·yeur´** *n.* one who is sexually gratified by observing sexual objects or acts; one obsessed with the viewing of sensational or sordid events **–vo·yeur´ism** *n.* **–voy·eur·is´tic** *adj.* **–voy·eur·is´ti·cal·ly** *adv.*

**vul´can·ize** *vt., vi.* to process, as rubber, in order to increase strength and elasticity **–vul·can·i·za´tion** *n.* **–vul´can·iz·er** *n.*

**vul´gar** *adj.* lacking manners, taste, etc.; offensive or obscene; of or pertaining to the common people; pertaining to a common language or dialect **–vul·gar´i·ty** *n.* **–vul´gar·ly** *adv.*

**vul·gar´i·an** *n.* a person of vulgar taste or manners, especially a wealthy person prone to ostentatious display

**vul´gar·ism** *n.* a word or expression generally considered to be in poor taste

**vul´gar·ize** *vt.* to make common or coarse; to popularize **–vul´gar·i·za´tion** *n.*

**vul´ner·a·ble** *adj.* open to attack or injury; open to criticism; susceptible to temptation **–vul·ner·a·bil´i·ty, vul´ner·a·ble·ness** *n.* **–vul´ner·a·bly** *adv.*

**vul´ture** *n.* a large bird that feeds on carrion; someone who preys in others **–vul´tur·ous** *adj.*

**vy´ing** *adj.* that vies or competes

**w, W** twenty-third letter of the English alphabet

**wack´y, whacky** *adj.* extremely irrational; erratic **–wack´i·ly** *adv.* **–wack´i·ness** *n.*

**wad** *n.* a small mass; a roll of currency: *–vt.* to press, roll, fold, etc. into a wad *–vi.* to form into a wad

**wad´dle** *n.* a rocking walk like that of a duck *–vi.* to move awkwardly **–wad'dler** *n.* **–wad´dly** *adj.*

**wade** *vi.* to walk through something that offers resistance, such as water; to proceed laboriously: *wade through a mountain of paperwork –vt.* to cross by walking on the bottom, as of a river

**wad´er** *n.* one who wades **–wad´ers** *n.* high waterproof boots

**wader, wading bird** a variety of long-legged bird that feeds in shallow water, such as a crane or stork

**waf´er** *n.* a thin, crisp cookie, cracker, etc.; a disk of gum used for sealing, as papers, etc.: *a wafer seal*

**waf´fle** *n.* a crisp batter cake *–vi.* to be evasive **–waf´fler** *n.* **–waf´fling·ly** *adv.* **–waf´fly** *adj.*

**waft** *vt.* to bear gently through the air or over water *–vi.* to blow gently *–n.* lightly passing air, sound, or aroma **–waft´er** *n.*

**wag** *vi., vt.* to move or cause to move rapidly, as a dog's tail *–n.* a wagging motion; a droll person; a wit

**wage** *n.* payment; reward or consequence *–vt.* to engage in, as *to wage war*

**wa´ger** *vt., vi.* to gamble *–n.* a bet; the thing bet on or the amount of a stake

**wag´ger·y** *n.* mischievous joking

**wag´gish** *adj.* humorous; said or done as a joke —**wag´gish·ly** *adv.* —**wag´gish·ness** *n.*

**wag´gle** *vt.* to swing with short quick motions —*vi.* to move unsteadily —**wag´gling·ly** *adv.* —**wag´gly** *adj.*

**wag´on** *n.* a four-wheeled vehicle for carrying heavy loads; a child's cart; a small food or beverage cart; a vehicle selling prepared food: *a lunch wagon*

**waif** *n.* a homeless child; a stray animal

**wail** *vi.* to make a mournful, crying sound —*vt.* to mourn or lament; to cry out in sorrow —**wail´er** *n.* —**wail´ful** *adj.* —**wail´ful·ly, wail´ing·ly** *adv.*

**wain´scot, wain´scot·ing** *n.* paneling for inner walls

**wain´wright** *n.* a maker of wagons

**waist** *n.* the narrowed middle of the body or object

**waist´coat** *(Brit.) n.* a short, sleeveless garment worn over a shirt; *(US)* a vest —**waist´coat·ed** *adj.*

**wait** *vi.* to anticipate; to pause; to delay; to remain in readiness —*vt.* to remain in expectation of; to delay: *wait for us*; to work as a waiter or waitress: *to wait tables* —*n.* *(Brit.)* musicians employed to play at a public function; street carolers or musicians

**wait´er** *n.* a man employed to serve, as in a restaurant; one who awaits; a tray for serving food

**wait´ing** *n.* expectant; remaining inactive

**wait´ress** *n.* a woman hired to serve, as in a restaurant

**waive** *vt.* to forego a claim to; to put off temporarily

**waiv´er** *n.* voluntary relinquishment; the instrument which evidences relinquishment

**wake**[1] *vi.* to emerge from sleep; to become alert —*vt.* to rouse from sleep; to make aware of or alert to —*n.* a watch or vigil, especially over the body of a deceased person; *(Brit.)* an annual parish festival; *(Brit.)* an annual vacation from work —**wak´er** *n.*

**wake**[2] *n.* the trail left by a vessel moving through the water; the track or turbulence left by anything that has passed: *the truck left a cloud of dust in its wake* —**in the wake of** following immediately after: *cheers were heard in the wake of the announcement*

**wake´ful** *adj.* not sleepy; watchful, alert; restless —**wake´ful·ly** *adv.* —**wake´ful·ness** *n.*

**wak´en** *vt.* to rouse from sleep; to stir up: *the speech wakened his patriotic fervor* —*vi.* to wake up; to become active or animated —**wak´en·er** *n.*

**wak´ing** *adj.* characterized by consciousness or awareness

**wale** *n.* a ridge or rib on cloth —*vt.* to raise welts by striking; to manufacture cloth with ridges

**walk** *vi.* to advance by moving the feet; to behave in a certain manner: *to walk in peace*; to leave abruptly: *they walked out* —*vt.* to force or help to walk: *walk the bicycle uphill*; to escort on a walk; to cause to move as though walking: *walk the refrigerator away from the wall, walk them through the procedure* —*n.* the act of walking; a distinctive manner of walking; a place for walking; status in society: *she was supported by people of all walks* —**walk all over** to mistreat —**walk off with** to steal —**walk on air** to feel exhilarated or euphoric —**walk out on** to abandon —**walk´er** *n.*

**walk´out** *n.* a labor strike

**walk´-up** *n.* an apartment located above the ground floor in a building with no elevator

**wall** *n.* a structure designed to enclose or divide an area; something resembling a wall: *a wall of silence* —*vt.* to provide with a wall; to enclose or separate with a wall —*adj.* attached to or built into a wall —**drive up a wall** to frustrate or distress —**off the wall** unconventional; eccentric —**wall´less** *adj.* —**wall´like** *adj.*

**wal´la·by** *n.* a small kangaroo

**wall´eye** *n.* an eye with a light-coloured iris; a condition in which the eyes diverge; a type of fish —**wall´eyed** *adj.*

**wall´flow·er** *n.* one who is shy or unpopular

**wal´lop** *vt.* to beat soundly; to strike a hard blow —*n.* a hard blow —**wal´lop·er** *n.*

**wal´lop·ing** *adj.* very large —*n.* a beating; a defeat

**wal´low** *vi.* to roll about in mud, snow, etc.; to be plentiful: *wallowing in profits*; to indulge oneself: *he wallowed in self-pity* —*n.* the act of wallowing; a depression or hollow —**wal´low·er** *n.*

**wall´-to-wall´** *adj.* completely covered: *wall-to-wall carpeting*; completely filled: *wall-to-wall people*

**waltz** *n.* a ballroom dance —*vi.* to dance a waltz; to move quickly —**waltz´er** *n.*

**wan** *adj.* pale, as from sickness; faint or feeble —**wan´ly** *adv.* —**wan´ness** *n.*

**wand** *n.* a slender rod waved by a conjurer; a staff symbolizing authority; a musician's baton

**wan´der** *vi.* to roam; to go casually or by an indirect route; to meander; to stray —*vt.* to meander across or through —**wan´der·er** *n.* —**wan´der·ing·ly** *adv.*

**wan´der·lust** *n.* an impulse to travel; restlessness

**wane** *vi.* to diminish; to decline or decrease gradually —*n.* a decreasing; a period of decline

**wan´gle** *vt.* to obtain by indirect or dishonest means —*vi.* to resort to irregular methods —**wan´gler** *n.*

**want** *vt.* to feel a wish for; to desire; to lack; to request or require: *wanted on the phone* —*vi.* to have need; to be destitute —*n.* a lack scarcity; poverty —**want´er** *n.* —**want´less** *adj.* —**want´less·ness** *n.*

**want´ing** *adj.* missing or lacking; not coming up to some standard, need, or expectation

**wan´ton** *adj.* licentious or lewd; heartless; unrestrained; capricious or unprovoked —*vi.* to act in a wanton manner —*vt.* to squander —*n.* a lewd or licentious person —**wan´ton·ly** *adv.* —**wan´ton·ness** *n.*

**wap´i·ti** *n.* the American elk

**war** *n.* armed strife between nations, states, etc.; any conflict or struggle; warfare —*vi.* to wage war; to fight to be in opposition or contention —*adj.* pertaining to war or its aftermath: *war orphans*

**war´ble** *vi., vt.* to sing with trills, tremulo, etc. —*n.* the act or sound of warbling —**war´bler** *n.*

**war chest** a fund set aside for a purpose, such as for a political campaign

**ward** *n.* a section of a hospital: *maternity ward*; an administrative division of a city; one in the charge of a guardian or the state; the act of guarding or being guarded —*vt.* to repel or turn aside

**war´den** *n.* a supervisor or custodian; *(Brit.)* an executive or administrative officer; *(US)* the chief administrative officer of a prison

**ward´er** *n.* a person who guards or protects; *(Brit.)* a prison guard —**ward´er•ship** *n.*

**ward´robe** *n.* a cabinet for storing apparel; the costumes belonging to a theater or theater group; the room where theater costumes are kept; collectively, all the garments that belong to a person, or those suited to a particular season: *winter wardrobe*

**ward´room** *n.* eating or living quarters for commissioned officers aboard a warship

**ward´ship** *n.* the state of being a ward; custody

**ware** *n.* articles of the same type collectively, as *glassware, hardware,* etc.; dishes or pottery, especially those of a particular kind; merchandise displayed for sale

**ware´house** *n.* a place where goods are kept awaiting sale or use; a storehouse; *(Brit.)* a large retail store —*vt.* to keep in a warehouse —**ware´house•man** *n.*

**war´fare** *n.* the waging of war; struggle or strife

**war horse** a veteran of many struggles, as a politician

**war´like** *adj.* fond of war; threatening war

**war´lock** *n.* a male witch; a sorcerer

**war´lord** *n.* a military commander who governs; a militaristic head of state —**war´lord•ism** *n.*

**warm** *adj.* moderately or relatively hot; imparting or preserving warmth: *warm clothing*; heated, as from exertion; cordial or friendly; recently made, as *warm from the oven*; suggesting warmth, as of a color —*vt., vi.* to make or become heated, interested, or excited: *she warmed to the idea of redecorating*; to become friendly; to fill with or feel pleasure: *it warms the heart* —**warm´er** *n.* —**warm´ly** *adv.* —**warm´ness** *n.*

**warm´-blood´ed** *adj.* having a nearly constant, warm body temperature; ardent or passionate —**warm´-blood´ed•ness** *n.*

**warmed´-o´ver** *adj.* reheated, as of leftover food; stale or hackneyed; made ineffectual by overuse

**warm´-heart•ed** *adj.* kind; sympathetic; generous —**warm´heart•ed•ly** *adv.* —**warm´heart•ed•ness** *n.*

**warm´ish** *adj.* somewhat warm

**war´mon•ger** *n.* one who tries to provoke war —**war´mon•ger•ing** *adj., n.*

**warmth** *n.* a sense of being warm or comfortable; ardor or excitement; friendliness or understanding

**warn** *vt.* to alert to danger; to advise; to give notice to go or stay away —*vi.* to give warning —**warn´er** *n.*

**warn´ing** *n.* the act of giving notice or being alerted; that which alerts or advises —*adj.* serving to give notice or warn: *a warning light* —**warn´ing•ly** *adv.*

**warp** *vt.* to twist out of shape, as for a piece of wood; to corrupt or pervert; to divert from a proper course; to arrange strands for weaving so as to run lengthwise —*vi.* to become twisted; to go astray —*n.* a condition of being twisted out of shape; a distortion; an abnormality; a mental or moral aberration; woven strands that run the length of a fabric —**warp´er** *n.* —**warp´ing** *n.*

**war´rant** *n.* an order that provides legal authorization for arrest, search, etc.; a guarantee; a sanction or justification —*vt.* to assure the quality of; to guarantee against loss if a product does not perform as advertised; to give legal authority; to guarantee clear title to property —**war•rant•a•bil´i•ty, war´rant•a•ble•ness** *n.* —**war´rant•a•ble** *adj.* —**war´rant•a•bly** *adv.*

**war´rant•ee´** *n.* the person to whom a warranty is given

**war´ran•tor´, war´rant•er** *n.* one who makes or issues a warrant or who gives a warranty to another

**war´ran•ty** *n.* a guarantee by a seller that whatever is sold is as represented; an official authorization or warrant; justification for a course of action; legal assurance by a seller of property that the title is free and clear

**war´ren** *n.* a place where rabbits are kept; an enclosure for small animals; an overcrowded living space

**war´ri•or** *n.* one engaged or experienced in warfare

**wart** *n.* a small, hard growth on the skin; any of various natural growths on certain plants and animals —**wart´ed, wart´y** *adj.*

**war´y** *adj.* watchful: *be wary of easy money*; marked by caution; shrewd —**war´i•ly** *adv.* —**war´i•ness** *n.*

**wash** *vt.* to cleanse with a liquid; to cover with liquid; to soak or rinse; to flow against or over; to coat with a thin layer of pigment —*vi.* to bathe or launder; to be removed or drawn off by a liquid; to bear close scrutiny: *his alibi won't wash* —*n.* the process of wetting or cleaning with liquid; clothes set aside to be laundered; a surge of water or the turbulence caused by rushing water: *wash from a boat's propeller*; removal or deposit of topsoil by rushing water; an area periodically covered by water; a preparation for washing or coating; a thin coating of pigment: —**come out in the wash** to be revealed —**wash one´s hands of** to renounce —**wash out** to be removed, damaged, or destroyed by moving water; to be eliminated, as from school or a sports team

**wash´a•ble** *adj.* that can be laundered without damage —**wash•a•bil´i•ty** *n.*

**wash´ba•sin, wash´bowl** *n.* a water container for washing the hands and face

**wash´board** *n.* a board having a corrugated surface for

scrubbing laundry
**washed´-out´** *adj.* faded; exhausted
**washed´-up´** *adj.* finished; no longer capable
**wash´er** *n.* one or that which washes; a small, flat disk used to tighten a nut or a joint
**wash´out** *n.* erosion by the action of water; a failure
**wash´room** *n.* a lavatory
**wash´stand** *n.* a cabinet for holding a pitcher, washbowl, etc.; a bathroom sink
**wash´tub** *n.* a large vessel used for laundry
**wasp** *n.* an insect with a slender segmented body, related to the bee
**wasp´ish** *adj.* like a wasp: having a slender figure; irritable **–wasp´ish·ly** *adv.* **–wasp´ish·ness** *n.*
**wasp waist** a slim, narrow waist **–wasp-waist·ed** *adj.*
**was´sail** *n.* an ancient toast; a spiced drink of ale and wine; a celebration *–vi.* to revel or carouse *–vt.* to drink to the health of **–was´sail·er** *n.*
**wast´age** *n.* that lost by leakage, etc.
**waste** *vt.* to use thoughtlessly; to squander; to make weak; to fail to use or take advantage of; to devastate *–vi.* to lose vigor, etc.; to diminish; to pass gradually, as time *–n.* thoughtless or unnecessary consumption; failure to benefit; a desolate place; a gradual wearing away; something discarded **–wast´er** *n.*
**wast´ed** *adj.* needlessly depleted; useless or excessive: *wasted effort*; frail or feeble, as from illness; inebriated or under the influence of a narcotic
**waste´ful** *adj.* prone to or causing waste; extravagant **–waste´ful·ly** *adv.* **–waste´ful·ness** *n.*
**waste´land** *n.* a barren or desolate land
**waste pipe** a conduit for carrying off waste
**wast´er** *n.* a spendthrift or squanderer; an idler
**wast´ing** *adj.* destructive; enfeebling **–wast´ing·ly** *adv.*
**was´trel** *n.* a spendthrift; an idler
**watch** *vi.* to observe closely; to be on the alert; to wait expectantly; to function as a guard; to keep a religious vigil *–vt.* to look attentively; to keep informed: *watch the course of the election campaign*; to be alert for; to guard *–n.* careful observation; an attitude of alertness; one in service as a guard; the time of being on guard duty; a small timepiece, as worn on the wrist or carried in a pocket; a religious vigil **–watch´er** *n.*
**watch´case** *n.* a covering for a watch
**watch´dog** *n.* a guard dog; a person who serves to protect against waste, unlawful or prohibited acts, etc.
**watch´ful** *adj.* vigilant; alert **–watch´ful·ly** *adv.* **–watch´ful·ness** *n.*
**watch´man** *n.* one who guards and protects
**watch´word** *n.* a password; a slogan
**wa´ter** *n.* the colorless liquid that is an essential constituent of all organisms; a body of water; a supply of water; preparation of water holding a substance in solution, such as urine *–vt.* to provide with water; to dilute with water *–vi.* to discharge water **–keep one´s head above water** to stay out of difficulty **–water down** to dilute in some manner, such as by increasing shares in a corporation without adding to assets **–watered-down** *adj.* **–water under the bridge** a past event that is to be forgiven or forgotten **–wa´ter·er** *n.*
**wa´ter·bed** *n.* a bed with a water-filled mattress
**wa´ter·borne** *adj.* floating on water; transported on a ship, etc.
**water clock** a timepiece operated by water
**water closet** *(Brit.)* a toilet
**wa´ter·col·or** *n.* a water-soluble pigment or coloring matter; a painting rendered in watercolors *–adj.* painted with watercolors **–wa´ter·col·or·ist** *n.*
**wa´ter·course** *n.* a flow of water, as a river, stream, etc.; a channel for water
**wa´ter·fowl** *n.* a swimming game bird
**wa´ter·front** *n.* property abutting or overlooking a body of water; an area of docks, warehouses, etc.
**water gap** a deep ravine permitting passage of water, usually the course of a river or stream
**wa´ter·glass** *n.* a drinking vessel; a gauge for indicating water level; a bucket-like device with a glass bottom, used for examining objects under water
**watering hole** a pond or pool frequented by wildlife; a tavern or pub
**wa´ter·ish** *adj.* resembling water: clear; watery
**water level** *n.* the relative elevation of the surface of a body of water; a ship's waterline
**wa´ter·line** *n.* a line on the hull of a ship which shows where the water surface reaches; a mark showing the level to which water has risen, as during a flood
**wa´ter·logged** *adj.* soaked with water; so saturated as to be unmanageable and barely able to float
**water main** a primary conduit for carrying water
**wa´ter·mark** *n.* a waterline; a design impressed into paper when it is made *–vt.* to impress with a watermark
**water mill** a mill with water-powered equipment
**water nymph** a mythical being that dwells in a stream, lake, etc.
**water pipe** a conduit for water; a tobacco pipe designed so that the smoke is filtered and cooled by water
**wa´ter·pow·er** *n.* energy derived from flowing or falling water
**wa´ter·shed** *n.* the region from which a river receives its supply of water; a decisive turning point
**wa´ter·spout** *n.* a moving, whirling column of water; a pipe for discharging water
**water table** the upper level of saturated subterranean rock
**wa´ter·tight** *adj.* so closely made that water cannot leak through; that cannot be misunderstood, found illegal, or in error **–wa´ter·tight·ness** *n.*

**water tower** a tank used as a reservoir to maintain water pressure
**water vapor** moisture below the boiling point mixed in the air
**wa´ter·way** *n.* a river etc., especially when navigable
**water wheel** a wheel turned by flowing water, used for power or for raising water
**wa´ter·works** *n.* a system of pumps, pipes, etc. for furnishing a water supply
**wa´ter·worn** *adj.* worn smooth or eroded by running or falling water
**wa´ter·y** *adj.* like water; diluted **–wa´ter·i·ness** *n.*
**watt** *n.* a unit of electrical power
**watt´age** *n.* a measure of power expressed in watts
**wat´tle** *n.* a woven framework of poles and twigs; a fold of skin hanging from the throat of a bird or lizard
**wave** *vi.* to move freely, as a flag in the wind; to greet or signal with the hand; to have the shape of a series of curves or curls, as of the hair *–vt.* to cause to move freely; to flourish; to signal by waving; to give a curved appearance to; to form into curves or curls *–n.* a ridge, as on the surface of a liquid: *the ocean waves pounded the shore*; a motion with the hand; a series of curves, as *a hair wave*; an upsurge, as *a wave of nausea*, a somewhat prolonged condition, as *a heat wave*; the pattern formed by the transfer of energy, as *a sound wave* **–wav´er** *n.*
**wave´form** *n.* the curve produced by recording the movement of a wave of energy
**wave´length** *n.* the distance between two like points, such as the crests or troughs, in consecutive cycles of an energy wave
**wa´ver** *vi.* to move one way and the other; to be uncertain; to falter *–n.* a wavering **–wa´ver·er** *n.* **–wa´ver·ing·ly** *adv.*
**wav´y** *adj.* full of curves, as *wavy hair*; undulating **–wav´i·ly** *adv.* **–wav´i·ness** *n.*
**wax** *n.* a pliable substance that is insoluble in water and that burns in the air; a waxlike product, as paraffin etc. *–adj.* made with or from wax *–vt.* to coat or polish with wax *–vi.* to gradually increase; to express oneself: *he waxed poetic on the joys of love*
**wax´en** *adj.* consisting of or covered with wax; pale or pallid; malleable or pliant
**wax´er** *n.* a person or machine that applies wax
**wax museum** a place that exhibits life-size wax figures
**wax paper** paper coated with wax, used in the preparation and preservation of food
**wax´work** *n.* something sculpted in wax **–wax´work·er** *n.*
**wax´works** *n.* an exhibit of wax sculptures
**wax´y** *adj.* resembling wax; abounding in wax; pale or pallid **–wax´i·ness** *n.*
**way** *n.* a direction; a passage from one place to another; space or room: *make way for the king*; a process or means: *a way to solve the problem*; a customary or habitual manner: *the way we live, do it your way*; a condition: *in a bad way* **–go out of the way** to be inconvenienced **–in a way** to some extent **–out of the way** taken care of; completed; remote *–adv.*
**way´bill** *n.* a document providing particulars about a shipment of goods
**way´far·er** *n.* one who travels, usually aimlessly and on foot **–way´far·ing** *n., adj.*
**way´lay** *vt.* to lie in ambush; to meet on the way **–way´lay·er** *n.*
**ways and means** methods for defraying costs or accomplishing something
**way station** an intermediate station, as on a railroad
**way´ward** *adj.* willful, headstrong; not predictable **–way´ward·ly** *adv.* **–way´ward·ness** *n.*
**weak** *adj.* lacking strength, energy etc.; not effective, as of an argument; lacking mental power; lacking skill or experience; deficient in something
**weak´en** *vt., vi.* to make or become weak or weaker **–weak´en·er** *n.*
**weak´fish** *n.* any of various marine food fishes
**weak´ling** *n.* a feeble person or animal
**weak´ly** *adj.* sick or feeble *–adv.* in a weak manner **–weak´li·ness** *n.*
**weak´-mind´ed** *adj.* not resolute; lacking conviction; foolish; unable to comprehend **–weak´mind´ed·ly** *adv.* **–weak´mind´ed·ness** *n.*
**weak´ness** *n.* the quality of being fragile; a slight failing; a strong liking; something that strongly attracts
**weal** *n.* a welt, as from a blow
**wealth** *n.* riches: an abundance of assets or goods; the state of being rich; great abundance of anything: *a wealth of knowledge*
**wealth´y** *adj.* possessing riches; characterized by abundance; more than sufficient **–wealth´i·ly** *adv.* **–wealth´i·ness** *n.*
**wean** *vt.* to end dependence on mother's milk for nourishment; to withdraw from a detrimental habit or association
**wean´ling** *adj.* freely weaned *–n.* a child or animal freshly weaned
**weap´on** *n.* any implement that may be used against an adversary **–weap´on·ry** *n.*
**wear** *vt.* to have on the person, as a garment or ornament; to display, as an aspect; to damage by constant use; to exhaust *–vi.* to be diminished by use; to withstand the effects of use, time, etc.: *to wear well*; to have a tiring effect: *the trip was wearing* *–n.* the act of wearing or being worn; articles of dress; destruction from use or time; durability **–wear´er** *n.*
**wear´a·ble** *adj.* suitable for wear
**wear·a·bil´i·ty** *n.* the ability to withstand the effects of use or time
**wear´ing** *adj.* tiresome; exhausting; designed to be

worn —**wear´ing·ly** *adv.*

**wea´ry** *adj.* tired; fatigued; discontented or bored; indicating fatigue —*vt., vi.* to make or become weary —**wea´ri·ly** *adv.* —**wea´ri·ness** *n.*

**wea´ri·some** *adj.* causing fatigue; tiresome —**wea´ri·some·ly** *adv.* —**wea´ri·some·ness** *n.*

**wea´sel** *n.* a small, slender carnivorous animal; a sly or treacherous person —*vi.* to renege, as on a promise: *weaseled out of the deal*; to equivocate

**weath´er** *n.* general atmospheric conditions, as temperature, moisture, wind, etc.; unpleasant conditions —*vt.* to expose to the elements; to show the effects of exposure; to pass through and survive —*vi.* to undergo changes from exposure; to resist the action of weather —*adj.* facing the direction of the wind

**weath´er·beat·en, weath´er·worn** *adj.* showing the effects of exposure to weather

**weath´ered** *adj.* damaged by or as if by the elements; visibly improved by exposure or intended to emulate exposure, as *weathered brick* or *weathered siding*

**weath´er·ing** *n.* the process by which materials exposed to the elements undergo changes; the appearance of materials that have been exposed to the elements, often produced artificially for effect

**weath´er·proof** *adj.* capable of withstanding the effects of exposure to harsh weather —*vt.* to make weatherproof —**weath´er·proof·ness** *n.*

**weather station** a place from which meteorological observations are made

**weath´er·strip, weath´er·strip·ping** *n.* material applied in or over crevices to exclude drafts, rain, etc. —*vt.* to attach or apply weatherstripping

**weave** *vt.* to make something by interlacing thread, yarn etc.; to produce by interlacing elements: *weave a tale*; to advance by moving from one side to another —*vi.* to make by weaving; to become interlaced; to make one's way by weaving —**weav´er** *n.*

**web** *n.* the network spun by a spider; an artfully contrived trap; an entanglement: *a web of deceit*; any complex network: *the world-wide web for computers*; the membrane connecting the digits of aquatic birds, frogs, etc. —*vt.* to create a web; to trap in a web

**webbed** *adj.* of or having a web

**wed** *vt., vi.* to marry

**wed´ding** *n.* the rite of marriage; the anniversary of a marriage

**wedge** *n.* a tapered piece of metal wood, etc. used to create pressure in a fissure, such as to split a log or tighten a joint; something in the form of a wedge; something that facilitates entry, intrusion, etc. —*vt.* to force apart or fix in place with a wedge; to crowd or squeeze —*vi.* to force oneself in

**wed´lock** *n.* the state of being married

**wee** *adj.* very small

**weed** *n.* an unwanted plant, especially of growth among cultivated plants —*vt., vi.* to remove unwanted growth; to remove anything considered undesirable: *weed out the useless information* —**weed´er** *n.*

**weed´y** *adj.* abounding in weeds: *a weedy garden*; of a weed or weeds; gawky or lanky —**weed´i·ly** *adv.* —**weed´i·ness** *n.*

**week** *n.* a period of seven calendar days, customarily Sunday through Saturday; a period described by an event or cause: *Christmas week, Teacher Recognition week*; the portion of a week dedicated to business: *a five-day week*

**week´end** *n.* the time at the end of a work week, usually Friday evening to Sunday evening —*vi.* to visit over the weekend: *we'll weekend at the beach house*

**week´end·er** *n.* a vacationer or weekend visitor; a small bag designed to carry clothing and incidentals sufficient for a few days needs

**week´ly** *adj., adv.* occurring every week or once a week; pertaining to a week: *a weekly wage* —*n.* a periodical issued once a week

**weep** *vt.* to show grief or remorse by shedding tears; to form liquid in drops, as condensation —*vt.* to weep for; to shed liquid —*n.* the act of weeping; an exhudation of liquid, as from a running sore —**weep´er** *n.*

**weep´ing** *adj.* that weeps; shedding tears; having branches that curve downward

**weeping willow** a tree notable for long drooping branches

**weep´y** *adj.* weeping or inclined to weep

**wee´vil** *n.* a small destructive beetle —**wee´vil·ly, wee´vil·y** *adj.*

**weigh** *vt.* to determine the weight of; to measure according to weight; to consider carefully: *to weigh the consequences* —*vi.* to have a specified weight; to have importance: *to weigh heavy on one's mind*; to be burdensome: *weighed down with guilt* —**weigh´er** *n.*

**weight** *n.* heaviness; a measure of heaviness; a piece used as a standard in weighing; a unit of heaviness; burden or pressure: *the weight of responsibility*; importance or consequence; a heavy object used in competition or for exercise; an object used to hold something down; *a paperweight* —*vt.* to make heavy; to oppress or burden

**weight´ed** *adj.* adjusted so as to correctly reflect the ratio of elements, as *a weighted average*

**weight´less** *adj.* having or experiencing little or no heaviness; free from the pull of gravity, as in outer space —**weight´less·ly** *adv.* —**weight´less·ness** *n.*

**weight´y** *adj.* of great importance: *a weighty decision*; effectual: *a weighty argument*; oppressive; heavy —**weight´i·ly** *adv.* —**weight´i·ness** *n.*

**weir** *n.* a dam across a waterway to raise or divert the water; a fence in a stream, used to catch fish

**weird** *adj.* odd or bizarre; pertaining to the supernatural —**weird´ly** *adv.* —**weird´ness** *n.*

**wel´come** *vt.* to greet hospitably; to receive with pleasure —*n.* a warm reception —*adj.* received cordially; producing satisfaction; free to useor enjoy —**wel´come·ly** *adv.* —**wel´come·ness** *n.* —**wel´com·er** *n.*

**weld** *vt.* to unite, as two pieces of metal, by the application of heat; to bring into close association —*n.* the joining of metal by welding; the joint formed by welding —**weld´a·ble** *adj.* —**weld´er** *n.*

**wel´fare** *n.* well-being; prosperity; money or other assistance given to those in need

**welfare state** a system by which the state assumes responsibility for the welfare of its citizens, as for health insurance, retirement, etc.

**well** *n.* a shaft sunk into the earth; a source of continued supply; a depression or cavity used to hold or collect water; a vertical opening through a building for light, ventilation, stairs, etc. —*vi.* to rise to the surface —*vt.* to gush or pour forth —*adv.* satisfactorily: *performed well*; in a correct manner; to a considerable extent: *well known*; quite, positively: *well worth the money* —*adj.* suitable or proper; fortunate; in good health; prosperous: *well off*

**well´-ad·just·ed** *adj.* suitably adapted to surroundings or circumstances; mentally sound

**well´-appoint´ed** *adj.* properly equipped

**well-bal´anced** *adj.* correctly proportioned; mentally sound

**well´-be´ing** *n.* health, happiness, or prosperity

**well´born** *adj.* of good family; titled; aristocratic

**well´-de·fined´** *adj.* having distinct features or limits; unambiguous

**well´-done** *adj.* performed skillfully; thoroughly cooked

**well´-fa´vored** *adj.* attractive; comely

**well´-found´ed** *adj.* based on fact

**well´-ground´ed** *adj.* properly schooled or taught

**well´-in·ten´tioned** *adj.* meaning well; having good intentions

**well´-man´nered** *adj.* courteous; polite

**well´-mean´ing** *adj.* having good intentions

**well´-nigh´** *adv.* almost

**well´-off´** *adj.* in comfortable circumstances; wealthy

**well´-round´ed** *adj.* having many interests, abilities, etc.

**well´spring** *n.* the source of a stream, spring, etc.; a source of continual supply

**well´-timed´** *adj.* happening at a favorable time

**well´-wish·er** *n.* a supporter —**well´-wish·ing** *adj.*, *n.*

**welt** *n.* a raised mark on the skin resulting from a blow; a strip of material used to cover or strengthen a seam —*vt.* to decorate with a welt; to flog so as to raise welts

**wen** *n.* a cyst

**wend** *vt.* to go on; to proceed

**were´wolf** *n.* in folklore, a person changed into a wolf or able to take the form of a wolf

**west** *n.* the direction in which the sun sets —*adj.*

**west´er·ly** *adj.*, *adv.* in, toward, or of the west —**west´er·li·ness** *n.*

**west´ern** *adj.* of, in, directed toward, or facing the west; from the west —**west´ern·er** *n.*

**west´ern·ize** *vt.* to adapt to the customs of a western nation, such as the US or Europe; to adopt the trappings of the American west, especially in manner of dress —**west·ern·i·za´tion** *n.*

**wet** *adj.* moistened or covered with a liquid; marked by rainfall; not yet dry, as paint —*n.* moisture; rainy weather —*vt.*, *vi.* to make or become wet —**all wet** completely wrong —**wet behind the ears** inexperienced —**wet´ness** *n.*

**wet blanket** one who discourages or disparages taking part in festivities; one whose presence diminishes the enjoyment of others

**wet´land** *n.* a land area such as a swamp or marsh that is saturated or partly under water

**whack** *vt.*, *vi.* to strike sharply —*n.* a resounding blow

**whale** *n.* a very large marine mammal; something very good, large, or impressive: *a whale of a party* —*vi.* to engage in hunting whales —**whal´er** *n.*

**wharf** *n.*, *pl.* **wharfs, wharves** a place or structure for the docking and loading or unloading of ships; a pier or dock

**what** *pron.* which specific thing, amount, circumstance, etc.: *what is this?, what does it cost?, what happened?* that which: *take only what is yours*; whatever situation or contingency: *able to take what comes* —*adj.* which one: *what color is it? what show did you watch?* —*adv.* how much: *what does it matter?* —**what for** a strong reproof or denunciation —**what it boils down to** the gist of the matter; essentially

**what´not** *n.* an article of furniture designed to hold and display small objects; a small decorative object

**wheal** *n.* a small pimple on the skin

**wheat** *n.* a cereal grass, esp. one ground into flour

**wheat germ** the nutricious embryo of the wheat kernel

**whee´dle** *vt.* to persuade by flattery, cajolery, etc.; to obtain by cajoling or coaxing —*vi.* to use flattery or cajolery —**whee´dler** —**whee´dling·ly** *adv.*

**wheel** *n.* a disk or rim that turns on a central axis; a turning or rotating movement; a person of influence —*vt.* to move or convey on wheels; to cause to turn, as though on an axis; to provide with wheels —*vi.* to turn, as on an axis; to change one's course; to move on wheels

**wheel´bar·row** *n.* a one-wheeled vehicle with opposing handles used to move small loads —*vt.* to convey in a wheelbarrow

**wheel´chair** *n.* a chair mounted between large wheels, for the use of one unable to walk

**wheel´er-deal´er** *n.* one who acts freely, aggressively, and often unscrupulously, as in arranging a business or political bargain
**wheel´wright** *n.* a man whose business is making or repairing wheels
**wheeze** *vt., vi.* to breathe with a husky, whistling sound —*n.* a wheezing sound —**wheez´i·ly, wheez´ing·ly** *adv.* —**wheez´i·ness** *n.* —**wheez´y** *adj.*
**whelp** *n.* one of the young of a dog, wolf, etc.; a worthless young fellow —*vt., vi.* to give birth
**when** *adv.* at what or which time; at an earlier time; under what circumstances —*conj.*
**whence** *adv.* from what place or source —*conj.*
**where** *adv.* at or in what place or situation; to or from what place —*conj.*
**where´a·bouts** *n.* an unspecified location: *we don't know his whereabouts*
**where´with·al** *n.* the necessary means or resources
**whet** *vt.* to sharpen, as a knife; to excite or stimulate: *the smell of food will whet your appetite*
**whet´stone** *n.* a fine stone for the sharpening of knives, etc.
**whey** *n.* a clear liquid that separates from the curd when milk is curdled, as in the making of cheese —**whey´ey, whey´ish** *adj.*
**which** *pron.* what thing: *which is larger?* that previously indicated: *take the red car, which is mine* —*adj.* what specific one: *which car do you want to take?*
**whiff** *n.* a gust of air; an aroma; a puff
**while** *vt.* to pass time pleasantly —*n.* a span or amount of time —*conj.* during the time that; at the same time; whereas
**whim** *n.* a sudden, capricious idea or notion
**whim´per** *vi., vt.* to cry or utter with a plaintive sound —**whim´per·er** *n.* —**whim´per·ing·ly** *adv.*
**whim´si·cal** *adj.* capricious; marked by erratic or unpredictable conduct; odd or quaint —**whim·si·cal´i·ty, whim´si·cal·ness** *n.* —**whim´si·cal·ly** *adv.*
**whim´sy** *n.* a whim or caprice; odd or quaint humor
**whine** *vi.* to utter a high, plaintive, nasal sound expressive of grief or distress; to complain in a fretful or childish way; to make a steady high-pitched sound, as of a machine —*vt.* to utter with a whine — *n.* — **whin´er** *n.* —**whin´ing·ly** *adv.* —**whin´y** *adj.*
**whip** *vt.* to strike with a lash; to beat to a froth; to seize, throw, etc. with a sudden motion —*vi.* to move or turn suddenly; to thrash about —*n.* a lash attached to a handle; a whipping or thrashing motion; a legislator appointed to enforce discipline, attendance, etc.; a dessert containing whipped cream or beaten egg whites
**whip´lash** *n.* the end of a whip; a neck injury caused by a sudden snapping of the head
**whip´per·snap·per** *n.* a pretentious but insignificant young person
**whipping boy** one who receives undeserved blame
**whir** *vt., vi.* to fly or move with a buzzing sound —*n.* a whizzing sound; confusion or bustle
**whirl** *vi.* to turn or revolve rapidly; to move or go swiftly; to have a spinning sensation —*vt.* to cause to turn or revolve rapidly —*n.* a swift rotating motion; a state of confusion; a round of activities: *the social whirl* —**whirl´er** *n.*
**whirl´pool** *n.* an eddy or votex of rapidly whirling water
**whirl´wind** *n.* a rapidly spinning column of air such as a tornado or waterspout; a destructive force —*adj.* extremely swift or impetuous: *a whirlwind tour*
**whisk** *vt.* to brush or sweep off lightly; to beat with quick movements —*vi.* to move quickly and lightly —*n.* a light sweeping motion; a kitchen utensil made up of wire loops for whipping or blending cream, egg whites, sauces, etc.
**whisk broom** a small hand broom
**whisk´er** *n.* the hair of a man's beard; long bristly hair near the mouth of some animals —**whisk´ered, whisk´er·y** *adj.*
**whis´key, whis´ky** *n.* an alcoholic beverage —*adj.* pertaining to or made with whiskey
**whis´per** *n.* hushed speech; a secret communication; a low, rustling sound —*vi.* to speak in hushed tones; to speak furtively; to make a low, rustling sound —*vt.* to utter or speak in a low tone —**whis´per·er** *n.* —**whis´per·ing·ly** *adv.* —**whis´per·y** *adv.*
**whist** *n.* a card game similar to bridge
**whis´tle** *vi.* to make a sharp, shrill sound; to sound a whistle —*vt.* to produce a sound by whistling —*n.* a sharp, shrill sound; a device for making such a sound: *a steam whistle* —**whis´tler** *n.*
**whis´tle-blow´er** *n.* a person who exposes wrongdoing, often one with strong links to the organization cited such as an employee —**whis´tle-blow·ing** *n.*
**whistle stop** a town along the course of a railway where a train stops only when signaled to do so: a small town, or one of little importance; a brief stop in the course of a political candidate's tour
**whit** *n.* the smallest bit
**white** *n.* the color produced by reflection of all the visible colors of the spectrum; the condition of being white; anything white or nearly white; the white part of something, as of an egg; the lighter-colored pieces, as of chess men, or the one playing those pieces —*adj.* lacking hue, as new snow; relatively light in color, as *white wine, white hair,* or *white skin*; relatively unmarked or clean: *white paper*; relatively harmless or innocuous: *white noise* —**white´ness** *n.*
**white blood cell** cells of the blood that help the body stave off infection and disease
**white´col´lar** *adj.* designating salaried employees
**white dwarf** an extremely dense star that glows faintly

due to its relatively small size

**white elephant** anything that is a burden and expensive to maintain; something of uncertain value

**white flag** a symbol of surrender

**white heat** the temperature at which heated metal turns white; a state of intense emotion **–white-hot** *adj.*

**white knight** a rescuer; a person or organization that buys or merges with a company in order to rescue it from a hostile takeover

**white´-knuck´le** *adj.* marked by or causing severe uneasiness or apprehension: *a white-knuckle flight*

**white lie** a harmless, trivial fib

**whit´en** *vt., vi.* to make or become white, as by bleaching **–whit´en·er** *n.*

**white paper** an authoritative report, especially one prepared by a government agency

**white sauce** a sauce of cream or broth, thickened with a butter and flour mixture, used especially as a base for a variety of flavored sauces

**white´wash** *n.* a thin mixture of lime, water, sizing etc. used for coating walls or other structures; a suppressing or concealing of faults or failure *–vt.* to coat with whitewash; to suppress or gloss over, as wrongdoing **–white´wash·er** *n.*

**whit´ish** *adj.* somewhat white or nearly white **–whit´ish·ness** *n.*

**whit´tle** *vt.* to make or shape by cutting bits from; to reduce or wear away a little at a time: *he whittled away at his inheritance until there was nothing left* *–vi.* to cut or shape wood **–whit´tler** *n.*

**whiz** *vi., vt.* to make or cause to make a hissing and humming sound while passing rapidly through the air *–n.* a whizzing sound; a person of extraordinary ability

**whiz kid** a relatively young person who is extremely clever, talented, or successful

**who·dun´it** *n.* a mystery story

**whole** *adj.* complete or entire: *she read the whole book*; not broken or defective: *a whole walnut*; being the full amount: *tell us the whole story* *–n.* collectively, all the parts or elements that make up a thing **–whole´ness** *n.*

**whole´heart·ed** *adj.* complete and unreserved enthusiasm, energy, dedication, etc. **–whole´heart·ed·ly** *adv.* **–whole´heart·ed·ness** *n.*

**whole´sale** *n.* the sale of goods in bulk, usually to a person or company that resells to consumers *–adj.* pertaining to the buying or selling of goods in bulk; made or done on a large scale *–adv.* in bulk, extensively: *wholesale slaughter* **–whole´sal·er** *n.*

**whole´some** *adj.* tending to promote health; advocating mental or moral righteousness: *wholesome entertainment* **–whole´some·ly** *adv.* **–whole´some·ness** *n.*

**whol´ly** *adv.* completely, totally; exclusively, only

**whoop** *vi.* to utter loud cries *–vt.* to call or chase away with loud cries *–n.* a shout of excitement, joy etc.

**whooping cough** a contagious respiratory disease marked by violent coughing

**whop´per** *n.* something large or remarkable; an outrageous lie

**whop´ping** *adj.* unusually large or remarkable

**why** *adv.* for what cause, purpose, or reason *–n.* a cause or reason

**wick** *n.* a cord or strand that conveys fuel to a flame, as of a candle or oil lamp *–vt., vi.* to convey or be conveyed by capillary action **–wick´ing** *n.*

**wick´ed** *adj.* evil; mischievous or roguish; mean or troublesome **–wick´ed·ly** *adv.* **–wick´ed·ness** *n.*

**wide** *adj.* relatively broad; spacious; distant from the desired point: *wide of the mark*; having great scope *–adv.* extensively **–wide´ly** *adv.* **–wide´ness** *n.*

**wid´en** *vt., vi.* to make or become wide or wider **–wid´en·er** *n.*

**wide´spread´** *adj.* extending over a large area; happening or accepted extensively

**wid´ow** *n.* a woman whose husband has died

**wid´ow·er** *n.* a man whose wife has died

**width** *n.* the dimension of an object from side to side

**wield** *vt.* to use, as a weapon or tool; to exercise authority, power, influence, etc. **–wield´a·ble** *adj.* **–wield´er** *n.*

**wield´y** *adj.* easily handled or managed

**wie´ner, wie´ner·wurst** *n.* a kind of smoked sausage

**wife** *n.* a woman who is joined to a man in marriage **–wife´dom, wife´hood** *n.*

**wife´ly** *adj.* of or suitable to a wife **–wife´li·ness** *n.*

**wig** *n.* a head covering that replaces part or all of the wearer's hair, constructed from real or artificial hair *–vt.* to furnish with a wig

**wig´gle** *vi., vt.* to move or cause to move from side to side *–n.* **–wig´gler** *n.* **–wig´gly** *adj.*

**wild** *adj.* living or growing in a natural state; uncivilized; undisciplined; reckless or imprudent; extremely odd, strange, or bizarre; disorderly or disarranged; far from the mark: *a wild throw* *–n.* an uninhabited or uncultivated place *–adv.* in a wild manner **–wild´ly** *adv.* **–wild´ness** *n.*

**wild´cat** *n.* any of various feral cats, as the lynx, cougar, etc.; an aggressive, quick-tempered person; a tricky or unsound business venture *–adj.* unsound or risky; unofficial or unauthorized *–vt., vi.* to drill for oil **–wild´cat·ter** *n.*

**wildcate strike** an unauthorized walkout

**wil´der·ness** *n.* an uncultivated or uninhabited area

**wild´fire** *n.* a raging fire, difficult to extinguish

**wild´fowl** *n.* a wild game bird

**wild-goose chase** pursuit of the unknown or unattainable

**wild´life** *n.* wild animals collectively

**wild rice** an aquatic grass of North America or its edible grain
**wild´wood** *n.* natural forest land
**wile** *n.* a trick – *vt.* to lure, beguile, or mislead
**will** *n.* the power to make deliberate choices; a specific purpose, choice, etc.; strong determination; self control –*vt.* to choose; to resolve upon as an action or course; to decree –*vi.* to wish or desire
**will´ful** *adj.* deliberate, intentional; stubborn or headstrong –**will´ful·ly** *adv.* –**will´ful·ness** *n.*
**will´ing** *adj.* favorably disposed; readily and gladly acting, responding, giving, etc. –**will´ing·ly** *adv.* –**will´ing·ness** *n.*
**wil´low** *n.* a tree or shrub with flexible shoots often used in basketry –*adj.* made of willow wood
**wil´low·y** *adj.* tall and graceful; lithe or flexible; supple; abounding in willow trees –**wil´low·i·ness** *n.*
**will´pow·er** *n.* strength to control one's actions or desires; determination
**wilt** *vi.* to lose freshness; to droop –*vt.* to cause to lose freshness, energy, etc.
**wil´y** *adj.* sly or cunning –**wil´i·ly** *adv.* –**wil´i·ness** *n.*
**wimp** *n.* a person regarded as a weakling: a sissy; one who whimpers –**wimp´ish, wimp´y** *adj.*
**win** *vi.* to be victorious –*vt.* to be successful in; to gain victory; to influence –*n.* a victory
**wince** *vi.* to shrink back; to be startled; to recoil, as in pain –*n.* a startled motion –**winc´er** *n.*
**wind** *n.* any movement of air; breath; idle chatter –*vt.* to catch a scent of; to exhaust the breath of: *the short run winded him*
**wind** *vt., vi.* coil or twine
**wind´bag** *n.* an overly talkative person
**wind´break** *n.* an anything, such as a hedge, fence, etc., that protects from the wind
**wind´break·er** *n.* an outer jacket with close-fitting waistband and cuffs
**wind´ed** *adj.* out of breath
**wind´fall** *n.* something, as ripened fruit, brought down by the wind; unexpected good fortune
**wind gauge** a device for measuring the speed of the wind
**wind´ing** *adj.* turning about an axis or core; having bends or turns –*n.* a bend or turn
**wind instrument** a musical instrument sounded by blowing
**wind´jam·mer** *n.* a sailing vessel
**wind´lass** *n.* a device for hoisting or hauling
**wind´mill** *n.* a mill turned by the wind to power a pump, etc.
**win´dow** *n.* an opening to admit light or air
**window dressing** an arrangement in a store window; a means by which something is made to seem more attractive or plausible than it actually is
**win´dow-shop** *vi.* to look over goods without intention of buying –**win´dow-shop·per** *n.*
**win´dow·sill** *n.* the ledge beneath a window opening
**wind´shear** *n.* a strong rapid change in wind direction
**wind´swept** *adj.* exposed to or brushed by wind
**wind tunnel** a device that artificially produces winds, used to study the effects of the force of wind on the design of airplane wings, etc.
**wind´up** *n.* a conclusion
**wind´ward** *adj.* toward the direction from which the wind blows; being on the side exposed to the wind –*n.* the direction facing the wind –*adv.* against the wind
**wind´y** *adj.* stormy; tempestuous; boastful or talkative –**wind´i·ly** *adv.* –**wind´i·ness** *n.*
**wine** *n.* fermented juice, especially of the grape; the color of red wine –*vt.* to entertain or treat with wine
**wine cellar** a storage space for wines
**wine´press** *n.* an apparatus for extracting grape juice; a place where grape juice is extracted
**win´er·y** *n.* an establishment where wine is made
**wing** *n.* an organ of flight; anything resembling or suggesting a wing; an attachment or extension, as of a building, a stage, an organization, etc. –*vt.* to pass over in flight; to accomplish by flying; to disable by wounding slightly –*vi.* to fly
**winged** *adj.* having wings; sublime, lifty
**wink** *vi., vt.* to blink or cause to blink; to signal by closing the eyelid of one eye; to twinkle –*n.* a fleeting time; a twinkle; a hint conveyed by winking –**forty winks** a short nap –**wink´er** *n.*
**win´na·ble** *adj.* attainable; possible to accomplish –**win·na·bil´i·ty** *n.*
**win´ner** *n.* one who prevails; a victor; someone or something likely to succeed
**win´ning** *adj.* successful; charming –**win´ning·ly** *adv.* –**win´ning·ness** *n.*
**win´now** *vt.* to separate; to eliminate that which is bad –*vi.* to separate grain from chaff –*n.* a device used to separate grain –**win´now·er** *n.*
**win´some** *adj.* charming; attractive –**win´some·ly** *adv.* –**win´some·ness** *n.*
**win´ter** *n.* the coldest season, between autumn and spring; a year: *a man of ninety winters* –*vi.* to pass the winter –*vt.* to protect during the winter –*adj.* suitable for or characteristic of winter
**win´ter·green** *n.* a small evergreen plant or the flavoring oil extracted from its leaves
**win´ter·ize** *vt.* to prepare for winter –**win·ter·i·za´tion** *n.*
**win´ter·y, win´try** *adj.* of or like winter: cold, stormy, bleak, etc. –**win´tri·ly** *adv.* –**win´tri·ness** *n.*
**win´y** *adj.* having the taste, color, etc. of wine
**wipe** *vt.* to rub; to remove or apply by rubbing –*n.* the act of wiping –**wip´er** *n.*

**wipe out** to destroy utterly

**wire** *n.* a slender rod or strand of metal; something made of wire; a telegram *—vt.* to fasten with wire; to equip with wiring, as for providing a building with electricity; to telegraph *—vi.* to telegraph **—wir´er** *n.*

**wired** *adj.* fitted out for electricity, telephones, etc.; keyed up or excited

**wire´less** *adj.* having no wires; requiring no wires *—n.* a device such as a telephone or computer mouse that operates without wires; *(Brit.)* a radio

**wire´tap** *n.* a device for listening in on or recording a telephone conversation *—vt.* to connect or listen with a wiretap *—vi.* to use a wiretap **—wire´tap·per** *n.*

**wir´ing** *n.* a network of wires such as installed within a building to provide electricity, telephone service, etc.; the process of connecting or installing wires

**wir´y** *adj.* lean, but tough and sinewy; stiff or bristly, like wire **—wir´i·ly** *adv.* **—wir´i·ness** *n.*

**wis´dom** *n.* the ability to make sound judgements; insight or intuition; extensive knowledge; an accumulated body of knowledge

**wise** *adj.* having insight, common sense, or knowledge; shrewd and calculating **—wise´ly** *adv.*

**wise´a·cre** *n.* one who claims to know everything; a smart aleck or jokester

**wise´crack** *n.* an insolent or supercilious remark *—vi.* to utter a wisecrack

**wish** *n.* a desire or longing; something desired *—vt.* to have a desire or longing for; to request or entreat *—vi.* to feel a desire; to express desire **—wish´er** *n.*

**wish´ful** *adj.* having or indicating a desire **—wish´ful·ly** *adv.* **—wish´ful·ness** *n.*

**wishful thinking** believing that what one wants to be true is true

**wish´y-wash´y** *adj.* lacking in purpose; indecisive or ineffective

**wisp** *n.* a small bunch, as of straw or hair; a mere indication: *a wisp of perfume*; a delicate thing: *a wisp of a child* **—wisp´y** *adj.* **—wisp´i·ly** *adv.* **—wisp´i·ness** *n.*

**wist´ful** *adj.* wishful, yearning; musing, pensive **—wist´ful·ly** *adv.* **—wist´ful·ness** *n.*

**wit** *n.* intelligence; mental acuity; guile: *to live by one's wits*; a clever or amusing person

**witch** *n.* a woman who practices sorcery; an ugly or cruel old woman; a fascinating woman *—vt.* to work a spell upon; to fascinate or charm **—witch´y** *adj.*

**witch´craft** *n.* black magic, sorcery; extraordinary influence or charm

**witch´er·y** *n.* witchcraft; the power to fascinate

**witch hazel** any of a genus of small trees and shrubs; a mild astringent containing an extract from the bark and leaves of the witch hazel plant

**witch hunt** investigation or harassment of dissenters

**witch´ing** *adj.* able to enchant **—witch´ing·ly** *adv.*

**with·draw´** *vt.* to take away or move; to take back or rescind, as an offer; to prevent from using, selling, etc. *—vi.* to retreat; to remove oneself **—with·draw´a·ble** *adj.* **—with·draw´er** *n.*

**with·draw´al** *n.* an instance of taking back, removing, retreating, etc.; the process or effects of overcoming an addiction

**with·drawn´** *adj.* not responsive; introverted; isolated

**with´er** *vi.* to become limp or dry, like cut flowers; to waste, as flesh *—vt.* to cause to become limp or dry; to disconcert or humble, as by a scornful glance

**with·hold´** *vt.* to hold back; to refuse to grant, permit, etc. *—vi.* to refrain **—with·hold´er** *n.*

**with·stand´** *vt., vi.* to resist, oppose, or endure

**with·stand´** *vt.* to resist, oppose. or endure

**wit´less** *adj.* lacking intelligence; fatuous; silly or foolish **—wit´less·ly** *adv.* **—wit´less·ness** *n.*

**wit´ness** *n.* one who is competent to testify by virtue of having seen or learned something; one who attests to the authenticity of a document, signature, etc *—vt.* to see or know personally; to give testimony; to subscribe to the authenticity of a document, signature, etc *—vi.* to testify

**wit´ti·cism** *n.* a clever or humorous remark

**wit´ting** *adj.* knowing; aware; purposely done **—wit´ting·ly** *adv.*

**wit´ty** *adj.* displaying cleverness or humor **—wit´ti·ly** *adv.* **—wit´ti·ness** *n.*

**wiz´ard** *n.* a sorcerer; one exceptionally skillful or clever *—adj. (Brit.)* extraordinary: *he's a wizard pianist* **—wiz´ard·ly** *adv.*

**wiz´ard·ry** *n.* the practice or methods of a wizard

**wiz´ened** *adj.* shriveled; dried up

**wob´ble** *vi.* to sway unsteadily; to show indecision *—vt.* to cause to wobble *—n.* unsteadiness; instability **—wob´bler** *n.* **—wob´bli·ness** *n.* **—wob´bly** *adj.*

**woe** *n.* overwhelming sorrow; suffering

**woe´be·gone** *adj.* mournful; sorrowful

**woe´ful** *adj.* accompanied by or causing sorrow; paltry or mean **—woe´ful·ly** *adv.* **—woe´ful·ness** *n.*

**wolf** *n.* a wild, carnivorous mammal related to the dog; a cruel or rapacious person; a man devoted to the pursuit of women

**wolf´ish** *adj.* rapacious, savage; suggestive of a wolf **—wolf´ish·ly** *adv.* **—wolf´ish·ness** *n.*

**wom´an** *n.* an adult human female; a female attendant *—adj.* of or characteristic of women; female

**wom´an·ish** *adj.* characteristic of a woman; feminine **—wom´an·ish·ly** *adv.* **—wom´an·ish·ness** *n.*

**wom´an·ize** *vi.* to aggressively pursue women *—vt.* to endow with female characteristics **—wom´an·iz·er** *n.*

**wom´an·kind** *n.* women collectively

**wom´an·ly** *adj.* having qualities suited to a woman **—wom´an·li·ness** *n.*

**womb** *n.* a place where anything is engendered or brought into life; a sheltering space or area

**wom´bat** *n.* a burrowing marsupial of Australia

**won´der** *n.* a feeling of mingled surprise, admiration, and astonishment; something causing wonder *—vt.* to have a feeling of curiosity or doubt *—vi.* to marvel; to be curious or doubtful *—adj.* spectacularly successful **—won´der·er** *n.* **—won´der·ing·ly** *adv.*

**won´der·ful** *adj.* astonishing; very good **—won´der·ful·ly** *adv.* **—won´der·ful·ness** *n.*

**won´der·ment** *n.* astonishment or awe; something marvelous; puzzlement

**won´drous** *adj.* wonderful; extraordinary *—adv.* surprisingly **—won´drous·ly** *adv.* **—won´drous·ness** *n.*

**wont** *adj.* accustomed *—n.* an ordinary manner of doing or acting

**wont´ed** *adj.* commonly used or done; accustomed **—wont´ed·ly** *adv.* **—wont´ed·ness** *n.*

**woo** *vt.* to seek the affection or approval of; to entreat earnestly *—vi.* to pay court **—woo´er** *n.*

**wood** *n.* the hard fibrous material that constitutes the bulk of a tree; a forest *—adj.* made of or using wood; living or growing among trees

**wood´craft** *n.* knowledge of survival in the wild as to making shelter, finding food, etc.; the art of fashioning articles of wood **—wood´crafts·man** *n.*

**wood´cut** *n.* an engraved block of wood used for making prints; a print made from a woodblock engraving

**wood´ed** *adj.* abounding with trees

**wood´en** *adj.* made of wood; stiff or awkward **—wood´en·ly** *adv.* **—wood´en·ness** *n.*

**wood´land** *n.* land covered with trees; timberland *—adj.* belonging to or dwelling in the woods

**wood nymph** a forest sprite

**woods´y** *adj.* of, pertaining to, or like a woodland **—woods´i·ness** *n.*

**wood´wind** *n.* a musical instrument that uses a wood or woodlike reed

**wood´work** *n.* things made of wood; the interior trim in a house, such as door and window frames or molding **—wood´work·er** *n.***—wood´work·ing** *n.*

**wood´y** *adj.* made of or containing wood; resembling wood; wooded **—wood´i·ness** *n.*

**wool** *n.* a soft, durable fiber from the fleece of certain animals; yarn, fabric, or garments made from the fibers *—adj.* made of or pertaining to wool

**wool´en** *adj.* of or pertaining to wool; made of wool *—n.* cloth or clothing made of wool

**wool´gath·er·ing** *n.* idle daydreaming

**wool´ly, wool´y** *adj.* consisting of or resembling wool; not sharply detailed **—wool´i·ness, wool li·ness** *n.*

**wooz´y** *adj.* befuddled; nauseous **—wooz´i·ly** *adv.* **—wooz´i·ness** *n.*

**word** *n.* the smallest meaningful unit of a language; speech; a brief remark, message, comment, command, etc.; a promise

**word´age** *n.* words collectively; verbiage

**word´ing** *n.* a style or arrangement of words; phraseology

**word´less** *adj.* unspoken; silent **—word´less·ly** *adv.* **—word´less·ness** *n.*

**word of mouth** oral communication **—word-of-mouth** *adj.*

**word´play** *n.* clever repartee

**word´y** *adj.* expressed in too many words; verbal **—word´i·ly** *adv.* **—word´i·ness** *n.*

**work** *n.* physical or mental exertion; labor; employment; one's profession, trade, etc.; the place where one is employed *—vi.* to perform work; to be employed; to prove effective *—vt.* to cause or bring about; to make or shape by toil or skill; to cause to be productive; to make or achieve by effort **—work´er** *n.*

**work´a·ble** *adj.* capable of being worked, developed, etc.; practicable, as a plan **—work·a·bil´i·ty** *adv.* **—work´a·ble·ness** *n.*

**work´ing** *adj.* employed; occupied by work; that performs its function; sufficient for use or action: *a working agreement*

**working capital** the finances of a business available for its operation

**working class** those who work for wages

**work´man·like** *adj.* like or befitting a skilled workman; skillfully done

**work´man·ship** *n.* the art or skill of a workman; the quality of work; the work accomplished

**work of art** something considered to be fine art, as painting or sculpture; anything made or done with great beauty or skill

**work´out** *n.* an activity to improve skills, physical fitness etc.; strenuous or intense activity

**work sheet** a schedule or record of an employee's work times; a copy of preliminary notes or calculations; a spreadsheet

**work´shop** *n.* an area set aside for light tasks or projects; a meeting or seminar for training or discussion in a specialized field or on a specific subject

**world** *n.* the earth; the universe; a celestial body; a part of the earth: *the Third World*; a division of time, things, etc.: *the ancient world, the animal world*; a large amount: *a world of knowledge*

**world´ly** *adj.* pertaining to the world; devoted to secular, earthly things; sophisticated **—world´li·ness** *n.*

**world´ly-wise** *adj.* schooled in the ways of the world; sophisticated

**world´-wea·ry** *adj.* dissatisfied or discontented with life and its conditions **—world´-wea·ri·ness** *n.*

**worm** *n.* an elongated, limbless, soft-bodied creature; a despicable or despised person; something seen to be like a worm *—vt.* to proceed in a wormlike manner; to draw forth by artful means: *worm the information out of him*; to rid of intestinal worms *—vi.* to progress slowly and stealthily

**worm gear** a toothed wheel that meshes with a shaft having a spiral prominence

**worn** *adj.* frayed, damaged, etc. by wear; showing the effects of worry, anxiety, etc.; hackneyed

**worn-out** *adj.* having lost all value or effectiveness, especially from long use; tired or exhausted

**wor´ri·ment** *n.* a source of concern or anxiety

**wor´ri·some** *adj.* causing concern or anxiety **—wor´ri·some·ly** *adv.*

**wor´ry** *vi.* to be uneasy; to feel anxiety *—vt.* to cause to feel uneasy; to bother or pester; to bite, pull at, or shake with the teeth *—n.* a state of anxiety or uneasiness; something causing such a state **—wor´ri·er** *n.*

**worse** *adj.* bad to a greater degree; less favorable circumstances, etc. *—adv.* in a less favorable manner, way, etc.; with greater intensity, severity, etc.

**wors´en** *vt., vi.* to make or become less favorable

**wor´ship** *n.* adoration, homage; rituals, prayers, etc. used in paying tribute to a diety; excessive or ardent admiration *—vt.* to venerate; to have intense admiration or love for *—vi.* to perform acts of veneration **—wor´ship·er, wor´ship·per** *n.*

**wor´ship·ful** *adj.* feeling or showing great reverence, etc **—wor´ship·ful·ly** *adv.* **—wor´ship·ful·ness** *n.*

**worst** *adj.* extremely bad or ill; least favorable *—adv.* to the extreme degree of inferiority, badness, etc. *—vt.* to defeat, vanquish

**wor´sted** *n.* a type of woolen yarn, or a fabric made from such yarn *— adj.* mades from worsted

**worth** *n.* the value of something; the quality that makes a thing estimable or desirable; the amount obtainable for a specific sum: *two dollars worth of gas*; wealth *—adj.* equal in value to; deserving of

**worth´less** *adj.* having no value **—worth´less·ly** *adv.* **—worth´less·ness** *n.*

**worth´while´** *adj.* sufficiently important to occupy the time; of sufficient value to repay the effort **— worth´while´ness** *n.*

**wor´thy** *adj.* having valuable qualitites; deserving *—n.* a person of worth **—wor´ thi·iy** *adv.* **—wor´thiness** *n.*

**would´-be** *adj.* desiring, professing, or intending

**wound** *n.* an injury, any cause of pain, as to feelings, etc. *—vt., vi.* to inflict a wound; to injure the feelings or pride of **— wound´ed·ly** *adv.* **—wound´ing·ly** *adv.*

**wraith** *n.* an apparition of a person seen shortly before or after death; any specter

**wran´gle** *vt.* to argue noisily and angrily *—vt.* to argue, debate; to get by arguing stubbornly; to herd, as livestock *—n.* an angry dispute **—wran´gler** *n.*

**wrap** *vt* to surround and cover, as with paper, a blanket, etc.; to wind about something *—n.* an outer garment

**wrap´per** *n.* material enclosing something, as a gift, etc.; a woman's dressing gown; one who wraps

**wrap´ping** *n.* a covering: material enclosing something

**wrath** *n.* violent rage or fury

**wrath´ful** *adj.* extremely angry; expressing or resulting from rage **—wrath´ful·ly** *adv.* **—wrath´ful-ness** *n.*

**wreak** *vt.* to inflict or exact, as vengeance; to give free expression to, as passion

**wreath** *n.* a circular band of flowers, etc. as for a crown or decoration; a curling or spiral band, as of smoke

**wreathe** *vt.* to form into a wreath, as by twisting or twining; to adorn or encircle as with wreaths *—vi.* to take the form of a wreath; to twist, turn, or coil

**wreck** *vt.* to cause the destruction of *—vi.* to suffer destruction; to engage in destroying, as for plunder or salvage *—n.* the act of destroying; that which has been ruined; broken remnants or remains

**wreck´age** *n.* broken remnants from a wreck

**wreck´er** *n.* one who causes destruction; one employed in tearing down and removing old buildings; a person or machine that clears away auto wrecks

**wrench** *n.* a violent twist; a sprain, twist, or pull of a part of the body; *(US)* a tool for turning, etc. *—vt.* to twist forcibly so as to cause injury *—vi.* to give a twist

**wrest** *vt.* to pull away by violent twisting; to seize forcibly; to gain by great effort

**wres´tle** *vi.* to engage in wrestling; to struggle or contend *—vt.* to contend in wrestling *—n.* a difficult struggle **—wres´tler** *n.*

**wres´tling** *n.* a sport in which unarmed contestants endeavor to force each other to the ground

**wretch** *n.* a vile person; a miserable person

**wretch´ed** *adj.* marked by misery or poverty; despicable or contemptible: *it's a wretched approach to health care for the aged* **—wretch´ed·ly** *adv.* **—wretch´ed·ness** *n.*

**wrig´gle** *vi.* to twist in a sinuous manner, to make one's way by evasive or indirect means *—vt.* to cause to wriggle; to advance by evasive or sly means *—n.* the motion of one who or that wriggles **— wrig´gly** *adj.*

**wrig´gler** *n.* someone or something that wriggles; a mosquito larva

**wring** *vt.* to squeeze or compress by twisting; to force out, as water, by twisting; to acquire forcibly; to distress *—n.* a twisting or forcing **—wring´er** *n.*

**wrin´kle** *n.* a crease; a modification, as *a new wrinkle* *— vt., vi.* to make or become creased **—wrin´kly** *adv.*

**wrist** *n.* the part of the arm between the forearm and hand; the part of a garment that covers the wrist

**write** *vt.* to inscribe on a surface with pen or pencil; to communicate by letter; to be the author or composer of; to leave evidence: *guilt is written all over his face* *—vi.* to inscribe on a surface; to communicate in writing; to be occupied as an author **—writ´er** *n.*

**writhe** *vi.* to twist or distort the body, as in pain; to suffer, as from embarrassment, sorrow, etc. *—vt.* to cause to be twisted or distorted **—writh´er** *n.*

**wrong** *adj.* mistaken; inappropriate; not moral or legal; not working properly; unintentional *—adv.* in